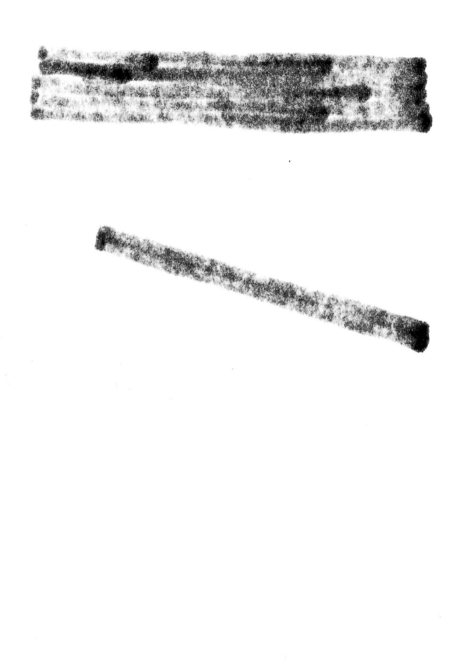

Contemporary American Theater Critics:

A Directory and Anthology of Their Works

compiled by

M.E. Comtois

and

Lynn F. Miller

The Scarecrow Press, Inc.
Metuchen, N.J. & London
1977

Library of Congress Cataloging in Publication Data

Comtois, M   E   1927-
    Contemporary American theater critics.

    "Selected bibliography of books and articles on
American theater criticism, 1900-1975 (James Williams)":
p. xxiv.

    Includes indexes.
    1.   Theater critics--United States--Directories.
I.   Miller, Lynn F. , joint author. II.   Title.
PN1707. 9. C6   792'. 9   77-23063
ISBN 0-8108-1057-3

DEDICATED

to the memory of our mothers, Helen Jones Hart and Helen Friedman Fieldman; to the future of our children, Kate and Liza Comtois and Jennifer and Jonathan Miller; and to our supportive husbands, Dr. Richard Comtois and Arthur H. Miller, Esq.

CONTENTS

*A sample biography, with key,
will be found on page 2.

v

INTRODUCTION

Contemporary American Theater Critics fills an information gap
about the lives and work of American theater critics. It is designed
to answer the questions: who are the critics, especially those outside New York City and other major urban centers; what are the
educational and professional backgrounds of the critics; and where
and how do they work now?

No conceptual or qualitative questions about the role of the critic in
society, the aesthetic standing of theater criticism as an art form,
or the relative merits or failures of critics are addressed in this
reference book. Such questions are valid and need to be addressed;
they are implied by the material gathered here, and the reader or
user of the compilation may no doubt be able to proceed to confront
these issues based on data collected here.

The compilers have proceeded on the firm belief that theater criticism is important to society, does serve a valid function in every
community (even if simply that of consumers' guide), and that theater criticism can be, should be, and often is an art form in itself.

The compilers' goal has been to gather biographical information and
sample pieces of criticism from as many well-regarded theater
critics as possible in the time allowed between initial concept and
publisher's deadline. The focus is on "regional" critics; the work
of the "tastemakers" who operate in and around New York is, though
included here, already available and well-known to those with access
to mass circulation magazines indexed in The Reader's Guide and to
the New York newspapers.

Among the users of the data, it is expected, will be students of
theater criticism who may learn who their future colleagues will be,

what media employ critics, and what the ordinary writing of these critics is like. Educators will refer to the directory as a resource for course work in theater criticism. Librarians will find it a useful source for answering specific questions about theater critics' lives and work. Practicing critics will want to know who their colleagues around the country are. Publishers and broadcasters will find the book a tool to evaluate the market of employable critics.

The main entries are alphabetical by critic's last name. A sample entry in the standardized form chosen for this work appears on page 2 along with a key to the numbered biographical elements of each entry. The provision of a geographical index, alphabetical first by state and then listing the critics within that state alphabetically (and with Canada following, in one sequence), facilitates the location of critics by region. An index of newspapers, journals, and radio and television stations employing the critics entered here, the Publisher/ Broadcaster Index, follows; the third index is of titles of plays or musicals that were reviewed in the works of criticism anthologized herein. All index entries refer the reader to the critics involved.

We began compiling this work in 1974 by sending letters to over 450 artistic directors of professional theaters, resident repertory companies and university theater centers throughout the United States, and some of Canada, asking them to recommend the best, in their estimation, theater critics regularly reviewing the productions of their theaters. These artistic directors were requested to rank these critics, supplying an educated guess about how many people each reached via his or her medium, to determine the sphere of impact of each critic. From the replies to these letters, the compilers made up lists of those critics considered significant in their regions, and contacted them for inclusion. Subsequently, the American Theater Critics Association lent its support to the project, contacted its membership and urged them to be included. Henry Hewes, secretary of the Association and theater critic for Saturday Review, graciously contributed his thinking and guidance to the development of the data-gathering.

At first, the compilers had aimed simply to gather files of the biographies and sample reviews as a resource for the use of criticism students and faculty in the Rutgers University Theater program. The project began as a joint effort by the Theater Department of Douglass College, Rutgers University, and the Mabel Smith Douglass Library, Douglass College, to form an information resource that had been totally lacking, even at the otherwise eminently complete Library for the Performing Arts at Lincoln Center. The development into book form came when the Scarecrow Press responded with interest to the need for such information to exist on a widespread basis. It is in the nature of librarians and scholars to find information gaps and be moved to fill them.

After drafting a simple format for biographical data and deciding to request two sample reviews of the critic's own choosing from each, we sent a "data kit" to each critic on our list, the American Theater Critics Association list, and the first- and second-night lists of critics supplied by the League of New York Theaters. It took us about two years to elicit and compile the responses.

With regard to scope, we are fully aware that this is not the complete list of working theater critics in America. Several important critics of whose work we are fully cognizant simply did not respond. Also, several of the entries do not include a sample review. This was usually because no reviews were submitted by the critic, but in some cases permission to reprint could not be obtained. We do aim for fuller coverage in planned supplements to the main volume as the quantity of continued response merits them in the future. The book is published but the data-gathering goes on and the file builds. Those critics not now included may want to be considered for inclusion in a supplement.

The cooperation and support of the entire Douglass College Theater Department made the carrying out of the entire project possible. The gracious cooperation of Daisy Brightenback, director of the Mabel Smith Douglass Library, Douglass College, was a great asset. John Bettenbender, dean of the School of the Creative and Performing Arts, Rutgers University, also lent support to the project.

The Rutgers University Research Council provided a grant to assist partially in the development of the project. We heartily thank all of these for their assistance. The dedicated help and hard work of research assistants James Williams, Robert Ludera, Ralph Leary, Kathryn Yaros, and Esther Blachford made it possible for the work to be completed; without their perseverance and assistance it would not have happened.

Lynn F. Miller
Highland Park, New Jersey
September 1976

ACKNOWLEDGMENTS

All reviews in this volume are fully credited on the page where they begin and are reprinted by permission of the owners. All rights are reserved. The following notices are specified: Albright's "Marceau..." and "Tobacco Road," copyright © 1975 by The Houston Post. Bannon's "Progressive Character Focus..." and "Julie...," copyright © 1974 by The Buffalo Evening News. Bardacke's "The Dybbuk" and "A New Look at Hamlet...," copyright © 1975 and 1974 by San Diego Magazine. Bermel's "The Iceman Melteth" and "Grape Juice and Wine," copyright © 1974 by American Labor Conference on International Affairs, Inc. Brukenfeld's "A Gadfly..." and "Piran-Jello," copyright © 1974 by The Village Voice, Inc. Bunke's "'Bridegroom'..." and "Guthrie Just Gets Better," copyright © 1976 by Des Moines Register & Tribune Co. Chapin's "The Limits of Satire" and "The Theater of Berrigan," copyright © 1970 and 1971 by Christianity and Crisis, Inc. Colby's "'Equus'..." and "New York Humor...," copyright © 1974 by Park East News, Inc. Constant's "Theatre: Cyrano" and "The Bolshoi Ballet...," copyright © 1973 by Trocadero Publishing, Inc. C. Davis's "Theater," reprinted by permission of Tanner Publications Co., Inc. Drake's "A New Twist ..." and "Marceau...," copyright © 1975 by The Los Angeles Times. Edwards's "A Streetcar..." and "Seagulls of 1933," copyright © 1973 and 1975 by Daily Variety Ltd. Elkin's "The Jockey Club Stakes" and "Raisin; Jacques Brel," copyright © 1973 by The Jewish Exponent of Philadelphia. Feingold's "It's Older..." and "Is There Hope...," copyright © 1976 by The Village Voice, Inc. Feldman's "Surprises..." and "Reality Conquers All...," copyright © 1975 by Kosco Media, Inc. Friedman's "Eliza Slams the Door" and "Fighting Vainly...," copyright © 1974 and 1973 by The Real Paper. Fuller's "Playwright and Play...," copyright © 1973 by Black World, and his "What the Wine-Sellers Buy," copyright © 1974 by Woodie King, Jr. Gilder's "The Iceman Cometh" and "Leave It to Me," copyright © 1946 and 1939 by Theatre Arts, both copyright © 1950 by Theatre Arts Books. Gold's "A Rare Evening..." and "A Shell of a Play," copyright © 1975 and 1976 by the New York Post Corporation. Gottfried's "A Double Meaning 'Seagull'" and "Shakespeare...," copyright © 1975 by the New York Post Corporation. Griffin's "Stage [Butley...]" and "Stage [Jumpers...]," copyright © 1973 and 1974 by Passionist Mission, Inc. Hawthorn's "Show's a 'Dandy'" and "Rep's 'Meeting'...," copyright © 1976 by the Seattle Post-Intelligencer. Herridge's "Stuttgart..." and "Bresson...," copyright © 1975 by the New York Post Corporation. Hughes's "Of Dolls, Dreams and Duds" and "Albee's 'Seascape'," copyright © 1975 American Press, Inc. Joslyn's "Quint Carries..." and "'I Do' Promise...," copyright © 1975 by the Milwaukee Sentinel. Kalem's "Delta Wildcat" and "Freudian Exorcism," copyright © 1974 by Time Inc. Kareda's "Canadian Play..." and "Stratford's 'Twelfth Night'...," copyright © 1975 by the Toronto Star. Kauffmann's "The Lady from the Sea" and "A Chorus Line," copyright © 1976 and 1975 by Stanley Kauffmann. Kelly's "St. Joan Opens..." and "Measure for Measure" reprinted courtesy of The Boston Globe. Kincaid's "Rigoletto" and "Der Frei-schütz," copyright © 1974 and 1975 by The Metropolitan Opera Guild Inc. Lahr's "Orlando Furioso," copyright © 1970 by The Village Voice, Inc. Lord's " Delight Abounds..." and "In Praise of 'In Praise of Love'," copyright © 1974 and 1975 by The Long Island Catholic. Marranca's "Quo Vadis..." and "There, There and There," copyright © 1975 by SoHo Weekly News. Merin's "Heartbroken Shaw" and "TNT Baltimore," copyright © 1976 by SoHo Weekly News. Mootz's "National Theatre of the Deaf..." and "Comedic 'Measure' ...," copyright © 1975 and 1976 by The [Louisville] Courier-Journal. Norton's "Carnovsky As Lear..." and "Shakespeare Theater Presents 'Our Town'," copyright © 1975 by the Boston Herald American. Novick's "No Play's Like 'Holmes'" and "Scenes from Another Marriage," copyright © 1974 and 1975 by The Village Voice, Inc. Plant's "Measure for Measure" and "Scenes from a Marriage," copyright © 1974 by Jon Plant. Plutzik's " Capote Adaptation..." and "Antony, Cleopatra...," copyright © 1973 and 1976 by the Buffalo Courier-Express. Richards's "An Explosion of Invention" and " 'Waiting for Godot'...," copyright © 1974 and 1976 by the Washington Star. Ridley's "Betrayal..." and "The Musical's Future...," copyright © 1975 Dow Jones & Co., Inc. J. Ruth's " 'Tobacco Road' Triumphs" and "The Crucible," copyright © 1974 the Sunday News, Lancaster, Pa. Sainer's "We Cease to Be Victims..." and "A Dream Production Falls," copyright © 1976 by The Village Voice, Inc. Shorey's "Lenny Bombs Again" and "Oil Lamps Is Coming," copyright © 1975 and 1974 by The Birmingham News Co. D. Smith's "Top Cast ..." and "Musante's Purr-fect...," copyright © 1975 by the Courier Express, Buffalo, N.Y. Sobel's "Shenandoah" and "The Wiz," copyright © 1975 by Billboard Publications, Inc. Stasio's "All About Evil" and "Lucky Cat," copyright © 1975 by Cue Magazine. Steele's "Measure for Measure" and "What the Butler Saw," copyright © 1976 by the Minneapolis Tribune. Sullivan's "Night of the Iguana" and "Eloquence of a Man...," copyright © 1976 and 1975 by the Los Angeles Times. Syna's "Ethnic Theater Flowers..." and "The Perils of Broadway...," copyright © 1976 by Wisdom's Child. Takiff's " 'Gravity'..." and "This 'Hedda Gabler'...," copyright © 1975 and 1976 by the Philadelphia Daily News. Thompson's "Jacques Brel..." and "Where's Charley," copyright © 1973 by Kosco Media, Syracuse, N.Y. Titcomb's "The Country Wife..." and " 'Macbeth' Intrigues...," copyright © 1973 by The Harvard Crimson, Inc. Trevens's "Drama and Dance," copyright © 1975 by H. Prim Co., Inc. Walsh's "Three Sisters" and "Dancing in One Mind," copyright © 1975 and 1974 by New Times, Inc., Tempe, Ariz. Watts's " 'Seascape': Albee at Top..." and "A Plunge to the Depths," copyright © 1974 and 1975 by the New York Post Corporation. Wealer's "The Stage," copyright © 1975 by Commonweal Publishing Co., Inc. Wetzsteon's "Harsh, Bitter, Brutal ...," copyright © 1976 by The Village Voice, Inc. Wilson's "The Uncluttered Style..." and "Fun and Games...," copyright © 1972 and 1974 by The Wall Street Journal--Dow Jones Co. Inc. M. Young's "God's, Maybe..." and "Casting a Vote...," copyright © 1974 by The Hearst Corporation.

THE AMERICAN THEATRE CRITICS ASSOCIATION

Henry Hewes

Twenty-five years ago there were only three or four non-profit professional theatres operating in this country. Today there are 137 such theatres in 66 cities in 32 states, and in recent years such non-profit professional theatres have been the originators of many of the best plays produced in the United States. Almost without anyone's noticing it we have built a truly American theatre.

However this changing shape of the art was noticed by 24 critics from around the country who, on August 3 and 4, 1974, met and formed the American Theatre Critics Association in order to initiate an approach to providing more responsive coverage of the American Theatre as a whole. The meeting took place at the Eugene O'Neill Theatre Center in Waterford, Connecticut, where the National Critics Institute under the leadership of Philadelphia critic Ernest Schier had for several summers been assuming the task of teaching critics there as fellows from newspapers around the United States. Indeed it was the National Critics Institute and the O'Neill who were the hosts for this founding meeting.

After a discussion of the needs of those present, two committees were formed. The first (Richard L. Coe, Rosamund Gilder, Otis Guernsey, Elliot Norton and Dan Sullivan) wrote a statement of purposes:

> To make possible greater communication among American theatre critics.
> To encourage absolute freedom of expression in theatre and in theatre criticism.
> To advance standards of theatre by advancing standards of theatre criticism.
> To increase public awareness of the theatre as an important national resource.

and
To reaffirm the individual critic's right to disagree with his or her colleagues on all matters including the above.

A second committee, (Clara Hieronymus, Ted Kalem, Tom McElfresh, Norman Nadel, Corbin Patrick, David Richards) wrote a set of by-laws that attempted to create a non-bureaucratic organization that would be guided by an executive committee, with no formal officers. The original by-laws called for a five-critic executive committee and two classes of membership. These items were subsequently amended to increase the executive committee to seven and to provide only one class of membership. The revised by-laws are:

ARTICLE I: EXECUTIVE COMMITTEE

Section 1: The business and organizational responsibilities shall be entrusted to an elected executive committee consisting of seven members, any four of whom shall constitute a quorum. The committee may choose its own chairman and its own secretary. Members of the executive committee will be elected at the annual membership meeting. The executive committee will serve without compensation. The executive committee members as much as possible shall represent different geographical areas. Two members of the Executive Committee shall be elected for three year terms, three members of the Executive Committee shall be elected for two year terms, and two members of the Executive Committee shall be elected for one year terms.

Section 2: Meetings. The executive committee shall meet at least three times a year, at a place and time of its choice. Written notice of any meeting of the executive committee shall be given at least two weeks previous thereto.

Section 3: Removal. Any member of the executive committee may be removed by a majority vote of the members of the association, whenever in their judgment the best interest of the association will be served thereby. A majority of the remaining members of the executive committee may initiate such action.

Section 4: Vacancies. A vacancy in office for any reason may be filled by a majority vote of the executive committee members for the unexpired portion of the term.

Section 5: Other committees shall be appointed by the executive committee when required.

ARTICLE II: FISCAL YEAR

The fiscal year of the organization shall begin on the first
day of July and end on the 30th day of June.

ARTICLE III: ANNUAL MEETING

The association's annual full membership meeting shall be
held at a time and place selected by the executive committee.

ARTICLE IV: AMENDMENTS TO THE BYLAWS

These bylaws may be amended or repealed by a majority
affirmative vote of the members in attendance at the annual
meeting and by proxy vote on an authorized form.

ARTICLE V: DUES

The annual dues shall be determined by the executive committee, but shall not exceed twenty-five dollars.

ARTICLE VI: MEMBERSHIP

Eligible for membership is any professional writer who is
now or has been actively employed reviewing theatre on a regular, continuing basis for at least two years by a newspaper,
magazine, TV or radio station. Applications for membership
shall be considered and acted upon by the executive committee,
which may make exceptions as they deem advisable.

One of our first tasks was to find out who were the critics
around the country, and the kind of reviews they wrote. Luckily
Rutgers University was already contemplating the project of collecting
this information in a file at Rutgers, and the newly-formed ATCA
happily joined with Rutgers to create not only a file at Rutgers, but
a copy of that file at the Theatre Collection of the Lincoln Center
Library for the Performing Arts in New York City. At the Theatre
Collection there are two ways for the reader to read the work of
critics around the United States. If, for instance, one wishes to
read the criticism being written in Los Angeles, one goes to the
card catalog under the heading DRAMA--CRITICS--U.S.--LOS AN-
GELES. There will be a cross-reference list of those critics working in the Los Angeles area whose biographical sketches and sample
reviews are available in individual folders under each critic's name.
The American Theatre Critics Association will try to keep these fold-

ers current by asking its members to mail to the Theatre Collection recent reviews of important theatre events as they occur. And of course, as new critics come along, new folders will be added to the collection.

The Theatre Collection project is an essential step toward the ATCA's goal of greater communication among American theatre critics. The second step was to enroll a substantial number of these critics as members. And once enrolled we have attempted to bring them together with a newsletter published four times a year, and by spring meetings in New York City, and annual summer meetings at Waterford, Connecticut.

As for our other purposes we have under development an annual publication which would reproduce reviews that have with some success tackled challenging problems in theatre criticism, and hopefully reading these will jog both critics and editors out of routine approaches to their methods of theatre coverage. The ATCA is also the official American affiliate of the International Association of Theatre Critics and through attendance of IATC conferences, our representatives will be able to compare notes with foreign critics and report back to the membership.

Perhaps the most compelling need among critics and editors located around the United States was for increasing the public's awareness that the theatre had become a truly national resource, and that local activity was not merely Broadway's stepchild. Accordingly the ATCA persuaded the American Theatre Wing and the League of New York Theatres and Producers to award an annual Tony to an outstanding resident professional theatre operating outside the New York City area. The first Tony was awarded in 1976 to the Washington, D. C., Arena Stage and its artistic director, Zelda Fichandler.

Then beginning with the 1976-77 season, the ATCA will select a best play, to be included in the Burns Mantle Best Plays annual. The play selected must be a world premiere regular professional production in the United States, between June 1, 1976, and May 31, 1977, that has not been produced in New York City before May 31, 1977.

We are still a very young organization, and our potential for making progress toward our goals seems strong. What is needed now is a recognition by editors and publishers that it is important to underwrite critics' trips to cover theatre in cities other than their own and one or two annual trips to enable them to come together with their colleagues, and explore their dedication to the purposes they have proposed. The ultimate beneficiaries are the readers, viewers, and listeners.

At the time of this writing, the executive committee consisted of Clara Hieronymus, The [Nashville] Tennesseean; Ann Holmes, Houston Chronicle; Tom McElfresh, Cincinnati Enquirer; Elliot Norton, Boston Herald-American; Ernest Schier, Philadelphia Evening & Sunday Bulletin; Dan Sullivan, Los Angeles Times; and Henry Hewes, Saturday Review. The foregoing statement was prepared with their assistance. --H. H.

A PROFILE OF THE
AMERICAN THEATER CRITIC

M. E. Comtois

Theater criticism, as a profession, is largely a 20th-century phenomenon. Men of letters--Sir Philip Sidney, John Dryden, Dr. Johnson, even Samuel Pepys--wrote about the theater upon occasion, but to make a career of going to the theater and writing about it, no. It took George Bernard Shaw and Max Beerbohm, in London in the first decades of this century, to establish a reputation for the theater critic as a professional writer and sometime artist. Stark Young, in America, was such a critic-artist, as was James Agee in film criticism.

The question of the theater critic as artist (and as a scholar and a gentleman* for that matter) is a qualitative judgment, much disputed. Theater critics are vilified (indeed that is the occupational hazard for critics), but they also vilify themselves and each other. Matters of taste, disparate visions of the world and of their task, further confuse the issues. Since the theater production is long gone before the critical judgments about it can be viewed in any historical perspective, there is not even the test of time to resolve such matters.

Generally accepted standards for theater criticism will emerge only when those who perform it are recognized as having a professional identity and a body of common practices. This collection was designed to provide such recognition and to allow that sort of qualitative evaluation to begin. What we now know, as a result of the

---

*Gentleman/Gentlewoman: Use of masculine designations reflects the "unliberated" state of the profession. Seven women influence national theater opinion; 62 women in all write theater criticism.

collection, are the facts and figures of the profession. We know that nearly 300 men and women in the mid-1970's are professional playgoers and writers who command a sphere of influence, and are paid to share their personal responses to a theater event with a populace. The biographies of these critics (collected in this volume) considered together, build a structure of fact about the theater critic, which will at the very least dispel false myths about critics and which may raise the consciousness of the critic as theater expert.

Of course these statistical data do not in themselves define the critic, whose work is nothing if not the product of his sensibilities, his thought, his experience. What it can address is the confusion about expectations, mostly erroneous, of what a theater critic is supposed to do. After all, theater critics address many different audiences. There are nationally syndicated critics and local critics; those who write for daily papers, for weekly art or entertainment magazines, and for literary journals. There is a new breed of theater critic emerging from the background of talk shows on radio and television. All these theater critics are consumer guides for a theater product; they also generate a climate of opinion which defines and qualifies the standards, professional and/or artistic, by which theater is judged in our time. The muddling of these two functions alone has given rise to contradictory images of the theater critic as a know-everything know-nothing, a perceptive executioner of what he advocates, a spurious power.

There has been a gulf between the mightiest and the lowliest in this field. Like the M. D. who disavows the chiropractor, some "critics" dismiss "reviewers" as better never to have writ at all, but it is hoped that study of the reviews in this collection will illuminate this point; the supposed inferiority of mere reviewers could prove to be yet another fallacy. The first service to the field to be performed is to separate facts about reviewers/critics from various fictions about them. The fallacies of the critic as sportswriter, or chronic dyspeptic, or frustrated actor may be dispelled by the facts of his or her career, education, and publication. For now, it is enough to identify those who write professional criticism and bring their careers into focus, one with another.

*   *   *

One half of the over 290 working critics entered in this Directory are in the Northeast, and of these, nearly 100 are in the New York City area. About 25 are in the South, about 50 in the Midwest and close to 30 in the Mountain and Pacific areas. This of course follows the concentration of theater activity in the large metropolitan centers, but towns and cities from less than 500,000 up to a million support more than 135 local critics, or 45 per cent of the profession. There are 40 critics writing for national consumption whose work is accessible anywhere in the country. The Christian Science Monitor, The New York Times, The Washington Post, syndicated reviews, and periodicals account for most of these. However there are 20 more critics who may not reach a national audience, e.g., the critics on the trade papers, and those like Elliot Norton on The Boston Herald American, who nonetheless clearly influence the professional theater as it evolves each year. These 60 critics seem to dominate national opinion by virtue of their insight, or their circulation, and/or their geographic location. Their biographies have been compared to those of local critics throughout this analysis and geography clearly tells. It appears necessary to be a frog in the big pond--whatever your own stature--if you wish to influence the theater as a whole.

About 90 per cent of the critics write for publication, as opposed to broadcasting. Of these 250 who write, slightly more than half are critics exclusively; the rest also edit and write feature articles. Of the more than 130 who are critics only, around 80 write theater criticism exclusively. The rest cover films or the arts in general in the course of their reviewing. All theater critics write some criticism outside the theater, and among the most prominent theater critics are those with reputations for film and dance criticism as well.

Theater criticism, broadcast on radio and television, has received only the sparest recognition in the American Theater Critics Collection. About 30 have been identified and only nine of those are theater critics exclusively. There are surely more, but the ephem-

eral nature of their review, and the parochial appeal of theater for
the vast radio and television audience may keep media theater
critics "in the closet," discussing theater performances and affecting
opinion accordingly, but fading into "columnist" or "commentator"
identities.

Of critics who write, more than 150 write for daily newspapers, about 45 for weeklies, and 35 to 40 for magazines. A question about the quality of the reviews, given the short time to reflect
and write (the complaint of the daily reviewer who must have his
copy in by midnight), arises here, but at least 15 of the 60 or so
national critics have two-to 12-hour deadlines also. The greater the
critic's influence, the greater his option to deliberate, though Clive
Barnes and Morton Gottfried are notable exceptions. Output for
most critics ranges from 50 to 150 reviews a year. They also write
a certain number of special pieces on film, books, and other events
in the arts. Of the two-thirds who reported specific figures for
plays and musicals reviewed, 50 publish up to 30 reviews a year,
112 publish from 40 to 125 reviews a year, 27 publish over 125.
The average output is over 60. This implies there are nearly
18,000 reviews circulating each year about theater events.

A third of the prominent critics have been writing criticism
for over 20 years--a sixth of all theater critics have. Only one in
every eight critics has been writing less than five years. If the
years of writing theater criticism are measured in consequence of
output, and assuming that most critics will have seen more than they
review, the average critic would appear to have attended about 900
productions. If theater-going experience is the basic qualification
for the critic, most critics do bring a prodigious background for comparison to each new production they see. It is a stable, long-lived
profession. In an audience of 10 critics, it can be statistically expected that one critic will be under 35, three will be younger than
45, four will be between 46 and 60 and three will be over 60.
Across the country, less than a quarter of the critics have been at
their job five years or less, and more than a half, from 10 to over
20 years.

Though most theater critics have long, continuous careers, only half of them have a full-time commitment to one employer. Across the country at least 115 report one income, but nearly 40 are also professors. Nearly 50 are freelance writers, and 30 or more do other things to balance out their professional critic careers. Among the nationally prominent critics, 25 have full-time commitments, 17 freelance for second income, 11 teach and eight have various other outside commitments. Does this independence of employer imply an independence of opinion expressed? Theater critics are assumed to be autonomous; At least one half of the critics herein are not totally dependent upon one publisher for their livelihood.

Critics are well-educated; 95 per cent have some higher education and every critic younger than 35 has a bachelor's degree. A third have had some graduate study and 10 per cent have doctorates or masters of fine arts degrees. The undergraduate background is in liberal arts, chiefly English, and graduate studies are divided between English and the theater as chief areas of study. The prominent critics differ from their local colleagues chiefly in that two-thirds went to Ivy League schools as undergraduates. Nationally, most theater critics went to state universities, although a third of all graduate study has been at an Ivy League institution. There are more than 20 Phi Beta Kappas, at least 17 prize winners for theater criticism, nearly 40 recipients of newspaper/media awards, about 20 grant or fellowship award-winners and 35 or 40 honored by other citations and special recognition. The number who have advanced degrees in theater (a more current phenomena since theater has only recently become an established academic discipline) may be reflected in the fact that 38 per cent of the critics under 35 start right out writing theater criticism. The first job held, as reported across the country and over the years, other than theater critic, was: reporter (47 give this reply), editor and teacher (38).

Most theater critics are writers, not performers. Three in 10 have done some acting at some point, and one in six has a play produced or published to his credit. Nearly 40 (or not quite one in eight across the country) have written at least one book. Half of the 60 critics who influence national opinion have published at least one book, which may also be a cause as well as effect of their eminence.

One in five is single, three out of four who are married have children, though only one half of those under 35 are married and one in three of these have children. The independence of thought of theater critics in general is reflected in their religion and politics where the majority are uncommitted.

The details in the lives of working theater critics are available, in the pages that follow, and can go far to flesh out the profile that emerges from the statistics of the profession. The theater critic has been basically described. It is now possible to consider the inner vision from which the criticism itself arises.

SELECTED BIBLIOGRAPHY
OF BOOKS AND ARTICLES
ON AMERICAN THEATER CRITICISM, 1900-1976

James Williams

The Bibliography is divided into the following parts:

Books by Practicing Critics
Performance Observations
Play Analysis
Books by Non-Critics
Indexes to Reviews
Digests of Reviews
Periodical Articles
1900-1925: By Critics;
About Critics
1926-1941: By Critics;
About Critics

1942-1951: By Critics;
About Critics
1952-1961: By Critics;
About Critics
1962-1976: By Critics;
About Critics
Special Materials... Lincoln Center Library
Periodical Issues Devoted to Theater Criticism

BOOKS BY PRACTICING CRITICS

PERFORMANCE OBSERVATIONS

Anderson, John. The American Theatre. New York: Dial Press, 1938.

_____. Box Office. New York: Jonathan Cape and Smith, 1929.

Atkinson, Justin Brooks. Broadway. New York: Macmillan, 1970.

_____. Broadway Scrapbook. New York: Theater Arts Books, 1947.

Bentley, Eric Russell. The Dramatic Event. Boston: Beacon, 1954.

_____. Theater of War. New York: Viking, 1972.

_____. What Is Theatre?. New York: Atheneum, 1968.

Brown, John Mason. The Art of Playgoing. New York: W. W. Norton, 1936.

_____. Broadway in Review. New York: W. W. Norton, 1940.

_____. Dramatis Personae. New York: Viking Press, 1963.

_____. The Modern Theatre in Revolt. New York: W. W. Norton, 1929.

_____. Two on the Aisle. New York: W. W. Norton, 1938.

_____. Upstage. New York: W. W. Norton, 1930.

Brustein, Robert Sanford. The Culture Watch. New York: Knopf, 1975.

_____. Revolution as Theater. New York: Liveright, 1971.

_____. Seasons of Discontent. New York: Simon and Schuster, 1965.

_____. The Third Theatre. New York: Alfred Knopf, 1969.

Clurman, Harold. The Divine Pastime. New York: Macmillan, 1974.

_____. Lies Like Truth. New York: Macmillan, 1958.

_____. The Naked Image. New York: Macmillan, 1966.

Eaton, Walter Prichard. The American Stage Today. Boston: Small, Maynard and Co., 1908.

_____. At the New Theatre and Others. Boston: Small, Maynard and Co., 1910.

_____. Plays and Players. Cincinnati: Stewart and Kidd, 1916.

Fyles, Franklyn. The Theatre and Its People. New York: Doubleday and Page, 1900.

Gaver, Jack. Season In, Season Out 1965-1966. New York: Hawthorn Books, 1966.

Gilman, Richard. Common and Uncommon Masks. New York: Random House, 1971.

Gottfried, Martin. Opening Nights. New York: Putnam, 1969.

_____. A Theater Divided. Boston: Little, Brown, 1967.

Hammond, Percy. But--Is It Art?. Garden City, N.Y.: Doubleday, Page and Co., 1927.

_____. This Atom in the Audience. New York: Ferris Printing Co., 1940.

Hapgood, Norman. The Stage In America 1897-1900. New York: Macmillan, 1901.

Isaacs, Edith (ed.). Theatre: Essays on the Arts of the Theatre. Boston: Little, Brown, 1927.

Kauffman, Stanley. Persons of the Drama. New York: Harper and Row, 1976.

Kerr, Walter. God on the Gymnasium Floor. New York: Simon and Schuster, 1971.

_____. Pieces at Eight. New York: Simon and Schuster, 1957.

_____. The Theatre in Spite of Itself. New York: Simon and Schuster, 1963.

_____. Thirty Plays Hath November. New York: Simon and Schuster, 1969.

Kirby, Michael (ed.). The New Theatre. New York: New York University, 1974.

Lahr, John. Astonish Me. New York: Viking, 1973.

_____. Up Against the Fourth Wall. New York: Grove Press, 1970.

Lewis, Emory. Stages, the Fifty-Year Childhood of the American Theatre. Englewood Cliffs, N. J.: Prentice-Hall, 1969.

MacGowan, Kenneth. Footlights Across America. New York: Harcourt and Brace, 1929.

Nathan, George Jean. Another Book on the Theatre. New York: B. W. Huebsch, 1915.

_____. Art of Night. New York: Knopf, 1928.

_____. Comedians All. New York: Knopf, 1919.

_____. The Critic and the Drama. New York: Knopf, 1922.

_____. Critica Materia. New York: Knopf, 1924.

_____. Entertainment of the Nation. New York: Knopf, 1942.

_____. Encyclopedia of the Theatre. New York: Knopf, 1940.

_____. House of Satan. New York: Knopf, 1926.

_____. Intimate Notebooks of George Jean Nathan. New York: Knopf, 1932.

———. Mister George Jean Nathan Presents. New York: Knopf, 1917.

———. The Morning After the First Night. New York: Knopf, 1938.

———. Passing Judgements. New York: Knopf, 1935.

———. The Popular Theatre. New York: Knopf. 1918.

———. Since Ibsen. New York: Knopf, 1933.

———. Testament of a Critic. New York: Knopf, 1931.

———. Theatre Book of the Year 1942-1943. New York: Knopf, 1943.

———. Theatre Book of the Year 1943-1944. New York: Knopf, 1944.

———. Theatre Book of the Year 1944-1945. New York: Knopf, 1945.

———. Theatre Book of the Year 1945-1946. New York: Knopf, 1946.

———. Theatre Book of the Year 1946-1947. New York: Knopf, 1947.

———. Theatre Book of the Year 1947-1948. New York: Knopf, 1948.

———. Theatre Book of the Year 1948-1949. New York: Knopf, 1949.

———. Theatre Book of the Year 1949-1950. New York: Knopf, 1950.

———. Theatre Book of the Year 1950-1951. New York: Knopf, 1951.

———. Theatre of the Fifties. New York: Knopf, 1953.

———. Theatre of the Moment. New York: Knopf, 1936.

———. The Theatre, the Drama, the Girls. New York: Knopf, 1921.

———. The World in Falseface. New York: Knopf, 1923.

Novick, Julius. Beyond Broadway. New York: Hill and Wang, 1968.

Bibliography

Oppenheimer, George. The Passionate Playgoer. New York: Viking, 1958.

Ruhl, Arthur. Second Nights. New York: Scribner's, 1914.

Sainer, Arthur. The Radical Theatre Notebook. New York: Discus Books, 1975.

Simon, John. Acid Test. New York: Stein and Day, 1963.

_____. Singularities. New York: Random House, 1975.

_____. Uneasy Stages. New York: Random House, 1975.

Towse, John Ranken. Sixty Years in the Theatre. New York: Funk and Wagnalls, 1916.

Winter, William. Other Days. Freeport, N. Y.: Books for Libraries Press, 1908.

_____. Shadows of the Stage. New York: Macmillan, 1906.

_____. Vagrant Memories. New York: G. H. Doran, 1915.

_____. The Wallet of Time. Freeport, N. Y.: Books for Libraries Press, 1913.

Woollcott, Alexander. Enchanted Aisles. New York: Putnam, 1924.

_____. Going to Pieces. New York: Putnam, 1925.

_____. Mrs. Fiske: Her Views on Actors, Acting and the Problems of the Stage. New York: Century Co., 1917.

_____. Shouts and Murmurs. New York: Putnam, 1922.

Young, Stark. The Flower in Drama. New York: Scribner's, 1955.

_____. Glamour. Freeport, N. Y.: Books for Libraries Press, 1925.

_____. Immortal Shadows. New York: Scribner's, 1948.

_____. The Theatre. New York: Hill and Wang, 1954.

PLAY ANALYSIS

Bentley, Eric Russell. Life of the Drama. New York: Atheneum, 1967.

_____. The Playwright as Thinker. New York: Harcourt, Brace and World, 1967.

_____. The Theatre of Commitment. New York: Atheneum, 1967.

Bermal, Albert. Contradictory Characters. New York: Dutton, 1973.

Brustein, Robert Sanford. The Theatre of Revolt. Boston: Little, Brown, 1964.

Gardner, Rufus Hallette. Our Splintered Stage. New York: Macmillan, 1965.

Gilman, Richard. A Confusion of Realms. New York: Vintage, 1969.

Hamilton, Clayton Meeker. Problems of the Playwright. New York: Holt and Co., 1917.

_____. The Theory of the Theatre and Other Principles of Dramatic Criticism. New York: Holt and Co., 1910.

Huneker, James Gibbons. Iconoclasts. New York: Greenwood Press, 1905.

_____. Selected Essays. New York: Scribner's, 1929.

Kerr, Walter. Tragedy and Comedy. New York: Simon and Schuster, 1967.

Krutch, Joseph Wood. The American Drama Since 1918. New York: Braziller, 1967.

_____. "Modernism" and Modern Drama. New York: Russell and Russell, 1953.

Lewisohn, Ludwig. The Drama and the Stage. Freeport, N.Y.: Books for Libraries Press, 1969.

McCarthy, Mary. Sights and Spectacles. New York: Farrar, Straus, and Co., 1956.

_____. Theatre Chronicles 1937-1962. New York: Farrar, Straus, and Co., 1963.

Matthews, Brander. Principles of Playmaking. Freeport, N.Y.: Books for Libraries Press, 1919.

_____. A Study of the Drama. Boston: Houghton Mifflin, 1910.

Skinner, Robert Dana. Our Changing Theatre. New York: Dial
    Press, 1931.

BOOKS BY NON-CRITICS

Altshuler, Thelma, and Janero, Richard Paul. Responses to Drama:
    An Introduction to Plays and Movies. Boston: Houghton
    Mifflin, 1967.

Bladel, Roderick. Walter Kerr: An Analysis of His Criticism.
    Metuchen, N. J. : Scarecrow Press, 1976.

Engel, Lehman. The Critics. New York: Macmillan, 1976.

Smith, Samuel Stephenson. Craft of the Critic. New York: Crowell,
    1931.

INDEXES TO REVIEWS

Salem, James T. (ed.). A Guide to Critical Reviews. Part I:
    American Drama, 1909-1969, 2d ed. Metuchen, N. J. : Scare-
    crow Press, 1973.

_____ (ed.). A Guide to Critical Reviews. Part II: The Mu-
    sical, 1909-1974, 2d ed. Metuchen, N. J. : Scarecrow Press,
    1976.

_____ (ed.). A Guide to Critical Reviews. Part III: British
    and Continental Drama from Ibsen to Pinter. Metuchen, N. J. :
    Scarecrow Press, 1968.

DIGESTS OF REVIEWS

Beckerman, Bernard, and Seigsman, Howard (eds.). On Stage: Se-
    lected Reviews of the New York Times 1920-1970. New York:
    Arno Press, 1973.

Marlowe, Joan, and Blake, Betty (comps.). New York Theater
    Critics. New York: Critics Theater Reviews, Inc. , vol. 1-
    (1940-). (Weekly, with annual cumulations; two comprehen-
    sive cumulation volumes have been published--1940-1960, 1961-
    1972.)

Moses, Montrose Jonas, and Brown, John Mason (eds.). The Amer-

ican Theater As Seen by Its Critics 1752-1934.   New York:
W. W. Norton, 1934.

PERIODICAL ARTICLES, 1900-1925

BY CRITICS

Clapp, H. A. "Reminiscences of a Dramatic Critic." Atlantic, 88:
    155-165, 344-354, 490-501, 622-634, Aug.-Nov. 1901.

Colby, F. M. "Doubts of a Dramatic Critic." Bookman, 18: 603-
    5, Feb. 1904.

_____. "Model for Dramatic Critics." Forum, 39: 550-60,
    April 1908.

"Confessions of a Dramatic Critic." Independent, 60: 492-7, March
    1, 1906.

Dale, Alan. "Can a Dramatic Critic Be Quite Honest?" Cosmo-
    politan, 41: 397-404, Aug. 1906.

_____. "Impersonal Note in Criticism." Cosmopolitan, 47: 347-
    352, Aug. 1909.

_____. "Sufferings of a Dramatic Critic." Cosmopolitan, 50:
    61-4, Dec. 1910.

"Dramatic Critic and the Trust." Independent, 67: 770-1, Sept. 30,
    1909.

Hamilton, Clayton. "Function of Dramatic Criticism." Bookman,
    35: 26-31, March 1912.

Hammond, Percy. "Transplanting the Chicago Critic." Bookman,
    54: 142-43, Oct. 1921.

MacGowan, Kenneth. "Corrupted Dramatic Critics." Dial, 64: 13-
    15, Jan. 3, 1918.

Matthews, Brander. "Is Dramatic Criticism Necessary?" Book-
    man, 42: 82-7, Sept. 1915.

Metcalfe, James S. "Dramatic Criticism in the American Press."
    Atlantic, 121: 495-9, April 1918.

Moses, Montrose J. "America's Dramatick Criticks." Theater
    Arts, 9: 470-7, July 1924.

Nathan, George Jean. "Hamlet in the Hamlets." Bookman, 34: 290-3, Nov. 1911.

_____. "Lamentation, Op. 4329." American Mercury, 5: 499-501, Aug. 1925.

Street, J. "Confessions of a Reformed Dramatic Critic." Harper's Weekly, 58: 9-11, Aug. 16, 20-22, Aug. 23, 1913.

Winter, William. "Biography and Dramatic Criticism." Harper's Weekly, 55: 18, Jan. 28, 1911.

ABOUT CRITICS

"Critic's Word to His Critics." Literary Digest, 45: 421-2, Sept. 14, 1912.

"Cudgeling the Dramatic Critics." Literary Digest, 48: 321-2, Feb. 14, 1914.

"Do Critics Know Anything About Acting?" Literary Digest, 58: 24-5, July 20, 1918.

"Dramatic Critics Unmasked." Literary Digest, 68: 33, Jan. 29, 1921.

PERIODICAL ARTICLES, 1926-1941

BY CRITICS

Krutch, Joseph Wood. "How I Stand It." Nation, 150: 222-4, Feb. 10, 1940.

_____. "Philosophical Criticism." Nation, 134: 407-8, April 6, 1932.

McCarthy, Mary. "Actors and the Critics." With reply by J. W. Krutch. Nation, 144: 536, 566-7, 573, May 8-15, 1937.

Miles, Carlton. "Provincial Critic." Theater Arts, 11: 199-202, March 1927.

Nathan, George Jean. "Credo in Recollection." American Mercury, 8: 372-4, July 1926.

_____. "Every Man His Own Critic." Newsweek, 14: 24, Aug. 21, 1939.

_____. "Theatrical Journalism." Newsweek, 12: 26, July 11,
1938.

Skinner, R. Dana. "On the Curious Art of Playgoing." Commonweal, 14: 130-1, June 3, 1931.

Woollcott, Alexander. "How a Critic Gets That Way." Collier's,
81: 12, Feb. 28, 1928.

Wyatt, E. V. "Critical Confidences." Catholic World, 126: 526-7,
Jan. 1928.

Young, Stark. "Tale of Critics." New Republic, 81: 106, Dec. 5,
1934.

ABOUT CRITICS

Brown, Ivor. "Dramatic Criticism: Is It Possible?" Theater Arts,
24: 803-7, Nov. 1940.

"Down With the Critics." Nation, 125: 671-2, Dec. 14, 1927.

"Dramatic Criticism: The Personal Equation." Theater Arts, 20:
129-34, Feb. 1936.

"Dramatic Critics Fight Shy." Literary Digest, 112: 19, March 19,
1932.

"Failing Plays and the Critics." Theater Arts, 25: 777-8, Nov.
1941.

"Is Brooks Atkinson a Literary Gunman?" Theater Arts, 19: 3-6,
Jan. 1935.

O'Casey, Sean. "Pontiffs of the Theatre." Fortnightly, 146: 411-7,
Oct. 1936.

"Profession Dying of Its Own Vices." Theater Arts, 14: 96-8, Feb.
1930.

"Seed-Bed for Dramatic Critics." Theater Arts, 21: 158-60, Feb.
1937.

"These Critics." Literary Digest, 94: 27, July 2, 1927.

"Three-In-One: the Ideal Critic." Theater Arts, 21: 478-82, June
1937.

"Wherein Dramatic Critics Are Blind." Literary Digest, 117: 23,
Feb. 24, 1934.

PERIODICAL ARTICLES, 1942-1951

BY CRITICS

Anderson, John.   "The Circle."   Theatre Annual, 1: 17-28, 1942.

Brown, John Mason.   " Concerning the Jukeses. "   Saturday Review
     of Literature, 29: 38-40, April 20, 1946.

_____. "Critical Stumbling Block. "   Saturday Review of Litera-
     ture, 28: 24-5, March 17, 1945.

Gibbs, Woolcott. "Two-in-One: The Reviewer Critic. "   New York-
     er, 18: 28, April 4, 1942.

Hutchens, John K.   "Third-Stringer. "   Saturday Review of Litera-
     ture, 28: 24-5, Sept. 1, 1945.

Isaacs, Edith.   "Critical Arena. "   Theater Arts, 26: 104-11, 191-6,
     257-65, 754-62, Feb. -April, Dec. 1942.

Kerr, Walter.   "Good Intentions. "   Commonweal, 54: 333-4, July
     13, 1951.

Nathan, George Jean.   "Case Against Critics. "   American Mercury,
     54: 203-8, Feb. 1942.

_____. "Clinical Notes on the Critical Art. "   American Mercury,
     59: 108-11, July 1944.

_____. "Personal Blueprint. "   American Mercury, 70: 414-19,
     April 1950.

_____. "Theater: A Critical Vocabulary. "   American Mercury,
     72: 607-10, May 1951.

Watts, Richard, Jr.   "Critics: Cheerleaders or Cranks?"   Satur-
     day Review of Literature, 31: 6, Sept. 25, 1948.

ABOUT CRITICS

"Agony on the Aisle. "   Life, 29: 59-60, Dec. 18, 1950.

Collins, Ralph L.   "The Playwright and the Press: Elmer Rice and
     His Critics. "   Theatre Annual, 7: 35-58, 1948.

"Critics Versus Playwrights. "   Life, 21: 49-50, Oct. 7, 1946.

"Failing Plays and the Critics. "   Theater Arts, 25: 777-8, Nov. 1941.

Gibbs, Woolcott. "Broadway Garland: Parodies of Dramatic Reviewers." New Yorker, 23: 33-6, Nov. 22, 1947.

Houseman, John. "Critics in the Aisle Seats." Harper's, 203: 16, 58-66, Oct. 1951.

Lewis, Robert. "Three-Way Critics: Professional, Amateur, College Performances." Theater Arts, 26: 451-52, July 1942.

"On Rising to Appreciation with Discrimination." Theater Arts, 30: 621-2, Nov. 1946.

White, E. B. "Drama Critics." New Yorker, 23: 78, March 1, 1947.

PERIODICAL ARTICLES, 1952-1961

BY CRITICS

Atkinson, Brooks. "Anatomy of Newspaper Criticism." Theater Arts, 44: 8-9, April 1960.

Bentley, Eric. "Do We Believe in Discussion?" New Republic, 135: 22, July 2, 1956.

Brustein, Robert. "Criticism and Journalism." New Republic, 144: 22-23, Jan. 23, 1961.

Calta, Louis. "One Man's Opinion Is Another Man's Poison." Theater Arts, 40: 65, April 1956.

Hawkins, William. "The Critic." Theatre Annual, 14: 19-27, 1956.

Kerr, Walter. "The Dictatorial New York Critics." Theatre Annual, 10: 20-27, 1952.

Krutch, Joseph Wood. "A Defense of the Professional Reviewer." Theatre Annual, 17: 68-75, 1960.

Young, Stark. "Art of Theater Criticism." Young-Harper's, 220: 26, March 1960.

ABOUT CRITICS

Brockett, Lenyth. "The Newspaperman as Critic." Educational Theatre Journal, 5: 240-246, Oct. 1953.

Crane, R. S. "Varieties of Dramatic Criticism." Tulane Drama

Review, 1: 22-38, 1955.

"Critics in the Act." Theater Arts, 37: 13, July 1953.

"Critic's Rights." Time, 63: 95, May 17, 1954.

Guiness, Alec. "Artist Views the Critics." Atlantic, 191: 51-5, March 1953.

Hecht, Ben. "Wistfully Yours." Theater Arts, 36: 12-13, July 1951.

Morehouse, Ward. "America's Dramatic Critics." Theater Arts, 40: 29 Sept.; 63 Oct.; 33 Nov. 1956; 41: 65 April; 75 June; 73 July; 25 Aug.; 55 Sept.; 33 Oct.; 76 Nov.; 78 Dec. 1957; 42: 56 Feb.; 71 March; 73 April; 47 July; 56 Aug.; 57 Sept. 1958; 43: 90-1 Dec. 1959.

"Seven on the Aisle." Time, 63: 44, March 1, 1954.

Spelvin, George (pseud.). "Criticizing the Critics: How to Be Really Helpful, or Second-Guessing at First Nights." Theater Arts, 45: 12-13, Feb. 1961.

_____. "Criticizing the Critics," cont. Theater Arts, 45: 16-17 July; 64-65 Nov. 1961; 47: 64-65 Jan. 1963.

_____. "Memoirs of a Snake-in-the-Grass." Theater Arts, 37: 22-3, April 1953.

_____. "Mr. Spelvin Criticizes the Critics." Theater Arts, 36: 32-3, Aug. 1952.

_____. "Mr. Spelvin Criticizes the Critics," cont. Theater Arts, 37: 72-3 May; 68-9 July 1958; 38: 70-1 Feb.; 25 March; 62-3 April; 77 May; 80-1 June; 81-2 Nov.; 79 Dec. 1954; 39: 28-9 Jan.; 59-60 Feb. 1955.

Tucci, Nicholai. "Observer Observed." Saturday Review, 44: 44, Oct. 7, 1961.

Wheelock, Dorothy. "Unsung Heroes: Second-Nighters." Theater Arts, 36: 46-7, April 1952.

PERIODICAL ARTICLES, 1962-1976

BY CRITICS

Brustein, Robert. "Where Are the Repertory Critics?" New Republic, 173: 23-5, Sept. 13, 1975.

Clurman, Harold. "Critic's Credo." Nation, 199: 120-2, 147-8,
      Sept. 14, 21, 1964.

_____. "Rave Notice as Menace." Nation, 219: 185-8, Sept. 7,
      1974.

Gilman, Richard. "Necessity for Destructive Criticism." Theater
      Arts, 46: 23-4, Sept. 1962.

Gussow, Mel. "Amiable Springboard." Newsweek, 70: 96, Dec.
      18, 1967.

Kronenberger, Louis. "Return to Civilian Life." Theater Arts,
      47: 14-15, Feb. 1963.

Richardson, Jack. "On Reviewing Plays." Commentary, 42: 79-
      82, Sept. 1966; 57: 71-3, April 1974.

Simon, John. "Once More unto the Breach." New York, 6: 60,
      July 30, 1973.

Stasio, Marilyn. "Nights the Critics Lost Their Cool." Ms., 4:
      37-8, Sept. 1975.

ABOUT CRITICS

Cooper, Albert. "Critic as Superstar." Newsweek, 82: 96-8, Dec.
      24, 1973.

"Critics, Critics, Critics." Newsweek, 59: 79, March 5, 1962.

"Divided Men on the Aisle: Review System Under Reform?" News-
      week, 67: 84, Jan. 17, 1966.

"Dear Kerr: You Sir!" Time, 88: 68, Sept. 9, 1966.

"Doctor in the House: Drama Critic Elliot Norton." Newsweek,
      65: 76, April 12, 1965.

"Enter Clive Barnes." Newsweek, 69: 109, March 20, 1967.

Hirsch, F. "Apostle to the Gentiles: John Lahr." Nation, 211:
      600-1, Dec. 7, 1970.

Kazin, Alfred. "Useful Critic." Atlantic, 216: 73-4, Dec. 1965.

"New Man on the Aisle: Stanley Kauffmann." Newsweek, 66: 92,
      Dec. 20, 1965.

"Reviewers." Newsweek, 74: 76, Aug. 11, 1969.

Shayon, Robert Louis. "Critics on the Critics: Harris Survey."
      Saturday Review, 53: 52-3, March 21, 1970.

Bibliography   xxxviii

"Two Hundred on the Aisle." Newsweek, 67: 92, Feb. 14, 1966.

"View from Women's Wear: Drama Critic Martin Gottfried." Time,
    86: 109-10, Nov. 5, 1965.

SPECIAL MATERIALS AVAILABLE
in the Theater Collection of
the Lincoln Center Library for the Performing Arts

SCRAPBOOKS

The Robinson Locke Collection of Dramatic Scrapbooks.   (Turn-of-
the-century clippings by and about critics.)

THESES AND PAPERS

Norton, Elliot. Puffers, Pundits, and Other Play Reviewers: A
    Short History of American Dramatic Criticism.   Text of paper
    read at first American College Theater Festival, Washington,
    D. C. , 1969.

Rothman, John.   The Origin and Development of Dramatic Criticism
    in the New York Times 1851-1880.   Master's thesis, New York
    University, 1949.

Taylor, Jo Beth Boyd.   The New York Drama Critics Circle; Its
    Activities, Procedures, and Achievements.   Thesis, East
    Texas State University, Athens, Texas, 1968.

PERIODICAL ISSUES Devoted to Theater Criticism

Kirby, Michael (ed.).   The Drama Review (New York University),
    vol. 18, no. 3, Sept. 1974.

Landesman, Rocco (ed.).   Yale/Theatre (Yale University), vol. 4,
    no. 2, spring 1973.

THE DIRECTORY

An alphabetical listing of
291 theater critics giving
biographical data and sample
reviews.

[1] WELLINGTON, Stanley Robinson; (2) Theater critic; (3) b. Cleveland, Feb. 22, 1921; (4) s. Walter and Louise (Robinson) W.; (5) B.A. Ohio State U., major subj.: journalism, 1943; (6) m. Anita Howland, Aug. 3, 1943; (7) children --Mary Ellen, Susan Louise; (8) News assistant, Lakewood (Ohio) Journal 1947-1951, Staff writer, Lakewood Journal 1951-1958, Drama critic, Lakewood Journal, 1959- (9) Apprentice: Warren (Ohio) Music Circus, summer 1938; Actor: Lakewood Comm. Theater, 1940, 1942; Acting associate: Great Lakes Shakespeare Festival, Lakewood, Ohio, summer, 1946; Prod. and dir. Emperor Jones, Karamu Playhouse, 1952; Lect., John Carroll Univ., 1966-1968; Cleveland State, 1970- ; (10) Mayor's Council for the Arts 1972-3; (11) Memb., Cleve. Dist. Park Bd., 1964-5; (12) Memb., Advisory Board for the Theater, Ohio State Arts Council 1970- ; (13) Cpl., U.S. Army, 1943-1945; (14) Cited for Service to the Theater by the Midwestern Theater Conference, 1971; (15) Memb., Nat'l Arts Club; (16) Republican; (17) Methodist; (18) Mason; (19) Shady Knoll Country Club (Cleve.); (20) Contrib. articles to Parade, Theatre Crafts, Encyclopaedia Britannica; "Highroad," a one-act play in Best Short Plays of 1965; author, Potluck, a TV drama series presented on WGBG (Cleve.), 1969; (21) 220 Bluff Hills Rd., Cleveland, O. 44188, Ph. 216-524-4387; (22) Lakewood Journal, 11 Main St., Cleveland, O. 44188, Ph. 216-751-5000; (23) Circulation: 100,000; (24) 50 plays and musicals, 50 motion pictures, 5 dance, 5 miscellaneous.

KEY TO NUMBERED ELEMENTS ABOVE

1 Name (numeral 1 excluded from actual entries)
2 Position
3 Vital statistics
4 Parents
5 Education and major area(s) of study
6 Marital status
7 Children
8 Career
9 Career-related activities, including any practical theater experience
10 Civil activities
11 Political activities
12 Non-professional directorship
13 Military record
14 Decorations and awards
15 Professional and other memberships
16 Political affiliation
17 Religion
18 Lodges
19 Clubs
20 Writings
21 Home address and telephone number
22 Office address and telephone number
23 Circulation and/or audience reached
24 Approximate number of reviews annually, in one or more of the arts

ABELS, Joel M., (2) Theater Critic and Editor and Publisher; (3) b. New York, April 6, 1926; (4) s. John and Florence (Abels); (5) B.S. Wharton School, University of Pennsylvania, major subj.: industrial engineering, 1947; (6) m. Lenore Lewis, March 7, 1948; (7) child--Nanette Linda; (8) Joined Travel Trade Publications in 1958 following brief career in industrial engineering and as reporter on several small trade publications; (10) member of President's National Tourism Resources Committee: Chairman, National Travel Committee for Regional Tour Development: Secretary, Larchmont Association of Presbyterian Men; (11) Chairman of Travel Industry Committee to Re-elect the President; (12) Director of Discover America Travel Organizations; (13) Sergeant U.S. Army 1944-1946: Awarded Bronze Star, Combat Infantry Medal, Arms of Colmar and four Battle Stars; (14) Gold Medal of Austria; Travel Writer of the Year Award: Discover America Award for Contribution to Domestic Tourism; (15) Member American Society of Travel Agents: SKAL: Bon Vivants: Discover American Travel Organizations; (16) Republican; (17) Presbyterian; (19) Capital Hill Club (Washington): Bankers Club (Miami): Rockefeller Center Club (New York); (20) Package Tour Handbook published by Discover America Data Institute: Weekly editorials in Travel Trade Publications: monthly feature articles in both Travel Trade and Discover America Publications; (21) 22 Normandy Lane, Woods of Larchmont, New York, 834-5515; (22) 605 Fifth Avenue, New York, New York 10017, 752-3233; (23) Circulation: 21,000 covering the entire U.S. travel industry; (24) 20 plays and musicals.

AFRICANO, Lillian Tabeek, (2) Critic and freelance editor-writer; (3) b. Paterson, N.J., June 7, 1935; (4) d. John and Nadwa (Gorab); (5) Douglass College, 1953-55, B.A. Barnard College, summa cum laude, special honors program, major subj.: history-political science, Columbia Univ. graduate school, 1957-58; (6) m. Arthur L. Africano, M.D., June 28, 1958; (7) children--David, Nina, Arthur; (8) Teacher: Union City (N.J.) public schools 1957-59, Drama Critic, The Villager 1969- , Theater Editor, The Villager 1973-75, Drama Critic, Asbury Park Press 1973- ; (9) News Editor, Feature Editor Caellian 1954-55; (10) Regional Director, National Sec'y W. A. to Student AMA; (14) Phi Beta Kappa, 1956; (15) Vice-President Drama Desk; (16) Democrat; (17) Catholic; (20) Cont. Articles to Worldview, Viva, Ms., Chicago Sun-Times Showcase, Christian Science Monitor, Boston Phoenix; (21) 45 W. 10th St., New York, N.Y. 10011, Ph. 212-475-4091; (22) Office, 45 W. 10th St., New York, N.Y. 10011, Ph. 212-475-4827; (23) Circulation: The Villager: 20,000, Asbury Park Press: 100,000; (24) 100 reviews, plays, films, miscellaneous.

"Kid Champion" Is No Knockout
(by Lillian Africano, The Villager, February 27, 1975)

"Kid Champion," Public Theater's newest production, has
a catchy title, a borderline hero and an occasionally ironic sense
of humor. It treats, with some uncertainty, and at great length,
the life and psyche of one Kid Champion, pop superstar and
Grade A brat.

Playwright Thomas Babe attempts an ambitious and episodic account of several transitional months in the Kid's
life. They take the singer through a series of emotional and
physical crises and demonstrate, for those who haven't heard,
that life at the top is lonely. Like any other rock star of
sterotype and legend, Kid Champion is a heavy user of drugs,
sex and money. None of these, however, eases the pains
of what seems to have been a conventionally deprived childhood and a terminal case of adolescence.

Since his problems are fairly routine, it is the talent and
success factor that endows the Kid with whatever appeal he has.
But aside from some random and predictable observations (like
the one which differentiates between the worship he gets and the
love he doesn't), the success phenomenon isn't really explored
in any new or engaging way.

Mr. Babe tries to probe and illuminate every facet of his
subject's personality; in doing so he inadvertently buries Kid's
flashes of humor and his antic behavioral irregularities under
some heavy overwriting. Director John Pasquin compounds the
feeling of excessive length by allowing the material to amble
along at a leisurely pace. His use of film projections doesn't
add much to the production, and when the projector malfunctions
(as it did one evening last week), the effect is particularly unfortunate.

Christopher Walken, a New York Shakespeare Festival regular, plays the superstar with overtones of Michael Moriarty, another N.Y.S.T. alumnus. He coils and uncoils his body in a
dazzling variety of poses, some of which suggest the presence
of a real human being. Mr. Babe hasn't given Walken the wher-
withal to go any further, meaning apparently to say that the Kid
is all surface glitter, unloved because he doesn't know how to
love.

David Margulies turns in a solid performance as Harvey,
the Manager. Christopher Allport, Matthew Cowles and Don
Scardino give good support as the Kid's back-up, even if their
dialogue is excessively devoted to words of one syllable. Kathryn Walker is meticulously glacial as the press agent who finally takes control of Kid Champion, and Kenneth McMillan is the
academic who studies and tries to love him.

Maybe Arthur Conan Doyle Is Trying to Tell Us Something
(by Lillian Africano, Chicago Sun-Times, January 8, 1975)

Some three quarters of a century after Sir Arthur Conan
Doyle sent him to his death in the churning waters of Reichenbach
Falls, a victim of the fiendishly clever Professor Moriarty,
Sherlock Holmes appears to be alive and well, enjoying his big-
gest revival in 40 years.

"Why now? According to Dr. Julian Wolff, commissioner
of the Baker Street irregulars--a group dedicated to puzzling over
and theorizing upon the Holmes stories--the current commercial
success of the saturnine detective comes out of some devilishly
clever timing, a little serendipity and the joint efforts of several
good press agents.

First, a world famous company like Britain's Royal Shakespeare Company launches a major revival of the play, "Sherlock
Holmes," on two continents. Currently it is being performed at
the Broadhurst Theater on Broadway. Then several of what the
publishing industry considers important books are given release
dates to coincide, and the advertising copywriters start announcing a revival. Before you know it, the revival is really on.
Reincarnations of Holmes and Dr. Watson appear on network television, selling a variety of products and theatrical producers begin scrambling for Holmes properties and big stars to play in
them.

Holmes has been giving profitable employment ever since the
day he was born; Conan Doyle often referred to his brainchild as
"my banking book." The play bears the strong mark of William
Gillette, the actor who made an entire career of it. Conan
Doyle, who had begun to tire of Holmes, gave the play over to
the actor with no artistic strings. Gillette altered the original
concept to create a stage character that would do justice to his
own professional abilities. He played Holmes for 36 years, beginning in New York in 1899 and ending, at 82, with a radio
broadcast in 1935. His farewell tour lasted three years instead
of one season, by popular demand, and Booth Tarkington wrote
of it: "I would rather see him play Sherlock Holmes than be a
child again on Christmas morning."

But it was Basil Rathbone who brought to life the magic of
Holmes for several generations of nonscholars. Sardonic, lean,
otherworldly in his nasal pronouncements, Rathbone found in Nigel
Bruce the perfect foil for his humorless intensity--a lovable,
bumbling, excessively human Dr. Watson. For many Holmes
fans, these two were the only possible representations of the
sleuthing team, although such great actors as John Gielgud
(Holmes) and Ralph Richardson (Watson) had a successful version
on radio. Representing an "official" point of view, Dr. Wolff
said of the Rathbone-Bruce duo: "The public simply got used
to an extraordinary counterfeit."

If the popular favorite gets a learned thumbs down, so does the Royal Shakespeare version, a hot Broadway ticket anyway. "Good theater, but not good Conan Doyle" has been the expert consensus. To a fan not absolutely committed to some ideal, however, the play is brilliantly staged and fascinatingly acted.

For the title-character and star, John Wood, it was Rathbone's image that affected his characterization as much as the scant direction left by Conan Doyle. "I feel that his shadow hangs over me," he says. "Basil Rathbone is the one to beat, not to give in to." Wood fits nicely the existing physical descriptions, as well as Sidney Paget's classic illustrations for the "Adventures" in Strand magazine: He is a tall, thin man with an aquiline nose. Wood's Holmes is giddy at times, morbid at others, balanced somewhere between the perfection of his deductive reveries and a distressingly untidy reality. He is cheerfully matter-of-fact about his drug habit, resigned to an early end, dying of boredom generated by his own infallibility and by his premature exhaustion of whatever surprises the world has to offer--barring, of course, romance, a part of this production though not of the original stories or of Rathbone's ascetic interpretation.

Wood's principal problem is the same weakness found in many revivals--the lack of a totally successfully idea for handling vintage material that people once took very seriously. Rathbone himself faced a similar problem when he tried, without much success, to revive his film self on the stage in 1953, seven years after his last cinematic adventure. He found that too much time had passed, that important ingredients had been altered. (Nigel Bruce was too ill to play Watson and the material, written by Ouida Rathbone, was not up to Conan Doyle's standards.)

A serious contribution to the current revival is the kind of scholarship found in Samuel Rosenberg's book, "Naked is the Best Disguise" (Bobbs Merrill, $8.95). It involves the kind of detective work officially approved by the Baker Street irregulars and concerns the secrets Conan Doyle concealed in his stories, a la Jacqueline Susann.

Using techniques he learned as a literary detective (spotting plagiarisms for Warner Brothers) Rosenberg does some delightful who's who-ing. Among his deductions. The infamous Professor Moriarty was none other than ... Friedrich Neitzsche! Conan Doyle, he says, was tired of Holmes, bored with writing about him, even though the tales were his principal means of financing the spiritualist explorations that cost him a fortune, as well as a peerage. He went to Switzerland with the idea of destroying Holmes, but without a specific villain in mind. Nietzsche, Rosenberg discovered, was staying at the same hotel near Reichenbach Falls. What better villain could there be than the notorious anti-Christ of Victorian society? Point by point, Rosenberg compares Moriarity's biography with Nietzsche's. Both were

university professors at 21; Nietzsche became syphilitic, while
Moriarty suffered from an inherited "blood taint"; both were
alienated from their particular societies, and so on.

Rosenberg picks out other recognizable personalities in the
stories--people with noticeable foibles, like Oscar Wilde and
George Sand. It took Rosenberg some 20 years to mull over his
discoveries and just one and a half years to write his book, confident that there would be the same kind of enthusiasm that
prompted Conan Doyle to resurrect Holmes 10 years after he
killed him (at a time when his funds were dwindling).

That kind of confidence seems well placed. Crowds of young
people have only recently turned out for a seminar on Holmes in
New York, some playing tapes of old radio broadcasts on port-
able machines. When asked why interest is so strong in a generation that wasn't even born when any of the great characterizations were being done, experts replied that Holmes satisfies
a longing for style, that he represents an appeal to logic at a
time when life seems increasingly illogical, that he represents
a sense of security in an age when it is rare to see something
through from beginning to end or, simply, that Holmes is a
gentleman.

And from Ken Saunders, a spiritualist author who says the
spirit of Conan Doyle has made numerous attempts to contact
him: "Who knows, perhaps it's he who is responsible for all
these books and revivals. Maybe he's trying to tell us something. "

ALBRECHT, Ernest Jacob, (2) Theater Critic; (3) b. Carteret, N.J.,
Nov. 6, 1937; (4) s. Emil and Helen (Weber) A.; (5) B.S. Rutgers
Univ., Educ. major: English and Theater, 1959; M.A. Northwestern
Univ., 1960; Post graduate work, Northwestern Univ., 1964-65; ma-
jor: theatre (6) m. Pearl Czere, Mar. 30, 1963; (7) children--Chris-
topher Ernest, Eric Jacob; (8) Theater Critic, New Brunswick (N.J.)
Home News, 1966- ; Asst. Professor, Middlesex County College,
Edison (N.J.), 1967- ; Teacher, East Brunswick (N.J.) High School,
1960-1966; (9) Director - approximately 65 productions of plays and
musicals at Parkway Playhouse, Burnsville (N.C.), Summer 1962 &
1963; Asst. Director, Cape May Playhouse, Cape May, N.J., 1964;
Director, Surflight Summer Theater, Beach Haven, N.J., 1964-1972;
Lakewood Musical Theater, Barnesville, Pa., 1967-68; Club Bene
Dinner Theater, Morgan, N.J., 1969-71; Producing Director, Plays-
in-the-Park for Middlesex County Parks and Recreation Dept., Edison, N.J., 1972- ; (10) Middlesex County Cultural & Heritage Comm.
1974-75; (15) Drama Desk; (16) Democrat; (20) Contributed articles
to N.J. Suburban Life, Theater Crafts magazines; (21) 43 Ainsworth
Ave., East Brunswick, N.J. 08816, Ph. 201-247-7923; (22) Office;
The Home News, New Brunswick, N.J., 08903; Ph. 201-246-5500;
Middlesex County College, Ph. 201-548-6000, ext. 421; Park Office,
Ph. 201-246-6900; (23) Circulation: 70,000 (24) 165 theater reviews.

"Skin of Our Teeth" Production Lacks Bite
(by Ernest Albrecht, Home News, September 10, 1975)

When Thornton Wilder's "The Skin of Our Teeth" first played
New York City and won the Pulitzer Prize in 1943, the theater
at which it played got a reputation among cab drivers as a spot
to pick up some early fares as audiences left during the first or
second intermissions. Since the play is about mankind's repeated
narrow escapes from extinction, acts two and three are pretty
much like act one, except for the particular catastrophe descending upon the Antrobus family.

Since man hasn't learned too much from his own history and
made this planet any more peaceful, it must have given Wilder
some ironic satisfaction to see those leaving his play early. They
got the message in act one, learned their lesson and were able
to exercise an option often seldom invoked. Long before Anthony
Newley, they were able to say "Stop the world I want to get off"
and do something meaningful about it.

My sympathies tend to lie with those audiences of 30 years
ago. "The Skin of Our Teeth" is a sometimes amusing, sometimes charmingly anachronistic, but essentially, for all its and
man's progress, static work.

Wilder must have understood the problematic nature of the
play's subject matter. He has created, as a kind of surrogate
voice for the audience's uneasiness, the character of Sabina, the
Antorbus's maid, who is besides that a spoof of the well-made
comedy, a sometimes stage manager, commentator and the eternal other woman.

It is the star part and to help her survive, Wilder has to
finagle with the Noah story a bit and get her on board the ark
as a kind of stowaway.

In this production, staged for the Kennedy Center in Washington by Jose Quintero, Elizabeth Ashley plays the role as the
sterotypical bubble-headed floozie, adding dash of what seems to
be a leftover from the Southern accent she used in "Cat On A
Hot Tin Roof." For the most part Miss Ashley reads her lines
as if she were pulling taffy. It is at first rather a charming
caricature, particularly since she makes no secret of her contempt for the play. Somewhere around the middle of the second
act, it gets to be a bit wearing and one must wonder if she hates
the part so much, why doesn't she say the lines a bit faster and
skip all the sighs, heavenward glances and elongated vowels of
the last syllable of every word she pronounces.

Alfred Drake is more successful in keeping his detachment
from becoming a distraction. He is a rather grand George Antrobus, with quite a bit of the matinee idol about his performances.

Martha Scott, on the other hand--and by the nature of her role as the perennial mother--plays Mrs. Antrobus with complete conviction. She does not stand aside of her character for the character is too absorbed in looking out after her children.

Charlotte Jones makes a good bit of the cameo role of fortune teller, although her performance does not seem to be up to the melodramatics and chilling theatrics the role could display.

This production of "The Skin of Our Teeth" may be appropos the Bicentennial interest in American playwrights and particularly one who felt so sure America and mankind would come out all right.

Well, the facts are not all in on that last point. As to the play itself, it just misses being a total bore by the skin of its own teeth.

O'Neill Play Refreshing Look at Bygone America
(by Ernest Albrecht, Home News, September 19, 1975)

In the tangled and tortured landscape of Eugene O'Neill's plays there is one sunny glen. "Ah, Wilderness" is the playwright's one effort at comedy, a valentine to his youth.

Set in a small Connecticut town on the Fourth of July, 1906, the play depicts the growing pains of an adolescent as he simultaneously discovers love and romantic poetry. Unlike most of the playwright's other works, this one is set in a stable home, with loving, secure parents.

There are, nonetheless, elements here that became central concerns in other more serious plays. Booze and low women, guilt and shame are not unknown even in the Miller home--but here they have a bittersweet quality that turned to pure bitterness elsewhere.
The revival of the play being presented by The Circle-in-the-Square has been mounted in association with the Long Wharf Theater, where the play was staged previously.

Arvin Brown has directed the production, emphasizing the nostalgic Americana of the piece. Firecrackers, patriotic favors, lobster dinners, antique colloquialism and period pop music give the production an air of attic rummaging.

The large cast is charmingly domestic, playing in a style as comfortable as an old slipper. Geraldine Fitzgerald is most appealing as the mother hen, amused and scandalized by the goings-on in her household. She manages the evening meal--with all its drunken disruptions, clumsy service and hilarity--with the grace and good nature of a queen on vacation.

Teresa Wright is somewhat restrained as the old maid Aunt

Lily, but the wound and waste is always apparent. And with William Swetland as Uncle Sid, she provides some of the evening's more emotional moments.

But essentially it is an evening of pleasantries, and amusement with the change in morals and manners. Richard, the middle son, has his first flirtation with unrequited love, loose women and liquor. He is lectured on morality, endures a father-and-son heart-to-heart talk, a hangover and an insipid girl friend.

Richard Backus portrays Richard with an emerging air of dignity and a flair for personal dramatics. It is a pleasing performance that avoids the excesses of gangling adolescence which could turn the role into a cloying caricature.

Paul Rudd is a nicely stuffed shirt as the elder son, Yale man whose new-found maturity and wisdom must be handled with great care.

And Ralph Drischell provides an amusing portrayal of the dour Puritan--as the girl friend's outraged father.

"Ah, Wilderness" may not rise to the heights of drama found in the rest of O'Neill's work, nor be as intensely engaging as his other family portraits, but it was never meant to be more passionate or heated than a front porch on a still summer's evening. One can almost hear the crickets chirping. Here all is as right with the world as anyone could ever hope for it to be. So we can only smile, sigh, sink into a deep easy chair, and relax with contented amusement.

ALBRIGHT, William Robert; (2) Theater/Music Critic; (3) b. San Diego; (4) s. Harvey L. and Velma (Schnase) A.; (5) B.A., U.C.L.A., major subj.: English Lit., 1967; (6) Single; (8) Theater/Music Critic, La Jolla (Cal.) Light and Journal 1969-1972, Music Critic, San Francisco Chronicle 1972-1973, Theater/Music Critic, Houston Post 1973- ; (9) Fellow, Rockefeller Foundation Project for the Training of Music Critics, 1971-1973, Fellow, Kennedy Center/Music Critics Association Music Critics Institute, Summer 1972, Fellow, Association of American Dance Companies Dance Critics Institute, Summer 1973, Actor/Board Member, New Heritage Theater, San Diego, 1971-72; (15) Mem. Music Critics Association, Dance Critics Association, American Theater Critics Association; (16) Democrat; (20) Program notes for various San Diego theater groups and for Houston Grand Opera, liner notes for London Records; (21) 1966 West McKinney, Houston, TX 77019, Ph. 713-526-0159; (22) Office: Houston Post, 4747 Southwest Freeway, Houston, TX 77001, Ph. 713-621-7000; (23) Circulation: 300,000; (24) 55 plays and musicals, 55 classical concerts, 20 films, 10 dance, 10 miscellaneous, 52 records (150-200 records total).

11 ALBRIGHT

"Tobacco Road"
(by William Albright, Houston Post, April 11, 1975)

An important aspect of most comedy is that the audience is
meant to feel superior to the characters onstage. This is certainly true in "Tobacco Road," which opened a five-week run at
the Alley Theater Thursday night.

Jack Kirkland's grimly comic 1933 play (based on Erskine
Caldwell's novel of the year before) holds up Jeeter Lester's
rural Georgia kith and kin and finds them wanting in solvency,
piety, humanity, fidelity, honesty, chastity, ambition and nearly
every other quality we, their "betters," take to be virtues.

The brutishness of the Lesters is almost childlike in its
lack of malice or remorse. If hate rather than poverty and
ignorance prompted Jeeter's starvation of his mother, or his
woundingly blunt remarks about his daughter Ellie May's hare-
lip, or his emotionless reaction to his wife's death, "Tobacco
Road" would horrify, not entertain.

As it is, we are able to laugh heartily (if at times uneasily
and guiltily) at the characters' ugly behavior.

The most captivating performance at Wednesday's preview
was the Dude of Rutherford Cravens. Energetically disrespect-
ful, Jeeter's youngest son was shrilly vivid and downright repulsive yet perversely winning. With so little to eat, one wonders
where Dude got all his abrasive drive.

In his Alley Debut, John Newton worked to play down Jeeter's sloth and communicate the heroism and nobility implied in
Jeeter's conviction that it is better to starve to death on the im-
provident land than to move to the city and a job in a mill. One
almost began to sympathize with a man who gets what he knows
he's asking for as Newton sought traces of warmth and strength
in Jeeter.

Lillian Evans played Ada Lester with a hardness bred by
years of deprivation and hopelessness. Clenched teeth and a
deep voice transmitted a strength hard to reconcile with her ac-
quiescence to Jeeter's worthlessness. But it made her selfless
death all the more moving.

As Sister Bessie, the joyously carnal woman preacher who
embodies the noisy religion that is the last refuge of down-and-
outers, Shirley Slater lacked the total, iron-lunged hokum of the
species. Inhibition certainly didn't weaken Mimi Carr's performance as the lusty Ellie May, however (her serpentine flirtation
with David Wurst's distraught Lov was spectacular).

William Trotman occasionally let excess creep in (Grandma
Lester was doubled over like a jackknife, the third act opened

with Jeeter urinating contentedly against his house). But his direction was aptly simple and direct, with the play's grimness
and laughter nicely fused.

Jonathan Duff's lighting cast ironically rosy dawns on Jack
Kenny's brilliantly detailed set of the Lester shack, and Barbara
C. Cox provided the scruffy costumes that rightly looked like they
came in at slightly under the record-holding (3,180 performances)
original production's costume budget of $12.

Marceau Says a Lot Without Talking
(by William Albright, Houston Post, January 30, 1975)

I have just returned from Marcel Marceau's "concert" in
Jones Hall. In the next several hundred words, I will try to describe the wonderful spell this superb artist cast without using any.

In the first part of the program, Marceau performed style
pantomimes. These usually demonstrate basic techniques of pantomimes such as walking, climbing stairs and the like. But
Wednesday, Marceau concentrated on situations involving either
just one person or, in "The Public Garden," a whole parkful of
characters.

Marceau became a latently artistic bill poster who hangs
posters with an eye for composition, a gambler with only a passing acquaintance with Lady Luck, the murderous Cain, a pickpocket whose nightmare gives him arms that streeeetch like
Plastic Man's and hands that multiply like nothing you ever saw,
and a woman wistfully recalling a lost love.

The last three numbers were brand-new, but not nearly so
effective as a familiar one, "The Public Garden." Taking the
air in Marceau's fantasy world, we meet sighing lovers, garru-
lous benchwarmers, stuffy clerics, mischievous children, and
even living statues. Delightful.

More serious but also more bewildering was "Contrasts,"
new to Houston. Here, Marceau juxtaposes military drill and
tango dancing, a factory and a party, a carnival midway and a
firing squad.

After intermission, Marceau treated the large audience to
his Bip pantomimes, peopled by a character as much his lovable
property as Chaplin's Tramp.

In "Bip as a China Salesman," he is fired for breaking a dish
and retaliates by smashing the entire inventory. He then becomes
"Bip the Matador" and, after several timid veronicas, follows the
coup de grace by milking his "bull."

Even better was "Bip Travels by Train," an extended litany
of mishaps aboard a train. After that came "Bip at a Society

Party," and even though I have seen it before, I hated to leave
to put this on paper.

The program will doubtless be different at his final performance Thursday night. But the performer will be the same, so
it's hard to go wrong.

ALTMAN, Peter, Alexander; (2) Theater Critic; (3) b. Washington,
D. C. , June 3, 1943; (4) s. Oscar L. and Alberta (Smith) A. ; (5) B. A.
University of California, Berkely, in English, 1963, M. A. University
of Pennsylvania in English, 1964, Other Study, Harvard, Georgetown,
Columbia, Urbino (Italy) Universities; (6) Single; (8) Minneapolis Star,
1966-75 (critic, 1966; columnist from 1968; arts editor from 1971);
Lecturer at University of Minnesota, 1965-75 (English); (9) Guthrie
Theater (Minneapolis) Literary Manager, 1971; (13) Army Reserve;
(14) Bush Fellowship, 1973, Fellow, National Endowment Dance Critic's Seminar, 1973, American Political Science Association Prize
for Reporting series, Twin Cities News; (15) Guild for Reviews;
(20) freelance writing commissions for Musical Newsletter, Philadelphia Inquirer, Houston Post, Minnesota Orchestra Program; Broadcast interview/series, KSJN-FM, Minneapolis, leader in symposium
on criticism; (22) Minneapolis Star, 425 Portland Place, Minneapolis,
Minn.   55415, Ph. 612-372-4380; (23) Circulation: 250,000; (24) approximately 160 reviews, 40 columns annually.

ANDERSON, George Walter; (2) Entertainment editor and drama critic; (3) b. Arnold, Pa. , Jan. 21, 1932; (4) s. Francis and Margaret
(Crytzer) A. ; (5) B. A. Duquesne University, major subj. : journalism, 1955; (6) m. Nancy Link, Nov. 11, 1961; (7) children--Scott
Elliott, Holly Kathleen; (8) general assignment reporter, New Kensington Daily Dispatch 1958-59; assistant city editor, Valley Daily
News, Tarentum, Pa. , 1960-69; part-time duties as drama critic
and entertainment columnist, Valley Daily News, 1960-69; drama critic
entertainment columnist, Pittsburgh Post-Gazette 1969-74; drama critic
and entertainment editor, Post-Gazette, 1974- ; (9) entertainment reports nine times weekly on WWSW radio, Pittsburgh, 1973- ; reviews
on WQED community television; critic on WTAE-TV, 1971; reviews
for the Pittsburgh Point, 1965; president Allegheny Valley Concert
Association, 1967-69; founder and president Allegheny Classic Film
Society, 1963-66; instructor in film Duquesne University, 1972-73;
instructor in film University of Pittsburgh, 1974; (10) member of
Allegheny County Fair Advisory Commission; (11) member of West-
moreland County Citizens for Johnson, 1964; (12) board of directors
Variety Club Tent No. 1; (13) Lieutenant, U. S. Army field artillery,
1955-57; (14) Golden Quill Award for best newspaper column 1962;
Keystone Press award for best column 1963; Variety Club Award for
outstanding entertainment critic, 1974; (16) Democrat; (19) Variety
Club, Pittsburgh; Pittsburgh Press Club; (20) instructional series
WQEX; (21) 440 Locust St. , Pittsburgh, Pa. 15218, Ph. 412-243-6543;
(22) Pittsburgh Post-Gazette, 50 Boulevard of the Allies, Pittsburgh,
Pa.   15222, Ph. 412-263-1577; (23) Circulation: 250,000; radio

audience, 150,000; (24) 100 movies; 25 plays; 15 concerts; 10 miscellaneous.

Osborne Drama Revived at Pitt
(by George Anderson, Pittsburgh Post-Gazette, May 30, 1975)

Nearly two decades of social and cultural upheaval have tended to soothe some of the abrasive qualities of John Osborne's "Look Back in Anger."

But it remains not only an engrossing drama in its own right, but one of the seminal theater works of our time. It is the progenitor of much of the important, often revolutionary drama of the 1960s and '70s.

The work is the final production of the University of Pittsburgh's three-play series of revolutionary dramas, and concludes a commendable season in which the theater tried to reach out to the community at large in order to fill partially the theater vacuum that has existed this year in our city.

We can salute the quality of Pitt's work and express gratitude for the scope of their vision in serving the public.

Under the sensitive direction of Richard Mennen, a fine production of Osborne's play has been mounted in the Stephen Foster Memorial.

The story of rebellious Jimmy Porter, lashing out articulately but futilely at the world around him, especially at those closest to him, is vividly realized by a well-cast group of actors.

William Wendt, although starting a bit uncertainly as the relentlessly cruel Jimmy, grew impressively in the part. His sarcasm is best in his quieter moments, but he always demonstrates genuine acting skill and an understanding of this large and difficult role.

Kate Young, as his abused wife who represents the fading class system of Britain and is, therefore, the target of Jimmy's hostility, is superb. With three sharply contrasting performances this past year--the title role in "Gigi," Sally Bowles in "Cabaret," the current Allison Porter--she establishes herself as one of Pittsburgh's best young actresses.

David Kuhn as the rather neuter friend of Jimmy and Allison, Polly Bolton as a woman whose presence becomes a catalyst for action in the Porters' one-room flat in the Midlands and Ronald Stanley Sopyla as Allison's old-school father are also praiseworthy.

Interestingly, in its plot "Look Back in Anger" has some of the character of a British rewrite of "A Streetcar Named Desire," although its story is resolved differently.

The emotional weight of its principal characters corresponds fascinatingly, however: Jimmy is a more articulate Stanley Kowalski; Allison is his pregnant Stella from a higher class of society; Polly intrudes like Blanche, although she goes to bed with him more willingly; friend Cliff is similar to the ineffectual Mitch.

But, "Look Back in Anger" stands on its own as a strong, if talky and slightly overlong drama that fully justifies revival, particularly when done as well as it is here.

<u>Pitt Studio Theater Offers Original Play</u>
(by George Anderson, Pittsburgh Post-Gazette, June 2, 1975)

One of the most adventurous theater programs in the city, especially noteworthy in this year in theatrical limbo, is that of the University of Pittsburgh's Studio Theater.

It offers a kind of workshop atmosphere for offbeat plays, complementing the three major productions of the University of Pittsburgh Theater.

Buried deep in the bowels of the Cathedral of Learning, two flights down from street level, the Studio Theater is currently housing a premiere of a drama by Shubert playwright Larry Myers, a doctoral candidate in the university's department of speech and theater arts.

The play is called "Hannah," and it bears the clear imprint of a gifted playwright.

Myers has a remarkable knack for writing bitchily comic dialogue in the vein of Edward Albee and Mart Crowley.

He also has an eclectic style that is eminently theatrical. One can easily visualize "Hannah" stunning audiences in a powerhouse production.

The present production only hints at the potential of the play, although it has a strong lusty performance in the title role.

Viewed within the limitations of a student production, however, there is still enough strength evident to make "Hannah" a promising work of a genuine if nascent talent.

The author describes the play as "a tragicomedy of the Broadway myth." It concerns a woman with every characteristic of a has-been but two: age and career.

Hannah is only 30 and she has never achieved even a fleeting moment of success in the theater.

The total professional and personal failure of her life has turned her into a foul-mouthed virago flailing out at everyone and everything around her.

Alone, she ranges from self-abuse to self-pity.

The characters in Hannah's life are a collection of emotional or physical cripples. They include a bisexual lover, a blind brother, a stultifying mother, a transvestite friend, a vacuous teenybopper--even a prospective roommate turns out to be a lesbian.

Myers shows the interest in castoffs and freaks that mark so many contemporary plays, particularly those abrasive modern dramas that Joseph Papp's company specializes in.

It is not surprising to learn that Myers has worked with Papp's favorite playwright, David Rabe. The brother in "Hannah" seems directly related to the younger son in "Sticks and Bones." A relationship also seems to exist with such other contemporary works as "Rosebloom" and "Mert and Phil."

Myers himself declares his work has been influenced by Vonnegut, Warhol, Godard and Artaud.

Certainly, he is a writer of his time, given to the kind of outrageous, irreverent humor that would have been unthinkable even just a few years ago.

Dramatically, there are weaknesses, notably a sort of religio-narcotic ritual by candlelight. Monologues that frequently interrupt the proceedings are sometimes distractingly ambiguous. Are they flashbacks or fantasies?

Myers' greatest success is with dialogue:

"You've got a face only Fellini could love."

"Wouldn't you know he'd be from some tacky state starting with a vowel?"

"We have nothing in common except a Zip code."

"You're one long Norcross greeting card."

"My nymphomania must be subsiding. I walked two blocks without seeing a single thing that interested me."

"I always suspected I was inclined to bisexuality. As a boy I read both the Hardy Boys and Nancy Drew."

Jocelyn Johnson is an uncompromising force in the title role. Her impressive performance would be even better had she someone equally strong to play against.

As it is, she's like Albee's Martha without a George.

Director Toby Beckwith and his technical crew acquit themselves well, especially with the elaborate slide projections used
throughout the play.

APIKIAN, Nevart; (2) Theater-movie critic, The Post-Standard, Syracuse, N.Y.; (3) b. New York City, April 4; (4) d. Minas and Satenik
(Serabian) Apikian; (5) B.A. Syracuse University, liberal arts-journa-
lism; (8) Reporter, city desk, The Post-Standard 1943. Theater-movie critic, 1953; (15) Member Women in Communications, Inc. , formerly Theta Sigma Phi; Central New York branch, National League
of American Pen Women; (16) Independent; (17) Armenian Apostolic
Church; (19) Syracuse Symphony Women's Guild associate member and
the Everson Museum; (21) 125 Parkway Drive, Syracuse, N.Y.
13207, Ph. 315-476-4326; (22) The Post-Standard, Clinton Square,
Syracuse, N.Y.   13201, Ph. 315-473-7931; (23) Circulation: 100,000;
(24) 30 to 35 plays and musicals a year; 55 films; 5 miscellaneous.

"Frustrated" Hedda Alive on City Stage
(by Nevart Apikian, Post-Standard, November 23, 1974)

Henrik Ibsen's "Hedda Gabler" reveals the ultimate frustrated
woman with her envy, boredom, glory in unrealistic romanticism
and finally her concern with "what people will say."

In the person of Sara Croft, she came alive on Syracuse
Stage at the Regent Experimental Theater last night to an opening night audience of 200--a full house.

This version, as adapted and directed by John Dillon, is
tightened up into three acts, with only one intermission to place
the emphasis even more sharply on Hedda, daughter of Gen. Gabler, and a woman obsessed with his pistols as toys.

The scene opens on the turn-of-the-century residence in the
Norwegian town of Christiana at the end of the 19th century.   Hed-
da has just returned from a six-month honeymoon in Europe with
George Tesman, research fellow in cultural history.

James Secrest, as Tesman, a "file and index" type who loves
his books, plays it affectionately with his Aunt Ju-Ju who raised
him and is absolutely infatuated with the beautiful Hedda.

A not-unexpected laugh comes from a Syracuse University-
oriented first-night audience at the line: "Headmasters don't
make the most amusing company," as Hedda complains of boredom with her husband she married to have a fine house and to
become a brilliant hostess.   She has the house but not the money
for a butler nor a horse to ride in style.

The return of her former companion, the brilliant Eilert

Loevborg with his well-received new book sets the scene for
Hedda's ultimate resolution of her life.

Virginia Kiser plays Mrs. Elvsted ... [and] is just right as
the woman who must take care of someone. Her obvious delight
when she learns that Hedda is pregnant is well done as is her outburst when Hedda makes fun of her new bonnet.

Anne Ives simply is Bertha, the Tesmans' maid, somewhat
in awe of her fashionable new mistress, Hedda.

Above all it is Sara Croft who must carry this play which
revolves about her impossible demands on living her life through
her husband's position in life.

Miss Croft displays the personality of Hedda beautifully. She
has the airs of a woman used to demanding and getting the best.
She will flirt--just so far. In burning the manuscript her frustration and jealousy flare up. Yet, for all her modern airs, she
is too concerned with the opinion of others to live her own life.
Smoking a cigarette is just an empty gesture. In the 20th century, she would be a prime subject for a psychiatrist's couch.

All this goes on in a hothouse atmosphere of a dwelling heavy
with dark furniture, palms and ferns, "smelling like a corsage
the morning after the ball." The stage looks as if the contorted,
twisted fern-like forms rising up to the lights are an extension
of the plants below, stifling Hedda, who yearns for freedom but
hasn't the courage to live it. As devised by David Chapman it's
an exciting set.

Meet Hedda at Syracuse Stage; she's a woman to remember.

Shaw's Wit, Honesty Given Life in "Arms"
(by Nevart Apikian, Post-Standard, February 15, 1975)

George Bernard Shaw's "Arms and the Man" goes down as
smoothly as chocolate creams--a favorite of the play's hero, the
famous Chocolate Soldier.

Syracuse Stage players last night, directed by Thomas Gruene-
wald, brought alive the wit of the famous playwright who delighted
in tearing away pretense to reveal true heroism, true station in
life and true love.

The audience, somewhat smaller than usual on opening night,
laughed heartily at the antics of the fine cast.

Robert Moberly as "the Man," the Chocolate Soldier, is a
standout whether trying to stand up after being awake for 48 hours
and in danger of being caught as an enemy soldier in a lady's
boudoir, or as a cleaned-up version, complete with medals, who
calmly recites his financial assets in a proposal of marriage.

He's a professional soldier, a romantic, a practical man who sees no sense in killing and above all, a "free citizen," which is Shaw's ideal. Moberly is excellent--a joy for theater-goers who enjoy a Shaw hero.

The young lady of the play, which takes place at her father's house in a Bulgarian town in 1885, is played by Eren Ozker. Although she sometimes overreacts and displays anger rather than merely pretending to sulk, she is charming in the role. Though she is engaged to a handsome, romantic soldier who leads a cavalry charge in the battle, she finds herself attracted to the old pro of a soldier--the Man--who carries chocolates instead of cartridges into battle.

The two servants in the family are the pert and spirited Louka, well acted by Kelly Wood, and the servile Nicola, brought to life by Merwin Goldsmith. He can offer a low bow, always deferring to his betters to help his own station in life.

Catherine Petkoff, who fancies herself a fine lady, is delightfully played by Patricia O'Connell, while her forthright husband, the major, is boldly played by Ben Kapen. His surprise is fine, following that clever bit of stage play when Raina "rescues" her autographed picture.

Richard Yarnell is the handsome Major Saranoff as he glories in never saying he's sorry or twisting around comically to write his name with a hand more accustomed to the sword. It's an engaging portrait of the handsome hero.

David Kagen rounds out the cast of the very military Russian soldier.

Settings by David Chapman reach to the height of the Regent Experimental Theater stage. A wire sculpture of a cavalry charge serves as backdrop for bedroom, garden and library.

I would have preferred keeping the proscenium arch from the previous drama for this comedy, using a mountain backdrop, more naturalistic, as Shaw described. Four walls would have given it that box feeling.

Shaw fans, and I am one, can look forward to good ensemble playing and a great showcase here for his witticisms. It's another in the string of outstanding hits from our professional theater, Syracuse Stage, and will be playing through March 8.

APTER, Andrew William; (2) Theater critic; (3) b. New York City, June 20, 1947; (4) s. Samuel L. and Marilyn (Silverman); (5) B.A. Tufts U., English, 1969; M.A. Indiana U., 1972, Theatre & Drama; Ph.D. Cand. 1974, Indiana U., Theatre and Drama & American Studies; (6) Single; (8) Drama critic, Bloomington Herald-Telephone,

1973- ; Associate Instructor, Department of Theatre and Drama,
Indiana University 1972-1975; (9) Actor, Tufts U., Harvard U., In-
diana U., Brown County Playhouse; Director, Tufts U., Indiana U.,
Community Theatre, Ice House Theatre (Hannibal, Mo.); (14) Critic
Fellow, Eugene O'Neill Memorial Theater Center, 1974; (21) 1516
Dorchester Dr. #1, Bloomington, Ind. 47401, Ph. 812-336-6738;
(22) Bloomington Herald-Telephone, 1900 S. Walnut St., Bloomington,
Ind. 47401, Ph. 812-332-4401; (23) Circulation: 25,000; (24) 50 plays
and musicals, 6 opera, 6 dance.

Play Strindberg
(by Andrew Apter, Bloomington Herald-Telephone, October 4, 1974)

Staging a play in T-300 is precarious. If the countless obstacles and limitations of that performance space atop the IU
Theatre & Drama building can be met, it can offer rare theatre
experiences.

"Play Strindberg" is just such a unique experience. A team
of three actors under the sure direction of David Lloyd Chambers
transforms the tiny black room into a rich theatrical world.

The basic idea of Friedrich Duerrenmatt's ninety minute
"choreography" suggests the ponderousness that too often under-
cuts the powerful vision of this most notable contemporary dramatist.

In this case, Duerrenmatt draws directly from the material
of dramatic literature's all-time great misogynist, his inspiration
being August Strindberg's "The Dance of Death." Strindberg's
is a tragedy of out and out warfare. The battle is pitched on
the marital front.

What Duerrenmatt derives, happily, is a play that is eclectic
without being an intellectual exercise. Marvelous epigrams and
a distinctively unStrindbergian objectivity color the play's probing
of human insufficiency and failure.

The situation in "Play Strindberg" is simple, what one would
expect from a three character play. Edgar and Alice have been
married for 25 years. Into their life comes Alice's cousin Kurt,
to whom she has long been attracted.

To offset the typical, Duerrenmatt organizes his play into
rounds. No ordinary fray is this. "Play Strindberg" goes the
full fifteen, the great heavyweight championship of the world.

Director Chambers attacks this unusual stylistic framework
courageously. In the opening round Edgar and Alice strike with
a flurry of verbal jabs. The haymakers are rightly held in reserve. The final rounds are exhausted pawings.

Edgar and Alice are machine-like in their encounters. After

all, they've been at it for a quarter of a century. In one brilliant sequence, typical of the production's admirable execution,
the couple hisses a slur simultaneously. They know it by rote.

To contrast, Kurt is casual to the point of exasperation.
He assures us that we are allowed to laugh. In the laughter the
play is all the more tragic. Alice's contempt finally reduces
Edgar to a vegetable. Now she can love him.

The performances of P. Bradley Armacost (P. Bradley Armacost?), Nerrida King and Patrick Young are superlative, particularly notable in their handling of the play's difficult style.
Armacost's transformation of the original play's dance of death
into a fiendish jig is beautifully true to the tone of the production.

As the wife, King is impeccably icy, a neat complement to
Young's noncommital goo in the role of Kurt. For once the diction is flawless, the action wedded to the word.

Excluding Sunday, this bout will be re-enacted every night
through Wednesday. And you don't have to fly to Zaire to see it.

Edward II
(by Andrew Apter, Bloomington Herald-Telephone, October 12, 1974)

Men who make history long for the freedom to answer only
to themselves. Those in the private sector futilely endeavor to
make their mark in history.

Such are the concluding images of two first-rate productions
given at the IU Auditorium by the City Center Acting Company.
In Christopher Marlowe's "Edward II" an entire social order is
demolished because a monarch selects to satisfy his passions
rather than be politic. In Anton Chekhov's "The Three Sisters"
an engulfing void gapes before people who are desperate to justify the value of their existence.

The two plays also bring forth two conflicting but equally
devastating visions of time. Marlowe's play digests 25 years of
English history into one, which in turn is boiled down to 150
minutes of stage time.

The compacted time forbids introspection. Everything is immediate, life is to be burned up. It is as if Edward's life was
passing before him in a furious flurry of painful remembrances.

Director Ellis Rabb has not merely staged the Marlowe drama.
The production is carefully orchestrated, finely choreographed.
Like the warring factions in the play, the audience is allowed no
time to ponder.

Instead, it is pummeled with a barrage of visual and aural
stimuli. The loose gowns and open gestures of Edward and his

marble sculpture-male lover Gaveston intertwine with their cruel deaths, by disembowelment and castration respectively.

These horrors have other counterpoints. The Elder Mortimer, as he observes on Edward's behalf that "The mightiest of kings have had their minions" is underscored with an atypical dose of harmony from Bob James' music. The final curtain call itself was an elegant combination of music and dance which still emphasized a world too fast-paced, distinctively out of breath.

Chekhov's world is completely opposite. Since time hangs so heavily there is all the more opportunity to consider the pathos of his characters.

"The Three Sisters" is exquisite and saddening beyond expression. Aspirations are undercut continually by the reality of the moment, a reality no one is competent to grasp. Inappropriate couples find themselves wed. Others seek work to fight boredom, then discover they are too exhausted to live.

Boris Tumarin's direction is respectful of the play's idiosyncratic humor, rendering the all-prevailing emptiness all the more poignant. In one instance, however, a major decision backfired.

Tumarin elected to play against the reticence and quiet appeal of Tusenbach. Norman Snow in this role was obnoxious rather than clumsy. The lamentable result was the utter failure of Tusenbach's farewell scene with Irina which lacked the muted desperation of his tragic life.

The degree of disappointment this scene engendered is magnified because, as they have proven in the past, the CCAC is as fine a company as one could hope to see. Again this year they brought to the IU Auditorium an expertise and a professionalism true to the best purposes of the theatre.

ATKINSON, Justin Brooks; (2) Retired journalist; (3) b. Melrose, Mass., Nov. 28, 1894; (4) s. Jonathan Henry and Garafelia Atkinson; (5) B.A. Harvard, 1917, English major; (6) m. Oriana Torrey, Aug. 18, 1926; (8) Reporter, Springfield Daily News, 1917; English instructor at Dartmouth, 1917-18; U.S. Army, Development Battalion, 1918; Reporter and assistant to drama critic of the Boston Evening Transcript, 1918-19; Associate editor Harvard Alumni Bulletin, 1919-1922, also continuing as assistant to drama critic of the Transcript; Editor Book Review, New York Times, 1922; Drama critic New York Times, 1925-1942; War correspondent, China, 1942-1944; News correspondent for the Times in Moscow, 1925-26. Resumed drama critic of the Times, 1946-1960; Writer of Critic at Large column, New York Times, 1960-1965; Retired 1965; (14) Received Pulitzer Price, 1948; Honorary degrees from Williams, Clark, Dartmouth, Washington,

Adelphi, Long Island University, Franklin and Marshall, Pace; (15)
Member The Players, American Academy of Arts and Science;
P. E. N. , Critics Circle; (20) Author: Skyline Promenade, 1925;
Henry Thoreau, the Cosmic Yankee, 1927; East of the Hudson, 1933;
The Cingalese Prince, 1935; Broadway Scrapbook, 1947; Once Around
the Sun, 1951; Tuesdays and Fridays, 1963; Brief Chronicles, 1966;
Broadway, 1970; This Bright Land, 1972; The Lively Years (with Al
Hirschfeld), 1973; (21) Durham, N. Y. 12422.

New O'Neill Aspects: Recent Developments in the Art of a Native
              Playwright--Producing in Orchestrated Form
          (by J. Brooks Atkinson, New York Times, December 20, 1925)
                         [His first review]

        Nothing has been more apparent in the plays of Eugene
O'Neill during the past year or two than his withdrawal from what
the pundits call "the contemporary scene" and his preoccupation
with his own states of mind. "Welded," "All God's Chillun Got
Wings" and "Desire Under the Elms," coming after the productions of "The Emperor Jones," "Anna Christie" and "The Hairy
Ape," are Mr. O'Neill at war with shadows, his own shadow in
many respects; and they are Mr. O'Neill none too intelligible for
his audiences. His technique has grown looser and has begun to
lean over more heavily upon the scene designer for the projection
of recondite themes. And now comes "The Fountain," written in
1921, an evening of pageantry, badly proportioned, diffuse and
wearisome, despite the poetic beauty of its conception. With a
gentle thrust at his former critics, Mr. O'Neill swears that this
is not "morbid realism. " In two of the three acts neither is it
drama.

        Ever since the production of "Beyond the Horizon," in 1920,
Mr. O'Neill has been increasingly acclaimed in extravagant pane-
gyrics as the most promising of the younger dramatists, as the
greatest of the young American dramatists, or even as the greatest American dramatist with no further reservation. Such praise
is not mere flattery: Mr. O'Neill's equipment for the writing of
drama is quite extraordinary. In discussions of the superlative
in drama the convention is to draw comparison with the Greek
tragedies, the works of poets concerned with universal principles.
If Mr. O'Neill's choice of subject-matter does not bear up well
under that examination, the treatment of his material does. For
Mr. O'Neill is also a poet at heart, and he has that rarest genius for interpreting characters as symbols. In "The Hairy Ape"
Yank is no less a character in his own right because he speaks
for an entire social group or for all mankind at times; the major
persons in "Anna Christie" likewise interpret universal points of
view while they are speaking for themselves in the play. Mr.
O'Neill's dramas, moreover, throb with emotion. For certain
types of people Mr. O'Neill displays the keenest sympathy and
understanding; and his treatment of them in drama illuminates
their hopes and despairs beyond anything seen on our stages. To
limit his achievement in this respect to the pungency of charac-

terization in "S. S. Glencairn" would be to underestimate the emotional force, the sensitiveness and the translucence that may be discovered in various degrees in all of his plays.

Even in "The Fountain" Mr. O'Neill deals profusely in poetry. Here, again, his sympathy for mankind colors his dialogue and shapes the course of his play. Ponce de Leon seeking the spring of eternal life, to renew his youth and recover the freshness of life itself, represents Mr. O'Neill's most common thesis. For, like Robert in "Beyond the Horizon," Ella in "Different" and Anna Christie herself, Ponce de Leon has a vision of beauty and is eager to defeat life, to pass through the gloomy barriers that separate mortal existence from happiness. By many signs this sort of romance fits Mr. O'Neill's genius. In the program note, in which the author disclaims any pretense at historical accuracy, he declares he "has sought more to express the urging spirit of that period." In many respects "the urging spirit" of life generally to fulfill its destiny, to throw off the fetters of arbitrary circumstances, to live hard and deep, facing the sources of human existence--in many respects this "urging spirit" motivates the characters in all the O'Neill plays. The "morbid realism" so often ascribed to them indicates the author's preoccupation with the immediate fetters rather than the sweetness of life "beyond the horizon."

Part of the essential equipment of the poet and dramatist is simple expression. Teeming with the emotions and beliefs that are within himself, he must break through to the audience and set them vibrating at the same intensity. Those who believe that Mr. O'Neill has something fine to say are eager to understand him. And the fluidity of his technique often becomes the channel through which he pours out his emotional philosophy completely. The technical construction of "The Emperor Jones," for instance, is the perfect expression of that psychological theme. But despite the sympathetic embellishments of the scene designer, "The Fountain" does not transport the audience to the dramatist's plane. Six preliminary scenes weave the medieval beauties of those times into a tapestry of all the theatre's arts, and consume fully two-thirds of the play. Five much briefer scenes record Ponce de Leon's foreordained failure and record the playwright's supposed meaning: "There is no gold but love; no heaven but youth." Each one of the scenes, moreover, by virtue of its imagination, the poetic quality of the dialogue and the scenic investiture, reveals its own particular beauty.

But except for one or two group scenes and an eerie scene in which Mr. Jones has blended lighting and screening in a luminous stage picture, "The Fountain" rarely stirs the emotions or gives spur to the imagination. No dominant emotion binds the fragments of the play into an entity. Instead of trimming his play of non-essentials, Mr. O'Neill has rather filled it with a profusion of irrelevant ornaments that clog the action and imprison the meaning. The tendency toward prolixity and arbi-

trariness apparent in "All God's Chillun Got Wings" and "Desire
Under the Elms" has quite overwhelmed this drama, written at
an earlier period. In fact, the austere self-criticism that has
prompted Mr. O'Neill to destroy sixteen of his dramas as un-
worthy of production has in this instance indulged him too freely.
He seems to have ignored the audiences he has sought to instruct
before.   And the distinction of "The Fountain" is not of the script
but of the scene designer.

The records of the past year or two confirm the opinion that
Mr. O'Neill's best work is the "morbid realism" distasteful to
many playgoers who take their plays literally, but precious in
the American theatre none the less.   When he writes of the riff-
raff of the sea or the provincial people of the coast, he writes
of what he knows, with a robust elemental strength unmatched
by any native playwright.   Dialogue, characterization and humor
blend as themes and movements in a symphony.   And always
there is some equally elemental force shaping the course of the
drama.   In "Anna Christie," old Chris Christopherson speaks
the final words: "Fog, fog, fog, all bloody time.   You can't
see vhere you vas going, no.   Only dat ole davil, sea--she
knows!"   In that play Mr. O'Neill succeeded in his symbolic
character interpretation, and his audiences understood him.

Producing as a Fine Art.
No sooner had the Moscow Art Theatre Musical Studio revealed
the classic beauties of orchestrated acting on Monday evening in
a superb production of "Lysistrata," than our own Neighborhood
Playhouse, in a remote corner of the east side, applied similar
principles to a performance of "The Dybbuk" on Tuesday.   According to their respective degrees, both productions resolve the
multiplicities of stage art into a single instrument upon which
the conductor may play the stops as an individual and supply uniform expression.   In "Lysistrata" group emotions rise and fall
throughout the performance as though the players and choruses
were an individual responding to an idea.   In "The Dybbuk" group
emotions pass through similar modulations; but instead of an idea
they express the soul of a people--superstition, reverence, fear,
joy and the supernatural.

Among the Philistines, the acclaim of foreign actors, when
they set up their paraphernalia in this country, is put down as a
species of artistic snobbery, reflecting superior attitude toward
native players.   Sometimes that comes close to the truth; sometimes the foreigners patronize us with arrogance and feminine
duplicity.   But the Moscow company has developed the art of
group production beyond any group in this country.   To see them
in "Lysistrata" is to be convinced.   Scenery, individual and choral acting become an entity, and the beauty of the production
transcends the actual expression of the play.   As the supreme
transcendentalist of this country, Emerson makes that point in
an exalted passage: "The artist who is to produce a work which
is to be admired, not by his friends or his townspeople or his

contemporaries but by all men, and which is to be more beautiful to the eye in proportion to its culture, must disindividualize
himself, and be a man of no party, and no manner, and no age,
but one through whom the soul of all men circulates, as the common air through his lungs. He must work in the spirit in which
we conceive a prophet to speak, or an angel of the Lord to act:
that is, he is not to speak his own words or to do his own works,
or think his own thoughts, but is to be an organ through which the
universal mind acts." Applying that definition to the Moscovians
does not overestimate their abilities. For it is the essence of
all the theatrical arts.

Now, another critical snobbery, often bruited about to the
disgust of the layman, is the ostentatious talk of rhythms. No
one has difficulty in recognizing the rhythms of music and poetry,
dividing the phrases into units. Even prose develops an audible
rhythm and constitutes in large measure the writer's style. But
what of the rhythms of painting, sculpture and architecture; and
what of the rhythms of acting? Here we tread the quicksands of
intellectual definition, or stand in the position of carrying theories
forcibly into practice, of inductive reasoning. But the incredulous ones who, in this respect at least, come blatantly from
Missouri, will discover the rhythms of acting for themselves in
the Moscovian productions. Inasmuch as these players speak in
the Russian language, the ordinary playgoer will find his attention more concerned with the form of the performance as a whole
than with the individual lines. And he will discover that the performance expresses shape, color and eloquence quite apart from
the verbal detail of the play, and that all these qualities flow in
rhythm.

The comparison of the Moscovians with the Neighborhood
Players becomes most interesting in the matter of choral acting.
Aristophanes's comedy provides for the conventional chorus of
Greek drama to echo the dramatic idea and to give it vocal substance. And the Moscovians have restored to it its use as an
integral part of the comedy. "The Dybbuk," however, a modern
drama first produced after the war, has no specific chorus, but
the beggars, wedding guests, minyan and followers perform a
similar function. Directed by a Russian in association with Alice
Lewisohn, they serve the purpose of chorus admirably.

The nature of Ansky's drama leads itself to that sort of
dramatic treatment. A program note by Henry G. Alsberg explains the theme of this play: "In Ansky had grown up a great
yearning to show the ghetto as it existed up to the last quarter
of the nineteenth century, from its best, its spiritual aide.
The kernel of this existence lay in their religious life, their belief in the absolute reality of everything written in the Bible and
the Talmud, and even their belief in the derived superstitions,
in the great wonder-rabbis, who could do 'miracles,' conjure
up the great 'antagonist' with a spell, and create golems, and
even revive the dead. The charm of all this and its sweetness

and sacredness Ansky wished to transmit to future generations
before they should be wiped out by onmoving Marxism and the
'materialistic interpretation of history'."

To set off this folklore portrait a thread of story runs through
the play concerning a departed spirit that enters into the body
of a maiden, controls her actions and speaks through her lips.
At length the Tsadik, or Holy Man of Chassidism, communicates
with the spirit beyond this world and by incantation casts him
out of the maiden's body.   Thus "The Dybbuk" runs away from
reality into the hush of mysticism, with omens, portents, rituals
and symbols.   The professional prayer men intoning chassidic
chants or dancing, like whirling dervishes; the wedding guests
dancing exotic, traditional steps, claiming the honor of turning
the bride around, and threatening her when she resists; the minyan with Rabbi Aesrael communicating with the world beyond--
all invoke in choral form the folk emotion of the play.   Admirably directed, they too, create a rhythm for the performance
modulating the key according to the course of the play, moving
at times in unison to express mass emotion.

After such performances the "Star" system seems a mere-
tricious thing indeed.   For the ordinary balderdash of the stage,
the "star" of course supplies the personal element that appeals
to undiscriminating theatregoers.   The apotheosis of the stage
art, however, is the coordination of play, setting and acting into a form as unified and as vibrant as a Manet canvas or a Beethoven symphony.   Incidentally Eugene O'Neill's plays, discussed
at the head of this article, require the same orchestrated expression.

<u>Theatre: "Romeo and Juliet" in Canada</u>
(by J. Brooks Atkinson, New York Times, July 1, 1960)
[His last review]

Since Julie Harris has a unique personality, it follows that
her Juliet is unique.   During three and a half centuries, the part
may have been played as modestly as she plays it, but certainly
not in the last quarter of a century.

As performed last evening in the Festival Playhouse, her
Juliet is fragile and infinitely touching.   Although the scale is
diminutive, the workmanship is dainty like the design in a piece
of old jewelry or on an ancient vase.   Most of us are happily
familiar with Miss Harris' carefully modeled portraits in other
parts, the softness of the lines balanced by the resolution of
spirit.

Now she has brought the same magic to a part that is commonly played with torrid passion.   Her Juliet is a defenseless
child who lives in an aura of stillness, her raptures shy, her
anguish poignant.   Although the character is young, Miss Harris'
acting has the maturity of an artist who knows how to express

the elusive emotions of an imagined maiden.

Everything in the production blends with her characterization. This is Michael Langham's most sensitive and resolved piece of direction. Although his attention to detail is meticulous, his command of the story is firm and knowing. He holds it off at a distance, like a rare and beautiful legend out of the past and far away, a source of wonder and pity in modern times.

Like Juliet, the Romeo of Bruno Gerussi is young and defenseless. Love does not fill him with ecstasy. A reserved, distrait youth, he is caught up in a wild passion he does not understand. It precipitates him into situations that he cannot control.

He is in a daze of horror when Tybalt and Mercutio draw their swords. Although his instincts are good in the emergency, his response to them is fatal. When he is banished he cannot cope with the consequences. When he makes his way by night to Juliet's tomb and kills Paris in the darkness, he is a bewildered youth lost in a maze of grief and blind devotion. Mr. Gerussi is an excellent actor. Unlike Romeo, he knows what he is doing and has the perception and technique to do it. His Romeo provides the perfect counterpart to Miss Harris' Juliet.

Not that this is a mournful "Romeo and Juliet." Christopher Plummer's swaggering, witty Mercutio is an exciting person, gallantly humorous when he staggers off the stage after Tybalt has wounded him. Douglas Rain's implacable Tybalt--contemptuous and hot-headed but well-mannered--drives through the play as recklessly as his rapier. Kate Reid's coarse, clumsy, leering, warm-hearted nurse is original and funny. The Capulet by Jack Creley, the Prince by Robert Goodier, the Paris by Leo Ciceri, the Montague by John Vernon are vigorous characerizations.

But the distinction of this "Romeo and Juliet" is the uniformity of style adhered to by an excellent company that respects the minor parts as well as the big ones, and applies to each the same taste and skill. In Tanya Moiseiwitsch's vivid costumes that convey by color and design the rhythms of the drama, the actors provide a "Romeo and Juliet" that is unusual and illuminating. Fulfilling the promise of the prologue, it compassionately records the fearful passage of a death-marked love.

BACON, Ed. , Ledger-Star, Norfolk, Va. 23501.

BANNON, Anthony L. , (2) Critic; (3) b. Hanover, N.H. , Dec. 6, 1942; (4) s. Robert E. and Frances A. B.; (5) B.S. St. Bonaventure U. , major subject: biology, 1964; M.A.H. , State University of New York at Buffalo, 1975, major field: film and criticism; (6) m. Susan J.

Clark, Sept. 14, 1974; (7) children--Nicholas, Brendan (by previous
marriage); (8) Teacher, Father Baker H.S., Lackawanna, N.Y.,
1964-66; apprentice critic and general assignment reporter, Buffalo
Evening News, 1966-69; staff critic, Buffalo Evening News, 1969- ;
(9) Independent film and video artist, commissions for Buffalo area
television in documentary and experimental works, 11 titles; lecture-
showings and workshops in film, video and criticism; critic fellow,
Eugene O'Neill Memorial Theater Foundation, 1969; writing instructor, Calasanctius Preparatory School for Mentally Gifted Children,
1968; section leader, Buffalo Black Journalism Workshop, 1970;
Allentown Arts Lab; film teacher, 1971; director, film studies, New
School of Performing Arts, 1972-74; consultant, Allentown Community
Center film series, 1974; (10) Member, SUNY/Buffalo Select Commit-
tee on the Media, 1969; (14) Western New York unit, The Newspaper
Guild, Page One awards for feature writing, 1968, 70, 71; Page One
award for opinion writing, 1971; Best feature story, American Asso-
ciation of Commerce Publications, 1970; Bunis award for best Western
New York magazine article, 1972; member, American Seminar in
Film, 1974-75; (15) Chairman, education committee, Greater Buffalo
Press, Radio and Television Association, 1969; member, Sigma Delta
Chi; (16) Democrat; (20) Cont. articles to more than 20 national publications, including The Writer, Presbyterian Life; author, The Personal Film, Niagara University's Film Repertory Center Film Study
Guide; (21) 408 Ashland Ave., Buffalo, N.Y. 14222; Ph. 716-886-
1303; (22) Buffalo Evening News, One News Plaza, Buffalo, N.Y.
14240; (23) Circulation: 270,000 M-F, 300,000 S.; (24) 25 plays, 60
motion pictures and video, 25 still photography, 6 dance, 10 pop music, 50 news and feature stories on the arts.

Julie: Powerful, Painful Theater
(by Anthony Bannon, Buffalo Evening News, October 18, 1974)

Strindberg is stripped of the cover of polite, 19th Century
language, and his play, "Miss Julie," exposed.

Thought raw in 1888 for its rugged treatment of sexual and
social material, the play, since then has been immunized by the slogan, "Battle of the sexes."

But the Paris Theater Project, directed by former Buffalo
actor Thom Sokolski, has unmasked the work of the Swedish dramatist, pared its words, added the tension of violent physicality
and made the play hard to look at again. They call the adaptation "Julie" and perform it in the American Contemporary Theater at 11:30 PM this week-end and next.

The play is tough because it tackles taboo without flinching.
Society, and its individuals, quickly cover the threat of destruction by the animal within, and only artists, and rare men of the
mind such as Freud and Reich, dare to venture.

Sokolski's work deals with two people, an aristocratic woman
and her family's male servant, who cannot accept themselves,

both shamed by their position, both using the other to change their
state and free their repression.

Contemporary Freudians have suggested repression is a
denial of the body and an assent to death over life--the death
wish.   Sexuality, it has been argued, may either be the vehicle
to bodily recognition or a weapon in its destruction.

For Strindberg, who precursed these notions by nearly half
a century, and more poignantly for Sokolski, sex, believed by
the characters to be a tool for change, becomes rather a vehicle
for violence and death.   And that, by normative standards, is a
profound taboo.

Sokolski's theater then, is one of cruelty, which seeks by
its savage assaults, to cleanse like classic tragedy.

Thus, the play is less to honor Strindberg, than it is to respect his idea.

The set, instead of Strindberg's naturalism, is void of that
pretense, now the domain of film.   The performance area here
is lit by a single bare bulb and equipped with the props of bond-
age: a knife, boots and birdcage, and a chair and glass.   The
walls are bare.

The language, mostly though not exclusively Strindgerg, is
delivered in chant, song, natural rhythms, superimposed and non-
verbal structures.

The performance is attentive to movement and to design.   It
is at once highly stylized and painfully realistic.   It is meant to
serve, in waves of pleasure and pain, the destructive cycle of
the two actors, who approach each other with eroticism fulfilled
without touching, but exploded to brutality when they do.

It is as if each character uses the other to inflict a psychic
suicide, the woman raging against the possibility of love yet
seeking it with an impossible lover, commanding him to beat her
while slapping herself until her face reddens and she crumbles,
sobbing.   And the man, dreaming about becoming a master of
servants, pounding himself with his master's boots, signifying
where the medals he will win will be worn.

At the end, however, it is the audience which is punished for
its own participation in the psyche of death.

Julie, who had been passively watched, walks toward the
audience with a knife at her throat, asking her lover to order
her to death, but by her look, more properly asking the audience.

At arm's length from the first row of seats, she presses
the knife against her flesh.

She removes the knife, but not the tension, turning and leaving the performance space.

By so powerfully ending the play, removing the mask of performance, she exposes the audience as voyeur.

Lynne Greenblatt is Julie, an extraordinary performance carried across the width of woman as child, mother, lover and aggressor.

John Martin is the servant, a more exterior performance than Miss Greenblatt's convincing interior justification.

In all, however, a powerful, painful theater.

Progressive Character Focus Built Among Politics, Puns in "King John" (by Anthony Bannon, Buffalo Evening News, July 24, 1974)

This is his show, as is Hamlet's or Lear's or, more properly, Richard's. And Edward Atienza in the title role of Shakespeare's "The Life and Death of King John" gives a slowly built, quite rightly theatrical performance which stretches from dignity to madness as it does from life to death.

It is a big swallow for an actor, maybe bigger than the play itself.

Not found in the collections of Shakespeare's major plays, King John is given credence here as an illumination to "Richard III" and "Richard II" between which two it falls in the cycle of history plays. And it also is given attention as an undying metaphor for political corruption.

The festival theater, however, has a better argument reasoned from performance.

John will carry his England to war. His stance and language are the familiar cloaks--of dignity when wrong is the rule, of right when there is none, of power as the measure of justice. That he shares this shaky position with another king, with the mother of a prince and with the emissary of the Church in Rome is the promise the play offers as its beginning. But it is not a promise kept.

Instead, the focus is crisply applied to John and how he changes. Atienza holds focus: At first in the low key of his office's confidence, securely handling his state and only giving slight portents to the havoc which follows--a turn or flourish of cloak that with their quickness belie the fluidity of his reign. And then, once decisions too quickly made to cover previous errors collect and sum his collapse, he moves with the threat of a man become less than human.

Words at this point catch in Atienza's throat and lock insensibly upon themselves. He prowls the stage like a creature stalked, slinking like a cat, lurching to stop and claw at his robe, a little man whose puffery has been punctured, frightened.

He'll die soon, somewhat overdone in loincloth and resurrection lighting, and that will be the end of it--full circle.

More than politics, in fact, the play is about circles, or at least arcs. With his familiar and by now a little tedious use of miraculous coincidence to turn the corners of plot in his lesser plays (such as "Pericles" also in repertory here), Shakespeare with "John" makes verbal miracles, circles and arcs, with puns.

The punning is a match for the curious swings of plot, which moves like an errant pendulum from England to France, from dual promises of war and peace skewed across a course of passion, madness, marriage, ambition and death of legions, a king and a child prince.

The punning ranges from the facile "Cut him to pieces; ... Keep the peace, I say"--to the more sensible--"Our griefs, and manners, reason now; ... But there is little reason in your grief; therefore 'twere reason you had manners now." For its showiness, however, it becomes all show and an encumbrance to understanding.

Director Peter Dews takes the audience with John by dropping inflection on the play's curiosity pieces into the tone of conversation and raising the volume on the moments of psychological truth which mean more on the stage than words.

He is given a commentator, Philip The Bastard, who by his birth both royal and shamed, can play the fool in knight's dress, speaking as an equal to kings while carrying their messages and order and with them the drama. Douglas Rain plays him with puckish humor and grand gesture, his voice when raised an unmistakable signal to listen and get a message.

And director Dews is given Martha Henry, always a pleasure. She plays Constance, an aggressive, pompous, self-congratulating stage mother to young Prince Arthur, rightful owner of John's crown and the ostensible reason for all the fighting.

Really, though, Constance is the reason. She rails throaty invocations to war and later cries her grief for a son stolen-- lost advantage--as if the world were at her disposal. What happens is that the theater is hers for those moments.

With these fine actors, director Dews leaves the contemporary portent of the play alone, the significance of war's folly, the use and constraint of power, and the consequence of corrupted ambition left pretty much for audience conclusions. The closest

he comes to comtemporaneity is a sword struggle under strobe
light and that is the closest to serious mistake.

BARBER, William, Long Island Press, 92-20 168th Street, Jamaica,
N.Y. 11404.

BARBOUR, John; (2) "Critic-at-Large"; (3) b. Toronto, Canada, Apr.
24, 1937; (5) High school drop out; (8) TV producer, and commentator,
KNBC Burbank, Cal., 1970- ; (9) Actor: Castle Theater Repertory
Co., Farnham, Surrey, England, 1960; produced Chucko the Clown,
KABC; host for "Barbour's People," KNXT; guested on "The Dean
Martin Show," "The Tonight Show," "The Steve Allen Show," "The
Joey Bishop Show"; (14) Emmy, host KABC "AM" Program, 1972;
Emmy, "The 19" Variety Show, 1975; Golden Mike, Radio & TV
News Association of Southern California, 1972 commentary on the
Munich Massacre during the 1972 Olympics; (20) Wrote and recorded
album: "It's Tough to Be White"; (22) NBC News, 3000 West Ala-
meda Ave., Burbank, Cal. 91505, Ph. 213-845-700, 849-3911.

[Review of Chuck Heston]
(by John Barbour, over KNBC radio, Los Angeles, January 29, 1975)

It's not true when they say the truth never hurt anyone. I've
found, as a critic, it can hurt the one who tries to speak it.

Especially when you try to point out that some of the emperors
in our society have no clothes. Movie stars in our society are
sort of emperors. Chuck Heston is a movie star. This year
he appeared in two of the biggest disaster films "Airport '75 "
and "Earthquake." And now at the Mark Taper he can also be
seen in disaster theatre "Macbeth '75." It hurts me to tell
you that while clothes can make an Emperor, Shakespeare can
unmake an actor, and as Macbeth Heston shows he has no talent
for it. The genius in the writing of Shakespeare's characters
is that even with the incredible imagery and poetry in the language, the characters are real; Macbeth, like Hamlet, is at once
indecisive and resolute.

That requires a sensitivity that is missing in a film personality which seems resolute only falling out of 747s. When he
tries to 'act' Macbeth, he loses whatever ease and charm he may
possess on the screen, and ends up sounding unnaturally like
Ted Baxter in hiphuggers.

In one scene he even behaved like Ted Baxter. The actor
playing MacDuff worked with a crutch. It was announced he'd
hurt his foot in rehearsal. In a big swordfighting scene, this
actor accidentally dropped his sword. Instead of having the presence to hand it back to him, Heston started to swordfight against
the guy's crutch.

Heston is Chairman of the Board of the Center Theatre, and
as such he deserves the major portion of the blame for allowing
Director Peter Wood to ruin both Shakespeare's "Macbeth" and
Vanessa Redgrave's reputation in the worst production I've ever
seen.

As for Heston's trying the stage, how can you applaud anyone
who doesn't know his own limitations?

One good thing about it; it only runs till the 23rd!

[Review of Give Em Hell Harry]
(by John Barbour, over KNBC radio, Los Angeles, May 21, 1975)

If he sees James Whitmore in Give Em Hell Harry, I bet
Rich Little kicks himself for not spending more time doing Truman and less time doing Nixon. Not only is it unlikely that in
15 years or so that there'll ever be a show called Give Em Hell
Dicky, but if an entertainer like Rich does the voices of 20 live
people in half an hour, he is still called an impressionist; but if
an actor like Whitmore does the voice of someone who's no longer
with us for two hours, he's called an artist. That's the kind of
irony I think the Harry Truman that James Whitmore shows us
at The Ahmanson would have enjoyed. Give Em Hell Harry,
written by Samuel Gallu is called a play. But it is not. What
the Music Center is really presenting is James Whitmore in an
Evening with Harry Truman. Regardless of what it's called,
though, it's a hell of an evening. It is a much more stimulating,
informative, entertaining and human evening than even Whitmore's
Will Rogers, primarily because Truman's position as President
was much more important. We hear Harry give Hell to big
business, big labor and big politicians. He said no politician
can get rich without being a crook! We hear him in pre-civil
rights days tell a crowd of whites that blacks must be free because in order to keep a black in the gutter some white is gonna
have to stay in the gutter to hold him there. When asked about
his decision to drop the A bomb on Hiroshima, he says he's still
waiting for someone to apologize for Pearl Harbor. And in the
early 20's when Jew-hating Klansmen threaten his life because
they think he has Jewish ancestry, he tells them the Klan must've
been organized by a Jew; who else could sell them those crummy
$1.95 sheets for $16.00.

Truman felt America would survive if we stuck to our Con-
stition and sense of humor; in this terrific show the latter balances beautifully the wonderfully revealing moments that are human
or historic.

The supreme compliment you can pay Whitmore as an actor
is he's getting more respect and laughs for Truman now than
Truman got for himself; and one of the compliments we can pay
Harry Truman as President: Whitmore is probably making more
money!

BARDACKE, Frances Lavender; (2) Theater and book critic; (3) b.
Antwerp, Belgium, Nov. 19, 1919; (4) d. Franklin and Catherine
(Woodward); (5) B. A. Upsala College, East Orange, N. J., major
subject: English Literature; (6) m. Theodore Bardacke, June 29,
1939; (7) children--Franklin Joseph, Paul Gregory; (8) Poet, playwright, critic; (9) published privately Moving Melody, a book of
poems, 1948; wrote and produced April Forever, Redlands University,
1952; wrote and produced Anniversary, San Diego, 1961; wrote and
directed The Ferry, San Diego, 1962; wrote and acted in An Evening
with Frances Bardacke, San Diego City College, 1966; wrote and produced The Ballad of Yankee Jim, 1967; Eldorado and John Phoenix
Esq., San Diego Old Town, 1968; Adopted and co-produced The Frogs,
California Western University Summer Festival 1967; co-authored
with John Sinor Slightly Higher on the West Coast, Cassius Carter
Center Stage, 1970 (Old Globe) San Diego, California; (14) Director's
Prize at Old Globe, One Act Play Contest, San Diego, 1962; (21)
815 Manhattan Ct., San Diego, Ca. 92109, Ph. 714-488-4561; (23)
Circulation: 30,000; (24) twelve theater reviews, six book reviews.

Theatre: "Macbett" and "The Dybbuk"
(by Frances L. Bardacke, San Diego Magazine, March 1975)

At the Carter Stage Ionesco's Macbett, directed by Floyd
Gaffney of UCSD, was a strange treat. Macbett is Eugene Ionesco's essay on Shakespeare's tragedy of perverted ambition, Macbeth. Of course, the French absurdist has his own special things
to say and way of saying them. In the first place, he makes
Macbett and Banco anti-heroes, or anti-villains, as you wish.
They are simply warlike, stupid ordinary men who repeat phrases
about war, loyalty, tyranny and revolt. They could be substituted
for each other, the men they kill or the men that will eventually
kill them.

There is no great and loyal subject in this play to be subverted by the desire for power. Duncan is an equally empty ruler as befits old heroes brought down to their modern images.
The difference is in the women. Lady Macbett is not Lady Macbeth, but Duncan's Queen abetted by her Lady in Waiting (or their
magical counterfeits). They are only sometimes disguised as
the witches of Shakespeare's original. Lady Macbeth may have
been a dark power in Macbeth's drive, but she was flesh not an
evil spirit and her feelings of guilt and remorse go further and
deeper than her husband's.

But in Ionesco's Macbett the distaff is all evil. Direct from
the master (Satan) they are seducers, adulterers and murderers,
completely remorseless. If Macbeth's sin has become minimized
with his character, his lady's sin comes direct from the Evil one
himself. So much for Male Chauvinist drama.

The language of Ionesco's play suffers from being translated
from another language, particularly into English. The aural
quality of a language can't be translated and its English version

seems especially awkward because it is the language of Shakespeare. I don't mean that Macbett should have Shakespeare's
poetry but rather that there is something lacking in the contrast.
It should have been translated into better anti-poetry.

The production at the Carter Stage was slow and too static
for the excitement of the sets and costumes by Peggy Kellner.
It was an interesting evening visually and intellectually but no
more.

At the Mission Playhouse That Championship Season by Jason
Miller, directed by Edith Pirazzini, was well presented with an
especially fine performance by William Quiett as Tom Daley, the
alcoholic iconoclast. But the drama is a cliché. There may be
times when I could believe that sports fans are Peter Pans (Howard Cosell might well be Captain Hook), that wars are won or
lost in college gymnasiums or that mature men are morally circumscribed by how they were taught to play the school games.
But I don't often, and I have not once blamed Watergate on Richard Nixon's erstwhile football coach. As a result, Mr. Miller's
play about the rotten core of men still dominated by their old
coach, a cliché-ridden bigot, never becomes real for me. But
it was well done and the players seemed to believe it.

Next at the Mission Playhouse will be Hot 1 Baltimore, a
comedy about a rundown residence for crazies, whores and inge-
nues. A series by the same name has just been introduced on
TV as a new situation comedy, an event that I wouldn't have believed possible five years ago. There was a time, once, when
the theatre had the corner on risqué comedy. Then the movies
went far beyond the wildest burlesque. And now TV exploits the
whore with a heart of gold on a weekly series. Perhaps the oldest profession will get overexposed.

At the Mark Taper Forum in Los Angeles a very important
event is taking place. A presentation of The Dybbuk in English.
The Dybbuk was written by S. Ansky after he had studied first
hand the folk tales and legends of the Jewish settlements in Eastern Europe. Ansky wrote his play in Russian and called it Between Two Worlds then later The Dybbuk. It was first produced
in Vilna in 1920, a month after its author died. It was translated
into Hebrew, Yiddish and several other languages including English. It is not often produced and although I have read the play
(and I can remember seeing a movie of it some 35 years ago; it
had subtitles, but I can't remember what the spoken language
was), The Mark Taper Forum production was the first stage
performance I have seen. It was directed and choreographed by
John Hirsch from his own adaptation. The translation I had read
was from the Yiddish by Alsberg and Katzin in a Modern Library
Collection. It seems to differ from the one at the Mark Taper
mainly in that Hirsch's adaptation has enlarged on and explicated
the mysticism and added a bit of familiar, wry Jewish humor.

Now that Fiddler on the Roof has made the precarious survival in the shtetel picturesque, and The Exorcist has made the
confrontation of possession a best seller, The Dybbuk, which pre-
dates both of them, is a most fortunate revival being more genuine than either Fiddler or The Exorcist.

A dibbuk/dybbuk (derived from the Hebrew to cling or cleave)
is either an evil spirit that possesses a man or the soul of a
dead person who enters and lives in another's body. In the play
The Dybbuk the possession of a young bride on her wedding day
takes place because her wealthy father has opportunely forgotten
an old promise to a dead friend that their children should marry.
The marriage contract has been made in heaven and the poor
scholar and heiress meet unbeknownst and feel their destiny. The
father finds a wealthy bridegroom and the poor scholar, who has
become a student of the mysteries, dies and possesses his bride
on the day of the wedding. The great Rabbi Azrielke discovers
the truth and exorcises the spirit (dibbuk) but he cannot change
the lovers' destiny and the maiden elects to go with her true
bridegroom into the unknown.

It is a fascinating production, set against a magnificent display by designer Maxine Graham which emphasized the mystical
rather than the folk quality of the play. It was beautifully acted
by the whole cast with Marilyn Lightstone and Melora Marshall
doubling in the difficult role of Leah. It is an evening of both
religious and theatrical magic.

A New Look at Hamlet: God's Vengeance
(by Frances L. Bardacke, San Diego Magazine, May 1974)

At the Mark Taper Forum, Stacy Keach made his essay at
Hamlet. As far as I'm concerned it was a disappointing production. Of course, any Hamlet is an event and a full length Hamlet
is always worth the going. When it is at the Mark Taper Forum
and under the direction of Gordon Davidson, if it doesn't come
off "great" it is a disappointment. Yet, it has been a well attended production that has had its run extended by audience demand.

Mr. Keach is an actor with the best credentials for Shakespeare, but his Hamlet, although refreshingly clear in the soliloquies was never ambivalent nor involuted enough. No matter
how you interpret Hamlet he is a man at war within himself and
it is his internal conflict that is the crux of the play.

Mr. Keach talked well, but in crisis was either flat and monotonous, or, as when confronted by the ghost, fell into strange
physical gyrations as if to disguise his lack of subtlety. It is
surprising that director Gordon Davidson did nothing to help.
There were times when it seemed that without too great an effort something distracting or emphatic could have happened, but
it didn't.

Some of the direction was inspired and problem-solving, as in the dumb show, but at other times it was incredibly awkward such as the trap door fire in the night watch scene which slammed shut for a sound effect, but violated stage reality.

The various actors were equally uneven. Harris Yulin seemed a particularly good Claudius giving time and meaning to his role as a covert villain. The production was not as fortunate in Salome Jens as Gertrude. There are many interpretations for Gertrude and, I suppose, one is being so sweet and passive that one king within a month's time gets to look pretty much like another. Ms. Jens played her role with almost non-existent passion.

Jeff Corey's Polonius was a delight and Peter Nyberg's Laertes one of the best. He slyly showed himself his father's son in his advice to his sister and threw into relief Hamlet's ambivalence towards revenge by being so easily subverted into dishonor by the King. Kitty Winn's Ophelia was sweet but understated. Avery Schreiber's gravedigger was a brief moment of delight.

But such a weighing of roles can't help but reflect how I particularly respond to Hamlet. It is one of those plays that so abstracts emotions and judgments that it becomes a Rorschach to its interpreters.

My reaction to Hamlet, I am afraid, is not the usual. I rebel at the assumption almost everybody makes that revenge for his father's death by the murder of his uncle is Hamlet's proper course, and that it is his "indecision" that throws the play into tragedy. I see him as everyone does as an introspective man caught in an ambivalence to the point of both disguised and real madness (for in his fake madness we see shreds of insanity just as Polonius and the King see traces of sanity). My difference is that I see the drive to revenge and murder as the fatal flaw rather than his inability to act.

Hamlet is a deeply religious play suffused with the laws of God, often in opposition to the passions of man. In his first soliloquy Hamlet describes a depression so deep he has only rejected suicide because of God's "canon." In such a state it is easy to converse with spirits (also biblically proscribed). The ghost confirms Hamlet's blackest thoughts yet his demand for violent revenge goes against Hamlet's nature. The ghost's warlike garb and demeanor emphasize his message of violence, so much so that the uniformed guards take him to be a herald of war. Denmark is threatened by Fortinbras (Norway) who seeks to regain land lost by his father to the late King Hamlet in a fatal duel. Thus he becomes one of three sons in the play seeking to avenge his father's death.

Hamlet seeks final proof of his uncle's guilt in the play within a play because he himself is suspicious that the apparition may be a combination of his melancholy and the devil. In his descent toward tragedy he begins by brooding on evil and finds it everywhere in the world, in friends and even in his love for Ophelia. He becomes so callous toward murder the death of Polonius barely troubles him and his gratuitous sentence of death for his former firends Rosencrantz and Guildenstern is "not near his conscience."

When Hamlet finds he can not kill the King at his seeming prayers, it is not because he wants a greater revenge as he rationalizes, but because he can not bring himself to do what Laertes later gives voice to, "cut his throat i'th church." And in that almost irrelevant episode to the play when he reflects on Fortinbras' armies on the march and uses the episode to shore up his own resolution to murder, it is ironic that he never realizes that while Fortinbras has been diverted from his revenge upon Denmark he has merely shifted one violent attack to another senseless war.

Laertes, who has none of Hamlet's sensibilities, comes back from France hellbent for the murder of his father's murderer and in his passion is easily perverted by the King into as despicable an act of treachery as exists. Yet so involved are we with "honorable revenge" that we tend to overlook the unbated, poisoned foils as the epitome of dishonor.

At the end of the play, Hamlet, despite his better nature, kills the King, taking in the process seven other lives; his own, and those of Laertes, Polonius, Rosencrantz, Guildenstern and inadvertently Ophelia and his mother. All persons whom at one time and to various degrees, he had loved.

What no one seems to remark, despite Claudius' soliloquy at his attempted prayers, Act III, Scene III, when he speaks of his kinship to Cain: "O, my offense is rank, it smells to heaven; it hath the primal eldest curse upon it, a brother's murder ..." is that the play's seven unnecessary deaths are directly related to that "primal curse" when God proclaimed to those seeking vengeance on Cain, Genesis IV:15: "Therefore whosoever slayeth Cain, vengeance shall be taken on him sevenfold."

BARNES, Clive Alexander; (2) Drama and dance critic; (3) b. London England, May 13, 1927; (4) s. Arthur Lionel and Freda Marguerite (Garratt) B; (5) B.A., U. Oxford (Eng.), 1951; (6) m. Patricia Amy Evelyn Winckley, June 26, 1958; (7) children--Christopher John Clive, Joanna Rosemary Maya; (8) Co-editor Oxford dance mag. Arabesque, 1950; asst. editor Dance and Dancers, 1950-58, asso. editor, 1958-61, exec. editor, 1961-65, editor, N.Y.C., 1965- ; writer music, dance, drama, films Daily Express, London, 1956-65; dance critic The Times, London, 1962-65; The Spectator, London, 1959-65, New York Times, 1965-67; drama and dance ·critic, New York Times, 1967- ; (9) adj. professor, dept. journalism, N.Y.U., 1968-75.

(13) R. A. F. 1945-48; (14) Decorated comdr. Order Brit. Empire; knight Order of Dannebrog (Denmark); (15) Mem. Critics Circle London (past sec. , chmn, ballet section), N. Y. Drama Critics Circle (pres. 1975-75); (20) Ballet in Britain Since the War, 1953; Frederick Ashton and his Ballets, 1961; (with others) Ballet Here and Now, 1961; Dance Scene, USA, 1967; editor: Best American Plays, 6th and 7th series; (21) 450 West 2nd Ave. , New York City, N. Y.   10024; (22) New York Times, 229 W. 43rd St. , New York City, N. Y. 10036.

BASS, Milton Ralph; (2) Entertainment editor, critic and columnist; (3) b. Pittsfield, Mass. , Jan. 15, 1923; (4) s. Philip and Lean (Brunell) B. ; (5) B. S. University of Mass, major subj. Biology, 1947; M. A. Smith College, English and Comp. Lit. 1948; two years doctoral study, Columbia U. 1948-50; (6) m. Ruth Mary Haskins, May 27, 1960; (7) children--Michael Jon, Elissa Allen and Amy Brunell; (8) Entertainment editor and critic, Berkshire Eagle, Pittsfield, Mass. , 1950- ; (9) Program director, educational television 1965-66; Consultant on television to Ford Foundation, 1966; Consultant to New York State Council on the Arts, 1971-73; (13) Pfc. , United States Army, World War II; (14) Silver Star Medal and four battle stars; (15) Member of Authors Guild; (16) Democrat; (17) Jewish; (20) Three novels: "Jory" 1969, "Force Red" 1970, "The Doctor Who Made House Calls" 1973; magazine articles; (21) View Drive, Route 49, Pittsfield, Mass.   01201, Ph. 413-698-2271; (22) Berkshire Eagle, 33 Eagle St. , Pittsfield, Mass.   01201, Ph. 413-447-7311; (23) Circulation: 30,000; (24) 25 plays and musicals, 50 movies, 10 books, 30 TV shows, 5 miscellaneous.

"The Body & the Wheel"
(by Milton R. Bass, The Berkshire Eagle, April 5, 1974)

There are some 73 actors and a further 30 to 40 people working behind the scenes of "The Body & the Wheel," the dramatic presentation of the Gospel blended together by William Gibson at the Pierce Chapel of Cranwell School in Lenox.

From these core hundred there radiate innumerable families and friends who have been laboring with love for weeks for the showings tonight, tomorrow, Sunday and on April 19. From these laborings have come a community of spirit that will live with them for a long period, perhaps forever, of what can be accomplished by desire, dedication, togetherness, amateur eagerness and professional skill.   There are some, especially the young ones, who might not recognize for a long time what they experienced, but it was obvious at the dress rehearsal witnessed last night that it was definitely there.

Mr. Gibson reportedly put his talent to bear on the Gospels after an experience in Transcendental Meditation awakened in him the desire to return to the Catholic faith of his youth.   The hand that produced "Two for the Seesaw," "The Miracle Worker" and especially "John and Abigail" deals smoothly with the one who came "to seek and to save that which was lost."

But, Mr. Gibson's professional skill is most noticeable in what he was able to accomplish with a huge cast of eager amateurs, who invariably are willing to do anything but who usually don't know how to do it. In this case, they mostly do it.

The other major factor is the casting of Spencer Louis Trova in the role of Jesus. Mr. Trova's great talent and solid acting background furnish a rock on which all the other characters, from disciples to street urchins, can safely perch. The role is a back-breaking one on which the focus and the pressure never waver, but Mr. Trova is able to handle it all carefully with just the right modulation to keep the impossible from being impossible.

And it is amazing how well the pace is kept in this long production, how attuned each person is to everyone around him and to what is being attempted. It was obviously a great pre-Lenten experience for all who participated and should be as much for most of the audience.

The title of the work is taken from the writings of the late Dr. Albert Schweitzer:

"In the knowledge that he is the coming son of man, Jesus lays hold of the wheel of the world to set it moving on that last revolution which is to bring all ordinary history to a close.

It refuses to turn, and he throws himself upon it. Then it does turn and crushes him. Instead of bringing in the eschatological conditions, he has destroyed them.

The wheel rolls onward, and the mangled body of the one immeasurable great man who was strong enough to think of himself as the spiritual ruler of mankind and to bend history to his purpose, is hanging upon it still.

That is his victory and his reign."

"Jacques Brel Is Alive and Well and Living in Paris"
(By Milton R. Bass, The Berkshire Eagle, February 15, 1975)

First of all, the real-life situation. Jacques Brel is alive but definitely not well and definitely not living in Paris. The 46-year-old composer-singer is a victim of lung cancer and reportedly has sailed out to sea on his yacht to spend his last days where he has been happiest in the past.

Now for the background. Seven years ago two bright men named Eric Blau and Mort Shuman put together an off-Broadway revue based on the songs and spiels of Brel, who was little known outside his native Belgium. The revue was not one of those overnight sensations, but it ran and it ran and it ran until

it achieved 1,847 performances.   In 1972 it moved to Broadway
for six weeks and then it took off on a road tour of the United
States and Canada.   It has since become the rage in most of the
countries of Europe, and now it is being produced all the way
down to the high school level.

Eric Blau wrote a screenplay he considered suitable for the
songs and it was filmed in France, from whence it was purchased
by Ely Landau for his American Film Theatre series.   It is the
second production of the season and opened yesterday afternoon
at the Little Cinema of the Berkshire Museum.   Its final performance will be tonight at 8 p.m.

Now for the opinion.   The only other time I have seen this
production was a live one (in every sense) put on by the Riggs
Players of Stockbridge last year.   You couldn't understand half
the lyrics and those you could understand were not very earth-
shaking, but Brel and his collaborator have a fine sense of melodic sweetness, and the acting and direction were ingenious enough
to carry the rest.   I enjoyed it tremendously.

The film version, unfortunately, does the opposite.   It takes
away all the liveness and it permits you to pay attention to the
lyrics, which suffocate you with their banality.   In addition, the
frenetic musical accompaniment steals from Brel's gentleness and
makes everything sound like French honky tonk, of which there
is no honkier and no tonkier.

Writer Blau was trying for a wild, surrealistic trip through
the imagination of the three characters in the revue--a housewife, a taxi driver and a Marine--but the final effect is more
kooky dull than imaginative.   Director Dennis Heroux, a Canadian
comer, doesn't come up with anything that sticks to your mind.

The cast of three is quite accomplished but they are not able
to rise above the "bittersweet" sameness of the music and lyrics.
Elly Stone, who is Mrs. Blau, is most effective in "The Old
Folks" and "Carousel," Joe Maisiel in "Middle Class" and Mort
Shuman in "Funeral Tango" and "I Drive a Cab."   Ironically,
Brel himself, in a brief appearance, is the most moving in de-
livering his "Ne Me Quittes Pas."   You don't have to understand
French to know what is affecting him.   He gets it all across in
the phrasing and tonal modifications.

There are some 25 songs in the production, two of which
are new.   The most familiar one to radio listeners is "If We
Only Have Love," which is sung with moderate effectiveness by
all three principals as a finale.

The photography, which was done in Paris, Nice, the French
Alps and on the cold shores of the Mediterranean, is rather blatant and unappreciative of the natural grandeur.   In his desperation for movement, director Heroux grabs at closeups as much

as possible, and it is the first time I have seen nasal passages
so clearly and been transmogrified by wobbling larynxes.

Those of you who have never seen "Jacques Brel" or heard
the songs still might find the hour and a half entertaining. I
hope so.

BEALS, Kathie Stahl; (2) Arts writer; (3) b. Seattle, Wash; (4) d.
Kathleen George and Gustav Richard Stahl; (5) Northfield (Mass.)
School, Mills College, Ca. , (theater major), College of New Rochelle
(N. Y.), English major B. A.; (6) m. Frederick H. Beals; (7) chil-
dren--Hellock, Dexter, Frederick Jr. , Gordon; (8) Financial copy,
Merrill Lynch; editor, Club Life in Westchester; Fashion copy, Sears
Roebuck and Best and Co. ; Reporter, Daily Times (Mamaroneck,
N. Y.); Feature writer, arts editor, visual and performing arts writer
and critic Westchester Rockland Newspapers (member Gannett Group)
in Westchester County; (9) Professional children's theatre actress;
(10) Director, local Head Start; chairman, March of Dimes; president,
PTA and college alumnae club; (14) Award Associated Press Association of New York for news feature; (15) Director, Sigma Delta Chi
Society of Professional Journalists; National Press Club; (17) Episcopal; (20) Free lance speeches, articles; (21) 400 Carroll Ave. , Mamaroneck, N.Y.   10543, Ph. 914-698-0617; (22) One Gannett Drive,
White Plains, N. Y.   10604, Ph. 914-694-9300; (23) Circulation:
about 200,000 in Lifestyles section of eight dailies; (24) visual art
and dance.

<u>Street Theater: What Is it, Really?</u>
(by Kathie Beals, Westchester Rockland Newspapers, August 8, 1975)

Old time street theater was clowns and songs and Punch and
Judy.   Today it is something else.

Every summer a non-profit group called The Street Theater
tours Westchester prisons and low income areas with a new play
from the drama workshops of New York State prisons.   The cast
includes former inmates, actual inmates let out for the evening
and professional actors.   The message is, "Brother, we're in
this thing together."

On the evening when The Street Theater was to present "Get-
in' Over" in White Plains 11-year-old cousins Nina Harper and
Jeffrey Blair were ready long before the big yellow truck rumbled
down Fisher Avenue.

They and a swirling, cheerful crowd of other black youngsters
who live in the Winbrook Housing Project romped on the grass,
threw balls high in the air and chased each other across the space
between buildings while they waited.

"Live shows are much better than television--T. V. , is phony,"
Nina remarked seriously as she smoothed her neat blouse and

shorts. "I've seen lots of free shows in Baltimore--that's where I really live--and I even saw a jazz opera but I don't remember the name of it."

"Yeah, there's plenty going on in Baltimore," Jeffrey echoed, "But I'm afraid to go out at night there. There's fires and fights and once a rat ran right over my foot, Boy!"

"We get a lot of shows right here," he said with pride. "I've seen music and dancing and puppets and last night we had a big block party in the lot across the street.

"Do you 'spose they'll have dancing in this show? Nina and I couldn't tell from the poster we read."

When the Street Theater truck arrived nearly an hour late-- it had broken down en route--producer Gary Smith and his crew worked as fast as they could to let down its sides, all the time sweeping children off the cab and stage with good-humored patience.

Then, suddenly, there was music, there were actors--black and white--doing a loose-limbed shuffle on stage as about 75 children crowded in front, their faces staring up hopefully.

It wasn't easy to follow the plot, even though the actors donned character masks at one point--"a good idea," Nina said approvingly, after an involuntary start of fright.

There was a crazy-looking white woman in ragbag clothes ("Is that a housewife?" Jeffrey wanted to know) telling a sweet-faced black man that she understood his problems, that he needed help in adjusting to the outside world after getting out of prison. Then there was a groovy looking black man passing out something to be sniffed and something else to be smoked by their hero. There were songs, too, by a handsome young black woman who also played bongo drums.

But for a long time there were no adults in the audience. Middleaged women sitting on benches behind the stage truck continued to chat. Men lounging on the steps of the nearest building stayed there. A snappily dressed fellow carrying a full golf bag and a pair of shiny, fringe-flap shoes walked past briskly, heading for the street.

Finally, a small group of teenagers and 20-to 30-year-olds joined the crowd in time to hear a rough dialog between a prostitute and her pimp.

"That's cursing," little Jeff said suddenly. "I don't want to stay." And he ran off toward a distant ice cream wagon.

Nina lingered a few moments. Then she decided, "That's

not nice," and she, too, disappeared.

Two young mothers, one dressed as if she had just come home from an office job, were standing nearby discussing the play when it ended abruptly, taking them by surprise.

"Is this an intermission or is this all?" the woman in T-shirt and slacks called to Gary Smith as he hurried past.

That was all.

"Well," she said, "I think it is a good thing for those men to have to memorize all those lines. It probably kept them busy in prison."

Now the sky was dark blue all over and the street lights were yellow in the summer night. The truck had been driven off and the two white people, Gary Smith and his wife, tired and disheveled, their sleeveless knit shirts and blue jeans sagging and dusty, prepared to go home.

"This wasn't a typical performance," Smith said apologetical-ly. "For one thing, we were missing an actor, an inmate who didn't show up, so we had to cut three scenes in the beginning of the play."

Looking equally disappointed, his wife added, "This is always a difficult place to perform in because it is so noisy and there are so many children."

"The Runner Stumbles" into Priest's Home

(by Kathie Beals, Westchester Rockland Newspapers, December 31, 1975)

The time is 1911. The place, an isolated village in northern Michigan. The chief characters: a recalcitrant priest, a joyful nun, a careful convert. The event--murder.

These are the bare bones of Milan Stitt's hypnotically absorb-ing play, "The Runner Stumbles," which received its world pre-miere by the Hartman Theater Company in Stamford Tuesday night.

Up in Solon, Mich., where all they do--says the lawyer for the defense--is drink and spit and plant and swear, Roman Catho-lics are an exotic minority. What really went on in the priest's house? A prosecutor, an unseen jury and the audience find out as the play unfolds in a series of flashbacks and comes to a hor-rifying climax on the witness stand.

The play slowly opens with a lantern-jawed young jailer (Morrie Piersol) telling his prisoner to remove his belt--"so you won't try to hang yourself"--an inexperienced lawyer--"I never actually tried a case before"--humbly asking if the prisoner will accept him.

The prisoner is Father Rivard, and he is accused of murdering Sister Rita, the sole teacher in his tiny parochial school.

As the priest, Stephen Joyce has a special charisma arisen from his handsome appearance and a justly praised acting style.

He carries the play beautifully, but in the same key throughout; one wonders if director Austin Pendleton was deliberate or careless in not showing more contrast between the despairing priest on trial and, in flashback, the priest living the events that led to the trial.

Nancy Donohue is a perfectly realized Sister Rita: beautiful and bubbling with enthusiasm--"I'm a person who's a nun, not a nun who used to be a person." She wants to communicate and be loved; she almost hopes her pupils will stumble now and then so they can come to her for loving and comforting. And she's a born trouble-maker, as only the very very innocent can be; Miss Donohue is superb.

Superb is also the word for Sloane Shelton, who completes the rectory trio as Mrs. Shandig, the housekeeper. Respectful, strong and quietly righteous, Miss Shelton is a power to be reckoned with.

Bernard Frawley is Monsignor Nicholson, emissary of an annoyed bishop. One would expect him to be more curt than soft--even indifferent--considering what he has to say. But soft is Frawley's style, and that style has its merits.

In smaller roles, Eren Ozker is nicely intense as Louise, the star pupil; William Bogert properly overbearing as the prosecutor, Katina Commings appropriately bewildered as James Noble, a touching Abe Lincoln figure as the country lawyer.

"The Runner Stumbles" has been in progress and in workshop production for 10 years. Some faults remain--a love scene is curiously wrong--but it is easy to see why the Hartman Theater Company could hardly wait to produce the play, with Robert Verberkmoes to design the sets; James Berton Harris, the costumes; and Cheryl Thacker, the lighting.

BEAUFORT, John; (2) Drama critic, New York, retired; (3) b. Edmonton, Canada, 23 Sept. , 1912; (4) s. Ernest Beaufort and his wife Margaret Mary (Crawley); (5) Private and public schools in Canada and the United States, and Rollins College, Florida; (6) m. Francesca Bruning; (8) Copy boy, news and feature assignments to 1939 when became Monitor's resident N.Y. drama critic; war correspondent, 1946-1950 Chief of News Bureau in New York; Editor of the Arts and Magazine Section, 1950-51; resumed position as New York dramatic and film critic, 1951; appointed Monitor Arts-Entertainment editor, 1959; chief of London Bureau, 1962-65; Feature Editor in Boston

1965-70; New York drama critic, 1971-75, retired; (9) Lectured extensively on the theater for college and community audiences; (15) Players, Garrick; (20) Cont. Broadway reviews for The Times (London); (21) 588 Fifth Avenue, New York, N.Y., Ph. 212-757-1222.

BECK, David, Salt Lake Tribune, 143 South Main Street, P.O. Box 867, Salt Lake City, Utah 84110

BERMEL, Albert; (2) Free lance critic; (3) b. London, England, Dec. 20, 1927; (8) Critic, New Leader, 1964-1968, 1973-1974; Professor in Theatre Arts Division of Columbia, 1966-1972; Professor Speech and Theatre Department of Lehman College, and Ph.D. program at Graduate Center of CUNY, 1972- ; Visiting Professor at Rutgers, 1966-67; at the Julliard School, 1972-1973; at Purchase, 1974; (14) Guggenheim Fellowship in Playwriting, 1965-66; (15) Obie Awards judge, 1966; Tony Awards judge, 1974; (20) Books: The Genius of the French, The Plays of Courteline, One-Act Comedies of Molière, Contradictory Characters, Three Popular French Comedies, Artaud's Theatre of Cruelty, The Comic Agony: Masks of Wit and Humor in the Modern Theatre; Contributing editor for Arts in Society, Performance, Twentieth Century Literature, Reader's Encyclopedia of World Drama; Seven original full-length plays and seven original one-acts; Screenplay for motion picture Run; Cont. articles to Harpers, The Nation, The New Republic, Arts in Society, The Drama Review, New York Times Book Review, and "Arts in Leisure" section, Midstream, Columbia Forum, The Shaw Review, Boston University Journal, Twentieth Century Literature; (21) 5 Pershing Avenue, New Rochelle, N.Y. 10801, Ph. 914-636-2131.

The Iceman Melteth
(by Albert Bermel, The New Leader, January 21, 1974)

Maybe it's time for The Iceman Cometh to go back in the freezer until some imaginative director turns up and liberates it from its author. With O'Neill and his guardian-wife both dead, why keep deferring slavishly to his stage directions? He thought he could safeguard his work by piling up all those explicit instructions for costumes, sets, period touches, gestures, and vocal inflections; he even explained how to grin, whisper and stare ("almost mockingly," "with a grim smile"). To honor these things may seem like loyalty, but a director's first loyalty is to the play's possibilities, not to the author's notorious distrust of actors.

Harry Hope's West Side bar and its denizens are brought into richly detailed relationships by the dialogue; they do not need a literal set and activities to duplicate what the play already gives us in abundance. Unyoked from its burden of visual authenticity, Iceman would become much larger than an assortment of social castaways who slump over tables and take turns at raising their heads and voices.

As they wobble between their sodden recoveries from whiskey, their fitful memories of a better past that never was, and their hopes for a better future they mean to do nothing about, these bleared, lost spirits add up to a portrait of purgatory. O'Neill painstakingly worked his limbo out in a musical form. It has two major themes, sounded by the two main antagonists.

Larry Slade is a former Socialist who grew disillusioned with "the Movement" and left it; he now wishes to die and escape from the guilty feelings of having let down his old comrades. His passive retreat into "foolosophical" self-contemplation has infected the other drunks and landed them in a collective lethargy. But the arrival of Hickey the salesman needles them all, Larry included, out of their boozing and whimpering. Before they know it, each of them is making plans to change his life.

The twin themes are scored for the minor characters too, so as to give the play plenty of instrumental and tonal variety. O'Neill brings his motifs together at the end when Hickey confesses that he murdered his wife, while Parritt, a young man associated with Larry, confesses at the same time (in counterpoint) that he betrayed his mother--a leading figure in the Movement--to the police. The two principals swap roles as their themes tangle. Larry, who has desperately tried to keep out of everybody else's life, feels compelled to sit in judgment on Parritt, his "son," and urge him to atone for the betrayal by killing himself; Hickey, the gabby, self-appointed conscience for everybody else, surrenders to the law.

O'Neill has thus composed a tone-poem about Americans. He pits our innate psychological conservatism, our inclination to be thankful for what we have and to protect it from specified and unspecified threats, against our inner Dale Carnegie or Elmer Letterman, who is convinced that he can improve himself infinitely if he simply sweats hard enough. The struggle between self-preservation and the urge to proselytize (a mask for the urge to succeed) allows the American soul no peace. O'Neill knew that struggle at first hand and, like other superior American writers-- Thornton Wilder, for example, and Hemingway--strove to illuminate, to personify, its two sides, not merely in Iceman but in a string of other plays, such as Dynamo, The Great God Brown and The Hairy Ape.

O'Neill a composer? It sounds improbable. We have been taught to look on him as the Last Utter Realist. Iceman, however, had its realistic day in José Quintero's version at the Circle in the Square some years ago, the one that launched Jason Robards and kept cometh-ing around on educational TV; and the recent filmed treatment with Lee Marvin and Robert Ryan similarly took no "unrealistic" chances.

Theodore Mann's revival (Joseph E. Levine Theater) puts a black actor in the role of Hickey--this is the extent of its

novelty--and, as one would expect, James Earl Jones exerts his
formidable gifts to the play's advantage. Otherwise, Mann does
little more than recapitulate and reblock the staging by Quintero,
his former partner. In spite of some good back-up performances
by Tom Aldredge as Jimmy Tomorrow the journalist, Joseph
Ragno as Rocky the bartender, and David Margulies, who lends
Hugo the Viennese anarchist an unaccountable Russian accent,
this production does not let the play sing or soar, only roar.

The favored adjective in O'Neill criticism is "powerful."
This means, in Mann's production as always, that the actors
noisily harangue one another (and the audience) or else transpose
frequently from murmuring to shouting in order to "dramatize"
the material. But high-decibel counts do not reach O'Neill's
music, much less his realism.

We have moved into a new era of directing, abandoning the
notion articulated by Nigel Dennis in 1963 (very late in the game)
when he wrote, "The highest praise a director can receive is
congratulations for appearing to have contributed nothing whatever
to the play." We now realize that a director cannot avoid contributing to a play, even if it be no more than his ineptitude.

Not long ago in England I saw The Shrew, a drastic remod-
eling of The Taming of the Shrew undertaken by the Open Space
company led by Charles Marowitz, an American-born director
and critic. Kiss Me, Kate it isn't. Marowitz has pared down
his cast to six actors, squeezed out the banter in the comedy,
and conceived the action as the brutalization of Katharina by a
sadistic, mercenary Petruchio.

With its many stylized elements The Shrew left some London
critics uneasy; they saw it as a taming of the Bard. I found it
a first-rate interpretation. Thelma Holt's acting as an oppressed
yet defiant heroine opens the play up and acidly comments on
arranged marriages and paternal intimidation. The last scenes,
where she publicly vows to take her husband as her master, present her as a brainwashed prisoner, reminiscent of a Moscow-
trial victim in the 1930s; she mouths the ordained words but her
eyes tell us that, like Brecht's Galileo, she lives to fight another day.

Clearly, O'Neill is less pliable a writer than Shakespeare is,
and therefore less susceptible to refashioning. Still, only 20
years after his death we can see that directors will need to reckon with his musical structure and theatrical poetry if his plays
are to live and not just be exhibited like so many fossils.

By way of contrast, Jay Broad's revival of Eric Bentley's
Are You Now or Have You Ever Been (Riverside Church Theater)
is a model of conceptual daring on the part of a director. I
missed the initial production of Are You Now at Yale last year
but got the impression from reviews of a fairly straightforward

"theater of fact" treatment, a mock-up of actual hearings of the House Committee on Un-American Activities.

Broad takes his cue from the play's subtitle, "The Investigation of Show Business" from 1947-58, and surrounds the playing area with sequentially blinking marquee bulbs, which have the further benefit of simulating the atmosphere of lighted hoopla--kliegs and strobes--created by the press and television contingent. Photographs of the participants flash on to three separated screens; one compares them with the faces of the actors, a uniformly excellent cast that includes Albert Hall, Allan Miller, Arnold Soboloff, and Peter Thompson, who take on multiple roles as witnesses and Committee members. The sense of reconstrution, rather than a pretense at enactment, gives the material the feel of live documentation.

Indeed, that is the play's purpose. As Jules Chametzky points out in the current issue of Performance magazine, to study the hearings as strictly historical events means missing the connections down to the present, the formative political years, say, of Richard Nixon.

Broad's artifice goes beyond reminding us that there were heroes and villains among the witnesses; it displays the United States during a liberalizing period, when its unity and liberal ideals were nevertheless being steadily undermined by the Committee's racism and anti-Semitism. For instance, by announcing the original Russian-Jewish or German-Jewish names of movie celebrities Edward Arnold and Danny Kaye, the Committee members behaved as if they were conducting a ritual unmasking.

Anybody who lived through those times cannot help being fascinated and troubled by the wearing-down of Larry Parks, the comic self-abasement of Abe Burrows, the tremendous rage of Lionel Stander, and the insinuations directed at Paul Robeson, with whose indignant testimony the play suddenly ends. For a last tableau, Broad cuts the lights off and on; the actors stand transfixed like gargoyles but brimming with potential energy, as if one word from the Director Above would start the proceedings all over again.

As the only person in New York who has never before seen a Neil Simon play, I don't know whether to feel disappointed or justified by The Good Doctor (O'Neill Theater), which has a poster title set in quasi-Cyrillic type and is drawn (through a long straw) from some stories by Chekhov. René Auberjonois, Frances Sternhagen and Barnard Hughes collaborate variously and pleasantly. Christopher Plummer, as narrator, plays a Simonian Chekhov, or Chekhovian Simon, who worries about getting writer's block, yet never about exuding overdoses of easy charm. A small orchestra bumps out painless, peasanty tunes by Peter Link. A. J. Antoon directs. Exposed to so many names redolent of commercial triumphs, one recalls with a pang (who knows why?) that Anton Chekhov was a very sick man.

Grape Juice and Wine
(by Albert Bermel, The New Leader, June 10, 1974)

Ever since early 1957 when Candide, "a comic operetta
based on Voltaire's satire," ended a brief run at the Martin Beck
Theater, fans of Leonard Bernstein's score have drooled over
their deteriorated LP recordings and yearned for a resurrection.
About five years ago I heard one Candide-lover, who had just
transferred the music to a cassette, insist that the show would
never come back: It was too classy for a large public; the ac-
tion--hopping about from Westphalia to Lisbon, to Paris, Buenos
Aires, Venice, and home to Westphalia--was too bitty and remote;
the theme was too dispiriting; the hero too bland; the heroine too
penetrable.

His arguments illustrate our habit of attributing a flop to ex-
cesses, rather than to deficiencies. (A hit is self-explanatory.)
That Broadway bromide, "Give the public what it wants," means,
"Don't give the public more than it can take."

I remember enjoying the original show, which had stamina,
verve and all the other glossy qualities a musical is supposed to
display. Although its program notes seemed unnecessarily defensive about Voltaire's novel ("a beloved and international best seller for 200 years"), Lillian Hellman's adaptation presented sliv-
ers of the tale with sharp edges; so did the lyrics by Richard
Wilbur, John LaTouche and Dorothy Parker. Barbara Cook and
Richard Rounseville sang Cunegonde's and Candide's numbers me-
lodically and intelligibly; Max Adrian was funny doubling as Pangloss and his opposite, Martin the Pessimist. The staging by
Tyrone Guthrie lacked none of the rapidity and expansiveness that
had characterized his previous work on Broadway, Tamburlaine
and The Matchmaker, both of them money-spinners.

If this better-than-competent musical failed, I conclude it did
so because of its deficiencies. From a commercial viewpoint, it
made the mistake of excluding those moments of sloshy reconciliation that give theater-partygoers their obligatory lump in the
throat. As an artistic endeavor, it did not do justice to its
source, that story of mutilations, murders, rapes, and assorted
other horrors: Guthrie and his teammates could not reproduce
Voltaire's chilly-scrivener tone. For his objectivity and uninvolved reporting they substituted flipness and arched eyebrows.

Harold Prince has now picked up the challenge, scraping together fragments of the first Candide and adding some novelties.
The result is, in both senses, a sell-out. As a producer who
has forged an effective career for himself in directing, Prince
has become the David Belasco of recent decades. Following
Belasco's example, he consistently keeps a jump ahead of the
competition. For Superman, Cabaret, Follies, and A Little
Night Music he styled embroidery that concealed the worn fabric.

In this instance, Prince began by junking Lillian Hellman's
book and replaced it with one by Hugh Wheeler, the author of
Big Fish, Little Fish and Look, We've Come Through! (According to a letter Prince sent the New York Times, he first asked
Ms. Hellman to collaborate on the revival, evidently not thinking
that to invite an artist of her caliber to refashion her own script
is to proffer an insult, however well-meaning.) Wheeler thinned
out the story and, among other changes, excised the character
of Martin the Pessimist.

Next, Prince commissioned an environment, rather than a
mere set, from Eugene Lee and his wife Franne, who specialize
in environments and have already created two for Peter Brook,
one indoors (Paris) and one outdoors (Persepolis), another for
André Gregory's Alice in Wonderland, and yet another for a
Broadway extravaganza called Dude, which folded swiftly last
year after dropping about a million dollars.

Would the new Candide be another Dude, a veritable Candude?
Cannily avoiding a straight plunge into the big time, Prince tried
out his revamped show under modest circumstances, the Chelsea
Arts Center in Brooklyn--and came up with a certified winner.
In short order he transferred it to Manhattan, gutting the gigantic Broadway Theater, to make way for the Lees' environment,
now vastly enlarged. At the Broadway an actor prefaces the
evening with a statistical warning: Please keep your fingers,
coats and peanut shells away from the 10 separate stages, run-
ways, and drawbridges.

Environmental theater has its appeals. I am susceptible to
them, having especially savored the most impressive one of our
time, Orlando Furioso, where you raced around an arena, pursued by wagons with episodes being enacted aboard them. The
Broadway, however, has numbered seats, all anchored to the
floor; they consist of individual padded stools at $12 each for
aristocrats, big spenders or critics, and benches and bleachers
for the hoi polloi. The actors swarm around the house but you
must sit trapped on your number. Thus the pride of this production, its environment, remains static and decorative.

For Broadway regulars this seems to be enough of an attraction. They help themselves to free peanuts in the lobby; enter
the auditorium alongside wooden screens scribbled over with
harmless graffiti; and sit in exquisitely cramping togetherness
with their knees in other people's backs or laps. The genteel
slumming has allowed Prince once again to modify--and so pre-
serve--the hallowed formula for musicals.

Prince's directing resembles his producing in disguising
sackcloth as silk, grape juice as wine. The performance abounds
in distractions and speed. One incident played at your elbow
follows hard upon another that reaches you from a remote corner.
A soprano voice acquires a Doppler effect as it rushes past.

Candide gallops the length and breadth of the building. Curtains
keep rising to reveal Cunegonde on one of the 10 stages. The
narrator, "Dr. Voltaire," interrupts the action repeatedly by
materializing at some new entrance.

When you see the acting close up, though, its details look
unfinished, if not shoddy. Mark Baker as Candide and Maureen
Brennan as Cunegonde have nice smiles, steel-rimmed singing
voices, and not much else. After one song, "Glitter and be
Gay," Ms. Brennan wins applause not for her singing, but for
having plucked jewelry out of the headpiece of an actress who
sat in front of her fingering an imaginary harmonium--for no
conceivable reason. Many reviews praised Lewis J. Stadlen, who
essays Voltaire, Dr. Pangloss and several lesser acting chores.
Stadlen works like a demon and sweats like a fountain. Yet his
Voltaire drops lines--surprisingly pallid ones--in a standardized
stage-old-man's quaver, while his Pangloss is a familiar, lip-
smacking lecher with scholarly pretensions.

And so Candide flourishes. Possibly it was once 17 years
ahead of its time. Now it seems, like most Broadway musicals,
to be 200 years behind.

Find Your Way Home (Biltmore Theater) goes further back,
as far as the first story about the tart with a heart. Only this
time around, there is a twist. The girl is a man.

"The first serious play about homosexuality," said the reviews. "Honest" and "abrasive" and "scorching." When you hear
words like these you know you're in for a play in which characters keep screaming at one another to tell the truth or face the
truth, or, better, face up to the truth.

Julian, a man of 22, is desperately in love with Alan, a man
of 48. So is Alan's wife--at any rate, she is determined not to
let him go after umpteen years of marriage and two teenaged
children. During most of Act I and Act III the young man berates
the middle-aged man for his dishonesty. In Act II it's the wife's
turn to do the same. Why does the middle-aged man stand there
like a squeezed lemon, instead of grabbing his hat, booting them
both in the teeth, and hastening off, like Candide, to Buenos Aires
or some place?

Answer: He is requiting the young man's love. As he pleads
near the beginning, with an eloquence typical of the play at its
moments of crisis: "I want to live with you. Live here with you.
Live--anywhere." To which Julian smartly replies, "You don't
know what you're saying. No! Don't touch me!" Later, Julian
softens: "I want to live somewhere nice, I want to make a home
for you." Then, to demonstrate the play at its peak of abrasive-
ness, he asks politely, "Do you want to fuck?" And, within a
couple of minutes, as the two men clutch each other and kiss
thirstily, he cries, "Love me, please, make love!"

A playwright friend of mine once wrote an authentic-seeming scene between two gay men by picturing one of them as a woman. The author of Find Your Way Home, John Hopkins, exploits this device to the limits--and beyond--for the sake of easy laughs. "Am I supposed to squeal with delight?" says the young man. Or "I used to cry all the time." The dialogue improves not at all when the wife and husband have a strictly hetero quarrel: "Where was [were?] the understanding and help I needed? The love, the tenderness?" When Hopkins gets subtle he perpetrates such exchanges as: "Julian: Didn't you say I'd never see you again? Alan: No, I said I'd never see you again. There is a difference."

The acting of Michael Moriarty (who won a Tony) as the young man, Lee Richardson as the older man, and Jane Alexander as the wife, combined with Edwin Sherin's staging, is appallingly sincere. On your favorite channel any afternoon you will find wittier directing, more lathery soap, and more challenging situations than in this impoverished descendant of Camille.

BISHOFF, Donald Brian, Jr.; (2) Drama reviewer (and assistant city editor); (3) b. Martinsburg, W. Va., Dec. 30, 1936; (4) s. Donald and Helen (Hudgel) B.; (5) B.S. in Journalism, 1958; M.S. in Journalism, 1959, both from Medill School of Journalism, Northwestern U., Evanston, Ill.; (6) Divorced; (8) Reporter, City News Bureau of Chicago, 1959; Reporter, Richmond (Va.) Times Dispatch, 1959-60; Reporter, Eugene (Ore.) Register-Guard, 1960-1968; Assistant City Editor, Eugene Register-Guard, 1968- ; Drama Reviewer, Eugene Register-Guard, 1967- ; Columnist, Eugene Register-Guard, 1961- ; (9) Professional Journalism Fellow, with emphasis on drama, Stanford University, 1966; Actor, Very Little Theatre, Eugene, Ore., 1961, '62, '63, '72, '73; Member, Very Little Theatre of Eugene, 1961-67, including serving on board of directors; (12) A/1C, Air National Guard and Air Force Reserve, 1960-65; (14) Oregon Newspaper Publishers Assn. award for Best Local Column, 1967; (16) Democrat; (20) Misc. articles in Los Angeles Times' "West" magazine and in various newspapers, including Los Angeles Times, Oakland Tribune, Washington Post, Chicago Tribune (none, however, relating to drama); (21) 1735 Minda Dr., Eugene, Ore. 97401, Ph. 343-0892; (22) Eugene Register-Guard, P.O. Box 10188, Eugene, Ore. 97401, Ph. 503-485-1234; (23) Circulation: 55,000; (24) Approximately 50 plays and musicals.

"Laffing Man" Not Up to Expectations from a Professional
(by Don Bishoff, Register-Guard, February 1, 1975)

If Jerome Kilty were a student playwright, "The Laffing Man" might be charitably dismissed as "the unsuccessful effort of a young author who, nonetheless, shows promise."

But Jerome Kilty is a professional theater veteran. And he should be capable of better writing--and directing--than he has

delivered in his drama, which had its "world premiere" Friday
night at University Theatre.

The play, as conceived by playwright Kilty and director
Kilty, is a disappointing venture into the Kitchen Sink theory of
dramatic writing. That is, you create a bizarre setting for your
play, give it mythological overtones, people it with the widest
possible assortment of strange and sometimes-mad characters,
weave together several disparate themes which are supposed to
evolve into a philosophical whole, insert an occasional bit of
dialogue which has the veneer of profundity, and punctuate the
whole mess with both threatened and actual violence. And--
voila! --you have a hit play.

Sorry, Mr. Kilty. Not this time.

Kilty's bizarre setting is an about-to-be-razed San Francisco
funhouse. To it comes an American ambassador who was raised
in the back rooms of the place and escaped its poverty years ago
to rise to fame.

The ambassador has lately suffered a nervous breakdown over
having to peddle a dishonest foreign policy. When he arrives
back in his boyhood haunt, he (1) discovers it's a criminal hide-
out and (2) falls and breaks his leg.

Soon he's surrounded by a couple of old loonies who may or
may not have some connection with his past, a young punk hood,
a black gang leader, and a teenage moll with a heart of gold--
although maybe not 24-karet.

Kilty works in periodic flashbacks to the ambassador's boyhood by giving him a recurring nightmare about incidents that
happened then.

The biggest nightmare for the audience is trying to make
some sense of it all.

In the last-act confrontation between ambassador and gang
leader, Kilty appears to be trying to make a point about the lust
for power that corrupts both great nations and petty crooks. But
it's a strained point at best--and it's almost lost in the welter
of dramatic elements which playwright Kilty clumsily tries to make
a tapestry of, and which director Kilty frequently tries to jack up
with overacting by his performers.

Perhaps one of the biggest faults of all is Kilty's tin ear for
dialogue. People simply don't talk to one another in the stilted
way that Kilty's characters do.

One line of dialogue often doesn't seem to logically follow
that which came before it. Some lines seem inserted only for
cheap laughs and others only for dime store philosophical effect.

(Says the gang leader, trying to explain why he couldn't communicate with a judge sitting on his bench: "Half our society is sittin' down, the other half is standin' up. You can't have no argument that way.")

Subtlety is also not one of this play's virtues. Having selected the Theseus-slaying-the-Minotaur-in-the-labyrinth story as his mythology peg (the funhouse mirror maze being the labyrinth, the gang leader the minotaur, etc.), Kilty keeps working the word "labyrinth" into the conversation, lest we forget.

Clumsiness is another hallmark of this work. Kilty clumsily takes care of some of the first-act exposition by having the ambassador talk to himself about his background. Or the name of one of the characters is clumsily explained in the second act by having the ambassador say, "That's why they call you Mort-- in the Latin language, that's the word for death."

There's obscurity. A trapeze performer who lives in the funhouse dies during a flashback scene when the protagonist's sister cuts the rope of her trapeze. Why? And what does that have to do with what eventually happens? The answer may lie in the jumble of events which follow, but the audience will need a labyrinth map to find it.

And there are plot elements that are just dumb. Why would a big dope dealer also be involved in such petty crime as stealing TV sets? Or why doesn't the ambassador escape during the several opportunities Kilty's Swisscheese plot gives him--certainly the broken leg doesn't stop him from moving about the stage a great deal.

The UT production does feature a couple of good actors. As the ambassador, Rich Hawkins gives a solid performance in trying to give a believable characterization to a character who's not particularly believable. Hawkins is simply one of those actors whose acting skills and recognizable self-confidence enable him to command an audience's constant attention.

As "Pop," the wino ex-con who hangs around the funhouse, Lou Salerni gives a restrained-and-polished performance in a meaty part which would be easy to overdo. His raspy voice and shuffling walk abet a sure ability to deliver lines in just the way his character should.

Jerry Williams' complex set, which must serve for three different locations, is quite well designed and constructed. It is particularly good in capturing the musty atmosphere of the deserted funhouse--and the huge fluorescent drawing of the funhouse's "laffing man" in the background is striking.

However, as costumer, Williams has gone awry in at least one instance--the attire given the young punk is a laughable caricature of hoodlum attire.

Kilty's track record as both performer and playwright is a
good one. And there's a feeling that some of the things he's
tried in this play are good--there are some characters who could
be interesting, and some of the plot elements are potentially intriguing.

But he's tried to cram too many of them together, and he's
fallen victim to too many of the problems you might associate
with a fledgling playwright. So, unfortunately, University Theatre's chance for a theatrical plum--the first performance of a
major work by a "name" playwright--turned out to be a lemon.

Long Night's "Journey" Well Worth It
(by Don Bishoff, Register-Guard, June 23, 1975)

"Long Day's Journey into Night," as done by the Oregon
Shakespearean Festival, is one of those plays and productions
that personify what powerful dramatic theater is all about.

It is long: 3 1/2 hours. It demands much from an audience:
concentration, a willingness to watch individuals inflict deep psychological pain upon themselves and others, and a durable pos-
terior.

But the rewards are great: a chance to view one of the
greatest works by one of America's greatest dramatists, a chance
to peer into the souls of troubled people rarely available outside
a psychiatrist's office, and an opportunity to watch four actors
and a director show that they truly know their craft.

In the latter sense, "Journey" probably ranks alongside "A
Man for All Seasons" and "Rosencrantz and Guildenstern Are
Dead" as the best of the festival's non-Shakespearean productions
of the last half-dozen years.

Playwright Eugene O'Neill wrote "Journey" as a slightly fic-
tionalized version of his own troubled family life--fading-actor
father, morphine-addicted mother, wastrel older son, and con-
sumption-stricken younger son (O'Neill himself). The play simply follows the family through one day in its Connecticut summer
home.

The family members quarrel violently, love each other with
almost equal passion, tell funny stories and sink into morose
despair. When they quarrel, they pick at each other--pulling
loose scabs of bitterness and self-hatred--then rush in just as
quickly to bandage up the wounds that they have created. Moods
change in mid-sentence and alliances shift rapidly as any two of
the family members combine to attack a third.

Most of this incredible, fascinating, turbulent interplay occurs in the first act of this two-act production, and it is here
that the play is most interesting. The second act is devoted

more to long, self-examining monologues--and it was in that part,
frankly, that I occasionally found my attention wandering. But
the monologues are a necessary part of O'Neill's scheme of
things, a sort of delayed exposition, as each character in turn
reveals how he or she got to this point in life.

The play is not all gloom, incidentally. There are many
funny lines--some black humor, some just funny, as when the
eldest son angrily accuses his father of believing that Shakespeare
was really an Irish Catholic.

Director Jerry Turner and his four principal actors have a
real sense of what O'Neill apparently intended with this play, and
they go about providing it with skill and insight--both in their
individual characterizations and in their sharply honed interplay.

As the father, James Tyrone, Michael Kevin Moore doesn't
so much talk as he does growl his lines, like a slightly irate
bear, biting off his words with measured irony or almost erupt-
ing into quick rages. There's a touch of George C. Scott in the
miserly, irascible--and yet at-times-tender--character he creates,
but it's still very much Moore's own creation.

Perhaps the most striking thing about Jean Smart, who plays
Mary Tyrone, the mother, is not her line delivery, but her mannerisms. At first she seems a quiet, calm individual, but then
you gradually become aware of her way of tugging at herself or
her clothes, gently rubbing her hands, or patting her hair as
the tensions grow within her. Her line delivery is suberb, also,
particularly in the rambling, morphine-haze rememberances she
has in the second act.

Denis Arndt gives a ruddy faced glow to the part of Jamie,
the heavy-drinking older son. Arndt can pump venom with the
best of them in the family quarrels, but he's at his best when
his character is masking his own despair with a happy-go-lucky
approach to the world. Arndt's best scene is a very funny recounting of his evening with Violet, the fat whore, a badly needed
scene which breaks the gloom of the second act.

Edmund Tyrone, the son who is really O'Neill himself, is
troubled more with physical than psychological ailments, and he
seems the only one with any real hope of breaking out of the
snare of despair that encircles the rest of the family.

It's a role that calls for underplaying, for quiet understanding, and this is what William Hurt gives to the part. He has a
way of talking in quiet rushes that convey the feeling and understanding that Edmund feels for the other members of his family.

Katherine James is quite good in her relatively brief appearances as the family's servant.

Richard Hay captures the murky existence of the Tyrone family in his dusty-bookshelf-and-drab-wicker-furniture set. And
Steven Maze's lighting is most effective, particularly in the highlights it gives to individual characters just before the fadeouts.

Craftsmanship seems an insufficient word to describe the
skill and care which Director Turner, his cast, and the Festival
Technical Company have invested in this production. But it is
stage craftsmanship of the highest order, and this is a production
which should be seen by anyone who really cares about good theater and who finds a great happiness in seeing it done well.

BLACK, Ira J.; (2) Theatre critic and broadcaster; (3) b. Brooklyn,
N.Y., Feb. 20, 1943; (4) s. Emanuel D. and Ray L. (Kooperman)
B.; (5) M.A. City University of New York-Hunter College, theatre
and cinema, 1974; M.A. Ohio State University, English literature,
1965; B.A. Brooklyn College, English 1963; (8) Assistant professor
of speech/theatre, Texas Southern University, 1972-74; Booking/Pro-
motional Manager, Texas Opera Theatre, 1974-75; Theatre critic,
Cultural Affairs Director and Staff Announcer, KLEF-Houston, 1974- ;
(9) Actor and member of the board, Main Street Theatre, 1975- (have
appeared in seven featured roles); (10) Member of Performing Arts
Committee, Main Street-'76 (Houston Chamber of Commerce), 1976;
(15) Mem., American Theatre Critics Assoc., American Theatre
Association, American Assoc. of University Professors; (20) Cont.
articles to KLEF Program Guide, reviews broadcast regularly on
KLEF-Houston, review published in Educational Theatre Journal;
(21) 3131 Timmons Lane, Houston, Tex. 77027, Ph. 713-960-1616;
(22) KLEF-Houston, 1401 South Post Oak Road, Houston, Tex. 77056,
Ph. 713-622-5333; (23) app. audience reached 10,000+; (24) 25-30
play reviews, 6-10 monthly articles.

The Fall and Rise of Bertolt Brecht
(by Ira J. Black, over KLEF radio, Houston, April 5, 1976)

Robert Frost once described himself as "having a lover's
quarrel with the world." This is most likely true of most artists as social commentators. Bertolt Brecht was one and he
wore the chips on his shoulders like epaulets. As he wrote in
a poem to Danish worker-actors:
You ... can make the experience of struggle
The property of all
And transform justice
Into a passion.
Of course, life in Germany between the world wars was the ideal
stimulus for this passionate genius, and while most people know
him only as the author of Three-Penny Opera, his output of plays,
poetry and prose essays was prodigious.

The Fall and Rise of Bertolt Brecht, the UH Drama Department's new production, is a Weimar cabaret-style pastiche of
songs and Brechtian patter, adapted for the occasion by Director

Sidney Berger. The work is ambitious in both conception and
execution--and eminently successful in both. The first half,
called "How to Survive," is pretty much a picture of life after
the debacle of World War One, with everyone going to Hell in a
wheelbarrow--full of Deutchmarks. The second, "To the Next
Generation," is a lesson in the tyrrany that filled the Weimar
void--the Third Reich. In all, there are thirty-four individual
pieces, mainly songs, cemented together into a cohesive picture
of Brecht's artistic vision with brief comments by Brecht or
about him and his work. Each element is perfectly matched to
its neighbors and the segues are near-seamless, giving the work
a flow and propulsive force that carries the audience along with
neither lapses of energy nor sacrifices to flashy freneticism.
Berger has taken the whole Brechtian literature and created a
multifaceted kaleidoscope with an always visible central focus,
in the person of an on-stage Bertolt Brecht.

As to the production itself--it does ample justice to its inspiration. Within the confined spaces of Cullen Hall's Attic
Theatre, tricked out like a bistro with tiny tables, tinsel and a
runway, the company of sixteen, accompanied by a piano and
drums, seems to be all over the place yet working with clocklike
precision. So much of this work's success depends on the fine
distinctions made among the strong emotions expressed--the ease
with which the transitions are made and the clarity with which
they are shown. Again, no concessions were made here.

In keeping with the cabaret atmosphere the company was costumed and made-up like George Grosz caricatures. That is,
everyone except Robert Bruce Linn as Brecht himself. In leather coat, short hair and cigar, he is a dead ringer for the play-
wright--as the incorporated slide show dares us to notice. So
complete is his impersonation, the passion and sense of commitment he projects as well as the physical image, that we accept
him as the echte-Brecht. His reading of the poem "Song About
My Mother" is particularly affecting, especially within the context of his more strident acerbidity.

Within the overall superb ensemble work, several individual
pieces are worth mentioning. Cindy Beall and Sidney O'Keefe
Dorf did their several "feature" pieces with the razor-sharp delivery of a Brechtian fallen woman, while Dallas Purdy's renditions of two of Brecht's most popular lyrics, "Pirate Jenny"
and "Surabaya Johnny," made Lotte Lenya sound the soul of sweetness and light.

One of the few extended non-musical pieces is the dramatic
monologue "The Jewish Wife" which encapsulates the experience
of the suddenly de-assimilated German Jews under Hitler. Marilyn Rogers' performance of it was particularly arresting.

Two hours of Brecht can be a wrenching experience. He
made no concessions nor allowed his audience any. The com-

bination of comedy, poignance and anger in the set pieces, joined
by the aphoristic commentary of Brecht himself in rapid succession is heady stuff, keeping the audience alert--and entertained--
throughout. The Fall and Rise of Bertolt Brecht, as conceived
and produced by Sidney Berger and his UH company, is one of
the most fascinating and enjoyably provocative evenings I've spent
in the theatre.

Review: 1776
(by Ira J. Black, over KLEF radio, Houston, June 28, 1976)

At the risk of becoming as "obnoxious and disliked" as John
Adams, let me say right off the bat that 1776 is one of the sor-
riest excuses for musical theatre, popularized history and patriotic fervor I've yet encountered. Of all the really good American musicals--and America is the acknowledged home of the art--
why did TUTS have to choose 1776 for its Bicentennial bid?
More than just pandering to the same sort of mentality that thinks
that all the Bicentennial means is red-white-and-blue beer mugs
and fire plugs, it is a demeaning picture of the men who wrangled
over starting our experiment and equally demeaning for those of
us who take our Americanism seriously. It seems to me the per-
petrators of 1776 have used the one trick to guarantee large un-
thinking audiences--a watered-down, gossipy version of American
history--no one's going to knock apple pie and Mom, right?   Maybe Voltaire was right--"Patriotism is the last refuge of the
soundrel."

One failing of most societies is that they monumentalize their
heroes and thus lose touch with their reality. Neither more nor
less, we are guilty of this hyperveneration ourselves. Let us
have no pedestals--our heroes were giants. As men among men,
Franklin, Adams and Jefferson were outstanding. Their wit, their
intelligence, their commitment--their humanity--are impressive
without exaggeration. Perhaps their very superiority made it necessary for the creators of 1776 to reduce them to caricatures in
order for them to be popularly palatable. Are we so small that
we cannot accept our Franklins unless they're dirty old men with
gout, our Adamses unless they're prim little Boston prudes, or
our Jeffersons unless they're silent back-benchers whose sole interest is bedding their wives? In order to vivify the musty portrait of that eventful Continental Congress, must it be perverted
into a vaudeville chorus? I think not. The moments of serious
purpose serve only as self-conscious intervals between lamely
funny, mediocre musical numbers--like the redeeming social significance of a pornographic novel, except that here it's the pornography that's lame too.

Perhaps more disturbing to me is that 1776 lets us sit back
on our complacency without re-evaluating--or even understanding
--the momentousness of that occasion. How many of us today
would go with the status quo of John Dickinson rather than the
traitorous madness of John Adams? We are allowed to accept

the melodramatic--and foregone--conclusion without realizing
that, as a body, we'd probably lynch the lot of them--or vote
them out of office, at the least. The ballad of "The Cool, Cool,
Conservative Men" is the only song with a touch of reality about
it. That lovely anti-war song "Momma, Look Sharp" is sentimental clap-trap--a calculated, tear-jerking palliative for es-
pousers of fashionable causes. "Molasses to Rum," the South's
answer to Northern anti-slave sentiment has dramatic validity--
but not in this play.

With the likes of the Adams Chronicles, An American Primitive, and Kingsley's The Patriots, to name just three Bicentennial productions of the past several months, why are we wasting
our time with schlock that cynically assumes we're all Archie
Bunkers who are as stupid as Edith?

Now to the TUTS production which is not outstanding in either
direction but, perhaps appropriately, middle-of-the-road. Michael Miller tried for a very frenetic, angular, gravelly John
Adams in keeping with history, if not the playwright. All the
boffo throwaway lines go to Ben Franklin, played by Kevin Cooney
as a Colonial Jack Paar. It's effective, to be sure, but suffers
from the grotesque make-up job which makes Franklin look like
a victim of one of his own experiments. Since no one else gets
such a portraiture job, he's even more out-of-place. The most
satisfying performance of the lot is Charles Krohn's as Dickinson
the leader of the anti-independence faction. Instead of the melodramatic villain twirling imaginary moustaches, this Dickinson
would have been a worthy adversary to the real Adams. As for
everyone else, it would serve little purpose running down the
list, assigning plusses and minuses. Perhaps my antipathy toward the work itself makes looking too long at this production an
act of diminishing equanimity. One last note though, in fairness
to the cast and Mr. Miller especially--if Conductor Charles
Rosekrans had been marking time for our forefathers, we'd probably be celebrating the 12th of August!

That's 1776--perhaps Franklin had this show in mind when
he suggested the turkey as our national bird.

BLANK, Edward L.; (2) Drama editor; (3) b. Pittsburgh, Pa., Oct.
26, 1943; (4) s. Albert and Gertrude (Sullivan) Blank; (5) B.A. Duquesne U., major: English, 1965; (6) Single; (8) The Pittsburgh
Press (1967-); City Desk reporter 1967-68; News and features copy
editor 1968-69; TV-Radio Editor 1969-71; Drama Editor 1971-; (13)
Lieutenant, U.S. Army, 1965-67; (22) 34 Blvd. of the Allies, Pittsburgh, Pa. 15230, Ph. 412-263-1525; (23) Circulation: 300 daily;
700,000 Sunday; (24) App. 275 stories/columns per year, roughly 40%
of which are reviews. These include both stage and screen. The other
stories are interviews and straight news stories relating to the stage
and screen.

Hilarious "Young Frankenstein" Spoofs Karloff Monster Classic
(by Edward L. Blank, Pittsburgh Press, February 5, 1975)

Young Dr. Fred Frankenstein pokes his head out the window
of the train and asks innocently:

"Pardon me, Boy. Is this the Transylvania Station?"

"Yah," comes the reply. "Track 29. Can I give you a
shine?"

Not all the humor in "Young Frankenstein," opening today
at the Chatham, is quite so inspired, but the bon mots are so
numerous, the picture is almost audience-proof.

This is the fourth and most polished film by director Mel
Brooks ("The Producers," "The 12 Chairs," "Blazing Saddles"),
who contributed to a screenplay by Gene Wilder.

Brooks plays no roles himself this time, but Wilder does--
he's the young contemporary doctor who visits Transylvania to
claim the estate of his grandfather, the legendary grave digger
and creator of the monster in Boris Karloff's "Frankenstein."

One needn't love the Karloff picture to get a kick out of this
one, but it won't hurt. Brooks' film is a comic gem when it's
being original as well as when it's spoofing Karloff's.

Consider the motley crew on hand:

Marty Feldman as Igor ("That's Eye-gore," he says), a
hunchback with a moveable hump and big, unfocused eyes.

Cloris Leachman as Frau Blucher, housekeeper of the Transylvanian Frankenstein estate. At the mention of her name, horses
rear and whinny in terror--no matter how softly it's spoken and
how distant the horses.

Teri Garr as Inga, the lucious lab assistant with the liquid
lips. Blonde, brainless cotton candy.

Madeline Kahn as young Frankenstein's chaste vamp of a
sweetheart. "Don't muss me," she says, warding off a goodbye
kiss. They rub elbows instead.

Peter Boyle as the seven-foot, zipper-necked monster with
a passion for violin music.

Kenneth Mars as Inspector Kemp, a Prussian takeoff on
Peter Sellers' Dr. Strangelove.

And Gene Hackman in a hilarious unbilled bit as a blind
monk into whose cabin the monster unwittingly stumbles.

Because Brooks and Wilder cram so many gags into the picture, one can't help being aware of many which don't work. The whole Mars role, for example, misses--partly because it's staged and played too stridently.

More often than not, "Young Frankenstein's" zingers come off. At least one scene--a "Puttin' on the Ritz"' parody--is convulsively funny.

Parents will be in more of a pickel than usual about the (appropriate) PG rating. There's scarcely any doubt children will find some scenes hilarious. On the other hand, sex is never far from the foreground, and there are a handful of implications regarding the monster's oversized attributes.

"Nash at Nine" Warms Playhouse with Wit, Wistful Moments
(by Edward L. Blank, Pittsburgh Press, February 12, 1975)

"Nash at Nine" is unexpected in two respects: in its booking here, on only seven days' notice, and in its effect.

It opened a seven-performance engagement at The Pittsburgh Playhouse last night, direct from Washington, D.C., where its national tour started two weeks ago.

The production, a musical-comedy revue, has a peculiar, understated impact. For most of its 1-hour-and-40-minute running time (including intermission), it involves the audience in an assortment of songs, quips and rhymes.

Suddenly it's warm and serious, and it works because the performers have succeeded in ingratiating themselves during the lighter moments.

"Nash at Nine" is a compilation of verses and lyrics by the late Ogden Nash, with a Milton Rosenstock score which won the Outer Circle Critics' Award a couple of seasons ago.

The four singer-actors (Craig Stevens, Jane Summerhays, John Stratton and Harvey Evans) are accompanied on stage by pianists Rod Derefinko and Brooks Morton.

There's no pattern to what they do, as the material is varied and changes continuously.

Word games are highlighted early, as when Stevens (frequently playing a Nash figure) defines himself as "a versifier trying to achieve the perfect rhyme."

But there is no rhyme for orange--short of a Miss Gorange. Lucrezia Borgia? Comin' toward ya.

The versifier is not above mocking bad verse ("I think that

I shall never see a billboard lovely as a tree").

Miss Summerhays speaks of the only two Hagens she knows: Walter and Copen.

Stratton and Evans play name games. They know their Kims, for example: Kim Stanley, Kim Hunter, Kim Novak, Akim Tamiroff ...

If the first half of the show only glitters nicely, the second works up to a sparkle.

The latter half begins with the most uproarious sequence-- a New York cocktail party which bores its dutiful host--and works toward a sad, pensive and finally optimistic conclusion-- much in the manner of "Jacques Brel."

In one of the more wistful moments, a woman turning 30 stares at herself apprehensively in a mirror. "How old is spring, Miranda?" she's asked at last. And a faint, relieved smile surfaces.

The Players, all eager to please, found an appreciative opening night audience applauding with increasing enthusiasm.

For a small show, it's surprisingly busy. Martin Charnin's direction keeps the players in perpetual motion--modified only during the thoughtful moments near the end.

David Chapman's set involves virtually all wooden props-- and many at that. Thankfully we're spared the pretensions of a bare stage--all too common these days.

Martin Aronstein's lighting, complicated by the continuous movement, and Theoni V. Aldredge's costumes, ranging from natty suits to saddle shoes, serve the production well.

Other performances are slated at 8:30 p.m. today through Saturday, with matinees at 2 p.m. Thursday and at 2:30 p.m. Saturday.

Oh, that The Playhouse would house more professional productions this season.

BONE, Harold MacPherson; (2) Theatre Critic, show business correspondent; (3) b. New Haven, Ct., Oct. 15, 1896; (4) s. George Drummond Bone, Sr. and Agnes McLay Bone; (5) Graduate, West Haven, Ct., High School (1914), general ed.; (6) Widower, following 1971 death of Marie Keenan Bone (married 41 years); (7) children-- Muriel Lou, Cynthia Harma; (8) Critic, New Haven Theatre News (weekly) 1937-40; Play reviewer, New Haven Morning Journal-Courier, 1945; Display advertising staff, N.H. Journal-Courier (approx.

1945-52); Part owner job printing shop (approx. 20 years); Editor and
Advertising Director, New Haven Info Magazine (monthly) (1953-1975);
New Haven Correspondent, Variety (1930--still serving in 1975). (For
Variety, I have reviewed the world premieres of Oklahoma!, My
Fair Lady, South Pacific, Sound of Music, Skin of Our Teeth, Time
of Your Life, All My Sons, Raisin in the Sun, Tea and Sympathy,
Shenandoah, Funny Thing Happened, Mary Mary, Sunshine Boys, Pris-
oner of Second Avenue, No Time for Sergeants, Mr. Roberts, and
countless others.); (10) Treasurer and Member Board of Dir. New
Haven Council of Churches (103 organizations); (13) Seaman U.S.
Naval Reserve Force, World War I; (15) Member American Theatre
Critics Assn.; (16) Republican; (17) Congregationalist: served 31
years as secretary of a Sunday School at one period having 800 members; also, over 20 years as a member of Board of Deacons, First
Congregational Church, West Haven, Ct.; (20) Freelance material to
various publications (moderate success); (21) 324 Elm St., West Hav-
en, Ct. 06516, Ph. 203-933-1791; (22) office address, same; (23)
range from statewide (Ct.) to international (Variety). I have covered
as many as 58 plays in 10 weeks (for review and factual purposes),
also as many as 400 motion pictures in one year. I have reviewed
virtually everything from a Chinese opera to a Russian drama, without knowing either language, as well as night club acts and three-
ring circuses.

"Away We Go!"
(by Harold M. Bone, Variety, March 11, 1943)

Having tried practically everything else this season, from
fantasy ("Mr. Sycamore") to stark realism ("Russian People"),
The Theatre Guild is now offering a package of nostalgia neatly
wrapped in a talented cast and tied up with a blue-ribbon score.
They've jigsawed Lynn Riggs' "Green Grow the Lilacs" and re-
assembled it as "Away We Go!", a tune-dance concoction whose
title is indicative of the show's potential marathon. It got off
to a good start here and should stretch into a sizeable stay on
Broadway. Film possibilities are bright.

Boasting a pretty-ditty, fancy-prancing combo, the production
lacks only editing to weld it into a first-class tuneshow. It's not for
the modern, whoopdedoo, blatant appetite, but it packs an escapist
appeal that should find a healthy response among those who go for
quality rather than clamor in their entertainment. Not that "Away"
is conservative: it's just that its liveliness is built on an old-fashioned foundation that seemed to ring the bell with first-nighters here.

Book sticks pretty close to the original, and in so doing provides a story with better-than-average tunes and terps. Through
play's unorthodox opening (girls do not come on for 35 minutes),
audience is made aware early that "Away" is not the conventional
type of song-and-dancer. Roles are played straight rather than
operetta fashion, which enhances the script angle of the production. Locale is Oklahoma at the turn of the century and book
retains the lusty outdoor flavor that punctuated "Lilacs" originally.

The new cleffing teammates, Richard Rodgers and Oscar
Hammerstein 2d, have turned in a capital job in their combined
maiden effort. Songs are appropriately sentimental, peppy and
comic, as situations require, and score as a whole comprises
a succession of melodious moments. Due for an early play on
the hit parade are "Oh, What a Beautiful Morning," "People Will
Say," "Boys and Girls Like You and Me," "The Surrey with
Fringe on Top," and "Many a New Day," Comedy clicks are "I
Can't Say No" and "All or Nothin'." A satirical ditty, "Pore
Jud Is Daid," is particularly nifty. Overall high calibre of score
augurs well for future possibilities of the new tune-smith duo.
Rodgers, or course, has achieved notable prominence as half of
the team of Rodgers and Hart.

Paced on a par with the fine music are the superb dance
creations of Agnes de Mille. Though dance angle absorbs a bit
too much running time, it's all sterling stuff and may present a
problem in cutting. Contributing prominently, on the ballet end
are Marc Platt, Katharine Sergava and George Church. Ensemble standouts are Joan McCracken and Bambi Linn, latter a per-
sonality-plus 16-year-old who shows considerable promise. Some
fast tapping is turned in by Lee Dixon, George Church and Eric
Victor. (In a rowdy straight scene late in preem performance,
Victor broke his wrist in a fall.)

In the vocal department, leads are carried by a fine boy-and-
girl team, Alfred Drake and Joan Roberts. Drake has been
around, largely in straight plays, but in this, his first major
musical, he comes through nicely on both personality and voice.
His opening solo, "Oh, What a Beautiful Morning'," is a quick
click and his vocal pairing with Miss Roberts blends well. Latter has come from midwest smaller productions to her initial
big-timer hereabouts with a combination of charm, grace and
singing ability that should demand, and get, attention. Her work
here drew enthusiastic approval. Other vocal tidbits are added
by Celeste Holm, Lee Dixon, Edwin Clay, Joseph Buloff and
Howard da Silva.

On the thespian end, Betty Garde draws the role of Aunt
Eller, a major item in the original play but somewhat submerged
in the musical version. Miss Garde goes through the paces with
her customary skill, but the role leaves much of her talent un-
cultivated. Howard da Silva gets a good break as the heavy,
Jud, and does okay by the job. His duet with Drake is something. Buloff sells himself aptly as Ali Hakim, the Persian peddler; and wrings out a number of lusty laughs. Miss Holm is
a surprise click as a singing comedienne, registering in a solo,
"I Can't Say No," and teaming with Dixon on "All or Nothin'."
Her straight stuff scores, too. Jane Lawrence handles a bit
easily.

Guild has dug into the sock to put this one on. Although
not so sumptuous as the golden era extravaganza musicals,

there's quality in the trappings for "Away." On costumes, Miles White has succeeded in making his feminine contingent attractive even though swathed in early century dress--no small trick in these days when female allure depends more or less on a certain amount of exposure. Sets by Lemuel Ayers feature a water-color effect with a simplicity that makes them distinctive. Backdrop perspectives are cleverly done. Staging by Reuben Mamoulian is expert and largely responsible for smoothness of performance.

Capsule Critiques: A Midsummer Night's Dream
(by Harold M. Bone, New Haven Info, June 1975)

Yale Repertory Theatre, in association with the Yale School of Music, presentation of William Shakespeare's fantasy with music from "The Fairy Queen," by Henry Purcell. Staged by Alvin Epstein; music adapted and conducted by Otto-Werner Mueller; scenery, Tony Straiges; costumes, Zack Brown; lighting, William B. Warfel; associate music director and conductor, Gary Fagin; choreographic associate, Carmen de Lavallade.

Cast: Jeremy Geidt, Franchelle Stewart Dorn, Robert Nersesian, Ralph Drischell, Kate McGregor-Steward, Stephen Rowe, Peter Schifter, Meryl Streep, Jerome Dempsey, Charles Levin, Joe Grifasi, Frederic Warriner, Paul Schierhorn, Ralph Redpath, Linda Atkinson, Joseph Capone, Lizbeth Mackay, John Rothman, Michael Lassell, Christopher Lloyd, Carmen de Lavallade, Danny Brustein, Brian Drutman, Evan Drutman, Chris Erikson.

Singers: Nansi Carroll, Renee Santer, Martha Bennett, Sue Lefebvre, James Bell, Rinde Eckert, Frank Lezzi, Robert McMahan, Susan Goldberger, Priscilla Warren, Alma Cuervo, Nancy Nelson, Kenneth Hamilton, Scott Persons, David Albert, Mark Hewitt.

Orchestra: conductor Otto-Werner Mueller, associate conductor Gary Fagin, Marion Egge, Gerry Elias, Scott Hankins, Tim Kidder, Mary Jane Levin, Nicholas Neuman, Bruce Patti, Mike Selman, Paula Sisson, Jim Wallenberg, Barbara Hanna, Linda Sanders, Marilyn Smith, Madalena Marx, Christina Soule, Jean-Eves Benichun, Alan Rickmeyer, Randy Cook, Frank Lynch, Garrett Bennett, Ben Aldridge, Dale White, C. J. Everett, Beth Ravin, Ian Hobson, Robert Weirich.

Shakespeare couldn't possibly have envisioned what the Yale Repertory Theatre would do to it when he penned "A Midsummer Night's Dream."

The YRT has taken the Bard for a ride ... a sort of rump tobogganing ride down a hillside in a forest ... and the outcome is a glorious mixture of mirth, music, and make-believe. It is a constantly ingenious, constantly surprising, and constantly

rewarding production. The pity is that too few people will be
able to enjoy it this year in its brief May 9 to 31 existence.
There is a promise, however, of reviving it two years hence
as the probable season-opener of 1976-77. Opening night bravos
were well deserved all around.

Shakespeare and melody have been combined in earlier presentations of "Midsummer Night's Dream" over the years, but
perhaps never so successfully as the present collaboration unquestionably turns out to be. There are times when the present
Henry Purcell vocal-instrumental contribution seems to blend
successfully with what the story is trying to tell us, and other
times when it seems to contribute equally successfully despite
having apparently disassociated itself from the story per se.
But whatever the case may be, the music is a very definite in-
gredient in the overall enjoyment of the work.

Some of the most prolonged laughter in the history of YRT
productions emanates from the antics of a group called "The
Rustics," who stage a play within a play. Composed of Jerome
Dempsey, Charles Levin, Joe Grifasi, Frederic Warriner, Paul
Schierhorn, Ralph Redpath, this troup is hilarious in its planning,
rehearsing, and performing of its own little version of Thespis.

YRT has tapped its till (with a contributing hand from the
Corbett Foundation) heavily in the matter of scenery and costumes. A picturesque set of hanging drapes and artwork cutouts
creates a good image of regal quarters in Athens, while an ingenious arrangement of a wooded area, opens up to disclose
scenes taking place within a hillside, as well as the aforementioned tobogganing locale that is put to brilliant use with a variety of pictorial action. A number of the costumes can best
be described as lavish. The exceptional visual effects are the
combined efforts of Tony Straiges (scenery), Zack Brown (costumes), William B. Warfel (lighting).

Ballet sequences are prominently on the asset list. They
lend beauty and graceful complement to mobile scenes of the
play. Carmen de Lavallade has done outstanding double duty in
both choreography and glowing performance, with Christopher
Lloyd as a valued ballet partner.

Regarding the score, some 20 selections have been woven
into the proceedings with effective results. Vocal numbers range
from solo to ensemble, with the bulk of the delivery emanating
from a ponderous balcony setup irrelevantly fastened to a side
wall of the auditorium. Otto-Werner Mueller has brilliantly
blended this happy wedding of singing (Yale Music School) and
acting (YRT) talent.

Alvin Epstein's staging of this monumental work is something
in the nature of phenomenal. To sort out the countless elements
and give each particular element the emphasis it warrants has

been a gargantuan assignment that Epstein has met with superlative merit. Dull moments in the three hours and a quarter span of entertainment are conspicuous by their absence. Among the acting personnel, standouts are Jeremy Geidt as Duke of Athens and his betrothed Franchelle Stewart Dorn; Kate McGregor-Stewart (Hermia), Stephen Rowe (Demetrius), Peter Schifter (Lysander), Meryl Street (Helena), the constantly-tiffing lovers; Linda Atkinson as the spritely Puck; Christopher Lloyd and Carmen de Lavallade (King and Queen of the Fairies); and the aforementioned riotous Rustics.

"Midsummer Dream" is one of the more (if not actually the most) resounding success of the YRT to date.

BORAK, Jeffrey; (2) Arts editor and drama critic; (5) B.A. University of Wisconsin, English; M.A. University of Washington, Drama, 1966; (8) Editor, Beacon newspaper, Dutchess County, 1970; News reporter, and Theater reviewer, Poughkeepsie Journal, 1971- ; Art editor and drama critic, 1974- ; (9) Asst. director of Creative Arts Center, Haile Selassie University, Addis Ababa (Peace Corp) 1966-68; Teacher, English, Ethiopia, 1968-69; Hyde Park, N.Y. 1969-70; (22) Poughkeepsie Journal, P.O. Box 1231, Poughkeepsie, N.Y. 12602, Ph. 914-454-2000; (23) Circulation: daily 37,000; Sunday 40,000.

"Mass" A Dazzling Theatrical Adventure
(by Jeffrey Borak, Poughkeepsie Journal, April 21, 1975)

The Poughkeepsie Ballet Theater production of Leonard Bernstein's "Mass" offers an object lesson in what a handful of professionals can do with a company of largely non-professional performers committed to their art.

Working with members of his own ballet company, Arthur Bloom and members of the Hudson Valley Philharmonic, a professional, Michael Hume, in a pivotal role, and a company of over 100 singers and players, Tom Adair has taken Bernstein's extraordinarily complex work and created out of it a dazzling theatrical adventure.

Bernstein has subtitled his work "A Theatre Piece for Singers, Players and Dancers." Through his choreography and staging, Adair has taken Bernstein literally, fashioning, in the process, a swift two-hour entertainment which constantly bombards the senses with flashes of sound, color and movement, played against the background of a simple, but nonetheless stunning J. Newton White setting done in rope and string.

I suspect that what really makes this production work so effectively for the most part is its sense of discipline both in Arthur Bloom's certain, tightly-controlled conducting of the piece and in the execution of Adair's staging.

It is a feeling which filters down to even the children's chorus, no mean accomplishment in itself.

The dynamics of the performance range from the obvious to the very subtle. Punctuated by Christiane Langer's superb costuming, the constant tension in the score between the Celebrant and his leaderless flock of congregants is reflected time and again in countless visual images and the myriad expressions in the faces and eyes of the more than 150 singers and dancers on stage.

His cherubic face fringed by a modest halo of hair, Michael Hume's Celebrant is a stark and dramatic contrast to the more calculatedly garish congregants who swirl around him.

He is the essence of innocence, offering the spiritually tortured masses the sanctity and peace of a formalized religious worship which can no longer meet their needs.

Surrounded in a circle of children, Hume's Celebrant seems safe and protected in the warmth of innocence which is later ripped apart by a restless flock searching desperately for answers. it cannot find from an unseen and silent God.

Led by a series of preacher-soloists, the company of singers and dancers follow the Celebrant's moving insistence that the Word of the Law cannot be defiled with a cynical gospel-sermon deriding man's constant violation of that very same Word.

"God said it's good to be poor, Good men must not be secure," one preacher sings. "So if we steal from you, It's just to help you stay pure."

"God made us the boss, God gave us the cross," another chants. "We turned it into a sword to spread the Word of the Lord, We use his holy decrees, To do whatever we please," they sing against a tawdry background of frosted lightbulbs and shimmering silver foil.

Fed up with asking questions which have no answers, the congregants over the Celebrant's insistence at completing the Mass, move across the stage and out onto the two platforms jutting into the audience with increasing agitation.

"We've got quarrels and qualms and such questions," they chant, "Give us answers, not psalms and suggestions. Give us peace that we don't keep on breaking, Give us something or we'll just start taking!"

Pressed by questions and growing self-doubts he himself cannot resolve, the Celebrant smashes the sacraments, tears off his vestments and hurls them at the crowd, dances on the altar in bitter, agonized fury waving the altar cloths like tattered remnants of a battle flag and then, his spirit completely broken, vanishes.

Out of the stunned silence which follows, a flute, then a boy soloist, then each of the congregants and, finally, the Celebrant himself, join in a swelling wave of love and peace as each one, shattered by the Celebrant's own trauma, discovers a peace and awareness from within; a peace which makes them reach out first to one another and then to the audience.

Surrounded on the altar steps by his newly-found flock, the Celebrant says simply: "The Mass is ended. Go in Peace."

The certainty of Hume's compelling performance, Adair's staging and choreography and Bloom's musical direction generally offset some very regrettable weaknesses in the production.

The key to the work's theme lies not only in the dramatic tensions and contrasts in Bernstein's music, but also in the libretto he fashioned out of the Liturgy of the Roman Mass together with Stephen Schwartz.

Despite the on-stage presence of numerous microphones, it was frequently difficult to hear, let alone understand, most of the soloists. The choruses, particularly the classical choir, were uneven in tone and one often yearned for more strength from them.

And, as odd as it may seem to mention it, there were moments when the production seemed to be over-choreographed; when, despite the presence of dramatic forms and images, the presence of dancers on stage really was not needed and I am thinking here of one particular moment between the Celebrant and the classical choir.

With its direct debt to other musical forms, passages from a variety of classical composers and the complexities both of its musical and dramatic themes, Bernstein's work really ought to be heard more than once. An intellectually challenging piece, it is apt to leave one strangely uninvolved emotionally; a feeling which, despite the brilliance of its concept and execution, crept over me often during its performance.

Still, whatever one may feel about the work itself, and there is certainly considerable room for debate, there can be little doubt that its Poughkeepsie Ballet Theatre production, under the guiding hands of Messrs. Adair and Bloom, remains an impressive achievement.

Cat Has Problems On Its Hot Tin Roof
(by Jeffrey Borak, Poughkeepsie Journal, August 12, 1975)

Tennessee Williams's "Cat on a Hot Tin Roof" is a summer play, filled with seething passions, hatreds, loves and life which bubble beneath the languid rhythms and tempos of a hot summer day.

It is a lacerating study of a family slowly being eaten away by greed, mistrust and deception, peppered with a cutting acerbic wit which casts a finely honed, cutting edge around the play.

The occasion is the 65th birthday of the family patriarch Big Daddy Pollit who has received word from his clinic that his acute physical condition is the result of a spastic colon instead of cancer; a carefully calculated lie his doctors and family have fabricated to ease Big Daddy's final days.

Big Daddy is master of a 28,000-acre estate, "the finest bottom land in the South," he roars. It will be his legacy to one of his two sons: one, an avaricious corporation lawyer who has kept his wife in a continual state of pregnancy, siring an obnoxious brood of "no neck monsters;" the other, his favorite, an alcoholic former athlete who drowns his guilt over his responsibility for the death of a close friend in bourbon.

There are the wives: Big Mama, herself shielded from the truth about Big Daddy's condition, bravely running around after her massive husband, drowning in the wake of his abuse and scorn; the eternally pregnant Mae who shares her husband's relentless ambition to gain the acceptance from Big Daddy he has so long been denied; and, at the center of it all, Maggie: cool, cunning, poised, who, with all the shrewd cunning of a feline which has been denied what it wants, systematically sets out to win back the love her husband Brick has denied her.

Deceit and self-illusion are not new themes to Williams. They fertilize the soil in which Williams's characters feed. But in "Cat," Williams uses these themes with all the artistry of a knife-thrower in a carnival sideshow.

The late autumnal production which has been mounted at Candlewood Theatre has little to do with the play Tennessee Williams wrote. Beyond some rather interesting cuts, the playing style of this production is curiously detached and glib.

There is nothing but technique all over the Candlewood stage. Gestures, vocal gimmickry are in abundance and they are used, for the most part, with little dramatic effect.

The main victim of all this is Williams. It is a one-level verbose production which glides over the script's mordant humor and turns itself into a meaningless exercise in rhetoric.

Sandy Dennis's Maggie is a dull, uninteresting harridan with a flat, one-tone line delivery which serves her well in her encounters with Mae but in no way suggests the passionate nature of the woman. She rarely smiles and when she does smile, it smacks of pretense and artifice. The air of cool calculation, softened by an abiding love for Brick and passion for survival which are so essential for Maggie is nowhere in evidence. It robs the play's final scene between Brick and the triumphant Maggie of its force and power, bringing this production to an abrupt halt rather than a dramatic resolution.

David Selby, who is physically right for the role of Maggie's husband Brick, fares no better than Miss Dennis. His Brick has the air of a laconic hayseed humorist who accidentally wandered on stage during a break in the taping of "Hee Haw" and can't find his way back.

Ronald Bishop is a massive Big Daddy roaring his way across Tom Barnes's superbly atmospheric set with a great deal of sound and fury which frequently touches base with the character but which, for the most part, signifies very little.

James Murtaugh and Peggy Cosgrove are acceptable as Gooper, Big Daddy's attorney son, and Mae, Gooper's wife. Geraldine Kay as Big Mama seems more like a Jewish mother at a bar mitzvah, running around making sure the guests have everything they want and need.

The show has been directed by Porter Van Zandt with no particular sense of style or nuance.

This is one "Cat" which has a great deal of trouble staying on its hot tin roof.

BOWMAN, Pierre L.; (2) Entertainment editor; (3) b. Honolulu, Hawaii, March 17, 1944; (4) s. F. Moffett and Ida May (Larson); (5) B.A. University of Minnesota, major subj: journalism, 1968; (6) m. Lee Ann Holmberg, Feb. 20, 1965; (7) children--Cassandra Annina, Samuel Kuikahi; (8) Reporter, United Press International, Minneapolis, 1968-1971; Staff writer, Honolulu Star-Bulletin, 1971-74; Entertainment editor, Honolulu Star-Bulletin, 1974- ; (9) Visiting associate journalism professor, University of Hawaii, 1975-76; (14) Named critic of the year for 1975 by Honolulu Magazine; (17) Protestant; (20) Articles for the Readers Digest, Weight Watchers Magazine; (21) 156-B N. Kalaheo Ave., Kailua, Hi. 96734, Ph. 808-262-8577; (22) Circulation: 120,000; (24) 60 plays and musicals, 60 motion pictures, 30 nightclubs, 12 recordings, 10 miscellaneous.

"Fiddler" Survives Its Star
(by Pierre Bowman, Honolulu Star-Bulletin, June 30, 1976)

"Fiddler on the Roof," which opened last night at the Concert Hall, is a musical so heartwarming and worthwhile that it survives flaws in its Honolulu production which would be fatal to nearly any other play.

The show is blessed with a fine score, galvanizing characters and a universal theme about man's ability to change, survive and continute to love. These blessings remain at the Concert Hall.

But another blessing inherent in the show--the vibrant role Tevye, the milkman whose nubile daughters shatter tradition and change his life--is sorely missing.

Jan Peerce has been cast as Tevye. He seems less like the girls' father than their grandfather. He shuffles around, barely lifting his feet from the stage, and is literally helped into the wings on some of his exits.

Tevye is the element that elevates "Fiddler" from pleasure to greatness. The role must brim with energy and give an audience a man who is burdened but still ready--and capable of--dancing to the metaphorical fiddler, who represents traditions which must be simultaneously changed and embraced.

Peerce sings well and occasionally creates a believable moment through his acting, but mostly, his performance is tired and threadbare.

Happily, the rest of the cast is in much better shape.

Dolores Wilson, as Golde, Tevye's wife (and as director of the show), delivers a generous performance of encompassing warmth. Her acting is impeccable (with the possible exception of a bit too much brow wiping) and her singing is rich and full-bodied.

Fritzi Burr delivers a lavishly comic Yente the Matchmaker, and fires off her lines so that they bounce off the back walls of the cavernous concert Hall.

The women playing the three eldest daughters--Jane Bergere, Carole Leslie Propp and Barbara Turner--each do well both singing and acting. Bergere exhibits a particularly full lyric soprano in the snatches of "Matchmaker" she gets to sing, and one wishes she had more to do in the vocal department.

Alvin Kupperman, playing Motel, the tailor who woos and wins the eldest daughter, is winning and touching.

Most of the time, the chorus delivers a nice, full sound, although it seems amazing that the men didn't know some of the lyrics to "L'Chaim, L'Chaim, To Life" last night.

In the pit, musical director Philip Ingalls does a fine job of conducting an orchestra that delivers a Broadway-quality sound.

There are other areas, however, where the quality strays rather far from Broadway, which is something worth pointing out because the Broadway business has been very freely used in promoting the show.

Most of the time, the choreography is a mess, with members of the cast literally bumping into one another.

There has been some very shoddy work fitting costumes for the Honolulu production.

The scenery has borrowed and copied the style of the economical elements of the original New York production--mainly painted drops--and does not include the essential (and expensive) on-stage turntable that can give "Fiddler" a kind of fluid grace almost unprecedented in the musical theater.

But missing turntables and messy hems and shaky scenery are of scant importance compared with performance by the artists on the stage.

And all through "Fiddler," genuine artists deliver fine work.

They swirl around the bare spot that is Jan Peerce.

It is probable that Peerce has been cast in the tradition that name performers sell tickets. It seems clear that the performance, and not the name, is of much greater importance.

<u>"Equus:" Rich, Powerful and Cool</u>
(by Pierre Bowman, Honolulu Star-Bulletin, July 7, 1976)

"Equus," Peter Shaffer's much-acclaimed drama, opened last night at the Leeward Community College Theater in a production by San Francisco's American Conservatory Theater that is highly theatrical, intellectually engrossing--and curiously remote emotionally.

The play ventures into a maze where everyone knows the entrance intimately. It is the human mind.

Nobody, however--perhaps not even Shaffer, knows the way out of the maze.

His play, then, twists and turns, maneuvering around tortuous angles, posing baffling questions and suggesting answers that are extremely difficult. It is theater as a forum for ideas.

On the surface, "Equus" deals with a psychiatrist's therapy sessions with a 17-year-old boy who put out the eyes of five horses with a sharp spike.

In Shaffer's program notes, the playwright explains that he built his play around the atrocity, which a friend had related to him. Shaffer notes that the act had no coherent explanation.

"I had to create a mental world in which the deed could be made comprehensible," he writes.

Drama often tries--and rarely succeeds--to create a vicarious emotional response in an audience, to make an audience not merely a witness but a participant in terms of its feelings.

"Equus" does just the opposite.

Shaffer has chosen to build his play around an incident so bizarre, horrifying and arcane that it would be improbable that any member of the audience would identify with the situation.

It is eventually clear that the boy's deed is one of human action taking passion to its outer limits. Shaffer's intent seems to be intellectual explanation rather than emotional understanding, but his work reaches heights of power because it ultimately erases the line between the intellectual and the emotional.

If all of this sounds like heavy going--and it is--it must be noted that the play is put together in a totally compelling fashion. It flips back and forth in time with fluid grace, giving the audience a chance to let its imagination range wide and free, filling in details mentally, accepting five brown-clad men with marvelous sculpted equine heads and hoofs as genuine horses.

Early in the play, the boy's mother says that "what the eye does not see, the heart does not grieve over."

Gradually, however, it is apparent that one does not necessarily see with the eye. The heart itself has a capacity for vision.

Gradually, the psychiatrist sees more and more, and perceives that there is more and more to grieve over. And gradually, the audience sees that, too.

The weighty questions are posed: What is the role of pain in the life that is really being lived? What is the role of worship? What is the role of acting out of complete passion, whether for good for evil? And are those who act with that complete passion the only souls who are living fully?

The psychiatrist cries out for worship of the "murderous, indispensible god of truth."

He cries that "life is only comprehensible through a thousand living gods," and that men must "worship as many as you can see--and more will come."

And if more gods do come, and they are seen, is there more for the heart to grieve over? In Shaffer's scheme of things, the answer seems to be yes.

With that answer, the play shakes an audience powerfully, rattling value systems to the core.

Under William Ball's direction, however, the emotions are not deeply touched.

Raye Birk delivers a fine performance as the psychiatrist. The role goes to soaring dramatic heights, and Birk ascends to some of them. He seems to lack the vocal power, however, for a totally consistent performance that would define greatness.

Daniel Zippi, as the boy, is a remarkable amalgamation of distracted--but not distracting--mannerisms which create a memorable character that is sustained until the climactic nude scene.

Under Ball's direction, the nude scene (between the boy and the girl who tries to seduce him, played with easy unself-consciousness by Janice Garcia) seems almost extraneous and part of the play more for shock value than for artistic considerations.

The boy's fixation with the horses, as objects of both sexual and religious passion, is fully developed, but his passion for the flesh of a young woman is almost incomprehensible in Ball's staging.

In spite of these shortcomings in the two crucial roles, however, "Equus" has devastating power and incomparable intellectual richness.

BRANCHE, Lewis W. (Bill); (2) Editorial writer, theater critic, Niagara Gazette; (3) b. Cape Vincent, N.Y., Aug. 15, 1927; (4) s. Lewis and Doris (Grimshaw) Branche; (5) B.A. Syracuse U., Major subj: English-education, 1949; (6) Single; (8) Reporter, Watertown, (N.Y.) Daily Times, 1957-59; Reporter, Niagara Gazette, Niagara Falls, N.Y., 1960-66; Free-lance theater and music critic, Niagara Gazette, 1966-69; Full-time editorial writer, free-lance critic, Niagara Gazette, 1970- ; (9) Inveterate theater-goer; (13) YN1 U.S. Navy, 1944-45, 1950-54; (16) Democrat; (17) Roman Catholic; (21) 519 Memorial Parkway, Niagara Falls, N.Y. 14301; (22) Niagara Gazette, 310 Niagara Street, Niagara Falls, N.Y. 14302, Ph. 716-282-2311; (23) Circulation: 36,000; (24) 70 amateur and professional plays, musicals, concerts, dance, and other programs.

"Devil's Disciple" Launches Shaw Theatre's 13th Season
(by Bill Branche, Niagara Gazette, June 1, 1974)

"The Devil's Disciple" is a play about the American Revolution written by that heretical (he admitted the Americans won the war) Irish-Englishman, George Bernard Shaw, who is more respectful of Americans in this play than he ever is of Englishmen in his other plays.

For this reason, if for no other, Americans should flock to
the Shaw Festival Theatre here to see "The Devil's Disciple,"
the opening production in the Festival's ambitious 13th season.

But there are many other reasons why anyone of any nation-
ality would enjoy this production. The most important is the
play itself, for it is both entertaining and enigmatic, in Shaw's
accustomed manner. The Revolution is actually only an incident
in the play, the hook on which Shaw hangs a quite profound study
of the way some men and women behave under the threat of
death.

In addition, there is something quite special about "The Devil's Disciple"--it is one of the few Shaw plays in which the heroine does not see through and stand superior to the world of
masculine follies. Judith Anderson, the minister's wife, does
not understand why her husband would leave Dick Dudgeon to die
for him at the hands of the British, or why Dick would consent
to die for her husband rather than for love of her. Judith is no
Candida, no Hesione, not even a Liza Doolittle; she is a brave
but bewildered woman in a man's world, and she accepts the ar-
rangements the men finally make among themselves.

Nevertheless, she is a splendid character, and she is splendidly played in this production by Domini Blythe. Miss Blythe
makes her a crucial but discreet presence, fearful, brave, passionate, a bit willful, but never dominant. Judith cannot dominate; this is a play about men, and only out of her confusion and
discretion can the men--her husband and Dick--reveal themselves
for what they are. It requires an actress of superb skill and
tact--Miss Blythe--to keep Judith's presence both crucial and discreet.

Now I've taken so much time on the play and Miss Blythe
that I must hurry over the many other good things in "The Devil's Disciple." It is a witty comedy, full of good lines, though
the most typical Shavian repartee is reserved for the long, wonderful third act. It is handsomely and wittily mounted, as most
Shaw Festival productions are. It is wonderfully cast--Tony Van
Bridge as the genial, gentlemanly General Burgoyne, Alan Searfe
playing Dick with a kind of meditative restraint, Norman Welsh
as Judith's surprisingly hearty minister husband, Eleanor Bee-
croft as the savagely virtuous Mrs. Timothy Dudgeon, Stuart
Kent as a good-natured British sergeant, and the rubber-faced
bassoon-voiced James Valentine playing a stiff-necked British
major with such relish that one understands immediately why
the British lost the war. The minor parts are equally well cast
and well acted.

Brian Murray's direction seems just right--generously proportioned to the Festival Theatre's big stage, leisurely enough to
let us think about what is happening, but never slack.

"The Devil's Disciple" will play in repertory, first with
"Charley's Aunt" (which opens tonight) through July 28, and then
with Shaw's "Too True to Be Good" through the end of the season on Sept. 1. (In addition, two plays--Ibsen's "Rosmersholm"
and Shaw's "The Admirable Bashville"--will be given at the old
Court House Theatre in July and August.) People who want to
see any of the plays would be well advised to make reservations
soon because most of them are already more than half booked
and a few performances are already sold out--as they deserve
to be if they're as good as "The Devil's Disciple."

Shaw Theater Offering Fails to Entertain, Is also Boring
(by Bill Branche, Niagara Gazette, August 6, 1974

"Too True to Be Good," the final offering of the Shaw Festival's 1974 season, might be subtitled, "The Artist as a Querulous Old Man"--or perhaps "A Querulous and Tedious Old Man."

It is Shaw, long after the great theatrical successes of his
life, complaining about the state of the world in a tone that is
no more than half jocular, and forecasting (accurately enough)
that there is worse to come. (The time was 1932.)

More than one eminent critic considers "Too True to Be
Good" a rough-hewn masterwork. Perhaps I could be convinced
they're right, but it would take a better production of the play
than Douglas Seale, the director, has mounted for the Shaw Festival.

The production suffers from being too slow and too static.
After the charmingly bouncy first act, nothing much happens on
stage to distract us from the fact that talk is going on and on and
on and not getting anywhere. To be sure, Shaw hasn't given a
director much to hang any action on, but surely it would have
been possible for Mr. Seale to do something more dramatic with
his actors than have them nibble on fruit or hand a copy of
"Pilgrim's Progress" back and forth. I am seldom bored in the
theater, but the endless preachments and posturings of the third
act left me near paralysis.

Still, I'm inclined to put the blame principally on Shaw. The
Shavian sermons he puts in the mouths of the characters are
querulous. He complains that Einsteinian physics has destroyed
the stability of the physical world he had once understood, and he
complains that the "Newtonian" conventions that propped up the
old social world have similarly been replaced by flux and chaos.
This is old man's talk, and like most old men's complaints, it
is dull stuff.

Perhaps it's true, as the souvenir program tells us, that Shaw's
earlier works "had spoiled everyone." If I had not gone to the Shaw
Festival expecting a Shavian play, I might have been less disappointed
at this un-Shavian play. Maybe I should have been looking for some-

thing else--adumbrations of Beckett, perhaps, as the program suggests. "Too True" does foreshadow Beckett's sense of the absurdity of life, and one might therefore see this late Shavian play as an early venture into the avant garde theater of the 1950s and 1960s.

I find this thesis weakened (though not demolished) by the fact that the first and parts of the second acts have the ambience of the commercial Broadway theater, and some episodes made me think poor old Shaw was trying very hard to emulate the smartness that was the mark of successful theater in the 1920s and 1930s.

But this is so much speculation. The fact remains that "Too True"--at least in this avatar--is a failure as entertainment and a bore as a tract.

There are some bright moments: Tony van Bridge enlivens the second act, along with Heath Lambers (but then, they have good reliable Shavian parts to act); Domini Blythe is frequently charming and so is Elizabeth Shepherd, though Miss Blythe becomes strident at times and there's a limit to what any actress can squeeze out of the simple-minded character of Susan Simpkins; John Horton's imperturbably crushing preaching is perversely admirable; and Maurice Strike's witty sets do more than Mr. Seale's direction to set the moods of the three acts.

It seems to me that neither Shaw nor the Shaw Festival has ever done anything that was without merit. I can't, therefore, recommend that anyone stay away from "Too True." But I'm sorry to say I can't make any more positive recommendation than that.

BROCK, Charles, Florida Times-Union, 1 Riverside Ave., Jacksonville, Fla. 32202, Ph. 904-791-4111.

BRODE, Douglas Isaac; (2) Theatre and film critic; (3) b. Long Island, Aug. 4, 1943; (4) s. Joseph and Irma (Lichenstein) B.; (5) B.S. Geneseo State U., major subj: English, 1965; M.A. Syracuse U., maj. subj.: Literature, 1969; (6) m. Sue Anne Johnson, July 22, 1967; (7) children--Shane Johnson Brode; (8) Critic, The Nickel Review (Syracuse), 1967-70; Critic, Show Magazine, 1970; Critic, The Syracuse New Times, 1970- ; Critic, WHEN Radio, 1973- ; (9) Apprentice actor, Gateway (Long Island) Summer Playhouse, 1962; Actor-writer-director, Experimental Theatre Group, Geneseo 1963-64; Teacher, Central Islip High School, Long Island, 1965-66; Teaching Assistant, Syracuse University, 1966-70; Prof. of English, Onondaga Community College, Syracuse, 1970- ; (10) Host, Everson Museum Film Program, 1971-72; (11) Campaign volunteer for Eugene McCarthy, 1968, and George McGovern, 1972; (12) Critic's Corner Host for Syracuse Stage, 1973-75; (14) Lucy Harmon Award for Outstanding

Contribution to Creative Fiction, 1963; Cothurnus Dramatics Society,
1963; Alpha Psi Omega Dramatics Honors Fraternity, 1964; Who's
Who Among Students in American Universities, 1965; (15) The Independent Film Critics Association; (16) Democrat; (17) Jewish; (20)
Numerous articles to Show Magazine and the Syracuse New Times on
theatre, film, and related arts; Crossroads to the Cinema, a text-
book published by Holbrook Press in 1975; forthcoming volume entitled
Films of the Fifties to be published in 1976 by Citadel Press; (21)
104 Longdale Drive, Liverpool, N.Y.   13088, Ph. 315-457-4032;
(22) Circulation: reach approximately 25,000 readers (Syracuse New
Times) and 150,000 listeners (WHEN); (24) Twenty plays and musicals,
100 motion pictures, 10 miscellaneous.

Prisoner of Second Avenue
(by Douglas Brode, over WHEN Radio, Syracuse, July 4, 1975)

The Summer Theatre Season opens with a hit--this is Doug
Brode--This year, the Skaneateles players have shifted their
home from the old Stone Mill Playhouse to the lovely midlakes
Country Club.   The Dinner Theatre package begins with a bountiful buffet including such exciting dishes as New England clam
chowder, shrimp Louisiane, homemade Lasagna and all the roast
prime ribs of beef you can eat--along with all sorts of salads and
sidedishes.   After the feast, the players perform Neil Simon's
ultra dark comedy, the Prisoner of Second Avenue, an excellent
farce about the insanity of trying to survive in Manhattan.   As
Mel, the harried husband, Dana Robinson is passable--nothing
more, nothing less.   But as Edna, his indomitable wife, Debbi
Armani proves herself to be a showstopper--she's a born actress,
with a terrific sense of comic timing and a marvellous ability
to move us to laughter and, sometimes, almost to tears.   Her
presence is what makes this show a definite hit.

Ten Little Indians
(by Douglas Brode, over WHEN Radio, Syracuse, August 14, 1975)

A stylish whodunit--This is Doug Brode--Agatha Christie's
Ten Little Indians is the grandaddy of all murder mysteries.   A
group of total strangers meets at a handsome mansion on a deserted island, but their host doesn't show up and, one by one,
they begin to die.   Which of the ten is actually the murderer?
That's the question you'll be asking as you watch the production
of this play now on view at the Playhouse on the Hill, in Clinton.
The company was clearly aware that the show's a compendium
of cliches, with cardboard characters and a charmingly contrived
story, so they wisely chose to do a slightly campy interpreta-
tion--instead of an aura of suspense, they create a handsome
setpiece, in which the occasionally ludicruous dialogue is made
to work--as comedy.   In fact, they've created an ensemble style
of acting that's very close to what we see in the recent film Murder on the Orient Express, adapted from another of Agatha
Christie's chillers.   If you enjoyed the grand guignol style of that
film, and would like to see a live production of similar material,
I'm sure you'll find Ten Little Indians to your taste.

BROOKS, Elston, Fort Worth Star Telegram, Carter Publications, Seventh & Taylor Sts., Forth Worth, Tex. 76102.

BRUKENFELD, Dick; (2) Theater Critic; (3) b. Brooklyn, N.Y., Dec. 22, 1933; (4) s. Carl and Helen (Ackerman) M.; (5) B.A. Harvard, major: history of fine arts, 1960; (6) Divorced; (8) Reporter and columnist, Lowell, Mass. Sun 1956-57; Copy editor, Paterson, N.J. Call, 1964; Theater critic, Village Voice, 1969- ; (9) Actor, Lyric Theater, Boston 1955; (10) Theater Committee of New York City Cultural Council, 1973- ; (11) Press staff for Committee for Stevenson at Los Angeles Democratic Convention, 1960, Press staff for McCarthy for President, New York 1968; (12) Vice President, Off Off Broadway Alliance, 1973-74; (13) 4F; (15) Director, Theatre Development Fund, 1974; (16) Democrat; (17) Jewish; (20) cont. chapters to Famous Artists Annual 1, Theatre 4, Theatre 5; "Big Game," a one-act play presented on WHDH TV Boston in 1968; "The Big Broadcast on East 53rd," a full length play presented at the Manhattan Theatre Club, March 1973, and again in a revised version at La Mama in 1974; (21) 610 West End Ave., New York, N.Y. 10024, Ph. 212-724-9911; (22) Village Voice, 80 University Place, New York, N.Y. 10003, Ph. 212-741-0030; (23) Circulation: 155,000; (24) 48 theatre columns, covering two plays each.

A Gadfly Is a Bad Fly
(by Dick Brukenfeld, Village Voice, November 7, 1974)

If that curmudgeon S. J. Perelman were truly in high dudgeon, "The Beauty Part" might be a cause for joy. But the man who wrote this show is merely playing the role of Perelman the peppery picador of pretentiousness. A revue without music, "Beauty Part's" sketchbook of American vulgarity needs a fresh-felt indignation to fuse its many parts. Unfortunately the author has created it in a gadfly fashion, dropping a Perelmanesque notion here and a Perelmanesque character name there. The notion of a national magazine's sponsoring a golem (monster) contest and such names as Milo Weatherwax, Kitty Entrail, and Roxanna DeVilbiss are funny as they drop. But a gadfly is a bad fly when it comes to creating two hours of theatre.

His verbal buckshot scatter in too many directions, even though Perelman starts with a target. Opening in the New York home of those gross arrivistes the Weatherwaxes, "Beauty Part" draws a bead on their callow son, Lance, and his quest to find himself as an artist--a writer, a painter, anything to live that precious mystical life. After following this youth a few steps on his odyssey the show puts him on the shelf and directs its fire at a variety of artistic and moral sell outs, mostly in Hollywood. But Perelman's buckshot plink off the surface because his projectiles are too verbal. It's magazine stuff lifted onto the stage without a proper rebirth. The angry, living edge is neither fresh nor sharp enough.

But enough of Perelman. I have bones to pick with James Hammerstein's direction and the producer, the American Place Theatre.

Where the script sags in stage reality, it does offer a gallery of cartoon characters puffed up with foolishness. Yet the characters we see in Hammerstein's production are too small, too bland. It's as if in trying to make these cartoons live on stage, the director has neglected their essential grotesqueness.

In a parade of roles, ranging from a middle-aged culture vulture to a nicely bosomed go-go girl, Cynthia Harris makes a notable exception to this blandness. Giving each of her parts a distinct flavor, she puffs each one big enough to be comic, yet roots it in a believable reality, giving you the confidence to laugh. Miss Harris works from life as does Bobo Lewis, who makes great fun out of a woman who sculpts in soap. I don't know where Ron Faber works from, but he is zany. The rest are efficient and serviceable but need stronger comic attitudes.

In the role Bert Lahr originated when "Beauty Part" opened on Broadway in 1962, Joseph Bova has a tough act to follow. If he lacks Lahr's inventiveness and the ability to puff himself into a comic bullfrog, Bova is engaging and amusing, although never hilarious. His humor isn't fiendish or obsessive enough for that. I like him best as the stingy old millionaire Nelson Smedley, but even this fine moment just trails off into vagueness because of Perelman's refusal, or inability, to write a workable dramatic scene. A fellow critic who saw the original production tells me that even Bert Lahr couldn't make the play work. I believe it.

But even if you wanted to see "Beauty Part," you couldn't buy a ticket. You would have to buy a four-play, season's subscription to the American Place Theatre, a kind of coercion which I think is terribly wrong. Why should a theatre which receives public funding --your tax dollar--operate like a private club?

Several years ago theatres like La Mama operated as private clubs to escape police harrassment. But even then you could cheaply "join" to see a single show. Until "Beauty Part," I had assumed the American Place opened their shows to the public after the critics came, which is in the final weeks. But after some friends tried to see this play, I discovered their productions are open to the public only by subscription.

Other institutional theatres, like the Public and Chelsea, offer subscriptions, but you can also buy tickets to single productions. You can even buy tickets to individual shows at the Metropolitan Opera. Although I like the American Place's goal of developing an American theatre, I see no reason why their efforts should be affirmed and commented on in the public press when they are not truly open to the public. Thus I personally

will not write about any more of their productions until tickets are
available in a way that is normal and healthy for a public art.

Piran Jello
(by Dick Brukenfeld, Village Voice, December 23, 1974)

Instead of Pirandello's "Rules of the Game," the Phoenix
Theatre is serving a wobbly trifle called Piran Jello, the Italian
master's play with its backbone removed. The dialogue is the
same, but the acting is disconnected. Although Pirandello wrote
a grotesque drama with moments of humor, Stephen Porter has
staged "Rules" like a drawing room comedy with sprinkles of
seriousness. And the jello begins to ooze in the opening scene
where, in an elegant art nouveau living room, we find a fetching
Joan Van Ark and a Valentinoish David Dukes bantering as if
they were bored young married's in Noel Coward land.

But Miss Van Ark is married to another man, and Mr.
Dukes is her lover, and both, rather than bored, are frustrated.
Mr. Dukes is frustrated because his girl friend hasn't allowed
him a visit for a week and isn't allowing him anything now. But
Miss Van Ark's frustration has little to do with Mr. Dukes.
She's locked into a power struggle with her cleverly obliging
husband. Not only has he moved out of the apartment but he
stops by each day for a half-hour just to maintain appearances--
both at her request--so she is not only free to have her lovers
but so she also keeps her respectability. ("Rules" takes place
in Italy in 1918.) Despite this arrangement, Miss Van Ark is
frustrated because she can't break through her husband's shell.
So long as he remains obliging and unflappable, he's in control.

The working out of this bizarre struggle is the central action.
Each time wife Van Ark asks for something, husband John Mc-
Martin plays by the rules of the game and does what a good Italian husband should. He agrees. Yet he never really gives in.
Controlling his emotions, he waits for the moment the game
turns to his advantage to make his kill. It's the kind of drama
Strindberg might have written had he grown up in Sicily as Pirandello did. As is so often the case with plays about death struggles between men and women, however, the actors make nice
what should be nasty. "Rules" is gelatinous and boring because
the leads, Van Ark and McMartin, sidestep its specialness.

The beings they bring on stage misfit the action. Miss Van
Ark shows us a conventional and sometimes flighty ingenue, when
she ought to be an impetuous, driven woman, much more unba-
lanced. And Mr. McMartin makes the fatal mistake of playing
a man who controls his passions as if he had no passions to control. The husband is disciplined, not lackadasical. From Mc-
Martin we need an overpowering, calculating intelligence and/or
the sense of a passionate nature struggling to control itself.
Bigness not beigeness. As his wife's pawn of a lover, David
Dukes is more convincing, yet he too could be more passionately

into the situation, especially in the beginning.

It's no accident that "Rules" is the play being rehearsed at the beginning of Pirandello's masterpiece, "Six Characters In Search of an Author." Both deal with husbands who live separately from their wives, a situation clearly close to the author. Pirandello and his wife married by arrangement of their parents. She became increasingly disturbed and made increasingly unreasonable demands on him--which, like a good Italian husband, he performed to the point of giving her everything but his pocket money.

This is worth noting, because "Rules," a so-called play of ideas, is rooted in passionate and often frustrating experience. And unless those passions are played, both ideas and actions turn to jello, and audiences like me want to junk it.

BUNKE, Joan Elizabeth; (2) Critic-at-large; (3) b. West Bend, Wis., Jan. 5, 1934; (4) d. Ernest and Rosaline (Bruessel); (5) B.A. U. of Wisconsin, journalism, 1955; (8) Assistant state editor, Lafayette (Ind.) Journal & Courier, 1955-58; from 1952, copy editor, assistant telegraph editor of Des Moines Tribune, then Picture magazine editor, and editorial writer, in succession of Des Moines Register; currently columnist-critic-at-large, of paper, The Des Moines Register; (14) Phi Beta Kappa, 1954, U. of Wisconsin; (20) 4525 Woodland Ave., Unit 7, West Des Moines, Ia. 50265; (21) Des Moines Register, 715 Locust St., Des Moines, Ia. 50304, Ph. 515-284-8000; (24) Approx. no. of theater, film, music, etc., reviews annually: scores.

"Bridegroom" a Good Ol' Country Time
(by Joan Bunke, Des Moines Register, March 16, 1976)

The big take-off in the Acting Company's "The Robber Bridegroom" Monday night in C.Y. Stephens Auditorium here turned into the big put-on. The touring repertory company played its hour-and-45-minute, country-music adaptation of Eudora Welty's fey Mississippi folk tale as cornpone camp.

Having warned its Celebrity Series ticket buyers that this production contained some nudity--inspired, of course, by "necessities of the plot"--the Acting Company proceeded to delight its audience of about 1,000 with square dancing, raucous singing and audacious corn, updating the 1942 Welty tale with Seventies satire and bawdiness.

Alfred Uhry contributed the sometimes-hilarious, sometimes-suggestive lyrics for Robert Waldman's mixture of country music, country ballads and country kidding. But though the show is spritely clear through, it's the company that deserves the greater share of the praise.

As in their Iowa opening in Cedar Rapids last week, company

members displayed the kind of professional polish that touring companies--the few that there are--rarely have. Director Gerald Freedman has designed a show without intermission that uses its cast to change sets and act as an audience as well as sing, dance and play assorted roles.

In a uniformly excellent cast, outstanding performances were delivered by Kevin Kline as Jamie Lockhart, the Bandit of the Woods; David Schramm as the Rich Planter; Mary Lou Rosato as Salome, the Wicked Stepmother; and Patti LuPone as the Fair Rosamund, who is robbed of her beautiful green dress and everything that goes with it by the Bandit of the Woods.

The "nude scene" became a delightful joke on the voyeur in each audience member as actress LuPone mocked the coy poses of nudie magazines and played the scene for total camp.

The advertising was directed at "mature audiences" as much for the graphic language as for the bare skin--but there wasn't a pornographic bone in the production's body.

One of the show's few flaws was its accent, which was more twang than drawl, the wrong kind of "south in the mouth" for a tale of legendary Mississippi. Its twang aside, the show as a piece of undiluted, totally meaningless fun, paced with barely a minute between laughs.

Those who came to see the sights got more in entertainment than they bargained for--and not every "nude show" can make that claim.

Guthrie Just Gets Better
(by Joan Bunke, Des Moines Register, June 20, 1976

It's competition that keeps improving the Guthrie Theater's quality. Competition with itself.

Over the years, as the season has lengthened and the number of productions has grown, the faithful theatergoer might have expected a decline in standards. It hasn't happened. Even the most eccentrically conceived or thoroughly dated plays have received lovingly detailed, professional productions full of ideas and imagination.

This year, the production gloss is shinier than ever--at least by the evidence of the Guthrie's opening last week of "The Matchmaker" and "Doctor Faustus," the first two plays in its eight-play repertory season.

The productions are first-class, combining all of the necessary elements of excellence: Astute casting of old and new members of the 25-member company; spare, elegant sets; subtle, imaginative lighting; and clean, clear shaping by Directors Michael Langham and Ken Ruta.

Both faces of the Guthrie, comic and tragic, are now on display. A funny, beautifully played production of Thornton Wilder's "The Matchmaker," full of skillful timing and rough-and-tumble slapstick, opened Monday. It was followed Wednesday by an electric, engrossing version of Christopher Marlowe's Elizabethan morality play, "Doctor Faustus." Of the latter, the Guthrie has made something of a modern miracle play; Director Ruta and his actors take Marlowe's blank verse and make it play intelligibly to modern ears, no easy achievement. "Marlowe's mighty line," as Ben Jonson called it echoes through the theater with clarity as well as power.

"Faustus" is the more interesting, the more adventurous piece of theater, but it's "Matchmaker" that will draw the crowds the Guthrie needs. This comedy about adventure, security and the machinations of matchmaker Dolly Gallagher Levi and merchant Horace Vandergelder is Wilder's most enjoyable piece of theater preaching. The main characters' addresses to the audience opening night drew lively feed-back, including predictable hissing at Vandergelder's male-chauvinist lines. Newcomer Tony Mockus plays the self-satisfied, pinchpenny blockhead with aplomb.

Guthrie mainstay Barbara Bryne does the "original" Dolly--the before-"Hello-Dolly!"-Dolly--with pithy, polished delivery. (It's important to forget all those sashaying, singing Dollies to appreciate this plotting, speechifying character.)

The only Bryne drawback opening night was the actress's almost unplaceable accent, partly Irish, partly New Yorkese. But then, what kind of accent does a Dolly Gallagher Levi have?

In this case, the accent is on slick, smooth theater entertainment.

The "Matchmaker" cast is gold clear through, including Guthrie returnee Helen Carey, who plays the milliner Irene Molloy with a flair for Irish spirit as well as Irish accent.

Concentration on a total concept, on unity of cast and production, on attention to detail make both plays work. In the comedy, Desmond Heeley's sets and costumes are detailed, colorful, but not fussy; the eye is engaged but not distracted.

Lighting designer Duane Schuler's art serves both productions well. For "Matchmaker," his design is mostly high-lighting. In "Faustus," the lighting design is integral to the action. The magic created by Marlowe's young Doctor Faustus after he has traded his soul for power and pleasure needs the precision and subtlety of Schuler's skill with light, dark, and shadow.

Mark Lamos plays Faustus with intensity and control, essential qualities. But, more, he takes the measure of Marlowe's meter--and conveys the meanings to us with a clarity that is all

the more effective because his performing polish conceals the
mechanism of how he does it. (The text cuts seem, at first
hearing, to have advanced the cause of intelligibility.)

The golden, spidery-Gothic set, by Ralph Funicello, contributes to the play's unity. It takes advantage of the Guthrie's
"second-story" set capability by giving the mighty Lucifer a kind
of flying bridge from which to oversee Faust's magic and his futile efforts at repentance.

Another Guthrie newcomer, Michael Gross, provides fresh
evidence that the company's new blood mingles well with the old.
Gross's Mephistophilis uses a superbly controlled voice to create a monster of malevolence.

One of Director Ruta's--and the Guthrie's--less attractive
devices is the hokum created by the play's student-servant, Wagner, and the Clown. The "comic relief" works too well--cutting
the tension Ruta and company have created so meticulously. In
the midst of the general excellence, however, it is a small flaw,
as is the raucous end to the Helen of Troy scene and its famous
lines: "Was this the face that launched a thousand ships and
burnt the topless towers of Illium?"

BURLEY, George Joseph; (2) Arts & Entertainment editor; (3) b.
Bottineau, N. Dak., Jan. 31, 1939; (4) s. Arthur and Malthide (Ro-
berge) B.; (5) B.A. University of Washington, major subj.: journalism, 1965; (8) Staff writer, asst. News editor, arts editor, Longview (Wash.) Daily News 1965-68; Arts & Entertainment editor, Everett (Wash.) Herald 1968- ; (10) Arts Council of Snohomish County
(Wash.); (13) USMC 1956-58; (16) Democrat; (17) Catholic; (20) co-
author "Roche Harbor: A Saga in the San Juans"; (21) 1422 88th Dr.
S.E., Everett, Wn. 98205, Ph. 206-334-7222; (22) Everett Herald,
P.O. Box 930, Everett, Wn. 98206, Ph. 206-259-5151; (23) Circulation: 52,000; (24) 150 reviews annually on concerts, operas, plays,
ballets, musicals.

SET's Version of "Camelot" Staging for Eye, Ear, Heart
(by George Burley, Everett Herald, March 30, 1975)

The troupers of Sound Expression Theater have not previously had reason to feel so good about an opening show as they did
when they concluded their performance of "Camelot" last night.

Their audience in Edmonds Auditorium was the largest they've
experienced so far on an opening night. This one was stuffed
with patrons and eager with deserving applause. SET, furthermore, was the best prepared it has ever been (the only real exception being some hesitation in lighting cues).

The polishing this production needs is minimal, so don't plan
to wait for the final weekend. The remaining seven performances

in fact, approach the two-thirds mark in being sold out (the April 11 show is completely gone).

SET has climbed to an impressive height already in its short life of five stagings. It is setting a stride of well done entertainment the community must not lose. Their "Camelot," directed by Ron Daum, is the latest reason why.

Alan Lund conducts a show which has the highly melodic score typical of Lerner and Loewe; well over half of its songs have entered the popular repertoire. But more, the show is adeptly staged with a unit-set concept within which imagination abounds. The principal performers are superb vocally and dramatically. And the performance flows with considerable grace.

It's a show for the eye, for the ear, for the heart. The whole family will enjoy it, will be moved by it, will very likely talk about if for long afterward.

With the opening of the show curtain, the audience is led into a crystal cave, an illusion Designer Christian Wagener created by large green, red and blue illuminated shapes imbedded in a succession of wings and overhead borders. At rear is a blue scrim. It's like peering into a magic time tunnel, in which the audience's attention can fall only upon the players.

The Arthurian legend of this 1960 fantasy can be traced back to the sixth century in its various strands. Popular interest in it remains constant: it is a legend and a vision for the ages. No period of literature is without its entry; as late as 1958 T. H. White retold it in "The Once and Future King," and it is that version on which "Camelot" is based.

It deals with the marriage of Arthur and Guenevere, the establishing of the Round Table as an instrument of peace, Lancelot's arrival from France and subsequent relationship with Guenevere, Mordred's attempt to unseat Arthur and the collapse of the Round Table. Lerner and Loewe halt the story on the eve of the great battle (in which Arthur was killed), instead have Arthur knight a young boy and send him off to spread the vision of Camelot, an optimistic ending which significantly influenced President John F. Kennedy.

Vocally the burden of "Camelot" falls almost entirely upon the two lead players, Betty Martin and Tony Lee as Arthur and Guenevere. Both veterans of many a musical production, they display strong, carrying voices and their skill at characterization provides intensely human figures.

As Lancelot, newcomer Eric Hanson does admirably in "C'est Moi" and "If Ever I Would Leave You." Michael McKee, another newcomer, makes a satisfying evil Mordred, carries "The Seven Deadly Virtures" with a flair.

A major highlight of the staging is the playing of J. A. Murphy in the role of visiting King Pellinore (he also plays Merlyn). A character player of considerable reputation in the area, Murphy is a walking case study in extracting a strong comedic character from little more than thin air. He drew hearty applause in mid-show, something rarely won by a player in a non-singing role in musical theater.

The costuming for the production is unexpectedly detailed for the heavy demands of such a period piece with a large cast. There are gowns and cloaks galore, with a good deal of detail. The props too, are interesting, the horses, the banners, the broadswords (Excalibur is a gem: a large, black-handled blade of internally lit lucite).

Rep Offers Evening of Laughing with Pair of Stoppard Farces
    (by George Burley, Everett Herald, April 2, 1975)

You can just about laugh youself sick right now at The 2nd Stage where the Seattle Repertory Theater has just opened a pair of one-act farces by Tom Stoppard, "After Magritte" and "The Real Inspector Hound."

Though the Czech-born English playwright has been heavily influenced by theater-of-the-absurd, neither of these plays is of the abstract or tragic variety of Edward Albee et al, but are instead absurd in the high comedic sense that makes a joke funny-- their construction of exaggeration, reversal, juxtaposition. And these are very funny plays.

Lead players Robbyn Stuart, Pamela Burrell, Marjorie Nelson, Edwin Bordo and John Brandon--all double-cast--return in a group from "Biography," the first production at The 2nd Stage, to play under the direction of William Glover. Joining them are John Gilbert, veteran of A Contemporary Theater, and newcomer Amelia Lauren. Glover has them all busy with zany characterizations and split-second timing.

"After Magritte" (1972) concerns a bickering husband and wife and the tuba-playing mother of one (they're not sure which) who have just returned from an exhibit of surrealist art by one Magritte. Now they are preparing in domestic disarray for an evening at a ballroom event, all of the while sharply debating the details of an individual they all haphazardly observed as they were leaving the museum.

Like the Indian folk tale of the seven blind men and their encounter with an elephant (Stoppard was raised in India), each interpretation is different. And wrong. The audience is assisted in following their twisted exchange by overhead slide projections.

In barges Police Inspector Foot to question them about a robbery near the museum which, it eventually comes out, never took place. And all the supporting evidence he and his uniformed Bobby previously spied through the flat's windows proves also to have been misinterpretation.

Though everything going--hip waders, body on the ironing board, the real person outside the museum--seems a bit kooky, there is a simple, logical explanation for each tidbit. The distance some of the wrong interpretations travel is hilariously outrageous.

"The Real Inspector Hound" preceded "Magritte" by four years (1968) but is longer and exhibits more readily Stoppard's virtuosity in clever plot construction. This one is really two plays going on simultaneously--one a whodunnit, the other a pair of drama critics watching it--and eventually they merge into an interdependent whole.

The whodunnit has every cliche of the English gothic-mansion thriller; it outright pokes fun at them; and it includes the host of stage bugaboos which might afflict a matinee troupe actually performing the play, along with their inept attempts to cover the flubs (the radio coming on before the player's hand reaches the knob, the veranda doors pushed instead of pulled).

Synchronized with the dialog of the rake, the ingenue, the beautiful widow, the elderly man-in-wheelchair and the police inspector is that of the two critics in theater seats at one end of the playing area, watching the everyone-gather-in-the-parlor plot. When not trying to out-do each other rhapsodizing this jaded turkey into a regal peacock, they chat about their private lives.

Moon, a second-string reviewer who is substituting tonight, voices thoughts about the first-string slot and its current occupant. Birdboot reveals his back-stage philanderings and philanderee, whom he replaces, goggle-eyed, in mid-play. Before you know it, everything is one big stew, with three bodies on the floor. And the real Inspector Hound finally stands up.

Played by the Rep's slick cast, the farces make a great evening.

BUTLER, Ron, Tulsa Daily World, P.O. Box 1770, Tulsa, Okla. 74102.

CAHN, Irving W.; (2) Theater critic; (3) b. New York, N.Y., Oct. 20, 1903; (4) s. Harris and Emma (Cahn); (5) B.S. New York U., 1927; Post Graduate studies N.Y.U., C.C.N.Y., Columbia lectures. English, journalism, drama, economics; (6) m. Mary Margaret Young, Nov. 29, 1938; (7) children--Ellen Patricia and Jill; (8) Covered high school events for N.Y. Morning World, N.Y. Evening Post 1921-22, as high school student; New York Inquirer, radio - theater 1931-35;

Drama critic-editor Pace Publications, 1932-36 (a group of
society magazines); Drama critic, N.Y. Informer 1933; Reviewed plays and interviewed actors for radio station WHOM,
N.Y. 1932-34; A member of Second Nighters (Second Night
Theater Press) appeared regularly on radio Station WMCA,
N.Y. 1935-36; Started as drama critic for Host, Nov. 1935
and still functioning in that capacity (40 years at post for
Host in Nov., 1975); Doubled as drama critic for the Hellenic News, 1972 with permission of Host publisher; (9) Interviewed
many times on "Luncheon at Sardi's," WOR radio, by Bill Slater,
1946-52; Interviewed frequently on the Joe Franklin Show, WOR radio
and WOR TV (TV program previously on Channel 5 (Metromedia)
and Channel 7 (ABC-TV) and other programs); Write for television
personalities and production for "20 Questions," radio and television
programs; "Take a Number," Mutual radio, "Best Girl," WOR radio;
(10) Shepherded star-studded shows to camps and hospitals during
WW II; (11) Wrote slogans, speeches for politicians/Independent; (15)
Member of the Drama Desk, The Outer Circle; (17) Hebrew; (20)
Have written for Charm, Magazine Digest, Actors Magazine, Silver
Screen, TV World and other magazines; (21) 98-76 Queens Blvd.,
Forest Hills, L. I., N.Y. 11374, Ph. TW 6-9152; (22) Host Office,
415 East 53 St., N.Y. 10022; Hellenic News Office, 117 W. 57 St.,
N.Y. 10019, Ph. 581-6555.

Theatre
(by Irving W. Cahn, The Host, February 8, 1975)

We were almost lyrical in praise of Terrence McNally's
"Bad Habits" last season and anticipated a return by the gifted
playwright. The other evening at the Longacre, Adela Holzer,
First Lady of Broadway Producers, who sponsored "Bad Habits,"
presented "The Ritz," by McNally, with Robert Drivas, who directed the earlier item, at the helm.

"The Ritz" is a thin, but hilarious comedy about a fat man
hiding out in a raffish "gay" bath from a "contract" on him, the
death order of a bemused ganglord. The frightened fatty didn't
know it was a notorious homo hangout and that the mob had
steered him there for the kill. No more of the plot (pun intended).
Flimsy, granted, but the eruptive happenings were frantic and
funny and that's what farce is all about!

Drivas raced the action, with never a slowdown. A pause
never refreshes in farce, it only invites examination and scrutiny
is a guest a farce should never invite.

The dialogue is rowdy and ribald and the acting of Jack Weston, the blubbery innocent on the lam, Rita Moreno, a tacky,
vulgar entertainer, Jerry Stiller, the "hit" man (see what we've
learned from "Kojak?") and the others in the company were just
swell, but the deliriously daffy direction and shrewd staging of
the amusical bits by Drivas is the raison d'etre for "The Ritz."
We're still laughing at the outrageous scenes between paunchy

Weston and raunchy Rita, who thinks he's Joe Papp and Jack accompanied by two "Queens" doing the Andrews Sisters.

We haven't roared as much since the recent news that Raquel Welch won the "Best Actress" Golden World Award over Helen Hayes in the Hollywood Foreign Press farce. We mean competition. Next year that organization may vote the Sex Symbol Statuette to Miss Hayes over Raquel Welch.

Theatre
(by Irving W. Cahn, The Host, February 22, 1975)

Nocl Coward's 45-year-old "Private Lives," which has become a civilized comedy classic was revived at the 46th St. Theater by Arthur Cantor last week with Maggie Smith and John Standing as the mercurial Amanda and Elyot, created by Gertrude Lawrence and Noel Coward and as the stuffy new mates introduced by Laurence Olivier, a promising neophyte and a blonde patrician, Adrianne Allen, Remak Ramsay and Niki Flacks.

The London cast was imported to Broadway in 1931, where "Private Lives" captivated critics and audiences. The film rights were bought for Norma Shearer and Robert Montgomery and it is doubtful whether Miss Lawrence and Mr. Coward ever recovered from the traumatic experience of viewing the motion picture. We saw the original play and the movie and still shudder at the cinematic rape.

"Private Lives" has been renasced many times. Tallulah enjoyed a 1947 fling and 22-years after we paid obeisance to Tammy Grimes and the impeccable Brian Bedford.

Altho patently artificial, "Private Lives" was written with such daft craft that it remains artful and amusing after almost half a century and comedy styles have changed in that time.

Maggie is magnificent and Standing outstanding as the divorced couple honeymooning with new partners who meet their old spouses and their newly acquired mates at a Deauville hotel the evening they both arrive. The jilting is obvious, but the circumstances hilarious.

Miss Smith's precise timing and droll delivery of Coward's brittle banter and biting ripostes are howlingly funny and Standing is a clever farceur. Miss Flack and Ramsay lend ample and able support. The direction by John Gielgud is deft and delightful and Anthony Powell's sets quite attractive.

CALDER, Ethan; (2) Theatre critic; (3) b. New York City, N.Y., March 17, 1922; (4) s. Abraham and Rose R.; (5) B.A. New School for Social Research, major subj: English; M.A. Columbia U., in English; (6) m. Elaine, Sep. 3, 1950; (7) children--Joanne, 22,

Holden, 14; (8) Managing editor, Aviation Magazine (now defunct);
(9) Theatre critic for several local Long Island weeklies; (13) Pfc,
US Army, 1942-45; (15) Member, Aviation Writers Association; Eastern Ski Writers Association; (16) Democrat; (17) Hebrew; (18) Knights
of Pythias; (20) Several plays and novels, none produced or published;
(21) 1 Windsor Place, Melville, N.Y., Ph. 692-9512; (22) Jewish
World of Long Island, Box 812, Melville, N.Y. 11746; (23) Circulation: 16,000; (24) approx. 24-30 reviews published annually.

Pacific Overtures
(by Ethan Calder, Jewish World of Long Island, Jan. 30-Feb. 12, 1976)

Producer-director Harold Prince is more intent than anyone
else working in the theatre today to push the plasticity of the American musical to its outermost limits. His best musicals have been
among the most imaginative and have made striking and original
comments on modern existence. This time Prince has put the
musical to the services of history to tell the story of Commodore
Perry's opening of Japan to Western trade and mores, telling it
from Japan's side and using the devices of the Kabuki Theatre to
do so. An ambitious undertaking, to be sure; would that it war-
ranted all that attention.

Several things are wrong in this show. Mainly, even by telling the story from Japan's side, there is nothing new or illuminating to tell. It illustrates history, but the main purpose seems
to be the devices used rather than the story itself. The means,
therefore, do not justify the end: they are the end. Similarly,
the blend of Broadway with Kabuki is not always smooth and even
becomes a drawback: Patricia Birch's choreography, for instance,
seems inhibited and limited by the imposed restrictions. And
John Weidman's book has nothing to say that we don't already
know: Perry's visit helped turn Japan from a backward, feudal
country into a modern, aggressive and "hip" nation. Period.

But if the book fails to be illuminating or even exciting, one
expects more from the pen and mind of Stephen Sondheim. But
Sondheim is not at his best here. Only one song, Four Black
Dragons, contains any musical punch. Another, Chrysanthemum
Tea, shows glints of Sondheim's clever way with words and
rhyme, and Pretty Lady has an appealing lilt to it, but that's it.
For the most part, his attempts at humor seem desperate and
fall flat. A madame and her girls, welcoming the Americans,
resort to pornographic pictures on their fans; some people rant
interminably about not seeing Perry's meeting with the Japanese
officials, and a Russian admiral goes on at length about not
touching his coat, presumably because it got a laugh the first
time. In fact, he mentions it so often, you wonder whether
there's a special meaning in it. There isn't.

Actually, the best parts of the show are visual: Boris Aronson's striking sets and spectacular effects, Florence Klotz' lovely
costumes and some of Prince's side effects on a runway leading

to the stage. These are splendid but somewhat like a fancy, luscious icing that dresses up a very small, plain cake underneath.

In short, Pacific Overtures is something to look at but nothing to see.

A Chorus Line
(by Ethan Calder, Jewish World of Long Island, March 26-April 8, 1976)

If, heaven forbid, you can see only one Broadway show this season, that show must be the smashing, dramatic musical A Chorus Line. Brilliantly conceived, directed and choreographed by Michael Bennett, the show is a tribute to the gallantry, courage, persistence and often sheer chutzpah of those talented persons who try out for a job in a show's chorus.

Most theatre goers give little thought to such people or to the often desperate circumstances surrounding their efforts. From such circumstances--perhaps typical, perhaps not--this show was formed. Broadway has come up with nothing this season to equal its impact. By comparison, the other musical offerings--and most of the dramatic ones--seem pale and artificial.

It is not likely that so much drama and anguish unfold each time some people try out for a show. Nor is it likely that so much pain, so many secrets or such inner conflicts are so easily and publicly revealed. Some of the material that emerges would take a good psychoanalyst years to uncover. In this show, they spill out with the drop of a hat.

One need not, and probably does not, accept everything that is revealed--that long monologue by the homosexual, though well done, is out of place and unbelievable for the time and place; it belongs in a confessional. There is also a song about not having the proper physical attributes that borders on the tasteless. And are we to believe that there is no meanness or spite in these people, especially when so many persons are contending for so few jobs?

Obviously the portraits are presented with love and admiraation, most of which rubs off quickly and perhaps indelibly on the audience. We come to admire them all and to root for them all. We want them all to get the job and nearly weep for those who don't.

Few shows involve the audience so completely, and therein lies its magic. Bennett has done a superb job in giving us this backstage glance, and his cast is almost uniformly perfect. All of them sing, dance and act effectively; they are indeed a uniquely talented bunch. Most outstanding is Donna McKechnie as the chorine trying to get back into show business and Sammy Williams as the homosexual. Carole Bishop is most striking in appearance,

and Priscilla Lopez is amusing as a drama school dropout. It
is certainly unfair not to mention all the others, but the cast is
large, and space allotments unfortunately must prevail.

For his Broadway debut, composer Marvin Hamlisch has
concocted an agreeable score. For the most part, it does what
it has to do; it fills the bill but is not, on the whole, very distinguished. Edward Kleban's lyrics are even less distinguished.
But that hardly matters when all else is so good. This show
overcomes the shortcomings that would be fatal to most musicals,
and emerges triumphant. It is tremendous!

CARR, Eugenie Waddell; (2) Arts reporter; (3) b. Wilmington, N. C. ,
Dec. 16, 1946; (4) d. James Dickson and Rosalie Watters Carr; (5)
A. B. , Sweet Briar College, major subj. : American Studies, 1968;
(6) Single; (8) Media assistant, Provandie Eastwood & Lombardi Inc.
(advertising), Boston, Mass. , 1968-69; editorial assistant, Boston
Sunday Advertiser (later Herald Advertiser), 1970-72; Staff reporter,
The Sentinel, Winston-Salem, N. C. , 1972- ; (14) First place, Columns
and Criticism, 1974 N. C. Press Association Awards; (16) Democrat;
(17) Episcopalian; (19) National Society of the Colonial Dames in the
State of North Carolina; (20) cont. articles to Dictionary of North
Carolina Biography (not yet published); (21) 1608 Northwest Blvd. ,
Winston-Salem, N. C. 27104, Ph. 919-725-6071; (22) The Sentinel,
P. O. Box 3159, Winston-Salem, N. C. 27102, Ph. 919-725-2311;
(23) Circulation: 40,000; (24) 15-20 plays and musicals.

Human Evils Portrayed; "Crucible" Bewitches Audience
(by Genie Carr, Sentinel, January 25, 1974)

When cast members of Arthur Miller's "The Crucible" took
their bows at the Summit School theater last night, there was
scarcely a smile among the 24 faces. For the audience, applause
was as much a release of tension as of appreciation.

It was that kind of play, and the players did it beautifully.

Although the story is set entirely in Salem, Mass. , during
the witch trials of 1692, Miller wrote "The Crucible" when Mc-
Carthyism was doing its best to re-create those days.

The play has been called weak in characterization, and indeed it is tempting to look for more in the characters than is
there. But Miller's object was more to show the wide-reaching
social implications of surrendering one's conscience than to examine specific victims of that surrender.

The players from the North Carolina School of the Arts generally did an excellent job of showing how men and women, good
and evil, live in a time when "those who are not for this court
are against it," as Deputy-Governor Danforth declares.

Leslie McConnell played the hero, John Proctor, in low-key fashion, proper for a farmer who wants only to be left alone to farm.

McConnell gave him no histrionics, just quiet stubbornness in letting his honesty take him to his death.

Danforth was played forcefully by Glyn O'Malley, who refrained from overdoing either the evil side of the deputy-governor or the signs of compassion that Miller uncharacteristically for that moralist, allowed him to have near the end.

Lucius Houghton was the perfect innocent, Giles Corey, who provided what passed in this exhaustingly serious play for comic relief. And Lesley Hunt as Rebeccah Nurse--a small part, but a woman crucial to John Proctor's fate--shone in her dignity, fearless honesty and goodness. The aged stoop was perfect, not the caricature it could easily have been, and the quiet line, "I have not had my breakfast," revealed the authorities for the devils they were.

Pam Reid's Tituba was a perfect foil for the cold New Englanders, whose stony faces contrasted with her uninhibited emotion.

It has been argued that the play's credibility is damaged when all those supposedly intelligent people believe Abigail Williams, a child and not highly well regarded in the first place. But in Salem, in 1692, they believed her. And Margot Dionne does quite a good job of portraying the nasty Abigail in her straight-faced prevarications.

The only serious reservation--and it was later mostly dispelled--was the Rev. Samuel Parris, played by Philip de Marco. He seemed at first less overbearing than he should be; his bluster was revealed too soon as bluster, not as the authority it first seems. But it very soon caught up with itself.

There was also some difficulty in hearing some of the lines, but that was overcome by the end of the first scene.

The sets, designed by John Kavelin, were just right: austere, rather gloomy, but reminders of honesty in the craftsmanship. The costumes by Maureen Trotto were fine, as was John W. McKernon's lighting, which was especially effective in the last scene.

All the scenes were powerfully directed, and the tension became nearly unbearable in the last.

The director, Robert Murray, probably took chance with that long, long walk Proctor and his wife Elizabeth (Wrenn Goodrum) take from the middle of the cell to the bench. It's a minute or so of absolute silence, and it worked. The tension was upheld from then until the last light was darkened.

The program notes make a bid to relate the terrors of Salem (and McCarthyism) to the evils of today. The horrible thing is of course, that though it's been nearly 300 years, the fight between man's conscience and some leaders' efforts to suborn that conscience is still with us.

It is largely the Puritans' heritage in us that causes us to see things in black and white. With strong reminders such as this production of "The Crucible," we may be able to remind ourselves to watch out for ourselves.

Rollicking Musical Fun Yet Respectful
(by Genie Carr, Sentinel, August 21, 1974)

"Godspell" is often called a "rock musical," although it doesn't bill itself that way. Since the term often calls up images of "hippies" and excruciating loudness, it is an unfortunate one for this gently rollicking, enchanting musical based on the Gospel According to St. Matthew.

"Godspell," which opened last night at the Arts Council Theater, is, quite simply, a joy. From the first mouthings of "Socrates" (we can tell it is he; it says so on his tee-shirt) in "Tower of Babble" to the wine break at intermission to the final beaming renditions of "Prepare Ye" and "Day by Day," there are gentleness, humor, pathos, wisdom and excellent performances.

What there is not is piousness. There is respect for the subject matter--Jesus' life and teachings--and there is good theater. The Broadway musical, brought here by Playmoore Productions Lts. of Salisbury, was conceived by John-Michael Tebelak, with music and "new lyrics" (not Matthew's?) by Stephen Schwartz.

There are the parables and the preachings; but Jesus' listeners are a sassy lot, and it takes some powerful gentleness to hold them down.

The script and music are delightful, but their success depends particularly heavily on the performers. They introduce their own visual and verbal gags, a collection of show styles (evangelism, musical comedy, vaudeville, burlesque) and a profusion of talented imitations, including Ed Sullivan, Mae West, W. C. Fields, Groucho Marx, Nixon and John Wayne. Even a reference to Old Salem makes it in.

The performers are thoroughly professional, though non-Equity. Scott Holmes as Jesus and Michael Reynolds as John the Baptist and Judas are excellent. But to single them out is to recognize only that they have the leading roles. There is an evenness of high quality in the performances that is not often seen here.

The other performers, whose vitality never wanes, are Helen Bollman, Judi Ann Coles, Tom Demenkoff, Debbie Hackett, Selma Hazouri, David Hughes, Mary Murray and Doug Williams. They perform the 14 songs, some well-known hits among them, with good voices and liveliness under the direction of Hoyt McCachren, director; Pam Harres, choreographer; and Gil Pirovano, musical director.

Robert Weidner has provided an effective set using only a sturdy chainlink fence, a couple of sawhorses and some planks. The colorful costumes, replete with stripped suspenders and lace-trimmed overalls, are by Ellen Davis.

The fine music is by Pirovano in piano and organ, Graham Carlton Jr. and Sandy Hoffman on guitar and Grey Barrier on percussion.

From start to finish, "Godspell" is a treat, just the right thing for a last-of-the-summer evening.

CARR, Jay, Detroit News, 615 Lafayette Blvd., Detroit, Mich. 48231, Ph. 313-222-2000.

CASSIDY, Claudia; (2) Newspaper-critic-at-large; (3) b. Shawneetown, Ill.; (4) d. George Peter and Olive (Grattan) Cassidy; (5) A.B., U. Illinois; (6) m. William John Crawford, June 15, 1929; (8) Music, drama critic, Chicago Journal of Commerce, 1925-41; Chicago Sun, 1941-42; Music, drama critic, Chicago Tribune, 1942-65, critic-at-large, 1966- ; (9) Weekly program Critic's Choice, WFMT, Chicago; Film critic the Chicagoan mag. (now Chicago mag.), 1973-74; critic-at-large Chicago mag., 1974- ; (21) 33 E. Bellevue Pl., Chicago, Ill. 60611; (22) Chicago Tribune, Tribune Tower, Chicago, Ill. 60611.

CEVETILLO, Lou; (2) Music, theatre, entertainment critic and columnist, "Vocal Scoops"; (3) b. Yonkers, N.Y., July 25, 1945; (5) B.A. Iona College, MA Fordham University, New York University Certificate Admin. Super.; (6) m.; (7) 2 children; (8) 1967-72 taught foreign languages, history, classical lang. and English; 1973-present, administrator in the field of education; 1972-present, music critic etc. for Westchester Rockland Newspapers; since 1975 has written a syndicated column on the vocal arts, "Vocal Scoops." This column included interviews with singers and conductors, historical notes, mini critiques, announcements of future performances and inside gossip about the goings on at the Met. and New York City Opera; (9) 1966-76, operatic tenor with several companies in the New York Area, Connecticut and New Jersey. Sang the title role of Mascagni's Opera, "L'Amico Fritz" in its New York City revival at Town Hall after more than a forty year absence, April 25, 1971; 1966-71, singer entertainer on cruise ships and in nightclubs in the New York Area includ. New Jersey and Connecticut; performed more than 25 lead

tenor roles in the French and Italian repertory; performed fifteen
comprimario roles in operatic products; member of the National
Thespian Society; appeared in Sheridan's "The Rivals" as Captain
Absolute, Miles Gloriosus, "A Funny Thing Happened on the Way to
the Forum" and first gangster in "Kiss Me Kate."; taught appreciation courses in theatre and opera; has directed community theatre
and opera companies; (22) One Gannett Drive, White Plains, N.Y.
10604, Ph. 914-694-9300.

Stars still Shine on Ann Miller
(by Lou Cevetillo, Westchester Weekend, August 2, 1974)

"I'm an Aries with a rising Taurus and Moon in Pisces,"
boasts Ann Miller star of the current production of the 1934 hit
Cole Porter musical "Anything Goes" at the Westchester Playhouse on Palmer Avenue in Yonkers.

"My interest in astrology came from reading a book, "Pursuit of Destiny." I read all the character readings of all my
friends and found an uncanny accuracy in them. I figured that
if the Egyptians and Greeks believed in it, how bad could it be?"

Miss Miller, who admits to being 53 years old is in wondrous condition. She is the only star of the 30's and 40's who has
kept some semblance of her heyday beauty. Ponce De Leon
should have consulted Ann before setting out to find the Fountain
of Youth. She obviously has found it.

"It was in "Anything Goes" that I was seriously injured 2
years ago. In the first act during the "Friendship" number I was
hit by a falling steel curtain. It has been two years since I have
danced and it just had to be in the same show. The doctors
warned that I might never be able to dance again after that accident, but I'm glad to say that they were wrong.

"I realize that I have been closely associated with the Hilton
Hotels as being the star who has opened more of them than any
other. This is simply because Conrad Hilton loved to dance and
I was his favorite dancer; and partner for that matter."

Ann Miller has based a career in this business on the energy
and vivacious style of her dancing and singing. Her fabulous legs
and big, singing voice have thrilled audiences since her early
days in the mid 30's.

"I travel with two dressers, (there are 12 changes in "Anything Goes") and my hair dresser: (the person most responsible
for keeping up the Ann Miller visual image, jet black shoulder
length hair coiffed in late sixties style and those ruby red lips).

"The most important stage production I have been in would
have to be "Mame." The show was about to close when I got
the offer and after I took over we ran for another year. I love

the theater and that was the first play I had done in many
years. "

Harry Rigby, producer of "Irene" and "No, No, Nanette" has
offered me the lead in his new Broadway production of "Girl Crazy," his latest revival for this fall. I tried to talk him into
"Anything Goes" because I think it is the best of the old musicals.
The songs are great and the dialogue can almost stand without
a refurbishing. That is the main problem with it not appearing
on Broadway as a revival vehicle. The widows of the authors
of the book refuse to let anyone rewrite or update any of the
lines and this is a must for a Broadway production. "

"I only hope this revival craze hits the film industry. I was
offered a part in a new film but I turned it down. I feel that the
part must be right if I'm to make a comeback in the film industry. "

Carlos Montoya Enthralls Audience
(by Lou Cevetillo   Westchester Rockland Newspapers, August 12, 1974)

It is rare that a Westchester audience has the opportunity to experience a living legend in performance in its backyard. Sunday
evening at the Westchester Playhouse, this experience was afforded an almost sold out house in the person of the greatest
living flamenco guitarist, Carlos Montoya.

Montoya presented nearly 20 examples of the art which had
its beginnings in the Gypsy Quarter of Andalucia, in southern
Spain. Flamenco is a mixture of Western European music and
North African styles and harmonies brought to Spain and nurtured
there during the Moorish invasion and occupation from 711 to
1492 A.D.

With crimson cape-like curtain behind the small figure of
Montoya, who bears an uncanny resemblance to Spain's General-
isimo Francisco Franco, and his singing guitar in front, Montoya
recalled all the splendor and pageantry of a corrida on a hot
Sunday afternoon in Madrid.

Montoya's fingering of the strings can be compared to the
agile grace of a matador going through the elegant moves in the
ring. His rendition of the "Macarena," a traditional bull fight
composition, stirred the soul as it did the tapping feet of the
audience.

A recital of Montoya's flamenco is always without dancers,
but no one misses the tapping "zapateado" of the dancers' boots.
In fact, Montoya's fingers move so quickly, he still has time to
tap the wooden base of the guitar to simulate the sound of clicking heels.

The absolute climax to this evening of Spanish beauty was

Montoya's rendition of the "Saeta," a guitar arrangement of the
familiar melody of the processional of "La Semana Santa" (Holy
Week). In this number, Montoya simulated the sounds of the
horns and the drums used in this festival. The tonal likeness
of his guitar to the drums and horns and the final fading of the
melody to signify the procession moving away from the listener
brought cheers of "Bravo" and "Ole" from the excited and
amazed audience.

Montoya stands above the other practioners of this instrument
in that he has a warm stage personality that comes over the
footlights. His air of knowing all there is to know about his art
and the cordial waves to his appreciative audience bring him
closer to the listener than mere playing could ever do.

The Spanish are a patriarchal people, who consider the title,
"Papa," as one of the highest. In that case ... "Viva Papa
Montoya, El Rey de los Guitaristas."

CHAPIN, Louis Le Bourgeois, Jr.; (2) Theater and arts critic, teacher, consultant; (3) b. Brooklyn, N.Y.; (4) s. Louis Le B. and
Julia (Tuckerman) C.; (5) B.A. Principia College, English and art
major, 1939; A.M. Boston U., in art history; (6) m. Mary Lee
Smith, Dec. 15, 1966; (7) children--Julia Wyche; (8) English and arts
teacher, Principia Upper School, St. Louis, 1939-41; 1945-46, radio
announcer and director at Boston and Worcester (Mass.) stations,
and at CBS-NY, 1941-45, Instructor, Asst. Prof., Assoc. Prof.
Fine Arts at Principia College, 1946-60, Staff Critic, Christian Science Monitor, Boston, 1960-63; N.Y. Theater and Film Critic,
Christian Science Monitor, 1963-66; Free-lance writer, critic, broadcaster, numerous publications and stations including WNET-NY and
NBC Radio, Director Earl Rowland Foundation, N.Y., 1968- ; (9)
Undergraduate, graduate, faculty participation in and direction of
theater productions; Direction of radio drama segments (CBS), Participation as critic, seminar leader at Eugene O'Neill Memorial Theater Foundation Playwright's Conference and Critic's Institute, 1966- ;
Course in Modern European Drama, Wagner College, 1967-68; Tutor
and Consultant in Writing, Empire State College of SUNY, 1974- ;
Course re-exploring nature of the masterpiece, Daycroft School,
Greenwich, 1976- ; Church Organist; (10) President, St. Botolph Citizen's Association, Boston, 1961-63; (15) Treasurer, Drama Desk,
1967-75, AFTRA; (17) Christian Scientist; (20) Cont. reviews and articles to Art News, Christian Herald, Christian Century, High Fidelity,
National Observer, North American Newspaper Alliance (NANA) and
elsewhere, and art catalogue and book introductions including Chaim
Gross and Abraham Rattner; (21) 7 Dandy Drive, Cos Cob, Ct.
06807, Ph. 203-661-4220; (24) In 1975 some 70-75 reviews, mostly
book and classical record reviews on radio.

Drama: The Limits of Satire
(by Louis Chapin, Christianity and Crisis, June 22, 1970)

The voice of the artist, if I read some of the current

criticism correctly, can no longer be trusted to comfort us--nor can we be trusted to deal honestly with the comfort. (I use the word in the sense of its Latin original, confortare, "to strengthen much.") The English writer Muriel Spark, in an arresting speech at the annual ceremony of the American Academy and National Institute of Arts and Letters, could see "no other living art form for the future" but those of satire and ridicule. Literature of sentiment and emotion, she pointed out, "however beautiful in itself, however striking in its depiction of actuality, has to go. It cheats us into a sense of involvement with life and society, but in reality it is a segregated activity.... Ridicule is the only honorable weapon we have left."

Miss Spark's points were made thoughtfully and without ridicule, and I find it pertinent to consider them before turning to two new musicals.

These are times, as she says, in which speech itself "has become sharper and more ready on everyone's tongue"--which does make it logical and inevitable for the arts of language, in particular, to embrace more satire than previously, more perhaps than they have since the 17th and 18th centuries. Today's black theatre, for instance, shows this kind of a flair.

Yet I wonder at the implied exclusivity of Miss Spark's recommendations. They could bring about (if enforceable) a segregation of styles--a class system--at least as dubious as that segregation she decries in the relation of the arts and society. Furthermore, to cauterize actualities, in the way of satire, without an availability somewhere of art that affirms possibilities is to pull weeds without reseeding, to defoliate.

Be all this as it may, a new "weapon" is appearing in the theatre, and while it is not necessarily satirical, neither is it escapist; I think it deserves to be called honorable. Sometimes it is a rock musical such as The Me Nobody Knows, which recently arrived downtown at the Orpheum. This is a genuinely heartening instance, a simple, skillful and sensitive compilation of writings by school children from 7 to 18 years in Bedford-Stuyvesant, Harlem, Jamaica and other regions of New York City that have not often been looked to for literature.

Stephen M. Joseph is the teacher who originally gathered it into book form. And the other people who wrote music (Gary William Friedman) and staged its numbers (Patricia Birch), added a few lyrics (Will Holt and Herbert Shapiro), designed the tall, accommodating unit set (Clarke Dunham) and rinsed it admirably with kid-devised projections (Stan Goldberg) have realized under Robert H. Livingston's direction the best-conceived, most self-consistent rock musical yet. Its ghetto's-eye view of the world is made up of what 12 mostly black and Puerto Rican characters dream, fear, hate, hope for and laugh at.

The Me Nobody Knows contains such moments of satire--or
sharp irony at least--as the film clip watched quizzically in
which Mummy tucks little Barbara into her crisp-sheeted suburban bed for the night.   It also contains many invitations to match
these children's gifts with ours.   It shows an insight capable, for
instance, of imagining man's passage through life in terms of a
disused railway station, or his remnant of hope in a fruitless
apple tree saved from the axe by a shroud of fog, so that "the
following Sunday, a baby apple was hanging on it."

The words seem often to have pushed up--perhaps awkwardly
--through the cracked pavement of adult neglect: "I keep on
knocking; no one is there.   I stand in darkness...." "Nowhere
can I go and break these bonds [drugs] which have me in an illusion." "Mother and Father, can't we come in?" "Try and dig
it before you damn it." "Sometimes I walk very alone."

There's other theatre, and not always musical, in which people with a common urge to say something or identify a situation
do so.   A still more direct, less theatrically finished instance
is The Concept, which in its long stay at the Pocket Theatre describes and discusses the liberative drug rehabilitation program at
Daytop House.   It was originally improvised by and is still performed here and elsewhere by young "graduates" of the intensive
course of self-discovery and mutual help.   Though The Concept
is firmly directed, no one in the changing casts is ordinarily a
professional actor; as a result the technical range and control
is often uneven.   But a cast so full of inward reasons for what
they are saying and doing rides easily over the outward inexperience.

It seems to me we should give theatre credit--especially in
the baleful light of Miss Spark's comments--for being able to
communicate from inside problem situations, whether a play is
written that way or simply used that way.

Admittedly, the camera does it more easily.   Near the end
of The Me Nobody Knows, listening to the crescendo rock of
"Let Me Come In" and staring back at these sober, unblinking
faces, I suddenly thought of certain group photos in that unique
Museum of Modern Art show of a mere half-generation ago, "The
Family of Man," for which Edward Steichen had articulately assembled 503 pictures from around the world.   Through them, unknown people spoke for themselves as only folk song, photography,
film--and now maybe the theatre--will let them.

None of which seems to be exactly what Miss Spark has in
mind for the future of the arts, though the presence of it helps
make the future itself conceivable.   One of our newest satirical
exhibits is that witty, uninhibited, bitterly resourceful and ultimately self-defeating "space age musical soap [opera]" Mod Donna,
which is quite passionately staged by Joseph Papp at his Public
Theatre.   He assures us in the program that Myrna Lamb's book

and lyrics are "not ... about the feminist movement." The
sharp impression I got from the Village-Brechtian, come-as-you-
are Chorus of Women is that they are the feminist movement,
its very vanguard.

This show, whose mean, stylized little plot satirizes the
kind of ultimate exploitation that can happen within and between
marriages is full of excellences and is great for controversy.
Susan Hulsman Bingham's music fits the sometimes enigmatic,
sometimes searing, never ordinary words like a tight leotard
and accommodates a limber rhythmic and harmonic idiom.   And
it's a particular joy, among the performances, to see the kind
of total actress that Sharon Laughlin (as the vicious wife) has
grown into.

Yet you gather from this skilled evening that the only con-
sequential ways that men and women can relate are the sexual
and the punitive, and usually both; that marriage is a more or
less mutual slave-pit (the master's fallen in too, and is doing
badly); and that the home is a kind of private brothel.   A child
is planned as the ultimate murder-weapon.

I realize that satire isn't meant to spell out the desirable alternatives.   But it sometimes leaves a little room for them.
Mod Donna is total, smiling, savvy self-sabotage--an exercise in
defoliation.   What's to be done with the land next?

Having been brought up, partly in England, under the rosy,
Rupert Brookean glow of virtuous necessity that hung over the
memory of World War I, I no doubt needed the better-aimed satirical correction of Joan Littlewood's Oh, What a Lovely War!
just as much as I did the profound, non-satirical ironies of Benjamin Britten's War Requiem, which drilled further in with its
twisting together of the Wilfred Owen poems and the Liturgy for
the Dead.   Neither work contaminates the other.   If compassion
and comfort are poison, then the courteous frame of Miss Spark's
address is poison.

In Edward Steichen's "Family of Man," the caption under a
Nazi photo of men, women and children being herded out of the
Warsaw ghetto quotes George Sand: "Humanity is outraged in
me and with me.   We must not dissimulate nor try to forget this
indignation which is one of the most passionate forms of love."
Satire, as a form of love, must burn down what it can of the
stubborn facades of cruelties and counter-cruelties, stupidities
and counter-stupidities.

But for building, even out of the ashes, we'll need more.

Drama: The Theater of Berrigan
(by Louis Chapin, Christianity and Crisis, April 19, 1971)

An extraordinary theater event--one that I suppose we should call "environmental theater"--began taking place in certain parts of Catonsville, Maryland, in May of 1968, moved for its second act to a Baltimore courtroom, and is playing out the third not only in the Danbury, Conn., Federal Penitentiary, but in informed consciences everywhere. So much has been written about that performance and its main actor, Father Daniel Berrigan, that to discuss its current, overlapping adaptation for theater audiences at the Good Shepherd-Faith Church in New York might seem superfluous. Would it reach any non-believers in the Berrigan cause, for one thing; and if it did, could it convert them by merely repeating parts of the trial itself?

My own experience may answer--at least it must for me. Though I left, as I came, unprepared to share all conclusions or to imitate the protest, the play introduced me, through the actors' persuasive proxy, to the particular humanity feeding the conclusions and generating the protest. (The difference of approach, from one to another of the seven non-Berrigans, gave some breadth to the protest.) As theater it reached where the news media hadn't reached, nor even the reading of Berrigan's own comments.

To describe that "first act" (the taking and burning of the draft files) as theatrical is not therefore to question its sincerity, but to credit, for one thing, its built-in irony (the use of a crude form of napalm and of metal containers "about as big as baby caskets"). If anything is questioned here, it is our niggardly use as a country of what we quarantine off as "legitimate" theater--a medium capable of doing for us all, and through us all, more of the conscientious rumpling that the Berrigans and their friends felt it necessary to do in their way at Catonsville.

Far underlying all such projections is a fact so fundamental that it drops easily out of sight in most debates on theater development and stage strategy. While some of us cling to the pictureframe of the proscenium and others swing the environmental wrecking-ball at whatever divides actor and audience, there remains that final and only definitive arena for any play in any theater in any "style"--the one which, like war in Marianne Moore's poem, is wholly inward.

To reach and seize that arena of consciousness, usually a play must with its own tools radically reshape the event. On the other hand, the "theater of conscience" may be most crucially needed for a play designated "theater of fact" (and therefore intolerant of much reshaping).

The current staging of The Trial of the Catonsville Nine by Gordon Davidson and an eminently right cast from the Phoenix Theater, has been revised and tightened, with a bit of reshaping in the sequence of testimony, by Saul Levitt, from last summer's more complete version at the Mark Taper Forum in Los Angeles. Yet it still duplicates the trial closely enough to have allowed defense attorney William Kunstler give his actual summation to the jury at a benefit performance in place of the actor David Spielburg. (Much more difficult, though intriguing to contemplate, would be for Daniel and Philip Berrigan, once out of prison, to step in for actors Ed Flanders and Michael Kane.)

As we recall the earlier "theater of fact" pieces in our time (almost invariably, beginning with Hochhuth's The Deputy, they conduct some kind of explicit or approximate trial), Catonsville turns out to be the least separated from its generative event by time, place or dramatic shape. It not only comes, relatively, on the heels of the trial itself, but its New York opening follows by only three weeks the indictment of Philip Berrigan for conspiring against governmental buildings and personnel in Washington. This must make it as nearly as any such poetically tempered play may ever be, a direct extension in time and exposure of the "first version," intensifying the reverberations while they are still spreading. (Some of what Berrigan has written about the play, I must admit, seems to turn and reverberate inward, rather like sound in an echo chamber.)

The play needs those reverberations to stand up, being far less structured, for instance, than In the Matter of J. Robert Oppenheimer. But it is uniquely qualified to test the theater's access in depth to any measurable segment of the public conscience, working somewhere between the illegal demonstration of conscience and the merely "legitimate" rehearsal of it. To succeed in this test it must thrust into many inward theaters and provoke many individually improvised dramas.

As to the thrust, Marilyn Stasio told in Cue magazine of being blocked on her way up the exit aisle by a quartet of theatergoers "so moved that they stood looking at each other in stunned silence.... Finally, one of them broke both the hush and the bottleneck by shrugging his shoulders and saying, 'But as theater, it's not much of a play, is it?'"

Agreed. Since the play tells us less about the outcome than we can read in the program, we find no suspense in the usual sense--it is really less of a play than the act of Catonsville. And the innate courtroom antagonism, slight to begin with, more or less dwindles under the judge's patient guidance until the contention that survives is not over the immediate innocence or guilt but over the court's inability to participate in the larger guilt. (And by the end, Berrigan feels uncomfortably close to negotiating even that: "I don't want it honed down to a gentlemen's agreement.")

Visual interest could of course be added. The entirely verbal texture of the court record could be opened up so as to reach around somewhat in time and space and dramatic image, and film could be used in addition to the shots of the burning that are screened at the end.

Whatever the shrug meant, it is not keeping audiences from filling the house and extending the run; nor, in some individual cases, from being visibly moved at what they see. People are evidently providing their own visuals, and using in their own ways the imagery of oppression, of an ardent commitment and of great courage in these nine witnesses' testimony.

But how many people? Any perceptible minority of the silent and non-theater-oriented majority? Hardly ... yet. Many of this majority, no doubt, see the whole undertaking as scandalously subversive, and the play, if they should see it, might not coax them very far towards approval. Yet it would take them up to questions too human to be subversive. (They might find themselves, as do many in the audience, glad to say the Lord's Prayer with the people on stage; and any rancor they found in the play would have to be their own.)

The Berrigans have abandoned the American judicial system as a hopeless, bureaucratic bog, and have found little encouragement within their church. The theater, itself the despair of many, is their principle voice at the moment. Still, there is available truth at the roots of each of these institutions, and that truth has to do in the churches and in the theater with breaking temporary laws in order to honor and clarify the unbreakable ones.

When Christ raised Lazarus, the prescribed causality of disease crumbled. When Bach wrote a fugue, the little legalisms of the form were scattered by the onrush of music. Picasso switched in 1907 from the comfortable customs of figural and facial representation to the sudden no-man's-land of Les Demoiselles d'Avignon, and so moved decisively towards the Guernica of 30 years later, one of the definitive war protests of all time. As for theater and public opinion, Ibsen thoroughly roiled his fellow Norwegians by questioning, if not breaking, in a given play the very axiom he had promoted in the previous one.

Our inclination as a country, however grudging, is still to obey governmental law. It seems to me that Daniel Berrigan's performance in Catonsville and his non-play in New York both recognize that inclination, and in a secondary way respect it (in the difficulty, rather than the final exuberance, of his decision). However, if we can bring anything approaching his love and joy and sheer guts to the shattering of those folk laws that describe theater as an elite, luxurious communion of escape, and let it be the voice of our concern as well--then it may be that we can leave the rest of the draft records to turn yellow and useless where they are.

CHRISTIANSEN, Richard Dean; (2) Critic at Large; (3) b. Berwyn, Il. , Aug. 1, 1931; (4) s. William and Louise (Dethlefs) C.; (5) B.A. Carleton College, Northfield, Minn. , major subj.: English, 1953;

(6) Single; (8) Reporter, City News Bureau of Chicago, 1956-57; Reporter, Chicago Daily News, 1957-64; Editor of Panorama magazine and arts & amusements for Chicago Daily News, 1965-73; Editor of The Chicagoan magazine, 1973; Critic at large, Chicago Daily News, 1974- ; (9) College and community theater work, theater apprentice at Chevy Chase Summer Theater, 1949; (10) Member of Governor's Commission on Financing the Arts in Illinois, 1972; (12) Director, Arts Club of Chicago; (13) Cpl., U.S. Army, 1954-56; (14) Marshall Field Award for journalism, Chicago Newspaper Guild special award, 1971; Chicago Emmy award for TV Show, Panorama, 1969; Chicago Newspaper Guild award for service to journalism, 1974; (15) Mem., The Cliff Dwellers, Chicago Press Club, Sigma Delta Chi, The Arts Club of Chicago; (16) Republican; (17) Lutheran (Missouri Synod); (19) The Whitehall Club; (20) Wrote and served as host for shows on theater and film on Chicago TV stations WTTW (public television) and WFLD; (21) 2901 King Drive, Apt. 1809, Chicago, Il., 60616, Ph. 312-842-2682; (22) Chicago Daily News, 401 N. Wabash Ave., Chicago, Il., 60611, Ph. 312-321-2183; (23) Circulation: 450,000 plus newspapers serviced by Chicago Daily News-Sun Times wire service; (24) 150 plays and musicals, 50 dance, 50 arts-related features, 20 films, and a little of this, a little of that.

Young Author Scores in First Play
(by Richard Christiansen, Chicago Daily News, May 10, 1976)

"All I Want," which arrived this weekend at the Victory Gardens Theater, is a vibrant first play written and directed by Bruce Hickey, who is 23 and a former caseworker for the Department of Public Aid.

The play, which Hickey calls "an urban tragicomedy," mirrors both its author's youth and his experience, being on the one hand a sentimental melodrama and on the other a touching human drama firmly rooted in the realities of the lives it depicts.

The story concerns one unhappy family in the physical and spiritual wasteland of Chicago's Uptown neighborhood: the mother, desperately trying to fight off old age with boozed-up good times; her son, a street punk dropping out of high school; and her daughter, a waitress struggling to be free of the drug habit imposed on her by a sadistic boy friend.

These three could be considered typical cases in a social worker's file, but Hickey does not classify them. To his credit, and to the play's great strength, he treats them as individual human beings endowed with a spark of dignity.

Hickey has all the surface details of his characters down cold: the clothes they wear, the food they eat, the rough language they speak. The blood they shed seems real; when they're hooked on drugs, they look it.

Caught up in a familiar plot of violence, the characters

nevertheless seem fresh and original, because their creator has such feeling for and understanding of these people.

The play moves almost like a movie. Michael Merritt's lighting dissolves from one playing area to the next in the extended setting he has devised for the small third-floor theater at 3730 N. Clark. Some effectively recorded songs by Hickey and Paul Joseph (who portrays the villainous boy friend) also help bridge the emotions of each scene.

The all-stops-out climax is shrewdly prepared and skillfully staged, yet the play actually is strongest in its quiet moments, when the simple rhythm of human interaction takes over.

There's a very poignant moment when the son (Bobby DiCicco, in a stunning performance) and his mother (Linda Clink-Scale) almost, but not quite, express affection for each other.

And the scenes between the daughter (Lynn Longos, a lovely 19-year-old) and the kind hillbilly cook who loves her (David Mink) are handled with moving grace and tenderness.

All five players, under Hickey's direction, appear in truth, to be living their roles.

This makes them halting and rough around the edges at times, but what they lose in facility, they more than gain back in hard-earned honesty.

Character and compassion, in the end, win out over cardboard plot. "All I Want" gives us what we hope for in the theater: people we care about.

"Sitcom" a Savage Satire
(by Richard Christiansen, Chicago Daily News, June 23, 1976)

Julian Barry's "Sitcom," which had its premiere Tuesday night in the St. Nicholas Theater, is a sociological-political-philosophical-economic-religious-historical-theatrical-science fiction satire that plays as if it had been dreamed up by Lina Wertmueller, Orson Wells, Tom O'Horgan, Chevy Chase, Norman Lear, Lenny Bruce, Ralph Edwards, Abbie Hoffman, Bertolt Brecht and anybody else who happened to be around at the time.

Clearly (and sometimes not so clearly), Barry has bitten off more than he or his cast of 29 actors or his audience can chew.

Nevertheless, though alternately appalled and agape at the whole incredible concoction, I was fascinated.

The three-act drama, which takes place in a TV studio where a situation comedy (sitcom) is being taped, is set sometime in the near future, when the state has taken complete control.

The show being presented before a live audience is The Horowitz House, a hateful kind of All in the Family that is produced
and enacted by a full panoply of slimy show-business types.

By the end of Act I, a young heckler in the audience has
identified himself as the new Messiah--and the son of the show's
leading lady.

By the end of Act II, Israel has been bombed and invaded,
forcing the producers to change their show to The Beiruti Bunch,
for the benefit of the victorious Arabs.

And by the end of the play, still another Messiah has emerged as a John F. Kennedy look-alike to declare a new state
of fascism in which the entire cast winds up behind the barbed
wire of a concentration camp.

There's much more, including the reincarnation of Joan of
Arc.

The total effect, however, is that of an immense flood of
disgust washing over the entire rotten range of contemporary
society.

In Barry's vengeful view, our media-sated world, where progressive action has been drowned in cynicism and circuses, is
ripe for a new Hitler. The liberalism of past generations has
atrophied; the Jesus freak faith of the present generation is leading to a blind alley.

What's left? Totalitarianism. And who will survive? The
same sniveling hypocrites and cowards who have come through
all the other holocausts.

This is raging paranoia in full cry, almost shrieking in its
anti-humanism.

I can't say that I like it; but, in between its high-flown outrage and its crude show biz shticks, "Sitcom" has more theatrical coherence than its sprawling contents would at first indicate.

The St. Nicholas company--which went ahead with this production over the objections of its former artistic director, David
Mamet--has given the play all the manpower and technical facilities it can muster.

Julie Nagel's costumes, David Emmons' setting, Robert
Shook's lighting and a complex array of blinking "Applause" signs
and closed-circuit television sets are perfectly on target.

In the huge cast, the three featured Equity actors are Nes-
bitt Blaisdell as a drunken actor, Patti Wilkus as a spiteful parody of a Jewish mother and Sidney Eden, superb as the craven,

slick-spieling author of the TV show, Leonard Poetry.

As director, Barry has performed incredibly well in unifying all the diverse characters on stage in his play within a play.

He has done less well in integrating all the various ideas that swarm through his script. Half the time, it's difficult to tell whether the obscenities on stage are purposeful satire or unconscious vulgarity.

Yet for every instance of lame foolery, there is a striking moment of sharp insight.

"Sitcom" is a blatant, noisy, nasty play. It practically screams with a death wish, but it overflows with life. It is repulsive and engrossing--and you will not see anything like it for some time to come.

CLAY, Carolyn Elizabeth; (2) Theatre critic, contributing arts editor; (3) b. Baltimore, Md., May 31, 1948; (4) d. Dr. Richard and Madeline (Murray) Clay; (5) B.A. Denison U., major subj: Theatre Arts, 1970; M.F.A. Boston U., major subj: Theatre Arts, 1972; (6) m. Douglas Trees, Nov. 22, 1973; (8) Freelance Theatre and book reviewer, Boston After Dark, 1971-1972; Theatre Critic, Boston After Dark 1972-1973; Cultural reporter, film and theatre Reviewer, Boston Globe 1973-1974; Theatre critic, contributing arts editor, Boston Phoenix 1974- ; (9) Actor, Southern Shakespeare Repertory Company, Coral Gables, Fla., summers 1965, 1966; Apprentice, Asolo Theater Festival, Sarasota, Fla., summer 1968; Instructor, Introductory acting, Denison U., 1969-70; Guest Instructor, Dramatic Criticism, Boston U., 1975; (16) Independent; (21) 84 Cherry St., Wenhem, Mass. 01984; (22) Boston Phoenix, 100 Massachusetts Ave., Boston, Mass. 02115; Ph. 617-536-5390; (23) Circulation: 110,000; (24) 125 plays and musicals, 10 books, 10 miscellaneous and news stories.

Theatre
(by Carolyn Clay, Boston Phoenix, December 3, 1974)

"Shenandoah" is the mushiest thing I've been through since Mrs. Walton learned to walk again. Like the grandiose Jimmy Stewart movie from which it sprang, this new musical (on its way to Broadway after a much-heralded summer opening at the Goodspeed Opera House) is as unabashedly sentimental as a Judy Garland tearjerker, as highminded as a Christian martyr and as irresistible as Noah's flood (a deluge not unlike the one set off opening night, the audience sniffling audibly as magnificent Andersons fell like flies).

As for the nobly envisioned but actually gruesome Civil War against which the "Shenandoah" saga unfolds, I categorically refuse to take seriously any war in which the fightin' boys wear

taps on their boots. Yet despite the seeming incongruity of song-
and-dance and bayonets-and-brutality, "Shenandoah" is a surprisingly good musical. The score is excellent and the star, John
Cullum, more overpowering than the war.

"Shenandoah"'s story hasn't been altered--James Lee Barrett
adapted the book from his own screenplay. Charles Anderson
(a man's man, probably the model for the Dinty Moore beef stew
ads) is still tilling his own precious soil, feeding his large family by the sweat of its collective brow. Mrs. Anderson, we
learn, died (probably in self-defense) giving birth to the seventh
of their sickeningly wholesome offspring, and Charlie, who obviously believes in marriage and motherhood, even after death
doth us part, wanders out under the Spanish moss from time to
time and spouts senile philosophy at her tombstone.

Because he has no slaves (with six sons, who needs slaves?)
and doesn't believe in it anyway, Anderson has no intention of
sacrificing his sons to the questionable cause of the state of Virginia. The musical chronicles his highminded if unrealistic effort to stand aloof as the war rages all around him. Inevitably
if sadly, the Andersons are swept into it when the Yanks take
the youngest son prisoner.

"Shenandoah," despite the sentimentality so often attributed
to women's entertainments, is a man's musical permeated by the
masculine mystique, right down to the lusty choreography with its
pocket-flask-and-hoedown flavor. Except for Jenny, who can out-
shoot her brothers when she isn't mooning over the cowed Confederate who weds and beds her, women are agreeable baby-ma-
chines. And the men even take credit for that in "It's a Boy,"
a macho number ripped off, tune-wise, from "Carousel."

But the appeal of this musical will be tremendous. In addition to having a better than average score, "Shenandoah" plays
on the now modish yearning for a return to the joys of family
life and the old-fashioned stability of yesteryear. The wedding
of Jenny Anderson is right off a Valentine, embellished with
twinkling lanterns, tinkly music and a humming accompaniment
to the marriage vows. The whole flowery scene drifts, finally,
into a moony number with lyrics like "Love is the recipe that
flavors a life." One has to admire the guts behind this kind of
go-for-broke gooiness. Rod McKuen would be hard put to top it,
and his music can't compete with that of Geld and Udell.

I hate myself for having succumbed to the emotional crush
of "Shenandoah," but there's no denying it. And I'd sit through
it all again, if not to marvel at the power of Cullum's lungs,
then to see if this time I couldn't remain steeled in my cynicism,
immune to the tearful return of the littlest Anderson (believed
dead), who hobbles into the meetin' house on a crutch. Tiny
Tim lives! Aw shucks, I'm misting over just thinking about it.

Stoppard Jumps to Clever Contusions
(by Carolyn Clay, Boston Phoenix, December 24, 1974)

Someday Tom Stoppard may make that final jump, from the
craggy cliffs of reductio-ad-absurdum into an unsettled sea, there
to bodysurf on the froth of his own delightful lunacy.   Until then,
we Stoppard devotees may continue to marvel at his lucid teeter-
ings on the brink.   We may continue to argue that his plays'
making no sense makes no difference.   Critics, academics, and
Agatha Christie nuts will, meanwhile, continue to fume, as the
Czechoslovakian fruitcake makes mincemeat of their most precious
postulates.

Stoppard, who has given us the Beckett-borrowed but much
celebrated Rosencrantz and Guildenstern are Dead, as well as
The Real Inspector Hound, wrote Jumpers in 1972.   While it
can't be said that this daffy juxtaposition of mental and carnal
gymnastics laid the biggest egg that Broadway has ever nested,
it was by no means a Rosencrantz and Guildenstern.   Jumpers,
which bounces from genuine metaphysical muddling to metaphysical spoof and back again, is a talky play.   Though not as intricate an exercise as Hound, it is a bit coy.   There are problems.
But the ones that have not been solved in the wild and glittery
production currently mounted in Providence at Trinity Square are
treated with enough hoopla that no one cares.

The Stoppard script is scattershot, action taking place (often
simultaneously) in three square rooms, lined up on the tiny stage
like back-to-back train cars.   Robert D. Soule's setting looks
like Mae West's boudoir, a Harvard library and the cookie house
from Hansel and Gretel squashed together on the display floor at
J. Homestock.   But the competing action in each of the three
rings only adds to the circus effect created in the opening scene,
in which a sultry songstress croons a comeback while a mousy
nude swings from a chandelier and eight of the Trinity actors
make their debut as acrobats.   Confetti and spangles are dispensed with abandon as the distracted singer tries to get her
moon-tunes mentally sorted out and the "jumpers" caper and cart-
wheel to the strains of "Shine On, Harvest Moon."   Suddenly a
shot is fired from somewhere, one of the acrobats falls, and the
play gets underway.

As it turns out, these are not circus performers at all, but
party-guests at an academic soiree.   Most of them are professors
of philosophy.   The dead one, stashed in the crooner's closet,
holds the coveted Chair of Logic and had been scheduled for a
debate that very evening on the weighty subject, "Man: Good, Bad
or Indifferent?" with one George Moore, a Professor of Moral
Philosophy in whose home both shindig and shooting have taken
place.   Mrs. Moore is a dotty (that's her name, no coincidence)
former nightclub singer, whose retirement and neuroses hinge
on an inability to cope with the Space Program and its callous
destruction of the moon's romance.   She spends her idle days

behind the satin curtains of her canopied bed, rolling on the shiny sheets with a gymnastic psychiatrist by the name of Jumpers.

Stoppard's most effective feat lies in the playful contrast of Moore's longwinded philosophical blundering as he labors over his lecture on the moral condition of man and Dotty's more reasonable madness, her realization that man, like it or not, has been altered by his walk on the moon. He has peered through space at the tiny earth from God's vantage point. This contrast could, I believe, be achieved in about half the time, were George's metaphysical meanderings trimmed down some. But Jumpers is still a mysterious as well as a very funny play. And Richard Kneeland pulls out every device in his actor's bag to combat George's verbosity, from shameless punning to prop tricks and pratfalls. Some of the ham is sandwiched into the script, I suppose, but a lot of it is served up a la carte (and beautifully, too) by a sheepish yet charismatic Kneeland.

The actor is not alone responsible for saving George Moore from the doldrums of his own dullness. While spoofing philosophy in general, Stoppard bats around some fascinating moral notions. And Word Baker, who states in his pocket program biography that as a director he prefers to "keep out of the way" of his material, has made an astute choice. Superimposing directorial craziness onto what Stoppard has already proscribed would probably take the bounce right out of Jumpers. Baker has cast the show very creatively, making use of his actors' personalities in ways that, though they mayn't have occurred to Stoppard, are extremely workable. And Baker's handling of the close of Act I, in which the corpse is danced with immaculate grace into a large, beribboned plastic bag (all to the tune of "Sentimental Journey"), is perfect.

George Martin practically drips urbanity as the debonair doctor who is as rambunctious in Mrs. Moore's boudoir as he is unctuous in Mr. Moore's study. And Margo Skinner brings to the retired prima donna, a role created by the cool-as-a-cucumber Diana Rigg, a crazy, sexy vulnerability that is marvelous-- a Monroe-esque counter to the icy glamour of her trimmings. Mina Manente, who follows her naked ride on the chandelier with two hours of wordless hangover as she both records Kneeland's blathering in shorthand and nurses a bromo, ought to get a decoration of sorts. Thank God I'm above remarks like "Where would she pin it?"

CLOSE, Roy M., Minneapolis Star, 425 Portland Ave., Minneapolis, Minn. 55488.

CLURMAN, Harold; (2) Stage director, theatre critic, university pro-

fessor and lecturer; (3) b. New York City, Sept. 18, 1901; (4) s.
Samuel & Bertha (Saphir); (5) Columbia University, 1921; University
of Paris, 1923--Literature; (6) m. Stella Adler, divorced; m.
Juleen Compton, divorced; (7) Step-daughter: Ellen Adler Oppenheim; (8)
1931-41, Co-Founder, The Group Theatre; 1937-41, Managing Direc-
tor, The Group Theatre; 1941-46, Film Producer and Director, 20th
Century Fox, Paramount, RKO; 1946-52, Critic of Arts, Tomorrow
Magazine; 1949-52, Theatre Critic, The New Republic; 1959 & 63,
Guest Theatre Critic, The London Observer; 1953-present, Theatre
Critic, The Nation; (9) Actor and Stage Manager, Theatre Guild,
1924-29; Play Reader, Theatre Guild, 1929-31; Co-Founder of Group
Theatre, New York 1931-41; Productions directed: Awake and Sing
(Odets), Golden Boy (Odets), Member of the Wedding (McCullers),
Autumn Garden (Hellman), Bus Stop (Inge), Tiger at the Gates (Girau-
deux-Fry), Touch of the Poet (O'Neill), Incident at Vichy (Miller);
(14) Donaldson Award for Direction (A Member of the Wedding),
1950; Chevalier, French Legion of Honor, 1956; George Jean
Nathan Prize for Dramatic Criticism, 1958-59.   Honorary Doc-
tor of Literature, Bard College, 1958; Honorary Doctor of Fine
Arts, Carnegie Institute, 1963; Andrew Mellon Lecturer in Drama, Carnegie Institute, 1963; Sang Prize for Dramatic Criticism,
Knox College, 1968; Honorary Doctor of Fine Arts, Ripon College, 1969; Honorary Doctor of Fine Arts, Boston University,
1969; Brandeis University Medal of Achievement for Distinguished
Contribution to American Arts, 1976; (20) Published Works: The
Fervent Years, Knopf 1945; Lies Like Truth (Theatre Reviews
and Essays), Macmillan 1958; The Naked Image (Observations on
the Modern Theatre), Macmillan 1966; On Directing, Macmillan
1972; The Divine Pastime, Macmillan 1974; All People Are Famous, Harcourt Brace Jovanovich 1974.

Theatre
(by Harold Clurman, The Nation, May 22, 1976)

The Brecht-Weill Threepenny Opera is surely one of the
masterworks of the 20th-century theatre.   It is peculiarly ravish-
ing: it enchants with sweet sickness.   Its impudent snarl de-
lights--most strangely.   It is defiant and yet very nearly funereal.
The mournful alternates with the heroic.   Heartbroken, it manages
to laugh.   The wretchedness of Germany after World War I, its
baleful future, its hope and failure are all here.   Beneath the
mockery and challenge, it presages the approaching defeat.   There
is a sense of doom in it, yet it inspires elation by a consciousness of the living moment.   It is a play of a befouled time
struggling to express its malady and to overcome it.   Much of
its music has a heavy, dragging beat of depression, but along
with this we hear in it a will to fight the way to courage and
light.

That was the Germany of the time, and Brecht was wholly
of it.   As certain artists in the past sought refuge from dark
days of social and personal disease by turning to the Church,

Brecht found salvation in a humanistic Marxism. But in 1928, when The Threepenny Opera was produced, he was not yet there; he was intellectually convinced of his dawning belief but not yet possessed by it. Much of his skepticism (never altogether dispelled) and a masochistic anguish which the war's aftermath had instilled in him still remained. This ambivalence is what makes the play an enduring work. It is not "propaganda," though the political Right as well as the Left saw it as such and made its first production an occasion for scandal and riot.

If without preconception one leaves oneself open to the full effect of The Threepenny Opera, one senses that Brecht was himself infected with the romantic glow of decay, even as he reviled it and aspired to liberate himself from it. Hence the pervasive irony of the work which, together with Weill's telltale score, at once embraces and jeers at the schmaltzy lubricity of the surrounding scene. This side of the duality is sounded in the words and music in which the gangster Macheath and his consort Jenny sweetly recall (with acid admixture) the wonderful time (literally translated) "in that bordello where we kept house." The opposing note is struck in the foreboding of the play's last lines: the rich (again literally) "eat up the poor man's bread. For they [the poor] are in darkness and the others are in the light. And you see the rich in brightness, those in darkness drop from sight." Between these antipodes there is the guying denunciation of Macheath's self-defense which, in Eric Bentley's translation, reads: "We artisans of the lower middleclass, who work with honest jimmies on the cash boxes of small shopkeepers, are being ruined by large concerns backed by the banks. What is a picklock to a bank share? What is the burgling of a bank to the founding of a bank? What is the murder of a man to the employment of a man?"

When Kurt Weill, whose music marvelously matches the originality, wit and poetry of Brecht's writing, undertook his first American assignment with the Group Theatre's production of Paul Green's Johnny Johnson, he told the acting company that, for him as much as for Brecht, understanding each word of the verses was more important than an appreciation of vocal quality. For this reason Brecht and he preferred actors who enunciated clearly to singers who were chiefly concerned with the tones they emitted.

Perhaps the most distressing thing about the production now playing at the Vivian Beaumont Theatre of Lincoln Center is that no more than half of the lyrics are readily intelligible. The producers call special attention to the new translation by Ralph Manheim and John Willett. It may be excellent, though for those who know the extraordinary terseness of the original German, no translation can be altogether satisfactory. But if we fail to hear it quite distinctly, pleasure in the play is well-nigh lost.

Directed by Richard Foreman, the production is certainly

"different" from any I've seen in New York, Berlin, Tokyo and
Moscow, but not happily so. One immediately striking difference
is Douglas Schmidt's setting, which has a stimulatingly modern
look. It consists of a naked stage framed by a metal structure
to which are appended rotating, rising and descending wheels; a
black background with sectional panels, and a battery of lights--
all lending the stage a feeling of industrial environment. (It is
reminiscent, for those who have seen them, of Meyerhold's con-
structionist settings between 1920 and 1925.) We soon perceive
that the production indeed is "different" but entirely misconceived.
The basic tone is grim, lapidary, with some resemblance to that
of a demonstration in the 1960s.

The actors make "big" points by shouting. Brecht's style es-
chews this: shouting is counterindicated. His whole method can
be summed up in the phrase, "Cool it." Brecht rarely proclaims: he is insidious, sly. He lays on slush--along with
Weill--as a device to heighten the sting of his intention. His
characters usually address the audience with an unctuous plausibility, as if to woo it. In this production, several songs are delivered in strident wrath. The Threepenny style is no secret:
listen to the German recording made in 1958 under Lotte Lenya's
supervision. She herself, the Jenny of the original Berlin production, is delicate, sprightly, a cunning soubrette. There is a
veiled mystery about her, and when she declares that she will
kill all who had failed to recognize her worth she flicks the word
"all" from her lips in an easy whip of contempt. (Jenny at the
Vivian Beaumont--Ellen Greene--has been turned into a brazen
horror.) To roar Brecht because he had revolutionary convictions is to equate him with the most guileless of American "art-
is-a-weapon" amateurs.

Richard Foreman is a talented director. I like several of
his previous essays: Dr. Sealevy, for example. But here he
distracts us from a number of songs by having all sorts of "mysterious" by-play going on behind and beside the singers, adding
to our difficulty in understanding what they say. Finally the elaborate and complex scenic scheme becomes a hindrance to enjoyment: it is all too busy.

So gifted and delightful a comedian as Raul Julia suffers a
loss from this treatment. One can't make out how to view his
Macheath. He is not funny, not raffishly attractive, not representative of anything except a fake macabre, which is the chief
stylistic attribute of the production.

So much ability and effort have been expended to give us a
new, tough, and to those not previously acquainted with it, puzzling Threepenny. As Brecht has written, "Between producing
a shock and getting on people's nerves there is a difference...."

Theatre
(by Harold Clurman, The Nation, June 19, 1976)

Fernando Arrabal's The Architect and the Emperor of Assyria is a "big" play (La Mama Annex, 66 East 4th St.). I do
not refer to its length--in a cut version it runs three hours--
but to its sweep. It is a vast "send up" of modern civilization--
"Christian capitalism"--a play of gargantuan blasphemy.

It is not to be readily categorized. Arrabal himself has referred to it as a panel in his "theatre of panic." He and his audience are under a similar spell. He saves himself and us from
its brutal blows by a sort of hideous humor; his total disgust is
spewed out in raucously derisive laughter. It may be called a
sado-masochistic farce. But no conventional epithet quite fits it.
It is surely an original play, even if for pigeonhole purposes we
invoke the names of Ghelderode, Genet, Goya and Buñuel.

The influence of Spanish Catholic atmosphere and upbringing
are strong in Arrabal. "In Spain," he wrote, "children are
cruel ... in my childhood, everything was sin and I wonder to
what degree the idea of sinfulness does not still haunt me." It
certainly does! But added to this there is the actual experience
of the Franco years, during which his father disappeared from
jail never to be heard from again. Arrabal's investigation into
the condition of Franco's prisons and his brief incarceration in
one of them contributed to his education in horror.

Because his father had been a traitor to the regime, Arrabal's
mother abjured her husband. It was on a search for his father that
Arrabal set out for France, where he settled in 1960 and began to
write most of his plays in French. First produced in Paris in 1967,
when he was 35, The Architect and the Emperor was not an easy
play for me to grasp when I than saw it. Nor is it now wholly trans-
parent--one may ask oneself why the "Architect," why "Assyria,"
etc.? --but its mood, its sentiment, its special eloquence and
its basic thrust make it unmistakably powerful. Like it or not,
it is one of the signal plays of our time.

A "gentleman" falling to earth from an airplane accident,
lands on an unknown island of which the sole inhabitant is a savage. In that isolation the man of the world teaches the native
barbarian the speech and facts of the outside world. The instruction is a process of fun and games: the games of justice,
war, religion, love, marriage, filial attachment and duty. Our
culture's representative becomes the "Emperor" as the native is
the "Architect," the creature of work and constructive action or,
if you will, master and slave. And what does the Architect gather from the Emperor's discourse? At first the Emperor speaks
of the blessings of the world which made him. "Ah philosophy!
Ah music! Ah monuments!" he periodically exclaims. "Civilization? What a wonder!" he goes on. "During thousands of centuries man has stored knowledge and enriched his intelligence

until he has attained this marvelous perfection that has become
life. Everywhere, happiness, joy, tranquillity, laughter, understanding. All is conceived to render man's life easier, his happiness greater, and his peace more durable. Man has discovered
all that's necessary to his well-being and today he's the happiest
and most serene being in all creation."

But around the very ecstasy of his praise there is nothing
but destruction, frightfulness, venom, slaughter, obscenity. "All
that is atrocious, nauseating, putrid and vulgar is contained in
one word: God." As for justice: "What justice? What is Justice? Justice is a certain number of men like you and me who
most of the time escape this very justice by hypocrisy or subter-
fuge--I don't give a damn for your courts, your operetta judges,
your puppet tribunals and your prisons of vengeance." He quotes
a great poet: "Little bastard, big bastard, we are all bastards."

These are the least of his imprecations. The hot line between Kennedy and Khrushchev is alluded to, the unspeakable
curse of the bomb is part of the panorama, the ghastly idiocy
of war reports in which the casualties of the opposing powers are
triumphantly trumpeted, are given their due in this message from
hell. The Emperor recalls the memory of his adored mother,
reviled and decapitated! With all this there is an ambiguous savor of the homosexual. And the play ends in a satanic ritual
of self-immolation. The Emperor bids the Architect to kill and
eat him. "I want you to be you and me at the same time."
Perhaps, to begin with, they were two sides of the same entity:
humankind. For at the end we witness the repetition of the initial pattern: the Architect returns in the person of the Emper-
or, the Emperor in that of the Architect.

The writing is sometimes cast in the mode of surrealist
"automatic" composition, widly incoherent and yet astonishingly
lyrical, with a sort of madly orgiastic afflatus and hurricane giddiness in which everything from Coca-Cola to world literature
revolve in a giddily grotesque dance: "We'll erect palaces with
labyrinths," the Emperor shouts, "we'll dig pools for sea turtles
to bathe in, I'll give you an automobile so that you can tour
through all my thoughts and pipes steaming liquid smoke in spirals that change into alarm clocks. I'll drain the swamps and
out of their mud will emerge a flock of pink flamingos with tin-
foil crowns, etc. etc." Everything is desecrated in an appalling
circus.

Yet one cannot say the play's ferocity voices an all-consum-
ing nihilism--no work of art ever does--for even the Emperor
says to the Martian of his imagination, "I want to stay on earth.
... We have just reached the point where we can sustain grief....
What, I'll die an atrocious death during a war, burnt by radia-
tion? ... In spite of the fact that I don't know and have no desire to know Mars, I a thousand times prefer to live on earth
in spite of our wars and difficulties, rather than on your dream

planet." The play, is at once a howl of anguish, a hysterical prayer, and a protest.

Tom O'Horgan has directed the play with epic glee on Bill Stabile's fantastic set, which we look down on from the height of several tiers. There is picturesqueness and ingenuity in his direction though his extravagance leaves too little to the imagination. He errs in matters of taste and his desire to find a physical equivalent for the author's every idea and metaphor sometimes obscures the text, which in this case is of the first importance. For all that, I consider his production one of the most outstanding of several seasons. Lazaro Perez as the Architect and Ronald Periman as the Emperor (all the other "characters" are mimed as part of the games played by the two principals) are loyal to and efficient in their formidable tasks.

COCHRAN, Marsha Rabe; (2) Theatre critic, interviewer, arts feature writer; (3) b. Dubuque, Iowa, Jan. 24, 1948; (4) d. William L. and Ruth (McCormick) Rabe; (5) B.A. Yale University, major subj: English literature, 1975; (6) m. John R. Cochran, April 20, 1968; (8) Free-lance journalist and critic, New Haven Register, 1971- ; (9) Property manager, LaMama production of Leslie Lee's Elegy for a Down Queen, 1971; (14) Eleanor H. and Andrew J. McGlinchee Playwrighting Prize, Hunter College, 1972; Henry P. Wright Prize, Yale University, 1975; (15) Phi Beta Kappa; (16) Democratic; (17) Roman Catholic; (20) Clio Magazine; (21) 13 Eighth Ave., Branford, Conn. 06405, Ph. 203-488-4573; (23) Circulation: 130,000; (24) 12 plays and musicals.

At Goodspeed: Familiar Porter Sophistication
(by Marsha R. Cochran, New Haven Register, July 9, 1974)

In 1939, when "DuBarry Was a Lady" opened its pre-Broadway run in New Haven, a local critic, reacting with a "guardian-of-the-public morality" mentality, called Cole Porter's sophisticated and somewhat risque lyrics, "comfort station poetry."

That was 35 years ago, and although the double-entendres and naughty one-liners are played to the hilt in this new production at the Goodspeed Opera House, it's likely that the audience is going to be a good deal more entertained than offended.

Early Broadway musicals are infamously short on plot, and "DuBarry Was a Lady" is no exception. By comparison, however, it's a bit more ingenious and creative than most. Louie Blore has just hit the jackpot in the Irish sweepstakes and, like a school of good-natured piranha, his friends are all waiting for a share. Louie quickly discovers that the stripper of his dreams, May Daly, is in love with Alex Barton, dashing Hollywood correspondent. Hoping to slip Alex a mickey and thus slip away with May, Louie accidentally slips himself and drifts away to dreamland. The rest of the play takes place in Louie's foggy

head which is filled with images from a movie about the notorious
Madame DuBarry and her romantic liasons.

It's a drugged dream combining elements of 52nd Street
striptease with 18th century France and the court of Louis XV.
Characters from the strip joint take their corresponding places
in the court.   May is DuBarry, Louie is a much beleaguered
and very frustrated Louis, and Alex is Alexandre, a revolutionary songwriter who falls for DuBarry.   The jokes depend on the
absurd incongruity created by the meeting of vaudeville with royalty, and when they work, they're fine.

Further narrative explanation at this point is unnecessary.
Suffice to say, Louie, in his stupor, comes to see that money
can't buy love.   And the lovers, in true romantic fashion, prove
that love can make happiness.

Joey Faye, a familiar face who's been on the boards since
Minsky's, has some very funny moments as Louie-Louie.   His
"Friendship" duet with Susan Waldman and his foot-shuffling attempts at seduction are both fresh and funny.   However, a very
long and mismashed "latrine" scene with John Lemme in Act I
lacks the vitality and energy to make it work.   Faye's obvious
gift for "schtick" needs a bit more control, so that when the
grimaces and double-takes happen they relate to the material.
When it comes to comedy, less is sometimes better.

As May-DuBarry, Susan Waldman combines the right amounts
of sensuality and honky-tonk charm.   Her "Give Him the Oo-La-
La" solo, with its riotous reference to Eleanor and Franklin
Roosevelt, is a clever, well-delivered Porter classic.   Her duet
with Faye "But in the Morning, No" is also ribald and raunchy
and very witty.

Bonnie Schon and Richard Cooper Payne provide a nice, innocent little subplot as the bickering lovers and their "Well Did
you Evah!" is pure Porter poetry, a witty, wicked and very telling spoof on the pretensions of high society.

The sets by Fred Voelpel, while fanciful and attractive,
seemed to be giving people more than their due problems.   Scenes
were obviously held up while panels were moved from left to
right for no apparent reason.   Perhaps director Neal Kenyon,
who, for the most part, handles his actors ably and well, might
simplify some of the scene changes and thus shorten the hour
and 45 minute first act.   But these are technical difficulties which
will no doubt be ironed out.

The costumes by David Toser are dazzling and the dance
numbers, even the "Danse Tzigone" (which may or may not have
been intended as humor) are imaginatively choreographed by Bick
Boss.

Musical director Lynn Crigler presents some very interesting Porter. The music itself is often uneven and sometimes nondescript, but when Porter's going full-steam, it's delightfully sophisticated and great fun.

Play Set in '30s: "Biography" Is Frothy Fun
(by Marsha R. Cochran, New Haven Register, August 8, 1974)

S. N. Behrman's "Biography," a bittersweet comedy written in the early 1930s, is a curious little period piece. It is certainly not a classic. Its scope is both limited and time-bound. Its characters seem like phantoms, charming and likeable anachronisms, as provocative and remote as the discoveries in an archeological dig. Like a good Cole Porter song, there is always somehow less there than meets the eye and ear. There is much talk and many ideas. But in the end, it all boils down to a diverting nothing.

The third production of the Summer Theatre of Greater New Haven's first season, "Biography" pits that special 30s brand of sassy, sophisticated, world-weary tolerance against that equally special 30s brand of starry-eyed, breathlessly indignant idealism. The main characters in combat are Marion, a Tennessee-born adventuress who has painted them, loved them and left them in all the capitals of the world: and Richard, a young journalist of obscure and meager beginnings who dishwashed his way through Yale and is now the editor of a barely middle-class magazine, "Everyweek."

Richard approaches Marion with the proposition that she publish her memoirs in his magazine just as her old lover, Leander Nolan, now a Senate hopeful, drifts back into Marion's life. If Marion agrees to publish her biography, she will probably hurt Leander's election chances, for the book must include their youthfully idyllic liaison. However, if she knuckles under to the pressure, she will betray Richard's hope and trust. Naturally, Richard falls in love with Marion, while despising her uncommitted way of life. Just as naturally, Leander harbors a nostalgic affection for his old sweetheart. And to add the transparent to the predictable, Marion, in her seemingly boundless capacity for affection, loves them both, each according to his due.

The plot resolves itself with Marion optimistically going on, sacrificing her love for Richard for fear of destroying in him those very qualities she most loves, and rejecting Leander because, in spite of what he may feel, for her the past is as charred and dead as her burned manuscript. Although she can sympathize with Richard's Utopian vision, she cannot make it her own.

The set for this production, by Tom DiMauro, subtly captures the casual bohemian sophistication of the action. Marion's New York studio is littered with paintings, prints and canvases.

A wastebasket spills over with discarded papers. Flowers and plants decorate the corners. Valerie Neale's costumes are also accurate and attractive, making fanciful use of handkerchief skirts, ropes of pearls and billowing sleeves.

Under J. Robert Jennings' smooth direction, the acting is, for the most part, confident and polished. Sharon Alpert is very good as the flippantly coy Marion. When she incredulously asks Leander, "Do you really want to be a Senator or can't you help it?" she brings down the house. Kirk van der Swaagh, as the hulking, awkward Leander is often touching in his confusion. And Roy Callendrella is hilarious as Leander's newspaper-mogul, prospective father-in-law. His pompous lectures on the healthful benefits of "roughage," and his finger wagging moral hypocrisy are perfect.

Darlene Ranno is also fine as Leander's tough-talking fiancee, and Tony Amendola as Feydak, Marion's old friend and confidant; and Pat Flynn, as her maid, are both excellent in their Old World characterizations. Although Gary Jerolman is a bit too obvious and hysterical as Richard, his performance provides a good foil for Alpert's calmly amused Marion.

At one point in the play, Marion wonders whether or not to go on with her memoirs, "Who cares about the confessional ravings of an obscure woman?" After all, the only reason her life has any value as "copy" is because she has had the good taste, or good luck, to have been the mistress of some very important and famous men. In the end, one cannot help but echo Marion's question, Who does care? Although "Biography" provides a good glimpse of what the 30s thought it was, it is ultimately the Late Late Show, amusing, entertaining, but trivial.

COE, Richard Livingston; (2) Theater critic; (3) b. New York, N.Y., Nov. 8, 1916; (4) s. Elmer James Secor Coe and Lillie Musgrave C.; (5) George Washington U., English, 1938; (6) m. Christine Sadler, May 4, 1946; (8) Radio editor, assistant drama critic, The Washington Post, 1938-42; United States Army Air Corps, 1942; columnist-editor, Stars and Stripes, Cairo, Egypt, 1943-46; Public Service Reporting, Washington Newspaper Guild, 1949; (14) Citation of the District of Columbia, D.C. Board of Commissioners, 1957; Certificate of Community Action, The Washington Board of Trade, 1957; Award of Merit, General Federation of Women's Clubs, 1957; Critic of the Year, Directors Guild of America, 1963; American Theater Association Silver Citation, Mobile Award, 1974; (17) Episcopalian; (19) National Press Club; The Players; (20) Contributor to London Chronicle, London Reynolds News; Egyptian Mail; Egyptian Gazette; Palestine Post; Shakespeare Quarterly; New York Times; The New Republic; The Nation; Ambassador; The Smithsonian Magazine; The Washingtonian; Grolier's Encyclopedia; Amerika; Commentator for WRC-NBC-TV 1969-75; (21) 2713 Dumbarton Ave., N.W. Washington D.C. 20007, Ph. 202-338-8730; (22) The Washington Post,

1150 15th St., N.W. Washington D.C. 20071, Ph. 202-223-7563;
(23) Circulation: 585,900; (24) 200 plays and musicals, 48-50 Profiles or Interviews. Plus 48 for TV or other.

"1600 Pennsylvania": A Musical Address to the Nation
(by Richard L. Coe, Washington Post, March 25, 1976)

"1600 Pennsylvania Avenue," the highly touted new musical
play about White House occupants of the 19th century, finally
"opened" officially last night at the National, where its run
through April 17 has long been sold out.

If this means a gap in your theater going, consider that a
pause that refreshes.

It may well be that "1600" will yet make a show that knows
where it's going; it certainly is not so messed up now as reports
of its Philadelphia premiere indicated. What it lacks is a determined tone. When it preaches it is fatuous. When it tries for
pure history it is often off the mark badly. When it tries for
satire it sometimes works. But its focus is undetermined.

There are strong points: Leonard Bernstein's score, which
includes several bouncing tunes and has been eloquently orchestrated by Sid Ramin and Hershy Kay; some exceptionally fine,
strong singing voices, especially in the chorus, and three tip-top
starring performances by Ken Howard, Gilbert Price and Patricia
Routledge, who, so far as the house was concerned, could go on
singing a duet with herself as both Julia Grant and Lucy Hayes
forever.

The basic problem is the insistence of the story line, which
I gather was as much Bernstein's notion as that of his librettist,
Alan Jay Lerner. Having determined that they want to contrast
the white presidential families with the lives of the Blacks who
serve them, they are more or less stuck with finding ways to
dramatize the white-black conflict from the John Adams administration to that of Teddy Roosevelt. It is a sensitive, imaginative
ambition, but history is not so accommodating.

This is curious because both men have worked closely with
classic sociological material which disguised their purpose. What
could be stronger than "Pygmalion's" point about how accents destroy human chances, which Lerner used so cleverly in "My Fair
Lady?" Didn't Bernstein learn from the original Lillian Hellman
"Candide" adaptation that Voltaire was too clever to appear to be
lecturing?

The preaching is partially excused by using the device of a
play-withing-a-play. A modern cast is rehearsing a 19th-century
panorama of the White House as a home. During the period,
leading man Howard will start as Washington (false teeth) and
touch on Jefferson, Adams, Madison (only Dolley sees him),

Monroe, Buchanan, Lincoln, Andrew Johnson, Grant, Hayes, Garfield, McKinley and the 20th century's Rough Rider, Teddy R. This scheme allows cleverness for Tony Walton's costumes and not too much of heavy scenic maneuvering.

But the basic concept now is obviously reduced from what it was and the play is still in a state of flux. It's own history is pertinent.

The advance interest in "1600" is understandable, the first collaboration between Lerner who adapted such works as "My Fair Lady," "Camelot" and "Brigadoon" (all from previous sources), and Bernstein, composer of such scores as "West Side Story," "Wonderful Town," "Candide" and "Mass," which opened the Kennedy Center Opera House. From this record our success-hipped culture expects, at least, the moon. Small wonder that for its welcome initiation as a theatrical angel, Coca Cola embraced the chance to contribute the full $900,000 budget to producers Roger L. Stevens and Robert Whitehead.

The White House as setting, however, is no guarantee of success. There also was a record-setting advance sale in 1962 for a National tryout, "Mr. President," with a book by Howard Lindsay and Russel Crouse and music by Irving Berlin. They were as firm a collaborative team as this one for a dozen years earlier they had collaborated on Ethel Merman's long-lived hit, "Call Me Madam" (which didn't venture into the White House, though an actor had a walk on as President Truman).

For the gala "Mr. President" premiere, President and Mrs. Kennedy arrived late and separately, while Vice President and Mrs. Johnson, early and together, headed the flossy audience while the curtain was held. For all its promise, "Mr. President," starring Robert Ryan and Nanette Fabray, ate up its fancy advance and expired unmourned, costing its producer, Leland Hayward, a small fortune.

The first of these modern Presidents-in-Someone-Else's-Flesh musicals was the Pulitzer-winning "Of Thee I Sing" of 1931, by George S. Kaufman and Morrie Ryskind to music by the Gershwins. The team tried again two years later with "Let's Eat Cake," but it was no go. The most vivid of New York-bound White House tryouts the National has seen was "I'd Rather Be Right" in 1937, by Kaufman and Hart to a Richard Rodgers score. This boasted George M. Cohan's marvelous mimiery of Franklin D. Roosevelt and that jovial gentleman in the White House enjoyed it immensely, as did everyone else.

Perhaps because of its collaborators' previous record "1600" has had an extra rocky road. Star Ken Howard, who was Thomas Jefferson in another National tryout, "1776," was not signed for his presidential roles until the day before rehearsals started. When it gave its first performance four weeks ago in Philadelphia, it ran three hours and 45 minutes, shorter at that, than "Show Boat's" historic 1927 premiere at the National. Everyone quaked at the critical notices in Philadelphia, but the public broke the Forrest Theater's box-office record.

Director Frank Corsaro was fired "for artistic differences" and choreographer Donald McKayle left with him. Replacing them, respectively, are Gilbert Moses and George Faison, the team that turned "The Wiz" into a Broadway smash for the past 60 weeks after five months of alterations. They're credited with a 75 per cent change since the first performance.

"1600" has been cut by one hour since Philadelphia, but the original list of eight visible Presidents has been extended to 13, give or take the dead McKinley.

What with complex scenery, the problems of rewriting some scenes, rehearsing others and performing earlier versions and the need to handcopy orchestration changes, musical tryouts are notoriously costly, iffy periods. Some improve under the hectic life-saving treatment; others expire.

The unifying factor of the successful White House musicals, then, has been a certain, uniform attitude, the assured point of view.

This does not refer to Bernstein's usually varied score "Rehearse!" the opening and the final number, boasts "If we keep on our toes and we don't close, it's gonna be great. "Take Care of This House" is practically a hymn and "The President Jefferson Sunday Luncheon Party March" is a beaut. The Routledge show-stopper, "Duet for One: First Lady of the Land," displays her comic genius, however unfair it may be to Julia Grant and Lemonade Lucy. Reid Shelton leads the British crisply while Washington burns.

The Buchanan number, miserable as that period was, falls fairly flat and the wind-up of Act I suffers from the basic preconception. Guy Costley as Little Lud who grows up into Lucy handles the not-easy "If I Was Dove" with such accomplished ease that the lad matures naturally into Price, whose full-throated voice is pleasure, though one wished his song were better. Maybe some will be?

No, the variety of songs should be there, including the minstrel style used for a strong portion of Act I but they do voice either familiar or reiterated themes. There is acid here and too much is too much. It's as though the creators could think no further.

After so chaotic a period, one does find zest and spirit in the staging and playing, probably ascribed to the fresh guidance of director Moses and choreographer Faison. Some of the dance

numbers already have the stretching vitality Faison poured into
his musicals here and "The Wiz." The Moses challenge now is
to determine a strong, decisive tone in favor of a cause that
digresses.

"A Texas Trilogy": In Affirmation of Wonder
(by Richard L. Coe, Washington Post, May 9, 1976)

"A Texas Triology" is far and away the most creative theater yet offered by the Kennedy Center: new, compelling, affirmative plays by a sensitive observer of the human comedy, richly staged in myriad detail. Not since the late '40s, when Miller
and Williams were breaking in on us, has one heard so assured,
so American a dramatic voice. Whatever else the future holds
for Preston Jones, he has written three gorgeous, actable plays.

It doesn't matter much which of the three you see at the
Eisenhower. There will be differences as to which is the most
satisfying. Washington's introduction to them came last year
with Alan Schneider's Kreeger staging of "The Last Meeting of
the Knights of the White Magnolia," an incisive dissection of one
of those get-together organizations so deeply embedded in the
American tradition.

In that one you meet some characters who reappear in the
other two. "Lu Ann Hampton Laverty Oberlander" allows, at
last, a dazzling, demanding role for a star actress. Diane
Ladd's performance is a marvel of character building and she
proves herself a dynamic star of the first rank. "The Oldest
Living Graduate," set further up on the social scale, is a study
of the upwardly mobile in a dying world and offers Fred Gwynne
a part comparable to Ladd's. Gwynne is making the most of it.

My admiration for the plays stems from their strong affirmation of character. There are no villains. There are simply
people reacting, bumbling along, doing what they can with what
they've been given. From the lines, short, concise and sounding so true, stem characters whom actors must find a joy to
flesh out.

With this accuracy of lines and tone, the characters seem to
unfold like artichokes, each leaf stripped away to bring us closer
to the concealed heart within. A character may seem to be,
say, greedy or impatient, but once Jones has stripped away the
leaves, the person may turn out to be giving or long-suffering.

This is a writer's attitude which takes living to reach. To
understand this about humanity shows a philosophical maturity
our recent playwrights have not revealed. To make these seemingly humdrum, humble people dramatic takes a true theatrical
gift.

During Lu Ann's 20-year span she develops from an empty-headed high school cheerleader into a woman who may be frazzled but has not been afraid to grapple with her world. She survives and at least has the treasure of a remembered, shared love to bolster her spirits.

Jones gets at this not so much by showing the traditionally dramatic meeting, but what came of it. Having met Dale Laverty, we know what kind of husband he must have made--and while we never see him again, we see him reflected through Lu Ann's attitudes in Red Grover's bar. When their daughter pays a secret visit to her father and tells us about it, we can see Dale in middle age, though he's not visible. Everett McGill's mime (learned, perhaps, as the first horse in "Equus") is uproariously funny and we can imagine how he bloated. The same technique is used to introduce Lu Ann to her second husband, the curiously romantic Oberlander, voiced with telling excitement by Baxter Harris as he dreams of the truck-filled highways. James Staley's Billy Bob of 20 years apart is a striking effect.

In a sense, Lu Ann's play is three one-acters, each an authentic slice-of-life episode. What makes them so playable and the playwright's choices so rewarding is that each act is a sustained scene. With its chips of this and that, influenced by film techniques, modern theater has been forgetting the values of the sustained scene. They give players time to build character and to lead an episode to a dramatic punctuation.

"Knights" is a wholly different approach, consuming the same amount of time as its action. The members have no idea, when their meeting begins, that this will be the last one. While some tend to think of the members of this fraternal organization as caricatures, they are not played that way nor do I find them so. By golly, there are people like this--doughty, wandering individualists who have no trouble whatever with their identities. They may seem crazy as loons, but so far as they are concerned, they know exactly who they are and have no truck with that overworked, introspective vein of contemporary drama.

The point is that they have things to learn. In their varied ways, Rufe, Olin, Red, L. D. , Skip and Milo learn that their world has changed. To that they will react in their individual ways. The give and take in these parts is grand, thanks to Walter Flanagan, Thomas Toner, Patrick Hines, Henderson Forsythe, Graham Bickel and Josh Mostel.

In the fascinating internal balances common to all three plays, "Knights" has its age extremes: the old, dazed colonel, relic of the past, and the appealing, non-compus Lonnie Roy, who somehow is going to have to cope with a future in this arid town. Just what future, Jones and that neat actor Paul O'Keefe leave up to you. The fitting keystone to the "Knights" architecture is black Ramsey Eyes, the hotel porter, supposed to know

nothing whatever about this Ku Klux Klannish band.   But he knows
all about it and his quiet, amused chuckles as the curtain falls is
gloriously right.   The veteran John Marriott repeats his Kreeger
performance.

That I found "Graduate" the most moving may be just personal.   This shows the coming generation taking over from the
elder.   Crass Floyd knows nothing of the romantic reason his
old father, Col. Kinkaid, has for holding on to the Genet property
Floyd wants to turn into an "exclusive" real estate "manor."
Maureen, Floyd's wife, appears to scorn the cantankerous, near-
senile old colonel and has a sharp, bitter tongue.   Developing
these parts, their only roles in the three, Lee Richardson and
Patricia Roe make outstanding contributions.   As the real-estate
partner, Henderson is totally different from his "Knights" role
and Kristin Griffith is deliciously oozy as his vacuous, ambitious
wife.   Major Kethum and Cadet Turnbull suggest hip educators
and their victims.

The play is about life's graspings and letting-go.   As we
realize the situation, explained through the crusty old duffer's
confidence to a handyman, the essential characters emerge.
Childless Maureen is not heartless.   Floyd is not despicable.
Gwynne's colonel becomes a true romantic.

Again, then, in quite another way, "Graduate" has its architectural shape, something like the Hampton Court maze.

Finally, after exposition to the three, they merge into a
larger form.   Though this indeed is West Texas, for the plays
are defiantly regional, it also is life itself, with change as the
essence of living.   The "Knights" day is long gone.   "Lu Ann"
somehow has survived 20 years dominated by frustrations.
"Graduate" sees change and, reluctantly but firmly, lets go.

This overall theme--all plays ending with expiring life--has
a final turn not of anger but of affirmation of wonder.   What a
comment, that laughter from Ramsey Eyes!   What determination,
that acceptance of Lu Ann!   What a peace, that understanding of
father, son and daughter-in-law as Schneider lets the scene drift
from our vision!   Without saying, so, Jones is murmuring,
"Aren't people amazing?"

This is that tone of affirmation our stage too long has been
missing.   Jones' method of getting to it is earthy, sharp, mocking humor spiked with honest sentiment.   To laugh unrestrainedly
while tears well up is a rare theater experience.

In almost every aspect the three productions are definitive,
thanks to Alan Schneider's commanding grasp of the plays as a
whole, their characters and joinings.   Such details as the settings
and lighting by Ben Edwards and the costumes of Jane Greenwood
are exactly satisfying without ever fighting for attention.

To stage three such plays simultaneously is an immense achievement. To do one at a time is the usual route, but with eight weeks to get three onto a stage for successive opening nights takes professionalism of the highest order from all involved.

We owe Jones' first step to Paul Baker of the Dallas Theater Center, where all were introduced. As a member of the company, searching for plays to produce, Jones was irritated to realize that many of today's plays are, in Baker's words, "about a love triangle with settings in pads of New York, Los Angeles or San Francisco, but that little had been written about the country he knew so well from his own roamings, Middle America." Feeling that he would at least make a stab at getting away from those cities, Jones wrote "Knights," then "Lu Ann," finally, in the spring of '74, completed "Graduate." All in all, three full-length plays in 20 months.

Here Audrey Wood seems to have entered the picture. Back in the late '30's, this tiny, doughty literary agent discovered Tennessee Williams. Later she came across William Inge. Then she found Arthur Kopit. And there were more. Now, at a time when most people would be winding down, Miss Wood has uncovered Jones, surely a high batting average for her unusual profession.

And, rushing down to Dallas, always on the alert, curious Schneider quickly recognized the plays' values, prevailing on his longtime Arena Stage associate, Zelda Fichandler, to give "Knights" a whirl. Simultaneously, the American Playwrights Theater chose it for its members this past season, accounting for scores of "Knights" productions around the country.

Miss Wood's next step would be critical, to choose the right New York producer. They were at her heels, evidently, for word travels fast, but she decided this producer had to be special. "I thought about that long and hard and offered them to Robert Whitehead because he treats plays carefully, like the fragile things they are. With his longtime partner, Roger Stevens, I felt confident Whitehead would make the right, troublesome choices to get these on stage."

The cast echoes Miss Wood's appreciation of Whitehead. They agreed when one remarked, "I've never enjoyed the atmosphere of a company more, nor, I guess, have I ever worked harder, but this has been a sharing experience, watching the plays grow with each rehearsal and performance."

Besides the stars, Ladd and Gwynne, there are those first-rank players already mentioned as well as Ralph Roberts' beamish eagerness as the listening handyman, William Le Massena's p. r. -minded educator and Kate Wilkinson's touching mother to Lu Ann. At one time or another, most of these players have worked

before with Schneider, or in the Kreeger version, and there is
an ensemble feel throughout, uncommon to most commercial theater ventures.

What will come of all this after the Eisenhower on June 27?

The Edwards sets were made for the Eisenhower's movable
stages, which slide at the press of a button. They will have to
be reconstructed, at some expense to "fly" up to the wings of
other theaters. Whitehead is considering a Boston visit after the
Washington finale. New York is known to be clamoring but
Whitehead has no intention of just rushing to a still risky venture.

New York is a risk on two counts. The repertory scheme,
trail blazed this season by the London import "The Norman Conquests," is confusing to the usual New York Pattern. And there
is little New York likes better than to sniff at what the rest of
the land finds admirable. So there will be both habits and pre-
conceptions to overcome.

More importantly, there is the playwright himself. Oceans
of publicity and attention now are breaking over Jones' head.
Since these three, Jones has written another, "A Place on the
Magdalena Flats," already produced in Dallas and to be revived
there May 17 as part of director Baker's annual "Play Market."

How can Jones keep his head? He likes fishing and that's
one way out of the storm and back to earth. At 40 he also has
been working in theater as actor, stage-manager or box-office
attendant long enough to be wise to the theater's transitory adula-
tions. Most vital, it seems to many observers, is Mrs. Jones,
Mary Sue.

A lean, electric-looking woman, she is Baker's top assistant
at the Dallas Theater Center, where she also acts and is a professor of theater at Trinity University. She hasn't appeared in
her husband's plays "because I don't want to ruin them. One
first night in a family is bad enough." She too, is theaterwise
and quietly conscious of her responsibilities as chief keeper of
the flame. It's not an easy spot, but if anyone can fill it, Mary
Sue Jones, perceptive, critical and tender, can.

Backstage these nights at the Eisenhower there's a rare atmosphere of professional excitement. The challenge of a different play almost every one of the 11 performances a week, the
unanimous absorption to polish the playing and the swift reactions of the audiences conspire for a rare contagious unity.
Everyone seems to sense that something special is happening.
It is.

COLBY, Vineta; (2) Professor of English, theater reviewer for Park
East (weekly newspaper); (3) b. New York, N.Y., Mary 12, 1922;

(4) d. Walter and Vineta (Rolls) Blumoff; (5) B.A. New York U.,
1942; Ph. D. (English), Yale, 1946; (6) m. Robert A. Colby, May 8,
1947; (8) Instructor-Assistant Prof. Eng., Roosevelt College, Chicago, 1947-51; editor, H. W. Wilson Co., N.Y.C., 1951-57; Instruc-
tor-Prof. Eng., Queens College, CUNY, 1957- ; Theater reviewer
Park East, 1960- ; (14) Member, Phi Beta Kappa; (15) AAUP, MLA;
(20) Editor, American Culture in the Sixties (1963); (with S. J.
Kunitz) European Authors (1967); author, The Singular Anomaly: Women Novelists of the 19th Century (1970); Yesterday's Woman: Domestic Realism in the English Novel (1974); co-author (with R. A.
Colby) The Equivocal Virtue: Mrs. Oliphant and the Victorian Literary Market Place (1966); (22) Dept. of English, Queens College,
Flushing, N.Y. 11367; Park East, 401 East 79 St., New York, N.Y.
10021, Ph. 212-535-5106.

New York Humor in "Dreyfus"
(by Vineta Colby, Park East, October 24, 1974)

Dreyfus in Rehearsal comes to Broadway so carefully cali-
brated for commercial success that one wonders why the dialogue
isn't Fortran or some other computer language. With a theme
as moving as anti-semitism, with actors as endearing and enduring as Sam Levene and Ruth Gordon, and with a director-
adaptor as solidly professional as Garson Kanin, how can it fail?
Very easily.

Playwright Jean-Claude Grumberg has already been highly
honored for a successful run of his play in Paris last year.
What his Dreyfus in Rehearsal was like before Garson Kanin took
it over, we have no idea. The tendentious speech-making of the
young playwright-director in the play itself suggests that it was
one of those earnest, deeply felt European social dramas that
succeed by their sheer unabashed editorial journalism. In America we have had only glimpses of what such drama can be--from
Brecht at its best to, maybe, WPA Federal Theatre.

The conception is not without interest. In 1931 a small company of provincial Polish Jews--ordinary workers by day, amateur actors by night--are rehearsing a play about the court martial of Capt. Dreyfus. That notorious scandal of thirty-five years
earlier means nothing to them. They'd be happier playing Jewish
vaudeville. But the young playwright persists and they rehearse,
while outside, first distantly then ominously closer, anti-semitism
spreads. A silly ineffectual lecturer bumbles away about Zion-
ism--remote and meaningless to his listeners. The playwright
himself spouts platitudes about brotherhood. They are finally invaded by some foul-mouthed drunken village louts, and after a
scuffle they give up the play. In the end the young people have
gone off to begin life anew--one, ironically, to communism (where
there's no anti-semitism, he reports!), the others to Berlin
(where they discover there are a lot of vacant apartments in the
Jewish quarter.) This leaves the older folks with their vaude-
ville--and fearful hearts.

Perhaps if Mr. Kanin had retained the hard core of brutal truth which a play like this must have, he would have achieved a measure of artistic success. But in slicking it up with a mixture of tones, acting styles, and cheap commercialism, he has thrown it away. One is never sure where Dreyfus in Rehearsal is going. Boris Aronson's fanciful Chagallish drop curtain and some background Yiddish music suggest an arch ethnic comedy. The homely wise-cracking and shoulder-shrugging strictly New York humor.

The shifts then to the serious matter and to the intellectually complex issue of Dreyfusism (a very special and sinister kind of anti-semitism, different from the coarse racism of Polish pogroms) are disconcerting. The shifts in acting--from the mellow professionalism of Sam Levene and Ruth Gordon, to Avery Schreiber's stand-up comic routines, to clumsy amateur performances-- are equally disconcerting.

Nevertheless, with this subject, these starts, and the advance ballyhoo, Dreyfus in Rehearsal may breathe some life into the Broadway scene. But it will be artificial respiration.

"Equus" Is a Theatrical Feast
(by Vineta Colby, Park East, November 7, 1974)

Like an unused muscle, one's theatrical imagination becomes flabby and atrophied. There once was a theatre of illusion--of sheer, dazzling make believe, staggering us with a power not of real ideas or great language, but of mind-boggling fantasy. It was a bubble. After we left the theatre, the lights, the masks and the music, we looked back and saw the play stripped quite undistinguished and ordinary in its nakedness, but while it lasted it was theatre--not the play we read and analyze and remember as literature, but the spectacle that delights because it fools us and makes us innocent again.

Peter Shaffer's Equus, coming to New York after a triumphant run in London, is precisely the sort of fantasy that our under-nourished theatrical imaginations have been craving. To be sure, this is not the imagination department of whimsy or innocence as we ordinarily know them. Equus is a commercial shocker, exploiting all the trendy, pseudo-intellectual vogues of psychiatry. Peter Shaffer--some of whose earlier ventures in theatre like Five-Finger Exercise were pretentious bores--has moved up only a few rungs on the ladder of ideas. Madness is fashionable and saddism is in, and the current quizzer is who is mad--we or they?

But Equus is a brilliant entertainment because it makes exploitation itself stylish, elegant, and fascinating. Shaffer handles his shoddy material with such professional confidence, John Dexter has staged it with so much vigor and inventiveness, and Anthony Hopkins and Peter Firth act the leading roles with such total absorption that we are willing captives of the illusion.

Here is the--alas--not untimely subject of a juvenile who has committed a crime of unspeakable horror--the blinding of six horses--and a psychiatrist who probes the mystery of why. Actually there isn't much mystery--the erotic urges of a sensitive boy, complicated by the not unusual parental pressures--an educated, religious mother and a socialist, working-class father.

Far more interesting is the solution--the slick professional diagnosis--by the psychiatrist. Here is the physician who cannot heal himself--a man with the guilty suspicion that his "cure"-- a tranquil, adjusted, "normal" patient--demands a sacrifice of the passion, the Dionysiac "splendor" that the presently "sick" boy knows. The psychiatrist, in his own sterile marriage, lives vicariously in Greek history and legend. The boy, in his "madness," really lives.

As our sprinkling of quotation marks indicates, Shaffer is playing with words. The jargon of popular psychiatry gets a shiny new coat here, but it's only a veneer. Still, shabby old things come alive under polish, and what polish we have in Equus! The stage is almost bare, except for a few benches and some scaffolding of seats for a spillover of the audience. Yet with the flick of a few wrists it is a psychiatrist's office, a boy's bedroom, a barn, an arena. And the horses themselves--six actors in wire head pieces and wire platform horseshoes--are brilliantly executed.

Young Peter Firth is intense, full of explosive destructiveness, yet pathetic in his troubled agonized innocence. Anthony Hopkins, who was the superb Pierre in the recent TV War and Peace, transcends his role--the thinking-man's Exorcist--and turns it into a wonderfully complex and vulnerable character.

For its performances and its staging Equus may well make theatre history. And in what has been until recently a theatrical famine, it is a feast.

COLLINS, William B., Philadelphia Inquirer, 400 North Broad St., Philadelphia, Pa. 19101.

CONSTANT, Yvonne; (2) Theater critic; (3) b. Paris, France; (4) d. Constantin and Suzanne (Brogard) Coronakis; (5) Baccalauréat (Paris, France) Philosophy; (6) m. M. A. Lanin, April 2, 1969; (7) child-- Gérard Pinguet; (8) Actress-singer on Broadway (4 shows); TV, To- night Show (45 lines), Merv Griffin Show (12 lines); Night clubs, 2 American films Drama critic for "France-Amérique" since 1969; (9) Lecturer at the "Alliance-Française" around the U.S., subject: "Theater, Both Sides of the Footlights"; (14) Tony Award "La Plume de ma Tante" Broadway 1960, N.Y. drama critic citation as one of

season's most promising actress; (15) Alliance Française/French
Institute; (17) Catholic; (21) 20 Sutton Place South, New York, N.Y.
10022; (22) Howard Lanin Prod., Ph. 212-752-0960; (23) Circulation:
distributed throughout the U.S.; (24) 80 plays, musicals and ballet
in 1974.

Cyrano
(by Yvonne Constant, France-Amérique, June 14, 1973)

Et voici notre (Cyrano de Bergerac) à Broadway! et en musique ... Je vous dirai d'abord que la production du spectacle
est très belle, que les costumes, les éclairages, les décors lui
donnent des airs de tableaux de maîtres flamands. Je vous dirai
encore que l'adaptation d'Antony Burgess suit de très près le
texte original, encore qu'il le (mette au goût du jour) par 2 fois
au moins, en ajoutant des répliques d'un goût plus que douteux
et dont le romantisme délirant de Rostand aurait frémi.   Ceci
dit, nous retrouvons ligne pour ligne la tirade des (Non, merci!)
et celle des (Nez) et nous vibrons sous leur panache, mais hélas,
elles sont mises en musique, (par Michael J. Lewis) et telle-
ment mièvrement que celle-ci devient une insulte au débordement
lyrique du texte.   On a également fait de Cyrano, une sorte de
Figaro de Rossini, l'instant d'un couplet. Il n'y avait vraiment
aucun besoin de faire une comédie musicale de (Cyrano de Bergerac) si c'était pour l' assaisonner à cette sauce insipide.

Dirigé par Michael Kidd, Christopher Plummer est le héros
avec fougue, grâce, tact, et émotion.   Cet acteur canadien est
certainement un Cyrano idéal, de ce côté-ci de l'Atlantique.   La
direction de la dernière scène le tourne tout à coup en (Man of
la Mancha), ce qui est une surprise gratuite.

Roxanne, devenue (Roxana) est interpŕetée par Leigh Beery,
qui est jolie, chante bien, mais est sans grande personnalité;
Mark Lamos, Christian, est jeune et beau comme le veut le
rôle.

(Cyrano) à Broadway, une gageure, dont le lyrisme fait encore mouche, 76 ans après sa création.

The Bolshoi Ballet and the Bolshoi Dance Academy
(by Yvonne Constant, France-Amérique, July 5-11, 1973)

Absolument extraordinaire! Stupéfiant! Le Ballet Bolshoi
amène pour la première fois son Académie de danse qui présente
(Ballet School) avec 8 petities filles d'environ 7 à 10 ans, un
minuscule petit garçon et des éléments plus avancés en âge et
en technique.   Mais, quelle merveille que celle-ci, quelle discipline, quelle pureté dans la ligne, que de genoux tendus à
l'extrême, de parfaites cinquièmes, quelle rigoureuse propreté!
Ces élèves sont si fabuleux que bien des étoiles d'autres grandes
compagnies rougiraient de leur propre technique! Il faut remercier
pour leur méthode de travail Sofia Golovkina, directrice de

l'Académie et Maxime Martirosyan, maître de ballet.

Malheureusement, (Chopiniana) qui fait directement suite, est un désappointement. C'est un peu comme être transporté 40 ans plus tard ... Nous sommes désenchantés par l'interprétation des étoiles, le style est sauvegardé mais ce n'est pas suffisant après les grands espoirs de l'ouverture.

En revanche, la troisième partie, qui est composée de pas de deux de ballets célèbres, nous donne l'occasion de retrouver notre enthousiasme et notre exaltation. Dans (Flames of Paris), Nina Sorokina est rapide et enjouée, Yuri Vladimirov fait un incroyable manège de sauts qui nous fait, nous, tomber à la reverse... Dans (Le Cygne noir), Ludmila Semenyaka est belle, sa technique est superbe et altière, Alexandre Godunov réussit sa variation magnifiquement. Dans le gopak de (Taras Boulba), Shamil Yagudin met une note de danse de caractère dans une soirée presque exclusivement classique, (Spartacus) est parfaitement beau et parfaitement dansé et enfin, dans la variation de la Fée Dragée du (Casse-Noisette) de Tchaikowsky, apparaît Nadezhda Pavlova, la reine, la grande découverte de la soirée. Avec ses dégagés trop hauts pour être réels, des équilibres d'une facilité déconcertante, Mlle Pavlova, âgée de 17 ans, fera parler d'elle mondialement. Son partenaire Yvacheslav Gordeyev est tout à sa hauteur, ses manèges de jetés et ses sauts sont spectaculaires.

Il y a des failles dans le programme du Bolshoï, elles consistent dans l'interprétation des membres les plus anciens ce la troupe ce qui tend à donner un aspect vieillot à (Chopiniana) (Raymonda) et (Etude), mais ceci mis à part, la brillance de la compagnie est incomparable et nous assistons à des solis inoubliables.

COOK, J. David; (2) Theater and music critic; (3) b. Delray Beach, Fla., July 29, 1927; (5) ABJ U. of Georgia, major subj: journalism, 1950; (6) m. Mariam Katiba, Jan. 14, 1953; (7) children--Dana, Maclyn, Lisa, Lori; (8) City editor, Ocala Star-Banner, 1956-1962; editor, Ocala Star-Banner, 1963-67; Associate editor, Tallahassee Democrat, 1968-; (16) Democrat; (17) Presbyterian; (19) Tallahassee Kiwanis; (21) 1309 Piedmont Dr., Tallahassee, Fla. 32303; Ph. 904-385-6201; (23) Circulation: 45,000; (24) 12 plays, five musicals, 10 misc., 25 musical concerts.

A Not-So-Funny Caper
(by David Cook, Tallahassee Democrat, May 30, 1975)

The current offering of the FSU School of Theater, Jean Anouilh's "Thieves Carnival," is a farce that draws sharp targets. The problem is that it usually misses the target the author has so clearly erected.

Where there should be laughter, there is only quiet amusement. Worst of all, exchanges of dialog designed to be funny, provoke no response at all.

With that much said, it should be pointed out the talented cast works hard to pump life into proceedings. Neither the cast nor the direction (by Richard Fallon) is to be faulted. The technical aspects are handled superbly.

Anouilh has mixed fantasy, nonsense and irony with some pungent observations of life. Two sets of thieves, both inept in their own way, go after a rich, aristocratic family to pick it clean.

Out of boredom, aging Lady Huff invites three thieves into her home, where they enjoy luxury of a type that makes two of them forget why they came. Meanwhile, a father and son of some substance are trying to woo a daughter in order to get their hands on the family's money.

Two love stories run concurrently, one fresh and youthful; the other cynical. Mixed up in the play are ironic comments on society as well as a startling lack of realism in portraying rogues.

Standing aside, observing the proceedings, is a musician, Danny Lliteras, whose facial expressions and music offer commentary.

Wendell Collins gives an excellent characterization as Peterbono, the thief who works with debonaire Hector and beginner Gustav. Chris Ceraso fits the part of Hector ideally, and Tom Lantzy is appealing as Gustav, the youthful apprentice who falls in love with Lady Huff's daughter Juliette.

Penny Key gives a warm portrayal of a girl in love and is convincing in her willingness to run away with Gustav.

Sherrie La Rue matches Collin's performance as the aging, bored Lady Huff who knows she is dealing with thieves but cherishes the excitement of what might happen--and does.

Barry Lessinger has some funny moments as the inept Lord Edgard. Bill Barnes and Jon Claridge work hard as father and son, the Dupont-Duforts, who never come close to their mark.

Candice Carnicelli is the bored divorcee, Eva, who is unable to strike up a meaningful love affair, despite willing cooperation from Hector. She does a fine job with her role and certainly makes a striking stage appearance.

The set designs are most impressive. Designer John C. Hunter produces a remarkable representation of Lady Huff's drawing room. The opening also is well executed. This is effective stagecraft.

Director Fallon has done well with an experienced cast from

the School of Theater.   The failure is not his but in the material.

Still, it is a moderately entertaining show, well worth seeing for it is diverting and sometimes funny.

Little Theater Offers Warm "Majority of One"
(by David Cook, Tallahassee Democrat, December 10, 1975)

There is an appealing warmth about the Tallahassee Little Theater's production of Leonard Spigelgass' play, "A Majority of One."

Performances resume at 8:15 tonight at the Playhouse off Thomasville Road at Betton Road and will continue through Saturday night.

Among other things, the play is a sensitive portrayal of middle-age love.   But with a twist.   There is a distinct clash of cultures when a wealthy, urbane Japanese widower begins wooing a practical but very orthodox Jewish widow from Brooklyn.

This often humorous story also offers a lesson in the inconsistences of racial prejudice.   It is all very low key, but the message packs a wallop.

The characters are well cast, and the direction by Ralph Cook is generally good.   There were some jitters and a few fluffs on opening night, but generally, everything went well.   It was a pleasant evening.

Inge Schwarz, a native of Germany, makes her American stage debut as Mrs. Jacoby, the Brooklyn widow.   Her colorful but human performance is matched by the warm depth of Bill Swain as the Japanese gentleman, Mr. Asano.

Mrs. Jacoby and Mr. Asano meet aboard a ship bound for Japan where her son-in-law has been assigned in the American diplomatic service.   It takes Mrs. Jacoby awhile to put aside her hatred for the Japanese which dates back to the death of her soldier son in World War II.

Despite her interest in Mr. Asano, she drops him because of the opposition of her daughter and son-in-law.   And when she resumes her relationship later, she does so only to help her son-in-law.   She rebuffs Asano's proposal but his charm cannot be escaped.

Jan Sownie does a good job as the daughter.   Thomas Walker is every inch the stiff diplomat worried about mistakes that might hurt his career.

Donald Roy Shebs gives a remarkable performance as the house boy Eddie.   A. Geoffrey Maylan literally takes over the stage with a brilliant cameo appearance as Captain Norcross, the policeman who shows up on the occasion when Mrs. Jacoby is missing.

Miriam Venger is quite good as Mrs. Jacoby's friend in Brooklyn who almost comes unhinged upon meeting Mr. Asano when he comes to call.

The success of the production, however, falls heaviest on the shoulders of the two principals, Mrs. Schwarz and Bill Swain. Fortunately, they have the ability and strength to carry the show. They are quite believable and often touching in their cautious exchanges as a depth of feeling between them grows.

The stage design is simple but serviceable. A scene in Mr. Asano's deceptively simple house is most effective.

The Japanese costumes are well done. In fact, most of the technical aspects are handled well. All is not perfection, of course, but it adds up to a pleasurable evening of theater.

CROSSETT, David Allen; (2) Entertainment editor, theatre critic; (3) b. Jamestown, N.Y., June 6, 1941; (4) David Weston and Jean (Allen) C.; (5) B.A. Upsala College, major: psychology, 1965; Trenton State College, major: teaching, 1967; H-B Studio, New York City, 1974, playwriting; currently candidate for PhD, New York U., drama; (6) m. Dorothy Ellen Sandell, June 26, 1965; (7) children--Jennifer Ann, Laura Ellen; (8) Circulation dept., Recorder Publishing Co., 1968; Staff writer, Recorder Publishing Co., 1969; Theatre critic, Recorder Publishing Co., 1969 to present; Entertainment editor, Recorder Publishing Co., 1972 to present; English teacher and director of dramatics, Bernards Twp. Bd. of Ed., Basking Ridge, 1967 to present; (9) Actor, Technical director, business manager, Upsala College Workshop 90, 1962-65; Director, Chester Theatre Group, Little Murders, Black River Playhouse, Chester, 1972; Founder and artistic director, New Lord Chamberlain Co., Midsummer Night's Dream, Our Town, Spoon River Anthology, from 1973; (10) Deacon, Peapack Reformed Church, Gladstone; (11) Commissioner, Peapack-Gladstone Environmental Commission, 1970-1973; (15) New Jersey Drama Critics Assn., National Education Assn.; (16) Republican; (17) Dutch Reformed (Presbyterian); (20) The Miracle Machine (children's musical produced at Stony Hill Playhouse, Hunter, N.Y., 1963, Dearly Departed (unpublished), 1973, Scotty (unpublished), 1974, Shady Rest (projected for showcase, spring 1976); (21) 219 Mosle Rd., R.D. # 1, Far Hills, New Jersey 07931, Ph. 201-234-0216; (22) Bernardsville News, 17-19 Morristown Rd., Bernardsville, N.J. 07924, Ph. 201-766-3900; (23) Circulation: Shopping and Entertainment Guide carried in Bernardsville News, Observer-Tribune, Echoes-Sentinel, Hunterdon Review, all weekly newspapers of the Recorder Publishing Co., combined circulation 23,000; (24) 50 plays and musicals, 15 art, 5 film, 20 related features.

Epic Staging Used at McCarter for Brecht's "Mother Courage"
(by Allen Crossett, Bernardsville News, February 20, 1975)

At a time when it is so painfully obvious that the peace is
being threatened by economic considerations, it is not surprising
that theatre artists wishing to make a political statement turn to
the works of Bertold Brecht.

At Princeton's McCarter Theatre producing director Michael
Kahn originally intended to stage "Exiles" by James Joyce, but
instead he has switched to Brecht, perhaps in response to the
growing ease with which government leaders in this country are
considering war as a solution to the oil crisis.

Whether intended or not, the parallels between Mother Courage and her suffering through the Thirty Years' War in Europe
and the forces at work pushing the United States into a more
militant political position are impossible to ignore.

Eric Bentley's translation is being used for this production
and I suspect that Kahn, in an effort to reproduce accurately the
staging of the Deutsches Theater, has freely used Brecht's written and photographic notes.

Brecht's play is heavily ironic, and naming his title character Mother Courage is one of the many beautiful ironies. Although
she has borne children she is no mother, for she manages to
sacrifice both sons as well as her only daughter because of her
unfailing desire to profit, to keep her business going.

And she is not courageous, for she admits rather proudly
that she got her name while trying to escape a bombardment
which threatened her business.

Brecht wrote the play in the epic style and the McCarter production reproduces this style most accurately. The stage revolves,
making possible the beautiful image of Mother Courage and her
children pulling the Canteen Wagon, and while the wheels turn and
people appear to walk, the stage moves beneath, keeping them
relatively stationary.

Slides are projected to indicate the location of the following
scene as well as the essence of the action, an important device
for producing the "alienation effect" Brecht wanted. White light
(no colored gels) is used for illumination.

And frequently the play is stopped for a song, performed in
a cabaret style accompanied by accordian, trumpet, and percussion.

Academy-award winning Eileen Heckart appears in the title
role, a part which is extremely difficult, for Mother Courage is
on stage throughout most of the three-hour performance. Miss

Heckart beautifully captures the raspy quality of the character.

Her suffering, when she hears the news that her youngest
son has been killed because she bargained too long over the price
on his freedom, is a most famous moment, the time when Mother Courage releases the "silent scream," demonstrating her internal anguish while outwardly maintaining her politically expen-
dient indifference.

But as the years pass, and the suffering continues, none of
the characters show increased age, and none indicates any sign
of being beaten down by year after year of continued hardships.
Mother Courage, especially, one would think, should show some
change, but in the McCarter production she is essentially the
same at the end of the performance as she was at the beginning.

Philip Yankee portrays a gentle Swiss Cheese, with Charles
Sweigart as his swaggering older brother, Eilif.   Tom Poston is
seen as the Chaplin, with Lee Richardson as the cook.

The character who manages to create the most vivid image
of suffering as well as heroism is Mother Courage's daughter,
Kattrin, played by Maria Tucci.   Kattrin is dumb, and the only
sounds she can make are hysterical cries.

Miss Tucci takes this role and with her face, especially with
her eyes, makes the character speak a language which transcends
the limitations of words.   She gives an unforgettable performance.

The McCarter production is an excellent example of epic
staging for those with an historical interest in theatre, the play
is politically relevant for those seeking entertainment with a
message, but most important of all, it is a most intelligent and
successful staging of a work of art.   Brecht speaks universal
truths through the use of poetic images, and at McCarter these
images have been recognized and projected.

Not for many years have I been so impressed by the brilliance of a production, but Michael Kahn's staging of "Mother
Courage" is one of the finest I have ever had the pleasure of
witnessing.

Paper Mill Revives Moss Hart Comedy
(by Allen Crosset, Bernardsville News, March 6, 1975)

You can't go wrong when you're working with such talents as
Vivian Blaine, Celeste Holm, Sam Levene, Kay Medford and Wesley Addy.   And, of course, Moss Hart.

Maybe all those young people who so enthusiastically supported
the Paper Mill production of "Godspell" have never heard of these
performers, but if they returned to Millburn to see "Light Up The
Sky" these names would never be forgotten.

Written by Moss Hart, "Light Up the Sky" is a warmly funny comedy about show-biz, about a young writer who pens an allegory and suffers through the opening try-out in Boston. Suffering with him are the star actress, the producer and his wife, among others. Plot, however, is not at the heart of this production.

Moss Hart creates characters, and characters they are! At the Paper Mill Playhouse a collection of show-biz "technicians" are recreating a time when theatre was simply a joy. Here are performers who were mastering their technique before the method had actors mumbling their lines with their backs to the audience. Here are performers who are perfectionists with timing, with gesture, with subtle nuances of acting ... technique.

For about two minutes during the performance I attended, I sat with my eyes closed and just listened, and I heard merriment rolling like gentle waves, with laugh after laugh building and building to a crescendo after which the process would immediately begin again.

Kay Medford has most of the fun and most of the good lines as she plays the down-to-earth mother of the star. Sam Levene, who created the role of the producer in 1948, is still just as tough and demanding, with Vivian Blaine as his beautiful and brittle wife.

Celeste Holm plays the glamorous actress with Wesley Addy as the smooth and experienced writer who recognizes both the talent of a young writer and the demands that writing makes.

Director Harold J. Kennedy, who deserves special credit for making this production really zing with vitality, appears as the director in the play. Skipp Lynch is unfortunately weak in the part of the young, insecure playwright but the role makes up for some of this weakness.

Pegge Winslow, Donald Barton, Jack Collard and Earl Bangert Sr. complete the cast.

Designer John Pitt has beautifully created the setting, a luxurious suite at the Ritz-Carlton Hotel.

These days there is no telling what you might find in the sky over Millburn, but on stage at the Paper Mill Playhouse, Moss Hart's "Light Up The Sky" is dazzling and the performers are radiant.

CURRIE, (Donald) Glenne; (2) Critic and editor; (3) b. Hamilton, Ont., Mar. 1, 1926; (4) s. Donald and Winnifred A. (Spaul); (5) U. of Toronto, Faculty of Forestry, 1943-46; (6) m. Irene Ramsay Wilson, Jan. 10, 1953; (8) Editor-reporter The Canadian Press, Toronto,

1947-51; Editor, Reuters Ltd., London, 1952-54; Editor, Paul Pop-
per Ltd., London, 1954-56; Editor-correspondent, United Press (latter United Press International), London, 1956-60, Johannesburg 1961,
New York 1961-68, Manila 1968-70, Hong Kong 1970-73, New York
1973-75; UPI Lively Arts Editor 1975- ; (22) 372 Central Park West,
Apt. 8R, New York, N.Y. 10025, Ph. 212-662-5025; (23) United
Press International, 220 East 42nd St., New York, N.Y. 10017, Ph.
212-682-0400 ext. 451; (24) Reviews and articles distributed to more
than 1,100 newspapers and 3,650 radio stations in the U.S., plus
2,000 other UPI clients in Canada, Europe, and Asia. Also reviews
dance, opera and music, and directs coverage of films, archeology,
art, architecture.

<u>All Things Being Equus, Burton Is a Winner</u>
(by Glenne Currie, UPI, March 5, 1976)

Richard Burton is one of our finest actors, a "gut" performer with a tragic face and an heroic voice, whom we do not see
often enough on stage.

For his first Broadway appearance since his 1964 "Hamlet,"
Burton has chosen the role of the psychiatrist Martin Dysart in
Peter Shaffer's "Equus." He officially assumed the role Feb.
26 at the Plymouth Theatre, from Anthony Perkins.

"Equus" deals with a psychiatrist in a small English town
who is called on to treat a 17-year boy who for a combination
of religious and sexual hang-ups, has blinded six horses with a
knife. The psychiatrist, unhappily married and instead in love
with classical and mythical Greece, helps the boy relive the experience and puts him on the road to recovery.

But Dysart's self-doubts make him question the morality of
returning to dreary normality a youngster who has been "trying
to become a centaur in a Hampshire field."

Burton and director John Dexter have dug deep into Dysart's
psyche to present a tired, tortured man who despairs of his job
"in the adjustment business," and who in this particular case is
damned if he does and damned if he doesn't.

At the same time they have lost sight of Dysart the psychiatrist, who must retain a modicum of objectivity if he has any
chance of helping the boy, Alan.

Anthony Hopkins, another Welshman with a hypnotic voice,
who originated the role of Dysart when the show opened at the
Plymouth Oct. 24, 1974, trod the delicate line between professional objectivity and personal involvement superbly. He played
from both heart and mind.

Burton makes no pretense at standing outside Alan's predicament. He is involved from the beginning, reacts immediately

and sharply to everything the boy says, does or reveals, and
unbalances the play toward the psychiatrist and away from the
boy.

He is abetted in this, unfortunately, by Keith McDermott's
underplayed performance as Alan. The first of his two big
scenes, in which he abreacts his midnight communion with the
equine god Equus, in the person of the stallion Nugget, is a
pale shadow of the original performance by Peter Firth.

Burton, however, is a delight to watch and hear. At 50,
he is at what should be the peak of his career, and the combination of his expressive voice, face and body make everything he
does worth watching.

He will play the role for at least 10 weeks, and probably
will make the film of "Equus."

"My Fair Lady" Still Sparkles
(by Glenne Currie, UPI, April 4, 1976)

Blow the trumpets! Break out the Champagne! The world's
greatest musical is back, with (church) bells-a-chiming!

The 20th anniversary Broadway production of "My Fair Lady"
has begun its run at the St. James Theatre.

"My Fair Lady" is as delightful as ever: the songs, the
wit, the dances, the costumes, all are as good as you remember. The cast, with a couple of exceptions, is as fine as the
original, which was well-nigh perfect.

Unless future costs get out of sight--the present production
cost more than twice the $400,000 of the original--the Alan Jay
Lerner-Frederick Loewe masterpiece may well reappear every
20 years as long as the language of George Bernard Shaw remains recognizable.

It is a work of joy throughout, and if it drags slightly in the
last couple of suddenly sentimental scenes, that only emphasizes
the qualities of the rest of the show.

It's as concentrated as "The Marriage of Figaro," and the
one scene which provides us with "Just You Wait," "The Rain
in Spain" and "I Could Have Danced All Night" in quick suces-
sion is nearly as full of invention as the first act of the Mozart.

Everyone connected with the production deserves a medal:

Producer Herman Levin, whom the original show made rich;
director Jerry Adler; scenic designer Oliver Smith, who has
made new sets on a more intimate scale than the original and
only lapses in a couple of scenes; Cecil Beaton, whose costumes

vary little from his original designs; and choreographer Crandall Diehl, who has recreated Hanya Holm's dances from his memory as leading dancer 20 years ago.

Of the new cast, Christine Andreas as Eliza Doolittle merits a special tip of the hat. She not only has a great voice, but she is more believable as the curb-side flower seller than the lady-like, Cinderella heroine portrayed by Julie Andrews.

Miss Andreas is more human than Julie Andrews, and thus the romantic denouement more genuine.

George Rose has the unenviable chore of trying to erase the memory of Stanley Holloway (and of Wilfred Lawson) as Alfred Doolittle, and does magnificently.

He's not the veteran musical hall comedian that Holloway was, but he's a thoroughly professional stage artist and creates a comic character that would have warmed the cockles of Shaw's heart.

Robert Coote is even better than he was in the original role of Col. Pickering. His Dr. Watson-like bumbling is combined with perfect timing and delivery to wring every laugh from the script.

Ian Richardson as Henry Higgins has an even harder act to follow than Rose; the suave, total ego of Rex Harrison. He doesn't even come close.

His performance is cramped; he pushes the songs where Harrison caressed them; his performance is full of business which Harrison didn't need; above all, he doesn't have the dominating personality demanded by the role.

It is not his fault he is miscast but it is his misfortune he is being misused.

CUTHBERT, David, Times-Picayune, 3800 Howard Ave., New Orleans, Louisiana 70140.

DAFOE, Christopher Grannis; (2) Drama Critic; (3) b. Winnipeg, Manitoba, July 25, 1936; (4) s. John and Marjorie (Metcalfe); (5) U. of Winnipeg, Stanford; (6) m. Nancy Cosgrave, Sept. 24, 1960; (7) children--Christopher, Sarah, Alexander; (8) Copy editor, reporter, assistant features editor, Winnipeg Free Press 1955-60, drama critic, editorial writer Winnipeg Free Press, 1960-68; Drama critic, columnist The Vancouver Sun 1968- ; (9) Actor, Canadian Broadcasting Corp. radio and television 1955-60, actor, Manitoba Theatre Centre and other stage groups 1955-60. Play Two Friends staged at Manitoba Theatre Centre 1962; (12) Board of directors,

Winnipeg Symphony Orchestra, 1967-68; (14) Canada Council Award 1968, Canada Council Travelling Critic Award 1972, Fellowship at Stanford University, 1966; (15) Member, Toronto Drama Bench; (17) Church of England; (20) Cont. articles to London Times, Manchester Guardian, Montreal Star, Tamarack Review, Jerusalem Post, Yorkshire Post; scripts and commentaries for CBC radio and television; plays, poems and short stories produced on CBC radio; (21) 3486 Greentree Lane, North Vancouver, British Columbia, Ph. 985-0164; (22) The Vancouver Sun, 2250 Granville Street, Vancouver, B.C., Canada V6H 362, Ph. 604-732-2111; (23) Circulation: 250,000; (24) Approx. 150 reviews, 150 miscellaneous columns.

Camino Real Less Than Royally Played
(by Christopher Dafoe, Vancouver Sun, March 30, 1972)

The Camino Real is a crowded street on which dreams and harsh realities mingle. One is never certain where the dreams end and the realities begin; cold light and soft shadow touch and blend and those who find themselves at the darkest and most dreary corner of the road must pause in their journey and undergo a period of adjustment before moving on into the unknown.

Tennessee Williams' dramatic journey down to the dead end of the Camino Real is a long and difficult one, and it should be undertaken only by those equipped to take risks. Valor is never enough.

Members of the West Vancouver Little Theatre Guild--displaying a full measure of bravado but very little discretion--set off down the rocky road at the North Vancouver Centennial Theatre Wednesday night and almost at once came to grief in a deep ditch.

Let me say it as gently as possible: Camino Real by Tennessee Williams is far beyond the scope of the West Vancouver Little Theatre Guild.

The cast is a large one and the West Vancouver company--in common with many amateur groups--simply lacks the personnel to give each role the attention it deserves. What can one say, for example, of a production in which the opening scene--and a rather important opening scene at that--is so badly spoken that it is impossible to make out a single word?

This state of affairs persisted with depressing monotony throughout the first act; that is, as long as I was on hand to endure it. It may have improved after the interval. Miracles have been known to occur, even in these latter days, but I, for one, was not tempted to remain in my seat to find out. One can take only so much, even in the line of duty.

Camino Real is a play that demands a strong guiding hand to give it shape and focus. The script is like an orchestral score or a paint box waiting for a wet brush and an inspired hand to blend the colors. Interpretation is everything. A strong mood must be established. The deep wells of emotion under the lines must be helped to flow.

What we see is as important as what we hear. Technical facilities must be used to enhance and underline the thrust of the text. In this production one could admire only the memory-work of those involved. They had the text at their finger-tips, but the implications of the text eluded them.

Bad sets, bad acting and an insufficient understanding by those involved of what the play means combined to make the early hours of Wednesday evening pass by like a painful vigil. The West Vancouver Little Theatre production is, I regret to say, one that only a mother, an aunt or an understanding spouse could possibly appreciate and love.

Much of it is simply laughable. The whores of Camino Real, for example, seem to have something of the Junior League Follies about them. On the other, more favored side of the street, the inhabitants of the posh but cursed Siete Mares hotel exist like cardboard cutouts.

Not a breath of life rustles the potted palms.

In the no-man's-land between the whorehouse and the house of doomed privilege, confusion reigns. Director Ed Collier has yet to find a way of making incidents stand out from the mass. When his stage is full of actors he has only a stage full of actors to offer us. He fails to zero in on events, to make personalities stand out in sharp relief. There is much more than a question of blocking involved here. Focus is required as well as tension and significant movement.

It is also a good idea to start a play at the announced time. The opening night performance was called for 8 p. m. It finally got underway at 8:35. One has only so much patience to spare. Mine ran out at about 10:30--and the end of the dusty road was not yet in sight.

Frontier Bard a Clever, Dashing Figure
(by Christopher Dafoe, Vancouver Sun, March 7, 1975)

Ben Jonson was one of the first to notice that his colleague William Shakespeare was "not of an age, but for all time." Since then, every generation has seen Shakespeare with its own eyes and found a point of contact in keeping with its own attitudes and needs.

During the 18th century, they gave happy endings to his tragedies and indulged contemporary tastes by creating long musical interludes to "enhance" the original texts. The actor-managers of the 19th century responded to the popular fancy for melodrama by producing broad, bombasting productions of the plays.

Our own century has the gift of hindsight, and we are able
to respond to Shakespeare in many forms and variations, from
William Poel's Elizabethan-style revivals before the First World
War to the wildly imaginative and up-dated versions popular during recent years.

The plays themselves are so strong, so resilient that they
have endured and survived all the fantastic interpretations that
have been heaped on them. Somewhere, somebody is playing
Hamlet stark naked or attempting Macbeth in plastic kilts, and
yet the essential spirit of William Shakespeare shines through
like a beacon. Most plays tend to vanish under heavy burdens
of eccentricity. Shakespeare refuses to be upstaged.

The central theme of The Comedy of Errors--a monumental
mix-up of twins--was already old when Shakespeare took The
Menechmi, by the Roman comic poet Plautus, and refurbished it
for the Elizabethan stage. Since then the Shakespearean version
has been regarded as the final word on the subject, although his
play has appeared in many settings.

The latest revival, staged by members of the Stratford Festival Company at the Queen Elizabeth Theatre Thursday night,
finds that celebrated double brace of twins--Antipholus of Syracuse and Antipholus of Ephesus and Dromio of Syracuse and Dromio of Ephesus--cavorting on the North American frontier in the
shadow of a giant covered wagon.

Directors Robin Phillips and David Toguri have taken full
advantage of the singular ability of the 20th century audience to
feel comfortable in any period.

The "old West" is a home from home to anyone who has
ever been to the movies, and so it is not too difficult to imagine
the Anthipholi as a pair of dudes and Solinus, duke of Ephesus,
as the "boss man" of a one-horse town.

When the play begins, a sort of lynching is about to take
place, and as the drama proceeds one is almost tempted to suppose that Mark Twain served as co-author, with a measure of
help from Charlie Chaplin.

In short, the Phillips-Toguri transformation works beautifully.
The text fits easily into the concept and the Shakespearean body
cuts a somehow dashing figure in its curious garments. There
has been no need to pinch or strain in order to get the garment
to fit; every detail has been carefully attended to: when, for example, swords are called for, sword-canes appear. Even the
place-names sit easily in a continent that has traditionally borrowed place-names from the old world.

Philips and Toguri have taken certain liberties in an audacious and pleasing way, such as the moment when Adriana--
played with a full measure of spice by Jackie Burroughs--sudden-
ly becomes carried away in the middle of an impassioned speech
and bursts into vigorous song.

One might also mention the clever and effective device of
having certain emphatic utterances underlined by melodramatic
music supplied by Alan Laing.

A few spoil-sports might feel obliged to suggest that this
production of The Comedy of Errors sounds like a brazen sendup of The Bard. In fact, it is a clever and entertaining exploitation of a sturdy comic play. The Comedy of Errors invites
fanciful and imaginative interpretations. As the play unfolds, we
laugh with Shakespeare, not at him.

Members of the company employ a charming variety of accents with which to utter the Shakespearean verse, from the traditional "voice beautiful" of the Stratford Festival stage to the
sonorous drawl of the old frontier. Both styles of speech are
employed to full comic effect.

The members of the company perform with a briskness that
might easily have been inspired by Mack Sennett. Nicholas Pennell and Barry MacGregor are both spruce and attractive as the
brothers Antipholus, and Bernard Hopkins and Richard Whelan
provide highly comic mirror-images as the brothers Dromio.

Jackie Burroughs--who is certainly the most elegant comic
actress that Stratford has seen since the brief engagement of Zoe
Caldwell several seasons ago--plays the tart wife Adriana to the
hilt, and Gale Garnett is pleasingly dim and demure as Luciana.

Eric Donkin makes a brief but spectacular appearance as Dr.
Pinch, attired in mouldy buffalo robes and brandishing a water-
divining rod. The various supporting roles are well filled by
members of this refreshingly bright stage company.

The younger generation has opened the door at Stratford and
let in a welcome rush of fresh air.

DANIELS, Robert Laurence; (2) Drama and Music Editor, North Jersey Suburbanite, 12 William Street, Englewood, N.J. 07631; Theatre
critic, The Week Ahead, 38 W. Oakland Ave., Oakland, N.J. 07436;
New Jersey contributor, Variety; (3) b. Port Chester, N.Y., Jan 1,
1933; (4) s. Leslie and Odaline Daniels; (5) Passaic Valley Regional
High School, Little Falls, N.J.; (6) m. Marilyn Tintle, Aug. 16,
1954; (7) children--Marc Laurence, Lisa Allyn, David Laurence; (8)
1972, began "Applause" column in No. Jersey Suburbanite; 1975
"Stage Door" in The Week Ahead; 1974 Dani. in Variety; (9) Acted:
Barn Theatre, Montville, community theatre, Man for All Seasons,

House of Atreus, 1968; Theatre of Riverside Church, N.Y., Boy
with a Cart, The Gospel Witch, 1965; Directed: Barn Theatre,
Montville, N.J., The Subject Was Roses, The Desperate Hours (winner Barn Theatre Arthur award for Best Director), Private Lives,
The Lion in Winter; Wyckoff Village Players, Franklin Lakes, N.J.,
Company, 1973. Professional magic act, various clubs, churches,
schools, private parties, U.S. Army Special Services; (17) Protes-
tant-Reformed; (21) 5 Cedar Street, Oakland, N.J., Ph. 337-4530;
(22) 3 E. Palisade Ave., Englewood, N.J. 07436, Ph. 568-4455;
(23) Circulation: 30,000 North Jersey Suburbanite, 15,000 The Week
Ahead; (24) 100 plays and musicals, 10 concerts, night club, dance,
5 book, 5 movie, 10 interviews.

Love from Mother
(by Robert L. Daniels, Variety, August 28, 1974)

"Love from Mother," trying out at the Theatre in the Dome,
a summer stock venture on the site of St. John Terrell's Old
Music Circus on the hilltop just outside this old Delaware River
town, is an absurd farce about a family inheritance and the welfare of a deceased's neurotic son. The situation involves the
eavesdropping by the maternal ghost, valiantly played by Cathryn
Damon.

It's generally a one-joke show, with amusing moments as the
spook vainly attempts such supernatural feats as haunting, flying,
moving objects, etc. Short of expanding and strengthening the
plot, the futile spiritualism stuff might be better exploited.

Patti Perkins has a brief spree doing a "Me and My Shadow"
routine, unconsciously accompanied by the invisible shade of mama. But the cast frequently seems uncomfortable with the dull
material and tacky production. The theatre's acoustics don't
help. --Dani.

Liv Ullmann Carries "A Doll's House"
(by Robert L. Daniels, The Week Ahead, March 19, 1975)

The American theatrical debut of Liv Ullmann in "A Doll's
House" at Lincoln Center has been properly greeted with a great
deal of attention. She has been photographed, interviewed and
showered with well-deserved plaudits. Last week her face illuminated newsstands and magazine racks bringing a new distinction
to corner candy stores as Newsweek's cover girl. Critics have
likened her to one's mother, lover, child, sister and friend.

Her film performances have left us with such vivid memories
that it often seems we have shared a great portion of our life
with her. The pioneer bride and mother in the two-part epic,
"The Emmigrants" and "The New Land," the myriad facets of
her housewife in "Scenes from a Marriage" and her haunting, indifferent sister in "Cries and Whispers" are montaged forever on
a private canvas in my brain.

Ibsen's "A Doll's House" is an accepted masterpiece and comparisons are inevitable. I much prefer the 1971 production which starred Claire Bloom and was directed by Patrick Garland and their subsequent film. Miss Ullmann makes this her own production of the N. Y. Shakespeare Festival very much her own. As Nora, the child wife of the arrogant Torvald Helmer, she is much less fragile than Julie Harris, who played the role for television's Hallmark Hall of Fame. Though less kittenish than Claire Bloom's Nora, the necessary playfulness remains. Bloom's kitten had a cold panther-like quality, whereas the blue-eyed Norwegian beauty adds a warming touch that makes her Nora altogether cuddly.

Miss Ullmann is a stunning actress. Her movement is poetically lovely without looking stagey. Her natural presence is so magnetic, it is difficult to watch other players. She has framed several little pictures to treasure and her long final grasp for independence is softly underplayed with a quiet strength.

Sam Waterston, who is quickly emerging as one of our most respectable talents, is an admirable Helmer. He plays the pampering husband with a rigid military crispness that offers a taut contrast to Ullmann's frivolity. Tormod Skagestad's direction is cold, depriving the show of proper atmosphere. The simple Santo Loquasto set doesn't help and the supporting cast is not strong enough to make some of the famous scenes come alive. Michael Granger's Dr. Rank is so wooden and unfeeling that it just gave me enough reason to return my undivided attention to Liv Ullmann.

The excitement surrounding the casting of an international star in a classic play has prompted producer Joseph Papp to book more of the same next season. Already there is talk of Ullmann's "St. Joan" and Waterson's "Hamlet." I would suggest subscribing early, as the entire engagement of "Doll's House" is completely sold out to the last seat. I feel guilty having seen it twice, but I can recommend checking the bulletin board for ticket exchange in the Vivian Beaumont Theatre lobby or waiting around for cancellations. Liv Ullmann is worth the wait.

DASGUPTA, Gautam; (2) Theater critic; (3) b. Calcutta (India), July 1, 1949; (4) s. Medini and Jharna (Dasgupta); (5) B. M. E. Jadavpur U. , Calcutta, Major subj: Mechanical Engineering, 1969; M. A. U. of Connecticut, Major subj: English, 1972; Ph. D. (in progress) C. U. N. Y. Graduate Center, Major subj: Theater; (6) m. Bonnie Marranca, Aug. 1, 1975; (8) Film and theater critic, Frontier (Calcutta) 1967-70; Theater critic, Soho Weekly News 1975- ; Publisher and co-editor, Performing Arts Journal 1976- ; (9) Adjunct Lecturer, Brooklyn College, 1974-75; Actor, Ontological Hysteric Theater, 1975-76; (14) Best Speaker, All-India Debating Competition, 1969; (15) ex-officio member, Calcutta Film Society and Cine Club of

Calcutta; Assoc. member, Asian Program of the American Theater
Association; (17) Hindu; (20) Cont. articles to Asian Theater Bulletin,
Film (London), Margins; (21) 92 St. Marks Place, Apt. 4, New York,
N.Y. 10009; Ph. 212-260-7586; (22) Performing Arts Journal; P.O.
Box 858, Peter Stuyvesant Station, New York, N.Y. 10009.

Mystic Theatre from Tibet
(by Gautam Dasgupta, Soho Weekly News, November 21, 1975)

To many of us in the West, knowledge of Tibetan culture is
confined either to the Tibetan Book of the Dead or to their philosophical pursuit of and writings on Mahayana Buddhist doctrine.
Commonly viewed as a theocratic state, in spite of its falling
under Chinese rule in 1959, we are wont to look upon Tibet as
a somber hermitic kingdom where the joys and miseries of daily
living are sacrificed at the altar of spiritual aggrandizement.
That this is but a myopic assessment of a richly varied culture
is now brought home to us in a rare and delectable treat by
Lhamo: Folk Opera of Tibet.

Performing for the first time in the West, the company of
over 25 artists was formed in India in the Sixties under the pa-
tronage of His Holiness the Dalai Lama with the intent of preserving the mystique and unique artistry of traditional Tibetan
forms of entertainment. The lhamo (opera), secular in origin,
dates back to around the Sixteenth Century and was rooted in the
epicurean ethics of its founder Thangtong Gyalpo. Under the
pressures of a predominantly religious national sensibility, the
lhamo gradually incorporated canonical themes into its largely
frivolous and realistic structure. Eventually, its form crystal-
lized around a basic plot, episodic in nature, that freely drew
upon national history, mythological tales, Buddhist tenets and,
most significantly, on the lives and passions of Tibetan peasants--
an aspect that not only makes a lhamo performance universally
acceptable but imbues it with a naivete and rustic charm that is
not to be found in the more refined, regimented and unsullied
performances of other Asiatic art forms.

The current troupe belongs to the Chungba school of lhamo
art (the other two being the Kyimulunga and Gyangara schools)
and one that is characterized by an unassuming attitude to theatrical form and stylization. Bringing to bear upon their flamboyant dramatization of "The Story of Pema Wemba" a free-flowing and deceptively simple artistry, the dancers and singers cast
a hypnotic spell as they draw us into a joyous celebration of life
in all its ecstasy and wonderment. A complicated tale of heroic
deeds and miraculous escapes, which result in the young Pema
Wemba's victory over the evil King, is conveyed with a child's
vision and trust in the world of make-belief.

Partly because of its playful theatricality, the lhamo, traditionally done in the open, does not suffer within the confines of
a closed auditorium. Bedecked in colorful silk robes with

overflowing sleeves, the dancers traverse the stage with broad
movements overjoyed, as it were, by the rediscovery of a newly
found theatrical space. Devoid of the rigidity and symbolic representations of the classical mudras, these Tibetan dancers reveal an interest in movement that is mostly functional--not so
much in the sense of being quasi-realistic but as organic exten-
sions of physiognomical traits. It is perhaps closest to the
movement patterns of American Indian dances.

Informing all aspects of this production is a naive and engaging esthetic duality between a near-realistic approach on the
one hand and a semi-realized stylization on the other. While
the main characters remain on stage visible at all times, no
attempt is made to render them "invisible" as in the Japanese
theater. The actors react to events on stage taking place at other
times or in distant lands with as much interest as if they were
participants in those events. Within specific scenes, however,
the acting retains a curiously naturalistic flavor although the
actors appear in masks or cardboard cutouts. And elsewhere,
the actors are left free to improvise.

The lhamo libretto, likewise, is a conglomerate of similar
artistic tendencies. Part dramatic and part narrative, the arias
are sung to the accompaniment of a large drum and a cymbal.
A single dominant motif governs the rhythmic construct of the
libretto that builds essentially through repetition. The choral
portions are carried by the nymphs and fairies who frame the
stage picture on both sides. The verbal arias are at times offset by highpitched sounds (non-verbal arias), the infinite modulations tenderly recalling the echoes from the mountains that
must necessarily intrude upon these outdoor productions when
performed in their native land.

One of the most thrilling theatrical experiences to be witnessed in our time, the Lhamo: Folk Opera of Tibet presents
radicalization of the concept of total theater. Theirs is a remarkable achievement that gains in strength and vitality from a
simplicity and unpretentiousness that has always been, and will
remain, a criteria of good art.

Burning Bright
(by Gautam Dasgupta, Soho Weekly News, January 15, 1976)

Jack London was born in 1876, a hundred years after this
fledgling nation had come into its own. The American ideal
called for rugged individualism and a sense of adventure, a frontier mentality that formed the life and breath of Jack London.
Starting off his boisterous career as a boozing and fighting out-
law on the San Francisco waterfront, he was to emerge as one
of the foremost adventure story writers of this century. Tormented by delusions of grandeur and fame, his rise from a poverty stricken youth in Oakland to a well-respected "millionaire"
novelist aptly captured the essence of the American Dream.

His fictions of romance and exploration were tinged with a sense of despair and understanding that grew out of his confrontations with The Communist Manifesto. Darwin, Haeckel, Nietzsche and, eventually, the philosopher-athlete of Shaw's Man and Superman. Central to his novels were an irresolute idealism contorted by the demands of modern day economism and Darwinian determinism. In retrospect, the cynicism of his outlook renders him as one of the archetypal popular novelists of the 20th century.

That such a varied and dramatic life should one day emerge as a fit subject for the stage was to be expected; and now, in a superbly conceived one-man show written, directed and acted by William Shepard, the passionate trials of this real-life Ahab "broiled in hell fire" returns to commemorate his birth centennial. A powerful portrait culled from Jack London's diverse and professional life, Shepard has given us an absorbing and complete picture of the novelist full of the tragic scars that penetrate the surface of an outwardly happy-go-lucky adventuresome spirit.

Sustaining the dramatic intensity of his character in a tightly-knit and fine performance, he has expanded London's personal and moral vision to include those of his predecessors and contemporaries. Having captured the poetic essence of Hawthorne, Melville and Kipling in London's life and work, Shepard has not only documented the "true story of Jack London" but offers a period in history that is the result of the expansiveness of his directorial vision. An informative evening in the theater, the adaptation never loses sight of the dramatic touch that endows this one-man show with an intensity charged with purpose.

Drawn with compassion and beauty, Shepard has set his show on a bare stage with minimal props enshrouded in white sheets. As the evening races on, the ghost-like, faraway reality of the situation gradually dissolves under the warmth of London's exuberance. The "burning daylight" of his temperament spills over on to the stage and the audience in a dazzling display of imaginative theater for which William Shepard is owed our thanks.

DASSYLVA, Martial; (2) Theater critic; (3) b. La Malbaie (Québec), Dec. 25, 1936; (4) s. Antoine Dassylva and Anita Gagné; (5) B. A. Laval U. , 1956; superior studies in philosophy and theology, Ottawa Dominican Collegium, 1956-61; (6) Single; (8) Journalist, assistant deskman and drama critic, le Soleil, Québec, 1961-65; Drama critic and theater reporter, la Presse, Montréal, since 1965; (20) Several books and articles, on theatre in Quebec and other drama topics, including Un Théâtre en Efferverscence (Critiques et Chroniques de Théâtre, 1965-1972), Montréal, 1975; (21) 4466, Girouard Avenue, Montréal, Québec, Canada, H4A 3E4, Ph. 1-514-481-6526; (22) Journal la Presse, 750, Saint-Laurent Boulevard, Montréal, Québec, Canada. H2Y 1K9, Ph. 1-514-285-7070; (23) Circulation: 180,000 on weekdays; 220,000 on Saturday; (24) From 100 to 150 plays and musicals (French and English). About the same number of interviews and information papers on theater activity.

Paralysie du corps et de l'âme
(by Martial Dassylva, La Presse, January 8, 1973)

Le tableáu que nous présente "Creeps" des handicapés phy-
siques et de leur réhabilitation n'est ni beau ni rassurant. De
plus, il dérangera sûrement les consciences assoupies et tous
les bénévoles, permanents ou occasionnels, qui avec ou sans
arrière-pensée travaillent dans ce secteur.

Freeman n'est pas tendre pour les Shriners, les membres
des clubs Rotary et Kiwanis. Sans doute l'économie de la pièce
a-telle besoin de ces pauses-arrêts au cours desquelles l'auteur
illustre à sa façon tout ce déploiement de ce que l'un des cinq
handicapés de la pièce appelle la "pityshit" qui assomme les
handicapés et leur rappelle indirectement leur impuissance et
leur état de dépendance. Mais cela va beaucoup plus loin et
remet en cause des formes de charité et d'entraide trop facile-
ment admises et pratiquées. Comme John Herbert nous avait
fait entrer avec "Fortune and Men's Eyes" dans l'univers des
institutions de détention et de correction mieux connues sous le
nom de prison, David Freeman nous introduit dans l'univers d'un
atelier-refuge pour personnes atteintes de paralysie cérébrale.

Ce n'est d'ailleurs pas pour rien si le souvenir de la pièce
de Herbert nous revient en mémoire lorsque l'on assiste à une
représentation de "Creeps." Les deux oeuvres ont beaucoup de
points en commun, notamment une même attention aux frustrations sociales et psychologiques d'un groupe minoritaire, une
même compassion pour la misère humaine et, finalement, une
même passion pour retrouver le langage direct et imagé d'un
milieu donné, même au prix de blesser les chastes oreilles.

Thérapies inutiles?

"Creeps" ne dure qu'une heure et quart et toute son action
se passe dans une salle de toilette d'un atelier-refuge dirigé par
un monsieur Carson. C'est là que se retrouvent les cinq principaux personnages de la pièce lorsqu'ils en ont marre de "jouer
avec des blocs," de "réparer un tapis," de "faire de la peinture,"
en d'autres mots de s'occuper à tuer le temps sous prétexte de
réhabilitation.

La thèse capitale de "Creeps," si l'on peut évidemment parler de thèse lorsqui'il s'agit de jauger et d'examiner des sentiments et des réactions humains, c'est qu'en définitive ces théra-
pies dites occupationnelles, menées contre tout espoir, sapent
dangereusement le moral des handicapés et leurs motivations
profondes.

Dans quelle mesure cette thèse est-elle juste? Dans quelle
mesure cette situation des ateliers-dortoirs est-elle catastrophi-
que et pour les premiers intéressés et pour la société dans son
ensemble?

Je ne saurais le dire.

Mais la pièce de Freeman, en engendrant le doute et en forçant l'interrogation, oblige du même coup à une salutaire réflexion.

Et parce qu'elle le fait en termes hautement dramatiques, parce qu'en l'espace d'une heure elle parvient à nous faire saisir, par petites touches successives à la fois discrètes et fortes, la qualité tragique de la frustration qui sousentend et justifie le comportement de chacun de ces cinq handicapés, en somme, parce qu'elle nous fait presque toucher du doigt cette paralysie de l'âme qui accompagne jusqu'à un certain point toute paralysie ou atrophie du corps, "Creeps" sort vraiment de l'ordinaire et va beaucoup plus loin que le simple théâtre à thèse.

Au Centaur, la production, dont le tempo est parfois un peu trop lent, est interprétée par un groupe de comédiens bien choisis, à qui le metteur en scène Maurice Podbrey n'a pas demandé, heureusement, des excès de composition. Dans les principaux rôles, tous observent une discrétion remarquable qui ne nuit aucunement à la vraisemblance des caractères et braque plutôt les projecteurs sur l'essentiel: la difficulté de vivre, une difficulté qui n'est pas exempte d'humour et de moments très drôles, mais une difficulté quand même déchirante.

Les Bas et les Hauts de la Ménard
(by Martial Dassylva, La Presse, November 7, 1974)

Pour un bon spectacle, c'en est un bon et c'en est même un bon de bon!

Non seulement le texte des "Hauts et les bas d'la vie d'une diva: Sarah Ménard par eux-mêmes" indique-t-il que Jean-Claude Germain a retrouvé sa forme des grands jours, mais encore la musique créée spécialement pour cette production par Jacques Perron estelle tout simplement extraordinaire, je le répète tout simplement extraordinaire, exécutée qu'elle est, d'ailleurs, au piano par Gaston Brisson, un accompagnateur de premier ordre qui se révèle, de surcoît, un fort convenable comédien.

Et puis, on a des éclairages très élaborés et un décor en tous points fantastique de Claude-André Roy et des costumes excellents de Diane Paquet.

On peut, aussi, voir à l'oeuvre Nicole Leblanc qui, pendant deux heures, se dépense sans compter, se multiplie et montre avec éclat la souplesse exceptionnelle de son métier et les immenses ressources d'un talent qui trouve ici une occasion rêvée de s'exprimer.

Ces ressources, elle s'en sert pour rendre toutes les nuances d'un texte difficile et toutes les contradictions d'un personnage à la vie mouvementée, remplie et diverse.

Le texte de Germain est difficile en ce qu'il ne se contente pas de développer l'anecdote ou la situation de base suivant un mode linéaire classique. Ce n'est, par exemple, qu'à la toute fin de la pièce que l'on apprend que la grande diva Sarah Ménard a été invitée pour inaugurer dans sa paroisse natale, Sainte-Marthe-surmer, un centre culturel qui portera son nom.

Elle apprend que ce centre n'est, en fait, qu'une "piscine culturelle." Constatant qu'elle entre de son vivant dans une espèce de passé culturel et que les "chèvres basses sur pattes" du haut de la côte de Sainte-Marthe-sur-mer associent aussi naïvement le nom d'une chanteuse classique à un centre d'activité sportive, Sarah Ménard prend soudainement conscience de la situation curieuse des Québécois, de céux qui ont réussi et des autres, et se penche sur son évolution personnelle.

Fidèle à la technique, qu'il a employée déjà à plusieurs reprises, de la construction contrapuntique à partir de flashes, Jean-Claude Germain retrace les différentes étapes de la carrière de la diva Sarah depuis le temps de la fête du curé et des guides jusqu'aux voyages dans les grandes capitales, en passant par les études chez le professeur Ildebrando Bruchesi, l'épisode du dépucelage et la longue suite des amours tumultueuses.

J'aimerais disposer de plus d'espace pour examiner en détail les différents aspects des hauts et des bas de la carrière de la Ménard. Disons tout simplement que l'humour de Germain et de sa création, Sarah, tombe généralement pile et que la pièce, malgré quelques longueurs occasionnelles, comporte de magnifiques trouvailles verbales et comiques.

Cela apparaît plus spécialement dans les chansons, dont quatre ou cinq sont absolument remarquables et qui, si elles étaient endisquées, deviendraient rapidement des succès populaires.

Je songe ici à "La chanson d'la séduction des instruments" qui permet à Nicole Leblanc de réussir un numéro de cabaret éblouissant, alors que la musique passe du tzigane à l'espagnol avant de devenir jazz, boogie-woogie, rock, etc.

Plus tôt, on avait eu droit à un "Aria d'Eurydice au téléphone" tout à fait crevant et à une "Chanson du lever des guides catholiques" exécutée avec brio par Gaston Brisson.

Le spectacle se termine d'ailleurs par une gigue dont la musique étonnante vous cloue sur votre siège. Cette scène est précédée par l'évocation des études chez le célèbre professeur Bruchesi et par "La chanson du bottin de l'opéra italien" pendant laquelle la Ménard se moque des morts d'opéra.

L'un des couplets de la chanson se lit comme suit: "Rossini,

Bellini, Puccini, Mascagni/L'opéra j'aillis ça j'aillis ça ça sdit pas/Caccini, Cavalli, Scarlatti, Piccini/J'aillis ça l'opéra, j'aillis ça ça sdit pas/ (...)/ L'opéra, l'opéra, l'opéra ça speut pas."

DAUPHIN, Susan Helfrich; (2) Theater critic; (3) b. Baltimore, Md., Sept. 1, 1928; (4) William and Elsie (Lipps) Helfrich; (5) U. of Maryland, Boston Museum of Fine Arts, U. of Houston, major subj.: English; (6) m. Vernon M. Dauphin, Jr., Feb. 7, 1959; (7) children-- William Mayfield, Eva Kate; (8) Free lance writer 1968-pres., feature writer Friendswood (Tx.) News 1971-pres, Theater critic and columnist (Friendswood) News, Mar. 1974-pres; Theater writer: Community News, Dickinson Bulletin, League City Bulletin, Hitchcock Bulletin, Beaumont Enterprise, Houston Town & Country Magazine, Zone One Magazine, current. Clear Lake Report, KLYX radio Oct. 1974-Mar. 1975; Curtain Call Radio Program (Reviews, etc.); KUHF Radio, Nov. 1975-pres.; (9) Member (actor, director etc, also sec'y) Brevard Players, Melbourne, Fla. 1956-59, Judge; Bob Hope Talent Contest 1974, Annual Awards Judge, Pasadena Little Theater 1976-77; Staff, Southwestern Writer's Conference, 1976. Wrote, produced and performed TV segments for Channel 39, 1975; (10) Friendswood POPS Committee, Friends of the Library; (14) Five Annual Awards, Texas Press Women (TV, Radio, Newspaper scripts and criticism) 1976; (15) National Press Women's Assoc. (& Texas Press Women); (16) Democrat; (17) Episcopal; (19) Writer's Club of Pasadena, Rayburn Country (Tx.); (20) Contribute articles to Sportfishing Magazine, Texas Churchman; (21), (22) 111 Royal Court, Friendswood, Tx. 77546, Ph. 713-482-7355; (23) Circulation: Newspapers 40,000+, Radio 50,000+; (24) Ballet, opera, motion pictures, restaurants, general entertainment.

"Subject to Change"
(by Sue Dauphin, Dickinson Bulletin and over KUHF Radio, May 2, 1976)

The Cabaret Theater productions group has really got a winner in its new show at the Balinese Room in Galveston. Jules Tasca's play, "Subject to Change," is a solidly funny show to start with and Director Charlie Bailey has put together a can't-miss cast.

Dixie Taylor will own the role of Madeline from henceforth, at least as far as the Houston Area is concerned. She has the character down to a science and the audience in the palm of her hand. Madeline is one of a pair of spinster sisters who are complete opposites but who have shared a home in silent misunderstanding for thirty years. Sort of a female odd couple. Now the efficient, community pillar sister, Gertrude, has reached out for a last grab at life in the form of romance and marriage with a middle-aged bowling alley owner. Boy friend Erwin Leeds, as played by Kenn Cullinane, comes equipped with wide-eyed innocence, a driving desire for Gertrude, and an eighty-year-old, alcoholic mother. Kenn puts a Charles Nelson Riley air to his

characterization as he strives to carry out his romantic aims
over the opposition of both mother and future sister-in-law.

Lois Fleck gives Gertrude a human warmth and vulnerability
to the demands of those around her that contrast sharply and hilariously with Madeline's insensitive helplessness. Madeline cannot even operate the electric can opener without help, nor locate
the car keys carefully pinned to her housecoat.

Barbara Wilson Jones gives a fillip to the otherwise bland
part of the neighbor who is the mainstay of each sister in turn
as the crises mount. Whether she's crawling across the stage
on her knees trying to hem a restless bride's gown or gleefully
pushing a phoney cripple to her entrapment, Barbara does it
with a flair.

Ron Jones, yes, Barbara's husband, portrays the handyman,
Pignitelli, with farcical enthusiasm, pouring on the Italian accent
and mannerisms, playing his best scene when he, too, is down
on his knees, but in his case it's to thank the Lord for the supposed miracle of Madeline's sudden recovery.

Madeline lets the audience in on her deception from the very
beginning with deliciously malicious chuckles. She is determined
to hang on to her supportive sister at any cost, going even to the
lengths of committing her considerable cursing vocabulary to note
paper after her fake stroke. As Dixie does it, you can almost
see the scratch pad scorching.

Norma Holland Jones, no relation to Barbara and Ron, uses
both makeup and acting skills to age herself to the not-so-sweet
little old lady who considers the afternoon well spent if she's
just left alone in a room with ten whiskey sours. Norma has
the drunkenly wispish motions perfectly down as she raises bemused, hazy, but very persistent objections to her son's marriage.

Put them all together, with Charlie directing and you have
a terribly funny show that really shouldn't be missed.

"Caliban" Ballet
(by Sue Dauphin, Beaumont Enterprise and over KUHF Radio, May 7, 1976)

One of the most maligned creatures in all literature finally has
a fan club. And its founder and president is James Clouser. Jim
believes that Caliban, the monster-slave from Shakespeare's play,
The Tempest, has always been mistreated and he thinks it's high
time to set the record straight. So he has created a ballet as
seen from Caliban's point of view.

The Houston Ballet's premiere production of "Caliban," as
seen from the opening night audience's point of view was superb.
It is not a traditional ballet, so don't expect to see one. What

it is ... is the product of a group of talented and dedicated young
artists who have come together with the necessary chemistry to
produce a new and electrifying work.   Start with Clouser, himself, who had the vision of a humanized Caliban ... And the
sense to add St. Elmo's Fire to express his vision musically.
Mix in the dancers of the Houston Ballet company who were inspired to really consider their interpretation of the characters
they portrayed.   Blend it all together with fine costume, set and
lighting design and you have something truly exciting.   Though
this is ballet, and it is based closely on Shakespeare, it doesn't
take a knowledge of The Tempest or even a great understanding
of ballet to appreciate "Caliban. "

The ballet is an almost overwhelming series of visual and
musical delights.   It is Caliban himself coming across as a human being in love, hopelessly over his head ... or cringing before the torments of his master ... or dreaming of the future with
himself the master.   It is the beautiful princess Miranda, innocence personified in the first act; wickedly capricious in Caliban's second act nightmare; and ignoring him in the third act ...
or Ariel the favored slave who can fly as Caliban dreams of doing, who carries out his Master's orders with impish glee ...
and Prospero, the master; cold, imperious, and protective of
his beloved daughter.   It is the dancers, Jory Hancock, Denise
Smokoski, Rodwic Fukino, and Whit Haworth expressing their
roles as clearly as if they had endless pages of dialog.   And Robert Raimondo, beautifully dancing the triple role of the three
usurpers of the throne of Naples.

Sonja Zarek has costumed the dancers in everything from
their everyday blue jeans to gossamer wings, but I'll guarantee
there's not a tutu in the whole show.   There is a cow girl ...
and a seven foot viking.   And there is humor ... and romance
... and music.   All kinds.   A jig ... a ballad ... country
western ...

Although "Caliban" has been labeled a rock ballet, the group,
St. Elmo's Fire, makes music that would better be called 'eclectic'.   They have collaborated with Clouser to create an original
score that utilizes many different sounds and instruments, all of
them good.

"Caliban" as a production, couldn't miss ... and shouldn't
have been missed.   The only bad thing I can say about it is that
the Houston Ballet only scheduled three performances.   "Caliban"
deserves more performances and national recognition.   I predict
they will get both.   Actually it is true that a repeat of the ballet
has been scheduled for next season, February 10 thru 12, 1977.
Public opinion should insure that the Houston Ballet keeps that
promise to us.

DAVIS, Curtis Harrison (Curt); (2) Entertainment editor, theater and
film critic, interviewer, columnist; (3) b. Orange, N.J., Sept. 21,
1949; (4) s. Robert and Frances (Hackett) D.; (5) A.B. Hamilton College, major subj.: English, 1971; (8) Reporter, (Newark, N.J.)
Star-Ledger, 1968-71, reporter-writer, Time Inc. house organ and
People magazine, 1972-75, entertainment editor, critic, Encore magazine, 1975- ; (9) Critic fellow: National Critics Institute, Waterford, Conn., 1971; Observer: Actors Studio, 1972-73; (15) Member:
Drama Desk, 1971-74, Outer Critics Circle, 1974- , National Academy of Television Arts and Sciences, 1974- , International Radio
and Television Society, 1974- ; Board director: Triad Playwrights
Company, 1975- ; (16) Democrat; (17) Baptist; (19) Delta Phi fraternity, Williams Club; (20) Contributed articles to Nomad, In the Know,
Library Journal, Ebony, Promenade; People story condensed in Reader's Digest; (22) Encore, 515 Madison Ave., New York, N.Y. 10022,
Ph. 212-593-2223; (23) Circulation: 600,000 nationally; (24) 50 plays,
70 motion pictures, 50 cabarets, 30 records, 50 miscellaneous critical commentary.

Professor George
(by Curt Davis, Encore American & Worldwide News, November 24, 1975)

When Tennessee Williams gets into his snits and Lillian Hellman gets more lines in her face, their mortality is reinforced.
When they no longer write, when they're no longer here even to
make comment or to directly inspire, such playwrights as Marsha Sheiness will take over.

Marsha Sheiness's one-act Professor George had a limited
run at the off-off-Broadway Playwrights Horizons and played a
week later at the Queens Playhouse in the Park. That was its
first New York exposure, and it mustn't be the last. This play
about the undiscovered identity within us all may be the finest
piece of theater writing in the past two years.

Set in a present-day college classroom, Professor George
opens to the Staple Singers' "Respect Yourself" blaring offstage.
Students come in one at a time, waiting for yet another semester
to start in the same, ordinary way. But this year will be different. This year they have Professor George in what is essentially Think 101, what they will discover to be the lowest common
denominator in the human learning experience. A tall, spinsterish woman enters the room and begins--sternly, bitingly, harsh-
ly, lifelike--to act as catalyst for the students to change from
their caterpillars into their potential butterflies. Professor
George, through a series of aesthetic-philosophical-social exercises, shames, inspires, and instructs her students to wake up
and to keep moving so they'll know they're alive. This sudden,
undirected thrust is confusing and painful for the students. She
has penetrated their shells, but consummation is still to come.
Not everyone can do it. Not everyone can "throw yourself into
space," not everyone can "do more than manage," not everyone
can stop "letting it go until tomorrow [which] makes it harder,"

not everyone can say, as she does, "I am what I am," not everyone is strong enough not to "just walk out on himself."

The play is not all abstract semantics, not a second-grade
Beckett or Pinter exercise. It's situation and character drama--
hilarious and so moving one can only gasp--and it, as does the
professor, instructs. It's probably an actor-proof play, too, for
despite the fine performances by Professor Victoria Boothby and
Students Paul Lieber, Maria Cellario, Robert Burke, Steve Pom-
erantz, and Alice Elliott, and Sheiness's own driving direction,
it can be given a staged reading (as at the O'Neill Memorial
Theater Center four summers ago) and be just as alive and dynamic. One of the exercises Professor George has her students
do is clap someone else's personal rhythm. Each character has
his own rhythm that is visible and viable and most applause-
worthy.

Professor George was performed with Sheiness's Clair and
the Chair at the Playwrights Horizons. It too, is about the
awareness of one's sensitivities and the part of a person kept
hidden; everything that is in Clair is in George, but direction
(by Hillary Wyler) and performances were far below those for
George. But Marsha Sheiness's talent can burst through any
barriers. As long as she is not locked into a search inward,
she will no doubt continue the walk down that path to dramatic
glory.

Very Good Eddie
(by Curt Davis, Encore American & Worldwide News, November 24, 1975)

The dedication of Goodspeed Opera House in East Haddam, Connecticut to the preservation of the American musical has spawned
Man of La Mancha and Shenandoah, both of which went on to Broadway acclaim. Very Good Eddie, as its predecessors, deserves
New York success.

Very Good Eddie was written in 1915 the first non-operatic
musical to have a book. After seeing the show, one may ask,
"Oh. It has a book?" The book is its feel--of a vaudevillian
situation comedy of marital melee, with all imaginable plot complications. It's its own entity, a period piece uprooted intact
and transplanted in time. Under Bill Gile's direction, it's a
dandy time.

For missed light cues, a look at the wrong side of a hotel
register, a ballad a bit too long--sloppiness--a plethora of delights compensates. Lively choreography by Dan Siretta breezes
alongside pretty Jerome Kern tunes and witty lyrics by nine
writers. Characters are named Lily Pond and Chrystal Poole,
Always Innit, Dyar Thurst. Dialogue by Philip Bartolomae and
Guy Bolton has kernels of corn, but much of it is charming and
pointed. Best of all is the acting. As Eddie, a small, apron-
strings newlywed who bemoans his size 13 collar and size 3

shoes, Charles Repole is simultaneously funny and poignant.
Going up on tiptoe to sing a note or to kiss his wife's cheek,
Repole richly combines a boyish desire to please with a determination to approximate his true self. As a college buddy's new
wife mistaken for Eddie's, Virginia Seidel strikes a series of
poses (necessary for showing the character's submission and
naïveté) and deserves a garland of posies. She in her way is
as wide-eyed in performance as Repole and the ayes for those
eyes have it. The rest of the cast, particularly Joel Craig,
James Harden, Travis Hudson, and Cynthia Wells, bursts with
rightness.

The curtain call brings the cast together, singing "We've
done our best to make you smile." By the end of the show, the
audience has either smiled or it hasn't; cowtowing with a lyric
like that is distasteful. But so much of Very Good Eddie is
sweet and spicy that the stomach purrs.

DAVIS, James, New York Daily News, 220 East 42 St., New York,
N.Y. 10017, Ph. 212-682-1234.

DAY, Richard Wrisley; (2) Performing arts critic-editor; (3) b.
Rhinebeck, N.Y., Jan. 25, 1936; (4) s. Herbert Britain and Katherine
Wrisley (Day); (5) B.A. Academia di Minerva, Bari, Puglia, Italy,
major area study: ancient civilizations-European history, 1957;
graduate courses drama, dramatic literature & music, Bard College,
1958; private study operatic singing w. John Nichols (Manhattan
Opera), d., and Jean Wells (NYC Opera), ret.; private study acting
w. Stuart Brush-Henry Robinson, NYC; summer study London School
Journalism, 1969; under-graduate study history, Hartwick College,
1954-56; (6) m. Michele Carpenter, July 25, 1970; (8) Arts Critic,
The Woodstock Review (NY), 1958 (concurrent with study at Bard
College); Arts Editor & Critic, the Landers Suburban Newspaper
Group (mid-Hudson Valley, N.Y.) 1959; Music-Theater Critic, The
Bridgeport (Ct.) Post-Telegram Newspapers, 1960-65; Performing
& Graphic Arts Critic & Music Editor, The Bridgeport (Ct.) Post-
Telegram, 1966 to date; lecturer on Theory & Practice & History
of Arts Criticism at various educational institutions and cultural as-
sociations; have written critical studies on Munich Opera Festival,
Wagner Festival, Edinburgh International Arts Festival, "London;
Performing Arts Capital" & regularly critique opera, concert, recitals & ballet in New York City for The Bridgeport Post; (9) Acted
and sang in collegiate drama and opera productions; frequently judge
music competitions and have appeared on Educational Television &
Radio symposiums on the arts; (11) Special Assistant to the late William R. Williams, Member Congress, R-NY, 1952-53; (12) Board
of Trustees, Greater Bridgeport Symphony Orchestra; Member of
Music Committee, Greater Bridgeport Symphony Society; former member Woodstock (NY) Arts Council; (13) Seconded to USN (SB) by W.
R. Williams 1952-53 for special temporary assignment; (14) Naval
Expedition Award & Order of Merit; (15) Critics Association; Society

Amateur Archeologists & Explorers; Bards, Balladeers & Cynics,
London; f. mem. New York Historical Association; (16) politically
Independent; (17) Anglican (n. p.); (19) f. mem. Union League, New
Haven, Ct. , Hudson River Sailing Club, University Clubs of Poughkeepsie (N. Y.) & Bridgeport, Ct.; (20) "History of Arts Criticism"
(in ms. form); (21) 765 Laurel Ave. , Bridgeport, Ct. , and "Rokeby
Farm," Barrytown, N. Y. , Ph. (Ct.) 366-9449; (22) 765 Laurel Ave. ,
06604, (main business address) & c/o The Post, 410 State St. , Bridgeport, Ct. 06602, Ph. 203-366-9444 and 203-333-0161 (Post Bldg.); (23)
Circulation: 100,000 (Approx.); (The Post largest daily & Sunday newspaper between NYC & New Haven, Ct.); (24) Approx. 200 plays, ballets, operas, concerts, recitals, etc ... per winter season; estimated 40 plays, concerts, etc ... each summer season. First full-
time arts critic to be employed in Connecticut.

Barrie's Finest Romance Given Admirable Revival
(by Richard Day, Bridgeport Post, December 30, 1975)

Gently mirthful, warmly romantic, reflecting wisdom gained
through experience, James M. Barrie's affectionate bow to wo-
mankind, "What Every Woman Knows," possesses vitality and
charm in the Long Warf theater's timely and admirable revival.

Written during a critical phase in the playwright's matrimo-
nial-domestic life, "What Every Woman Knows" provides an
adroit exposure of the erroneous presumption of masculine superiority, while commenting via contrast on the shallowness and
folly of humanity's penchant for equating mere surface appeal with
quality and depth. Characteristically, Barrie developed his script
without recourse to the fanaticism and-or bitterness, I suppose
we might say overkill, common in dramas of human relations
now being written. In fact, recent dramatic literature does not,
to the best of my knowledge, contain a work wherein the role of
woman is paid fuller or more sincere tribute.

Not only has Kenneth Frankel's production realized and sustained the warmth and whimsical humor of the play through the
portrayals of a first-rate cast, the sets and costumes of Steven
Rubin and Jania Szatanski, aided by Judith Rasmuson's lighting,
have facilitated the recreation of atmosphere from the solidarity
of a middle-class Scots house to the classic grace and summer
warmth of the garden terrace at a British country home during
the reign of Edward the VII.

Heading a company whose Scots and British accents are
firmly (though modified) in place, Joyce Ebert and Christopher
Lloyd were a pleasure to observe and hear as the loyal intelligent and warm-hearted wife and her intense, humorless spouse,
who realizes at the eleventh hour that his rise from uncouthness
and obscurity to political prominence and eloquence on the speakers' platform, have in large measure, been the product of her
unobtrusive way of refining his thoughts and utterances.

In conveying his character's magnetism and gradual develoment from raw youth to smugly confident, experienced politician, Mr. Lloyd was rarely less than entirely convincing; and the same can be said of Miss Ebert, whose selfless dedication, quiet humor and confidence rang absolutely true, instead of acquiring an aroma of falsity and cuteness, which easily could have transpired in the hands of a less capable and experienced actress.

Supporting roles were executed with equal distinction: Blair Brown was appropriately lovely and empty-headed as the flirtatious Lady Sybil; Mildred Dunnock played the scheming elderly Comptesse with that finish born of much practice and Emery Battis was the epitome of the shrewd, suave and commanding elder government official of yore.

Good though this production was at the onset, my expectations are that it will gain in quality as the run progresses, and surely its timely theme, warmth, and instructiveness without didacticism, combine to make a most satisfying evening at the theater. If you possibly can, go!

Bitter Drama Conjectures Bard's Discontent, Death
(by Richard Day, Bridgeport Post, February 4, 1976)

In the American premiere of Edward Bond's "Bingo: Scenes of Money and Death," Yale Repertory theater patrons are presented with a strikingly original, conjectural drama recounting William Shakespeare's final, bitter "winter of discontent," wherein he discovers that the peaceful, secure retirement anticipated is instead a period of guilty anguish, unwilling compliance in the cruelty of property Enclosure, estrangement without escape, and suicidal despair.

Fashioned in six economic, vividly illustrative and effectual scenes, the stark drama, staged with a simpleness somewhat reminiscent of the stage in classic times, depicts characters and events with the knife-edged clarity of a playwright sure in craft and design.

An exacting script demanding strong ensemble playing, "Bingo" summons the best concerted and individual characterization of which the theater's personnel are capable, with Alvin Epstein heading a splendid cast as the weary, anguished master of New Place.

Face, mannerisms, voice and movements eloquently conveying a notable portrait of burdensome disconsolation and increasing physical infirmity, Mr. Epstein gives a profoundly complete and touching depiction of a man whose flames of greatness have at last burned-out, leaving only an empty husk awaiting the flail, and ultimately going down before it willfully, with repeated lamentings of utter despair.

It is as fine an interpretation as I can recall over the years of familiarity with the actor's work. And, as has been previously indicated, he is by no means alone.

Philip Kerr is the epitome of cool, poised inconsequential reasonability as the Stratford magistrate whose sole interest is reserved for profit and to whom the unjustly displaced small farmers and their women are but vermin in need of extermination.

Jeremy Geldt adds another to his memorable list of portrayals, stirring smiles and pity with the role of a kindly villager and gardener to Shakespeare whom a long-ago injury had reduced to a quasi-simpleton; one supposes he is symbolic of the innocents of this world.

During the second act, Tom Hill enacts the frustration and envy-ridden Ben Johnson with a fine show of bursting rage; the intensity of his performance matches that of Mr. Epstein's momentarily roused Shakespeare, overmastering his old rival.

Shakespeare's daughter, Judith, face a frozen mask of righteous disapproval, hard-tongued bitterness, voice taut, overbearing of manner, is played right convincingly by Linda Atkinson.

And one cannot fault the understanding, sympathy and loyalty which Anne Gerety brings so warmly to the role of Shakespeare's solicitous old housekeeper, or the skill of Marcell Rosenblatt's character acting as the wretched, vagrant girl whose hand-to-mouth existence ends on a gallows.

Last, though by no means least, mention should be made of the manner in which Don Daniels, the British director who did "Afore Night Come" at Long Wharf last season, has unobtrusively, capably exercised his skill to insure a smooth, natural exposition.

This writer has not always found Mr. Bond's dramas entirely satisfactory; however, all that has come before, and between four and five of his plays have been done at the YRT, bow to this continually absorbing, masterfully executed work. My injunction, go!

DELAUNOY, Didier; (2) Theatre critic; (3) b. Arcachon, France, Dec. 8, 1937; (4) s. Leopold (Deutsch) and Simone (Gruot); (5) grad. Bordeaux (France) U. , major subj. : philosophy, literature, politics, 1957; (8) Publicity Director, CTI Records, 1973-75; free-lance writer; (13) QM2, French Navy, 1958-61; (15) Mem. N. A. R. A. S. (Nat'l Acad. Recording Arts & Sciences); (20) regular contributor to The Black American, Soul, Encore; articles in Stereo Review, The New York Times, After Dark, Players; liner notes on Columbia, United Artists, Philips albums; (21) 155 East 34th Street, Apt. # 2G, New York, N. Y. 10016, Ph. 212-889-4478; (22) CTI Records, 1 Rockefeller Plaza, New York, N. Y. 10020, Ph. 212-489-6120;

(23) The Black American, 200 West 149th Street, New York, N.Y. 10031, Ph. 212-286-4132. Circ.: 165,000; Soul, 8271 Melrose Ave., Los Angeles, Ca. 90046, Ph. 213-653-7775. Circ.: 175,000; (24) 65-80 plays and musicals, 10-25 films.

Of Mice and Men
(by Didier Delaunoy, Black American, January 16-22, 1975)

John Steinbeck's "Of Mice and Men" is one of those powerful dramas that stick with you forever. I still can vividly remember the film version made in 1939, with Lon Chaney and Burgess Meredith in the leading roles.

The impact of this forceful play is further enhanced in the sensational production currently at the Brooks Atkinson. The stage is almost bare: only a few details suggest here a bunkhouse, there a hayloft. But in these simple settings designed by William and Jean Eckart, the play has ample room to unfold, to stretch and reach out. The effect is almost unbearable.

And whereas the movie version--which is, at this point, my only other frame of reference--offered perhaps more intimacy in the way it searched the inner thoughts of the characters by exploring their faces in close-ups, the stage beings in more immediacy to the entire story.

James Earl Jones gives a fantastic performance. As originally conceived by Steinbeck, Lenny is white. The casting of Jones in the part brings in a whole new set of thoughts and motives. His relationship with George takes on a totally different meaning. The whole idea itself would have been an explosive one in 1937, when the play was written. Today, it still is an intriguing concept, one that draws on more than the mere relationship and friendship between Lennie and George.

Jones, of course, is superb, fumbling and bumbling, always seeking something soft to caress, and being veritably gauche. The murder of Curley's wife is a rapid act, beautifully staged, almost a balletic moment where the strength of the actor is quickly displayed, and almost immediately replaced by a sorrowful reaction.

The last scene, in which Lennie is killed by George, again is one of those poignant moments that can't be erased from one's memory. If only because Jones' extraordinary acting makes it such an emotional scene.

As George, the focal point in Lennie's life, Kevin Conway is a perfect companion. His performance is almost as extraordinary as that of James Earl Jones. Both actors play splendidly against each other. In a sense, they're both so good and so strong that they tend to overshadow the other members of the cast, all excellent, which include Stefan Gierasch, David Clarke,

Mark Gordon, Pamela Blair, David Gale, Pat Corley, James
Staley, and Joe Seneca.

The direction by Edwin Sherin is flawless. All in all, "Of
Mice and Men" is a play one should see at least once. The current production is well worth catching!

Theatre
(by Didier Delaunoy, Soul, March 3, 1975)

More than ever, this season, the theatre is thriving. In a
recent report, "Variety," the Bible of Show Business, gloated
over the fact that by every possible standard, the 1974-75 season
was one of the best Broadway had seen in years.

Not only are the new plays good, new productions of old plays
are also generally excellent. And, of course, the contribution
by actors and actresses is such that many people along the so-
called Great White Way predict it will be extremely difficult to
pick up the next Tony winners.

The lure, of course, is that you can admire some of the best
talent in the country doing what they can do best. Where, for
instance, would you expect to see in the flesh actors like James
Earl Jones, Cleavon Little and Rex Harrison? Or, on the distaff
side, superb actresses such as Rita Moreno, Rosetta Lenoire or
Virginia Capers?

"Of Mice and Men"

At the Brooks Atkinson, for instance, the extraordinary James
Earl Jones does a grander-than-life reading of the part of Lennie in a sensational revival of John Steinbeck's "Of Mice and
Men." If you have seen the 1939 television film version, which
is most people's only frame of reference, you probably remember Lon Chaney's portrayal of Lennie, the feeble-minded giant,
happy when he is permitted to stroke the soft, furry back of a
mouse or a puppy, and utterly disconsolate when his hand has
crushed it.

As originally conceived, Lennie is white. The casting of
James Earl Jones in the part is a real coup: he brings to the
part, almost inevitably, an extra dimension. Lennie's relationship with George, the intelligent, good-natured man who always
pulls him out of trouble, because of its Black-white undertones,
becomes more profound, more significant. When Lennie accident-
ly kills the Boss' son's wife, the men who set out to find him
and lynch him do so for more reasons than one (remember that
the action of the play takes place in 1937).

Throughout the play, James Earl Jones is nothing short of
superb. He dominates the stage, physically and emotionally,
and his presence elicits awe and admiration. His acting is so

rich, his technique so right that he can suggest scores of meanings with only a glance or a gesture.

As George, Kevin Conway is equally at ease, and an excellent foil for Jones. His reading is well balanced, superbly shaded and beautifully restrained.

Together, both men manage to create such vibes that this revival is bound to be remembered as one of the most exciting evenings offered on Broadway this season.

"The Member of the Wedding"

At the Helen Hayes Theatre, for a brief moment, Marge Eliot graced the stage in another superlative revival, this time Carson McCullers' "The Member of the Wedding." The play itself is concerned with an awkward, hot-tempered, and highly imaginative ugly duckling of twelve, Frankie, who feels that the world should take notice of her, who longs for companionship, and essentially finds it difficult to make the transition to adolescence.

She spends most of the time with the house cook, Berenice Sadie Brown (Ethel Waters created the role in the original production), and because the play is set in the South in the 1940's, some of the comments and attitudes between Blacks and whites have taken a more poignant significance.

As Berenice Sadie Brown, Marge Eliot provided a true revelation. This was her first starring role on Broadway, and brief as the run of this revival was, she proved a worthy successor to dramatic actresses such as the late Diana Sands and Cicely Tyson.

"The Member of the Wedding" is now in Washington, D.C. for a four-week engagement, and if you happen to live there or are visiting, try to catch it. As for Ms. Eliot, I was extremely privileged; she granted me an interview which will appear in a future issue of Soul.

"The Wiz"

All the glitter of a Hollywood premiere is what awaited theatre goers at the opening of "The Wiz," the soul version of "The Wizard of Oz." On hand were some of the biggest names in show business, including Stevie Wonder, Melvin Van Peebles, Micki Grant, Vinnette Carroll, Dustin Hoffman, Cleavon Little and Esther Rolle. It was an evening to be reckoned with, with New York's "Who's Who" out for a special treat.

The treat indeed proved to be very special. "The Wiz" is everything a Broadway musical should be--colorful, imaginative, opulent, and above all, musical.

What impresses one immediately is the quality of the staging, the beauty of the settings, and the unusual appeal of the costumes. The creators involved, Geoffrey Holder, Tom H. John and George Faison, have let their imagination run wild, and in so doing they have given Broadway one of its most attractive shows in years.

As Dorothy, the little girl from Kansas whisked away to the enchanted land of Oz by a hurricane, Stephanie Mills is dynamite. Her performance is uniquely powerful and convincing.

On the way to Oz, she meets The Scarecrow, The Tinman, and The Lion (respectively Hinton Battle, a footloose and fancy free gem of an actor, Tiger Haynes, and Ted Ross, who manages to steal the show in a couple of scenes).

In the Emerald City (one of the most gorgeous sets you're likely to see on Broadway these days), they meet The Wiz, played with dash by Andre de Shields, who orders them to go and kill Evillene, the wicked witch of the West, grossly caricatured by Male King.

The entire show is seasoned with a sensational score out of which hit tunes emerge one after the other, beginning with "The Feeling We Once Had" (splendidly performed by Tasha Thomas), "Ease on Down The Road," "Mean Ole Lion," "To Be Able To Fell," "Everybody Rejoice" which is an exhilarating showstopper, full of dash and vibrancy, "Believe In Yourself," "Y'all Got It," and "A Rested Body Is A Rested Mind."

In its every superb facet, "The Wiz" is a fairy tale come true, one that is bound to attract kids and their parents for many years to come.

DENTON, Jon, Daily Oklahoman-Oklahoma City Times, Oklahoma City, Okla. 73125.

DETTMER, Roger; (2) Theater critic; (3) b. Cincinnati, O., Aug. 2, 1927; (4) s. Christian H. and Cornelia (Van Schouwen) Dettmer; (5) U. of Cincinnati, 1945-47; Columbia U., N.Y., 1947, advertising; U. of Michigan, 1948-50; B.A., English/Music Theory; (8) Asst. Mgr., Cincinnati Symphony Orchestra, 1950-51; music writer, New York Herald Tribune, 1951-53; theatre, music and audio editor/critic, Chicago Today (formerly Herald-American, American, 1953-74; theatre critic, Chicago Tribune, 1974-); (9) Pers. mgr. Stomu Yamash'ta (percussionist, 1968-70). Pre-Bway play-doctor (Sing, Man, Sing; Ziegfeld Follies; New Faces 1956 and 1960; Night of the Iguana, et al., 1956-61). Instr. Rockefeller Foundation trng. music critics, U. So. California, 1965-68; Radio and TV programs, Cincinnati, Chicago; 1950-64; (10) Mem. Illinois Arts Council theater advisory panel, 1970-73; (14) Phi Beta Kappa, Phi Kappa Psi, Theta Alpha Phi (hon. mem.); Corecipient Feature Div. Award A.P. (1965); (15) orig. Amer. Music

Critics Assn. (founding mem., v. p. 1957-58); mem. Music Critics
Assn., Inter-American Music Critics Assn., American Symphony
Orchestra League, A. F. T. R. A.; (16) Protestant; (17) Independent;
(20) Contributor to Bel Canto, Cincinnati Enquirer, Cincinnati Times-
Star, Helsinki Sanomat, Toledo Blade (1946-50); New York Times,
San Francisco Chronicle, Honolulu Morning Advertiser, Theatre Arts,
Musical America (1959-64); High Fidelity (1959-60); Stereo Review
(1974-); Opera (London 1959-74), Recordo Geijitsu (Japan, 1968-69).
(21) 415 W. Aldine Ave., 9/B, Chicago, Ill 60657; (22) Chicago
Tribune, 435 N. Michigan Ave., Rm. 414, Chicago, Ill. 60611, Ph.
312-222-4282; (23) Daily & Sunday; (24) Reviews: ca. 125 theater, 15
recordings and audio, 48 Sunday theater features, misc. film and
music annually.

A Tragic Revival of an O'Neill Soaper
(by Roger Dettmer, Chicago Tribune, Feburary 14, 1975)

Eugene O'Neill waited two years for a Broadway production--
at a February matinee in 1920--of his first full-length play,
"Beyond the Horizon," portentously described as "An American
Tragedy in Three Acts." It didn't star John Barrymore, who
he'd hoped would create the role of a book-loving dreamer with
tubercular lungs, trapped on a family farm in New England by a
neighbor girl who claimed to love him but didn't.

Richard Bennett--father of Constance and Joan and Barbara--
found the script in his producer's office and insisted upon playing
it, as a consequence of which O'Neill won his first Pulitizer
Prize. It was revived [no, disinterred is the verb] Thursday
night by the St. Nicholas Theater Company, in Grace Lutheran
Church on West Belden Avenue, and what is there to say of this
misguided enterprise after the fact?

Well ... for starters, they don't write plays like this today.
Not even for installment performances on afternoon television.
By any contemporary measure, it is soap opera and melodrama,
with line after line like "O Ruth, our love is sweeter than any
distant dream." Before his death in 1953, O'Neill was to write
timeless tragedies for the stage; and after his death to be judged
our greatest playwright to date.

But the early works do not sustain. Not "The Emperor
Jones," nor "Anna Christie," nor "Desire Under the Elms," nor
"Strange Interlude" [except as a showcase for a tour-de-force
company such as the Actors Studio presented on Broadway in
1963]. "Beyond the Horizon" predated all of these.

Had he written nothing other than "The Iceman Cometh" and
"Long Day's Journey Into Night," O'Neill's reputation as a titan
would be secure. But to write these, he had to write other
plays.

Out of respect for the man's indelible achievements, his

earliest plays ought to be allowed their eternal rest. Occasionally in "Beyond the Horizon," like flashes of lightning, a future
landscape is momentarily illuminated. But even with editing by
director David Mamet [including a child of the visionary and his
fickle wife who really loved a brother gone to sea, tho he was
truly the man of the land], this relic of 1920 is turgid, awkward
to speak, humorless, and gesticular.

The St. Nicholas Players are nowhere nearly ready to attempt O'Neill--at any stage of his development. The performance was amateurish, this said more in sadness than exasperation. Yes, Mary Frances Farrell [as the wife] and William H.
Macy [as the farmboy who goes to sea] have promise, but not
yet a control of technique, or the craft to externalize internal
moments credibly. Byrne Piven in one scene belonged with his
own--elder and better--elsewhere than we found him to be.

"Philanthropist" Offers Rich Insights
(by Roger Dettmer, Chicago Tribune, February 19, 1975)

At Goodman Theater Center Tuesday night, on the main
stage, "The Philanthropist" by Christopher Hampton opened--a
play of such finesse, insight, distinctiveness and purpose that,
right now, it has erased from the mind [as from a blackboard]
memories of a comparable achievement.

Certainly an abstemious description by Peter Roberts in
"Theater in Britain" had not prepared us: "... a two-act comedy
of manners in a realistic setting," with the further note that
Hampton, born in 1946, had it first produced five years ago!
One must be on guard constantly against hyperbole, and take care
not to undervalue what a cast, director, and designers of set,
costumes, and lighting can contribute to the success of such an
occasion.

But I am no more able at this moment to restrain enthusiasm for an experience simultaneously entertaining and enriching,
than I am able at this moment to recall a playwright remotely
as precocious as Christopher Hampton.

From an author twice his 23 [at most 24] years when "The
Philanthropist" was composed, it would be superb: literate without sounding a "literary" note, hilarious yet heartfelt to the extent of poignancy, satiric but not cynical, withal supremely well
made. There are elements of absurdist farce, yet a smooth
modulation into comedy [the best of which have vulnerable hearts]
that uses manners--not an exageration of manners--to reveal a
human condition.

I can't expect everyone will respond as wholly--yet wish at
the same time all might. Playgoing is a subjective experience,
whether or not one carries a press pass and pen. But when one
can recognize as life what is seen and heard, subjectivity is

is intensified; and with it appreciation. In "The Philanthropist,"
Hampton has created an antonymous contemporary of Moliere's
storied "Misanthrope." Philip is a college lecturer in philology
who admits, even volunteers, "I have no critical faculties. I
love the sound of words."

He composes anagrams, gives awkward dinner parties, lives
in ivory tower isolation from the unpleasantness of real life [ex-
cept when, as in a brilliant first scene here, it intrudes comi-
cally]. And Brian Murray plays him as bewitchingly, brilliantly,
with a technique used for surprise, as Hampton has written this
childlike, lonely, even terrified man, who thinks everyone to be
like he is.

It astounds him to be told by a copping-out colleague, Donald,
that "most people live on the desperate hope that everyone else
isn't like them." It dismays him when Araminta brazenly attempts his seduction; or that his fiancée, Celia, lies to make
life "different," loving only men who will hurt her; or that Bra-
ham, a glib novelist who talks in paradoxes, is suspicious of a
presumed sublety; or that "quiet" Liz can be a passionate sexual
partner.

All these are multi-dimensional as Hampton has created
them--and, furthermore, as they are played by [in order] David
H. Leary, Judith Ivey, Swoozie Kurtz, Richard Clarke, and Ver-
onica Castang. To this ensemble, add Jarlath Conroy as a
failed playwright in the first scene.

Michael Montel's cumulative direction could hardly be improved upon, tho Clarke would be even more effective as the novelist if less oratorical. I'd like to live in Peter Wexler's set,
with Ken Billingston's lighting design [tho I'd turn down the volume level on cunningly selected music between the scenes], and
have costumer John David Ridge as a personal tailor if I could
afford him.

But these finally are the servants of Hampton--at last a British playwright who, under a burnished veneer and with wondrous
wit, cares and can feel; who transcends anger and contempt; who
has written a play neither Shaw nor Anouilh would disdain as their
own. If it does not, by intermission, already entrance you,
please stay to the end--for your own sake and enlightenment. And
try not to mind the forthright use of certain X-rated expletives:
"civilized" people do use them just as here, to make an effect.

DeVINE, J. [oseph] Lawrence; (2) Theater critic; (3) b. New York
City, N. Y. , Sept. 21, 1935; (4) s. John Justin and Hazel (Tippit);
(5) Georgetown U. , 1954; U. of Michigan, B. S. in journalism, Medill School of Journalism; Northwestern U. , 1957; (6) m. Jane Christian, Aug. 18, 1959; marriage diss. 1967; m. Lucy Memory Williamson, July 26, 1968; (7) children--John Justin II, Ellen Morse; (8) Staff

writer, columnist, The Miami Herald, 1962-65; theater critic, The
Miami Herald, 1965-67; Entertainment editor, drama and film critic,
The Los Angeles Herald-Examiner, 1967-68; drama critic, entertainment editor, The Detroit Free Press, 1968- ; (9) Critic Fellow,
Critics Institute, Eugene O'Neill Memorial Theater Center, Waterford, Conn. , 1971; teaching faculty, Eugene O'Neill Theater Center,
1973-75; (10) Instructor, drama criticism, the University of Detroit,
1974; (11) special agent, U.S. Army Counter Intelligence Corps,
1958-62; Russian-German language specialist; (12) "Outstanding Citizen
of Florida," award of Florida Association of Architects, AIA, 1965;
(13) Member, Outer Critics Circle, American Theater Critics Association; (16) Independent; (17) Roman Catholic; (20) Cont. articles to
Grolier's Encyclopedia Yearbook, film section, 1969-70-71-72, The
Los Angeles Times, New York Magazine, Knight Newspapers Inc.
wire service; (21) 1050 Van Dyke, Detroit, Mich. 48214, Ph. 313-
499-0348; (22) The Detroit Free Press, 321 W. Lafayette Blvd. ,
Detroit, Mich. , 48226, Ph. 313-222-6517; (23) Circulation: 628,000
daily, 743,000 Sunday; (24) 100 plays and musicals, 50 films, 25
miscellaneous.

"Misanthrope" Well-Played: Crisp and Starchy

(by Lawrence DeVine, Detroit Free Press, February 1, 1975)

Of all of Moliere's plays, only "The Misanthrope" might have
been written by Shakespeare. It is the most serious of Moliere's
popular plays, knottier and less obvious than his farces. It also
is so insightful, even socially conscious, that it comes right to
20th-century life in an updated, first-class new production at the
Meadow Brook Theatre.

Its heroine, Celemine, is right out of Shakespeare--a modern
flirt, selfish, with a mind of her own. She is a straightforward
minx, alongside a Beatrice or a Rosalind. To play her and the
title's dour Alceste, director Terence Kilburn arranged an interesting pair of talents in Susanne Peters and Guy Stockwell. But
the overpowering art is in the play and the natural respiration it
gets from Kilburn's innovative staging circa 1913.

The original version's Louis XIV isn't king anymore in Kilburn's bright transition, admittedly inspired by the 1974 Tony Harrison production in London with Diana Rigg and Alec McCowen.
They don't have Louis to kick around anymore.

But rocketing "The Misanthrope" ahead from 1666 to 1913
places it in France's hectic pre-war government of musical premiers. Aristide Briand and Jean Louis Barthou met each other
coming and going out of the Elysee Palace, and high-level gossip
was just as piquant as ever.

Kilburn could not secure the rights to the brilliant new translation by Harrison, so he employed the trusty Richard Wilbur
over the years, over "Tartuffe" mainly. But his "Misanthrope"
is straight to the point and plays very well in the hands (or lips)

of this tasteful company assembled by Kilburn.

Stockwell's Alceste, all in all, is a rather likeable sourpuss. He is up to here with gossip and flattery, and he says so.   But Moliere is shotgunning his wit.   He pokes fun twice--at Alceste's targets, and then, with the second barrel, at Alceste himself, a peckish, rather narrow man.

Alceste's utter candor earns him a lawsuit for slander.   Rather than argue about it, at play's end he dispiritedly flees Paris, either in high dudgeon or an Hispano-Suisa.

His blind spot is Celemine, a snappy 20-year-old whose means of support is all that is not highly visible.   Will she flee along with him?   She will not, though she might sincerely miss him.   The intriguing character is introduced by Susanne Peters in a knockout brown and peach silk gown and some artfully applied make-up at the decolletage which immediately gives her a whiff of the Diana Rigg insouciancy.   She is well-spoken, crisp as celery and reason enough for the starchy Alceste to give her a wrinkle.

Stockwell's Alceste is burly in looks and a little heavy with the light touch.   Stockwell plays a pretty humorless character, true.   But an actor of his proven substance might approach Alceste a bit less stiffly.

No little part of the Meadow Brook "Misanthrope's" success is due to the costumes by Mary Lynn Bonnell and a subtly witty set by Nancy Thompson.   The set is almost fantastical: A gilded sea-shell of a Parisian drawing room in plum, toast and aqua, outlined in leaded glass.   Getting rid of that too-real showroom sofa would help it.

Among the supporting players, Joseph Shaw is back (good news) as the feckless bad poet Oronte.   They ought to give Joe Shaw a home and a deed at Meadow Brook.   William Halliday is just one of Celemine's gallants, looking like a giddy George Brent or a manly Billy DeWolfe--take your choice.   Elisabeth Orion as the catty Arsinoe (a wonderful name) has one of her best roles in a long series of them there.   Robert Grossman is good in two roles.   One of them is the valet, Basque, drolly envisioned by Kilburn as a Real Basque, complete with spiky sideburns and Cuban-type accent.

A Good Look at Some Bad Old Days
(by Lawrence DeVine, Detroit Free Press, February 7, 1975)

There are, naturally, two main kinds of labor: Maternal and organized.   Historically there have been as few men able to talk reasonably about one as the other.

The poet Donald Hall figuratively crafted them both into a

new evening of theater called "Bread and Roses" given its world
premiere at the Power Center for the Performing Arts on the
University of Michigan campus, where Hall teaches and writes.

"Bread and Roses" is more pageant than play.

It celebrates the noisy and bleeding birth in the U.S. of uni-
field labor, the Industrial Workers of the World. "Bread and
Roses" is an invigorating parade of the IWW's member of "Wobblies," good old unabased left wing theatre about the bad old days.

The long one-act event is put before us in a "lest we forget"
sort of spirit, recapitulating the tumultuous reaction of Americans
when someone oppresses them.

Hall discards the stricter conventions of a play, which require leading characters, a plot and a discernable path toward
an evening's progress. "Bread and Roses" has none of those.
It is a panorama with fists and banners, a lively mural, and who
misses plot anyway, when he's having a good time?

Hall candidly borrowed some 90 percent of his show from
printed histories of the Wobblies, including the best guess about
how IWW members got the nickname. A hospitable West Coast
Chinese restaurant owner's asking "Are you IWW?" came out:
"All loo eye wobble wobble?"

"Bread and Roses" emerges as a professor's-dream sort of
play, an illustrated lecture on the IWW catapulted out of the
classroom onto the capacious stage of the Power Center. There
20 actors--illuminated with vitality, their necks and veins throbbing as they sing the old Wobbly songs--relive the unarguably
dramatic moments of the struggle of the early 1900s.

Out of the shadows, on a simple set with an elevated platform
and stairs, appear the mythic Joe Hill, the old Buffalo Big Bill
Haywood, mill owners, maltreated children, and hot-blooded
heroines like Elizabeth Gurley Flynn, Emma Goldman and the
cantankerous "Mother Jones," a gritty Irish woman who was on
the barricades at 95.

To bring them all together, Hall created a narrator, an old
actor who remembers how it was. He is played by the show's
lone professional, Walter Rhodes, a wonderfully sympathetic host
who moves among the fresh-faced student cast like a comfortably
rumpled Melvyn Douglas. The others on stage are not credited
by role--there are too many roles--but Evan Jeffries as both
Clarence Darrow and Joe Hill, and Susan Wall as a series of
spunky creatures, deserve any trouble it takes to learn their
names.

Richard Meyer's direction is muscular in the way that a big
project like this one cries out for. The show insists upon

continual episodes, a sudden electric song, numerous characters
... in short, a Very Big Picture. Meyer's direction reminds
one of the subtly organized clamor, for "Hope" in that way.

"Bread and Roses" inspires some reverence for, or at least
knowledge of, another period when times were bad and Americans' answer was individual gumption. Hall also avoids any extrapolated bitterness about today, when union men may be led by
knaves (a Dave Beck, a felon like Jimmy Hoffa) instead of working for them.

It truthfully is very stirring to hear "The Internationale"
sung by fervent young actors when they are playing workers bent
on recognition, not subversion. What inadequacies the show may
have lie in its exposition. A time frame at the beginning is neglected; a statement is needed at the outset of the IWW's aims
for an industrial union versus trade unions.

But quibbling is easily lost in the hubbub of "Bread and
Roses" and its music. In a master stroke of staging, the music
is supplied by an upright piano, guitar, kazoo, an older drummer and the white-haired Mr. Percy Danforth, who plays the
bones. His sound echoes bygone America, high-stepping feet,
ghostly applause.

DIBBLE, Pater Davis; (2) Theatre, movie and especially opera critic;
Feature Editor; Eye Columnist; (3) b. Englewood, N.J., July 12,
1927; (4) s. Winston Chase and Vadna Raymond (Davis) Dibble; (5)
A.B. Harvard College 1948, major: English; (6) unmarried; (8) Wo-
men's Wear Daily, New York, 1955 to present; Amateur Cinema
League, New York (film consultant and associate editor Movie Makers
magazine), 1953-54; Cue magazine, editorial service, various dates;
(9) business manager, Martha's Vineyard Playhouse, summer 1948;
actor, Clayton Playhouse, Clayton, N.Y., summer 1950; actor,
Mountain Playhouse, Jennerstown, Pa., summer 1950; (13) S/Sgt,
U.S. Army, 1945-47, sergeant-major Fort Dix, N.J.; (15) Actors
Equity Association 1950-55 (honorary withdrawal); American Federa-
tion of Radio and Television Artists, 1950-55 (honorary withdrawal);
Drama Desk, New York, 1965-present; Outer Critics Circle, New
York, 1970-present; (17) Protestant-Episcopal; (19) Hasty Pudding-
Institute of 1776, 1947-present; (20) Contributed articles to Ladies
Home Journal, U.S. Camera, in addition to regular features in Wo-
men's Wear Daily and W; (21) 21 Stuyvesant Oval, New York, N.Y.
10009, Ph. 677-3218 and 777-5514; (22) Women's Wear Daily, 7 E.
12 St., New York, N.Y. 10003, Ph. 741-4042; (23) Circulation:
Women's Wear Daily, 74,590; W, 164,000; (24) 25 opera, 12 theater,
12 books, 12 reviews as features interviews.

DISSEN, Mary, Ledger-Star, Norfolk, Va. 23501.

DORAN, J. Terence; (2) Arts editor, theater critic; (3) b. South
Bend, Ind., Jan. 25, 1936; (4) s. James R. and Lorene (Nees); (5)
B.A. Dartmouth College, major subj: physics and English, 1959;
(6) m. Carolyn Suwalski, Oct. 17, 1964; (7) children--Jennifer J.,
James R II, Nicholas T.; (9) Dir. Chekhov farces for Courtyard
Theater, Buffalo, N.Y., 1970; co-director documentary film "Citizen
of What Country?" 1970; Dir. "Pilk's Madhouse" for American Contemporary Theater, Buffalo, N.Y., 1972; Dir. "Six Comedies" for
American Contemporary Theater, Buffalo, N.Y., 1973; author, "Internal Combustion" prod. by American Contemporary Theater, Buffalo,
N.Y., 1975; (13) honorable discharge; (16) Independent; (20) Professional criticism, play "Internal Combustion" and "Trajectory"; (21)
171 Highland Ave., Buffalo, N.Y. 14222, Ph. 716-886-0432; (22)
1 News Plaza, Buffalo Evening News 14240, Ph. 716-849-4506; (23)
Circulation: 300,000; (24) 50 films, 25 plays, 25 other.

"Saint Joan": Not Much at Stake
(by Terry Doran, Buffalo Evening News, June 10, 1975)

Shaw was not backward about it. He described his "Saint
Joan" as high tragedy. With this in mind, expectations for one
of Shaw's major works here [Stratford, Ont.] might have been
said to be pretty well set. And solidly disappointed.

The performance, directed in eccentric fashion by William
Hutt, starts with low comedy and bogs down thereafter. It's the
one rut to be avoided at all costs. Shaw is sparingly humorous,
without additional outside aid, and at the right moments.

It's all the more bewildering for reasons unconnected with
Shaw. It's no secret that the Stratford Festival had degenerated
in the past several seasons. Sitting in on any one performance
you would have classified it as a tourist attraction. Not a bad
designation, though not the stated aim.

So the nomination of Robin Phillips as the new artistic director brought about equal amounts, approximately, of hope and controversy. The former because Phillips possesses an admirable
record in British theater. The latter caused by his not having
been born and bred Canadian.

Canadians thrashed that one out last year, leaving Philips
winded and holding the fort. Now the heavy guns of professional
critics are swinging in Phillips's direction. How he'll fare remains to be seen, for "Saint Joan" is only the first of many productions under his leadership. "Saint Joan," however, is a notably limp beginning.

The sweeping artistic changes implied in all Phillips' remarks and demeanor are all but invisible in "Saint Joan." The
identical relapses into pseudo-comedy and noisy declamation are
again present. I wouldn't want to be misunderstood, but it's all
fairly brazen audience-grabbing gimmickry.

In any case, behind "Saint Joan" is the puzzling figure of William Hutt. Hutt is one of the few actors nurtured at the festival over the years who has claim to be called one of Canada's leading actors. Lately his performances have veered into the bizarre, a quality now discovered in his direction as well.

Looking around for something, anything, to recommend this production I find myself at a loss. A smattering of spectacle: A coronation procession, or black-robed figures in deep shadow with heavy liturgical refrains. Maybe the all-purpose opportunity to hear one of the finer plays in the literature recited by live performers, a mixed blessing here.

Sounds harsh, I know. And cannot possible be true every inch of the play. There are moments, then. How couldn't there be with Shaw? There are reasonably good performances, Pat Galloway as Joan, creditable is the extent of it. Leslie Yeo, excellent as the Earl of Warwick, and along with William Needles in the role of inquisitor, a minority in the cast aware that Shaw's parts are not expressly for civilized buffoons.

However, the overarching drama is left in shambles. Primarily, it seems, due to a willingness, eagerness, to throw it all out the window for a big laugh here, puerile stage business there and thrusting, unignorable unreality everywhere.

A letdown, as I say, and one that may be rectified in the next several evenings when productions of Shakespeare directed by Robin Phillips open to public view. Last year at this time, when an especially soggy season was unfolding, Phillips was able to talk an inspired artistic game as director-elect. It may be that "Saint Joan" is a ringer and not the artistic standard. We'll report tomorrow.

Brilliant "Measure for Measure" Tips Scale for Phillips
(by Terry Doran, Buffalo Evening News, June 12, 1975)

In all probability, the test [at Stratford, Ont.] in everyone's eyes was to be "Measure for Measure." It would have been, at any rate, surprising if it hadn't. In this one, the third production to adorn the Festival Stage in as many evenings, Robin Phillips was to go on view (or trial) as a director.

It all sounds overly dramatic no doubt. The point is that Phillips got a very chilly welcome when he came over here from England to assume the position of artistic director of the Stratford Festival. The complaint was that there are plenty of Canadians who could do the job, and perhaps there are.

Moreover, Phillips is young and his reputation, while good enough, was made in Britain and is not monumental like that, for example, of Tyrone Guthrie. Phillips plunged ahead, attempting to rescue the repertory theater from the doldrums. Scuttlebutt had it that his position remained beleagured and unsettled.

It appears, though, that he is no mean hand at sly politics. The contesting faction of mostly veteran performers wonder the inplicit banner of William Hutt were given as much rope as might hang them. Which they did a fair job of opening night with a paralytic version of Shaw's "Saint Joan."

"Measure for Measure," then was Phillips' official debut on the big, and in many ways difficult Festival Stage. The debut is brilliant. One might want to play it safe by adding comparatively, but I'm not sure that's necessary.

It is, you see, quite easy to champion Phillips. For from the beginning he announced himself as enemy to the torpor and empty theatrics that had come to characterize performances at Stratford. And in a single stroke last evening, he substituted deed for word and established the quality of work he is out after.

At the conclusion, many in the audience leapt to their feet and shouted bravo and noisy approval, and for once it seemed they had every reason to be pleased. Anyone with any sense ought to be very happy Phillips is here.

An interesting irony concerns William Hutt, thought by many to be the heir-apparent displaced by Phillips' arrival. Hutt's performance as Vincentio is probably his finest in years on this particular stage. It also says a good deal about Hutt's dedication to his craft.

Overall the company outdoes itself. Actors not unfamiliar with the lacklustre performance shine in this one. I'm thinking perhaps of Richard Monette as Lucio, who is outstanding. Others who have done quite well in the past do even better under intelligent guidance. Martha Henry as Isabella comes immediately to mind.

Hand in hand, however, with everything Phillips' has talked about goes Brian Bedford's performance. Bedford plays Angelo, the central figure susceptible to law, power and corruption, and and an arch bureaucrat in Phillips' interpretation.

Every utterance by Bedford comes as though from the thoughts of Angelo. So that the vaunted diction required in Shakespeare evaporates as an issue. One is left listening in pure clarity to the mind of the speaker. Difficulties of comprehension simply go away.

In this--the temptation is to say feat, in light of all the flighty articulation usually flapping around in a Shakespeare production--Bedford raises goals for the company as a whole and lets the audience know they needn't fall into a sweat trying to pierce antique garble delivered at lightning speed. It's really a revelation.

DOWNEY, Roger Bayard; (2) Theater critic; (3) b. Princeton, British
Columbia, Canada, Aug. 18, 1937; (4) s. Ralph and Mina (Neuert)
D.; (5) U. of Chicago, 1957-61, no degree; U. of Washington, B.A.
1966, political science; U. of Washington Drama School, 1967-68,
no degree; (8) Actor, director, general manager, The Empty Space,
Seattle, Wa. 1972- ; columnist, The Argus (weekly newspaper),
1972- ; general purpose reviewer, The Everett Herald (daily newspaper), 1972-1974; Kulcher editor for a string of ephemeral "underground" papers; The Helix (1968-70), The New Times Journal (1971),
The Seattle Flag (1972); (9) writing, acting in, composing music for,
translating and directing plays at intervals since 1957; (10) Member,
Allied Arts Ad Hoc Committee for the Arts, Seattle, 1974 (lobbying
for state support for arts); (13) U.S. Army, RA 19708505, 1961-64;
Good Conduct medal (lost); (16) (libertarian socialist by upbringing
and disposition); (21) 1505 Lake Washington Boulevard, Seattle, Wa.
98122, Ph. 206-329-3033; (22) 6654 W-H-S Bldg., Seattle, Wa. 98101,
Ph. 206-682-1212; (23) Circulation: 7,500, 22,000 reached; (24) 50
screeds annually.

Staging of Pirandello Outstrips Play Itself
(by Roger Downey, Everett Herald, February 8, 1973)

A philosophical debate about the nature of truth--what could
be less effective in the theater? So you might think, until you
see Luigi Pirandello's "Right You Are! (If You Think You Are)"
in the production staged by Edward Payson Call.

In fact, I have a shrewd idea that there really isn't anything
very theatrical about the Italian author's play. The entire plot,
theme and point is summed up in the title: truth is relative, and
if you think you're right about something, you are right, and no
one has any business arguing with you.

Doesn't seem like much on which to build a 2-1/2-hour play,
does it? But wait until you see what Call--and the actors of the
University of Washington's Professional Training Program--do
with it.

It's Madame Aguzzi's day "at home" in a small provincial
Italian town, and the gossips are gathering. As the hot afternoon
sun seeps in through the curtains on Robert Dahlstrom's wonderful set, the townspeople gather to talk about the latest local mystery: a new clerk at the town hall who lives with his wife in a
tenement on the edge of town, and keeps his mother-in-law in a
fancy flat downtown ... and next door to his own superior's
apartment, at that!

When the neighborhood gossips have finally got the mystery
settled to their own satisfaction, who should turn up but the mother-in-law herself, to tell them that their solution to the problem
is all wrong. As soon as she leaves, in comes the son, to tell
everybody to forgive the old lady, because she is a little, well
... weak in the head, and ...

So it goes, for the three full acts--mysteries inside mysteries, like chinese boxes. It could be terribly thin, but, in
Call's capable hands the suspense grows and grows. Even though
we know that the author is playing philosophical games with us,
the dramatic tension grows to a climax.

Call's specialty may be suspense (he directed the fine version of "Child's Play" for the Seattle Repertory Theater), but
here he has outdone himself, giving body and substance to a
thesis drama, and a thin one at that. He has a wonderful gift
for finding exactly the right grouping of figures, just the right
stage picture, to express the meaning of the moment. The climax of the play--when the walls roll back and display The Truth--
is simply terrific.

Call's actors do him proud, especially Demetra Pittman as
the mother-in-law and Tom Spiller as the son, with Donald Bear-
don fine as the sardonic mouthpiece for the author, Laudisi.
Pirandello, at least as far as this play is concerned, has gotten
better than he deserved.

AFT Bill "The Homecoming" Lavish, Disguised Meringue
(by Roger Downey, Everett Herald, December 8, 1973)

Harold Pinter's "The Homecoming," the third in the series
of eight plays-made-movies presented by the American Film Theater, runs four performances Monday and Tuesday at the Everett
Theater and the Lynn Theater in Lynnwood. Purely as a production, it is the best so far.

Both of the AFT's earlier films--Albee's "A Delicate Balance,"
and O'Neill's "The Iceman Cometh"--fell somewhat short of their
high aspirations. Both contained weak performances in central
roles--Hepburn and Remick in "Balance," Lee Marvin in "Iceman"--and "Balance" suffered as well from a distracting and zom-
bie-like camera technique and abominable sound. "The Homecoming" was shot by Peter Watkin, the same man who has to be
blamed for "Delicate Balance," but his work here is at the top
of his very able form; and the cast, much the same one which
director Peter Hall assembled for his Royal Shakespeare Company
production of the play a few years back, is magnificent. Even
more important, it is consistent, with no one performance standing out or falling short.

It's a good thing, for Pinter is above all an actor's playwright; you have only to read through a paragraph of his dialog
to feel the urge to recite it aloud. And "The Homecoming" is,
more than any of his other plays, totally dependent on great
acting to pull it off. There is almost literally nothing else going
on beyond acting.

Pinter, an actor himself, is stage-wise enough to know that
actors require a situation, too, not just words. So he gives

them situations: eerie, melodramatic confrontations, in which
hate and fear and loathing sizzle between the characters like heat
lightning.

Unfortunately all they are is situations. They don't arise
out of any human relationships between the characters, or even
any moral pre-occupation of the author. Pinter's plays are
value-free as well as plot free. The ways his people behave have
nothing to do with the way you or I do, but only with what will
make theatrically effective "moment."

The effect of this is that the looming menace of each scene
seems wildly exaggerated compared to the situation which produces it, so behind every curse and innuendo that the five men
in Pinter's North London family utter lurks potentially the snick--
er of farce.

Actors realize this instinctively, and protect themselves:
Pinter performers nearly always "camp," ever so slightly. In
"The Homecoming," Paul Rogers is wonderful as the old Dad of
the family, spewing contempt impartially among his sons ... so
wonderful that you don't notice at first that from time to time he
is also playing Mum, going into drag without changing his costume.

And so on, throughout the cast: Michael Jayston, as the
Ph. D. brother back from America on a visit, maintains a fixed,
faint smile straight through events so humiliating and repulsive
that he becomes fascinating. Each time another blow falls we
look over at him to see if this will make him crack. Buster
Keaton knew the same trick.

Terence Rigby gets his effects by playing the boxer son as
someone so dumb that he could ignore an earthquake, and Ian
Holm by putting elegant, invisible quotation marks around every
word he says. Cyril Cusack seems slightly uncomfortable as
the chauffeur uncle, but uses his discomfort like that produced
by an itch which cannot be scratched without a breach of etiquette.
His discomfort is understandable: the part is something of a
fifth wheel. Even Pinter seems aware of that, in his vague way.
He has the character spend the last 15 minutes of the play lying
inexplicably on the floor.

Vivien Merchant (Mrs. Pinter) repeats the performance for
which she became famous as Ruth, the slut-prophetess-wife of
the professor. It's very well done, but the most remarkable
thing about the performance is how well she does in a part 20
years too young for her. The camera is cruel.

In sum, then, "The Homecoming" is stylish entertainment
of no substance at all--a lavish-looking meal which turns out,
on tasting, to consist entirely of cunningly disguised meringue.
Light, but not filling.

DRAKE, Sylvie (nee Sylvie Franco); (2) Theater critic; (3) b. Alexandria, Egypt, Dec. 18, 1930; (4) d. of Robert Franco and Simonette (Barda); (5) English Girls' College, Alexandria, Egypt; immigrated to the U.S., Aug. 1949; MTA Pasadena Playhouse; (6) m. Ken Drake, April 29, 1952, divorced in 1972; m. Ty Jurras, June 16, 1973; (7) children--Myriam Jessica and Robert Ira; (8) acted Off Broadway 1950; acted and directed at Stage Society in Los Angeles 1953-56; translated Claudel's "Tidings Brought to Many," Anouilh's "Traveler without Luggage"; joined the Writers' Guild of America in 1960; wrote for television 1960-67; drama critic for the Los Angeles Canyon Crier 1968-71; worked on assignment for the Los Angeles Times 1969-71; joined drama staff as full-time columnist and critic for the Los Angeles Times; (21) 4901 Densmore Ave., Encino, Calif. 91436, Ph. 213-986-1362; (22) L.A. Times, Times Mirror Square, Los Angeles, Calif. 90053, Ph. 213-625-2345; (23) Circulation: over 1 million; (24) Reviews approximately 75 plays and musicals per year in addition to about 100 columns and periodic features and interviews.

A New Twist to "Old Times"
(by Sylvie Drake, Los Angeles Times, January 20, 1975)

The Actors' Studio's on-again, off-again promise of a season of productions seems finally seriously on. The lovely old William S. Hart home on De Longpre (West Hollywood), where the group of Strasberg disciples is headquartered, has been spruced up. Some parking is now offered at the top of the steep driveway (and handled well by attendants with flashlights). The entrance to the theater has been moved to the east side of the building--past the box office and up an inviting garden path. And intermission hospitality is dispensed warmly in the main house beside a roaring fire.

Things would seem off to a good start--until time comes to see the play. It happens to be Harold Pinter's "Old Times"-- perhaps his most spare and most intriguing piece, richly layered with unexpressed meaning, double-entendre, enigmatic silences, lean, long pauses that speak more than words, even when their meaning is not clear--indeed, often because their meaning is not clear. It is, viewed from this corner, Pinter at his rarefied best--a magnetic jigsaw puzzle with pieces that don't quite fit, cerebral in concept, emotional in impact, witty, wistful, angular and open.

That is, at any rate, how I remember the play. It's not what actors Sandra Seacat, Will Hare and Hildy Brooks are serving up on the Studio stage--a difference, I hasten to add, in which these actors take considerable pride.

Supervising director Arthur Penn states in a program note that, in this production, "at last 'Old Times' makes sense. It is," he goes on, "the richness of the inner life between these people that makes this play ... so extraordinary--not the emptiness that critics always seem to emphasize."

What the actors have done here (Penn insists the performers must take major responsibility for their work) is fill in those long pauses and gaps with concrete information--a specific "inner life" dredged up via the "method" (a Studio hallmark) from the actors' own horizons--and with junky clutter: busy business, a sea of superfluous props in perpetuo mobile and specific sullen "meaning."

Far from elucidation, this "Old Times," imported from the New York branch of the Studio, provides only a narrow and largely Freudian imitation of that exciting, elusive shadow play that Pinter wrote and, I believe, intended. This production is the deadly subjugation of imagination to explicit, dull events--the shackling of inspired possibilities in favor of uninspired fact.

The imagination is robbed blind, beginning with Marc Meyer's set, which is a cluttered, homey living room in Act I and, in Act II, a seedy bedroom dialogue to the contrary, with a pair of Salvation Army single beds separated by tables covered by a glut of pillboxes. Lest the deeper significance of this dredged-up inner life should escape even the brightest member of the audience, Anna (Hildy Brooks) shakes a disapproving head, not once but several times, at that barbituric sea.

Worse yet, the production is singularly unpleasant to experience, its poor judgment often compounded by bad taste. The fleeting, erotic innuendos of the Pinter text are reduced here to the gaucherie of Will Hare (as Deeley) impulsively dropping his pants with a coarse, raucous laugh. It's an extreme example but it epitomizes the demoralizing choices made at the Studio.

From the point of view of craft, Hare's thick British dialect (Northumberland?), not matched by the ladies, seems curiously out of place, although technically there is no rule against it. Both he and Hildy Brooks, who have some singing to do are so tentative about it that it is hard to tell whether they are merely timid or cannot carry a tune. In any case, it doesn't work. Sandra Seacat as Deeley's wife Kate is so understated that the smile becomes vacant instead of enigmatic.

Miss Brooks is the strongest, or at least the most subtle performer of the three, but given the interpretation they have all opted for, her potential is never fully realized. (I'd love to see her in another production.) Rarely does one believe that Kate and Deeley are husband and wife. They relate to one another only superficially--another reason why they lack interest.

A psychologist I know was asked once if he practiced in the Freudian or Jungian tradition. He answered that he had learned to use whatever theories worked best, including plain horse sense.

Perhaps it's time for some of this wisdom to infiltrate the

Actors' Studio.   Many more productions like this one could give
the "method" a bad name.

Marceau: That Says It All
(by Sylvie Drake, Los Angeles Times, February 27, 1975)

Like a Santa Claus stripped of paunch, of habit, of clumsy
jollity, Marcel Marceau is back in town, his languid arms laden
with new gifts, his soul on an ever-ascending spiral of grace.
Another step, another silent measure upward and this man of
blood and sinew must surely become spirit.

There were moments Tuesday, during his opening performance at the Shubert, when he almost did.   It felt as if the
transmutation--eerie, dazzling, inscrutable--were about to begin.
That it did not, that Marceau was still solidly there at the end
to bow respectfully at the intense and genuine standing ovation
that greeted him, seemed the true miracle.

The unexpected aspect of Marceau's current appearance at
the Shubert is that it is different: in content to a large degree
(he has indeed brought much excellent new material), but also in
emotional texture, which is harder to explain.   It seems as
though Marceau is practicing his eloquence on a new spiritual
wavelength.   Call it a mystical maturity, a deepening sense as
well as expression of grace.   The poetry in the motion has gone
from Shelley to Keats, remaining inexorably precise and inextri-
cably woven into the humane antics of such early models as Chaplin, Keaton, Langdon.

How does one break it down?   The first half, devoted to
what Marceau calls "Style pantomimes," is overwhelmingly new--
at least to this writer.   It offers tone poems ("The Dress--
Memories of a Past Love," "The Creation of the World"), a remarkable free-form composition ("Contrasts"), a brilliant new
bit of existential fantasy ("The Pickpocket's Nightmare") along
with a balancing assortment of light verse ("The Bill Poster,"
"The Dice Players," "The Small Cafe").

The second half, as usual, is given over to the misadventures of Marceau's alter ego.   Bip--part Little Tramp, part
Walter Mitty.   A splendid train sequence ("Bip Travels by Train")
and a delicious encounter with figment of his imagination ("Bip as
a Matador") accompany the more familiar "Bip at a Society Party".

Also present are the perennial anchors of the repertoire:
"The Maskmaker" and "David and Goliath"--both, if possible,
more astonishing than ever.

But more than what he does, it's how he does it that you
want to talk about, because Marceau has achieved a virtuosity of
execution that seriously borders on perfection.   Is it conceivable,
for instance, that in a drunk scene he manages to express his

queasiness by such a barely perceptible loss of balance that you actually see the stage moving and Marceau standing still? Yet it happens and this must be the stuff genius is made of--an exaggeration of reality so knowing, precise and controlled that it makes an imprint far greater than the reality itself.

These exceedingly subtle refinements are what project Marceau's extraordinary physical vocabulary beyond the mere pleasurable massaging of the senses into a far more remarkable exhumation of the soul--yours, along with his. You do not observe Marceau. You experience him--every contortion of the nimble body, every darting look, or compassionate gesture, each wan retraction of the lips, each undulating motion of the languorous, liquid hand.

Costume, the clean bare stage, the precise and loving prologues of cardbearer Pierre Verry, even the size of the black space around him, serve merely to set off the laser presence of this unparalleled master.

There is a Japanese distinction I have long admired that the French would now be well-advised to beg, borrow or steal; it is the tradition of honoring their great artists by designating them National Living Treasures. Marcel Marceau is an International Living Treasure--and he's only at the Shubert for three weeks.

Hurry.

DRESSER, Norman; (2) Theater-movie-TV-book critic; (3) b. Mine La Motte, Mo., Nov. 18, 1916; (4) s. Clarence G. and Katharine (Thorpe) Dresser; (5) Attended U. of Iowa and U. of London (England); majors: journalism and literature; (6) m. Josephine Walsh, Feb. 19, 1959; (7) children--David S., Andrew; (8) Cub reporter, St. Louis Post-Dispatch, 1944-45; rewriteman, Columbus (Ga.) Ledger, 1945-46; state editor, Sunday editor, Mansfield (O.) News Journal, 1946-48; Sunday section editor, Peach section editor, Toledo (O.) Blade, 1948-66; entertainment editor, The Blade, 1967- ; (19) Mem. Press Club, Toledo, and Sigma Delta Chi; (21) 2860 Inwood Dr., Toledo, O. 43606, Ph. 419-474-4167; (22) The Blade, 541 Superior St., Toledo, O. 43604; Ph. 419-259-7280; (23) Circulation: 175,000 D., 210,000 S.; (24) 30 plays and musicals, 150 movies, 100 television, 40 books, 10 miscellaneous.

A Strayed "Love's Labour's Lost"
(by Norman Dresser, The Blade, June 24, 1974)

"Love's Labour's Lost" has been led astray from the Shakespearean period to the 19th century French Second Empire in the new Stratford Festival production. The result is an opulent but too precious comedy of manners.

Not that the evening is a complete failure for the discriminating playgoer. It's always a pleasure to renew acquaintances

with the thoroughly professional Stratford players and to let the
senses luxuriate in the lovely Festival Theater on the banks of
the Avon, flowing softly through the little Ontario town which has
become a major theatrical capital of the world.

But, let's face it, "Love's Labour's Lost" is a rather curious choice for one of the major productions at this year's festival. It is an extremely dated comedy with a fanciful plot of little appeal to the contemporary audience, its only saving grace
being patches of witty dialogue amid the labored romanticism of
the tale.

As if recognizing the essential antiquity of the plot, director
Michael Bawtree has dandied up the piece with the transition to
a flossy Second Empire period. He has also blended in some
lushly romantic music which also helps camouflage the aridity
of the basic idea. The result is a comedy that is all style and
little substance.

It is a tribute to the talented Stratford performers and the
incomparable backstage crew that this comedy is more fun to
watch then to write about. Such players as William Hutt, Nicholas Pennell, Pat Galloway, and Pat Bentley-Fisher are incapable
of delivering bad performances.

And the show was a visual delight, with the ladies fetching
indeed in swirling Second Empire gowns, gay hats, and pretty
parasols and the men in colorful coats, skin-tight pants, and
silk top hats or plumed headgear.

Hutt, an actor of great style and wit, was a standout as Don
Armado, a quixotic, slow-moving, stately old Spanish soldier.
In the romantic lead, Pennell was an improbably handsome courtier who delivered his lines with such flair you almost forgot the
silliness of many of them. Pat Galloway, Pennell's inamorata,
was impressive. And in the small role of a lusty country wench,
Miss Bentley-Fisher was a delight, rolling her saucy eyes and
waving her little red tongue between her lips.

Powys Thomas, a usually dependable actor, was disappointing
as Holofernes, the dandified schoolmaster, and Brian Petchey
seemed miscast somewhat as the king of Navarre. Mervyn Blake
was far from dull as Dull, the constable.

The ornate plot, not one of Shakespeare's better comedy vehicles, concerns what happens when King Ferdinand persuades
three of his friends in court to take a vow of monastic celibacy
and devote themselves to study for three years.

Their intentions are almost immediately put to the test when
the Princess of France arrives with three beautiful ladies of the
court, and romance flowers.

Love letters are exchanged, complications follow when letters are delivered to the wrong swains, and there is a masquerade in which each of the princely cohorts pays court to the wrong masked lady.

The play ends on a rather sober and inconclusive note as the impetuous suitors are told they must hie off to a hermitage "and there stay until the 12 celestial signs have brought about their annual reckoning" (a flowery phrase for one year) before learning if the ladies return their love.

It is dialogue such as that just quoted which all too often makes "Love's Labour's Lost" a dull exercise. There is enough genuine wit about the eternal battle between the sexes sprinkled through this comedy to make it occasionally enjoyable. But there are long stretches of tedium, especially in the 1-1/2-hour first act.

Dinner Theatergoers Enjoy "I Do! I Do!"
(by Norman Dresser, The Blade, January 3, 1975)

"I Do! I Do!" does very nicely indeed, thank you.

This witty and sentimental musical chronicling the joys and tribulations of marriage opened New Year's eve at the Westgate Dinner Theater and it was truly cause for celebration among theater lovers. A near-capacity audience greeted the show with delight.

Although "I Do! I Do!" is a simple musical in concept and design, with but a single set and a cast--count 'em--of just two, it's by no means an easy show to stage. Its very simplicity poses artistic challenges for the director and cast.

It is, therefore, a pleasure to report that the production is virtually flawless, and the cast, in the persons of Stephen Arlen and Gaylea Byrne, turn in superb performances. Arlen and Miss Byrne won the hearts of the audience with their fine acting and singing. The standing ovation they received at the end of the show was thoroughly deserved.

Arlen and Miss Byrne are not big names in show business, although each has a rich and varied theatrical background. But they're strictly pros, and interesting chemistry was bubbling between them from the opening scene to the final blackout.

"I Do! I Do!" is adapted from Jan de Hartog's heart-warming comedy, "The Fourposter," and covers 50 years of a marriage, from the wedding night a century ago to the 50th anniversary celebration. The single set is dominated by a fourposter bed.

In mood, the show ranges from joyous exuberance to poignant sadness. It's a mark of the stars' talents that they struck
the right note throughout in a show with a wide range of emotions.

Tom Jones' book and lyrics and the music by Harvey Schmidt
mirror accurately de Hartog's original drama. Jones and
Schmidt, who created that smash musical, "The Fantasticks,"
have written some lovely tunes for this show, ranging from the
rather sad "Where Are the Snows?" to the richly comic "Flaming Agnes."

Perhaps the most memorable song is "My Cup Runneth
Over," which has become something of a pop classic. Worthy
of mention also are the haunting "What Is a Woman?", sung with
sweet charm by Miss Byrne; "I Love My Wife," robustly performed by Arlen, and "Someone Needs Me."

Arlen, a native of Wales, has the rich, strong voice pro-
verbially associated with Welshmen. His diction, both when
singing lyrics and speaking his lines, is clear and fluid.

Miss Byrne vocalizes with feeling and radiates a sweetness
and charm which makes her perfect casting for the role of
Agnes. Her voice and acting reflect years of training and professional work on Broadway and throughout the world.

"I Do! I Do!" ranks as an excellent vehicle for dinner theater. It is an intimate show, ideal for the thrust stage and the
small house of the Westgate.

The excellent set was designed by Ray Pentzell, associate
professor of theater at the University of Toledo. Musical direct-
or Steve Skorija worked with two other musicians, including Toledo's John Thone, at the rear of the stage, separated from the
stage by a cunningly designed set of folding doors. The three-
piece combo was just right for this intimate production.

"I Do! I Do!" marks the second production by Ken Shaw's
Westgate Dinner Theater and clearly proves that Shaw's new theatrical venture has class written all over it. I didn't believe
that Shaw could top his first show, "Once More, with Feeling,"
but he has.

Theatergoers with good memories may recall that Shaw
opened the Masonic Auditorium in October, 1969, with his American Theater League production of "I Do! I Do!" starring Mimi
Hines and Phil Ford. The current show is in many respects a
better one.

DREW, Michael, Milwaukee Journal, 333 W. State St., Milwaukee,
Wis. 53201.

DULZER, Marie Ann; (2) Theater Critic; Professor of Speech and
Theater; (3) b. Cleveland, July 10, 1935; (4) d. Edward and Sophia
(Grill); (5) B.A. Marymount College, Salina, Kan., maj. subj.:
speech and theater, 1958; M.A. U. of Arizona, maj. subj.: speech,
1963; (6) single; (8) Music and Drama Editor, Times Herald Record
(Middletown, N.Y.) 1973- ; Assoc. Prof. of Speech and Theater,
Orange County Community College, Middletown, N.Y. 1966- ; (9) Apprentice, Cleveland Playhouse, 1958-59, Director of over 20 college
productions, 5 children's productions; Director College Lyceum Cultural Series 1970-72; Producer - Director College Summer Theaters,
1972, 1974; Founder, Producer, Director "Jelly Bean Playhouse" for
children 8 - 12, 1973- ; Consultant to Orange County Recreation Program 1970- ; (14) Who's Who in American Colleges, 1958; Who's Who
in Education, 1969; (15) American Theater Assoc.; (16) Democrat;
(17) Roman Catholic; (20) Articles to National Thespian, Arizona
Speech Assoc. Jrnl., 1962, 1964; reviews, weekly cultural calendar
listings, op. ed., analyses, features; (21) 42 Mountain Ave., Middletown, N.Y. 10940, Ph. 914-342-5718; (22) 40 Mulberry St., Middletown, N.Y. 10940, Ph. 914-343-2181; (23) Circulation: 60,000; (24)
40 plays and musicals, 20 entertainment (arena - night club), 5 dance.

He's Come a Long Way from "The Nutty Professor"
(by Marie Ann Dulzer, Times Herald Record, August 7, 1975)

"First time I ever got a starting ovation," quipped Jerry
Lewis when the Candlewood Theatre crowd stood up to cheer the
comedian at his Monday night opening. His start however proved
better than the finished product.

The modified night club act presents an open, nice guy entertainer who quickly turns into an amplified, ear-splitting human
noisemaker. When he is funny, he is very funny, and when he
is bad, he is horrid. The real question of the evening turned
out to be material.

Lewis' overall comic spritz is lacking in this show, for his
material is more often geared to bathroom style humor, rather
than his forte, creative slap stick. The entire show from lead-
in singer Cathy Carlson to the back up big band lacks class, and
often taste.

Red-haired Miss Carlson's alternately gusty belt-sensual
purr song renditions are interspersed with poorly handled spontaneous comments. What should be easy, casual chatter comes
off as forced banter. It's always difficult to play warm-up for
a top name, but there is more strain in Miss Carlson's performance than can be attributed to the heat wave.

The Candlewood Theatre Orchestra is made up of the Hudson

Valley Philharmonic musicians recruited for the occasion. Their musical capabilities are certain, but their stage presence generates little rapport or response for the show. Strike two.

Lewis won his international reputation for his comic genius so evident in his early films. In 1959 he was a screen writer, producer, director and actor. Jerry Lewis Productions signed a contract with Paramount Productions which is still the biggest single transaction in film history for the exclusive of one star. The payment was $10,000,000 plus 60 per cent of the profits to star in fourteen films. His initial films such as the one about the joint U.S.-Russian space venture displayed a comic who could perform wild slap stick, quickly adapt to gentle pathos, and as quickly go to warm charm. Candlewood press releases call him a 20th century phenomenon.

He can sing, dance, throw out one-liners, play spontaneously off his audience, and make great use of surprise props. He snatches a giant flashlight to spot an audience member carried away with laughter; he assures you he can handle anything, then sucks on his king size pacificer. But his current material plays minimally to his strong points. This act is no challenge for Lewis' creativity.

The thin line between night club and theater entertainment is not the issue here. Sophisticated audiences now take most anything, but they are equally adept at recognizing tasteful entertainment. Lewis can get away with ogling a well endowed young singer in a "what's up front that counts" sketch. But the bathroom humor that keeps popping up throughout the evening is more suitable to a commercial for a personal product than theater entertainment.

Old pro Jerry Lewis is 50 years old, looks 30, and has the energy of a teenager. Surely his acknowledged slapstick talent can find better material for his remarkable creativity.

<u>Woodstock's "Prague Spring" an Unusual Musical</u>
(by Marie Ann Dulzer, Times Herald Record, August 15, 1975)

"History will freeze its golden moment," says Alexander Dubcek in the new musical "Prague Spring," now at the Woodstock Playhouse. In a very true sense, the rise and fall of Czech leader Dubcek is the golden moment authors Lee Kalcheim and Joseph Raposo have captured in this script.

The subject may seem unlikely for a cabaret style musical, but the script and lyrics by Kalcheim (a TV, film and theatre writer who's won an Emmy Award) supported by Raposo's music (Raposo composer of "Sing," many popular songs, and much of the "Sesame Street" music), does deliver its message.

Kalcheim said in an interview that the plight of Dubcek, and the marvelous Czech sense of humor, so often self depre-

cating, are major points in his script. Both these ideas were
projected in the production which opened Wednesday.

If anything, Dubcek the man, and the outside forces to which
he is subjected, are overemphasized, especially in the first act.
The build of events in duration seems more the problem than
number of events.

The Czech sense of humor is delightfully handled and the
clever lyrics of "The Guilty Song" and "Ivan Come Home" make
the play's message more easily palatable. These two songs are
marvelous, laughing-at-oneself pieces, but with emphatic meaning, basic to the script.

The Woodstock production of "Prague Spring" brings out the
best in the new script. The episodic work (it could be a find
movie) is performed cabaret style, with soft shoe, song, and
serious drama. Director Isaac Schambelan has exquisitely staged
the play, and it is his diversified movement and the fine acting
that often lets the overemphasized scenes be accepted by the audience.

Lewis Arlt, Joel Brooks, David Berman and Elliot Cukor are
expertly versatile in their many faceted roles with sufficiently diversified touches to make characters distinct. These young men
are adept at acting, and singing, and transform the Paster-Prian-
ti set of levels--into whatever locale is needed.

Linda Geiser, as the sole female performer, is adequate,
but was much too one-level and unsure in her performance opening night.

Dubcek is portrayed with great energy by Ben Slack. He
plays to the inner struggle of the man who expects political leaders to communicate with people, and laments when no one listens.
In trying to emphasize the human qualities of Dubcek, Slack often
energizes almost melodramatically in vocal emphasis and repetitious gesture. There is no doubt, however, that his performance
is moving and does evoke sympathy for Dubcek.

But shouldn't the audience feel more than sympathy for Dubcek's plight? He is so close to realizing his dream of a demo-
cratic-socialistic government for Czechoslovakia. He has loyalty
to his Russian ties, yet sees their dominance as a threat to his
government.

Dubcek resigns. He knows the score, but is forced to with-
draw from the game. How can the score change if one is not
playing, yet what alternatives if any, existed? "Leave me alone,"
says Dubcek.

The two-hour Kalcheim script has been performed at The
University of Rhode Island, and was read at the Eugene O'Neill
Playwright's workshop in Connecticut. It will next go to the

Cleveland Playhouse, one of the nation's first regional theaters.

It is exciting to see a promising new script, and experience the impact of the theatrical message, and whatever its problems, "Prague Spring" does make an impression.

ECKERT, Thor, Jr.; (2) Theater critic; (3) b. New York City, Nov. 14, 1949; (4) s. Thor and Jacqueline (McGowan) E.; (5) B.A. Colgate U., major: English, 1971; (6) single; (8) Head Copy Kid, The Christian Science Monitor, 1971-71; Communications Asst., Monitor Wire room, 1972-74; Boston Theater Critic, 1974 (started Jan.); adding Music Critic, Nov. 1974 as well; (15) Member, American Theater Critics Association; (16) Independent; (17) Christian Scientist; (21) 199 Massachusetts Ave., #514, Boston, Mass. 02115, Ph. 617-267-3473; (22) Christian Science Monitor, One Norway St., Boston, Mass. 02115, Ph. 617-262-2300, ext. 2320; (23) Circulation: 200,000; (24) 68 theater reviews; 65 music reviews; 11 movie reviews; 9 interviews; 12 misc. (appx. figures). Critic's Choice column every week.

EDWARDS, William J.; (2) Legit editor, critic, columnist; (3) b. Vincennes, Ind., Feb. 2, 1930; (4) s. Henry W. and Irene P. (Turner); (5) B.A., Indiana U., major subj: creative writing, 1957; (6) Divorced; (8) Staff writer, Evansville (Ind.) Courier, 1954-55; staff writer, Bloomington, (Ind.) Herald-Telephone, 1955-56; engineering writer 1957-63; Sports Editor, Anchorage (Alaska) Daily News, 1963-64; assistant sports editor, Bakersfield Californian, 1964-65; staff writer, wire editor, asst. managing editor, Alhambra (Calif.) Post-Advocate, 1965-66; staff writer-drama critic, 1966- ; (9) Iroquois Summer Theatre, Louisville, Ky., 1954; actor, Theatre-americana, Altadena, Calif., 1959-60; established Thiokol Theatre, Logan, Utah, 1962; independent stage actor, 1964-65; wrote book and lyrics for "Springtime and Stephanie," produced, 1957, at IU; currently studying musical comedy writing with Lehman Engel at BMI Musical Comedy Workshop; president, three terms, of L.A. Drama Critics Circle, 1971, 1973, 1974; (11) Ward work in Democratic Party; (13) U.S. Navy, 1948-52, yeoman second class; (15) Founder and member, L.A. Drama Critics Circle; (16) Democrat; (17) Roman Catholic; (20) Write crossword puzzle for Daily Variety; Mankind Magazine; West Coast Review of Books, freelance articles in Show Business, Mannikin; (21) 754 Maltman Ave., Los Angeles, Calif. 90026, Ph. 213-663-1485; (22) Daily Variety, 1400 N. Cahuenga Blvd., Los Angeles, Calif. 90028, Ph. 213-469-1141; (23) Circulation: 13,225-14,500; (24) Approximately 200-250.

A Streetcar Named Desire
(by Bill Edwards, Daily Variety, March 21, 1973)

Center Theatre Group Ahmanson has come up with the right combination of names for a boxoffice success, but those "names" have put together not much more than an artistic mediocrity. However, the play, Tennessee Williams, Jon Voight and Faye

Dunaway will doubtless sell the tickets.

"A Streetcar Named Desire" is such a special commodity, one of the truly great American plays that is so frequently done by all types of theatre groups, that it has become a classic on its own merits. And Williams' subsequent output has kept his name and reputation in the front ranks of American theatre, where it should remain.

Consequently, one wouldn't think much harm could be done to this play. Miss Dunaway is fascinating--at times--as the superdelicate Blanche DuBois whose nerves, or the lines in her face, cannot stand the stark light of an unshaded bulb. Miss Dunaway achieves the right balance of delicacy for certain scenes and becomes the timid, caged animal Blanche is. But in the next few scenes, she loses that balance and is Faye Dunaway acting at being Blanche.

Her confession about losing Belle Reve, the family home, is so matter of fact that Blanche might have been the woman down the street. But in her recollection of her lover and the few tender moments she has with Mitch, Miss Dunaway gives a heart-crushing performance. At times her portrayal is as beautiful as a southern belle dancing the varsoviana at a cotillion; at others it is like a competent actress reading cold for an audition.

Voight, on the other hand, has managed, with the help of director James Bridges, to make Stanley Kowalski insignificant. As written, Stanley is a crude, vulgar, wallowing, rutting animal whose interests are limited to poker, beer and uncontrolled sex; he is disgustingly fascinating.

Voight underplays him to the point of being a nice guy--completely alien to the character. Stanley Kowalski probably wouldn't have any patience with nice guys. Voight and the whole production are as soft as the lights Blanche tries to make by putting paper Japanese lanterns over the bare bulb in the Kowalskis' bedroom.

This characterization of Stanley is gutless. It's unbelievable that he could terrorize Blanche as played by Miss Dunaway. In her weakest moments, she could chew him up--in her strong moments, she could chew up the whole production and use her curtain call for a toothpick.

Miss Dunaway's unevenness might not be so noticeable, however, were it not for Lee McCain who is so precise and exactly right as Stella Kowalski. Miss McCain doesn't push her characterization, nor does she have to stretch to reach the right stride. Hers is a fine performance. Earl Holliman as Mitch doesn't have much of a chance. Against Voight he seems to have been restrained by Bridges; against Miss Dunaway he doesn't stand a chance.

Peggy Rea is outstanding as the woman upstairs and Jerome Guardino good as her husband.   Scott Colomby adds a nice touch as the newspaper delivery boy.

Bridges is to be blamed for the awkwardness and weaknesses of this production.   He has to shoulder the responsibility of such things as using the upstairs balcony as an entrance from the street--unless there's a stairway in the back of the house no one could get there without being seen.   It's also his fault that the highs and lows of the show are not properly spaced.

It is not his fault, however, that the audience laughed as if they were watching a farce.   Part of these unexpected laughs might have been the reason for Miss Dunaway's falling in and out of character.   But she has to take full responsibility for not selling Blanche's most poignant moment--when she fantasizes her death at sea, "a sea as blue as my first lover's eyes."   By no stretch of the imagination should that segment be funny, but part of it got laughs.

CTG has pulled out all stops on the physical production.   Robert Tyler Lee's unit set is one of a whole section of New Orleans' Latin Quarter--complete with utility poles looming up over rooftops.   Attractive though it may be, set could use an overhead cyclorama to keep some of the speeches from going up into the fly loft.   Ahmanson has enough problems with acoustics as it is.

Theodora Van Runkle's costumes are superb.   Not only do the Southern flimsy gowns fit Miss Dunaway's lithe figure, they personify the character of Blanche.   And the 1940s fashions are just right--even down to Stella's maternity middy.

H. R. Poindexter's lighting is quite complimentary and incidental music by Fred Werner, supervised by Gerhard Samuel, works very well.

Williams, who was in audience Monday night must have been appalled at what has happened to his play.   For those who've never seen a professional production of "Streetcar," this is an unfortunate introduction to a classic.   For the knowledgable theatregoer or thesp who's hankered after one of the meaty roles, this is a travesty.   But the irony is--it will probably make money.   Edwa.

Seagulls of 1933
(by Bill Edwards, Daily Variety, February 24, 1975)

Attention all legit producers.   Good theatre is still being written and scripts can be found being done in out-of-the-way houses like the Sherman Oaks Playhouse.   Tenants Actors Alley has unearthed a comedy by Frank Salisbury with the unlikely title "Seagulls of 1933" that cries out for a good commercial production.   With the proper treatment, this show could excel a lot of commercial pap that is taking Tonys and Drama Desk awards.

Although Actors Alley's production is tacky and in too many cases not well enough performed, one can see under the surface and find a genuinely human comedy with characters experiencing real emotions and relationships.

Salisbury's characters (not necessarily those portrayed by the actors) include an extremely wealthy brother and sister, he confined to a wheelchair only because his practical nurse treats him as if he's dying, and she swooping down on whatever beach they might be living at to sexually devour young men.

There's also an aspiring opera singer black maid who's instructed to act French, a crass school-teacher from Texas, an ingenuous hustler who's willing to please everybody, a designing blind daughter and a tres gay count who says of his yacht, "He's a very sturdy ship."

They're all found at a villa at Cap Ferrat where the nurse and the brother are about to be married because she's engineered it--not because of love. Schoolteacher has brought one of her stud students to Europe to broaden his horizons, but has been careful enough to pretend he is her son. The rich sister, of course, gloms on to him right away and they start bedding down behind teacher's back.

The practical nurse's practicality works against her when she brings her blind daughter from blind boarding school for the wedding. Invalid brother takes a shine to her and immediately starts walking. Sister's sexual sorties with the stud are put to a halt when the gay count proselytizes his services. And the maid just observes all these comings and goings.

Logan Ramsey directs show with a flair that keeps the pace brisk. Arthur Peterson is quite good as the invalid, Margaretta Ramsey excellent as the sexy sister whose motto seems to be "There's nothing like a good night's lack of sleep." George Cederberg shows much restraint with the role of the hustler, not letting the role get out of hand. And Carrie Dieterich gives a solid performance as the blind daughter. Vivian Tann has fun as the maid and shares that with the audience.

Less effective are Ruth Marcus as the teacher (whose role is the least defined); Doris Martin as the bland, unimaginative nurse who's never allowed any excitement in her life and when some happens around her she ignores it as it's not for her; and Sandy Ignon as the count who poses with a Count Dracula pout.

Salisbury writes intelligent comedy with poignant moments, allowing his characters a realness not often found in such comedies. When Dieterich says "Being blind is not all it's cracked up to be," it's not an outrageous black comedy line. It's a statement with meaning, but still gets a laugh. When the count, a miserably dissipated sybarite, confides to the hustler, "I'm going to tell you something I've never told anyone before--very often," it seems to be just what he would say--a snow job born out of loneliness.

Even the hustler, who recognizes his limitations (he'll be old and his body unsalable when he's 25), genuinely believes his mission in life is to serve those who need him most. To the count, he replies: "People like you are just as good as lepers."

Script is not 100% finished, but well on the way to being. None of the characters is a pasteboard-cutout, each is solid and three-dimension.

Production values are at a minimum. Makeshift sets and lighting with existing board at the rented theatre can tend to drag the show down, but with least amount of effort can be ignored. In this case the play's the thing.   Edwa.

EICHELBAUM, Stanley; (2) Journalist; (3) b. N.Y.C., Oct. 5, 1926; (4) s. Sam and Rebecca (Rosen); (5) B.A. magna cum laude, Coll. City N.Y. 1947; M.A., Columbia, 1948; Certificat d'Etudes, Sorbonne, Paris, France, 1949; (6) Unmarried; (8) Editorial researcher reporter New Yorker Mag., N.Y.C., 1949-58; with San Francisco Examiner, 1958- ; drama editor, critic plays and movies, 1961- ; (9) Membership selections com. San Francisco Internat. Film Festival; (10) Lectr. on arts, various colls., univs., clubs, 1961- ; Instru. workshop in critical writing U. Cal. Extension, San Francisco, 1968- ; (12) Mem. program San Francisco Art Inst., 1968-70. Mem. Cal. Hist. Soc.; (14) Phi Beta Kappa; (16) Democrat; (20) Reviews in San Francisco Examiner (daily); (21) 333 Green St., San Francisco, Cal. 94133; Ph. 415-434-2840; (22) San Francisco Examiner, 110 5 St., San Francisco, Calif., Ph. 415-781-2424; (23) Daily Circulation: 180,000; Sunday Circulation: 670,000; (24) 200 film reviews and 100 theater reviews.

A Bizarre Travesty of "King Richard III"
(by Stanley Eichelbaum, San Francisco Examiner, October 14, 1974)

Words are inadequate to describe William Ball's flamingly different production of "King Richard III," which opened ACT's new season Saturday night at the Geary and left the play and cast limp from heat exhaustion.

The bizarre travesty of Shakespeare's interpreted history of Richard's murderous ascent to the British throne is the boldest and wildest revisionism we've had from Ball. It's certain to provoke violent controversy.

While there's never a dull moment, I can't say I liked it and I suspect many are going to loathe it.

A Ball production in spades, it slashes the play to the bone, omitting whole scenes and reducing important characters to shadows, yet it reaches beyond the text with all sorts of exotic invention.

You might call it Ball's personal vision of "Richard III," for he's moved the bloody melodrama into a psychosexual dream world enclosed in a black void below which sits an armor-plated battleship turret. Above this hangs a huge metal sculpture symbolizing the British crown.

What transpires in Robert Blackman's setting is a Felliniesque freak show, a carnival of carnage also suggesting samurai and kung-fu films, and filled with weird and fantastical creatures.

Costume designer Robert Fletcher threw caution to the wind, presumably at Ball's instigation. The play's royal personages parade and prance about in a mad blaze of low-camp fashion. The men are mostly fops who wear cod-pieces the size of grapefruit. And the women are either frizzy-haired grotesques who flash more breast than hookers, or raving hags, like the witches in "Macbeth."

Portraying the deformed, villainous Richard is Randall Duk Kim, a compelling and accomplished Korean-American actor, whose effectiveness is sharply curtailed by Ball's baroque staging.

Kim, for example, must signal Richard's determination "to dream upon the crown" by stretching toward the symbolic sculptured crown. And if that weren't already excessive, Ball later makes him jump up and swing from it.

The coronation scene is something else again. Richard's throne is a metal ladder, and the treacherous king's new wife, Lady Anne (Hope Alexander-Willis), crouches beneath him at the end of a long chain, a hideous dog collar around her neck.

A flashier example of how the plag is vulgarized is Richard's karate duel with Richmond, immediately following the doomed king's cry, "My kingdom for a horse."

Richmond trots in bare-chested, looking like a unicorn, and since Randall Smith, who plays him, is a dead ringer for Marc Singer, we're right back in last season's "Taming of the Shrew."

As in that production, Ball hasn't resisted burlesque comedy. Even the subtle Richard and his clever henchman, Buckingham (Raye Birk), turn into vaudeville clowns.

The acting level is very uneven, with some atrocious work by young newcomers to the company. But Ball's direction is in black-and-white terms of good guys and bad guys, not the most suitable approach to Shakespeare's ingeniously written play.

We are privileged, in any event, to have the unusually talented Kim in ACT. He won high acclaim with the New York Shakespeare Festival. And his commanding presence in the role of the tyrant-king gives Ball's production a powerful lift.

Ball graciously dedicated the opening-night performance to Paine Knickerbocker, my worthy colleague and good friend, whose retirement as the Chronicle critic two weeks ago filled me with great sadness.

A Potent Dirge for the Sixties
(by Stanley Eichelbaum, San Francisco Examiner, December 16, 1975)

"Kennedy's Children," one of the more rewarding entries of the current Broadway season, is a strange, spellbinding play with a strange history.

It originated off-off-Broadway and disappeared after a two-week run in 1973, re-emerging the next year in London, where it's been a major hit.

The play is an American examination of shattered hope in the aftermath of the Kennedy sixties. And its success may be attributed to veteran British director Clive Donner, whose films include "Nothing But the Best" and "What's New, Pussycat?" He staged the London and New York productions--no small feat because of the tricky format utilized by author Robert Patrick.

Patrick is a Texan who worked at odd jobs in New York's coffee-house theaters before he turned to playwriting. He made little impact with his early experimental works ("The Haunted Host," "Camera Obscura"), but came to full realization with "Kennedy's Children," a powerful, beautifully written barroom drama that's unusual for letting five characters speak their mind without ever speaking to each other.

The setting is a well-stocked East Village bar named Phebe's, where the protagonists congregate on a rainy afternoon in 1974. They drink and talk, but their words are meant only for the audience and reflect the shared disillusion of these onetime Kennedy children, whose monologues are cross-currents of personal memory about the decline of the sixties into a hell of moral, political and social decay.

Patrick's play is remarkable for the shattering honesty of his viewpoint. He doesn't hesitate to lay the blame on his own generation for some of the horrors that befell this country after drugs and commercial interests took over the counterculture and obliterated the idealism of the Kennedy era.

His dirge for the sixties is a thoughful, affecting, poetic and droll comment on people's vulnerability and failure to come to grips with their own neurotic tendencies.

Four of his characters are losers and loners. The exception
is a buxom, sad-eyed woman, played by Barbara Montgomery,
who did not at least drop out (she works for an ad agency) when
her dreams of Camelot crumbled. She nonetheless grieves for
those halcyon years and regrets the passing of "a time when
everyone loved someone."

The most ravaged of the five, Michael Sacks, is a junkie
Vietnam veteran, whose burned-out mind is filled with the guilt
and paranoia of his war experience.

The other characters are better drawn and more interesting
and are made especially memorable by three outstanding performances.

Shirley Knight is smashingly effective as a would-be sex god-
dess--a failed actress whose downfall began not with John Kennedy's assassination, but with Marilyn Monroe's death.

She sought to replace Marilyn, but her world collapsed when
film stars went out of style and she became just another piece
of "automated, undulating, available, eager meat." Describing
her downhill slide from go-go dancer to whore, she reeks of self-
pity and suicidal despair. Yet she's able to toss off amusingly
bitchy gibes, like her crack about the gay men she's known, who
became the drag queens of today's new femininity.

Miss Knight gives one of her finest performances as the
pathetic sexpot. And equally brilliant is a young actress named
Kaiulani Lee, who movingly plays a sixties' hippie transformed
from a Haight-Ashbury flower child to an East Village misfit.

She tells how she read Allen Ginsberg when she was "just
a little kid," how she was a charter member of SNCC and the
SDS and how she fought with the activists in Chicago, only to be
rejected by the new militants. "The blacks don't need us," she
sighs. "The Indians don't want us. And the Haight-Ashbury,
where I once pushed speed during the day and worked for a drug-
rehabilitation program at night, has turned into an urban slum."

Finally, she shouts, "I hate the sixties!" and dissolves into
tears for her wasted youth.

The last of the quintet is Don Parker, divertingly cast as
a homosexual actor whose remarkably unsuccessful career has
taken him from the off-off-Broadway coffee houses, where he
was somebody, to nothing more noteworthy than an all-male musical of "Lysistrata."

The play, in essence, is a touching, funny collage of disenchantment with the damned decade that has so strongly influenced
the present one. It's written with sure, solid skill and Donner's
staging of the monologues is resourceful and even quite ingenious,
there being no moment when the private talk falters in interest.

ELKIN, Michael; (2) Critic and entertainment editor of Jewish Exponent; (3) b. Philadelphia, June 7, 1949; (4) s. Harry (deceased) and Rose (Kramer); (5) B.S. Journalism, Temple U., 1970; (6) m. Maxine Edelson, Aug. 11, 1974; (8) Religious editor, Jewish Exponent, 7-72 to 9-72; editor-in-chief, Greater Philadelphia Publishing Co., 10-72 to 11-72, entertainment editor, Jewish Exponent, 12-72 to present; (16) Democrat; (20) Contributed articles to "Discover Magazine" and to entertainment section of "Evening Bulletin," book reviewer for "Philadelphia Inquirer"; (21) Meadows at Lower Gwynedd; (22) 1513 Walnut St., Phila., Ph. 569-4100; (23) Circulation: 70,000 weekly; (24) 65 reviews.

"The Jockey Club Stakes"
(by Michael Elkin, Jewish Exponent, January 12, 1973)

"Theeeere they go. It's the Marquis on the outside, followed by Lord Cloverly. And running last is the Colonel. Headed toward the stretch, the Colonel is moving up, here comes the Colonel. And the winnah ..."

Wilfred Hyde-White, Geoffrey Sumner and Robert Coote are a lovable, bumbling, devious triumvirate of jockey club nobility in a race for laughs, devoted to keeping England's racing world scrupulous. And as "The Jockey Club Stakes" bears out, this triumvirate rivals only the Roman triumvirate of Caesar and firends for back-handedness, sly maneuvers and surprise followed by shock.

How these three old men, who by the looks of them either should have been put out to pasture or shot, control this English import with their stylish humor and tactful use of the play's witty dialogue, even while the show gets bogged down in sub-sub-sub-plot, attests to their talent.

In past seasons, trans-Atlantic flights of humor have somehow lost control of the fun on the way over. American audiences, who have heard critics rave about "the West End smash that should be a must for every legitimate theater-goer," have sometimes found the raves to be, at the least, illegitimate. "There's a Girl in My Soup" brought yuks in London and yawns here. "Pajama Tops," a show dedicated to June Wilkenson's top-heavy performance, proved to be a worthless bit of comedic foreplay, climaxing in nothing but wasted money.

So, after bouts with clipped words and pauses for laughter which never came American audiences grew weary of shelling out money for plays which could not transverse provincialism.

Discouraged by American critics such as William Goldman, who had said the best English play cannot approach a good American play, American audiences expected boredom from English shows which arrived here described as "comedies of manners." After all, this country's theatergoers have been bred on quicknes fast changes of scenery, fast-paced comedies, rapid changes of characters--"Golden Boy," "Star Spangled Girl" and "Fiorello" are prime examples. But maybe recent English successes, such as "Sleuth," a slowly-evolved mystery of horrors which so fascinated the American public, proved an English play can slow down the audience's tempo a bit and succeed.

Home, like "Sleuth's" author Anthony Schaeffer, uses time as a tool of trade, interspersing words with pauses to allow the dialogue to take full effect, allowing characters to draw out reactions, as the audience draws out the laughs. It is a fascinating use of timing.

Reactions to this play by English and American audiences differ only in the Englishman's "ho-ho"s and the the American's "ha-ha"s, for the play's humor and style are universal.

William Douglas Home, whose brother, Sir Alec Douglas Home lost a prime ministership, has received an overwhelming vote of applause wherever he has taken "The Jockey Club Stakes," and Philadelphia is no exception.

"Raisin," "Jacques Brel"
(by Michael Elkin, Jewish Exponent, September 21, 1973)

Shout hallelujah and shake the walls with the power of your shouting, 'cause the Walnut Street Theater has itself a winner.

"Raisin" has the air booming with supersonic blasts of energy and dynamite. Savor the booms of explosions of excitement in your soul and don't try to stop the feet from tap-tapping out the music because you'll find they have souls of their own.

The swinging sensitive musical adaptation of Lorraine Hansberry's "A Raisin in the Sun" starts the season with a snap of the fingers and high-kicking high Cs. The opening number, beautifully choreographed by Donald McKayle, who also directed, is a frenzy-paced account of life bursting in the ghetto streets and sets the story line for a smooth production of a black family's struggle in a white man's world. McKayle has instilled black magic into his high kicks, turns and pirouettes, conjuring up images of years of struggling and tension to the span of two and one half hours and the confinements of the stage's street.

"A Raisin in the Sun" was a successful literal transposition of the black's life from street to stage. James Baldwin said, "Never before in the entire history of the American theater had so much of the truth of the black people's lives been seen on the stage." Miss Hansberry's play introduced a new black audience to the Great White Way and opened doors for future black dramatists, such as Jones, Ward and Elder, to express their anger, rather than keeping their words to themselves in the darkness of isolation. Recent theater has not had that many master-

pieces to tamper with and anything short of a masterful musical
version would have detracted from a significant play and would
have been demeaning to the memory of Miss Hansberry.

However, her husband Robert Nemiroff, who produced and
co-authored "Raisin" and linked Miss Hansberry's letters and
ideas into the successful "To Be Young, Gifted and Black," has
built "Raisin" as an energy-packed memorial to his wife, whose
energy could only be stopped by the cancer she died from in
1965. Although some of the situations in the show that existed
at its writing in the '50s no longer are as relevant, and the show
needs some tightening, "Raisin" is a musically and literarily
poignant expression of the black experience.

Lyricist Robert Brittan, who wrote the English lyrics to the
Israeli song "Bashana Haba'ah," and composer Judd Woldin wove
the words and music into a fine tapestry of soft beauty.   The
lyrics are so well integrated that they are really part of the
script and it just so happens that some pretty funky music has
come along to accompany them on their way to the audience, although the songs too often blend into each other.   "Not Anymore," concerning the black family's (Younger) "welcome" into
an all white neighborhood is caustically funny and provides bittersweet afterthoughts.

Joe Morton is a dynamic Walter Lee Younger, whose fight
against working and bowing to the Man is a tense bout of a man
swinging blindly in a ring without ropes.   His voice adds power
to already searing lyrics and his answer to his mother, "You
Done Right," is a chilling reflection of a man who also has lost
out to his family.   His anger is chained down by his inadequacies
to defeat life and Morton plays him beautifully.

Virginia Capers, as Mama, adds a wonderful dimension of
tenderness in scenes scripted with tears in mind.   Her vision of
"Measure the Valleys" belongs to every mother who will not lose
faith in her child no matter the problem or disappointment.   Deborah Allen adds comic relief as the sister whose dreams of escaping her roach-infested home center around going to medical
school.   Ernestine Jackson does well as Younger's wife.

How can Ralph Carter pack so much acting know-how into 11
years of bounciness? He plays Younger's son and has an amazing knack for knowing how to steal scenes.   He is a joyous plus
in a plus-abounding show.

"Jacques Brel"

If we only had love, Jacques Brel tells us, then the world
would be so much more beautiful.   Plenty of presidents, admin-
istrators and officials have said the same thing.   But how come
it sounds so much more convincing when Brel says it?

Because Jacques Brel is a poet who has found music to complement his words and the French composer has a way with words that make living seem worth the struggle and the beauty around us more apparent. His works are alive and well in the repertoires of Johnny Mathis, Judy Collins, David Bowie and a whole list of vocalists who have taken Brel's French words to sweet music and turned them into grooves of their own. And one thing about a Jacques Brel song. Its beauty transcends language.

"Jacques Brel Is Alive and Well and Living in Paris" is a splendid evening of his songs with minimum staging, the emphasis on the soft aura his songs create. The Continental Dinner Theatre, 7511 Coventry Ave. , Melrose Park, has assembled four performers who afford viewers a delightful evening, begun by a delicious dinner. Dean Bennett's rendition of "Next" is moving and disturbing and his voice carries the message across in powerful thrusts. Ed Williame's "Statue" is effective and the whirling dizziness of "Carousel" is effected by Sallu Lou Nation. Caroll LaCasse rounds out the cast.

The quartet's finale, "If We Only Had Love," is a warm and suitably soothing ending to one of the best locally staged dinner theater presentations in the last two years.

EUREKA, Leonard, Fort Worth Star Telegram, Carter Publications, Seventh and Taylor Sts. , Fort Worth, Tex. 76102

FEINGOLD, Michael; (2) Theatre critic, The Village Voice: Literary Consultant, Yale Repertory Theatre; (3) b. Chicago, May 5, 1945; (4) s. Bernard and Elsie (Silver) Feingold; (5) B.A. , Columbia U. , 1966, maj. subj: English; M. F. A. in Criticism and Dramatic Literature, Yale School of Drama, 1970; (6) Single; (8) Critic, Columbia Daily Spectator, 1963-66; Founding Editor, yale/theatre, 1968 (member, editorial board, 1968-70; now consulting editor); critic, Village Voice, 1970-present; (9) A variety of plays and translations produced at Yale Rep. and other theatres; directing for various off-off Broadway groups; presently Artistic Director, Theatre-at-Noon, St. Peter's Church, New York; (10) Member, Theatre Advisory Panel, Nat'l Endowment for the Arts, 1973-present; (11) translating Brecht; (14) BMI Varsity Show Award, Book and Lyrics, Best College Musical, 1966; John Gassner Prize in Criticism, Yale 1968; (15) Member, Theatre Communications Group Advisory Panel; (17) Private; (20) Trans. of Brecht, Mahagonny and Roundheads and Peakheads in Collected Plays of Brecht (Random House); trans. of Der Jasager in yale/theatre, Winter 1975; unpublished trans. of Brecht, The Little Mahagonny, Happy End, The Berlin Requiem; Diderot, Rameau's Nephew; Moliere, The Bourgeois Gentleman; Ibsen, When We Dead Awaken; Offenbach, Two Blind Beggars, Two Fishermen, Marriage By Lanternlight; Donizetti, Viva La Mamma (Le Convenienze Teatrali); articles in Village Voice, New York Sunday Times, New Republic, Saturday

Review, yale/theatre, Plays & Players, etc. Edited seven volumes
of American plays for Winter House Ltd. (now distributed by DBS
Publications); contributed prefaces to volumes of Kenneth Bernard,
Tom Eyen, Jacobs & Casey's Grease. Plays: The Bawd's Opera
(Columbia Univ. 1966); The Pill (ditto, 1967); Red Shoes (children's
play, produced Yale 1969, with Carmen de Lavallade); etc.; (21) 17
W. 74 St., N.Y.C. 10023; Ph, 212-787-7428; (22) Village Voice,
80 University Place, N.Y.C. 10003, Ph. 212-741-0030; Yale Repertory Theatre, 222 York Street, New Haven, Conn. 06520, Ph. 203-
436-8492; (23) Circulation: Voice, 150,000; other audiences for
other works; (24) 100-150 plays, musicals, and performance pieces
annually.

It's Older, but Still Glorious
(by Michael Feingold, Village Voice, April 26, 1976)

I complain a great deal about the American Place Theatre,
and I suppose I am a dreadful nag, but the plain fact is that the
American Place Theatre asks for the complaints, by setting its
sights higher than any other theatre in New York, and deserves
them, for so often missing the high mark it has set. Or to put
it another way, a bad theatre doing bad work does not surprise
a critic, who learns in the course of time to expect such things;
its mediocre work may even be taken as a pleasant surprise and
an improvement. But the American Place set itself up to be the
very best contemporary theatre in New York, and on half a dozen
or so occasions in the last 12 years, it actually has been that--
so noticeably that I don't even feel the need to list the playwrights,
actors, designers, directors, who at one time or another stunned
us there with their abilities and the force of their revelations.
Naturally, when the theatre that wants to be the best, and has
proved it can be, shirks its mission, and gives us markdowns
instead, the critical sledgehammer comes down with exceptional
fervor and velocity.

The American Place made its debut in 1964, with one of those
few occasions: Two thirds of Robert Lowell's trilogy "The Old
Glory," directed by Jonathan Miller. Two years later, they completed the occasion with a production of the longest and least
wieldy of the plays, "Endecott and The Red Cross," featuring
Kenneth Haigh. Now they have revived all three plays in new
productions, as a deeply ironic tribute to this dismaying Bicentennial year, and for the first time it is possible to see all three
plays in one evening and discover that the full scope of Lowell's
imaginative exercise, though 12 years older, is still glorious.
We would not have had these plays if the American Place Theatre had not been there to produce them; and we would not be
able to see them now in their proper sequence if that theatre
were not still producing All these facts should be borne in mind,
as witness to the great debt we owe the American Place, while
the critical sledgehammer descends, as it will do a few paragraphs from now, on the current productions, which, as I have
already suggested, are not as good as they should be, and--

except in a few performances--not up to the standard the American Place itself has set. At the same time, I should make clear that the productions, which are modestly inadequate rather than maniacally wrong, are not a great obstacle to the enjoyment of some of the best dramatic writing done in America in the past 12 years (or in the past 50, for that matter), and that no play in New York at the moment is more worth seeing than these.

What Lowell tried to do in "The Old Glory" was take some of the more expressive moments in American literature--three short stories by Hawthorne and a novella by Melville--and transmute them into an American mythology. The proverbial American innocence is seen as a mask for the unease of alienation, the snobbery and intolerance of zealots, and the terrifying violence that erupts in the new race bred of the zealous and the alienated.

Governor Endecott of Massachusetts, in "Endecott and the Red Cross," is a turncoat Cavalier who has become an uneasy Puritan. Thomas Morton, the politicking, compromising boss of the Merry Mount settlement, which permits Maypole dancing and bawdry, and sells liquor and firearms to the Indians, thinks he can save his colony from Endecott's persecution by playing on his loyalty to England. But when Morton produces his trump card--a High Church courtier with a royal message commuting Endecott's governorship--Endecott chokes down his loyalty, rips down the British flag (the Red Cross), and burns Merry Mount. American independence, then, is born out of a tragedy of divided motives, for Endecott, a sophisticated man who despises Puritan pietism and knows that some of the Puritan hatred of Merry Mount is envy of Morton's financial success in trading with the Indians, nevertheless needs to sacrifice himself to a cause, and cannot find one in the wildness of America or in the pagan licentiousness of the Caroline court. He gives himself up to Puritanism, allowing his men to take orders from the fanatical Elder Palfrey (whose father has been killed by the Indians), and makes the burning of Merry Mount the symbol of his own sacrifice, just when the Puritans are beginning to doubt his devotion.

In the second and shortest piece, the phantasmagorical "My Kinsman, Major Molineux," the motives of the revolutionaries-- this ... time ... in Boston roughly a hundred years later--are even more divided. Molineaux is the despised and feared commander of the British troops in Boston ("lobsterbacks"), and his kinsmen are two young boys from the frontier settlement of Deerfield, who come in search of him and find, instead, a conspiracy to overthrow him in progress, the significance of which they are too young to understand. Boston, in their naive eyes, is an urban hell out of a Gillray cartoon, in which the most fervent revolutionaries are the people with the most moral corruption to hide: a prostitute, the powder-puff aristocrat whom she "converts" to revolutionary manliness, a shady and bellicose tavern keeper, a hypocritical clergyman. And the commander the boys keep meeting is not their kinsman--when they finally see Molineux, he is being ejected from the city, tarred and feathered, on a cart--but the pox-ridden turncoat, Colonel Greenough, who wants to destroy Molineux so he can have Molineux's house and goods.

The least dramatic of the three plays in the strict sense, "Major Molineux" is the most exciting and richest poetically, with its squirming, vital grotesquerie, its thousand allusions and satirical jabs, and its opportunities for visionary spectacle. And the vision of innocence as the conductor of all these sparks, a seeming error in terms of structure (the boys are protagonists who take no part in the action), turns out to carry the moral burden of the play, which is that passivity in the face of violence can be a form of spiritual deadness: Robin and his brother have seen Boston, and seen the murder of their kinsman, and done nothing about it; guided there by a Charon-like ferryman, in some sense they belong in the hellish city.

"Benito Cereno," the trilogy's concluding play, is its best-known and strongest dramatically. Lowell's feat here is chiefly to take themes that are dormant in Melville's original novella, and bring them up to full contemporary relevance without sacrificing the historical factuality of the original. The argument of the play is too familiar to synopsize. Innocence ("Who would want to murder Amasa Delano?") once again leads to violence, and the representative of the land of independence finds himself destroying the misunderstood independence of others. As with the first two plays, the sting is even stronger now than at the time of the first production. Among other aspects, now that a dozen years of racial turmoil have died down, we can see that Babu and the rebel slaves in some way deserve their fate. They have chosen to puppetize their former master, fly the black flag of piracy, and threaten Delano into giving them supplies and guidance, instead of standing on their own rights and addressing him as newly independent men. If this were the only side to Babu's case, the play would be a racist melodrama with a happy ending. As things stand, we see that it is made up of two interlocking tragedies: that of the murdered black man, who wins his dignity and loses his life, and that of the murdering white, whose life is saved but whose moral sanity is lost.

While the history of the last 12 years has been branding Lowell's prophecies into our foreheads, production standards in the New York theatre have gone steadily downhill, or, at least, so one would conclude from the revival "The Old Glory" has gotten. In actual fact, there is still enough acting talent in New York to man a battleship or two, though very little of it is on display at the American Place--a puzzling fact, since both of the directors involved are well-known and extremely good actors. The most that can be said for the performance overall is that everyone speaks clearly, so that Lowell's precious words come through, and it is possible to attend the trilogy and, while hearing it have

a dream performance of it come to life in your head. Not much
else can be said for it, overall--with one major exception I will
get to shortly.

Brian Murray's staging of "Endecott and the Red Cross" is
the drabbest sort of stock-company work, weakly imagined and,
in the crowd scene, amateurishly executed. Kenneth Harvey
snivels his way through Endecott, rising only to a brief flicker
of rhetorical fire at the end, and to tragedy nowhere, while
Richard Clarke twitters monotonously as the royal emissary.
Only Jerome Dempsey, as the conniving Morton, carries any
conviction, and New York has seen too many good performances
by Mr. Dempsey (most recently his Telfer in "Trelawney") to
be satisfied with this disheveled one. Nowhere is there a sense
that people actually lived in the 17th century, or that anything
like this might conceivably have happened. Mr. Murray's Maypole ceremony is the cutest little Kate Greenaway illustration,
and John Wulp, one of the two gifted designers being misused
here, might at least have explained to him that trees in Massachusetts are green in May.

That the failure of imagination involved is Mr. Murray's,
more than the actors', is borne out in "My Kinsman, Major Molineux," in which the same company shows some spirit and va-
riety--dulled, however, by the action being even more messily
and clumsily staged than in "Endecott." Willa Kim's costumes
come into their own here (though I remember them as being
still more Gillrayish and two-dimensional in 1964), and Herbert
Kaplan's tingly music is helpful, but the production is badly in
need of focus, in spite of nice efforts by Josh Clark and Scott
Sorrel as the two brothers, and by Mr. Dempsey again (Greenough), Gloria Rossi (Prostitute), and particularly George Hall,
as the two-faced minister.

The staging of "Benito Cereno" by Austin Pendleton is at
least a little better--efficient in its handling of the crowd, though
one of the black slaves keeps up a crosseyed twitch, during other
people's scenes, which would seem vulgar and amateurish even
in a Broadway musical. Mr. Pendleton has some idea of the
shape of the play, and of the psychological currents underneath
it; his groupings are more or less appropriate, and his use of
the mainsail as a scene curtain for both Babu's "entertainment"
and the scenes in Cereno's cabin is an ingenious one.

What the production lacks, curiously for a director whose
acting is so sensitive to emotional nuance, is any sense of feeling. There is a lack of tropical atmosphere; long stretches
which were hypnotically languorous in Miller's production (aided
by Yehudi Wyner's tension-building music, not used here) are
merely blank in this one. The psychological subtexts--as in the
scene in which Delano fondles his bosun, halfway through the
play--seem poured on superficially. Some of it may have to do
with the stiffness of the acting: Nicholas Coster, the Delano,

starts authoritatively but never changes or develops, and John
Getz's attempts at naivete, in the role of the bosun, come out
uncomfortably as Mickey Rooney brashness.   Alan Mixon, generally a crude but powerful actor, makes a partial success by
suggesting that the crudity is the element in Benito Cereno's
character which kept him alive when his friends died, but it is
hard to fight off memories of Frank Langella's sick, tremulous
suavity in the role.

Fortunately, "Benito Cereno" has Roscoe Lee Browne, recreating the role of Babu, the seemingly obsequious slave. Browne's
original performance was one of those great moments, when a
supremely skilled actor comes into possession of a role so good
even an idiot could win praise in it, and lifts it off the ground
and into theatre history with the simplest and most telling strokes
at his command.   To the unpracticed eye it may look as if Mr.
Browne is doing nothing, as he leaps sunnily over pools of dangerous rhetoric and pits of hidden menace in the character.
What he is actually doing is called underplaying, and it is some
of the finest underplaying ever seen on the New York stage.
When Babu says "How would you like to shake hands with the
Queen of Heaven?" to Captain Delano, it is impossible to locate
any death threat in the velvety politeness of his expression.
The highest tribute one can pay to Mr. Browne's acting is in the
fact that the threat is there, all the same, and the moment re-
verberates for days after the performance.

Is There Hope in Soap?
(by Michael Feingold, Village Voice, May 17, 1976)

What, after all, is soap opera?   The juxtaposition, you
might say, of the most extreme melodramatic situations with the
most banal and everyday surface behavior.   To the cynics who
see the disparity, soaps are comic, but millions of American
housewives, having been taught to expect nothing from art (or
life either, for that matter), take the banality as a true representation of human behavior, and thrill to the melodrama the
way their ancestors thrilled to Dion Boucicault.   Of course, if
you offered them the melodrama on the surface, all open and
aboveboard, they wouldn't touch it; the laggard pace, the expressionless conversation, the musical pairing-off of the characters
for coffee and revelations, are talismans of the soap's reality,
the way Victorian novels became more convincing by pretending
to be bundles of somebody's letters.   In this country only the
most sophisticated citizens can waive the pretense of reality and
accept the conventions of drama for what they are.

Lanford Wilson's new play, "Serenading Louie," is either a
soap opera, or a play about the same things soap opera is about,
and about the soap opera as well.   If the former, it is another
flat piece of Off-Broadway commercial drama, with good acting
opportunities in it; if the latter, it is what the Player calls the
real ending of "The Beggar's Opera," which is "a downright deep

tragedy," and a great one at that.   But it will take us 10 more
years of social turmoil to decide which, and I don't pretend to
be a futurologist.   My suspicions, however, are always on Mr.
Wilson's side, and so I conclude that, if "Serenading Louie" is
revived 10 years from now, it will be received in awe and spoken
of as A Classic.

What Wilson has done is to discover a link between the banality and the melodrama, the one thing his master Chekhov, who
invented the combination of elements we call soap opera, never
quite did: Chekhov's characters sit around, mooning about love
and life, until the mortgage-melodrama happens offstage and they
find themselves turned out of the house.   In "Serenading Louie,"
the melodrama violence happens onstage at the end--with all the
discretion a master craftsman can bring to the soap form--and
happens because of the everyday monotony and the mooning about.

Wilson's characters are two young couples--three of the
four, old college friends, looking back sentimentally on the days
when they sang the Whiffenpoof Song and life was simple--who
have become successful and suburbanized, and now find that life
has dried up for them.   One couple has a daughter and an adultery to deal with, the other a burgeoning political career on the
husband's part and utter lack of interest on the wife's.   The
sameness of the lives is such that, metaphorically, they live in
the same place, and John Lee Beatty's spacious suburban split-
level serves for both households, often simultaneously.   Eventually the sameness and the purposelessness get to the characters,
with a creeping finality that builds, stroke by stroke, in their
dialogue, and there is divorce, and worse.

Exploring the emptiness of an average American life is a
risky business for a playwright, and Wilson comes very close to
getting caught in the brambles of bathos.   The scenes his subur-
banites play with one another--"Don't drink any more." "How did
it happen to us?" "Your wife is seeing someone else."--are the
typical ones, redeemed, the way Chekhov's scenes are redeemed,
by the playwright's sensitivity to the turns and discontinuities of
real conversation, and by the inexorability with which the scenes
increase in pitch till the awful climax is reached, each one throwing its straw on the camel's back of the two shaky marriages.

Marshall Mason has staged "Serenading Louie" with the quiet
exactitude that always accompanies him when he is working on
Wilson's plays (or say, on Wilsonish plays) and seems to desert
him in Feifferland; it's good to have him back at home.   The
four actors are Tanya Berezin, Trish Hawkins, Edward J. Moore,
and Michael Storm.   Miss Hawkins has grown tremendously in
skill since her charmingly awkward days in "Hot L Baltimore,"
and gives a fully rounded portrait here.   I always like Miss
Berezin--I uncritically adore Miss Berezin, in fact--but I have
to own up that I am tired of always seeing her cast as tart-
sweet know-it-alls; either it's time for her to play Ophelia, or

she should take her sassy stage persona all the way into Restoration gallantry, where it started. Mr. Moore, an intelligent actor of slightly crude technique, cleverly uses the crudity here--blurting and abrupting all his big points--to suggest the man's confused state of mind, and his immense physical stature is cleverly used by Mr. Mason for hints of the impending violence: Towering, once over Miss Berezin and once over Mr. Storm, he nearly suggests Frankenstein's monster, and a Mary Shelley adaptation may be in order for him. The young politician is the easiest part, for no one in America knows what politicians are really like off camera; Mr. Storm plays it with great sense and seriousness, and looks convincing when the play has him study legal papers, not the easiest trick for a handsome actor. It being the Circle, the quartet naturally plays together as though they had been rehearsing as long as the Budapest Strings, so that, even if the play is a soap opera, the performance touches emotions considerably deeper than Mary Hartman's.

FELDMAN, David Edward; (2) Theater critic--newspaper and television; (3) b. Yonkers, N.Y., Feb. 8, 1939; (4) s. Samuel A. and Edith R. (Friedman); (5) B.A. State U. of N.Y. at Albany, major subj.: English; M.A. Syracuse U., Modern Lit.; M.F.A. Brandeis U., Theater Arts; (6) m. Norma J. Schoenfeld, Aug. 29, 1965; (7) child--Jessica Beth; (8) Copy boy, N.Y. Daily News, 1960; Ass't. Ed., Life Insurance Courant; UPI Stringer, Cortland, N.Y., 1966; Theater Critic, Syracuse New Times, 1972-present; Theater Critic and Commentator, WCNY-TV (Public Broadcast Service), Syracuse, N.Y., 1974-present; (9) Stage Carpenter, Brandeis U., 1968-69; produced playwright; Asst. Prof. of Eng. (Creative Writing, Journalism, Dramatic Lit.) Onondaga Community College, 1972-present; (10) Judge, Salt City (Syracuse, N.Y.) National Black Playwrights' Competition, 1975; (13) PFC (twice) U.S. Army Nat'l Guard; (20) plays produced: "The Fifty Year Game of Gin Rummy," Brandeis Univ., 1971, Berkshire Theater Festival, 1971; "Steinberg," WBRS-FM, 1969; Berkshire Theater Festival, 1971; "Georgie Porgy," Brandeis Univ., 1970; (21) 102 Euclid Terr., Syracuse, N.Y., Ph. 315-474-3208; (22) Syracuse New Times, Box 95 University Station, Syracuse, N.Y. 13210, Ph. 315-476-3143; (23) Circulation: approx. 25000 for newspaper; television audience unestimated; (24) 40 plays, musicals, articles of theatrical interest for newspaper; 20 television reviews & interviews.

Surprises from the Students
(by David Feldman, Syracuse New Times, February 16, 1975)

In its own way, Syracuse is a genuine theatre town, and the diversity of its drama scene is a continual surprise. Consider, for example, two presentations of the last week:

The first was at the Salt City Playhouse and Performing Arts Center (SCPPAC), with the inauguration of their new 50-Cent Theatre. The presentations were three intense, original one-act plays about the black experience by two young, local playwrights.

The second was The Steadfast Tin Soldier, a children's play
by the students and staff of Onondaga Community College's Theatre Department. It will soon go on the road to delight elementary school students throughout the area, and will be featured
at the Everson Museum's Children's Festival Week, Feb. 15 to 23.

The 50-Cent Theatre at SCPPAC is a new concept for the
area--a showcase theatre in Salt City's second playing area.
Along with the three new short plays, several interpretative
dances and readings of two poems were featured for the premiere presentation Feb. 2.

The first play, One Way or the Other, by Central Tech student Thomas Grimes, is a tight piece about a slum mother's defiance of her mother and friends in order to keep her illegitimate child. There is power and perception in the characterization of the strong-willed mother who announces, "I'm a woman
and a mother, and I got a job to do whether I'm married or not."

The strong conflict engendered by the opening moments is
weakened by some unnecessary repetition of exposition and by an
undramatic curtain speech, but the characters are vividly and
realistically drawn. Phyllis Holmes, who appeared in all three
plays, was both strong and tender in the lead role.

The second play, No School Tomorrow, also by Grimes, deals
with a high school student who has helped start a race riot in his
school. Like One Way or the Other, it is a family drama. Here,
the mother (Holmes again) convinces her son (Grimes) to return
to school, saying that it's better to "raise a few bucks in your
paycheck than rasing hell."

Donnie Brown as her other son, out of work because he has
no high school diploma, helps convince his brother. Like Grimes'
other play, this one starts with good, strong conflict and rises
quickly, without unnecessary dialog or action, to its climax.

Both are primarily thematic pieces and resort to curtain didacticism to get their point across, rather than having the climax arises out of the action. But that's almost inevitable in such
short pieces. For both plays, Grimes evidences a nice sense of
drama, a keen appreciation for the realities of life, and a warm
understanding of human nature.

The third one-acter, There's More to Life by Roderick Tor-
rence, is a longer and more complex work. It's about a young
black who, despite the protestations of his sister and brother,
gives way to the temptations of an exciting but short and violent
street life. It is a tightly plotted work, quickly paced and forceful. When it relies upon exposition and speeches instead of action and dialog, much is said, novelistically, but little achieved

in terms of character development. The characters, however, are interesting, and the situation is realistically and powerfully drawn in short, clear strokes.

Profits from the 50-Cent Theatre will go to buy musical instruments for Salt City's performing arts school, and to provide funds for the organization's upcoming black playwrights contest. The organizers of the new theatre hope to continue it on a steady basis and welcome plays, poems and other suitable material, along with actors and technical people. Those interested should contact SCPPAC.

While the OCC production of The Steadfast Tin Soldier deals with subject matter that is a far cry from ghetto life, it is no less valuable an asset for the development of interest in local theatre. It is replete with a pretty paper doll, two Teddy bears, a Raggedy Anne, several tin soldiers and a grumpy, nasty jack-in-the-box who practically steals the show.

It has some humans, too, adding to an involved plot centering on a young boy's birthday, a toy soldier unceremoniously pushed out a window, and a certain amount of interaction between actors and audience.

The audience loved it, cheering the soldier and paper doll and booing the jack-in-the-box. The costumes, designed and executed by Terry LaVada, are accurately enlarged, delightful versions of standard children's room equipment, and David Conely has directed it in a manner to make even the most hard-hearted third-grader cheer for the side of goodness and decency.

While that production is pretty well hooked for its school tours, it will appear at the Everson's festival, and OCC offers several productions for local high schools, including a scene from America Hurrah!, a new production of Feiffer's People with original music by local composer Mike Markowitz, and a mime lecture-demonstration-workshop.

Reality Conquers All in Shaw Play
(by David Feldman, Syracuse New Times, February 23, 1975)

George Bernard Shaw's Arms and the Man was the British dramatist's first play to be done in America. That 1894 production, while not a notable success, did establish Shaw on these shores, and the play has become one of the most popular works of the crusty, iconoclastic playwright. Syracuse Stage's current production of it is pleasant and almost always enjoyable, but it does little to enhance Shaw's reputation.

The story is simple enough: It is 1885, and an officer in the Serbian Army, his regiment defeated, takes refuge in the home of the fiancee of the Bulgarian officer who led the attack. The fugitive turns out to be a prosaic Swiss mercenary named

Bluntschli who prefers chocolate candies to cartridges and a secure life to martial heroics. His unidealistic realism eventually
conquers both the lady's romantic idealism and her heart. In so
doing, he converts her soldier lover who confesses his passion
for the serving girl, and he wins the hearts and minds of the
lady's parents as he convinces them that his five hotels, dozens
of carriage horses, closets full of linen and silverware and his
sturdy middleclass republicanism are worth far more than their
aristocratic pretentions.

All this is served up with heavy helpings of Shavian charm,
wit--and didacticism. The play has the flaw of presuming that
those things which are intellectually imaginable, even logical,
are also capable of being accepted and done by blood-and-guts
people with emotions. Shaw always had the proselytizer's mis-
belief that everybody was capable of doing what he himself could
achieve. The result is that the characters here tend to stand for
something before they are full, real human beings. In the best
play writing, things work in just the opposite direction.

Thomas Gruenwald's direction works against the didactic emphasis of the play, heavily stressing the characters. Thus,
Bluntschli, marvelously underplayed by Robert Moberly, comes
out unexpectably warm and charming--and we find ourselves liking him for his personality rather than for his ideas.

Ben Kapen as Petkoff, the father, is a delightful, hearty,
devoted father, not a caricature of aristocratic bumbling and be-
fuddlement. Even the servant, who wishes to leave his position
someday to set up shop in the city--and who is another representative of Shaw's anti-romantic theme--is a rather fetching and
sympathetic person as played by Merwin Goldsmith.

Not only have they all been directed to be quite pleasant, but
there is also a strong emphasis upon hand gestures, double takes
and sight gags--to the point that too many of Shaw's themes are
underplayed and unstressed. As a result we often have the sense
of knowing that something important has just been said without
being sure just what it was.

This is not to say that Gruenwald's direction is heavy-handed
or obtrusive. Nevertheless, in the emphasis upon character and
manner, we tend to lose sight of the theme. David Chapman's
flexible, handsome set and Jerry Pannozzo's excellent costumes
encourage this tendency.

As for the rest of the cast, there is a certain vague unevenness. Patricia O'Connell as the mother is more lovable than
shrewish, but her performance is restrained and subtle. Raina,
the young girl, as played by Eren Ozker, seems to seesaw back
and forth from pert charm to sputtering nastiness, and we are
not sure what the stolid, reasonable Bluntschli sees in her.
Richard Yarnell does yeoman service as the soldier-fiance, but

he lacks presence, being too frequently awkward. The scene where he manhandles and, in his own way, shows his love for Kelly Wood, the serving girl, just does not ring true. She fights him off as if he were some hesitant mugger in the park, not as the ambitious girl with love in her own heart for this handsome soldier.

Some of these moments of unsteadiness will tighten up as the production continues its run through March 8. This is not superb Shaw (and the problems are as much within the writing as within the production), but it is very good Shaw, nonetheless. And, as we have come to expect of Syracuse Stage--now completing its first full year at the Regent Experimental Theatre-- it is skilled, well-executed, professional theatre.

FISHER, Edward A. (Eddie); (2) Executive Entertainment Editor, Columbus (Ohio) Dispatch; (3) b. Columbus, Ohio, June 8, 1920; (4) s. Samuel and Ada Fisher (deceased); (5) Education: through senior high school; (6) single; (8) Part-time reporter for sports departments, Ohio State Journal and Columbus Dispatch, 1939-46; editor, Columbus Bowling News, 1947-49; editor, Ohio Jewish Chronicle, 1949-53; sportswriter, assistant editor sports department, Columbus Dispatch, 1954-70; appointed executive entertainment editor, Columbus Dispatch, May, 1970; (9) Reviewed nightclubs, concerts and films on contributory basis for Columbus Dispatch, 1940-70; (17) Jewish; (20) Annual contributor to Street & Smith Baseball Yearbook, 1963-70; correspondent, The Sporting News, 1958-70; (21) 380 S. 5th St., Apt. 209, Columbus, O. 43215, Ph. 614-221-0080; (22) 34 S. 3rd St., Columbus, O. 43216; Ph. 614-461-8836; (23) Circulation: daily, 225,000; Sunday, 330,000; (24) 15 editorial columns, 8 film reviews, 10 stage shows (Columbus and New York), 10 night club shows (Columbus, Miami, New York, Las Vegas).

Aisles of Manhattan Invaded Again
(by Eddie Fisher, Columbus Dispatch, May 30, 1976)

In a time capsule starting at 8 p.m. May 20 and ending exactly 70 hours later, this daredevil/glutton (read that masochist) clocked four full stage shows and a segment of another on and near Broadway, plus an unscheduled movie, the Saturday Night Live television airing and three Woody Woodbury-type comics at the piano in a lively joint called the Monkey Bar.

The coup in this latest invasion of the aisles of Manhattan would be in catching two of the hottest numbers in town on the same day--A Chorus Line on stage at the Shubert and the Emmy Award-winning Chevy Chase and the Saturday Night Live TV-er in NBC's RCA studios.

The madcap mini-marathon also included Chicago, My Fair Lady and Pacific Overtures.

(The segment of a show referred to previously was Let My
People Come, a trashy concoction off Broadway, authored by columnist Earl Wilson's son, Junior. We could abide only about
20 minutes before getting the message and escaping. Oh yes,
the show's making big money.)

But there's important territory to cover, so let us away.

Our biggest surprise was Chicago on 46th St. It's doing capacity business, probably more for individual achievement than
as a package.

The show seems to be by and for its director and choreographer, the esteemed Bob Fosse. He was responsible for the
monumentally successful Cabaret and has merely changed the time,
place and names and moved it to Chicago.

It's a rework of an old play about a Chicago murderess
(Roxie Hart) and her sensational jury trial in the mid-1920's.
The show has A-1 dancing (it being Fosse's, what else?), stunning sets (Tony Walton) and lighting (Jules Fisher), many funny
moments and a hurry-up pace.

What Chicago doesn't have is substance ... if that really
matters.

What it also doesn't have is music to remember. Now that's
a surprise, for the collaborators are John Kander and Fred Ebb,
whose pre-Chicago achievements are led by the Cabaret smash.

Gwen Verdon, no spring chick by now, nonetheless manages
to be sprightly and entertaining. Her dancing partner, another
time-tested trouper, Chita Rivera, is considered by many as
being the show's star.

My Fair Lady hasn't aged a bit. She's as gorgeous as when
she made her glorious debut 20 years ago. The "all time" words
and music of Lerner and Loewe, the ultra ultra costumes of
Cecil Beaton and the general concept of the musicalized Pygmalion are all as lustrous today as then.

Unfortunately for most of the 1976 cast, roles are constantly
being compared--which seems fair enough.

Ian Richardson is the new Prof. Henry Higgins. We'll take
the old one, sexy Rexy Harrison. Britisher Richardson does
not have the wherewithal. With such a meaty role he should do
more with what author George Bernard Shaw and musicmen Lerner and Loewe gifted him. Now if Ian was the first 'enry 'ig-
gins and Rex came along 20 years later, Harrison would be acclaimed, Richardson forgotten.

Then there's the Covent Garden flower girl, Liza Doolittle,

whose function was to be converted into a duchess by her ice-
watery mentor, Higgins.   Now if the new Liza, Christine Andreas,
were the original, and Julie Andrews came along, there would
less apt to be a resentment.   Miss Andreas is much eaiser to
accept.

Kenley Players customers should remember Chris Andreas.
She was one of the New Christy Minstrels who was given an acting part in a disaster of a musical here about three years ago,
Good News (a misnomer).   Then, because of her beauty and crystal-clear and pure voice, she was given a co-starring role by
producer John Kenley.   He plucked her from the Minstrels and
thrust her into the Burt Bacharach hit, Promises, Promises,
with Rich Little.

As the scroungy flower girl early in Fair Lady, Chris doesn't
seem to belong--because of that bel canto front and that Miss
America glow.   But when the transformation to princess arrives,
the role fits like an undersized body stocking.

By the way, her beauty wasn't marred, merely scratched
superficially, when a piece of dressingroom plaster came loose
ten minutes before curtain time one night a few weeks ago.   The
chunk of ceiling struck Chris on the forehead and required stiches
and sedatives.   "My first reaction," she recalled during a be-
tween-shows interview at Sardi's, "was how my understudy would
respond on such short notice.   But she did fine and of course I'm
happy to be back."

Pacific Overtures, the latest collaboration of the twin geniuses,
director Harold Prince and songsmith Stephen Sondheim, may go
down in Broadway history as the most under-rated, under-appre-
ciated presentation the musical theater ever has known.

A shame.

Prince and Sondheim probably figured they had a loser, only
because their product would soar so far over the average audience's
heads.   True.   But here's a fervent hope that Hal and Steve won't
regress to lower level of commercialism--even if it is a matter
of survival.

Pacific Overtures is a musical documentary concerning Japanese culture, specifically Commodore Matthew Calbraith Perry
and his bulldozing visit to Nippon in 1853.   It's an all-male, all-
Oriental cast.

Chorus Line has been contracted for an open run.   It's scheduled to play through Oct. 17, but if business demands, the L.A.
bookers (Shubert Theater) have the option to extend the run.

"Right now," explains Deeds, "I can only guess when we'll
have the show--either in late December, early January or next
March or Ap-ril."

Danny projects an estimate of upwards of 40,000 will see Chorus Line ("I look for a lot of repeat business, too, and a good response from towns as far away as Cincinnati," he adds).

It will be interesting to see how a giant of a vehicle as this will do if it's booked around Christmas time. Deeds has had other biggies booked here at that time of the year, and they didn't draw well. Chorus Line is supposed to defy all excuses.

The show also is causing a minor problem for Deeds in that he has five other items scheduled on the subscription series but can't even pencil in the dates yet until he knows when Chorus Line lines up.

Price Is Right, So "Damn Yankees" Is Darn Good
(by Eddie Fisher, Columbus Dispatch, July 21, 1976)

You can enjoy Kenley Players' version of Damn Yankees here this week--if you're not a stickler for accurate detail, if you're not a baseball buff and if you can accept (or ignore) a bush-league excuse for a plot.

Our so-called national pastime, often maligned (and occasionally justifiably so) for being a drag or bore, moves too quickly on stage at Veterans Memorial to be labeled dull.

Captained by that old Devil Vincent Price, this Kenley team has many all-stars on its roster--enough to offset some of the weak positions, such as the lamentable story line, the bland, unimaginative scenery and some of the words and music.

Damn Yankees in 1954 was adapted for stage from a book called The Year the Yankees Lost the Pennant. Bob Fosse did the choreography, Jerry Ross and Dick Adler wrote the score. Gwen Verdon danced her way to fame and helped the show last through more than a thousand performances on Broadway.

If nothing else, Damn Yankees has come as close as anything to becoming a hit as a baseball story on stage, screen or television.

The story concerns a middle-aged fan who lives and dies with his beloved, hapless Washington Senators. In despair, he murmers that he'd sell his soul if the Senators could win the pennant and stop those "damn Yankees." (Back in the monopoly days of the for-real New York Yankees, most of the country hated them.)

Anyhow, Satan, that fiendish buyer of lost souls, appears. He's dressed in civvies and his mortal name is Mr. Applegate. Mr. Price wears the horns and tail well.

The plot then thickens, but it doesn't jell. The Devil converts the old fan (Joe Boyd) into a 22-year-old superstar ball player, Joe Hardy.

Eventually, the seventh-place Senators catch and pass the despised Yankees to win the pennant. It wasn't easy, however, considering the shenanigans of the Devil and his little playmate, Lola the vixen, vamp, scamp, siren and baseball's original groupie.

Damn Yankees offers the reprise of the charming Oliver! duo for Kenley Players of two years ago--Price and young Russ Thacker.

Vincent hams it up delightfully and effectively. He all but steals the show with his Good Old Days solo in the second act. And if there's a moment when a lull is brewing, there's Price to make it right, to keep the faith and the pace.

Rusty Thacker isn't built like a home-run hero (neither is the Reds' Joe Morgan) but who cares? He has a strong throwing, er, singing voice, and does at least an adequate acting job as the Devilmade Joe Hardy.

It probably isn't fair to equate Pia Zadora's Lola to the role created by Gwen Verdon two decades ago. John Kenley has transformed the original Lola from a 30-ish, overpowering seductress to a cutesy teeny-bopper who should be dealing with junior-high pip-squeaks, not major league bruisers. Audiences will neither love nor hate Lola; and they're supposed to be moved one direction or the other.

Perfect casting is Lawrence Vincent as the fan who would sell his soul. If ever anyone looked like an old third-baseman and current manager or scout, it's Vincent. He does a commendable job.

So does his suffering spouse, Providence Hollander as Meg Boyd. Her soulful musical interpretations are strong and she's obviously a fine actress.

And if ever you see a sportswriter with the legs of a Paige Massman, the inquiring reporter with the dumb questions, let me know. I'll apply for renewal of my baseball writer's card. She dances up a tornado in the Shoeless Joe number. Soon you get the message: this gal is the reincarnation of the Verdon/Lola vintage.

Laura Waterbury and Carol Trigg are sharp, funny and realistic as the rabid fanettes who just love baseball and the people who play the game--but not necessarily in that sequence.

Something nice should be said too about the musical conductor Dick Patton. He swings the baton with the fluidity of a prime-time Ted Williams.

Unless the upcoming Shenandoah prevails later this season,
Damn Yankees just might be awarded the Kenley championship for
1976--maybe not at the box office but at least in the ratings.

FOREMAN, Thomas Elton; (2) Theater critic; (3) b. Forsythe, Mont.,
May 13, 1918; (4) s. Thomas B. and Dora (Regester) F.; (5) A.B.
Fresno State College, Fresno, Calif., in English and Journalism,
1946; M.A. in American History, Fresno State College, 1957; (6)
m. June E. McNeil, Apr. 2, 1949; (7) children--Steven Thomas,
Rebecca June, Kimberly Annette; (8) Reporter, Fresno Bee, 1939-41;
public relations assistant and public relations director, Fresno State
College, 1946-51; teacher English and drama, Tranquillity Union
High School, Calif., 1951-52; teacher English and journalism and
public relations director, College of the Sequoias, Visalia, Calif.,
1953-57; feature writer and theater critic, Riverside, Calif., Press
& Enterprise, 1957-present; (9) Active with community theater groups
in Fresno, Visalia and Riverside, winner best actor award, Riverside Community Players, 1965-66 and 1966-67 seasons; president
Riverside Inter-Church Drama Group, 1968-69; co-founder and director Brotherhood Players repertory drama group, 1970-present; (13)
Cpl. U.S. Army, 1939-45; (15) Member Los Angeles Drama Critics
Circle; (16) Democrat; (17) Methodist; (20) Author several locally-
produced one-act plays; (21) 4773 Newbury Ct., Riverside, CA. 92507,
Ph. 714-684-7775; (22) Press & Enterprise, Box 792; Riverside, CA
92502, Ph. 714-684-1200; (23) Circulation: 90,000; (24) 75 plays and
musicals.

UCR Presents Cliché-Turned-Classic
(by T. E. Foreman, Daily Enterprise, November 29, 1974)

Since there is no hard-and-fast rule on when a play goes
from being a classic, it is entirely arbitrary to say that Thornton Wilder's "Our Town" has now reached classic status.

Certainly it was a cliche long enough. Wilder's folksy drama
of small town life in the early years of this century has been a
favorite of high school and community theater groups for several
generations.

But a current University of California, Riverside, presentation of the play makes it apparent that Wilder's work has out-
lived that status.

The daily life of the folks in Grover's Corners, N.H., and
the romance of George and Emily still makes for an interesting,
entertaining and moving dramatic experience.

It is entirely conceivable that, as the Stage Manager suggests
in his early remarks, people will be reading this play a thousand years from now to learn how people lived in the early part
of the 20th century.

The basic message of "Our Town" will probably hold as true then as it does now--that the world is beautiful, life is wonderful and we should look at each other and appreciate what we have.

That's not to say that "Our Town" is the definitive picture of life in America in the early part of the century. We might get an entirely different picture if we were to shift our attention just a few blocks, to the Polish sector of Grover's Corners. We would certainly get a different and less idyllic picture if we looked in on a sweat shop worker in the New York City of that period, or a black sharecropper family in the deep South.

Nevertheless, on his own chosen grounds, Wilder's work rings true.

The UCR production admirably brings out the values of the play under Richard Risso's direction.

Michael C. Scahill has a fine relaxed command of the proceedings as the Stage Manager, while Cathy De Cuir and Jeffrey Ellis, as Emily and George, nicely capture the painful coltishness of adolescence growing into adulthood.

Lynette Godsey, William T. Sutherland, Rebecca Leah Nachison and James Harbour as their respective parents are convincingly parental.

Some nice touches among the supporting players include Karen Stewart's Mrs. Soames, Robin Pollock's Rebecca Gibbs and John Cooper's Professor Willard. And as the Stage Manager notes, the cast includes "many others, too numerous to mention." All are fine.

A curmudgeon might quarrel with the variety of versions of a New Hampshire accent, or lack of one, exhibited, and there seems to be a certain amount of walking through walls as the Studio Theater stage becomes overly crowded at times, albeit with imaginary scenery.

But these are minor flaws which do not detract from the enjoyment of what is an estimable, excellent American play--a classic, you might say.

Charlton Heston's "Macbeth" Is Competent but Not Memorable
(by T. E. Foreman, Daily Enterprise, January 31, 1975)

The production of "Macbeth" currently at the Ahmanson Theater of the Los Angeles Music Center is a splendidly staged version of Shakespeare's historic tragedy.

It moves along at a brisk but not breakneck pace, it is as gory as you suspect Shakespeare intended it to be and director Peter Wood has introduced some ingenious touches which generally enhance the show.

It is also a production marked by a series of highly competent but not memorable performances, including that of Charlton Heston in the title role.

Heston has achieved a sort of middle ground in his performance which does not irritate you into throwing rocks at him, but also does not inspire a search for superlatives.

There are a number of different interpretations of Macbeth's character possible: as an essentially bloodthirsty villain who would have been likely to go ahead with his murder of the king and the subsequent outrages even without the prompting of the witches and his wife, as a basically decent man led astray by ambition, or as a weakling pushed into villainy by a domineering wife.

Heston doesn't make a strong statement for any of those, or any other definite interpretation of the character.   He gives you a little of each, and the result is not a bad performance just not a memorable one either.

More memorable is Vanessa Redgrave as Lady Macbeth. There is no question about her interpretation.   Her Lady Macbeth is a scheming bitch who does not blink an eye at murder as a means to get ahead, and is not at all hesitant to use her considerable sex appeal to help achieve her ambitions.

Some of her early speeches are in the British Shakespearean tradition--speak rapidly but enunciate clearly, and don't worry about such subtleties as inner feelings or emotional motivations. But she soon establishes a firm grip on the character, and by the sleepwalking scene she is a Lady Macbeth in a class with the best.

The rest of the roles are all in expert hands, with nobody making an especially vivid impression.

Major assets of the production are H. R. Poindexter's sets and lighting.   Twisted columns that move in and out, stairways that slide on and off and backdrops lighted with imaginative inventiveness give variously the feel of a battlefield, the castle interior or a haunted woods, with a nice balance between the abstract and the specific.

Wood has used the settings with vivid effect, although it is possible to quarrel with some of his directorial touches.

One of the most original of these has the three witches make their first appearance as dead bodies on a battlefield, who come eerily to life when Macbeth and Banquo enter.

It's an interesting idea--but wouldn't it be even more striking if these supposedly dead soldiers turned out to be women? And wouldn't that make it more reasonable, then, for Macbeth and Banquo to refer to the witches as the "weird sisters?"

Wood's idea of having the witches also appear as Macbeth's hired murderers is also an interesting one, although it could be argued that this touch makes it appear too much that the whole tragedy is the result of diabolical manipulation and not of human failings.

Another quibble is that Banquo's makeup, when he appears as a ghost, makes him look more like the Creature from the Black Lagoon than a disembodied spirit.

Richard Jordan, who plays Macduff, sprained an ankle late in rehearsals and played the early performances with a crutch. Presumably once the ankle is mended he will discard that prop, and he will not have the grotesquerie of his crutch besting Macbeth's sword in the final battle.

And, unfortunately, that severed head of Macbeth in the final scene is probably always going to draw snickers, even when the audience is not largely made up of students.

But those quibbles aside, it is an excellent production. With a few reservations, including a possible exhortation to Heston to give a stronger performance. Shakespeare would probably have liked it.

FORSBERG, Helen, Salt Lake Tribune, 143 South Main St., P.O. Box 867, Salt Lake City, Ut. 84110

FOWLER, Giles Merrill; (2) Theater and Motion Picture Critic; (3) b. Kansas City, Mo., Jan. 3, 1934; (4) s. Richard B. and Elinor (Montgomery) F.; (5) B.A. Westminster College, Fulton, Mo., major subj.: English, 1955; M.S. in Journalism, Columbia U., 1956; (6) m. Jane Pecinovsky, Jan. 17, 1959; (7) child--Stephen Carr F.; (8) Reporter, Kansas City (Mo.) Star, 1956-57, 58-62; Motion Picture Editor, 1962- ; Drama and Motion Picture Editor, 1964- ; Reporter, Times of London (Eng.), 1957-58; (9) Frequent lecturer in theater, films and drama criticism at area colleges and universities; cast musician, Gilded Cage Theater, Kansas City, Mo., 1959-61; (10) Mem. Mayor's Theater Planning Committee (Kansas City, Mo.) 1965-66; mem. Film Advisory Committee, Missouri Council on the Arts, 1965- ; mem. Film Advisory Committee, Kansas Arts Commission, 1971- ; (15) Mem. Motion Picture Assn. of Kansas City, Mo., 1962- ; mem. Friends of Art, Kansas City, Mo., 1960- ; mem. Beta Theta Pi, Phi Alpha Theta (pres. Westminster chpt., 1955), Pi Delta Epsilon; (19) Carriage Club; (20) Articles in Cultural Affairs Magazine and Kansas City Fine Arts Calendar; plays (unpublished,

unproduced, unmourned); (21) 810 W. 57th St. , Kansas City, Mo.
64113, Ph. 816-333-3253; (22) Kansas City Star, 1729 Grand, Kansas
City Mo. 64108, Ph. 816-421-1200; (23) Circulation: Morning,
325,000; Evening, 315,000; Sunday, 410,000; (24) 50 plays and musicals, 80 motion pictures.

Theater in Mid-America
(by Giles M. Fowler, Kansas City Star, March 5, 1974)

New York's City Center Acting Company, touring the Midwest
with a small repertoire of large productions, unveiled one of decided interest Monday night in St. Joseph. It is Chekhov's "The
Three Sisters" (the same the company will offer March 13 in
Kansas City), and an affecting piece it proved to be on the stage
of the Missouri Theater here.

Under Boris Tumarin's direction, this "Three Sisters" seeks--
and mostly finds--the peculiarly Russian contrasts within the tragicomedy. The play is just that: Tragic and comic, touched
with absurdity and anguish, drollery and pain. It is in one sense
a static drama, yet life abounds in its interplay of moods that
shift like the fickle breezes of an autumn afternoon.

Three sisters pass the years of ennui and frustration in a
small garrison town, their hopes kept alive by the dream of fleeing one day to Moscow. Moscow--to go to Moscow! It is a
yearning endlessly repeated, and it will never come to anything
more.

Meantime the concerns of family and provincial society circulate around them, lending momentary illusions of purpose.
There are parties, friends, work, domestic crises, a tentative
romance to mitigate a boring marriage. And always talk--talk
of Moscow, of better times past and desired. So ineffectual, so
silly, so bravely, achingly human and redeeming are the passions
at play in Chekhov's confined world.

Is the drama as bleak as all this makes it sound? Not at
all, and least of all in this sharply tuned production, with its
gusts of humor and gaiety between the darker passages.

For a time in the first act I suspected the company had gone
too far for comedy at the expense of other tones. The early bits
of manneredness, jesting and fatuity at a birthday luncheon are
almost too broadly stated. Yet taken with the full range of
moods gradually introduced, the comic falls into balance. It is
never far off, but neither is the heartbreak.

There is a special boldness in the production's sudden pivoting of emotions, sometimes with a gesture, an inflection, at
other times with an impromptu song (melancholy or joyous) or
some wafting breeze-change in the atmosphere on stage.

The young Irina, exquisitely played by Patti LuPone, can bubble with pleasure one moment, then reveal with a crack in her voice that "we've been choked." Her homely suitor, the Baron Tusenbach performed with endearing, gawky-debonair ardor by Norman Snow, can play the buffoon and the figure of gallant sensibility with scarcely a change of manner.

Masha (Mary-Joan Negro) alternates convincingly between the edgy, arctic bitterness of the discontented wife and the glowing yet guarded ecstasy of the mature woman in love for the first time. Peter Dvorsky is a rueful, likeable Colonel Vershinin, the married officer who engages Masha in futile romance, and Richard Ooms is at once absurd and pitiful as Masha's schoolmaster husband.

The third sister, Olga (Mary Lou Rosato), has one of the production's more painful moments when her spinsterish cheerfulness gives way to near-hysteria before the cruelties of her sister-in-law (played to peak bitchiness by Sandra Halperin). The weakling brother, Andrey, develops rather uncertainly in the performance by Benjamin Hendrickson, but his outburst of defensiveness and despair in Act III is wrenching indeed.

Though the ensemble acting is almost always impressive (one never doubts this is a "company" in the full sense), not all the portrayals work as well on their own. David Schramm as the boozy old Dr. Chebutykin never quite finds the depths of the character's self-contempt, and the Captain Solyony played by Sam Tsoutsouvas somehow misses the role's full, dangerous instability. The ancient Anfisa (Gisela Caldwell) is no more than a set of standard, old-age mannerisms.

I might add that the costumes are far handsomer than the sets, which have a rather tatty, road-worn look.

But overall the production shows both troupe and drama to strong advantage, and Kansas Citians may anticipate with pleasure the company's visit (with this play and two others). The 4-state tour is co-ordinated by the Mid-America Arts Alliance, which deserves a share of the applause.

Theater in Mid-America
(by Giles M. Fowler, Kansas City Star, March 6, 1975)

Appearing here before its visit next week to Kansas City, the City Center Acting Company has introduced another of its touring productions, "The Time of Your Life." Despite entertaining parts, the sum of the show in my view does not deliver what the title promises.

About the best Kansas Citians can expect of William Saroyan's saloon comedy, due March 14 at the Lyric Theater, is the once-removed amusement of a play now faded into a quaint period piece. The performance Tuesday night at the Missouri Theater here pointed up problems inherent in script and production.

Even as bright a company as this New York troupe is hard put to cope with the play's slack design, not to mention the author's weakness for sentimental whimsey and stereotypes. Until Act III, when "The Time of Your Life" suddenly does spring to life, the show tends to limp between stretches of sporadic humor.

Saroyan wrote his play as a microcosmic slice of humanity as seen among the habitues of a waterfront saloon in 1939. The author's concerns are '30s concerns: the "little man" with big hopes, the innate virtues of the proletariat, the tyrannies of petty meanness, the approach of war.

A band of dreamers, drifters, floozies and bar-stool philosophers is presided over by a "student" of life, Joe, who tipples champagne while indulging his whims and playing moral interlocutor. He sends a pal on oddball errands just for the hell of it, becomes a matchmaker for his chum and a woebegone hooker and resorts to the kind of Comments on Life that are only heard in saloons on stage.

Around him the other characters circulate with their private obsessions, yearnings or caprices. Saroyan deals out his people one or two at a time, giving each his dramatic moment before shuffling him back into the deck. Only in Act III does the show stack a playable band in terms of melodrama (a showdown between good and evil) and also draws its best Jokers.

The production picks up when the play does, and there are some truly funny bits involving, among other things, a gum-chewing contest, a rousing Salvation Army hymn and the world's most dazzling pinball machine.

Especially I welcomed the entertaining presence of David Schramm as an old-timer whose tall tales are bizarre to the point of surrealism. But even this character is a variation on a type. And few other portrayals are spectacular enough, beyond the merely workmanlike, to make us forget how glibly conventional Saroyan's ideas really are.

Norman Snow has an ingratiating sweetness as the simple-minded Tom, and Patti LuPone has a wounded appeal as Kitty Duval, the bawd with loving heart. There are a few other standouts, among them Mary Lou Rosato as the enigmatic Mary L., Sam Tsoutsotivas as a patriotic pinball freak and Benjamin Hendrickson as the tough-sentimental proprietor.

Some other performances are dull or worse (others simply adequate), and there is little point belaboring the weaker members of a cast that is stretched too thinly for its own good.

What the show misses most, however, is a Joe of sufficient presence to anchor this drifting play. Nicolas Surovy is pleasant enough in the part, but somehow he lacks the quirky style and raffish eccentricity to make Joe very interesting. His own lack of focus becomes the production's as well.

Also missed is the consistent vitality and depth of detail that the director, Jack O'Brien, should have imposed. The saloon setting is excellent but much that happens within it seems shambling and haphazard. Players around the rim of the action seem uncertain of how to pass their unoccupied time, and often their upstage business has an aimless, uncertain look as though it were hardly directed at all.

In fairness, the production should not be taken as a true gauge of the company's abilities. A fine staging of Chekhov's "The Three Sisters" has shown how well the troupe can do with a far more interesting script.

FRATTI, Mario; (2) Theater Critic, Playwright, College Professor; (3) b. L'Aquila, Italy, July 5, 1927; American citizen; (4) s. Leone and Palmira (Silvi); (5) Ph.D. in Foreign Languages and Literature; (6, 7) m. Lina Fedrigo, children: Mirko and Barbara; m. Laura Dubman, child: Valentina; (8) Teacher, interpreter, drama critic, playwright, Assoc. Professor at Columbia University, Adelphi College, Hunter College; (9) Actor at ten, once; (13) Lieutenant in the Italian army; (15) Drama Desk, Outer Critics Circle, American Theatre Critics Association; (16) Democrat; (17) Agnostic; (20) Over 1000 drama reviews in Paese Sera, Ridotto, Theatron, Arcoscenico, Sipario, Artepiu, Tempo Sensibile, Costume, Parola del Popolo, Drama & Theater; plays: Cage, Suicide, Academy, Return, Bridge, Mafia, Duse, Refusal, Brothel, Family, Gift, Chinese Friend, Wish, Refrigerators, Races, Che Guevara, Victim, Chile 1973, Seducers, Madam Senator, Dialogue with a Negro, Originality, Patty Hearst, Kissinger were produced in over 300 theaters in 17 languages; published by Dell, Colliers, Macmillan, Enact, Breakthrough, Proscenium, Edgemoor, Crown, McGraw-Hill and Prentice-Hall; (21) 145 W. 55, Ph. Ju 2-6697; (22) Hunter College, 695 Park Ave. , Ph. 360-5550; (23) Circulation: at least 200,000; (24) I often review films; sometimes, books.

"Knock Knock": Where Is Our Old Jules Feiffer?
(by Mario Fratti, Ridotto [Venice-Rome], February 18, 1976
[here translated])

A few years ago I went to see "Little Murders" on Broadway. Arthur Miller was sitting across the aisle from me. We both roared with laughter. It was a good, funny play.

Last week, at the Biltmore Theater, I went to see "Knock Knock." Nobody laughed. I'm surprised this kind of play reached Broadway. (Feiffer must be surprised too.) It is so unreal it may bore you to death.

Two old men--a Jewish "Odd Couple"--are arguing. Abe
(Neil Flanagan) drives Cohn (Daniel Seltzer) crazy by saying,
absurdly, "I see two fingers but I say five because I prefer
five; there is no bedroom there because I only see the curtain
hiding the bedroom." Pirandellian jokes I found highly resistible.
Cohn wishes Abe would disappear. He does. Wiseman (Judd
Hirsch) pops up in his place. He is worse. He deserves dying
in a trunk.

Fortunately, Our good Lord sends Saint Joan of Arc (Nancy
Snyder) to rescue them. She is a new Noah looking for "two of
every kind" for her spaceship (Ark). They discuss and fight ad
nauseam. St. Joan seems to give up on her mission and becomes
their maid. Being a lousy cook, she faints a few times.

At the end, after a rather funny monologue (a sarcastic game
of words), she ascends to Heaven and the odd couple is left alone.

The pace is slow and exasperating; the mood is forcedly funny. (The actors often wait for laughs that never come.) Feiffer's
emphasis is only on word-games, unfortunately; not on structure
and plot. The actors work hard but their ebullience often carries them overboard into caricature.

The production is satisfactory and the gimmicks work. It
is the play that disappoints. I like Feiffer's cartoons (realistic,
precise, to the point); I desperately tried to like "Knock Knock."
I could not. A gloomy spectator outside uttered his ferocious
condemnation: "spectacularly unfunny." I think he was being
wordier than Feiffer. It was just "unfunny."

Anyhow, I think some spectators with a special sense of hu-
mor--those who like apparitions--might enjoy it. "Everything is
possible," Abe tells Cohn. Everything.

Beautiful Italian Songs. Fun in Many Languages.
(by Mario Fratti, Paese-Sera [Rome], June 6, 1976 [here translated])

At the Provincetown Playhouse (133 MacDougal Street), Peter
Copani has presented some more of his songs. Street songs that
have the unusual flavor of a dramatic reality. Strong, polemic,
pleasant. The emphasis is on a sense of humor typically Italo-
American (especially "L'America ha fatto per te" and "Pairs of
One.") Beautifully sung by Susan Friedman, Jose Vega, Val Reit-
er and Gwen Sumtree. Vigorous staging by Don Signore. An
emotionally charged evening. Worth seeing. At the Circle in
the Square (159 Bleecker Street), fun in many languages. "The
Primary English Class" by Israel Horovitz, directed by Edward
Berkeley. A classroom, at night. The students have nothing in
common except the name "Wastebasket" in Italian, French, German, Chinese and Japanese. The implication is that, being

foreigners, they are a minority worthy of garbage cans. They
don't know a word of English. Wild misunderstandings ensue.
Funny, at first. But predictable. The teacher (exciting Diane
Keaton) is a neurotic American who does not know how to teach
(read: "rule the world"). She teaches absurd rules in absurd
terms. She tries to be the policewoman of the world; she does
not succeed.

She is funny; even when she is terrorized by an alleged rapist who in reality is only looking for his mop. (He can only
speak Polish, adding confusion to confusion.)

There is a moment at the end when it seems that--magical-
ly--the Italian student has learned some English. This moment
is unfortunately not clarified and exploited. It could have been
a perfect curtain.

Metaphors speak for themselves. We cannot rule the world
any longer because foreign countries are no longer in tune with
our language. (Rapists come from the East.)

The situation has great possibilities but here we have only
an unnecessarily stretched-out one-acter. It needs a companion
piece.

Mr. Berkeley keeps things moving forward briskly. Excellent performances by Diane Keaton, Richard Libertini, Tom Ku-
biak, Sol Frieder and Atsumi Sakato.

FREEMAN, Charles K.; (2) Critic, director; (3) b. Birkenhead, England; (4) s. Bernard and Rebecca (Goodman) Freeman; (5) Malden
H.S. (Mass.); (6) m. Letty Cooper, 1943; (7) children--one daughter;
(8) 1954-65, drama critic for the Westchester-Rockland County (N.Y.)
group of 10 daily papers; 1965 theater writer-critic, Tri-State Suburban Group; (9) directed Girls in Uniform (1934); Merry-Go-Round
(1935); Sixteen (1935); with the Federal Th. (WPA) Project, directed
The Life and Death of an American (1939); was a supervisor for the
Federal Dance (WPA) Project; staged a production of Hellzapoppin
(1942); was a member of the War Writers Board (WW II); and dramatized See Here Private Hargrove for the USO Camp Shows. Directed Song of Norway (1944); adapted with Gerald Savory, Hand in
Glove (1944); The Great Waltz (1945); directed I Like It Here (1946);
for the American Negro Th., directed The Washington Years (1948);
directed 20 weeks of stock (Montclair, N.J., 1948); directed the revival of Diamond Lil (1949). At the Sombrero Playhouse (Phoenix,
Ariz., 1955); directed Oh, Men! Oh, Women!, Dial "M" for Murder, Stalag 17, My 3 Angels, The Caine Mutiny Court Martial, and
Picnic; was resident director of the Amer. Th. Wing Studio Co.
(Cane Playhouse, Dennis, Mass., Summer 1958), and directed Arms
and the Man. Stage adapter of Warner Bros. "Calmity Jane" musical,
1965; Annual Panelist, Theatre Symposiums, Max Reinhardt Archives,
Harpur College, Univ. State of N.Y.; (13) Mem. War Writer's Board

1941-42; producer U.S.O., World War II; (14) Edith Rockefeller Director award, 1934; (15) Outer Circle, 1958-68, now hon. acting president; Soc. of Stage Directors, Dramatists Guild, Actors Equity; (21 & 22) 18 Overlook Road, Ossining, N.Y. 10562.

A Memorial to Eugene O'Neill
(by Charles K. Freeman, Tri-State Suburban, 1970)

Generously spread out on some verdant acres in the Connecticut countryside is the Eugene O'Neill Memorial Theatre Center. One reaches it by heading for Waterford (adjoining New London), then following well-marked roads until you are directed smack in front of where the action is.

A snooping summer theatre reporter found out that what goes on there boggles the mind. For no matter in what direction one looks there are actors, directors, writers, stage designers and administration hands attending to the business of the day. And business is booming.

Consider some of the projects encompassed by the Center. (And note there are no reins on your wandering be you theatre buff or just plain John Doe, citizen.)

Currently in active session is the National Playwrights' Conference, July 6 to August 2. Three stages as well as marked-off areas in fields are occupied. Pause to catch the tense attention paid by some tyro playwright as his dialogue comes to life. Listen to a director's admonition to an actor. He may gently suggest to the playwright that such and such a line doesn't serve the character. "Think of something else, here."

Or "This speech is overlong, I'd suggest a cut." And the writer promises to come up with a revision. The rehearsal proceeds.

Move along, past a company of Nigerians experimenting with bongo counterpoint to some bit of a playscene. The Nigerians have been brought over to work on a new play. A complement of 16 together with writer Wole Soyinka. They'll soon be presenting the result of their creation towards the end of the conference.

There's no pressure here. No aura of Broadway "show-biz." And plenty of room to work. The stages are a 300 seat amphitheatre carpentered in the main by volunteer labor. Adjoining is a handsome barn restored to its new dignity with the aid of Foundation funds.

The cost to manage the barnseating which can expand from 150 to 350 ran upwards of $100,000. But there's a gallery for the exhibition of theatre memorabilia and blueprints to set up a puppet show.

A good stretch-of-legs walk away is an Instant Theater
roughly built with an arena stage and three levels-high bleacher
seats for onlookers. Neither audiences or actors are being cod-
dled here. Total emphasis is on the writers' work. Fourteen
to be exposed during the conference weeks chosen from some
300 submissions.

Performers are urged to devote their talent to role clarification; memorization of lines is of secondary need. All players
during performance carry manuscripts; move as directed with
only simple staging aids and once through with the performances
take on another assignment. The O'Neill scene is midwived by
invited critics who sit in on post performance analyses. The
critics are not there for review purposes ... all is directed toward the playwright and his vision.

The Playwrights' Conference is but one tributary of the O'-
Neill conglomerate. The center is also the home of the interna-
tionally famed Theatre of The Deaf. It guides the Professional
School for Deaf Theatre Personnel, also the Little Theatre of
The Deaf.

There is a Secondary School Teachers Theatre Program; a
Critics' Institute; a New Playwrights Catalogue; a Community
Theatre Council; and in the fall there will be a National Theatre
Institute funded by the Rockefellers with a $300,000 grant. This
latest project will select students for a resident semester in all
areas of theatre studies practically applied. A string of participating colleges are already lined up.

Does Broadway and Theatre benefit from these Connecticut
incubations? Indeed, yes. A fellowship program gave Ron Co-
wen his opportunity to develop "Summertree" produced in New
York (now being filmed); John Guare got his innings with "Mu-
zeeka" and "Cop Out" here; Jeff Wanshell's Lincoln Center produced "The Disintegration of James Cherry" was burnished under Center Guidance.

The man responsible for the O'Neill Memorial is George C.
White, a tireless theatre enthusiast.

Starting with an insurance policy loan of $1200 to underwrite
his first conference, Mr. White kept after the Waterford town
fathers until they turned over an aging mansion of 26 rooms that
now houses the administration rooms. With unflagging tenacity,
he convinced the Rockefellers, Fords and U.S. Arts endowments
to, at latest count, fund him to the extent of $2 million over
the last six years.

Mr. White is a man of many sights and great energy. His
imagination took hold of the New London O'Neill family home and
from there soared. The Waterford happenings now explore every
avenue towards expanding the theatre's horizons.

"American Theatre ... Who Cares?"
(by Charles K. Freeman, Tri-State Suburban, 1970's)

I was saddened to read the above quoted phrase in a Sunday
Times' piece by the distinguished dean of the Yale School of Drama. It was clear, about three sips down my morning cup of
coffee, that Robert Brustein was piqued by the state of the contemporary Broadway landscape. And he was expressing himself
sourly on the subject. (Not a new one.)

The acrid smoke from hotted phrases curled upwards from
the printed page. "Musical anodynes," "Neil Simon tranquilizers"
and "pep pills" from London. Thus the diet the theatre survives
on. Other posies: "arrogance," "lunatic innovation," "revolutionary posturing" and "noisy calisthenics" with "nowhere in the
last six or seven years any achievement."

Nor was that all. The Black Theatre caught it. Also nudity
(of course) as well as audience participation, the avant--garde,
the "new" theatre and the "counter culture." Now my breakfast
toast was as ashes in the mouth. Strange, I had been under the
impression that a lot of the above had at one time or the other
silted down from New Haven.

Don't think for a moment that the critical fraternity (maternity, too) escaped. They were skin-flayed with: "ravenous
press" ... "grown craven sloppy or shrilly partisan" hungering
(no less) "after new theatrical saviours." To paraphrase an
award-winning TV commercial: "Mama mia, those are some
tasty phraseballs!"

As the piece continued, fingernails were sheathed and a modicum of calm followed. That was about when the Yale Drama
Works came up for appraisal.

The tidings were more con amore. "Animating vision," "experimental energy," "imaginative power," "plays of serious consequence." On the subject of the survival of the Repertory Theatre there: "assuming the survival has been achieved with hon-
or." Affirmation and TLC from Mr. Brustein to his worthy shop.

I wonder though if the Yale unit was set down in the middle
of New York whether the multimedia demands of the art-enter-
tainment industry (which it is, like it or not) would be met.
Would, say, "No, No Nanette" or "Fiddler On the Roof" never
have happened?

It requires no special perception to conclude that there is
no major American playwright. (Where, incidentally is the ma-
jor American statesman ... or for that matter ... European.)
And if what is imported from London as "pep-pills" (Peter
Brooks' "A Midsummer Night's Dream," "The Homecoming,"
"Sleuth, " etc.) why contend, as he does, that we had best learn

fast from the English and European cultures?

There are indeed a few top-rank financially assured companies abroad to be envied. But there are some here too that need not count out the till every night, yet they are sorely wanting in artistic completion.

The theatre has been a sitting duck for centuries. It is the most vulnerable of the arts to pummel, blackeye and accuse of evil and malfeasance. But for all the ills its flesh is heir to it is not quite the shabby vessel it is made out to be.

The recent handsomely produced Tony Award show in a rundown of musicals demonstrated there is a wide range of writing and acting talent. A similar catalogue could be shown of plays produced here not without esteem. Even Mr. Brustein cares: "Where else except the theatre can we enjoy living encounter, a vital confrontation with the unexpected." And there are a host of Broadway sector workers (and off) who care and are (without resorting to abrasive denunciation) seriously dedicated to the American Theatre.

FREEMAN Jayne Stewart; (2) Arts reporter and critic; (3) b. Fairfield, Ia., Aug. 17, 1933; (4) d. Wilson and Frances (Hardie) Stewart; (5) B.A. State University of Iowa, Major subj.: dramatic arts, 1955; (6) m. Richard L. Freeman, May 29, 1954; (7) children--Patricia Lynn, Alison Jayne, Richard Lewis, Jr.; (8) Producer and Hostess: "Artscene," WNED-TV, 1967- ; Arts reporter and critic: WBEN-TV, 1971- ; Arts reporter: WBEN radio, 1975- ; Actor: Ryukyus Theatre 1955; Actor, director: Amherst Comm. Theatre, 1956-1972; Producer, Director: Calvary Epis. Musical, 1966; Writer, Producer: Buffalo Comm. Musical, 1969; Freelance radio and TV commercials: 1964- ; Radio and TV specials: WBEN-TV, WBEN radio, WNED-TV, 1971- ; (9) Substitute teacher of drama and speech: 1956-1973; (10) Jr. League of Buff., Millard Fillmore Jr. Bd., Operation Good Govt.; Honorary mem.: Patteran Artists; mem.: Friends of the Buffalo Theatre, Inc., 1975- ; Director: Associated Arts Organization, 1968- 1973; (14) Best supporting actress: Eastern Play Festival, 1967; Best director: Corning Play Festival, 1966; (15) Charter mem.: National Theater Critics Assoc.; Mem.: Phi Beta Kappa; Mem.: Delta Gamma; Mem.: Philharmonic Women's Committee; (16) Republican; (17) Episcopalian; (19) Park Country Club, Four Seasons Racquet Club; (20) Cont. articles to: Buffalo Evening News, Video 17 Fan Magazine; (21) 182 Le Brun Circle, Buffalo, N.Y. 14226, Ph. 716-836-0260; (22) WBEN-TV, 2077 Elmwood Ave., Buffalo, N.Y. 14207, Ph. 716-876-0930; WNED-TV, 184 Barton St., Buffalo, N.Y. 14213, Ph. 716-885-1000.

"Desire Under the Elms"
(by Jayne S. Freeman, over WBEN television, Buffalo, N.Y.,
January 9, 1975)

The plot, briefly, is this: a 35 year old woman marries a 75

year old New England farmer; she wants a home of her own.
Then she finds her husband plans on willing it to a son by another
marriage.   She subsequently falls in love with the son, has a
child by him and things don't get any better after that.

A critic of 50 years ago called this play, "an ode to greed
and lust and murder without remorse." But as played by the
Studio Arena, that burning greed and lust are missing from the
first part, so that when the murder without remorse comes about,
it just looks like a severe case of post-partum blues.

The obviously low-budget set is a problem.   The one-dimensional elms aren't much to have desire under, and, although I
know the five required sets are tough to handle on the Studio
Arena thrust stage, something should have been done to make it
look more like a New England farmhouse and less like the second
floor of the Goodwill.   Then, none of the leads is quite right for
his part; the earthy characters and down-East accents don't come
naturally.

However, the atmosphere is right.   The pace of the show, the
action scenes, the lights and music all contribute to a production
that is surprisingly good considering all the minuses ... and
that's a tip of the hat to director Warren Enters.

The show he's put together isn't brilliant, but it's sound.
In other words, it may not be O'Neill at its best, but it is Studio
Arena at its better.

Joan Rivers and John Davidson
(by Jayne S. Freeman, over WBEN television, Buffalo, N.Y.,
June 17, 1975)

I first saw John Davidson seven years ago at Melody Fair
when he was just a kid.   And I must say he's matured.   In fact,
Arthur Godfrey might even say he's lost his humility.   He was
always good, always charming; now seven years later he knows
it.   I liked him better in the days before he did.

Anyway, he still tosses his head like a young colt, melodizes
even better than he used to on songs old and new, clowns around,
and ends the evening with a musical comment as he sings the best
songs of 1975 ... commercial jingles.

Davidson gives a stagewise and cocksure performance.   Joan
Rivers is also stagewise and cocky, but maybe not so sure.   Remember, she may be loved and desired now, but she was a fatty
when she was young, and in her intense performance, there's always that fat kid screaming to get out.

Her routine stems from that youthful lack of assurance,
mixed with her mature female attitudes.   Now I don't know how
you men felt about her subject matter of self-image, marriage

and her gynecologist, but when she talks to the audience about
how tough it is to be a woman, we women laughed and said
"amen. "

Someone commented last night he hadn't felt this kind of electricity on opening night for a long time, and I agree. John Davidson, clowning singer; Joan Rivers, singing clown ... separate
but equal on that Melody Fair stage ... create the kind of excitement between performer and collective audience that can't
happen in the one-to-one basis between you and your TV screen.
Theirs is the kind of act that will keep live theatre living, no
matter how dependent we grow on that small electronic stage.

FRIEDMAN, Arthur; (2) Theater critic; (3) b. New York, Dec. 21,
1935; (4) s. Morris and Rose (Morson); (5) B.A. City College of New
York, major subj.: English, 1957; A.M. Boston U. , major subj.:
English, 1959; Harvard U. Graduate School of Arts and Sciences
1959-67; (6) Single; (8) Drama Critic, Harvard Drama Review 1965-
67; Boston Spectator 1966-67; The Phoenix 1969-72; The Real Paper
1972- ; (9) Actor, Harvard Summer School Repertory Theater 1966,
1968; Harvard Dramatic Club Summer Players 1967-69; Dir. "The
Pooh Players" 1966-69; Taught at Boston University 1957-63; City
College of New York, summer 1969, 1961-64, Harvard University
1962-66, Lowell State College 1966- ; (14) Carnegie Fellow, C.C.N.Y.
1959; Leon Pin, C.C.N.Y. 1957; (15) Mem. American Federation of
Teachers; (16) Independent; (17) Druid; (20) Cont. articles to Educational Theatre Journal, Prime Time, Boston Magazine, Shakespeare
Newsletter; (21) 1200 Massachusetts Ave. , # 59W, Cambridge, Mass.
02138, Ph. 617-876-8221; (22) The Real Paper, 10B Mt. Auburn St. ,
Cambridge, Mass. 02138, Ph. 617-492-8101; (23) Circulation: 100,000
weekly; (24) 60 plays and musicals; 5 miscellaneous.

Theatre: Fighting Vainly the Old Anouilh
(by Arthur Friedman, The Real Paper, August 22, 1973)

Taking playwrights at their word is a tricky business. Jean
Anouilh, for example, assures us that his "Dear Antoine" is presented "with no other object" than to entertain us for a moment.
Quelle chinoiserie! Anouilh's got something other than entertainment up his sleeve. And when he says of his central character
that "under his surface levity, Antoine was a very enigmatic
man," Anouilh might just as well be describing his play.

A typical reaction to "Dear Antoine," especially on the part
of those whose sense of negative capability is underdeveloped, has
been to complain that the play's "surface brilliance" does not
justify its length and lack of substance. Such viewers are, in
Keats' words, unable to accept "mysteries, doubts, without any
irritable reaching after fact and reason." If a playwright promises us momentary entertainment, dammit, it's unfair of him
to "baffle us for weeks!"

But in "Dear Antoine" Anouilh means to show that great theatre (as opposed to the sort of potboilers and melodramas his
character Antoine writes) is an accurate mirror of life's ambiguities and confusions only when it itself is ambiguous and complex. What is life, after all, but "a secret play hidden behind
so many theatrical effects"?

Anouilh's Antoine, an aging playwright who has achieved considerable success on the popular stage, has not been quite so
successful in life. Though he has thrice married, kept mistresses galore and retained the friendship of distinguished men--has,
in other words, seemed to have lived life to the hilt--Antoine
has never understood the nature of their relationship to him.
What role has he played in their lives? Have they loved him?
Or is love merely a demand of the ego?

So Antoine summons the "characters" of his life to the Ba-
varian retreat where he has secluded himself for three years.
Their arrival, he hopes, will finally enable him to "write the
real script" of his life, to fashion a semblance of unity from
the remnants of his unruly past, to create his lasting memorial.

There is, however, one complication. Either through accident or suicide, Antoine is dead.

Thus, his former wives, children, mistresses and friends
(a critic, a doctor, a professor) assemble--at Antoine's posthumous request--for his funeral. And, as in one of his own contrived plots, a timely avalanche maroons them in his mansion.
A recording of Antoine's voice sets the stage for the last egotistic assertion of this minor playwright directing the final scene
of his life from the grave. The characters of his past must do
the rest: exhume the truth of their feelings for him.

So far, so good. A conventionally interesting plot for comedy or melodrama or mystery--what with its echo of a dead
man's voice, its snowbound guests, even the howling of a forlorn
dog.

But Anouilh has only begun his trickery. A flashback takes
us three years into the past, to Antoine's 50th birthday party at
which he announces to the same houseguests his plans to write
a play called "Dear Antoine" about a dead playwright, his assembled family and friends, an avalanche ... and so on.

In the following act, a group of Parisian players descend
on the mansion to take up their roles, under Antoine's direction,
in a private performance of "Dear Antoine." (We've already
met these "actors" as the characters of Act I.) The rehearsal
breaks down completely: the players cannot improvise the emotions Antoine expects of them; they cannot find satisfactory motivation nor understand the people they are to represent. Antoine's masterwork, then, if it is to be a success, must await
his death.

Next--if you are still following me--we are whisked forward
to the present, or, if you will, back to where we began. Antoine is dead again. Each of his guests, in a series of charged
encounters, tries to straighten out his or her past relationship
with him. Then ... departure to a Chekhovian Gotterdammerung
of shutters being hammered shut, dimming lights, luggage being
carted off. Antoine's guests leave the past behind them (like old
Firs, forgotten in "The Cherry Orchard"), a few with a greater
understanding of what this final "act" of Antoine's life has meant.

Well, where does this leave us? In a Chinese box--with
doors opening onto other doors, questions onto other questions.
Has a funeral reunion really taken place? Or, from the outset,
has what we have seen been a private performance for an invisible, self-indulgent playwright somewhere behind, beyond us in
the darkened theatre? Are the onstage actors portraying figures
from Antoine's life, or are they actors playing actors playing
figures from Antoine's life? We are never sure--nor meant to
be.

For the meaning of "Dear Antoine," like the meaning of most
human experiences, never sorts itself out with clockwork precision. Only in lesser arts--as Antoine's career illustrates--are
uncertainties perfectly resolved, loose endings neatly trimmed
at the edges, emotions and relationships clarified beyond all ambiguity.

The Harvard Summer School Repertory production of "Dear
Antoine" is in every way worthy of this play. I have only the
highest praise for Kent Paul's restrained direction of Anouilh's
menage-a-treize, especially of those half-dozen or so roles that
might easily have developed into caricature. From a uniformly
capable group of players, too numerous to mention individually,
I must single out Sharon Spelman as Antoine's resentful former
mistress, Estelle, whose "eyes are dry for life." Here is an
actress to watch and relish; she has style and depth, particularly in her long opening scene, where every gesture and intonation
reveals a new aspect of this unhappy woman's biography.

Kudos, too, for Patricia Falkenhain's monstrous Carlotta
(Antoine's first wife), a salty old harridan of the theatre, whose
foghorn voice, painted face and red fright-wig belie her underlying soundness of spirit; Robert Gerringer's bone-dry etching
of Lapinet, the academic Boswell to Antoine's Dr. Johnson (what
a splendid Tesman Gerringer could play--to Falkenhain's Hedda
Gabler, naturally); Amy Nathan's softly appealing Maria, Antoine's
last wife, who is strong enough to leave him for a man she does
not love because she no longer wants her life to be stage-man-
aged by her husband; and, finally, Robert Pastene's theatrical,
commanding, strangely distant Antoine.

The baroque setting of Ralph Funicello, whose drapery and
scaffolding rightly suggests that we may be watching a performance

of a performance, is eminently suitable, as are the richly understated costumes of Linda Martin.

In all, this "Dear Antoine" is as fine an example of ensemble stagework as you'll be likely to find during these long summer nights.

Eliza Slams the Door
(by Arthur Friedman, The Real Paper, September 4, 1974)

Cinderella stories with happy endings are all very well for
musicals. So playgoers young enough in mind to like "My Fair
Lady" accept its conventional romantic theme (ugly duckling into
swan) and its conventional happy ending (student marries teacher)
as entirely in accord with the natural laws of musical comedy.

But something about the conclusion of "My Fair Lady" nags
at our consciences. It does seem inevitable that Eliza Doolittle
should bestow her body and soul on the crotchety Professor Higgins who, after all, has stitched her together from cockney shreds
and gutter patches and fashioned a socially acceptable lady.
Torn up by her roots and transplanted into the alien soil of respectable society, she has nothing but her body and soul to give.
What else is there for Eliza to do but serve her Dr. Frankenstein as slipper-bearer, pipe-lighter and experimental showpiece?
She's grown accustomed to his face because, in her new incarnation as an artificially created lady of leisure, his is the only
face she knows. So Messrs. Lerner and Loewe, to keep Eliza
off the streets, have her fall in love with Higgins. The real
world, you see, always disappears in fairy tales; Cinderella never
goes back to her stepsisters.

Fortunately, the successful London revival of "Pygmalion"
(the source-play for "My Fair Lady") proves that Shaw had something other than fairy tale endings on his mind.

Because director John Dexter chooses the least romantic conclusion of this multi-ended comedy, "Pygmalion" seems to have
grown more timely during its long exile from the stage. After
the final breakdown of nuptial negotiations between Eliza and Higgins, Eliza walks out of her life as a guinea-pig and into a real
life of her own--A Shavian Nora slamming the door of her doll's
house. "Pygmalion" thus becomes the story of her liberation.

Dexter is helped in this interpretation by some clever casting against type. Wisely sidestepping the definitive models established by Rex Harrison and Julie Andrews in the musical version, he has chosen Diana Rigg for Eliza and Alec McCowen for
Higgins.

Those who know her from "The Avengers" or from her Cordelia and Lady Macbeth, understand that Rigg is no grimy angel-
of-the-streets waiting for a chance to unfurl her golden wings.

Rigg's eyes are never dewy with romance. This actress is too svelte, too calculating to get a convincing cockney dander up, so she opts for a tamer and more workable reading of the early Eliza. Her Covent Garden flower-girl is a clumsy, gangling, mush-mouthed smudge of a woman, less tough than pathetic, less fiery than self-pitying. But there is a latent strength in her desire to be "elevated" by Higgins' lessons in oral "self-presentation," a sense of determination that prepares us for Eliza's later independence.

In Eliza's second stage, after Higgins' hard schooling in speech, movement and social demeanor, Rigg gives us an isolated and bewildered woman miserably ready to test her new role as a lady of quality. During the famous tea scene at the home of Higgins' mother, Rigg plays Eliza as a marionette fresh from the painter's workbench--still sticky, a little tight in the joints, numbly unsure of her mechanical words.

Her third stage comes when Eliza must deal with Higgins' insensitivity (he still thinks of her as a social reclamation project, not as a woman). Thanks to the professor's instruction, Rigg's Eliza is now a bold, precise and graceful beauty--a Shavian "new woman." At last she can bargain with Higgins from strength. Their marital negotiations fail because Higgins cannot shake off his fixed notions of what role a woman should play in his life (she will become another "old bachelor") and because he is afraid of his feelings for her. So Eliza bids him a tearless goodbye.

This "unhappy ending" is made dramatically acceptable--even necessary--by the incompatibility of Rigg's Eliza and Alex McCowen's Higgins. McCowen does not project the sexual charisma and brisk authority of a Rex Harrison. A less expansive and more contrived actor than Harrison, McCowen cannot play Higgins as a Svengali-like shaper of Eliza's destiny through sheer force of will. So McCowen uses the strength he had to create a Higgins different from (and more complex than) any we have seen before.

His is the very model of the antiseptic scientist, a man of fastidious mind and spirit. McCowen's Higgins has plenty of problems of his own, problems no less delimiting than the social handicaps of Eliza. He is insecure in crowds: he doesn't know what to do with his hands or where to rest his eyes. He is uneasy with women, cowed by men. A mama's boy, he depends on old Mrs. Higgins' sly wisdom to pull him through difficult times. He escapes into his phonetic experiments to avoid feeling for, and communicating with, others.

In the great last act of "Pygmalion," McCowen's Higgins comes to understand, in a befuddled yet not unprideful way, that his finest student has surpassed her master in the very art of self-assertion he is licensed to teach. Eliza, in short, has learned to outplay him at his own game. So there is no sadness at Eliza's abandonment of Higgins, merely the bracing reassurance that she is setting out to win the world, perhaps to do for her callow suitor Freddie what Higgins has done for her.

So fresh and timely a reading of "Pygmalion" proves that the long road back from a musicalization has not been as rough or weary for Shaw's great comedy as we feared. Thanks to Dexter, Rigg and McCowen, "Pygmalion" is with us again on its own terms.

FULLER, Hoyt W.; (2) Exec. Editor; (3) b. Atlanta, Ga., Sept. 10, 1928; (5) B.A. Wayne State U., Detroit, Mich. (English Lit. - Journalism); Advanced Study, Wayne State U.; (8) Assistant Ed., Colliers Encyclopedia; West African Correspondent, Haagse Post, Amsterdam; Associate Ed., Ebony Magazine; Feature Editor, Michigan Chronicle; Reporter, Detroit Tribune; Exec. Editor, Black World; (9) Teaching Experience: Fiction Writing Seminar, Columbia College, Chicago, Ill.; Afro-American Lit., Northwestern University; Afro-American Lit., Indiana University; Afro-American Lit., Wayne State University; (14) John Hay Whitney Opportunity Fellowship, 1965-66; (15) Member, Detroit Actors Guild; Board of Directors, Kuumba Theatre Workshop; (20) Editor, Annual Theatre Issue, Black World Magazine; author, Journey to Africa; published in: Black Expression: Essays in the Creative Arts by and about Black Americans, ed. Addison Gayle Jr.; American Negro Short Stories, ed. John Henrick Clark; The Black Aesthetic, ed. Addison Gayle Jr.; Black Literature in American, ed. Houston A. Baker; Points of Departure, ed. Ernece Kelly; Beyond the Angry Black, ed. John A. Williams; The Black American Writer, ed. C. W. E. Bigsby; Cont. articles to: The New Yorker, The Nation, the New Leader, The New Republic, Midstream, Southwest Review, North American Review, The Chicago Defender, Chicago Jewish Forum, Book Week (New York Herald Tribune), Book Week (Chicago Sun-Times), Books Today (Chicago Tribune, African Forum, The Detroit News, The Christian Science Monitor, The New York Times Book Review; (21) 3001 S. Martin Luther King Dr., Apt. 1902, Chicago, Ill. 60616, Ph. 312-842-5370; (22) 820 South Michigan Ave., Chicago, Ill. 60605, Ph. 312-786-7682.

Playwright and Play: Joseph A. Walker and The River Niger
(by Hoyt W. Fuller, Black World, April 1973)

Joseph A. Walker lives in Harlem. The window in his work alcove overlooks busy 132nd Street and a stretch of Fifth Avenue that makes no claim to fashion. His house is comfortable, and busy, and relaxed. The books on the shelves are wide-ranging in subject, but the heavy emphasis on The Theater brings no surprise; for both Mr. Walker and his composer-musician wife, Dottie, are deeply involved in theater. And for Mr. Walker, that involvement suddenly has projected him into the national spotlight. His play, The River Niger, mounted in a superb production by the Negro Ensemble Company downtown, is one of the most

exciting plays to be presented anywhere in this country in the
past year.

Mr. Walker is a large man, gentle of face and bearing,
possessed of a calmness of manner and an appealing tonality
which, one suspects, he brought with him at the onset of his
career in the theater. That career began at Howard University
in Washington, D.C., although little of note happened to it there
beyond exposure and rudimentary experience. Following a stint
in the Air Force, Mr. Walker studied for a master's degree in
drama at Catholic University. While there, he received addi-
tional--though limited--experience as an actor in university productions.

Mr. Walker moved to New York City in the mid-Sixties, obtained a regular job as mathematics and English teacher in a
junior high school, and joined a theater group under the direction
of actor Lou Gossett. His first substantial part was in The Believers, an Off-Broadway musical that ran several months in
1967. Other roles followed, including a part in comedian Woody
Allen's film, Bananas.

Acting, however, proved undependable as a means of livelihood, and Mr. Walker found himself affronted by many of the
conditions under which actors must seek work. He chose the
security of teaching, preferring not to submit to the conditions
he found harrowing and demeaning. At the same time, he continued to write and, in 1969, the Negro Ensemble Company produced his play, Harangues. The play received encouraging notices. A year later, the Negro Ensemble Company produced another of his plays, Ododo, which won more encouraging notices.

With The River Niger, the playwright's collaboration with
the Negro Ensemble Company has proved a perfect union. The
play, which is rich in theme and traditional in form, was directed with brilliant insight by Douglas Turner Ward and performed with near faultlessness by a supremely talented cast.
The play deals, on a fundamental level, with the eternal struggle of Black men to forge a whole life for their progeny in a
society whose basic institutions are organized against the probability of the struggle ever bearing fruit. This theme, simply
stated, says almost nothing of the play, however, for the playwright has handled the theme with such grace and care that the
theme blends magically with the story, culminating in a human
experience which, though familiar in its contours, is fresh and
illuminating in its effect.

There are three generations in the Harlem household of
Johnny Williams--Grandma Wilhelmina Brown, the mother of
Johnny's wife, Mattie; Johnny and Mattie; and Johnny and Mattie's
son, Jeff, home from the wars. Johnny's best friend is Dudley
Stanton, a bachelor physician for whom the Williamses constitute
a surrogate family. And there is Ann Vanderguild, the South

African nurse who descends from Canada, unexpected and unan-
nounced to claim her man, the Williamses' homecoming son. The
other characters are less notable, though no less important to
the action of the play, particularly to the violent dénouement.
As these characters relate and interrelate, they reveal much of
the essence of the Black reality, always as men and women confronting the complexity of their total being, and they emerge with
the full-dimensioned clarity of memorable characters, strong,
weak, funny, pathetic, and always pulsatingly alive.

As Johnny Williams, Doug Turner Ward is the central character of the play, and it is difficult to imagine the role played
better. He is all gruffness and loud talk and bluff, but underneath it all vulnerable and tender at the same time. As Grandma, the versatile Frances Foster is a gem, formidable and funny, proud and prejudiced, carrying in her ancient bosom a terrible memory which ties her, forever, to the truth Black people
deny at their peril. Roxie Roker, as Johnny's wife and Grandma's daughter, is the Strong Black Woman, with a difference:
it is clear that she knows that point at which her man's striving
collided with the wall he is powerless to move, and she cushions
his lifelong fall with tireless compassion. And Grenna Whitaker,
as the South African exile, is marvelous. Simply that. A lovely young woman, she has the eloquence of voice and movement
which seems ideal for her role as the daughter and sister of Black
men crushed in their fight against oppressive racism in South
Africa. Perhaps her talent creates the illusion, but her mastery
of the South African accent--the Afrikaan-flavored English imposed on Bantu--is uncanny. And Graham Brown as the philosophical doctor, ready with cash and quips, seems just right in
his understated role as the family friend, the symbol of that
racial resourcefulness which never fails.

In The River Niger, playwright Walker touches on all bases.
The play is integrated, complete. If it has any faults, they are--
in the judgment of this writer--first, a tendency towards con-
trivancy in the treatment of the "militants" who first invade the
Williams home and, then, later, bring tragedy into it; and second, in the violent shoot-out ending of the play which, because
it seems melodramatic, clashes with the sustained simplicity and
honesty of the first two-thirds of the play.

But Mr. Walker, of course, rejects the suggestion that the
play's ending is "melodramatic." He feels that the gunplay is
in keeping with the motion of the play, the natural culmination
of the events taking place on and off stage.

At press time, The River Niger run at the Negro Ensemble
Company's theater had been extended, and there was talk of trans-
ferring the production uptown to Broadway. It also reliably was
reported that Ossie Davis, busy at the time filming Gordon's
War in Harlem, was interested in translating The River Niger to
the screen.

Meanwhile, Mr. Walker, who supports his family by teaching speech at City College (and at his alma mater, Howard University, to which he commutes), pursues a Ph. D. degree in films at New York University and promotes the Demi-Gods, a music, dance and drama group he and Mrs. Walker founded. He recognizes that, with a "hit" on his hands, more will be expected of him next time around. And there is every reason to suppose he will be prepared to give it.

"What the Wine-Sellers Buy"
(by Hoyt Fuller, a solicited opinion assured of publication without regard to views expressed, appearing in an advertisement in New York Times, February 15, 1974)

There is a moment early in "What the Wine-Sellers Buy" when Rico the pimp makes a profound observation on the Black experience in America. It is at the beginning of Rico's campaign to recruit the young hero Steve as his protege, and Rico, the master psychologist, zeros in on Steve's healthy preoccupation with school and sports.

Rico, released from prison, is established as a tenant in the same house occupied by Steve and his mother, Laura Carlton. She knows what Rico is and her hostility to him is unyielding. A widow, she must work hard to support her son and herself in a rundown Detroit community. Her antagonism and fear of Rico is heightened by the memory of her late husband's tragic brush with the underworld. The way to make something of himself, she assures Steve, is through study, hard work and keeping out of trouble. But in the battle for Steve's mind, Rico holds the aces. He puts down school, arguing plausibly that a Black man's best education is available in the streets; he throws around money as if it is merely paper; his clothes are expensive and dazzling; glamorous women are at his command; he is in control; he is his own man.

Rico takes the classic dilemma of the Black in America and reduces it to terms which suit his simple purposes: there are only two kinds of people in the world--the takers and the taken, the exploiters and the exploited--and that American society is organized to permanently fix Black men in a position of impotence. And, Rico argues, Black women like Laura Carlton, seeking to protect their men, ensure their impotence by insisting that they obey the rules which are designed to emasculate them. The choice before him, Rico preaches to Steve, is to be a "punk" like all those hard-working, debt-ridden Black clods or else to be a man like Rico.

Rico, played with serpentine cool by actor Dick Williams, is the kind of creature a cold and manipulative system deserves. But it is the burden of Milner's rich and insightful play that man's need to love--that human impulse--is his ultimate defense against total corruption. "What the Wine-Sellers Buy" deals with

the crucial weeks in a young Black man's life when he must decide whether there are things in his life which are not marketable, and if so, what they are.   Steve has a mother who wants
to protect him, and a girl who wants to love him, and his decision can betray the one and destroy the other.

"Wine-Sellers" is a play with many strengths.   First, it
sweeps the viewer into the urban Black community where life,
though always hard, is sparked by a unique buoyancy and energy,
laced with mocking laughter.   It focuses on plain people, coping
in their own ways with the limited alternatives at hand.   The
play illuminates the beauty and will to survive of men programmed for defeat and the unflagging spirit of the women who love
and need them.

The play's performances range from adequate to superb.   The
roles acted by Marilyn B. Coleman and Loretta Greene seemed
to suffer from periodic inattention, but both women are superior
actresses.   The talented Gloria Edwards added a dimension to
her role by subtly portraying the flashy whore as a heroin addict;
and Jean Du Shon, as the young heroine's embattled mother,
brought an extra measure of poignancy to her role.   Glynn Tur-
man, as Steve, was excellent.   The young character's gradual
and reluctant transformation from average student to neophyte
pimp was masterful.   But the play belongs to Dick Williams,
whose resourcefulness and attractiveness as an actor, aided by
the prominence and centrality of his role, make him the villain
the audiences love to hate.

The play was strikingly staged, the setting cleverly conceived
by Santo Loquasto, and the costumes by Judy Dearing--particular-
ly the flamboyant outfits worn by Mr. Williams--were imaginative.

The direction, by Michael Schultz, was sensitive and expertly
paced.   The play is episodic, the dialogue sometimes drawn out,
and a director--not familiar with the lifestyle of the characters
and not attuned to their rhythm--might have been tempted to
quicken the movement, which would have been disastrous.   Still,
Mr. Schultz and Mr. Milner might have served the play better
by making Steve's final transformation less abrupt.   While it is
true that the audience is pulling for a happy ending, the too rapid change in attitude does a kind of violence to a well-drawn
character.

FUNK, Nancy Melich; (2) Theater reviewer and feature writer for
Art Section and Home Magazine; (3) b. Moab, Ut., Nov. 10, 1942;
(4) d. Doris (Snyder) and Mitchell Melich; (5) B.S. U. of Utah, major: journalism, 1970; (6) m. Timothy J. Funk, Sept. 19, 1970;
(7) children--Shelly Lynne, Christopher Bryan; (8) Salt Lake Tribune
1970 to present; (9) movie extra "Rio Grande" and "Airport 1975";
(21) 1236 Roosevelt Ave., Salt Lake City, Ut. 84105, Ph. 801-466-
7186; (22) Salt Lake Tribune, 143 South Main, P.O. Box 867, Salt

Lake City, Ut. 84110, Ph. 801-524-4581; (23) Circulation: 102,000 daily, Sundays 180,000; (24) 65-70 plays and musicals, occasional motion picture and miscellaneous concerts.

I Can't Hear You When the King Is Singing
(by Nancy Funk, Salt Lake Tribune, May 23, 1974)

If medals were awarded for perseverance, five of them should be ceremoniously given to five actors currently appearing in the Babcock Theatre's production of "Long Day's Journey Into Night." And David Jones, the play's director, should receive a half dozen!

For certainly the strangest and most incongruous production of the Eugene O'Neill classic, Tuesday's opening night presentation will long be remembered.

You must bear in mind, the Babcock Theatre is housed in the basement of Pioneer Memorial Theatre--two flights down from the main lobby and PMT's mainstage.

Eugene O'Neill may be downstairs but Rodgers and Hammerstein didn't let that interfere. Their musical, "The King and I," was carrying on for all its lovely worth upstairs, while down at Babcock the distraction was immense.

The odd thing about all this was the timing, totally unintentional, between the songs of "The King and I" and the dialogue in "Journey."

The story begins in the familiar way, with mother and father in conversation and the two sons entering shortly thereafter. Talk eventually comes to "mama's problem" and all of a sudden, from out of the ceiling flows the lilting strains "Whenever I feel afraid, I hold my head erect and Whistle a Happy Tune," etc., etc., etc.

I was somewhat jolted for the moment, but decided not to let it bother me--concentrate more deeply on the play--get involved with the intensity of O'Neill and the music won't distract.

It worked for awhile, but not long. Music is heard off and on throughout Act II. When the March of the Children is happening upstairs, James Tyrone, the father walks emphatically into his living room; when mother and dad become engrossed in conversation, it's "Hello, Young Lovers" overhead.

But the worst of all occurs in Act IV, during the most dramatic and draining moments of the play.

Edmund has just undergone a tiring, emotional moment with his father when the door slams and Jamie drunk, arrives home. Father leaves and the two brothers are left alone. Jamie tells of his night out and then begins to elaborate on his love for his brother. He walks toward Edmund, stumbling and crying, and embraces him. They part. And yes, you guessed it. There goes the music again--this time louder than previously and of course what else but "Shall We Dance?"

It was totally unnerving and I wouldn't have blamed the actors if they had stopped right then and walked off the stage.

Anyone who has read or seen the play knows how terribly, terribly difficult a piece it is. The demands placed on both actor and audience are of incredible magnitude. O'Neill is like that and this of all his works commands that attitude. To have a distraction such as this one is unforgivable.

It is hard to say to what extent the cast was bothered. Some lines were noticeably flubbed and the rhythm of the play was certainly damaged. I am reluctant to criticize the production, per se, because of the strange circumstances under which it was performed.

Aside from the previously mentioned disturbances, the most difficult aspect to this "Journey" was the age of the mother and father.

Jodee Steffensen has a fine voice and the physical size of a Mary Tyrone but she looks scarcely more than 20. Not at all like a woman addicted to drugs for several years and the mother of two grown sons.

Scott Peacock as her husband James presented the same problem for me. He just wasn't convincing.

Michael Stark as Jamie and Craig Ferre, the afflicted Edmund, were both good. Ferre's portrayal was the most consistent throughout and the strongest, while Stark lost control of his Jamie in Act IV when acting drunk. But then who wouldn't with all that whistling and drum pounding going on overhead?

Carla Hawkins was also good in her brief part as the maid.

The show will continue through Saturday with a 7 p.m. curtain. It's very long, nearly four hours and unless your concentration is far better than mine or unless the show adjourns to the PMT lawn or unless you like your O'Neill flavored with Rodgers and Hammerstein, you might think twice before going to this production.

Is Frank Perry's Latest Film Really a Comedy?
(by Nancy Funk, Salt Lake Tribune, March 23, 1975)

Frank Perry is a stocky, dark-haired man with kind eyes. His first film, in 1962, "David and Lisa," earned him an Academy

Award nomination as best director of the year.

Since then he has directed "Diary of a Mad Housewife," "Last Summer," and "Man on a Swing" to mention a few.

He was in Salt Lake City recently to discuss and promote his latest film, "Rancho Deluxe" billed as a "wildly imaginative western comedy," starring Jeff Bridges, Sam Waterston, Elizabeth Ashley, Slim Pickens and others.

The picture is easily the worst film I have seen in the last five years, maybe ever, and it was curiosity as well as a sense of fair play that compelled me to talk with Mr. Perry.

The film, for me, is not a comedy, but rather a hateful, degrading stab at American ranchers and the way they live.

Made in Livingston, Mont. , it is basically concerned with two cattle rustlers and their escapades which include carving up a steer with a chainsaw just for the fun of it and sleeping around whenever they get the chance. Filled with gutter talk and unnecessary violence, the picture is anything but a comedy.

Mr. Perry, a man who says he's "deeply concerned about the condition of today's society," said he did intend the film as a comedy, that he had made "statement" films in the past and was interested in doing something else. He said perhaps he hadn't succeeded with this picture.

However, Mr. Perry did say the film had received praise from Judith Crist, a standing ovation at a five-day film festival in Dallas, raves from a woman writer for the Denver Post as well as from the editor of the paper in Livingston, Mont.

"The only other reaction like yours I've received was from Vogue's movie critic," said Mr. Perry. "He hated the film and said he planned to do a two-page spread on how terrible it was."

The amiable director intently and patiently listened to the criticism waged against his film and in no way tried to change my thinking on the subject.

He believes movies are a very personal thing and that there is no right or wrong interpretation on what someone decides, merely a difference of opinion.

He deplored the decadent society he found in Livingston but said he consciously tried to avoid making another "statement" film.

"I was not trying to be cynical nor was I trying to make a comedy in the sense of Mel Brooks' 'Blazing Saddles'."

The most serious objection I have is the way in which the
film is being "sold" to the public.

There is nothing funny to me about unnecessary killing of the
animals, young men who get their kicks from threatening the
lives of old men, or offensive language flowing freely from teen-
age girls.

The picture is unnecessary and I find it difficult to believe
anyone could or would consider it entertaining.

GAGNARD, Frank Lewis; (2) Journalist; (3) b. Kerrville, Tex.,
Nov. 8, 1929; (4) s. Frank and Leona Jo (Bevins); (5) B.A., N. Tex.
State U., 1951; (8) Amusements staff Dallas Morning News, 1951-57;
critic, fine arts editor New Orleans Item. 1957-58; critic amuse-
ments editor New Orleans Times-Picayune 1959- ; (21) 538 Madison
St., New Orleans, La. 70116; (22) 3800 Howard Ave., New Orleans,
La. 70140.

GALE, William Keene; (2) Theater critic; (3) b. New York City,
Nov. 9, 1940; (4) s. William and Ida (Gillis); (5) B.A. Ohio State U.,
major subj.: History, 1965; (6) m. Peggy Bican, May 19, 1963; (7)
children--Susan Moore, Jeffrey Keene; (8) News reporter, magazine
editor, Providence Journal, 1966-72, entertainment writer, 1973-75,
entertainment editor, 1976- ; (9) College theater, teacher of journalism, Rhode Island College, Providence; (13) Sergeant, air traffic
controller, USAF; (14) Several local journalism; (16) Independent;
(20) Free lance writing in Yankee, other magazines; (21) 9 Sixth St.,
West Barrington, R.I. 02806, Ph. 401-245-5968; (22) Providence
Journal-Bulletin, 75 Fountain St., Providence, R.I. 02902, Ph. 401-
277-7267; (23) Circulation: 200,000; (24) Also review movies.

"Rex" Needs More Than Glitter
(by William K. Gale, Providence Journal-Bulletin, March 24, 1976)

Rex at the Shubert Theater is a 16th Century Ringling Brothers, Barnum & Bailey show, sumptuous--with gorgeous sets
and fine music, but overdone--too often substituting glitter for
substance and dramatic excitement.

You must admire the lovely and effective sets and costumes
and the songs that flow so easily from the story.   But this pre-
Broadway musical, which purports to be the story of Henry VIII,
is weak at its base.   The book simply does not match the music,
the staging or the performances.

But there is still a good deal to enjoy.   Henry is played with
great life and bravura by Nicol Williamson, a splendid actor who,
in taking King Henry from a roistering, wenching, tyrannical
despot to a wretched, sad old man, gives a huge performance.

He imbues Rex with intensity and a feeling of life lived on
the edge that you don't often get in a big "Broadway" musical.
He's an actor with the skills to match the life of Henry VIII.

His singing voice is pleasant, but not outstanding and his
dancing--well it's a good thing he wore a mask which hid the
pained expression he showed before beginning his one attempt.

Richard Rodgers' music is splendid.   At 74 he has not lost
his touch.   Songs like As I Once Loved You and In Time flow
through Rex as gently as a country stream.

The elaborate and beautiful sets by John Conklin, who is
familiar to theatergoers here from his designs at the American
Shakespeare Festival in Stratford, are clever and almost breathtaking in application, not to mention expense.   He also did the
colorful Camelot-like costumes which, if they occasionally rival
those once worn by the Denver Broncos football team, are lovely
to look at.

The lyrics to go with Rodgers' music are generally pleasant
and appropriate.   They were done by Sheldon Harnick who has
written in collaboration with others Fiddler on the Roof and Fiorello, not to mention the immortal Boston Beguine from New Faces
of 1952.   For work like that he can be forgiven occasional lyrics
in Rex such as "... the world starts to glow like a stained glass
window ..."

So, despite all the good things, Rex lacks a dramatic intensity.   Sherman Yellen's book concentrates on Henry's wives (although we see nothing of a couple of them) and shows us a version of Henry VIII which begins as a sort of Peck's Bad Boy and
runs through despotism and beheadings to old age, but is concentrated on his character and ignores the consequences of his acts.

Cardinal Wolsey is dismissed like a bothersome fly and Henry's effect on Europe after his break with Rome is hardly seen
at all.   Perhaps they can't get all this in a musical but more
substantial history and less theatrical posing would help Rex a
good deal.

Still, while it's not the greatest show on earth it is a huge,
spectacular presentation, an old fashioned Broadway musical which
you admire for what it does well and wish it had maintained a
high level all the way through.

Julie Harris as Poet Dickinson in One-Person Show
(by William K. Gale, Providence Journal, April 8, 1976)

The actress is on stage alone for almost two hours.   Her
character is a reclusive woman who never goes out and almost
never sees anyone in the dusty, small town of her birth and 56-
year-long life.

But all of this works, dazzlingly at times, making The Belle of Amherst a wonderfully gratifying one-woman production.

The reason it works is that the actress is Julie Harris, the character is Emily Dickinson and the town is Amherst, Mass. They have been woven together by a young author, William Luce, and directed by Charles Nelson Reilly into brilliant theater at the Colonial Theater.

Miss Harris gives the best one-person show I've ever seen. She is an actress of such wide range that she can sweep you completely along with her as she shifts instantly from the impish delight of a little girl to a full-grown woman mourning the death of her parents.

Her performance in the The Belle of Amherst is astonishing, filled with intelligence, good humor, pathos, all the bittersweet of life. She propels the feeling of being ready to burst with joy or anguish or both at once. You should not miss this performance.

In addition, she has one of the finest voices imaginable. Every word she says--even when she has her back to the audience--comes over clear and precise. No mumbling for Julie Harris and calling it acting.

The words she has to speak are to a large extent Emily Dickinson's. For a good portion of the show Miss Harris recites Miss Dickinson's work, poems in part or in full, words from letters or notes discovered after her death. The playwright has skillfully interwoven all this into a picture of a woman alone in her passion, living an eccentric life by the standards of most people. But she was a woman whose homebound observations filled her world with a fuller life than most people will ever know.

The Belle of Amherst tells the story of the revolutionary poems and reclusive life of Emily Dickinson from 1845 until 1886 when she died. It shows us that she was a woman who constructed her own world in her poems. Only about seven were published in her lifetime and that was probably just as well because her work was far ahead of its time, dissonant, off-rhyme and ambiguous. It was undoubtedly more attuned to the 20th Century, when it was read, than to the 19th, when it was written.

At 15, Emily said she anticipated being "the belle of Amherst when I reach my 17th year." But at that age she realized she was plain and that there might be no suitable suitors. She studied for a year at Mt. Holyoke under "the dragon," stern headmistress Mary Lyon. But she was too free a thinker for that institution in 1847 (she believed in a Diety but not in the trappings of religion) and returned home to her stern patriarchal father and a house in which all trembled when he approached.

Emily Dickinson apparently had two male suitors but for varying reasons (one was married) they fell away and she moved more and more deeply into her own world. The poems she showed to "experts" were downgraded. Efforts were made to improve her writing style, to fix up those "imperfect" rhymes.

More and more she enjoyed being the mysterious "woman in white," Squire Edward Dickinson's half-cracked daughter. "Tell the truth but tell it slant," she wrote.

The truth in The Belle of Amherst leans heavily on Emily Dickinson's lighter side. The play would have you believe she was an impish recluse, alone and happy. No one knows the absolute truth here and the script for The Belle of Amherst makes its version most palatable.

The sets are plain and handsome, the lighting a bit noticeable and Reilly's direction provides a flow on stage that like Emily Dickinson's poetry, wastes no motion.

But Miss Harris overwhelms all. The only thing with a chance to stand up to her are the words of Miss Dickinson. Together, they are a magnificent combination.

Some people can't go home again. The Belle of Amherst, by portraying Emily Dickinson's life, shows that some people never need leave home to know the world.

GARDNER, R. H. (Rufus Hallette III); (2) Drama and film critic; (3) b. Mayfield, Ky. , July 25, 1918; (4) s. Rufus Hallette and Kathleen (Moorman) Gardner; (5) B. A. Texas Christian U. , double major: History and English, 1941; (6) divorced; (8) Aircraft engineer, Glenn L. Martin Co. , 1941-49; reporter and feature writer Baltimore Sun, 1951-54; drama and film critic 1954; (9) Guest lecturer in modern drama, Goucher College, 1968; (10) Member of Mayor's Committee on the Theater, 1974; (12) Board of directors Baltimore Film Festival, 1975; (13) Baptist; (14) Democrat; (15) Member Dramatists Guild, American Newspaper Guild; Author of two produced plays; (20) "I. O. U. Jeremiah" (1950) and "Christabel and the Rubicon" (1969), also one book "The Splintered Stage: The Decline of the American Theater," published by Macmillan in 1964; (22) The Sunpapers, Baltimore, Md. 21203; Ph. 301-332-6453; (24,25) Write three columns a week for The Sun, a morning paper with a circulation of 350,000. Inasmuch as I sometimes review more than one production at a time, I would estimate that I cover approximately 200 shows a year, with possibly a 60-40 split between films and plays.

A Film Hard To Stomach
(by R. H. Gardner, Baltimore Sun, February 1, 1974)

Last Sunday's Times carried a story on the reaction of New Yorkers to "The Exorcist. " After standing in line for hours,

many people were alleged to have vomited, fainted or left the
theater trembling before the film's conclusion. "Several people
had heart attacks, a guard told me," wrote reporter Judy Klemesrud. "One woman even had a miscarriage, he said."

I have never been in a theater when a woman had a miscarriage, but I was in one once when a man had a heart attack.
The commotion was so pronounced, as an ambulance crew hustled
in with a stretcher and other emergency equipment, that everyone quite forgot about the movie. And against a multiplicity of
such interruptions, people dropping and gagging all over the place,
no film, however horrible, could sustain its impact.

It's apparent, though, that director William Friedkin--who,
I am told, declared on a recent television show that Greek women often miscarried while watching "Oedipus"--likes the idea
that some find his work too strong for their stomachs. So, one
concludes, does Warner Brothers, which expects to make more
money on "The Exorcist" than on "My Fair Lady." Press agents
used to hire girls to swoon over Sinatra back in the Forties.
David Merrick once hired a woman to go up on the stage and hit
the actor playing the unpleasant Jimmy Porter in his production
of "Look Back in Anger." And it's not inconceivable that some
un-disinterested party might pay people to throw up during exhibitions of "The Exorcist."

Not only do such goings-on, fully publicized in the newspapers, make for the kind of turn-out colorfully described by Ms.
Klemesrud as "the longlonglonglonglong movie line"; they create
a mystique for the picture that, as much as the effort put into
it by the writer, director, actors, etc. is part of its power.

Nothing particularly shocking occurs in "The Exorcist" until
almost half-way through; yet the spectators at the screening I
attended had been so programmed by publicity that footage that
in any other film would have seemed dull (and a lot of "The Exorcist" is precisely that) held them in suspense. They had come
expecting to be frightened, and, by Beelzebub, they were ready!

Nor were they disappointed, for "The Exorcist" is a scary
film, but no more so than "The Haunting" or any other well-done
ghost story. Its shock value lies not so much in its supernatural
theme as in the foul language screenwriter William Peter Blatty,
working from his best-selling novel, has put into the mouth of a
12-year-old girl. That and the vomit she, as an instrument of
the devil, keeps spewing all over everyone who comes within spitting range.

Apart from these matters, the film is pure gimmickery. I
couldn't help thinking, while watching it, how much fun old Cecil
B. DeMille would have had with it. He loved to part the Red
Sea and light up the Burning Bush; and "The Exorcist," with its
God-vs. -Satan struggle, bouncing bed and flying bric-a-brac,

would have been right down his alley.

The child, powerfully played by Linda Blair (who mouths the obscenities actually spoken by Mercedes McCambridge), is the product of a broken home. Her divorced actress-mother (Ellen Burstyn) is in the process of making a movie in Georgetown when the demon, for reasons known only to God and Mr. Blatty, decides to move in with them. His coming is heralded by crashing sounds in the attic, the flickering of the house lights and the inability of the daughter to hold her urine. Finally, when the latter's bed begins to bounce around, the mother, suspecting that something is wrong, consults a physician.

The series of examinations to which he and his colleagues subject the child were for me the most harrowing part of the film. Portrayed in glaring detail and involving all kinds of ghastly machinery, they suggested nothing so much as the tortures of the Spanish Inquisition--which, I suppose, was Friedkin's intention.

Unable to find any physical cause for her disturbance, the doctors recommend psychiatric care, and when this, the last resort of medical science, fails, a priest is brought in.

We have already seen this worthy, played with his customary intensity by Jason Miller, on various occasions--in the crowd watching the shooting of the mother's film, running the track behind the seminary where he is in charge of mental health, going to New York to visit his aged mother. At the time his services are sought as an exorcist, the mother has just died under circumstances particularly painful to him, as a result of which he is beginning to lose his faith.

Loath at first to take the case, he finally agrees when the child--or, rather, Miss McCambridge--begins to speak Latin and other recondite languages to him. At this point, a character we have not seen since the film's brief introductory sequence, set in Iraq, enters the proceedings--an elderly priest-archeologist, played with imposing dignity by Max von Sydow. It is he--again for reasons never clear--who has accidentally loosed the devil on the little girl, and he takes to the task of exorcism like a duck to water (holy, that is).

Recognizing his enemy at once, the devil, as the old man approaches the bed, squirts a great glob of vomit (actually pea soup) into his eye--a good example of the director's taste, since the effect is unavoidably comic--and follows up this coup with a stream of grotesque obscenities, which the elder priest advises the younger not to listen to.

And so it goes. All in all, a pretty rough exorcism in which the forces of God win only a pyrrhic victory over their demonic foe. Presumably, this was not true of the actual case, occurring in Mt. Rainier, Md. in 1949, upon which Blatty based his novel.

As to whether I recommend seeing "The Exorcist," which
is appearing at the Tower and Strand Theaters, the answer is
"Yes, if after reading this review, it strikes you as something
you'd enjoy." But, if you are hell-bent on seeing it, please
ignore the fact the film has an "R" rating and leave your children
at home. They might learn a couple of new words.

New Stoppard Play Jumps High Despite Built-In Handicaps
(by R. H. Gardner, Baltimore Sun, February 22, 1974)

Tom Stoppard told me during an interview last week that his
objective in "Jumpers" was to write a profound farce. And to
the extent that the play, which opened this week at the Kennedy
Center's Eisenhower Theater in Washington, is a wildly farcical
treatment of a profound theme he has succeeded. It is a brilliant,
one might also say brave, concept; and I admire it almost as
much as I admire him for giving it form. My only reservations
relate to how the result works on the stage.

An Englishman, Stoppard is virtually unique among the young
playwrights growing up since the war in that, while strongly attracted to Samuel Beckett, he regards the God-is-dead dogma as
too glib a philosophy for anything so mysterious as human life.
Reduced to essentials, "Jumpers" amounts to an argument aimed
at refuting this philosophy. Not since Archibald MacLeish's
"J. B." has there been such a straightforward, unashamedly affirmative polemic.

But action, not philosophy, is the stuff of drama. Stoppard's
problem lay in making his argument dramatic and entertaining.
The solution he came up with was to present it in a framework
incorporating elements of the music hall and circus. This framework was not original with him, having already been employed by
Beckett, John Osborne and others. But the particular use to
which he put it was.

Atheistic members of the philosophy department at an uniden-
tified English university were depicted as gymnasts, whose tumbling symbolized their agility at rationalizing God, morality or
anything smacking of the absolute out of existence. As the one
to play David to these bounding Goliaths, Stoppard chose a physically unprepossessing, mentally befuddled professor named (not
to be confused with the man whose "Principia Ethica" is said to
have changed the course of English philosophy) George Moore.

George's wife, Dotty, is a former showgirl, given to ridiculing George and entertaining Archibald Jumper, the school's
vice-chancellor and leading gymnast, in her bedroom at lunch-
time. ("Either he should come after lunch," observes George
peevishly, "or you should get up before it.") She is also given
to singing sentimental songs about the moon ("Harvest,"

"Carolina," "Over Miami," etc.) at parties, as Jumper and his colleagues are jumping. During one of these combined vocal and acrobatic orgies, McFee, her husband's principal opponent in a philosophical debate to be held as part of a future symposium, becomes a murder victim when he is shot out of the middle of a human pyramid. At this point, the play begins.

There is a political theme and a bit about the first English astronauts to land on the moon (one of the problems is that Stoppard tries to do too much), but the body of the work falls into three main sections: the acrobatic sequences, which are pure theater; the scenes in Dotty's bedroom, dealing with the murder-victim and Jumper, and the scenes in George's study, where he is dictating his symposium speech to a deadpan secretary, introduced at the party as a naked redhead swinging on a chandelier. It is in the ideas wittily expressed during these dictating sessions that the essence of the play lies.

George, whose mind works in a bumbling, zig-zag, yet ultimately logical fashion, starts by asking, "Does, for the sake of argument, God--so to speak--exist?" Telling his secretary to "leave a space," he proceeds to point out the inconsistencies of some of the arguments used by those taking the negative view.

For example, the theory that the number of fractions, progressing backwards from the numeral one to zero, is infinite--which is but another application of the theory propounded by the Greek philosopher Zeno that, since an arrow shot at a target, travels halfway to its destination, then halfway through the remaining space, then halfway again ad infinitum, "it never gets there. And," George adds with a lunatic grin, "St. Sebastian died of fright."

George, as a professor of moral philosophy, is endeavoring to arrive at an understanding of what "we mean when we say something is good or something is bad," and he feels that the source of such meaning must be in God. "Good" and "bad," he tries to explain to Inspector Bones, who comes around to investigate McFee's murder and get Dotty's autograph on a record album, are terms unacceptable to his opponents, who have been known to argue that there's nothing "wrong" in killing people.

"And what," asks the shocked inspector, "kind of philosophy is that?"

"Mainstream I call it," says George.

As for the acrobats, about whom the inspector seems curious, they are "Logical positivists, mainly, with a linguistic analyst or two and a couple of Benthamite Utilitarians ... lapsed Kantians and empiricists generally ... and, of course the usual Behaviorists ... a mixture of the more philosophical members of the university gymnastics team and the more gymnastic members of the philosophical school."

To the question why he doesn't jump with the rest, George replies that he belongs to a school that regards all sudden movement as ill-bred.

Though taking the form of outrageous puns like "Zeno evil," Stoppard's humor generally is of a very high order, and through it he manages to make most of George's fuzzy-headed grappling with the abstract entertaining and sometimes--as when he compares the relationship between man and God to that existing between a polygon and a circle--intellectually stimulating as well.

As the sides of a square are increased to a pentagon, octagon, hexagon, etc. , the figure becomes more and more like a circle. Hence, George argues, had the circle never existed, it could be deduced from the polygon and concludes "It seems to me life is a polygon."

So what is wrong with "Jumpers?" For one thing, its three parts--the gymnast, Dotty and George themes--do not meld smoothly: and, in its alternate jumping back and forth between her bedroom and his study, the action after a while becomes repetitious--a condition emphasized by the way director Peter Wood and designer Josef Svoboda have chosen to present it.

Moreover, while three hours is not as long as four ("Long Day's Journey into Night") or five ("Hamlet"), it is quite long enough for a play that is essentially a lecture broken intermittently by circus acrobatics and vaudeville turns. It is true that Stoppard has a lot to say, most of which I not only respect but applaud. But couldn't we dispense with a little of Dotty, played with enthusiasm but without real inspiration by Jill Clayburgh, or some of the gymnastics--which, after the initial impact, soon cease to be interesting?

Brian Bedford is another matter. He brings to a most challenging role the technical gifts and human understanding necessary to make it a triumph, both for himself and the playwright. I do not know who played this part in the original English production, but I can't imagine it without Bedford. Whether weaving unsteadily about the stage with a tortoise in his hand or theorizing, he is superb.

In conclusion, let me say that, during a seemingly endless period of fashionable negativism, it is refreshing, not to mention reassuring, to come upon a work so brilliantly positive as "Jumpers." I would not have missed seeing it for the world, and I feel that whatever weakenesses it possesses as a staged production can in no way detract from its strength as total work. Bravo!

GILDER, Rosamond Janet deKay; (2) Writer, editor, lecturer, executive; (3) b. Marion, Mass. , July 17, 1891; (4) d. Richard Watson

Gilder, Helena deKay Gilder (father poet editor of the Century magazine; mother painter). (5) Attended Brearley School, N.Y.C.; (8) Theatre Arts Monthly: Assistant Editor, Drama Critic and Editor 1924-1948; Barnard College, Instructor in English 1949-1955; American National Theatre and Academy, Secretary 1945-1950; Board Member and Vice President 1946-1968; Vice-Chairman, International Cultural Exchange Program ANTA - State Department 1954-1963; National Theatre Conference, Editorial Secretary 1932-1936; Federal Theatre Project: Director, Bureau of Research and Publication 1935-1936; New York Drama Critics Circle, Secretary 1946-1950; Honorary Member Critics Circle 1950-present; International Theatre Institute, Founder, Vice-President, President and Honorary President 1947-present; U.S. Centre, ITI, Director, President 1948-present; National Commission for UNESCO, Chairman, Panel on Dramatic Art 1948-1954; (14) Antoinette Perry Award, 1948; AETA Award of Merit, 1961; Kelsey Allen Award, 1963; ANTA Award, 1965; USITT Award, 1967; Prague CSMS Gold Medal, 1969; from France, Officier de l'Ordre des Arts et des Lettres, 1965; Honorary Degree; L.H.D., University of Denver, 1969; (20) Publications: Letters of Richard Watson Gilder (Houghton Mifflin); My Life by Emma Calvé (Appleton) translation; Enter the Actress; The First Women in the Theatre (Threatre Arts Books, 1960); John Gielgud's Hamlet (Oxford 1937); Theatre Arts Anthology (Theatre Arts Books, 1950) editor; articles in theatre subjects for theatre magazines in Europe and U.S. (21) 24 Gramercy Park, New York, N.Y. 10003; (22) ITI, 245 West 52nd St., New York, N.Y. 10019

"Leave it to Me!"
(by Rosamond Gilder, Theatre Arts Monthly, January 1939)

The incredible ineptitudes, the waste of money and talent, the stupidities, commercial and artistic, of nearly half the winter's offerings can almost be forgotten, if not forgiven, in rejoicing over the restoration of song and dance to the bosom of a doting public.

Victor Moore leads the way, his body borne precariously ahead of his unwilling legs, his moon face riding high over a wrack of packages, his smile tentative, ingratiating. He is, as always, in a tough spot. Through the machinations of Bella and Samuel Spewack who evolved Leave It to Me! from their own comedy, Clear All Wires, and Vinton Freedley who produced it, Victor Moore, in the guise of Alonzo P. Goodhue, a mild middle-western business man, finds himself heading for Moscow where he is to take up his duties as American Ambassador. This in itself is bad enough, for Alonzo is a home-body who cares nothing for foreign affairs, but the plot is seriously complicated by the fact that one J. H. Brody covets the honor Goodhue despises, and is determined to do him in. He is aided and abetted in this intention by Buckley Joyce Thomas (alias William Gaxton), an enterprising newspaperman who blithely undertakes to ruin Goodhue and get him recalled. The resulting international imbroglio brings Victor Moore and William Gaxton together again

in a riotous evening of unalloyed delights for which Cole Porter
has written some of his gayest tunes and lyrics, Albert Johnson
has designed two memorable railroad stations and some acceptable interiors and Raoul Pêne du Bois has whipped together a
frothy collection of colorful costumes.

"For God's sake, can't you do the wrong thing?" Gaxton
asks Moore in a sudden fury of despair when his efforts to get
the Ambassador into hot water have all failed.   As far as the
audience is concerned the answer is no.   Whether he is Vice-
President or Public Enemy Number 13, whether he is Throttle-
bottom, Goodhue or just plain Stinky-to-his-friends, Victor
Moore can do no wrong.   His attack on that section of the human anatomy which harbors idiot laughter is infallible.   The
mirth he provokes is unorthodox, as far as the philosophers are
concerned, for it is not thoughtful as Meredith would have it,
nor does it spring from any desire to instruct or correct as the
learned doctors insist it should.   It is a laughter born of sympathy, compound of smiles and chuckles.   Victor Moore is the
Timid Soul in person, terrified by a bustling, competent world,
browbeaten by his womenfolk.   He is friendly among the ruthless, trusting among the predatory--eager for simple joys.   "I
want to go back to old Topeka" is a plaintive wail, a parody of
all home and mammy songs, an exquisite caricature, which has
yet a spark of eternal truth.

Like all great comedians, Victor Moore has the gift of projecting without words a sequence of thought and mood.   In the
scene with the Nazi emissary his face is a comic battleground.
On it are registered in lightning succession a series of conflicting emotions: his dislike of the paunchy bully who stands at attention before him; his desire to give him a swift kick in the
belly; his terror at the mere thought of such an action; his growing excitement as he glances from Gaxton who is silently urging
him on, to the tempting, khaki-clad midriff before him; his despairing appraisal of his own weakness, in contrast with the
other's rigid strength; his mischievous appreciation of the ludicrous effect of making that complacent balloon collapse and his
sudden resolution.   The black-out comes before Moore moves,
but the projected action and its ridiculous consequences have already been seen by the audience, mirrored in his expressive
face.

The genius of comic acting lies largely in the skill with
which such moments are elaborated.   Sometimes it is a matter
of business: packages that fall to the ground and have to be
picked up, mechanisms that refuse to work, the malice of inan-
imate objects.   Moore's performance abounds in these bits of
completely lunatic entertainment, comic cadenzas embroidered
on a simple theme.   In the scene following that with the Nazi
envoy he has received a cable from Washington which he bliss-
fully hopes will contain his recall.   Aided by Gaxton, he proceeds to decode the telegram, looking each phrase up in his

book and writing the message syllable by syllable on a large
blackboard. The code is made up of first lines of familiar songs
and as he turns the pages of his little book he bellows out the
line again and again until he has found the right place and written
the decoded word on the blackboard. All the elements of masterly clowning are used in this brief scene--perfect timing, exactly the right amount of reiteration, concentration, contrast and
frustration. He plays the whole scene with consummate skill,
sensing to a nicety just what volume of voice, what amount of
repetition, will land his laughs. His many years in vaudeville
have give him a sixth sense with which to gauge his audience and
carry it with him through these moon-struck moments.

Sophie Tucker also has the sure vaudevillian touch. One line,
one simple musical phrase, is enough for her. Before she has
finished with that little lyric beginning, "Most gentlemen don't
like love," every possible (and impossible) variation on the theme
has been juggled in the air and tossed across the footlights.
Rubicund and hearty in her robust maturity, her very presence
is a guarantee against gloom. She is the perfect foil for Moore,
and their rendering of a travel ditty entitled "From the USA to
the USSR" provides the happiest combination of two expert talents.
Gaxton brings his familiar cheer-leader drive to enliven proceedings, and Mary Martin, on this her first appearance in New York,
hits the bull's-eye with an edifying strip tease executed on the
Russian Steppes, during which she explains, quite clearly, that
her "heart belongs to Daddy." With plenty of plot involving
"Buck" Thomas and Colette (sung by Tamara), Dolly and her
Daddy, Mrs. Goodhue and her five daughters, and some unusually good dancing on the part of the Buccaneers and Les Girls, the
new Cole Porter ticket, carrying those old Presidential teammates Gaxton and Moore, is already running up a heavy vote.

"The Iceman Cometh"
(by Rosamond Gilder, Theatre Arts Monthly, December 1946)

Eugene O'Neill's return after twelve years of absence has
done more than give the new season a fillip of interest: it has
restored to the theatre something of its intrinsic stature. O'-
Neill's gift for puzzling, infuriating and delighting his audiences
makes everything he writes important even to those whom it ex-
asperates. The Iceman Cometh presented by the House of O'-
Neill, the Theatre Guild, in an admirable production directed by
Eddie Dowling has stirred Broadway from its daydreaming even
as his hero Hickey stirs the bums in the backroom of Harry
Hope's dump from their alcohol-ridden fancies. Sardi's and
Twenty-One, Walgreen's and El Morocco seethed with indignant
argument after an opening "night" that began at 4:30 in the afternoon and continued until 10--an opening for which the theatrically knowing and those who like to be seen at important events
turned out in force. Though baseball and the movies may draw
greater crowds, the theatre can console itself with the fact that
in the end playwrights last longer in man's recollection. And

certainly Eugene O'Neill will, because his plays, and this one in
particular, exist on more than one plane. The Iceman Cometh
is made of good theatre substance--meaty material for actors,
racy dialogue, variety of character, suspense and passion--all
within the strait-jacket of a rigid pattern. It is also primarily
an allegory of man's pitiful estate, a parable of his search for
redemption.

O'Neill has gone back to the saloons and gin-mills of his
early days--and plays--for the setting of The Iceman, which he
wrote in 1939. Harry Hope's bar and the backroom behind it is
a composite of the dives he himself used to frequent in his restless youth. Hope's place is, according to one of its "inmates,"
the No Chance Saloon, Bedrock Bar, the End of the Line Café
where five-cent whiskey--"cyanide cut with carbolic acid to give
it a mellow flavor"--is sold to a motley collection of down-and-
outers by an amiably boozy proprietor. The whole action of the
play, such as it is swings between the bar itself with its half-
door on the street and the dingy backroom where, as the curtain
rises, a dozen assorted drunks sit at round tables drinking and
dreaming of that golden tomorrow which will see them restored
once more to a living world. They are waiting for Hickey, a
traveling salesman, who comes to them from time to time to
live out a "periodical," a fabulous bender in which they share
his whiskey and listen to his jokes, particularly that one about
his loving wife whom he has treated so badly but who is all right
now because he left her safely at home in bed--"with the iceman." While waiting for Hickey, Larry, the philosophic ex-anar-
chist tells the newly-arrived Parritt (who is the son of a famous
woman anarchist now under arrest for participating in a bombing
episode on the West Coast) all about the other members of his dead-
end club. Each has a story of fraud or failure behind him; each lives
in an alcoholic "pipe dream" of future hope--till Hickey arrives.

Then the trouble starts. Hickey has reformed. He is off
the booze; he has found salvation and he intends to make all his
friends follow his path to peace and happiness. They are to face
their dream tomorrows in actual fact. But the results of his pro-
selytizing are disastrous. Hate, fear, anguish and despair descend on the inhabitants of the erstwhile fools' paradise. Hickey
finds to his horror that his gospel of disillusionment does not
work. He is forced to explain the cause of his own reform in
order to prove he is right. He pours out the story of his life,
of his relations with his wife whom he loved and who loved him
too well--and whom he killed to save her from the suffering he
was forever inflicting. He had left her that very morning safe
in bed--"with the iceman," Death. And then as Hickey tells the
story of the woman he murdered for love he realizes with a sudden blinding flash that this too was illusion, that he had killed
her because he hated her; he killed her and cursed her for her
intolerable, overwhelming love. This last confession brings a
final reversal. The murder and the cursing were madness. "I
must have been crazy," Hickey cries out in despair. The bums

who had been listening to his story in a sort of horrified stupor
stir at the words. Hickey was crazy all the time! His reform
was a pipe dream too. They can go back to their old illusions,
their whiskey, their dreams; they reach thirstily for their bottles. Only the boy Parritt, Larry and Hickey himself are changed.
Hickey gives himself up to the police for murder, Parritt commits suicide realizing he is as guilty of mother-murder as Hickey of wife-murder and Larry the philosopher faces the fact that
for him too death is the only answer. The cycle is complete.
If this is life then indeed "The best of all were never to be
born."

Like Peer Gynt's onion, the story of The Iceman has its layers
and layers of meaning. It touches on a dozen different themes and
relationships. While the subsidiary characters are separate mi-
crocosms of despair, the three chief figures, Hickey, Larry and
Parritt, are three aspects of man--each element loving and loathing the other. The play is in a very special sense a summary of
much of O'Neill's past writing. Superficially it goes back as far
as the vigorous sea plays with which he made his debut. Its
frank barroom talk, its conventional tarts, its amiable drunks,
its passion and violence are reminders of the impact of his first
writing. Don Parritt, the boy rejected by his mother, haunted
by the guilt of his betrayal of her, which is nothing less than
matricide, recalls O'Neill's days of absorption in psychoanalysis
while Larry the philosopher is the O'Neill who attempted a detachment and objectivity never native to him.

But it is through Hickey who has known the love that passeth
understanding and has rejected it that we glimpse O'Neill's ultimate meaning. Blind, besotted and misguided, man haunted by
death lives by lies. "The lie of a pipe dream is what gives life
to the whole misbegotten mad lot of us, drunk or sober," Larry
says at the opening of the play. But there is a truth which is
not the truth of alcohol or political shibboleths, or psychology
or philosophy, or even the truth of "facing the truth" which Hickey preaches. The greatest illusion of all is to believe that dis-
illusionment--the unaided processes of the intellect--can solve
man's dilemma. There is a force that, like the love that Hickey's
wife bore him, is made of understanding and forgiveness. Man
finds such love intolerable. "I couldn't forgive her for forgiving
me," Hickey explains. "I caught myself hating her for making
me hate myself so much. There is a limit to the guilt you can
feel and the forgiveness and pity you can take." And so man
denies, destroys and blasphemes such love, only in the end to find
that this too will be forgiven. The denizens of Hickey's world
and of the world at large find a simple answer to Hickey's final
revelation. The man is mad! Hamlet to the contrary notwithstanding, there is nothing more in heaven and earth than can be
compassed in any current philosophy. Pass the bottle. Drink
up. What the hell! It's a good play, brother, why bother.

And it is a good play, excellently acted and directed, full

of substance. It would seem that it could readily be compressed
into a more reasonable running time, but O'Neill has a tendency
to shirk the task of selection and condensation. He has so much
to say that even this four-and-a-half-hour play must seem short
to a man who thinks in terms of trilogies and nine-play cycles.
For the onlooker, however, a shorter play would have brought
into sharper focus the conflicting and merging elements of the
three chief figures of the fable. The subsidiary characters are
not sufficiently important or rounded to demand the time and attention they absorb. They are each set in their groove in the
first half hour. They never emerge from the pattern to take on
human proportions. The reiterated pattern of their false redemption and its death-dealing effect becomes tedious. Mr. O'Neill
seems to underestimate the ability of the audience to grasp his
idea, or perhaps more truly he has so fond a remembrance softened by time and distance of these denizens of his kingdom of
despair that he cannot bear to tear up the sketches he has made
in his mind's eye as he sat with them at marble-topped tables or
leaned against mahogany bars in a hundred saloons the world over.

But the length of The Iceman, though it adds very little to
the characterizations so boldly sketched in the first scenes, does
permit an interesting orchestration of effects which Mr. Dowling
has developed in his direction. The stage is almost continuously
peopled by all the characters in the play at once. There is little
movement; there is only an antiphonal development of themes.
Besides the pipe-dream motive, which is developed in turn by
each of the characters playing in groups of threes and fours,
there is also the predominant, haunting theme of Death. O'Neill's
bums are all in pursuit of forgetfulness, of sleep, of death. They
spend most of their time in blissful or tormented alcoholic slum-
ber. O'Neill uses this device to bring them in and out of the
action without making them leave the stage. As the play progresses, the way the tables are grouped in the backroom and bar
and the manner in which actors are grouped around them--
slumped over asleep or sitting in a deathly day dream--provide
a constant visual comment on the developing theme.

Mr. Dowling and the Theatre Guild have gathered a fine cast
which gives as integrated a performance as has been seen in
many a long day on the New York stage. Robert Edmond Jones
has managed the miracle of making visible and at the same time
expressive a sordid environment which is essential to the play
but would lose its power were it merely photographic. Harry
Hope's bar and backroom is indeed the very home of oblivion,
a Sargasso Sea of human flotsam. It seems etched in dirt, dusty
with despair--a place where wrecked mariners are kind to each
other because this is the end and there will be no rescue. The
derelict ship is captained by Harry Hope, superbly played by Dudley Digges to whom the role of this genial, testy, irascible, kindly saloon keeper is a mine of histrionic possibilities. James
Barton has a more difficult assignment in Hickey, the genial
salesman peddling a false redemption among his bottlemates. He

acquits himself with vigor of a task that might conceivably be
more subtly handled, doing full justice to the speech in which
he tells his life history--the longest soliloquy yet heard on any
New York stage. Larry, the philosophic bystander who discovers
that he is not really as much in love with easeful death as he
thought, is given substance and authority by Carl Benton Reid,
while a young actor, Paul Crabtree, does a sound, workmanlike
job with the role of the distraught youth tormented by a virulent
Oedipus complex. Nicholas Joy and Russell Collins catch the
essence of their simpler and more boldly sketched parts and present them with delightful clarity. Indeed it would be only fair
to list the entire male cast, not excluding the explosive Italian
barkeep (played by Tom Pedi) who strikes a welcome note of
crude common sense and raucous humor in an atomosphere of
boozy self-delusion and introspection. Ruth Gilbert as the youngest of the tarts contributes her shrill giggle and high sharp staccato chatter to a symphony played in a minor key. She is the
most effective of the three girls, who, as is often the case in
Mr. O'Neill's plays, lack reality. The Iceman Cometh, in fact,
has many of Mr. O'Neill's old faults as well as his distinguished
virtues--it shows his complete lack of humor, his sententiousness
and sentimentality--but it is immensely rich and rewarding to the
playgoer and serves the welcome purpose of stirring argument
and contention in the theatre, as Mr. O'Neill has done all his life.
It is good to know he has not lost his cunning and that we are to
have other plays from him this year and next to remind us that
the theatre is not all dumb show and noise.

GILL, Brendan; (2) Writer; (3) b. Hartford, Conn. , Oct. 4, 1914;
(4) s. Michael Henry Richard and Elizabeth (Duffy); (5) A. B. , Yale,
1936; (6) m. Anne Barnard, June 20, 1936; (7) children--Brenda,
Michael, Holly, Madelaine, Rosemary, Kate, Charles; (8) Contributed
to New Yorker, 1936- , film critic, 1960-67; drama critic, 1968- ;
(10) Chrmn, bd. for Art and Urban Resources, N.Y.C.; v. p. Film
Society, Lincoln Center; pres. , Inst. Cinemateque; pres. Landmarks
Conservancy of N.Y.; mem. N.Y.C. Commn. Cultural Affairs; mem.
Mayor's Com. in Pub. Interest, N.Y.C.; mem. Irish Georgian So-
ciety (dir); Victorian Society Am. (v. p.); (19) Grolier, Coffee House,
Century Assn (N.Y.C.); (20) The Trouble of One House, 1950; The
Day the Money Stopped (adapted play with Maxwell Anderson, 1958),
1957; Fat Girl, 1971; Tallulah, 1972; (with Robert Kimball) Cole,
1971; (with Jerome Zerbe) Happy Times, 1973; Ways of Loving, 1974;
Here at the New Yorker, 1975; (21) Bronxville, N.Y. 10708; also
Norfolk, CT 06058; (22) 25 W. 43rd St. , New York City, N.Y. 10036.

GILMAN, Richard; (2) Author, educator; (2) b. N.Y.C. , Apr. 30,
1925; (3) s. Jacob and Marion (Wolinsky); (5) B. A. , U. Wis. , 1947,
L. H. D. , Grinnell College, 1967; (6) m. Lynn Nesbit; (7) children--
Nicholas, Priscilla, Claire; (8) Free lance writer, 1950-54; asso.
editor, drama critic Newsweek mag. , 1964-67; lit. editor New Republic 1968-70; prof. drama Yale, 1967- ; (9) Vis. Lect. English,

Columbia, 1964-65; vis. prof. drama Stanford, summer 1967; (13) Served with USMCR, 1943-46; (14) Recipient: George Jean Nathan award for drama criticism, 1972; (20) The Confusion of Realms, 1970; Drama, 1974. Contributing editor Partisan Rev. , 1972- ; (21) 333 Central Park West, New York City 10025; (22) School of Drama, Yale, New Haven, CT 06520.

GLACKIN, William Charles; (2) Arts editor and theater and music critic; (3) b. Sacramento, July 10, 1917; (4) s. William M. and Anita (Derr) G.; (5) B.S. St. Mary's College, California, 1939, major subj: Physics; graduate study, U. of California, Berkeley, English, 1939-41; (6 & 7) m. Helen Bateman, Aug. 8, 1941, children--Christine Anita and Nancy Alene; div. 1961; m. Sandra Littlewood, Jan. 27, 1962; son, Brendan Patrick, July 23, 1973; (8) Teacher, drama, stagecraft and other subjects, Sacramento City Schools (high school level), 1941-43; Assistant editor and editor, The Adakian, Army daily newspaper, Adak, the Aleutians, 1943-46; staff correspondent, International News Service, United Press, State Capitol, Sacramento, 1946-48; directed plays professionally, Sacramento Civic Theater, 1948; Arts Editor and principal drama and music critic, Sacramento Bee, from early 1949 to present; (13) U.S. Army 1943-46; (15) First president, Alaskaleutian Press Association, 1945; president, Sacramento Local American Newspaper Guild, 1952; (16) Democrat; (20) Author, "Anita," a historical play with music, produced by Lewis and Young Productions with Vincent Price and others, Santa Barbara County Bowl, four performances, 1955. Articles on theater in Theater Arts and N.Y. Times Arts and Leisure section; (21) 4835 Alturas Way, Sacramento 95822, Ph. 916-457-8445; (23) Sacramento Bee Circulation: 178,000 daily, 220,000 Sunday; articles also appear Fresno and Modesto Bees occasionally; (24) 150 reviews/ yr. (theater, music, occasionally movie, dance and opera).

A Funny, Brilliant "Seascape"

(by William C. Glackin, Sacramento Bee, April 13, 1975)

If you insist on having a message from Edward Albee, he's got one in Seascape. It's fundamental and fascinating and you'll be glad to have it. But if you just want to have a good time, go. This is a very funny play, full of fine surprises, many of them wearing scales.

Scales? Well, there are these two huge lizards, named Leslie and Sarah. But first you had better take a look at a couple of married human beings named Nancy and Charlie, sitting at a picnic on the shore.

In the superb reality of the setting James Tilton has designed for the play--which has moved from New York to the Shubert Theater here with its Broadway cast intact for a final run-through May 4--it is a bright blue day in a very solid world. Nancy likes it so much that, as she paints and chatters away at her laconic husband, she proposes, half-seriously, that they make picnicking a way of life. Now that their children have grown up and they have nothing else to do, why not take up a life of beachcombing around the world, in "all those places fancy people go to?"

The proposal may be only half-serious, but the disagreement that springs from it is clearly the result of a profound split.

"I don't wnat to do anything," Charles says. "I'm happy doing nothing. I just want to do nothing."

Nancy is indignant. "Is that what we came all this way for-- nothing? To lie back down in the crib again?"

Albee pursues these two opposing life-views down the avenues of their two memories. It appears that they had a full, faithful, reasonably happy life together, although Nancy does remember that once, at a gloomy time when he turned his back to her, she thought of divorce and other men.

Rather more interesting are his memories of a boyhood game, diving slowly down in the water until the sandy bottom received his still form. "I used to go way down and try to stay there," he says, smiling as he remembers the undulations and the silence. "It was very good."

But when she tries to get him to do it again, his "Let it go!" has a savage, anguished force. And so, Albee brings them to the ultimate disagreement in a simple exchange: Charlie says they've earned a rest. Nancy says, "We've earned a little life, if you ask me."

In this progress of revelations, Deborah Kerr and Barry Nelson are partners any author ought to be glad to have. At once cheerful and relentless, she is attractively full of the vitality he seems to shrink from and yet, by the very insistence of her attack, helps him gain some sympathy from us, if a puzzled sympathy. As for Nelson, he has little to say at first, and when he does say it, holds himself from us. But eventually the half-hidden look on his face as he remembers the underwater paradise of his lost youth reveals something like desperation.

"Are you telling me you're all caved in, Charlie?" she asks. "All closed down?" His "Maybe" is the answer of a man in trouble.

Enter the lizards.

You may have heard they were in the play, but to see them actually there, looming high above Nancy and Charlie on a ledge of rock, looking down with a round-eyed interest that seems definitely threatening, is a theatrical shock of spectacular proportions.

In the first place, thanks to the marvelous makeup and

costumes (skin-tight and tailed) which Fred Voelpel has designed
for Frank Langella and Maureen Anderman, they really look liz-
ardy. And the force of the illusion is doubled by the way they
move--lifting a graceful foreleg in slow motion in one instant,
scuttling to a new position with startling rapidity in the next.

Albee is his own director this time, and a superb one. He
has paced the quarrel up to this point with great skill and sensitivity, but now, with the brilliant collaboration of Langella and
Anderman, he adds a lively, unexpected dimension to the movement of the play. He also, in the vision of these so-far silent
monsters towering above the terrified couple, has thought up one
of the best first-act curtains in years.

The Act Two opener is pretty great, too. Picking up exactly where we left the four, it begins with a moment of silence.
Then the bigger lizard says to the smaller one, in the most
thoughtful and cultivated tones, "Well, Sarah, what do you think?"

The play now moves into an area of pure fun, as Leslie (for
that is the big lizard's name), Sarah, Nancy and Charlie gradually lose their fears (for the lizards are as scared as the people
are) and exchange information--about hands and handshakes, offspring, love and bigotry. "I don't want you looking at my wife's
breasts!" Charlie says angrily to Leslie as Nancy shows them
to Sarah. "I don't even know what they are!" Leslie protests.

Leslie also proves to be bigoted about fish. ("There's too
many of them. They're all over the place. Moving in to where
you live.... And they're stupid.")

It is all extremely funny, but eventually we learn that Leslie
and Sarah came up from the water out of a vaguely felt impulse
for change: "We didn't feel we belonged there any more." And
so Albee brings us to a climax which returns us to the argument
we began with: Action versus rejection, open versus closed.

Anderman and Langella, who have established not only their
lizardness but their personalities in deft, clever ways (his voice
is particularly artful), now move us with the pathos of their
plight, which is at once personal and primeval. Shall they take
the next step, and stay on dry land? Nancy points out that she,
for instance, leads a more interesting life than what her husband calls (not very tactfully) "brute beasts." But Charlie, grim
Charlie, is determined to convert them to his own view of life,
to warn them of the worst. In teaching Sarah, he makes her
cry, which moves Leslie first to wrath and then to fear.

I do not have to tell you what Leslie and Sarah decide to do
for you to know, by now, what the message of the play is. It
is: Live. Albee has told us before to open up, to act, to say
yes, but never, it seems to me, more clearly. This is one of
his simplest plays, and one of his best.

Noel Coward At His Best
(by William C. Glackin, Sacramento Bee, June 15, 1975)

The new show at the Geary Theater is aptly called "Noel Coward in Two Keys," for it gives us two notes in that remarkably rich chord, his talent, which were sounded intermittently throughout his extraordinary career.

One of these two short plays, called "Come into the Garden Maud," is merely facile, and leaves us pleasantly but mildly entertained.

The other, "A Song at Twilight," is the work of a master playwright at the top of his form, and leaves us reverberating to its art long after we leave the theater.

The two originally were part of a trio first produced in London in 1966 under the title, "Suite in Three Keys," a reference to the fact that all three take place in the same lavish hotel suite in Switzerland, although the stories and characters are not connected.

Coward himself acted all the male leading roles in the original production. The first New York production--in February, 1974, not quite a year after Coward died--starred Hume Cronyn, Jessica Tandy and Anne Baxter, and these same performers are now enacting the roles in San Francisco. "Noel Coward in Two Keys" is well worth the trip not only to experience "A Song at Twilight" but also to see these three skillful, seasoned performers at work--most especially Cronyn, whose portrayal of an aged, acerbic, world-famous writer named Hugo Latymer in this play is a rare masterpiece in itself.

When we meet Sir Hugo he is in something of a tizzy, although doing his best to disguise the fact. The cause is an imminent dinner date, there in the hotel suite, with a former mistress, Carlotta Gray, an actress, from whom he parted "centuries ago" in "a blaze of mutual acrimony." His wife and former secretary, Hilde, a faintly Teutonic lady who maintains a steady equanimity in the face of his nastiest remarks, has determined to go out for the evening, leaving him to face alone the question: Why does Carlotta want to see him?

In the course of this introduction Cronyn establishes, by a brilliant combination of exterior and interior touches, large and small, a character both fascinating in his wit and threateningly disagreeable. For his part, the playwright has given him a rich mine to work, but Cronyn's art adds measurably to the size, color and complexity of the result.

Prowling crabbily around, white hair awry as if refused even the run of a hand through it, lower lip set in a lifetime pout, mouth restless with irritation, face pallid and movement none

too sure, he is at first a picture of aged, petulant infirmity.
But some of this proves to be only one of the several poses of
a deceptive personality.

For when Carlotta arrives, the Latymer who emerges from
the bedroom is a strikingly--and hilariously--different figure.
His hair sweeps smoothly and handsomely back from an unfur-
rowed brow, his step is quick and graceful, his hand rests deb-
onairly in the pocket of a green velvet coat.

The edge of his wit remains dangerous, but he uses it with
some caution as he works toward the point that concerns him
most: "Why are you so suddenly curious? What is it you want?"

Miss Baxter, meanwhile, has been giving us a Carlotta who
is attractively relaxed, intelligent, realistically frank and agreeable.   It appears she has written her memoirs--he wrote his
some years ago, with something less than charity for all--and
wants permission to print his love letters to her.

The mere idea draws a bristling rejection.   Which brings
her to the bombshell which ends the play's first scene: she also
possesses a series of letters from Hugo to a man named Perry
Sheldon, who died in her care a few years back.   "What do you
know about Perry Sheldon?" Hugo says, suddenly still.   "Among
other things," she replies, "that he was the only true love of
your life."

In this new area the playwright and all three actors move
with increasing brilliance and subtlety.   For her part, Hilde (Miss
Tandy) returns to give us a touching insight into her own life
with Latymer and a moving demonstration of her loyalty.

The complexities of Latymer's dilemma are also a measure
of the subtlety and truth of the play.   It is deeply more than
simply a matter of defending his "carefully sculptured reputation"
as a Grand Old Man of Letters.   His tragic flaw is ultimately
revealed as more than a sexual variance; it is rather his unyielding defense of his vulnerability.   "You would prefer to be regarded as cynical, mean and unforgiving," Carlotta tells him,
"rather than as a vulnerable human being, capable of tenderness."
And it is this same impulse, Hilde later implies, which has
driven away every friend he ever had.

The personality as well as the play are resolved, at the end,
by Coward and Cronyn in some marvelous, silent moments, as
Hugo sits in his chair alone, regarding the letters which are at
last in his hand.   An actor himself, Coward wrote the simplest
of directions here; Cronyn gives us the man whole, with all the
feelings fighting in him against each other, the heat of their battle at last melting his defenses.

An hour and 20 minutes long, the play seems to me, in its

wit and human interest, equal to the best of Coward's work.
"Come into the Garden Maud," while pleasant and amusing,
seems merely that. It is about a rich, likable and unpretentious
American of perhaps 55, his harridan of a wife and a fortyish
Sicilian princess who appreciates him. The situation is explored
with effective humor but few surprises. The characterizations
are all skillfully made, and in the case of Cronyn and Tandy
quite strikingly different from those in the longer play. Joel
Parks acts the young waiter in both plays with a poise and intelligence that make him likeable and real. It has been smoothly
and powerfully well directed by Vivian Matalon, who staged the
London original. William Ritman's setting is handsome and solid and Ray Diffen's costumes are richly suitable.

GLOVER, William; (2) Theater critic; (3) b. N.Y.C., May 6, 1911;
(4) s. William Harper and Lily P. (Freir); (5) Litt. B., Rutgers U.,
1932; (6) m. Isobel M. Cole, Oct. 26, 1936; (8) City Editor Asbury
Park Press, 1935-39; news editor A.P., newsfeatures, 1941-53, the-
ater writer, 1953- ; drama critic, 1960- ; (13) Served as Lt. (j.g.)
U.S. Maritime Service, 1943-45; (15) Mem. N.Y. Drama Critics
Circle (pres.), Drama Desk (v.p.), N.Y. Newspaper Reporters Assn.,
Phi Beta Kappa, Sigma Delta Chi; (19) The Players, Overseas Press
(N.Y.C.); (20) Cont. periodicals; (22) Associated Press, 50 Rockefel-
ler Plaza, New York City, N.Y. 10020.

"Hamlet"
(by William Glover, AP, December 18, 1975)

Sam you've made the part too wrong.

Sam is an actor, last name Waterston, whose penchant for
tackling roles beyond his art direly flaws the "Hamlet" which officially opened Wednesday night at Lincoln Center's Beaumont
Theater. In blame, though, he is not alone.

The melancholy Dane is changed by Waterston into a peevish,
screechy schoolboy who obviously hasn't listened to his own famous bit about not tearing a passion to tatters.

Sudden bursts of excessive shouting, stiff face-front posturing
and such eccentric phrasing of the poetry as "shuffled off this
(pause) mortal coil," add up to a tiresome, wasteful and irksome
performance.

Other conspirators in this shredding Shakespeare are Director
Michael Rudman and a generally undistinguished assemblage of
performers.

Essentially, it is the same concept Rudman did last summer
in Central Park, also under the auspices of Producer Joseph
Papp. The staging involves one clumsily protracted mixup with
props.

Then it was free, now one must pay for the erratic three
and a half hour rendition.   Since no improvement was perceptible
over the previous al fresco event, this spectator departed at the
single intermission.

For the record, some replacements have been made in the
supportive ensemble.   Larry Gates continues as a blimpish Polonius.   Jane Alexander has taken over as a still pallid Queen
Gertrude, nor does Charles Cioffi's stolid Claudius better the
earlier one by Robert Burr, demoted now to just being a stolid
Ghost.

Maureen Anderman, though, is an attractively girlish Ophelia.
In debut with the Papp organization she shows understanding but
needs to improve projection.

The austere setting, a raked, wooded circle with separately
articulated pie segments, is by Santo Loquasto.   Hal George
clothes the women in floorsweeping gowns of indefinite vintage,
and costumes the men mostly in puffy-shouldered uniforms apparently trimmed with marshmallow epaulets.

Memorable "Hamlet" it isn't.

"Pacific Overtures"
(by William Glover, AP, January 11, 1976)

East is East and West is West, and now they've been brought
together on Broadway in a stunning, novel musical "Pacific Overtures."

The captivating fable, about what has happened to Japan ever
since Commodore Perry ended its isolation in 1853, sleekly
blends Main Stem expertise with Oriental exotica.

Produced and directed by Harold Prince, who tries something
different in every venture, and composed by Stephen Sondheim,
his chronic collaborator, the show officially opened Sunday night
at the Winter Garden following a weekend of press performances.
Audience jubilation was rampant at the Friday display attended.

"Pacific Overtures" is staged as though it were indeed being
performed in some Nippon city by a native company.   The players, in fact, with the exception of possibly a few minor participants, are all of Asian birth or ancestry.

Many of the devices and conventions of Kabuki theater have
been skillfully used, giving the quasi-historic charade the charm
and challenge of the colorfully unexpected.

A program note asserts that "except for a degree of dramatic license the incidents and characters are true."   The loophole
seems to have been freely used at some points, but with care

for the essential theme, which is to show how "a land of change-less order floating in the sea" was drawn, at first reluctantly and then imperiously, into global affairs.

The story was written by John Weidman, son of playwright-novelist Jerome Weidman, with additional material by Hugh Wheeler. "Madame Butterfly" or "The Mikado" it isn't, but un-folds an episodic account with satiric edge and much incidental humor.

Sondheim's music is his most interesting to date, combining Oriental tonal colors, rhythms and instruments that do not alien-ate the Western show-tune ear. His lyrics tend to couplet vari-ations that in a few instances could be lessened.

Especially lovely to hear are "Someone in a Tree," sung by four eavesdroppers at the first secret treaty meeting, and "Please Hello," in which other nations join the commerce race. The first act ends with a spectacular solo, "Lion Dance," and the cur-tain falls finally with "Next," wherein traditional costumes and man-ners are abandoned for a powerfully poignant ensemble procession.

The cast, with a single reservation about some muddy choral vocalizations, is totally delightful. Most of the principals enact multiple parts, the greatest including Mako, who switches from narrator to shogun to mikado to militant modern admiral.

Other worthies are Alvin Ing, Isao Sato, Soon-Teck Oh and Ernest Harado, a Godunoff Basso. In line with Kabuki tradition, the males double in most feminine roles.

Boris Aronson and Florence Koltz, respectively set and cos-tume designer, have teamed for wondrously delightful visual ef-fects.

"Pacific Overtures" has a bittersweet tang along with im-mediate excitement. A show for many seasons, for young and old, first-timer and the constant fan. Dai Ichi as they say along the Ginza for the very best.

GODDARD, Bob; (2) Theater Critic; (3) b. Madison, Mo., March 11, 1913; (4) s. Frank and Florence (Goddard); (5) B.J.U. of Missouri Journalism School, 1935; (8) Assistant Editor, St. Louis County Lead-er, 1935-37; On St. Louis Globe-Democrat staff ever since starting as reporter, later assistant feature editor, feature writer, currently Amusement Editor, daily around-town columnist, feature writer and theater critic; (13) PFC. in U.S. Army Air Force public relations, 1934-44; on staff of Stars and Stripes in France and Germany, 1944-45; (16) Democrat; (17) Methodist; (20) Wrote Children's book, "The Little Jester Who Couldn't Laugh," published by Steck Vaughn Co., contributed articles to Modern Maturity, Christian Science Monitor, is St. Louis correspondent for Variety; (21) Forest Park Hotel, 4910 West Pjne, St. Louis, Mo. 63108, Ph. 314-361-3500; (22) St. Louis

Globe-Democrat, 12th and Delmar, St. Louis, Mo. 63101, Ph. 314-342-1368; (23) Circulation: 298,500; (24) 30 plays and musicals; 6 miscellaneous.

Witchcraft Bubbles Hotly at Loretto
(by Bob Goddard, Globe-Democrat, January 6, 1975)

The Loretto-Hilton Repertory Theatre troupe is consorting with devils and witches these nights and doing a powerful job of it by way of a superb production of Arthur Miller's searing drama, "The Crucible."

Miller tore his vivid tale of hate and bigotry from the dark pages of the history of the Salem (Mass.) witch trials of 1692, writing in anger, not just for a time long gone but as an indictment of man's continuing inhumanity to man centuries later.

At any rate, aside from whatever relevance it has to the modern world, "The Crucible" stands on its own as a stark, churning drama of harsh times when mass hysteria sent innocent people to the gallows wholesale.

Pivotal roles in the seething center of the witches' brew are played with grim realism by Robert Darnell as John Proctor, a staunch, idealistic farmer charged with witchery for a moment of lechery, and by Margaret Winn as his dignified wife, Elizabeth, also falsely accused of witchcraft by the vengeful young girl whom Proctor trifled with.

They are excellent throughout but particularly, memorable in the climactic scene when they are faced with their moment of truth, a deeply moving scene on anybody's stage.

Renee Tadlock plays the vengeful Abigail with frightening abandon, stirring up other girls of the town to a frenzy of wild-eyed writhing in the spell of imaginary sorcery, thus turning Salem into its bloody days of iniquity.

Arthur A. Rosenberg struts and fulminates in an outstanding portrayal of the deputy governor presiding at the trials, an archetype of the domineering magistrate, clothing his machinations in the guise of justice and the fear of God.

Lewis Arlt gives a finely etched performance as a preacher who gradually faces up to reason in the wave of hysteria; Wil Love brings the fire and brimstone touch to a different sort of preacher, vengeful to the end, and Henry Strozier is in fine fettle as a crotchety old townsman who even manages to stir up some laughter in the generally dour proceedings.

Among others in all-around gifted lineup, gratifyingly on hand as assorted town types, sacred and profane: Louise Jenkins, Trinity Thompson, Patrick Desmond, Joneal Joplin, Vance

Sorrells and Judy Meyer. They're all fine, just fine.

Gene Lesser put it all together for maximum impact as director, and Grady Larkins matched the mood of the times with simple, austere sets as did John David Ridge with his drab, Puritan costumes.

American's Show Lives Up to Name
(by Bob Goddard, Globe-Democrat, May 28, 1975)

There is really no way to adequately explain Peter Cook and Dudley Moore except to say that they may well have escaped from some amiable lunatic asylum and are out to have as much fun as possible until somebody with a net comes to fetch them back to their proper haunts.

The two blithe British spirits, who opened a week's run Monday in "Good Evening," a series of slightly mad sketches at the American Theatre, are a highly diverting duo and as contrasting as day and night. But they are as attuned to each other's varying moods as gin is to vermouth, and the results are sometimes just as devastating.

Cook is long and lean with an air of imminent doom. Moore is impish, bright-eyed and deceptively innocent. You would never expect to see the two of them hobnobbing arm-in-arm in the ordinary course of affairs, but that's show biz.

On stage they are two of the reasons why there will always be an England, a jolly old England, quite comfortable in its fumbling Col. Blimp manner and always able to chuckle at its own vagaries.

There are 10 or so sketches in "Good Evening," some of them indulging in atrocious puns, some verging on under-understatement and some too infernally long, but all entertaining.

There's the little comedy classic, "One Leg Too Few," in which a one-legged actor auditions for the role of Tarzan; "The Gospel Truth," featuring Matthew, ace reporter for the Bethlehem Star, interviewing Arthur Shepherd, on-the-spot witness of angelic pronouncements, and "The Frog and the Peach," in which the proprietor of a restaurant that serves only frogs and peaches tells why he is so unsuccessful.

Cook is also charmingly idiotic as a coal miner with literary aspirations, and Moore is a further delight as the doddering father of a movie star and as a gay hotel serviceman who entices a barrister-guest into playing Desdemona to his Othello in the handkerchief scene from "Othello."

They are both engaging chaps in the foregoing and in other sharply honed sketches, but lest the talk get too much for you,

Moore is a handy man with a piano and has some antic fun taking
off on madrigal singers and classical composers.

"Good Evening" is a very good evening indeed.

GOLD, Sylviane; (2) Drama Assistant; (3) b. Paris, France, Feb. 17,
1948; (4) d. Jack and Annette (Movermann); (5) Queens College, 1964-
68; comparative literature, major subject; (6) m. Lawrence Simon-
berg June 30, 1972; (8) Joined N. Y. Post drama dept. in June, 1970;
20 freelance articles for Village Voice, Far East Traveler; (21) 315
Hicks St., Brooklyn Heights, N. Y. 11201, Ph. 212-UL5-3569; (22) 210
South St. , N. Y. , N. Y. , 10002, Ph. 212-349-5000; (23) approximately
500,000 circulation; (24) I also review films, folk troupes and spectacles on a stand-by basis.

A Rare Evening With "Three Sisters"
(by Sylviane Gold, New York Post, November 5, 1975)

The pieces in the jigsaw puzzle finally fell into place last
night, as The Acting Company presented its final production of
the season at the Harkness Theater--a moving and wonderfully
complete production of "The Three Sisters."

Since it arrived at that powder-blue house early last month
with "The Robber Bridegroom," the company's productions have
displayed its considerable talents, but also its weaknesses--a
lack of depth here, a misconceived or miscast performance there.
But last night's play contained not a single false note, not a moment's uneasiness. And while such evenings of theater are rare,
such evenings of Chekhov are rarer still.

His three sisters, pining for Moscow yet incapable of escaping from the stultifying garrison town that imprisons their
spirits, can be rather stultifying themselves. But Mary Lou
Rosato, Patti Lupone and Mary-Joan Negro--especially Mary-
Joan Negro--bring them to heartbreaking life on the stage, and
keep them alive for nearly three hours.

Miss Negro plays the supremely bored Masha, whose supremely boring husband has driven her into an affair with an officer. The baleful glances she throws at her sisters from a
chaise lounge as they discuss the "duty" of marriage speak ironies that no writer could put in a play.

Miss LuPone, playing Irina, matures before your eyes: The
playful, shallow young girl of Act I becomes a dim-eyed, practical woman, willing to accept a man she does not love as a husband, and equally willing to accept his death.

As Olga, the oldest of the sisters, Miss Rosato becomes pro-
gressively more spinsterish, acquiring neurotic mannerisms and
steely strength in equal proportions as her youth slips away.

While the sisters can be quite miserable all by themselves, their despair is intensified by the failure of their brother to fulfill the hopes they hold for him, and Benjamin Hendrickson captures a note of impending collapse from the very start of the play. Even as he asks, "Isn't it strange, how life lets you down?", he is dimly aware of how he has let life down.

The woman he marries and grows to despise is played with just the right kind of nasty vulgarity by Sandra Halperin. The smiling insincerity with which she slowly takes over the household is one of Chekhov's triumphs, and Miss Halperin does the character justice.

There isn't space in which to mention each actor, although all deserve it--Peter Dvorsky's sweetly philosophical colonel, whose love affair with Masha is cut short by the vagaries of military life; Norman Snow's lovelorn baron, who believes in work but never quite gets around to it; Richard Ooms' pathetic schoolmaster, who goes around giving "zero for conduct" while his wife carries on under his nose.

The care with which each character is fashioned and the precise way they interlock are not just happy accidents. The Acting Company has been doing this production of the "The Three Sisters" for two years now, and while Boris Tumarin's direction, Douglas W. Schmidt's setting and John David Ridge's costumes provided a firm foundation from the start, the perfection of the ensemble work can only be the result of time, time, time.

And time, time, time is running out if you have not yet seen The Acting Company do its stuff--or even if you have, "The Three Sisters" plays only through Saturday. After that, the group resumes its endless touring, hopefully to polish some other gem for next year.

A Shell of a Play
(by Sylviane Gold, New York Post, March 25, 1976)

Isolated in one of those uncanny time-warps that bedevil cultural historians, the work of Georg Buechner is generally conceded to be the drama's first expression of 20th-century angst. And "Woyzeck," constructed from fragments found after Buechner's death in 1837, gave literature its first genuine antihero.

Based on the trial records of a soldier who was beheaded in 1824 for having stabbed his unfaithful mistress, Buechner's scenes show us a Woyzeck whose only connection to reality is his relationship with the woman who has borne him an illegitimate son. To earn money for her and the child, he races from one small chore to another in the frenetic way that so disturbs his captain.

He is a man in retreat, hounded and derided by the captain
for whom he does odd jobs and by the doctor who's using him
for "scientific" experiments.

Mysterious voices tell him truths that he can barely make
out, much less repeat, while the captain tells him he should be
moral and the doctor advises him to be more rational but Woyzeck isn't stupid, and he knows that he is too poor to be respectable and too human to subjugate his nature to his reason.
He is adrift and aware of it, and that, in a nutshell, is the modern dilemma.

That in a nutshell, is also the reason "Woyzeck" has become
such a popular item on the off-off-Broadway circuit. And maybe that's the reason the Shaliko Company's version (which opened
yesterday at the Public Theater's Martinson Hall, 425 Lafayette
St.) deals less with the modern dilemma than with how to do
something different with "Woyzeck."

The result is almost gothic--Woyzeck as a bewildered, bisexual madman--and it's a conception that might serve if Buechner shared the romantic outlook of his contemporaries de Musset and Hugo. But Buechner's point of view is more properly
compared to Strindberg's or Beckett's; director Leonardo Shapiro
seems to have gotten no further than Grand Guignol.

Joseph Chaikin is an actor of uncommon presence, and his
Woyzeck takes over the stage from the rest of the company whenever he steps out on it. But his is a Woyzeck bereft of humanity,
an automaton, a lobotomized stutterer whose words are shouted
in a monochromatic voice that can only lecture an audience, not
move it. He walks as if in a dream, heavy-limbed and distracted
and understanding nothing. But Buechner's Woyzeck understands
too much, and that's his problem.

Jane Mandel plays Woyzeck's mistress with a sullen coldness
that has nothing to do with the passionate abandon written into the
role; Ray Barry struts with conviction as the macho drum major who seduces her. Ron Faber as the obnoxious captain and
Jake Dengel as the absurd doctor confuse burlesque with satire,
in still another indication of the wrong-headedness of this production.

The best example, however, is probably the brief program
note that calls Buechner a "contemporary of Marx and Darwin."
Buechner, of course, had been dead some 10 years when Marx
wrote "The Communist Manifesto" and some 20 years when Darwin published "The Origin of Species." Although all three were
born in the first quarter of the 19th century, thinking of them
as "contemporaries" leads to false conclusions about the source
of Buechner's radical spirit. Those false conclusions have eliminated the complexities of "Woyzeck" and left only a recitation,
a shell of the play.

GOTT FRIED, Martin; (2) Theater critic; (3) b. New York City, Oct.
9, 1933; (4) s. Isidore and Rae (Weitz); (5) B.A. Columbia, major
subj; English; 1955; (6) m. Jane Lahr, April 15, 1968; (7) child--
Maya; (8) music critic, Village Voice, 1961; off-Broadway drama
critic, Women's Wear Daily, 1962; senior drama critic, Women's
Wear Daily, 1963-1974; senior drama critic, New York Post, 1974-
present; (9) playwright, The Director, produced by Herbert Berghof
Theater, 1972; (13) U.S. Army, Military Intelligence, Frankfurt,
Germany, 1957-59; (14) Rockefeller Foundation Fellowships, 1968
and 1969 renewal; George Jean Nathan Award for Dramatic Criticism,
1969; (15) N.Y. Drama Critics Circle; (16) Democrat; (17) atheist;
(20) "A Theater Divided," Little, Brown and Co., 1968; "Opening
Nights," G. P. Putnam's Sons, 1970; also contribute articles to Sunday New York Times, Vogue Magazine, Yale Theatre/Quarterly and
various theater programs; (21) 17 East 96 Street, New York, N.Y.
10028, Ph. 722-3976; (22) N.Y. Post, 210 South Street, Ph. 349-
5000; (23) Circulation: 500,000; (24) Approximately 2,500 reviews
of theater productions.

A Double Meaning "Seagull"
(by Martin Gottfried, New York Post, January 31, 1975)

The Manhattan Theater Club's presentation of "The Seagull"
is a special event not just because of the production. That is
very good and often wonderful but, because of an uneven company,
not great.   This is an event because of the people involved, their
histories, and how the production relates to them and to our contemporary theater.   These aspects make this "Seagull" especially
moving.

Ten years ago, Joseph Chaikin was a very fine actor with
The Living Theater and Jean-Claude van Itallie was a young playwright of exceptional promise.   The movement toward company
theaters was just beginning.

Chaikin left The Living Theater when it became more interested in radical politics than in pure theater.   He founded the
Open Theater and van Itallie joined him.   Their company was to
become the best of the type because Chaikin, while innovating,
never forgot his professionalism, because The Open Theater,
while abandoning play scripts as its counterparts did, had not
abandoned playwrights.   In fact, in van Itallie it had a superb
one.

The Open Theater was the best American group theater because Chaikin was not a self-styled messiah; not a bourgeois
bohemian; but a truly dedicated and skilled artist and his company gave off feelings of purity and beauty.   Out of the van
Itallie-Chaikin collaboration came the wonderful "America Hurrah," and subsequently, "The Serpent."

Several years ago, van Itallie wisely (and I'm sure sadly)
left The Open Theater because its minimal interest in words

and play structure were too limiting for a real writer. Last
year Chaikin even more sadly, I'm sure, disbanded The Open
Theater sensing, I'd guess, the movement's demise. This long
but necessary chronology brings us to his staging of van Itallie's
adaptation of "The Seagull."

Think of the ironies! For all his reputation and experience,
it is Chaikin's professional debut as the director of a conventional play and it's a naturalistic one. Being a play by Chekhov, it
is the most perfect of naturalistic plays. The adaptation is by
van Itallie himself and what is the play about? A theater ex-
perimentalist coping with a traditional theatrical world! "The
Seagull" is about the flaming ideas of youth and how the corrupt
adult world tries to douse them. It is about the struggle of that
flame for survival.

As Chekhov himself has a character say toward the end,
"I'm beginning to think it isn't a matter of old or new forms.
What matters is to write without thinking of any forms ... al-
lowing what you write to come straight out."

This is Checkhov speaking across 80 years to Chaikin and
van Itallie. It is van Itallie, in the adaptation, speaking to himself and Chaikin. This relevance is what makes the production
of "The Seagull" an event and a thrilling one.

Chaikin's staging proves Chekhov's point. An artist is an
artist. His loving production has none of the "avant garde" to
it. It is sublimely understood Chekhov. The story moves directly through its pathways, each character grasped and fit into
the picture, all relationships marked and set. Though this is
the youngest of Chekhov's four masterworks, it definitely belongs
among them. The detail is awesome, the compassion engulfing,
and it all seems so simple under Chaikin's guidance. He understands just as van Itallie's tender adaptation does.

Philip Gilliam's scenery is of great help, its simple pine
paneling miraculously opening from a bare first act to ever fuller
sets. Leueen MacGrath is marvelous as Madame Arkadina--an
egotistical actress, a selfish mother and pathetic beneath. Thomas Barbour, as the doctor who speaks for the author, is wise
but human, and Margo Lee Sherman makes the lovelorn Masha
the soul of frustrated Chekhovian humanity.

The critical roles of Madame Arkadina's playwright son,
her second-rate lover and Nina, the "seagull" he victimizes,
are amateurishly played and this hurts the production--almost
crucially in its final scene. But because of the beautiful direction,
excellent work by most of the cast and the striking relationship
between the play and those involved in doing it, this "Seagull"
has a very special emotional power.

Shakespeare by the British
(by Martin Gottfried, New York Post, February 14, 1975)

The Royal Shakespeare Company may well deserve its reputation as the world's finest producer of Shakespeare, but it is
still an institution and it still runs the risk of institutionalizing
its work. This is exactly what has become of its "Love's Labour's Lost," which took its turn last night in the company's
season at the Brooklyn Academy of Music.

The play is one of Shakespeare's loveliest and most wise. The
physical production is gorgeous: a green canopy sweeping up toward the audience and a lush, grass carpet raking down; the costumes, also designed by Timothy O'Brien and Tazeena Firth, are
rich beyond anything we ever see in America: a rainbow of
colors, broken down into the most subtle of tints, in an array
of materials.

But the performance is sterile, an example of the cold and
uninspired professionalism so dangerous to the comfortable institution. Perhaps the Royal Shakespeare Company is spreading itself too thin. It has one production ("Sherlock Holmes") presently running on Broadway, another ("London Assurance") that just
closed, and is presently conducting two British seasons--one at
Stratford-on-Avon and another at its Aldwych Theater in London.
How many first string teams can it have?

The team playing "Love's Labour's Lost" is impeccable by any
standard, but by impeccable standards it is ordinary. It is also
short. Susan Fleetwood, as the French Princess, so towers over
David Suchet's King Ferdinand that every time he approaches her
(which he does as seldom as possible), he does it from five feet
away leaning toward her on his toes. Confronting her at last, he
confronts her chin.

I suppose it is perfectly all right to have a short production
with a tall princess, but not if that is the first thing you notice.
As David Jones has directed it, the play is filled with character-
less characters. This wonderfully written romantic comedy never
seemed so colorless. One character is no different from another,
and it is obvious as it never was before that Shakespeare could
leave characters on stage all night without giving them any lines.
To notice this with a company proud of ensemble work is to notice a bland production.

The pity, of course, is the play. "Love's Labour's Lost" almost unfortunately has contemporary relevance. Its women are
as liberated as any in the theater's 400 years since. I say "unfortunately" because it is one play that doesn't need relevance to
be justified. It has few lines that aren't exquisite. Its appreciation of education and wisdom is civility itself. It has an understanding of the difference between men and women that most people today do not approach.

For the men in this play are as foolish with women as all men seem to be; and the women seem to grow more sensible as the men grow more emotional. Moreover, the women in this particular production are especially interesting because Jones has them played with great sensuality. Shakespeare provides them with brains enough.

But that is as interesting as the production ever gets. Susan Fleetwood is a far cry from the usual, pristine and classy Princess. She is earthy and lush and, with her brains, someone to contend with. But Suchet's romancing of her is silly--he looks so much like Dudley Moore you think he must be kidding. Ultimately, the whole company fades into a general lull of competence or even less, occasionally even sing-songing the rhymed couplets.

It is the kind of Shakespeare born of too many festival companies and the Royal Shakespeare, no different than any other, is obliged to keep its energies flowing if it is not to become a museum.

GRAHAM, David Victor; (2) Theater Writer; (3) b. Flint, April 17, 1948; (4) s. Gordon and Eunice Graham; (5) B.A. Eastern Michigan U., major subjs.: history, political science, literature, 1970; (6) m. Linda A. Bennett, Sept. 6, 1975; (7) no children; (8) Reporter, Flint Journal, 1970, theater writer, Feb., 1974; (9) Author, director, five religious plays; (10) treasurer, Flint American Civil Liberties Union, board member, Life Enrichment Center; (13) Sp-4, Michigan National Guard, Medical Platoon, 1970-1976; (15) Mem., Flint Institue of Arts, American Theatre Critics Association; (16) Democrat; (17) Reformed Church of America; (20) see # 9; (21) 2820 Clement, Flint, Mich. 48504, Ph. 313-767-7765; (22) Flint Journal, 200 E. First St., Flint, Mich. 48502, Ph. 313-767-0660; (23) Circulation: 110,000; (24) 50 plays and musicals.

Cronyn is Spiny Shylock
(by David V. Graham, Flint Journal, June 15, 1976)

Hume Cronyn is not likely to win any awards from the B'nai B'rith for his portrayal of the Jewish Shylock in this season's "The Merchant of Venice" here. But it is a powerful performance that demands respect.

"Merchant," at the Festival Theater, is one of 11 productions the Stratford Festival is staging producing in its 24th season.

Shakespeare's play is about a young man who gets an older friend, a Venice Merchant, to borrow money from a Jew, Shylock. The money is needed so the young man can finance his pursuit of a rich young woman who requires unusual courting.

Cronyn, in this play's most engrossing performance, plays Shylock as a bitter, demanding usurer who insists on his pound of flesh when the merchant defaults on his loan.

His characterization is decidely different from the sympathetic but tragic figure usually staged in this century.   And it is
far removed from the comic interpretation the role received until the 1900s.

This Shylock is a militant Jew who even offends his rabbi and
friends in his claims.   Yet, by the end of play, Cronyn's performance begins to elicit sympathy as Cronyn goes beyond a portrayal of a villain and develops into a pathetic creature wronged
by a hostile world.

No, this character is not an anti-Semitic figure.

Some writers have claimed that Shakespeare couldn't have
been anti-Jewish because he probably didn't know any Jews because they were banned from Elizabethan England.

Those same writers believe that Shakespeare was just expanding on a stock literary character that had been around for
centuries.

It is undeniable, though, that this play seems to have been
created in the wake of an anti-Semitic scandal that had swept
England at the time of its writing.

A Jewish physician was apparently framed to make it appear
that he tried to poison Queen Elizabeth.   His execution fanned the
flames of anti-Jewish feeling in England and contributed to the
climate for several anti-Semitic plays.

Shakespeare went beyond a simple villain piece or stock
character.

Was Shakespeare being anti-Semitic when he had Shylock saying this to the Venice merchant? :

"Fair sir, you spat on me on Wednesday last; you spurned
me such a day; another time you called me a dog; and for these
courtesies I'll lend you thus much money?"

But what about this Stratford production, one of the three being presented on the Festival stage?

Although Cronyn's performance is the only enduring one, several other actors make substantial contributions.

Jackie Burroughs as Portia, an heiress who is the reason
for Shylock's loan, doesn't exactly create a vision of desirable
beauty as the female lead, but she comes across strongly when
she pretends to be a young lawyer to defeat Shylock's claims in
court to save the life of her suitor's friend.

Nick Mancuso, as her suitor, is successful in creating the

image of a man trying to save his friend.   His romantic ambitions seemed too restrained.

James Hurdle as his friend creates laughs with his flippant behavior, and Bernard Hopkins adds more comic relief as Shylock's low-breed servant.

Despite all this quality work, there is too much missing to make this a first-class production.

Bill Glassco's direction seems to suffer from insecurity.

Glassco, making his first attempt at the Festival stage, is a director of some note in Toronto's underground theater.

Here, though, he appears to be undecided whether to follow Stratford stage traditions or to break out with the newer forms of theater.

So, we have some characters doing small snatches of brilliant stage business followed by moments of monotony.

It is as though Glassco restrained himself after coming up with a few good ideas for fear of offending the Festival's largely middle-class audiences.   But, as artistic director Robin Phillips has already demonstrated, audiences will appreciate innovative, quality productions.

Unlike previous Stratford productions, this play gains little if anything by its revised setting.

Most annoying is the idea of having a packet of giggling harem girls and an Arabic "holy man" as servants to the heiress. It looks and sounds silly.

"My Fat Friend" Travels Here at Sluggish Pace
(by David V. Graham, Flint Journal, June 30, 1976)

Star Theater is billing its current production of "My Fat Friend" as the "hilarious new comedy."

This play is neither new nor hilarious.

Written by British television writer Charles Laurence, this comedy surfaced in London's West End in late 1972.

The following year it was one of the many English imports to play Broadway, where it did fairly well its first year.   It reopened the following year.

In December of the same year, it appeared at Detroit's Fisher Theater with Lynn Redgrave in the leading role.

Now playing at Whiting Auditorium with TV entertainer Vicki Lawrence, this play is a sad little effort to cash in on cheap homosexual jokes and jibes about fat women.

With a faster pace and dynamic acting, it might be more than just an extended Weight Watchers lecture.

An apparently nervous Miss Lawrence doesn't take advantage of her few chances to demonstrate her considerable charm, and Laurence's writing is the chatty kind that passes for cute in some circles.

The only saving grace in the show is Bob Moak's valiant efforts to improve its sluggish pace.

He plays an aging homosexual who is trying to help his overweight landlady lose weight so she can trap a prospective boyfriend. He receives assistance from an aspiring writer who doubles as the "family" cook.

Moak does as much as he can with this thin plot, but he has some problems too. Most troublesome is his affected English accent, which just sounds awful coming from this native of Ohio.

Unfortunately, Moak is forced to go with the accent because of the English expressions he must use. Director Richard Michaels should have made a better effort to revise the script so such a silly accent wouldn't have been necessary. He made some efforts to localize the script, so why not go all the way with it?

Everyone else in this small cast, including Miss Lawrence, is either so stiff or given such poor direction that the audience clearly starts becoming uncomfortable, especially in the second act when the platitudes about identity and other sociological nonsense begin.

The audience, which probably numbered 1,000, didn't get its first hearty laugh until well into the second scene. The first scene is strictly a sleeper.

Perhaps the cast will loosen up before the week's run is over.

GRANT, Darryl Clarence; (2) Theater Critic; (3) b. Detroit, Mich., Aug. 14, 1953; (4) s. Clarence and Lenore (Grant); (5) B.A. Michigan State U., major subj.: History; (6) single; (8) Student, upon graduation, hope to have career in Journalism and Arts management; (9) Departmental Aide, for the Lecture-Concert Series, Cultural Activities Office, acted in experimental prod. of Hamlet at M.S.U. Drama, dance, music critic WMSN student radio, plus drama critic for Michigan State News (dates respectively are as follows: 1) 1973-75 2) Feb. 1973 3) 1973, 74, & 75; 1974-1975 cont'g to present); (15) Member of Theta Delta Chi Fraternity; (16) Democrat; (17) Roman

Catholic; (20) Cont'd articles/reviews to Michigan State News, Oba-
tala Arts Review; (21) 1015 N. Capitol, #1, Lansing, Michigan 48906,
Ph. 517-487-0637 or 8231 Wisconsin, Detroit, 48204, Ph. 313-834-
1939; (22) Michigan State News, 345 Student Services Bldg. , MSU
East Lansing, Michigan 48824, Ph. 517-355-8252; (23) Circulation:
44,000; (24) 30 plays; 6 of which are musicals, 6 dance, about 8
miscellaneous.

Dinner-Theater Combination Succeeds
(by Darryl Grant, Michigan State News, January 30, 1975)

The Players Gallery dinner-theater presentation of "Blithe
Spirit" is a wonderful delight to both the palate and the mind.
The beef jardiniere dinner was delicious and well served, and
the play is entertaining and well portrayed by a gifted cast.

The Players Gallery production is supple in its treatment of
Noel Coward's brittle British humor. This dexterity is vitally
important in drawing room comedy, but it is especially important in British drawing room comedy where dialog tends to be
politely witty and dry. This distinctly British flavor can seem
vague and reserved in comparison to the wackiness that American
audiences are accustomed to seeing.

"Blithe Spirit" concerns the plight of novelist Charles Con-
domine when the ghost of his deceased wife appears at a seance.
The genius of Noel Coward's talent lies in subtle dualism that
produces highly entertaining comedy on one hand and insightful
social commentary on the other. The true theme of "Blithe
Spirit" is personal liberation and its realization.

Charles is a seemingly easily dominated man, controlled by
his first and second wives. After death strikes wife number two,
he realizes that both wives had the same intent in life--to satisfy
their insecurities by dominating him. At the end of the play he
realizes the truth and strikes out in a path of personal freedom
and responsibility.

Charles is played with casual and humorous flair by William
B. Shipley. Although his performance contains wonderful moments of facetious facility, there is an irritating struggle in evidence. Shipley is unable to feel entirely comfortable with Charles'
effeminacy. Effeminacy is one of the characteristics of the 1930s
British male and Shipley has difficulty displaying enough of it or
maintaining it when he has caught it.

Carol Rosenblaum gives a superb rendition of Charles' wife,
Ruth. Her performance catches the subtle characteristics of
an upper-class British lady. Her caustic crustiness, her vocal
inflections and indignant laugh are funny and memorable.

Susan Rosenthal as Madam Arcati is undoubtedly best where
slapstick humor is concerned. Her portrayal of the wacky

medium is sheer joy. Rosenthal's characterization is a store-
house of hilarious gestures like sniffing the air, looking in her
sleeve or lifting the tops of sandwiches. All of this is generally
done in mid-delivery, which grasps the funny bone even more
firmly.

Leslie Page is successful as the ghostly Elvira. She maintains the necessary amount of saccharine bitchiness that is a
main feature of the character.

Paul Kanter and Diane Royce make the most of their roles
as Dr. and Mrs. Bradman, exuding the proper air of stuffy respectability. Special kudos must also go to Barb Thorne for
her engaging portrayal as the maid Edith.

An important part of "Blithe Spirit's" success is owed to the
marvelous special effects designed by Craig Collins and executed
by Lee Andrews and Jack Flower. Their unique agility allows
vases to fly through the air and pictures and bric-a-brac to shatter by ghostly hands.

Director Stan Gill and Suzie Weissler have assembled a talented cast, and guided them with a knowing hand. Thus the
Players Gallery production becomes a memorable delight.

PAC's "Henry" Uneven in Disjointed Production
(by Darryl Grant, Michigan State News, April 25, 1975)

"Henry V," Shakespeare's play of noble sentiment and patriotic fervor, suffers under a laborious and unfulfilling treatment
by the Performing Arts Company.

Granted, "Henry V" is not one of Shakespeare's greatest
plays, yet it does reap certain rewards under careful direction
and treatment, which are not garnered under the auspices of director Frank Rutledge.

The watchful eye discerns the character of a man whose
mind is as fantastic as a mechanical toy, who is all truth and
sincerity on one hand and false and prying on the other. Seemingly boundless with Machiavellian wisdom, Henry is an interesting fellow with his chameleon-like personality.

Unfortunately, this character is hampered to the modern eye
with too many intricate subtleties that are not readily apparent.
There is too great a wealth of historical data and triumphal ora-
tories and scenes to make comfortable drama. However necessary these were to an audience in Shakespeare's day, they only
belabor a modern production.

Together with this awkwardness, is the disjointed treatment
by Frank Rutledge. In an attempt to bolster or reawaken the
mood of the Globe Theater, we are given an intellectual cheer-

leader in the person of Brenda Nickerson. Nickerson in the part
of the chorus, and also the modern mistress of ceremonies, does
a fine job, but one that would be better appreciated in solo. She
leads the audience into preperformance and postintermission activities, activities such as shouting contests, singing and joking--
things that are a nice attempt to alleviate the stiffness of traditional theater but here serve to distract and weaken the play's
impact. It is an impact that even in its original form was surely a little weak.

Weak is a kind term to apply to this production. Disjointed
is the more accurate. There are some good scenes, some very
poor ones, some bright moments and some dreary ones.

An interesting device that at times is rewarding, though not
completely, is having four actors portray Henry. This is a fine
way to show the multifacetedness of the character, and the different persona his psyche creates--his cruelty, his gentleness, his
nobility and his malice. But if there is to be a multiplicity it
should be displayed in one even show of strength and talent. One
can not quite be sure of the worth of the device when it is im-
balanced. Brian Carpenter, Fran Guinan, Bill Hutson and John
Schmedes are given the difficult task of portrayal. Carpenter
and Hutson are masterful with a careful and rich awareness of
their roles that is wonderful--Carpenter in his tactful pursuit
of Katherine, Hutson with his martial and humane wisdom on the
battlefield. Surely Hutson's soliloquy as the too human Henry on
the war plane is one of the definite glories of this season. Rich
and vibrant yet humble, he comes close to the original Shakesperian concept of the character.

However, the finesse of Carpenter and Hutson is marred by
the weakness and verbosity of Guinan and Schmedes. Guinan gets
carried away with the exigencies of his role, mainly the sound
of his voice. Schmedes becomes verbose in his obscurity.

There is also the problem of direction, which at times seems
invisible or little more than posing. There is no tightness or
clarity. Dramatic matter becomes a pile of indistinguishable
dung. Timing seems to have been ignored, and energy at a loss.
One could hope for a more virile, energetic tone considering the
pageantry and patriotism, but alas, there is none. It just drags
interminably on.

There is some satisfaction to be garnered from the rubble,
such as the imaginative costumes designed by Gretel Geist.

GRAY, Farnum Moore (Jr.); (2) Entertainment writer (theater and
film critic); (3) b. Miami, Fla., July 19, 1940; (4) s. Farnum M.
and Mattie Mae Gray; (5) B. A. U. of North Carolina at Chapel Hill,
major in English, 1962; (6) m. Wanda Davis, June 2, 1961; (7) chil-
dren--Daniel Farnum, Holly Patrice; (8) Reporter, Rocky Mount (N. C.)

Telegram, 1962-64; reporter, Winston-Salem Journal, 1965-67; writer
Pennsylvania Advancement School, Philadelphia, 1967-70; freelance
writer, 1970-71; director, Aspen (Colo.) Community School, 1971-72;
senior editor, Learning Magazine, 1972-73; freelance writer, 1973;
writer (theater and film critic), Atlanta Constitution, 1974- ; (14)
Award for influential writing about treatment of poor people in courts
from National Legal Aid and Defender Assoc., 1967; honorable mention from American Psychological Foundation for magazine article in
1974; (16) Ind. Demo.; (20) Co-author of Liberating Education: Psychological Learning Through Improvisational Drama, McCutchan Pub.
Co., 1973; cont. articles to The Nation, Psychology Today and other
magazines; chapters in books: Radical School Reform, Will It Grow
in a Classroom? and Teaching Social Studies in the Urban Classroom; (21) 1475 Kay Lane, Atlanta, Ga. 30306, Ph. 404-874-2904;
(22) The Atlanta Constitution, Box 4689, Atlanta, Ga. 30306, Ph.
404-572-5467; (23) Circulation: 260,000; (24) 75 plays, 120 motion
pictures, 25 concert and nightclub entertainers.

Masterful Handling of Pinter
(by Farnum Gray, Atlanta Constitution, January 18, 1975)

Harold Pinter's play, "The Birthday Party," offers an unusually stimulating experience, with its humor, terror, stunning
use of language, and thought-provoking, enigmatic view of the
senseless conditions in our lives.

The Academy Theatre's current production of the play is the
best-acted, most intelligently directed version I've seen, and
therefore the most absorbing.

Joining Frank Wittow in the cast are a group of mature performers who have studied at the Academy over the years. Under
Wittow's direction, they have gotten deeply into their characterizations, and they work beautifully together.

It's an excellent show and a fine reminder of how lucky Atlanta is to have the Academy. You can see it through Feb. 15.

Returning to the Academy stage after a 10-year absence, Edward Lee plays Stanley Webber, a hulking slob who plays the
piano. He has sought refuge from the world, which holds unexplained terrors for him, in a drab, seaside boarding house.

The boarding house is run by a wary old man named Petey
and his dotty wife, Meg. In those roles, Chris Curran and Gay
Griggs play some marvelous scenes.

Stanley's refuge is shattered by the arrival of two new guests.
These representatives of an undefined organization, Goldberg and
his henchman, McCann, have come to break Stanley and take him
back to whatever he was escaping from.

They stage a birthday party for him, though it is not his

birthday, and use the highly theatrical scene to exploit Stanley's guilt and other weaknesses.

As Goldberg, Wittow superbly maintains a constant air of menace, even while he is being a folksy, amiable fellow, telling stories of his Jewish upbringing.

Each character has a depth that adds to the play's riches.

As McCann, Larry Larson creates a picture of mindless corporate conformity. Though sometimes amusingly puzzled by Goldberg, he does what he is told.

Completing the cast is Yvonne Tenney as Lulu, an English working-class good-time girl.

Curran, as Petey, masterfully provides a viewpoint that enriches the play's meaning. A tired, subtle movement of his eyes is sometimes enough to draw giggles from the audience.

Meg is concerned with niceness. As often happens with unperceptive, nice people, she becomes the most effective aide to the evil Goldberg. Miss Griggs is fascinating in the role.

Ivey Shines in "Crucible"
(by Farnum Gray, Atlanta Constitution, March 22, 1975)

A strong Alliance Theatre Company cast--with Dana Ivey standing out in one of the best performances by an actress of this Atlanta season--opened Thursday night in "The Crucible," Arthur Miller's powerful melodrama of the Salem witch hunts.

The production, directed by Fred Chappell, is exciting, despite having too many fluffs and stepped-on lines even for an opening night.

The story--essentially true--takes place in 1692. A few girls, suppressed by Puritan rigidity, have been letting off steam by dancing in the woods at night, sometimes naked.

When they are caught by the Rev. Samuel Parris, a fearsome hell-fire preacher, their hysterical alibi is that the devil made them do it. They begin accusing innocent women of witchcraft. The theocratic state gives the accused women a choice of being hanged or confessing.

The community becomes a frenzied mob, with the witchcraft trials being used by the greedy and spiteful.

The central figures in the story are John Proctor, an honest farmer, his wife Elizabeth, and Abigail Williams, the leader of the girls who gain immense power by making the accusations of witchcraft.

Abigail, who once seduced Proctor, accuses his wife of witch-craft, intending to eliminate her and marry Proctor.

Howard Brunner does a fine job as Proctor, conveying his tormented ethical conflicts and nobility of character without losing the simplicity of this uneducated man.

Dana Ivey gives a stunning, masterful portrayal of Elizabeth Proctor.

She and Brunner bring off a great theatrical moment late in the play when they converse alone at the front of the stage.

Susan Harney gives a polished performance as Abigail.

Especially effective is the achievement of Miss Ivey and others in the cast in conveying, physically and otherwise, the changes that take place in their characters.

One of them, Mitchell Edmonds, gives a sensitive performance as the Rev. John Hale, whose pomposity and confidence in the system melts away in the face of his gradual realization that he has been wrong.

As the hell-obsessed Rev. Parris, Philip Pleasants increases the evil in his demeanor with each appearance.

In one of the well-cast supporting roles, Kay Creel is perfect as Mary Warren, the only one of the troublemaking girls who wavers in her story.

Mary Nell Santacroce is moving as Rebecca Nurse, an old woman of simple dignity who would rather die than give in to the court.

Presiding over the appalling court is Deputy-Governor Danforth, a monstrous combination of theologian and bureaucrat. Even when the court's errors become apparent, he rationalizes that he must go on killing people, because a change of policy would cast doubt on the guilt of the 12 he has already hanged.

In this rich role, Ed Holmes has only a few good moments. As Danforth's associate, Judge Hawthorne, Howard Zielke doesn't help matters.

Melissa Haney, an elementary school student, plays an ostensibly possessed girl, reminiscent of "The Exorcist."

Miller's play, first produced in 1952, was often associated with the political witch hunts of Sen. Joseph McCarthy. However, Miller's script does not call attention to contemporary parallels.

Miller kept his story close to what actually happened, even

using the names of the real people.   For dramatic efficiency,
there is some fusing of characters.

After the performance is over, the Alliance adds a nice
touch by handing out an epilogue telling what happened to the
characters later in their lives.

GREATOREX, Susan Marian; (2) Amusements editor/theater critic;
(3) b. Passaic, N.J., Nov. 3, 1948; (4) d. Tom Richard and Marian
Koyt (Misner) Greatorex; (5) B.A. U. of Delaware, major in International Relations, 1970; (6) single; (8) Reporter/copy editor, Manchester (N.H.) Union Leader, 1970-73; business, amusements and
real estate editor, The Herald-News, Passaic, N.J., 1973- ; (9)
Drama critic for The Review, University of Delaware Undergraduate
newspaper, 1968-70; (15) Executive board member, New Jersey Drama Critics Association; (17) Methodist; (21) 36 Mapes Ave., Nutley,
N.J. 07110; (22) The Herald-News, 988 Main Ave., Passaic, N.J.
07055, Ph. 201-365-3104; (23) Circulation: 90,000; (24) 50 plays and
or musicals, mostly at New Jersey Theaters, some in New York.

Andrews, Whiting Put the Show Back on Track
(by Susan Greatorex, Herald-News, January 26, 1976)

What ever you do, don't leave your seat when the curtain
comes down.

The best part of "Over Here," the current attraction at Playhouse on the Mall, is what happens when Maxene Andrews and
Margaret Whiting play themselves.

While they do a bang-up job of portraying the DePaul sisters
in the musical, the two are just too good for the tacky vehicle.
The show does its best to bring back the swing of the '40s with
the kind of jokes popular then, but wouldn't make it without the
two ladies who really know what it was all about.   It's also
helped by an audience filled with people who remember.

"Over Here" throws a cross-section of America on a train
trip from California to New York in the war years.   It mixes
some new recruits with girls, parent-types, a wacko lady spy
and the aforementioned singing sisters who run the canteen.
Holding it all together is a narrator-drill sergeant and a black
crewman who lets the passengers and audience know how far the
train has gone.   Enough for the story.

Miss Andrews, the one responsible for the distinct sound of
the Andrews Sisters, is responsible for keeping the musical on
its nostalgic trip.   Miss Whiting gives it class, especially when
she sings "Where Did the Good Times Go" in act two.

The cast also includes Dolly Jonah as the singing spy; Peter
Walker as Norwin Spokesman, the narrator; W. M. Hunt, Danny

Taylor and Scott Stevensen as the new recruits; Ilene Graff, Edie Cowan and Deborah Rush as their girls; Kenneth Frett as the trainman; and Jack Naughton, Nina Dova and Robert Nichols as the "adult" passengers.

The show, with music and lyrics by Richard M. Sherman and Robert B. Sherman and book by Will Holt, is not great but it does have some good moments. The old guys have fun remembering when they went off to World War I in "Hey Yvette," and Frett has a good time shuffling to "Don't Shoot the Hooey to Me, Louis." Another number, "Wartime Wedding" pretty well sums up all the wartime bride movies.

John Mineo staged the musical numbers and dances, which according to the program, follow Patricia Birch's Broadway choreography. Christopher Hewett directed.

Maxene Andrews and Margaret Whiting saved it, in spite of costumes by Brooks-Van Horn, Inc. One could understand and forgive the army attire the two wear throughout most of the show, but never the unflattering red and white performance costumes they wear as the singing sisters. They could have at least been given an opportunity to change into something pretty for the after-the-show bit when the two sing their hits. That part is well worth a short wait.

"6 Rms Riv Vu" Has What It Takes
(by Susan Greatorex, Herald-News, February 12, 1976)

The current show at the Paper Mill Playhouse has everything going for it.

"6 Rms Riv Vu" which opened Wednesday night has a name star, a terrific script and precise direction which makes for a good production.

The star is Tab Hunter, once the fairhaired boy of Hollywood, who transfers his talent to the stage with a nice portrayal of a nice guy.

The play by Bob Randall is a thoughtful comedy. It isn't a kneeslapper--there are too many poignant moments for that--but it does have warmly funny characters and a comic situation.

Translated, the title is the opening line of a classified advertisement for a New York rent-controlled apartment with six rooms and a view of the Hudson River. What the ad fails to mention is that one has to hang out the bathroom window and look sideways to get a glimpse of the river. It also omits any reference to the odd lady who lives next door with her doberman pinscher, Trixie, and the Hispanic superintendent who only fixes plumbing problems when a flood is underway.

However, the ad is enough to attract the attention of two married people (not to each other) who come to see it.

Hunter plays Paul Friedman, an advertising copy writer who has one son and a wife interested in women's lib. He's always stayed on the straight and narrow career/marriage path, but now, in his 30s is beginning to wonder what he's been missing.

Winsome Monica Moran is cast as Anne Miller, a college graduate and mother of two who now finds the most exciting moments of her life come when she's folding socks. She'd go crazy if it wasn't for a stray argyle every now and then.

It sounds like a perfect set up for an affair, right? The couple is helped by a missing doorknob which keeps them locked in the apartment, but hindered by their own moral backgrounds.

Those interested in learning more and laughing about it should go see the show.

Harvey Medlinsky did an admirable directing job which was apparent even opening night, the first time the cast did the show for an audience. Scenes that were slightly blurry Wednesday will undoubtedly come into focus with another performance or two. There are no real problems.

The cast also includes Christine Baranski as Paul's wife; Randall Robins as Anne's husband; Ernesto Gonzalez as the super; Alice Beardsley as the Woman in 4A and Janet MacKenzie and Gregory Nicholas as other prospective tenants. Their roles add a little color to what is basically a two-character play for Hunter and Miss Moran.

Billy Puzo created the appropriate empty-apartment set and lighting.

GRIFFIN, Henry William; (2) Theater critic; (3) b. Boston, February 7, 1935; (4) s. Henry Fr. and Margaret M. (Burke); (5) A. B., Boston College, 1960, majored in philosophy and English; M. A., Catholic U., 1962, history of dramatic literature; (6) m. Emilie Russell Dietrich, August 31, 1963; (7) children--Lucy Adelaide, Henry Francis, Sarah Jeannette; (8) Book editor: Macmillan 1962-64; Harcourt Brace Jovanovich 1964-68; Macmillan 1968 to present; (9) A Fourth for the Eighth, a play presented at the Evergreen Playhouse, Hollywood, 1964; Campion, a play presented at the 1971 Eugene O'Neill Playwrights' Conference, Waterford, Conn.; (15) The Drama Desk, Outer Critics Circle, Dramatists Guild, Authors League of America; (16) Democrat; (17) Catholic; (20) A dozen plays; (21) 110 Audley St., Kew Gardens, New York 11415, Ph. 212-846-5898; (22) Macmillan Publishing Co., Inc., 866 Third Ave., New York, N.Y. 10022, Ph. 212-935-2035; (23) Circulation: Sign Magazine, 175,000; (24) 40 plays and musicals; 2 original essays.

Stage
(by William Griffin, Sign Magazine, February 1973)

Butley is a play about an English professor in one of the colleges of London University whose life comes apart on stage. He is an extremely intelligent man (his witty puns and literary references leap like impalas from the dialogue), but he doesn't appear to be very diligent (he avoids his obligations as a teacher, and he estimates that it will take him twenty years to complete a book on T. S. Eliot). During the course of the play, calamities hit him with the regularity of a Greek tragedy observing the unity of time, but at the end, Ben Butley is about the same as he was at the beginning: psychologically selfish and sartorially sloppy. His trouble is that he cannot form a meaningful, lasting relationship with his wife, from whom he is now estranged, with his infant daughter, whose name he can't remember, or with his male lover, who is also a professor at the college. And it's all his own fault. In fact, Butley is more a case history with quite specific symptoms than a character whose makeup has some general relevance to mankind.

Alan Bates is superlative in the title role, blowing up the character as though it were a balloon, then letting the air out slowly, whistlingly, wheezingly.

Simon Gray, the playwright, himself a teacher of English in London University, writes with unerring accuracy of professors and their professorial folderol.

Pippin is a brassy, sassy musical about a young man who wants to do something fulfilling in life. The young man is an actor in a group of traveling players belonging to no particular century, and the part he plays is Pippin, one of the sons of Charlemagne, a ninth-century king of France.

The one most responsible for this musical is Bob Fosse, who is credited with directing and choreographing it. He is also responsible for reconceiving the material that was originally given to him by Roger O. Hirson (book) and Stephen Schwartz (music and lyrics). What he gave birth to after a year's gestation was a monster musical of dazzling dance and visual virtuosity.

The theme of the show is, if I may use Fosse's own words, "that life is pretty crumby, but in the end, there stands the family--pretty ugly, stripped of costumes and magic but holding hands." And that is how this big battleship of a musical ends. Not all that new, but nevertheless quite profound. It's a shame that so much of what precedes the ending is just loud and dull.

Special mention--very special mention--should be made of Ben Vereen, the playmaster or leader of the traveling acting troupe who put on the Pippin work for us. He is an actor,

singer and dancer of blazing talent and skill. See him in Pippin
and watch for his name, which is sure to appear again.

Enemies, by Maxim Gorky, the first play of the season for
the Repertory Theater of Lincoln Center, is a triumph. The
huge stage of the Vivian Beaumont Theater is filled with the facade of an enormous country house in provincial Russia, a lawn
of rich, green grass spreading before it. This is the backdrop
for the leisurely unfolding--perhaps I should say, undoing--of the
aristocracy's losing their grip on a society that has not only supported them but also made them wealthy. Before the play has
ended, the family has fallen, and the workers of the factory
owned by the family have won another victory in their march onward toward revolution.

The playwright is Maxim Gorky; he wrote the play in the
first years of the twentieth century. Overshadowed by such other
Russian writers as Chekhov, Tolstoy, and Dostoevski, he is becoming more widely known, and his plays are being more frequently produced.

The Lincoln Center production was immaculately directed by
Ellis Rabb. And the acting company distinguished itself for a
smooth, natural, superbly modulated performance.

My one reservation is that Enemies, like the other Russian
plays I've seen, moves so slowly. Russian society must have
died of its dead weight. However, in this production, the slow
pace of the plot was barely noticeable.

6 Rms Riv Vu is a play about a young, going-on-middle-
aged man and woman who discovered a six-room, rent-controlled
apartment of irregular shape and extravagant dimension with a
view (by hanging out the window) of the Hudson River. In it,
they also discover each other. The complication is that they
are both married, but not to each other. When they are unwittingly locked into the apartment, they are forced to face up to
each other, to review their lives, to try to escape--all of which
they do with an abundance of good humor. Before the play is
over, they have discovered their lost selves, made love once,
abandoned their youth forever, and returned rightfully to middle
age and their spouses.

Although the man and woman do knowingly violate their marriage vows, the play is not a libertarian tract on the beneficial
effects of random adultery. Rather, it is a warm, funny story
about two people--one Jewish, one Catholic--who find themselves
in a very odd predicament and work hard to extricate themselves
from it. Jerry Orbach and Jane Alexander and a handful of
others act extremely well in this modest little work.

6 Rms Riv Vu is obviously an apartment comedy. But if
the playwright Bob Randall may be said to have an apart-

ment in this popular genre, then it is Neil Simon who is superintendent of the building; the play is a pale, albeit pleasant, reflection of such blazing comedies as Barefoot in the Park, The
Odd Couple, and The Prisoner of Second Avenue.

Much Ado About Nothing, by William Shakespeare, has been
revived and Americanized by the New York Shakespeare Festival,
whose producer is Joseph Papp. Originally set in sixteenth-cen-
tury Messina, the play takes place now somewhere in Smalltown,
U.S.A., during the administration of Teddy Roosevelt. Straw
hats, draft beer, victrolas, a band in the park, a canoe on the
lake, and a couple of couples who, after a lot of verbal fireworks,
finally fall in love. If you can't see this superlative production
in person, watch for it on network television sometime during the
month of February.

The Lincoln Mask is a play about the several faces, the several personalities, that the playwright thinks Abe Lincoln had.
It opens with scenes from Our American Cousin, the play Lincoln
was watching when he was shot. From there, there are flashbacks of Lincoln's life, from his first political steps to the inevitable assassination.

The work reminds me of Robert Sherwood's Abe Lincoln in
Illinois or of the several Maxwell Anderson re-creations of English and French history. It is a stilted historical play whose
scenes are nothing but slices of chronology.

Fred Gwynne, very well known for his roles in two television
series (Car 54, Where Are You? and The Munsters), was splendid as Lincoln. He looked tall, awkward, and a trifle ugly; yet
he was handsome in an angular sort of way, and he has a deep,
resonant voice that he projected quite easily.

Eva Marie Saint, who has been seen in a variety of movie
and television roles, played Mary Todd, a southern belle who
hoped to ring in Washington with her Yankee husband. Unlike
a number of Broadway actresses, Miss Saint acted with skill;
her voice was audible and had a wide range, and her movements
around the set were easy and natural. The love scene between
Abe and Mary was worth more than the whole canonization of
Elizabeth I in last year's cultural bombshell Vivat, Vivat Regina!

The Last of Mrs. Lincoln is a play I thought would never
end. It covered the years in the life of Mary Todd Lincoln
from the assassination of her husband in 1865 until her own death
in 1882. What made the play seem interminable was the fact
that most of the scenes had no dramatic value; they were either
expository or declamatory and therefore dull. If it weren't for
Julie Harris, who played Mrs. Lincoln, the evening would have
been a total loss. She did a valiant job against overwhelming
odds, two of whom were the playwright (James Prideaux) and the
director (George Schaeffer). She may even win the Tony Award

for the season's best Broadway actress.

The Creation of the World and Other Business is a comedy by Arthur Miller. At least he intended it to be a comedy. Most critics found the humor leaden and his re-creation of several episodes from the book of Genesis lethargic. I found the play amusing enough, but I found myself quarreling with several of his theological premises. That man's sexuality can be a source of humor I can readily enough accept, but that sex--specifically intercourse between Adam and Eve--is the cause of man's downfall, his original sin, I find ludicrous. A liberated intellectual like Arthur Miller should know better.

None of the actors distinguished themselves. The set designer, Boris Aronson, put a little bit of Eden on stage. And the director, Gerald Freedman, kept everyone hustling around paradise.

Arthur Miller is remembered for his plays Death of a Salesman and The Crucible. If his reputation had to rely on his current offering, he'd soon be forgotten.

Mourning Becomes Electra, by Eugene O'Neill, is the first play to be presented at the new Circle in the Square Theater, which is located, not in Greenwich Village, but on West Fiftieth Street. This battleship of a play, which retells some episodes in Greek mythology in 1865 America, may have been gleaming when it was first presented in 1931. Now, some forty years later, the play has all the aura of the Monitor or the Merrimac-- a rusty, irrelevant antique. The production of the play is splendid, and the actors give very good performances, but I'm afraid that O'Neill's psychology of character development is an overwhelming obstacle.

Stage
(by William Griffin, Sign Magazine, November 1974)

Would you attend a play if you knew in advance that sometime during the course of the evening a young lady would disrobe while swinging from the chandelier?

A reader of Sign Magazine recently put this question to me in letter form. He or she felt that I should have mentioned that such an incident occurs in Jumpers, a play by Tom Stoppard. Attendance at such a play, the writer said, is tantamount to support of nudity on the stage.

First of all, my apologies for not having mentioned the incident in my review. Second, on reflection, I'm not sure I should have mentioned it. It occurred at the beginning of the play; six, or was it nine, acrobats were forming a human pyramid; lights were flashing blindingly; music was blaring deafeningly; one hardly knew where to look or listen; then it happened.

Since the incident took no more than a minute and was barely visible and had no relevance to what followed, I promptly forgot about it.

What I can't forget, however, is the basic point of the reader's letter. That is, should a reviewer of plays and musicals, besides telling what happens and what, if anything, it means, also give consumer guidance to potential patrons? Should the reviewer point out that attendance at certain theatrical presentations may be hazardous to one's morals or one's moral system?

On looking over the plays, and musicals I've attended during the last several seasons, I found that many of them are all too categorizable as hazardous to someone's health. The black English in such musicals as Ain't Supposed to Die a Natural Death and Inner City and in such plays as What the Wine-Sellers Buy and The River Niger is a case in point. The vocabulary is colorful and dynamically expressed, but it is often so earthy and elemental that shell-pink ears will surely be blistered by the end of scene one.

Homosexuality is not an easy subject to discuss in conversation, let alone on the stage. But it has emerged in three recent English plays, Butley, in which a college professor whose life is in a shambles retrogresses from heterosexuality to homosexuality. My Fat Friend, in which a middle-aged homosexual is an extremely well-adjusted and hilariously funny member of society. And Find Your Way Home, in which one man whose life with his wife is at an end finds hope and perhaps love with another man.

Alcoholism is too difficult a subject for many to swallow. Consequently, how does a critic describe Sir Toby Belch in Shakespeare's Twelfth Night or Dylan Thomas in Sidney Michaels' Dylan or Frank Elgin in Clifford Odets' Country Girl? All three are drunkards. The divinity of Jesus was challenged, many thought, in Jesus Christ, Superstar and diminished, some thought, in Godspell. A general lewdness and suggestiveness ran through A Funny Thing Happened on the Way to the Forum and galloped through Scapino. The choreography in such musicals as Pippin and Seesaw has intimations, almost imitations, of sexual intercourse. Anti-Semitism stalks the scenes of Shakespeare's Merchant of Venice.

The theater, as one can readily see, is an unholy, unwholesome place. Man's basest emotions are mirrored, even magnified, sometimes distorted beyond belief. Sometimes what the theater mirrors is an accurate reflection one way or another of what man is and does. And perhaps one reason why people continue to patronize the theater is that they sometimes see reflections of themselves and others through the artistry of playwrights and actors and directors and dancers and musicians. Even in so scatterbrained a work as Jumpers, the central character is trying to find a proof for the existence of God.

All things considered, perhaps it's wiser, safer, and not so
hazardous to one's health not to go to the theater, to stay at home
and read books or watch television. Or is it? One thing is certain: staying at home is cheaper!

GROSS, Marjorie P. (Marge); (2) Theater & music critic; (3) b. Gt.
Barrington, Mass., June 28, 1924; (4) d. Axel and Gertrude (Cook)
Peterson; (5) Searles School, major art, 1941; (6) m. Robert L.
Gross, Jan. 8, 1943; (7) child--Radford Lyell Gross; (8) Public relations, Gt. Barrington, Pittsfield, Leominster, Mass., 1943-51;
staff writer, theater, art, music critic, Fitchburg, Mass., Fitchburg Sentinel, 1952-62; drama, art, music critic, ass't women editor,
Ontario Daily Report, Ontario, Calif., 1967 to present; counselors'
secretary--public relations--Upland High School, 1963-67; (9) Theater
dancing since 5 yrs. --Drama Club, Searles--actress, production mgr.
Barrington Players and Leominster Little Theater; (10) Publicity
chrm. West End United Way, 1970- ; swimming and ballet water instructor 1945-71; (15) The Press Club of Southern California--bd.
member, sec. 1971- ; (16) Republican; (17) Episcopalian; (21) 8223
Tapia Via, Cucamonga, Calif., Ph. 714-982-3487; (22) Ontario Daily
Report, 212 E. B St., Ontario, Calif., P.O. Box 593, Ontario,
Calif. 91761, Ph. 714-983-3511; (23) Circulation: 30,000; (24) 40
plays, musicals, operas, symphonies from San Bernardino to Los
Angeles.

<u>Jane Reilly Superb in VCT Play</u>
(by Marge Gross, Daily Report, January 27, 1975)

Superb is the only way to describe the performance of Jane
Reilly in "The Prime of Miss Jean Brodie" now playing at the
Valley Community Theatre.

The combined talents of Miss Reilly and Jim Gardner as director brings to the little third-floor show place one of the most
provocative and vital productions since "Lion in Winter" was
staged in November of 1972.

Miss Reilly portrays the intense and compelling teacher
with incredible understanding. She makes every emotion
of Miss Brodie ... and all the Miss Brodies of the world ...
vivid, warm, exciting and compelling.

"The Prime of Miss Jean Brodie" is about a teacher "in her
prime" at a private girls' school in Edinburgh, Scotland, in the
1930s. Miss Brodie's story is told by a young nun who turns
out to be one of the students whose life was greatly influenced
by the teachings, passions and dreams of her teacher.

Miss Brodie lived for her girls who she refers to as her
"la creme de cremes." The story is complex with marvelous
overtones of humor, passions and a bevy of high emotions.

But the cast gives her excellent support, especially the four young students, Donna McCormick, Cecily French, Colleen Schultz and Carol Spencer. The direction of these girls has been well handled and each becomes a "creme de creme" in her own right.

Playing the men in the life of Miss Brodie are Joe Boydell as Gordon Lowther, the choir director. Boydell turns in a good performance. The character is limp and weak and the performance supports that character.

Jim Stanley plays the philandering artist, Teddy Lloyd. Teddy has a wife and six children but that doesn't stop his interest in love on the side. His yen is for Miss Brodie and every painting he turns out is the lovely teacher. Stanley is convincing in his love scenes with Miss Reilly, but as the lover of a teen-ager, he appears most uncomfortable.

Martha Fuller, always the trouper of the VCT, stepped into the role of Miss Mackay, the head mistress of the school, at the last minute due to the illness of Nancy Humphreys. Miss Fuller did an amazing bit of acting while carrying the script in her hands so she could read the lines.

The play opens with Sonya Urquhart as Sister Helena telling Mr. Perry, played by Bill Himebaugh, the story of Miss Brodie. It's a weak opening, but as the play rolls along, the two characters draw strength and assurance from the fabulous Miss Reilly.

The staging of "Miss Brodie" is handled in a clever manner since the sets include a schoolroom, office, art studio, recreation room and a living room area for the nun's story telling scenes.

"The Prime of Miss Jean Brodie" is a play worth seeing. It gives one faith and assurance that good theater has not been lost to trivia and musicals.

"Godspell" a Spirited, Refreshing Musical
(by Marge Gross, Daily Report, February 19, 1975)

"Godspell," the stage production now being presented through Saturday at the California Theater of Performing Arts is like manna from heaven.

The story is old, but the presentation and interpretation is now.

Basis of "Godspell" is according to St. Matthew as written in the New Testament. The story line follows the text, but St. Matthew might swallow a bit hard, as he chuckled, could he see the show.

The production side of this San Bernardino Civic Light Opera spring musical has been apprehensive about the audience reaction. Would it be appreciated, accepted?

Certainly, anyone with a child's Sunday School background would understand the plot, but would they dig it? Would it be considered rock and keep away the predominately mellow years theater-goers?

For what it is worth, this reviewer of solid, conservative New England stock and raised by the Good Book found "Godspell" the most thorough entertainment seen in these parts for a long time.

Don't be misled and think "Godspell" is in the "Jesus Christ Superstar" category. Jesus does play the lead, but it is done in such a refreshing way, only the pure of the purist could be offended.

The 12 young thespians (obviously that number as representing the disciples) and their leader, Jesus, present the show in a spirited, bright, funny and thoroughly entertaining manner.

Oh, there probably will be those who can't accept Jesus in red, white and blue striped pants. There could be those who can't take the parables in modern ... but clean ... language. Yet the whole show comes out inspirational and reverent. There are spots when your sides ache from laughing, and others when tears fill your eyes.

After all, what could be better than a combination of 13 energetic youths and the perfect script? Brad Murdoch leads as Jesus and the other cast members are Alan Martin, Anne O'Donnell, Jeffrey R. Winner, Sherry Landrum, Dorothy Holland, Nat Jones, Barbara Turvet, Pam Vilbert, Joe Fletcher, Greg Atkins, Debbie Abbatiello and Art Mendoza. There is no way to single out any one for praise. All are excellent.

The way the "plot" runs, the cast pulls off vignettes of parables in the language, music and gestures of now--Today, Tomorrow. Words can't adequately describe how it all jells. It just does.

The opening is confusing. It's a prologue on the Tower of Babel. It comes off as a nutty basketball game by a bunch of kids. Then the "plot" thickens and one begins to see what is happening as the cast cavorts in clown-like, wild outfits. With their direction through mime, antics, songs and dialogue, the mind looses up, the barriers fall away with the first chuckle. From then on, it's a lark ... until the end. Dramatic, Beautiful, Soulful.

Vibrant youth is bringing Good News to this sad world through Saturday in a vital musical. It's a show for doubters and believers.

GUERNSEY, Otis Love, Jr.; (2) Critic, editor; (3) N.Y.C., Aug. 9, 1918; (4) s. Otis L. and Margaret (Henderson); (5) Taft School, Watertown, Conn.; B.A., Yale, 1940; (6) m. Dorianne Downe, Dec. 11, 1943; (8) With New York Herald Tribune, 1941-60, successively copy boy, reporter, assoc. film and drama critic, film critic, and drama critic, arts editor, 1955-60; story cons. CBS 1957-59; free lance writer, 1960- ; editorial cons. New Eng. Guide, 1960- ; drama critic and sr. editor Show mag., 1963-64; arts editor Diplomat mag., 1965-57; Editor, The Dramatists Guild Quarterly, 1964- ; Best Plays series of theater yearbooks, 1965- ; (15) Mem. N.Y. Newspaper Guild, Phi Beta Kappa; (19) Coffee House, Century Assn. (N.Y.C.); (20) Author original film stories, also articles on stage and screen.; (21) North Pomfret, Vt. 05053.

GUNNER, Marjorie Janet; (2) Theatre Critic; (3) b. N.Y.C. Mar. 29, 1922; (4) d. Gertrude and Harry Grohman; (5) B.A., Cornell U. and N.Y.U., major subj.: drama, 1943; (6) m. Morris Gunner, Oct. 2, 1943, widowed 1966; (7) children--Holly and Rochelle; (8) Wrote "See-Lebrities I See" for Town & Village 1966, interviewing first night celebrities, became their drama critic 1966; wrote "On and Off-Broadway," weekly theatre coiumn and at various periods during 1967-76, reviewed Broadway and off-Broadway plays for the following newspapers: Bronx Home News, Long Island Examiner, Nassau Star, Matzner Publications, Floral Park and Franklin Square Papers, Brooklyn Shore Record, Ridgewood-Herald News, Gramercy Herald, Rockaway Record and Uptown Sentinel; (9) 1935 Art Scholarship-Central School of Allied Arts, 1939 won Luise Rainer Award sponsored by Loew's Theatres, via Radio station WHN, won acting scholarship to Carnegie Hall Drama School, Wolter Academy; 1939-43 state scholarship, Cornell U.; 1955 lyrics published to popular songs; 1964 became BMI (Broadcast Music Inc.) lyricist; 1971 edited and reported news for Bronx Home News over WNYC; (10) Member executive comm. Cornell Council for the Performing Arts 1968-70, executive board mem. ICCY (International Cultural Centers for Youth), 1972 American Theatre Wing mem.; (11) Member, Jefferson Democrat Club; (15) Drama Desk 1967-74, Outer Critics Circle 1968-76; (16) Democrat (17) Jew; (19) Atrium Club; (20) Cont. articles on musical comedy to Music Journal, an international magazine; (21) 276 First Ave., New York City 10009, Ph. 212-Or 3-9272 & 212-Or 7-8089; (22) "On and Off-Broadway" M. Gunner, 276 First Ave., NYC, Ph. 212-Or 3-9272; (23) Circulation: roughly 100,000; (24) Occasionally I review restaurant entertainment if talent relates or is destined for theatre.

On and Off Broadway
(by Marjorie Gunner, Bronx Home News, January 28, 1972)

The roll your owns are in, and at the experimental Forum of the Lincoln Center a conundrum is current. "The Ride Across Lake Constance" is a dream walking, parading perhaps after an intellect has been fed too much at Alice in Wonderland's mad tea party. Alice, you know, became exasperated but stayed on any-

way, fascinated as this play fascinates because explication is always on the verge of happening. Here is a weird mental exercise
contained in a single act, extremely well performed by a fine
cast, especially Stephen Elliot, Salome Jens and Kenne Curtis
who express a kaleidoscope of human feelings. Subliminal attitudes of love, anger, domination, docility, eagerness, trust and
anxiety enmesh and melt like in a Salvador Dali painting. The
6 main characters walk on the thin ice of social mores always in
danger of drowning by a cruel cut. If the "enfant terrible" Peter
Handke as translated from German by Michael Roloff sees reality
this grimly, he has our sympathy. He seats two extravagantly
exaggerated men of manners next to each other. One with white
powered face and ruffled shirt dominates the other who dwindles
to a nondescript. Their disjointed chatter is haughtily spoken
and servilely answered. The arrogant one makes the weaker re-
arrange his cigar box. There are servants and masters. Other
elegants formally attired sweep down a staircase, and sex enters
the games people play. Two ladies, one in red and one in silver
are alternately fondled by Kenne Curtis, a dandy. Previously preferred by him, Salome Jens the silver lady is suddenly coming
apart at the seams. Her make-up is spotty. She drops her compact, seems lost and is helped by the lady in red ostrich feathers.
Calm and reassuring, the cool red lady alters sharply when she
relates to her chosen man. Now she frets about her looks and
wants only to please him. Again, there are masters and servants, and both can be either.

Two identical stewardesses arrive with the fresh eagerness
of all society upon first introduction. Similing and gracious, they
dance and skip about serving drinks, picking up glasses, with that
polished politeness reserved for paying strangers. The surrealism
continues without pause. Handke sprints his frisky colt of ideas
so that you can pick your own theme. Tho his brilliance wins the
race he gradually loses some literal minded audience. Clearly
this is not a play for the masses. Rather it is for the absent-
minded or the intellectually gifted; the former because they can
forget it; the latter because they cannot.

GUSSOW, Mel, New York Times, 229 W. 43rd St., New York, N.Y.
10036.

HALE, Lewis David; (2) Arts Writer, Critic; (3) b. Oakland,
Calif., Oct. 7, 1930; (4) s. Fred and Esther Hale; (5) B.A.,
California State U. Fresno, 1960, journalism; (6) unmarried;
(8) Staff reporter Bakersfield Californian, 1960-61; Fresno
Bee reporter since; staff reporter Fresno Bee, 1961-65, arts writer
(theater, dance, art, music, films) since; (15) Newspaper Guild mem-
bership; Fresno Press Club; (16) Democratic; (17) Lutheran; (22) The
Fresno Bee, 1626 E. St., Fresno, 93721; Ph. 209-268-5221; (23)
Circulation: 110,000-135,000 (daily, Sunday); (24) 50 art reviews;
25 plays and musicals; 5 dance; 10 miscellaneous.

"Ernest in Love" Proves to be Fresh, Lively Show
(by David Hale, Fresno Bee, December 12, 1975)

"Ernest in Love," which is being given what is ostensibly
its California premiere at Theatre 3 is a musical retelling of
Oscar Wilde's "The Importance of Being Earnest."

Don't be put off by the unfamiliarity of the piece; there's a
good chance it may strike you as one of the freshest, liveliest
most enjoyable shows you've seen lately.

"Ernest in Love" has music by unknown Lee Pockriss and
book and lyrics by the equally obscure Anne Croswell. As a
spoof of drawingroom comedy of England's Edwardian era, it
manages to cherish the absurdities of another age even while it
pokes fun at them. The result is an entertainment which is sunny, charming good fun. Director Gordon Goede seems to have a
taste for staging these period pieces with clarity and simplicity.
The concept of the production suits for the most part the gentle
absurdity of the theatrical style and the situation, and the performances of the principals generally suit both the required mannered
approach to acting and the director's interpretation of the comedy.

The activity in "Ernest in Love" concerns the adventures of
a pair of aristocratic and lusting young blades. Particularly the
story revolves around one Jack Worthing who has discovered a
nifty scheme for disguising his ah, spirited, social life:

He establishes the idea that he has a younger brother who
periodically requires his counselling; the brother, obviously, is
either in London or in Shropshire, depending on which location
Jack needs to escape, to engage in some discrete womanizing.

Jack's equally irresponsible friend, Algenon, is involved. So
is "Algy's" snooty aunt, Lady Bracknell, and her delightful daughter, Gwendolyn--ostensibly engaged to Jack--and Jack's virginal
but willing ward, Cecily, whom the rakish Algy very much wants
to meet for naturally dishonorable reasons.

Most commendable of the actors, in the view of this spectator, are James Turnmire, as Algy, who seems most at home in
the stylized acting required, and Jayne Smithson as the delicately
pretty yet headstrong Gwendolyn, who doesn't seem to mind so
much Ernest's unfaithfulness as the innocuous nature of his name.

Randy Stump fits the script's specification as "a very earnest
young man intent on marrying Gwen:" he is not quite so comfortable as Turnmire.

Bette Engstrom, the social-climbing Lady Bracknell, has an
appropriate hooty voice and billowing stature, though the night we
saw the show she was stumbling over lines.

As the lovely Cecily, symbol of the English blueblooded girl
who has always dreamed of a "wicked man," Jane Kent appears
at times too obviously calculating to be the flighty maiden whose
fantasies anticipate the arrival of Algy.

Linda Hubbart is appealing as the very proper, but potentially passionate governess, and Derek Trimble is mostly effective,
doubling as Ernest's man Perkins and the stuffy professional celi-
bate, Rev. Chausble.   The songs are bright and brittle with lyrics that have an artificial air suitable to the comedy's nature; the
dialogue is full of witty, seemingly quotable lines you'll never remember once you leave the theater, and Goede's setting has an
elegant simplicity that is in tune with the play's upper class environs.   John A. Osborne's costumes are crisp and ornate, adding immeasurably to the graceful quality of the atmosphere.   The
only accompaniment is a sprightly piano, with Brian Hall as the
musician.

"Red Hot Lovers"
(by David Hale, Fresno Bee, July 23, 1976)

In the theater, where there is sex after 40--especially when
it comes to talking or fantasizing about it--there is laughter and
the formula works just fine with the Good Company Players' version of Neil Simon's "Last of the Red Hot Lovers."

Even after several years of exposure on stage or the screen,
the play has lost none of its ability to produce guffaws.

Indeed, this show, which just opened in the Fresno Memorial
Auditorium theater, is a more successful "Last of the Red Hot
Lovers" than the last one we saw, though we like that one, too.
It, too, was staged by Dan Pessano, for Fresno Community The-
ater.

Well, sure, the plot is simple-minded, though this play was
credited as Simon's first to contain serious writing.   And the
characters act like idiots.

But you'll still recognize them, and the plotline is loaded
with the gaglines--the kind of mouth-drying sarcasms for which
Simon is so famous.

The story, to refresh the memory, is about a middleaged,
successful, reasonably contented married man with an itch for a
fling with a lady other than his wife.

His naive but reasonable object is to escape the deadly routine of his life, to know "just one experience, so rewarding and
fulfilling it will last me the rest of my life."

The humor revolves around the fact that our hero is so in-
trinsically the homebody personality: Utterly dependable, indis-

putably faithful--sex isn't really the biggest thing in his life in any case--scrupulous in language and habits, shy of liquor or even cigarets.

Bob Rodgers fits the role of the errant husband to a tee: smallish, a bit portly, bustling, and full of adolescent naivety and nervousness about women.

In the play's three acts, his Rodgers' Barney Cashman invites three women--one at a time, naturally--for mid-afternoon trysts. The Love Nest, fittingly, is the neat little 1930s modern apartment of his mother, away afternoons working as a hospital volunteer.

Rodgers and his predicament are very funny, with his tentative, awed approach to his women, especially with an off-the-wall, would-be actress who introduces him to the wondrous sin of marijuana, and his wife's best friend who frustrates him with the sheer weight of her melancholia.

Probably the show's best lines go to Nancy Miller, as Cashman's first assignation: She's a carnivorous sophisticate with an insatiable craving for cigarets, scotch whisky, and a suicidal interest in men other than her 6-feet-2-inch, 220-pound husband.

Miss Miller has the right dry delivery and empty pose, but Rodgers did not seem comfortable and the segment did not come over convincingly the night this viewer sat in.

The final two acts, however, were as appealing and funny as any Simon we've seen:

Happiest is the one with Rodgers' Cashman confronted by Sindi Goldman as the unemployed actress, nonstop talker and undoubted psycho. Miss Goldman was a delight, with her ridiculous Gypsy-style costume, her metallic voice and a way of uttering the most wide-eyed inanities as if they had just occurred to her.

Then there's Doris Randall, as the wife's girlfriend, a desperately depressed woman who has known happiness perhaps 8.2 per cent of her life.

Miss Randall is quite possibly the most convincing Jeannette we've seen anywhere, a zombie with a voice like a whining drone, perfectly appropriate for a woman determined to dispel the last hope or joy from life.

The staging by Dan Pessano is smoothy rendered and Howard Bolter's setting is exactly right for a middleclass grandmother's dwelling. Deadly for romantic meetings.

HAMMERICH, Dick, Springfield Union, 1860 Main St., Springfield, Mass. 01103

HANSEN, Linda, Rochester Times-Union, 55 Exchange St., Rochester, N.Y. 14614, Ph. 716-232-7100.

HARADA, Wayne, Honolulu Advertiser, P.O. Box 3110, Honolulu, Ha. 96802

HARRIS, Jessica B.; (2) Theatre Critic; (3) b. New York, March 18, 1948; (4) d. Jesse B. and Rhoda A. (Harris); (5) A.B. Bryn Mawr College, major: French, 1968; Licence ès Lettres. Université de Nancy, Nancy France, Major: French, 1969; M.A. Queens College, major: French Theatre, 1971; Ph.D. work to be completed 1977; New York U. major: drama. Dissertation The Theatre of Sénégal; (6) single; (8) Theatre and film critic, Black American, New York, 1973-74; Theatre critic New York Amsterdam News 1974-present; (9) High School of Performing Arts, major-drama; (15) Second Night Critics List, New York, Outer Critics Circle; (16) Democrat; (17) Presbyterian; (19) Bryn Mawr Club of New York; (20) Cont. articles to Drama Review, Black Creation, Encore magazines, Third Press Review of Literature, Essence and Black Enterprise; (21) 32 Jane St., New York 10014, Ph. 212-741-3918; (22) New York Amsterdam News, 2340 Eighth Ave., New York 10027, Ph. 212-222-7800; (23) Circulation: sales-100,000, reader, 400,000+; (24) 65 plays, 10 dance, 15 feature and miscellaneous, 45 book reviews.

New Play--"Complicated Words"
(by Jessica B. Harris, N.Y. Amsterdam News, January 11, 1975)

"The Black Picture Show" is a problem drama. It presents the problem of the artist in society, but it also presents the audience with a very real problem of comprehension. For "The Black Picture Show" is a convoluted word maze in which the unwary, and even the aware, can become hopelessly entangled.

At the beginning of "The Black Picture Show," J.D. (for Jesus Delivers) announces in ringmaster fashion that the play will present the last days of his father, Alexander.

The play goes on to show the psychiatric unit of the Bronx Hospital where Alexander is a patient. From there Bill Gunn, the playwright, using a game that Alexander plays with his companion, Norman, as the device, transports the audience back to Alexander's young adulthood and then to an episode in his second marriage.

These levels of time and reality present the obvious Pirandellian problems as the audience is never truly aware if it is watching the "reality" of the event, or the "reality" of Alexander's mad perception of the event, or the "reality" of J.D.'s perception of Alexander's mad perception of the event.

These multiple levels of time and reality are further com-

plicated by the language of the play.   Bill Gunn, in his dialogues
uses colloquial, free-flowing speech.   But the play is punctuated
by self-conscious "serious" monologues in which the role of the
artist in the society is discussed.   These moments do not work,
for their self-consciousness and their pretense of enlightening,
when in fact they simply restate some very basic problems, interrupt the vital flow of the play.

However, Bill Gunn has some extraordinary observations and
his insights, when not overly underlined-either by the script or
by the direction are astonishing.

The acting on the whole is very fine.   Dick Anthony Williams,
aside from some momentary mannerisms as the mad Alexander,
slides through the multiple levels of time and reality with all of
the sinuosity of a panther.   When not fettered by the "musing
monologues" of the playwright, he brings the many facets of Alexander and his torment to life.

Carol Cole, as Alexander's mother, creates an amazing Black
Blanche DuBois of a grand dame.   Her performance as Rita is a
veritable tour-de-force.   Albert Hall, as J. D. is the proper foil
for Alexander, constantly taunting and examining.   Linda Miller
and Paul-David Richards are properly obnoxious as the white producer and his wife and Linda Miller even manages to create the
feel of a person under so obvious a caricature.

Graham Brown, as Norman, portrays the faithful companion
in all of his incarnations with proper concern and circumspection.
Sam Waymon's fine music combines so well with the action that
it unfortunately becomes lost.

"The Black Picture Show" is a problem like a Chinese puzzle.   It must be unravelled to reveal at its core either a treasure
or emptiness, but it must be unravelled.

Another View: "The Wiz" Is Great
(by Jessica B. Harris, N. Y. Amsterdam News, January 25, 1975)

The American musical theatre originated with Black people;
with the Broadway production "The Wiz" it has been reclaimed
by Black people.   "The Wiz," a new musical version of "the Wonderful Wizard of Oz," is soul food.   It is not only food for the
soul, but a theatrical version of the impulse that created soul
food.   Just as Black people took cast offs from white kitchens
and turned them into something uniquely theirs so William F.
Brown and Charles Smalls have taken a mediocre story (The
Wizard of Oz, by Frank L. Baum) which has been canonized by
the memory of Judy Garland, and created something uniquely
Black.

First "The Wiz" has nothing to do with Judy Garland--let
her rest in peace.   "The Wiz" has something to do with Black

people. From the moment that Aunt 'Em (Tasha Thomas) opens
her mouth, it is clear that the people who wrote and the people
who perform this musical know all about grandmothers and aunts
and Aretha and Love. The danced tornado that carries Dorothy
(Stephanie Mills) off to Oz only serves to further illustrate the
innovation of Black people in this musical where things are suggested, subtle and superb. Once in Oz the fun begins, Dorothy
meets Addapearl, the feel good girl, Good Witch of the North,
played uproariously by Clarice Taylor and "eases on down the
road" to see the Wiz. As in the well known story, Dorothy meets
the scarecrow, the tinman and the lion, but in "The Wiz" the
characters all say something about Black life and life styles: The
scarecrow (Hinton Battle) who asks for some spare change so
that he can get his head together, the tap dancing tin man (Tiger
Haynes)--alleluia Bojangles and the profiling lion who touches up
his mane (Ted Ross). They set off down the yellow brick road
to see the Wiz, passing through Kalidah country and a field of
soliciting poppies, where the lion is picked up by the mice squad.
They arrive at an Emerald City that is perpetual cocktail party,
and meet the Wiz (Andree De Shields) who is the ultimate con man.
The Wiz sends them off to kill Evillene (Mable King) a big mama
wicked witch of the West. When they succeed at this mission and
return to Oz they find that the Wiz is a charlatan and that it is
only with Glinda's help that Dorothy can get back to Kansas. (For
those of you who don't remember Glinda is the good Witch of the
South--but be assured that you have never seen a foxy witch like
this before.) Glinda arrives and Dorothy arrives home as the curtain falls to a standing ovation-every night it seems.

"The Wiz" is an explosion of color and sound. The sets by
Tom H. John are inventive and can transform the stage into anything from Evillene's fortress castle to a poppy field. Goeffry
Holder's costumes draw their inspiration from Black American
and African sources, from the lion's 125th street to Glinda's
Queen of Sheba. His direction maintains a constant pulse on Black
sources for the characters at all moments. This detail and precision constantly delights and astounds. George Faison's dances
are marvelous, transforming everyday gesture into powerful statements of a people (Mr. Faison has the dancers doing every Black
dance form from the Buck and Wing to the bump!)

The cast is flawless with special kudos going to Stephanie
Mills, a little girl with a big voice; Ted Ross, a stylin' lion who
has not forgotten that the lion is just a big pussy cat; Clarice
Taylor, a witch who leaves you in stitches; Mabel King, a Bessie
Smith of a Wicked Witch of the West whose song "Don't Bring
Me No Bad News" stops the second act; Andree De Shields, a Wiz
with more than a touch of Reverend Ike for inspiration; and Dee-
Dee Bridgewater who is simply beautiful. "The Wiz is a micro-
cosm of Black survival in America, it must be seen in all of
its splendor and richness to be truly believed--and "Over the
Rainbow" hasn't got a chance.

HARRIS, Sydney J. , Chicago Daily News, 401 N. Wabash Ave. ,
Chicago, Ill. 60611.

HARRISS, Robert Preston; (2) Art, Music and Drama Editor
(critic); (3) b. Fayetteville, N. C. , Aug. 19, 1902; (4) s. Frank
MacCulloch Harriss and Harriette Anderson Harriss; (5) B. A.
Duke U. , major subject English lit. , 1926; graduate study,
the Sorbonne (drama), Paris, 1931; (6) m. Margery Oren Willis,
1936; (7) child--Clarinda (Mrs. Clarinda Lott, teacher, poet.); (8)
Reporter, cont. signed articles to editorial page, assist. theater
critic, Baltimore Evening Sun, 1927-28; New York Herald Tribune,
Paris Herald staff, 1929-1933; Baltimore Sun, 1934-36, assoc. ed. ,
senior assoc. ed. and acting editor. Editor, Gardens, Houses and
People (magazine) 1947-57. Columnist, critic, arts editor, Baltimore
News American, 1947 to date; (15) Mem. American Theater Critics
Assoc. ; (16) Democrat; (17) Episcopalian; (19) Maryland Club, Balti-
more Country Club, Hamilton Street Club, Walters Art Gallery, Bal-
timore Museum of Art, Peale Museum, Md. Hist. Soc. etc. ; (20)
Contributor to magazines--short stories, essays, poems. Author:
novel "The Foxes" (Houghton Mifflin, in U. S. , Methuen, London)
which won British Book Society award and made U. S. best-seller list.
Short stories in various anthologies. Closely associated with H. L.
Mencken in newspaper and magazine work; (21) 306 Suffolk Rd. , Baltimore, Md. 21218, Ph. 235-7690; (22) Baltimore News American,
Baltimore, Md. 21203, Ph. 752-1212-ext. 402; (23) Circulation:
280,000.

Coward to Perfection
(by R. P. Harriss, Baltimore News American, February 25, 1975)

Noel Coward in "Two Keys," a presentation of two late--
perhaps the author's last--plays, arrived Monday night at the
Morris A. Mechanic Theater, where an avid audience welcomed
his bright talent that defies oblivion.

Under the "Two Keys" rubric was presented "Come Into the
Garden, Maud," and "A Song at Twilight," each starring Anne
Baxter, Hume Cronyn and Jessica Tandy, with Joel Parks in a
minor but indispensable role. The performances were in all instances excellent, and in the final scene of the second and more
important play, that of Hume Cronyn was superb.

The setting of the plays is a private suite in a luxurious
Swiss hotel. William Ritman's handsome set design serves for
both.

The curtain-raiser takes its mocking title from a love poem
of Tennyson's, specifically from the lines:

"Come into the garden, Maud,

For the black bat, night, has flown. "

The Maud of the play is Maud Caragnani, a Roman adventuress with minor-nobility connections plus warmth and sense of
decency. The plot concerns equally a rich, unpretentious, golf-
playing, self-made American, Verner Conklin, and his cold,
domineering, social-climbing American wife, Anna-Mary.

The three have a slight acquaintance from a previous meeting
in Rome. Mr. Conklin remembers Maud as an attractive woman,
Mrs. Conklin recalls that "she practically threw herself at you."
Maud arrives for cocktails, to which she was invited by Mrs.
Conklin--who had forgotten she was giving a very important party
that evening for a prince she is sedulously cultivating.

When one of Mrs. Conklin's invited guests telephones he's ill
and can't come, she implores Maud to fill in--otherwise there
would be thirteen guests, a situation to be avoided at all costs.
Maud declines because, frankly, she thinks the prince a bore and
a boor.

Mrs. Conklin gets rid of Maud and commands Mr. Conklin
to eat his dinner alone in their suite--she will tell her guests
he is ill, too, and thus there will not be thirteen present at her
party.

But it turns out she hasn't really got rid of Maud, who returns to keep Mr. Conklin company. The upshot is that she offers to relieve his loneliness permanently. He gladly sheds his
henpecked-husband role and they leave for a life together in
Rome.

Following this posthumus gift of laughter comes further and
more impressive proof that Noel Coward's bright talent defies
oblivion. "A Song at Twilight," ironically based on a popular
tune of Victorian sentimentality, cuts much deeper. It provides
drama worthy of high talent, and gets it.

"A Song at Twilight" concerns Sir Hugo Latymer, a famous
British author (the part somewhat suggesting Somerset Maugham
in old age); his devoted German wife; and his former mistress,
an actress he has not seen in many years.

The ex-mistress has requested an interview with him, which
he grants. She threatens to publish certain of his love letters--
not those written to her but the ones he wrote to his male secretary and lover, who is now dead. Her motive, it develops, is
not blackmail, but revenge for the male lover, who in his old
age became her friend. I will not here reveal further the work-
ings of the plot.

As the slinky, surgically rejuvenated, vulgar ex-mistress,
Anne Baxter stalks the hapless Sir Hugo with relentless conviction.
As Hilde Latymer, Jessica Tandy plays to perfection the sensitive,
selfless, protective wife.

As the eminent author whose long career has been tormented by his desperate effort to keep his homosexuality hidden, Hume Cronyn gives what may well be the most sensitive and moving performance of his notable stage career. In the final-scene climax--which is wordless--he holds the audience spellbound.

Everything about this production is first-rate, including Mr. Parks' portrayal of the Italian waiter Felix.

How exhilarating to have such theater downtown again!

"Magic Show" Arrives with Music and Dance
(by R. P. Harriss, Baltimore News American, April 23, 1975)

"The Magic Show," which arrived Tuesday night at the Morris A. Mechanic Theater, is a pleasantly different kind of musical-comedy confection: Cheesecake and youthful verve, studded with glittery magician's tricks, plus a whipped-cream topping of song and dance.

Like the oldtime magic shows, this one aims at nothing more than entertainment--and it succeeds very neatly. But unlike Thurston and the other shows our naive yesteryears, "The Magic Show" proceeds at a fast, mock-serious pace.

Though some of the tricks are as illusive as those of the magicians of yore, they are presented with an air of insouciance rather than heavy mystery. Peter DePaula, who heads this national touring company cast, looks like a skinny teenager who has always wanted to make it with his magic to the professional stage--and that's the theme of the show.

The story line proceeds like a modern fairy tale. The young magician and Cal his adoring girl assistant--played with appealing teenage earnestness by Baltimore's own Pippa Pearthree--get their big chance when Mr. Goldfarb, a big Broadway promoter, comes to see their act at a sleazy nightclub.

They are threatened by Feldman, a boozy oldtime rabbit-out-of-a-hat magician who--under pretense of providing "style, flair, and je ne sais quoi"--attempts to steal their best tricks.

Feldman is out to rout. For a time however, it looks as though faithful Pippa is going to lose Peter to the bewitching Charmin as the girl who gets sawed in two. But as in all good fairy tales, the virtuous young girl triumphs over the wily witch.

And so the final illusion turns Charmin into a lionness and Cal becomes, what she has yearned to be, a lion tamer. And that trick is just about the best in the show.

"The Magic Show" is a small-scale musical, and with everything, including the magic, crisp and bright and frisky. The

music is propulsive if not memorably melodic, and happily lacking in ear-shattering rock raucousness.

The songs by Stephen Schwartz, that tie together Doug Henning's magicianship and Bob Randall's book, have some catchy
lines--when the audience can catch them.   In the faster numbers
the singers' dictation is not too clear.

Patrons in the middle and back rows of the cavernous Mechanic strain their ears.   A pity, that, for some of the singing
lines are the kind that a master such as Ogden Nash might have
proved.   For instance, a couplet in which "hat trick" is rhymed
with "Geriatric."

There are some nice bits in the spoken lines, as when the
girl Cal, trying to bolster her wilting ego with claims that she
might have had a career in opera, announces that her music
teacher told her "I was the only pupil she ever had that could
be both Tosca and Scarpia."

Besides Mr. DePaula as the young magician, and Miss Pear-
three, as the teenage girl Friday, "The Magic Show" has other
performing assets, notably the shapely and brassy-voice Hester
Llewellyn as Charmin, Susan Eduward and Signa Joy as the
dancing team of Dina and Donna, and Paul Keith in the Low-
comedy role of Feldman, the fruity-voiced, bumbling has-been
magician.

"The Magic Show" runs just under two hours, without an intermission.   It is suitable for children, and there were many
young people in the opening-night audience.

It should also appeal to adults who are simply looking for a
pleasant way to pass an evening: The elderly who remember
the pompous magicians of their youth, and those in early middle
age, who have never seen such stage magic.   Certainly the large
mixed audience on the Monday night seemed to take to it wholeheartedly.

As a footnote: I regret to report that the Mechanic management has substituted a soft drink and confection concession for
its hat and coat checking service, an amenity no well-run theater
should lack.

HART, Thomas George; (2) Theater Critic; (3) b. Durham, N.C.,
March 3, 1949; (4) s. Thomas and Kathryn (Dunkelberger) H.; (5)
B.A Princeton U., major subject: English, 1971; M.A. and M. Phil.
Columbia U., major subject: English and Theater, 1972 and 1974;
(6) single; (8) Drama and art critic, Springfield Daily News 1974- ;
(16) Independent; (21) 130 School St., Springfield, Mass.; (22) Springfield Daily News, 1860 Main St., Springfield Mass. 01101, Ph. 413-
787-2480; (23) Circulation: 87,000; (24) 100 plays and musicals,

150 art shows, 10 movies, 10 local architecture, 30 interviews and misc.

Stage West's "Balcony" 'Pure' Entertainment
(by Tom Hart, Springfield Daily News, January 13, 1976)

Beggar, thief, forger, dope dealer and male prostitute, Jean Genet peoples his plays with obscene rituals of reality and illusion that assault the audience-society from which he has been an outcast.

"The Balcony," at Stage West through January 31, is the most popular of his plays, and I am delighted to see Springfield tackling it. While the play is now 20 years old, it remains one of the most baffingly experimental works available, as dazzlingly theatrical as it is cruel and absurd.

But I came away a bit disappointed. Gorgeous staging and fine acting have been enervated by an over-conscious attempt at pure entertainment, and the result is a chortling tameness that actually sounded rather dull.

Dull in part perhaps because the trumpeted "adults only" titillations I had looked forward to just weren't there. While no doubt offensive to some, neither lines nor limbs were any racier than one finds in R-rated flicks these days: not a bare bottom or bosom in sight, not a phrase unfamiliar to most sixth-graders.

We enter the world of Madame Irma's brothel, Le Balcon, where 38 studios cater to the play-acted perversions of a kinky clientele. A "judge" licks the shoes of a whipping-girl prostitute; a "general" rides his randy mare; an "archbishop" slavers after sins from a provocative penitent.

But revolution intrudes on this fantasy-world, and the roles become real, then roles again as the turmoil in the streets invades Madame Irma's mirrored domain.

Genet's work, then, mixes themes of reality and illusion into the tremendous theatricality of his sadomasochistic fantasies.

Director Rae Allen has chosen to emphasize this theatricality without bothering us with close exploration of the Pirandellian themes of false and real. To a certain extent she succeeds-- the first act in particular is a frantic mix of actors in the audience, choreography, and inventive entrances and exits.

With this in mind, the show's strongest performance is that of set designer Eugene Warner. Hidden doors, mirrored walls, tinsel curtains, and suspended metal walkways vie with images drawn from the grotesque girlies of Richard Lindner's paintings. Madame Irma's control-panel is a leopard-skin organ with flashing lights and phallic controls: this is a splendid set.

But the studied theatricality soon wears thin, and the atmosphere is more circus than brothel. Genet's potent obscenities, the hate that drives his work is lost in a thicket of Nixon imitations, sportcaster's commentary, tacked-on lines that tell us to "leave now if you're gonna" and burst of fire from toy machine-guns. Why not at least real machine-gun sound effects? Isn't the point that the revolution at least is real?

And as we progress into the later scenes, the intellectual poverty of this approach fails to carry us through the increasingly complex weavings of Genet's fabric of illusion and reality: only at the frozen curtain-call did I feel a touch of the role-playing magic that live theater can bring to this kind of art.

Perhaps this analysis is too clinically cruel. We still have the pageantry of a colorful production, and we still have some fine performances, even if they are played in a way that sees clowns rather than people. Barbara Tarbuck's Irma is tartly cynical, Yusef Bulos' General is pompously insecure, Michael Miller struts his Gestapo gestalt as the Police Chief, Franklyn Seales really seems to enjoy the whip as Ringmaster, and Nancy Sellin's low-key Carmen is the night's most humane portrayal.

But for all the theatrical fizz, the heady wine of Genet's fierce obscenity has been watered: I was not intoxicated by "The Balcony."

"The Estate" Powerful, Problematic
(by Tom Hart, Springfield Daily News, February 2, 1976)

"The Estate," a new play by Ray Aranha, enjoyed its world premiere Friday night with tremendous success. A bit long, yes, and wordy and weak in some roles, but this dramatization of Thomas Jefferson's relation to mulatto mistress and a black astronomer is loaded with beautiful language, constructed with taut skill, and above all deeply felt. I was fully engaged by this novel approach to the only real American tragedy, the relation of black to white. At the Hartford Stage Company through March 7.

Based on fact, Aranha's narrative could hardly be more juicily to the point in this Bicentennial year. Jefferson not only owned slaves while he wrote those ringing phrases about all men being equal, but he came to love one of them: Sally Hemings. Also real was self-taught astronomer Benjamin Banneker, a free black man.

We watch as Banneker is taunted by poor whites, as he visits Jefferson with Abigail Adams to prove the intellectual equality of blacks, as Sally Hemings and Jefferson's daughter wrestle with their love, as a racist neighbor slashes at Jefferson's hypocrisies, and finally, as Jefferson forces on himself the reluctant question "If not the intellect then it must be ...?"

The answer is racism, of course, but the great strength of Aranha's play is that it is not a simple tract. All the tangled aspects of American racism are treated with a compassion that understands how both races have been scarred by this historic evil.

And Aranha ties together the multiple facets with the central metaphor of oppression, the blow. The poor whites bludgeon a rich man's calf, and later the free black genius; Jefferson beats Sally almost as an act of love; the slaves mime the savage insurrection in Haiti with raised hatchets. The violent nub of racial oppression becomes an imprisoning, dehumanizing circle.

Aranha's language is both powerful and problematic--it pours forth in dazzling fountains of feeling, a kind of stream-of-consciousness with 18th-century eloquence. Here's Banneker describing his feelings at seeing his own hand at a Quaker meeting:

"I felt my white face crack, my lips thickening, the black tore through and the white face fell, smashing at my feet."

The problem is that first, one uncomfortably realizes at times that people simply don't talk like that, and second, that all the characters end up sounding rather alike when they do.

One may also fault the underdevelopment of Sally Hemings' character, though this is in part due to the subpar performance of Seret Scott. Where is her love, her rage, her sensuality? Certainly not in Scott's automaton movement and stiffly uninflected voice.

In the major roles, though, Aranha himself gives Banneker an exhausted dignity of age and effort, and Josef Sommer not only looks like Jefferson but mixes the politician's prevarications with the humanist's agony.

Anne Shropshire makes a biting Abigail Adams, Ted Graeber is stupidly arrogant with the honesty of the truly base as the neighbor, and William Jay's slave Cal is a poignant prefiguration of the enraged and emasculated black male.

The costumes are gorgeously colonial, and the single set combines with lighting to bring out Banneker's shabby cabin, the grounds and woods, and Jefferson's lithe Chippendale study.

When I think of the stunning confrontation scene that closes the first act, or the drawing-room wit of the scenes in the study, or the embracing metaphors that connect themes and characters, I am finally impressed by how well-crafted a play this is--for all the length, my attention was held. I will not be surprised if "The Estate" goes far beyond the Hartford Stage.

HARVEY, John Henry; (2) Music and theater critic; (3) b. New
Prague, Minn., Oct. 27, 1911; (4) s. William Lemuel and Eleonora
(Holub) H.; (5) B.A., Yale U., major subject: English, 1933; (6)
m. Irene Gorman, Aug. 21, 1939; (7) children--Eleonora Holub (Mrs.
Edward F. D'Arms Jr.), William Lemuel, John Henry Jr.; (8) Reporter, St. Paul Dispatch and Pioneer Press, 1934-45, music critic,
1945- , Drama critic, 1948- ; (9) Program annotator, Minneapolis
Symphony Orchestra, 1960-63; (15) mem. Music Critics Assn.,
American Theatre Critics Assn.; (16) Independent; (17) Roman Catholic; (19) Clubs: University, Minnesota (St. Paul); (20) Contrib. reviews to Musical America; (21) 445 Summit Ave., St. Paul, Minn.,
55102, Ph. 612-227-2201; (22) St. Paul Dispatch and Pioneer Press,
55 E. Fourth St., St. Paul, Minn. 55101, Ph. 612-222-5011; (23)
Circulation: Combined weekday 225,000; (24) 55 plays and musicals,
100 concerts, 18 operas, 15 dance events, 4 misc.

Guthrie Cast Takes Good Care of Pinter's "The Caretaker"
(by John H. Harvey, St. Paul Dispatch, June 5, 1975)

With its second opening of the new season, the Guthrie Theater, Minneapolis, got down to more serious and substantial business Wednesday night.

Harold Pinter's "The Caretaker" is, in a purely dramatic
sense, a sort of theater game. The author takes one character
with certain attributes, and brings into the same room with him
only one at a time, two other characters of entirely different
attributes.

With his clear private knowledge of each character, his keen
ear for common speech and his superb rhythmic sense, Pinter
develops through character interaction a play which is by turns
funny, horrifying and overall brilliantly theatrical.

For director and actors, this 15-year-old play is both a
challenge and a delight to explore. Among them, director Stephen Kanee and the three cast members have arrived at a taut,
powerfully rhythmed production of considerable virtuosity.

There is a good deal more to the play than a theatrical exercise, however. As the text gives the performers latitude in
dramatic interpretation, so the play offers the viewer scope to
find his own meanings in it.

The play takes place in a junk-filled room of an old, rundown house in London, and the basic plot is very simple. Davies,
a nasty old tramp of small-caliber cunning, is taken in by Aston,
a quiet kindly young man who is supposed to be fixing up the
house for his brother Mick the owner.

Davies seeks to assure himself a permanent refuge by playing one brother against the other and gets whipsawed.

The play turns on the tragedy Davies creates for himself--ejection from the mean little paradise he hopes he has found. Yet each of the three characters in his own way seems to be seeking a foothold in the world.

Davies is looking for the security represented by the room and by the identity contained in papers he left with "a man at Sidcup" and talks of retrieving.

Aston, a former mental patient, is seeking a grip on quiet, safe reality, and dreams of building a shed which can become a workshop for repairing and perhaps woodworking.

Mick wants to be a big shot, plays at being one by big talk, by confusing and tormenting Davies and by fantasizing about big business projects and living in a luxurious penthouse apartment.

Carrying the principal burden of the performance, Eric Christmas creates a portrait of Davies which is large in dimensions and richly filled in a shambling wreck of a man, vicious, insecure, narrow, contemptible and pitiably human.

Jeff Chandler imparts an eerie quality to the quiet introversion of Aston, and his long speech describing his mental breakdown and his experiences in the hospital is compellingly sustained and built.

Mark Lamos plays the role of Mick with a rather stagy quality, yet he is effective in the coiled-spring air he gives it. His sharp, jerky movements alternating with complete passivity, the febrile stare with which he delivers some of his speeches and the tremendous burst of violence in the last act suggest that Mick, in his own way, may have a share of mental disturbance.

Guthrie "Streetcar" Desirable
(by John H. Harvey, St. Paul Dispatch, June 19, 1975)

The writing in Tennessee Williams' "A Streetcar Named Desire" is such that the play will work effectively in less than professional situations.

At the same time, it offers wide scope for the ablest professional talents. The Guthrie Theater's new production, while it is not the best of all possible presentations, is an excellent one which shows to what heights the play can still rise after 28 years.

Principal credit for this can be assigned to two persons: Patricia Conolly, who plays the central role of Blanche DuBois, and Guthrie veteran Ken Ruta, making his debut there as a director.

Miss Conolly gives superb range and sensitivity to the part of the ill-fated Blanche, in flight from reality and the sordid rounds of alcohol and sexual promiscuity with which she has tried to drug herself against the world pressing in on her.

Her performance affectingly suggests, in its shudders, its simpers and affectations of old-fashioned Southern gentility, the flutters of a wounded bird vainly seeking escape. And she gives clean accent to the flashes of coarseness and stridency which come through when stress puts Blanche's guard down.

Richard Council gives considerable force and technical skill to the role of Stanley Kowalski, Blanche's brother-in-law, her unwilling host in his New Orleans slum flat and eventually her "executioner." Yet he does not fully hold up his side of the polarity between Stanley's primitive animalism and Blanche's affectation-armored vulnerability--of healthy barbarism vs. effete, decaying civilization.

He seems to present too cleancut a Stanley, and one does not find his insensitivity and loutish manners entirely convincing.

Karen Landry creates a well-considered and believable portrait of Blanche's realistic younger sister Stella, who accepts Stanley and his world and doesn't let dreams of past glory interfere with her relationship with him.

Peter Michael Goetz gives an effective account of the basically innocent man to whom Blanche looks for salvation, and the others in the cast play their roles ably.

Ruta's direction is distinguished by firm rhythm and flow, with hard-hitting accents, and he has obtained solid ensemble from his cast. It is a straightforward piece of work, dispensing with fancy echo and lighting effects which often were used in earlier productions of the play.

Jack Barkla's set captures both the sleaziness and airy attractiveness of the locale. The Guthrie's thrust stage is not entirely hospitable to such a play as this, but Barkla has solved the problems it presents with a good deal of success.

HATCH, Elizabeth A.; (2) Theatre critic; (3) b. Jersey City, N.J., 1897; (5) Attended Barnard College for 3 years; (6) Married 1921; (8) In Broadway production of "The Betrothal," 1918-1919; Devereux traveling Repertoire Co. , 1919; short vaudeville engagement, 1920; taught dancing 1925-29; taught speech and coached plays in Dwight School, Englewood, N.J., 1929-39; taught acting Sarah Lawrence College and acted with Morningside Players, Columbia University 1930-36; on Broadway 1932 "Life Begins"; taught speech and drama Beaver College 1944-45 and Latin American Institute, N.Y. City, 1945-46; (9) Directed many amateur theatre and dance productions over the years and taught speech and acting privately and in groups,

as well as English to the foreign-born in the U.S. , Germany and
Korea. Play critic for the Daily Hampshire Gazette, Northampton,
Mass, 1967- ; (24) In the past eight years have covered 249 produc-
tions at Smith College, Amherst, University of Massachusetts, Mt.
Holyoke, Hampshire College, Williston School, Greenfield Community
College, and three local civic theatre groups, as well as the pro-
fessional company "Stage West" in Springfield, Mass.

GCC and Pat Hingle Present "J.B."
(by Elizabeth A. Hatch, Daily Hampshire Gazette, December 6, 1974)

Throughout this week, in the Deerfield Academy Auditorium,
Greenfield Community College is presenting the poetic dramatic
fantasy "J.B. ," written by our distinguished local poet, Archibald
MacLeish.

Pat Hingle, the professional actor who created the part on
Broadway 15 years ago, plays the title role. It is a memorable
evening of fine theater. The large opening night audience welcomed it with sincere and warm acclaim.

As the locale for the production, historic Deerfield, with its
brave and bloody heritage, seems singularly appropriate. For
"J.B." is a timeless and universal drama. Modeled on the life
of the Biblical character Job, that good and blameless man who,
through suffering all possible trials, maintains his faith in God,
the work is, at the same time, a modern morality play, of the
"play-within-a-play" form.

In contrast to Job, J.B. shows modern man in a universe
whose God he cannot understand; while the "Voice from the Whirlwind" offers an answer, it is irrelevant to his needs and he must
find his solutions to the meaning of life as we must live it.

The drama is set "in a traveling circus which has been on
the roads of the world for a long time." A balloon man, Mr.
Zuss, and a popcorn vender, Nickles, put on masks and serve
as commentators on the action that unfolds. Mr. Zuss is God
and Nickles is the Devil. J.B. is a happy man, serene in the
company of his wife and children, healthy and rich. Nickles is
convinced that once J.B. is deprived of these things, he will
then curse God.

Mr. Zuss decides to put J.B. to the test and so gives Nickles power over him, J.B. 's children are killed, his money taken
away, he is tortured by painful disease. He cries out "Show me
my guilt, Oh God"; but his faith is not destroyed. "Comforters"
come to help him: a psychiatrist, a Communist and a cleric.
None of them can supply reason for God's indifference to J.B. 's
woes. But rather arbitrarily Mr. Zuss restores his wife and
his health, and J.B. hammers out his simple philosophy of love
and acceptance of life's suffering in an ending that is, incidentally, the weakest part of the play.

Under the able direction of George Johnston and with the magnificent performance of Pat Hingle who carries the bulk of the play on his stalwart back, the drama moved with smooth precision and fine pace; the setting, starkly functional, the lighting well-handled, the costuming appropriately unobtrusive, the sound effects helpful to the changing moods; the acting on the whole strongly supportive of Pat Hingle's obvious professionalism and, for amateurs (for the most part), amazingly good. But we are compelled, alas, to fault Louetta Atherton who, on opening night, in the role of Sarah, was markedly weak in projective power.

We liked especially the Nickles of Jim Girard which contrasted in its devilish virtuosity with the equally strong Zuss of Ralph Gordon Sr. who had fine voice and presence. We loved the five young children, played by Jim Moseley, Judy Butler, Jeff Gordon, Stephanie Greenblatt and Alexis Greenblatt, all extremely natural and poignantly accenting J. B. 's first great tragedy. The three Comforters, Bildad, Eliphaz and Zophar, all Biblical characters who reasoned with J. B. , were persuasively personified by Doug Vernes, Walter Banfield and Mike Brule respectively. And the smaller roles, too numerous to give separate credit, all furnished fine support for J. B. and deserve high praise.

As for Pat Hingle, he was J. B. We did not see his earlier performance but we believe that today he is probably a better J. B. than he was 15 years ago. He is more mature and therefore has profounder feeling for the role. His strong physique suggests the indomitable spirit of Man against all odds. His fine voice ranging the scale in emotional and poetic delivery, the variety of tone, the perfect timing, the controlled gesture, the meaningful pause, in short the fine technique of acting, moved his audience as in these hard-boiled days it is rarely moved. We thank you, Pat Hingle, for the experience.

The author, Archibald MacLeish, did not appear, but his was the "Voice from the Whirlwind" reciting the wonderful words from the Bible, in which the Lord admonishes Job, beginning: "Who is it that darkeneth counsel by words without knowledge? ," etc. Even Pat Hingle could not have read them more beautifully.

"Ah Wilderness": Faith in the Old Order Revived
(by Elizabeth A. Hatch, Daily Hampshire Gazette, November 25, 1975)

For its first production of the season, our professional theater in West Springfield, Stage/West, is presenting "Ah, Wilderness!" by the great American playwright, Eugene O'Neill. It is a happy choice, for it is a cheerful amusing serio-comedy of family life set in the early part of the century. It is also a realistic picture of our domestic society of that period, which in contrast to our present widening abyss between generations, is more refreshing. Besides being an amusing picture of "the good old days," it is, indeed, something of a revival of faith in the

old order--the order founded on the affection and respect our
fathers and grandfathers took for granted in family life in the
year 1906 and that we, today, have largely lost sight of.

The numerous gray-heads in the Wednesday matinee audience
enjoyed it all with nostalgic sentimental homage to the past,
while the all-wise teenagers present were highly amused by the
period piece with its dated cliches, many of which, strange to
say, still struck home.

The play was written and first produced in the 1930s, at a
time when O'Neill was on the point of creating the more famous
tragedy of his own family life, "Long Day's Journey into Night."
In this warm comedy, he presents an ideal family depicting
vividly the loving parents and siblings he never had. It is O'Neill's
most straightforward and most optimistic work, and the Stage/
West company have produced it with fine professional wisdom and
great charm.

The plot is simple, centering as it does on a large family,
the Millers, who live in a small town in Connecticut; all the action takes place on July 4 and 5 in the year 1906, on the side
porch and lawn of the family homestead and a nearby beer garden.   The Miller family consists of the father, Nat Miller, a
local newspaper publisher and a strong patriarchal figure, but
very human in kindliness and understanding; his wife, Essie, ef-
fusive and well-meaning but reactionary, a true woman of her
time; the children, Mildred, a pretty, teasing teen-ager, Arthur,
a proudly superior student at Yale, Tommy, the 10-year-old
youngest, and Richard, the second son, who is really the hero,
or nonhereo, of the piece. He is the only hint of the author,
Eugene O'Neill himself, for the boy is something of a renegade
and very bookish, quoting appropriate poetry on every possible
occasion.   In fact, the title of the play is from the well-known
Omar Khayyam verse which begins, "A loaf of bread, a jug of
wine and Thou," and ends "Ah, Wilderness were Paradise enow!"
which to the 16-year-old Richard expresses the ecstasy of his
love for his neighbor's shrinking violet daughter, Muriel.

Part of the household, also, is Lily Miller, the old maid
aunt and sister to Nat, who is half engaged to Sid Davis, Essie's
delightfully funny, dipsomaniac brother.   The light web of the
plot involves young Richard in a forbidden trip to a questionable
beer garden and his not too serious entanglement with the shady
nightlife there, which he is lured into by a Harvard man, as a
retaliatory gesture toward his sweetheart and to some extent his
family.

It is the return of the prodigal son theme that climaxes the
action--and a generally happy Biblical ending for nearly all concerned.   Carried with a light touch and homely humor, the play
is a comedy of decent family and neighborly life, which with the
basis of loving tolerance, is still our criterion.

The new director at Stage/West, Rae Allen, has done a masterful job of guiding the excellent cast through the gentle intricacies of the acting; pointing up the humor but never overplaying it. The timing, too, is perfect, and the character delineations consistently sustained. The single massive setting by Lauren King was impressive and well handled, with suggestive variation for the other scenes. The period costumes by Sigrid Insull, truly of the decade and worn with the air and ambience of the time.

The long cast of players was without fault. Most of the roles were vignettes and without much time for depth of character portrayal but all true and vital and smoothly relating. Lily Miller, played by Jane Lowry, was a dignified, attractive old maid aunt, strong in principle against the evils of Uncle Sid's drinking habits, which struck the only sad note in the play--sad because Uncle Sid, played by Tom Crawley, was such a lovable guy and very amusing in his cups. The Essie Miller of Elizabeth Parrish was the picture of the cackling but very kindly mother hen, and Chris Romilly's portrait of the eldest son, Arthur, was the paragon of the times, the typical Yale man and pride of the family.

We approved, also, Gwyllum Evans as David McComber, the strict father of the beautiful Muriel who, in his straight-laced pomposity, is no longer (we are glad to say) a type of father still extant. And Lisa Grayton we found charming as Mildred, the only daughter and prevailing popular coquette of the period, while Madonna T. Meagher added a tart edge to the scene as Nora, the sulky, unwilling servant. Philip Littell made a dashing Harvard student and attractive bad influence for a potential Yale man, while Nancy Sellin and Madonna T. Meagher were colorfully typical ladies of the evening.

Graham Beckel is a vitally persuasive actor and his picture of 16-year-old Richard was somewhat reminiscent of Tarkington's lovelorn Willy Baxter but with more subtle and interesting facets of character. One felt he would realize his father's faith in him--after his painful growing up.

But the star of the play was Nat Miller, the father. As interpreted by Robert Pastene with his fine stage presence, he was a dignified figure but at the same time, warmly understanding of his children, his wife and his neighbors, of life in general. Still, he was human, a little hurt by the teasing of his children, but with ever-ready humor enjoying their gaiety. He carried always, in our eyes, a touch of pathos as the good father Eugene O'Neill created from his own sad need.

A visit with the Miller family is recommended as a happy and worthwhile theater occasion for all ages.

HAUN, Harry, New York Daily News, 220 East 42 St., N.Y., N.Y. 10017, Ph. 212-682-1234.

HAWLEY, Michael James; (2) Entertainment Editor; (3) b. Trenton, N. J. , Sept. 1, 1953; (4) s. Philip C. and Anne J. (Fleming); (5) B. S. Southern Illinois U. at Carbondale, major: Journalism, minor: Cinema and Photography, 1975; (6) single; (8) Student writer, staff writer, Entertainment Editor, Daily Egyptian, SIU, 1973-75; (9) Program notes for art film series at Varsity Theater, Carbondale; (15) Southern Illinois Film Society; (16) Independent; (17) Catholic; (20) Article published in Lost Generation Journal; (21) Current through May 1975; 411 E. Hester St. , #16, Carbondale, Ill. 62901; after graduation: unknown; parent's: 9 Great Woods Drive, Trenton, N.J. 08618, Ph. 609-882-8796; (22) Daily Egyptian, Communications Bldg., SIU, Carbondale, Ill. 62901, Ph. 618-536-3311 ex. 241; (23) Circulation: 19,500; (24) 15 plays or musicals, 35 films, 20 concerts, 30 records, 20 miscellaneous.

"Tommy Allen Show" Whimsical, Biting
(by Michael Hawley, Daily Egyptian, ca. 1973-1974)

Reactions to "The Tommy Allen Show-Carbondale" will probably be as varied and intense as the hundreds of sensory-stinging stimuli the show manages to deal out.

Subjecting the audience to everything from whimsical fun and biting satire to raw confrontation with human emotion, "The Tommy Allen Show" is a theater experience Carbondale is unlikely to forget by next week. No matter what one's final judgment of the show might be, director Phyllis Wagner, the Southern Players and everyone else involved should be thanked for making this experience available to Carbondale audiences.

Written by open theater playwright Megan Terry, "The Tommy Allen Show" is divided into four unique parts which take place in varying locations throughout the Communications Building. Part two, which happens in the University Theater, is the main part of the production and deserves first attention.

With the University Theater believably transformed into a television studio by Randy Lockwood's set design, the show begins as a satire on late night television talk shows. While waiting for the show to begin, the audience listens to the orchestra warm up and a ballerina on roller skates demonstrates the electric applause and laughter cues.

After a lot of apprehensive ballyhoo by the "Tommy Allen Singers," Tommy Allen is finally cheered on stage for what starts out to be another "five-nights-a-week 52 weeks-a-year" show. Typically, musical numbers are performed and guests are introduced, each one representing a talk show host stereotype.

Gradually, the show departs from the plastic framework of television talk shows and attempts to say something about the hurting people existing behind the packaged images, and America's hero-worship relationship to its prominent entertainment

figures. Through selfish and compassionate interactions, the
characters come to realize they are only "pain, reflectors" for
a viewing public that has never "trained for intimacy."

Although the ideas "The Tommy Allen Show" tries to convey
are interesting and important, often the techniques used to demonstrate them are rough and questionable. Frequent use of reality departure and abstraction works brilliantly at times, but
these methods usually fit clumsily into the television talk show
framework.

But apart from all its heaviness, part two of the show is
also a lot of fun. Terry's script, which attacks everything from
sexism to commercialism, contains enough razor sharp humor
to last Carol Burnett an entire season--if she didn't have to worry
about censorship.

Most of the special bulletins, announcements and commercials,
some written by Terry and others written and localized for Carbondale by Lewis Bolton, are witty and delightfully shocking.
These are acted out on the sides of the stage by a company of
eight talented players. Cynthia Schramm deserves special note
for her imitations of Richard Nixon, a giant insect, and Carbondale's foremost dining hostess, "Betty Lou."

One commercial for the High Heaven Heroin Company ad-
vertises "needles and heroin bags for Barbie and Ken, a little
prostitute outfit for Barbie when she has to support Ken's habit,
and a drag outfit for Ken when Barbie is too sick to stroll."

Another fun part of the show is "Beat the Boys in the Band,"
where audience members try to stump the band with songs they
won't know. At Thursday evening's preview performance, Archibald McLeod, Chairman of the Theater Department, won ten free
games of pinball from Downstairs Arcade because the band couldn't
play "That's the Reason I Wear My Kilt."

A gallery of fine and sometimes brilliant performances are
given by nine actors who play the four Tommies and four guest
stars (Tommy IV is a vaudeville horse operated by two people).
Occasionally, however, their interpretations are weighted down
by a script which contains a lot of useless wooden words.

As Dan Daniels--The Queen of Comedy, Lewis Bolton is all
effeminate fire and fury. A Tiny Tim via Marjoe, Bolton creates
an atmosphere of tepid enthusiasm as he leads everyone on stage
in a session of wild repentance and testifying.

Christine Heins is mesmerizing as Tommy III, the glamorous
Hollywood star. Particularly impressive is her sensually icy
opening monologue and song, "The Night I Shot My Maidenform
Bra." Linda Invergo also turns in a good performance as Sally
Sommers, country and western singer and female chauvinist pig.

Her parody of female country and western singers is on target
as she whimpers lines like "When I killed your mother I was
only testing you to see if you'd be true."

The role of John J. Johnson, the child molester, is taken
on by John Olinick with more sleaziness than Peter Lorre's
"M." Christine Coyle plays Mrs. Florence Assbite, the middle
aged woman who is such a rotten performer that everyone just
loves her.

Every show has to have its host, and Robert Hollister is representative of all the smiling humanoids who sustain themselves
nightly on the warmth of audience applause. Rounding out the
cast is James Belushi in the unfortunate role of a militant rock
star, and Debbie Brown and Dave McCracken as Tommy IV.

Before the main part of the "Tommy Allen Show" begins,
the audience can anticipate in a sideshow of sensory experiences
and displays. Upon entering the Communications Building, a
gallery of huge promotion glossies greets you and gives a hint
of what's to come. Audience involvement with the show begins
immediately by watching rehearsal tapes and slides in the lounge.

Included in this interesting pre-show are scenes from Chekhov
plays which are performed in the courtyard. The green room
weapons display makes a statement about children's war toys,
particularly the video film of children actualy playing with these
toys.

A walk through the Laboratory Theater reveals a number of
crazy things to touch and play with. Among other things, newspapers are made available to make paper hats. Most people
chose to make paper cannon balls, and throw them at the women
singing opera on the elevated lighting bridge.

The most disturbing part of "The Tommy Allen Show" happens
in part three among the pipes and boilers in the Communications
Building's basement. Setting themselves up in various locations
around the cold metal apparatuses, cast members recite prepared
speeches in which they widly cry for understanding as people, not
as things.

Like walking through a zoo of bizarre animals, audience
members can elect to either laugh and quickly walk past each
cage--only seeing each person as an actor in a play, or listen
and try to understand them. The intense feelings created by
them makes it almost impossible to take the first route, and unbearably depressing to take the second.

Megan Terry was in Carbondale for the show, and said that
in another production cast members set themselves up in various
states of torture for this part of the show. Audience members
either helped them out or tortured them more, she said.

After leaving this hellish catacomb, part four consists of drinking coffee and watching tapes of the performance--a sort of "bringing back to earth" for everyone.

There are many things wrong with "The Tommy Allen Show." Some of the material is outdated, and many of its fuzzy concepts do not hold together well. Problems with technical cues and the orchestra also put a strain on the show, although these were taken care of during the weekend performances.

But much more is right about the show than is wrong. It reflects an awful lot of effort and care, and for $1.75 ($2.25 for the general public) it's a theater experience that shouldn't be passed up.

One Woman Creates 42 on Stage
(by Michael Hawley, Daily Egyptian, ca. 1973-74)

After brilliantly capturing the essences of 41 women in her show, "I Am A Woman," actress Viveca Lindfors used the words of a 42nd woman, French diarist Anais Nin, to accurately summarize and close the show.

"Emotional dramas which pass like storms, leave peace behind."

And the peace Lindfors left behind in Shryock Auditorium Saturday night was certainly a triumphant one. Her message was the diversity, pride and unity of all women, a message well-received by the largely feminist audience.

Revealing a portrait gallery that paid tribute to all women (there were undoubtedly a few she managed to miss), Lindfors used choice selections from literature, theater, essays, poetry and interviews to get her point across. As interpreted by Lindfors, women of all ages and time periods, from all classes and circumstances, made "I Am A Woman" a serious, but entertaining evening.

What word do you use to describe a woman who portrays 42 different people in two hours? Perhaps you could say that she changed like a chamelion, only faster. But that's much too ugly a description for someone as talented, beautiful and vivacious as Viveca Lindfors.

A very youthful 54-year-old Swede, Lindfors did justice to the majority of her characters, which ranged from Anne Frank describing the thrill of her first kiss, to Marilyn Monroe discussing what she wants to do with a life that has to mean more than just being a sex goddess. In between, her women were presented with compassion, humor and, often, bitterness.

It was particularly interesting to note the sequencing of the

performances. For instance, Barbara Seaman's hilarious discourse on that all-too-favorite subject, the female orgasm, was
followed by seemingly Victorian reading on the same subject
from D. H. Lawrence's "Lady Chatterly's Lover."

In another light moment, Lindfors lit a cigar to do a series
of biting impressions on the sexist theories of Freud. Totally
in contrast to this mood was her portrayal of a Vietnamese girl
giving horrifying testimony at the 1968 Paris Peace Conference.
A tape of the testimony spoken in Vietnamese was played against
Lindfor's translation, and the effect brought a solemn hush over
the auditorium.

Also outstanding was her too short excerpt from Ibsen's "A
Doll's House," a painful Hungarian poem titled "The Boy Changed
Into a Stag Clamors at the Gate of Secrets," and an eerie testa-
mony by Charles Mason's mother and girlfriend.

Before the evening ended, Lindfors also touched on Shakespeare, several selctions from Bertolt Brecht, Betty Friedan,
poetess Anne Sexton and Giradoux's "Mad Woman of Chaillot,"
among many others.

Three useful metal sculptures by Suzanne Benton were the
show's only sets, around which Lindfors gracefully worked her
art. In portraying the different women, Lindfors used simple
costumes and props--body stocking, wrap-around shirt, two
capes and wigs, handbag, umbrella, hat, scarf and drape--which
were hung on the sculptures and ready for use at the appropriate moment.

The numerous performances were smoothly linked by slight
changes in costume, lighting, recorded background music, sound
effects and state location. Occasionally, the changes were too
smooth, however, and following the program became difficult and
confusing. Lindfor's accent was also a small hinderance.

At times, it seemed that "I Am A Woman" could have been
improved had Lindfors narrowed her selections somewhat, and
expanded the more effective portrayals. There were also a few
interpretations, such as the aging actress from Tennessee Williams' "Sweet Bird of Youth," which did not meet Lindfors'
otherwise high standards.

Looking at "I Am A Woman" as a total piece of theater rather than 42 individual performances is, in a way, like looking
into a kaleidoscope. They both present a pattern of differently
colored, shaped fragments which blend to make a beautiful and
concise picture.

One of Lindfors' final moments on stage had her reciting
the lyrics to Helen Reddy's "I Am Woman," while the record
played in the background. When the song ended Lindfors

exuberantly swung her cape in the air above her head proclaiming the final, zealous statement, "I AM WO ..., WO ..., WO-MAN!"

HAWTHORN, Maggie; (2) Theater critic, jazz critic; (3) b. Seattle, Wash., 1929; (5) U. of Washington; (8) Down Beat Magazine; Ralph J. Gleason, San Francisco Chronical and syndicated columnist; A Contemporary Theater; New Directions in Music; Seattle Symphony Orchestra; Northwest Releasing Corp. Post-Intelligencer since November, 1972; (15) Washington State Press Women; Newspaper Guild; American Federation of Musicians; (22) Seattle Post-Intelligencer, Fifth and Wall, Seattle, Wash. 98121, Ph. 206-628-8332; (23) Circulation: 200,000 daily and Sunday; (24) 86 on theater; 53 on jazz and popular music; 29 on dance; 23 other.

Show's a "Dandy"
(by Maggie Hawthorn, Seattle Post-Intelligencer, January 12, 1976)

A frisky 89-year old is trotting around the boards at the Empty Space Theater, showing only superficial signs of age and exhibiting instead its class, flash and great good humor.

"Dandy Dick," the title character, is a race horse and although he does not appear he is the pivotal force in Sir Arthur Wing Pinero's 1887 farce about the manners and mores of his time.   The Space does a lusty, stylish and thoroughly delightful job with this bit of Edwardian stage dazzle, making of it a fast moving evening in which large and small parts are admirably taken and even the magical set transformation for Act II and the witty curtain calls were applauded.

Pinero was immensely popular during the early years of his career, although he later passed from favor when he seemed unable to adapt himself to the changes of the twentieth century. Early on, he turned out a steady stream of comedies for London's Court Theater and others, of which "Dandy Dick" is typical.

It was, and is, a model of craftsmanship: Pinero knew how to organize a plot, with contrasting and interacting subtales, and he knew how to move his actors about on stage to create a constant barrage of telling bits of business without anyone falling over another, unless it in some way furthered the sequence of events.   "Dandy Dick" is also a model of Pinero's recurrent examination of human frailties and the way in which the society of his day chose to circumvent accepted social standards.   Indeed, although minor details have changed, the principle is pointedly contemporary.   Although nobody would accuse Pinero of literary genius, his dialogue is sturdy, blunt and comic.

M. Burke Walker has directed an exemplary cast, keeping the large number of players and the confused story line remarkably untangled.   He has chosen to have his characters speak very precisely, not attempting the English accents, and the effect is both rewarding and appropriate. The exceptions, those who affect what is supposedly a "lower class" speech, do so uneasily and thereby call attention to the contrast.

Especially noteworthy were Jeffrey Steitzer as the Dean, all pasty-faced, sanctimonious rectitude; and Diane Schenker as his brusquely handsome sister, owner of the horseflesh in question. The sister, a racy widow with a sporting outlook on life, comes to stay with the Dean while she is down on her luck.

Wonderful complications ensue, having to do with various forms of wagering, romance, and with the administering of a surreptitious dose of medicine to the all-important nag. The Dean's two delectably frivolous daughters, played with skittish fizz by Lori Larsen and with sly charm by Marnie Mosiman, are courted by Tom Spiller and Robert Wright as two self-important soldiers. (Wright injects a wondrously excruciating violin exhibition during a parlor musicale.) Martin LaPlatney's portrayal of Blore, the larcenous butler, is a gem. J. V. Bradley, James Goodwin Rice and Kathy Lichter also figure prominently in the brou-ha-ha.

The set design was by Karen Gjelsteen, lights by James Verdery and costumes by the excellent Sally Richardson. As the Dean sighs, "Nothing like it in any other country--a regular, pure, simple English evening at home." Just so.

Rep's "Meeting" Is an Empty Statement
(by Maggie Hawthorn, Seattle Post-Intelligencer, January 16, 1976)

Much is made in the program notes of the fact that director Harold Scott, who guides "The Last Meeting of The Knights of The White Magnolia" through its paces at the Seattle Repertory Theater, is black. Supposedly, it is immensely significant that "a touching redneck comedy-drama should become a militant black-white manifesto."

Well, it isn't so. Mostly because "The Last Meeting" is a dim play, shallow and meaningless, and hardly provocative of any racial or even humane overtones at all. Stronger racial statements have been made on the stage for years, going back to such crowd-pleasers as "Raisin in the Sun" and continuing in an honorable line to today's plays by Athol Fugard, Ed Bullins and others.

Director Scott struggles to do a good job with what he has, but the all-male cast and the excellent technical support cannot make a denim purse out of a sow's butt.

"Butt" is the operative word, since it is so often used in the dialogue to invoke the atmosphere of "good ol' boy" horsing around which is the burden of this two act slice of life. "By god" and

"Jee'sus H. Kee-rist" turn up with painful frequency, as well, in speeches meant to give the flavor of small town West Texas. Playwright Preston Jones, himself a Texas resident and an actor at the Dallas Theater Center since 1962, wrote "Last Meeting" and two other plays in an earnest attempt to create truly American regional dramatic works. "Last Meeting" has been or is being produced by several regional theaters this year, through the American Playwrights Theater, and supposedly has been optioned for a Broadway production next season.

The "plot" is really only a situation; it never becomes more than a peek at a moment in the meaningless lives of these marginal people. Seven sorry men who are the last remnants of a white supremist group called the Knights of the White Magnolia are gathered in a rundown hotel owned by one of their number. They have, for the first time in years, a prospective new member with one of those double Southern names, Lonnie Roy McNeil.

These guys have nothing to hold them together except their mutual lack of direction or meaning and their excuse to play dominos, discuss geneology and the price of pipe, and drink cheap booze. An elderly black custodian appears now and again to offer oblique comments meant to hold heavy import. In the course of two acts, they squabble, drink, struggle through an initiation ceremony until the young subject finally bolts, and ultimately fall apart. It is, indeed, the last meeting.

Although Jones does have a good ear for the kind of speech his characters might use, it takes more than that for a good theater piece. His people, ignorant and bankrupt, are really never in contact with any dramatic purpose, either emotional or situational. In any case, they are all so trivial and empty that it is impossible to care one whit.

The script reads better than it plays; perhaps Mr. Jones has more future as a writer of novels for light summer reading than as a playwright. There are some easy laughs, about on the level of a mediocre sketch on, say, the Carol Burnett Show. There was frequent laughter in the theater but it resulted mostly from such infantile remarks as, "I hadda go pee." The sharpest scene was drawn as a parody of the lodge initiation, a wicked approximation of most fraternal organizations but still an easy shot.

The cast had a lot of trouble with the distinctive West Texas twang, and some managed better than others. Robert Donley did a good job as the colonel who is losing his grip on reality, and Bill Cobbs was a detached and knowing Ramsey-Eyes, the black observer. The others were Andy Backer, Henry Butler, Alan Zampese, John Wylie, Robert Sevra, Joseph Regalbuto and Michael Medeiros.

The dusty lodge room of the Cattleman's Hotel was designed by Robert Dahlstrom, the lights by Richard Devin and the costumes by Lewis D. Rampion. "Last Meeting" runs through Feb. 5.

HERMAN, George, Honolulu Advertiser, P.O. Box 3110, Honolulu, Ha. 96802.

HERRIDGE, Frances; (2) drama and film editor; (3) b. Troy, N.Y.; (4) d. Frederick and Elizabeth (Osgood) Herridge; (5) B.A. Smith College, 1933; post grad. N.Y.U., New School Social Research; (6) m. John Tull Baker, 1947 (div.); (7) children--George Henry Baker; m. 2nd, Adna H. Karns; (8) Asst. to Max Lerner, dance critic for PM, 1945-58; beauty and children's editor, N.Y. Post, 1949-54; drama editor, dance critic, 1954-64; drama and movie editor, dance critic, 1964- ; (21) 305 W. 28th St., New York City, N.Y. 10001; (22) New York Post, 210 South St., New York City, N.Y. 10002; (23) Circulation: 650,000.

<u>Stuttgart Changes Its Style</u>
(by Frances Herridge, New York Post, June 5, 1975)

The Stuttgart Ballet, which under John Cranko established its reputation with his evening-long dramatic ballets, last night showed its new face. It gave us our first look at two works by the Company's new director, Glen Tetley. And quite a change it is!

Not so much in "Voluntaries," a stunningly beautiful valediction to Cranko. That is ballet blended only slightly with the free flow of modern dance. But Tetley's "Arena" goes all the way into the modern field in a manner that is striking but will shock strict balletomanes.

"Voluntaries" gets its title from the musical definition of free-ranging organ improvisations played in the course of a religious service. The service here is in memory of founder Cranko whose death two years ago was such a blow to the company. The choreography, set to Francis Poulenc's Concerto for Organ, Strings and Percussion, is both sad and exultant, solemn and enlifting.

It is a shifting series of duets, trios and ensemble formations, entirely without story but throbbing with pure feeling. The vocabulary is balletic but sharpened with experimental lifts and holds and extreme overarcs.

There are superb duets for Marcia Haydee and Richard Cragun, sinuous and floating and radiantly danced. Birgit Keil, Reid Anderson and Jan Stripling make an equally lustrous trio. And the whole piece soars with tender sublimity. The costumes are uncluttered white leotards; the setting a projection of a pastel-dotted globe, designed by Rouben Ter-Arutunian.

In contrasting mood is "Arena" with its frenetic electronic music, its all-male sextet in briefs and bare feet, its taut unhappy world. Tetley describes it as "variations on the theme of might, dominance and pure power." And that will do as a generalization.

The setting hints of a gym with its drinking fountain, revolving fan and stacked chairs. The men, spotted with blood, strive for dominance over each other. Cragun topples Dieter Ammann from his pseudo-throne. But no sooner is Ammann downed than Egon Madsen grapples with Cragun, subduing him in turn. Eventually Ammann is driven to madness in the tension, throwing chairs about the stage and circling like a caged animal.

The movement is violent and restless, provocative in its slow-stretching explorations, its gutsy grappling, its acrobatic lifts. It is a vivid metaphor for the everlasting competition among men (and women), whether physically or psychologically, and the attempt of one to dominate the other in human relationships. It is hardly a pleasant work, but it is a powerful one and, along with "Voluntaries," shows Tetley's considerable talent and training in both ballet and modern dance.

The Stuttgart repertory will obviously not bog down in the classics. Tetley is a guarantee of new life, and the company has adapted itself remarkably well to the change of style.

The program also included Cranko's "Brouillards," a delicate lovely work--a series of divertissements set to Claude Debussy's "Brouillards." Those I like best are a playful duet with Melinda Witham and Hilde Koch, an exquisite trio with Birgit Kell, Heinz Clauss and Vladimir Klos, and a comic number with David Sutherland, Peter Connell and Patrice Montagnon.

Bresson Looks at Sir Lancelot
(by Frances Herridge, New York Post, June 5, 1975)

"Lancelot of the Lake," at the Art, is Robert Bresson's poetic vision of the days of King Arthur when knighthood was past its flowering. It is so rich in imagery of the time and the mores that if you can let yourself go with it you can be transported into that romantic land of idyllic honor and love. As such it is more accessible than most of Bresson's films.

As anyone knows who has seen "Diary of a Country Priest" and "Une Femme Douce," Bresson uses cinema as a good painter does his canvas, with no thought for the popular taste, but simply as a record of what he sees and feels. The result is totally his creation, which may or may not be communicable to the average viewer.

In "Lancelot," he has caught brilliantly the sights and sounds of knighthood, the immense loyalty to one's leader, the importance of honor, duty and bravery.

The story here is set at the end of the crusade for the Holy Grail. Returning empty handed, Lancelot feels that God is punishing him for his affair with Queen Guinevere and his consequent disloyalty to King Arthur. He tries to extricate himself but Guinevere won't let him go. Meanwhile the jealous Mordred reports him to the king, which leads to the destruction of Lancelot and the Roundtable.

Bresson screens the events with emotional detachment but with such accuracy of detail and atmosphere that you share in the tragedy.

You hear the constant neighing and hoofbeats of the horses, the clanking of armor which you see put on and taken off with a rhythm of its own. There is a striking scene of a joust--shot at saddle-high level where you know that each knight is downed by Lancelot only by the fallen shields. And there is the unforgettable end of a riderless horse still galloping amid a mass of crumpled armor.

Most impressive of all is the economy with which the story is told. A few lines of dialogue pierce the heart of the situation, and the film gets on to the next episode. No time is wasted on long arguments or background filler. You can sense the deep emotions each feels without their having to express them in words or action. And this stripped-down, understated depiction has surprising purity.

The cast, as in most of Bresson's work, is made up of unprofessionals or unknowns. There are no screen personalities to make you realize they are acting. But those used are completely real, particularly Luc Simon as Lancelot, Laura Duke Condominas as the Queen and Humbert Balsan as Gawain.

Little present-day relevance comes through. And Bresson's ultimate meaning is equivocal. But as a slice of Arthurian legend, it is a gem.

HEWES, Henry; (2) Drama critic; (3) b. Boston, Apr. 9, 1917; (4) s. Henry Fox and Margaret (Warman) H.; (5) B.S., Columbia, 1948; (6) m. Jane Fowle, Aug. 21, 1945; (7) children--Henry Fox, Tucker Fowle, Havelock; (8) Staff writer N.Y. Times, 1949-51; drama editor Saturday Review, 1952-73, drama critic, 1954-73; drama critic Saturday Rev. / World, 1973- ; drama critic Saturday Review 1975- ; lectr. Sarah Lawrence Coll., 1955-56, Columbia, 1956-57, Salzburg Seminar in Am. Studies, 1970, New Sch. for Social Research, 1972- ; (9) Adapter of play La Belle Aventure (produced as Accounting for Love), London, 1954; adapter-director Tennessee Williams' Three Players of a Summer Game, Westport, Conn., 1955; adapter-director (with Siobhan McKenna) Exptl. Hamlet, N.Y.C., 1957, Our Very Own Hole in the

Ground, N.Y.C., 1972. Adapter-director Watergate version Measure
for Measure, Great Lakes Shakespeare Festival, 1974; (12) Exec. sec.
Bd. Standards and Planning for Living Theatre, 1956-66, Am. Theatre Planning Bd., 1966- ; Mem. Pulitzer Prize Jury for Drama
1968; Chmn. Margo Jones Award Com., 1967- , Joseph Maharam
Award Com., 1965- . Consultant to Bicentennial World Theatre Season (1974-76). Bd. Dirs. Am. Theatre Wing, 1972- ; (13) Served as
tech. sgt. USAF, 1941-45; (15) Mem. N.Y. Drama Critics Circle
(v.p. 1969-71, pres. 1971-73), Drama Desk (pres. 1967-74), Am.
Theatre Critics Assn. (sec. 1973-), ANTA (exec. dir. Greater N.Y.
chpt. 1953-58), Internat. Assn. Theatre Critics, New Drama Forum
1974- ; The Critics Circle, London; (20) Editor Famous American
Plays of the 1940s; The Best Plays of 1961-62; The Best Plays of
1962-63; The Best Plays of 1963-64; (21) 1326 Madison Ave., New
York City, N.Y. 10028.

True Storey
(by Henry Hewes, Saturday Review/World, December 18, 1973)

British playwright David Storey is batting 1,000. Two of his
plays (Home and The Changing Room) recently won the New York
Drama Critics Circle awards as the best plays of their respective
seasons. Now a third work, The Contractor, which was written
before the other two, has been produced by the Chelsea Theater
Center at its new Chelsea Manhattan playhouse, and it may well
be the best of the three.

The Contractor takes place on two evocatively unimportant
days, the day before and the day after the wedding of a self-made
industrialist's daughter. On these days the "successful" Ewbank
comes to realize the sad fact that wealth has not freed him from
the disadvantages of class distinction and that it has prevented
him from achieving meaningful relationships with either the men
he employs or his "up-a-class" children.

The play begins easily, with Ewbank's workmen erecting before our eyes a wedding tent on Ewbank's lawn. Ewbank's attitudes are almost as coarse as the workmen's. (He laments to
them the necessity of educating a daughter when, after all, "women are only good for one damn thing. And for that you don't
have to read a book.") But his ownership of a fancy house makes
him overly concerned that the tent poles will mark up the lawn,
and his reluctantly acquired gentility makes him nervous that
some woman in the house might be shocked at the sight of a
workman taking a leak in the shrubbery.

The embodiment of Ewbank's absurd tragedy is his idle son,
Paul ("Oxford, Cambridge ... ask him anything and he'll come
up with the answer"). Paul detests the artificial values of his
parents and stubbornly seeks to establish a more "real" relationship with the world by helping erect the tent. Ewbank is upset
at the sight of Paul doing a six-shilling-an-hour job after spending thousands of pounds on his education.

As for Ewbank's daughter, Claire, her marriage to a young doctor seems a rather pallid venture compared with the elaborate and hard work that is going into its celebration. The before-our-eyes raising of the tent suggests the seldom-realized hopes for marriage and family life, and their beginning phase of hard work and first accomplishment. The second-act process of decorating the tent reflects the next phase of marriage: the tinselly enjoyment of what one has earned and achieved and the coasting along with less real work and more dependence on the sweat of others. And the third act, in which the tent is taken down, parallels the old-age descent into reality, when one sees the naked emptiness of the struggle.

There are also marvelous overtones about the failure of the Industrial Revolution, supplied by the senile, but nonetheless wise, comments of Ewbank's father. Old Ewbank was once a proud and talented artisan, who first made rope by hand and then became an expert rigger and maker of tents. In the old days such work was poorly paid. But in the machine age, his son, though far less good with his hands, was able to expand his father's craft into a lucrative business.

The workmen who make Ewbank's prosperity possible are no longer proud artisans but "the dregs of society," who work cheap for Ewbank because nobody else will employ them. In compensation for their low pay, the workmen retain the freedom to mock their employer to his face. The more extroverted, lively moments of the play are provided by their salty banter and edgy quarrels. Their foreman, Kay, is a monument of humiliation; though capable of taking responsibility, he has been forced into a life of indignity and endured subservience, both by his own weakness and by the necessity of providing for a wife and four daughters.

The four workmen are Bennett, a man destroyed by his wife's scornful infidelity; Glenny, a gullible moron cruelly teased but ultimately loved by the others; and Marshall and Fitzpatrick, a pair of Irish drifters, whose fantastical dialogues are more naturally entertaining than the interchanges of Beckett's allusively allegorical pair of tramps in Waiting for Godot. Fitzpatrick, in particular, is a master of the art of turning accusations and insults back on those who make them. His remarks are often caustic and destructive, but he has a fine sense of humor and a keen perception of who and where he is.

The New York production, which came to us via New Haven's Long Wharf Theater, beautifully realizes the play. The most indelible portraits are Joseph Maher's quick-witted Fitzpatrick and Kevin O'Connor's saintlike Glenny. But under Barry Davis's splendid direction, the entire company has succeeded in breathing life and truth into David Storey's indirect profundities and lovely landscape of luminous sorrows.

Stoppardfoolery
(by Henry Hewes, Saturday Review, November 15, 1975)

It's getting so Americans know nearly as much about the
British theater as they do about their own. Show Tour packages
bring thousands of travelers here each month to sample the good
British plays before they come to Broadway, and also allow the
visitors to enjoy a lot of theater that is either not strong enough
to pass critical muster in New York or not popular enough to
draw audiences for the kind of long run that would make it financially feasible on Broadway. Indeed, at the centrally located
Hotel Bristol, a visiting group of Americans that calls itself
Matinee could be seen in the elegant but intimate lobby happily
effervescing about the bountiful assortment of theater here. Certainly they--and an estimated 200,000 other adventurous Americans who will see British theater this year will return home to
tell 10 times their number about their pleasure.

But as estimable a disseminating force as their verbal reports may be, it is still probably the steadily increasing coverage of British theater by American critics that is most responsible not only for keeping millions of readers au courant, but
also for encouraging Broadway producers to import plays with
favorable reviews already in the bank. Four such London hits
have scheduled fall openings in New York.

Three of these will have casts substantially different from
those of their London predecessors. Alan Ayckbourn's domestic
trilogy, The Norman Conquests, which was judged the best play
of 1973 by the critics here, will be played on Broadway by Richard Benjamin, Paula Prentiss, Ken Howard, and Estelle Parsons.
Habeas Corpus, Alan Bennett's sex farce about an aging, adulter-
ous doctor, will star Donald Sinden instead of Alec Guinness,
who played the leading role here with impressive melancholy.
And Kennedy's Children, American playwright Robert Patrick's
oratorio of monologues in an East Village bar, will probably
benefit from an American cast. Patrick's play, which is being
performed all over Europe, is an amazing phenomenon. When
it was first performed Off-Off-Broadway in 1973, its only review,
by Michael Feingold in the Village Voice, was mildly unfavorable.
However, when produced at the King's Head--the London equivalent of an Off-Off-Broadway theater--it received favorable notices
from most of the English critics and was moved to a small West
End theater, where it has had capacity audiences and drawn enthusiastic praise from New York Times critic Clive Barnes.

The Fourth Offering, the Royal Shakespeare Company's production of Tom Stoppard's Travesties, will be imported in toto.
Travesties has already been called "a coruscating piece of pure
dramatic wizardry" by Clive Barnes, and "the most fascinating
new play I've come across in a long time" by Richard Watts,
and thus seems sure to be a critical success. I would like to

echo these paeans of praise, but there is reluctantly felt measure of exasperation mixed with my appreciation of this undeniably original and madly clever piece of work. Indeed, Stoppard's
all-encompassing trifle begins with such refreshing audaciousness
that it disarms the critic. In the reading room of the Zurich
Public Library, circa 1916, two literary revolutionaries and one
political revolutionary work side by side, completely oblivious of
each other. At one table sits James Joyce, dictating Ulysses
from scraps of paper fished out of his pocket. At another sits
Tristan Tsara, composing a Dadaist poem by drawing words out
of a hat at random. And scurrying about the shelves to make
notes about labor statistics is Vladimir Ilyich Ulyanov (later
known as Lenin). In what may be the play's most truly funny
moment, Joyce picks up a slip of paper he thinks will give him
his next line of Ulysses, only to find that it reads "G. E. C.
(U. S. A.) 250,000,000 marks, 28,000 workers. Profit 254,000,000
marks."   Lenin, hearing Joyce read these words aloud, recognizes the slip of paper as his. Without introductions, he takes
the slip from Joyce, and each goes back to his own work.

The incident is theoretically possible, because Joyce, Tsara,
and Lenin were in Zurich in 1916, but there is no evidence that
they ever met. What is known, however, is that a young British
consulate official named Henry Carr played the role of Algernon
in a semi-professional Zurich production of The Importance of
Being Earnest organized by Joyce. Carr subsequently became
involved in a trivial lawsuit with Joyce, who took revenge by
naming an unpleasant character in Ulysses after him. Now Stoppard, whose earlier success, Rosencrantz and Guildenstern Are
Dead, revealed his predilection for turning minor figures into
major characters, has chosen to add to Henry Carr's immortality
by making him the star of Travesties. Perhaps this choice, as
much as anything in the play, is the best clue to what Stoppard's
driving at in the disorderly parade of tomfoolery that ensues.

It is both the play's virtue and its curse that it says but
does not resolve a great many contradictory things, as it demean-
ingly ridicules the obsessions of its three revolutionaries. Joyce
is described as "an essentially private man who wished his total
indifference to public notice to be universally recognized," Lenin
is called "an intellectual theoretician bent on the seemingly impossible task of reshaping the civilized world into a federation
of standing committees of workers' deputies," and Tsara is told,
"You are an over-excited little man with a need for self-expression far beyond the scope of your natural gifts." Of course,
these are deliberate travesties of the trio, but within them Stoppard is expressing with uncommon intelligence and humor what
the common man's assessment might justifiably be. The common man's case is most neatly made when Carr, who lay wounded
for five days in no-man's-land during World War I, recalls for
the audience an apocryphal confrontation he had with Joyce. "I
flung at him, 'And what did you do in the Great War?' 'I wrote
Ulysses,' he said. 'What did you do?' ... Bloody nerve!"

While Stoppard recognizes that risking one's life might well be considered more of a commitment to society than comfortably writing a masterpiece in the library, he also offers us the opposite side of a coin he never stops flipping, when he has Joyce say, "An artist is the magician put among men to gratify--capriciously--their urge for immortality. ... What now of the Trojan War if it had been passed over by the artist's touch? A forgotten expedition prompted by Greek merchants looking for new markets. A minor redistribution of broken pots."

The form of the play is complicated. Supposed memories of Joyce, Tsara, and Lenin are related to us in digressive and uncertain retrospect by Carr, who confuses his fabrications with scenes from The Importance of Being Earnest, in which he played. Moreover, his memories frequently run off the track and the scene has to be wound back to the point where it went wild, and restarted. Also spliced into the script are mildly amusing parodies of "Jim Dooley" and of "Mr. Gallagher and Mr. Shean," and a mildly dull historical narration about Lenin that for no apparent reason stops using the same consistently comic capriciousness Stoppard applies elsewhere.

Travesties is flawlessly performed by the Royal Shakespeare Company, led by John Wood, who in my opinion gave last season's best Broadway performance in Sherlock Holmes. As Henry Carr he alternates between a portrait of the non-artist as an old man in a tattered long overcoat and the stunningly contrasted young fashion plate in Wilde's play. The constant shifts in time, and the intricacy of the excursive speeches Stoppard has written for him, would challenge any actor to the utmost, and Wood's mastery of the jocular role is quite a feat. Nevertheless, my admiration for Wood's achievement is bounded, because he seems to be trying to sell the role and the play for more than it is worth. This fault must probably be shared with the playwright and director Peter Wood. Their proud achievement is that they have fashioned an evening in which there is seldom a dull moment, but their ultimate nemesis is that there is seldom a true one either.

HIERONYMUS, Clara Booth Wiggins; (2) Journalist; (3) b. Drew, Miss., July 25, 1913; (4) d. Bruce Charles and Maude (Watson) Wiggins; (5) B.A. Cum laude, U. Tulsa, 1932; Master Social Work, U. Okla. 1936; (6) m. Senator Cleo Hieronymus, April 24, 1937; (7) children--Bruce Lee, Jane (Mrs. David) Piller; (8) Employment Sec. and counselor YWCA, Tulsa, 1936-38; labor market analyst Oklahoma Employment Service, also instr. sociology, U. Tulsa, 1938-50; free-lance writer Nashville Tennessean 1951-56, art and theater critic, home furnishings ed. 1956- ; Book Review radio KFMJ, Tulsa, 1938-1945; public speaker (on art, theatre, books, design, storytelling for children), 1950- ; (10) Bd. dirs. Samaritans Inc. 1967- , pres. 1967-69; bd. dir. Middle Tenn. Chpt. Nat. Arthritis Found., 1967-70; mem. Tenn. Fine Arts Center and Bot. Gardens, 1959- ; mem. adv.

Bd. O'More School of Professional Design, Franklin, Tenn., 1970- ;
(14) Dorothy Dawe Award American Furniture Mart, 1960,63,66,69;
Dallas Market Center Award, 1965; named Woman of the Year Communications, Bus. and Profl. Women's Club, Nashville 1966; citation
by Fisk U. for art crit., Apr. 1974; (15) Mem. panel jurors for selection American children's theaters to perform at Intern. Conf.
U.S.A., 1972; profl. theater critic at ASSITEJ, Int'l. Children's
Theater gen'l. assembly, Albany, N.Y., Feb. 1972.; profl. Theater
critic for American Theater Festival, Region VI, St. Louis, Feb.
1975, and American Theater Festival (National) at John F. Kennedy
Center, Washington, D.C., April, 1975; mem. Am. Soc. of Interior
Designers, Press Assoc.; mem. Nashville Children's Theater; mem.
Women in Communications; (16) Democrat; (17) Methodist; (18) Centennial, Le Petit Salon (Nashville); (20) Free-lance writer on country
music composers and performers with articles in BMI and elsewhere;
contr. Children's Theater Review; author (with Barbara Izard) Requiem for a Nun, On Stage and Off; in progress, book on Tenn.
craftsmen; (21) 2200 Hemingway Dr., Nashville, Tenn. 37215; (22)
The Tennessean, 1100 Broad St. Nashville, Tenn. 37202; (23) Circulation: 220,100; (24) 60-70 plays and musicals, at least 100 other
art forms reviewed.

Toad Hall Revisited
(by Clara Hieronymus, The Tennessean, April 29, 1975)

Cattails seem to grow from watery depths in the Childrens
Theater and rise in splendor above the stage floor. There is a
small row boat waiting at one side of the stage and a sign emphatically proclaiming that Toad Hall is off-limits to intruders.

When the curtain goes up and Toad Hall descends into view
nearly 700 children in the audience quiver with anticipation.
Their excitement, as they view The Wind in the Willows isn't
sustained at that level, unfortunately, though there are moments,
scenes, and bits of business to be savored along the way.

Those who have loved this Kenneth Grahame classic over the
years (when my daughter, now a mother herself, was a kinder-
gartener she proudly announced to the class that it was "the best
book I've ever read!") will not enjoy the smart alecky personality
this staging brings to Toad, nor the bright, slick cartoon style of
the production.

The sets, happily, seem to derive from the water's-edge
world of Howard Pyle's illustrations, and the costumes and make-
up are skillfully and charmingly designed. The latter uses Irene
Corey's techniques to create animal faces with make-up rather
than masks. Since the animals--toad, mole, rat, badger, variou
weasels and the otter mother and child--wear clothes like humans, the costumes suggest the personality and are blessedly
free of "cute" distractions like tails or other anatomical features.

David Kingsley, who is responsible for the costume and make

up designs, plays Toad, with a green moulded head covering and built-out chest. His kinetic green legs seem always either leaping or about to leap.

Jerry Winsett is a plump gray mole (though it isn't clear why his trousers are maroon) who is cheerful and clumsy and prone to bump into his friends, a mole's eyesight not being the best in the world.

Joseph Dunkel's Rat is something of a nervous dandy in plaid suit and big-heeled shoes; Michael Edwards is Badger, with big black and white head, walking cane and patriarchal manner.

The Weasel quartet is presented in the fashion of a slinky, skinny, wiry pack of thieving gypsies, given to stealing and fighting. They are an interesting bunch but it put my teeth on edge to hear them speaking with a cockney accent. Even more irritating is to have the jailer in black eye-patch with a Long John Silver inflection, complete with gutteral "H'r, Har, Har." Why?

Speaking of vocal patterns, the voice level for almost every actor is so similar in pitch and volume that it begins to be tedious, and one wonders if this is necessary.

The plot devolves around the efforts of the animal friends to find Mrs. Otter's son, Portly, with a sub-plot recounting Toad's personal misadventures that land him in jail and find him escaping with the help of the jailer's pretty daughter. He "thumbs" a ride on a charming little red train and makes his way back to his own neighborhood.

Portly, who says not a word throughout the play, is a born scene stealer, straight off the pages of a child's storybook in yellow boots and big-brimmed yellow straw hat with a ribbon streamer. Kenny Cathey played Portly in the cast that I saw; he alternates with Christopher Stevens during the run of the show.

The young audience at the opening performance reacted with obvious enjoyment to the yellow limousine, the clever device of the shadow puppet projection of utility poles and trees indicating the speed of the traveling car, and to the train. They grew restless, talkative and bored during the conversation in rat's office, but they clearly loved the action of the next scene--in Toad Hall--when the weasels get what they deserve--bruises and lumps in a zany duel scene in which sausages ultimately replace foils as weapons.

I'll hope teachers and mothers will read the book itself to these children, and encourage them to read it for themselves. They deserve to know that Toad is as kindly as he is curious, and as wisely philosophical as he is brash.

King Extends Domain
(by Clara Hieronymus, The Tennessean, May 3, 1975)

Anna and the King extended their domain to include every corner of Theater Nashville, which was virtually sold out for Thursday's opening performance, and could no doubt continue to add willing subjects to the citizenry of their musical kingdom all summer, were it possible to hold over that long.

Almost as if to prove once more that community theater can provide splendidly satisfying stage fare, The King and I is handsomely staged, free of self-conscious gestures and "cute" touches, and both absorbingly entertaining and moving.

George Schutt has directed and designed this perennially popular Rodgers and Hammerstein classic of the American musical stage, calling upon other professional talents to work with him in choreography, costuming, and performance.

I had the feeling that, in light of recent Asian turmoil and American focus on the status of women, The King and I was not 25 years old but newly minted as a reflection of 1975 cultural and social changes.

Anna seems very much a woman of today, and the clash of national pride between attitudes of East and West could not be more of the moment.

Anna is elegantly, delicately portrayed by Helen Hudson, her feminine exterior concealing her startlingly strong spirit. I could not always hear Miss Hudson over the orchestra, but admired her ability to stay in character as she sings. She is exquisite in her hoop-skirted costumes, and especially in the pale lilac gown she wears for the gala evening when the King proves to the English representative that he is not a barbarian.

As the King, Phillip Padgett is authoritative, undeniably regal and indeed the "Something Wonderful" his wife sings about. Padgett is a forceful character actor with a stunning stage presence; his change from the arbitrary little dictator to the troubled, introspective and charitable human being is believable and altogether touching. And speaking of regal authority, there is a marvelous moment early in the play which is the essence of memorable theater. It comes when the clutch of charming children is being introduced to the new schoolteacher and it is the turn of the young Prince, the eldest son, to meet Anna.

Dwayne Hood, in this role, enters the room, waiting his turn. There is such a surround of adolescent vulnerability and proud young arrogance that Anna automatically curtsies to this youth, subconsciously recognizing the royal perquisites in his angry stance. Like George Taylor, who plays Anna's son with appealing dignity, Hood had his acting training and experience in

Nashville's Children's Theater.

The famous ballet, "The Small House of Uncle Thomas," is a delight, done by attractive young dancers to choreography by Albertine.   I thought the choral reading technique employed by the wives in this scene extraordinarily pleasing, though I wondered at the capelets they wore over their pretty costumes. (They looked like those small shoulder covers used in hairdressers' shops to protect clothing under the dryers.)

Other small irritations include the fact that when Tuptim's sweetheart sings a love song to her ("We Kiss in a Shadow") he goes to center stage and sings it to the audience, and Lady Thiang, the head wife who sings the lovely "Something Wonderful," pitches it to the audience, concert-fashion, instead of to Anna to whom it is addressed.

These are all alterable, and even forgiveable, though in a production with so much going for it they ought not to be present. I should not neglect to commend Elaine Ganick as the sweet-voiced Tuptim, and Kay Carter as the lady-like, elegantly slender Lady Thiang.

HIRSCH, Samuel; (2) Critic at Large; (3) b. Trenton, N.J. , June 23, 1917; (4) s. of Albert and Anna (Fine) Hirsch; (5) B.A. 1947, M.A. 1949, U. of North Carolina, major subject: drama; Graduate of Neighborhood Playhouse School of Theater under Sanford Meisner, N.Y.C. (1939-41); (6) m. Rose R. Rabstein, Jan. 18, 1945; (7) children-- Ellen Gail, Martha Dale, Robin Eric; (8) Instructor, University of North Carolina, 1947-49; Ass't Prof. of Drama, University of Miami, 1949-53; Sam Hirsch School of Drama, 1954-58; Department Chairman (Acting & Directing), Boston University, 1959-66; Producer for "Stage Five Players", WHDH-TV, Channel 5, 1959-62; Theater and Arts Critic, WHDH-TV, 1966-72; Drama Critic and Arts Editor, Boston Herald Traveler, 1966-72; Lecturer and speaker, 1966-72; WTVJ, Critic-at-Large, 1973; Ass't to the President, Miami Philharmonic, 1973-74, 1975; Freelance Writer, 1974; (9) Professional Actor with Paul Green's Lost Colony; T.V. credits include U.S. Steel Hour, Edge of Night, 1958-59.   Producer/Director with following Actor's Equity companies: Casablanca Playhouse, Miami Beach, 1953; Biltmore Playhouse, Miami, 1953-54; Roosevelt Playhouse, Miami Beach, 1955; Musicomedy Festival, Miami, 1957; "Can-Can" Tour of South, 1957; "The Wizard of Oz" Ft. Lauderdale and Miami, 1957.   Managing Director, Falmouth Playhouse, 1961; Director, Hotel Bostonian, Boston, 1962; Resident Director, Berkshire Playhouse, Stockbridge, Mass, 1963; Artistic Director, Herald Traveler Repertory of Classical Drama, 1965-1972; (10) President and Member of Advisory Council, Boston Friends of Israel Arts, 1972-73; (15) Actor's Equity; Screen Actor's Guild; President, New England Theatre Conference, 1963-66; AFTRA; American National Theater and Academy, 1964; Outer Critic's Circle, 1967- on-going; (17) Jewish; (20) Articles: Journal of Social Issues, New England Theatre Conference Newsletter,

Art of Speaking, Boston Arts Magazine, Boston Magazine, Theatre 5, Boston Herald Traveler; (21) 711 Tiziano Ave., Coral Gables, Fla. 33143; Ph, 305-661-4757; (22) WTVJ-TV, 316 N. Miami Ave., Miami, Fla. 33128; Ph. 305-377-8241; (23) Circulation: 800,000; (24) 150-200 film, theater, art, opera, ballet, club act, book reviews.

Waiting for Godot
(by Samuel Hirsch, Boston Herald Traveler, April 12, 1968)

Samuel Beckett calls "Waiting for Godot" "a tragicomedy in two acts." It is a metaphor of man's fate, a serious play rife with derisive laughter, a profoundly original masterpiece, an elegy and a dramatic poem celebrating extreme hope and despair in our century.

Not since Henrik Ibsen wrote "A Doll's House" has a single play had such profound influence on drama. From its premiere production in Paris, January 5, 1963, it has puzzled, provoked and inspired audiences and theater people. Playwrights Harold Pinter and Edward Albee openly admit their debt to Beckett, and directors have staged plays in the style of his bleak world--as Peter Brook did in his version of Shakespeare's "King Lear," starring Paul Scofield.

Mystery exists at the heart of the play. Its meaning eludes easy answers and its overlapping hints only serve to increase the mystery. Story, plot--even character development--exist in a vacuum. There is no story. The action is passive, everything is circular, repetitive. Time passes. We watch it pass and the four major characters help it pass by occupying themselves with conversation, with games, with verbal encounters.

When the play ends we know it will begin as it began before, a ritual of repetition doomed to endless circling.

"Nothing happens," says Gogo, one of the two tramps who've come to a country road near a tree one evening--to wait for Godot, as they've been instructed. "Nobody comes, nobody goes. It's awful."

The play can be staged on various levels: as a vaudeville entertainment, as an unbridled circus entertainment--or, as in the case of Harold Scott's production currently concluding in repertory as part of a three-play season of the Harvard Summer School Repertory Theater at the Loeb Drama Center, it can be done as a serious psychological study of segments of our society.

Gogo, the forgetful one, the sleeper, always hungry, continuously obsessed with his physical comfort, despairing and querulous, is characterized as a Jew by Scott. Didi, his protector, a philosophizer and pessimist, suspicious and volatile, is a black man--an Uncle Tom type.

Lucky, the emaciated slave, is presented in this concept as

an Indian and Pozzo, his cruel, despotic master, is a portly white, Anglo-Saxon Protestant. The young boy, a shepherd who brings messages from Mr. Godot, is a Puerto Rican.

Thus, Beckett's abstract figures on a universal landscape are given deliberately strictured identities, and what was intended as a free metaphor takes on psychological over-tones that turn images of mankind into ideological stereotypes.

Whatever values Scott may have gained in this deliberate superimposition of ideas on archetypes are negated by his self-conscious casting. His Jew is hampered by frequent cries of "Oiy Vey," cliche utterances often used by virulent anti-Semites to brand an entire religious group. His black man shuffles and blinks, is afraid of pain and speaks with a Southern accent. His Indian wears a feather in his hair and a buckskin suit. The swarthy Puerto Rican boy speaks with an accent, and in both scenes in which he appears there's romantic Spanish guitar music playing behind his speech like musak.

Despite these directorial affectations (or are they indulgences?), the intellectual excitement of the play is undiminished. We're prodded to search for meanings within meanings. Dark, cryptic dialogue jumps out at us--and for a quick moment--reveals gloomy, partial answers.

While Didi sleeps, Gogo stands watch and worries. Like Hamlet, he broods and he wonders about the meaning of life and death. "Astride of a grave and a difficult birth," he grumbles. "Down in the hole, lingeringly, the gravedigger puts on the forceps. We have time to grow old. The air is full of our cries. (He listens.) But habit is a great deadener. (He looks at Didi.) At me too someone is looking, of me too someone is saying, He is sleeping, he knows nothing, let him sleep on. (Pause.) I can't go on! (Pause.) What have I said?"

Performances in this somber, sad and essentially humorless production, are generally competent. Roger Robinson is a nervous Didi, tense, high-strung, neurotic; his worried eyes are knotted in perpetual pain. Leland Moss is a soft and feminine Gogo, loose and ineffectual. He pouts and grimaces and manages to smother most of the comedy in his role.

The two most completely realized characters are George Sheanshang as Lucky and George Ede as Pozzo. Ede is an imposing actor, sadistic, maniacal, yet basically pitiful in his desperate need for power. Sheanshang is boneless and limp as the pack-horse slave, leaning against the rope around his neck like a worn-out scarecrow. His one speech, a masterpiece of metaphysical gabble and stream-of-conscious double-talk, is a litany of hopeless despair and his dance of thought is a pantomime of death.

Scott's use of the Loeb stage space is most remarkable. He opens the proscenium, combining the stage and the auditorium floor on one vast level, and seats the audience on three sides. The actors are made to look small and remote, heightening the sense of isolation embodied by the play.

An island in the center of the stage is created by designer C. Friedrich Oberle to look like the carcass of a giant dinosaur. An ancient rock, its flanks polished by wind, sun and rain, crouches like a square-backed turtle, and the one tree stands gaunt and tubular against a dead, grey sky. When the moon rises, it is splashed against the flat firmament and oozes into blackness.

The wonder is that "Waiting for Godot," no matter in what manner it is staged, despite any warping of its intention by a director's arbitrary concept, still breathes its own stubborn life. Unique, evocative, elusive, puzzling, as insoluble as its author, the terse tragicomedy is positively futile, ending not with a wimper but watchful waiting.

"The Dybbuk," "Equus" and "Born Yesterday"
(by Sam Hirsch, over WTVJ radio, Boston, May 19, 1975)

At season's end, there are three important plays on local stages. That's impressive, I think. Foremost drama is "Equus" at the Coconut Grove Playhouse. It's also playing Broadway and London, which makes a big coup for producer Bob Fishko ... and a first for Miami. Another impressive drama opened Saturday at Ruth Foreman's North Miami Playhouse.... The 55-year-old "The Dybbuk" by Yiddish playwright S. Ansky. They've simplified the romatic tragedy ... and given it a happy ending. Yet the sad story about the vengeful Dybbuk ... or spirit ... of the man who loved her possessing the body of a young bride ... and its exorcism by the chief Rabbi ... still has power to hold an audience transfixed. Arron Heyman's majestic as the Rabbi and Michael Pasternak plays the scholar-dybbuk with frenzied fervor. For balance ... and another happy ending ... there's Garson Kanin's "Born Yesterday" at the science museum. Funny and relevant, it has pert Wendy Dillon and portly Don Stout in the leads. So you see, live theater flourishes far from Broadway. See for yourself. I'm Sam Hirsch, your critic at large.

HODENFIELD, Jan, New York Post, 210 South Street, N.Y., N.Y. 10002, Ph. 212-349-5000.

HOFFMAN, William Lea; (2) Theater Critic, Arts/Entertainment Editor; (3) b. Ancon, Panama Canal Zone, May 10, 1943; (5) B.A. Eastern New Mexico U., English, American Studies 1969; (8) Critic, editorial page editor, Santa Fe New Mexican 1970-72; critic, Arts/ Entertainment editor, Albuquerque Journal 1972- ; (9) acting, technician

USO Theater Tour (Europe) 1964; two plays in ms.; opera chorus,
Albuquerque 1973-76; (12) co-editor, Eastern New Mexico Univ. literary magazine 1968-70; chairman, Eastern New Mexico Univ. Cultural
Affairs Council 1968-70; (13) Sgt., U.S. Army Europe 1963-66; (14)
First places: community services, editorial writing, New Mexico
Press Assn. 1971; (21) 9901 Leyendecker NE, Albuquerque, N.M.
87112; (22) Albuquerque Journal, P.O. Drawer J. Albuquerque, N.M.
87103, Ph. 505-842-2343; (23) Circulation: 110,000; (24) 20 plays
and musicals; 20 concerts; 20 films, dance, mime, visual arts.

Tennessee Williams
(by Will Hoffman, Albuquerque Journal, ca. 1970's)

Corrales Adobe Theatre's current production starts off like
a good many other local theater productions: It's a domestic setting with lots of jokes. But, two-and-a-half hours later, things
are much different. The oneliners modulate into cynical and ultimately destructive barbs. Reality and fantasy overlap into dis-
sonance. Simple domestic encounters in the kitchen and bedroom
crescendo into psychological--and real--stripteases.

It's the world of Tennesse Williams's "A Streetcar Named
Desire" and on the stage at the old San Ysidro Church, it all
hangs out. Every expression, line, gesture and nuance are uncovered, especially the brutal ones.

Director Louise Laval has wrought a sharply etched interpretation, most notably in the principal casting. JoAnn Muchmore
rightfully dominates the action as the fading Southern belle, Blanche
DuBois. She ranges across the emotional spectrum with lithe
facility yet bravura. Terrie Kreideweis seems rather too superficial as sister Stella. The men, on the other hand, seem a shade
too visceral. Bruce Katrcher as Stanley Kowalski almost gets
down on all fours to prove how animalistic he is. Manny Smith
as Mitch becomes a little too overbearing as Blanche's beau.

This generally "up-front" approach, welcome as it is, gets
slightly out of hand with the sporadic intrusions of the peripheral
characters, mostly neighbors. Rather than complementing or
heightening the growing domestic tension, these episodes seem
mostly sprawling hysteria.

Still, "A Streetcar Named Desire" is a powerful dramatic
sledgehammer, well worth the experience. And in the hands of
Corrales Adobe Theatre, it strikes loud and hard if a bit awkwardly.

"The Crucible": Severe Tests Stunningly Met
(by Will Hoffman, Albuquerque Journal, January 24, 1976)

As its title implies, Arthur Miller's historical drama, "The
Crucible" is a severe test; in fact, several severe tests.

All are stunningly realized in Albuquerque Classics Theatre's Bicentennial production tonight at 8:15 and closing Sunday at 2:15 p. m. in Popejoy Hall, UNM Fine Arts Center.

As contemporary drama, this play of thought and word is a masterpiece; as loose historical realization, it is a powerful, grisly chronicle; interpretively, CTC fully exploits this powerful drama in much of its best (and a little of its worst) work to date.

Like other profound 20th century dramatic masterpieces-- Miller's "Death of a Salesman," O'Neill's "Iceman Cometh" and Brecht's "Mother Courage"--"The Crucible" is a moving, gripping moral odyssey in which redemption and condemnation are fused. It's strong stuff but deeply moving and indelible.

Based on the Salem witch trials of 1692 and with contemporary overtones of the McCarthy era in which it was written, the just-under three-hour drama begins firmly rooted in history as the witch hysteria gathers force. But like other black chapters in American history (war atrocities, the Donner Party cannibalism and the McCarthy era), it demands intensive examination, unforgettably realized through dramatic and poetic license.

The characters and court proceedings are based on fact; Miller's lasting achievement is the weaving of profound characterizations with made-up real life dilemmas such as John Proctor's adultery to produce that malevolent psychological condition of mass-hysteria which can happen anywhere, anytime, forcing each to wrestle with the seemingly opposing forces of individual and collective responsibility.

Guest director Herschel Zohn, who has made "The Crucible" one of his signature pieces, elicits a powerful if sometimes hyperbolic realization, easily accepted in a script which demands intensive mutual reinforcment between dramatic vehicle and cast.

In one respect, the evening is a struggle and triumph over excesses; melodramatic shouting, pregnant pauses, dialog overlaps and needless gestures. As the drama takes shape, however, as the dilemmas and characters are defined, one forgets that the stage is make believe.

Backed by strong but unobtrusive stage movement and Ken Guthrie's stark, angular, framed set, the tragedy unwinds and all are caught in its path.

The large cast of 21 has no clinkers although there seems to be some inconsistency among too many characterizations which range from evocation to theatrics.

Mary Ann Smith as Elizabeth Proctor and Charles Driscoll as Judge Danforth are utterly wonderous and top-notch throughout. Achieving the same level are Patricia Springer as Abigail

Williams and Dane Hannum as John Hale.

In lesser roles but with equivalent skills are Katrina Person as Tituba, Linda Bergman as Rebecca Nurse, Bill Carstens as Giles Corey and Sharon McConnell as Sarah Good.

The others are sometimes plagued by excesses but all achieve poignant scenes.

As for Bruce Hawkinson as John Proctor, his is the one dominating, virtuoso, essential role. He has all the skills and often scales the heights. He tries too hard to be the pillar, the pivot; his crucial modulations and tempo shifts seem to lag and need more interaction.

For those who wait for Albuquerque's renaissance of serious theater-going, the time, again, is at hand. Productions like Classics Theatre's deserve a permanent and wide following.

HOGAN, William, San Francisco Chronicle, 905 Mission St., San Francisco, Cal. 94119.

HOLLOWAY, Anthony "Tony"; (2) Theater reviewer and Culture Editor; (3) b. Bloomington, Ill., July 2, 1922; (4) s. W. Rupert and Constance Gould Holloway; (5) B.A. University of Wichita, Kan., major subject: journalism; (6) m. Jessie Anne Croft, Sept. 9, 1946; she died December, 1954; m. Sara Rude, April 16, 1955; (7) children--Linda Kay and Dianne Kathleen and step-daughter, Nancy Gudlaugsson; Dianne died Aug. 19, 1955; (8) News Editor, Sedan, Kans., Times, 1949-51; Pryor, Okla. Times, News Editor, 1951-55; Bloomingon, Ill. Daily Pantagraph, 1955- ; (9) Active in Bloomington-Normal Community Players since 1957 as actor (14 plays), director (7 plays), executive board, president of board 1974-76; also active as actor with Conklin Players, dinner-theater group in B-N-; (10) Former member SPEBSQSA, Bloomington Chapter; former Lions Club member in Pryor, Okla. Served as president Unitarian Church Board; twice was president of Bloomington Pantagraphers Federal Credit Union; (13) U.S. Marines 1942-46, served in South Pacific; (16) Democrat; (17) Unitarian; (21) 1702 Hoover Dr., Normal, Ill. 61761, Ph. 452-2706; (22) Daily Pantagraph, Ph. 829-9411; zip code 61701; (23) Circulation: excess of 50,000; (24) 50-75 plays and musicals and miscellaneous.

"Cuckoo": Cast is "Professional"
(by Tony Holloway, Daily Pantagraph, November 15, 1974)

"One Flew Over the Cuckoo's Nest" just may be one of the best things done in many years by the Illinois State University Department of Theatre--and a fellow by the name of John Welsh has to be one of the most talented actors ever seen on the Westhoff Theatre stage.

The play by Dale Wasserman, which opened Thursday night, was superbly done by a cast that was remarkably well directed by Dr. Calvin Pritner.

The running time was two and a half hours, but I was so engrossed by the tremendous characterizations that the time fairly flew by and I was actually sorry to see the production end. I can't think of any play that I've seen recently that so completely held my attention.

If you think I'm exaggerating the great impact of the Wasserman play, I only can advise that you see it and judge for yourself.

One may be hard put to imagine that a play that deals with patients in a mental hospital can be really classified as "fun" entertainment. And yet, despite the subject matter, "One Flew Over the Cuckoo's Nest" was entertaining because it was done in such a professional manner that each character was not an actor on a stage--but a patient, a nurse or an attendant in a mental institution. The acting was that believable.

The plot deals with Randle P. McMurphy, a maverick who feigns mental illness to escape the drudgery of a work camp. McMurphy attempts to stir other patients in his ward to rebellion against the tyrannical Ratched, the head nurse on the ward. How well McMurphy succeeds is revealed in the final scene, which may come as a shock. I therefore decline to reveal the ending.

Despite the theme, most of the play is done in a comic vein. It is not depressing, although there is tension and stark drama in some scenes. It is not a play for children. Some of the language is raunchy and even may offend playgoers who want nothing but sweetness and light in their stage entertainment.

But no matter what the plot of a play is or how well or poorly it's written ("Cuckoo" is well written), in the final analysis it's the acting that counts--and in this respect Pritner and company should be mighty proud of their efforts.

Welsh is an actor who knows exactly what to do at every moment. His timing, his body movements and facial expressions are a director's delight. He is a tremendous asset to the ISU Department of Theatre. If "best performance" awards were given at season's end, he certainly would be a prime contender for the top honor.

Welsh is surrounded by a cast of top-notch supporting actors, not one of whom during the course of the evening, got out of character for a single moment. Even the two or three "patients" who had no lines to speak never once lost contact with what was going on about them. This is acting at its finest.

I could mention each of the 22 cast members by name and praise them all, but some, by virtue of having larger parts than others, stood out. There is Cyndi Adcock as Ratched, the nurse whose only motive in life seems to be to make others subservient to her and who will go to any lengths to beat down McMurphy; Doug O'Brien as Chief Bromden, the Indian who believes he is a nobody in a world that is alien to him; Thom Krueger as Harding, the intellect who is physically and emotionally unable to cope with life outside the institution; Terry Kinney as Billy, the stuttering virgin so dominated by his mother that he has completely lost confidence in himself; Terry Clark as Scanlon, who derives some sort of contentment in his sole possession, a supposed homemade bomb.

The nearly all white set, the multi-colored lighting between set changes, the eerie music--all enhance the overall effectiveness of the production.

"Long Day's Journey": ISU Play a Beautiful Job
(by Tony Holloway, Daily Pantagraph, February 21, 1975)

When the Illinois State University theater department staged "One Flew Over the Cuckoo's Nest" last November it, in my opinion, reached the top of the hill in a theatrical production.

And Thursday night in Westhoff Theatre another production joined "Cuckoo" at the top of that hill.

It was the superbly done "Long Day's Journey into Night" by Eugene O'Neill. What a beautiful job director Ralph L. Lane and his five-member cast did with the three-hour starkly realistic drama concerning O'Neill's own family.

While "Cuckoo" depicted a serious subject (life in a mental institution) in a light vein, "Long Day's Journey" was played with the seriousness that O'Neill must have intended in telling of one day's unhappiness and despair of the O'Neill family. In the play the name Tyrone is used.

The characters are James, the father, a famous actor whose miserliness has a telling effect on the health and welfare of his wife and two sons; Mary, his wife, a drug addict; Jamie, the eldest son who is an alcoholic, and Edmund, the youngest son, suffering from consumption. The fifth character is Cathleen, the slovenly maid and apparently the only sane member of the household.

Although the play has a plot, the drama is really a character study of each of the four members of the Tyrone family and the inability of each to cope with life's problems.

Ordinarily, three hours of dialogue (interrupted only by two short intermissions) would be intolerably long, especially when

the dialogue is of a depressing nature. But so expert are Lane's
charges in their roles, so intense do they become in their depic-
tions and so flawless are they in line delivery that I, for one,
was held spellbound by the sheer perfection of the entire production.

To say that one scene stood out above any other would be an
injustice. The play had an evenness about it--never once faltering.
Each of the five actors was in complete control at all times.
This takes stamina, deep concentration and remarkable memorization.

The cast? Director Lane couldn't have picked a better one.
I could rave on and on over their performances. But needless
to say, each person played exceedingly well against the others.
It was a closely knit, well disciplined quintet.

Leonhard W. Huber as James; Catherine A. Paxton as Mary;
Robert L. Maxey as Jamie; Michael A. Connolly as Edmund; and
Rebecca J. Arensman as Cathleen proved that with a good script,
good direction, an attractive set and many hours of hard work,
a drama such as "Long Day's Journey" can be a vibrant, exciting
evening in the theater.

HOLMES, Ann Hitchcock; (2) fine arts editor, theater, arts critic;
(3) b. El Paso, Tex., April 25, 1922; (4) d. Frederick E. and Joy
(Crutchfield) H.; (5) Whitworth College, Brookhaven, Miss., drama
scholarship; Southern College of Fine Arts Houston, music history,
theory, etc.; private study Georges Bridges studio, Birmingham,
Ala., sculpture; (6) single; (8) Fine Arts Editor, Houston (Tex.)
Chronicle, critic of theater, music, art and related arts 1948- ; assistant fine arts editor 1947-48; general news reporter 1943-47; (10)
Original member, City of Houston Arts Commission, 1967-74 (resigned); member, University of Texas Fine Arts Advisory Council,
1968- ; (14) recipient Ogden Reid Foundation (NY) grant for observation of the arts, their support and practice in 13 European countries,
1953; John Simon Guggenheim Fellow, grant providing for study of
theater, music and art in practice in America, 1961-62; Ford Foundation grant in the Criticism Program providing for behind scenes observation of major American theater directors at work, 1967; intensive attendance at theater and opera performances in West Germany
at invitation of West German government, 1968; winner of John G.
Flowers Memorial Award for outstanding architectural commentary,
given by Texas Society of Architects 1972 and 1974. (15) Member
American Theater Critics Assn., Music Critics Assn., and Dance
Critics Assn.; (17) Episcopalian; (19) Houston Yacht Club; (20) Thirteen half-hour shows "Expedition Houston" for ABC affiliate in Houston KTRK-TV; one hour TV show "The Man on the Moon" for KTRK-
TV; half hour show "Festival of the Bible in the Arts" for KTRK-TV;
half hour show about Alley Theater, Houston for KTRK-TV all from
1962-65; commissioned to write brochures for opening of Jesse H.
Jones Hall for the Performing Arts by donor of Hall; for arts in the

city's history by Houston Chamber of Commerce and a brochure to
launch Combined Arts Corporate Campaign, 1965-74; articles in New
York Times, Baltimore Sun, Art in American and Opera News; (21)
10807 Beinhorn Road, Houston, Tex. , 77024, Ph. 713-468-5803; (22)
Houston Chronicle, 801 Texas Ave. , Houston 77002, Ph. 713-220-
7670; (23) Circulation: 369,288; (24) 30 plays, 30 dance events, 30
symphonies, 12 operas, 20 art-architecture reviews, 4 film.

The Musical Show
(by Ann Holmes, Houston Chronicle, January 5, 1975)

With the national company of "Irene" headed this way for
seven performances this week, and with our local production of
"Promises, Promises" by Theater Under the Stars a huge success of last week, a question nags at us.

What is going on with our great American theatrical form,
the musical show?

It's changing in character and scale. Its fortunes hang, insecure.

If we can say without pursing a lip that jazz and soul and big
opulent musical shows are the American Bag, then why is it that
the National Endowment for the Arts which parcels out taxpayer
money to important cultural activities has none at all for the survival of musical theater of this kind?

We have the paradox of a stage form developed and perfected
in America, adored and copied (badly) by other nations, reaching
a new crisis point by being as good and popular as they have been.
What this says is that one tends to think of musicals as being as
commercial as popcorn--and thus needing no help.

But musical shows are in financial trouble time and again.

Syndicates back important new properties for Broadway, casting hopefully with prime talents who were successful in previous
shows. Riding on the long chance that the show catches on, they
more often see their money lost in a few performances.

In his revealing new book "Contradictions," producer Hal
Prince, one of Broadway's most successful and creative figures,
tells about his production of "Follies." It cost $800,000 to pro-
duce. It lost $685,000. There were 50 in the cast, 30 in the
orchestra and 28 backstage crew. "Follies" cost $80,000 a
week to break even and, at capacity, would have required 40
weeks to pay off the investment. But, as he points out, "Follies," which got sensational reviews, wasn't all that popular and
capacity didn't happen that often. "Follies" won seven Tony
Awards and turned in grosses as high as $91,000. But the box-
office pendulum fluctuated wildly--some weeks as low as $31,000,
other weeks tipping about $90,000.

Prince notes he's happy he did "Follies" but could never again in conscience go out for the money.

Musicals may be snubbed by serious theater lovers who prefer the spoken drama. But one can feel differently about them when they become an endangered species. You may not want to sing a duet with a whooping crane but you'd hate to see it head for the exit and never return.

"Follies" best moment is set in the shell of a theater about to fall under the wrecker's ball and brings back to the stage those long-stemmed follies girls, some of them the real article, and at its opening, Harvard Crimson hailed the show as a musical about the death of musicals, a more acute observation than may have been intended.

When "Irene" arrives this week with Jane Powell, it comes with what we understand is to be the full panoply you can expect from a "national company" with top stars, the full stage settings and a long-enough run to make the set-up worthwhile.

Productions of this caliber are becoming fewer and fewer. "Pippin" due here Feb. 15, 16 for two performances and "The Sunshine Boys" on Feb. 21, 23 for three performances, are "bus and truck" companies, capable of erecting their stage scenery quickly and moving out again to the next stop, and are usually less elaborate.

We should feel glad enough for the appearance of any musical, though nobody is planning to leave their fully sharpened critical judgments at home. But the complications these days of booking a major musical through the enormous reaches of America are discouraging.

Art Squires of the Foley's Southwest Concerts enterprise, when asked if he'd bring Colleen Dewhurst, and Walter Matthau from Los Angeles on tour with O'Casey's screenplay "Juno and the Paycock" (hardly a musical of course) said "I'd be ready, but we'd have to build a tour path to Houston and out of it."

The adventures of the recent musical "Mack and Mabel" which closed in early December after some 60 performances have provided a horrendous lesson. Apparently all musical theater producers are alert to it, too.

Frank Young of Theater Under the Stars thinks, as do others, "Mack and Mabel" may well have been the last of the big time musical shows that characterized what might be called the "Kismet" era.

The more successful policy is the musical geared close to a story and a star, for instance "A Little Night Music" based on an Ingmar Bergman film and "Promises, Promises" using

John O'Hara's "Apartment" as a basis.   In both cases big choruses are out.

As long as there is breath in Art Squires there is at least
hope of seeing touring musicals in Houston.   He is a member
of a syndicate of producers which has tried to interest stars like
Ingrid Bergman or George C. Scott in certain vehicles and then
to provide, for them, a tour route of cities through which they
could move.   This is the reverse of the long-time system we
have known.

So many musicals bite the tarnished Broadway dust that those
which might have shipped out in national or other companies are
not doing so.   The supply of touring shows is drying up.

Part of the killing cost of musicals in New York is bound
up in union demands.   Featherbedding is not unusual.

Since the practicality of presenting musicals is not in question, can we assume that the American people are, in fact, tired
of them?

Squires has no records to suggest this.   In fact his company
for "Irene," due to have arrived here today after a stand in Denver, has put it off a day in order to add more performances
there where the show has played to SRO crowds.

And Theater Under the Stars, the city's only full-scale musical theater group, has so much success it hardly knows what to
do.   Even so, it can't make ends meet.

Its last week's production of "Promises, Promises" has already been fully reviewed, but one can safely add that hardly
ever has the Music Hall stage been so professionally set.   Its
scenery was manipulated with professional skill, some sets moving into the wings as others flew down from the fly loft in admirable precision.   The company was first rate from the principals
Will MacKenzie (star material anywhere), Ann Cope and Jay
Stuart, to local specialist like Charles Krohn and Che Knight in
highly turned character roles.   The frenzied pitch is something
that might nicely have toned down in time, but here is a product
any theater could be proud of and audiences were virtually sell-
outs except for one matinee, Young said.

Season-ticket sales were 160 per cent above last year at
Theater Under the Stars--which has both free events in Miller
Theater in the park and a more formal winter season in the Mu-
sic Hall.

This season TUTS has staged "Camelot," "Promises Promises" and has "The King and I" coming up.   A questionnaire
filled in by patrons indicated that showgoers wanted TUTS to
add a fourth production in Music Hall next season, and nine out

of 10 said they would support them.

Last summer's "Oliver" in Miller Theater was such a TUTS success that one night 160,000 people attended, by park officers' estimates. The same production stimulated Kennedy Center to invite TUTS to collaborate on a new production of "The Odyssey" --with Yul Brynner--written about elsewere in this magazine. No dates were available for the venture in Houston's theaters.

Now, a new project may be forming up, but nothing was ready for announcement yet.

While such touring shows as "Irene" are major commercial attractions, TUTS is a nonprofit organization supported by Houston Endowment and the Moody Foundation which helped breach the chasm between earnings and production costs in its first two Music Hall seasons. Those grants end after this year.

What all these strands finally plait is a complex and tenuous existence for the unique art form of the American Musical-- whether the commercial item or the revived non-profit one.

Economic exigencies are forcing it to shrink in scale and to alter its character.

Its glamor is not unlike that of opera, in that people still want to see larger-than-life situations on a beautifully set stage with music.

Though I have personally felt many musicals were boring, redundant and downright silly, others obviously are bound firmly into our culture and contain rooted landmark occurences. "Oklahoma," "My Fair Lady," "West Side Story," "Cabaret," "Raisin"--all have superb reasons for being--as have others.

They are intrinsic to our American 20th century and they have pointed the way to the renaissance of opera in America. That they continue to attract audiences in such numbers proves something--if not about the theater, then about the need of people to extend their life styles or ease their burdens.

The support of the National Endowment ought to come along for the nonprofit institutions that are now attempting to place into firm American context the best works of our own musical-theatrical genius.

Meanwhile we may consider ourselves blessed to be receiving this week a national company playing "Irene" and to have seen the solid success of a local company in "Promises, Promises." Whatever the critical verdict of any of them, the survival has become remarkable and we are fortunate to experience examples of an American art form, which may be forced to change drastically if not vanish.

Scott Joplin Opera "Treemonisha" Exciting
(by Ann Holmes, Houston Chronicle, May 24, 1975)

Scott Joplin's opera "Treemonisha" got off to a slow start in
its Houston Grand Opera production in Hermann Park Friday
night.   But ironically by the time it had reached its finale in the
"Real Slow Drag," Miller Theater was ablaze with excitement.

The rare opera composed in 1911 and never before seen in
a fully professional production is being offered in seven perfor-
mances--free--in Hermann Park's al fresco stage, by Houston
Grand Opera as its Spring Festival offering.

The Joplin opera is not a ragtime work but indeed does break
into the 2/4 time with that steady bass beat and rattly syncopated
treble here and there.

And though some parts of this three-act opera about blacks
near Texarkana shortly after the Civil War is humdrum music,
there is a joyous open hearted melodic thrust to the show.

Though the blend of fairly harmonious European style music
and Joplin's own wonderfully vigorous and expressive ragged
writing makes for an uneven product, Gunther Schuller made a
beautifully integrated thing of it in his special orchestration for
this production.   And Schuller's conducting was marvelously supportive and responsive.

If we may quibble about the lack of finesse or even originality in the score, we miss the point.   It had freshness, high energy, an engaging naivete, even unexpected snatches of humor.

But above all else, Houston Grand Opera's "Treemonisha"
had a superb cast, a stunning production altogether, and three
absolutely show stopping numbers: The circle dance--"We're
Goin Around," early in act one; the rousing "Aunt Dinah Has
Blowed de Horn" that rings down the second act on shouts of
pleasure from the audience; and that superbly elegant "Real
Slow Drag" at the final curtain.

With the enormous company stretched out across the wide
stage carrying out Joplin's own special dance instructions--with
lyrical assist from the gifted choreographer Louis Johnson of
Washington D.C.--the emotional temperature built to the boiling
point.   It was a sensational finale that brought the whole company
back for a repeat of high kicking "Aunt Dinah" choreography.

In a richly gifted cast--all black--the young beauty Carmen
Balthrop of the cropped hair and the polished high cheekbones
as Treemonisha was clearly the standout.   Winner of this year's
Metropolitan Opera Auditions, Balthrop, who had been signed for
this role previously, sings like some sleek young divinity.   Her
voice is clear, steady--perhaps not big--but beautifully on center,

the production apparently easy. She is handsomely unmannered but modest and her long striding walk is attractive and refreshing.

Curtis Rayam's Remus, opposite her, was warm and sure and his manner just right as he saved the girl from the conjurers who had kidnapped her. Betty Allen, despite a sometimes intrusive vibrato, was a credible maternal figure as Monisha while Willard White's Ned was suitably gentle and encouraging in round bass tones. As Zodzetrick, the old con man conjurer, Avon Long was an amusing caricature while Donnie Ray Albert as Parson Alltalk and Darceal Duckens holding forth in the conjurer's camp offered mellow moments.

The somewhat simplistic libretto, Joplin's own, may not be a model of late day sophistication but it is a true period piece coming right out of the black composer's remarkable striving for growth. Frank Corasaro in directing and shaping the piece, has made a fine, stage success with it; Franco Colavecchia's decor is marvelously original, simple, workable and witty. The Johnson choreography is direct, unstrained and irresistible.

Prairie View A & M Chorus often filled that big stage with Joplin's excited and effective choral song, and altogether, this "Treemonisha" is a tonic show, a great delight bursting with talent. That the $140,000 spectacle is free is hard to believe.

HOWARD, Edwin; (2) Amusements Editor, Drama Critic, Memphis Press-Scimitar; Film and Drama Critic, WMC-TV; (3) b. Grand Island, Fla., July 26, 1924; (4) s. J. Zollie and Jessie (Magill) Howard; (5) Attended Southwestern-at-Memphis, Maj: English Lit., Philosophy, Languages; (6) m. Olivia LeMaster, July 11, 1946; div. May 15, 1975; (7) children--Meg, Heather; (8) Copy boy, Memphis Press-Scimitar, Aug. 1, 1942; reporter, Oct. 1942; Combat correspondent, 6th Armored Infantry Regiment, Italian campaign, May 1944-June 1945; co-founder-editor, 1st Armored Division Warrior, Italy and Germany, July 1945-December 1945; radio news writer, Associated Press, Memphis, Feb. '46-Sept. '46; amusements editor-drama critic, Memphis Press-Scimitar, Sept. '46 to date; film and drama critic, WMC-TV, Sept. '69 to date; guest commentator, WMC-TV, Jan. '73 to date; contrib. editor, The Delta Review, 1964-69; (9) Co-founder, member of board, Memphis Shakespeare Festival, 1950-65; (13) Pvt. 6th Armored Inf. Regt., Jan. '44; T/4, Hq., 1st Arm'd Div., Sept. '44; hon. dischge., Dec. '45; (14) Combat Infantry Badge, four battle stars, 1944-45; Boyd Martin Motion Picture Page Award, 1964, for Outstanding M. P. Pg. in the U.S. (circ. 100,000 to 250,000), given by Mot. Pic. Assn. of America; (16) Independent; (17) Presbyterian; (19) Wolf River Society; (20) Cont. articles to Theater Arts, Film Producers Journal, Photoplay, Movie Life, Modern Screen, Motion Picture, Theater Today and others; (21) 154 N. Cooper, Apt. 3, Memphis, Tenn., 38104, Ph. 901-725-4216; (22) Memphis Press-Scimitar, 495 Union Ave., Memphis, Tenn. 38101; (23) Circulation:

135,000 (Newspaper circ.); television--93,000 households; (24) 50
plays, 150 movies, (newspaper); 35 plays, 100 movies, 10 opera, 5
ballet, (television).

Rich Talent Matures in "Bernhardt"
(by Edwin Howard, Press Scimitar, January 21, 1975)

Four years ago, a talented young Memphis actress went to
Paris to study mime with Marcel Marceau. Last night, for the
first time since her year with Marceau and since winning the
Scotsman Award with her one-woman show at the Edinburgh Festival, she appeared on a Memphis stage, and lo! the talented
young actress had become an extraordinary artist.

"Stephanie Rich as 'Sarah Bernhardt,'" which played to an
enthusiastic sold-out audience in the Little Theater's Pink Palace
Playhouse last night and will be repeated there next Monday night,
is a remarkable evocation of the great French actress of the 19th
century at a crucial time in her life. It is a dramatic monologue
in the form of a press conference in her dressing-room at the
Comedie Française. Brilliantly constructed by Miss Rich from
Mme. Bernhardt's "Memories of My Life" and other researches
during the Memphian's stay in Paris, it is, in every important
sense, a one-person play. It is always dramatic, never merely
narrative, for Miss Rich knows how to make things happen on
the stage.

Sarah has just returned from a balloon ride and is still, figuratively, up in the air. She finds the Paris press (the audience)
assembled in her dressingroom for the press conference she had
almost forgotten, and proceeds to beguile, amuse, astonish and
lecture them (us) with her menagerie (parrot, monkey, lion, panther, etc), a re-enactment of her first audition, an explanation
of the "infamous slap" that started her on the road to stardom
at the Odeon Theater, and her encounters with Mrs. Patrick
Campbell, George Sand and Victor Hugo, all the while slipping
into her costume and make-up for her last performance at the
House of Molière in a stunning scene, which climaxes the playlet,
from Racine's "Phedre," performed in excellent French.

Utlizing the disciplines of mime as part of a formidable inventory of histrionic techniques, Miss Rich creates again and
again the living moments of Mme. Bernhardt's life. With extraordinary grace and rhythm and stunning changes of pace she
makes Bernhardt live, and makes theater, before our very eyes.

The climax is, indeed, so powerful, and the entire piece such
a vivid application of mime to acting that her ensuing mime show,
"Echoes Of:," should, it seems to me, be used as the curtain-
raiser.

This is not to say that the mime show is inferior to "Sarah
Bernhardt," but merely that it does not build to a dramatic

climax as "Bernhardt" does, and that it is a natural prologue to the full display of Miss Rich's vocal and pantomimic art.

In any case, she shows herself to be an impressive mime, proficient at the entire vocabulary of familiar realistic illusions, and innovative, too, with her own subtle abstractions and a humorous sketch in which a mime is interviewed--on the radio.

The two-part, one-woman show is an exciting demonstration of the maturing of a fine Memphis talent whom some of us saw begin to blossom in "Stop the World, I Want to Get Off" and "The Member of the Wedding" at Memphis State.

Latest Nostalgia Item--"Hair"
(by Edwin Howard, Press-Scimitar, April 3, 1975)

Move Over, "Irene" and "No, No, Nanette," and make room for "Hair." Even in a first-rate production, I suspect that the tribal love-rock musical of 1968 would seem old-hat and irrelevant today. In a production without either passion or precision, such as the touring one that gave a single Memphis performance last night in the Auditorium Music Hall, "Hair" is a nostalgia item that sends the audience home ho-humming.

Young people seeing the Gerome Ragni, James Rado and Galt McDermott show for the first time must have wondered what all the excitement was about. Even the nude scene--always pointless--now seems perfunctory.

The touring company of 16, plus five-piece band, is energetic, and a few of the cast, notably the girls playing Sheila and Crissy, are even talented. But Byron T. Cleeland's direction--or what's left of it--is totally devoid of anything resembling pace or unity and simply allows everybody to do his own thing.

The phallic gesture is most of the male performers' thing, and they indulge it in various manifestations with tiresome obsessiveness far beyond any of the other three productions of "Hair" I have seen. Berger goes through his anthropoidal motions and Claude through his more sensitive assignments without either ever engaging the audience's interest or sympathy. The performer playing Claude (I can't tell you any of the actors' names because no programs were distributed) has a pleasant singing voice but with his neat little mustache looks, but for his blond Dynel wig, more like a 30-year-old bank teller than an innocent flower child. Cleeland's staging of Claude's symbolic crucifixion when he submits to the draft is as mechanical as a light cue: "O.K. boys, turn on the symbolism."

The musical highlight of this production, with very little competition, is the Sheila actress's stirring rendition of "Easy To Be Hard." She is, strangely, not nearly so effective on "Good Morning Starshine," although performers in the aisles nagged and wheedled the audience into standing up and clapping their hands during it.

The Crissy performer's singing of "Aquarius," which finally got the show started about 8:15 after some desultory and generally unintelligible playing around, is also of a higher quality than most of the rest of the show.

Theatrical and cultural historians, forced to rely on recordings and such revivals as this, may one day look back and be hard-pressed to understand or explain the impact "Hair" had on audiences and the institution of theater when it first exploded on the scene. You had to be there. And you had to see it in the context of the turbulent times out of which it erupted.

Rado and Ragni put down random ideas for things to do in the show for two years. The main idea they had was to put down all the things they hated--war, the draft, racism, patriotism, conventional morality, cleanliness, and all those middle class values they felt were symbolized by neat short haircuts and shaved necks. But they also wanted to sing the praises of all the things they loved--other hippies of whatever sex, pot and other drugs, and peace.

There were several ways you could play "Hair" and still have it work. You could play the hatred and add the audience to the things you put down. That's the way the Broadway company did it. You could play the love, particularly of peace and each other, and enfold the audience in those good hope-for a-better-world feelings. That's the way Keith Kennedy's brilliant Memphis State University Theater production did it. Or, like the last road company that played Memphis, you could just play around the both approaches.

What you couldn't--and can't--do and get away with it was play "Hair" perfunctorily. But that's how this touring company plays it, may it rest in peace.

HOWELL, Chauncey; (2) Theatre critic and arts reporter, WNBC-TV, New York City; (3) b. Easton, Pa.; (4) s. Chauncey D. and Kathryn (Shirer); (5) B.A., Amherst College, 1957; major: Greek; (6) single; (8) Writer and columnist, Women's Wear Daily, 1965-73; writer and reporter, etc., WNBC-TV, New York, from August 1973; free-lance restaurant reviewer for "Playboy" magazine, 1968-to present; etc.; (9) Acting and producing at college and in the Army; off-Broadway productions in the early 1960s; (13) Sergeant, U.S. Army, 1957-59; recalled for one year, 1961; (14) None that I can remember outside of college; (16) High Church Tory; (17) Ditto; (18) Alpha Delta Phi, college fraternity; (19) Pomfret Club, Easton, Pa.; (20) Various articles in Holiday, McCall's, Playboy, Cosmopolitan, New York Times Sunday drama section, etc.; (21) 7 Charles St., New York, N.Y. 10014; Ph. WA 4-8353; (22) Room 724, 30 Rockefeller Plaza, New York,

N. Y. 10020; Ph. 247-8300, ext. 3610; (23) Have no idea; I hope it's
millions; (24) If you may describe my entertainment and arts pieces
as "reviews," which many people do, I do an average of three or four
a week on "News Center 4." Formal reviews average about one a
week during the theatre season. We do not customarily review, in
a formal sense, off-Broadway. However, we do many pieces on off-
Broadway productions.

HUDSON, Roy, Salt Lake Tribune, 143 South Main St., P.O. Box
867, Salt Lake City, Ut. 84110.

HUGHES, Catharine, Rachel; (2) Theatre critic; (3) b. Newark, N.J.,
Sept. 4, 1935; (4) d. John and Eleanor (Woodworth) Hughes; (8) Ass't
to the President, L. B. Herr & Son, 1952-57; Director of Publicity
& Advertising, Sheed & Ward, 1957-63; Merchandising Coordinator,
Praeger Publishers, 1963-67; American Theater Critic, Plays and
Players, 1969-75; Drama Critic, America, 1970-on-going; Consulting
Editor, Sheed & Ward, Seabury Press, 1970-74; (9) Assistant Direct-
or, Off Broadway productions; (10) Theatre Consultant for the New
York State Council on the Arts; (15) New Theatre Forum, Outer Critics Circle, American Theater Critics Association; (16) Democrat;
(17) Roman Catholic; (20) Articles in: Show Business, Publishers
Weekly, The Critics, New York Times, The Nation, Playbill, Ebony,
The Progressive, After Dark, Commonweal, Christian Century, Saturday Review, Antioch Review, Arts in Society. Books: Plays, Politics, and Polemics; and American Playwrights: 1945-1975. Edi-
tor/Photographer: The Secret Shrine, The Smokeless Fire, The Solitary Journey, Shadow and Substance. Editor and Contributing Photographer to "Mysticism and Modern Man" Series. Author of play,
Madame Lafayette, produced off-Broadway; (21) 79 West 12th St.,
Apt. 6B, New York, N.Y. 10011, Ph. 212-AL5-6896; (23) Circulation: 60,000; (24) Approximately 100.

Albee's "Seascape"
(by Catharine Hughes, America, February 22, 1975)

Edward Albee has described his new play, Seascape, as the
"life" part of a life/death play that began with All Over in 1971.
Regrettably, life is one of the things it most obviously lacks.

A middle-aged couple named Nancy and Charlie have been
spending some time by the sea. "Can't we just stay here forever?" she asks, for she loves the water as Charlie once did.
As a boy, he wanted to live under the sea, wanted to be "fish-
like." He used to go "way down, and try to stay." He hasn't
done it, however, since he was 17, and it has been "too long"
for him to go back again, as Nancy urges. He would rather
"remember." He would rather do nothing. And that is precisely
what they do for approximately 35 minutes of the first act: nothing but review their lives tediously and acrimoniously, though
their acrimony has none of the acerb bite and bitchy humor of

<u>Who's Afraid of Virginia Woolf</u>? and certainly none of its interest.

Just when tedium theatens to become numbness, two lizard-like creatures emerge from the sea. They are Sarah and Leslie, and they, too, are apparently middle-aged (though telling a middle-aged lizard from a young lizard is beyond me). At first, the two couples are afraid of each other, then gradually begin to develop points of contact, are alternately aggressive, responsive, patronizing, curious. What is one to make, for instance, of Nancy having had only three children and taken care of them for 20 or more years, when Sarah has had 700 and abandoned them?

But Albee is more concerned with similarities than with differences. "In the course of the play," he has commented, "the evolutionary pattern is speeded up billions of revolutions." Thus, it slowly evolves that Sarah and Leslie are, or have the potential to be, every bit as bigoted, every bit as middle-class in their values and behavior, as Nancy and Charlie. They, however, aren't put off by blacks or "foreigners," but by fish: "There's too many of them; they're all over the place ... moving in, taking over where you live ... and they're stupid!"

Why had they come up from the sea, these two green-scaled creatures? "We had changed," Sarah reveals," all of a sudden, everything ... down there ... was terribly ... interesting, I suppose; but what did it have to do with us anymore?" Charlie tells them that what has happened is called "flux." "And it's always going on; right now, to all of us." And maybe, he admits, he envies them, "down there, free from it all; down <u>there</u> with the beasts."

Envy or no, Charlie causes Sarah to cry at the thought that Leslie will one day die, go away forever. It is an alien concept, and Leslie attempts to choke him, for Sarah has never cried before.

"It's ... rather dangerous ... up here," Leslie decides. "Everywhere," returns Charlie. But they cannot return, and the process must go on, despite their anxiety. Nancy tells them she and Charlie could "help." As the curtain falls, Leslie has acceded: "All right. Begin."

As a course in elementary Darwinism, <u>Seascape</u> just might have some value. As a play, it is pretentious, simplistic, verbose and banal. As in <u>All Over</u>, the writing is presumed (by the author) to be poetic and profound, resonant, when in reality it is devoid of life and artificial, the producer of inertia. Sadly, <u>Seascape</u> would seem only to confirm what has become more and more evident with the passing years: that it is to such plays as <u>Tiny Alice</u>, <u>Malcolm</u>, <u>All Over</u> and <u>Seascape</u>, not the earlier, more vital and vibrant--and, yes more profound--<u>Zoo Story</u> and <u>Virginia Woolf</u>, that one must look for the "real" Edward Albee. It is a disappointing discovery to make.

Given what they have to work with, Deborah Kerr and Barry Nelson probably do about as well as could be expected as Nancy and Charlie, and Frank Langella and Maureen Anderman somehow manage to make the two sea creatures quite engaging. The play has been directed by the author, who has been known to criticize directors in the past, and this may possibly have been a mistake. Whatever the case, it must be accepted as the "definitive" version of what Albee had in mind, which makes its failure even more regrettable.

Of Dolls, Dreams and Duds
(by Catharine Hughes, America, April 19, 1975)

If America were Variety, this column might well carry the headline, "Beaumont Buys Biggies" or "Festival Faces Facts." For, after less than two seasons as the theatre constituent of New York's Lincoln Center (in the center's Vivian Beaumont Theatre), Joseph Papp and his New York Shakespeare Festival are tossing in the towel on their much vaunted "new-play" policy. It was the right idea at the wrong time in the wrong place, and Mr. Papp deserves nothing but credit for acknowledging and moving to rectify the situation, though clearly doing it with reluctance.

"We engendered a great deal of anger and frustration on the part of the audience, outright hostility," he said in a recent New York Times interview. "We began losing audiences. They could not bear endless obscenities. I did not want to alienate the audiences. But I could not help but alienate them."

Unfortunately, there was a factor beyond the traditional expectations of the Beaumont's subscription audiences: the new plays presented by Mr. Papp, with the exception of Miguel Pinero's Short Eyes, which was transferred from the Festival's Public Theatre (downtown) to substitute for another work, were in general from mediocre to poor. It was not only the subscription audiences that fell off. So did the rest.

Mr. Papp's own words suggest much of why this happened: "We are building a national theatre. Standards and quality will be the key words for next season." (One has to ask why, with five or six theatres available in the Public Theatre complex for experimental or less than fully developed works; those were not key words from the outset.)

Apart from the quality of the plays themselves, there has been another reason for the failure of the new-play policy (and the old-play revivals) staged by the NYSF at Lincoln Center. The quality of the productions has been inconsistent, at least partly because of Mr. Papp's penchant--to be admired elsewhere --for using untried directors given to whimsical, quixotic, deliberately gimmicky approaches, to say the least. Speaking of the Public Theatre, he says: "In our new plays there, we want experienced directors. We want more care and cultivation rather

than innovation and getting the young started. " Of Lincoln Cen-
ter, he notes that he is currently involved in obtaining the ser-
vices of such directors as Mike Nichols, Arthur Penn and Anthony
Page; that playwrights under consideration include Shaw, Chekhov,
Tolstoy and O'Neill, with such stars as Max von Sydow, Vanessa
Redgrave, Bibi Andersson, Al Pacino, Dustin Hoffman, Stacy
Keach and, for Shaw's Saint Joan, the star of the Festival's sin-
gle real success at Lincoln Center, Liv Ullmann.

There are a number of things to be said of Mr. Papp's
change of heart concerning Lincoln Center, the first being that it
is the right decision.   As the theatre constituent there, the Beaumont has been initially a stepchild, at times an embarrassment,
never on a level with the other companies: the New York Philharmonic, the New York City Ballet and City Opera, and the Metropolitan Opera, or with the visiting companies of international
stature that from time to time occupy the complex's other houses:
the Royal Ballet, Moscow's Bolshoi, the Boston Symphony and
American Ballet Theatre, among others.   The productions in the
Beaumont have seldom, and perhaps never, met this standard.

Too, if New York, or America, is to have a major theatre
company deserving of a national and international acceptance,
Lincoln Center today seems the only place for it, and Mr. Papp
is wisely intending to form such a permanent company, while
bringing in "guest stars" for individual seasons for productions.
As the British National Theatre and Royal Shakespeare Company
have proved time and again, being a basically "classic" theatre
does not necessarily mean being a museum (a fact that most
American classic theatres have managed to ignore).   One can
only hope Mr. Papp will yet prove that the Beaumont need not
be the theatrical graveyard it has thus far been for so many great
expectations.

It can hardly have been a coincidence that the announcement
of the new policy came just as Liv Ullmann was opening in A
Doll's House--sold out prior to opening for its entire eight-week
run, whereas previous productions had merely limped along.

Liv Ullmann came to New York already canonized for her
film work and for her out-of-town success in the role, and she
surely was the best thing about this otherwise inadequately conceived, generally ill-performed production, staged by Tormod
Skagestad, who has been artistic and managing director of the
Norwegian Theatre since 1960.

In several key roles--notably, Mrs. Linde, Dr. Rank and
Nils Krogstad--the acting bordered on, or achieved, the inept.
The production itself was dull to the point of tedium, with little
attempt made to do other than showcase the star.   The translation was the same one in which Claire Bloom triumphed several
seasons ago--Christopher Hampton's--but here it seemed oddly
deficient in the hands of a cast that was even more deficient.

Miss Ullmann herself was a considerable disappointment, despite her unquestioned beauty and radiance. She is an actress of enormous magnetism and talent, but here--dare I say it?--was somewhat miscast. Nora's character calls for evolution from the "squirrel," the child-wife, into the figure of the last scene who has experienced some measure of self-recognition and some degree of understanding of what her relationship with Torvald (Sam Waterston) has been and has become. Liv Ullmann's Nora is, in the early stages, largely unconvincing as she plays the skylark-squirrel Torvald conceives of. Despite her charm and presence, she is a trifle too sophisticated for it to emerge as other than superficial playing, at a time or two almost embarrassing. Nora should be seen to be one of two things; either genuinely naive and childlike or playing a role suited to Torvald's needs and vanity. Miss Ullmann's interpretation falls somewhere in between and is consequently less satisfying than it might have been within a more certain directorial conception. But, let it be said, the audience had come to see Liv Ullmann, not Nora Helmer or A Doll's House, and Mr. Skagestad made sure that they did.

HUNTER, Frank, St. Louis Globe-Democrat, 12th Boulevard at Delmar, St. Louis, Mo. 63101.

HUSTEN, Bruce H.; (2) Arts Editor and Drama Critic; (3) b. Troy, N.Y., July 16, 1948; (4) s. Judith and Sanford Husten; (5) B.A. Union College, Schenectady, N.Y., 1971, maj. sub.: Comparative Communist Studies; minor sub.: Drama; (6) Single; (8) Reporter, The Record Newspapers, Troy, N.Y., summers 1966, 1968; Reporter, Schenectady Gazette, 1967, 1968 part time, summer drama critic 1971, 1972; Reporter Evening Standard, London, Eng. part time 1969-70; Ed. Kite, Albany 1972; Reporter, The Times Record, Troy, N.Y. 1973- ; currently theater critic at Knickerbocker News-Union Star in Albany; (9) Prof. jazz pianist, 1967-71; publicity-promotion assistant, City Center Acting Co., Sarotoga Performing Arts Center, summer, 1973; (21) 400 Saratoga Court, Colonie East, Latham, N.Y. 12110, Ph. 518-783-1557; (22) Knickerbocker News-Union Star, Albany, N.Y., Ph. 518-272-200; (23) Circulation: 50,000; (24) 50 plays, musicals, 60 films, 10 misc.

Juilliard Job in "School for Scandal" Is Masterpiece
(by Bruce Husten, Schenectady Gazette, July 5, 1972)

Driving home from the Saratoga Performing Arts Center Monday night, where I had gone to see and review the Juilliard Acting Company's production of "School for Scandal," I thought and thought about the whole concept of the "rave review" in the world of drama criticism.

For the Juilliard company--which is now very much an official member of SPAC's team of summer artists-in-residence--

presented Sheridan's Restoration comedy so flawlessly that I felt
it my duty to out-race any and every other rave review that has
ever been written.

Even more than that, though, I felt the obligation to tell as
many friends and readers as I could muster up that they are
missing out on an unprecedented theatrical experience if they do
not go to SPAC to see this company in action. You've got to
be a heartless Philistine if you don't fall immediately in love
with them.

If comparisons are in order, let it be known that this critical evaluation is not based on a lifetime of seeing smalltown
amateur theater or even lavish productions of frivolous Broadway
musicals. I must confess to being something of a theatrical snob
with a penchant for "heavy" drama that is well done, and the
theatrical scene in America has disillusioned me to the point of
escape: I spend as many winters as possible now in London going to theater at its finest.

Just before returning here for the summer, in fact, I went
to see Laurence Olivier's National Theater Company--probably the
finest repertory company in the English-speaking world--in a production of this same play directed by Jonathan Miller, a young
British director whose bold, eccentric interpretations of classic
plays have set the London stage aglow.

And there is no doubt in my mind that Gerald Freedman's
Juilliard production puts Miller and Olivier and the whole National Theater Company to utter shame. The real irony here is that
the British have always scorned us for attempting Restoration
comedy (not to mention Shakespeare!), claiming it is part of their
blood and not ours and that any attempt to produce it is as
doomed from the start as any of their attempts to produce Albee
or Mike Weller or Terrence McNally.

"School for Scandal" is one of five plays written between 1775
and 1778 by Richard Brinsley Sheridan, an English playwright ordinarily regarded as Oliver Goldsmith's aid and successor in the
attempt to restore comedy to its own province of mirth. Sheridan
is best remembered for "The Rivals" and his creation of the in-
imitible Mrs. Malaprop, the bungling old lady-of-supposed-man-
ners who has a great deal of trouble with the English language.

"School for Scandal" is an equally-good but tragically-aban-
doned play and, like "The Rivals," one which represents a return to the ideals of witty, elegant comedy, purged of its Restoration impurities but one which preserves a hysterical consciousness of the sentimental absurdities of the times. Its dialogue has the exquisite precision of Congreve and its plot, the
irresistible hysteria of Farquhar.

Much in the play is familiar to other drama of this genre;

two brothers, one impulsive and feckless like Tom Jones and Joseph Andrews, the other spewing glorious sentiments while simultaneously plotting mischief; the "scandal club" of Lady Sneerwell;
and the quarrelsome couple, in this case the aging Sir Peter
Teazle and his young wife from the country. Sheridan, however,
invigorates an old formula with new life, while Freedman directs
the Juilliard company to make for a theatrical totality the likes
of which Restoration comedy has not seen for some time in this
country.

Other than Freedman (whose current production of "Hamlet"
with Stacy Keach and Colleen Dewhurst is faring exceedingly well
with Joseph Papp's Shakespeare-in-the-Park Festival in New York),
it is unfair to single out any other members of this company, for
it is the totality of the thing that needs lauding here, and without
exception every single actor, stage hand and tech man deserves
a share of the plaudits.

Douglas Schmidt's set is simultaneously elegant and multifunc-
tional, while John David Ridge's costumes are absolutely dazzling.

The cast of 23 functions together as if they were one, a rare
virtue to be found only with the best repertory companies. It is
only a good rep company, in fact, that is capable of pulling off
something like "School for Scandal" with aplomb, for the members of the company, having worked and studied together over a
period of months and years, know each other and can interact
with one another and are able to avoid the pitfalls of overacting,
camping and stage-stealing. And it is this virtue that now seems
certain to carve for the Juilliard Acting Company a rare niche in
the annals of the American theater.

What will be most fun now is to watch this same company of
actors in other roles throughout its SPAC season, and the program notes help us do this by giving us a list of repertory casting that names every member of the company and notes each of
the roles he will be playing.

Mary Lou Rosato, for example, whose Lady Sneerwell in
this play lives admirably up to her name, will give us the crippled Mme. Desmermortes when Juilliard presents Anouilh's
"Ring Round the Moon" next week, and it promises to be a trea-
surable treat.

At this stage of the game, in fact, we are likely to be watching for David Ogden Stiers, Gerald Shaw, David Schramm, Norman Snow and Kevin Kline whose respective "School for Scandal"
roles of Joseph Surface, Sir Benjamin Backbite, Sir Peter Teazle, Sir Oliver Surface and Charles Surface invite intrigue and
curiosity for the future.

Again, however, these are singled out only because they happen to have been cast in the major parts of the play. Every

single member of the cast, from Snake to the servants, is equally competent.

If fault must be found, one might quibble with Norman Snow's
hint of a southern accent as Sir Oliver Surface, a minor point
which would have gone unnoticed were it not for the perfection of
the English accent by the rest of the cast. He makes up for it,
in any case, when he puts on a thick Irish accent to disguise
himself to his nephew Joseph as Mr. Stanley.

The first and second scenes of the last act go on a bit, and
Freedman might have done well to edit the script there, but the
fault is Sheridan's and not Juilliard's.

Likewise, Charles Surface's almost-didactic monologue at the
end of the screen scene seems a bit heavy-handed after the fits
of hysteria created by the perfectly-timed revelation of Lady Teazle behind the screen.

When Charles says to his brother and Sir Peter, "What? Is
Morality dumb too? Brother, I'm sorry to find you have given
that worthy man (Sir Peter) grounds for so much uneasiness.
Sir Peter, there's nothing in the world so noble as a man of sentiment," we realize this is the essence and indeed the extent of
Sheridan's morality in this play, yet somehow it seems poorly
placed after the laughter that has preceded it.

We also wonder at the need for two intervals in this production, but we confess that when you have to quibble with something so trivial, you're dealing with a superlative piece of theater.

The secret to the success of this production (which continues
through Saturday at the Spa Summer Theater on SPAC's grounds),
actually, is that the Juilliard people have resisted the temptation
to camp up Sheridan's script. Of course we have caricatures
here, but they are never exaggerated more than they should be
and are more often than not underplayed.

A lesser company would find no choice but to camp it up for
all it was worth in order to extract some of the humor, but the
Juilliard people are masters of such expertise and so talented a
lot that they can afford to let the humor ooze out by itself. They
do, and it does.

Juilliard Acting Company, John Houseman (who's their artistic
director), Gerald Freedman, Margot Haley (who's their administrator), forgive my schmaltz, but I love you. Now how about
giving us Farquhar's "The Beaux' Stratagem," another piece of
abandoned, brilliant restoration comedy?

Where's Charley? Please--Don't Ask
(by Bruce Husten, Times Record, May 10, 1974)

Charley is counting on the arrival of his rich aunt, Donna

Lucia D'Alvadorez, to get him out of some rough fixes with his girlfriend, his roommate's girlfriend, and the girls' guardian.

Auntie never shows, though, so Charley has to don women's clothes and pretend to be Donna Lucia.

So throughout this play, which opened for a three week run at the Albany Civic Theater here last night, everybody's always running around asking "Where's Charlie?"

Watching this production, one wouldn't have the vaguest idea.

"Where's Charley" is a musical adaption of Brandon Thomas' original comic farce, "Charley's Aunt." I've seen the latter in several different London productions, each one successively as bad as its predecessor.

Take a bad play, add to it no-better-than-average music and lyrics and painfully embarrassing choreography, and give it a mediocre, amateur production.

I needn't tell you the results--and I don't suggest you venture out to discover them for yourselves.

While certainly there are some redeeming factors in the production, it never ceases to amaze me that a troupe could pick so shallow--and for that very reason, so difficult--a vehicle with which to work.

Director Maria Aronson sets the production in the England of 1892, and purports to satirize the social hypocrisies and languorous wealth of the Victorians.

The playwright's characterizations, however, are so hyperbolized, so cartoon-like and so caricatured that they present an insurmountable task for any actor.

You watch this production and you ask how anyone could present interpretations like that, but when you stop to think about it, what choice does a director or an actor have, given the script he has to work with?

There are two saving graces in this production--which is, by the way, about the worst thing I have seen the usually-reliable Albany Civic Theater come up with.

The first is the quality of the voices. There is some good choral work and there are several excellent soloists (notable, Peggy O'Neil as the real Donna Lucia, and particularly Gary Aldrich as Sir Francis Chesney, father of Charley's roommate).

And there is a quite-passable performance by Peter Salm in the lead role of Charley Wykeham, who must alternate from

Oxford student to rich aunt.

Salm reads Charley as a likeable, naive yearling, though he offers an interesting contrast--if admittedly somewhat incongrous --in his interpretation of the aunt as a conniving, experienced lady-about-town.

But he is always convincing, occasionally quite funny and generally a competent singer.

In one scene in Act I, Charley finally returns to his girl- friend Amy after having been disguised as the aunt.

Amy, not yet perturbed, sees him and mutters, "I feel cer- tain I must be having hallucinations."

I shared poor Amy's fate quite heartily.

JACAWAY, Taffy Marie; (2) Women's Editor and Arts/Entertainment Editor; (3) b. Brooklyn, Jan. 19, 1928; (4) d. Thomas and Kathleen Tavernor; (5) Scholarship to Lincoln College, majored in English and education at U. of I.; (6) divorced; (7) children--Marc, Charlyn and Martin; (8) Women's News Editor and Arts/Entertainment Editor; (9) Acted with Springfield, (Ill.) Opera Assn., Gallery Circle Theatre (New Orleans), New York Professional Children's Theatre, Burien Workshop Theatre (Seattle). Directed children's, youth and adult theatre, wrote children's plays; (15) Member Wash. Presswomen's Assn., Natl. Fed. of Presswomen; Sigma Delta Chi; (16) Democrat; (17) R. Catholic; (19) Kent Soroptimist; (20) Features, photos, cri- tiques and interviews for Fournier Newspapers; (21) 26310 135th SE, Kent, Wash. 98031, Ph. 631-4120; (22) Kent News-Journal, Renton Record-Chronicle, Auburn Globe-News, all box 130, Kent, Wash. 98031, Ph. 206-872-6672; (23) Circulation: 65,000; (24) 80 plays, musicals, 5 concerts, 10 interviews.

"Godspell" Tops ACT's Cake
(by Taffy Jacaway, Globe News, Record-Chronicle, News-Journal, September 20, 1974)

"Godspell" is the frosting on A Contemporary Theatre's 10th anniversary cake!

Opening Tuesday night to a sellout house of its scheduled run, "Godspell" has been extended at least until Oct. 13. My guess is it will be held over even longer, with some, like myself, go- ing back for seconds!

Topping an exciting season, the rock musical based on the Gospel by St. Matthew is a fresh, vibrant, if not cheeky, inter- pretation of the teachings of Jesus.

Controversial, yet acclaimed by many clergy, the circus-

styled revue gives very literal but light-hearted treatment to the
parables.

Wayne Hudgins as Jesus, blessed the audience with just the
right mixture of warmth and spark. A lesser Lord would have
smacked of too much sentimentality. His first act soft-shoe routine is a gem.

Michael Byron is almost a one-man show in himself--sings,
dances, acts his baggy pants off and cavorts acrobatically whenever the scene allows.

Strongest production number of the evening featured Gail Hebert singing "Day by Day." Gail zomps a song, sells it and
makes everyone love it.

William C. Witter has strong command of the stage both as
his John the Baptist scene "Prepare Ye the Way of the Lord,"
and in lesser spots later, including the Judas scene.

Pert Kathryn Luster is a Jill-in-the-box. Every muscle of
her trim body seemed to spring her from one spot on the stage
to the next.

Director Gregory A. Falls has succeeded with the show by
his finicky attention to detail. The little details are what make
this show Big.

Musical direction by Stan Keen deserves special mention.
Musical cues jumped right on the action, leaving no dead spots
in the show.

Drummer Bill Kotick of the Overton Berry Trio makes the
show a field day for toe-tappers.

"Godspell" speaks sanctity sans sanctimony--Amen to that!

"A Doll's House" Furnished with Great Theatrics
(by Taffy Jacaway, Globe-News, Record-Chronicle, News-Journal,
February 9, 1975)

Jeannie Carson is a spirited Nora in Henrik Ibsen's A Doll's
House, now on stage at Seattle Repertory Theatre. She romps,
curls up on a couch arm like a kitten, becomes withdrawn at a
moment's notice and fills Doll's House with lively theatrics!

Directed and translated by the inimitable Eva Le Gallienne,
the Rep production wrings every nuance from the Ibsen script.

Doll's House has lost its initial shock value of a woman
daring to assert herself, daring to get a loan of money through
forgery of her father's signature. Never mind that the money
was needed to save her husband's health.

Throughout the performance tiny titters of laughter from the audience punctuated lines whenever Torvald, the husband played by Curt Dawson, uttered funny passe lines about HIS ability, strength, duties and privileges.

At times, one thought Doll's House might better have been named The Aviary, since Torvald is always referring to his Nora as some type of bird--the Spendthrift Bird, "my little lark" and such. Little did he fathom his little bird would fly the nest!

David Hurst as Nils Krogstad, poor desperate, wronged man and Nora's nemesis, turned in a strong performance. In one scene of utter dejection his posture told the whole story--even with his back turned.

Margaret Hilton handled the role of Mrs. Linde with great sensitivity.

Hurd Hatfield added maturity to the role of Dr. Rank, terminally ill with tuberculosis. His softly lit, tender scene with Nora was most touching, showing great restraint in his confession of love.

Next to the fantastic performance turned in by the actors, the set design and lighting deserved a round of bouquets. Set designer Eldon Elder created an intricate masterpiece of a set, masterfully lighted by Richard Nelson.

Costume designer Lewis D. Rampino kept his costuming soft and subdued, so as not to detract from set or the theatrics of the cast.

Doll's House is well furnished with skillful theatrics--a "must see" of this season's Rep program.

JACOBI, Peter Paul; (2) Educator and writer; (3) b. Berlin, Germany, March 15, 1930; (4) s. Paul A. and Liesbeth Jacobi; came to U.S. 1938, naturalized, 1944; (5) B.S. Northwestern U. Medill School of Journalism, 1952, M.S., 1953; (6) m. Harriet Ackley, Dec. 8, 1956; (7) children--Keith Peter, Wyn; (8) Faculty journalism Northwestern U., Evanston, Ill., 1955- , professional lecturer, 1955-63, assistant professor, 1963-66, associate dean, 1966-74, associate professor, 1966-69, professor of journalism 1969- , also special arts consultant for university 1974- ; Editor, Chicago Lyric Opera News, 1958-61, Music Magazine/Musical Courier, Chicago 1961-62; news assignment editor, newscaster, theatre-music reporter, NBC, Chicago, 1955-61; news editor ABC, Chicago, 1952-53; radio commentator music and opera 1958-65; theatre, film critic WMAQ-TV, Chicago 1964-74; arts critic, Chicago Public Television WTTW 1974- ; critic Hollister Newspapers of suburban Chicago, 1963-70; music columnist Chicagoan Magazine, 1973-74; Chicago correspondent Opera magazine, 1974- ; theatre contributor, Christian Science Monitor, 1956- ; script consultant, Goodman Theatre, Chicago, 1973- ; (15) Member theatre advisory committee Illinois Arts Council; Member Chicago's Jefferson Theatre Awards committee; Member National Academy TV Arts and Sciences (board of Governors, Chicago), Radio-TV News Directors Association, Association for Education in Journalism, Sigma Delta Chi; (20) Contributor of articles on arts to Chicago Daily News, New York Times, Saturday Review, others; (21) 2042 Wilmette Ave., Wilmette, Ill. 60091; (24) Approximate number of reviews annually: 50 in theatre, film, music, art.

"Grease" Romps Happily Back into Town
(by Peter Jacobi, Chicago Daily News, September 13, 1973)

The homecoming was like cool, man. "Rama-lama-lama, kadinga da ding-dong," as the lyrics say.

"Grease" completed its round trip Wednesday night, arriving for what probably will be a lengthy run at the Blackstone.

It has been a long and heady journey for two Chicago boys, Jim Jacobs and Warren Casey, since three summers ago when they sat down to write a musical based on some high school memories.

They expected the Kingston Mines premiere production, on Lincoln Av., to last a handful of performances. But it ran and ran. Then it got to New York, all spruced up and professionalized. Again it ran and ran. Then it went on national tour with another company of actors. That ran and ran. A version sprang up in London, another in Mexico City. These ran and ran.

Finally, it got back to Chicago.

It has changed as it prospered. What began as an overly talky, Chicago-oriented, and somewhat amateurishly performed show has become more musical, snappier in tempo, and glitzily produced.

Basically, however, "Grease" is still the same: a raunchy-crude, silly, joyful evocation of a time not long past, the rock-rollicking late '50s when Presley and Bill Haley's Comets ruled a teen-age world.

Too bad some of the Chicago jokes couldn't have been replaced for our consumption. Too bad some of the almost improvised horseplay of the original cast--so freewheeling and loose-- couldn't have been recaptured.

Too bad that some of the current performers, good as they are, lack the genuine youthfulness of high school kids very simply because they haven't been high school kids for too long a time. Too bad that faulty microphoning and overly amplified and electrified musical instruments combine to fuzz out too many of the happy lyrics.

But still "Grease" is a welcome returnee, rockily tuneful, imaginative yet direct in its approach to an audience, and just enough different still from the formula Broadway musical to make it stand out.

It will never be every person's show. At intermission a friend of mine waved from his seat across the theater and then put his thumbs down while pouting at the mouth. Just to the right of me stood two young ladies in delighted delirium, one of them exclaiming, "I could see this a million times."

Well, I couldn't. But I thought "Grease" a rather vital show at Kingston Mines. It remains so. My nostalgia dates back another 10 years, to the late '40s. Yet the good-natured journey back to a specific era can be fun for anyone who is able to relax and let it wash over him.

"Grease" returns on the heels of that very good film, "American Graffiti." Both celebrate the same period, the same youthful rituals of hot rodding and wising off and teen-age mating games.

"Grease" contains more graffiti than the film. It's lighter-hearted, too, without a thought about growing up and unhappier times ahead. Yet, strong similarities there are.

The songs are sort of boffo, from a parody of a sirupy Alma Mater to the Burger Palace Boys' wowie hymn to a car called "Greased Lightnin'," from "Shakin' at the High School Hop" to the satire song of the liberated gal who heads the Pink Ladies, "Look at Me, I'm Sandra Dee, Lousy with Virginity."

The pace never slows. "Grease" has been ably directed by Tom Moore to bring out all possible sweaty energy in his performers. A couple of the girls overact outrageously, but Judy Kaye is firm of voice and bristling with sarcasm as Rizzo, the girl who mocks Sandra Dee.

Marilu Henner, once with the original Kingston Mines company, has joined this Chicago company as another Pink Lady. She's new to the professional stage, but doesn't seem so.

Another original is James Canning as the most innocent of the Burger Palace Boys, all of whom are genuine characters, rowdy, grease-laden, crummy-dirty, and very funny.

Funniest and most effective is the hero of the tale, Barry Bostwick as Danny Zuko, a loyal gang member, full of the devil and yet with a gentler streak that attracts him to a girl more goody than the rest. Bostwick is all oooh-oohs and ah-ahs, breaking his voice like the best of the rock stars. He can bluster and stammer, dance with the furies, and make the most of an Elvis pelvis.

The dances are virile.

Rama-lama-lama, ka-dinga da ding-dong. I didn't understand
all of it.   The sounds overwhelmed.   But Sha-na-na I'm ready.
Chang chang-a changitty to go along.   "Grease" is fun.

The Free Streeters Reach Out--with Love
(by Peter Jacobi, Chicago Daily News, December 4, 1973)

There's a welcome at the door; people say hello.   At the
end, they offer popcorn.   In between, we're asked to "Celebrate
the City."

And so we do, watching the exuberant performers who are
the Free Street Theater.

They've taken over a concrete cavern in the Newberry Plaza,
1030 N. State, for a three-week gala season that's meant to
elicit financial support from the community.

No longer allowed to be dependent on the Illinois Arts Council,
which was instrumental in nurturing it between 1969 and last
spring, Free Street Theater is reaching outward, toward the
many thousands it has enraptured during seasons past.

But no beggars are they who work for their pay and who deserve support.

I've long been entranced by the spells the Free Street Theater
weaves through the guiding genius of director-creator Patrick
Henry.   Entranced not only because it touched my sensibilities,
but because it reaches an audience, all kinds of audiences in all
sorts of spaces and places.   I'd rather see it in a park or street
corner or community center.

But no matter where the Free Streeters work, they establish
an envelopmental environment.   So they did at this past weekend's
opener.

First there were marionettes off at the side: an airplane-
flying elf, a magician, and a lazy dragon scared skinless by a
sneeze.

Then came the Free Street Theater's emotion-oozing "Can
the Human Race Survive Itself?" in which music and dance re-
create the history of the city, from the place where man first
sought to live close to other men to the place it became, a world
of "no" rather than "yes," of dreams decayed, where living "is
one long life of dying."

Its various parts hold varying levels of effectiveness, but
the total bops the mind.

Two men wrestle, struggle in a magnificently choreographed combat. A city is described as "them zones, them zones," with school zones connected to safety zones, and safety zones to o-zones. Other songs decry greed and plead love. And one can even experience the united sounds of a timpani and a washboard.

Quite frankly, Free Street Theater is difficult to evaluate. This critic usually just gets wrapped up in what's going on and forgets he's there to analyze. But then isn't that what art is all about: the momentary building of a fantasy world which in one way or another enriches those who come in contact with it?

"Can the Human Race Survive Itself?" does that. To be quite cornball about it, I felt love. And I saw our crazy world in a glow that made things clearer, just a bit.

All of Patrick Henry's performers are good. They're an ensemble, versatile and easy to appreciate.

Each evening during the gala season, a special guest is showcased to conclude the goings-on. At the opening it was amazing Amanda Ambrose, from Mister Kelly's.

Wednesday the special guests will be folk singers from the Old Town School of Folk Music; Thursday, Milawi, the jazz group, and comedienne-songstress Liz Torres whose intense voice is lava and firestorm as she sings of loving a man and loving all men.

Friday, the guests will be the Precious Blood Church choir; the Saturday matinee, Second City's Comedia Players; and Saturday night, the Southern Illinois University dance company. (No performances Tuesdays.)

It all amounts to a pleasurable and meaningful gift for the holiday season. Pardon my rapture, but I was delighted.

JENNINGS, Robert Maurice; (2) Theater-Music Editor; (3) b. Nashville, Tenn. , Nov. 1, 1924; (4) s. Robert Maurice and Ethel (McHughes) J.; (5) B. A. Univ. of Missouri, major subj. : social sciences, 1949; B. Journalism, Univ. of Missouri, Major subj. : news, 1949; (6) m. Betty Ann Prall, May 14, 1956; (7) child--Elizabeth McHughes; (8) free-lance writing, California, 1949; staff writer, Clarksdale, Miss. , Press Register, 1949-58; staff writer, Memphis Commercial Appeal, 1958-66; theater-music editor, Memphis Commercial Appeal, 1966-present; (13) Staff sergeant, U. S. Army, 1943-46; (14) Silver Star for gallantry in action, 1944; (15) Phi Beta Kappa, Univ. of Missouri, 1949; (16) Disenchanted Democrat; (17) Baptist; (20) Newspaper columns, reviews, news stories; (21) 918 East Drive, Memphis, Tenn. 38108, Ph. 901-FA3-6588; (22) Commercial Appeal, Memphis, Tenn. 38101, Ph. 901-JA6-8811; (23) Circulation: 288,743 (Sunday), 218,721 (daily); (24) 40 theater productions, 10 operas, 40 concerts and recitals, 12 ballet, 12 other.

Williams "Descents" to Low Ebb
(by Robert Jennings, Commercial Appeal, April 2, 1968)

If "Tobacco Road" had been written in the late 1960s instead of the early 1930s, if the locale had been the Mississippi Delta instead of back-country Georgia, and if it had been written by Tennessee Williams, the result might be very much like Mr. Williams' new play.

Each deals in the grotesqueries of rural American types, subspecies Dixie. Each reeks of sex. Each has moments of a kind of poetic, almost inadvertent effectiveness in the middle of primitive comedy.

Mr. Williams' play is titled "The Seven Descents of Myrtle," producer David Merrick having prevailed in a difference of opinion with the author. He preferred "Kingdom of Earth." The title is verbally ambiguous, one theatergoer confiding to me that on first hearing she thought it was "The Seventy Cents of Myrtle." Another, perhaps with a judicial turn of mind, said he thought it was "The Seven Dissents of Myrtle."

The production is newly resident at the Ethel Barrymore Theatre as the 17th Williams' opening since his Broadway debut with "The Glass Menagerie" 22 seasons back. Jose Quintero is director.

Harry Guardino, Estelle Parsons and Brian Bedford give performances of stature and charm, which are among qualities in which the play itself is, alas, deficient. The cast, and presumably Mr. Quintero, not only fills the written specifications of Mr. Williams, but often goes far beyond to supply dimensions not explicit in the play.

Mr. Guardino and Mr. Bedford are half-brothers (same father) disdainful of each other. They live on Delta acres in the Friars Point vicinity. The Mississippi River threatens to put the region under 10 feet of water as Mr. Bedford, an advanced tubercular, returns from a Memphis hospital escorting Miss Parsons as bride in a highly singular matrimony.

The wedded state is not intended to be blissful for Mr. Bedford, whose momism is even more advanced than his tuberculosis, except that it offers him a chance to bilk Mr. Guardino of his inheritance. Mr. Bedford became the land's owner on his mother's death, Mr. Guardino being what is euphemistically called in those parts "a woods colt." He was the product of a liaison not consecrated by marriage.

Mr. Bedford, however, found himself unable to run the farm, his gifts inclining more toward bleaching his hair by deft application to the roots with an orange stick dipped into a secret formula passed on to him by his mother, Miss Lottie. (Clever Mr. Williams names her effete offspring Lot.)

In helplessness, Mr. Bedford has appealed to the older Mr. Guardino to come back from a Meridian saw mill and run the old home place. Mr. Guardino agreed only on condition that a paper be signed making him heir to the property on Mr. Bedford's rapidly approaching death.

But Mr. Bedford rankles under the knowledge that the inheritance, especially Miss Lottie's little parlor and its pretties, will go to so uncouth a man. In a strategic ploy in Memphis he marries Miss Parsons, a stripteaser down on her luck, to set up a widow as heir to the farm.

The basic confrontation is between Miss Parsons' Myrtle and Mr. Guardino, whose name, I am sorry to say, is Chicken. He acquired it after having climbed to the roof of the house to sit with the chickens while riding out an earlier flood.

Mr. Bedford retires from the arena early, after the first act mainly occupying the upstairs bedroom of Jo Mielziner's fine, two-story representation of the farm house. Mr. Guardino's stronghold is the kitchen downstairs, to which Miss Parsons periodically repairs to war and finally to woo with him. Her downward negotiations of the stairs are the descents of the title, although I do not think there are seven of them.

Mr. Williams writes with more polish than did the Jack Kirkland-Erskine Caldwell "Tobacco Road" writers, but there is little space for the lyricism which often glows in his plays. Only a touch creeps through.

But he never has had truer ear nor clearer perception for the phrases, inflections, vocabulary, humors and very thoughts of the Deltan represented by Mr. Guardino.

One-Man Show Gives Harry Well
(by Robert Jennings, Commercial Appeal, May 7, 1975)

It must have been during Eisenhower's campaign for re-election in 1956 that a slightly disparaging sticker appeared on some anti-Ike bumpers: "If We're Going To Have A Golfer In The White House, Let's Have A Good One: Ben Hogan For President."

Well, in the election a couple of presidential campaigns before that it turned out that Harry Truman needed no help. But after seeing James Whitmore's one-man show, "Give 'Em Hell Harry!," a paraphrasing bumper sticker comes to mind:

"If We're Going To Have A Comedian In The White House,

Let's Have A Good One: Truman For President."

For in Whitmore's engrossing portrayal of Samuel Gallu's
"play" about Truman, Harry emerges as a fellow of infinite jest.

He is not only one of the great stand-up comics, he's also
funny sitting down. He's even funny mowing the grass. The audience last night, at the first of two sold-out performances in
The Auditorium Music Hall, lapped up the Truman wit, the Truman ribaldry and the jolly Truman habit of being undeterred by
any old notions that if you can't say something good about someone, don't say anything.

Truman says a great many bad things about lots of people--
just repaying them in kind, of course--and now and again he even
says some good things about somebody, usually General Marshall.

It is all very diverting, even when the script is shamelessly
rigged, as in an imaginary White House conversation between
Truman and the ghost of Franklin D. Roosevelt.

All is not comedy, nor persiflage, nor venom, however, in
this Truman representation. He also comes through as a man
scrapping for survival, both for himself as a President and politician and for his country as the land of the free. Perhaps a
sense of humor, even as unbuttoned a one as Truman's, is necessary for survival in that pressure chamber of an office.

Whether giving hell to MacArthur, or McCarthy, or the Ku
Klux Klan, or just to Republicans in general, Whitmore is a
lively, totally convincing Truman. It is basically an evening of
hell-giving, so much so that only Whitmore's clever pacing and
rapid-fire delivery ward off tedium and an overdose of raised
voice.

If Truman ever had any quiet, restrained, pensive moments--
Harry? Pensive?--they are scarcely noted here. As a result,
it is an evening without as many facets as it might have. But
those it does display are capitally shown and sparkle brightly.

Whitmore is visually remarkable, looking a good deal the
way we remember Truman appearing in the 1940s and 1950s.
Acoustically, he achieves a passable duplication of that flat Missouri twang, which would have been much more effective without
the everpresent amplification actors use nowadays.

The applause, which punctuated the show and welled up loudly at the intermission and the end, seemed equally for the sentiments which Truman voiced and for Whitmore's skill in voicing
them.

JOHNSON, Wayne Eaton; (2) Theater Critic; (3) b. Phoenix, Ariz.,

May 9, 1930; (4) s. Roscoe and Marion (Eaton) J.; (5) B.A., Colorado
U., English lit.; graduate study in drama at Duke U. and U. of
Vienna (Austria); M.A., U.C.L.A., journalism; (6) divorced; (7) children with subject, Katherine and Jeffrey; (8) Editorial writer and
critic, The Denver Post, 1960-65; Arts and Entertainment Editor,
The Seattle Times, 1965- ; (13) Army Counter Intelligence Corps
agent 1954-56; (20) Author of numerous theater pieces, the most notable being "The Indian Experience," presented throughout Pacific
Northwest 1972-73, presented in Playhouse II Off-Broadway 1973; also
dozens of pieces for national magazines; (21) 11303 Durland Pl. N.E.,
Seattle, Wash. 98125; Ph. EM2-0141; (22) Seattle Times, Fairview
N. and John, Seattle, Wash. 98111, Ph. MA 2-0300; (23) Circulation:
daily, 230,000; Sunday, 300,000; (24) Approx. 150 per year.

Tandy, Cronyn Great at 2nd Stage
(by Wayne Johnson, Seattle Times, December 3, 1975)

Experiencing the performance of a true virtuoso is always a
great treat, and when two perfectly matched virtuosos perform
together, the treat is not simply doubled but increased by a quan-
tum leap.

Such a rare, memorable treat was provided by Jessica Tandy
and Hume Cronyn last night when they opened their two-person
show, "The Many Faces of Love," at the Seattle Repertory Theater's 2nd Stage.

The most important thing to say immediately about this show
is: See it! The Cronyns (they have been married for 33 years)
have been performing "The Many Faces of Love" in one-night
stands in large auditoriums across the nation. For this week,
they are settled into the intimate 2nd Stage for seven more performances.

Don't miss them! You're not likely to see better acting anywhere, any time.

Using only a small platform on which are an oriental rug,
two lecterns and two chairs, Miss Tandy and Cronyn create the
whole wonderful world of the theater, and with their remarkable
skills, honed to a fine edge by many years of experience, they
bring to vital life the many attitudes about love and the infinite
varieties of love.

The Cronyns rank high among the theatrical royalty of our
time. It is a privilege to have them here.

Their two-hour show is an almost seamless compilation of
poetry, prose, speeches, letters, and dramatic scenes; all dealing with some aspect of love. The material, compiled and edited
by Eleanor Wolquitt, is sometimes sad, sometimes funny, now
poignant, now acerbic, and in at least one instance--Caitlin
Thomas' agonizing over the death of her poet-husband, Dylan--

almost unbearable in its intensity.

The material is good, and it has been well arranged for variety and pacing. The arrangement creates some unusual juxtapositions: for example, the show begins with an amusing poem about middle age by Ogden Nash, and this is followed immediately by Dostoevsky's intense and acute examination of the nature of love and then by Edna St. Vincent Millay's touching poem, "God's World."

Light and wickedly funny verses by the likes of Judith Viorst, Richard Armour and Dorothy Parker are interspersed throughout the show to act as a lightening counterpoint to the heavier, more dramatic sections.

There is one particularly delectable scene in which Miss Tandy half-recites, half-sings the words of "Tea for Two," and then Cronyn responds with a Thurber fable about what would happen if the wife really did get up at 5 a.m. to "make sugar cakes for me to take for all the boys to see."

But the most impressive, most moving sections of the show are those which are most serious and most dramatic.

Cronyn's reading of an excerpt from Thomas Wolfe's "Of Time and the River"--in which Ben gives his 12-year-old brother Eugene a watch for a birthday present--is deeply affecting, as is Cronyn's interpretation of an Alan Paton short story, in which a black man and a white man have a poignant meeting in South Africa.

Miss Tandy, who was the original Blanche in "A Streetcar Named Desire," delivers with spine-tingling intensity the speech in which Blanche describes the love of her young life, her marriage, and the eventual suicide of her husband.

The Cronyns also do scenes from plays in which they have starred together: a scene from Edward Albee's "A Delicate Balance," in which Cronyn disguises his lack of love for his daughter by describing how he killed his pet cat; and a scene from Jan de Hartog's "The Fourposter," in which Miss Tandy tells Cronyn she is leaving him after 26 years of marriage.

There is also a lively scene from James Goldman's "Lion in Winter," in which Cronyn as Henry II engages in a spirited sparring match with Miss Tandy as his wife, Eleanor of Aquitaine.

Another juicy bit of comic relief comes when Cronyn reads a letter, in which Benjamin Franklin, with wonderfully explicit detail, lists the compelling reasons for marrying an older woman.

For any theater buff, it is a joy to watch the Cronyns work. Their acting is consistently informed with intelligence and economy, and their timing--whether in an intensely dramatic scene or in frivolous verse--is impeccable.

The Cronyns were last here when they performed "Promenade All" for the Seattle Rep at the Playhouse in 1972.

Classical Theater Survives in Japan
(by Wayne Johnson, Seattle Times, May 13, 1976)

The young woman at the information desk in the Royal Hotel here was friendly and eager to help, but she was baffled by my request for information about the Asahiza ("za" means "theater" in Japanese).

"Asahiza?" she said. "I don't know it."

I told her that the Asahiza in Osaka had the reputation of being one of Japan's finest theaters for performances of Bunraku, the Japanese puppet drama that dates back to the 17th Century.

"I've never seen Bunraku," said the Japanese woman who was in her middle 20s.

I asked if she had ever seen the other forms of classical Japanese theater--Noh and Kabuki.

"No," she said. "Never. People of my generation don't go for that. We like, well, Dionne Warwick and that sort of thing."

She then obligingly telephoned the Asahiza, found out that day's performance times (noon and 4 p. m.), and wrote out directions to the theater which I could give to a taxi driver.

At the Asahiza, good tickets (at about $8) were easily available for the noon performance. A good many audience members had arrived at the theater early enough to sit in their seats and eat lunch from small wooden boxes.

Much in Japan has changed dramatically in the past two decades, but the quality of the traditional Japanese theater has remained unaltered: superb, detailed performances presented by remarkably disciplined actors.

Bunraku at the Asahiza in Osaka is nothing short of sensationally good theater work, and the same is true for Kabuki performances at the Kabukiza in Tokyo and Noh performances at Kanze Kaikan in Tokyo.

Also unchanged from 20 years ago is the fact that audiences for the traditional Japanese theater range from middle-aged to old. For the younger generations, there's "Dionne Warwick and that sort of thing."

During my previous stay in Japan, I became completely hooked on the aristocratic, elegant, poetic understatement of Noh (which dates back to the 14th Century) and on the colorful, spectacular, wildly extravagant overstatement of Kabuki (a form which began in the 17th Century). My experiences with Noh and Kabuki on this trip confirmed that I am forever hooked on them.

Until this trip, I had never seen Bunraku in Japan. (A visiting Japanese troupe presented Bunraku at the Moore Theater in Seattle some years ago, but the performance was less than memorable because the theater was not really suited for Bunraku performance.)

The Bunraku performance I saw at the Asahiza was indelibly memorable. By a lucky chance, I saw a performance of what the program described as "one of the three masterpieces of Bunraku."

The play was "Sugawara Denju Tenarai Kagami" ("Sugawara's Secrets of Calligraphy"), which was written in 1746.

There is no need here to detail its fascinating and complicated plot, but it does seem in order to describe the Bunraku style, which--like the styles of Kabuki and Noh--is characterized by mind-boggling discipline and artistry.

The Bunraku puppets, fashioned with incredible detail and color, are about two-thirds life-size. Each puppet is manipulated by three men who are dressed entirely in black, including black hoods over their heads (the Bunraku masters, however, do not wear the black hoods).

During the first 10 minutes or so of the performance, I was captivated by watching the astounding coordination of the puppets' manipulators. The puppets, in a sense, seemed incidental to the complex work of the men who were moving them.

Then a particularly handsome, white-cloaked puppet appeared at stage left. I know it sounds ridiculous, but I swear I saw that puppet tell his manipulators to remove his white robe, which the manipulators dutifully did.

From that moment on, I barely noticed the black-clad puppeteers. My concentration was entirely on the puppets themselves, which seemed to have a life independent of any human manipulation. The illusion was completely believable.

There were many fine, exciting moments in the play, including a hair-raising ritual suicide. But my favorite scenes were when an old man (he didn't seem like a puppet by then) toked on an opium pipe and got delightfully high, and when three wives prepared dinner in one of the most charming pas de trois I've ever seen on any stage.

The action of the puppets is accompanied by handsomely gowned speakers on a side stage. The speakers (who seem to read from a script, but they have obviously memorized it) provide the voices of the puppets, and their range of vocal sound and their discipline are as remarkable as the expertise of the puppet manipulators.

There is also shamisen music and drumming to accompany and underscore the dramatic action of the puppets.

I am now as hooked on Bunraku as I am on Noh and Kabuki. Bunraku is clearly high theatrical art, which requires a kind of training and discipline that is apparent in the work of only the very best Western actors.

I suspect that Bunraku will survive for many centuries after "Dionne Warwick and all that stuff" have completely faded from anyone's memory.

JONES, Bruce, Tampa Tribune, P.O. Box 191, Tampa, Fla. 33601.

JONES, John Bush; (2) Special Drama Correspondent, Kansas City Star, and Associate Professor of English, U. of Kansas; (3) b. Chicago, Ill., Aug. 3, 1940; (4) s. Aaron J., Jr. and Dorothy (Bush); (5) B.S. Northwestern U., major subj.: theatre, 1962; M.A. (English) Northwestern U., 1963; Ph.D. (English), Northwestern U., 1970; (6) m. Sandra Carson, May 18, 1968; (7) child--Aaron Carson; (8) Theatre critic, Lawrence (Kansas) Journal-World, 1970-72, Special Drama Correspondent, Kansas City Star, 1970- ; (9) Apprentice, Music Theatre (Highland Park, Ill.), summer 1959; assistant house manager, McVickers Theatre (Chicago), 1959-60; assistant stage manager, Happy Medium Theatre (Chicago), 1960-61; lighting designer and stage manager, Wagon Wheel Playhouse (Warsaw, Inc.), Summer 1962; instructor of English, Northwestern U., 1965-68; assistant professor of English, U. of Kansas, 1968-71; associate professor of English, U. of Kansas, 1971- ; founder and first stage director, Northwestern University Gilbert and Sullivan Guild, 1968; co-founder and co-stage director, Mount Oread Gilbert and Sullivan Company, U. of Kansas, 1968-70; director of opera workshop productions, U. of Kansas, 1973, 1975; (14) Newberry Library Grant-in-Aid, 1971; American Philosophical Society Grant, 1972; (15) Modern Language Association, American Theatre Association, Malone Society, (16) Independent; (17) Jewish-Unitarian; (19) Savage Club (London, Eng.); (20) Scholarly and critical articles in Educational Theatre Journal, Quarterly Journal of Speech, Victorian Poetry, Victorian Newsletter, Western Humanities Review, Proof, Studies in Bibliography, Papers of the Bibliographical Society of America, The Library, Encyclopedia Americana, etc.; Editor, Readings in Descriptive Bibliography (Kent State U. Press, 1974); Editor, W. S. Gilbert: A Century of Scholarship and Commentary (NYU Press, 1970); (21) 315 Mississippi St., Lawrence, Ks. 66044, Ph. 913-842-9028; (22) Dept. of English, U.

of Kansas, Lawrence, Ks. 66045, Ph. 913-864-4391; (23) Circulation: Kansas City Star, 325,000; (24) 10-15 plays and musicals.

Theater in Mid-America: "Celebration"
(by John Bush Jones, Kansas City Star, February 2, 1973)

Let's face it, "The Fantasticks" is a hard act to follow. Despite some qualified successes ("110 in the Shade" and "I Do! I Do!"), Tom Jones and Harvey Schmidt have yet to come remotely near the brilliance of their first and nearly perfect musical.

Certainly "Celebration" misses that mark by even greater distance. Yet the current K.U. production is about as successful as possible considering the material.

What is chiefly wrong with the script and score of "Celebration" is--everything. Except for the title song and "Where Did It Go?" the musical numbers are exquisitely undistinguished--as stale as those in "The Fantasticks" were fresh. Most of the tunes are little better than amateurish imitations of the authors' earlier triumphs. And of the uninspired lyrics, the less said the better.

Like the music, the script appears to be a feeble attempt to cash in once again on the successful "Fantasticks" formula. But what was elegant simplicity there has become heavy-handed clutter in "Celebration." Both plots are essentially allegories of innocence and experience, but in "The Fantasticks" this was dramatized with poetic charm and theatrical subtleties. In "Celebration" the allegory is nakedly obvious and tediously explained.

What's more, the authors no longer seem content to show a single simple aspect of the life cycle. No, here we have not only innocence and experience but youth and age, excitement and boredom, artificiality and genuineness, and seemingly every other pair of opposites that one could ladle out of the great pot of myth. What's lacking, in a word, is focus.

Nevertheless director Kathleen Nicolini and especially the choreographer, DeeDee Clark, have somehow managed to make a fast-paced evening's entertainment from a seemingly hopeless script. And this is no small praise for even professionals, let alone theater students. It's the rare bad play that receives a good production.

The direction, significantly including many cuts in the script, is intelligent, and Miss Nicolini does her best to bring clarity out of the play's chaos. Miss Clark, however, is most responsible for making the show move. Her dances are imaginative and varied, and she has her company performing them with more flair and precision than I have seen at K.U. in years.

The cast of four principals and chorus is competent though
uneven. No doubt part of the problem again lies in what the
script demands of them. In Potemkin, a combination narrator
and con man, Jones and Schmidt have perpetrated a watered-
down El Gallo, even mouthing speeches about the passing of seasons. Such a part does not give Tom Tucker much to work
with, though his fine baritone voice somewhat compensates for a
tendency to overact.

More successful is Michael C. Booker as the wide-eyed innocent who is the hero of the piece. Booker's innocence is there
all right, as well as another fine singing voice, but I generally
saw in him more sheepishness than earnestness. Least successful is Marilyn Michael as the potentially corruptible girl who
comes to value innocence. Her initial hardness never really left
her, and her breathy soprano is unequal to the demands of her
numbers.

The reverse can be said for the villain, as portrayed by Jeff
Cyronek, an actor with a slick command of stage comedy and real
knowhow in executing his vaudevillian song and dance routines.
Complementing the polished staging is an extremely handsome set
by Stephen A. Meriwether. But one question still remains: Is
a bad theatrical property worth all this effort and energy?

Theater in Mid-America: "Half-Eaten Heads"
(by John Bush Jones, Kansas City Star, December 1, 1973)

The best thing about "Half-Eaten Heads" is the title. Also
the most original. In a press release on the play, the author,
Dan Duling, acknowledges his indebtedness to James Dean, Faustus, Norma Desmond ("Sunset Boulevard," lest you've forgotten),
Othello and Jack Webb, among others.

He may be serious or partly jesting. In any case he would
have been more accurate and honest to acknowledge his blatant
borrowings from Albee's "American Dream," Kopit's "Oh Dad,
Poor Dad," Durrenmatt's "The Visit," Mrozek's "Tango," and
Stoppard's "Real Inspector Hound."

With greedy relish for all the now-too-familiar theatrical
gimmickry surrounding the also-too-familiar fantasy-reality gam-
bit, by the end of the play, so to speak, Duling pulls out all the
Stoppards. Least palatable is the final moment directly reminiscent of "Tango," itself so brilliantly produced at K.U. last
year.

And, seemingly in keeping with the play's title, the borrowings aren't even subtle, but disgorge themselves in great, raw,
undigested lumps. Oh that this too, too obvious flesh would resolve itself into a play.

Aside from lack of originality, the chief trouble with "Half-

Eaten Heads" is the nature of its deliberate ambiguity. There's nothing wrong with the confusion of reality and illusion as a dramatic technique, of course (it's practically been done to death). But the mere fact of the ambiguity should at least be made clear to the audience. It isn't here: it's simply fuzzy.

Marcia Grund in her staging and Don Essmiller in his occasionally too symbolic lighting have done what they could to bring some kind of ordered structure to this chaos, but the formlessness of the script nearly gets the best of them and almost swollows them alive.

Few of the actors fare much better. The trouble is that nearly everyone is playing on one level--affectation--so that the truly intended affectation of Aunt Leatha, a has-been actress, falls flat; she has nothing with which to contrast her theatricality. Only Richard Moses and Jean Averill manage to escape this quality in their acting, playing out their brief scene with refreshing toughness and concrete characterizations.

Late in the first act last night, one character asked another, "You're not bored now, are you?" And I silently answered, "You wanna bet?"

JONES, Welton H. Jr.; (2) Entertainment Editor; (3) b. Fort Worth, June 18, 1936; (4) s. Welton H. and Sarah Mabel (Elder) J.; (5) B.A. Texas A & M U., journalism and English, 1958; (6) Divorced; (7) children--Diana Ellen, Welton H. III; (8) Reporter (intern) Lubbock (TX) Avalanche-Journal, 1956, reporter (intern) Houston Post 1957, copy boy New York Herald Tribune 1958, reporter Houston Post 1960-61, amusements editor Shreveport (LA) Times 1962-65, staff writer and reviewer San Diego Union 1966-72, entertainment editor San Diego Union 1973- ; (9) College and little theater work 1957-60; founded Juneau (Alaska) Little Theater 1960, dir. "Our Town"; founded and produced for Major Productions Inc., Houston, 1961; co-founder New Heritage Theater Inc., San Diego, 1970, dir. "The New Black Crook," "Chinchilla!" and Shaw's "The Bolshevick Empress," served three terms as president of board; (no civic, political or non-pro directorships); (13) officer, US Coast Guard Reserve, 1959 to present with current rank of Commander; (14) Various minor awards; (15) Member Music Critic's Association 1963-65, member Sigma Delta Chi 1956-60, member American Newspaper Guild 1966-present, member American Theater Critics Association (pending); (16) Democrat; (17) no religious affiliation; (19) Member San Diego Press Club; (20) Articles for Variety, Copley Press, various daily newspapers; (21) 2331 E St. #12, San Diego, CA. 92102, Ph. 714-239-0509; (22) The San Diego Union, Box 191, San Diego, CA. 92112, Ph. 714-299-3131; (23) Circulation: 170,000 daily, 300,000 Sundays; (24) 60 plays, 5-10 each dance, popular, classical music, etc.

Film Giants Meet with Varied Success on Stage
(by Welton Jones, San Diego Union, February 16, 1975)

Two major screen talents are currently involved in stage projects here, one trying much and mostly failing, the other aiming modestly and succeeding grandly.

At the Ahmanson Theater in the Music Center through March 8, Charlton Heston is wrestling manfully with "Macbeth," surrounded by a turgid production staged by England's Peter Wood with a confusing assortment of concepts betrayed here and there by casting.

Across town at the Shubert Theater, Ingrid Bergman moves with languid grace through a trifling comedy by Somerset Maugham, "The Constant Wife," tightly directed by John Gielgud to yield all its small cargo of insight and amusement.

Which is the more interesting enterprise? A difficult question. "The Constant Wife" is not constantly intriguing, due to long stretches of quasi-Shavian discourse in the play and a certain mustiness inherent in the decor, but it is a gleaming, well-tooled gem of a show. The "Macbeth," on the other hand, is subject to fits of excellence, mostly involving Vanessa Redgrave's presence as Lady Macbeth, but encumbered with a lack of focus and insight.

Central to any consideration of these two shows is the presence of the star, in each case near-legendary personalities from another medium. It is doubtful if either project would have been even considered had they not been available, so their status must be put into perspective.

Film stars on stage is not a new phenomenon, here or elsewhere, but the nature of these two productions suggests that something more than exploitive showcasing was intended. "The Constant Wife" can be considered a vehicle for an accomplished high-style actress in an ensemble situation but a certain willingness to submerge one's ego in the demands of the work is required of the star. "Macbeth," needless to say, is nobody's vehicle.

So, what we have are two enormously successful performers working outside their customary surroundings and doing so with a certain willingness to extend themselves in the face of undoubted economic losses and possible audience disappointment.

Neither performer deserves any particular acclaim for deciding to find the time for an extended stage assignment. The theater in no way requires such efforts for survival. Apparently, the reverse is true--electronic artists in all areas find refreshment in the demands and disciplines of live performances.

The names Bergman and Heston may bring people into the theater but two players named Ingrid and Charlton must take it from there, working in association with many others, sustaining the demands of a continuing run.

Comparing the two roles is like comparing apples and oranges. Any attempt at playing Shakespeare is exhilarating and perilous, an opportunity to succeed or fail on a grand scale, or to reach a level of compromise respectable or otherwise. Therefore, Heston's undertaking Macbeth is a laudable deed for an actor whose chiseled profile and manly intensity has been quite enough so often.

On the other hand, Miss Bergman has perhaps been more realistic in her ambitions, opting for a creation which logic puts within her means and then achieving it with a minimum of fuss.

It's doubtful that either of these productions will form a large part of anybody's fond theatrical memories but it's certain that each project is enriched by the presence of its star.

The "Macbeth" is curiously slow and detached. Despite the liberal use of stage blood, there is little horror evoked by the play's primitive savagery. As crime piles on crime, Heston plants his feet, clenches his teeth and digs in like an ox before the gale.

He and most of the other players are dogged by the notorious acoustics of the Ahmanson. Shouting and the ghostly misdirection of electronic amplification are the inevitable results.

The single shining exception to inaudibility is Vanessa Redgrave, whose gorgeous diction and peerless projection throw the whole show slightly out of balance. Her Lady Macbeth is not a model for the role but it is a most regal, feminine and intelligent performance by a splendid actress.

Wood's idea of the play dwells heavily on the predestination implied by the witches' prophecies. There are many an arch look exchanged as events transpire and Heston clings doggedly to his supposed invulnerability right up to its collapse.

Toward this end, Wood uses men (including the excellent Benjamin Steward) as the witches and has these same actors double as the various murderers, wretches seemingly in thrall to some power they only dimly perceive. It's an interesting idea not carried far enough. Ellis Rabb did much more with the same approach in a haunting 1969 version at San Diego's Old Globe in which the witches carried all the way through to the penultimate scene where they showed up as the household servants who arm Macbeth while informing him of his lady's death.

The remainder of the Ahmanson cast was notable chiefly

for the passionately youthful Malcolm of William Ian Gamble, the strangely held-in Macduff of Richard Jordan and the flashy combat scenes credited to Anthony DeLongis (who also performed some of them) and Joe Canutt.

John Ireland walked through Duncan with little more than dignity and maturity, not quite enough; William Rhys played the Porter (combined with the minor role of Seyton) with poignant physicality not properly integrated into the production, and John Devlin struggled to little effect as Banquo.   The rest blended in blandly with H. R. Poindexter's sets, which can be described as six towering Styrofoam parentheses, semicircling upstage of a raked pancake playing area and stabbed now and then by stair-units--the whole thing a stage manager's nightmare.

Miss Redgrave's presence is the single factor that raises this production significantly above the level of the ordinary.

At the Shubert, practically everything was at least slightly above the ordinary. Miss Bergman, who manages to radiate ani-mal magnetism even in drawing room comedy, is surrounded by an excellent cast of experienced actors manipulated by Gielgud with a precision bordering on arrogance.

The Maugham play is elegant, a one-joke affair suggested by the title in which a British surgeon's wife refuses to acknowlege the clumsy affair going on between her husband and her scatter-brained best friend. As the proceedings unfold--an old beau of hers returns from abroad with passions undamped, another friend offers her an employment opportunity which will make her finan-cially independent and the affair is finally exposed with only the wife's aplomb and quick lies forestalling unpleasantness--Miss Bergman constructs an early feminist, disdainful of conventional mores, realistic in her demands upon others and ultimately able to bring about a delicious denouement in which she assures the best worlds possible for everybody.

The cast seems to have been chosen at least partly for their ability to suggest uppercrust English without specifically using the accents, perhaps due in part to the charming but unmistakable Scandinavian edge that still creeps into Miss Bergman's speech.

Brenda Forbes is a lusciously accurate dowager who espouses the double standard and discreetly mourns Queen Victoria (the time is the late 1920s); Delphi Lawrence is a steely spinster; Carolyn Lagerfelt plays the aging flapper adultress right at the edge of proper taste; Jack Gwillim and Paul Harding provide the well-tailored males to be used and fondly demolished by Miss Bergman, and Marti Stephens, Donald Silber and Richard Marr complete the company.

Alan Tagg provided the white and airy drawing room (with a photomural or projection of London just outside the French windows) and Beatrice Dawson designed the smashing costumes.

"Tempest" Opens Old Globe Season in Glorious Style
(by Welton Jones, San Diego Union, June 4, 1975)

Craft and art in the service of a master conjurer, onstage and off, have united to provide the Old Globe Theater with one of its most glorious productions in a decade--Ellis Rabb's staging of "The Tempest."

This majestic, throat-catching spectacle, seemingly born of a deep love for their labors on the part of all involved, opened the Globe's 26th San Diego National Shakespeare Festival last night and set a new, higher standard for the second quarter-century of this happy institution.

Rabb, a theatrical creator at the heights of his power, dominated the production as a director of unflagging invention and purpose and as an actor in the central role of Prospero, the deposed Duke of Milan whose enemies fall into his power on his deserted island of exile.

Prospero, Rabb and Shakespeare merge into one sharp image as the actor-director focuses the poet and his creation. His eyes seeing beyond the mortals and spirits surrounding him, Rabb's Prospero, steeped in learning both natural and super-natural, seems to watch himself grow yet further beyond revenge, beyond frustration and towards a peace and harmony as rare in nature as in art.

Rabb's Prospero is a father-figure of stunning force. His daughter Miranda, played with a lovely balance of innocence and womanliness by Terrence O'Connor, is serene within his sphere, ripe to bestow her purity upon the shipwrecked son of Naples' king, Ferdinand, played with textured gallantry by Patrick Duffy.

The other shipwrecked nobility--the king of Naples, his scheming brother, Prospero's own brother who plotted his ruin-- find an almost religious experience in Prospero's ultimate stern but unqualified forgiveness. John-Frederick Jones, Barry Kraft and Forrest Buckman play the three, respectively, with style and presence.

Ronald Long, as the old and honorable councillor to the king who suffers fools stoically, makes touching the virtues of constancy. And, speaking of fools, the production has a finely matched pair in the person of the grossly blustering G. Wood and the dry, straight-faced Joseph Bird, who are not above a bit of song-and-dance to the catchy tunes devised by Cathy MacDonald.

But it is Prospero's special relationships with the two creatures native to the island--the sprite Ariel and the monster

Caliban--which continually revive the awe and mystery of this production.

As Caliban, Ronnie B. Baker is encumbered with a crab costume which, no matter how accurate to the lines in the play, is one of the few less-than-successful creations of designer Peggy Kellner.

And Tom DeMastri's Ariel is perhaps one of the most successful interpretations of this difficult role that one could wish for. The actor is young, and the voice shows it, but his physical beauty and grace and his dignified, sober purposefulness mesh poignantly with the visions of Prospero.

Rabb has done practically no tinkering with the text, even including the masque which Prospero stages for Miranda and Ferdinand. This is a stunning spectacle, at once sensual and chaste, classic and baroque, elaborate and transitory, always joyous.

Ms. MacDonald's music contributes greatly throughout but never as much as it does in the masque, where Marian Mercer as Juno presides regally with grandiose song.

Ms. Kellner's designs are likewise inspired, in the masque and throughout, her costuming accurate and fantastic as appropriate. And her setting, a deep, soft cave pierced by a raked platform and bordered by eccentric stairs, is a complete and welcome departure from the familiar psuedo-Elizabethan wood veneer.

This is a production to cherish, one which should take its place in the memory of perennial festival-goers for at least the next 25 seasons.

JONES, William Dennis; (2) Entertainment Editor; (3) b. Indianapolis, Ind., June 11, 1942; (4) s. Marshall W. and Katie (Price) Jones; (5) Attended Phoenix (Ariz), Mesa (Ariz.) Colleges, and Clarion State College (Pa.); English Major; (6) m. Donna Walter Apr. 23, 1966; (7) children--Christopher and Jason; (8) News Editor, Arizona (Phx.) Weekly Gazette, 1967; Police Reporter, Evening Outlook (Santa Monica, Calif.) 1968; free-lance writer, 1969-72, southern California and Pennsylvania; Entertainment Editor, Mesa (Ariz.) Tribune, 1972- ; (13) Sp4 (Cpl.) 1961-1964; (16) Independent; (21) 55 S. 94th Place, Chandler, Ariz., 85224, Ph. 602-963-7446; (22) 120 W. 1st Ave., Mesa, Ariz. 85201, Ph. 602-833-1221; (23) Circulation: 25,000; (24) 25 plays, 5 books

Bach: Pretty Darn Quippy
(by William Jones, Mesa Tribune, March 13, 1974)

"The Intimate P.D.Q. Bach," which was staged, or at least showed up, at Gammage Auditorium in Tempe Monday to perform

its musicological madness before a crowd which left few seats
unweighted and not a single parking place unfilled--an inconstancy
which makes exasperated late-comers like myself believe that
either the planning of the Gammage seating-parking ratio was in-
efficient or that more cars are arriving than people--is either a
study in "Originality Through Incompetence," as the bearded, bedraggled Professor Peter Schickele is wont to theorize from behind his podium stationed before his class of 5,000, or it is a
sophisticated rip-off designed to slake the youthful thirst for dis-
sonance, garbed as it is in hair and barbed as it is in puns,
antics and spoofing machines which clank, bump, grump, toot and
floot their way to barking laughter hung in blasted silence--but,
on the other hand, and more possibly, "P.D.Q." is a --- (please
fill in the blank) which introduces an era of order and structure
to an era of chaos and frustration--a la, Johann Sebastian Bach
meets Alice Cooper--and lets the audience decide subconsciously
which era it's laughing at: that which argues the merits of the
Handelian 4-4 time and diatonic harmony against Bach's chro-
matic idiom, or "Toot Suite for Calliope, four hands," played
by a likeable madman dressed in a rumpled tux, dun-colored work-
shoes and white socks, who occasionally takes karate chops at
his instruments when he is not pontificating to the audience about
P.D.Q. 's four periods of development: (1) the Plunge, (2) the
Soused, (3) the Period He Skipped, and (4) Contrition, informing
the world that Rosemary Woods may be hired as the recording
engineer for the fifth upcoming P.D.Q. album, leaving his piano
to go to the bathroom, accompanying himself in an opera entitled:
"Hansel and Gretel and Ted and Alice," or being otherwise as
absurd as a runaway sentence.

"Boys in Band" Has Clout
(by William Jones, Mesa Tribune, June 12, 1974)

The first thing you will discover about "The Boys in The
Band," to be staged another stint Thursday through Sunday at
Arizona State University's Lyceum Theater, is that the play is
not a musical.

The second thing you will discover is how grateful you are
for leaving your children at home.

And the third thing you will discover is that "Band" is a fine
drama with lots of clout.

Brutal from beginning to end--and employing a language that
would make the late Lenny Bruce grin--the story takes place in
an apartment in New York City where seven homosexuals hold a
very unhappy birthday party for another fellow traveler.   Enter
an old college friend, a heterosexual--of the host, and the groundwork for a plot bristling with conflicts has been laid.

The subject of the play is clearly one which many people find
repugnant--either out of fear or moral principle; however, it is

equally clear that the author, Mart Crowley, has used homosexuality only as a device to explore a human condition, and not as a theme in itself.

It's Crowley's concern with that fine line between illusion and reality, self-deception and truth, which gives "Band" its substance and its clout.

The instrument used to tear away all the guests' false illusions is the party's host, Michael, played brilliantly by Bill Fahlgren.   Unwittingly spurred on by an inherent dissatisfaction with his own lifestyle, the cynical, acid-tongued Michael devises a "truth game" intended to make all the guests victims.

The outcome of the "game" is a shocker, magnificently unexpected, but not at all inappropriate to the characters.

The savagely serious mood and language of the play is given intermittent relief by a sense of humor which, although bloodthirsty, is not without wit and tact.

Too much praise cannot be heaped upon the stunning performance of Fahlgren.   Unlike the "flat" sterotyped roles of most of the other cast, Fahlgren steps believably into the role of the host, whose character is measurably more difficult because he must convey to an audience an individual capable of surprise, one who is living on the edge of uncertainty--about himself.

Fahlgren, by getting into a character of Michael's complexity successfully, demonstrates a rare ability for empathy, which hopefully will find more exercise in an acting career.

JOSLYN, Jay, Thomas; (2) Arts Critic; (3) b. Minneapolis, June 13, 1923; (4) s. William Jay and Hazel Mae (Howlett); (5) Student journalism, Marquette U. , 1941-47; (6) m. Ana Julia Blodgett, June 19, 1948; (7) children--William, Thomas, Lyn (Mrs. Kevin Blackston), Julia, Jennie, Sarah; (8) Reporter, North Shore Publications, Shorewood, Wis. , 1945-47; reporter, editor, Superior (Wis.) Telegram, 1947-50; Associate Editor, Torch Magazine (Milwaukee), 1950-51; Reporter, state, farm, and Sunday Editor, Twin City News Record and Arts reviewer, Menasha and Appleton (Wis.) Post-Crescent, 1953-65; Arts Reviewer, reporter, Milwaukee Sentinel, 1965-present; (13) Served with USAAF, 1943-45; (14) Certificate of Merit Wisconsin Historical Society 1963; (15) Member Menasha Historical Society (Present, 1965, founding member); (17) United Church of Christ; (19) Fox Valley Glass Club (President 1964), Kiwanian (President of Menasha 1963); (21) 8709 W. Spokane St. , Milwaukee, Wis. 53224.

"I Do" Holds Promise of Blissful Stay
(by Jay Joslyn, Milwaukee Sentinel, March 19, 1975)

With Ken Berry playing "I Do, I Do," Centre Stage Dinner

Playhouse is going to enjoy some good business through April 6.

Berry, the engaging star of TV's, "Mayberry, R. F. D." series, is a superb dancer, a pleasant singer and a personality actor who really communicates with an audience.

Tom Jones and Harvey Schmidt's timeless adaptation of Jan de Hartog's "Fourposter" is an ideal vehicle for Berry.

The story of 50 years of a marriage is a light hearted recital that needs Berry's sure touch to carry off the spots of corny sentimentality, moments of truth and episodes of pretention.

Bouncing back Berry's energies as the distaff side of the two person cast is Jeannine Ann Cole, a comedienne with good timing and the ability to react.

Tuesday, her opening night performance might have been enough on the vacuous side to cause a dedicated women's libber to bridle a bit. When she gives her role a bit more moxey, sparks will fly.

Two pianos and a drum kept in hand by Jack Quigley at one of the grands served up a tasty accompaniment for the plum of a show.

Quint Carries Skylight Show as Schweik
(by Jay Joslyn, Milwaukee Sentinel, March 27, 1975)

"Schweik, Schweik. The kind of fellow other fellows like" is a role that made tenor Robert Quint a star in the eyes of members of the Skylight Theater audience Wednesday night.

Active in Milwaukee in comprimero and revue roles for some time, Quint qualifies as an overnight success thanks to the title role in the Skylight's "The Good Soldier Schweik."

Quint's friendly face and outgoing personality made him the perfect Schweik and his true voice and enunciation made him a clear hit with the audience.

While Robert Kurka's jazzy score makes a few strenuous demands on the central character, Quint is given little rest. He carries the show and it could not be in better hands.

The hero of Jaroslav Hasek's satirical post-World War I novel is the kind of Pollyanna character who escapes the consequence of his bungling because of the warmth of his personality.

Librettist Lewis Allen's adaptation of the Czech novel is a loosely assembled string of episodic beads that rush a multitude of characters across the stage to let Schweik defeat as many bureaucratic evils as possible.

Designer-director Clair Richardson has solved the shifting scene problem with a few boxes, a few props and the willing help of the audience's imagination.

The scruffiness of Schweik's life is emphasized by using long john underwear as the basic costume for both men and women.

Richardson has assembled a cast of haphazard sizes and shapes but, happily, competent voices, to handle the 30 roles. Chicago tenor Michael Kalinyen makes a memorial debut.

The end result is a low key improvisation resting on Quint's unflappable characterization that demonstrates the senselessness of bureaucracy and war but muffs the satirical bite.

KALEM, Theodore Eustace; (2) Theater Critic; (3) b. Malden, Mass., Dec. 19, 1919; (4) s. George and Urania (Stoeriades) K.; (5) B.A. Harvard, major subj.: sociology, 1942; (6) m. Helen Newlin, Aug. 26, 1953; (7) children--Marina Helen, Theodore Eustace Jr., John Howard; (8) Book reviewer, Christian Science Monitor, 1948-50; Book reviewer, Time, 1951-61; Drama Critic, Time, 1961- ; (13) Staff Sergeant, U.S. Army, 1942-45; (15) Mem. New York Drama Critics Circle; American Theater Critics Association; (16) Republican; (17) Protestant; (19) The Players, The Coffee House; (20) Article on Eugene O'Neill in the Encyclopedia Britannica; (21) 135 East 18th St., New York, N.Y. 10003, Ph. 212-AL 4-6741; (22) Time & Life Bldg., Rockefeller Center, New York, N.Y. 10020, Ph. 212-JU 6-1212; (23) Circulation: 4,307,638 (Domestic), 5,821,439 (World-wide); (24) 60.

Delta Wildcat
(by T. E. Kalem, Time, October 7, 1974)

Great playwrights differ in their gifts, but they possess one attribute in common. They create great characters, people who live long beyond the run of the play and stalk the corridors of the mind. Hamlet the play is 373 years old; Hamlet the character is immortal.

Among living playwrights, none has created more such characters than Tennessee Williams. Actors and actresses rise to these roles with peak efforts, sometimes giving the most memorable performances of their careers. The present revival of Cat on a Hot Tin Roof is just that sort of triumph.

Elizabeth Ashley left the New York stage slightly over a decade ago as a lovely ingénue. She returns, still ravishingly beautiful, as an actress absoluta. Her Maggie the Cat is sensuous, wily, febrile, gallant, and scorchingly Southern.

Her heart belongs to Brick (Keir Dullea), who spurns her in bed and is drowning in alcohol out of fear that he may be a homosexual. Brick's father, Big Daddy (Fred Gwynne), is dying of cancer, and the childless Maggie is in a steely duel with Brick's brother Gooper (Charles Siebert) and his fecund wife Mae (Joan Pape) for the imminent inheritance of "28,000 acres of the richest land this side of the valley Nile." What evolves is a series of con-

frontations that would reduce the forthcoming Foreman-Ali fight
to a game of patty-cake.

Gwynne's Big Daddy is a man of cutting cruelty, but he lacks
the roguish animal magnestism of Burl Ives in the 1955 original.
Dullea is much too nerveless as Brick; his crutch upstages him.
Stalwart Kate Reid rates a special citation for her earthy, grieving, raging Big Mama. But it is Elizabeth Ashley, purring,
clawing, fighting for her man, who gives the play a mesmeric,
electrifying intensity.

<h3 style="text-align:center">Freudian Exorcism</h3>

(by T. E. Kalem, Time, November 4, 1974)

> Shining, it was Adam and maiden ... / So it must
> have been after the birth of the simple light/ In
> the first spinning place, the spellbound horses walking
> warm/ Out of the whinnying green stable/ On to
> the fields of praise (Fern Hill, Dylan Thomas).

In Equus, it is the Old Adam and night, and six horses are
wheeling in terror. They have been blinded by a 17-year-old
boy wielding a metal spike. Spurred by this lacerating image,
Peter Shaffer has fashioned a galvanizing psychological thriller.

It is also a Manhattan cocktail-party play, the sort of drama
that shoots adrenaline into people's tongues and makes ticket
scalpers' fingers itch in anticipation. T. S. Eliot's The Cocktail
Party was just such a play. So was J. B. and A Man for All
Seasons and Who's Afraid of Virginia Woolf? These plays have
one thing in common. They roar through an evening with blazing
dramatic pyrotechnics. On the following dawn, the embers of
their dubious intellectual premises will scarcely bear analysis.

But playgoers dearly cherish a theatrical hypo, and Broadway desperately needed an Equus. Almost as desperately as did
Richard III. Why has this boy done this horrendous thing? The
structure of the play is like that of a trial in which the witness
and culprit, Alan Strang (Peter Firth), is coaxed, tricked and
thundered at by a prosecuting psychiatrist, Martin Dysart (Anthony Hopkins). In a way, Dysart is a physician who cannot heal
himself. At the Rokeby Psychiatric Hospital in southern England,
he is a skeptical practitioner of Freudian exorcism. He is a
devotee of reason yearning for Dionysian revels. He has a loveless marriage with a wife he has not even kissed in six years.
He pores over pictures of Greek gods and tries to get close to
pagan worship on vacations in the Peloponnesus.

At first, all that Dysart can get out of Alan is inane TV
commercial jingles. But as the interrogation proceeds and Alan
relives key aspects of his life, Dysart realizes that the boy has
not only a passion for horses but also a consuming belief that
they are gods. Thus to relieve the boy of his guilty torment
will simultaneously rob him of his deity. What price normality?

At the end of Act I, Alan is riding his favorite steed, Nugget (Everett McGill), in an orgiastic frenzy that could be defined as a sexual climax or as "union with God," depending on the way one chooses to look at it.

The horses, by the way, are simply tall men in chestnut track suits. On their feet are strutted hooves about 4 in. high. Over their heads are airy, stylized masks of interlaced leather and silver wire. These possess such hieratic dignity and beauty that a special citation should be awarded Scenery Designer and Costumer John Napier. How could these noble animals be maimed by a boy who revered them? For answers, Playwright Shaffer digs into his rather voluminous bag of stereotypes. Alan's mother is a frigid religious hysteric, compellingly played by Frances Sternhagen.

Alan's father is a do-gooding socialist printer and a self-righteous authoritarian moralist who gets his after-hours kicks at skin flicks. At the stable where he works on weekends, Alan is sexually aroused by a pert, enticing co-employee (Roberta Maxwell). In a nude scene that precedes the play's climax, they try to make love but Alan falters. He feels that the eyes of his gods watch and condemn him. Then the horror begins.

With consummate theatrical brio, Shaffer has attuned the audience to some of its deepest desires--sin, guilt, confession, atonement and a degree of redemption. Dare one say that he has also blinded the audience to his exaltation of deranged violence as religious passion and his derogation of civilizing reason as hollow passivity?

In a superb cast, two performers are in the megaton range. Peter Firth makes Alan a fallen angel of anguish, and Anthony Hopkins' psychiatrist is a tour de force that should make any other Tony contender blanch.

KAREDA, Urjo; (2) Theatre critic; (3) b. Tallinn, Estonia, Feb. 9, 1944; (4) s. Endel and Helmi (Urm) K.; (5) B.A. and M.A., U. of Toronto, English Literature, Doctoral thesis for Cambridge U. (England) uncompleted, subject: modern tragicomedy; (6) m. Shelagh Hewitt, Oct. 4, 1969; (7) children--daughter Maia; (8) 1966-68, Staff writer, Entertainment Department, the Globe and Mail, Toronto; 1968-70, columnist, writing on arts in England, Toronto Star; 1970-71, film critic, Toronto Star; from 1971, theatre critic, Toronto Star; also, 1970-75, Department of English, Erindale College, University of Toronto; (9) Freelance writer, New York Times, Opera News, Maclean's Magazines; freelance broadcaster, Canadian Broadcasting Corporation; 1971, directed Pinter's Landscape and Silence, Firehall Theatre, Toronto; (12) advisor, Province of Ontario Council for the Arts; (14) Canada Council Doctoral Fellowship, 1967-70; Harvard Doctoral Fellowship, to start from 1967 (declined); (15) Member, Toronto Drama Bench; (16) Information unavailable; (17) Information

unavailable; (20) Cont. articles in The Toronto Star, as well as occasional pieces in New York Times and Opera News; (21) information
unavailable; (22) Toronto Star, 1 Yonge St., Toronto, Ontario, Canada M5E 1E6, Ph. 416-367-2000; (23) 500,000 (daily), 755,500 (Saturdays); (24) 200 plays, 25 movies, 10 operas.

Canadian Play a Spectacular Hit on Broadway
(by Urjo Kareda, Toronto Star, April 2, 1975)

The most spectacular new hit on Broadway is a Canadian
play.

It's true that Same Time, Next Year is in some ways the
definitive Broadway comedy, immaculately attuned to and written
for its audiences. But indeed, the author, Bernard Slade, is a
Canadian, a St. Catharines native and ex-Torontonian.

Several years ago he had plays produced on the CBC, at the
Crest and the Manitoba Theatre Centre, all of which are mentioned in his program biography.

More recently, he moved to California where he created such
TV series as The Partridge Family and Bridget and Bernie, none
of which is even whispered in the program.

Same Time, Next Year marks Slade's Broadway debut, and
the play, which he wrote during a two-week Hawaiian holiday, has
been greeted with mostly enthusiastic reviews, long lines of ticket
buyers and even a Tony Award nomination.

It's a two-character work of the most engaging attractiveness,
with acting roles--taken superbly on Broadway by Ellen Burstyn
and Charles Grodin--so generous that there couldn't be a thirtyish
acting couple anywhere in the United States who isn't fighting for
a chance at the touring company.

Slade's premise is simple, mechanical and slightly inspired.
He takes a couple, Doris and George, each happily married, who
have a chance sexual encounter in a California inn in 1951.
George, an accountant, was on his way to help a friend with taxes. Doris was on her way to a Catholic retreat. They decide to
continue meeting just once a year, at the same time and in the
same place.

The play observes six of their illicit weekends between 1951
and 1975, and it doesn't take the audience long to catch on that
most of the play's fun lies in the radical, vaguely improbable but
theatrically effective changes that the couple undergoes from
scene to scene.

Doris is seen, elliptically, as a gauche, shy young housewife,
then a dissatisfied suburbanite, then a suddenly liberated student

at Berkeley, and finally, a successful businesswoman and possible political candidate.

George, too, shifts from a guilt-ridden, ambitious young accountant to a stuffy, what's-the-country-coming-to conservative (timed, of course, to coincide with Doris' frank, free-wheeling radicalism) and at last to a cocktail pianist in a singles bar.

The backdrop to these transformations includes childbirth, separation, illness, economic decline and even death, but it's the nostalgic romanticism, the muted, friendly ecstasy of the foreground, with its once-a-year enchantment, that we're told to hold onto.

The pattern, then, is very thin, and Slade is liable both to overload the couple with clever jokes which don't always spring from character, and to flinch from more difficult emotions. There's a scene, for instance, in which George tells of his son's death in Viet Nam, which is cut off before it's really begun.

On the other hand, Slade's structure is heady with a genuine, deeply-felt romanticism, rich in comic possibilities, and most important, extraordinarily playable. Same Time, Next Year is a gorgeously satisfying evening in terms of its opportunities for actors. Under Gene Saks' most skillful direction, Ellen Burstyn and Charles Grodin accomplish wonders.

Grodin may be a bit short of charm initially, but he's a fine physical technician and the character grows beautifully into middle-age. The magnificent Ellen Burstyn reveals again that gift for making emotions and situations seem truthful--as in her Oscar-deserving performance in Alice Doesn't Live Here Any More-- and her Doris is breathtakingly shaped and shaded, a complex, tremendously moving characterization.

Thus it's possible both to overrate and underrate Bernard Slade's play.

It does lack depth at the times when we need it, and it does perhaps play too callously on nostalgia for the past. But it is also very funny, very touching and very skillful.

Ellen Burstyn, after all, couldn't have built her memorable performance from nothing. One doesn't begrudge Bernard Slade a single handclap of his success.

Stratford's Twelfth Night Distinguished by Its Clarity
(by Urjo Kareda, Toronto Star, June 11, 1975)

After the glum opening night Saint Joan peopled by some of Stratford's most familiar actors, it was fascinating last night to watch Twelfth Night, in which virtually every major role was performed by an actor making a Festival Theatre debut this season.

The resultant freshness wasn't merely the effect of novelty but of an insistence upon proportion and sensibility, encouraged obviously by director David Jones, on loan from the Royal Shakespeare Company.

Hence the general upsurge in quality was no coincidence. This was a Twelfth Night distinguished by its truthfulness, clarity and unaffectedness.

This isn't a production of startling revelations or independently brilliant performances, with the exception of Brian Bedford's extraordinary Malvolio. Its substantial satisfactions come from the intelligence with which its elements have been measured out, and the balance within the acting company.

Even with a play as dangerously familiar as Twelfth Night it is interesting how much can be achieved by scrupulous fidelity.

Director David Jones, designer Susan Benson, lighting designer Gil Wechsler and composer Harry Freedman, all generously supporting the actors, have laid out an Illyria of understated langor.

It is a believable context for the complexly erotic, sometimes cruel events which follow, a world in which almost everyone is a bit too selfish, a bit too vain, in which there is too much money and too much unfilled time.

The native Illyrians, like the storm-separated twins Viola and Sebastian who are drawn into this world, dally and play at games whose consequences they can never imagine. All their fantasy is turned inward; the logical progression from one action to another is beyond their comprehension.

In some ways, this may be Shakespeare's most maddening comic crew, more or less all afflicted with the steward Malvolio's chronic self-love. But in this production we are nevertheless able to perceive them as human and worth caring for.

So pervasive in fact is Jones' stress upon character that some of the more mechanical plot turnings go a little flat, and the second half in particular has slack stretches in which Shakespeare, also not altogether convincingly, trots out some farce tricks, sets up duels and muddles recognitions.

In this performance, one is far less interested in the turn of events than in the response to events and how events transform behavior:

Marti Maraden's Olivia moves compellingly, for instance, from a not very likeable haughtiness to an urgent, dangerous passion. Kathleen Widdoes' Viola is at first impishly delighted with

her disguise until the confusion about her sexual identity draws
forth feelings she cannot manipulate.

Stephen Macht's Orsino, artifice looking for substance, finds
reality in apparent betrayal. All these roles are finely drawn
with an eye to the inner personality.

Equally fully developed are the characters from the comic
sub-plot, who for once are not exaggerated beyond bounds, but
retain their social credibility as members of a countess' household.

Leslie Yeo's Sir Toby Belch is still authoritative and a vigorous swordsman; he just happens to be a drunk.

Denise Fergusson's Maria is no coarse ninny, but a spinster
whose romance with Sir Toby is a precarious thing.

Frank Maraden's Sir Andrew Aguecheek is a victim of his
own headlong and innocent enthusiasms.

Tom Kneebone's Seste is a professional clown still, but with
panic, depression and malice creeping at the edges.

None of them is unaware of time's passing and its effects.
(What with Kneebone, Fergusson and Widdoes--what a memorable
collection of huge, melancholy eyes!)

On a level all its own--not inappropriately, since the character is the play's true outsider--is Brian Bedford's Malvolio,
a preening, pontificating booby on intimate speaking terms with
the Deity.

The actor's collection of condescending smirks and self-as-
suring smiles is miraculous and the detail in his performance
of the letter scene, manipulating the audience with deadpan
amazement, is a consummate achievement in comic invention.

And there has to be a final word in praise of the production's
sensual beauties, most memorably isolated in the exquisite feeling for color and texture in Susan Benson's costumes and in
resigned melancholy of Harry Freedman's songs.

KAUFFMANN, Stanley Jules; (2) Author; (3) b. New York City, April
24, 1916; (4) s. Joseph H. and Jeannette (Steiner) K.; (5) B.F.A.,
N.Y.U. 1935; (6) m. Laura Cohen, Feb. 5, 1943; (8) Memorial
Washington Sq. Players, 1931-41, assoc. editor Bantam Books, 1949-
52, Editor in Chief Ballantine Books, 1952-56; Editor Alfred A.
Knopf, 1959-60; film critic, New Republic, N.Y.C., 1958-65, 67- .
Assoc. editor of lit., 1966-67, theater critic, 1969- ; drama critic
N.Y. Times, 1966; (9) Condr. program The Art of Film, channel 13,
N.Y.C., 1963-67, vis. prof. drama Yale, 1967-68, 69-73; Distinguished

prof. City U. of N. Y. , 1973- ; (14) Ford Found. Fellow for Study
abroad, 1964 & 1971; hon. Fellow Morse Coll. , Yale, 1964; (20) Author:
The Hidden Hero, 1949; The Tightrope, 1952; A Change of Climate,
1954; Man of the World, 1956; A World on Film, 1966; Figures of
Light, 1972; Editor (with Bruce Henstall) American Film Criticism:
From the Beginning to Citizen Kane, 1973; (21) 10 W. 15th St.
N. Y. C. , N. Y. 10011.

A Chorus Line
(by Stanley Kauffmann, New Republic, June 21, 1975)

Credit where credit is certainly due. I haven't been shy
about criticizing Joseph Papp adversely, so I underscore at the
start that his hospitality and support helped to make A Chorus
Line possible. Apparently he had little to do with the creation
of the show (and hasn't claimed it), but he provided the place
for Michael Bennett and his collaborators to evolve it over a
period of months as a workshop production. Many of the Public
Theater workshops never see the light, or much light. Once in
a good while, as with Jack Gelber's version of Mailer's Barbary
Shore, the results are as interesting as any in Papp's far-flung--
and still flinging--empire. A scattershot policy occasionally pays
off if you keep it up long enough. Papp persists; and this is one
of the happier results.

Michael Bennett is a Broadway choreographer and director
whose previous work, as I've seen it, has ranged from fair to
foul. His choreography for Company was smart, for Follies less
smart; his direction of Neil Simon's play God's Favorite was a
mistake. Most of his work has been in musicals--he began as
a chorus dancer at 17 and is now only 32--and the experience
of the chorus call has been central to his life, the process of
trying out for jobs in a show, getting and not getting them. That
experience is a microcosm of cultural comment. Out of it Bennett has made a good show, using a method that is a further
cultural comment.

The Broadway musical performer is a special, rarefied
breed. He (please also read "she") was much in demand in the
first half of this century when musicals were produced in great
numbers. It's paradoxical that, as the number of musicals has
drastically declined, their job requirements have risen in strin-
gency. Formerly a show might have a singing group, a group
of show girls (who only had to be tall and gorgeous), a dance
group whose work was mainly tap, and occasionally some ballet
dancers as well. From about the time of Oklahoma! (1943) and
Agnes DeMille's choreography therein, the character of Broadway dancing has changed; this, combined with money tightening,
has made it necessary for fewer and fewer people to do more
and more. The same ensemble must now do the dancing (tap
and ballet), sing, look sexy, and also play small parts when
necessary. The competent Broadway musical performer is one
of the best-trained people in the American theater--and has

become so just as his job opportunities have dwindled. ("Don't tell me that Broadway is dying," wails one of the girls in this show. "I just got here.")

With all that's required and with so few chances to us it, the chorus call for a Broadway show has become a special circle of hell. To explore it, to explore why some people insist on preparing and heading for it, Bennett conceived the idea of A Chorus Line. His helpers, all skillful, were the co-choreographer Bob Avian, the writers James Kirkwood and Nicholas Dante, the lyricist Edward Kleban and the composer Marvin Hamlisch. Robin Wagner's setting is just black drapes with a huge mirror as backdrop which splits into sections on pivots and can disappear--not a fresh idea but useful for a dance show. Tharon Musser's lighting is highly responsive to situations and does more to "dress" the show than any other element.

The strikingly different fact about A Chorus Line, and its most illuminating cultural aspect, is that it was evolved through months of rehearsal. Bennett has said that the entire cast--a very talented group--was engaged before the show was written. The book, the songs and the dances were worked out as they went along, from materials that came out of rehearsals, including the lives of all the participants. This is clearly the appropriation by Broadway musical people of a method that has been developed, not by Off Broadway but by Off Off Broadway--in "matrix" groups, such as Joseph Chaikin's now disbanded Open Theater, which evolve their productions out of the contributions in rehearsal of all the participants, with writers and composers (if used at all) as collaborators in the evolution. In fact one moment near the beginning of A Chorus Line--when a dance ends with the line of dancers holding up their photographs in front of their faces--is strongly reminiscent of a similar device in the Open Theater's Mutation Show (1973). In further fact this show's over all method, winnowing out the performers' autobiographies to juxtapose them against what they are now, is also reminiscent of The Mutation Show.

As the lights come up on A Chorus Line (no curtain), a group of 23 men and women--called "boys and girls"--are dancing in rehearsal clothes, led by the director and his assistant. The director soon eliminates six. Then, seated at the back of the auditorium, he tells the remaining 17 that he will finally select eight, "four and four"; that he wants a strong unit who can also play small parts; and that he must know more about them. This public self-revelation, not exactly run-of-the-mill at chorus calls, is the central device. Each of them steps forward in turn and talks, and/or sings and dances, about "himself." Each of them is actually dealing with a fictional character, but all of this material has obviously been mined from firsthand observation or experience, worked over and "set" by Bennett and his colleagues. Finally the director chooses eight.

Two common denominators apply to most of the stories. First, these dancers hated their families and hometowns. (One of the boys grew up in Buffalo which so depressed him that he once thought of killing himself; but "to commit suicide in Buffalo is redundant.") Second, as one number says, "everything is beautiful at the ballet." They are mostly refugees who dread having to return to the outside world either by failing or by aging. The border between psychic needs and creative impulse is always fuzzy; and this show makes clear that most of these people are here, have suffered to get here, are suffering to stay, at least as much out of hatred of their pasts and past selves and the glare of daylight as out of their love of dancing and the theater.

None of this is startling or deep, some of it is show-biz corn, but most of it is authentic, even some of the corn. And almost all of it is well done. Carole Bishop as an aging dancer, Priscilla Lopez as a cockily clearheaded Puerto Rican, Sammy Williams with a riskily sentimental scene about a homosexual who has finally been acknowledged by his parents, are outstanding. The low point is a plotty scene between the director and his ex-girl, who was almost a star and now needs a chorus job, but Donna McKechnie dances the part with dazzle.

Bennett's problem with these successive "case histories" was variety of presentation, which he handled so well that we're never conscious of the problem. Hamlisch's music, though there are no hummable tunes, is sculpted to its occasions neatly and danceably. And there is an ironic payoff. In the latter part of the show (two hours plus, no intermission) the dancers learn a number from the new show for which they're trying out. For the curtain call of A Chorus Line all 17 come out in the new show's costumes and do that new number. The costumes are pure Busby Berkeley; the song is peppily inane. This, Bennett and friends seem to be saying, is what these people were dying to get into, what they have trained for.

So A Chorus Line is the result of a Broadway institution going to Off Broadway to examine itself, using Off Off Broadway methods to do it (whether or not Bennett saw the Open Theater), and finding some futility to report. The irony is compounded because this show, a smash success, will move up to Broadway in July. Well, the successful move of Candide from Off Broadway to a huge big-time house proved that there was big money in unconventional staging of conventional material. Now this good new musical, made by a process absolutely antithetical to big-time procedures, is going up to be a big-time success. It's no news that commerce feeds on art, but the joke here is that this show, which fundamentally tells us how sterile the whole Broadway business is, is going up to help sustain it.

The Lady from the Sea
(by Stanley Kauffmann, New Republic, April 10, 1976)

Vanessa Redgrave, lovely, a light upon the stage as she is
on the screen, joins her sister in the New York theater season.
Four weeks ago I wrote of Lynn Redgrave's sturdy performance
in Mrs. Warren's Profession which (principally) made the production a pleasant surprise.   Now Vaness R. 's lyric performance
of Ellida in Ibsen's Lady from the Sea is that production's only
stay against disaster.

I admit that I went to this play with considerable fear.   Quite
apart from its intrinsic quality (of which more later) I've always
thought it so allusive and rarefied as to be virtually unactable.
(This is even more true, I think, of Ibsen's vastly superior When
We Dead Awaken.)   I knew something of the stage history of the
piece, including Duse's success.   But Duse's very success confirmed my feelings.   If one can rely on theatrical history at all,
then she was an actress who specialized in Soul and Beauty, both
spelled with capitals, and she performed for a society that spelled
them the same way.   I found it hard to imagine how, for a contemporary audience, one could authenticate--with real, physically
present people--this drama of a woman who is in the thrall of
a mystic marriage to the sea.   Despite Redgrave's gifts, and
even speculating about improvements in other roles, I still can't
imagine it.

Ellida is the young second wife of Dr. Wangel, a gentle middle-aged physician who has two teen-age daughters.   (The younger one, Hilde, reappears in The Master Builder.)   Before she
met Wangel, Ellida, herself the daughter of a lighthouse-keeper,
had a romance with a mysterious sailor, and they "wed" each
other by throwing rings into the sea.   He disappeared; eventually she allowed herself to become Mrs. Wangel and came to live
in this house above the fjord, still near the sea, still "belonging" to the sailor.   She had one child, who she thinks had the
sailor's eyes (though the man had been gone for years).   Since
the child's death she has had no marital relations with Wangel,
feeling that she has betrayed the sailor.   The sailor suddenly
appears one day, claims Ellida as his own, and says he will return next day to take her away.   Wangel refuses to "release"
Ellida, for her own good.   But when the sailor reappears, Wangel does "release" her so that she can choose freely between
him and the sailor.   With the choice now entirely hers, she
chooses her husband (a foretaste of Candida here), and the sailor
disappears forever.

The central idea--a woman enslaved by her past who is freed
by being given freedom of choice--is a blank symbol which can
be colored any hue that the reader-spectator brings with him.

Many distinguished critics have commented on The Lady from the Sea and have found in it everything from analogies with Dante to prescience about Freud. (It was written in 1888.) I have no special quarrel with any of the analyses I know and will even offer the lame tribute that their variety is a compliment to Ibsen. My difference with them is in value judgment, not in analysis. Just because the play is varyingly analyzable; just because many interpretations of Ellida's enslavement and release are possible; just because there is a contrast in the play between a safe pool in which carp live and the wild sea in which people drown; just because the sailor killed his captain long ago and would say only that it was the right thing to do (which Ibsen never clarifies even as metaphor); just because there's a parallel between Ellida and her older stepdaughter who accepts the proposal of an older man; just because many other patterns can be winkled out--it doesn't necessarily follow from all these "becauses" that The Lady from the Sea is a good play.   One affliction of serious criticism is the belief that if a work can sustain analysis, it's good.

Esthetic experience is something else.   The evaluative truth, for me, is that this play is tenuous, strained, and even arbitrarily cobbled in places.   A young would-be sculptor, now wooing a Wangel daughter, just happens to have been on a ship with the mysterious sailor and just happens to have heard him make a revealing remark which he now just happens to remember, a device (like others in other realistic Ibsen plays) right out of the 19th-century theater of carpentry where the author had labored for 11 years.   Tenuousness and strain dominate the subplots of The Lady.   It's patent that they are meant analogically to the central story, but they are simply not very interesting in themselves; they are mere padding to bulk out a full length play. As for that central story, Ellida spends most of the first three acts remembering something that happened long ago.   This is a very different theatrical conception from Hedda Gabler; she too is in the thrall of her past, doomed by it, but with the very start of the play, that doom begins to be dramatically articulated.

Another point--a criticism that Strindberg might have made in the vein of his criticism of A Doll's House.   It seems to me that the crucial action of the play is Wangel's, not Ellida's.   It is he who goes through the greatest transformation, a conventional and deeply loving husband who is moved to grant his wife her freedom so that she may make a free choice between him and another man.   True, it is she who then has to make that choice; but she has been shown as a person of greater imaginative reach, so the making of that choice is little temperamental wrench for her, even though it's an emotional one.   The real character enlargement is Wangel's, not hers; the whole play can be seen as a drama of his belated maturation--possibly it should be called The Husband of the Lady from the Sea.   The reason that A Doll's House and Hedda Gabler end so much less happily than this play is that the husbands in those two plays are incapable of growth.

Agree with my estimate of The Lady or not, still you would
likely agree that any performance of it runs a constant risk of
slipping into the unbearably precious. That, at least, does not
happen: because of Vanessa Redgrave's purity, concentration,
grace. It's not possible to believe in Ellida any more than one
can believe in a character in Everyman or The Faerie Queene.
Redgrave's job is harder than it would be in (figuratively) those
works because Ibsen has surrounded her abstraction with detailed
realistic characterization. Redgrave seems to realize this and
seems to abstract herself without any touch of posing. She speaks
quietly and moves gently, confiding her story to Wangel rather
than displaying her delicacy. (She never really raises her voice
until the last act.) Redgrave is a large woman with immediate
stage command; I've rarely seen that command used so easily
for intimacy and sensitivity.

But then there is Pat Hingle, the Wangel--pedestrian and
trite, just another slice of Dear Old Dad in any domestic American play. One of the problems in using an English actress in
America is how to surround her with accents that don't make her
sound alien; in this regard Hingle was an especially poor choice.
The others in the cast range from the bearable--George Ede as
the jack-of-all-arts Ballested, Kimberly Farr as the older daugh-
ter--to the utterly unbearable--Richard Lynch as the Stranger
(the sailor). It's a hellishly difficult part: he has to walk in
and immediately justify everything poetical that has been said
about him. Christopher Walken at his best might be able to do
it, if he would accept such a small part. Lynch simply hasn't
any of the requisite powers.

And Tony Richardson, the director, has handled him especially badly by plunking him into the middle of that wretched Circle
in the Square playing oval. Earlier, Richardson has staged the
first act at the far end, an effect something like watching a tea
party at the distant end of a small race-track. When he comes
to an actor who should be kept distant, Richardson whams him
at us, pores and all. To put it kindly, Richardson is one more
director beaten by that theater, which should be razed and re-
built.

Michael Meyer's translation leaves some flexibility to be desired. When Ellida says at the end that she was blind to Wangel's love, he says: "Your thoughts were directed elsewhere."
Couldn't Meyer at least have left out "directed"?

KAYE, Joseph; (2) New York Theater Correspondent for the Kansas
City Star; (3) b. Odessa, Russia; (5) Primary school in Glasgow,
Scotland; (6) m. Frances Balub; (7) child--Judith Reed; (15) United
Nations Correspondents Association; Music Critics Assoc.; Dance
Critics Assoc.; Outer Critics Circle; (21) 405 East 54th St., New
York, N.Y. 10027; Ph. 212-PL5-1932; (22) Kansas City Star, Kansas
City, Mo. 64108.

Kansas Citian Portrays a Horse
(by Joseph Kaye, Kansas City Star, December 17, 1974)

Everett McGill, an actor from Kansas City, has a unique part in a new Broadway super-hit, "Equus." McGill plays the First Horse, a silent role, but an important one. The play, by an English dramatist, Peter Shaffer, deals with the passion of a boy for horses, and, McGill is one of several horses but the one symbolic of the boy's attachment and the one he rides on secret visits to the stable.

Stylized horse's heads and hoofs are worn by the men who enact the horses, and the illusion is remarkably realistic. The men have to be tall, and with muscular, but slender bodies, particularly the First Horse, who is dominant throughout the drama. That is how Everett McGill got the part. He had been in a flop Off-Broadway show but was noticed by an agent, and when casting began for "Equus" the agent remembered him and McGill hurried back from a vacation in Canada for an audition. The director, John Dexter, was happy to get him. McGill is 6 feet, 2 inches tall and of just the right physique.

McGill also doubles in a speaking part, but it is his First Horse that draws attention. The boy, Alan, mounts and rides him in one of the crucial scenes, and the effect is astonishingly realistic.

"Equus" is a strange, sometimes horrifying, but always fascinating play. It is based on an apparently little-known English crime committed by a stable boy who blinded a number of horses.

Shaffer had no knowledge of the details of this extraordinary incident, but he was intrigued by what possibly could have been the reason for this act. After considerable research in psychiatry and legends concerning horses, he created "Equus." In it a similar act is committed by a boy (Peter Firth) who attends horses in a stable, and a psychiatrist (Anthony Hopkins) who attempts to probe the boy's mind to discover the reason for the crime. What is revealed is a boy's passion for horses that is so deep that in his distorted mind he almost deifies them.

In a way, "Equus" is a mystery, with the doctor's persistent painful examination, the boy's resistance and final yielding, and flashbacks providing the background, forming an emotional suspense story.

In the process of this sleuthing the doctor, a fully mature, married man, realizes that he has never felt the enveloping quality of passion that this boy possessed.

"Equus" is a complex play, and audiences must draw certain conclusions for themselves. But so compelling is it, so brilliant the acting and staging, that the response from critics and audiences was enthusiastic and the production is one of the biggest hits of many season.

Everett McGill is a graduate of the University of Missouri-Kansas City and while he attended Kansas City, Kansas, Junior College, he formed a jazz band, the Dell Shays, which was quite popular in the area. He had dramatic experience when he was at Rosedale High School. His drama teacher, James Shepherd, gave him roles in plays "from Ionesco to Shakespeare." Later these early theatrical adventures led him to study in London and attempt to break into the New York theater. After "pounding on many doors" here, he was engaged by the late Repertory Company of Lincoln Center.

McGill is married to Mrs. Linda Ruzich McGill who studied dancing at the University conservatory. He is the son of Everett and Ollie McGill, of 1898 S. 7th, Kansas City, Kansas.

South African Hits on Broadway
(by Joseph Kaye, Kansas City Star, January 22, 1975)

When theater award time comes along, John Kani and Winston Ntshona are among the most likely to be honored--along with the plays they act in, "Sizwe Banzi Is Dead" and "The Island."

Kani and Ntshona are players from South Africa. "Sizwe" and "The Island" are successes at the Edison Theater here, performed alternately. They are unusual plays, having been devised as improvisations. They were evolved in so remarkable a manner that both plays with their 2-man interpreters have been hits in Africa, in Britain and now on Broadway.

Those who see "Sizwe" and "The Island" marvel at the acting of Kani and Ntshoma. They are as natural as men you may meet on the street, but the naturalness has the artifice and the quality of genius. They are members of what may be termed pure theater.

Kani and Ntshona belong to a theater company in Port Elizabeth, South Africa, the Serpent Players, whose leader and inspiration is Athol Fugard, the famed South African white dramatist whose works have been presented here. "Sizwe" and "The Island" were created with Fugard's collaboration.

"Sizwe Is Dead" is about a black African who comes to Port Elizabeth to find work but cannot because his passbook, which all blacks are requred to carry, does not allow him to work there. He and a friend find the body of a black man who was killed and whose passbook permits work in Port Elizabeth. Sizwe, being actually an official number, adopts the dead man's passbook and so becomes a dead Sizwe but a live man to work and send support to his family.

In "The Island," which refers to Robben Island, a maximum security prison for political offenders, some of the blacks there stage the classic Greek tragedy, "Antigone," which stresses the duty to humanity above the laws of a state.

A strange element in the production of these plays is that although they expose the globally condemned practice of apartheid (racial separation) in South Africa--and the laws concerning apartheid are severe--the two plays were allowed to be performed in South Africa (with white actors for white audiences and black actors for the black theater).

That may be a sign of hope.

KELLY, Kevin; (2) Theater and Film Critic for The Boston Globe; (3) b. Boston, Aug. 5, 1934; (4) s. St. Clair and Joan (Sinnott) Kelly; (5) M.A. Boston U. , subject: English Literature; (8) Staff member The Boston Globe, 1958, theater critic 1962, critic-at-large 1966, film critic 1970, local theater critic for Show Business Illustrated, 1960-62; (14) Elected Collegium of Distinguished Alumni of the College of Liberal Arts of Boston University 1974, elected to Phi Beta Kappa for Distinguished Achievement as Theater and Film Critic 1975, elected to the National Society of Film Critics; (21) 39 Mount Hope, Norwell, Mass. , 02061, Ph. 617-659-7761; (22) The Boston Globe, 135 Morrissey Blvd. , Boston, Mass. 02107, Ph. 617-929-2783; (23) Circulation: daily 475,346; Sunday 583,787; (24) 250 film reviews, 50 theater reviews, 50 miscellaneous.

"St. Joan" Opens Season at Stratford
(by Kevin Kelly, Boston Globe, June 15, 1975)

The Stratford Festival's 23d season opened Monday night with George Bernard Shaw's "Saint Joan" in a thoroughly routine production that did little or nothing to indicate the sweeping changes supposedly taking place under the festival's new artistic director, Robin Phillips. Whether or not Stratford, like Joan, is up for burning is still to be decided. The bold Phillips policies announced last year (a blitzing of Stratford's old theatrical ways, including the restructuring of the neo-Elizabethan stage which has long been the theater's working, yet symbolic, cornerstone) are to be tried in "Twelfth Night" and "Measure for Measure," which follow the Shaw. Yet, if Phillips really is the fresh wind of the future, why so little breath expended on "Saint Joan?" Why, in the premiere production of his debut season, a guarded return to the old ways he has steadfastly sworn to escape?

As perplexing as these questions are, they stray slightly from the immediate point which is, or should be, "Saint Joan." The play has been directed by William Hutt, a member of what must now be considered Stratford's vanishing regime. Written in 1923, Shaw's work collects the known facts of Joan's life and puts them to a distinct Shavian purpose. We are not meant

merely to be present at a religious inquest, an idle auto-da-fe,
nor are we meant merely to be present at the fitting of a halo
on a headstrong heroine. We are meant, instead, to witness
the whole historic continuum perpetuated by ignorance and bigotry.
Joan's life is important to Shaw only for its philosophic cause
and effect. Although he indicates that she may be nothing more
than a self-deluded peasant, he doesn't rob her of saintliness
that makes "Saint Joan" the brilliant play it is.

After Joan's death at the stake, the victim of fantastic inner
voices in collision with the stupidity of the Church and the law,
Shaw ressurects her for an epilogue in which she's surrounded
by friends and foes. Twenty-five years have passed since her
body crumbled to ash and her heart refused to burn. Her un-
proved guilt has driven balmy some of her persecutors while
others have waited in hope for the beginning glimmer of her halo.
Shaw brings on a dapper "20th-Century gentleman" who announces
to the assembled ghosts that Joan, declared venerable in 1904 and
blessed in 1908, has been canonized at last in 1920. There is
congratulatory gladness among the ghosts who honor themselves
with self-justification for their guilt and genuflect at the feet of
their new saint. But when asked if they are ready now to receive her fully, to accept her as a woman on earth, they all, to
a man, back off. A soldier, who offered Joan a ready-made
cross just before she burned, is the last to leave, called back
to a 12 o'clock curfew in Hell, and Joan is left alone, almost
as she began, whispering a final line to heaven: "Oh, God, that
made this beautiful earth, when will it be ready to receive Thy
saints? How long, O Lord, how long?"

Shaw's epilogue often has been criticized as unnecessary, an
anti-climactic tag line, a witty but self-indulgent afterthought. On
analysis, however, it contains his real purpose. It's what the
play is all about. It gives Joan's life a relevance far beyond
toadying to her sainthood. Joan, the maverick finally proved
"right," is no more acceptable to the world than Joan the maverick thought "wrong." The honor lately hung on her by the church,
like most honors early or late, is hollow and has nothing to do
with her unquenchable spirit which, when tried, is forceful enough,
in its peasant wisdom, to withstand the supposedly sophisticated
knowledge of her superiors. To Shaw, Joan is a national child
of God (I guess his Day of the Supreme Force). She may be
momentarily duped by her fear of torture but it is through her
essential will that she triumphs.

What is principally dismaying about the Stratford production
is that, for all its talk of burning, it never catches fire. Hutt
has arranged some scenes very well, mostly the hard-headed,
ironic exchanges between Church and State. He evenly sustains
Shaw's intellectual line, but what he seems unable to balance is
the play's emotional tone. As played by Pat Galloway (in an approximation of the semi-Cockney accent Shaw specified for Sybil
Thorndike, which was later Dublinized by Siobhan McKenna, Joan

is an ingenue older than some. Miss Galloway is not exactly over-the-hill but her Joan, while physically short-cropped perfect, simply lacks the drive of youth. Her occasionally hoydenish behavior is scratch-work on an unyielding surface. She does some very skilled things, but she exists well beyond the parameter of the truly gifted, far beyond, for example, the intimate and sorrowing corner where Miss McKenna was able to bleed all our hearts white. Miss Galloway's emotional range is either sorely limited or, in Hutt's direction, inadvisedly curtailed. Although she strains her eyes heavenward, she keeps Joan earthbound, as though her real terror were not a fear of burning but a fear of flying. There are good and bad performances around her.

The overall production design by Maxine Graham is sparse but effective, with a brief but opulent processional for the crowning of the Dauphin in Rheims Cathedral neatly contrasting with the dark severity of Joan's inquisition. Gil Wechsler's lighting is superb and Berthold Carriere's music is atmospheric. "Saint Joan" has not altered my concept of Stratford's tradition at all.

"Measure for Measure" at Stratford
(by Kevin Kelly, Boston Globe, June 16, 1975)

"Measure for Measure" is sometimes regarded as second-rate yet, in the full canon, I find it one of Shakespeare's most engrossing plays. Although unnecessarily filibustered in the elaborate descant of its plot, it is a work of startling insight. And further, in the remarkable production it's now being given, as the third opener in the Stratford Festival's 23d season, it's a mind-rattling experience. As staged by Robin Phillips, Stratford's new bolshevik wonder boy, "Measure" is dramatically, as well as philosophically, charged. While it doesn't fully indicate a total swerve from Stratford's traditional path, it does, at least, indicate the scope of Phillips' directorial range. The scope is panoramic.

The first of Phillips' innovations seems a sly come-on, only to develop into something more. Faithful to the text, the play has been set in Vienna but in Vienna at the turn of the century. Before the action begins, we are in a beckoningly nostalgic world of fog-swirling streets and lamplighted corners. Maids and menservants come and go, dusting the furniture in the office of Vincento, the Viennese Duke, then moving silently backstage to reappear and arrange the props.

As the play deepens, the Duke, for all the ribbons on his uniform, for all his regal bearing, could be any hierarchical authority in any century, just as Angelo, his self-servingly corrupt Deputy, could be any latter-day Nixon flunky. The distance Phillips sets from the Elizabethan Age, although specifically distanced to 1910, extends right into the 1970s. While theatrically setting a tone, what Phillips has done is to write us Shakespeare's message about the abuses of power and authority as though, in effect, it came on a postcard from a not-too-distant past.   The resonances in this "Measure" are so loud they can't be mistaken.

The kindly Duke supposedly abandons Vienna, which is swirling in corruption, to the authority of Angelo.   The Duke wants to see what happens when certain lax laws against unchaste behavior are put into effect.   He disguises himself as a priest and calmly observes Angelo's reign of Terror.   Angelo, who is steadily revealed as an immoral fraud, a zealous, lascivious dictator, orders the death of a young man, Claudio, who has impregnated the woman he intends to marry.   Claudio's sister, Isabella, who plans to become a nun, begs Angelo for her brother's life.   Her entreaty is so eloquent, her beauty so shining, Angelo is moved.   He will spare Claudio if Isabella will accede to his sexual wishes.   Like a patient spider, the Duke watches what happens, constructs a thick web and traps his prey.

Phillips reads "Measure" for the dark comedy it is, and has made it wintry bleak.   This approach is usually worked around Angelo, who's a combination Tartuffe and Scarpia (and, within our own contemporary echo, Nixon and Agnew), in other words, evil passing itself off under the twin guises of power and virtue. Phillips has characterized Angelo within a clerk-like, Puritanic rigidity, so Puritanic, in fact, that the revelation of his lurking lust comes as a shock.   However, Phillips doesn't just settle for Angelo.   He sees the Duke with an odd twist, has given him a streak of pederasty, a fondness for a gardening boy and one of his own lieutenants.   This homosexual undertone scotches the play's usual happy ending, the intimation of a romance between the Duke and Isabella.   The complications are fascinating.   They extend even to the re-thinking of the slanderous Lucio, who is here characterized as a brash boulevardier, not at all shamed when he is publicly humiliated by the Duke.

The performances are memorable: William Hutt's Duke, a good man whose goodness is humanly flawed; Brian Bedford's Angelo, a purse-mouthed martinet shocked pale, finally, by his own awareness of his warped soul; Stephen Macht's manly but terror-stricken Claudio; Richard Monette's snappy, cane-twirling Lucio; and Martha Henry's plain, spinsterial Isabella.   Miss Henry wears the white habit of a novice and steel-rimmed spectacles and, at first, she looks like a librarian playing a nurse in a World War I movie, but she develops Isabella with such perception the image becomes the woman.   In Phillips' concept the bawdy comedy of Mistress Overdone is down-played but not enough for me because Sheena Larkin's bawd is a cartoon that belongs in a fun-house.

Anyway, a "Measure for Measure" at Stratford is without equal.

KELLY, Martin Patrick; (2) Theater critic; (3) b. New York City,
April 20, 1925; (4) s. Martin and Rose (Mawe); (5) B.A. Siena College, major subj. English, MFA, Catholic U. of America, major
subj. theater directing; (6) m. Margaret Ashman, Jan. 29, 1949;
(7) child--Margaret Mary; (8) Sports writer, Albany (N.Y.) Times
Union 1948-49; city desk, Albany Times Union, 1949-51; press agent,
Albany Playhouse, 1953-54; drama critic, Albany Times Union, 1967-
present; (9) Instructor in drama, Siena College and College of Saint
Rose, 1954-59; director, Slingerlands Community Players, others,
1961-65; resident playwright, Playwrights Production Company (Albany),
1971-present; Consultant, New York State Community Theater Asso-
ciation, 1973; (13) Cpl. U.S. Marine Corps, 1943-46; (14) Annual
Award for Contribution to Community Theater by New York State
Community Theater Association, 1971; (15) Mem. Lambs Club; (16)
Republican; (17) Roman Catholic; (20) Three full-length plays pro-
duced by Playwrights Production Company, "The Awakening" (1971);
"By the People" (1972); "Home to the Greenhorn" (1974); (21) 512
Bradford Street, Albany, N.Y. 12206, Ph. 518-482-8356; (22) Albany
Times Union, 645 Albany-Shaker Road, Albany, N.Y. 12201, Ph.
518-453-5458; (23) Circulation: 80,000 daily, 140,000 Sunday; (24)
100 plays and musicals, 25 Sunday articles.

Mountebanks' "As You Like It" Spirited
(by Martin P. Kelly, Times-Union, March 3, 1975)

"As You Like It" is probably Shakespeare's most complete
romance, filled with all the wondrous joys and despair of young
love playfully examined in a plot that almost defies description.

The Mountebanks at Union College unveiled a light, airy but
overlong, production of the pastoral comedy this past weekend
and will offer it again Thursday through Saturday nights at the
Nott Memorial Theater on the Union College campus.

Director Barry K. Smith succeeds in gaining much of the
fun of the script once it gets involved in the various love affairs
of the numerous young people. The pace drags and the lack of
real command of Shakespeare's metre is most evident in the
earlier scenes when the plot hinges on banishment of young people and possible death because of disobedience to an autocratic
ruler.

This play introduced one of Shakespeare's most self-assured
comic heroines, a precursor to the ladies of the Restoration, in
the character of Rosalind who pursues the object of her affections
to the forest of Arden where she assumes the disguise of a boy
and tricks her swain into proposing to her. Helena Binder captures much of the joy of love-starved youth in her portrayal and
makes the most of the witty dialogue given the character.

Smith has been most successful in the several love scenes in
picturing Shakespeare as the witty writer he was. The cast at
Union, as Miss Binder demonstrates, displays a command of the

tricky play with words. It is a full-blown romance and the actors play it that way. The women of the cast are particularly
good with gamin-like Jody Stollmack ably supporting Miss Binder
as Celia, the confidante of Rosalind and herself an ardent lover
of a would-be villain.

Karen Bernhard adds a neat portrait of a country girl smitten with the hero while fending off the ardent petitions of a country bumpkin; and Wendy Solovay combines with Leo Bloomrosen
who plays Touchstone, the clown, to offer a more earthy romantic interlude.

Bloomrosen gains much of Shakespeare's character in his
playing of the wise Fool who can laugh at his betters while
making them laugh. Peter Sobol is good also as the somewhat
cynical observer to the proceedings. The actor does well with
the the famed "Seven Ages of Man" speech ("All the world's a
stage, and we are mere players etc.") keeping the comic mixed
with the serious observation of the human existence.

After a slow start, Michael Sherer as Orlando the hapless
hero of the piece, grabs a hold on the character, principally in
the love scenes with Rosalind. He is a pleasant dupe of the
young woman and physically offers all that a young woman would
desire, making the role believeable.

David Lederkramer has the more difficult job of being villainous at one time (he wishes his brother dead or banished),
and then romantic later when he courts Celia. It doesn't quite
ring true but then realistically little in the play does anyway.

The large cast moves with alacrity but in the lesser roles
lacks the true command of the language which can make the lines
sing and fill the theater. The set by Charles N. Steckler captures quite excellently the airiness of the plot and recreates the
Elizabethan thrust stage in the arena auditorium without the bulk-
iness of heavy scenery. It is done with curtains that offer a
main stage, and several inner stages, and it is all quite effective.

An orchestra and some original music is added to the production but its presence seems to promise more than is offered,
particularly when recorded music is presented along with the live
musicians. It serves more to confuse than illuminate.

Generally, the youth and exuberance of the young performers
do justice to the script that seems the youngest in spirit of all
Shakespeare's plays.

"London Assurance:" A Promising Future for an Old Hall
(by Martin Kelly, Times-Union, March 10, 1975)

For the audiences transported this past weekend back into
the 19th century at the Cohoes Music Hall when the opening

performances of the first show in 70 years were given, the experience was a mixed blessing.

The hall has been recreated almost exactly as it was 100 years ago when it first opened as a theater, and considering that most of us are taller and larger than our ancestors, the permanent seating already in place never lets you forget that you are sitting in architecture designed for another era.

But the play's the thing, and "London Assurance," which is the first offering of the season, is a handsome relic of 130 years ago that remains a bridge between the comedies of Sheridan and Goldsmith of the 18th century and Oscar Wilde of the late 19th century. Dion Boucicault, an Irishman who made his name in England and later in America, has written of the foibles of the English gentry with wit and wisdom. What he lacks is the highly stylized form of Sheridan, and the extreme cleverness of Wilde, but he remains a satisfying writer of the comedy of manners.

The company formed at the Cohoes Music Hall for this brief season is an expert troupe, but one which is still several steps away from the ensemble playing so vital to a play such as "London Assurance."

James O'Reilly, the artistic director for the Music Hall who selected the company, has also staged the production, and is most successful in the second act when the complicated plotting reaches its most confused state for the characters involved.

Boucicault takes aim at a vain elder citizen who thinks and acts young with little conviction except upon himself. He becomes betrothed to a young woman whom he has never met but his son, a young man about town, manages to outwit his father and marry the girl instead.

In the meantime, there are a whole of assortment of stock characters who aid the plot or become dupes in its unraveling. Generally, the cast has a high time with these roles but the difficulty with the production lies with the opening. The pace doesn't really take hold, primarily because the comic tone is not established soon enough. For example, Curt Richardson, a young intern in the company, plays the valet for the errant son, and must open the play by stating his plight. The actor is too straightforward and frankly not sufficiently mature as a character who must continually lie about his master's activities and still be comic.

When the vain old man appears, the audience is treated to a character who is more fey than foppish. Peter Murphy is a good actor who surely knows the intricacies of the character but his physical stature and early manner does not establish sufficient command of the stage. His early delivery is measured when it

should be brisk and self-assured. The audience is asked to
laugh at his ridiculous physical costuming and makeup, including
a red wig, when it should be convulsed by his outrageous attitude,
his vain posture. One had difficulty wiping away the image of
the late Ernie Kovacs' character "Percy Dovetonsils" while watching Murphy perform.

The production clearly reaches its full potential in the second act romantic duel between Julia Fremon as the young girl
in question, and Dan Diggles as the young man out to trick his
father. This is an obvious forerunner to Wilde's proposal scene
betwen Jack Worthing and Gwendolyn in "The Importance of Being Earnest." The two actors fence with words and make the
cagey courting a delightful experience. Diggles has an infectious
manner about him that carries through the play, and Miss Fremon gains the full impact of all the sharp barbs of the liberated
woman.

Pauline Brailsford presents another facet of the liberated
woman as the huntress who rides to hounds and forces her husband to cower. She swaggers yet conveys the woman who would
rather be bossed. Miss Brailsbord is also credited with editing
of the script used in this production.

KEOGH, James Edward; (2) Editor and theater critic; (3) b. New
York City, Oct. 18, 1948; (4) s. George and Gloria Keogh; (5) B.S.
Business Management and Finance 1975, Fairleigh Dickinson U.;
Juilliard School of Music 1969; (6) m. Anne (Ceda) Keogh; (7)
child--Sandra Colleen; (8) Radio reporter WHBI Radio Newark 1969-
70; Freelance writer, New York Times Denver Post; Editor, Business Week; reporter WNBC TV; Freelance reporter WINS Radio;
United Press International and Associated Press; Bergen Newspapers,
editor in chief; (9) Musical arranger and composer; Musical director
for theater company; (14) Nominee, Pulitzer Prize 1972; Distinguished
Public Service Through Journalism Award, Sigma Delta Chi, national professional journalism society; (15) Catholic Actors guild; Sigma
Delta Chi; New York Business Press; American Business Press;
(17) Catholic; (20) Burglarproof: Complete Guide to Home Security
(McGraw-Hill book); Police Public Relations (American Federation
of Police book); syndicated radio feature on security; (21 & 22) 11
Preston Street, Ridgefield Park, N.J. 07660; (23) Circulation: 130,000
(24) 52 plays and musicals, 60 motion pictures and 20 miscellaneous.

Joey Heatherton Not to Be Missed
(by James Edward Keogh, Bergen News, May 1975)

If you would like to give your husband and yourself an early
Father's Day gift, then I would bring your attention to The Wal-
dorf Astoria's Empire Room where Joey Heatherton is playing.
The show should not be missed.

The room was packed last Tuesday night with everyone

waiting to see Joey Heatherton. Like many television viewers,
the image she projects on the tube was expected during her performance. But Joey Heatherton proved that she has more than
a figure.

As a true professional, she controlled the mood of the show
from the moment Joey Heatherton placed her feet on the stage.
One minute an up tempo number and then a delicate ballad without losing the audience for a second.

The public's impression when her name is mentioned is that
of a woman selling mattresses. What is sometimes overlooked
is her dancing, singing and overall entertainment ability.

If you want to enjoy yourself with good wholesome entertainment, Joey Heatherton is the person you should see. She will
have you dancing in your seat and you will be leaving with a
smile on your face.

Joey Heatherton will be appearing twice nightly at 8:30 and
11:30 p.m. Tuesday through Thursdays and at 9 p.m. and midnight Fridays and Saturdays from May 13 through the 24. Attend and you will be surprised.

At Lunch with Dina Merrill
(by James Edward Keogh, Sun-Bulletin, May 18, 1975)

One of the many jobs a reporter is assigned involves luncheon interviews with important theatrical people. Usually, the
pretentious performer is willing to tell you how great she is and
how important the role she is playing is to her career.

Well, this week it was my turn to conduct such an interview
with Dina Merrill. So armed with a press release containing
her background, I drove to the Playhouse on the Bergen Mall
where she is starring in "Angel Street" and I was taken off
guard.

Dina Merrill who is also Mrs. Cliff Robertson and grand-
daughter of Charles Post of the Post Corp fame, turned out to
be more down to earth than could be expected.

While sitting in on rehearsal before lunch, what appears
simple to the audience during a performance was found to be
hard work for the performers. Dina Merrill and the other actors rehearsed the play without any props. For most people,
picking up a pot that isn't there would appear difficult but not
for Dina Merrill, a true sign of professionalism in the theater.

With a call for lunch, the interview began. Having lunch
with the performer enables a relaxed atmosphere where the true
personality outshines the actor or actress. Although most would
anticipate lunch at an expensive restaurant, not so with Dina

Merrill.   The surrounding was a snack bar on the mall.

Over a hamburger and milk, Dina Merrill talked freely about
her family life with Cliff Robertson and their six-year old
daughter.

The glamorous picture of a star's life most people imagine
is just not real, at least for the Robertsons.   By 9 a. m. , Dina
Merrill has left her Connecticut home to drive her daughter to
school.   From there it's off to rehearsal in Paramus.   Dina
Merrill was glad the toll increases on the George Washington
Bridge and other river crossings did not effect the commuter
who crosses at the Tapanzee Bridge.

Although rehearsals start at 11 a. m. at the mall, for Dina
Merrill 9:30 a. m. is the time she spends with the stage manager
going over her lines.   Then it's on with the play.

Most readers would expect that since rehearsal started late,
there is little work to be accomplished and the actors and actresses would break early.   Not so!   For Dina Merrill, work does
not stop until about 6 p. m. and then, as with all commuters, it's
back across the bridge to Connecticut in time for 7 p. m. supper
with her family.

Following supper, she and her husband play with their child
until bed time, for their daughter that is, which is around 9 p. m.
Now, according to what has been written in the entertainment
column, most would think the Robertsons would be off to night
clubs in New York or to a party.

However, as Dina Merrill put in, those performers attending
parties are usually "between" jobs.   For Dina Merrill, as with
most American families, it's time to take a shower, wash up and
relax for a moment.   And that is really all she has, a moment.
By 10 p. m. , Dina Merrill claims she has difficulty holding her
eyes open and off to bed she goes.   After all, she is one of the
many commuters and 8 a. m. comes very fast.

Dina Merrill, who will be at the Playhouse at The Bergen
Mall from May 16 through the 25, is gearing her performance
of Angel Street for Broadway.   Current plans call for the show
to play in other areas of the country before moving on Broadway
by next year.

"I want to experience everything in my profession, "   Dina
Merrill remarked.   She has never starred on Broadway.   Her
performance in Angel Street, Patrick Hamilton's thriller, marks
the first time she has performed in a play in seven years.

Before recently appearing on Cannon, Marcus Welby and
other television series, Dina Merrill was president of the Dina
Merrill Cosmetic Division of Coty.   However, her division was

designed to capture the high price cosmetic line which was later dropped. Dina Merrill claims that although her heart is in acting and with her family, she would consider a similar situation with another firm.

KERR, Walter; (2) Drama critic, author; (3) b. Evanston, Ill., July 8, 1913; (4) s. Walter Sylvester and Esther (Daugherty) K; (5) B.S. in Speech, Northwestern, 1937, M.A., 1938; (6) m. Jean Collins, Aug. 9, 1943; (7) children--Christopher, Colin, John, Gilbert, Gregory, Katharine; (8) Drama critic Commonweal, 1950-52; N.Y. Herald-Tribune, 1951-66; Sun. drama critic N.Y. Times, 1966- ; (14) George Jean Nathan award, 1964; award, National Institute Arts and Sciences, 1972; (20) Books: How Not to Write a Play, Criticism and Censorship, Pieces at Eight, The Decline of Pleasure, The Theater in Spite of Itself, Tragedy and Comedy, God on the Gymnasium Floor, Thirty Plays Hath November; (21) 1 Beach Ave., Larchmont, N.Y. 10538; (22) N.Y. Times, Ph. 212-556-1234.

KESSLER, Leonard Irwin; (2) Drama critic; (3) b. September 14, 1942; (6) m. Paula Lynn Kessler; (7) children--Jonathan Eric, July 1, 1970; Joshua Elliot, April 14, 1975; (8) Drama Critic with "Entertainment Eye" since Spring of 1971; (9) Started motion picture column (approx. thirty movies a year) using pen name Eric Lind; (15) Member New Jersey Drama Critics Association Historian, 1973-75; (21) 70 Amsterdam Ave., Passaic, N.J. 07055, Ph. 201-778-6625.

New Dimension Theatre Studio Participates in Festival 70
(by Leonard Kessler, Entertainment Eye, Spring 1971)

The New Dimension Theatre Studio will participate in the Bergen County Professional Arts Festival by presenting the Jean-Claude Van Italie collection of three short plays called "America, Hurrah." The one-acters, which found Off-Broadway acclaim five years ago, will be performed on Saturday evening, April 17 at 8:30 p.m. at Fairleigh Dickinson's Becton Hall in Teaneck.

After generating considerable artistic and pecuniary success since its initial presentation at the Hackensack YM-YWHA's "Twelve Evenings of Theater," the director and leader, Dr. Richard Imundo would naturally like to continue the triumph with this road-show engagement.

However, it seems just being invited to perform is an honor in itself. The sponsor of this area's cultural event-par excellence is the North Jersey Cultural Council. New Dimension is a founding member of the organization and even with this chartered status the Theatre group still had to prove its excellence.

And, apparently, the hurrah for the play was one of the factors. After speaking with Dr. Imundo, one can see why NDT qualified. Imundo has a firm and daring philosophy and his

productions are stamped with this quality. With its present
home base at the "Y", the director is grateful to have found
complete freedom to choose and direct plays which he feels say
something about our lives today.

Dr. Imundo explains his mod direction by explaining that "I
am certainly not opposed to the classics of yester-year, but I
also want to create works that hopefully will be the classics of
tomorrow." With that belief in mind, and "good" drama in his
heart, Imundo apparently does not compromise, either in his
choices or his style, which he describes as "eclectic-at its best."

In "America, Hurrah" and its sardonic outlook, he has discovered a tone which works perfectly with his dramatic values.
Van Italie's pessimistic view of our non-communicative society
is given the Imundo touch. He has been able to update the contest of the play, but as he says, "strangely enough, I did not
have to alter the pertinent dialogue." Using the zoom lense and
a projector with colors, the innovative stage manipulator feels
he made his MOMENT: when he sees the playwright, the actors
and the audience as one; understanding and seeing life together.
And this is, after all, what the Dramatic Arts is all about.

Unfortunately, the financial aspects of New Dimension are
not the best. Its predicament is two-fold. The studio works
with a paid, proficient company who can not be members of New
York City's Actor's Equity since they do not work in Manhattan.
Because of this many people feel that NDT is community theatre
where dedicated amateurs use their leisure time to produce plays.

On the contrary, as part of the Studio's training program and
school, all members must serve an apprenticeship first. A long
tenure may not mean automatic stardom, for, again, the Imundo
credo means that only the best people get the parts, not necessarily the long runners. This loss of the slighted, knowledgeable actor does not help.

Going into the community with strong thespians means money.
The lack of a steady subsidy appears to be the biggest drawback.
"With a grant which will pay for a business manager, as well as
myself, I can just worry about putting on the best possible theater because if the stage techniques work, the patrons will come.
Then the actors can be paid," says Dr. Imundo, commenting on
the financial. Thus Imundo would rather direct a substantial
Edward Albee drama and not have to concern himself with the
box office.

The theater-goer has a perfect opportunity to witness this
sane and sober philosophy at work at Festival '70. Also he may
wish to contact Mrs. Mildred Reicher at CO 1-6338 to arrange
a different kind of fund-raising event for his league, organization or religious group. In any case with its serious philosophy
and dynamic leadership, NDT should create excitement at Becton
Hall. New Dimension Theatre, hurrah.

Critics, Criticism and Kudos
(by Leonard Kessler, Entertainment Eye, June-July 1975)

Periodically it has been asked what the function of the critic is. Criticism abounds from reader, producer and player alike. The subscriber often finds himself annoyed at the writer because they do not agree on what constitutes an evening's entertainment. A reviewer tries to see everything and his historical retrospect makes him--hopefully--an expert on what is good, bad or indifferent.

The impresario wants to give his audience their money's worth so he can make enough pecuniary matter to sustain the next presentations. Therefore, he is not so much interested in the artistic merit, as much as he wants his product to sell. If it is meritorious, as well as productive, so much the better.

A drama scribe likes to see sell-outs, but it does hurt when the dramatic elements appraised critically are lacking, and yet, the playgoers are obviously moved enough to buy tickets. The right star in a weak vehicle, misleading publicity, or even a sensational scene (i. e. the now innocuous bit of nudity in "Hair") are all factors toward helping achieve a successful run. Occasionally, a play opens that is satisfying to everyone, dramatically and commercially.

The actor is very fearful of reviews, more times when he is just at the start of a potentially fruitful career. However, there is the situation where the established performer banks his reputation on a perilous venture (in New York, Mary Martin brought in a disasterous musical called "Jennie" many years ago to no critical éclat).

Whatever, it seems that everyone concerned in the theatrical community is not going to agree with one another. But in the middle is still the good, old reliable critic. He really does try his best, with the material he has at hand. And much of the time, it is more than difficult, when he (or she, let us never forget the female correspondents) must sit through two different presentations of the same show at two playhouses. Or the nights when the curtain opens to still another version of a popular play. And, what about having to watch "The Fantastiks" five times in as many years.

So what, it might be said! That's the job. Alas, this is true. Occupational hazards are found with every position. The compensations are great for the person who truly loves the theatre, and can convey this through intelligent writing.

Unfortunately, it does not always follow that writers who write well are good arbiters of thespic taste. In the writing fraternity are those who can compose a competent piece but do not really care.

If one examines further there are public relations people
acting as critics; newspaper editors whose first allegiance is to
their paper; and, sadly enough, writers who fawn over producers
and performers just because the latter are nice to them. Happily, they are all in the minority.

For the most part, critics are honest and devoted to their
readers. Of course, they do not always agree, for audiences
are usually not patrons of the arts. They are people out for a
special night and want to be just "entertained."

The writer finds that he must detail his opinion, as well as
the audience's reaction to the proceedings. Countless shows have
met with critical applause and never found a ticket-buyer. The
counterpart, of course, is the mediocre fare turning away the
crowds. It appears to be a paradox which is patterned on life
itself. And while it is incomprehensible, as long as the actual
play is based on actual life then that is comfort enough, at least
until the next vagary comes along.

The New Jersey theatrical scene, of late has contained all
the above-mentioned discussion about the triumvirate and their
peculiarities--the stub-holder, the producer and the actor in tandem with the critic.

Discussing the best is always the easiest. McCarter Theatre in BiCentennial-oriented Princeton is to be congratulated for
their last two plays, even though one was intolerably awful. It
seems that Tennessee Williams wanted another chance with a
failure originally titled, "The Seven Descents of Myrtle." His
association with Producer-Director, Michael Kahn, is now theatrical legend, as they both brought to Broadway this season a much
improved "Cat on a Hot Tin Roof." Apparently hoping to succeed
again, Mr. Williams re-wrote "Myrtle" into "Kingdom of Earth"
and Mr. Kahn produced it.

For giving this Williams work another chance, hats off. But
hats on the chest in respect and mourning as we gaze in dismay.
This is a work that is not worth rewrites. Criticized initially
as almost a parody of his talented way with the down-trodden,
Princetonians did not know whether to snicker or be serious with
this supposed "comedy."

Kahn's "Romeo and Juliet" was another story entirely. Capturing the double-entendre and dazzling dismay of young love, this
was a fresh and honest approach to the most familiar love story
of them all. What was basically Kahn's American Shakespeare
Theatre's presentation worked as well in Jersey as it did last
year in bucolic Stratford, Connecticut.

The cast changes were just fine. Richard Backus played a
lovesick Romeo, at times overwhelmed with the realities and
consequences of his passion for Maria Tucci's Juliet. Ms. Tucci

was obviously not the fourteen year-old she is supposed to be,
yet her transition before she takes the potion was powerful
enough to dispel any casting peculiarities. Backus and Tucci on
the balcony made for memorable "star-crossed" lovers.

Tom Poston as Friar Lawrence, Charlotte Jones as the
Nurse, and Brian Petchey as Mercutio addressed themselves admirably.

With John Conklin's believably attractive settings, Jane Greenwood's impressive costuming (updating the proceedings to 1866)
and Marc B. Weiss' technical lighting skill, the entire experience,
under Kahn's firm hand, makes one look to next season. Finally
American plays will be recognized to celebrate 1976 and from the
outlook, subscriptions should be immediately obtained.

Jersey theatre is often criticized for its reliance on revivals.
This is no doubt true, but when premieres are to be found, they
deserve notice, even when they do not live up to expectations.
The Playhouse on the Mall has tried to give fine presentations
in different areas of theatrical endeavor. The World First of
the Rock Musical, "Lucifer" was efficient with its pronouncement
that the Devil is not that bad a fellow. Capsuling the biblical
stories with Lucifer singing his way into our hearts was not a
bad idea.

Though promising, the events start off badly with an inept
ballet. Ironically enough, it is only with the appearance of Jesus
Christ that the tempo picks up to a dilly of a first act finale.

Strangely, this "Lucifer" is not truly a rock-style musicale.
The music is eclectic, containing a soft-shoe routine and even
a hoedown.

The Mall came up with an old Broadway flop with a touch
of the marital "Fourposter." Called "Peter-Pat" when it starred
Dick Shawn and Joan Hackett, this two-character exercise presented Patty Duke Astin and husband John in cliche-ridden situations. It seemed to make little difference to the delighted spectators who roared with delight. This is a perfect example where
critics and patrons disagree. And with the "name" to bring tic-
ket-purchasers, it made a tedious critical evening, but most entertaining buyers market. The most interesting part of the
"marriage gambol" was Frank Desmond's use of the unit set culminating in a lovely farmhouse bedroom suite. At least everyone was pleased in one little way or another.

The fact remains that Perry Bruskin is succeeding in bringing to his public different bill of fare, whether charming to one
or another or all. His reprise of "Angel Street" should delight
seekers of suspense entertainment, even those familiar with the
classic Bergman-Boyer flick. Bruskin has made an attempt and
he is to be praised for making everyone happy. Here's to some

better choices. By the way, whatever happened to the under-
rated "Cuckoo's Nest?"

For those wondering about the University theatrical scene it
is presently trying its best at William Paterson College where
the theatre is most professionally equipped. The chairman of
the theatre department, Dr. James W. Rodgers tells us that the
two productions ("The Time of Your Life" and a musical premiere "Gambler's Paradise") were the products of the integration of professionals with college and community theatrical elements.

The latter showed it. Starring Alfred Drake, one of the
most accomplished leading musical stars of Broadway fame, it
was a trivial evening that teetered on the amateurish. Of course
there were moments, but one missed the expressive baritone of
Drake's "Kean." It is still there but he seemed to be saving it
for another night. It was a good "college try" to warm up for
a New York run, but to little entertaining avail.

William Saroyan's Pulitzer Prize Comedy, "Life," has some
left in it. Actually a mood piece, it spotlighted Pat Hingle in
the key part of a drinking, generous soul who delights in helping
others. Hingle is a sensitive actor, embodying the pathetic and
the decent of humanity. In a cameo role, as one of the inhabitants of the saloon, Tom Brennan, late of Montclair's Whole Theatre and Drew's Shakespeare Festival, was perfection as a loud-
mouth named Kit Carson. Of course, the student element was
not on par with the leading players, but somehow Paterson's
venture deserves praise for trying something different.

The Whole Theatre Co. ended on an ambivalent note. Garcia
Lorca's "The House of Bernarda Alba" is downbeat all the way,
and predictable. The acting in the lead role, Marjorie Fierst
was first-rate, as were the daughters, particularly, Judith Del-
gado, who possesses a fiery magnitude to her playing. Though
Lynn Clifton in the pivotal maid part was lifeless, the ensemble
was good in Ernie Schenk's imaginatively thought-out settings.

The play was much too monotonous in feeling, achieving little
power by the bloody conclusion. But, once more, Whole is right
there, attempting to produce what they consider provocative works.
Certainly their "Waiting for Godot" came full circle in presenting
the best pro theatre since the new year began.

This can not apply to the Paper Mill Playhouse in Millburn.
Their presentations have been uncommonly poor. "The Fantasticks" needs a fantasy atmosphere and Jay Hampton's direction
was heavy-handed on John Pitt's crowded set. John Gavin was
wooden and only Kurt Peterson and Marti Rolph as the Roman-
tics were able to spark life here. True, though, the stub-holders
seemed to enjoy themselves immensely.

Presenting "The Marriage-Go-Round" for another go-round
is inexcusable, no matter how well-done. This is a tried, fifties
comedy with ho-hum laughs. Why this was chosen was a mystery.

In candid fact, The Paper Mill has not had a show that one
could really exclaim about. Last year was "Anything Goes,"
"Music Man" and "South Pacific." Surely financial considerations could not be so low as to descend to the depths with old
hat.

"Irene" is a conglomeration of songs put on because it's
trying to cash in on "Nanette." Surprisingly though, it does not
pretend to be anything but what it is--old-fashioned corn, with
light-hearted music and dance. It's the only hope for artistic
salvation at the Mill.

Critics are there to warn or beckon. But it is only one
person's opinion. We always want theatres to take a chance on
doing the different. Perhaps the reader should do like-wise and
not let anyone tell him what to do. The last productions in Jersey have shown us more than ever that the critic does not have
the last word. Audiences seem to like what they do not. And
they're entitled, after all, it is their money. But it's always
comforting to see if what you're seeing is liked by "the man on
the aisle."

KINKAID, Frank Eugene; (2) Theatre and Opera Critic; (3) b. Gainesville, Fla. , Oct 5, 1922; (4) s. R. H. and Letitia Kinkaid; (5) B.A.
U. of Washington 1949, major subj: Drama; (6) m. Marilyn Saul
Nov. 19, 1960; (7) children--Toby and Sean; (8) KOIN-TV Portland,
Ore. , 1958-present; since 1966 fully assigned to TV news coverage
of the arts. Since 1966, Portland critic for New York Metropolitan
Opera Guild's Opera News; (9) Equity actor 1950-58; (14) In a recent national survey conducted by Argus Magazine of Seattle in behalf of the Seattle Arts Advocates, was given honor as covering the
arts in greater depth than any TV person in the U.S.; (15) Member
County-City Arts commission; (20) Feature article "Ernest Bloch and
His Macbeth" May 1974; (23) KOIN-TV is a basic CBS outlet with a
coverage area of 2 million; (24) Review 5 operas per year, 50 movies,
10 touring dance, 5 local dance, 10 musicals 5 Shakespeare, 2 Festivals. Three 30-minute specials per year on arts.

Rigoletto
(by Frank Kinkaid, Opera News, November 1974)

Verdi could not be called popular in Portland. His music was
heard here three seasons ago, and the trio of performances of
Rigoletto which began on September 26 are hardly likely to contribute to a local revival.

The unit set, consisting of fragmented arches and building
facades (from the Canadian Opera), proved as inept for Rigoletto's

house as it did ideal for the Duke's ballroom.   Later, as Spara-
fucile's "palace," it made the whole idea of unit sets ludicrous.
The low-key lighting appeared to remain constant.

Vocally, neither of the Italian singers making U.S. debuts
caused much excitement.   Kino Puglisi's lyric baritone too often
fell short of Verdi's line, though he acted the jester with style
and understated power.   Ruggero Orofino as the tall, virile Duke,
hobbled by drum-tight vocal production, proved an indifferent actor.   Performing her first Gilda, Patricia Wells was trill-less
but scored with her lyric singing.   Archie Drake's superb Spara-
fucile, along with Alyce Roger's Maddalena and Donald Drain's
hearty Marullo, added much.   Director Frans Boerlage's strong
point was balanced stage pictures that unhappily had little dramatic tension.   His first act had the wholesome look of a junior
prom.   Stefan Minde, faced with stage surprises, conducted carefully.

Der Freischütz
(by Frank Kinkaid, Opera News, January 11, 1975)

Der Freischütz made a rare American appearance as the
Portland Opera scheduled three performances starting November
21.   Carey Wong constructed an isolated village of weather-
beaten planks, couched under impressionistic rope branches that
were intensified by scrims and projections for the Wolf's Glen,
allowing a swirling fog cover that proved mysterious and frightening.   The spoken dialogue, which could have been a burden to
Portland audiences, was pruned drastically.   Director Frans
Boerlage kept the stage action simple and uncluttered.   But his
attempts at pace were often negated by the languid tempos imposed by Stefan Minde; Agathe's "Leise, leise" barely moved,
to the distress of Johanna Meier's radiant work.

The towering German bass Manfred Schenk poured forth torrents of black voice, portraying the doomed, haunted Kaspar with
enormous skill.   Karl-Walter Böhm, a chesty heldentenor, found
the lyric portions of Max's music trying, but Michael Gallup's
Kuno became a major role with this young bass' luscious sound.
Gwenlynn Little, a pert and accurate Aennchen, deserved her
success.   Der Freischütz, the latest novelty in the POA's current emphasis on German opera, found polite acceptance but little evidence that locally unfamiliar singspiels will become a
fashion.

KISSEL, Howard William; (2) Arts Editor; (3) b. Oct. 29, 1942, Milwaukee, Wis.; (4) Leo and Ruth Kissel; (5) B.A., Columbia College
(English and Comparative Literature), M.S. Northwestern (Journalism)
(6) m. Christine Buck, May 5, 1974; (8) Reporter, Daily News Record; Feature Writer, Gentleman's Quarterly; Arts Editor, Women's
Wear Daily; (15) Member, New York Film Critics Circle--Chairman,
1976; (21) 275 Central Park West, New York, N.Y. 10024, Ph.

212-873-9141; (22) 7 East 12th St., New York, N.Y. 10003, Ph.
212-741-4043; (23) Circulation: 80,000; (24) Films, Books.

"Who's Afraid of Virginia Woolf?"
(by Howard Kissel, Women's Wear Daily, April 2, 1976)

Edward Albee's "Who's Afraid of Virginia Woolf?" is about the fictions people create to manage their lives. Some couples live by the fiction of happiness; George and Martha, on the other hand, have created a more complex, twisted set of fantasies to sustain what is in many ways a durable marriage. When the play was first produced, the intention seemed to be to play for the emotional reality behind the fictions so that the audience would be surprised and sometimes puzzled by what was real and what was not. Because we are now familiar with the play, and, more important, because we have learned that you can't make such neat distinctions between what is real and what is not, we can now enjoy watching George and Martha deliberately creating fictions for themselves and their guests, Nick and Honey. We can find just as much drama--perhaps even a more truthful drama--in this act as we did in the earlier actors' fabricating the intense emotions behind the "fun and games."

Seen in this light, Albee's marvelous play almost has the air of a classical comedy. Even the language, which 13 years ago was considered shocking, now seems merely banter--pungent sallies in an ongoing war conducted in carefully articulated and modulated verbiage. Albee has directed the current revival at the Music Box in a way that emphasizes its brittle wit, its verbal elegance and, in the final act, when Martha acknowledges her love for George, her dependence on him, its eloquent poetry.

Albee has a magnificent cast. Colleen Dewhurst, with her elemental sensuality and her special voice--at once poetic and gravelly--gives us a powerfully sculpted Martha, at her most impressive when the sculptor's chisel she and her husband wield strikes too hard and the surface shatters. Ben Gazzara, whom we tend to think of as earthy and moody, plays George with the assurance, the restraint, the strength and the grace of a classical actor, a dazzling accomplishment. Richard Kelton and Maureen Anderman give strong, subtly nuanced performances as Nick and Honey, roles that are easy to do as caricature.

Albee's play, which translates many prototypical American fears and fantasies into timeless, abstract drama, is as vital and exciting as it was when it opened.

KLAIN, Jane; (2) Associate editor, theatre and film critic; (3) b. New York City, Jan. 5, 1947; (4) d. Seymour and Carolyn (Danziger); (5) B.A. University College, N.Y.U., major subj: English lit., 1968; M.A. New York University, major subj: theatre and film, 1975; (6) m. Stephen H. Klain, July 18, 1971; (8) assoc. editor

International Motion Picture Almanac and International Television Almanac 1970-71, film critic Motion Picture Daily and Motion Picture Herald 1969-71, currently associate editor and entertainment critic Where Magazine, New York edition; (9) Member stage crew Hall of Fame Players N.Y.U. 1964-68; member Cooperative Film Society, Inc.; (15) Phi Beta Kappa, 1968; (21) 54 West 16th St., New York, N.Y. 10011, Ph. 212-989-5709; (22) Where Magazine, 135 W. 50th St., N.Y., N.Y. 10020, Ph. 212-977-8387; (23) Circulation: 20,000; (24) 30 plays and musicals, 25 films.

Refreshing Breeze
(by Jane Klain, Where Magazine, March 15, 1975)

During its past seven seasons, the Negro Ensemble Company has presented some of America's finest theatre. Leslie Lee's extraordinary family drama, "The First Breeze of Summer," currently at the St. Marks Playhouse, heralds an auspicious eighth season. It tells of an ordinary yet important weekend in the lives of the Edwards family. Gremmar has come to stay with her son Milton, a plasterer, and his wife Hattie, and during her birthday weekend the old woman relives memories of her early life.

Mr. Lee interweaves Gremmar's visit with her son and grandchildren Nate and Lou with the tale of her youthful days when she was known as Lucretia, when three men fathered her children and then left her. Despite Lucretia's hard life, she created her own set of just values and passed them on to her family. Grandchild Nate has dropped out of school, while Lou has become a bookworm who hopes to deny his black heritage. He emulates his grandmother's religiosity but rejects sex as frightening and sinful. When the puritanical boy learns that his grandmother never married her lovers, and worse, that one of them was white, there is an explosive confrontation.

The play tells its many tales with humor and compassion. There is the porter Lucretia loves who loses his job defending an elderly porter who had once been a doctor. There is Harper Edwards, a miner who aspires to the ministry but turns to alcohol after he seduces Lucretia. An enthusiastic religious meeting becomes an hilarious affirmation of Lou's love for his grandmother.

Artistic director of the N.E.C. Douglas Turner Ward, who plays Harper, has staged the work vividly and the acting is flawless. Frances Foster gives a strong, moving performance as Gremmar and Janet League in the flashbacks plays her with sparkling spirit. Reyno is outstanding as Lou, suggesting thoughtful intelligence and repressed passions. Moses Gunn adds stature to the upright character of the father and as Nate, Charles Brown makes a wonderfully natural contrast to his prudish younger brother.

"The First Breeze of Summer" is an exceptionally enjoyable play, richly textured with humor, warmth and wisdom.

Hollywood Holocaust
(by Jane Klain, Where Magazine, May 10, 1975)

Hollywood with its many mysteries has always held a strong fascination for writers, filmmakers and audiences alike. Perhaps one of the most cynical and poetic dissections of the movie capital, is "The Day of the Locust," Nathanael West's horrific vision of Hollywood in the 1930s.

Director John Schlesinger ("Darling," "Midnight Cowboy") has now brilliantly translated West's classic American novel into a powerfully hypnotic film, currently at Cinema I.

More than just an extremely faithful re-creation of period costumes, hairdoes and living quarters (the San Bernadino Arms in which the principal characters reside almost takes on a seedy life of its own), the film is peopled with the grotesques whom West called "The people who come to California to die ... all those poor devils who can only be stirred by the promise of miracles and then only to violence." There are also those like Faye Greener (played by Karen Black with a rapacious gusto and moving poignancy), a vivacious, self-centered film extra, who has internalized all the illusions Hollywood has manufactured.

Into this tinderbox world of frustrated false dreams comes Tod Hackett, a young artist fresh out of Yale. As West's spokesman he becomes involved with Burgess Meredith as Miss Black's pathetic, has-been vaudevillian father; an aging midwestern bookkeeper, Homer Simpsom (played with great compassion by an almost unrecognizable Donald Sutherland) and the ruthless studio executives.

A bizarre relationship develops between the artist, the bookkeeper and Miss Black to whom they are both foolishly and fatally attracted. Frustrated hopes turn into a bitterness which culminates in the film's climax, a nightmarish movie premiere marked by mass violence.

Hollywood as a land of excess has been magnificently photographed by Conrad Hall. Everything, from the oranges that drop from their branches to the freaks and the beauties like Faye, is overripe here, the sunlight more than golden. Waldo Salt's excellent screenplay has fleshed out West's symbolic novel in cinematic terms. And the vivid performances are uniformly compelling.

Like Tod Hackett we are intrigued by the vision "The Day of the Locust" presents.

KLEIN, Gerald Louis; (2) Arts critic; (3) b. Peoria, Ill. , Dec. 19,
1926; (4) s. Erwin and Louise (Lammers) A. ; (5) B.Mus. (piano ma-
jor) Bradley U. , 1949; Grad work, U. of Illinois; (6) m. Mary E.
Dudas, June 4, 1955; (7) children--Jerry, Jeffrey, Lisa, Marilou,
James, Jean, Barbara; (8) Peoria Journal Star, editorial writer,
Sept. 1953;   Music-drama critic, March, 1972; (9) Part-time faculty,
Bradley University, Critical writing course; (13) U. S. Navy, 1944-46;
(14) Pacific Theater; (17) Catholic; (20) Three fiction works to Red-
book, and various articles and features to New York Times, Reader's
Digest, Family Circle, Ford Times, Chicago Tribune; (21) Rt. 2, Meta-
mora, Ill. 61548, Ph. 309-383-4562; (22) 1 News Plaza, Peoria, Ill. 61601,
Ph. 309-686-3116; (23) Circulation: Approx. 130,000; (24) 50 plays, 40
concerts, 60 movies, 5 dance, 5 opera, 10 misc.

"Bus Stop" Material Suffers Inertia Problem
(by Jerry Klein, Journal Star, date unknown)

I have the uncomfortable feeling that William Inge's plays
have faded into a kind of lower case status in which the focus
is so tight and the human potential so limited that there is not
so much a growth of awareness as a constriction of it.

One need not have titans for heroes and there is, to be sure,
grandeur in wayside diners, on company picnics, in the meanest
of dives.

But I find myself growing impatient while watching Inge's
characters, waiting in vain for some illustration of the truth that
Leon Bloy touches on when he compares the soul, even that of
the lowest concierge, to a raging inferno.

Little of that in Inge, however, for his characters remain
for the most part pathetically stunted, showing only a glimmer
of something that is usually extinguished in despair.

Given such a preamble, it might seem absurd to bestow the
least jot of praise on Peoria Players production of William Inge's
"Bus Stop," which opened Friday.   Not so.

This group has taken Inge's pathetic characters and rather
pedestrian situation and sustained a show that remains fascinating
without precisely igniting its audience.

Let's face it, the play has an enormous amount of inertia
to overcome.   Here is the bus out of Kansas City stopped in
the snow and its handful of passengers forced to spend much of
the night at the combined diner-bus stop.   There is probably as
much sheer drama in your corner McDonald's on a slow Friday
in Lent.

The play is people with recognizeable types; a predatory
grass widow, a young girl eager for life, a sheriff who must
have been the model for Rooster Cogburn, a vaguely amoral bus

driver, a professor who laments the waste of his life, the romantic couple, the much-used nightclub singer and the virginal cowboy whose amatory technique is like that of the black bear.

There is rich drama here, but somewhat surface.

The characters are sketched instead of limned and probed and they seem capable of the most minimal growth. The only real show of heroism is that of Virgil, who chooses loneliness, but it is a puzzling choice at that. The Montana ranch, it would seem, is big enough for a newly married couple and Virgil, too.

But no matter. This production excels in a number of respects and not the least is its setting, a marvel of time and place right down to the chrome and plastic-covered seats at the snack bar, the elaborate juke box and the price of milk shakes.

There is also an ingenious and most effective snowfall going on outside the window, done by a process which ought to be patented and sold. It involves styrofoam and fans and a clever recycling system.

Eleanor Ruethe as Grace Hoylard presides over this bus stop with a performance that is brisk and properly busy, for she is a simple woman, this Grace, with only a few needs. Mary Kerrigan plays Elma Duckworth, her helper, with the unaffected guile of a high school girl who can't wait to grow up and it is a job well handled.

The action erupts when the bus arrives and Cheri Stillson as Cherie races in seeking protection from Bo, a western version of Stanley Kowalski. She is a faded nightclub singer on her way out, with but one last chance. But it must not be by force of the kind that Eldon Beever applies as Bo. He is unable to understand why the first girl he has ever wanted and had doesn't feel the same. This is a forceful and finally winning performance.

Jack Lawless is excellent as the professor who finds, perhaps, in his encounter with the high school girl, a way towards salvation and Charles Welch is Carl, the bus driver whose upstairs rendezvous with Grace serves the added function of clearing the room slightly and tightening the drama.

Bruce Leipold is Virgil, a role that calls largely for a silent presence, but it is done skillfully and he emerges as one of the real, sympathetic people in the play.

I have saved Robert Smith as Will Masters for last because he brings in here another imposing performance, solid and assured as the sheriff and touched lightly by a subtleness and humor that makes it into a most appealing role.

Teckie Metzel is assistant director. Gary Betts designed

the excellent set and doubles as stage manager.   Special effects
are by Seth Glen.   Jo Roberts is chairman of the detailed properties, Allan Geier did lights and costumes are by Audrey Poole.

"The Man Who Came to Dinner" A Brilliant University Offering
        (by Jerry Klein, Journal Star, April 25, 1976)

Two plays opened here this past week within a dozen or so
blocks of each other, both comedies, but miles apart in theme
and years apart in time, but both illustrating pointedly what university theater ought to be.

Illinois State University's Westhoff Theater is the setting for
that grand old Moss Hart and George S. Kaufman comedy, "The
Man Who Came to Dinner" and it is an absolutely first-rate production.   Donald E. LaCasse Jr. has spared no horses in this
splendidly detailed and beautifully acted show.   It is the kind of
thing with a cast list so long that it gives directors nightmares
and half the people in the drama department a shot at something
or other.   There are, unless my computer has failed, 34 in all,
and not a weak sister among them.

"The Man Who Came to Dinner" quite obviously needs strong
leads to be good.   It has however, so many character actor parts
that one bad one can nearly bring down the whole thing.   This
has, to put it unblushingly, an incredibly good cast, many of
them even unfamiliar.

I am not sure whether the effects of last year's ISU triumph
with "Cuckoo's Nest" at the Kennedy Center is having an effect
yet on the quality of students coming into the theater department,
but it is part of the school's most gratifying upward mobility.
And this is perhaps the best display yet of a massive production
with unerring excellence all the way down the line.

Michael Connolly's Sheridan Whiteside is an outsized character, the kind of man who is easily hated and feared at the
same time.   There may be a trace of warmth here someplace,
but Connolly keeps it well hidden beneath a lofty, glacial exterior that is reminiscent, somehow, of Alexander Wolcott.   His
first words on emerging into the Stanley living room are, "I
may vomit," and it is an air of superiority and disdain he maintains brilliantly.

Who next from this virtual telephone book?   Nan Wade as
Maggie Cutler has a fascinating rightness about her as the efficient and worldly secretary who finds love in the small Ohio
town.   She has abundant poise and presence and an extraordinary
appeal.   As the newspaperman Bert Jefferson, Steve Harker
brings an old-fashioned kind of innocence to his part and considerable expertise.   Janet Nawrocki is excellent as the fuddled
wife and Craig Huisenga as the husband is required to display
consistent outrage, and does.

Then there are Mark Pence and Laurie Metcalf as the appealing kids out of this Andy Hardy era comedy, both fresh and well presented, and Robin Tammer in a vibrant part as the extravagant actress Lorraine Sheldon, and a whole host of small comic roles, some of them absolute gems.

Nicholas Ruggeri as Beverly Carlton nearly stops everything with his too short appearance, and there are Tobi Baer as the prim Miss Preen, Jay Clark as the doctor, Susan Stringer as nutty Aunt Harriet and Alan Wilder in a nifty part as Banjo, plus William Hastings and Karen Vaccaro as John and Sarah ... and many more.

Bruce Brockman's setting is nice middle America Georgian and Frank Vybiral's costumes are good enough to stir memories for anybody who was alive and seeing things in 1939, right down to baggy trousers, hosiery with seams and the kind of hair styles reminiscent of Ginny Simms and Claudette Colbert.

Altogether, brilliant! It runs tonight and repeats Wednesday through Saturday at 8 p. m. nightly.

Wesleyan's Skits Wickedly Funny

Meanwhile, Terrence McNally's "Bad Habits" at Illinois Wesleyan University's McPherson Theater is a blackly absurd, wickedly funny pair of skits about two different cuckoo's nests that are inhabited, on and off, by discontented couples of various persuasions, alcoholics, fetishists, and so forth. The one is witty and incisive and the other on somewhat a lower level, but John Bergstrom has given them a properly breakneck pace that was put off on opening night, I suspect, by repeated volleys of shrill and raucous laughter, which might be as disconcerting to the players as to most members of the audience.

The opening act takes place at Ravenswood, a resort of sorts that resembles a Forest Lawn for the Living. Michale Burke is the proprietor, Jason Pepper, M. D. (Dr. Pepper) who tools around in an electric wheel chair smoking vile cigars and inhaling martinis as he tries to liberate various partners with his quackery.

These include a couple of outrageous queers, wonderfully played by Thomas Koehler and Michael Cooper, a couple of actors who are married to and competing with each other continually, done with a fine edge of genial phoniness by Dyane Karp and James E. Mosiej, and Thomas Richards and Heidi Wagner as the Scupps, a battling couple trying to kill one another since 1963. Forever lurking about in the shrubbery is the very correct Otto, an insolent German maitre'd done so well by Stan Hayes that his repeated query, "Rrrrubdown?" will probably become a campus joke.

In the second portion, Dunelawn, all the actors from Ravinswood reappear except the girls. Here, in what is apparently some wierd psycho sanitarium, nurses Ruth Benson and Becky Hedges (Anna Randall and Anna Swanson) philosophize over their search for perfection as they zap patients into blissful tranquility with Dr. Toynbee's marvelous serum.

The doctor is Michael Cooper again, who wanders about muttering either gibberish or Swedish and inspiring a mad reverence from his nurses and patients, who insist he is a saint.

The patients include Thomas Koehler as a prodigious alcoholic with lyrical dreams of the perfect drink, James Mosiej whose bible is Frederick's of Hollywood catalogue, and Thomas Richards as Mr. Yamadoro, an ingenious sado-masochist. Michael Burke has been transformed from the urbane doctor in part I to Hugh Gumbs, a character whose vice is so unspeakable it is never revealed. And this time, Stan Hayes is Bruno, the leering gardener.

There is almost too much here to chart or make much sense of, save for its sometimes pointed and sometimes low humor. And yet, "Bad Habits" is widly nutty stuff, a mad and wonderful lampoon of the smart and expensive asylums and marriage centers with their quack remedies.

The comedy does not name names, but the targets are recognizeable enough, at least at the outset. Afterward, they are left virtually bludgeoned to death and the audiences quivering with laughter. Who under the circumstances, can ask for anything more?

Gary Burton did the costumes and the scenery and lighting is by Roger Drake with the special dance staged by Thom Cobb.

KLEIN, Stewart Roy; (2) Theater & Film critic, Reporter; (3) b. Phila. Apr. 8, 1933; (4) s. Joseph and Minnie (Heller); (5) Temple U. 1951-55, major subj.: journalism; (6) m. Helen Kocsko, Nov. 26, 1961; (7) children--Marjorie, JoAnn, Joseph; (8) Copy boy, Phila. Inquirer, 1951-55; Reporter, Doylestown (Pa.) Daily Intelligencer; Reporter, Editor, Phila. Daily News, 1955-60; Reporter, News Director, WCAU, Phila., 1960-61; Network News Writer, Editor, ABC, N.Y., 1961-63; Network Newscaster, "Flair Reports" ABC, N.Y., 1963-64; Reporter, Critic, WNEW, 1964-67; Co-host, "New Yorkers," daytime talk show, WNEW-TV, 1967-68; Critic, Reporter, WNEW-TV, 1967-present; (9) Lect., Nat'l Critics Inst., O'Neill Memorial Theater Ctr. 1974, U. of Pitts. 1973; (10) Member, Amer. Theater Cong; (11) Skeptic; (13) Pfc, U.S. Army 1956-58; (14) Phila. Press Club, Feature Award, 1959; (15) Mem. Drama Desk; (16) Ind.; (17) Jewish; (19) Tenafly Racquet; (21) 18 Crestwood Pl., Hillsdale, N.J. 07642; (22) 205 E. 67th St., N.Y., N.Y., 10021, ph. 212-535-1000; (23) Circulation: Approx. 1.5 million viewers nightly; (24) 60

plays and musicals, 75 motion pictures, 10 dance, 15 club & concert
performers, 15 books, 10 misc.

"Don't Call Back"
(by Stewart Klein, over WNEW-television, New York, date unknown)

"Don't Call Back" is a mystery thriller, and do not tell its
ending. Matter of fact, do not tell its beginning, either. And
I certainly wouldn't say a word about the middle, which might
be the worst of the 3, although it's hard to say. I can tell you
that the person who did it tonight was not the butler, but Russell
O'Neill, a first-time playwright, who according to the program
is the author of eight published novels. One of them is called
"Jonathan," the tale of a Hollywood screen writer turned into a
horse by a Mexican witch. If I were Mr. O'Neill I would not
tempt fate.

For his play is shallow, silly, ridiculously plotted and it
has all the tension of tapioca pudding.

For the record, it concerns a star actress held captive in
her Park Avenue apartment by her son's three alleged friends,
a trio of ghetto murderers on the lam. They plan to escape
using the star as a hostage.

There is an idea here, but there are mile-wide holes in the
plot, not a single character is believable, and the dialogue had
the audience laughing in the wrong place.

As for the acting, it is generally awful, with Miss Frances
doing her usual log number. Although a black performer, Dorian
Harewood, showed promise.

The best I can say about "Don't Call Back" which runs all
of 70 minutes, is that with sharp editing, it might make a four-
minute TV special.

"Doll's House"
(by Stewart Klein, over WNEW-television, New York, date unknown)

Ibsen's Nora Helmer, of course, is one of the classic feminist heroines of the stage. In this drama, she is regarded by
her husband in typical Victorian fashion: like an amiable idiot,
a child's toy to be possessed and then ignored ... A doll to play
with and then toss aside.

And after eight years of marriage and three children, Nora
realizes after a financial crisis that her life and marriage are
pointless. And she leaves home and hearth to stand on her own
two feet.

A couple of seasons back, when the bra fires of women's
lib burned their brightest, "A Doll's House" was revived and

it fanned the flames--thanks in large part to a superb performance by Claire Bloom.   Today the feminist issue has lost some
of its urgency.   But this production is still as relevant as tomorrow morning's newspaper.

As Nora, Liv Ullmann, in her American debut, gives a radiant performance.   She is a statuesque beauty who commands
the stage.   But at the outset she overplays the girlish, unawakened
Nora.   And this lessens the impact of her transformation.

Sam Waterston as husband Torvald is strong but also a bit
too obvious.

Ibsen is not the most subtle playwright and "A Doll's House"
requires an extra light touch.   This production leans the other
way.   But it is sturdy, intelligent and recommended.

KLEINMAN, Louis; (2) Theatre critic--now retired; (3) b. N. Y. C. ,
Jan. 25, 1912; (4) s. Barnett and Millicent (deceased); (5) B. Sc. ,
M. Sc. , New York U. , major subj. :   science, performing arts, 1935;
(6) m. Jeannette Kalish, Dec. 25, 1934; (7) children--Bert, Mark;
(8) Producer-director: Chester summer theatre (N. Y.), Writer:
night club comics, Producer: WNYE radio; Actor: TV, channels
11, 13, 25 (N. Y.), Drama Critic: WRVR, WNYE; Production Manager: WNYE-FM; (15) Member: AGVA, NAEB; (17) Hebrew; (20)
Articles in: Catholic Educator, Book: "Science Experiments"; (21)
6784 Groton St. , Forest Hills, N. Y. , 11375, Ph. 212-BO 8-4251;
(22) 29 Fort Greene Place, Brooklyn, N. Y. 11217, Ph. 212-596-
5690; (23) Circulation: Metropolitan New York City; (24) 75-100.

"The Night That Made America Famous"
(by Louis Kleinman, over WNYNE-FM radio, Brooklyn, N. Y. ,
February 28, 1975)

If you visit the Ethel Barrymore Theatre one of these days,
you'll come away with the feeling that Harry Chapin is a very
talented fellow.   That's because he's the star, the composer and
the lyricist of a new Broadway offering called "The Night That
Made America Famous."   This is a musical and accompanying
multi-media presentation which, on the whole, is entertaining,
occasionally arresting, seldom ecstatic, but always interesting.

This musical melange explores the life styles of young
Americans in the 60's and 70's and throws in a few extraneous
matters for insurance.   Harry Chapin catches the essence of
the struggle of the young people much as Pete Seeger was able
to immortalize the American scene of the 40's and 50's.   Chapin's music is in the contemporary vein, eschewing the pop for-
mulas and embracing the modal harmonies so prevalent among
the guitar playing composers today.   He is the star of his show,
and, as such, I find him singularly uninteresting.   Chapin sings
to himself, almost within himself, seldom making any visual

contact with his audience, and his delivery alternates between two decibel levels--high and low. But he is surrounded by a few delightful performers--Kelly Garrett, most compelling personality in the show, and a gorgeous singer, to boot, Gil Price, whom I remember so well from Newley's "The Roar of the Greasepaint," has an intensity in performance which is stunning and what a voice!   Then there are Delores Hall and Bill Starr-- both seasoned entertainers and it shows!

The production leaves much to be desired. Gene Frankel, the director, seems to believe that a singer and a song cannot stand by themselves. He invests almost every one of the 25 numbers with so much movement, so much media projection, so much trick lighting that the message of the lyrics and the beauty of the music are frequently smothered by all the activity on stage.

"The Night That Made America Famous" certainly winds up on the plus side, with much to commend it. I would have hoped that it could have been even more effective than it is--but nonetheless, it's a welcome addition to the Broadway scene, and if only the tickets were less expensive, then the high school and college kids could flock to the Barrymore Theatre on West 47 Street.

"The First Breeze of Summer"
(by Louis Kleinman, over WNYE-FM radio, Brooklyn, N.Y., March 3, 1975)

The Negro Ensemble Company opened this season with a fascinating study of the inter-relationships among the members of a black lower middle-class family in an urban center in the Northeast. The play bears the title "The First Breeze of Summer" and it's a maiden effort off-Broadway for its author, Leslie Lee--someone we shall be hearing from again.

Mr. Lee takes his time drawing his characters and painting them into real flesh and blood people.   During the two and a half hours of playing time, you get to know intimately each member of the Edwards family--the reflective grandmother, the strong father, the patient mother, the ebullient aunt, the older volatile son and the younger ambitious son.   You join them in their moments of exhilaration and weep for them in their travails.

The fairly large cast is almost uniformly excellent.   The veteran actor, Moses Gunn, is especially effective as the father and Charles Brown, as the older son, gives an utterly magnificent performance.   Douglas Turner Ward, who directed this play, appears near the end in one scene and he scores as a brilliant actor.   A young actor, Reyno, illuminates the stage with one of the most exciting performances I have seen this season.   The one jarring note in "The First Breeze of Summer" is struck by Frances Foster to whom is entrusted the pivotol role of the grandmother.

The Negro Ensemble Company is appearing in its home, The St. Mark's Playhouse, on 2nd Avenue near 8th Street, just a stone's throw from the New York Telephone Company building, which was burned out a few days ago. Because of the situation, the Negro Ensemble Company has an emergency telephone number--575-5860.

I commend to your attention, "The First Breeze of Summer" without reservation.

KLOTEN, Edgar Lawrence; (2) Professor of Theater, Theater Critic; (3) b. Buffalo, N.Y., May 21, 1912; (4) s. Cassius and Frances (Bauer) K.; (5) Ph.B. Canisius College, 1934; M.A., Catholic U., speech and drama, 1941; Columbia U., doctoral studies, theatre history and criticism, 1950, 1967-68; (6) m. Norma Leuthner, attorney, Aug. 16, 1952; (7) child--Gregory Vincent, b. July 31, 1953; (8) Teacher, theatre director, prior to 1942, Ass't. Prof., Fordham University, 1946-52, Professional theater, actor, director, 1952-56, Assoc. Prof., theater director, Univ. of Hartford, 1956- , Drama Critic, West Hartford News, 1960- ; (9) Actor, producer, director: Grand Island Playhouse (N.Y.), summer 1952-53, Glens Falls Arena Theater, (N.Y.) 1953, 1954, Ivy Tower Playhouse (N.J.), summer 1954, 1957, Gateway Playhouse (N.J.) summer, 1955, 1956, Wagon Wheel Playhouse (Ill.) 1955-56, Producer-Moderator, "Eye on Conn." T.V. series, 1957-58, Berkshire Playhouse, summer, 1958, Southbury Playhouse, summer, 1959, Member, Univ. Drama Trio, (over 100 programs); (10) West Hartford Senior Cit. Advisory Comm., Chr. 1974- , W. Htfd. Cultural Prog. Comm., Trustee, 1968- , Mark Twain Memorial Centennial Comm. 1974; (11) Delegate, Sen. Lowell Weicker's Sr. Intern Prog., Wash., D.C., 1975; (12) Mem. Conn. Arts Educ. Comm. 1974- ; (13) Lieut., U.S. Coast Guard Reserve, 1942-46; (14) Moss Hart Memorial Award, 1971, nominated again, 1975; (15) Am. Th. Ass'n., N.E. Th. Conf., Children's Th. Conf.; (16) Democrat; (17) Roman Catholic; (20) Articles: N.Y. Times, Players, Theatre U.S.A., Show Business, Shakespeare Newsletter, Catholic Theatre (ed.), Drama Critique, Co-author, dramatization "The Man That Corrupted Hadleyburg" by Mark Twain, produced, 1974, one-acts, produced and unpublished; (21) 19 Red Top Drive, West Hartford, Conn. 06110, Ph. 521-7777; (22) Univ. of Hartford, 200 Bloomfield Ave., W. Htfd. 06117, Ph. 203-243-4528; (23) Circulation: 15,000; (24) 100 plays and musicals, 15 dance, 10 miscellaneous.

"Elementary, My Dear Watson"
(by Edgar Kloten, West Hartford News, February 13, 1975)

There are a lot of reasons why you should see the Royal Shakespeare Company in the production of "Sherlock Holmes" now playing in New York at the Broadhurst Theatre.

The show is one of the most highly activated cloak-and-dagger plays of the last half of the 19th century, if not for all time.

It also has the superior acting skills of John Wood as the titular character and Philip Locke as the nefarious Professor Moriarty.

If you are turned on by scenery, "Sherlock Holmes" has a collection of stage settings that defy description. They turn into place on a pair of revolvers which proceed to show you rooms of intricate detail. They all seem to be double-storied with twisting staircases and corners and alcoves which must keep the stage hands busier than bees, ants and one-armed wallpaper hangers combined. And, I can guess that the actors must have needed a roadmap when they first encountered the backstage openings so as to get on at the proper time and through the correct aperture. They do, indeed, and it is all quite marvelous.

What might be another good reason for seeing "Sherlock Holmes" is that it was written by William Gillette with, of course, not a little help from author Arthur Conan Doyle who invented the whole thing in the first place.

William Gillette, his castle at East Haddam attesting to his immortality in Connecticut, was born in Hartford in 1855. It may not be very well known that his father occupied a seat in the U.S. Capitol as Senator from Connecticut.

Gillette wrote most of the pieces in which he played, with the Civil War play "Secret Service" and "Sherlock Holmes" being two of the most popular. The latter first appeared in 1899 and enjoyed tremendous popularity. Gillette, like his companion actor, Walter Hampden, was always making farewell tours: Gillette in "Holmes," Hampden in "Cyrano."

Anyway, what is going on at the Broadhurst with the estimable Royal Company from Britain behooves all lovers of melodrama and the pursuit of dastardly villainy to move fast.

"Sherlock Holmes," because of the laws of the American Actors Equity Association, will soon have Mr. Wood, alone of the English crew, surrounded by American actors. They may be just as good in the roles and as suitable, and I hope they are, but I'm inclined to think that it is Britannia to rule in this one.

Rip Torn Tears into Strindberg "Father"
(by Edgar Kloten, West Hartford News, February 27, 1975)

Yale Repertory Theatre in New Haven has a real winner with its production of August Strindberg's "The Father." Rip Torn heads the cast as the bedeviled captain in this play about the battle of the sexes, and although first written in 1887, it is as modern as today's headlines.

Strindberg's writings were so often based upon his own life

experiences and it is a matter of record that he fancied himself in the role of the husband and father who was taunted and tantalized by a wife who no longer loved him and who desired feminine power over him and his daughter. "The Father" is not completely autobiographical but it does reveal many of the probings of this fascinating playwright into his own mind, his interest in a form of alchemy and his abiding love for his children.

The story has Laura, the wife, who in the Yale production is played by Elzbieta Czyzewska, looking probably like Strindberg's first wife, Siri. Siri was childlike and baby-faced. Miss Czyzewska looks too young for the calculating female of the action with a daughter as that delineated by Meryle Streep but she manages to convey the basic outlines of the quietly vixenish woman. It is difficult to catch all of Elzbieta's lines, however, for her middle-European rhythms do intrude on intelligibility.

It is Rip Torn, however, who gives the illuminating and terrifying performance of the tragic figure of the Captain. He has been infused with the seeds of doubt about his paternity of the child and he then begins to doubt almost everything that has meant anything to him in this dubious marriage.

Mr. Torn gives a virtuoso performance, beginning the play in a loud and commanding vocal approach with his soldier's flare slowing at each turn. His readings are strong and somewhat intoned and suggest that his every idea is deeply ingrained within his very soul. It is an interesting technique. But the tones of Torn are still capable of the bewildered and the possessed and his final scene with Margaret, the Nurse are lovely in their beauty and childlike fantasy. I recommend that all actors take a look at "The Father" in the person of Rip Torn for lessons in control and discipline.

Elizabeth Parrish is the old Nurse, and, she too, is frightened, believing and believable. Meryl Streep as the daughter, Bertha, is completely competent as the pawn over whom the fight begins. Strindberg, it is said, argued over the education of his daughters just as does the Captain.

The other men in the play are Frederic Warriner, the wife's brother, a minister in the remote Swedish town, Ralph Drischell, the Doctor who does not suspect the scheming wife, Ralph Redpath, a soldier who sets up the idea as to "who really knows whether or not a father can tell his own child," and Stephen Rowe as an orderly. They are all fine.

This is the first time I have seen such a completely realistic set on the Yale Stage. Designed by Michael H. Yeargan, it suggests a vast lodge made of weathered wood and surrounds the action with a coldness and depth that is eminently successful.

Under the direction of Jeff Bleckner, this may be one of

the most satisfying productions seen at Yale in a long time. It certainly has a unity and drive that is most compelling. Utmost accolades should go to Rip Torn for a stirring performance.

KRAUS, Ted M.; (2) Publisher, editor and theatre critic; (3) b. New York City, N.Y., April 18, 1923; (4) s. Herman and Ruth (Weinberg); (5) M.A., Columbia U., N.Y.C., English; B.S. New York U., Economics; (6) m. Joanna Halpert, April 1, 1966; (8) Founder, publisher and theatre critic of Critical Digest, bi-weekly N.Y.C. and London theatre newsletter, 1948-to present; Contributing N.Y.C. editor to Players Magazine, Dekalb, Ill., 1972-to present; (9) Lecturer: Baruch College, N.Y.C., 1963-69, Univ. of Maryland, Baltimore County, Catonsville, Md., 1969-70, Dutchess Community College, Poughkeepsie, N.Y., 1973-present; (15) Drama Desk, secretary, 1963-69; American Community Theatre Assn., Board of Directors 1967-70; (16) Democrat; (17) Jewish; (20) Contributed articles: Theatre Arts, Players, N.Y. Times Travel, Southern Theatre; (21) 76 Fox Run, Poughkeepsie, N.Y. 12603, Ph. 914-452-6184; (22) Critical Digest, 225 West 34th St., Room 918, New York, New York, 10001, Ph. 914-452-6184; (23) Circulation: College and community theatre leaders, drama editors; (24) 150 theatre reviews of N.Y.C. and London.

Pros and Cons--London
(by Ted M. Kraus, Critical Digest, January 6, 1975)

LONDON: Christmas roses basking in England's "warmest" holiday season since 1940, security frisking of an entire audience (including the lifting of men's hats) prior to curtain-time, an unhappy shabbiness to streets, tubes and people, plus an absence of truly first-rate theatre fare (because London's "best" are busy raising dollars via Broadway hits) are the major impressions of a year-end holiday visit. A first day introduction to London's "participatory street theatre" resulted in being part of the 16,000 customers and employees politely escorted out of Harrods in 12 minutes flat, seconds prior to the final pre-IRA holiday cease fire bombing. All other theatrical experiences were anti-climatic.

Considering Britain's current problems of economics, politics and foreign policy, it is slight wonder that London theatre producers are looking nostalgically to diverse decades of the 20th Century for clues to satisfying entertainment. But it does become scary, on either side of the Atlantic, when the producers recall the good old depression days of the '30s, as several of London's current hits do. While many of last season's London productions delved into diverse combinations of marriage, several of this season's plays and musicals study the complexities of family relationships in a swiftly changing society. The IRA bombs seem too close for any playwright to yet study the problems.

All of the London plays and musicals seen were cast, played and directed expertly, every element done in quiet, understated taste.   Though the costumes in the period pieces were lovely, the extra-heavy flying set pieces in the musicals were too often extremely wasteful.

London's playhouses are lovely, warm palaces of red velvet, crystal and stained-glass lamps, cozy, inviting bars--all combined to provide a splendid, comfortable setting for theatrical enjoyment.   The New London, built on the site of the former Winter Garden, is an efficient, antiseptic multi-purpose auditorium that lacks the soft, warm, charming elegance that does make London theatre-going, even to see second best, such a joy.

WHAT EVERY WOMAN KNOWS is a beautifully staged, played revival of Barrie's witty 1908 play.   Though done with perhaps more love and sweetness than the author originally intended, Dorothy Tutin's "Maggie" is a lovely portrait of one woman's survival technique.

TABLE MANNERS, part one of Alan Ayckbourn's The Norman Conquest trilogy is an ingeniously conceived, expertly played comic commentary on the ultimate loneliness of compulsory family life, brilliantly set within the framework of a modern comedy of manners.   What is slightly annoying are the too obvious insertions to what is happening off-stage, and thus in the other two plays.   The result is more padding than interest.

CYMBELINE presented by the few remaining Royal Shakespeare Co. members left in England is a lesser try at one of the Bard's lesser works.   John Napier's ultra-lovely gowns are the highlights of the still longish confusion of mistaken identity cases.

BILLY, a super spectacular musical version of the Billy Liar play, is a magnificently over-produced "American" type musical, a current box-office hit produced by the American talent agent Peter Witt.   It features a remarkable tour de force song-dance-acting title performance by Michael Crawford.   But it is only in the musical's last 30 minutes, when presumably the production ran out of money for new costumes and more flying sets, that the basic strength of the script and of Crawford's performance can be measured.   Minus several thousand pounds (currency as well as weight) the production would be vastly improved.

THE GOOD COMPANIONS is a very warm, sweet, sentimental 1930 vintage "show business" musical that defies its use of dozens of film musical cliches.   It is the delightful portraits of Priestley's correctly titled troupe, lead by the impressive musical stage debuts of favorites John Mills and Judi Dench that rightly pleases its international audience.   Music and lyrics are strictly so-so, but at least one holiday audience did not want to leave the perfectly lovely onstage characters for the outside

"real" world. The entire audience enjoyed two musical encores
to such a degree that not a single person left his seat or made
an attempt to go home.

DEJA REVUE, a review of British musical reviews from
1939 to 1963, compiled by Alan Melville, is a gentle, humorous,
tasteful remembrance of some of the best and some of the
worst material of its kind. Shelia Hancock heads an easy-to-take
cast. For an overseas visitor seeing all of the material for the
first time, the concept of presenting a "typical review" (including
an awful "Manhattan Song" lullaby) is a questionable concept.

COLE, musical based on the songs of Cole Porter, presented
evenings at the Mermaid, is a classy, slick recital of the life,
times and work of the witty American composer who most naturally would appeal to English theatre fans. The talented cast present the material (again the good and the bad) with tremendous
skill, talent and charm. U. S. native Kenneth Nelson, now a London resident, is the best of the ten players.

TREASURE ISLAND, presented afternoons at the Mermaid
during the holiday season, is a rollicking adventure with enough
mystery, villainy and noble sentiments to satisfy any English
family audience on Boxing Day. The all male cast of pirates
and gentlemen swagger through the scenes with the assurance of
performers well-trained in speech, song, stage fights and
sword play. Before one's very eyes Admiral Benbow's tavern
becomes the Hispaniola. Projections on panels skillfully create
a stormy sea, a tropical isle and a benevolent sky at the journey's end. Although many of the musical numbers enhance the
production, the inclusion of comedian Spike Milligan does not.
His antics, his goats and his play to the audience provoke laughter out of place. The end of Act One destroys the tension and
the excitement that the theatre demands, that Stevenson intended,
and that children crave.

Pros and Cons
(by Ted M. Kraus, Critical Digest, February 3, 1975)

SEASCAPE is an interesting, affirmative philosophical play
(a rare American species) given a superb production featuring
the welcome return to the NYC stage of the talented, lovely
Deborah Kerr. James Tilton's magnificent three story high
Montauk sand dune looks ripe for either of the two plays the
script promises: the revealing, incisive play of ideas on the
meaning of life itself and/or an exciting fantasy discovering why
man progressed out of the sea. Instead the first act is devoted
to the petty sounding worries of the virtues of the wealthly elderly living near one expensive beach resort versus visiting many
expensive beach resorts. The second act limits, perhaps pur-
posefully, the discussion with two inquisitive lizards to cocktail
party probing. The unjustified ending is a hopeful, if undeserved,
tribute to the kindness of man. While it is always a joy to

listen to Albee's wonderful use of language, both man and lizard sound pedantic.

THE RITZ is a shallow, cheap, unfunny one-joke cartoon presented at a hysterical pace and sound level. This silly, shaky idea of "The Godfather" hiding in a homosexual Turkish bath might be a fun idea for a short skit at the next "Stunt Night" at your local Mafia headquarters, but it is not enough for a full evening of farce/satire/comedy.

BLACK PICTURE SHOW is an angry, complex battle cry against the dangers to an artist's integrity in a commercial world. Bill Gunn is a talented, articulate new playwright deserving of the expert Beaumont presentation. It would seem a mistake to have let the author of this still to-be-worked-on script direct it. The double confusion of race hatred and the escalation of the writer-in-the-attic myth to a black poet/film director living in an East Side townhouse requires the talents of a stern editor and an even stronger director to sort out.

PRETZELS is an intelligent, biting, often very clever, revue. The material, mostly concerning the built-in frustrations of middle-class urban existence, is given a polished presentation rightly recalling the best of the early "Proposition" and "Compass" revues. Three of the four performers were trained at the Boston based "Proposition." John Forster's music and lyrics are especially bright efforts set to some quietly wild ideas; though he should be excused from his acting chores.

KRIEGER, Robert, Hartford Times, Hartford, Conn. 06101, Ph. 203-249-8211.

LAHR, John; (2) Theatre critic, novelist; (3) b. Los Angeles, July 12th 1941; (4) s. Bert & Mildred (Schroeder); (5) B.A. Yale, B.A. Oxford, English; (6) m. Anthea Mander, Aug. 12, 1965; (8) Theatre critic Manhattan East 1966-67, Theatre Editor Evergreen Review 1968-70; Theatre critic The New York Free Press 1967-69, Theatre critic The Village Voice 1969- ; (9) Literary Adviser Guthrie Theatre, Minneapolis 1968, Literary Manager Repertory Theatre of Lincoln Center 1969-71; Theatre Editor Grove Press 1968-70; (12) PEN Club Board 1972-75, Board Choreoconcerts, 1966- ; (14) George Jean Nathan Award for Drama criticism 1969; (20) Notes on A Cowardly Lion (1969), Editor: Showcase 1 (1969), Up Against the Fourth Wall (1970), Acting Out America (1971), Casebook on Harold Pinter's The Homecoming (with Anthea Lahr) (1971), The Autograph Hound (1973), Astonish Me (1973), Life-Show (with Jonathan Price) (1973), Hot to Trot (1974); (21) 418 East 88th St. , New York 10028, Ph. 289-3533.

"Orlando Furioso"
(by John Lahr, Village Voice, November 12, 1970)

"Orlando Furioso" is wonderful. Epic, gigantic, operatic,

outrageous--it is like walking into your most heroic dream,
awake. Performed in Italian by the Teatro Libro di Roma, all
the chivalric myths of the Renaissance with their virgins and
voyages are incarnated on a scale as exaggerated and thrilling
as Donatello's St. George. The area (a geodesic bubble in Bryant Park at 42nd Street) is as large as a football field and
framed at either end by two mammoth, ornamental curtains--one
a formal russet, the other a dappled, blue Tintoretto sky. From
behind these two artificial "boundaries" swirls a world of monumental artifice: maidens and monsters, warriors and witches.
Propelled on wooden platforms which raise the actors above eye
level, the events surround the audience and hurtle among them.
Nobody sits at "Orlando Furioso," but patrons who like their
theatre to have a beginning, a middle, and an end will be satis-
fied--there are six of everything in this play. For the audience
as well as the knights errant, it is every man for himself. Theatre becomes sport. The audience, themselves transformed into
a new community of seekers, rushes to meet the action wherever
the stories unfold around them. They learn quickly how to dodge
the dangerous 20-foot steel horses caroming around the floor.
Caught up in the festival spirit of the event, they hiss the villains and bravo the flamboyant passion of the actors with all
their posturing and rolled "r's." I have never seen anything like
it!

"Orlando Furioso" is, like Ariosto's epic poem (1516) from
which it was adapted, about action, not character. Orlando
dreams that his beloved Angelica is in trouble. He sets out to
find her. After that, everybody is furioso. This is street theatre: the gestures and motives are broad. The medieval platea
which once creaked through town squares have been streamlined
and speeded up. What we need to know about the people is visible not only through their chestbeating, but by what is on their
backs. The wizard, Atlante, with his scaly, armadillo cape and
green skin; the female warrior, Bradamante, disguised in search
of her lover in a male tunic and massive gray boots; the tormented Orlando in black shirt; the Homicidal Females who "kill
all men who are not virile enough to enjoy at least 90 of them
in one day." (You'll have to imagine what they look like!) Like
a medieval pageant, the emphasis is on show not tell. While
the actors perform with eloquent sincerity (the cornerstone of
High camp), it is in the manipulation of space, the design of the
tableaux, and the use of the audience where "Orlando Furioso"
becomes truly breathtaking. Every moment has its tangible astonishment.

Platforms combine and divide as fluidly as rain drops. The
choreography is as elaborate as it is varied and precise. What
begins as Orlando's bed of dreams, splits to reveal a series of
cages where humans squat with only eyes and hands ominously
visible. The spectacle has the protean quality of nightmare.
Nothing holds its shape. Every moment is a startling visual
surprise. There is humor even in the familiar cliffs and scrub

pines of the painted backdrops. This is the Italian countryside
behind the Mona Lisa. But there is much more. A castle is
moved into the audience. Fabulous, glittering horses are
matched by a colossal bone structure called the Marine Bear.
When Orlando challenges the beast, he runs at it with an anchor.
The mammoth vertebrate opens as he charges full tilt. He ends
up inside it, flailing, and then swims (he is carried, kicking)
away. This is a moment of glorious astonishment. We watch
it with the same wide-eyed amazement and expectation that medieval audiences waited for the devil to fall through a trapdoor
with firecrackers tied to his tail. No less mind-blowing is the
Hippogriff, a magical beast with the diaphanous wings of a flying
fish and head of a griffon. To see it soar is to be able--for
that moment--to remember Icarus's dream and why he imagined
it. To turn and gape at the massive horses--five abreast--
charging at enemies across the field is to be caught, astounded
and almost helpless, in the vortex of violence.

Because most of the audience cannot fall back on English
to make sense of the production's myriad plot-lines, they must
either enter into the vectors of action, or walk away as disgruntled at real play as they are at real life. Experiencing "Orlando Furioso" is like finding the meaning of a Pollock painting:
you must accept it, find a place to begin, then follow the energy.
Thought, theme, and texture come after the initial commitment
of trust. And there is tremendous energy to lure the unwilling
into the world of the imagination. The production succeeds
through the genius of its design (directed by Luca Ronconi) in
making the audience feel drama not as words but as images in
space, not as explanations but unrepeatable experiences. Teatro
Libero guides the audience gently and in good humor, not in one
but many directions. The audience makes up its own event, by
discovering it; steered by the busy performers who frame them
and vie with such humor and guile for their attention. Life on
stage must be pieced together from the tapestry of events and
strands of logic.

There is method in this operatic madness. The endless
ritual battles, the disguises, the magical escapes have a repetition in performance which makes a comment on the idealization
of heroic legend. The ideals of loyalty, pure love, military
courage are not things we can respect in our betrayed, jaded,
modern imaginations unless they are swollen to such mythic,
Herculean proportions. Mystery has been sacrificed to technology. Renaissance folklore--its cultish violence parading as
valour, its alabaster virtue--is as preposterous and artificial as
the acting. The production is not simply Camp (although when
one maiden, Alcina, enters in a gold mask and a Degas tu-tu
with an attendant blowing bubbles, it seems too much of a wink).
At the end of the play a labyrinth weaves out into the central
playing area. The audience moves through it. Around them
are cages--now madhouses--where the central characters reenact
the play's main events. The moment is stunning: indicative of

the intellectual integrity of the evening. The visual images sardonically reveal the characters trapped in the madness of their tragic rhetoric and the melodramatic "logic" of their actions. Legends which have come off the page and into life are not paraded like a circus side-show before modern eyes. The audience strolls from cage to cage--staring, making faces, testing the energy of each performer as they recount their tales with obsessed passion. Suddenly, but on cue, each cage stops its performance. The actors leave. What is left of this fabulous event is the audience groping through the chicken-wire labyrinth looking for the next piece of the spectacle. They are in the cages. They are looking at each other, actors in their own drama. Their gestures, their clothes have an extravagance and exaggeration; their relationships are melodramatic and perhaps as hollow as the world they've enjoyed. In this harsh and final white light, dwarfed in the massive space, the reason for dreaming and playing is made clear. We are such small, timorous souls with such gargantuan appetites. What else is there for us but the imagined strength and the comforting evasion of myth.

LAMBERT, Virginia Van Houten; (2) Theater and Opera Critic; (3) b. Paterson, N.J., Nov. 1, 1938; (4) d. Edward Van Houten and Virginia (Mc Aleer) W.; (5) B.S., Seton Hall U., major subj.: English and education, 1959; (6) m. Raymond J. Lambert Jr., Nov. 26, 1959; (7) children--Eileen, Patrick, Kathleen; (8) Editorial Assistant, Paterson (N.J.) Morning Call, 1966-67, Staff Writer, Morning Call, 1967-68, Woman's Editor, Morning Call, 1968, Staff Writer, The Record (Hackensack, N.J.) 1968-1973, Entertainment Writer, The Record, 1973- ; (21) 29 Lincoln Place, Waldwick, N.J., 07463; (22) The Record, 150 River St., Hackensack, N.J. 07602, Ph. 646-4365; (23) Circulation: 150,000 daily; 200,000 Sunday; (24) 30 plays and musicals, 12 operas, 2 dance, 5 miscellaneous.

"Little Night Music" Big Night for Theater Lovers
(by Virginia Lambert, Sunday Record, January 12, 1975)

Ambition has gone rather out of fashion lately. But sometimes it can be a good thing.

Perry Bruskin, producer at the Playhouse on the Mall in Paramus, was ambitious. He decided to produce the Stephen Sondheim musical "A Little Night Music" there. The result-- which opened Friday--is a delight for everyone who walks into the theater.

Of course, Bruskin had help. "A Little Night Music" is a marvelous show. But it is also a very special show. There are no socko production numbers guaranteed to stun the audience into applause. A musical sophisticate will love the tunes, but he or she might have a bit of difficulty walking out humming them.

To make it come together requires taste, sophistication, style, and intelligence.   Fortunately, this production has them all.

Much of the credit must go to George Martin, who stage managed the original Broadway production and directed the production here.   Martin has had a long time to become familiar with the subtleties of this very subtle show, and it shows.   He has given it the slightly dreamlike ambience necessary to translate Ingmar Bergman's film, "Smiles of a Summer Night," to three dimensional reality without losing the flavor, but always it is like a touch of "fines herbes," never a clove of garlic.

The cast, too, contributes much.   Dorothy Collins is smart enough to know that Desiree Armfelt is a mature woman and never lets anyone forget it.   But she does not confuse maturity with hardness which makes her rendition of "Send in The Clowns" totally affecting.

Ron Holgate is equally successful as Fredrik Egerman, husband--for eleven months--of a virgin and anxious to resume a relationship with Desiree.   His recognition of his own faults gives them dignity and his mellow voice is marvelous for the music he has to sing.

Nancy Andrews, as the retired--with considerably more than a small pension--courtesan Madame Armfeldt, was a bit less satisfying.   She sings well, moves well, and looks well, but she lacks the cynical edge necessary to make the role come alive.

Linda Byrne was appropriately feckless and girlish as the virginal Anne Egerman, and Richard Cooper Bayne was nicely priggish as her stepson Henrik.   As Count Carl-Magnus Malcolm and Countess Charlotte Malcolm, Bob Gunton and Beth Fowler were delightfully jaded and nasty and Gunton's rich voice and meticulous diction were decided assets.

Fine voices and meticulous diction are particularly important in this show.   Sondheim's music has the intricacy and character of a Delius opera and frequently serves not as decoration or explication but to advance the plot.

Fortunately, again, the Playhouse production is well served. Like Holgate, Deborah Dean Walker, who plays Desiree's daughter Fredrika, and three of the four Lieder Singers, Patti Allison, Marsha Bagwell, and Dale Butler, have operatic training. The other cast members have experience in light opera as well as musical comedy.   When they get together, the voices almost make the walls of the theater swell.

Frank Desmond's marvelous set does make the theater expand.   It is a marvelous fantasy of Swedish country side with sliding birch trees, rolling beds, and a banquet table complete with candelabra that, combined with Leon di Leone's skillful lighting creates exactly the right atmosphere.

If you love theater, if you love music, if you love a good time, go to see it.

This Canto Wasn't So Bel

(by Virginia Lambert, The Record, February 21, 1975)

Bel canto loosely translated, means beautiful singing.

Given their banal and frequently ludicrous plots and the scant opportunities for interesting staging, the only reason to perform these early 19th Century works is, in fact, beautiful singing.

There was no evident reason for New York City Opera to offer Vincenzo Bellini's 1835 opera "I Puritani" as its opening work of the spring season last night at the New York State Theater.

"I Puritani" is rightly known as a tenor-killer. Written for the Italian tenor, Giovanni Rubini, the role of Arturo is sparked by high Ds and D flats--even an F. Rubini was a great success in the role. The New York City Opera used three tenors last night trying to duplicate his feat.

The first casualty was Enrico Di Giuseppe who won critical acclaim for his performance in the role when City Opera first presented the work last spring. Di Giuseppe bowed out before last night's opening curtain. There was a brief announcement that he was indisposed.

Instead, the company flew Pierre Duval in from Canada. It would have been better if he stayed there. From the moment he opened his mouth, Duval's pinched tone was irritating. When he reached for his first high note, irritation became pain. When the rest of the company took curtain calls at the end of Act I, Duval was conspicuous by his absence.

Arturo does not appear in Act II.

At the beginning of Act III, there was further brief announcement--Mr. Duval was indisposed and could not continue the performance: Roger Patterson, fortunately, was in the theater and would replace him.

Since Patterson is a regular member of the company, and since Duval has proved before to be a singer of little merit, one wonders why Patterson was not chosen as Di Giuseppe's replacement originally.

His is not a glorious voice, nor even a great voice, but it certainly proved a welcome relief after Duval's debacle.

Truthfully, the reason for presenting "I Puritani" is no mystery. The production is designed as a vehicle for the company's best known star, Beverly Sills. Unfortunately, Miss Sills was not in good enough voice last night to merit a vehicle.

She had pitch troubles much of the evening and the edginess evident in her voice over the last few years last night bordered on shrillness. It didn't seem to bother the legions of assembled Sills fans, however. They cheered, stamped, shouted, and gave her a standing ovation.

Di Giuseppe was not the only cast member plagued by illness. Richard Fredricks, scheduled to sing the role of Sir Robert Forth, also bowed out before the opening curtain. "I Puritani" has been a bad-luck opera for Fredericks. He begged not to be reviewed during early performances of the opera last spring because he was not feeling up to par.

The company was more fortunate in its choice of replacement for Fredricks. Pablo Elvira handled the role nicely after some early moments of difficulty in matching conductor Julius Rudel's tempi.

Some of the best singing of the evening was provided by Robert Hale in the role of Sir Giorgio Walton. His second act duet with Elvira was particularly effective.

Also adequate were Jerold Siena as Sir Bruno Roberton, Irwin Densen as Lord Gualtiero Walton, and Diane Curry in the relatively thankless role of Enrichetta, widow of Charles I.

Until New York City Opera unveiled this production of "I Puritani" last spring, the opera had not been staged in New York for almost half a century. In a way, that's a shame, because Bellini adorned it with some lovely music. But if last night's performance is the best we can expect to hear, it would be better if it disappeared for another hundred years.

LEBHERZ, Richard; (2) Drama Critic; (3) b. Nov. 3, 1921; (8) Freelance writer for Washington Post, Washington Star, and Queen and Nova Magazines (London). Drama Critic-Frederick News-Post, 1967-present; (20) Novels: The Altars of the Heart (1957), The Man in the White Raincoat (1965), The Nazi Overcoat (1967); (22) Frederick News-Post, 200 E. Patrick St., Frederick, Md. 21701.

Maggie the Cat Finally Reaches Washington with No Claws Barred (by Richard Lebherz, Frederick News-Post, February 17, 1975)

Even though Tennessee Williams had attended the opening last summer of the American Shakespeare Theatre's Revival of his lengthy "Cat On A Hot Tin Roof," he was there again Wednesday in the audience of the Kennedy Center's Opera House

for the Washington opening. He was dressed handsomely in a
beautifully (Italian?) tailored suit, wore glasses with rather thick
lenses, and seemed just as entranced with the play as the rest
of us were. And well he should be, because "Cat" is one of
the best of his plays, and one of the best American plays ever
written.

"Cat" explores a facet of American life that any worthy
American, anywhere, any time, will have to face up to and that
is looking at the truth or trying to avoid it. Lately, especially
in Washington, we have been trying to look at the ugly truth of
an Ex-President's betrayal and taking steps to rectify his un-
scrupulous and terrible behavior. As all of us know, it is not an
easy thing to accomplish. To this day, Nixon has never been
able to squarely face what he has done, and most probably he
never will.

But Williams is saying in "Cat" that it is best to face the
truth rather than live the lie. Mendacity is to be cut out of our
life patterns and thrown away as a dangerous cancer.

Curiously enough, right next door to the Opera House is another play written by Moliere called "The Misanthrope" whose
theme is not unlike "Cat." At the Eisenhower Theatre, Alceste
is very much in the same position that Brick (Michael Zaslow)
is in "Cat"--the position of hating life, hating its lies and with-
drawing from it. Both men are misanthropic, but for very different reasons.

Act I of "Cat" belongs to Maggie (Elizabeth Ashley) because
she literally sets the tone of the play, tells us where everyone
and everything is, then moves aside to let Act II lock into position. Act II belongs to Big Daddy (Fred Gwynne). You can look
at Act III as if it were a sort of verbal sextet, a skillful blending of Big Mama (Kate Reid) and Big Daddy, Brick and Maggie,
and his brother Gooper (Charles Siebert) and Gooper's wife, Mae
(Joan Pape).

As the play opens, Maggie has been dining with the family.
Mae and Gooper have brought along their "no neck" children,
as Maggie calls them, and one of the children has spilled something on Maggie's dress. She comes into her bedroom to change.
We find that Brick is there drinking heavily, apparently, and he
has broken his leg the night before. (The crutch is symbolic,
of course, as well as fact.)

He has withdrawn from life, so to speak. Certainly he has
withdrawn from Maggie both mentally, physically and spiritually.
He despises her as much as Big Daddy apparently despises Big
Mama. But Maggie won't let things the way they are not only
because she is deeply in love with Brick, (as Big Mama is with
Big Daddy), but also because Big Daddy is dying of cancer, and
his estate is literally up for grabs. Why else would Mae and

Gooper and their "no neck" children be there?

While everyone else knows that Big Daddy is dying of cancer, he is told by his doctor that he really has nothing more
dangerous than a spastic colon. Big Daddy is overjoyed at the
prospects of living without the black cloud of death hanging over
his head. But he makes one mistake. He tackles Brick and he
tries to get at the deep-seated reason Brick is drinking himself
to death. Or trying to.

Then we learn the story. Brick had a close relationship
with Skipper. They grew up together, played together in football
games, and the two boys were very much devoted to each other.
So much so, that their relationship had come to mean something
deep and necessary for the both of them. Maggie entered the
picture during this time, finely insisting that if Brick was going
to marry her, he would have to do it then. They married and
their sex life was good. As Big Mama puts it, banging her fist
down on the mattress of their bed, "When a marriage goes on
the rocks, the rocks are right here."

Well, the rocks were right on the mattress as far as Maggie and Brick were concerned. Maggie sensed that there was
something deep and "unhealthy" between Brick and Skipper, and
she was determined to end it. Their devotion to each other
frightened and threatened her own relationship with Brick. She
actually accuses Skipper of being a homosexual, which frightens
Skipper, so he attempts to make love to Maggie and fails. This
worsens the situation for Skipper because he now believes what
Maggie says is true. He is a homosexual because he loves
Brick.

Skipper starts to drink heavily. Finally, one night in desperation he calls Brick to tell him that he loves him, but Brick
hangs up on him. The next thing that Brick hears about Skipper
is that he has committed suicide.

Now Brick didn't know about what happened between
Maggie and Skipper but because Maggie believes in truth,
she finally tells him. From that day to this he has had
nothing to do with her. He loathes her and despises her
because in Brick's eyes she had demeaned a relationship
that Brick has held to be a fine relationship between he
and Skipper.

The question set up in "Cat" about Brick and Skipper is
really never answered. Is Brick a homosexual or is he not?
Will he ever go back to Maggie? Will he really ever sire a
son by a woman he says he despises?

"Cat On a Hot Tin Roof" sprawls across the stage like a
terrible Southern continent with its cast of characters caught in
a psychological puzzle. These are members of a family all

living more or less under one roof but knowing next to nothing about each other's personal life.

Big Mama is deeply in love with a husband who treats her as if she were part of the cattle he has enfenced outside in the fields. He accuses her of wanting to take over when he dies, an accusation, by the way, that is not remotely true. Big Mama has lived with Big Daddy only because she loves him.

After he has wounded her deeply by accusing her of wanting him dead so she can take over the plantation, she tells him that she has always loved him and that he has hurt her.

"Wouldn't it be funny if that were true?" says Big Daddy.

At the end of the play, when Maggie is trying to lure Brick back into her bed so she can have a son by him, Maggie tells him the same thing that Big Mama told Big Daddy. She loves him.

The last line of the play is Brick's. "Wouldn't it be funny if that were true?"

So, history is repeating itself.

There isn't any doubt that Elizabeth Ashley's remarkable and intuitive performance is one of those rare moments in the theatre when an actress steps into the role that she was created to play. She slips into it with apparent ease, like the silk slips she wears during most of Act I, but what looks easy has been carefully studied and created with care.

Michael Zaslow has recently replaced Kier Dullea, who played the original Brick in this production up at Stratford, Conn. and I found him to be much more effective. Both Ben Gazzara (who played the original Brick on Broadway) and Dullea approached the role of Brick as if they had sealed off the meaning of the Skipper episode, but Zaslow plays the role as if he can never get away from the possible meaning of it.

Kate Reid makes Big Mama into a monumental woman, a gross, fat, bejeweled, no-taste sort of Southern woman who has a heart bigger than she is, and whose one crusade has always been to love her husband deeply. She has been ill-used, mismanaged, and probably unloved but she is alive and fighting.

This is a solid, finely acted production directed by Michael Kahn. Like blazing fireworks on a hot Fourth of July night, "Cat On a Hot Tin Roof" explodes into a dazzling display of sizzling acting, exciting direction, and most of all, the splendid brilliance of Tennessee William's genius.

"Absent Friends"--Ayckbourn's Latest Play to Open in London
(by Richard Lebherz, Frederick News-Post, August 4, 1975)

When Alan Ayckbourn's "Absurd Person Singular" opened at
the Kennedy Center last fall, for a vast number of Americans
this was their first taste of this English playwright even though
just a few months before the Kennedy Center's pre-Broadway
opening Arena Stage had successfully produced Ayckbourn's "Relatively Speaking" in repertory.

"Absurd Person Singular" made it quite obvious that this
playwright had an absurd but delicious sense of humor, and much
like Neil Simon, whom he is often compared to, he could be
quite satirical and ironic with his cutting sense of humor.

On Wednesday, July 23, Alan Ayckbourn's latest play, his
11th, premiered at the Garrick Theatre. It was an occasion that
stimulated considerable interest because his "The Norman Conquests" is also playing in London. This trilogy of plays will be
coming to the United States within the next few months.

There was an almost Checkovian touch about his new play,
an almost light touch that caused the London Times critic to
dismiss the play as being far too light. He called his review
"Tea without Sympathy."

But while "Absent Friends" may deal with apparent frivoli-
ties, there is a deeper rhythm running throughout the play which
the Time's critic may have missed.

Diana (Pat Heywood) is unhappily married to Paul (Peter
Bowles) because he has been having it off with Evelyn (Cheryl
Kennedy) who is the wife of John (Ray Brooks). John, by the
way, is a very close friend of Diana and Paul's.

They also have another friend named Marg (Phyllida Law)
who comes to visit without her husband Gordon. Gordon, it
seems, is always sick with something so he never appears at
parties.

All of them are good friends and they are coming together
for tea so that they can be with Colin (Richard Briers). Colin
has recently lost his fiance, Carla, who died unexpectedly. His
friends have rallied round Colin to get him through this trying
period that they think he is in.

But when Colin does arrive the situation quickly changes.
He is not suffering from melancholia. He seems to have adjusted remarkably well to his fiance's death. He even believes
that his friends are happily married when it is perfectly obvious
that they are anything but.

Even though Colin will never realize it, says Ayckbourn,

he is far luckier to have lost his fiance, than to have married her. Their relationship won't have the chance to deteriorate like those of his friends. Boredom and adultery would have set in.

Colin keeps telling first Diana then Paul how much each loves the other. This completely unnerves Diana who at one point becomes absolutely unhinged and must be taken upstairs and put to bed under sedation.

John, who is already a nervous wreck, suffers from a sort of incipient St. Vitus Dance syndrome. He is terrified of death and all its implications. When Colin gets out some snapshots of his dead fiance for their approval, John starts bounding around like a Mexican jumping bean. Evelyn, his wife, is bored to death with being married (and having a baby to look after) but she is especially bored with John. Death she can cope with.

Apparently what Ayckbourn is pointing out is the complete vacuum that most middle class Englishmen and their wives live in.

Yes, the play is slight because the people he deals with are slight. They talk about everyday boring subjects and the only drama to come into their lives comes vicariously through Colin's appearance. After all, he has had a close encounter with death, and while John may be afraid of it, death is action of some sort.

But alas, Colin is oblivious to their oblivion. He does not realize that he has somehow miraculously escaped the deadly trap of marriage.

This is not the first time that Ayckbourn has fingered the relationships of husbands and wives who have nothing to do but disintegrate. He pointed this out in the hilarious "Absurd Person Singular." One wife tried to commit suicide under her husband's very nose and no one seemed to realize it.

Luckily, Eric Thompson who also directed "Absurd Person Singular" directed "Absent Friends." His direction is utterly perfect for this play. He never allows the maudlin to creep in and he never lets his actors slip carelessly out of their mundane characterizations. Thompson's undertaking of Ayckbourn's plays makes it possible for them to simmer comfortably on the same burner so to speak. And he has an excellent cast to bring it off.

Phyllida Law (Eric Thompson's wife off-stage) is perfect as a dizzy sort of woman who tries to hold their world together in her fluttering hands. Cheryl Kennedy (Tom Courtney's wife off-stage) has the difficult role of saying "Yeah" to almost every question addressed to her. She must find a way of making each "Yeah" mean something different. Ray Brooks as the St. Vitus

Dance expert is perfect with his bouncing gate. Richard Briers,
as poor Colin, has just the right bouncy optimistic lilt to set all
of the married couples crazy.

Pat Heywood's Diana unfolds like a quivering flower until its
petals start trembling to pieces.   Peter Bowles, as her husband,
is a perfect balance of indifference toward her problems.

I don't know if "Absent Friends" will break any records or
win any, but at the same time it does show Ayckbourn's certain
touch upon the pulse of England's middle class citizens.   The
play itself is very much like the smell of honeysuckle on a summer's night.   It's lightly scented yet slightly sickening for there
lingers underneath a certain decaying odor that borders upon the
beginning of putrefaction.

What all the characters in "Absent Friends" must do is not
inhale too deeply for marriage, apparently, like death, is a
booby trap that can explode right in their midst.

LEEDS, Dixie (Diane); (2) Theater Critic; (3) b. Urbana, Ohio, Sept.
5, 1934; (4) d. Albert and Bertha Auxter; (5) B.A. Michigan State
U., major subj.: Theater and Television Broadcasting, 1956; (6)
m. Peter Leeds, Aug. 25, 1956; (7) children--David, Derek, Devry,
Dorin; (8) News reporter Ch 13 (Toledo, Ohio) 1965-68, Women's
Editor, Feature reporter, Documentary Producer Co-Anchor, Theater
Critic Ch 8 (Indianapolis, Ind.); (9) Actress, Maumee Valley Civic
Theatre, Blithe Spirit 1963, Auntie Mame 1964, Bell, Book and Can-
dle 1965, Taming of the Shrew 1966, The Terrible Meek 1966; Di-
recting: The Chalk Garden 1967, Bell, Book and Candle 1965, Our
Town 1964, Under Milkwood 1963; (10) Member of the Board, Cen-
tral Ind., Nat'l Fdn. March of Dimes, 1974-75 Campaign Dir.,
M.O.D., Member of the Board Cystic Fibrosis of Ind.; (14) Outstanding Young Women in America, 1967; (21) [recently moved to:]
2505 Regent Ave., Minneapolis, Minn. 55422; (23) Circulation:
WISH-TV viewing homes 150,000; (24) 50 plays.

"The Rainmaker"
(by Diane Leeds, over WISH-television, Indianapolis, early 1970's)

Americana is touted in the program notes for The Rainmaker
at Indiana Repertory Theatre....   And curiously, the lack of
authentic human Americana is what is most missed in the production.

The actors in this drama are quality performers, as is
usual at I.R.T., but, in most instances, they wear their co-
coons of character too loosely.   The Father, full voiced and
unbowed by the vagaries of weather and time could as well deliver his lines from a Boston drawing room as a western farm.
As played by Russell Gold, the details of character are simply
not in evidence.   Some of that does not fault the actor.   He,

as the others who played "farmers," showed no wear marks on clothing ... and although the jeans were faded to a proper color for much wear.... There was no tell-tale lighter hue where a saddle or tractor seat should have stolen color.

It may seem downright "picky" to mention the lack of dust on boots.... But the premise of the play rests on the fact that a drought has been plaguing the area for some weeks ... and logic would presume dust ... and even a sweat stain or two on a stetson and a shirt. And why would a man emerge fully clothed from his upstairs bedroom in the middle of a 104-degree night to check on a family crisis? It's only because I. R. T. is usually so complete in attention to detail that these lapses stick out.

Ken Jenkins as the con-man rainmaker is attractively flamboyant, insincere and beguiling.... And Katharine Houghton is appropriately earnest though appehensive at her predicted spinsterhood. Robert Scogin as the deputy gives a gem of a performance, attaining consistently a low-key portrayal of rural America that others in the cast seem to deem only partly unnecessary.

The story deals with dreams and realities and how each fits into the scheme of several lives ... most centrally Lizzie Curry's. She, of course, opts for practical reality after a dalliance with a dream.... And even the dream ... in the person of Starbuck the Rainmaker, faces, for at least one or two moments the reality of himself.

The sets for The Rainmaker are gorgeous ... with the detail here lending credibility to the production. The show is not one of I. R. T. 's best in several areas.... But I. R. T. 's second or even third best is worthy of appreciative audiences through March fifteenth.

"The Miracle Worker"
(by Diane Leeds, over WISH-television, Indianapolis, early 1970's)

The new production at The New Civic Theatre falls into the must be seen category.

Played well by a fine cast, the show has a reputation of good reception whenever it's done.... But this time, the William Gibson play, The Miracle Worker, has connected with the right cast to bring a full theatre experience to the audience.... The best of Civic's season, so far.

The wonder of the production is young Cathryn Ferree who plays young Helen Keller with sensitivity, and the abandonment of a frustrated intellect lacking the tools of human communication.

Helen's mother is played very effectively by Tess Edleman

... who conveys the traditional Southern gentlewoman who manages to accomplish her aims despite a code that requires her to address her husband by his title ... Captain. Her thoughts ... even her life ... revolves around the young Helen.... Stricken by an unnamed "fever" as an infant and left, as a result, without sight or hearing.... And so without speech.

Into this unhappy and torn household comes Annie Sullivan played by Judith Cohn. Just graduated from a school for blind girls, Annie perceives Helen's major problem as one of discipline.... There has never been any. Through common sense, a battle of wills and sheer muscle, the teacher becomes a miracle worker as she finds the key and unlocks the trapped mind of Helen Keller.

Vivid portrayals by others in the cast include Margaret Eastridge as an indulgent aunt, and Roger Wooden as the almost grown half-brother who feels cheated of his father's affection by Helen's affliction.

But the real emphasis must remain with Mrs. Cohn and young Cathryn Ferree.... Because they are the wonder and the miracle of the play.... As were the real people they portray the wonder and miracle of their time.

LEHMAN, Jon Leonard; (2) arts page editor/ theater critic; (3) b. Columbus, O., Dec. 15, 1940; (5) B.A. U. of Chicago, major: English lit.; (8) Reporter, copy editor, asst. city editor, The Patriot Ledger (Quincy, Ma.) 1966-69; arts page editor/theater critic, The Patriot Ledger, 1969- ; (9) Dir. "Plaza Suite" (amateur) 1975.; (13) U.S. Army (Spec. 4) 1963-65; (22) Patriot Ledger, 13 Temple St., Quincy, Ma. 02169, Ph. 617-472-7000; (23) Circulation: Approx. 75,000; (24) 50 plays and musicals, 5 films, 5 television, 5 miscellaneous.

"Shenandoah": A Warm-hearted Success
(by Jon Lehman, Patriot Ledger, November 16, 1974)

Boston, and soon Broadway, has another hit musical of Americana, a sort of "1776" meets "Fiddler on the Roof." This one's about the Civil War, its name is "Shenandoah," and it opened at the Colonial Theater last night for a three-week stand.

It is a production of fairly modest pretensions fully and artfully realized: a tuneful and frequently touching score by the men who wrote "Purlie," a book based on the 1965 film "Shenandoah" which tells a simple and emotion-filled story of a Virginia farmer and his six sons and a daughter caught in a war the father wants no part of.

The cast is an exceptionally attractive one, which produces robust singing and lively dancing when it's called for, led by

John Cullum as the independent-minded farmer-father. Cullum, whom you may remember most easily as the delegate Rutledge who sang the powerful "Molasses to Rum to Slaves" in "1776" is a musical strongman in the Alfred Drake-Richard Kiley mold. His singing of the reflective ballad "The Pickers Are Comin'" and the impassioned "Meditation" are moving moments.

Although the emotions of war, the anger, the bitterness and the heartbreak are played to the full when they come, "Shenandoah" is always under control as sure and deft as the simple, suggestive sets and lighting of C. Murawski and Thomas Skelton.

After an overture which is little more than an introduction, the curtain opens quickly to a bare stage with red and blue lighting and opposing bands of blue and grey-clad young soldiers singing a martial air and countermarching till the scene dissolves in a slow motion ballet of rifles and bayonets. Out of the melee comes John Cullum as Charlie Anderson, delivering at his family supper table his message of fierce pacifism in a song titled "I've Heard It All Before": "the dream turns to ashes, the wheat to straw, what was it all for?"

Time and again in the course of the evening, director Philip Rose (who also coproduced and collaborated on the book) keeps emotions in close check. Cullum sings the reprise of his "Meditation" at the side of his wife's grave, culminating in a stirring declaration that he will defend his farm and his family before all else, and before the audience can begin the applause it is waiting for, the music changes into a quieter key and Cullum moves quickly into some contemplative lines which open to the following scene. It is one of many deftly managed moments in the evening.

The musical opens in spring, when Charlie Anderson believes he can keep his family from the harm of war. The season is suggested by profusions of willow-green boughs which hang like festoons from the flies. The farmhouse and later the village church where Anderson somewhat reluctantly takes his flock are suggested by outlines of roofs, windows and doorways lowered against lighted backdrops.

Outstanding among the cast are Penelope Milford as the daughter, Jenny, and Donna Theodore as a daughter-in-law. Both have strong, clear voices and they are well matched in a song which could make a country music hit, "We Make a Beautiful Pair."

The undoubted favorites of the audience were Joseph Shapiro as the youngest son, who is kidnaped by Union troops, and Chip Ford as the slave boy from a neighboring plantation. Young Ford shows off an enchanting story-telling style in his description of what it's like to be an "inventory," and the two boys are irresistible with their duet, "Why Am I Me?"

The five older Anderson boys are played with almost equal strength in line reading, singing and dancing by Ted Agress, Joel Higgins, Jordan Suffin, David Russell and Robert Rosen. Robert Tucker's choreography for them is in the clogging, high-jumping style of "Seven Brides for Seven Brothers" and all those Howard Keel movies, especially in a number about how "Next to Lovin'" they like fightin' best.

The music is by Gary Geld and the lyrics by Peter Udell, who besides "Purlie" have written numerous popular songs in the country and western, rhythm-and-blues and rock-and-roll fields. Mr. Geld's tunes are like the production as a whole--attractive, sufficient for the moment, but not, I'm afraid, apt to be long remembered.

"Peer Gynt" in Providence
(by Jon Lehman, Patriot Ledger, January 15, 1975)

It is trite to say that the things of imagination that astonished and excited our great-grandparents may require an equal act of imagination on our part to understand why. And it is, depressingly, as uncommon to encounter that imaginative and vital production which brings to the quaint and dusty "classic" the life force which got it remembered in the first place.

Henrik Ibsen's "Peer Gynt" is one of those quaint classics which I had never, frankly, expected to see staged. This early work of Ibsen's (his second "important" one, written in 1867) is packed full of the element of fantasy that is submerged so rigorously through his best-known naturalistic works. "Peer Gynt," which in its simplest terms is a tale of a boy who tells tales, is subtitled " A dramatic poem," and like the last plays of Ibsen, which keep soaring into supernatural realms, it seems to the naive reader unstageable.

Its action is wildly fragmented, leaping from Norwegian peasant cottages to the famous mountain king's hall to the pre-Civil War American South (by report) and a Cairo madhouse which prefigures the psychological theories of Freud. Its characters range from the trolls of Norwegian legend to gentlemen of the world embarked on an international cruise, and its images from campfire tales of reindeer hunting to the sphinx of Gizeh.

Its dramatic tone is equally discontinuous, alternating between the simple, sometimes lyric, sometimes brawling naturalism of the scenes of Peer's childhood and the shockingly "modern" cynicism of the 19th Century's equivalents of the jet set and the psychoanalyst. How in the world can all this be got onto the same stage?

But it is being done, astonishingly, by the Trinity Square Repertory Company in Providence, R. I.

This "Peer Gynt" is a new adaptation by Trinity Square director Adrian Hall and the company's resident composer-lyricist Richard Cumming, working from the Christopher Frye translation. Although it was worked out and first produced last summer at the University of Missouri at Kansas City, it bears the distinctive marks of the Trinity Square style: free-wheeling adaptation of the text, interpolation of contemporary material, borrowing from vaudeville and from screwball comedy, musical interludes, blatant sexuality and a fast-breaking ensemble style that capitalizes on the blackout and on isolating a bit of action for a moment and then merging it back into the swirl of events.

It is a style and approach calculated to stress the discordant modernity of "Peer Gynt"--to dust it off, to point out that even in this work often regarded as atypically poetic, Ibsen is the true father (perhaps grandfather is better) of modern theater.

One of the chief problems with "Peer Gynt," of course, is that very few people ever read it. As Richard Cumming remarks in a program note, most people think they know "Peer Gynt" from the familiar incidental music by Grieg (composed for the play's first, abbreviated production in Christiania in 1876). But Grieg's lyrical, sonorous Gynt is by no means Ibsen's.

It was the main objection of the contemporary Scandinavian critics that in the poem Ibsen had wasted his noble poetic powers on "thankless," ignoble material; that it was not, to speak plainly, uplifting to show as your main character a peasant lad who through arrogance and contempt born of rejection sets himself to become the embodiment of selfishness, the emperor of the world.

Grieg's score expresses that 19th-century yearning for idealization, the reluctance of his contemporaries to accept the bitter irony and psychological depth probes of Ibsen's vision. Cumming in his own incidental music has wisely avoided the romanticism of Grieg, striking instead an eclectic course that includes a lot of the wry, revue-ish tone, some patter songs, two or three pleasant ballads and a couple of plain-song hymns for the rock-ribbed congregation of townspeople.

This "Peer Gynt" is not a musical, but it is almost operatic in its staging, with the action ranging halfway round the audience on a rambling, circular ramp designed by Trinity Square's environmental genius, Eugene Lee. Constructed of rough timber, this globe-girdling ramp occupies about a fourth of the floor area of the huge upstairs playing space of Trinty's new Majestic Theater.

It has platforms for central scenes, a naturalistic millhouse for Peer's mother's farm, another naturalistic cottage for Peer's cabin in the hills where Solveig waits for him. A higher-level ramp serves for Peer's flight into the hills when he abducts the bride from the wedding.

In a particularly fortunate accident of environmental staging, the cottage where Solveig waits through all of Peer's travels is always before us, even while Peer is galloping across the desert, for instance, with his Arabian houri, Anitra.

Richard Kavanaugh's Peer Gynt is an attractive, impassioned youth, and when he is seen as the old, dying Peer returning home at the beginning and end of the play he is exceptionally striking. But it was his attractiveness, I guess, that gave me problems. I had trouble believing that he was the bad, frightening boy of whom mothers warned their daughters. In that respect, I found David Kennett's brief appearance as the young Peer in a flashback much closer to the elemental force of Peer.

There are some excellent contributions from Ed Hall in a number of sardonic roles, Barbara Orson as the bovine troll-princess, and Marguerite Lenert as the aged mother of Peer.

This is a production of striking visual images: a crowd of raincoated townspeople all huddled beneath a forest of black umbrellas; the old Peer in black coat, black hat and dark glasses peeling away the onion of his life; the mountain girls with gigantic plaster of paris mammaries applied to their fronts bumping and grinding with the wooly old troll men in the dance for the mountain king.

It is also a long production, and it fails to solve the problem that plagued Ibsen: how to get things wrapped up and get Peer's life over after the point of his incarnation of selfishness is made. It takes about 10 minutes too long.

Nonetheless, it is an overwhelming, full and various production of a play which is astonishing now as it was 100 years ago, and that's saying quite a bit.

LEOGRANDE, Ernest, New York Daily News, 220 East 42 St., N.Y., N.Y. 10017, Ph. 212-682-1234.

LEONARD, Roy; (2) Radio and Television Theatre & Arts Critic; (3) b. Redwood Falls, Minnesota, Jan 19, 1931; (4) s. Harold H. and Corinne (Stewart); (5) Drama Major, Emerson College, Boston, 1948-1950; also Radio & Speech; (6) m. Sheila Marie Finn (Oct. 11, 1953); (7) children--Kip 3/2/55; Kerry 8/3/57; Kent 10/17/58; Kyle 3/3/62; Kelly 8/6/66; (8) Staff Announcer, WESX Radio, Salem, Mass. 1950; Staff Announcer, WEIM Fitchburg, Mass. 1951-1952; Staff Announcer & Program Director, WKOX, Framingham, Mass., 1952-56; Radio Personality and TV Newsman, WHDH Radio & TV, Boston 1956-58; Radio Personality, TV Host, Newscaster, Critic WNAC Radio & TV, Boston 1958-67; Radio and TV Personality, Theatre and Nightclub Critic, Interviewer, WGN Radio & TV 1967 to date; (9) Actor Emerson College Drama Department Productions,

1948-50; Apprentice, Lake Whalom Playhouse, Fitchburg, Mass.
1950; Actor, Civic League Players, Framingham, Mass. 1953-57;
hundreds of interviews with actors, producers, directors, etc. in
Theatre Arts for Radio and TV since 1960; (13) USAF, Special Services, Armed Forces Radio Service, 1950-51; (15) Jefferson Awards
Committee and Sarah Siddons Society, Chicago; (16) Democrat; (17)
Catholic; (21) not available; (22) WGN Radio & Television, 2501
Bradley Place, Chicago, Ill. 60618, Ph. 312-528-2311; (23) Circulation: Radio audience, approximately 250,000; Television audience,
approximately 400,000; (24) approximately 50 plays and musicals,
25 motion pictures, 50 nightclub and concert attractions.

"A Little Night Music"
(by Roy Leonard, over WGN Radio, Chicago, October 28, 1974)

"A Little Night Music" is not the usual, run of the mill
show that we often associate with Broadway awards. The Tony
Award winning production that has opened at the Shubert Theatre
certainly won't be for everyone. But for those who really care
about the American musical theatre, it is a gem. Stephen Sondheim has written a musical score, closer to opera than we usually hear on the legitimate stage and Harold Prince has not
pandered to popular taste in producing and directing what is basically an adult fairy tale. The complicated story of love and
lovers has grace, charm and wit. Film star, Jean Simmons
is making her musical debut as the seductive Desiree and she
is captivating. Another familiar face is that of Margaret Hamilton, best remembered for her role in the "Wizard of Oz." The
setting and costuming are far above average. In fact, the entire concept and production of "A Little Night Music" puts it
into a very special class of its own.

"Private Lives"
(by Roy Leonard, over WGN Radio, Chicago, November 27, 1974)

Theatre goers in Chicago got their Thanksgiving turkey a
little early this year. You see, in show biz, a turkey is something that should be good, but isn't. This year's turkey is the
current production of "Private Lives" at the Blackstone Theatre.
I guess the blame must fall on the director, John Gielgud. He
has allowed his star, Maggie Smith to completely destroy one
of Noel Coward's most delightful characters. Her outrageous
poses and postures are nearly outdone by her vocal gymnastics
which try the patience of any lover of this fine play. For those
who may never have seen this sophisticated comedy, it's bear-
able. But the memories of Gertrude Lawrence, Tallulah Bankhead and even Tammie Grimes will serve you better.

LERMAN, Leo, Vogue, Condé Nast Publications, Inc., 350 Madison
Ave., New York, N.Y. 10017

LE SOURD, Jacques J. O.; (2) Theater Critic; (3) b. Neuilly-sur-
Seine, France, Jan. 6, 1950; (4) s. Olivier and Evelyne (Schanze)
L.; res. U.S., 1959- ; (5) B.A., U. of Chicago, major subj.: po-
litical science, 1971; (6) Writer, Encyclopaedia Britannica, 1971-72,
Staff Writer, Daily Times, Mamaroneck (N.Y.), 1973- , Drama
Critic, Westchester Rockland Newspapers (Gannett Co.), 1975- ; (19)
Club: U. of Chicago of Westchester; (20) 117 Library Lane, Mama-
roneck, N.Y. 10543, Ph. 914-698-3452; (21) Daily Times, 126 Li-
brary Lane, Mamaroneck, N.Y. 10543, Ph. 914-698-5500; (23) Circulation: 230,000.

"Hamlet" Opens at Beaumont
(by Jacques le Sourd, Westchester Rockland Newspapers
December 18, 1975)

Joseph Papp's new production of Shakespeare's "Hamlet,"
which opened Wednesday night at the Vivian Beaumont Theater
of Lincoln Center, has lots of surface chic. What it doesn't
have, unfortunately, is a satisfactory Hamlet.

Slight and strident, Sam Waterston's manic Hamlet lacks
the weight and substance, the profound dignity and nobility of
the character Shakespeare created.

Where Shakespeare's Hamlet, consumed by grief and the
need to avenge his father's murder, teeters between feigned and
genuine madness, Waterston's keyed-up, hysterical, high-pitched
Hamlet is just bananas.

There is irony in this, for Waterston has proved himself a
master of the subtle, the calmly intelligent and introspective
characterization in other roles. We don't expect shallow stridency from him.

So what went wrong this time? His concept of the role, and
that of director Michael Rudman missed the target. But beyond
that, there is such a thing as simple miscasting. Talented as
he is, Waterston doesn't have the voice, the face, the body of
a Hamlet. The part just isn't for him.

But this isn't just Waterston's Waterloo.

There's so much pizazz, so much self-conscious style for
its own sake in this "Hamlet" that the play itself is almost
smothered.

Before the first line is spoken our attention is commanded
by the massive wooden disc, slightly inclined toward us like a
platter being passed at a formal dinner, on which the entire
play is to be performed.

It's an elegant, ingenious thing designed by Santo Loquasto.
A corner slice of it rises occasionally to hold the king and

queen's thrones, and a center rectangle opens miraculously to serve as Ophelia's grave, chock full of real dirt and old bones, for the final graveyard bloodbath.

But we're conscious of it all the time, especially as the actors stagger about trying to keep their balance on the incline.

And against all this starkness director Rudman keeps his actors shouting their lines at a fevered pitch, until the unanimous hysteria begins to be tiresome.   There is some brilliant swordplay, though, for which due credit must be given both director and performers (Waterston and, as Laertes, James Sutorius).

Truly grand costumes by Hal George and some superbly modulated lighting by Martin Aronstein, with neo-Elizabethan music by John Morris, help give the whole its Bloomingdale's chic.

One fears the Bard himself has been quite forgotten.

Kipling's Dictum Bows to Sondheim
(by Jacques le Sourd, Westchester Rockland Newspapers, January 12, 1976)

East is East, and West is West, and the twain have met in "Pacific Overtures," a new musical from producer-director Harold Prince and composer-lyricist Stephen Sondheim that opened at the Winter Garden Theater Sunday night.

The show is a big gamble for Prince and Sondheim, but then we can't expect the men who gave us "Follies" and "Company" and "A Little Night Music" to take the safe route.

"Pacific Overtures" isn't safe, tired, tried-and-true Broadway fare; but it is original, refreshing and engaging.

Exotic enough to be new and interesting, it's also familiar enough to strike responsive chords in Broadway-bred hearts. What's more, it's a show with both beauty and brains.

For, in addition to being a lovely spectacle, "Pacific Overtures" is also an intelligent lament on the destruction of an ancient, fragile culture.

The show begins in July, 1853, with the fateful arrival in Japan of Commodore Matthew Perry of the United States, whose mission it was to pry open the oyster that was Japan, and to introduce Western trade.

It ends in the age of Toyota City and Sony TV, of Japan Airlines and Tokyo glutted with cars and pollution. Japan's present, erected on the wreckage of its past, is evoked with chilling intensity in the final song, entitled simply "Next."

A laudable sentiment, to deplore the obliteration of traditional Japanese culture, but how have Prince, Sondheim, and writer
John Weidman made it into a musical?

By looking at the whole theme--which of necessity is a sche-
matic version of history--from a Japanese perspective.   They
were clever to have tried it, and they have succeeded.

It is, to be sure, the point of view of a Japanese exposed
to the American culture, but that is totally appropriate.

The show blends traditional forms of Japanese Kabuki theater with those of the conventional Broadway musical.

To begin with, the actors, even those portraying Westerners, are Japanese.   Commodore Perry himself is played by
Haruki Fujimoto, looking every bit like the Japanese paintings
of Perry done at the time of his visits there.

Not incidentally, Perry also looks like an evil, demonic
personification of Uncle Sam in the superb "Lion Dance" that
closes Act I.

True to kabuki form, all women's parts are played by men.
There is narration from a "reciter" (Mako), who also speaks
some of the lines and utters some of the cries for performers
mouthing them on the stage.

"Pacific Overtures" is in great measure a visual spectacle,
but Stephen Sondheim's characteristically haunting and evocative
songs are an essential part of the mix.

Every one of them makes a point crucial to the show's
message.   And Prince's staging of them meets their tone perfectly.

The tale is practically told in "A Bowler Hat," during which
the clothing and furniture of a member of the samurai nobility
gradually become Europeanized, while on the other side of the
stage a newly dubbed samurai embraces the tradition with the
ardor of a convert.

But it isn't all somber, either, though the dark undertones
in Sondheim's songs are always there behind the mirth.

In one amusing number a series of delegates--from America, England, Holland, Russia and France--make characteristic
arrivals, and in the funniest song in the show ("Welcome to
Kanagawa"), Ernest Harada is a terribly funny Madam instruct-
ing her girls on the way to please American customers.

Interestingly, credits for scenery and costumes--both of
which are spectacular--do not list Japanese creators but Boris
Aronson and Florence Klotz. Both deserve high praise.

LESTER, Elenore; (2) Free lance critic; (8) Started as a film critic
and feature writer on the arts on the Newark Star-Ledger; quickly
drawn to the flourishing Off Broadway theatre of the 50's and helped
launch the first Off Off Broadway production, Ubu Roi, in 1960.
Began to review Off Off Broadway plays for the Village Voice and
in 1965 wrote the first major article on Off Off Broadway theatre
for the New York Times Magazine. Presently writes criticism for
SoHo Weekly News. Written on various aspects of the theatre for
New York Times; (9) Teaches theatre courses at New York University's School of Continuing Education; (20) Esquire, Ms. , and Viva.

LEWIS, Allan; (2) Theater Critic; (3) b. New York, N.Y. , June 30,
1908; (4) s. Barnett and Rebecca (Ehrlich); (5) M.A. Columbia U. ,
major subj. : English, 1929; Ph.D. Stanford U. , English, 1943;
Ph.D. Natl. U. of Mexico, Comp. Lit. ; 1954; (6) m. Brooke War-
ing, artist; (7) children--Anita Sorel, and Lanny Lewis; (8) Dir.
Shakespeare Inst. and Littlefield Prof. Shakesp. Studies, Univ. of
Bridgeport; 1965-75; Senior Member, Theater Arts Division, New
School, N.Y. 1960-76; Chm. Theater Dept. Briarcliff College, 1958-
60; Chm. Drama Dept. Bennington College, 1948-59; Chm. Theater
Division, Univ. of Mexico, 1951-58; Exec. Dir. New Dramatists
Comm. 1961-62; Director, Univ. Theatre, Mexico City, 1951-57;
Director and actor with Actors Lab. Theater, Hollywood, 1939-41;
Drama Critic, New Haven Register, 1967-76; (9) Radio, and TV
appearances with Ed. TV; NBC; (12) Trustee, American Shakespeare
Theater; (13) Lt. US. Air Force, CBI Theater, 1941-45; (15) Mem-
ber, AAUP; Mod. Lang. Assoc. , International Shakespeare Assoc. ;
(16) Democrat; (20) Author, The Comtemporary Theater (Crown),
American Plays and Playwrights (Crown), Ionesco (Twayne), El Tea-
tro Moderno (Spanish), articles for the Guardian, Social Research,
Nation, Contemp. Review, Art and Society, others; (21) Elwil Dr. ,
Wesport, Conn. 06880, Ph. 203-227-2462; (23) Circulation: 250,000;
(24) 50 plays and book reviews, 15 dance and music concerts.

"Jumpers" Pursues Nothingness
(by Allan Lewis, New Haven Register, March 17, 1974)

If God is dead, and God was good, what choices are left
to man to find valid guides for human conduct? Is there no
distinction between good and evil, or do values merge in vague
abstract linguistic arguments? How can a play be built around
philosophical discussion of the nature of existence? Tom Stoppard has done it and brilliantly in "Jumpers," now playing at
the Kennedy Center in Washington and soon to be shown in New
York.

George Moore, professor of Moral Philosophy at a British

university is preparing a debate on natural law with his colleague,
Duncan McFee.   All during the play he rehearses for his great
public moment by dictating to his bland emotionless secretary.
He is so completely immersed in his thoughts that he pays little
attention to a murder that is committed in his own house, even
though the dead body is hanging in his wife's bedroom closet
and the murdered man was his philosophical opponent for the
forthcoming debate.   He ignores reality to find the ultimate reality.   He interrupts his dictation walking in and out of his study
to see his wife, search for his missing hare, and be interviewed
by the inspector from Scotland Yard.   His colleagues who are
skilled in mental gymnastics are also proficient in physical gymnastics.   The play opens with an elaborate tumbling act, the
full philosophy team celebrating a party in George's posh May-
fair penthouse.   The elaborate quarters are not paid for from
his meager salary as professor, but from the income of his
beautiful wife, Dotty, who was a former musical star, and the
voice on a series of popular albums.

During the gymnastic exhibition McFee is shot.   Who killed
him?   Dotty who moved in and out of the jumpers singing "spoon-
ey, Juney, moon songs" as she did in the days of former stardom or the prim secretary who, totally nude, streaks across
the room on a swinging chandelier or perhaps Archie Jumper
who wasn't there at all?   Archie is the dapper Vice-Chancellor,
doctor, lawyer, psychiatrist, who though a mediocre philosopher,
is the ideal non-gymnasium jumper, bouncing from one muddled
concept or pretty woman to another with bland serenity.

When Scotland Yard's Inspector Bones comes to investigate,
Dotty easily distracts him with her bedroom prowess while the
dead body keeps jumping in and out of the closet door.   Archie
explains to Bones that McFee walked into the park "where he
crawled into a large plastic bag and shot himself. "   If Bones is
willing to forget the whole thing, Archie is prepared to offer him
the university chair in logic.   We never know who the murderer
is, nor is it necessary, for any positive solution would be subject to further analysis.

In a dream sequence which follows the play George's symposium does take place, the subject "Man--Good, Bad or Indifferent?"   The substitute for McFee is Archie himself, speaking
in totally disjointed nonsequiturs while the gymnasts leap on
trampolines, parallel bars, and flying rings, and Dotty sings her
farewell to moon songs.   The combination of gymnast and philosopher applies to all members of the department except Archie
who is too busy as God's substitute and George who is too busy
being anchored in the pursuit of the absolute.   They are the logical final opponents, Archie, summarizing all knowledge in an
explosion of gibberish and George, with an unfaithful wife; a
dead hare which he loved, a crushed tortoise which he accident-
ly stepped on, affirming that "life is better than death, love better than hate" and that there is no need to despair for "even

those deprived and cruelly treated, nonetheless grow up." At
the grave the undertaker doffs his top hat and "impregnates the
prettiest woman," close to Vladimir's line in "Waiting for Godot"
"down in the hole, lingeringly, the grave digger puts on his
forceps."

"Jumpers" is a mad, brilliant theatrical tour de force.
Tom Stoppard had displayed his intellectual prowess in "Rosencrantz and Guildenstern are Dead," his macabre, Joe Orton surrealist fantasy "Magritte" and "The Real Inspector Hound," which
is making a return visit to New Haven's Shubert March 25, and
now, he has created the zaniest philosophical murder play of the
decade much in the manner of Duerenmatt in "The Physicists"
and "The Deadly Game." The play is hilariously funny and
deadly serious. Peter Wood, the director, and the Kennedy
Center have adorned an intellectual monologue with high theatricality. Brian Bedford, as George, the one philosopher who
doesn't jump from existentialism to behaviorism to logical posi-
tivism in an exercise of bandwagon leaping is an unforgettable
professor lost in his ideas, searching for absolutes that can sustain action, resisting endless relativism, and caught in a murder investigation. He is a remarkable human, living with a distracting sex symbol that does not distract him at all, dictating
to an unattractive secretary who appeared most attractive in the
nude and turns out to be the mistress and possible murderess
of McFee, and forced to compete with an Olympic team of acro-
bat-priest-philosophers who persist in endless motion and hold
fast to nothing.

Then there is the moon, the key image of the play. Dotty
sings about the moon, the romantic symbol of love, poetry and
madness. But back projections of the astronauts landing, show
the moon to be another piece of barren real estate. Through
a mechanical malfunction of their space ship, one of the astronauts is left on the moon, moving endlessly in space. Science
too, has failed. The world of objective analysis, cause and effect, logical time space relationship is as void as God's shadow.
The play is a theatrical seminar in the quest for meaning, the
emptiness of philosophy and an unsolved murder. With Stoppard's inexhaustible cleverness, "Jumpers" is a fantastic display
of the exhausting pursuit of nothingness which leaves us at least
with the joy of having been part of it.

"Hamlet" in Central Park: Alive, Intense, Almost Great
(by Allan Lewis, New Haven Register, July 6, 1975)

For two hours--about the time it takes--until the first in-
termission--"Hamlet" was on the verge of becoming a major
contribution to contemporary interpretations of Shakespeare's
masterpiece. Sam Waterston, a most unlikely candidate for the
title role, provided a sharp and welcome break with tradition.
Nervous, highstrung, bold in utterance, active, shouting a great
deal of the time, he created a Dane who was less melancholy

than deeply disturbed and outspoken, a frail, excitable, endearing, sensitive Prince, speaking the lines with total disregard for traditional patterns, but endowing them with new found freshness and conviction, retaining the rhythmic patterns but giving the internal structure a different balance that shattered prevailing molds and made "Hamlet" into a new play, alive, intensely appealing, and of this decade.

Sam Waterston was not selected as a romantic hero. He had recently played the stuffy Helmer in Ibsen's "A Doll's House," was bashful Benedict in "Much Ado About Nothing" and the aspiring salesman, Tom, in "The Glass Managerie." His Hamlet is extraordinary, a revelation of an actor's versatility, an interpretation that is uniquely Waterston's, a boyish, outgoing Hamlet, wild and frenetic at times, calm and calculating at others, the trapped intellectual, pulled into the maelstrom of events, uncommonly gifted but always human. Waterston's Hamlet is a living man, not a literary parable. The variations in his voice are matched by the variety of graceful movements. He dances on all levels, emotionally, physically and mentally. It is the best Hamlet since David Warner at the Royal Shakespeare Company a few years ago presented the gangling, lost, reluctant Hamlet of the Sixties, a young man who didn't want to be involved but was forced into action by the corrupt society that surrounds him. Waterston is closer to this decade, alert, brash, shouting, violent, subdued, knowing he has to act, confident of his powers, but disturbed by its consequences. He rejects Ophelia because she is part of the enemy's camp. He faces the Ghost without hesitation. He is not sexually drawn to his mother and in the closet scene they sit at opposite ends of the huge stage to underscore the distance that is between them.

He is a man alone, under pressure to avenge his father's death who, after his first encounter with the Ghost, warns Horatio not to be disturbed if Hamlet should put on an "antic disposition." Waterston uses the madness of Hamlet in complicated variations. He feigns madness to confound Polonius and Rosencrantz and Guildenstern. But the pretense carries over into reality and Hamlet actually becomes mad as in his first encounter with Ophelia but quickly senses the danger, recovers his balance and proceeds with controlled calm.

This is a vibrating, stimulating, inspiring "Hamlet" and much is due to the director, Michael Rudman, a Texan by birth, but a British import who earned a reputation for avant garde experimentation with the Traverse Theatre of Edinburgh and later with the Hampstead Theatre Club of London. Like Waterston, he approaches the play with respect but not awe, anxious to avoid the well worn patterns and keep the play as though it were a new found script. Some of what he attempts fails, some works, but it is all part of an active imagination seeking to present the play as though it had never been done before.

The opening scene is indicative of the director's daring and the scene does not come off. We are accustomed to parapets, mysterious figures in the night, the Ghost's appearance. Rudman had a dozen soldiers in stiff military parade move on either side, standing guard on all corners. Horatio and Marcellus are center stage, reacting to an invisible Ghost. Central Park's Delacorte Theatre is much too light at 8 p. m. for ghostly carryings on, and what would have been effective at a later hour, fizzled.

The uniforms were severe military dress of a European country of the past century, evidently chosen to represent an indefinite period and provide the basis for universality rather than a specific time and place. The stiff military bearing of the soldiers, the heel clicking and smart saluting, was evidently the director's idea of a society living under a rigid, ordered discipline. Hamlet, the doubter, the one who questions, he who breaks the mold plays effectively against the surroundings of blind obedience. For the Court scene, two long tables were set at right angles and all the characters sat stiffly in military uniform as though at a council of war. Laertes rose smartly from his seat, begged permission to leave for France, and marched off. Hamlet likewise rose from his seat to answer the King.

This time the staging worked well, another perspective, another insight, and rarely did the director become gimmicky, the curse of the pursuit of originality. When Laertes and the King plot the death of Hamlet, prior to the final duel scene, they both have bows in their hands and shoot arrows into a dummy some twenty feet away. This is the sort of trickery that was unnecessary, playing too eagerly for obvious symbolism. But my sympathy was with the director. This scene is much too talky and generally can become a disastrous letdown at a key moment. The temptation was to add some movement to the scene but it didn't advance the play. One was more interested in the accuracy of the arrow shooting than in listening to the plot against Hamlet's life.

The set by Santo Loquasto was likewise a mixed blessing. Hard geometric lines of black and silver framed a series of mirrors as a unit set designed presumably to match the cold rigid stuffiness of the military court but it was too frail for the appearance of the Ghost and too cold for the closet used to show multiple figures of the elusive Ghost, or to create effects beyond immediate reality.

The cast, surprising for Central Park and for most American Shakespeare theaters, spoke their lines clearly and intelligently. Horatio was a dignified scholar, soft and well spoken by James Cahill. Larry Gates played a foolish, prating Polonius, and doubled as the Gravedigger. Claudius the King was strong and forceful enough to be a counterpart to Hamlet's revenge. Robert Burr as Claudius should know this well for a

few years ago he substituted for Richard Burton and took over
the role Hamlet himself.

The women were woefully weak. Neither Ruby Dee nor
the lovely Andrea Marcovicci as Ophelia could manage the lines
with clean intent. Laertes was too much the prig and too lacking in clarity. The second half drooped, mainly because Hamlet was gone off to England. Laertes and Ophelia took over and
couldn't hold the high level of the director's concept. Too much
was lost to build up again to the big finale. The duel scene
was splendidly executed, a tribute to the athletic accomplishments of both actors, but the tragic force had blown away. The
military court, the regimented society, the power of the king as
absolute evil, with Hamlet as the frail figure in violent revolt
against a heartless world, so strong in the first half failed to
find its full play of mighty opposites in the second half. But
this is a production well worth seeing. Sam Waterston is a
worthy addition to the long line of memorable Hamlets, a different Hamlet that came close to greatness.

LINDSTROM, Pia; (2) NBC-TV theatre critic; (3) b. Stockholm,
Sweden; (5) B. A. , Mills College, history and government; (6) m.
Joseph Daly; (7) children--Justin and Nicholas; (8) Reporter, WNBC-
TV News 1973- present; correspondent, WCBS-TV News, 1970-1973;
reporter, KGO-TV San Francisco, 1968-1970; co-host, A. M. Show,
San Francisco (ABC), 1967-1968; (9) Review books for N. I. S. Radio
(NBC); (15) Member of A. F. T. R. A. ; (22) NBC, 30 Rockefeller Plaza,
New York, N. Y. 10020; (23) Circulation: television audience reached,
approx. 1, 300, 000.

LITTLEJOHN, David; (2) Professor, Writer, Critic; (3) b. San Fran-
cisco, Calif. , May 8, 1937; (4) s. George and Josephine (Cullen)
Littlejohn; (5) B. A. University of California, Architecture and Eng-
lish, 1959; M. A. , 1960, Ph. D. , 1963, Harvard U. , English; (6) m.
Sheila Hageman, June 10, 1963; (7) children--Victoria and Gregory
David; (8) Spectrometer Applications Engineer, Varian Associates,
Palo Alto, Calif. , 1959-60. Teaching Fellow and Tutor in English,
Harvard U. , 1961-63. Asst. Prof. English, U. C. Berkeley, 1963-
69; Asst. Prof. Journalism, 1969-71; Assoc. Prof. , 1971- ; Assoc.
Dean, 1973- . Book Critic, KQED, San Francisco, 1964-65. Drama Critic, 1965-69. "Critic at Large," 1968- . "Critic at Large"
for Public Broadcasting Service TV network, 1971-72. (300+ televised reviews to date). (12) Consultant to Aspen Institute Program
on Communications and Society, 1974-75; (14) Rotary Club Scholarship, 1954. Woodrow Wilson Fellowship, 1959. Fulbright Lecturer
in American Literature and Civilization, Universite de Montpellier,
France, 1966-67. A. C. L. S. Research Fellowship for work in England and France, 1972-73; (15) Member, A. F. T. R. A. , Association
des Amis d'Andre Gide, The National Trust for Historic Preservation, University (of Calif.) Art Museum Council Board; (20) Dr.
Johnson: His Life in Letters (Prentice-Hall 1965); Black on White:

A Critical Survey of Writing by American Negroes (Grossman 1966;
Viking paperback); Interruptions: Essays Reviews and Reflections
(Grossman 1970); Gide: A Collection of Critical Essays (Prentice-
Hall 1970); Andre Gide Reader (Knopf 1971); Dr. Johnson and Noah
Webster: Two Men and Their Dictionaries (Book Club of Calif.
1971). Also over sixty essays, reviews, and articles (New Republic,
NY Times, Saturday Review, Nation, The Reporter, Commonweal,
Daedalus, etc.) of which 14 are reprinted in Interruptions. None
of these are on theatrical subjects. At present, regular book re-
viewer for New Republic and contributing writer for NY Times, Aspen Program, and KQED; (21) 719 Coventry Road, Kensington, Calif.
94707, Ph. 415-527-1554; (22) School of Journalism, University of
California, Berkeley, Calif. 94720, Ph. 415-642-3383; or KQED,
San Francisco; (23) Circulation: Perhaps 100,000 with KQED reviews; 300,000 with New Republic; 1 million with PBS network; (24)
Varies from weekly (52/yr.) on full-time TV years to 10-20 in
others. Currently concentrating on books, film, TV, and opera rather than the traditional theatre.

"Hot L Baltimore"
(by David Littlejohn, over KQED television, San Francisco,
November 5, 1973)

The "Hot L Baltimore," ACT's second offering this season,
is the worst production the company has offered us, since they
first came out west in the summer of 66. The play opened off
Broadway in New York just eight months ago, and won several
awards there, but it's a terrible play: lifeless, gauche, sophomoric, undramatic. ACT has made use of a number of second
and third rate scripts in the past seven years, but I'd venture
that this is probably the worst play they've ever done, as well
as the worst production.

I hesitate to blame the cast, because I know--any ACT regular knows--that several of them, at least, are capable of substantial, beautiful, even inspired characterizations. Ray Reinhardt is one of ACT's genuine stars. In Lanford Wilson's play, he
sits, a nonentity in a toupee, with virtually nothing to do. And
what they've done to Elizabeth Huddle is criminally obscene.
She struts and sprawls around as somebody's cartoon fantasy of
a whore: she all but has the word written on her bare buttocks
in rhinestones. She does have to scamper around screaming,
naked and wigless, at the end of Act I, which a big part of the
opening night audience thought the greatest theatrical event since
Oedipus poked out his eyes. Her neon-lit hooker reminded me
of ACT's perhaps second grossest production, a camped-up travesty of Brendan Behan's The Hostage back in 68 or 69. And
that leads me to lay some of the blame, at least, on the direct-
or, Allen Fletcher, who (though he's done some very honorable
things) also directed that mess. No actor seems to have been
given the least encouragement to think up a plausible human being who might be speaking his lines.

But there you are, really: the most ingenious director going would have had insuperable problems, I think, making anything plausible, anything human, anything dramatically viable
out of 80% of these lines.

The cashier at the Downtown Center Garage (a very keen
theatre critic) told us that Act III was even worse than Act I
and Act II. I believe him, but I'm afraid I didn't stay to see
it, so you'll have to take that part of my review 2nd hand.

"As You Like It"
(by David Littlejohn, over KQED television, San Francisco,
July 18, 1974)

I can think, offhand, of about 30 other productions I wish
the National Theatre of Great Britain had picked for their first-
ever visit to San Francisco. But Clifford Williams' seven-year-
old, all-male, mod/plastic version of Shakespeare's As You Like
It is still a very good show, far and away the best evening's
theatre I've seen since I came back from London myself a year
ago.

That still leaves it a peculiar choice for the NT's second
American tour. Although the cast is very good, very skillful,
there's no one in it you've heard of--so that's not going to sell
tickets. And As You Like It probably comes about 23rd or 24th
on the list of most-often-performed Shakespeare plays. It's a
very appealing, but very slight romantic comedy.

The seven-year-old production does show its age, however,
almost more than the 374-year old play. Nothing dates more
rapidly than mod men's fashions, and the courtiers' Mac-collared
suits and poly-vinyl-chloride capes are all but labeled "Swinging
London 1967." The villainous duke comes on in shades and
white fur, like Rock King Phil Spector at some private party for
the Beatles; his hired goon clomps around in black leather. The
show's one big mistake--it's incredibly gross, but it only lasts
a minute--is Hymen, the Marriage God, who "descends" for the
last scene Wedding Pageant: a skinny bearded counter tenor got
up all in gold, like someone's ludicrous caricature of a pop idol
of the 60s.

Most of this folly is reserved for the early Court scenes,
however. Once we move into the Forest of Arden, where the
play's genial comedy and intermingled romances all take place,
the strange costumes and comic anachronisms all begin to make
sense--especially against Ralph Koltai's prize-winning sets:
giant transparent straws descend from sliding, punctured sheets
of plastic sky to conjure up the very nowhere-anywhere pastoral
place I think Shakespeare had in mind. The good duke's banished
court trade jokes, pick on poor Jacques, sing all those great
Shakespeare songs to lute and guitar, and provide a warm-hearted
backdrop for the four pairs of lovers, of varying social class,

who all get married in Act 5. Each of the other pairs seems
so happily matched that you very quickly forget that Rosalind,
Celia, Phebe, and Audrey are all played by men, just as they
were in 1600. It's a conceit that comes off, in this case, not
the least bit giggly or campy and it happily resolves that old
Shakespearean comedy problem of the girl-disguised-in-men's
clothes. This time, for once, you believe it.

LONEY, Glenn Meredith; (2) Professor of Theatre/Theatre Critic-
Journalist; (3) b. Sacramento, Calif. , 24 Dec. 1928; (4) s. David
Merton and Marion (Busher) L. ; (5) B. A. , Univ. of Calif. , Berkeley;
M. A. Univ. of Wisconsin, Madison; Ph. D. , Stanford Univ. , Palo
Alto; UG Majors: Drama, Speech, English, and Journalism Group;
Grad. Majors: Oral Interp. , Dramatic Literature; (6) single; (8)
Drama-Speech-English Teaching: Univ. of Calif. , 1949-50; Stanford
Univ. , 1952-53; U. S. Army, 1953-55; San Francisco State, 1955-56;
Univ. of Nevada (Las Vegas), 1956; Univ. of Maryland (Europe &
Middle East), 1956-59, Hofstra Univ. & Adelphi Univ. , 1959-51;
Brooklyn College and CUNY Grad. Center, 1961--date; (9) Radio
Series: "Curtain Time in Europe," (1959-61); Contrib. Editor: The-
atre Arts (1963); Arts Correspondent: Christian Science Monitor
(1958-65); "In the Words of" Series for Cue (1968-71); Cont. Ed:
Players (1968-71); Drama Critic; Educational Theatre Journal (with
and replacing John Gassner) (1965-70); Cont. Ed: Theatre Crafts
1968-to date); Cont. Ed: After Dark (1969-to date); Cont. Ed:
Dance (1970-to date); Cont. Ed: Inter/View (1970-71); Drama Desk
(1961-74); Theatre Forum (1974-to date); Outer Circle of Drama
Critics (1965-to date); American-Scandinavian Foundation Fellow (1963)
to study Swedish Folk Drama; Holland Festival, advisor on American
theatre and dance groups; (10) TV Series: "Exploring Your Museums,"
"Meet the Professor"; American Theatre Museum Committee; Save
the Lyceum Committee; South Street Seaport Restoration; American-
Victorian Museum/Founding Member; Ad Hoc Committee to Save the
Forum; (13) U. S. Army (1953-55), Educational Specialist; (15) Phi
Beta Kappa, Alpha Mu Gamma, Phi Eta Sigma, SGA, ATA, UCTA,
CTC, USITT, ASTR, IFTR, ANTA; (16) Democrat; (17) Protestant
(20) Cont. to: Reporter, Life, Sat. Eve Post, Commonweal, Opera
News, Music Journal, QJS, NAEB Journal, Signature, Ramparts,
New York Times, New York Herald-Tribune, Variety, Show, Amer-
ican Scholar, Adelphi Quarterly, Modern Drama, Theatre Annual,
American-German Review, Rundschau, High Fidelity/Musical Amer-
ica, American-Scandinavian Review, Scandinavian Times, Theatre
Today, Theatre Design and Technology, Architectural Forum, Craft
Horizons, Smithsonian, Reader's Digest, American Artist, etc. ;
Books: Briefing and Conference Techniques (McGraw-Hill 1959);
John Gassner's Dramatic Soundings (Intro and posthumous editing,
Crown 1968); Freedly & Reeves' History of the Theatre (Rev. of
American Theatre, Crown 1968); Gassner & Quinn Reader's Encyclo-
pedia of World Drama (Essays on Operetta, Musical Comedy, Wag-
ner, Da Ponte, and Gilbert, Crowell 1969); with Robert Corrigan
Tragedy (1971), Comedy (1971), and Forms of Drama (1972) (Hough-
ton-Mifflin); Theatre Crafts Book of Costume (1973) and Theatre

Crafts Book of Makeup (1974) (Selected Chapters, Rodale); Peter
Brook/Royal Shakespeare Production of Midsummer Night's Dream
(Interviews and editing, Dramatic Publisher, 1974); with Pat Mac-
Kay The Shakespeare Complex (Drama Book Specialists, 1975); (21)
3 East 71st St., New York, N.Y. 10021, Ph. 212-TR 9-5386; (22)
CUNY Grad. Center, 33 West 42nd St., New York, N.Y. 10036,
Ph. 212-790-4464; (23) Currently free lance, so N/A; (24) Average
30 reviews and critical pieces.

Theatre Abroad
(by Glenn Loney, Educational Theatre Journal, March 1967)

"Oh to Be in England
--A London Theatre Album"

Mr. Osborne is an outrage,
   Mr. Pinter is obscene.
Let us clear the stage of garbage,
   Let us keep the party clean.

Peter Hall is steeped in squalor,
   Peter Brook quite frankly stinks.
Let's erase their filthy swearwords,
   Let's kick out their kitchen sinks.

Samuel Beckett deals in dustbins,
   Arnold Wesker's full of spleen.
Bertolt Brecht's a dirty Commie,
   Jean Genet is just a queen.

N. F. Simpson's awf'ly silly,
   Henry Livings should be shot.
Do you wonder that our theatre's
   Gradually going to pot?

What's the Aldwych but a haven
   For the poor and sick of mind?
Where the air is loud as thunder,
   With those ladies breaking wind†

[† "BBC Song 'Horrified' Littler," Daily Telegraph
       (July 6, 1966), p. 22.]

*   *   *

These inspired lines and other more piquant stanzas not reprinted here were the cause of a singularly curious libel suit
which enlivened the London theatre scene last summer. They
were penned by Herbert Kretzmer, an able and witty critic,
for the BBC feature, Not So Much of a Programme, More a
Way of Life. Clearly designed to mock Emile Littler, a well
known West End Producer, they suggested that an attack he had
made the previous summer on the "dirt plays" at the Aldwych

Theatre was not completely honest. Not one to take criticism
lying down, Littler brought suit against the BBC and Kretzmer.

During the desultory summer season of 1965, Littler had
provided welcome amusement for the more sophisticated playgoers by blasts of moral outrage against such productions at the
Royal Shakespeare Company's London house, the Aldwych, as
David Rudkin's shocker, Afore Night Come; Roger Vitrac's rediscovered Absurdity, Victor; and Peter Weiss's highly successful drama, Marat/Sade. It is true that a number of conservatives wrote their favorite newspapers in Littler's support, but
the majority of letters published in various daily, weekly, and
monthly journals either ridiculed the attacks or enthusiastically
endorsed Aldwych programs. Not a few were moved to note
that Titus Andronicus, Hamlet, Othello, among the classic fare
that Littler found suitable for the Royal Shakespeare, are even
more bloody and shocking than the efforts of Rudkin and Weiss.

In the witness box at the libel trial, Littler told the jury:

> I am and always have been a great lover of the living the-
> atre and anything I have had to say about the dirty plays
> or anything has not been so much for myself but for the
> way they have been driving the audiences away from our
> théatres in London and the country [ibid.].

For that reason, he wanted to clear his name, he said. His
attorney pointed out: "We complain of the words from 'What's
the Aldwych but a haven' [onward to the end of the lyric.] It
is obvious that this lyric was calculated to lower Mr. Littler
in the minds of right-thinking people" [ibid.].

Unfortunately for Littler, the ample reporting of the trial
gave him scope to provide further amusement for the judicious.
Regardless of the outcome of the trial, rehearsing his complaints
against current stage fare did not enhance his reputation as a
man of the theatre. Even the sober reporters of the Times and
the Telegraph could make readers laugh with straight quotes
from the courtroom. Headlines advised the public that the jury
was reading Roger Vitrac and Peter Weiss over the weekend.

One might have been more indulgent of Littler, even while
disagreeing with his judgements, had there not been some odd
circumstances connected to the 1965 outbursts of outraged morality. At that time, Littler was a board member of the Royal
Shakespeare. Apparently unable to prevail within the organization, he had decided to carry his battle to the public. That
may be questionable policy. In any case, it misfired, resulting
in greater publicity and popularity for the Aldwych and all the
"dirt" plays. Littler's chief supporter in his crusade for decency was Peter Cadbury, a major holder in the Keith Prowse
Ticket Agencies. Not only had the Aldwych, the National, the
Mermaid, and the Royal Court--all subsidized in one way or

another--been drawing away the once sizable West End audiences,
but the Aldwych and the National had also recently taken steps
to end the practice of booking agencies keeping a percentage of
the ticket price as a fee. Obviously Littler and Cadbury were
feeling the pinch.

That would have been compromising enough, but Littler was
at the time offering a spectacle at Her Majesty's: The Right
Honourable Gentlemen. Posters outside the theatre warned that
the play was not suitable for children. Private Eye, London's
bawdy and sophomorically rude journal for Mods, opined that it
was not even fit for adults. Aside from the suspicion that the
production was attempting to cash in on the morbid curiosity
aroused by the Profumo scandal, it dealt with putative sexual
hi-jinx quite as "swinging" as any on the Aldwych boards. The
essential difference seemed to be the silk-satin-plush period
quality of the Littler show, as opposed to the municipal trash
heap school of design sometimes favored by the Royal Shakespeare.

Recently it was announced that actor Paul Scofield will join
Peter Brook and Peter Hall as a director of the Royal Shakespeare, which operates on an almost year-around basis at both
the Stratford-upon-Avon and the London houses. Michel St.
Denis, long one of the managing triumvirate, is elevated to the
rank of Consultant Director. Some London visitors have been
puzzled to find a Shakespeare company so relentlessly dedicated
to introducing the newest and fartherest-out dráma, but the directors know what they are doing. This kind of renewal is good
for both audiences and actors. Peter Brook insists that it gives
leaven and balance and rare insights to playing Shakespeare--
which can become stale without new ideas and experiments.

During a lull in the creation of Brook's new opus, US, an
improvisation which vividly attacks the U.S. for its conduct of
the war in Viet Nam and, by extension, all of U.S.-British as
well [sic], this dynamic director took time out to discuss his
concepts of the Royal Shakespeare's work. A button with an
American flag and the slogan, "Keep God in America!" set off
his lapel.

"I don't always approve of what is being done," he said.
"But if I am overruled--well, that is our freedom: to do what
we want to do." And what precisely does the Aldwych, as a
company, want to do? "We are searching for a union of ritualistic and popular theatre. The Elizabethans found such a form.
But we cannot copy Shakespeare today. We have to experiment--
to find our own way of expressing these qualities." What this
means in practical terms is a reality with which the ordinary
man in the audience can connect, yet conveyed in a heightened,
condensed, formalized--ritual--expression that gives meaning
to the idea and the emotion.

"Weiss has largely done this with Marat/Sade. There, as in a film, the experience is a totality: language, action, emotion, spectacle." And what of the charges that Brook's production had distorted Weiss's play? "The text is not the play. Only a small part. Words change or say different things in another time and place. The director has to go beneath them and find the author's true intent." With Weiss nearby, Brook could ask. That was useful, he says, but he could still do Marat/Sade without Weiss on hand. "I have to do Shakespeare that way. Actually, a play is really a mass of material: thoughts, feelings, ideas, actions. The printed words are a very small part. Shakespeare's text is not what he did on stage. But the mass is still there. It's always there--and we have to find it."

What is the ritual answer? "Not Brecht's Epic Theatre. At the end of his life, Brecht was beginning to realize its real limitations. Within the boundaries of his theories, Brecht could never have written Hamlet. In Mother Courage, he shows us the outside; he cannot show what goes on inside. He oversimplifies. His theories caused him to have a biased view of humanity."

Brook agrees that with his season of Theatre of Cruelty, he had gone "far out." The present season, he believes, is not so extreme, but does continue the search for the ritual/popular equation in theatre. Among the plays on view at the Aldwych are Marguerite Dura's Days in the Trees, Slawomir Mrozek's Tango, and Friedrich Dürrenmatt's The Meteor. It is a measure of the company's excellence that it can play Duras as easily as Shakespeare, though some of each rubs off on the other.

Harold Hobson, Sunday Times critic and a great admirer of Marguerite Duras, insists that the crux of Days in the Trees is most relevant to modern England: "There is a latent feeling that a price must be paid for our current affluence." Unfortunately for that argument, it came shortly before Prime Minister Wilson began crying poor, cut back tourist spending, and suggested that unemployment might not be a bad thing. That from a Laborite! There is not that much affluence visible in England any way.

It is true that the Mother, brilliantly played by Dame Peggy Ashcroft, is far fonder of her ne-er-do-well son, George Baker, than she is of his prosperous brothers, who are only interested in money and possessions and power. But this son is clearly a wastrel who takes advantage of everyone, women in particular, and his mother--from whom he steals, since she seems to wish that--especially. Mother has a voracious appetite; she is constantly hungry. This can easily be taken as a metaphor for her cannibalistic appetite for her son, whom she has deliberately ruined. This is not exactly a re-write of The Silver Cord, but the fundamental and the overtones are all there. At least Dame Peggy gets a free dinner out of it.

Tango is a Polish import which is having a number of good
German productions currently. It is an extended metaphor of
the political tendencies of the 20th century, seen in one peculiar
household. Timothy O' Brien's direction and Trevor Nunn's settings do much to evoke the crazy world of this family, and the
cast, featuring Patience Collier as a very old lady, is uniformly
fine. The unbridled freedom of democracy verging on anarchy,
represented by the parents, results in family chaos. The totalitarianism of the son seems about to carry the day, when it
collapses. The curtain falls on the frightening alliance of the
old guard, representing tradition, with the family valet, representing a brutal animal dominance which can just as quickly become servile to any master not paralysed by intellect, sensitivity, or fairness. The play is not exact in its analogies, but
this ambiguity is refreshing and demands thought.

The Meteor was reviewed last issue in its Munich production.
The Royal Shakespeare has featured Patrick Magee, of Marat/
Sade, as Schwitter but neither he nor the rest of the cast is
able to suggest that Germanic flavor which explains and excuses
the darkly comic events. It is, however, a good try.

Soon work will begin on a new $3. 6 million "space stage"
in London's bombed-out Barbican district, a new home for the
Royal Shakespeare. The search for the popular/ritual formula
will continue. When the theatre is completed, it will be the
second new house to be built in the City of London in nearly
three hundred years. The comfortable Mermaid Theatre at Pud-
dle Dock is the other. Its moving spirit, producer-actor-direc-
tor-reader Bernard Miles, has tried to run it as a repertory
theatre several times, but lack of money and space have hampered him. Recently his production of Bill Naughton's Spring
and Port Wine moved to the West End, feeding the popular
taste for Naughton's familiar, friendly portraits of ordinary
folks. An off-beat Naughton fantasy, He Was Gone When They
Got There was a bit of lively juvenilia, richly laced with earthy
country humor--at which Miles excells. As Badger, the last
living man in all Britain whose name and number are not in the
central files of a vast computer--voice courtesy of Peter Sel-
lers--Miles was hilarious, but the groaning, grunting, twinkling
computer stole the show. The production was fun but not enough
for a transfer.

Robin Midgley's mounting of Sardou's Let's Get a Divorce
gave the Mermaid a handsome, wildly funny contender in the
current French farce revival. Fenella Fielding, Hugh Paddick,
and Barry Foster made this a stylised joy. Martin Lees and
Sheelagh Killeen, on sets and costumes, set the tone of high,
high camp. The show was promptly transferred to the West
End, to be followed by yet another Shaw revival. Every show
that transfers, though, depletes Miles' stock of available actors.

He has no company as such, and yet he likes to work with people he knows. He says there is little profit from commercial transfers, since the West Enders keep most of the profit, but it's either that, or kill the show to make room for his next production.

The Royal Court, also a tiny theatre, has been trying repertory. Director William Gaskill, late of the National Theatre, says somewhat ruefully that it costs too much to pay company members who may not be cast. The problems in moving settings and storing them that the Mermaid faces have also beset him. The Court has a hard time finding actors. Young, untried talents are plentiful, and aged players can be located, but those in the middle years, especially character actors are in very short supply. Gaskill can afford a £20-30 per week average, and even £40 for a seasoned actor. Most can get far more on TV. For Sir Alec Guiness' recent appearance in Macbeth, the wage was £50. Presumably, Simone Signoret was similarly rewarded for her Lady Macbeth. "Only a very rich actor can 'afford' to play the court," Gaskill sighs.

Critics were a bit testy with Gaskill in his first year as managing director, a year which saw the passing of George Devine, the founder of the English Stage Company, the Court's producing organization. "I started out to make the Court a pocket National Theatre," Gaskill recalls, "but that was aiming too high. The National has longer rehearsal periods, a real ensemble, skilled players. But it sets standards and provides competition which is stimulating."

There are 10,000 members in the Court's theatre club, but they only come when they are impressed by the critic's reviews. There is Gaskill laments, no real audience dedicated to the theatre regardless of what is produced. Oh, a small hard core of enthusiasts, he admits, but not enough to make a subscription program work. Programing is based on excellence and immediacy. Works by Simpson, Jellico, and Orton have been tried out in a special Sunday evening series. They may later be transferred, if there is response.

One of these was Christopher Hampton's When Did You Last See My Mother? That it dealt with the twisted inner life of an 18-year-old who first seduces his best friend and follows this up with the successful conquest of the boy's mother was cause enough for raised eyebrows. What really startled the critics, who almost to a man raved about the play, was the tautness of the action, the tension of the dialogue, the believability of Victor Henry as the young seducer. The author is now 20 and a student at Oxford. He wrote the play, news items revealed, when he was 18. Ah, youth!

The Court, of course, is the theatre that spawned John Osborne and many others who are now in the forefront of writing, directing, and acting in England and America. A current Gaskill favorite is Edward Bond, author of Saved. Even declaring the Court a private theatre club for the run did not save Gaskill and company from a prosecution for producing this shocker. The error, it seems, was that the play was not licensed, even for private production. The Lord Chamberlain, says Gaskill, had demanded too many cuts. Other plays have been staged "privately" without observing the license formalities, but apparently the Court was chosen for a test case. The result seems to be an even greater public sentiment against stage censorship.

Among recent fare were Harley Granville-Barker's The Voysey Inheritance, Arnold Wesker's Their Very Own and Golden City, and Alfred Jarry's Ubu Roi. The first was a handsome period revival, finely played. Oddly enough, the liberals Gaskill thought would come streaming in to warm their hands over the ethical fires of this drama did not appear. It is perhaps too decent and too dated, and its very real debt to Chekhov shows in every line--but not to its detriment. The theatre was packed with Tories who chortled happily during the intervals about plots, good dialogue, lavish settings--"and on such a small stage, my dear! How do they do it?"--and the good old days. Ubu was great, great fun, had a little of Jarry in it, and offered music hall comedian Max Wall a come-back worthy of his lively, bawdy ad-lib talent. David Hockney's wonderful designs were as important as Wall's quips, but this first of all Absurd plays--according to Martin Esslin's catalogue, at least--did manage to offend Tory ladies. Mère Ubu's breasts were made of pink plastic and protruded rudely through her basic black frumpish frock. When touched, as they were frequently, these swelling landmarks lit up. And that was only the beginning of the directorial inventiveness of Iain Cuthbertson.

Wesker's drama did not achieve critical or audience success. This is understandable both owing to the length and the unnecessary complexity of the story. Gaskill says it was Wesker's sixth draft. Nonetheless, it had much to recommend it in its telling of the dream and disillusion of a Labour-oriented architect who wants to build marvellous cities for the English workers. Their indifference, Labour's stubborn opposition, and the Tories' condescending assistance nearly break the architect's heart and his will. The play must surely mirror Wesker's own disillusion with a movement which has repaid his enthusiastic efforts to bring culture to the masses with coldness and lack of cooperation. Joan Littlewood has already discovered that merely showing a print of a Rembrandt to a chimney-sweep or Romeo and Juliet to a grizzled charwoman does not open up rich wells of native sensitivity nor spark instant art appreciation, though she consistently placed the blame for the demise of her Stratford East theatre elsewhere.

Kenneth Tynan is being close-mouthed about the plans of

the National Theatre. Perhaps he has learned a lesson from
Orson Welles, whom he once described as a man who used up
his genius in conversation. Work on the new home on the South
Bank of the Thames, near Festival Hall, is going forward. In
the meantime, the handsome productions on the Old Vic stage
are generally sold out. They speak the excellence of this troupe
far louder than press agentry could. Since relatively few Americans can go to London, it is a shame the National cannot come
to us, but the projected United States visit, in connection with
the Montreal Exposition, has had to be cancelled. Those who
can see this remarkable ensemble on its Canadian tour should
make every effort to do so.

While one admires and respects the Royal Shakespeare's
courage and experimentation, an evening at the Aldwych is occasionally disappointing--more because of the script than the
ensemble. At the National, however, it is difficult to remember any production that has not, in some way, been outstanding
and thoroughly enjoyable. The brilliance of such directors as
John Dexter, such designers as Motley, and such players as
Sir Laurence Olivier and Maggie Smith, supported by a magnificent company, is mainly reponsible for this, though the programing, which is not as adventurous as the Royal Shakespeare's,
is also involved. Yet, this season will see As You Like It with
an all-male cast, thanks to Dexter and Polish critic Jan Kott,
who will serve as advisor. Ostrovsky's The Storm and Strindberg's Dance of Death are also in the repertory.

A wonderful treat for theatre specialists is the revival of
Pinero's Trelawny of the "Wells." Although the plot is tears-
and-smiles melodrama, director Desmond O'Donovan, with Motley's valuable assistance, has recreated the backstage world
of 19th-century London theatre with remarkable warmth and
pathos. The settings are breathtaking evocations of another
era, and what Maggie Smith, Robert Stephens, Louise Purnell,
and Michael Byrne bring to life in them is good for many hearty
laughs and at least as many Kleenex. This production breathed
with that indefinable "joy" that Robert Brustein finds so regrettably lacking in the theatre.

Maggie Smith is in danger of becoming a National Institution.
Her supporting role as Avonia Bunn nearly overshadowed poor
Trelawny. In Franco Zeffirelli's Much Ado About Nothing, her
Beatrice--to Robert Stephens' excellent Benedick--is nearly definitive. In the midst of her high-spirited banter, she catches
her breath with, "... there was a star danced, and under that
was I born." It was almost heartbreaking.

Robert Stephens is also rapidly distinguishing himself as
one of the best young actors on the English stage. Among his
widely varied roles, in addition to Benedick and Tom Wrench,
in Trelawny, are Atahuallpa, in Royal Hunt, and the prissy
antique dealer in Black Comedy. He really seems to become

the character, so much so that one wonders who the real Robert
Stephens is.

Zeffirelli has created a turn-of-the-century Italian town for
this drama, complete with the ornate, twinkling street arches
which deck out every festival. All the stereotypes, played to
the hilt, are present, including a noisy brass band which makes
the whole evening a raucous carnival. Even Dogberry and Verges, for a change, are funny. RCA-Victor has issued a fine
album of the performance (VDM/VDS-104), with a sturdy text
so one can compare Robert Graves' alterations with the standard
version.

The changes are not violent--nor in most cases particularly important or useful. They did inspire some criticism from
the Bard's acolytes, so nothing was said in the program or in
the RCA-Victor album (VDM/VDS-112) of the National's excellent revival of Love for Love about the updating of Congreve.
Indeed, reviewers were delighted to find how topical and fresh
this Restoration great remains. Rumor has it that that is partly
thanks to playwright Peter Shaffer, whose Royal Hunt of the Sun
and Black Comedy are popular staples of the National Theatre
diet. Comparison of the Congreve script with the record album
text shows some interesting additions which are entirely in the
spirit of Congreve--he might actually have wished he'd thought
of them first--and some deletions of sub-plot material which
make the drama move more smoothly. As with Trelawny and
Much Ado, the production has so much delightful music and
dance in it, it verges on musical comedy at times. And how
remarkable that so many of the National's players are talented
singers and dancers! Peter Wood's direction and Lila de No-
bili's designs evoke the period richly, providing a perfect frame
for Sir Laurence Olivier's portrait of Tattle, and equally finely
etched pictures by Geraldine McEwan, Joyce Redman, John
Stride, Miles Malleson, Edward Hardwicke, and Robert Lang.
It is interesting that Sir Laurence, as the fop of fops, lets us
know with saucy impudence that he is, for all his affectations,
a man with a man's desire for women, whereas American actors
all too often add quite another dimension to the Restoration gentlemen when they attempt to tackle problems of style and manner. The National might do well to open a theatre school for
American Fulbright Scholars, since our acting schools have
failed so dismally in training students in style and diction. If
they cannot or will not bring us Love for Love, Trelawny, or
Much Ado, then we would do well to buy every available album.
One hopes for The Royal Hunt and The Recruiting Officer on
records.

Chichester is not exactly a London suburb, especially with
no festival train running now that the National Theatre has given
up operation of its space stage, but it still draws city people
to mingle with an increasingly "County" audience. Michael Ben-
thall's Macbeth was visually quite striking, with sets by Alan

Tagg and costumes by Michael Annals. Tom Courtenay, of film
fame, was a passable Malcolm, but John Clements' Macbeth was
merely puzzling. The man seemed hollow; the words came out
with good vocal power, but no force of meaning. Since Clements
has done many fine things in his career, this was disappointing.
Perhaps serving as director of the festival divided his energies
unduly. Lindsay Anderson staged The Cherry Orchard with Celia
Johnson as Madame Ranyevskaya. She made her a foolish woman, without the theatrical glamour so often generated. Anderson put so much emphasis on each role that valuable new relationships were revealed among the minor characters, but it
made the whole production unnecessarily diffuse. Good news for
festival planners everywhere is that Chichester, without the National name and company, managed to break into the black. This
despite some tepid reviews and empty seats. That argues good
management.

Although the commercial West End theatre is supposed to
be "in trouble," good shows and solid revivals seem to have no
difficulty in finding packed houses. Harold Hobson points out
a change in theatre-going attitudes, however. He says the Royal
Shakespeare, the National, and the other serious, subsidised
houses have polarized audiences: "We're feeling intellectual tonight. Let's go to the Royal Shakespeare." Or, he says, "Tonight, we're frivolous. Let's take in a musical." They expect
easy entertainment at the commercial theatre and are even offended when they encounter something more demanding. This
encourages producers to do more farces and musicals, as on
Broadway, avoiding new, serious drama. Hobson gloomily pre-
dicts: "We can expect a progressive decline in intellect in the
commercial theatre."

Vivienne Byerley, an old hand at press relations who has
consistently handled some of the best West End fare, does not
go that far. She feels, as do many, that the past season was
better than the previous one--which has not been true in New
York for some years now. She points to the highly successful
revivals of Shaw, Wilde, and Sheridan to prove that commercial
theatre can and does mount good work. As for entertainment,
she believes tragedy can be as effective in the West End as
comedy, if for slightly different reasons. "You go out of the
theatre saying, 'Well, I've got that out of my system!'" But
many of the Royal Shakespeare's plays, she believes, do not
offer Aristotelian purgation. "I'm not objecting to 'dirt' in plays.
I object to being bored. So much being written now is plotless
and artless." As for the art of Public Relations in London theatre, Miss Byerley finds her job a pleasant one. The rules
are known and ethics are observed. One or two typical American "press stunts," she notes, and an agent would be through.
Poor notices don't require dishonest culling of reviews for favorable adjectives, she insists. In fact, reviews don't break
a show. Lower production costs mean a play can run from
four to six weeks, finding its audience by word of mouth. Fleet

Street is quick to take note if a panned production begins to attract audiences, for that is news.

The West End never seems to tire of Shaw revivals. After only a couple of years, The Doctor's Dilemma was back, but not as good as with Brian Bedford. You Never Can Tell is all too dated in its thought, but Motley made it marvellously period, and Sir Ralph Richardson brought it a needed twinkle of humor. Man and Superman, played without the Don Juan sequence, needed some editing and adjusting. Both the production and Alan Badel's John Tanner suffered from tired blood. Ellis Rabb's APA could teach director Philip Wiseman some useful lessons.

From America came The Owl and The Pussycat--a palpable hit. Hello, Dolly! was not much admired and Mary Martin quickly deserted ship to be replaced by England's funniest comedienne, Dora Bryan--the mother in the film version of Taste of Honey. It was Hello, Dora all the way; the rest of the evening was utter boredom, even with the New York sets, costumes, and limp choreography. An Arsenic and Old Lace revival with Dame Sybil Thorndike and Athene Seyler delighted full houses, but too many amateur versions have dulled its edge. It is set in Brooklyn which surely never had as many English accents in the whole borough as on this single stage. The Bellow Plays premiered in London, later moving to New York as Under the Weather London loved them; New York did not. The Sound of Music--both the musical and the film--continues to play to capacity houses after all these years. Funny Girl had a short run, owing to Barbra Streisand's departure.

A revival of Wilde's An Ideal Husband was handsome to look at in Anthony Holland's settings, but the melodrama is all too dated. In an all-star cast, Margaret Lockwood stood out almost painfully. Most of the others seemed merely to be repeating lines with ill concealed distaste. More successful were revivals of Lady Windermere's Fan and Sheridan's The Rivals.

Oliver! closed at last. Sister George was still running strong, but Agatha Christie's The Mousetrap was far ahead, in its fourteenth year. Robert and Elizabeth, Boeing-Boeing, and The Black and White Minstrel Show showed no signs of retiring. Among new popular entries were There's a Girl in My Soup--promised for New York, alas; Charlie Girl, starring indestructible Anna Neagle; Noel Coward's interesting Suite in Three Keys, which proved a tour de force for Irene Worth, who hopefully will grace the forthcoming New York production; and female impersonator Danny LaRue, in Come Spy with Me, a knockabout espionage farce with turns worthy of the Marx Brothers. Indifferent offerings included On the Level, a so-called musical about the GCE exams, those tests which determine who goes on to higher education and who does not, a topic of little interest to Americans--and, as it turned out, to Britons as well. Benn W. Levy offered Public and Confidential which was no Springtime

<u>for Henry</u> dealing as it did with a high government official who
lusts for pretty women and gratifies himself with a girl he has
just met only minutes after his wife has died in the next room.
Shades of Emile Littler!   For John Gregson also played a Rt.
Hon. Gent. Constance Cummings was good as the secretary-
mistress who knows all and suffers much, but the fabric was
too much like TV soap opera.   Glynis Johns and Keith Michell
puffed and panted, but they couldn't blow life into Anita Loos'
labored adaptation of Jean Canolle's <u>The King's Mare</u>.   Henry
VIII and Anne of Cleves deserved better than this witless farce.
Despite Ralph Koltai's stunningly unusual settings, which made
the play seem to take place in a sheet metal factory, the whole
thing looked like a mixture of <u>Beckett</u> and <u>Man for All Seasons,</u>
liberally laced with <u>Luv</u>.

A high point in the West End theatre is Jay Presson Allen's
skillful adaptation of Muriel Spark's challenging novel, <u>The Prime</u>
<u>of Miss Jean Brodie</u>.   Vanessa Redgrave, as the unwitting Scot-
tish fascist schoolmarm, is superb, as are all the cast.   It is
a pleasure to see young actors who are believably teenage.
The moments of wild humor in Miss Brodie's battles for her
men and her girls were often cut short by the darker texture
of the Brodie character and the revelation of the depths of duplicity and self-ignorance in the human soul.

<u>Broadway in Review</u>
(by Glenn Loney, Educational Theatre Journal, December 1968)

Through a Glass Darkly:

It has been noted that those who do not study history are
condemned to repeat it.   To which the late Crane Brinton added
that those who <u>do</u> study it are <u>also</u> condemned to repeat it.
That is both insight and foresight.   It is Cassandra-intelligence
that is quite as specific as anyone could wish.   Further detail,
actual timetables of misfortune and destruction--these no one
wants.

But they are readily at hand.   As is the perception, the
fear, the realization, that we are living in a Gothic world, too.
A fantastic world of our own making.   Yet no one seems to
know how the giants came to be; who is clanking the chains and
ringing those distant bells; why the full moon has vanished behind blood-red clouds; or what we are to do about that clammy,
cloudy substance that is floating down the dim hallway to envelop
us.   The mirror reflects the cloud.   Instead of human faces, it
echoes images of vampires and strange Bosch-like brutes from
some unclean cavern in the subconscious.   Off its surface bounce
growled, shrieked slogans: "Destroy the Middle-Class!" or
"Lawnorder!" If the glass clears, it shows not what stands in
front of it, but what lies beyond in a dreadful wonderland only
a madman would wish to penetrate.

For once, however, this mirror, this image of the times, has in its thespian manifestation begun a new season with shock, concern, fright, power, outrage, and understanding that give hope both for the future of theatre--and even for man's survival.

That may seem unbelievable, perhaps impossible for an art form that has been so long and so thoroughly subjected to the commercial motive. Yet, it seems to be so. Even the more bizarre fragments of the New York theatre are saying something worth listening to, and occasionally, worth looking at, though not always.

Mao and Mary Shelley--a Mismatched Couple:

In selecting Mrs. Shelley's Frankenstein theme, the Living Theatre Company made an almost prophetic choice of a mythic framework to support the variety of things they wish to say about the nature of contemporary society. This work was being re-hearsed in Munich during their self-imposed exile as long ago as the summer of 1965, long before Dr. Christiaan Barnard ex-ploded into the headlines. But the heart transplant engineered by Dr. Victor Frankenstein, madly played by Julian Beck, is wildly different from those televised documentaries of what awaits you at your friendly neighborhood hospital. Both in the amusing-ly complicated gimmickry and the frenetic acting style, it is a close relative to the zanier exercises of the Playhouse of the Ridiculous.

Make no mistake, however. Frankenstein is a serious, positive statement. Its weaknesses are endemic to this group: attenuation, confusion, hysteria, superfluity of materials and/or ideas. For all the complexities of ideas and actions shown or discussed, the view is simplistic, just as are the visions of Beck and his wife and co-founder of the company, Judith Malina. They have seen the face of evil in the world and they rightly hate it. During the play, the cast repeatedly cries: "How can we end human suffering?"

One sullen square in the audience muttered: "Drop the cur-tain!" But that is a cheap laugh, and it is not relevant. No more so than saying that Frankenstein was better with Boris Karloff. This is an impressive production, but it runs danger-ously close to provoking laughter because of the self-indulgence of the company. Shouted Marxists slogans, deafening choruses of the thought of Chairman Mao, all obviously invoked as pos-sible formulae for solving the world's problems, do not enchant or transfigure the viewers. The exhausting energy level of the performers, the torrent of sound they generate does not succeed in dulling the intellect to possible inconsistencies or objections.

The protracted action, spanning three acts, includes a sado-masochistic revel of killing. It begins when a Yoga meditation fails to levitate a young lady. She is plunked in a coffin, and, soon, others are being garroted, beheaded, electrocuted, gassed, and shot with abandon. This image of humans destroying each other until they have almost wiped out the race is repeated later. Using the oriental shadowscreen, the troupe shows Dr. Frankenstein robbing the coffined corpse of its heart. Another dead body is chosen for the transplant. Rituals follow, rich in mythic power. The activation of the body is pursued by Frankenstein, with the aid of such notables as Paracelsus, Freud, and Norbert Wiener.

Inside the creature's head--outlined in colored lights and illustrated by a glowing backdrop indicating the various areas of brain control--actors recreate functions, passions, ideas, history, culture. But the forces of destruction and hate, the Four Horseman, are also raging within the brain. There is an outbreak of violence, killing. The authorities take over. Then arrests of actors are made in the audience. They are subjected to the humiliations of prison, progressing cell by cell, arrest by arrest, until they have filled the divisions of the three-story scaffold which is the setting. Their rages and ravings make M rat/Sade seem tame. A prison revolt breaks out, culminating in a destroying fire. But the creature is alive. And, as the elaborate action sequence in the program explains, "Man Lives."

This is a cyclic parable of birth, death, rebirth, or of creation, destruction, and recreation. Therein lies its hope, its positive quality. But its determined, detailed dissection of human evils is deliberate and important, whether one's solutions are the same as the Becks' or not. Visually, much of the production is excitingly theatrical. Lighting effects are brilliantly achieved, especially considering the financial limitations the company has, as well as its touring schedule. The burning of the prison is a splendid effect, as are the silhouettes of the prisoners. The concentrated variety of activity in the human brain is also played and lit with real skill. One effect stands out: the players, standing on three levels of the scaffolding, group themselves into a huge black monster, lit from behind, with strange, menacing glowing eyes.

Two very comic moments: (1) news items from the current day's New York Times are read aloud, contrasting so strangely with the stage action that even topics like Hubert Humphrey and the atom bomb seem obscenely amusing: and, (2) Brooklyn police, caricatures of the fat cop, search the Brooklyn Academy audience for smokers--to save the building from fire, not the inhaler from cancer--and are confronted by actor-police, busily arresting fellow actors. The real police retreat in confusion.

Once, doing an interview with the Becks for the New York Times, I thought to stress the quality and continuity of my interest in the work of the Living Theatre. "I've seen every show you've done at your 14th Street theatre," I said. "And, while there were some productions I really didn't like, it was always interesting!"

Beck looked at me with pity. "Well, I'm glad. If people like you liked our work, we'd <u>know</u> we were on the wrong track."

Fortunately, I still have reservations and misgivings, so the Beck train won't be derailed by my admiration. If <u>Frankenstein</u> were shortened; if the number of simultaneous incidents onstage were reduced; if the hysteria were better orchestrated, it would be overpowering.

How Now, Brown Mao?

Chairman Mao needs a New York agent. His Thought is being used not only by the Living Theatre, but also by Theatre 1969, the newest on-Broadway repertory company. As the virgin offering of the new troupe, organized by Richard Barr and Edward Albee, <u>Quotations From Chairman Mao Tse-Tung's Maidenhood</u> was slightly soiled by the fact of its previous playing in Buffalo. If visitors to the Billy Rose Theatre expect another <u>Virginia Woolf,</u> they are rudely disappointed. <u>Box</u> begins the evening. Onstage is the frame of an immense bo<u>x.</u> Offstage, a voice discusses the box and the possible failure of art forms. As a play without visible actors or action, <u>Box</u> is no match for Paul Foster's <u>Balls.</u> Foster, at least had his two invisible talking corpses represented by swinging balls onstage. Albee's box does not move. <u>Quotations</u>, which follows immediately, takes place within the box. Chairman Mao appears, wearing an inscrutable Asian mask. He promptly rips this off, revealing another one exactly like it underneath--his own face. He proceeds to recite his maxims from that little red book. He wanders through the audience, pausing in the stage boxes and elsewhere to study the spectators' faces and let them hear his analysis of history and society. Albee has chosen frightening quotes: the thought that these thoughts are being daily inculcated in millions of people is unpleasant, for, true or not, Mao's judgments and perceptions are antithetical to life as it is now lived in the United States.

The force of his condemnation of our system is sharpened by contrast. His quotes alternate with other phrases. Inside the box, on shipboard, a bored wealthy widow bores a clergyman with the more intimate details of her loves and despairs. She has money, time, wit, and seems both useless and empty as a person. She reads, she says, Trollope and James while travelling. Her dialogue suggests James, in its endlessly proliferating sentences and inconsequential content. Is she what Mao is inveighing against? An obligatto to these parallel but separate themes is the determined elocution of Will Carleton's <u>Over the Hill to the Poor House,</u> by Sudie Bond, in her archetypal role of an Albee old lady. The hackneyed sentiment and laborious verse, as delivered, stress rather than destroy the

image of pluck in the face of humiliation and betrayal by family
and friends. Repetitions are even used as defiant answers to
Chairman Mao's sweeping assertions about the doom that hangs
over the enemies of Marxism. Then, subtley, the voice of
Ruth White begins interweaving the script of Box with the strands
of the play underway. It is far more interesting to listen to
than it is to watch. And it is much more provocative to think
about its levels of meaning and its odd contrasts of character
and world-view than it is to see it on stage.

That certainly cannot be said of Albee's own mounting of
The American Dream. Thanks to Sada Thompson and Donald
Davis, as Mommy and Daddy, and to Sudie Bond, as Grandma,
this wittily acid family portrait seems better and funnier than
it did when it first appeared. The production owes something
to the original directorial conception of Alan Schneider, obviously, but Albee and his cast have explored new possibilities, so
that it is most achingly sad when its comedy is most hysterical.
There are those who handle the problems of this play--the
charges that it makes against American family mores and rela-
tionships--by labelling it "Absurdist" and then walking away.
This has, true, much of the nonsense of Ionesco's The Bald Soprano, but, fortunately, in Albee's play, it is more logical,
really a kind of viciously funny cartoon of reality. It may well
be that there is a lot of Albee's own youth tied up in this bitter
confection. It certainly rings true when applied to other lives
and families. The first part of this bill is The Death of Bessie
Smith, and the two plays match well. Rosemary Murphy's performance as the driven, frustrated, bitchy southern nurse is a
little classic. You hate her, but oh how you pity her, trapped
in that hatred, that longing, that desperate rage to throw off
ideas and patterns that destroy the heart--without the courage
or the knowledge to do it. Sex, rather than race, seems at the
core of her sickness, but there is much more to it than that.
Self-hatred is the secret. And that is a public secret which
cries out in almost all of Albee's plays. His people are not at
peace with themselves. They buy intellectual and emotional
breathing space by hacking away at others, usually those dear-
est to them. This play, some say, isn't about Bessie Smith
at all. They are shocked. They have been mislead, they say.
Nonsense. It is about her death; why she could be allowed to
die. It is also about the daily deaths of many of the seemingly
living. If anything, especially in Michael Kahn's tautly directed
new mounting, this drama is more relevant, more important today than it was when it first appeared.

Samuel Beckett's Happy Days and Krapp's Last Tape, which
is paired again with Albee's The Zoo Story, round out four repertory evenings which really challenge the typical Broadway audience.

The Quality of Mercy:

After its resounding success at Washington's Arena Theatre

last spring, Howard Sackler's <u>The Great White Hope</u> was brilliantly translated from the arena to the proscenium by the same
director, Ed Sherin.   If it was good in Washington, it was splendid in New York.   Seldom has there been such a spontaneous
standing ovation--and not just on opening night, when audiences
are capable of anything--for the entire cast, and especially for
the towering performance of James Earl Jones, as Jack Jefferson, the kind, generous fighter who is destroyed by a vengeful
white society.   Scene after scene was vigorously applauded.
There seemed no other way to work off the tension aroused by
the incisiveness of the writing and the skill of the playing.
Everything worked so well, so very professionally.   The image
of a swiftly-moving reality--despite the fragmentary settings and
the knowledge that <u>this</u> was not exactly what really happened--
was constantly invoked.

Ed Sherin had said that he was eager to do the show in a
proscenium frame.   Watching the effect of scenes that had first
been witnessed in the D. C. home of the Arena--a goodly number
of whose players are now on Broadway for what looks like a <u>long</u>
stay--it is easy to see why.   So much that was lost, visually
and audially, in Washington is so sharply controlled and focussed
in New York, that the impact and the meaning are enormously
increased.   Although the saga of Jefferson's pathetic degradation
as he scavanges for a living across Europe still seems too long
and involved, there are moments of rare pathos, and at least
one scene--where he meets the son of an African chieftan, studying law and politics in Germany--that is terribly important as
contrast.   The son of what Americans would then have called a
savage is receiving an impressive education, while the son of a
free American--albeit a black American--has virtually no education and is being hounded by agents of the U. S. Government, as
a result of a legalistic frame-up.   Of course, it is hard to believe that the American state would be a party to injustice or
prejudice, but then this play is set in the past when Americans
were less compassionate and enlightened than they now are.
Sackler's American Gothic landscape is pre-Chicago and pre-
Watts, but it holds the terrors of the unreal and the unexplain-
able--the more so because it was like that.

Jones' performances are a triumph, but those of Jane Alexander,
as his white beloved, Lou Gilbert, as his manager, and George
Mathews, as Cap'n Dan, a boxing power and his antagonist, have
improved remarkably since Washington.   Part of this, of course,
is the advantage provided by playing out from a proscenium
frame.   The grace, loyalty, affection, fear, anguish, and despair projected by Miss Alexander are remarkable to behold.
She has certainly grown in the role tremendously.   To see the
two lovers, so simply direct and generous in their love--and in
their reaction to those they meet, crushed so low that the dregs
are mutual disgust, is to wonder indeed: what a piece of work
is man?   Jefferson's crime, Sackler shows, was to be black ...
a crime he compounded by being strong, able, decent, and
friendly.

An Ordinary Man, the first-produced play of Mel Arrighi,
was handsomely and expensively staged at the Cherry Lane. It
did not last, and a number of critics took pains to dismiss it.
Which is curious since it was well acted and directed, with
sound plotting and interesting dialogue. It's perhaps in the content that sensibilities are aroused. The framework is a war
crimes trial for Andy Neff, the man who made those "documentary films" for the government, showing the inferiority of the
Negro. The films were the lever which made possible the arrest and confinement of the nation's entire black population in
concentration camps. The frightening story of the increasing
gap between blacks and whites is told in flashbacks. The parallels between Gothic Americ today and Nazi Germany in the 1930's
are all too clear in this play--just as they seem to be emerging
now, sharply focussed by the election campaign, school disturbances, and other strife-ridden social problems. This is a
cautionary drama. It suggests that fascism will not ultimately
triumph, even in the USA, but it does sketch a grim possibility
which many middle-class whites now discuss with some satisfaction. Perhaps no one wants to think about the dangers of Ex-
tremism?

We've All Got To Make Sacrifices:

At the Playhouse of the Ridiculous, the shoe is on the other
foot. In Kenneth Bernard's The Moke-Eater, a white salesman
has the misfortune to have his car break down in a nameless
southern town. The citizens, their faces painted with masks
reminiscent of the Peking Opera, claw at him like animals. He
insists his name is Jack, but they are determined he is Fred.
Soon, they have ripped off his clothing and are closing in on
him. A white chief, Alec--played, of course, by a woman:
Sirra Bandit, from Warhol's Factory--takes charge. If Jack-
Fred will amuse these oppressed folk, they will let him go.
For nearly two hours, he is subjected--in actual fact--to the
most vivid violent humiliations. Then his car is fixed, and the
happy natives wave goodbye. Five minutes later, he is back--
all roads lead, not to Rome, but to his death. He is clawed
to pieces--a clever color film projected on his nude body--and
his liver is literally stuffed in his mouth. Which makes concentration camps seem tame.

All this upstairs on an impromptu stage at Max's Kansas
City, where all the Beautiful People go now. And liver is occasionally on the menu, too.

This drama owes nothing to Euripides, but then Richard
Schechner's Dionysus in '69 will never have to fork over any
royalties to his estate either. It is true that some fine choral
passages and speeches survive, but encountering them in this
framework is a bit like looking at the ruins of Athens, covered
with American tourists. Obviously Schechner's Performance
Group spends a lot of useful time on gymnastic and vocal

limbering exercises. In fact, much of the performance--that
which is not specifically sensual or orgiastic in its pantomime--
is of this nature. It is rather like watching Army P. T. exercises done on the actors' own time. Diction, apparently, is not
one of the group's concerns. That is fine when they are being
themselves--Dionysus, it seems, is actually reincarnated in the
person of actor William Finley--but not so when they aspire to
poetic language in spavined speech.

It would be easy to be flip and destructive about this work.
In fact, there is a great deal of flip-ness in the performance,
as well as near nudity. But this is its own thing. It is not
Euripides' The Bacchae, and it should not be judged as though
it were. It goes beyond and behind that play. It tries to re-
create the Bacchic ecstasy, to show the forbidden rites. On
that basis, one may wonder why those Bacchantes were grappling with male chorus members--weren't men forbidden? Oddly
and successfully, the orgiastic quality is communicated, often
directly to audience members who find themselves involved in
the action--there are no seats, as such. To have a Bacchante
speak her lines, urging sensual joys, directly to one is a curious sensation. And it works, theatrically, as so much pseudo-
audience-involvement at La Mama and the Public Theatre has
not. On its own terms, this production is often amusing, frequently frank, occasionally exciting, even erotically so. It
works, and it is different. Most people over thirty hate it.

Robert Shaw's The Man in the Glass Booth deals with another kind of sacrifice: the impersonation by a millionaire
American immigrant German-Jew of an Eichmann figure at a
war crimes trial in Israel. Some viewers profess bafflement--
is the character really a Jew or a Nazi? Shaw is no Pirandello,
and he has made the point quite clear by the end of the play.
It has its melodramatic effects, and the customary collection of
Jewish jokes--a number of them obligatorily anti-Semitic, since
that is a special kind of suffering. Quite aside from all the
clever chatter and odd complications Shaw has introduced, the
material of this play is really rather thin. The best effect,
provoking critical raves, is the transformation of what seems a
darkened sanctuary into a magnificent Manhattan penthouse in an
instant. But this is old stuff. The Drottningholm Theatre has
similar transformations every performance.

Donald Pleasance has been extravagantly admired in the title
role. He is certainly an extravagant performer. Perhaps it is
this studied abandon that amazes people. "What an actor! I'd
feel a fool doing that." Quite right. And so should he, now and
then. He speaks most of the words, some of which are almost
poetic, with clarity and elevation occasionally worthy of Stratford-
on-Avon. Then, where "ain't" and other grammatical flat-tires
are scattered in his dialogue--apparently Shaw's way of showing
his essential vulgarity, despite his great wealth--he hits them
hard so that they jar against the rest of the line. The accent

flutters from music-hall Dutch to vaudeville Yiddish, from refined Cockney to Lambeth Palace precision.

Lighter Fare for Lighter Heads:

But Shaw at least has provided an alternative to The Megillah
of Itzak Manger, another musical imported from Israel.   Fortunately, there were a number of musical alternatives early in
the season: Marlene, even more triumphant and artificial than
last year; Gilbert Becaud, the French heart-breaker; and Noel
Coward's Sweet Potato, an updated salute to the Master.   This
didn't work out well, since Coward's material doesn't update,
not to LSD 1968.   George Grizzard, Dorothy Loudon, Tom Kneebone, Carole Shelley were fine troupers, however, even to the
point of beginning and ending in what was meant to look like the
nude.   Their theatre, of course, was next door to the Biltmore
and Hair.

Affairs of the heart were variously treated, for those who
yearn for escape from reality.   A Victorian Gothic interior,
quite handsomely built--why don't these carpenters get the chance
to take a bow with the setting?--was the chief attraction of Woman Is My Idea.   It was not the idea of the critics nor indeed
of audiences, aside from some stalwart members of Jesus Christ
Church of Latter Day Saints.   Two of whom fiercely defended
their enjoyment to any who would listen at the closing performance.   It featured John Heffernan who gave a good interpretation of a thankless role, that of John Rocky Park.   He was
called by his full name during most of the play, and one came
to think of him as one of those public recreation areas the Department of the Interior has created in the great state of Utah.
He was, it was artfully suggested, wrong in resisting marriage,
especially since he was to become first President of the University of Utah--or was it Brigham Young University?   Anyway,
Brigham was present--thanks to Hugh Marlowe--and polygamy
was an issue.   The complications and the jokes were so obvious
and mechanical, it was a chore to watch this to its end, despite
the local color tit-bits, fascinating to one who has lived in Mormon country.   Nevertheless, it should have a long career on
the community circuit, if there are no anti-Mormon bigots around.
It is that kind of playwriting.   Closed after five performances,
it lost $125,000.

Lovers, by Brian Friel, and Lovers and Other Strangers,
by Renée Taylor and Joseph Bologna, had disturbingly similar
titles.   Friel's two one-acts could have been written years ago
by Lennox Robinson.   They may have been.   Art Carney, much
admired, was the weak link; he substituted Gleason-type burlesque for honest comedy.   Fionnuala Flanagan and Eamon Morrissey, as young lovers, were quite moving, even endearing.   Friel,
using a stage manager device, lets the audience know half-way
through getting to know them that they will drown that very afternoon.   What a pathetic gimmick!   The Taylor-Bologna opus was

a lot of the latter. Four skits survived by the opening. They were essentially obvious one-line cartoon gags, stretched out to fifteen or twenty minutes. And painfully acted, though with great expenditure of energy.

LONGAKER, Jon Dasu; (2) Theater Critic and Professor of Art History; (3) b. Davos, Switzerland, Jan. 5, 1920; (4) s. Mark and Helene (Dasu) L.; (5) B.A., U. of Pa., major subj.: Fine Arts, 1941; Barnes Foundation, Marion, Pa., 1946-47; Columbia Univ. Grad. School, 1947-51; Belgian American Educational Foundation, Brussels, 1951; (6) m. Lyde Ramsey Arrott, June 18, 1955; (7) children--Eliza Dasu, Mark Ramsey, Jonathan Davis, Charles Ramsey; (8) Teaching: Barnes Foundation, 1950-51; Institute for American Universities, Aix-en-Provence, France, 1964-65; Randolph-Macon College, Ashland, Virginia, 1953- ; Criticism: Art Critic, Richmond (Virginia) Times-Dispatch, 1956-64; Theater Critic, Richmond (Virginia) Times-Dispatch, 1965- ; (9) Actor, community theaters 1953-59; Director, Randolph-Macon College, 1954-60; (10) Mem. Virginia State Art Commission, 1970-74; mem. Virginia Museum Fellowship Committee, 1960-1975; (12) Mem. of the board and former president, Virginia Film Society, 1960- ; mem. of the board, Hanover Arts and Activities Center, 1973- ; (13) US Naval Reserve, Ensign to Lieutenant, 1942-46; (14) Phi Beta Kappa; Fellowship, Belgian American Educational Foundation; (15) Virginia Writers Club; (17) non-denominational churchgoer; (19) Hanover Country Club; (20) Articles for Institute of Southern Culture and Arts in Virginia magazine, book: Art Style and History; (21) 133 Beverly Road, Ashland, Va., 23005, Ph. 804-798-6400; (22) Randolph-Macon College, Ashland, Va., 23005; (23) Circulation: weekdays 137,000; Sundays 208,000; (24) I also write occasional art and book reviews and a monthly column on the arts in Commonwealth magazine.

"The Deadly Delilah"
(by Jon Longaker, Richmond Times-Dispatch, April 13, 1974)

This has got to be the wildest spoof of a detective thriller ever written. Before the lights go up, a dozen people enter the darkened stage, slug, strangle and shoot one another, scream, groan, slam doors and jump out of the window.

When the lights go on, Matt Fallon, (Alan Krulick), feet on desk, sips straight whisky, blows cigarette smoke very meaningfully and generally acts like a private eye.

Matt has a devoted secretary, of course, who keeps telling him to take care of himself. To which admonition he always answers in a cool Bogart tone: "Sure, kid, sure." As the rest of the characters come on they recall their prototypes without actually imitating them exactly. The portly man in the wheel chair who likes to "collect evidence of man's baseness" (Steven Furst) reminds us of Sydney Greenstreet. His knife-wielding butler (Ron Duncan) is a Peter Lorre type. And so on.

Those who like to unravel complicated murder plots will enjoy the labyrinthine pattern of the story line. Those who don't can just laugh at the absurdity of the plot's sudden twists. The deadly Delilah of the play's title refers to a rare potted plant which has hidden in it a tape recording whose blackmail potential is so great that practically everybody in the play, even the most insignificant characters, are willing to kill to get it.

The fat man's wife, played by Barbara Crane-Baker in a way that reminds one of Lauren Bacall, switches her amorous inclinations according to her needs at the moment. Her stepdaughter (Lynne Salsbury) is a blonde sex kitten who takes her stepmother's lover away from her. One of these (Joseph Kelly) is in big debt to gambler Johnny Roulette (Frank McGinty). Actually Johnny was born Harry Krapp in the same slums that Matt Fallon came up from. Among the many other characters is the sadistic police lieutenant who hates Matt's guts and vows to throw him out with the garbage. And he does so literally several times.

There are lots of visual gags to go with the spoof. Matt takes a letter out of a corpse's hand and starts to pull the knife out of its back to open the letter with. Then there is corny dialogue of the 1940 Hollywood flick. "Life is a sad little merry-go-round when you can't catch the brass ring," says the daughter in a pensive mood. "You're a loaded crate of dynamite," says Matt in a passionate one.

Music of the period sustains the mood, Billy Holliday, Benny Goodman, and '40s costumes, long skirts and broad-brimmed hats. Harsh lighting, often dim and back-lit, recalls the wartime film and the drabness of the set is deliberate. Tom Crane-Baker's direction brings out the hilarity of the humor on levels ranging from slapstick to subtler satire. Some rough edges here and there, odd lapses of timing of the opening night variety, should clear up in subsequent performances.

All in all, "Delilah" is delightfully different.

"The Last of the Red Hot Lovers"
(by Jon Longaker, Richmond Times-Dispatch, September 20, 1976)

Whatever else Neil Simon may mean to future historians of of theater, he is certainly the stage chronicler of our time. Each of his plays--and he has had at least one on Broadway for the last dozen years--is a vivid snapshot of some aspect of life in contemporary America. And each one is hilariously funny.

In "The Last of the Red Hot Lovers" Simon examines three phases in Barney Cashman's strategy for having an extramarital affair. Barney has been married for 23 years, we learn at one point, and feels that this is his last chance to have a fling. It is also his first, for Barney is as square and wholesome as a piece of corn bread. He is the kind of man who pours an un-drunk drink of Scotch back into the bottle. He neither smokes nor drinks himself. He keeps putting lotions on his hands to kill the smell of the fish he handles in his restaurant.

He is also most unwise in his choice of would-be sexual partners. His first target is a barb-tongued maenad whose un-inhibited eroticism and derisive sarcasm dampen his lust. Act 2 brings on a screwball whom he has picked up in the park and whose wild tales of sex orgies and violence first fascinate and then terrify him. The scene of their smoking pot together is one of the funniest in the show.

Target number three is, of all things, a friend of his wife's, a depressed woman (her happiness quotient, she says, is 8.2 out of 100) who is obsessed with the world's immorality, who chews tranquillizers and turns the seduction into a confession.

The part of Cashman obviously requires an actor with a strong, warm and outgoing personality, and the person of Doug Hill fills the bill nicely. As the play progresses he grows in sophistication, switching from a blue suit and white socks in the first act to a red shirt and checked leisure suit in the third.

Director Paul Iddings has made use of other devices like this to establish character.

As for the ladies, Billie Jean Crawford has to work at the role of the hard-as-nails Elaine. The words are there but not the personality. Fran Broaddus as the paranoid Bobbi enlivens the second act with her breathless delivery and frantic stage movements. And as the sin-fraught Jeanette, Anne Costello turns in a superb performance, giving her tear-filled scenes enough variety to sustain her difficult, constantly emotional part with great effect.

Hill's performance tends to be on the static side, perhaps because of his years before the television cameras where the voice alone suffices and body movement is undesirable. It is only in the second and third acts, when the action becomes more volatile, that Hill begins to use his whole body.

A fortunate result of this situation is that the play, which moves a bit slowly in the first act, picks up in excitement as the evening progresses and the laughs come faster.

LORD, Howard Blaine; (2) Theater Critic and Educator; (3) b. Wash-ington D. C. , July 8, 1926; (4) s. Ernest Grier and Margaret Ellen (Blaine); (5) B. A. U. of Chicago, liberal arts, 1948; grad. work in hist. and phil. , U. of Chicago 1949-50; M. A. Catholic Univ. , drama maj. , English min. , 1956; grad work in theater, N. Y. U. 1961-63; (6) m. Lucille Patricia Vasta, June 28, 1958; (7) children--Margaret

Ellen, Elizabeth Anne, Teresa Marie, Michael Francis; (8) Actor, director, stage mgr. , company mgr. , business mgr. , Players Incorporated, Washington D. C. , 1953-58; asst. prof. and Head of Dept. of Speech and Drama, St. Mary's College, Notre Dame, Ind. , 1956-60; asst. prof. of speech and drama, St. John's University Jamaica, N. Y. , 1960-66; theater critic, Long Island Catholic, 1964- ; staff researcher, LIC, 1966; asst. prof. of drama and literature, 1966-74, assoc. prof. , 1974- , New College, Hofstra University, Hempstead, N. Y. 11550; (9) Director of Off-Campus Education, 1970- , Coordinator, University Without Walls, 1973- ; (10) Chm. English Advisory Committee, Northport-E Northport School District, 1974; (13) USNR, 1944-46; (15) AAUP, Society for Field Experience Education, American Theater Association; (16) Democrat; (17) Roman Catholic; (21) 319 Scudder Ave. , Northport, N. Y. 11768, Ph. 516-757-7498; (22) UWW at New College, Hofstra University, Hempstead, N. Y. 11550, Ph. 516-560-3651; (23) Circulation: 183,000; (24) 50 theatre reviews annually.

Delight Abounds in Playful Play about Faust-like Sherlock Holmes
(by Howard Lord, Long Island Catholic, December 5, 1974)

He's too honorable to sell his soul to the Devil. Besides, matching wits with the Devil, in the person of the fiendish Moriarty, is the only diversion for a man who has mastered and is bored with "the commonplace of existence. " But, in the end, the Eternal Feminine gets him.

Of course, Sherlock Holmes is not Faust, nor does the play by Conan Doyle and the American actor, William Gillette purport to offer a comprehensive statement about the human condition. But the similarities are remarkable.

He is, indeed, a master mind. Like Faust, he knows all there is to know. Consequently, his deductions are effortless and quick. What baffles the good mind lies revealed to his. There is nothing left to strive for in this world--except the apprehension of the only other master mind.

He sees himself as a tragic figure. He flirts constantly with death to relieve his boredom. He even resorts to cocaine.

Like Faust, he has become a figure of mythical proportions. He captures our imaginations.

Like Faust, he is both classical and romantic; romantic in his restless search for enterprises worthy of his talents, classical in the purity and precision of his intellect.

Ultimately, like Faust, he is redeemed by a good woman. His own goodness cannot resist the attraction of true virtue in another. He fights the impulse, but love conquers even Sherlock Holmes.

That ending, I'm sure, is pure Gillette. We know that Conan Doyle abandoned the play which Gillette had commissioned and
that the great showman completed it. I wouldn't be surprised if
the actor and the author parted company over that ending. Conan Doyle probably wanted his master mind to remain simply that.
Gillette, I suspect, developed the Faustian aspects.

The Royal Shakespeare Company's production of "Sherlock
Holmes," on view at the Broadhurst, is masterful. It seeks
only to entertain, to divert. It is playful. Holmes and Moriarty
have conversations like this: "Undoubtedly, all that I have to say
has already crossed your mind." (Pause.) "And my answer
has undoubtedly crossed yours." The stage is fog drenched.
The master lock to Moriarty's lair whirls and clicks, clanks
and clangs as if it were the most important actor on the stage.
There are delights around every foggy turn. Most are provided
by the intriguing Holmes, the cool center of all danger and manipulation.

John Wood must be having the time of his life as the nimble
sleuth. He has captured not only Holmes' dexterity, but his
passion. He is impatient with others' inability to see the obvious. He is impatient with his own humanity when it hints at
being non-rational. He is gleeful at his carefully contrived but
narrow escapes. He relishes his encounters with Moriarty.

If Wood's Holmes is light, wit and energy, Philip Locke's
Moriarty is ponderous, forceful and devastating. What a pair!

Frank Dunlop, director of the still running "Scapino," directed "Sherlock Holmes." After seeing these two plays, I conclude he is a master himself. He is inventive, but never exercises invention for its own sake. He uses the stage to illuminate the action. Carl Toms has given him ingenious and gorgeous Victorian settings to work with.

It is romantic and melodramatic theatre, frank and unabashed.
It is intended only to divert. It is evidence of a turn-of-the
century nostalgia for a time when tragedy was possible. Holmes'
boredom with humdrum existence was echoed, I suspect, in his
audience. One thing saves it from being merely melodramatic.
Melodramas are peopled by stereotypical characters. The characters of Holmes and Moriarty are larger than stereotypes.
They are indeed humanity and the archfiend locked in mortal
combat. The game's afoot at the Broadhurst. Don't miss it.

In Praise of "In Praise of Love"
(by Howard Lord, Long Island Catholic, January 16, 1975)

When was the last time you wept, or wanted to weep, bittersweet tears of joy in the theatre? When was the last time
you heard Rex Harrison devastate an audience with an astounded
and indignant, "Are you mad?!" When was the last time you

saw a comedy-drama not about cosmic absurdity and human futility but about people--rich, warm, quirky people, confronting disaster and acting their way, joyfully, through the worst of times? It's been a long time, right?

Rex Harrison and Julie Harris will make you weep, will make you roar with laughter and will captivate you when you see them in Terence Rattigan's new play on Broadway, "In Praise of Love." This is a play for people who value sentiment, wit, talent and craft in the theatre. How many of us are there left?

I must confess to a bit of discomfort in the first act, but the ending made all things right. Rex Harrison plays an erudite, crotchety and absent-minded book reviewer named Sebastian Cruttwell. The part is deliciously written, and Harrison not only savors every morsel; he adds his own sauce. When he leaves Martin Gabel and Julie Harris alone to develop some critically important exposition, the shift from elegant comedy to routine exposition creates a letdown. You listen attentively to the exposition, which is extended and seemingly cluttered with detail, and you wonder what on earth Rattigan had in mind.

Here are the facts. Julie, Harrison's wife, is a former Estonian Resistance Fighter. She has no country. She was discovered by Harrison in Berlin when he was with British Intelligence after the war. He married her so she could come to England. They remained together. They had a son. Harrison is an ardent Socialist; the son is working actively for the Liberal Party. Harrison wrote a fine novel when he returned to England after the War. He wrote another novel, which was panned. He abandoned creative writing and became a distinguished critic. Harrison and Harris met Gabel, a wealthy writer of sex novels, in America. Gabel fell in love with Julie and remains so to this day. Julie is in the last stages of a terminal disease, poly-arthritis, caused by youthful malnutrition. She is concerned about Harrison who is so utterly dependent on her that he doesn't know how to adjust the thermostate when his room is cold. Julie wants someone to take care of him after she's gone. She hopes it can be a Lady Prunella, with whom Harrison is having an affair, or, just conceivably, the son.

Get the idea? The exposition in the play is as enchanting as that paragraph was in this review. Rattigan tricks it up a bit by having Julie get drunk on American (ugh!) vodka as she unfolds the story, but it's pretty tedious, and it's difficult to see where it's supposed to lead.

But you've got to stick with this play, because Rattigan, Harrison, Harris, Gabel and a young actor who plays the son, Peter Burnell, compensate for the tedious half of the first act with an exquisite second.

Rattigan has an important point to make. It is best summed

up in one of Harrison's lines: "I've been in love with Lydia for six months, and I could have been in love with her for 28 years. Maybe I loved her when we were married. I can't remember." He discovered she was to die six months ago. That shattering fact called his attention to her, and he discovered she was radiant.

The point, I think, is not that we shouldn't take each other for granted. It's more basic and positive. It is that love needs exercise and expression. When we settle into routine relationships with those we truly love, we overlay that love with sediment. We can forget that love is underneath it all. All we see in our daily rounds is the mundane surface of something rich and rare. It takes impending loss to remind us of the value of a submerged love and an unconsidered partner. Yet that love and the devotion of that partner have given our lives and activities all the value that they have had. Rattigan is telling us we are only half alive if we are not actively aware of our blessings.

Fred Coe directed with intelligence and restraint. Mielziner's setting is perfect. Harrison has never been more brilliant. It is his performance, more than any other, which illuminates the play. Julie Harris looks marvellous and plays with her customary passion. Martin Gabel seems uncomfortable in a thankless, protatic role. And Peter Burnell is first-rate as the son.

The play has its problems. Such a keen craftsman as Terence Rattigan should have been able to be more engaging with his exposition. But all problems are resolved at the ending and audiences leave in a positive nimbus of good feeling.

LOY, Robert H.; (2) Reporter; (3) b. Brazil, Ind., Nov. 3, 1918; (4) s. Herman and Tonie J. (Payne) L.; (5) A.B. Indiana U., major subject, journalism, 1949; (6) m. Jeannette M. Davis, July 29, 1972; (13) U.S. Army 1941-45; (16) Democrat; (17) Methodist; (21) 1707 W. Harvard Ave., Muncie, Ind. 47304, Ph. 288-9844; (22) Muncie Evening Press, 125 S. High St., Muncie, Ind. 47305; Ph. 747-5733; (23) Circulation: 23,000; (24) 25-30 motion pictures; six symphonic concerts; 11 university theater productions including musicals; 10 traveling professional productions including drama, musicals, concerts and recitals.

Chekhov Would Have Liked City Center's Production
(by Bob Loy, Muncie Evening Press, November 12, 1974)

The City Center Acting Company of New York gave a performance of Anton Chekhov's "Three Sisters" in Emens Auditorium Monday apparently the way the playwright would have wanted it.

When the play was in rehearsal for its premier performance by the Moscow Art Theater in 1901, Chekhov threw up his hands and fled the city because he thought the players were giving it too "heavy" an interpretation. He accused the director, Stanislavsky, of ruining his play.

Chekhov thought his dramas should be played with a light touch. This is exactly how The City Center Company did "Three Sisters."

Some singing and dancing, apparently lacking in the original, was incorporated and attempts were made to invest some of the characterizations with humor despite the insistent aura of gloom and doom which pervades the drama.

"Three Sisters" is a story of blasted hopes, unfulfilled yearnings, unrealized dreams. Every character has a hang-up of some sort. Upon all these individual character shortfalls turns the drama.

In a broader sense, however, Chekhov was mirroring the malaise, the character disintegration of the Russian upper classes and he seemed to presage the Bolshivik revolution.

He has the character, Baron Tuzenbach, say, "The day of reckoning is here. Something formidable is threatening us; a strong, cleansing storm is gathering; it is coming nearer and nearer; it will soon sweep our world clean of laziness, indifference, prejudice against work, and wretched boredom."

Chekhov designed his drama with an equal division of labor among the actors. There are no "stars" and it would be vain to attempt to choose best performances among the young actors and actresses of the three-year-old City Center Company, all of whom are graduates of the Drama Division of the Juilliard School.

I thought Mary-John Negro as the sister, Masha, was outstanding although Mary Lou Rosato as Olga and Patti LuPone as Irina were excellent.

Richard Ooms gave a particularly touching performance as Kulygin, the patient, fatuous ass of a school teacher who always tried to keep up a bold front although he was bleeding inside because of the indifference of his wife.

Norman Snow as Tuzenbach seemed a shade too energetic at first but this overt mooning over Irina and his good-natured clumsiness added a spark of humor to the proceedings.

Others who might be mentioned are David Schramm as Chebutykin, the military doctor; Sandra Halperin as Natasha; Peter Dvorsky as Col. Vershinin and Benjamin Hendreckson as Audrey, all of whom gave solid performances.

"Seesaw" Is Slow-Paced and Lacking in Vitality
(by Bob Loy, Muncie Evening Press, February 4, 1975)

The musical "Seesaw" hit the Emens Auditorium stage Monday night with the vitality of a buzzsaw--with the teeth knocked out.

It was slow-paced, cliche-ridden and top heavy with its star, John Raitt. It was redeemed by some good chorus numbers and adequate performances by junior cast members.

The best music came after the final curtain when Raitt, as he did with "Camelot," last year, decided the tunes in the show did not do justice to his voice and sang some additional songs.

He gave us "Maria" and a medley from "Oklahoma" which were better than anything in "Seesaw."

"Seesaw" is based on the play "Two for the Seesaw" by William Gibson. It concerns a "square" lawyer from Omaha, Nebraska (Raitt) who comes to New York, meets and falls in love with hip, swing dancer, Gittel Mosca (Liz Torres).

Gittel is the sterotyped tough, New York Jewish gamin who lives in an apartment in the East Village (where else).

She and the lawyer are miles apart culturally. She is hypnotized by his use of the expression "local colloquialism" to describe the term "big apple" as applied to New York. She has him say it over and over.

They have a brief love affair but, alas, he is burdened with a wife back in Omaha who manages to lure him back in the end.

Miss Torres is a lanky, angular young woman with considerable talent for contortionist comedy. When she and Ron Kurowski, who portrays a "gay" dancer and choreographer, are interacting the pacing is good.

But most of her scenes are with Raitt and these are lifeless and monotonous. Even their love scenes are wooden.

Raitt tends to stand hulkingly around and his threatening presence seemed to intimidate the girl.

Although the dancers are not the best ever seen in a road company at Emens, they pick up the tempo of the show considerably and at least one member of the audience kept peeking at his program to try to estimate how long it would be before they were on again.

A particular crowd pleaser was the last chorus number in the second act, with Kurowski leading the way and the dancers bedecked in toy balloons. It was cute and perky.

Unlike that terrible orchestra he brought with "Camelot" last year, Raitt had a fairly good group this time which helped matters considerably.

Clever use was made of movable sets for instant scene changes and the backdrops and scrims of the New York skyline were impressive.

LOYND, Roy, Los Angeles Herald-Examiner, The Hearst Corp., 111 S. Broadway, Los Angeles, Cal. 90015.

LUELOFF, Jorie; (2) Theater critic; (3) b. Milwaukee; (4) d. R. T. and Marjorie (Kaltenbach); (5) B.A. Mills College, major subj.: Political Science; (6) m. Richard Friedman, May 1, 1970; (8) Feature writer, Associated Press, 1963-65; Newscaster and reporter, NBC News, Chicago, 1965-present, Drama critic, NBC News, Chicago, 1973-present; (10) Member, Joseph Jefferson Awards Committee, 1975-present; (12) Member Chicago Press Club Board of Governors, 1972-74; member Board of Governors, Chicago Chapter of National Academy of TV Arts and Sciences, 1973-present; Member Junior Governing Board of the Chicago Symphony, 1972-74; (22) NBC News, Merchandise Mart, Chicago, Ill. 60614; (23) Circulation: 500,000; (24) 100 plays.

Henry Fonda as Clarence Darrow
(by Jorie Lueloff, over WMAQ television, Chicago, April 10, 1975)

The Studebaker used to be one of the drabest, dingiest places in town, but that's being changed now. The new look is just as bright and shiny as the current production on stage. Henry Fonda is back as the famous trial lawyer Clarence Darrow.

The show, set in Darrow's old age, consists of a monologue, as the old lawyer looks back over his life. As he calls up memories--both personal and professional--Fonda moves easily through a well-designed three-part set representing home, office and, of course, courtroom. And in the courtroom some of his most colorful cross examinations and arguments are recreated.

The show is perhaps of special interest to Chicagoans. This was Darrow's home and, of course, the scene of some of his best known cases including his defense of Leopold and Loeb in the Bobby Franks murder. Fonda plays Darrow in an understated manner--perhaps a bit too understated for some tastes-- One might expect a bit more vinegar and crust. What does come across is the sharpness, humanity and decency of Darrow-- all well-laced with healthy humor. It's a nice evening.

Coward in Two Keys
(by Jorie Lueloff, over WMAQ television, Chicago, April 29, 1975)

I love Noel Coward's plays--the elegant settings, the sophisticated characters, the clever dialogue ... Nevertheless, I have
to admit that things dragged a bit last night. First of all, this
pair of plays aren't Coward at his peak. Secondly, they aren't
done with quite enough vinegar and zest.

The cast is distinguished--Jessica Tandy, Hume Cronyn, and
Anne Baxter. And the first half of the double bill works rather
well. It features the Conklins--the stereotype American couple
travelling in Europe. He's a rich businessman relegated to
serving as errand boy for his social-climbing wife. Jessica
Tandy epitomizes the American matron on the make, whose idea
of heaven is mixing with third rate royalty. When a seating
arrangement becomes awkward, her solution is to send her husband off to eat alone in his room.

Hume Cronyn has his fun in the second play--as a waspish,
aging literary lion enduring a reunion with his onetime mistress.
Confronted with a threat to his carefully contrived image, he
runs the gamut of tricks.

He sulks, he threatens, he quavers, he throws a tantrum.
It's a funny scene--but it could be funnier. The pacing's slushy,
the delivery not poisonous enough--and the net effect not quite
up to super-British Noel Coward snuff. Don't get me wrong.
There are some funny moments, and the evening on a whole is
pleasant enough. It's just that it could be so much sharper--in
the true Coward tradition.

McCASLIN, Walter, Journal Herald, 37 South Ludlow St., Dayton,
O. 45401

McELFRESH, Tom; (2) Drama critic; (3) b. Bracken County, Ken.,
Jan. 18, 1935; (4) s. Henry Edward and Esther (Perkins) McElfresh;
(5) A.B. Eastern Kentucky State College, 1956; (6) m. Joan R.
Scholle, June 23, 1956; (7) children--Victoria, Alison, Stephanie;
(8) copywriter/copy chief Leonard M. Sive & Associates, Advertising (Cincinnati) 1959-63; Sr. VP/creative Sive Advertising 1963-71;
consultant Sive Advertising 1971-present; contributed dramatic criticism and general articles The Cincinnati Enquirer 1968-71; theater
critic The Cincinnati Enquirer 1971-present; (9) Director, designer,
performer community theater productions 1960-71; appeared in Equity
productions 1960-65 and in Equity stock (hiatus from Enquirer) 1973;
lectured on critical journalism University of Cincinnati 1972, Thomas
More College 1972; Miami (of Ohio) University 1972-73; (13) Commissioned 2nd Lt. US Army Signal Corps 1956, resigned reserve
Captain, 1963; (15) Member Ohio Community Theater Association,

Ohio Theater Alliance; American Theater Critics Association; (21) 1026 Lower Jackson Road, Park Hills, Covington, Kentucky 41011; Ph. 606-431-7366; (22) The Cincinnati Enquirer, 617 Vine St., Cincinnati, O. 45202, Ph. 513-721-2700.

Playhouse Rightly Shows No Fear of Albee's "Virginia Woolf"
(by Tom McElfresh, Cincinnati Enquirer, November 22, 1974)

It is, I think, neither overly romantic nor light minded to relate "Who's Afraid of Virginia Woolf," the Edward Albee play which Thursday opened at the Cincinnati Playhouse, to a pop song Rob Reider sang on television the same day--one line of which states, "Any kind of love is better than no love at all." Any contact.

In the play's long scathing, searching evening we ultimately come to understand that--at least on the first name level--George and Martha require, desire, the baiting, the barking, the mutual psyche-battering they exchange. One, perhaps, of the wilder shores of love. But love.

For the few of you unfamiliar with the play--let me sketch quickly: Martha (52), daughter of a New England college president, is married to George (46). He is a history lecturer unlikely to gain further distinction in the halls of academe. After a late Saturday night party at the president's home, Martha invites Nick (30), a young, handsome, rapaciously ambitious and barely scrupled biology professor and his banal, balefully, ordinary wife Honey (26) over for some even later drinking. Most of two acts are a violent raveling and knitting up of Albee's multilinear themes, until in Act Three it is revealed that George and Martha's mysterious and much-discussed "son" is a fiction-- a figment of their mutually sterile bodies and fecund imaginations. For 21 years the "son" has remained a private battleground and solace; now, in going further than they've ever gone before in wounding each other, George announces that the "son" has been killed. In the play's single truly quiet moment, at the very end, George and Martha take a first step into a new un-games relationship: There is a hint of hope, but only the barest hint.

It is not, I think, accidental that the two leading roles are named George and Martha--any more than it is accidental that the college is supposedly located in a city called New Carthage, after that ultimately destroyed African city of light; but it would be faulty to read the play and the characters entirely as metaphor for perishing American culture.

The play is far richer in thematic material: Albee's jaundiced, jittery view of parent-child relationships is there; his allergy to many forms of marriage and its practitioners. The guise of academic quiet in American universities gets glanced beneath.

There is the tug-of-war between humanitarian-historian
George and biologist Nick about what's good for man and his
culture.   There's the sharp contrast between acerbic Martha and
banal Honey ... as portraits of "woman." Among many other
themes.

And, too, we might give Albee the benefit of a certainty:
That he knows about playmaking and about involving audiences--
that some aspects of the play may simply be there because
they're racketing good theater and carry no particular political
resonance.

Garland Wright has staged this lengthy and complex work--
Albee's first full length play, premiered in 1961--with a musician's ear for its delicately balanced dynamics--for the highly
strung quartet of chamber horrors.   Further, he has eased out
into view most of Albee's mordantly witty comedy without letting
it turn into high camp wisecrackery.

All four facile players manage Albee's quite literary language without letting it sound so and at the same time without letting it read out too slickly.

Bette Ford presents Martha's relatively flat character with
a progression that grows from caustic brio to full tilt rage.   She
worked very slightly better against the strong reaction of Wednesday's young and enthusiastic preview audience (when I saw the
whole play) than against Thursday's older, quieter, more thoughtful one (with whom I saw only Act One.)   A sound, planned performance.

James Ray plays George in a rush of dry, drawling cyni-
cism--a lucid, dangerous performance if a fraction removed.
If faintly petulant.   An utterly valid interpretation of the role
and something a bit new to it, I think.   His rage has a com-
prehending, almost theraputic quality about it--as he plays out
the games Martha invents for him.   There might be a fraction
more suggestion that their battles are mandatory to his continued
sanity as well as hers.   A fraction less amplitude of strange affection for his mate.   But, withal it's a marvel of a reading.
As we've come to expect from Ray.

J. Kenneth Campbell's Nick is square-fronted and assertive.
And Eda Zahl gives Honey a tuned blend of sweetened vapidity
and vituperative egocentricity.   I would fault her for some of
her comic drunken mannerisms as bordering on the cheap, however.

John Scheffler's set makes a bit too large an arena though
the cluttered Victorian tone is right as rain.   And the painting
might have been a bit better executed.   Susan Tsu's costumes
are fine as are Marc Weiss' lighting patterns.

Neither the play--as a play--nor the production quite meet the standards set by the Playhouse production of "A Delicate Balance." But it is in sum a sturdy, frequently quite electric exercise.

Actors Defeat Playwright 5-0 at Playhouse
(by Tom McElfresh, Cincinnati Inquirer, March 28, 1975)

There are manifold problems with the production of Jason Miller's Pulitzer prize play, "That Championship Season," which opened Thursday at the Cincinnati Playhouse, the fourth in the current six-play subscription season. And they're sins of comission, of excess.

Act One played tightly and securely enough, but by the beginning of Act Two staginess and an overabundance of histrionics from all five members of the company began choking the play. Director John Dillon has either staged in or failed to edit out a lot of very actory excess. It's too loud, too pausey, too fraught and too melodramatic. And, since the one role that is the play's chorus and conscience is being played as a glib, burlesqued drunk rather than a caring, whipped, sardonic one, the play is further denied both its heart and its mind.

Five men, the coach and four of the five starters who made up a state high school basketball championship team gather for their annual reunion; this is the 20th. The significance of the missing starter who knows they stole the trophy, that they won it with play that skirted the rules and violated the spirit of the game, is the play's climax.

In 20 years the team spirit has become a guilty shadow; it's maintained, whipped into a lather once a year because the coach can't stand to let go of it. It was his life. The players, paunchily near their forties are all past and no future; that championship season peaked their lives too early. George is a stupid Mayor; James is a mediocre school principal; Phil is rich on his father's money and bored with an excess of booze and money and women; he's even seduced George's wife; Tom is the drunk who should see too clearly but, as played by James Cook, sees only enough to pick at wounds.

Four men charged into their manhood magnetized into a desperate, dissolving friendship by what used to be and by their dog-blind loyalty to the Coach.

The Coach's terms are win at any cost, hurt, gouge, punish an enemy--and any opposition is adjudged a blood enemy--with any weakness. He's also bigoted, close minded and archly reactionary. He sets quite an example.

It should be tragic that men take to life with a simplistic, kill-or-be-killed attitude that pays even less than lip service to

the ideals of sportsmanship games are supposed to teach. It should
be tragic that men come to their adult state with blocked, adolescent
values. But in this production the tragedy gets swallowed up.

The play descends into a melodrama about whether George
will accept money from Phil for his re-election campaign after
he learns that Phil has taken his wife. The surface values of
the play get ranted at the expense of the submerged and valuable
levels.

Reid Shelton comes nearest a performance, but then the
Coach whose simplistic political view can inexplicably lump
John Kennedy and Senator Joseph McCarthy into one camp is
the simplest role. He, however, is capable of the most obvious acting. William Metzo's reading is full of mechanical,
one-two-three bravura as rich Phil. Raymond Thorne is guilt-
iest of all of showing us just how hard he can act. James
Cook, I've mentioned.

The sins are actors' sins, but the fault I lay with director
Dillon. All five performers proved themselves able in "Arsenic." Dillon could have coached some control into them.

McGOVERN, Bernard Francis; (2) Journalist; (3) b. Bklyn, N.Y.,
Jan. 19, 1940; (4) s. James Bernard and Burnadette (Mountain);
(5) Student U. Tampa, 1957-60; (6) m. Pauline Tourles, Sept. 24,
1961; (7) children--Jennifer, Victoria; (8) Program Director, WTUN,
Tampa, 1958-60; freelance 1960-61; theatre critic Tampa (Fla.)
Tribune 1962-66, staff 1966-68, theatre critic 1968-71, newsfeatures
editor 1972-73, editorial writer and asst. to editor 1974- ; (9) Cmml.
announcer for radio, TV, films; cons. in arts, entertainment and
commercial communications; (10) Cultural advisor Hillsborough Community College 1970-74; senior journalism seminar lecturer, Univ.
of South Florida 1972-73; special advisor, arts management program,
University of Tampa 1974, seminar lecturer U. Tampa arts management program 1975. Active auctions on and for Pub. TV and for
civic orgns. including Am. Cancer Soc., Gifted Children, Boy Scouts
of America. Mem. Nat. Acad. TV Arts, Sciences blue ribbon panels
1972-73, 73-74. (Judge - News. Doc. Emmy Awards); Mem. National Film Board of Review 1962-75; member, bd. of directors
Hillsborough Association for Gifted Education; (15) Sigma Delta Chi;
(16) Republican; (17) Greek Orthodox; (20) Regular contributor to
Variety; (21) 2107 Mariana St., Tampa FL 33612; (22) 202 South
Parker St., Tampa, FL 33606.

"Oh Dad ..." Too Bad to Be Sad
(by Bernie McGovern, Tampa Tribune, April 15, 1970)

"Oh Dad, Poor Dad ..." Asolo's taken you oh so seriously
and, worse yet, sophomorically, and it's all so sad.

"Oh Dad, Poor Dad, Mamma's Hung You in the Closet and

I'm Feelin' So Sad" is the State Theater's new and fifth-entry in its 1970 repertory on the grounds of the Ringling Museum.

It is the most disappointing outing of the Asolo's season, not only dull but dreary.

Arthur Kopit's wildly titled, vivid and biting comedy deals with a young man imprisoned within his mother's life.

She is a most formidable figure, keeper of venus fly traps that eat anything, and a purring piranha that is more selectively on a diet of Siamese cats, or, if available, kittens.

Mom is one big bad person who satisfies herself by devouring her son, repressing him, possessing him, protecting him from the evils of the outside world, a world she is past master of, and one she is fighting tooth and nail.

But when Sonny gets blue, tired of writing letters to strangers in the phone book, unfulfilled by his stamp collection, he seeks a greener pasture in the form of a sugar-coated trollop.

Mom has naturally arranged the match, sure it will fail after a brief case of overexposure. Naturally, Sonny likes the lady just fine and when she proves to be a match for Mom, the scene is set for the play's climactic big bed scene in which Sonny is given his choice between Mom and Unmom.

Other characters include a bevy of berated bellboys briefly, and a love interest for Mom, if such a thing is possible, which serves mainly to launch Mom into her prerogative: The Monologue, which backgrounds her and her afflictions and provides, along with the sexy finish, half of the play's high points.

Dad, stuffed, mounted and transported wherever Momma goes, tactfully keeps to his closet.

"Oh Dad ..." is admittedly not everyone's cup of tea. It is a ridiculous play which fully appreciated is a horrendously funny one, a rich, gaudy, erotic, truly fantastic satire.

But to Asolo guest director Peter Frisch, it is a stark, and most realistic tragedy, a dreadful dirge played straight. Humor, which is rampant, is relegated to such a minor role that it becomes comic relief.

There have been livelier wakes.

The play's somber tone can be chalked up to an unfortunate attempt, a nice try mistake, a lapse in judgement, in the long run a most excusable offense.

But the play's juvenile handling is something else again. It adds insult to injury.   It is inexcusable.

With all the finesse, faith, and, most importantly, contempt, of a born brat, the production actually expects laughable psuedo-shock to excite its audience.   But it is difficult to become excited, or even stay awake, for innovations that are not only dull, but worse, dated; for chronic illness that pretends to be emotion; for eroticism when it is reduced to adolescent sex fantasy.

Following through on its theme, the show's total effect is to present its audience with take it or leave it!

That really isn't much choice.

The Asolo's standard high production values and its company are up to professional par, i. e. , they are faithful to the director and nothing more.

Isa Thomas plays Momma, William Pitts is Sonny, and, Carol Williard is the girl.   Bradford Wallace and Henry Strozier are also featured.

Homes Easley has designed a cage for a set, most suitable.

"Faustus" Comes on Strong in Latest Version at Asolo
(by Bernie McGovern, Tampa Tribune, May 12, 1970)

The Asolo Theater's new production, "Doctor Faustus," is a feast for the eyes, ears, nose, throat, whatever; a super spectacular, a thoroughly theatrical experience.

Designed to mesmerize its audience, it does.

But after all, all that could be expected.   For "Doctor Faustus," the tale of the man who sold his soul to the devil, is Asolo's annual orgy, its big budget, big box office, knock 'en dead, where's a scalper when you really need one, hurry 'cause it's going fast, immediately optioned for New York, Bob Strane-Eberle Thomas extravaganza and collaboration.

The Strane-Thomas combination has come to be regarded, and rightly so, as the artistic high point of each Asolo season.   "A" Strane-Thomas combination occurs frequently since both are the resident directors and principal, if reluctant, actors of the state theater.   But "The" Strane-Thomas teaming up is the one-time pulling out of all the stops that stands audiences on their heads.

Based on Christopher Marlowe's version, "Doctor Faustus," written by Strane and Thomas, directed by Strane, featuring Thomas is a wonderful show, a technical marvel, designed by Holmes Easley, staged by Jim Hoskins, with lighting by John Gowans, and featuring the more subtle abilities of Robert Naismith, property master.

Property master?

Property master. Naismith has designed extremely effective
life masks that disguise all of the company's players, save two,
as they play anwhere from three to five parts. The two exceptions are Patrick Egan, who alone has one role, as Faustus, and
Isa Thomas, usually featured in Asolo production but this time
merely understudying all the feminine roles.

All of the technicals in the show are extremely effective.
Whatever thought cloyed in Asolo's "Oh, Dad ..." comes together
in " ... Faustus." Everything works. Holmes Easley's set is
beyond his usual top flight design standards. In addition, he gets
credit for designing all aspects of the show and he is as much,
probably more, responsible for its success as is anyone. The
play is set before a semi-circle of revolving panels and movable
platforms, the production moving in and out and around on a
stage built up, allowing rare underlighting, just one effect from
Gowans.

In short, "Doctor Faustus" ought to be set down in a text-
book and distributed to all those who aspire to work in the theater but not be seen in a theater.

Performances, by Egan; by Thomas, principally as Mephistopheles; Henry Strozier, principally as Lucifer; William Pitts,
principally as the servant Wagner; Macon McCalman, principally
as the comic character Robin, with Bradford Wallace, as his
henchmen Ralph and by David Mallon, Sharon Spelman, Stuart
Culpepper, Barbara Redmond and Carol Willard are excellent.

Clearly, "Doctor Faustus" is a show that shouldn't be missed,
a show that should be stood in line for, the show of the year.

But ... If "Doctor Faustus" is a marvelous show to watch, it is
a sad show to behold.

For the Asolo's production, probably quite unwittingly marks
the beginning of Faust's new decline.

Faustus is a curious entity. He regularly declines and falls,
not just in his play, but in the life cycle of his various plays
and versions. On a cycle, he grows popular as a tragic hero,
declines into being a pop character, disappears in a burlesque,
in which he is a fool. Of course, Faustus is a fool so perhaps
it is inherent, certainly not evil, but just as certainly, sad.

Faustus starts each cycle as a majestic tragic figure plagued
by a terrible, bizarre plight. It is this bizarreness that leads
to the first debasement of the tragedy, spectacularization, such
as Asolo's as the urge to jazz old Faustus up, sets in an an effort to broaden his appeal. The next step is burlesque.

How far can old Faustus sink? When Goethe found him he was the leading character in a puppet show.

Strane and Thomas, using the early and very playable Marlowe rendition as a basis, have taken Faustus down the garden path and come up with an extremely entertaining, but not very substantial, showcasing of the character.

Faustus is reduced to moving from one technical aspect to another to such an extent that one doesn't really care what happens to Faustus, only how it's going to happen. Reenforcing the reliance on technicals to tell the story is the script. While Strane and Thomas, or if you prefer, Thomas and Strane, have remained surprisingly faithful to the script, they have also simplified it, smoothed it out, and come up with a great book musical.

Asolo's production is not a musical, but it could have easily been one and that would be the next step to burlesque and then to skit, and then to puppet show or TV sitcom.

With apologies to "Damn Yankees," the last "Faust" musical, Faustus would kick the show off with the title tune, "Faustus," a good tune since it recurs through as the show's theme. It's a thoroughly legit number, consistent with the classics and with the suspension of dramatic action commonplace in musicals. Faustus is a doctor, of medicine, philosophy, theology, and sick of it. He's seeking new kicks, and since it is a musical, a brighter tomorrow. He's got friends who convince him to take up the deadly magical arts, make a pact with the Fallen Angel.

OK, he agrees, but he's still not convinced, and as he tries to come up with his first free spirit, he sings the inquisitive "The Devil, You Say?"

Successful in his effort, up pops the devil's rep, he signs away his soul and the next tune has got to be "Me and Mephistopheles."

Meanwhile, Faustus' colleagues at the university, a male chorus, sing the rousing tribute "He's a Helluva Guy."

But Faustus still harbors some doubts about his status and sings the plaintiff "I'll Be Damned."

Lucifer himself enters to reaffirm his contract with Faustus, because, the Devil says in the show's first rock song, "You Bet Your Sweet Soul." This is followed by a really big production number, "The Seven Deadly Sins," which is by the way already a production number, without a score, in the currently running drama.

Marlowe didn't have foresight for musicals so he didn't

provide a love interest. Back to Goethe to come up with a Gretchen who sings "Who'll Know?" The song has absolutely nothing to do with the show but it will make a good single.

Low comedy is provided for with "The Ballad of Ralph and Robin," two clowns who try to do some conjuring of their own.

Back at the plot, Faustus and his devilish friend are on tour and as the first act nears its end they head up the profusely illustrated production number, "Takin' in the Known World."

Since "Faustus" is not yet a comedy, intermission comes right after the somberly knowing "Misery Loves Company."

The second act opens with an irreverent show stopper, "Poppin' in on the Pope."

The female chorus comes on with "Hubbub, Beelzebub" and Faustus goes on to entertain the Holy Roman Emperor with the ghost of Alexander the Great. This scene isn't really needed, but it does provide the opportunity to present the one really class ballet number "Illusions of Grandeur," appropriately lit and set.

But so much for art, the show continues with a reprise of "Who'll Know" just so they'll know there is a love interest lurking there.

Robin and Ralph, meanwhile, are chasing the local tavern girl, Nan Spit, now a teenage Spitfire, but they stop long enough to watch her do a sexy single teen-age spitfire type dance. If there's too much dance in the second act, this sequence can be moved to Act One.

"Who'll Know" is reprised again, followed by a novelty number that gives Faustus' servant a number while they set up backstage. Learning that his boss will leave him his fortune when he's dead, Wagner sings "Thou Will Be Done."

Faustus, preceded by his reputation, comes across a troupe of players and in a play-within-a-play they lambast him with the wild "You're Not a Horse Doctor, You're an Ass, Doctor."

A mixed chorus of devils sings the big jazz number "Gotha" followed by Faustus' rendition of the second act lament, "Lament."

Lucifer re-enters to sing the inspirational "It's All a Lie" but before the curtain, Faustus discloses that he wrote the devil's contract in invisible blood and with his fingers crossed so it's all invalid; that Nan Spit is not his love interest but the beautiful runaway princess of Westphalia.

The entire company assembles to sing the title song as the

finale unfolds on the seashore where Faustus has gone to live
happily ever after.

MACKAY, Barbara Edith; (2) Theater Critic; (3) b. New York, Oct.
22, 1944; (4) d. Charles E. and Agnes (Talbot) M.; (5) B.A. Wellesley College, major subj.: English literature, 1966; M.F.A. The
Johns Hopkins University, Writing Seminars, major field: poetry,
1968; M.F.A., D.F.A., Yale University School of Drama, major
subj: dramatic literature and criticism, 1974; (6) single; (8) Drama
Critic, Saturday Review/World magazine, 1974-75; drama editor The
Denver Post 1975- ; film critic, Film International magazine, 1975- ;
(9) assistant editor and contributor to yale/theater magazine, 1968-
71; assistant editor, Performance and Scripts magazines, 1971-72;
part-time lecturer, Queens College, Department of Communications,
1973-75; (14) American Association of University Women Fellowship
for Advanced Studies, 1972-73; (16) Democrat; (17) Congregational;
(20) Cont. articles to yale/theater, Saturday Review, Film International; dissertation: "The New Woman in the writing of Büchner,
Ibsen, Strindberg and Brecht."; (21) 116 East 92 Street, New York,
N.Y. 10028; Ph. 212-369-7539; (22) The Denver Post, Denver, Colo.
80201; (24) 60 plays and musicals, 50 motion pictures.

Women on the Rocks
(by Barbara Mackay, SR/World, April 6, 1974)

Gigi and Lorelei still may be wooed with furs, diamonds,
and champagne, but in many of New York's Off-Broadway the-
aters--from Greenwich Village garages to the prestigious Brooklyn Academy of Music--female characters no longer measure
success in inches of mink. Yet even with the current interest
in women's liberation, much of the drama that purports to be
sympathetic still presents familiar sterotypes: woman as diaper-
changer, dishwasher, office functionary, cook, or sex kitten.
Presumably the intention of such caricatures is the exposure of
male brutality and insensitivity. In fact, they only reduce a
complex situation to a simplistic formula; All men are villains,
and all women victims.

In a revival of Elaine May's Not Enough Rope at Broodje's
Cafe Theater, a girl is preparing to hang herself. A young man
breaks down her locked door, not to keep the girl from killing
herself, but to take back the rope she borrowed for her noose.
The comedy gets steadily blacker until the lights fade out on the
girl sobbing hopelessly, clutching her landlady's corpse.

The main character is again a suicidal woman in Diane Kagan's High Time a short play produced by the WPA theater, a
back-room stage in New York's Bowery. Frustrated by loneliness and a meaningless job--pulling a huge brass handle on a
nameless, dial-studded machine--she contemplates the "big jump"
from her skyscraper office. Again a man happens along, a
mountaineer who has conquered all the world's mountains and is

reduced to climbing buildings. Concerned only with getting to the top, he ignores the girl's plea for some slight sign of human affection, and he climbs up as she plunges down.

Presumably, High Time and Not Enough Rope derive from the current interest in feminism. But neither one deals specifically with the problems of women as women. Both plays seem much more concerned with the fact that human beings can't communicate. In the same way, Avra Petride's and Diane Kagan's On the Rocks (also playing at the WPA Theater) would present no problem if the playbill had read, "Women! Men!" instead of "Women! Women!" It's a clever comic adaptation of the Prometheus story, in which Ms. Petrides, a gifted comedienne, slinks and lurches and writhes around the stage, a tortured would-be sculptress tied to a rock above an abyss. But her problem is more than physical: She's emotionally chained to the strutting, glutting bird that daily devours her liver. He's all she's got. But then, she's all he's got, and the play focuses on his problems (he's a bald-headed eagle with vertigo) as much as on hers. Finally, On the Rocks is just a witty dramatization of an old human, and not particularly female, dilemma: Some people can't live with or without each other.

Disquieting Muses, a recent presentation at the Theater at St. Clement's (in a midtown church), illustrates the basic problem again: It might just as easily have been about men's failure to come to terms with life. A "response to the suicides of women artists," conceived and directed by Betsey Shevey, Disquieting Muses lumps together Marilyn Monroe, Virginia Woolf, Billie Holiday, Diane Arbus, Janis Joplin, Sylvia Plath, and Judy Garland. Each of the characters, except for Plath, is dressed identically in platinum-blonde wigs and silver pasties. Each one goes through a series of monotonous rituals--being rejected by her parents, discovering art as an outlet for her frustrations, hiding her true feelings behind the artist's mask--and each ritual is followed by a standard chorus ("I am me," "I am here," "I am woman"). By the end, every move, every speech, every symbolic suicide is predictable. When the sensitive, vulnerable, loving self can't remain locked inside any longer, it destroys the outer professional shell: Billie Holiday covers herself with flowers and lies back to die, Janis Joplin swigs some gin and then collapses, Virginia Woolf covers herself with a blue sheet, representing the sea.

Even the set for Disquieting Muses promises more than it delivers. Cluttered with the stuff of woman's fantasies and nightmares--wedding gowns, dolls, baby carriages, grocery carts, an oven with two bruised legs protruding from it--the stage looks as though it could easily contain settings for seven different stories, instead of one story told seven times. But the really disquieting aspect of the production is the disservice it does to these artists. It reduces their art to a compensation for pain, ignoring the fact that what made Joplin and Garland and Holiday

great singers was precisely their ability to reflect extreme emotion, especially pain. Even worse, by making these seven women neurotic, schizophrenic children, searching for the love
mommy and daddy never gave them, Disquieting Muses gives a
simplistic analysis of their deaths. And, without adequate motivation, these women appear to have been supreme masochists,
bent on self-destruction, instead of the gifted, creative, unique
individuals they were.

Megan Terry's Hothouse verges on melodrama and ends with
the incredible suggestion that when all else fails, a woman can
run home to mama and get the only surefire remedies for heart-
ache--mother love and booze. But Hothouse deserves attention
for two reasons: First, it really is about women; and, second,
it admits the complexity of sexual relationships. There are no
clear villains and victims in Megan Terry's writing; men bruta-
lize men and women use women.

Produced in the Circle Theater, a loft on Manhattan's Upper
West Side, the play takes place in a house shared by grandmother, mother, and daughter. The paint is peeling off the walls,
the plants are dying, the grass is full of weeds, and the women
are alcoholics, perpetually losing their men. The main character is a loud, blowsy, buxom redhead, who shouts a lot about
what brutes men are and drinks a lot to forget how much she
misses them. While men are in the room, she dances, sings,
flirts, and keeps up a continuous, one-woman floor show. Yet
when she is with her daughter or mother, all the bravado and
apparent self-confidence slips away and she becomes a pathetic,
aging earth mother with no outlet for her lust or her tenderness.

Ms. Terry uses this contrast as evidence that woman is her
own worst enemy; she acts like a plastic, unbreakable doll, then
goes to pieces when she is treated like one. What Hothouse
shows, among many other things, is one woman's realization
that she has wasted her life in a useless race against wrinkles
and bulges, dressing up and performing for an audience that
finally doesn't care.

All of the plays mentioned so far show woman at the first
level of self-awareness, waking up to her social and sexual vic-
timization. In Viveca Lindfors's I Am a Woman, a traveling
adaptation of writing by and about women, there are a few fleeting glimpses of women who are already fully awake and beginning to rebel against oppression, women determined to compete
with men or to live without them.

However, the production as a whole is more concerned with
showing the entire spectrum of feminine attitudes toward life than
with making a case for women's liberation. And, as such, it
is a perfect vehicle for Ms. Lindfors's virtuosity. She swirls
onto the stage at the Theater in Space, wearing two capes, a
purse, a hat, and a scarf--basic props that she combines to

create forty distinct, colorful characters. She plays a romantic, adolescent Anne Frank describing her first kiss; Portia in Shakespeare's Merchant of Venice vowing her undying love; a Vietnamese woman telling of American soldiers' brutality to Vietnamese women; and Marilyn Monroe explaining her desire for happiness, not money: "I just want to be wonderful." Yet, as Ms. Lindfors whips through her catalog of characters, there is a strong emotional undercurrent binding the varied images together, a suggestion that woman's main strength is her passivity. Most of the selections imply that she will continue to adapt to, rather than transform society and that her primary objectives in life are marriage and children. Whether she is an unwed, pregnant girl without any way of supporting her child, an aging woman watching her beauty fade, a young girl aching for a perfect, passionate love, or an old mother mourning the death of her son, woman (as Ms. Lindfors sees her) is still primarily a loser, longing for the unattainable and bearing her burdens silently.

Only one recent production shows a woman designing her own life: the Cherry Lane Theater's Dear Nobody, co-authored by Terry Belanger and Jane Marla Robbins. Ironically, the play is based on the life and diaries of the novelist Fanny Burney, who's been dead for 134 years. Along with collaborating on the script, Ms. Robbins plays Fanny Burney, sketching episodes from her life as a teenage girl, a newly discovered novelist, an attendant to the queen at England's royal court, a wife, and a mother. She skillfully impersonates a variety of people whom Miss Burney knew and described in her journals: a hearty, earthy Samuel Johnson, a dapper Richard Brinsley Sheridan, various proper eighteenth-century ladies, and the notoriously improper Mme. de Staël. In the process, Ms. Robbins reveals Fanny Burney to be a witty, willful, unconventional woman who, in that decidedly anti-feminist time, managed to live and work as she pleased.

An increasing number of feminist drama groups and feminist playwrights are appearing all the time. They represent a broad range of political and sexual ideologies, involvement with the women's liberation movement, and dramatic technique. For example, the Westbeth Playwrights Feminist Collective works within a traditional theatrical structure. It consists of five women playwrights and hires directors, producers, actors, and technicians. The It's All Right to Be Woman Theater, on the other hand, is a true theater collective, which rejects the (supposedly masculine) notion of hierarchical organization in its very structure: There are no specified playwrights, directors, or stagehands.

Some groups--especially those who do improvisations or deal specifically with lesbianism--restrict attendance at certain performances to women, on the theory that men in an audience inhibit women's spontaneity. Most of the new feminist groups and independent playwrights are limited by lack of money or

performance space, and as a result, their shows are few and
far between.   But given time and the new public interest in feminist theater, they may eventually provide a revised image of
woman, proud of her sex and determined to solve her problems
by some method other than suicide.

Theater Without Words
(by Barbara Mackay, Saturday Review, February 8, 1975)

A candle burning, a chorus of women moaning, a body sway-
ing, a scream: For many contemporary playwrights and directors, such elements are afterthoughts, special effects tacked on
to enhance a scripted scene.   The text comes first, the texture
after.   Props, lighting, choreography, and music are secondary
to the play's words.

It is not a new attitude primarily in literary Western theater.
When Shakespeare gave Lady Macbeth a taper to carry during
her sleepwalk, he was capitalizing on the candle's practical and
symbolic potential: It could illuminate the actress's face while
it contributed to the generally eerie atmosphere of his scene.
But Shakespeare never intended the audience's attention to be
focused on the prop instead of on the lady's speech.

Antonin Artaud, the actor-writer-director-poet of the early
twentieth century, was probably the most flamboyant critic of
this literary bias in theater.   He envisioned a drama that would
appeal to the senses rather than to the mind, an organic, integral happening--a mise-enscène--in which all the sensual and
production elements would be equal in importance to the text.
Most important, Artaud dreamed of a new theatrical language
"foreign to every spoken tongue," an indecipherable stage-poetry
that could communicate experience and emotion without relying
on rational dialogue.

More recently, Jerzy Grotowski and his Polish Theater Laboratory brought a highly physicalized, anti-literary theater to
the United States.   Though Grotowski does use some established
texts as a basis for his productions, his approach is like Artaud's in that it minimizes the rational aspects of plot and language, while maximizing the importance of physical detail, movement, gesture.

But contemporary American theater does not have a Grotowski or an Artaud.   Nor does it have any playwrights of the caliber of Britain's Samuel Beckett or Germany's Peter Handke,
men who have rejected the notion of theater as a forum in which
ideas must be expressed in distinct, comprehensible monologues
and dialogues, each speech being made up of grammatically correct (or intentionally incorrect) questions and answers, statements, and exclamations.

There is, indeed, a resurgence of interest in mime, judging

from the number of classes in a variety of techniques offered
to actors and actresses in New York City. Although pantomine
is, strictly speaking, the ultimate in non-verbal theater, it does
not automatically offer a new or challenging alternative to conventional verbal theater. Lindsay Kemp's Flowers, for instance,
was an instant flop on Broadway: Decadence without words, it
seems, is not altogether that different from decadence with
words. And the beginning of Athol Fugard's The Island, during
which two laborers transform a bare stage into the torrid, dry,
buggy island on which they are prisoners, fades off into a moving, but conventional, spoken drama.

All of which contributes to my appreciation of two experimental productions that were offered, oddly enough, about three
doors away from one another this winter, on a littered, nondescript street off Manhattan's Bowery.

The New York Theater Ensemble is a scruffy little theater
that houses some of the best and some of the worst avant-garde
groups in New York City. When I went there in December to
see a small group called Mabou Mines, there were, five minutes
before show-time, three other people in the audience: I prepared for the worst. Instead, I watched not only the best production of Beckett's Come and Go I have ever seen or expect to
see but also a delightful exercise in absurdity, The B Beaver
Animation. In this collaborative work, the protagonist is a stuttering beaver that, "ssssummoning ssssangfroid," narrates what
seems to be the story of his daily life and his failure to construct, in reinforced concrete, the perfect dam.

I say "seems to be" because this is an extremely impressionistic playlet, with nothing like a conventional plot. Instead,
a series of visual and verbal suggestions gradually coalesce in
the mind to form a story. But the events onstage are so rich
and swift that there is no telling whether I got the whole, or
only, story. In fact, there are probably as many stories in a
Mabou Mines animation as there are audience members who have
seen it.

Nothing in B Beaver matches, from the odd scraps of material, wood, and metal that make up the set to the studiously
outlandish costumes: One of the five characters wears a silk
Japanese dressing gown, sneakers, and a pair of sunglasses
with only one lens. The language is equally incongrous. One
character begins a sentence; another ends it. Two or three or
four characters speak at the same time. Words overlap; images
irrelevant to one another are thrown together. Then suddenly
out of the general verbal hubbub, a phrase bubbles up to the
surface and bursts out, clear and comprehensible to guide the
audience along. At one point, for instance, the beaver says,
"I go under," which is as much a reflection on his general state
of mind as it is of his physical action. Then blue lights play
over the stage, a piece of metal is shaken, making a vaguely

liquid sound, the actors gurgle, and the scene continues underwater.

Superficially, B Beaver is simply an amusing mind-game,
a clever illustration of a confused, hapless existence. But at
the same time, it's an intriguing, successful theatrical experiment. Instead of dismissing words, as mime does, the group
transforms language into rhythmic patterns and creates offbeat
associations that demand an intuitive, rather than a rational, response. And the play's linguistic anarchy, in which "meaning"
becomes available only in periodic flashes, encourages a mental
engagement in the viewer--but a specifically imaginative, not an
intellectual, engagement--a willingness to let associations flow
freely and to let the play take shape slowly, if at all. After
being mentally numbed by many productions--on and off Broad-
way--that demand nothing more than a modicum of applause, I
found that a night with Mabou Mines could be exhilarating. As
I left the New York Theater Ensemble, my brain percolating,
even the bottle-strewn Bowery looked good.

Whether or not they dress their characters in long robes
and set them among Corinthian columns, most directors who
want to reinvigorate the Greek classics usually begin with a desire to be utterly faithful to the original. Andrei Serban, the
young Romanian director whose three Greek plays christened the
new La Mama Experimental Theater Company Annex this winter,
apparently begins with a zealous infidelity, at least to plot and
text. Although he uses the originals (the Medea of Euripides
and of Seneca, The Trojan Women of Euripides, and Sophocles'
Electra), Serban strips the plays to their bare outlines, then recreates the basic emotional states about which Euripides, Sophocles, and Seneca were writing.

The Trojan Women, the longest and most varied of the three
works, is made up of various highly animated incidents: A bare-
breasted Cassandra performs a mad dance before she is led into captivity; Helen of Troy is brought in, her hair symbolically
shorn, her clothes ripped off, and her body smeared with mud;
a Trojan virgin is raped by her lusty Greek captor. These episodes are interspersed with very subdued scenes--some so quiet
that they become visual tableaux--of Andromache bathing her son
before his death, of a weaver committing suicide, of the Trojan
women being transported from their homeland.

While all these highly charged emotional moments re-create
familiar emotions--fear, grief, pity, horror, love, despair,
hatred--they are distinctly unfamiliar theatrically, in part because the productions upset many of our expectations of what it
means to be an audience. In the Medea, for instance, the audience follows the actors into a small, dark area, the way lit
only by candles, then into a cavernous, rectangular hall; there
the play proceeds in a narrow path between banks of audience
members seated on benches and on cushions on the floor. In

The Trojan Women, too, the audience follows a procession of actors into the huge (100 feet by 38 feet by 40 feet) main playing area, where the first part of the play is performed in the spectators' midst: When Helen of Troy is wheeled in, in a tumbrel, the audience quite naturally becomes a crowd of Trojans watching her humiliation.

But the main explanation for the curious sense of theatrical newness at these plays is that they are presented in a rough approximation of the original Greek and Latin, the ancient languages having been distilled into an assortment of unfamiliar sounds--harsh guttural noises and strange consonant blends like KX and PTH. Under the direction of composer Elizabeth Swados, this language--or anti-language--is rarely spoken: It is sung, whispered, chanted, shouted, and often accompanied by a drum, a flute, or a single bell, so that speech itself serves as a kind of elemental music.

Using a great variety of instruments (including recorder, conch, mandolin, and gamelan) and an equally great variety of tunes reminiscent of everything from Near Eastern folk songs to Greek Orthodox liturgical chants, Ms. Swados creates more than a musical background against which some idea or emotion is presented verbally: Her music and lyrics becomes the precise expression of that emotion.

When Cassandra's captor leads her off like an animal with a rope around its neck, she repeats three notes over and over again, her voice quivering slightly; when Andromache washes her son's body, she kneels on a ramp above him (the audience stands below them both), wailing a harsh, monotonous, nasal chant, a sustained cry that seems to be ripped from vocal cords raw with weeping. Both scenes are theatrically very simple; yet they are evocations of grief and longing that burn into the memory. More than a month after I had seen The Trojan Women, I found it impossible to forget the sound of those laments.

Nor can I forget certain visual images. In one scene a weaver walks up a long ramp, plunges a knife into her stomach, then twists in slow circles down the ramp, her hair and gown billowing out around her as if under water, while blue-green lights dapple her drowning body.

It's virtually impossible, though, to talk about discrete visual or verbal effects in Serban's work. Much of the impact of the weaver's death scene, for instance, depends on the contrast between the slow, sinuous movements of her body falling, and the steady, light rhythm of flute, drum, and bells, suggesting a graceful underwater dance of liberation, rather than a macabre suicide.

Unlike so many "committee" productions, in which the physical properties, the lighting, the blocking, or the set are at odds with the play itself, apparently designed by experts who never seem to have so much as corresponded about the play, all the physical elements in the <u>Medea</u>, <u>Electra</u>, and <u>Trojan Women</u> are in perfect accord. When Aegisthus descends a ramp in <u>Electra</u>, he is personification of brutality and force: His low, guttural curse, the live snake wrapped around his neck, his heavy body advancing toward Electra in menacing, slow steps--everything about him symbolizes evil.

Serban's plays are also unlike much so called symbolic drama, which never really establishes the validity of its symbols and therefore remains flat and one dimensional. These productions work on several levels at once. At the end of <u>Electra</u>, the chorus and main characters walk in, each with a handbell of different size and pitch. Instead of detracting from my emotional appreciation of the scene, the fact that I associated the sound of the bells with Christian Easter celebrations added to it: I was put in mind of the ritualistic origins of the <u>Electra</u> and of the general connections between all spring rites of cleansing and regeneration.

In many ways, Serban is Artaud's perfect <u>metteur en scène</u>: He is interested in the mythic aspects of drama, he knows how to realize the theater's physical potential, he talks of appealing to "the intelligence of emotion" rather than to the intellect, and he has created a new language capable of expressing feeling rather than thought. Most important, Serban's productions accomplish something that directors and critics often talk about: something that is, nevertheless, rarely done. Instead of using theater realistically--as a photographic replica of contemporary life, giving us back a catalog of familiar thoughts, incidents, and human characteristics--Serban uses theater as a hazy mirror, reflecting a more elemental, archetypal reality, in which the "classic" emotions--love, hatred, jealousy, rage, pity--regain the massive proportions denied them in much modern, realistic drama.

Because <u>Medea</u> has returned once (the original was done at La Mama in 1972), there is reason to hope that all three Serban productions may return to New York again someday. They are currently scheduled to go on tour in Europe in the early summer. As for the Mabou Mines, they perform sporadically, whenever they find a vacant theater. A new animal animation (<u>The Shaggy Dog</u>) will probably be ready some time this spring, and there are rumors of a three-play Beckett evening. Anyone sincerely interested in New York's best experimental theater should keep an eye out for these productions, and--in the more distant future--for the return of Andrei Serban.

McKENNA, Timothy; (2) Film and Theater Critic; (3) b. Paterson, New Jersey, March 25, 1948; (4) s. Joseph L. and Anna T. (Kunitski) McKenna; (5) B. A. Montclair (N. J.) State College, major subj. :

mathematics, 1971; graduate study in linguistics, New York U.,
1971-72; (6) m. Marie Basile, Sept. 1, 1974; (8) Reporter, The
Paterson News, 1971-72; music critic, feature writer, The News,
1972-73; film-theater critic, The News, 1974- . Listed on First
Night Critics List, League of New York Theaters and Producers;
(9) Wrote story for tentatively titled American International film,
"Neighbors," 1973; (10-16) no civic activities, no political activities
no directorships, no military service, no awards, no memberships,
no political affiliation; (17) Roman Catholic; (18) no lodges; (19) no
clubs; (20) no other published writings; (21) 417 Valley Road, Uppe
Montclair, N.J. 07043; Ph. 201-744-0640; (22) The Paterson News
News Plaza, Paterson, N.J. 07509; Ph. 201-274-2000; (23) Circula
tion: 80,000; (24) 50 plays, 50 films; occasional concert and reco
reviews; interviews and feature stories on film and theater.

"Blasts and Bravos": Make-Believe Mencken
(by Timothy McKenna, Paterson News, January 17, 1975)

In many respects, "Blasts and Bravos: an Evening with
H. L. Mencken" is a fine one-man show.

Paul Shyre is an engaging actor and he seems very comfo
table playing Mencken. None of his mannerisms or gestures
seem exaggerated or unnatural, and none of the props he employs, such as a beer mug or cigar, are unduly prominent. T
show has a nice easy pace to it, the lighter anecdotes alterna
pleasantly with the more serious or pointed ones. Eldon Elde
set--designed to simulate the study in Mencken's Baltimore hc
--is modestly attractive and cozy in the tiny Cherry Lane The
atre.

In fact there is only one problem. The man that Shyre p
sents is not Mencken, not at least as I know him.

Now I'm not an expert on this famous writer and philolog
but I am familiar with some of his important work, and the s
face biographical details of his life. As Shyre presents him,
Mencken was all homespun wisdom and crackerbarrel humor--
sort of an urban Will Rogers. But the real Mencken was far
from this.

He was totally independent, he was self-educated, and he
hated pretension and pomposity as much as any salt-of-the-ea
philosopher. And he refused to come to New York to work;
spent his entire life in Baltimore.

But he was, throughout his life, a serious thinker who tc
his work and ideas seriously. Shyre would make you think tl
Mencken wanted nothing more out of life than clothing, shelte
and a good beer. But the man was a firm rationalist and he
spent his life pursuing the benefits of rational, even scholarl
endeavor.

Consider, for example, that one of Mencken's most important works is his "American Language," a book he originally
published in 1918 but revised and expanded throughout his life.
It's still considered a basic source of information on the varieties
of American speech.   He also wrote a volume on Nietzsche's
philosophy, a book which probably isn't a definitive work today,
but is in retrospect a noteworthy achievement, considering that
the German philosopher was not widely accepted by American
scholars before World War II.

But Shyre, who adapted the play himself, is content to present us a man who was obsessed merely with attacking propriety
and the Fundamentalist Christianity which was the established
religion of his day.   To be sure, Mencken delighted in ridiculing
"frauds" and sacred establishment figures, but his lasting accomplishments are based on his very sound thinking, not simply
his iconoclasm.   Lines such as "America's the greatest show on
earth" don't begin to convey the man's depth.   And unfortunately,
this quality is the thing "Blasts and Bravos" fails to capture.

A Stunning "Cat" Makes Its Bow
(by Timothy McKenna, Paterson News, March 28, 1975)

If this current Broadway season were to last another 10
years it still couldn't offer us a worthier production than its
first serious drama, the revival of Tennessee Williams' "Cat on
a Hot Tin Roof," which opened Tuesday at the ANTA theater.

This production deserves all the praise that was heaped upon
it this summer when it was first staged in Stratford, Conn. , and
all of us who missed it have to be supremely thankful that ANTA
and the American Shakespeare Theatre have decided to bring it to
Broadway intact.   You couldn't ask for more in an evening of
theater; the play is one of the most absorbing and thought-provoking of modern American dramas, and it's been given a flawless production, with direction, sets and lighting bringing out its
best qualities.   And most important of all, the cast is superb.

Let me begin at the logical starting-point: the performance
of Elizabeth Ashley, which is magnificent.   It is fitting that she
has gotten so much attention in the press since she began the
role in the summer, for it will take at least a dozen good reviews and interviews to fittingly describe her interpretation of
Maggie, the "cat" of the title who is burning with desire and
frustration over her loveless marriage to Brick.   Surely one of
the four or five most beautiful contemporary actresses, Ms.
Ashley uses her appearance to make Maggie irresistibly sexy.
When she adjusts a stocking in front of an imaginary mirror or
sensually combs her fine, shining hair, the effect is almost in-
describable; it makes Brick's neglect of her as he drinks himself into oblivion all the more exasperating.

But she doesn't stop with the surface aspects of the role.

Her characterization is extraordinarily multi-faceted. She is threatening and bitchy, and at times she appears to embody the exaggerated feminity which her latent-homosexual husband sees in her. She also seems to grow in strength and honesty as the play moves towards its climax and in the final moments a genuine sense of humor emerges once she has "talked away" her pain. And at the climax she becomes the one truly decent member of Big Daddy's family. You are not likely to see a better actress in this role ever again.

Though he understandably doesn't make the spectacular impression that Ms. Ashley does, Fred Gwynne is also excellent in the role of Big Daddy. His tall, lean figure gives him a naturally comic look, but he overcomes this with a masterful handling of Southern vocal mannerisms, and his Big Daddy is solid and even dignified in a blunt, unrestrained way. As he constantly repeats himself, relishing the feel and taste of his own words in his mouth, Gwynne expertly conveys the character's typically exuberant and outgoing nature.

This leaves us with Keir Dullea as the ex-athlete Brick and Kate Reid as Big Mama. Dullea has, perhaps, the play's toughest role, since he must simply hobble around on a crutch and silently anger everyone. He does the task justice. In his appearance and movements he is perfect.

Ms. Reid is possibly a bit too comic in such a negative play, but her role is much shorter than the others, and she, of course, had to breathe life into it.

There is just enough space to say that John Conklin's set is stunning, the supporting cast is fine, and the play itself grabs hold of you and doesn't let you go--it is that exciting. "Cat on a Hot Tin Roof" will be at the ANTA, 245 West 52nd St. only through Nov. 16. There's no excuse for waiting for something better; it's the real thing, as they say.

MacLEOD, Beatrice; (2) Theater Critic, Ithaca Journal, Ithaca, N.Y.; (3) b. Jan. 15, 1910, Bensonhurst, N.Y.; (4) d. William D. and Edith Waldo Beach; (5) B.A. Swarthmore College 1931, MFA Yale Drama School 1934, Major studies literature and drama; (6) m. Robert Brodie MacLeod, September 1936; (7) children--Ian Fullerton (deceased) and Alison Stuart (now Dvorak); (8) Teaching, Swarthmore College 1934-46, Ithaca College 1949-51; (9) Director of summer stock, The Forty-Niners at Chase Barn, Whitefield, N.H. 1933-41; Director, Montreal Negro Theatre Guild, 1946-48; Board member, Ithaca Festival of the Arts (abortive) 1965-70; (10) Co-founder, Parents' Committee for the Children's Ward, Tompkins Co. Community Hospital; Co-founder, Friends of the Ithaca Co-op, Inc.; Executive Secretary, Tompkins Co. Mental Health Society (3 years); (12) Executive Secretary, Telluride Assocation (an educational trust based at

Cornell University); (15) Phi Beta Kappa, League of Women Voters;
(16) Democratic; (17) None; (20) Children's book, "On Small Wings,"
Westminster Press 1959; (21) 957 East State St. , Ithaca, N.Y.
14850, Ph. 607-273-6654; (22) Telluride, 217 West Ave. , Ithaca,
N.Y. , Ph. 607-273-5011; (23) Circulation: Approximately 20,000;
(24) (All theatre including musical theatre): about 40 reviews/year.

"Imaginary Invalid"
(by Beatrice MacLeod, Ithaca Journal, October 2, 1974)

In a recent television showing of the British import, "Theater of Blood," London's drama critics, one by one, were appropriately done to death by a man of the theater who considered
himself wronged by them. Any viewing critic could not be
blamed for having a few tremors, and wondering at the temerity
of his own occasional harshness.

A good-sized audience at Ithaca College Tuesday night laughed
loud and long at the premiere of Molière's "Imaginary Invalid."
For the most part, however, they were not laughing at Molière,
but at a kind of sledge-hammer reading of Molière's plot that
works so hard at being funny that it's exhausting. There, I've
said it; now "come, sweet death," but let it be with a rapier?

This satire on the medical profession in 17th century France
is built around a hypochondriac who so delights in the attention
gained through his real and imagined ills that he is the prey of
quacks and the despair of his household. His stinginess gives
rise to the idea of marrying his daughter to a doctor, to save
on medical bills, and he picks a marvellously unsavory specimen.
His daughter, of course, has ideas of her own, as does his predatory wife,--and the household is saved from disaster only by
the wits of Toinette, the clever and indefatigable maid.

All of this absurdity, in Molière's hands, is a kind of comic
ballet--playful, sparkling, light-hearted, its thrusts at society
done with fencer's foils. The Ithaca College production does
not lack talent. Kip Rosser's Argan is endlessly inventive, agile,
and versatile at milking laughs; Joni Fritz in the role of Toinette
is a study in high-energy perpetual motion, and communicates
the sense of fun which should permeate the whole play.

And there are others who find, at moments, the grace of
style which is Molière's hallmark. But for the most part the
acting is burdened with too much business, too effortfully done.
The "silvery laughter" of the comic spirit is drowned in the
heavy guffaw.

The physical production is quite charming: Donald Creason's
set is tasteful and beguiling, nicely lit. Ritchie Spencer's costumes are attractive and work well. Joseph Tague's pleasant
harpsichord recordings announce the proper style even if the
performance gets its own way.

Molière, the acknowledged master of comic drama, had impeccable taste, and a sense of economy. The Ithaca College "Invalid" would do well to pare down its tricks of business by about half, and lower its decibels--closer to the range of the harpsichord.

"Anthony & Cleopatra"
(by Beatrice MacLeod, Ithaca Journal, November 15, 1974)

Of all of Shakespeare's great tragedies, "Anthony and Cleopatra" is probably the one least often performed. Its canvas is vast, its legendary leads captivating, quixotic, somehow larger than life. Among the tragedies, it is the only one which welds the themes of love and power, so bonding them that it's impossible to disentagle the strands. And its movement through history, as Octavius Caesar gathers in the victims of his wars--including Egypt--gives the play a density of texture not always easy to follow.

The Cornell production under James Clancy's direction is performed on a single set by Joan Churchill, and the visual experience is magical. Actors emerge from and disappear into labyrinthine ways; Doug Marmee's storybook costumes now glimmer, now blaze in the fitful, kaleidoscopic lighting. There are masks and antic movement, armor and plumed helmets, blood and ritual and death. All of this plus a vividly orchestrated pattern of sound held the opening-night audience quite mesmerized.

The most difficult stretch for young performers is the stretch to middle life, and it must be remembered that the Cleopatra and Antony of Shakespeare's play are mature people. Barbara Dean and Dana Mills are both strong and charismatic, even managing to convey something of the tarnish of experience--which makes the miracle of this late love poignant and finally ennobling.

Mills has tremendous vocal power, grace and energy of movement, and an intelligence which seems to clarify and focus the scenes in which he appears. Dean resists the impulse to let either the rages or the raptures of her Cleopatra become kittenish, maintaining a dignity in this astonishing woman that is compatible with mid-life.

Actually, Shakespeare has carefully characterized all of the portraits in his panoramic cast, though reading and close study make this more visible than the quick exposure of a single performance. Some whose clear individuality emerge from the crowd are the delightful Enobarbus of Patrick Husted, the warmly loyal Alexas of Rolf Hansen, the Soothsayer of Gary Frumess, and the Dolabella of Donavan Diez. The Octavius Caesar of David Savran is properly self-important, colorless and insensitive; and Timothy Baker plays a useless, shallow Lepidus, as written.

What the performance chiefly lacks is clarity--a sharp focus

on lines and actions which must be perceived for continuity.
Not that the narrative sequence is so important, but with all the
comings and goings and changes of scene, one needs a ribbon to
follow simply to avoid confusion.

One surprising bit is a scene showing the murder of Pacor-
us, son of the Parthian king. Beautifully and theatrically staged,
it's a happening which Shakespeare refers to, but does not include. To show it is an interesting notion, but it doesn't significantly forward the motion of the play.

There is much in this production of "Antony and Cleopatra"
which should encourage viewers to go back to the script--to
catch a missed bit of cause and consequence, to savor again
some of the most glorious poetry in the language. And they will
go back with a visual imagery not likely to be forgotten.

Campus and community deserve at least one Shakespeare a
season. This one will play through Sunday, and next Thursday
through Saturday, at the University Theater in Willard Straight
Hall. Read it first, if you can. If you can't, see it anyway.

McREYNOLDS, Janet; (2) Theatre and Film Critic; (3) b. Bluffton,
Ark., July 19, 1933; (4) d. Joe and Vergie (Jones) Ballew; (5) B.J.
University of Texas, major subj.: journalism, 1955; M.A. U. of
Oregon, major subj: English, 1962; Ph.D. U. of Minnesota, major
subj.: English, minor Theatre, 1970; (6) m. William McReynolds,
Sept. 1, 1962; (7) children--Jesse, Jill, Tristan; (8) Theatre and
Film critic, Town & Country Review, Boulder, Colo., 1972-73; The-
atre and Film critic, Boulder (Colo.) Daily Camera, 1974- ; (9)
Assistant director, Nomad Community Theatre, 1971; author of one-
act play, "Kathia" produced at The Changing Scene in Denver, Colo.,
1974; (16) Democrat; (20) A novel, I Have A Great Desire, Houghton-
Mifflin, 1962; poetry in many small magazines; doctorate disserta-
tion, "Image of the Theatre in Victorian Literature," on microfilm,
University of Minnesota; (21) 2990 18th St., Boulder, Colo. 80302,
Ph. 303-443-8566; (23) Circulation: 40,000; (24) 60 plays and musicals, 50 motion pictures, 3 dance.

"Miracles"
(by Janet McReynolds, Boulder Sunday Camera, March 2, 1975)

Germinal Stage Denver is presenting two short plays which add
up to as rich an evening of theatre as I have experienced this season.
The plays, under the canopy title "Miracles and Other Diversions"
are character studies of the down-and-out who somehow rise for
another bout with Life, the hopeless who, drinking their cup of
bitterness, find a brief and perhaps illusory reprieve at the bottom.

They are symmetrically balanced: two men in the first and two
women in the second.

John Mortimer's "The Dock Brief" has a whimsical, Dickensian flavor, with enough exaggeration to push it over the rim into the Absurd. Morganhall is an English barrister who has grown old while waiting for all the opportunity to try his first case. Fowle is a mild-mannered murderer who, being without hope, is "free to be kind." He enters wholeheartedly into the barrister's hope of launching a new life upon the successful conclusion of his case. In a frenzy they work up the case for the defense, with the adaptable Fowle taking the parts of judge, witnesses, and jury. But for Morganhall it is a repeat of his one love affair: when the time for action finally arrives, he is too exhausted.

Ed Baierlein gives a flawless performance as the unlucky Morganhall, walking a thin line between pathos and caricature, with his expired hopes and exploding fantasies. The fumbling gestures and wheezy voice suggest a ghost wandering the endless corridors of a deserted Victorian mansion.

John Seifert in his first major role at the Germinal is perfectly insane as the harmless wife-murderer, Fowle. He proves himself a comedian of the first order.

The second play, Tennessee Williams' "The Mutilated," has a symbolic framework. The action takes place on Christmas Eve, and explores the relationship between two women. Upstairs in the Silver Dollar Hotel sits Trinket Dugan, alias Agnes Jones, mutilated. Trinket's life is altered; her mutilation is more psychological than physical. She is trapped in unending spirals of loneliness. In the lobby and on South Rampart Street Celeste Delacroix Griffin prowls, her mind deranged, her body a foul sewer no man will touch. The two, typical of Williams' theme of the war between spirit and flesh, are estranged, and what it costs each of them is the burden of the play.

Nancy Yeager, as Trinket Dugan, is the perfect Williams heroine, frail, vulnerable, transparent in her hope and in her exquisite consciousness of being a wounded animal.

Melody Ann Page, who lives in Boulder, is making her first appearance at the Germinal as Celeste. She is a major talent, with her snapping black eyes and body like a rag doll whose stuffing is beginning to burst through the seams.

There is also a marvelous supporting cast which serves as a chorus. Vince Zaffiro gives an impressive performance as the night clerk at the hotel. Ed Baierlein is effectively cruel as the sailor temporarily snarled by Trinket. The costumes by Penny Stames are particularly good.

Scenes from Two Marriages
(by Janet McReynolds, Boulder Sunday Camera, March 9, 1975)

It is hard to explain the fascination of Ingmar Bergman's

S"cenes from a Marriage." There is little drama, no nudity, the subject is banal and for long periods there are only two people on screen. The film, which was originally a six-part television series, may be the ultimate soap opera: the weepy cliches elevated to a high art.

In spite of the subtitles pasted across the picture, "Scenes" is a peculiarly American experience. Liv Ullmann, with her china-doll prettiness, her upfrontness, her vulnerability and her breathtaking gift for life, is our new representative woman. Her statements in recent interviews indicate that her real-life personality is very close to the character she plays on the screen. The distinction between life and art is further blurred by our knowledge that she has lived with Bergman and is now raising their child.

The plot is almost a case history of the emerging American female, victim and heroine of the Sensuous Revolution. The script is being rewritten in bedrooms all across the country. The educated, careered, well-to-do are dropping out of marriage with as much compulsion as, a decade ago, they dropped out of the Establishment. To the liberated woman and the spouse who-- frequently--has supported her liberation, divorce seems the next logical step.

Johan and Marianne, the characters in Bergman's modern morality play, are the ideal couple. Their lives are perfect to the point of banality. They have a good income, a comfortable home, two children, cultivated friends, loving families, an interesting life. They each have a career. He is a scientist who writes (we are led to believe) mediocre poetry. She is a lawyer specializing in divorce cases. They have bought the myth of their own completeness. Their sex life is not what it once was, and affection takes more time than they can afford. Nevertheless they are forever telling each other how happy they are in their showcase marriage.

True to the soap opera genre, Erland Josephson, as Johan, is always seen from the woman's point of view. His face a register of weaknesses, self-conceit, evasions, regrets, Josephson operates from the feeling that his position as husband and father is basically ridiculous. He is always having to pump up his ego.

The film begins with Johan and Marianne being interviewed for a magazine article. He is a boastful, squirmy little boy reciting his list of accomplishments, adding with a facetiousness that is intended to embarrass Marianne that he is very good in bed. She is constrained, self-conscious, looking at him for approval of every phrase she utters. About all she can say about herself is that she is married to Johan and has two daughters.

Another couple comes to dinner and unleashes the dogs of matrimonial hell, while Johan and Marianne ooze concern and pity. Afterwards they wash dishes together, comfortable in the knowledge it could never happen to them.

Then one night it happens. He tells her that he has fallen in love with Paula and is flying to Paris with her the next day. Ullmann's face is a perfect mask of woe as she absorbs the shock. He is as repellent as a negatively charged pole, but she clings like a sticky burr, fighting for her very identity, her life. Further humiliation arises when she calls a friend and is told "they" knew all along.

The next Scene shows the emerging woman. Marianne, girlish in a new frilly blouse, is radiantly in possession of herself. He is a mixture of cockiness and guilt, a typical male on the loose. She wants him to be interested in her mind, her new discoveries about herself. She brings out the journal she has been keeping for her analyst and reads. "From my early years I was taught to be secretive and deceitful. I never knew what I wanted. I always thought 'what does he want me to want?.'" To him this is only a dreary prologue to love-making. He falls asleep while she is reading.

Then they are in his office to sign the divorce papers. She is confident, motivated, cruel, demanding immediate sexual satisfaction (on the floor). He responds to her hard, glittery gaiety, only to be repulsed as soon as the sex act is over. He strikes her, out of frustration and need. Their civilized ways have brought them to this?

This would be a miserably bleak film without the last Scene. Marianne and Johan are each married to other people. Like a pair of guilty children they sneak away for a weekend in the country. Freedom and self-enlightenment has not brought them happiness. Watching him build a fire, whistling, absorbed in the homely task, she sees that his frame has shrunken, he is showing his age, at the same time he is simple, like a child. She feels a new tenderness, seeing how he has accepted his limitations.

Past all the lies and entanglements, they at last have time to be merely human. Two people alone in a dark house in the middle of the night.

In John Cassavetes' film "A Woman Under the Influence," Gena Rowlands is Marianne without the education, career, understanding analyst: a woman with no identity of her own, nothing between her and insanity but her husband and kids. This view of a woman "going under" is stark and primitive, perhaps the most powerful film ever made about a working-class family. Rowlands, as Mabel, looms large and menacing on the screen, standing off doctor and family as her mind races like a runaway train, totally out of control. As the camera circles her, isolates her, she loses her humanity, becomes a trapped, potentially dangerous animal. Something to be subdued.

What has to be subdued, finally, is Mabel's sensuality, which is in conflict with Nick's sense of propriety. She is like an unstable gas, an unpredictable element in his solidly masculine world. Nick brings a crowd of his friends home. She is too anxious to please. They don't know what to make of her as she circles the table, asking each one to dance. When Nick is embarrassed he turns brutal. Mabel being seductive, being "turned on" by his friends, is a disturbing intrusion of the personal. She is beat down like a too-friendly dog, she sits cringing at the table. "I can be anything you want me to be, Nick. Just tell me what you want me to be."

Peter Falk gives a very fine performance as a man who misses all the signals, who hasn't for all his very real love the foggiest notion of who Mabel is. The existence of a real Mabel beyond the class structure they are both locked into is a threat. When Mabel is due home from the hospital he invites all his friends, fills the house with people, then has his mother send them all home. Just the family attends Mabel's coming-home party. Rowland's performance in this scene is almost unbearably painful, the rising terror in her eyes, the uncontrollable contortions of her face as the forces that drove her crazy in the first place begin to close in again. She runs to the bathroom and tries to kill herself.

Then the kids move in, a funny, tender bundle of resistance that ends in a new vision of family unity. They are as beautiful as any children I have ever seen on screen, and utterly convincing in their portrayal of the separate world of childhood.

MAHAR, Ted; (2) Drama Editor, The Oregonian; (22) The Oregonian, Portland, Ore. 97201, Ph. 503-221-8327.

MANCINI, Joseph, New York Post, 210 South St., N.Y., N.Y. 10002, Ph. 212-349-5000.

MANGOLD, Elva; (2) Film-Drama critic, short story writer, plays, lyricist, articles; (3) b. Phila., Oct. 2, 1919; (4) Rose & Henry Publicker; (5) U. of Wisconsin; Marjorie Webster College (secretarial); (6) m. Maxwell J. Mangold, May 16, 1945; (7) Three sons: Jon, Mark, Dan; (8) Drama-film critic or other columnist, at present for The Long Island Entertainer, Our Town, Queens Tribune and its four branch issues, Jersey Pictorial and its five branch issues, Jewish Journal, L.I. Jewish Press, Westchester Jewish Tribune, Twilight mag., The Synagogue Light, The New York Single ... all newspapers except Twilight; (9) Write interviews of theatrical personalities. Occult column for one year for Singles mag., now defunct. Write travel column and recipe column for Jewish Journal. Articles on various subjects like Condominiums; Health; Hotels; Restaurants. Did drama reviews on radio, L.I. stations (like WLIR-FM) for hosts

Bill Clark, Richard Hoffman, Alan B. Allan etc.; (14) First Prize
Short Story, Phila. Regional Writers' Conference, 1966. Winner
1965 lyric writing contest for newspaper L. I. Entertainer; (15) Overseas Press Club ... was only drama critic, male or female; (16)
Democrat; (17) Jewish; (19) Hadassah, life member; (20) First Story
Job, book of short stories under pseudonym E. P. Maxwell, 1961,
Pilot Press. Two anthologies of Broadway and Off Broadway play
reviews ... Calling The Plays, 1966 & 1967 seasons. Stories in
anthologies and text books of Dell (The Outnumbered); Delcorte Press
(same, hardcover); Scribner's (hardcover and paperback), Impressions In Asphalt; Holt & Rhinehart, paperback, Search for America;
Noble & Noble, paperback, Crossroads and now, January, 1975, Mc-
Graw Hill's Focus--Themes In Literature. Did book and lyrics of
children's play played in upstate N. Y. schools. Wrote lyrics for
musical, Castle On the Dee, by David Levitt which previewed upstate
New York school; (21) 40 Park Ave., New York City, N. Y. 10016,
Ph. 679-8282; (22) Same; (23) The nine papers reach a million readers. (Breakdown on request); (24) All Broadway and Off Broadway
plays (am on Second Night List) ... approximately 75 plays yearly.
100 motion pictures. Sometimes do dance reviews, cover animal
shows at Madison Square Garden etc.

Film Drama Reviews
(by Elva Mangold, Westchester Jewish Tribune, October 1974)

It isn't every play that can get a glowing review from one
critic and a devastating one from another! Unfortunately I agree
with the detractor. Cat on a Hot Tin Roof has had its day.

Although Tennessee Williams dominated the drama scene of
the Fifties and Sixties with his gift of making doom and defeat
palatable and theatrically powerful, his last four plays have shown
his magic to be rapidly disintegrating. Perhaps it started with
Cat on a Hot Tin Roof because it's evident in this story about a
doomed plantation family unable to communicate that Williams'
control of style and writing is dissipating. The three acts are
little more than monologues ... first by Maggie, the Cat and
Brick's shunned wife; secondly by Big Daddy and finally by Big
Mama. (Elizabeth Ashley, Fred Gwynne, Kate Reid.) It's extremely tedious watching Elizabeth Ashley (whose voice is much
too gentle to penetrate the massive Anta theatre) being allotted
no more action than combing her hair, taking off her stockings
or fixing her eye makeup. How long can you stand watching
THAT? Conversely, the stunning scenic platform, a cutaway of
a marble and draped bedroom, overwhelms the action
(John Conklin) and detracts from Maggie's Martha Mitchellish
babbling. Perhaps the lethargic pace of the play is due to Michael Kahn's direction or his reluctance to cut drastically the
times when the actors are repeating exposition for the third and
fourth times.

What dates this Williams drama whose other plays about
desperation and death hold up magnificently (witness last season's

Streetcar success) is the growth of sophistication or acceptance
society has covered in the twenty years since Cat's inception.
Cat's story is about plantation owner, Big Daddy, dying of cancer; about coverup tactics to hide Brick's alcoholism; about homosexuality and the guilt of sex.   The components of the tragedy,
mired in their own hells, lie to each other, not only unable to
speak of their hangups but unable to escape them.   Today all is
different.   Cancer, no longer considered like leprosy, is spoken
about openly; an alcoholic can go to a psychiatrist or A.A.; homosexuality is now mostly a way of life and either Brick or his
frustrated wife would today simply break up the relationship and
start new lives.   It is thus harder to relate to Cat's characters
than to, say, Streetcar's Blanche or Stanley and his wife.   Sexual enslavement, boorishness, desperation, disgust, are emotions
always with us and as long as Williams concentrates on degradation and cruelty, people will probably flock to his plays.   Cat
fails because of its flowery, overlong, rambling writing; because
it's dated and because Fred Gwynne, as Big Daddy, was sadly
miscast.

Playtime
(by Elva Mangold, Queens Tribune, February 14, 1975)

Elward Albee's new play isn't a good one.   Even interspersed
in the one glowing review calling it "a major event" are words
like "triteness" and "aimlessness" which tell the real truth of
the matter.   What is Seascape?   Certainly not a comedy.   There
are no witty lines.   The only humorous aspect is the appearance
of two lizards (Frank Langella and Maureen Anderman) who drift
in from the sea to the dunes where languish a restless, still attractive, middle-aged wife (Deborah Kerr) and her listless husband (Barry Nelson).   Unlike Virginia Woolf, this Albee married
pair don't converse, discuss or battle.   Nancy, the wife, a wa-
terfall of words, does all the talking.   Hubby, Charlie, does little more than grunt except when wistfully recalling childhood days
spent weighted by stones, on the bottom of a pond.   (This tactic
lost me altogether.   How can one hold one's breath more than a
few minutes, hardly enough time to indulge, as related, in rem-
iniscing?)

Nor is this a poetic or philosophical treatise on Life.   All
that's ascertained is Nancy's conclusion, in effect, "life is short.
Have fun while it lasts."   After the appearance of the lizards
and the ensuing discussion about what it's like for humans and
for serpents, both couples come to the trite conclusion that all
living creatures feel the same emotions and, shades of Merchant
of Venice, that old "do we all not bleed when stabbed?" chestnut.
Finally Nancy arrives at the profound conclusion that evolution
is inevitable and how about starting immediately?   The play ends
with Nancy helping the lizards begin life's evolutionary process
instantly as if, three weeks from Thursday they'd shed their
scales and grow appendages.   So much for common sense!

James Tilton's seaside set is ingenious and breathtaking and those brilliant lizard costumes (Fred Voelpel) should be donated to a ballet company. They will outlast the play. Or should.

This Day of the Lizard is no Night of the Iguana. Even if you can accept that lizards can reason and speak English, there's A Delicate Balance between fantasy and reality which Albee hasn't bridged in this lifeless jumble. I hope it's not All Over for America's boy wonder.

MARKOFF, Hildy (aka Jeri Michaels); (2) Theatre Critic; (3) b. New York, Sept. 12, 1929; (4) d. the late Joseph Friefield and Shirley Chall Friefield Karpf; (5) B. A. Hunter College, major subj. : English, 1951; (6) m. Gerald Norman Markoff, Apr. 6, 1952; (7) children--Michael Joseph, Steven Richard; (8) Model, New York, 1951; Crowell Publishing Co. , New York, 1952-2; Playwright on Staff, Hillcrest Country Club, N. J. , 1961-66; Social columnist, News Dispatch, N. J. , 1961-66; Drama Critic, News Dispatch, N. J. , 1964-71, Managing Editor, News Dispatch, N. J. , 1967-72; Managing Editor, Jewish Dispatch, N. J. 1971-72; Asst. Editor, Bergen News and Sun-Bulletin (separate papers) 1973-74; Theatre, Film, Variety, Restaurant Critic, Bergen News, N. J. , 1973- ; Theatre, Film, Variety, Restaurant Critic Sun-Bulletin, 1974- ; Theatre Critic, Tao, N. J. , 1975- ; (9) Co-producer, Hillcrest Country Club, N. J. 1961-66, Co-authored Industrial Show, 1965; Original Play produced ("Ticket to Tarboro") on Strawhat Circuit 1970; Lyricist of songs played and sung at Horizon East, N. J. 1974- ; Discussed Theatre on Cable TV, Ft. Lee, N. J. , 1974; Conducted Cable TV celebrity interviews, Channel 6, Westchester County, N. Y. , 1975; (15) Charter member Teaneck Theatre Guild, N. J.; First President of the New Jersey Drama Critics Assn. , 1973-75; Mem. No. Jersey Press Assn. 1975-; (16) Republican; (17) Jewish; (21) 228 Lakeview Terr. , Teaneck, N. J. 07666, Ph. 201-833-1026; (22) Bergen Newspapers, 113 Grand Ave. , Palisades Park, N. J. 07650, Ph. 201-947-5000; (23) Circulation: 50,000 homes; (24) 80 plays and musicals, 40 motion pictures, 90 miscellaneous.

Yours Truly
(by Jeri Michaels, Bergen News, August 15, 1974)

"Luther," the fourth presentation I've seen at the New Jersey Shakespeare Festival on the Drew University campus in Madison, is perhaps not the most enjoyable production on their repertory list, but probably one of the most difficult. This assessment is drawn from two facts: first, the subject matter itself is tremendously complex in that it deals with a quite controversial religious genius, Martin Luther: and secondly, approximately 43 years of complicated action must be covered in the short space of something less than three hours. My hat's off to them for trying and that they almost succeed is more to their credit than not.

Because the performances are, in general, of the highest
caliber, I suppose that my quarrel is less with the company than
with John Osborne's script.   However, Paul Barry, the troupe's
artistic director, as well as this production's director and star
may have to share some of the fault.   Further, I suspect that
he became so involved with the character and his own portrayal
that he somehow failed to detect a sloppiness in tying all the
myriad facts together logically and coherently for the audience.
That is, Mr. Barry may be thoroughly steeped in Luther and his
background, but his audience may not be, and thus, it is up to
him not only to dramatize, but to educate.

So, before you see it, let me fill you in briefly on what it's
all about.   Martin Luther, the central figure in a period of religious, political, economic and intellectual ferment known as the
Reformation, was born in Germany, and became a Catholic priest
in 1507.   A trip to Rome opened his eyes to the corruption of
the Church and was intensified when a Dominican, John Tetzel,
sold indulgences which, he claimed, would release the souls of
departed relatives from Purgatory; this being done in behalf of
the Archbishop of Mainz for the purpose of paying off debts ac-
crued from his purchase of titles.

Luther then wrote his famous "Ninety-five Theses" which he
posted on the door of the church in Wittenberg, and offered to
defend them against even the Pope unless proven wrong by the
scriptures alone.   He advocated a return to a simpler form of
Christianity, opposed the power of the Roman Catholic hierarchy
and defended the rights of the princes in their conflict with the
Pope.   While his original commitment was for more equitable
treatment of the common man, as he himself acquired more power, he adopted those very attitudes he had formerly fought
against.   After his excommunication his views prevailed enough
to encourage the establishment of national churches in northern
Europe.

True, this is an oversimplification of an enormously complicated individual in a difficult era, but an explanatory note such
as this with the program, might have helped some members of
the audience over the rough spots and given this show greater
mass appeal.

It would seem to ask a great deal for people to watch a play
concerned with materialism versus theology without some questions arising in their minds.   For myself, I questioned whether
Luther's father would have been so hostile to his son's monkhood
during a time when the Catholic Church was the font of all learning and
practically the center of the universe?   The supposed storm vision
which brought about Luther's hasty decision on monkhood is still at issue and this, I felt, was not brought out firmly enough.   And later, the
peasants revolted, but against whom, and for what?   Mercifully,
Luther's epileptic fits are kept at a minimum, but the author's

preoccupation with his bowels seems excessive. Why was his debt to Frederick of Saxony never mentioned--which might have explained his leaning toward the princes? Why was he never referred to as Knight George, the alias he used when he went into hiding? According to this play, at a time when heretics were burned at the stake, the biggest radical of them all was walking around loose and preaching rebellion to the church as it then stood.

Despite all this, the performances are excellent and Paul Barry's is almost unforgettable--though there were times that I wondered whether he was agonizing over his war with the devil or his constipation. Nevertheless, it is a brilliant performance and one worth seeing.

Peter MacLean as Tetzel won enthusiastic applause from the audience because he directly involves us in his portrayal by coming down from the stage to harangue us and entreat us to purchase indulgences for our sins. As a matter-of-fact, this was the second time this week I'd seen Peter since he is featured in the opening sequence of "Friends of Eddie Coyle" now playing in our local movie houses. There's an energy and vitality to this man that seems lost on screen and like Charleton Heston, he appears to be more comfortable in costume drama as a man of another age. Yet herein he provides the comedy relief, if you will, and that's another dimension to his talent.

Albert Sanders, Brendan Burke, William Preston, Richard Council, Kenneth Gray, Margery Shaw and Richard Rossome, all actors we've reviewed in other roles who here put forth their finest efforts--they'd have to in order to keep pace with Paul Barry. And watching them again is like visiting your family-- such is the warm feeling you develop from seeing these familiar faces time and again in repertory. And when combined with the intimacy of this theatre, there is a closeness between audience and player that I've seldom if ever seen. Bravos too for the cast of 40, who offer solid support for the principal players.

Treat yourself to this rare and wonderful experience with a trip down to Drew and one of the Shakespeare Festival's five presentations--it is well worth it.

Yours Truly
(by Jeri Michaels, Bergen News, November 2, 1974)

Imperfect Ideal. The challenge of seeking perfection is explored once more in the myths surrounding King Arthur and his Knights of the Round Table, this time set to music by Allan Jay Lerner and Frederick Lowe, and dubbed, "Camelot." Sadly the current Paper Mill Playhouse production is rather like a fabled beauty who turns out to be a mere Plain Jane. That is to say, the show is colorful and mildly entertaining, but more interesting for its players than its place or pace.

For one thing, it does drag in spots and for this, director Stone Widney deserves full blame. For another, the set design by John Pitt is far too realistic for an idealistic show. True, semi-spiral steps are quite utilitarian, but they do detract from the quality of illusion necessary to the story. And aside from being rather unattractive, they would appear to be dangerously steep for the actors to manage without a guardrail. My advice to them is never look down.

What the sets lack in eye appeal, costume coordinator Vida Thomas has supplied with lovely and elegant costuming. It's a pleasure to look at men's legs for a change (we females can be chauvinists too) and some of the costumes worn by Arthur and Lancelot are stunning indeed--most particularly, Arthur's avocado green outfit!

Those who have never heard of King Arthur may be somewhat enchanted by this tale, but those of us who are aficionados of old, will need Merlin to turn the trick. You remember of course, how this peasant lad became king by removing the sword Excalibur from the stone where it had been placed by the childless late king; how he married the beautiful Guenevere, created an Order of Knights for the preservation of Right through Might; how his favorite knight, Sir Lancelot dallied with the queen and through the connivance of Arthur's illegitimate son, Mordred, was brought into conflict with the king; and how this ultimately brought about the down fall of camelot--you do remember all this, don't you? Like it was yesterday, of course.

Well, here they all are--the whole lot of them, dashing about with swords and armor, listing, tilting, jousting, singing, dancing and occasionally joking. Michael Allinson is very Rex Harrisonish as King Arthur and I felt his discomfort with the youth of the role at the play's beginning, but as the evening progressed and the character aged, his performance improved dramatically (if you'll forgive the pun). Allinson makes no attempt to sing, but delivers his songs recitativo--which is a lovely and dignified contrast to the rest of the cast. This makes his character someone special--as well he should be!

As Guenevere, Leigh Beery is lovely to look at with a delicate and sweet soprano, but she seems to lack the charismatic quality that grabs an audience making them feel what's happening to the character is important. In other words, I don't believe anyone cared whether she went to the stake or not--in fact, a good fire might have warmed things up a bit.

And now we come to dandy Don Stewart who portrays Michael Bauer on the daytime serial "The Guiding Light" and Lancelot in "Camelot." Apparently, Stewart's effect on females is overpowering, but it oftimes embarrasses me to be one when the ladies are making a public display of themselves. However, he's fairly nice looking and brings a surprisingly good voice to the

role--and I say this despite the nightclub work I've seen him do.
His "If Ever I Would Leave You" receives the greatest applause
of the night.   He has a good deal of grace on stage and his attempt at a French accent does bring a certain flavor to the
part--even if both the accent and flavor slip at times.   But--and
this is a big but--he doesn't bring the kind of warmth to the role
that would make the romance credible.   Except for one moment
when he drops to a knee before the lovely queen, there seems
to be no relationship between them; they're each in love in their
own little world, separate and apart.   When he says "I love
you," I don't believe it.   Those are words that cannot be easily
said across a room, so imagine how much more difficult across
a stage!   And he could look happier about all his curtain calls,
after all, that's a lot of love coming his way.

The show's only light moments are delivered deliciously by
Michael Lewis as Pellinore, and if he has lived too long in the
shadow of his famous parents, Sinclair Lewis and Dorothy Parker, then this is his time to shine.   Shine he does.   The inclination of course is to dismiss this kind of performance by saying
that the part itself is a winner, but those of us who have seen
less of a performance in it can appreciate Lewis' value.

The villain of the piece, Mordred, is spirited and properly
whiny as played by Noel Craig.   Indeed, he's the sort you love
to hate!   The play really comes alive whenever he's front and
center plotting his villainy.

The rest of the cast is more than competent and a few more
chorus numbers like "Fie on Goodness" might have helped this
show tremendously.

And fie on less than goodness, for although there is no such
thing as perfection--only the ideal, the same is true of this show.

MARKS, Arnold; (2) Entertainment Editor; (3) b. Philadelphia, Au-
gust 4, 1912; (4) s. Morris Marks and Esther Joel Marks; (5) B. A.
U. of Washington, Journalism major, 1935; M. S. Columbia U. , 1939,
Journalism; (6) m. Isabelle Ruppert, Oct. 3, 1942; (7) child--
Rupert William Joel, deceased; (8) Oregon Journal, reporter, 1946-
48; Entertainment Editor, 1948-present; TV Editor, 1954-present;
(9) Press Secretary to Major Amos Peasley, 1939; Editor, Pasco
Herald, Pasco, Washington, 1946; NW correspondent Motion Picture
Boxoffice; (13) U. S. Army 1942-46; (15) Member Sigma Delta Chi,
Sigma Alpha Mu; (21) 15 Greenridge Court, Lake Oswego, Ph. OR 9-
7034; (22) Oregon Journal, 1320 SW Broadway, Portland, Ore. 97201,
Ph. 503-221-8275.

SRO's "Oklahoma!" Entertainment Magic
(by Arnold Marks, Oregon Journal. July 3, 1976)

Rodgers and Hammerstein's now-classic musical, "Oklahoma! ," emerges as entertainment magic as the opening production of the Portland Civic Theater's Summer Repertory Onstage fourth season on the main stage.

This newcomer, ably directed by Bill Dobson, has a lot going for it. "Oklahoma!" builds beautifully with an enthusiastic cast of alert, joyous, mostly blue jean and gingham-clad players headed by two standouts in the leads as Laurey and Curly--singers Carol McGilvra and John McEvoy.

The set is tops and the show is presented without an opening curtain. A thrust stage and wings of natural wood project the players closer to the audience--covering the orchestra pit. The 10-piece orchestra under direction of Norman Mikelson is barely seen by the audience behind a back stage scrim. So good is the music (about the best this writer ever has heard for a little theater production) that on first impression it sounded like an "Oklahoma!" soundtrack.

The effective set was designed by Glenn Gaurer, the SRO's artistic director. It is impressionistic with simple props, either lowered from overhead or put into position quickly during blackouts by ranchhand members of the cast. This is a curtainless show, with the decor providing the farm scene with windmills.

The entire cast is bright and on its toes. Dobson keeps them in lively movement with never a lag. Choreography deserves mention. Young Rachel Klevit, a Schumacher dancer, provides show-stoppers with her assortment of dance routines performed by lithe, young talent, both male and female.

McEvoy fits the Curly role. He is a tall, handsome young man with a rich, vigorous and audible trained voice. He is a pretty good actor as well.

A beautiful blend is Miss McGilvra as Laurey, the coy farm girl the cowboy loves. She performs brilliantly with a charm that matches her crystal-clear voice.

If the movie musical ever returns, this pair could turn the eyes of studio talent scouts. Even so, they don't overshadow others in the cast.

Richard Hurst and Patsy Maxson provide rich, lusty comedy as Will Parker, the lovesick cowboy, and Ado Annie, the little girl who just can't say no to her boy friends.

Hurst is a PCT all-around entertainer. He gives his Parker role the works. Miss Maxson, in her third season as a guest artist, gives the sexy role a wild comedy touch.

Standouts include Robert Nielsen as peddler Ali Hakim and

Edie Gunnar as the fun'loving Aunt Eller. Keep an eye on petite Vicky Vose. She's well-cast as the giggling Gertie.

"Oklahoma!'s" hit songs are done with expertise.

McEvoy's opening, "Oh, What a Beautiful Mornin'" and "The Surrey with the Fringe on Top," as sung by McEvoy, Miss McGilvra and Miss Gunnar, set the scene.

Hurst's "Kansas City" and Miss Maxson's "I Can't Say No," are rousing comedy numbers complete with dance sequences. Tops, too, is "People Will Say We're in Love," the pensive love song by McEvoy and Miss Gilvra.

But tremendously dramatic is "Lonely Room," sung by Gerald Morgan as the villain ranchhand who lusts for Laurey. Morgan sings with solemn sincerity in a deep, moving voice.

Some of those dance routines are as exciting as an old John Wayne saloon brawl--particularly "The Farmer and the Cowman."

Costumes by Margaret Ball are tremendous.

This is one production that has everyone on stage doing something--with each bit adding to the enjoyment.

This musical is highly recommended.

Producer Eyes Portland
(by Arnold Marks, Oregon Journal, July 15, 1976)

Gene Persson, Broadway, off-Broadway and London producer and director, is in Portland this week surveying the possibility of launching a professional theater.

Persson, no man to be discouraged, is a stage, movie and television veteran, perhaps best known for the hit Broadway musical, "You're a Good Man, Charlie Brown," now set for its 10th anniversary production.

Discussing the pros and cons of a small theater that would stage contemporary productions, some fresh off the Broadway or London stage, Persson outlined both his administrative and production abilities.

From the lineup of his credits, including the recent San Francisco staging of Tennessee Williams' latest, "This is an Entertainment," it is evident he has plenty.

It is his opinion that the future of the theater is the regional theater.

"This is where new plays emerge today," he said. "Broadway

has gone totally commercial. It is a matter of economics and only great plays make it there--the big musicals and the comedies. When people are willing to pay $17.50 a ticket for a musical and $15 for a play, they want to be pretty sure what they are going to see. That's Broadway."

A theater? He will want a 700 to 800-seat house. The problem is to find something suitable in Portland.

This could be a shopping center or a downtown location.

His cast? He wants to put together the strongest company possible, and this would mean stage names--not movie or television names, particularly.

Auditions would be held in Portland, in San Francisco or New York. In the course of his recent survey, he has found many stage personalities eager to do a "season" in Portland or elsewhere in a fresh-off-Broadway or new play.

In addition to players, there are name directors eager for such experience.

Persson has been working with Williams on "This Is An Entertainment" with about 80 per cent of the production rewritten. Even though it did play to near capacity at the Geary in San Francisco, the play received mixed reviews. Before it heads for Broadway, it will have a new treatment, he says.

He finds Williams a fantastic, highly disciplined writer and considers him one of the greatest living American playwrights.

This is one reason why he would like to name the new theater "The Tennessee Williams Theater." As a memorial to the living writer, he says the project would have immediate recognizability--an aid in getting theater grants on a national level-- funds that would be matched here.

Persson, producing for 18 years, says he has considered the possibility of a Portland theater carefully.

Not only is it the only large city on the West Coast where a professional theater could be developed, but he would enjoy living here as well.

He says he would continue his commercial stage, film and television production work, with Portland as his headquarters. He lives in the Los Angeles area at present.

In addition to Williams' play, Persson has introduced black playwright LeRoi Jones' controversial plays, "Dutchman," "Toilet" and "Slave" to the stage in the '60s.

His motion picture version of "Dutchman" won Cannes and Venice
Film Festival awards. Jones is now Imamu Baraka and lives in
New Jersey, Persson says.

It will be interesting to see how Persson develops his proposed new Portland professional theater.

MARRANCA, Bonnie; (2) Theatre critic for the Soho Weekly News
from March, 1975. Previously wrote for Changes; (3) b. April 28,
1947 in Elizabeth, N. J.; (4) d. of Angelo and Evelyn (Mirabelli);
(5) B. A. in English (1969) from Montclair State College, N. J. and
U. of Copenhagen. Currently a Ph. D. candidate in Theatre at the
City University of New York. Dissertation topic: "The Aesthetics
of Mabou Mines." (6) m. Gautam Dasgupta on Aug. 1, 1975; (8)
Theatre Critic: Changes (1974-75), Soho Weekly News (from March
1975); assistant to Broadway press agent Max Eisen, New York City
1968; co-Editor, Performing Arts Journal, April 1975; (9) Taught
theatre in the School of General Studies at Lehman College in Spring,
1974. Member of Who's Who in American Colleges and Universities
(1969); University Fellowship (1974-75) at CUNY-Graduate Center;
Administrative assistant at Theater in Education, New York City
1970; Assistant to Playwright-producer Irv Bauer, 1970-71; Assistant
in Street Theater Division, New York City Dept. of Cultural Affairs,
1973; Teacher, Lehman College, CUNY, Spring term 1974; Adjunct
Lecturer, Richmond College, CUNY, Summer 1976; (20) Editor of
The Theatre of Images (Drama Book Specialists, 1976) Essays and
reviews on theatre, books, and music have appeared in The Nation,
Village Voice, Arts in Society, Drama and Theatre, Margins, Rolling Stone, Jazz Magazine (Paris) and Jazz Nytt (Sweden), Stereo
Review, and others. Founder and Editor (with husband Gautam Das-
gupta) of Performing Arts Journal in 1976; (21) c/o Drama Book
Specialists, 150 W. 52nd St. , New York, N. Y. 10019; (22) Soho
Weekly News, 111 Spring St. , New York, N. Y. 10012, Ph. 431-3150.

There, There, and There
(by Bonnie Marranca, Soho Weekly News, October 23, 1975)

Heidegger once wrote, "The human condition is to be there,"
an observation which Samuel Beckett carries to its painful end.
For Beckett, man is there, and there, and there ... Life and
death are one long, continuous present.

In "Mabou Mines Performs Samuel Beckett" we are given
three glimpses of death-in-life in a trio of works that run the
rhythmic cycle of comedy, melodrama and tragedy. The program of Play, Come and Go, and The Lost Ones is less than
ninety minutes, but in that short amount of time the dramatic
impact of Beckett's language, combined with the powerful visual
settings given his works, have left us so moved that it is no
wonder no one can applaud when The Lost Ones, and the program
itself has ended.

Each work is dominated by a central image: gray faces that look partially decomposed peep out of funeral urns in Play; Come and Go is visualized in a stage-length mirror that reflects the shimmering image of three women; in The Lost Ones the audience sits in an environment that suggests in sound, light, texture and mood the "flattened cylinder fifty metres round and eighteen high for the sake of harmony" from which those lost to life vainly try to free themselves.

Lee Breuer, who directed these works, has captured the Beckettian landscape of lost souls in stunning mise-en-scenes. Front spotlights that first surface on the three horizontally alligned urns (designed by Jene Highstein) suggest the Byzantine icons of medieval art. The cascading flow of words that pour out of the mouths of husband, wife, and mistress in sequential monologues are interwoven and repeated endlessly, orchestrated by an inquisitory spotlight. The eternal triangle is doomed to repeat the banality of their soap-opera drama that only Beckett could give philosophical significance to by dividing it into two parts: the emptiness of the past and the now of recognition.

Ruth Maleczech, Joanne Akalaitis, and David Warrilow have trouble with Beckett's staccato rhythms of despair, and the technical co-ordination of the lights has not yet been perfected, but a few splendid new lighting touches have been added at the beginning, and the actors have grown more into their roles since I saw this same production last spring at TNC. With time and practice, the rough spots can be easily ironed out.

Come and Go is performed by Ellen McElduff, Maleczech, and Akalaitis to perfection. The mirror effect is the coup de maitre of this "dramaticule" about personal loss and illusions. The mirror allows the actor to come in and out of a "frame," as it were. For example, when one character leaves the bench two are left, another leaves and one comes back. Yet, the three actors are always there--if only in half-light. As in Waiting for Godot, Happy Days, Endgame, and so on through Beckett, characters always remain on stage to face their personal destinies, however many games they may devise to keep themselves going.

The Lost Ones is the most extraordinary piece of the evening by virtue of David Warrilow's extraordinary performance. The metaphysical impact of Beckett's prose chamber work ranks with the Divine Comedy and Book VI of the Aeneid as a vision of the underworld. In a murky, yellow village of the damned where temperatures waver from boiling to freezing point, 200 people search in vain, alternately looking to escape through a cylindrical niche, and hunting for their beloved. Philip Glass's minimalist score captures the longing of these doomed travellers in tingling electronic sound that echoes the sound of distant wind chimes.

Warrilow, dressed in shabby jacket and trousers is the lisping, Irish narrator of the piece, his complex execution of the role spanning shades of voyeurism, humor, clinical detachment, sensuality, anguish, and perversity. That Warrilow alone sustains a piece so demanding in its dry, archaic and convoluted language is a tribute to his technical giftedness. He is the finest actor to surface in an avant-garde ensemble since the Open Theatre gained prominence.

Warrilow uses a combination of commentary and motivational techniques in his characterization. At times he simply describes the frustrated attempts of the "lost ones," using the small spongy cylinder, ladders and figurines that are situated on the floor of the environment so imaginatively realized by Thom Cathcart. Or, he will act out the difficulties of men and women who try to make love after their bodies have desiccated. Arms akimbo, twisting and stretching against the sponge-rubber walls that line the room he recalls, in one of Beckett's rolling, measured sentences, the pleasure when a husband and wife unknowingly meet in the cylinder and copulate--"The spectacle then is one to be remembered of frenzies prolonged in pain and hopelessness long beyond what even the most gifted lovers can achieve in camera."

Aside from relishing Warrilow's remarkable portrait there are the temporal-spatial dynamics of the production to admire. Breuer has theatrically conceived The Lost Ones with at least four perspectives in mind: that of the narrator; the narrator in the role of a "lost one"; the model of the cylindrical world; the experience of the audience living through time in an environment that approximates the cylinder. Beckett's formidable work is thus vicariously felt by an audience which experiences fluctuations in light, darkness, noise and mood. When, at the end of the piece the recitation resounds in total darkness, it is like the end of the world. With the light snuffed out, only the sound of silence remains.

This evening of Beckett must be seen not only for the care and precision of its production, but also for its studied capture of Beckett's complex vision. It is also the most thrilling Beckett that has been done in New York since Hume Cronyn and Jessica Tandy's performance in Not I at Lincoln Center's Forum a few years back.

"Quo Vadis, Richard Foreman?"
(by Bonnie Marranca, SoHo Weekly News, December 25, 1975)

"Yes, my films do have a beginning, middle and end, but not necessarily in that order." The words are Jean-Luc Godard's but the sentiment can also be attributed to Richard Foreman, who in Rhoda in Potatoland (Her Fall-Starts) offers us a text which is inside out. In other words, what follows precedes so that "at the end you are at the beginning which is where you should begin." However, Foreman assures us, the contacts he

makes with his source are "very erratic." Indeed, it is difficult
to remember what happens in the first part, and to compare and
contrast that with the second, and vice versa. The effect is deliberately disassociational because Foreman is not interested in
memory or remembering--the way audience members keep in
mind parts of the theater event that correspond to their own past
experiences. He is more concerned with what he terms the
"moment-by-moment" experiencing of art in images, ideas, perceptions that flow in and out of the mind.

In Rhoda, whose most obvious literary ancester is Lewis
Carroll's Alice in Wonderland, the journey is used as a metaphor
for aesthetic distance, ie. , the intellectual and emotional distance
the spectator travels to the art object in an understanding of it.
The route of the journey is the charted landscape of Foreman's
mind, and Foreman, who has given the American theater perhaps
the purest form of psychodrama up to this time, now puts forth
another dream play. But this one is a nightmare. Like tiny
Alice, Rhoda's adventures unfold in a world of surrealism that
ignores all normal laws of time and space. Objects shrink or
grow to gigantic proportions, surroundings shift from indoors to
outdoors in quick succession, and musique concrete mixes freely
with jazz, classical and French cabaret music. Those who people this world roam like dazed strangers in a foreign land, encountering other people and objects whose value is purely symbolic. The performing space is defined by a long, deep series
of alternating steps, planes and inclines which is continually reorganized by sliding flats and props. Rhoda has the quality of
a ride through a funhouse, and it is no wonder that this play--
this realm of distorting mirrors--has so much of the grotesque
element in it, outwardly evidenced in the use of the masks and
trolls and inwardly depicted in thematic conflicts. There is a
nod to the influence of monster movies, too.

In a Foreman play the intellectual and the sensual are always in conflict. Thus, in Rhoda the landscape of the mind is
juxtaposed with the landscape of the body which he characterizes
in spatial terms as "a beautiful vista," and of himself he says,
"I live in an imaginary country." Foreman, taking the grand
tour is--to continue the tourism metaphor--trying to photograph
(via the stage) the unphotographable: the functioning of the human mind (thought process).

What results are snapshots--captured moments--of Foreman's life; in particular, his relationship to Kate Manheim, who
plays Rhoda in this production. Whereas in last year's Pandering to the Masses: a Misrepresentation, the focus was on Max,
this time it is on Rhoda. Rhoda/Kate functions as both Icon
and Idea, and her crucial place in the Ontological-Hysteric Theater is not to be underestimated. She also serves as Foreman's
double, but not only his double. In a "triple play" move Foreman at one point leaves his booth in the first row of audience
bleachers, where he sits throughout the production running its

organizing tape system, and goes on stage. His real-life double,
actor John Matturri, stands behind him while Rhoda (Kate) goes
to the tape; then, Matturri goes to the tape while Foreman faces
Rhoda.

Aside from the personal relationships that appear to be sub-
jectified in Rhoda, Foreman is very specific about his own feelings as an artist--his bourgeois feelings. "OK. I wanna be
famous," says Rhoda, who at times wears a laurel wreath.
Foreman's double asks, "Aren't you the famous Richard Foreman? It's an honor to meet you. I admire you very much."
Again, at the end of the play Foreman gives his obsessiveness
with his public image full rein: "Who am I? Why do I want you
in my audience? What will you say about me behind my back?"
he inquires in his own voice on the tape. A look at the theater's
newspaper advertisements and the program notes will reveal that
Foreman has adopted for the first time Broadway's personality
cult mannerisms in the part of his ad that reads "staring (sic)
Kate Manheim and Bob Fleischner." Though Rhoda is at times
a very witty piece of writing, this sort of advertising strikes
me as less a manifestation of playfulness than desperation or
frustration. The crucial question--suggested by the parentheti-
cal "Her Fall-Starts" is, What is Foreman trying to tell us?
One can't be sure whether he means private or public success.

It is ironic that at this point in his life Foreman has chosen
to write a play overtly concerned with success or failure. Rhoda is playing to full houses; in 1976 Foreman's plays will be
published in two anthologies, and he will direct The Threepenny
Opera at the Vivian Beaumont, as well as a film and a play in
France. Perhaps the real question is, Will Success spoil Richard Foreman?

Clearly, with Rhoda Foreman has reached a critical point
in his career. He appears to have gone as far as he can with
his particular thematic concerns (in the form he has chosen to
present them): from objectification of experience to subjectifi-
cation, from repressed sexuality to an embracement of eroticism,
from concern for the acquisition of knowledge to recognition of
the limitations of the human mind. While once rigorous observation of events on stage substituted for the viewer's personal
experience as the key to understanding a Foreman work, now
repeated viewing of his works is making many of the elements
of his theater predictable. There is a difference between repetition and style.

With Rhoda the gap between Foreman and his audience seems
to be closing. Though Foreman has been accused of elitism (or
writing plays that no one can understand), I think it is a fundamentally democratic impulse that operates in his theater which
seeks to level everyone, ie., makes artists of us all. (John
Cage is a similar case in the field of music.) Foreman's love-
hate relationship with the audience is indeed paradoxical: on

the one hand, he must train audiences to view his theater in the "moment-by-moment" unfolding of it (by scanning rather than gestalt approaches) and, on the other, he is repulsed by audiences' traditional viewing of theater--their selecting elements of it that reinforce learned patterns of emotion and response.

Foreman, in fact, may even be negating his own Brechtianism (a strong element in his theater) on one level by integrating the audience in the work and asking for the IDENTIFICATION (or at least empathy) of the audience with the artist. If he hasn't done this then he has at least succeeded in partly bridging the gap between the audience and the event by moving the dialectic from the stage (where it remained in Brecht's theater) to the relationship between the stage and audience as the play evolves (here he has surpassed Brecht). In my estimation, Foreman has truly created a theater of the moment; like Gertrude Stein, he has succeeded in creating an "actual present" in his work.

Theater-in-the-making has always been Foreman's chief concern. So, throughout the production the refrain sounds in the author's (the dominant voice in this production) taped voice: "Make a comparison. That's what I did." Foreman plays Wittgensteinian language games with us, such as comparing a boat and a shoe; at times, the stage functions as a laboratory in which the audience's perceptual abilities are tested; Kantian synthetic judgments are made of events on stage; finally, the audience is told to look for the space in the audience, a very eerie, moving experiment (derived from Paul Dirac's theories) best explained by Foreman's "Third Manifesto" in the current issue of The Drama Review. Teaching plays or consciousness-raising group encounters--that's what his plays are when they aren't serving as Foreman's actual diaries or carrying on a dialogue with Western epistemology.

A highly complex, multi-dimensional experience, the Ontological-Hysteric Theater. Yet, Rhoda is more accessible than any of Foreman's recent pieces. It is a more erotic work, too, whose languid women recall the fin-du-siècle decoration and eroticism of a Gustav Klimt painting.

Though I would place the Ontological-Hysteric Theater clearly in the Theater of Images tradition of the last dozen years (and a style that is strong in the current works of newcomers to the theater scene), Foreman's work is literary in the sense that one can read it for references to literature ("Look, look, the lamp lights up" is from Breton's Nadja), painting (Duchamp, Ernst, and others), philosophy (mostly German), and psychology (Ehrenzweig, Freud, and others).

There is no dialogue in this theater except what is internal-- among the elements, not the characters. How, then, is communication possible? Perhaps the question is best answered by one of Foreman's own statements from a short essay he has just published in Confrontation, entitled "The Future of the Theatre: The Theatre Falls, accurately, to Pieces:"

> ... our attention is FILLED by a
> morsel of
> the world that enters and exits,
> immediately
> superseded (and/or superim-
> posed upon) by another
> morsel entering from a different
> direction. And
> the theatre will capture that
> BEING THERE on stage
> of each item, and retiring into
> the wings of that same item,
> waiting for its next momentary
> re-appearance
> on the boards of consciousness.

Consciousness--it is the password by which one enters the special world of the Ontological-Hysteric Theater. The rewards are many and they do not come without effort but the effect can be exhilirating. This is an experience which affords the opportunity to experience the present in the present (not by reflection in the past). The journey to the self is equal to the aesthetic distance traveled by the viewer to the theater event.

MASTERS, Les, Phoenix Gazette, 120 E. Van Buren St., P.O. Box 1950, Phoenix, Ariz. 85004.

MASTROIANNI, Tony, Cleveland Press, 901 Lakeside Ave., Cleveland, O. 44114, Ph. 216-623-1111.

MAYER, Ira; (2) Assistant editor; (3) b. New York, June 10, 1952; (4) Ludwig and Trude (Mayer); (5) B.A. Hunter College, major subj.: communications, 1973; (6) single; (8) weekly contributor, Village Voice (New York) 1970-75, assistant editor, Record World (New York) 1974-present; (17) Jewish; (20) Freelance contributor: Village Voice, Sunday New York Times (Arts & Leisure section), contributing editor--Modern Hi-Fi & Music, articles to Country Music, Audio, New York Post; (21) 210 West 70th St., New York, N.Y. 10023; (22) Record World, 1700 Broadway, New York, N.Y. 10019, Ph. 212-765-5020; (23) Circulation: 16,000--trade; (24) 12-15 musicals, 100 popular music & jazz concerts.

"A Chorus Line:" A Total Musical
(by Ira Mayer, Record World, June 28, 1975)

While Broadway is currently experiencing its best season in several years, the bulk of the credit goes to straight drama and

comedy. "The Wiz" and "Chicago" have been two musical exceptions, but nothing in recent years has been the total musical
that "A Chorus Line" is. The show is now at the New York
Shakespeare Festival Public Theater and moves to Broadway's
Shubert Theater July 25. All too often stage musicals consist
of songs thrown in the middle of a not terribly cohesive book.
In "A Chorus Line" the music is a part of the story and actually moves the play thematically along.

Conceived, choreographed and directed by Michael Bennett,
"A Chorus Line" is the story of an elimination audition for eight
roles in the chorus line of a new Broadway musical. Each of
the contenders gets a chance in the course of the audition to give
his or her background; all dance in different size ensembles and
most have the opportunity for singing and dancing solo. The intensity of a scene during which one of the potential chorus liners,
Paul (played by Sammy Williams), describes discovering his own
homosexuality, and the development of his career in that context
is such that the audience is left in a stupor. It is one of those
rare moments when applause is completely out of place, and silence a true tribute to a stunning performance.

Marvin Hamlisch's score is just that. The music is always
there, a part of what's going on, and one could easily believe
that there are twice the 12 numbers listed in the program. The
melodies are very hummable and Edward Kleban's lyrics are intelligent and frequently witty. The music is not only accompanied to the dances; it provides an omnipresent pulse for the
entire production.

The unqualified rave is perhaps the hardest review of all to
write. The production now on view was six months in prepara-
tion at the Public Theater. Every detail has been carefully
worked out. But the flow, from the first minute, is overwhelming. There are no seams. The music, dialogue, dancing, humor and drama are completely integrated. And while Williams
and Donna McKechnie might be said to have the featured roles,
the entire cast is uniformly superb.

"A Chorus Line" revives interest in the musical as an art
form in a way that has for a long time been missing. See it.

"Chicago": An Entertaining Evening
(by Ira Mayer, Record World, July 19, 1975

If "Chicago" has its share of "Cabaret" influences, it is still
a fully entertaining Broadway evening. For while "Chicago," at
the 46th Street Theatre, lacks the strength of "Cabaret's" book
and the natural setting it provided for the John Kander/Fred Ebb
score, it nonetheless has an abundance of fine melodies and the
seemingly inexhaustible talents of Chita Rivera and Gwen Verdon.
Bob Fosse, director and choreographer, has given the production
a polish that painlessly glosses over plot inconsistency.

The heart of any Kander/Ebb/Fosse work is song and dance, though, and that is precisely what carries "Chicago" to the heights it reaches.   And it is not just Rivera, Verdon and Jerry Orbach who put in the starring performances.   Mary McCarty's Sophie Tucker number as the Matron, "When You're Good to Mama," and M. O'Haughey's "A Little Bit of Good" are as effective as the Rivera and Verdon duets, as with the Act I closer, "My Own Best Friend."   The show finale has Rivera and Verdon in a dance routine that leaves the audience panting.

For this writer, it is Chita Rivera who sets the standard for the rest of the cast--a standard not easily (or always) met. She is graceful in her movements and provides a spark that lifts everyone on stage with her to higher energy levels.   The twinkle in her eyes, the unity of facial and hand expressions with lyric or story lines are the marks of the real Broadway trooper.   Ms. Rivera is that and more.

Perhaps the full potential of "Chicago" was not met--in the sense that Chicago in the 1920s could have been a greater source of book material for a more fully integrated musical, as was the case in "Cabaret."   As a musical entertainment, however (and even the playbill lists the show as "a musical vaudeville"), it succeeds.   The original cast album is due shortly from Arista.

MERIN, Jennifer; (2) Theatre Critic, Essayist, Cultural Correspondent; (3) b. New York City, October 28th; (4) d. Samuel (deceased) and Eda Reiss; (5) B.A. Clark U., Worcester, Mass., Major: History, honors in Fine Arts (Painting), 1965; MFA in Theatre, New York U. School of the Arts, 1969; (6) Single; (8) Theatre Critic/Features Writer, Soho Weekly News (1975-present); Correspondent for Canadian Theatre Review (1974-present), Theatre Facts (1975-present), Toneel Teatraal (1973-present); (9) Instructor: University of Wisconsin-Green Bay (Dramatic Literature, Experimental Theatre, Acting, Directing) 1975; New Conservatory Theatre (Acting, Theatre History) 1974-75; Neighborhood Playhouse Junior School (Acting) 1973-present; Academy of Music & Dramatic Art (Voice & Speech) 1973-75; New York City Correctional Institutions (Drama Workshops) 1972-74; Children's Cultural Workshop (Acting) 1963-68; Workshops (Acting & Movement) Tokyo, Japan 1971 and Workshops (Voice & Movement) London, England 1970.   Actress: American Place Theatre, Long Wharf Theatre, National Playwrights Conference, La Mama, Cambridge Drama Festival, Theatre at St. Clement's, Clark Center for the Performing Arts; Elia Kazan's Splendour in the Grass, Arthur Hiller's Love Story, Toho Cinema's Operation: Escape (in Japanese), ATG Cinema's Throw Away the Books (in Japanese); All major TV networks; Tenjo Sajiki Theatre, Tokyo, Japan and tour to France & Holland; Wherehouse La Mama, London, England; Recordings: Holt Reinhardt Winston educational tapes, ELEC Language Tapes for English Conversation (Tokyo, Japan); (10) Consultant to New York State Council on the Arts Theatre Program, 1974-present; (12) Coordinator, National Critics Institute, 1974; (15) American

Theatre Critics Association, International Association of Theatre
Critics, Actors Equity Association, Screen Actors Guild, American
Federation of Television and Radio Actors; (20) Contributed articles
to The Drama Review, Theatre Quarterly, Christian Science Monitor,
Village Voice, Theatre Crafts, Catalyst, Il Dramma, Oxford Com-
panion to the Theatre (Fourth Edition), The New Drama (NYU Press).
Photographs published in above, plus Daily News, National Observer,
Sunday Observer, Plays & Players, Asahi Shimbun; (21) 15 Leroy
St. , New York, New York 10014, Ph. 212-924-1043; (22) Same as
above; (23) Don't know; (24) 150 individual performance events, 5
theatre festivals, 5 books, 5 miscellaneous.

Heartbroken Shaw
(by Jennifer Merin, SoHo Weekly News, March 25, 1976)

As theater critic, George Bernard Shaw sometimes gave
playwrights (even those long dead) the opportunity to comment on
contemporary performances of their plays. In the preface to his
first published volume of plays (1898), for example, he imagined
Richard Brinsley Sheridan addressing actress Ada Rehan (a contemporary of Shaw's, renowned for her interpretation of Lady
Teazle) as follows: "My dear Miss Rehan: let me congratulate
you on a piece of tragic acting which has made me ashamed of
the triviality of my play, and obliterated Sir Peter Teazle from
my consciousness, though I meant him to be the hero of the
scene. I forsee an enormous success for both of us in this fortunate misrepresentation of my intention. " Cleverly bitter, but
no doubt deserved. One wonders what Shaw would say for himself, given the opportunity to review Jerry Engelbach's production
of Heartbreak House currently on the boards at the SoHo Rep.
Not being gifted with the quickest qualities of Shaw's wit, I don't
intend to simulate a Shavian commentary. I am nonetheless a
fierce admirer and feel impelled to protest against what might
have broken Shaw's heart.

When Shaw began to write Heartbreak House, the majority
of the English populace hadn't even a faint presentiment about the
coming of World War I. By the time he finished the play, its
premiere had to be postponed for fear that German bombers
would realize the conflagration in Act III, possibly not even waiting for their written cues. As observer of social and political
climates, Shaw noted the end of an era, the fading of the pre-
war, well-to-do English gentry, and he cast many of his observations into the mold of Anton Chekhov who, claims Shaw, also
wrote several Heartbreak Houses, one of which is entitled The
Cherry Orchard. Shaw's collection of characters in Heartbreak
House includes Hesions Hushabye, the unconventional mistress of an unconventional manse and the wife of Hector,
a gentleman who adopts outrageously daring personalities in
order to attract lovers like Ellie Dunn, a practical young
woman with high social aspirations who has arrived at the
country house for a weekend party. Ellie's father, Mazzini Dunn,
is an improverished poet who manages factories for Boss Mangan,

Captain of Industry with very Victorian sensibilities and a contracted marriage agreement with Ellie. Captain Shotover, Hesione's father, invents things and refuses to recognize his other
daughter, Ariadne, because she married a conservative government man. Those are not-too-distant relatives of the cast of
The Cherry Orchard, in that they are similarly concerned with
wealth, influence, culture and social and moral values. But
mostly, they are cousins in their humanity, in the completeness
of their emotional and intellectual lives. In Heartbreak House,
Hesione, a most opinionated woman, realizes that even the two
men she thought most doltish have feelings. She learns that
Mazzini cares deeply about his daughter and Mangan is oppressed
by his image as an all-powerful figure because he has really
very little influence or money. Similarly Ellie discovers that
Captain Shotover, for whom she has the utmost respect and admiration, strives to attain the "Seventh Level of Centration" with
liberal quantities of rum, but she accepts him and loves him
just the same.

The Act III arrival of War, which literally drops in unexpectedly in the form of bombs, is sometimes seen as a flaw in
the play. But what Shaw wanted to demonstrate is the sudden-
ness of war and the absolute foolishness and naivete with which
the characters respond, welcoming the excitement of conflagration
instead of retreating from the threat and horror of the war. Hesione, child-like but cultured, exclaims that the thunderous noises
are like Beethoven. Soon after, Mangan is killed by a bomb.
It is a shocking and ironic Shavian scene.

The Soho Rep production fails in almost every way. First
there is the language. Shaw's concern for language, made legendary in Pygmalion, was popularized in My Fair Lady when
Henry Higgins sang out: "Why can't the English learn to speak?"
True, the company at Soho Rep are Americans, but that's no
excuse. Why can't they learn to speak? The variety of obviously affected English accents is distracting.

Furthermore, the play is cut mercilessly. Agreed, Shaw
writes long, but the length is the seasoning. And when (as is
often the case here) almost every other line is deleted, the meat
is there but not the flavoring. Points of characterization are
cut away like excess fat. The music of the language, consciously orchestrated by Shaw, is distorted and the humor damaged.

The physical elements of the production fail to capture the
atmosphere of the play. Shaw, who withdrew plays from production because they couldn't be physically realized in their
scheduled theaters, applied his lucid language to detailed descriptions of the settings for the plays. Shaw is not like Shakespeare,
who wrote exposition of place within his character's dialogue and
thus "set" a bare stage. Shaw's instructions are outside the
language of the scene, and must be realized visually within the
physical decor. In this production of Heartbreak House, Shaw's

insistence on the nautical fittings of Captain Shotover's house are virtually ignored. Also, Shaw states explicitly that there should be no rug, but for the first two acts of the Soho Rep production, actors are poised upon a Persian so tattered that it would shame even the Salvation Army.

The costumes, although not elegant, would have been acceptable had they been ironed.

I'm not entirely sure of just what Shaw, a kind of demanding man, would have had to say about this production. How would he have handled the Off-Off-Broadway reviewer's too frequent dilemma? The Soho Rep is a young theater with serious and ambitious aims. They exist in a difficult financial environment and bad reviews might mean bad business. But would that fact of life have provoked Shaw, the critic, to submit Shaw, the playwright, to this Heartbreak?

TNT Baltimore

(by Jennifer Merin, SoHo Weekly News, July 1, 1976)

Before boarding the Metroliner to Baltimore, I rechecked my supply of headache remedy. One bottle of aspirin tablets in my camera bag, another in my luggage. I was prepared.

It is almost impossible to predict what degree of chaos will rule proceedings at a theater festival, but I have traveled the festival circuit (traipsing to Poland, Iran, Venezuela and other such places) enough to know that fighting through crowds four times a day to see four shows a day, chasing after festival folk for interviews or conferences, and mingling with close friends whom you see once or twice a year, require stamina and devotion. With aspirin a much needed support.

And Baltimore. Friends laughingly knocked it as the cultural eight ball of the nation. Spiro Agnew's home turf. Straight up on belief, I trusted that his bad karma would not influence this event. And I was right.

It was, after all, Baltimore's resources, The Theatre Project and University of Maryland Baltimore County (UMBC) with the aid of the National Endowment for the Arts and the International Theatre Institute, that provided funds and facilities for TNT, aka The New Theatre Festival, a week long (June 7-12) theatrical blast designed to create lines of communication between colonies (aka theater groups) along the alternative theater routes of this country, and abroad. The 33 invited groups were housed and performed at UMBC, where they could meet each other through their work, could grow together in workshops led by resource people (aka Lee Breuer, Mel Andringa, Luis Valdez, Tina Packer, among others), could share information on the nuts and bolts (aka survival) of being a small theater.

Most festivals are designed, following one pattern or another, to inform the general public (frequently the rich general public) of current trends in theater. The emphasis is on performing; the rule of thumb for performers is perform and get gone. Not at TNT. It was a work space for alternative theater groups who have remained somewhat obscure to each other and to the rest of the world (including Big Apple Theater Town USA) because of their relative geographic isolation. So, the Free Southern Theatre, a black theater collective from New Orleans, and the ProVisional Theatre, a white collective from Los Angeles, discovered that they had been working independently on aspects of the same play, an alternative history of slavery and black citizenship in the United States. Their meeting resulted in a special, integrated performance of their productions. Where Is the Blood of Your Fathers? (Free Southern) and Voice of the People (ProVisional). Similarly, The Bear Republic, a men's theater group from Santa Cruz, California, sat down with Spiderwoman Theatre Workshop, a feminist theater group from New York, to contemplate a double bill of their works. Signals and Women in Violence, both of which were developed out of CR groups. Krishnan Nambudiri, a Kathakali dancer, and Tony Shearer, an American Indian translator of ancient myths and legends, tapped their special sources of magic to perform a wedding ceremony, out-of doors, under the full moon. Luis Valdez and Marvin Felix Camillo attended to some business over cigars and beer. The list goes on at length; the connections tie in to the future.

At the very moment of my arrival at TNT, I knew that I could safely abandon my bottles of aspirin. Festival Director Philip Arnoult clasped my hand and said, "Come with me. You gotta see this. It's just beautiful." Arnoult led me through UMBC's standard institutional cell-block brick halls, into a space pitched to obscurity through total darkness. As afterimages of dragons and other fearful beasts danced through the darkness before my unaccustomed eyes, I momentarily resorted to thoughts of my Bayer's back in the Press Office. But the event, the performance of A-non by the American Contemporary Theatre (ACT) of Buffalo, quickly claimed my vision and absorbed my thoughts. As my fanciful afterimages trudged off into the darkness, I perceived a long, straight luminescent line on the floor. The line, with its peculiar quality of absorbing light rather than emitting it, stretched out before me like an endless solid dividing line, night time on a country road. I was compelled to follow it ... into the void. But first, an experiment. I felt the surface of the light with my hand, which read like a flat cut-out against the pale surface glow. No reflection. Had the same reading of my foot. I inched along, crawling, determined to reach the other end and understand the space I was in. Suddenly, a black-robed figure loomed before me. Ten feet above me (it seemed more like a mile) a face, pale blue orb, peered down at me. Then it disappeared. But the robe was still there, so I crawled around it. In the distance, another face, this time slightly green in hue, flashed more brightly into view. I found

my way into a circle of observers moving in a silent, ritualistic
dance around the figure.   Our breathing sounded like great gusts
of wind.   We raised our arms and eyes to the lamp-like face,
now pulsating luminously above our up-turned faces.   I became
aware of other such clusters of beings throughout the space.   I
gravitated towards them.   Literary references momentarily took
hold.   I was in the middle of a Bread and Puppet recast of Lee
Breuer's version of Beckett's The Lost Ones.   Not really.   I
was in outer space.   Not really.   I was in the middle of a theatrical cosmic dance that lasted for a total of six hours, although I have no direct knowledge of exactly how long I kept the
step.   This was my introduction to TNT.

Later that night, some misguided soul phoned a bomb threat
into the UMBC dormitory where the majority of festival guests
were lodged.   We tumbled out of bed, in various stages of un-
dress, and followed our noses, roommates and neighbors out the
nearest exit and across the street to an expansive lawn.   For
almost two hours we froze our toes, bitched, gathered, mingled,
sang songs.   TNT.   Was this a practical pun?   Someone suggested that Arnoult was creating a festival happening.   He laughed
and said that it wouldn't have been a bad idea, but had he thought
of it, compulsory participation would have been limited to 30
minutes, at the very most.   Then it was over.   No bomb, and,
according to the police, the phoney phoner hadn't even known
that TNT was in progress.   Much to the credit of festival organizers and participants, the bomb event did not in the least bit
disturb the momentum or atmosphere of the festival.   The following night, Arnoult presented an alternative item, a grand
party, more in line with his idea of fun, and we danced with
abandon to the sounds of the Maryland Pace Makers, a West Indian steel band that we should be hearing more from.

TNT.   The New Theater.   What is it?   This question cropped
up among critical colleagues throughout the week-long meeting.
There were many answers, most of which succeeded in establishing only that new theater is not.   New clearly does not refer to
age because some of the groups are rapidly approaching their
chronological adolescence.   New does not refer to aesthetic because, with the exception of ACT's innovative approach to theatrical time/space, the groups employed fairly traditional conventions of performer/spectator relationship, of narrative line
of development, of revue format sustained through musical interlude of reexamined Grotowskian theatrical values.   New does
not refer to group organization because the theater has its own
long alternative history of creative collectivity.   New seems to
acknowledge some development in the spirit of theater, and in the
relationship between the groups and the communities they serve.
A social responsiveness and sense of responsibility.   For example, Chicago's Dream Theatre developed Heritage from old
people's dreams, recorded during theater games workshops conducted at senior citizens' centers in their city.   They perform
the play in these homes, acting out dreams and improvising on

dreams told by audience members during the performance.
Spectators who related dreams during festival performances
claimed that seeing their dreams acted out revitalized their
memories and gave the invaluable insights into their experiences.
Similarly, the Family, a group well known to New York audiences, conducted workshops and performed in Baltimore City
Jail during the festival. The highpowered forward drive of their
show, Straight From the Ghetto, successfully fulfills its intention
of energizing the community. Boston's Reality Theatre picks up
their community's political football of education in Class, subtitled "an hysterical drama in 12 grades." The groups that count
as kin in this category of new vary greatly in the quality of their
artistic vision and performance skills, but their commitment to
their audiences, to the spirit of their communities sets their
standard on a slightly different artistic course than that of avant-
gardists who, like Wilson and Foreman, follow the paths of their
personal visions. It might be accurate, then, to define new theater, in terms of the festival's primary thrust, as a populist
expression whose aesthetic, although sometimes following a less
than innovative theatrical form, is determined by the group's
need to respond rather directly to the social needs of the community.

TNT became a community of such groups. It was a time
of constructive encounter, with a thoroughly cooperative energy
and atmosphere of love. TNT's next dose of positive vibes is
already being planned for next year. I plan to go. I will, without trepidation, leave the aspirin behind.

METZ, Herbert Edward (known as Herb Metz on television appearances); (2) Associate Professor of English and Performing Arts, Head
of Drama Division of Performing Arts Area, Washington U., St.
Louis, Mo., Television critic (Channel 5, KSD, which is NBC's affiliate) of Theater and Films (occasionally, Radio critic as well);
(3) b. New York, N.Y., June 26, 1921; (4) s. Samuel and Rosa
(Adolf) M.; (5) B.A. City College of New York, major English--
M.A. State U. of Iowa, Major English--3 yrs. doctoral work, Louisiana State U. (one summer at U.C.L.A.), major Rhetoric and Drama; (6) Single; (8) Instructor, Auburn U. (Alabama) 1949-52, professor English and Performing Arts, Washington U., St. Louis, 1955-
present, TV critic of Theater and Films 1969-present; (9) Actor,
director and designer as University student; performed playwright;
teacher of all phases of theater (History, Theory, Literature, Playwriting, Acting, Directing, Phonetics, etc.); Active participation in
all areas taught (see 8 above); director of major mainstage productions annually, including Oedipus Rex, The Glass Menagerie (twice),
The Importance of Being Earnest (twice), A Streetcar Named Desire,
Salome, Look Back In Anger, Private Lives, The Cocktail Party,
The Homecoming, Romance Language (author, as well), Waiting for
Godot, etc.; (10) Frequent consultant and panelist (with John Houseman, Katherine Dunham, Andrew Sarris, etc.); have introduced, on
various occasions, theater notables Clive Barnes, Sir Tyrone Guthrie

and Vincent Canby for lectures and appearances; actively support local theatres (The Loretto-Hilton Repertory Co.) and Arts Organizations (Arts and Education Foundation); (11) Independent; (13) Sergeant,
U.S. Air Force, WW II, 1942-45; (14) Good Conduct Medal, Marksmanship Award; (15) American Federation of Television and Radio
Artists; Honorary Member of Thyrsus, theatrical organization; Honorary member ODK, Senior men's organization; (16) Independent;
(20) Many one-act plays, Romance Language, a full-length play; my
theatrical productions are considered my publications; theater critiques and essays; (21) 40 No. Kingshighway, St. Louis, Mo. 63108,
Ph. 367-3699; (22) Performing Arts Area, Mallinckrodt Center,
Washington University, St. Louis, Mo. 63130, Ph. 314-863-0100,
Sta. 4181; (23) Drama and film critiques are shown on two major
newscasts on those days shown--estimated viewing audience per day,
over 500,000; (24) Approximately 30 plays/musicals/miscellaneous
stage performances; approximately 25 films.

"Indians"
(by Herb Metz, over KSD television, St. Louis, October 30, 1974)

The Loretto-Hilton Repertory Company has opened its new
season not with a whimper but with a slightly hollow bang.   Arthur Kopit's celebrated play Indians is their vehicle, and it is,
as a play, more a theatrical exercise than a sustained drama.
But director Davey Marlin-Jones seems to like opportunities to
exercise his infatuation with theatricality, and his treatment of
Kopit's hymn to our ill-fated Indians permits his fervent talent
full play.

But to be infatuated with theatricality is not the same as to
be in love with it, and the perils of the former are evident in
this production.   Occasionally, however, dividends are to be
gained in visual and aural feasts, as, for example in the penultimate scene and in the striking final tableau.

Indians deals with our government's cruel, destructive treatment of the American Indian in the latter half of the 19th century.   Although the play is very "busy" in styles and characters,
it is basically structured on a triangle of conflicts, with Sitting
Bull and the U.S.A. at the base, and with Buffalo Bill at the
apex.   Alternating between debasing, tawdry Wild West Show de-
pictions of our Indian heritage and trenchant, serious scenes of
our "legal" murder of that heritage, Indians achieves a schizoid
(rather than a rich) statement on a horrendously grave subject.

The Loretto-Hilton troupe has spared nothing in its attempt
to do the Kopit script justice.   Perhaps it should have exercised
some reserve.   Why, for example, in a play on so rich a subject, should several precious minutes be devoted to a lavish display of Annie Oakley's legendary marksmanship?   Well, the prop
and lighting people had fun....

Nevertheless, despite some suffocating details of production,

Indians does manage to generate some simple-minded excitement (how can one resist strobe lights?--for me, the answer is "easily"). And some of the production elements--costumes, decor, etc. ,--are often inventive.

Of the many, many performers involved I particularly admired Robert Darnell as Sitting Bull and, in lesser roles, Henry Strozier, Don Plumley, Vance Sorrells and Patrick Desmond. Entrusted with the only rich character of the play, Joneal Joplin's Buffalo Bill presents us with a satisfactory external performance. His inability to get at--or to--the juicy interior of this hypocritical, not-very-bright but tortured man symbolizes both the script's and the production's lack of real guts, as well as its heavy reliance on richly-embroidered surfaces.

Thus, Indians, at the Loretto-Hilton, is more show-biz than history or drama. Therein may lie its popularity and appeal.

Meanwhile, downtown at the American, one can share someone's recollection of the 1950's in Grease. I saw this tacky mish-mosh in Chicago last year (thinking it was headed here last season). Grease will have to--as it evidently has done--capture its audience without my endorsement. Nothing can persuade me to sit through it again--even with its new cast which, of course, I cannot judge. Let's hope they're miracle workers!

"Murder on the Orient Express"
(by Herb Metz, over KSD television, St. Louis, February 19, 1975)

Lovers of the glamorous, old-fashioned genre of mystery stories, those high-fashioned whodunits that used to grace the stage and screen decades ago, can no longer say, "They just don't make 'em like that anymore." Murder on the Orient Express, now showing all over town and country, is a half-earnest attempt to re-create that kind of movie.

I say "half-earnest" because Murder on the Orient Express (also known as Murder on the Calais Coach) emerges, despite its fidelity to original author Agatha Christie's characters and plot, as faintly parodic. In short, its glittering facade and its glamorous gore manage to give of a faint aroma of high camp. Whether this was consciously or unconsciously achieved cannot be proved, but I'd guess the former--given the marvelously funny (over-lush) musical score, the splendidly over-done costuming and make-up, the sly over-acting, and the obvious glee it takes in being stylishly old-fashioned.

The set-up is a classic one. Load an exotic trans-continental train with an ill-assorted collection of characters (all of whom give off a slight stench of suspicion in their first close-up); throw in, unexpectedly and at the last minute, the internationally famed detective Hercule Poirot (one of Miss Christie's most masterful and popular creations) and start the train on its journey from Turkey to England. Murder one of the passengers; get the train stuck in a god-forsaken snow drift; and solve the mystery. Of course, anyone familiar with Agatha Christie's work will know that there are some fascinating complications and some ingenious twists along the way.

Once I recognized that element of affectionate, self-mocking camp in the movie, I settled back to enjoy it. Murder on the Orient Express is beautifully made, firmly directed by Sidney Lumet, and, despite the fact that it is a mystery, it will not tax your mind. It is entertaining, if I may use that over-used, much-abused word.

The cast reads like a who's who: Albert Finney is a very creditable Poirot; among the others (mostly suspects) are Lauren Bacall, Ingrid Bergman, Wendy Hiller, Anthony Perkins, Richard Widmark, Sean Connery, Vanessa Redgrave and, in a beautifully-wrought little characterization, the great John Gielgud. The funny little "curtain-call" taken by the stars ends this delightfully fake, eminently enjoyable trifle on just the right note.

MITCHELL, Patricia E.; (2) Entertainment Critic Eyewitness News at 11:00, Co-Anchor first four news at 5:30; (3) b. January 20, 1943, Georgia; (4) d. James and Bernice Edenfield; (5) A.B., M.A. U. of Georgia, Literature, Drama; (6) Divorced; (7) child--Mark, age 10; (8) Instructor of English, U. of Ga., 1967-70, instructor English, Film, Virginia Commonwealth U., 1970-71; Look Magazine Staff, 1971-72; Media Consultant Garth Associates, 1972; WBZ-TV, producer/entertainment critic, anchor, news reporter, 1972-75; (9) College Theatre, director of Community Theatre during 1967-70; (10) Task force for Urban Theatre, Boston 75, media advisor, Governor's Commission on the Status of Women; (11) Women's political caucus; (12) Board of directors, Women's Training and Resource Center, Portland, Me., 1973-74; (14) Phi Beta Kappa; (15) AAUP, AFTRA; (20) Numerous articles for English and literary publications during years as instructor. I write every day for TV--news and reviews; (21) 68 Pinckney St., Boston, Mass., Ph. 617-227-0146; (22) WBZ-TV, Soldiers Field Rd., Boston, Mass., Ph. 617-254-5670, 787-7000,-7019; (23) Circulation: 535,000; (24) Five a week.

Pocket Mime Theatre
(by Pat Mitchell, over WBZ television, Boston, January 22, 1976)

The Pocket Mime Theatre is a good choice for entertainment any night but in this bitter cold, the art of Mime seemed particularly warming--perhaps mime can be appreciated as a retreat in other ways too. In this noise-polluted world of TV, radio, traffic, and human voices, it's really nice to spend an evening in silence--but mime is of course a very special silence ... it can say more than words and create just as deep and affecting emotions and with the perfected mime talents of Boston's only resident mime troupe, mime is some of the all around best entertainment in town. This is the fifth season for Pocket Mime and they just get better and better--J. Tormey, Kate Bentley, Michael Atwell are true masters of this art which Marcel Marceau popularized for the masses ... but Pocket Mime has taken the art steps beyond Marceau's silent skits--their present program includes some mime character studies--Kate Bentley mimes the various stages of womanhood on a pedestal in a piece called sugar & spice supermarket. There are comic pieces--the pomp and pestering of the palace guard--the pick-up, the invisible person. But most memorable in tonight's selections, were the serious more complex pieces--those mimes which say so much about the society we live in thru the readily identifiable slices of life. The worker traces the tragedy of a man who works at the same job from youth to old age--or even more poignant is the breakdown of case no. 27395--a regular guy who begins a regular day snipping his face with the razor in the morning, killing an associate with a letter opener in the afternoon--but all this action happens without a word--only the faces, and bodies of these mimers which keep an audience hanging on every movement for its revelation--and never do I experience such a quiet audience as those at Pocket Mime--the reverence for the power and entertainment of silence is catching--it does take an active imagination to fully understand mime, but it only takes your attendance to appreciate the creative imaginations and talents of the Pocket Mime Theatre.

Equus
(by Pat Mitchell, over WBZ television, Boston, February 12, 1976)

I treated myself tonight to the very best theatrical treat this town has seen in a long while and fortunately, Equus has been here a long while--tonight, the Wilbur Theatre celebrated its 100th performance of this absolutely compelling play by Peter Shaffer--if you are among the few who haven't seen Equus, let me urge you to make plans to do so sometime before the end of March--tonight was my third time actually, and the second time with Brian Bedford and Dai Brandley--it is a masterpiece of theatre--so brilliantly constructed and executed. Certainly, the subject matter is shocking and unusual enough to keep an audience enthralled by its revelations alone. A story about a 17 year old boy who blinds six horses with a metal spike might have made a gruesome melodrama about madness--but Equus is not so much about madness as it is about passion. The set up of the psychiatrist patient relationship could have led to facile conclusions about any number of emotional complexities--but Shaffer offers much more than analysis or a crime--he has created an anatomy of passion, pain--both the patient's and the psychiatrist's. The connections between the boy's confusion of sex, religion, his worship of the slave-god, the horse--and the doctor's sublimated worship of ancient Greece dove-tail into some rather profound and disturbing conclusions about what is normal--is it any better to gallop naked through fields at midnight than to live in comfortable mediocrity? Equus is an exciting, beautifully written

discourse on the perils of life with and without pain. But it's
not all heavy musings--there is much humor, however black,
in this play and the performances of everyone are nearly perfect. I suppose the greatest compliment I can pay to this play
is to say that from the beginning to end of it, you have an in-
escapable feeling that you are involved in something important--
and you leave knowing something happened--let Equus's very
special entertainment happen for you.

MONSON, Karen, Chicago Daily News, 401 N. Wabash Ave. , Chicago,
Ill. 60611

MOOTZ, William Hoyt; (2) Drama and music critic; (3) b. Continental, O. , June 7, 1924; (4) s. Paul R. and Lenore E. (Simon); (5)
B. M. , University of Louisville School of Music (major: piano), 1946;
(8) Director of Music, Kentucky School for the Blind, 1946-61; teacher of piano, University of Louisville School of Music, 1948-56;
Assistant music critic, The Courier-Journal, 1948-56; Music editor
and assistant drama critic, The Courier-Journal, 1956-61; Drama
and Music Critic, The Courier-Journal, 1962- ; (9) Lecturer in the
arts, Indiana University Southeast, 1973- ; (14) Presented with Giovanni Martini Award for Outstanding Contribution to Louisville Arts
by Bellarmine College (Louisville), 1970; (21) 1430 Cherokee Road,
Louisville, Ky. 40204, Ph. 502-459-4790; (22) The Courier-Journal,
Louisville, Ky. 40202, Ph. 502-582-4011; (23) Circulation: 220,000
(daily) 360,000 (Sunday).

National Theatre of the Deaf Provides a Marvelous Evening
(by William Mootz, Courier-Journal, February 22, 1975)

The National Theatre of the Deaf has been touring the United
States and many other countries since 1967. During that time,
it has been recognized everywhere as one of America's outstanding theatrical companies.

Friday night, the troupe finally made a belated Louisville
debut at Spalding College Auditorium. But better late than never.
It was a marvelous evening these 15 players gave us, and an audience consisting of both local theater buffs and members of our
deaf community welcomed it with all but rapturous enthusiasm.

The National Theatre of the Deaf has developed a unique
dramatic form for its performances. But more about that in a
moment. The first thing a viewer notices about the company is
the extraordinary precision of its ensemble.

Most of these actors have been working together for the better part of a decade. During that time, they have developed an
acting style that is probably the most brilliantly polished of any
drama company in the nation. They work together with an ease
and sensitivity that comes only from long association and much

hard work. Such a finely tuned ensemble represents an ideal that most troupes in this country are still striving for, although it is one of the admirable achievements noted among the national theaters of England and Europe.

Friday night, the National Theatre of the Deaf presented a double bill--an adaptation of S. Ansky's famous Hebrew drama called "The Dybbuk," followed by a pop-art extravaganza titled "Priscilla, Princess of Power."

Both works were ritualistic in form, and both skillfully blended techniques that embraced straight acting and narrative exposition. Most of the players communicated through sign language, but there were also speaking actors present who not only took active roles in the two short plays, but who also supplied voices for some of their colleagues.

It sounds complex, I guess, but it works with incredible smoothness in actual practice. The gestures of performers using sign language were often of captivating grace, and a viewer quickly accepted as logical a spoken "translation" from another player on stage.

The results were hardly conventional theater. For one thing, the acting had a breadth of emotional range that one rarely encounters from American performers.

The entire evening was dazzling. "The Dybbuk" deals with a young bride whose body is possessed by the soul of a boy who once loved her. A religious rite is eventually performed by a rabbi to rid her of this demon spirit.

The combination of ritual, myth, and religious symbolism embraced by Ansky's play is of infinitely more dramatic richness than the cheap claptrap of a work like "The Exorcist." The performance, highlighted by Patrick Graybill's Rabbi and Freda Norman's Leye, was hypnotizing.

"Pricilla, Princess of Power," turned out to be an insolent romp, with Priscilla a kind of Captain Marvel saving the world from evil industrialists. It was all very bright, very swift, and very funny. The performance had a cartoon-like sassiness that made it constantly ingratiating.

The appearance of the National Theatre of the Deaf was sponsored by Spalding College, Actors Theatre, and the Greater Louisville Council for the Hearing Impaired, in association with the Kentucky Arts Commission. May it return to Louisville soon!

Comedic "Measure" Molded into Tragedy of Lust, Politics
(by William Mootz, Courier-Journal, February 12, 1976)

Producer Jon Jory often reserves his upstairs Victor Jory

Theatre for his most experimental, mind-stretching productions.
It's Actors Theatre's answer to New York's Off Broadway. At
its best, it's just about the most stimulating place in Louisville.

Last night, Jory opened one of the most challenging works
of his Louisville tenure in his Victor Jory showcase. It is
Charles Marowitz's adaptation of Shakespeare's "Measure for
Measure" and it's an evening that leaves a spectator feeling
challenged, rebellious, unsettled and eager to talk back.

In other words, ATL becomes an arena for intellectual ferment with this "Measure for Measure," and that's one reason
why ATL does itself honor with its production. It's an American premiere, by the way, marking the work's first Atlantic
crossing since its world premiere in London last summer.

Marowitz has placed all manner of difficulties in the path of
a theater which chooses to stage this "Measure for Measure."
To begin with, there are the problems of Shakespeare's original,
one of the most emotionally labyrinthian of all Sheakespeare's
comedies.

But Marowitz, paring the text and reshaping it into a tragedy
of lust and politics, has conceived an entirely different evening.

What he achieves is startling. If a contemporary architect
should take apart Canterbury Cathedral, stone by stone, and then
erect with them a monument to the mendacity of our times, the
effect might be somewhat the same. From the bricks and mortar of the ebony-hued, convulsive poetry of Shakespeare's "Measure for Measure," Marowitz gives us a universe rampant with
lechery.

Not for a minute do I believe, as Marowitz suggests, that
this is the play Shakespeare would have written, were it not for
the conventions that fettered his genius. Great writers, even
playwrights as great as Shakespeare, cannot escape the mores
of their times. Shakespeare exulted with the rest of Elizabethan
England at his country's emergence as a world power. Read
"Henry V" or nearly any other of his histories, if you doubt it.

So I don't think Shakespeare saw politics as quite the exercise in evil that emerges in Marowitz's play. But I'm fascinated
by the power of Marowitz's vision and stunned by the theatrical
virtuosity of his conception.

In Shakespeare, all wrongs are made right when justice and
Christian mercy prevail. Isabella, far from having to sacrifice
herself to the warped Angelo to save her unjustly condemned
brother, saves her soul and her brother's life through her wit
and virtue.

For Marowitz, the easy solutions of the play's final scenes
are false. So he leads the innocent to slaughter, as Isabella

cries in vain for justice.   Only the sensually base and morally
corrupt escape unscathed.

Marowitz, although he throws away Shakespeare's comedy
scenes, follows the original faithfully through "Measure for Measure's" first half.   But the rest is an abrasive, nightmarish departure, punctuated by rape, murder, and a final descent into
insanity.   In one of the production's most effective scenes, director Charles Kerr creates a bacchanalian Witches Sabbath,
with flickering light from gross phallic candles and the scent of
incense casting a depraved spell.

Still, ATL's production, resplendently costumed by Kurt
Wilhelm, strikes me as tentative.   The ending, with villains
whooping it up in orgiastic abandon, is facile, which may be the
playwright's fault.   But the evening, while ever so earnest, is
often turgid.

This is a play best performed by a company who've gained
familiarity with an author's style through long association with
him.   The present cast, lacking such familiarity, still is groping for the right tone and pace.   The production will find a
more secure shape as performances continue through the weeks
ahead.

Kerr's direction is most successful in its handling of Lucio,
who's on the periphery of the action but is a vivid commentator
and keen observer.   And Michael Thompson's performance in the
role breathes vitality into the evening.

I also liked Sarah Atkins' fragile Isabella, Michael Kevin's
hypocritical Duke and Eric Booth's vulnerable Claudio.

On the other hand, John Hancock is too stately, too round
of speech and too calculated in expression for Marowitz's despicable Angelo.   Hancock's a splendid actor, but he's here miscast.

Kerr's thoughtful direction of this complex script is reflected
in his musical background, a wonderfully effective compilation of
excerpts from Penderecki's "The Devils of Loudon."

MORGAN, Murray; (2) Drama critic; (3) b. Tacoma, Wash. , Feb.
16, 1916; (5) B. A. U. of Washington, 1937, cum laude, Journalism
major; M. S. Columbia U. , 1947, Journalism; (6) m. Rosa Northcutt,
1939; (7) children--one daughter, Lane, b. 1949; (8) Reporter, Grays
Harbor Washington, 1937-38; editor, Seattle Municipal News, and
Executive Secretary; Seattle Municipal League, 1938-39; Freelancing
in Europe 1939-40   (newspaper articles on kayak trip down Danube,
politics in Balkans);   City Desk, Spokane Chronicle, 1940; City Editor, Grays Harbor Washingtonian, 1940-41. (Columbia Graduate
School of Journalism 1941-42). Night News Editor, CBS World News,

New York, 1941-42; Editor, Time Magazine, 1941-42; Reporter, New
York Herald Tribune, 1941-42; Pulitizer Fellowship, Mexico, 1942-
43; Nijelski Consultants, Radio Research Project, 1946-47; Faculty,
University of Puget Sound, 1947-53; News Director KTBI/KTAC 1953-
56; News Commentary "Our Town, Our World" for Pacific First
Federal, 1956-71; Faculty, Tacoma Community College, History,
1970- ; Faculty, Highline Community College, History, 1970; Faculty,
Pacific Lutheran University, 1973; (13) U.S. Army Signal Intelligence,
Alaska--Pentagon, 1943-46; (14) Awards: Pulitzer Fellowship, 1942;
Seattle Historical Society Citations 1955, 1963, 1968; Governor's
Award, 1966, 1968; Washington Education Association State Achieve-
ment Award, 1963; Distinguished Community Service, National Asso-
ciation of Radio News Directors, 1952; Look Citation for Investigative
Reporting, 1956; Allied Arts Civic Achievement Award, 1966; John
Binns Distinguished Service Award, 1972; State Arts Award, 1974;
Municipal League Distinguished Citizen Award, 1974; (20) Books:
Novels: Day of the Dead 1946; The Viewless Winds 1949.   Com-
missioned: Century 21, 1963; The Hospital Women Built for Chil-
dren 1967; Non-fiction: Bridge to Russia (Those Amazing Aleutians)
1947; Dixie Raider, The Sage of the CSS Shenandoah 1948; The Co-
lumbia 1949; Skid Road 1951; The Dam 1954; Last Wilderness 1955;
Doctors to the World 1958; Northwest Corner 1962; One Man's Gold
Rush 1967; Contributed Magazine Articles to: American Heritage,
American West, Adventure, Argosy, Esquire, Coronet, Saturday
Evening Post, Saturday Review of Literature, Colliers, Readers Di-
gest, True, Woman's Home Companion, McCalls, Elks, Nation's
Business, Cosmopolitan, Holiday, Rotarian, Pacific Northwest Quart-
erly, Oregon Historical Quarterly; (21) c/o General Delivery, Trout
Lake, Washington; (22) Argus, White Henry Stewart Building, Seattle,
Washington 98101.

A Misdirected Hamlet
(by Murray Morgan, Argus, October 25, 1974)

Hamlet, which opened the Seattle Repertory Theater's 1974-
75 season, is a mitigated misadventure--an interesting experiment that proves the old way better.

Quirky and imaginative in portraying the pensive Dane as a
man of action, the production directed by Duncan Ross, reduces
Shakespeare's complex tragedy to the level of the play-within-the-
play, a murder melodrama.   There's something unripe in this
Denmark.

Christopher Walken, a handsome young man of enormous
energy, tackles undismayed the challenge of making the sweet
Prince into a contemporary man: rational, alienated and ruthless in this world he never made.

Walken's Hamlet is not mad, he's mod.   Decked out in a
golden jumpsuit that makes him look like a preshrunk Elvis Presley, he delivers the soliloquies head-on to the audience like a
politician selling a platform.   He horses around with his chums

like a tyro Hell's Angel, bangs people around like Mike Hammer. He has the modern hero's quick way with the ladies.   In conversation with Ophelia, he knocks her sprawling.   Visiting Gertrude's chamber, he climbs up on the bed with his mother and elbows apart her thighs.

Such novelties work as attention-grabbers.   In almost four hours there's scarcely a dull moment.   But Shakespeare's study of a man trapped by sensibility, a son who believes himself duty-bound to right a monstrous wrong done his father but hesitates to act, is turned into a case-history of an Oedipal young fellow who hates his stepfather.   That's reverse alchemy: the transformation of gold into a substance already common.

Innovation does not end with the concept of the prince. Marsha Wischlusen does Ophelia's mad scene as a reverse strip. She comes on naked but puts on a robe as she scatters the flowers.   There's nothing prurient about her nudity--she's built rather like the late Leslie Howard, but it does distract.   So does her makeup, early Hollywood; so do her gestures, early operatic.   And she is hard to hear.

The Rep's aim seems to be to give us a Hamlet for an age without heroes, a time of surface sheen and hollowness, an era of violence that fails to achieve its purpose.   This concept is emphasized by Eldon Elder's plastic Elsinore, Lewis Rampino's shiny, no-period costumes, Richard Nelson's lighting, which bounces distractingly off meaningless surfaces, and by the friezes of the Players, who as choreographed by Arne Zaslove project a sinister detachment.

These effects work.   They impel attention and seem to imply meaning, but down there, underneath the cosmetics, a great play is struggling to get out.

Two characters remain classic.   Ted D'Arms exploits to good effect his great physical presence; he creates a Claudius who lusts for power but is not despicable.   In the welter of accents and verbal rhythms, it is a relief to hear the lines read clearly.   We are reminded that Shakespeare wrote well.

Clayton Corzatte's delicate, measured portrayal of the platitudinous Polonius is a triumph.   He makes the old windbag so human that when he is accidentally killed while spying on the bedchamber, we feel guilt for having found him so tedious.

A week after seeing this idiosyncratic production, I find the gaudy set and costumes already going dim, the Prince a blur of action and loud talk, but Claudius and Polonius among the true pleasures I've had in years of watching plays.   And I wonder wistfully what might have been if all the money and effort and talent that went into putting more ham in this Hamlet had been concentrated on giving Seattle Shakespeare straight.

Brilliant Ensemble Illumines Chiller from Poland
(by Murray Morgan, Argus, November 8, 1974)

Tango, which closes this weekend at Cornish, is the funniest
serious play I can recall. It is a chilling but hilarious examination of the post-permissive age we are entering. In spite of the
handicaps of the tiny Cornish stage, the production is brilliant;
the cast, bellwethered by John Gilbert, works together for ensemble effect seldom achieved by local companies.

The play, first produced in Belgrade and Warsaw in 1965,
is the work of Slavomir Mrozek, a 43-year-old Polish satirist
and newspaper columnist who mixes Saroyan zaniess with Kafka
metaphysical gloom. He serves as a witty but mordant driver
for our present-day tumbril.

The story concerns an oddball family living by the rules of
Bohemian protest long after their demands for freedom to be
themselves have been too abundantly met. The senior generation,
Grandmother Eugenia (Jean Marie Kinney) and her brother Eugene, played by John Gilbert, have adjusted to the New disOrder.
Their son, Stomil (J.V. Bradley) and his wife Eleanor (Christine Healy) hold to revolutionary commitments to free love
against the tides of their personal affections in languishing hor-
mones. Eleanor on occasion sleeps with a slop named Eddie,
whose only charm is uncomplicated self-interest.

To this household returns Arthur (Mark D. Murphey), the
spawn of the rebels and heir of hardwon freedom. He craves
restraint. Longing for rules that might make protest meaningful, Arthur and Great-uncle Eugene stage a counter-revolution.

Arthur hopes to reimpose tradition or to establish formalism,
or belief in God, or sport, or awareness of death--some idea,
any idea, old or new, which might serve as counterweight to
anarchy. All fail. Arthur is left holding Power, symbolized
by a revolver; as a well-meaning intellectual he is unable to use
it speedily and selfishly. Power passes into the hands of the
man without principle.

In a curtain-scene without peer in comic horror, Mrozek
knots the strands he has woven. The brutal Eddie and the ac-
quiescent Eugene, those types who best survive revolution and
counter-revolution, dance the tango.

Tango is the only play I can recall seeing on a presspass,
then buying tickets to see again.

My thanks to Margaret Booker, Intiman's founder-director,
for introducing me to a new playwright and writer of such grave
and lively disenchantment; to Cornish School of Allied Arts for
its lashup with Intiman, which makes such plays accessible to
Seattle; to the entire cast for subordination of self to group-

effect; and, in order of my delight, to J. V. Bradley, for his performance as the father, especially when sliding from Bohemian assertion to bourgeois worry; to Carmi Boushey, for sheer loveliness; to Denis Arndt, for his sly, menacing portrayal of the brutish Eddie; and, above all, to John Gilbert, who as Uncle Eugene, that creature for all seasons, acts with eyebrow, tongue, spine and comic genius to maintain the tone of high farce which underscores Mrozek's seriousness.

MORRISON, Don, Minneapolis Star, 425 Portland Avenue, Minneapolis, Minn. 55488.

MORRISON, Hobe; (2) Author and critic; (3) b. Germantown, Penn., March 24, 1904; (4) s. of J. L. Morrison & Agnes (Millar) M.; (5) Public school in Philadelphia; (6) m. Elizabeth Augur (mar. dis.), m. Toni Darnay; (8) Drama editor and 2nd string critic of The Record, Phila., Penn. 1932-37; joined staff of Variety, Feb. 1937-current; (9) Freelance writer on theater; (19) The Players, New York Drama Critics Circle; (20) Daily columns for a syndicate of newspapers in Westchester, Rockland County, and New Jersey; (21) 7 West 16th St., NYC, N.Y. 10011, Ph. 212-989-0299; (22) Variety.

"A Matter of Gravity"
(by Hobe Morrison, Variety, February 11, 1976)

Katharine Hepburn is the main attraction and interest in "A Matter of Gravity," which opened Feb. 3 at the Broadhurst Theatre. Enid Bagnold's play, apparently a sort of summing up of her attitudes and ideas, is amusing, puzzling, perhaps too talky and a little too long for some tastes.

There is no question of the show's success. The production recovered its $160,000 investment and earned about 100% profit in its 15-week tryout tour and it is said to be virtually sold out through mid-April, when the star's verbal commitment ends.

There is no question, either, of the appeal of "Gravity" for Hepburn fans. The play keeps her onstage throughout almost the entire three acts. It presents her advantageously and she has lost none of her striking personality.

Hepburn, always strongly individualistic, is clearly becoming more and more her own self in her maturity. Her distinctive voice, manner of speaking, carriage and characteristics are seemingly becoming more pronounced. As an actress, she is unique, with a theatrical quality her public has found increasingly fascinating.

As for "Gravity," it's difficult to know exactly what it's supposed to be about or mean. It seems to be about almost everything. The 85-year-old author, a novelist as well as a dramatist,

is talking about age and youth, wealth and poverty, parenthood
and childlessness, tradition, good manners, race, love and sex--
a good deal about sex, including homosexualism, lesbianism and
even heterosexualism.

There's practically no plot or even physical action and the
outstanding occurrence, the heavyweight housemaid's unexplained
rise into the air, takes place offstage. Probably it's of no significance that that supernatural incident is a matter of gravity
in reverse.

The locale of the piece is a crumbling stately home of England, where a septuagenarian widow receives her adored grandson's four friends for a weekend. Relationships change and in
an audience-frustrating finale the imperious lady elects to live
in a private insane asylum. Does that reflect her opinion of
the guests?

Under Noel Willman's seemingly reserved direction, the performance is animated, occasionally a little rushed, audible and
not always entirely comprehensible. It is dominated by Hepburn's dynamic playing, which is undoubtedly what audiences
want and expect.

Charlotte Jones is suitably comic as the outsize, eccentric
maid, Christopher Reeve is presentable if not too forceful as
the grandson who takes a while to realize what the score is.
Wanda Bimson is decorative though a trifle vehement as the Jamaica girl who renounces a lesbian affair to marry the heir-
apparent to the mansion.

Paul Harding is comfortably relaxed and has plausibility and
good timing as a homosexual visitor who becomes the old lady's
devoted friend, and Elizabeth Lawrence is believable in the thankless role of an emotionally twisted heiress ashamed of her wealth.
Daniel Tamm and Robert Moberly are acceptable in minor roles.

Ben Edwards has designed a stunning living room setting
that suggests faded grandeur, Jane Greenwood's costumes are
theatrically appropriate and Thomas Skelton's lighting provides
proper mood. The producers of the already established hit are
Robert Whitehead, Robert L. Stevens and Konrad Matthaei.

"Mrs. Warren's Profession"
(by Hobe Morrison, Variety, February 25, 1976)

The passing years which ravage most topical plays have
dealt kindly with "Mrs. Warren's Profession," which opened last
Wednesday night (18) at the Vivian Beaumont Theatre in Lincoln
Center. Bernard Shaw's 78-year-old dramatic shocker is now
bland as to subject matter and dated in its technique, but its essential human values are still genuine and moving, at least in
the excellent revival by Joseph Papp's N.Y. Shakespeare Festival.

It's strange to realize that this attack on society's tacit acceptance of prostitution was once banned from public performance in London and that the producer and leading lady were arrested on a felony charge and prosecuted for its first presentation in New York. It's as though punishment had been imposed on the urchin who innocently mentioned the non-existence of the emperor's new clothes.

"Mrs. Warren" is actually a sternly moralistic play which exposed a truth that was offensive to the sanctimonious hypocrits of the Victorian era. In a broader sense, it condemns not only the corrosive influence of protitution profits, but the cant of the self-righteous in all levels of society, business and government. Finally, it was a fervent expression of the playwright's feminist convictions.

The play is one of Shaw's early works, written before he had learned to sugar-coat his serious messages with brilliantly witty dialog, and before his characters all became inescapably Shavian in their attitude and articulate logic. Although the text has evidently been cut considerably, it's still talky, with scenes that cause audience restlessness and coughing.

Despite the outmoded style, however, "Mrs. Warren" remains a surprisingly pertinent and vital work. A key element in its theatrical success is the eloquent performance of the present cast, headed by Ruth Gordon and Lynn Redgrave as the emotionally and rationally opposed mother-daughter leads.

The veteran Gordon is at her best as the indomitable, outspoken and proud woman who has climbed from agonizing poverty to wealth as the manager of an international chain of brothels. The actress has subdued the mannerisms--the strutting walk, the wagging finger and head-shake--that have sometimes marred her playing in the past, and offers a direct, authoritative and disciplined but not invariably audible portrayal. Even after 60 years on the stage, however, she retains traces of New England accent.

Redgrave also provides a distinctive, clean, clear and touching characterization as Shaw's conception of what used to be called an emancipated young woman--a no-nonsense, individual who scorns romance, compromise or equivocation.

Philip Bosco is believable as a blunt spokesman for bland acceptance of the profits from organized vice, Milo O'Shea gives a neatly detailed performance as a shallow local minister with a shady past, Edward Herrmann is plausible as his amiable, clear-headed but useless son and Ron Randell is acceptable in the thankless role of a blindly romantic friend.

Gerald Freedman's staging has skillfully, unobtrusive vigor, David Mitchell's three settings convey a sense of suburban

serenity, while Theoni V. Aldredge's costumes and Martin Aronstein's lighting convey appropriate atmosphere. As an example
of early Shaviana, "Mrs. Warren" is entertaining and revealing.
G. B. S. , it's clear, is still a dramatist of lively provocative
ideas.

Although the comedy was published in London in 1898, its
public performance was forbidden by an official known as the
Queen's Reader. However, it was given a so-called "private"
presentation in 1902 by the London Stage Society.

When the work was first done in 1905 by Arnold Daly at the
old Garrick Theatre in New York, there was so much public excitement over the event that the District Attorney had to pay $30
for a ticket. The producer, who also acted in the show, and
the leading lady, Mary Shaw (no relation to the author), were
arrested for presenting an "immoral play," but were acquitted
at a court trial.

So much for sinfulness or morality as a basis for drama
criticism.

MORROW, Sara Sprott; (2) theater and dance critic; (3) b. Nashville,
Tn. , Oct. 17, 1905; (4) d. Fred and Artie (Evans) S. ; (5) attended
Vanderbilt U. , and Wroxton College, Oxon. , England, Mills College,
Oakland, Calif. , subs. , drama and drama and dance criticism, Russian lit. , no degrees; (6) m. H. Paxton Morrow, June 1, 1929; (7)
child--Emily M. McCormick; San Francisco, two grandchildren, Car-
mack and Ashley; (8) Writer for Methodist Bd. of Ed. , 1950-70; drama critic for Nashville Banner since 1969; (14) Awarded fellowship
by Nat. End. Arts at Mills College, 1975; Award by Tenn. Hist. Soc.
1975, for best art. , 1974; (15) Panel judge for Int. Cong. of Child.
Theatre, 1972; mem. state, reg. and nat. theater confs. , American
Critics' Ass. ; (16) Democrat; (17) Episcopalian; (19) Club: Cheek-
wood; (20) cont. to Dramatics, Hist. quarterlies. , book reviews for
Nashville Banner, Nashville mag. , author book, "Make Bright the
Memories," a biog. , "Coming Events in Britain; (21) 304 Lynwood
Blvd. , Nashville, Tn. , 37205, Ph. 292-8600; (22) Nashville Banner,
1100 Broadway, Nashville, Tn. , Ph. 255-5401; (23) Circulation:
90,000; (24) 75-100 plays and musicals in U. S. and Britain, AFT
films, 6; dance, 4. Full color pages of theater and misc. , 4. Free
lance material.

"Jacques Brel" Was Alive but Not Well in Film
(by Sara Morrow, Nashville Banner, May 23, 1975)

Jacques Brel wasn't so well in the American Film Theater
(AFT) presentation Tuesday at the Belcourt Cinema. He needed
a doctor to replace Eric Blau, the screenwriter.

This final show of the series may best be described as an
exploration of the orifices in the facial structure by a camera

that seems to try to crawl inside the cranial cavity.

The insistence on gross close-ups has largely spoiled all of the films for me.   That is the trouble with attempting to transfer stage plays to film.   Exaggeration is necessary by living performers on stage; it is a fatal flaw to believe that audiences are clamoring for a look at Elly Stone's teeth (a few seemed to be missing), and Joe Masiell's epiglottis.

All three members of the cast, Miss Stone, Mort Shuman and Masiell have appeared in stage productions of Jacques Brel Is Alive and Well and Living in Paris along with Brel himself.

The original concept of Brel's lyrics and music, was marked by simplicity and disarming strengths.   The film is strapped with gimmicks and hokum which defy credibility.   A clutch of drug sniffers and pot smoking hippies in the cast adds to the confusion in an effort to update the action; the result is obfuscation to the point of delirium.

Brussels-native Brel wrote some plaintive, appealing lyrics. Whether part of this quality was lost in translation (French to English), I don't know, but false rhymes, news with shoes (unless you are among those that say "noos"), soldier and bolder, serve as irritants.

Miss Stone's voice range, at least in this film, is limited and the quality, less than persuasive.   I can only call her performance monotonous.

Masiell has a fine voice, but here, it lacked variety and resonance that viewers had a right to expect.

Platitudinous pretension (I've caught the disease) fits this medley of Brel songs.   The music, at times, hits with the force of an automatic drill boring into Nashville limestone.   If We Only Had Love, the final song by the trio, I found appealing.

What kind of symbolism was intended in Sons of, with three men hanging on crosses, escapes me.   I saw it "plain" in Next, the impersonalism of war, but even that became labored and sick as depicted in bordellos.

You didn't miss a thing if you failed to see the film.   It gets the prize for the worst production in the series of five offered by AFT.

Champions Presented at Ensemble
(by Sara Morrow, Nashville Banner, June 13, 1975)

An evening of champions was presented to the audience in Ensemble Theatre Company's That Championship Season Thursday night.

The play is about the 20th reunion of a trophy-winning high
school basketball team at the house of their coach, now a man
of 60.   Only four of the team's five members are present.
Martin, the absent player, is the ghost of season past whose
knowledge about the winning game becomes important as the action proceeds.

Meet the champs.   There is Tom, a chronic, sardonic drunk;
George, up for re-election as the small town's mayor and under
terrific pressure; Coach, himself, a dying bigot whose philosophy
is hate Jews, blacks and Communists, but revere Joe McCarthy
and Teddy Roosevelt; James, a mediocre high school principal
who has false teeth; and Phil, the only financially successful
member of the great team who boasts about his "Caddy," his
sexual prowess and his money.   No matter what Phil is, George
needs his support to win the mayoral race.

The play says that we are frightened to death to see ourselves as we are.   Cover up, lie, cheat on friends, but hide
beneath false theories, platitudes and forced gaiety.   Coach advises, "We've got to stick together for survival, boys."

This is a sad play; it points up as Ibsen often did in his
plays, that we do have to fight for survival in a hostile world.
Exaggeration of each of these men's problems is heightened to
let us see how phony they are as the thrust of the play reveals
their secret lives in the interaction with Coach trying to dominate and control as he did 20 years earlier.

Cecil Jones as Coach is fine in his role.   I loved his tacky
brown suit, shoes and socks, his attempts to force the tense
group into his own mold.   One by one, both he and the team
confess their loneliness, their numbing lives of misery.   Jones
is especially good in his scene of private revelation.   His hair
make-up is excellent, but a man with white hair would also have
a white chest mat.

Stephen Dees gives as convincing, casual performance of a
comic drunk as you're apt to see.   Shoddily dressed, sodden
with drink, he is acutely aware of the hypocrisy seething around
him.   It is he who tries to get the other men to admit that they
know very well why Martin is absent from all their reunions.

C. B. Anderson as George has a habit of nervous, mirthless
giggling that detracts from the opening scene.   Later, he stops
it and does some perceptive acting.

James, by David Landon, gets a good portrayal.   Terry
Alpaugh did not give me, at all times, the sense of feeling that
he was indeed a rich man of the world.

This is an excellent performance on the whole, but the play
is made up of strong language.   To me, this is essential and

fits the characters, but if you object to four letter words, it is not your cup of tea.

One sentence about the set. I do not believe that the coach's shabby quarters would have fresh, new wallpaper; it needs some water spots, some grime, to make it fit in with the tarnished silver trophy.

Ronnie Meek has done himself proud with his direction and may look forward to a good run of the play.

MOSSMAN, Josef, Des Moines Register and Tribune, 715 Locust St., Des Moines, Iowa 50304.

MOUNT, Betty Copsey; (2) Theater critic; Book reviewer; Drama Editor; (3) b. Nebraska City, Nebr., Mar. 6, 1919; (4) d. Maj. Gen. Robert L. and Vivian (McNamara) Copsey; (5) Duke U., journalism, 1940; Katharine Gibbs 1939; (6) m. Keith Bradford Mount, 1941; (7) children--Pamela, Patricia, Cynthia; (8) Theater critic, book reviewer and columnist, Summit (N.J.) Independent-Press, 1964- ; Drama Editor, Crossroads Magazine, 1966-69; Drama Editor, New Jersey Life Magazine, 1968- ; (9) Board of Governors, Summit Playhouse Association, 1965-73; Duke Players, 1936-38; actress; set decoration; (10) Chairman, playreading; Summit Branch American Association of University Women, chairman creative Arts, directed and acted in state-award winning plays; Girl Scout Drama Leader; Television appearances Ch. 52 for performing arts benefits; tours; (10) N.J. State Festival Play Judge; Teen Age Arts Festival Judge; (12) Ruling Elder New Providence Presbyterian Church, Sunday School teacher and Youth Fellowship Director 1950- 1975; Founder, Clearwater Swim Club, Director of Social Activities 1966-75; Overlook Hospital (Summit) Follies 1950-57; (14) B'nai B'rith Americanism Award for Distinguished Community Service 1974; YWCA Distinguished Service Award; (15) Kappa Alpha Theta; (16) Republican; (21) 1590 Valley Road, Millington, N.J. 07946, Ph. 201-647-3069; (22) N.J. Life Magazine, P.O. Box 40, Maplewood, N.J. 07040, Ph. 201-762-7030; (23) Newspaper circulation: 23,000; (24) 75 plays and musicals; 25 art-related review columns; articles on New Jersey, aviation, and architectural barriers as relate to the physically handicapped.

The Sunshine Boys
(by Betty Mount, Summit Independent-Press, June 1975)

When you've been in show business all your life, leaving the limelight doesn't come easily.

And the new play over at Paper Mill Playhouse, The Sunshine Boys, shows how hard retirement comes even to famous people. There are two of them, old vaudevillians based on the real characters of (Joe) Smith and (Charlie) Dale who were on the bill when Radio City Music Hall opened 43 years ago. Neil

Simon's latest hit to leave Broadway is a study of the reunion
of the two old-timers.

One is Willie, a Geritol Gerry who's still got his health but
that's all he's got.   What he needs, desperately, is an audience.
Still living in a molding hotel room (which costs as much today
as it did when it was elegant) Willie is still working on his
craft, never varying from his staccato oneline gag rhythm: "So
the first booking you get me in years is at the Old Actors'
Home!"

Jack Gilford plays Willie straight-faced, acid, shuffling
around; reading obituary columns, noting Sol Bloomstein has
died--"He was Roderigez of Carmen and Roderigez"--comment-
ing, "I knew him well.   He was a terrible person."

Lou Jacobi plays relaxed, really retired Al.   Al lives with
his daughter in New Jersey where he enjoys the trees, his
grandchildren and a rock garden.   Willie disdains suburbanity
such as a garden of rocks, saying he's sorry they ever finished
the George Washington Bridge.

Mr. Jacobi's patient description of how his daughter drove
him all the way into NYC in her car is a high point of hilarity
contrasting with Willie's belief that only a vacuum exists outside
Manhattan.

"Do you get any fan mail out there in Jersey?" asks Willie.
"Heck, I don't even get jury duty," Al admits.

The catalyst who brings them together is Willie's nephew,
a casting agent, played neatly with genuine, concerned sincerity
by Jeremy Stevens.   Mr. Stevens is also a writer for The Electric Company on Children's Television Workshop, for which he
received an Emmy Award.

Then there's Lee Meredith who plays every doctor's dream
nurse-receptionist ... wearing a white "uniform" which is exactly opposite of a bikini: instead of two tiny fabrics separated
by large expanses of skin, there's her middle area briefly attired.

Also Rosetta Lenoire, well-known TV actress, who plays
the editorial-we nurse (as in "How are we feeling today?") with
crisp authority.

I must take issue with Clive Barnes' remark that Neil Simon,
in this play, comes out "as a really serious writer."   Mr.
Barnes' snide semantics would have Mr. Simon's Willie rejoin
with "So who writes just for fun?"

Comedy is serious business and Mr. Simon has been highly
successful in polishing human characterization peculiarities ever

since The Odd Couple. Very young people, or older people who aren't interested in anybody but themselves, will not enjoy this show. But those who recognize the whimsical wheezing of real situations will find it delightful.

The Sunshine Boys are not Sunny. But they are Funny.

The Threepenny Opera
(by Betty Mount, Summit Independent-Press, March 1976)

Television fans of Channel 13's Masterpiece Theatre, which has recently given us glimpses of the strictly organized "class" society in England, will be further charmed by the live stage presentation the Craig Theatre in Summit is currently offering. But don't expect any crook'd pinkies waving teacups around ... TV's head parlour maid Rose would frown in distaste were she to describe the steamy, seamy characters in The Threepenny Opera: "Not proper sorts at all," Rose would dismiss them in clipped cockney.

And of course that's just what makes them so vivid. Based on John Gay's 18th century The Beggar's Opera, The Threepenny Opera is an insiders' look at 19th century London (during Queen Victoria's coronation) by 20th century playwright Bertolt Brecht.

Spiced with realism and expressed with satire, such a play is shocking in its revelation of organized crime at its low street levels, so it is not surprising that it was suppressed originally by Sir Robert Walpole in 1728, and in its adapted form, by the political powers in Nazi Germany. Some fifteen years ago it was still considered, in Greenwich Village! a daring production, while the lilting Kurt Weill music (English lyrics adaptation by Marc Blitzstein) hit the Top Ten Records List with bobby-sox idol Bobby Darin crooning the bloody ballad of Mack the Knife.

Harry Ailster is in charge of all musical details, right down to playing the piano and that is very good recommendation indeed; his accompaniment is without jazzy overtones, and devoid of sentimentality--which would spoil the effect. Mr. Ailster also has the singers pitched appropriately.

John Dunnell has achieved another monumental feat--staging the proceedings in the round. He has flanked the center arena with four ramps from where actors pose, leap onstage or simply enter; get chased, kicked or thrown out, or simply exit. The fast lighting effects serve as curtain for scene changes and the ramps are marked with fluorescent tape so stage hands and actors are ready when the blackout lifts.

The arena staging also allows for lovely pictorial effects like unto illustrations in a Dickens book, as well as eye contact with the audience. This is scary when a one-armed, ragged beggar approaches your front-row seat, as well as rewarding when the tasty trollops beckon tantalizingly. Their action and agility are equal to the professional gymnasts!

I must take issue with the length of the performance, however, since most of the audience has <u>not</u> been jogging all day. The play participants are in constant motion or in the spotlight. The audience, for all its engrossment, <u>sits</u> for hours. This undue length is partly due to actual running time, but also partly to slow cue-cutting in and some plodding entrances and exits. The first act has an even, heavy pace, unlightened by dancing or brisk rhythm.

The second act is a model of rhythmic variety, and then the third act drags again. Mr. Dunnell, who is a very good director to start with, is getting better all the time; he has introduced some real farce--as in the hobby-horse riding courier who is shunted from ramp to ramp for his climatic arrival--but not enough.

The costumes and makeup are expertly done, with performances of the crooks and tarts visually dramatic. Outstanding are Richard Barranger as the dashing highwayman, leering Macheath; Ronald Platt as ponderous, preachy, greedy head crook Peachum; Beatrice Conrad as sniveling Mrs. Peachum who nevertheless holds forth with gusto in the Ballad of (male) Dependency; Liz Dunnell the sultry Jenny whose pirate song and tango ballad are both highlights. Especially good contrast is portrayed by Phyllis Cohon as sweet, innocent Polly Peachum against the smoldering passion of Lucy, played by Irma Zehr.

The world these characters inhabit is admittedly mean, and "man is uncouth"--but why do the girls adore Macheath who insists he's a humble safe-cracker? Do the pickpockets get the nod from the Commissioner of Police to work through the coronation crowd? Does Macheath hang for all his sins? Or does President Ford--I mean Queen Victoria--come through with a pardon?

You really shouldn't miss this exciting piece of theater. The Craig Theatre has again chosen a vehicle worth seeing. Four of us had a delicious dinner downstairs at the New Hampshire House before curtain time--which was delayed because of an overflow house having to be seated. So reservations are definitely in order.

"That's not nice; that's art!" wail the cheerful, crippled casualties of industrial society who must lead unsavory lives ... Well, it's nice to have the Craig Theatre so handy, and the Craig Theatre has mounted an artful production.

NADEL, Norman Sanford; (2) Critic and cultural affairs writer,

Scripps-Howard Newspapers; (3) b. Newark, N.J., June 19, 1915; (4) s. Louis D. and Sara (Fiverson); (5) Denison Univ. (A.B. psychology, music, 1938), U. of Chicago (psychology, 1943); (6) m. Martha Smith, Feb. 8, 1941; (7) children--David William, Arlene Judith Hammer, Mark Alan; (8) Make-up editor, Columbus (O.) Citizen, 1939, radio columnist, 1940, music critic, 1942; drama, music, film critic and theater editor, 1947-61; drama critic, New York World-Telegram & Sun 1961 (also entertainment editor 1963-64), drama critic New York World Journal Tribune 1966-67, in 1967 named critic and cultural affairs writer for Scripps-Howard Newspapers, covering all visual and performing arts; (9) founder, board member and trombonist, Columbus Philharmonic Orchestra, 1940-47, taught journalism, Ohio State U., organized train and plane theater tours to New York (24) and Europe (4) under sponsorship of Columbus Citizen (26) and Theatre Guild (2), lectures extensively throughout the U.S. on theater and criticism, taught at University of Oregon, Wagner College, Florida State Univ., other schools; (10) Consultant to Theatre Guild 1967-70; arbiter of disputes between Actors Equity and the League of NY Theatres and Producers, 1968- , board member, American Community Theatre Assoc., 1972-76, New York City Cultural Council, 1970-74, Four Winds Theatre, Columbus Boychoir School; (13) Army of the U.S., 1942-45; (14) Variety Spotlight Award for outstanding service to the American Theatre, National Federation of Music Clubs citation for music criticism-1957, Denison U. Alumni Citation-1963, president of NY Drama Critics Circle-1966-67, honorary Doctor of Humane Letters degree from Denison U.-1967; Phi Mu Alpha Sinfonia (music honorary); (15) NY Drama Critics Circle, American Theatre Critics Assoc.; (16) Democratic; (17) Jewish; (19) clubs: Dutch Treat, Richmond County YC, White's Point YC; (20) Author of A Pictorial History of the Theatre Guild, 1970, articles for Saturday Review, NY Times, Bravo, Minutes, Theatre Arts, Yachting, Boating, Rudder, Cue, Together, The Best Plays of 1966-67, other publications; (21) 234 College Ave., Staten Island, NY, 10314, Ph 212-727-3693; (22) Scripps-Howard Newspapers, 200 Park Ave., New York City 10017, Ph. 212-867-5000; (23) Circulation: 1,900,000; (24) About 125 articles annually, including drama, music, painting, sculpture, literature, architecture, dance, opera.

New "Woolf" Confirms Stature, but ...
(by Norman Nadel, Scripps-Howard Newspapers, April 20, 1976)

Edward Albee's staging of his own "Who's Afraid of Virginia Woolf?" affords new evidence that a playwright-turned-director is not necessarily his own best friend.

But the Music Box theater's new production also confirms the stature of this brilliant and terrifyingly real comedy as a contemporary classic, and as one of the finest plays ever written by an American.

It would be hard to find a serious acting company, professional or amateur, anywhere in the world, which has not staged "Who's Afraid ..." since the original Broadway production opened Oct. 14, 1962.

This time around, George and Martha, the feuding faculty couple at a New England college, are played by Ben Gazzara and Colleen Dewhurst. The original stage couple were Arthur Hill and Uta Hagen, while the film version costarred Richard Burton and Elizabeth Taylor.

Albee can hardly be faulted for casting Dewhurst and Gazzara, considering their past performances and their proven excellence. Still, at some point during rehearsals he should have noticed that for all their individual virtuosity something wasn't working out quite as it should.

It is a matter of balance. George and Martha are the antagonists in perhaps the most merciless and articulate marital warfare ever brought to the stage. First one, then another, gets the upper hand. Even at the final curtain neither has really won; they've just exhausted themselves into a temporary truce. You know the war will go on.

Anyone who has observed the two star players in their separate performances over the years might have concluded, or expected, that Dewhurst would overwhelm Gazzara. She is an enormously outgoing actress; he is tightly contained.

However, the play and its corrosive contest are thrown out of balance for the opposite reason. For all the vulgar, vituperative vigor of her Martha, Dewhurst never seems to score a resounding victory against her spouse. Gazzara is always in command. He never shows defeat, dismay or tactical disorder.

Consequently, the delicate balance is not maintained, or even satisfactorily established, so the suspense is diminished accordingly.

"Who's Afraid of Virginia Woolf?" has a cast of four, the other two being a younger faculty couple who at first are the embarrassed observers of Martha's and George's slashing, eventually its participants and victims. This new staging presents Richard Kelton and Maureen Anderman as Nick and Honey.

The weakness here lies in the casting of Miss Anderman and in the way she has been directed. Excessive, grotesque mugging violates the painful reality which her role and everything else about the play require.

The world has undergone awesome changes since this play was introduced almost 14 years ago, but only one of the changes dates it at all, and that has to do more with the audience than with the script. Following that 1962 opening, I was one of the critics to protest the vulgarity of its language, even while admiring the play itself. "Obsessively vulgar, unnecessarily obscene," I wrote.

Now its language doesn't bother me as being unnecessary.

Nor does the rest of the audience seem disturbed. We might
not speak that way ourselves, but we recognize that such talk
belongs in a night-long blood-letting between George and Martha.

Whether this is progress or the opposite, it is the way of
the world in 1976 as opposed to 1962.

Henry VIII Musical English as Apple Pie
(by Norman Nadel, Scripps-Howard Newspapers, April 26, 1976)

"Rex," Richard Rodgers' new musical depicting the follies
and furies of Britain's King Henry VIII, is as English as apple
pie.

Only in the splendor of John Conklin's settings and costumes
is the pre-Elizabethan royal court evoked. Otherwise, lyricist
Sheldon Harnick and, to a lesser degree, playwright Sherman
Yellen have helped Rodgers create an ambiance closer to his
"Carousel," which was set in Maine, or "Oklahoma!".

So, in that respect, the lavish show which premiered last
night at the Lunt-Fontanne Theater, misses at least one of its
objectives by several thousand miles and by about 400 years.

It isn't that anyone seriously expects the 73-year old dean
of American musical theater composers and his fellow artists
to literally re-create England as it was back when the mercurial
Henry was wedding and beheading wives. After all, audiences
pay their $17.50 top for entertainment, not for a history lesson.

Nevertheless, if we are going to be caught up in the story
and the people, we need a measure of credibility which, in this
case, means that an episode out of English history should sound
English. Neither the music nor the speech does.

In fact, even Henry comes across as not particularly British,
and hardly in a way to suggest Henry VIII; rather, as an actor
making an off-hand mockery of the role. And Nicol Williamson
as Henry, was almost the sole true concession to the story's
Englishness. He was born in Scotland which is fairly close by,
and has acted for the past 16 years mostly in the English theater.

Penny Fuller manages to suggest the nature of Anne Boleyn
who charms Henry by her independence of spirit--until he decides
to get rid of her on the chopping block. She achieves an even
stronger characterization as the Princess Elizabeth. At no moment is "Rex" so stirring as at the final curtain when she plunks
herself down on the royal throne and looks off with a cold and
calculating eye into her own future of a half-century as England's
greatest queen.

Still, "Rex" entertains intermittently, if not consistently.
In lighting, sets, costumes and stage movement it is almost
invariably enjoyable to watch.

NELLHAUS, Arlynn; (2) General assignment reporter in the entertainment department; (5) B.A. U. of Michigan, music; U. of Paris,
political science; M.A. Radcliffe College, music; U. of Chicago,
music; Northwestern U. Medill School of Journalism; (8) Music teacher in various cities, reporter and music critic, both part-time with
The News, Skokie, Ill.; Zone correspondent for The Denver Post and
originator of Footlight Fanfare (community theatre) column in Zones
supplements; music critic for Denver Post on freelance basis; Denver Post Staff Writer (a) club editor, (b) general assignment reporter in Living section, (c) general assignment reporter in entertainment, specializing in theatre and music; (20) Articles in Essence,
the New York Times, the Philadelphia Inquirer, Playboy; (22) The
Denver Post, 650 15th St., Denver, Co. 80202, Ph. 303-297-1345;
(23) Circulation: 250,000 daily; 300,000 Sunday; (24) 30 plays and
musicals, 30 concerts and shows, 6 record reviews, 3 films, 1
miscellaneous.

Baldwin's Touch Shines Through in "The Moon"
(by Arlynn Nellhaus, Denver Post, May 15, 1975)

The Third Eye Theatre is offering a French pastry of a play
with Eric Baldwin's "The Moon."

Denverite Baldwin has come up with language and characters
that are strongly Gallic.

There is delicacy and intricacy in the lines as finely wrought
as the music of Satie. The characters have a touch of lunacy
and an individuality that smacks of Giraudoux.

And while Baldwin's cast waits in the forest in hopes of trapping the Devil, they unavoidably remind the theatregoer of Beckett's "Waiting for Godot."

All this may sound as if "The Moon" is completely derivative. Perhaps it is, but be that as it may, it remains a play
with considerable charm.

It is rife with humor--not the belly-laugh kind, but humor
that sneaks up on you for its subtlety and gentle playfulness.

The play is a trifle, a sweet moment, but it indicates that
young Baldwin is a writer of considerable talent, whose future
work should be anticipated with pleasure.

Wednesday night, the Third Eye cast did a fine job as Baldwin's assorted characters. John Meredith was excellent as the
dignified beggar, Bolivar.

Jerry Reitmeyer was the baffled condiment salesman, a role
that was a bit less clearly realized than the others. Barbara
Ulrich was loud and broad as his wine-loving wife.

Danny Woods plays Flowerweld, the grave robber, with elan,

and Jeannie Marlin flourished as mad Josefine.

Greg Boyle needs more voice projection to finish the job of getting across his role as Marco, Bolivar's beggar companion.

The choice of Satie's music was perfect for the play's mood, but the use of Wagner's "Ride of the Valkyries" and of "Red River Valley" was baffling.

Hearts Go Out at Scene for "Hagar's Children"
(by Arlynn Nellhaus, Denver Post, May 30, 1975)

Christmas is notorious as the season when so-called normal people tend to become distressed and anxious.

For the five children at Bridgehaven Farm, a home for emotionally disturbed children, Christmas is when they must look their loneliness straight in the face. The fragile threads that hold them together from sunrise to sunset snap, but the replacements are stronger.

Ernest A. Joselovitz' play, "Hagar's Children," which opened at the Changing Scene Theatre Thursday night, is set on Christmas Eve at the home.

The home's name tells what the place is and what it hopes to be. It is a haven for the children, who have been through the agony of mental hospitals and ended up totally rejected by their parents.

Whether or not the home is a bridge to a better life can be answered only by looking at what happens to each child, individually.

One thing that does exist for them at Bridgehaven is complete acceptance by the staff--a Jewish woman and a black man--two people who for other reasons are rejected by the world out there.

Joselovitz treats each of his characters tenderly and with respect. Despite his episodic first act, "Hagar's Children" becomes a deeply involving experience for the audience.

The playwright mixes laughter with sadness, most beautifully, perhaps, when Esther, the staffer, reads Rob a letter from his mother who tries to justify her reasons for not coming to see him this Christmas. The letter is signed, "Sincerely yours."

Another hallmark of Joselovitz's writing is his powerful sense of rhythm, sometimes haunting and sometimes thundering.

The Changing Scene cast, as directed by Richard Lore, ably serves the writer. Those who portray the children, especially, often present superb moments.

Rotund (but lovely) Cho Cho Castellano, waifish Diane Germain, fearful Paul Barner, Scott Le Duke and Ed Eyestone make up the tortured quintet of youngsters. Each of them presents a well-delineated characterization.

Madeline Kimmel and Jud Hart II are cool and self-possessed as the burdened staffers. A single criticism is that they could use more energy to keep their lines from going flat in the first act.

But in total, "Hagar's Children" is a play that stirs the heart and mind and clings to both. It is presented expertly with some fascinating performances.

NELSON, Boris, The Blade, 541 Superior St. , Toledo, O. 43604.

NELSON, Don, New York Daily News, 220 East 42 St. , N. Y. , N. Y. 10017, Ph. 212-682-1234.

NEWTON, Edmund, New York Post, 210 South St. , New York, N. Y. 10002, Ph. 212-349-5000.

NIELAND, Christine, Chicago Daily News, 401 N. Wabash Ave. , Chicago, Ill. 60611.

NIEPOLD, Mary Martin, Philadelphia Inquirer, 400 North Broad St. , Philadelphia, Pa. 19101.

NORKIN, Samuel N. ; (2) Newspaper illustrator of theater, opera and dance events. Also cultural writer and reviewer; (3) b. New York City, Jan. 10, 1920; (4) s. Harry and Jenny (Scotnevsky); (5) Art education: Scholarship winner-Pratt Institute, N. Y. and Metropolitan Art School, N. Y. Cooper Union, Brooklyn Museum Art School. Other: studied creative writing and political science at Washington & Lee U. and Queen College, N. Y. ; (6) m. Frances Silverman, Sept. 12, 1968; (7) Children--Richard Scott and Laura May; (8) Weekly newspaper illustrator of theater events, N. Y. Herald Tribune 1946-56. Same for N. Y. Daily News, 1956 to present. Also for newspapers across the U. S. where shows tour. Art Critic, Carnegie Hall House Program 1970-73; Theater articles and illustrations, Theater Magazine 1957-59; contributor of cultural articles and reviews, N. Y. Daily News 1971-present; Playfare, Off-Bdwy Illus. & Text 1970; (9) Contributed special sculpture and humor material to Cole Porter's "Can-Can" 1954; Exhibitions: 100 Theater Drawings at Lincoln Center, Museum of the Performing Arts, N. Y. 1970.

Theater drawings: Wright-Hepburn-Webster Gallery, N.Y. 1971; Theater Collection, Museum of the City of N.Y. 1950, 1951; Guild Hall, East Hampton, N.Y. 1969 and 1971; (13) Sgt. U.S. Air Corps 1943-46; (15) Member, National Cartoonists Society; President of Drama Desk, 1974-current. (Assoc. of N.Y. Drama Critics, Editors, Reporters); (16) Politically Independent; (17) Jewish - Ethical Culturist; (21) 205 W. 86th St., N.Y. 10024, Ph. 212-873-1695. Also 10 Shadow Lane, E. Hampton, N.Y. 11937, Ph. 516-267-6481; (23) Circulation: 3 1/2 million--N.Y. Sunday News. Also Washington Post, Phila. Inquirer, Boston Glove, Cleve. Plain Dealer, Detroit News, Chicago Tribune, Los Angeles Times, San Francisco Chronicle, etc.; (24) About 100 articles and reviews from 1972 to present.

Controversial "Mass" A Musical Milestone
(by Sam Norkin, Daily News, July 1, 1974)

Leonard Bernstein's "Mass," dedicated to the memory of John F. Kennedy and presented by the Kennedy Center and S. Hurok, opened a four-week engagement at the Metropolitan Opera House Wednesday.

Since its Washington premiere at the opening of Kennedy Center last September, it has been a subject of controversy and confusion as to its form and content.

Whether it is a mass, opera, oratorio or musical, I cannot say. It is definitely not "No, No Nanette." But I do believe that anyone interested in the directions the American musical theater is taking should not miss it.

"Mass" offers a fund of propulsive song and a firm central idea. Bernstein, who has composed intermittently on religious themes since his "Jeremiah" Symphony of 1943, is here concerned with the crisis of faith in our time. As a point of departure, he has us at a religious service based on texts from the liturgy of the Roman Mass.

A young leader, called the Celebrant, despairing of the cynicism of his congregation, renounces his leadership. Out of the ensuing chaos a new unity and faith emerges.

Bernstein has functionally applied a number of different musical styles all essentially his own and managed to unify them This variety is what makes "Mass" so constantly stimulating.

It was a grand amalgam of music with impassioned sequences like "The Work of the Lord," a pulsating revivalist piece for the Celebrant (vibrantly sung by Alan Titus) and chorus with a surging trumpet obbligato, that sweeps all before it. The musical episodes go from popular proclamations of faith by an earthy, impudent street band, through swingle-type singers, rock and blues to the most sensitive reverent song.

For defiance and cynicism there are rock, blues, electronic and quadraphonic sounds. Throughout, the inspired composer gives us the utmost craftmanship in his choirs and smaller vocal groupings. And some of Bernstein's very best passages are orchestral as in the deeply committed Meditation No. 1.

Conductor Maurice Peress is the masterly leader of a company of 175 that includes the splendid Alvin Ailey Dance Theater. From superb Alan Titus down to boy soprano Chris Cole, they do everything to realize the composer's intentions. Gordon Davidson managed the stage forces well.

The amplification was almost flawless, magnifying well produced, focused sound. Rock bands could learn much from "Mass."

Most of the text is well written by Stephen Schwartz and Leonard Bernstein. Some of the self-conscious lyrics of the original version have been improved. The renunciation sequence could be tightened to keep things moving.

"Mass" is a grand and memorable work.

Sholom Aleichem's Return to 2d Ave.
(by Sam Norkin, Daily News, October 22, 1974)

Something of value and pleasure is available down on Second Ave. at the Eden Theater, if you are at all familiar with Yiddish, for Harry Rothpearl's dedicated company has revived another Sholom Aleichem delight.

It is called "The Big Winner," a play with music, and as Sam Levene points out in the current "Dreyfus in Rehearsal," a play should have a song or two. Maurice Schwartz first produced it in 1922 under the title "200,000," starring himself and Paul Muni.

In spite of the fact that the story is old hat and its outcome predictable, the handsome production is full of surprises. This is attributable to David Opatoshu, who plays the winner of a 200,000 ruble lottery, but also transcribes his acting skill to his debut as a director. Scene by scene, whether hilarious or touching, he and his cast give persuasive performances marked by dignity and finesse. They are also supported by an authentic-sounding score, lyrical or virile as needed, by film composer Sol Kaplan with good lyrics by Wolf Younin.

Opatoshu, the poor tailor in a Jewish town in Russia 1910, vows not to let his winnings go to his head. He employs two apprentices (Bruce Adler and Stan Porter) who despair of marrying his daughter Diane Cypkin) now that she is rich.

We are then treated to a string of vastly amusing events in

the tradition of Moliere's "The Would-Be Gentleman." We crack
up at first sight of Jeffrey B. Moss' satirical costumes and
decor, acquired by the newly affluent family.

Then there is the Russianizing of the tailor's Jewish name
from Shimele Soroker to Semyon Markarovitch. And giveaways
of the Nouveau-Riche, like failure to bite the tip off a cigar.
A battle of wits with the new butler, (Elia Patron) over how to
serve preserves. Learning to tango, with well-turned dances
by Choreographer Sophie Maslow. An unforgettable screening
of early movies by two conmen, after which the ex-tailor and
his wife (Miriam Kressyn) stipulate that their family and friends
must get free passes to all showings, as a condition of investment in the new medium.

Inevitably, they are swindled out of their wealth as suddenly as they acquired it and have only their sound values to return to. So the daughter marries one apprentice, leaving the
other to take off sadly for America, destined to make his fortune and turn up now as our English narrator.

It all makes for a warm, entertaining evening of Yiddish
theater.

NORTON, Elliot; (2) Drama Critic; (3) b. Boston, Mass., May 17,
1903; (4) s. William Laurence and Mary E. Norton (Fitzgerald);
(5) A.B., Harvard College, 1926; English major; (6) m. Florence
E. Stelmach, Sept. 9, 1934; (7) children--Elizabeth Noel, Jane Flo-
rence, David Andrew; (8) Reporter, Boston Post, 1926-34; drama
critic, 1934-56; drama critic, Boston Daily Record, 1956-62; Boston
Record American, 1962-72; Boston Herald American and Sunday
Herald Advertiser, 1972- ; (9) Lecturer in English, Emerson College,
Boston College, Harvard Summer School; Adjunct Professor of Dra-
matic Literature, Boston University, since 1954; Moderator, "Elliot
Norton Reviews," WGBH-TV, Public Television, since 1958; (10)
Vice Chairman, Mass. Council on the Arts and Humanities, 1966-74;
President, Boston Press Club, 1950-52; (14) Honorary degrees from
Suffolk University (Doctor of Journalism) Emerson College (Litt.D.),
Northeastern University (D. Litt.), Boston College (D.H.L.), St.
Francis College (D. Litt), Fairfield University (D.H.L.); Boston Col-
lege Citation of Merit, 1947; Connor Memorial Award of Phi Alpha
Tau, 1956; Rodgers and Hammerstein Award as "the person who has
done most for the theater in Boston," 1962; George Jean Nathan
Award for "the best dramatic criticism written during the year,"
1963-64; Special Antoinette Perry (Tony) Award from the League of
New York Theaters, 1971; Humanities Award of the National Council
of Teachers of English, 1971; Gold Medal Award of Excellence,
American College Theater Festival, 1973; National Award of the New
England Theater Conference "for outstanding creative achievement in
the American Theater," 1974; (15) Fellow, American Academy of
Arts and Sciences; member (President, 1951-53) New England Theater Conference; executive committee, American Theater Critics

Association; (19) Harvard Club of Boston; (20) Cont. articles to New
York Times, N.Y. Herald Tribune, Theater Arts, Theater Annual,
Shakespeare Quarterly, Harvard Advocate, Boston University Journal;
Best Plays volumes for several years as Boston Editor; such books
as "A College in a Yard, Harvard"; "The Passionate Playgoer" (Viking Press); "The American Theater" (Forum Lectures); "The American Theater, A Sum of Its Parts" (Samuel French et al); (21) 126
Church St., Watertown, Mass. 02172, Ph. 924-7731; (22) 300 Harrison
Ave., Boston, Mass., Ph. 426-3000; (23) Daily Circulation: 340,000,
Sunday circulation 500,000; number of households reached by weekly
television show, estimated 15,000-20,000; (24) Number of written
reviews about 150 per year; television reviews, conducted with members of casts of plays, authors, directors, etc., about 30.

Carnovsky as Lear in Stratford, Conn.
(by Elliot Norton, Boston Herald American, May 17, 1975)

The English director Peter Brook once likened "King
Lear" to a great mountain, whose slopes are covered with the
bodies of actors who didn't make it to the top. The figure is
apt: this is one of the great plays of the world, and one of the
most awesomely difficult for those who try to play the title role.

Morris Carnovsky made the ascent ten years ago here at the
American Shakespeare Theater: he was grand then, a heroic
figure awesome and imposing in the great scenes of Lear's wrath,
tender and touching when the old King falls into madness and
eventually into death.

He is ten years older now, and that makes a difference.
Lear himself is old "fourscore and over" by his own reckoning.
But he is a giant, a colossus; terrible in anger, when he turns
away his beloved Cordelia and when he rages against the storm.

There is less power in Mr. Carnovsky's performance than
there was in the earlier production. There is pity but little
terror: grace and goodness, but a loss of grandeur.

The old actor looks the way the old King should. His hair
is a halo of grey and white around a heroic face that might have
been sculpted by Michelangelo. He gears himself like a king,
ay, every inch a king. He carries the woes of kingship and the
burdens of old age when he makes his first entrance, wearing a
vast drab robe and a tunic of metal discs.

His walk is heavy, his frown portentous. He begins abruptly, as the old man divides his kingdom, preparing to divest himself of its burdens by bestowing his lands on his three daughters.

The King is arbitrary here, of course. When he declares
he will give the largest share to the daughter who declares she
loves him most, he is unreasonable. When he cuts off Cordelia,
whom he loves most, because she cannot find the words he wants,

he is outrageous.   Mr. Carnovsky is not outrageous enough.

In denouncing and then disinheriting Cordelia, he is rash.
On the testimony of her sisters.   Lear has always been rash.
But he should be terrifying when the rashness is on him; his
anger is thunder and lightning.   Morris Carnovsky in this scene
seems merely peevish, and that's not enough for "King Lear."

Later, when Lear denounces his daughter Goneril and calls
down terrible curses on her and on her sister Regan, there is
a similar lack of power.

When Lear is turned out by his daughters and defies the
great storm in some of Shakespeare's most extraordinary
speeches, he speaks from Lear's heart but without Lear's lungs.

In his pride, Lear is a match for the elements; he shouts
them down.   Mr. Carnovsky merely conjures the wind and the
rain.

It is in the moments of pity and tenderness that this actor
reaches the Shakespearean level.

He finds himself when the old King is checked and harried
by his daughters, who challenge his need to surround himself
with armed followers.

Morris Carnovsky brings all his force and understanding to
bear in a great speech that begins: "Oh, reason not the need!"
There is nobility in his bearing here, and heartbreak.   He rises
to the old man's level of suffering.   In grief he reaches greatness.

He is great, too, when Lear's wits begin to turn and he
labors to understand the half-naked Edgar, disguised as a mad
beggar.

He is fearsome, frightening and heartbreaking as he conducts, in his madness, a mock trial in which the accused are
his evil daughters.   Later, when the King wanders into a field
and finds there the blinded Duke of Gloucester, he is a pitiable
old man with more than a hint of something noble still in his
poor cracked mind.

When Lear, now cured after a long rest, awakens from
sleep to find his beloved Cordelia standing over him in one of
the greatest moments in all drama, the great actor is at his
best: bewildered at first, then gradually beginning to piece
things together; humble now with this daughter so terribly
wronged: kindly, gentle and grateful.

He is grand, too, in the final moments when Lear stalks in
carrying in his arms the dead body of the murdered Cordelia and

kneels over her in grief that ends only when nature snaps his own lifeline and he keels over quietly, dead of grief.

In this new production, which will run all season at the American Shakespeare Theater in repertory with "Our Town" (which will be reviewed tomorrow) and "The Winter's Tale," which opens in July, the star is not well supported.

Except in the performance of Lee Richardson, who is strongly authoritative as the loyal Duke of Kent, most of the players are either not good enough for this great tragedy or they are not suited to the roles they play.

Anthony Page directed the production with some sense of spectacle. Jane Greenwood designed the costumes, which are bulky with wool and furs, to suggest the primitive times in which King Lear may have lived. The settings by David Jenkins consist of a great door of seeming bronze which opens ominously to disclose a painted backdrop representing a stormy sky: not very exciting, but fair enough.

Shakespeare Theater Presents "Our Town"
(by Elliot Norton, Boston Herald American, May 18, 1975)

What a beautiful play "Our Town" is! And what a good production the American Shakespeare Theater is putting on.

Michael Kahn, who has staged this drama of life and death and love and marriage in "Grover's Corners, N. H." and all the other corners of the world where good people live and die and love and get married, has cherished its truths, its humor and its wisdom and he has found the right actors and actresses for most, if not all, the great roles.

This is a simple play of profound meanings. It has to be simply acted without tricks or treats. Presenting the people of a small New England town in the early part of the century, it resists caricature and exposes the exaggerations of ham actors. At Stratford, Conn. , there are few hams.

Mr. Kahn elected Fred Gwynne to play the showiest part. As the Stage Manager, who conducts the audience through the three acts as guide and friend and philosopher, Mr. Gwynne shuns all temptations to be "cute" or "folksy." Nor does he push to get across his message, or that of Thornton Wilder. He plays it cool and lets the humor and the wisdom come through naturally.

He has, too, bless him, an authentic New England accent. He even knows how to say "ayeh," which few actors ever get to learn. And he knows that the old rural accent of this part of the world was not quaint, but colorful.

He is a modest narrator with an ingratiating manner that grows on the playgoer. Like any born New Englander, he makes no bid for popularity; he relies for favor on the good sense of his hearers. Thornton Wilder would be proud of Fred, who understands his play and makes it meaningful in a quiet, modest way.

The Shakespeare Theater presents Richard Backus and Kate Mulgrew as George Gibbs and Emily Webb, who live next door to one another in Grover's Corners and, as childhood sweethearts, unite their lives in marriage as most people in small towns and big cities do but with perhaps, little more feeling and a good deal more apprehension than most.

These are difficult roles. In George or Emily, any sign of quaintness or cuteness would be blasphemous, nothing less. Mr. Backus and Miss Mulgrew follow Fred Gwynne's example. They are both young, very attractive and endearing as they exchange notes on school homework, as they meet at Mr. Morgan's soda fountain to thrash out their differences and find they love one another, and as they struggle through the wedding ceremony.

The final act is a bold one: it takes place in the graveyard on a hill high over Grover's Corners, where the dead sit solemnly in their graves and watch the world of living people with cool indifference.

Emily, dead in childbirth, elects to come back from the dead, to live over one day in her life: her twelfth birthday.

The scene is one of the great ones, perhaps the greatest yet written by an American playwright, a scene of joy and sorrow almost unutterable, and of recognition.

Having "lived through" that day in her life as she was 14 years earlier, Emily turns back in grief to the Stage Manager to ask the key question of Our Town: "Does anyone ever really, fully realize the beauty of life while living it?"

The Stage Manager's answer is cryptic--and wise: "No," he says quietly: "The saints and the poets, mebbe--they do, some."

Miss Mulgrew is radiantly, heartbreakingly young at that moment, and very moving.

This second production of the American Shakespeare Theater's season is alternating with "King Lear," has some other good performances, some that are fair and one or two that suggest the actors think they are in "Aaron Slick from Punkin Crick."

There are good workmanlike--or should one say workperson-

like--performances by Eileen Heckart and Geraldine Fitzgerald,
admirable actresses, as the neighbors, Mrs. Gibbs and Mrs.
Webb. The acting of William Larsen, as Dr. Gibbs, is quietly
truthful in this production of the greatest American play, which
can be enjoyed, admired and cherished despite the shortcomings
of some supporting players.

NOTH, Dominique Paul; (2) Theater and Film Critic; (3) b. New
York City, Feb. 19, 1944; (4) s. Ernst Erich and Elena Fels Noth;
(5) Drama and English major, Marquette U. , semester shy of degree; (6) m. Louise Langley April 25, 1969; (7) children--Jeanne,
Felicia, Paul, Vincent; (8) Actor, director in New York and Washington, D. C. , 1964-66; editorial production, Time magazine, same
period; critic and feature writer, The Milwaukee Journal, 1967 to
present; Adjunct Professor in School of Fine Arts, U. of Wisconsin--
Milwaukee, 1973 to present; (9) Acting coach and lecturer, Marquette
University, 1967-73; guest lecturer English Department, Marquette
University, 1975; film critic educational Channel 10, Milwaukee,
1972 and 1974; actor, director with Marquette Players, 1960-65;
freelance writer early 1960s; (10) Evaluator, Wisconsin Arts Council; (14) Twice winner Milwaukee Press Club awards; (15) American
Theater Critics Association; (16) Democrat; (17) Catholic; (20) various; (21) 2865 N. Frederick Ave. , Milwaukee, Wis. 53211, Ph.
964-5612; (22) The Milwaukee Journal, 333 W. State St. , Milwaukee,
Wis. 53211, Ph. 224-2370; (23) Circulation: 540,000; (24) 30 plays
and musicals, 70 motion pictures, 5 dance, 25 music, 5 miscellaneous.

"Our Town" and "Three Sisters"--Distant Parallels
(by Dominique Paul Noth, Milwaukee Journal, January 27, 1974)

The time is one (turn of the century). The places are two
(rural New England and rural Russia). The works are "Our
Town" (currently on the Milwaukee Rep stage) and "Three Sisters"
(recently here on film in the American Film Theatre presentation
of Laurence Olivier and the National Theatre of Great Britain).

Two authors--Thornton Wilder and Anton Chekhov--separ-
ated by half a world have something in common besides artistry:
fading lifestyles, isolated portraits of life, informing conflicts.
They find in the past the future and the continuity of life, wasted
life and wishful life in "Sisters," unaware life and rockhard duties
in "Our Town. " But the humanism is alike, groping, aching.

It is the dream of Mrs. Gibbs' life to see Paris, France. It
is the dream of the three sisters to return to Moscow. But the
Russians are out of touch, educated beyond their circumstances.
Mrs. Gibbs dreams but goes back to making breakfast. The
sisters toss and turn, too delicate for such Puritan certainties.

The dead in "Our Town" are waiting for something. The
living in "Sisters" are, too. The New Englanders are only

casually aware of how beautiful life is--mostly they're content,
and afraid of the vast world beyond. The Russians feel the lack.
Wilder often is looking on. Chekhov is looking in.

Both plays are worlds dependent on actors and directors,
and both productions find their deepest resonances in the women.
Ruth Schudson's Mrs. Gibbs is so casually correct as to be
moving--characterization with ease and restraint. For contrasting color, Penelope Reed tinges the other mother, Mrs. Webb,
in edgy, busy motions.

But it is Judith Light--fulfilling the promise barely hinted
at in past Rep roles--who sweeps us and "Our Town" up to
heights. Her Emily, as few Emilys have, grows from an almost
comedic laying back in the first act, through girlish agonies in
the second act to a mature woman in the last act who must play
at being a child again. And it hurts. One may quibble here
and there, but this almost eccentric Emily vanquishes us with
her knowledge.

Rep director Nagle Jackson has seen "Our Town"--thankful-
ly--without the sentimentality attached to it in the past. This
produces virtues but also unwittingly exposes Wilder, the ob-
viousness of the symbols, the trickery of the bare stage devices,
Jackson has almost been too scholarly, too aware of Wilder the
agnostic. The production is amusingly wry, but only randomly
warm. Some roles are humorous or good--Jim Baker, William
McKereghan--but not real, too suave (though Robert Ground's
young man, George is straightforward).

The heaviness eventually saturates Durward McDonald's stage
manager, conceived with perfect New Englandese that becomes
unrelenting, though enlivened by sudden, booming moments of interpretation. But McDonald and that big, lowing voice, unwilling
to let an idea pass uninflected or unelongated, has confused creation of mood with creation of moo.

Chekhov's play is greater, subtler in symbol, closer to the
cosmic sense that Wilder so wants to get across. Jackson's
counterpart is Olivier, who is daringly simple in setting the reality of Chekhov against too spacious, too artificial settings.
Olivier is, like Jackson, obviously following a master plan, and
both sometimes hand us character behavior more style than substance.

But when "Three Sisters" is on target, it's great. Judith
Light's counterpart is Louise Purnell as ingenue Irina, who suffers constantly but struggles anyway. But what Emily might deteriorate into, in a different class and under different pressures,
is suggested by Joan Plowright's brilliantly sad and sudden Masha, and by Jeanne Watts' Olga, the eldest sister resigned to an
old maidish sense of loss.

But it is to Olga that Chekhov gives the final optimism,
"Let us live! Perhaps in a little while we will know why we
live, why we suffer." The dead Emily asks, "Do any human
beings realize life while they live it--every, every minute?"
Side by side the statements ring, and to see these works side
by side--failings and successes--is to touch the heart of art.

"Rehearsal" Falls Bit Short
(by Dominique Paul Noth, Milwaukee Journal, November 2, 1974)

The Milwaukee Repertory Theater Company went into "The
Rehearsal" Friday night with great care and high intentions.
Though certainly watchable, the production doesn't do justice to
one of Jean Anouilh's most moving and delicate plays.

Director William McKereghan has probed in both interesting
and strange directions, ignoring some possibilities, reaching for
others. His actors are facing roles so interlocked that the weak
drag down the strong or muddle the potentials.

This is a play within a play situation. Some charming but
shallow contemporary French aristocrats are decked out in 18th
century dress while amusing themselves with a love play. But
the count, their buoyantly frivolous leader, is falling truly in
love with the ingenuous working girl he has chosen to play the
ingenue.

While infidelity is the open norm among these idle rich,
such a departure from class--and from pleasure principles--
will not be tolerated by the count's clever wife, his mistress
and his best friend. They scheme to prevent it.

It is the disappointment of this production that, while the
wit works (heavily at times), the painful emotions of the piece
seem slight, as the finale. The outline is there, the focus is
not.

McKereghan, despite the intimacy of the Todd Wehr Theater,
allows some characters to react with broadness. There seems
to be a fear to trust the audience to enjoy a gentle laugh or
quiet realization.

The ingenue part is a difficult wisp of a thing to humanize,
and Leslie Geraci attacks it like a cheerleader for love matches.
Robert Lanchester, with biting punctuation and a masterful veneer of timing, plays the drunken friend, Hero, but in his scenes
with the straining Miss Geraci, he cannot hold the emotional
chords together.

As the countess, guest actress Margaret Hilton drenches her
lines in acid British delivery of much grace and some overplaying.

Next to her, guest actor William Cain seems too Americanized as the count, but he invests the repartee with hard work.
Drawling Tracy Friedman is mimicking elegant amorality as the
mistress, rather than personifying it. Nor is Andrew Miner
sure of his humor as the countess' insufferable "suffering lover."

"The Rehearsal" is a full grown play, and the performers
do have six weeks to grow into it. Several of them can.

NOTMAN, Edith (Wilkinson); (2) College professor/summer theatre
critic; (3) b. N.Y.C. April 14, 1937; (4) d. Cecil & Clara (Gubser)
Wilkinson; (5) B.A. Cornell U., 1959; major: English; M.A. U. of
Calif. at Berkeley, 1970, in dramatic art; Ph.D. expected 1975; (6)
m. John W. Notman (now dec'd) Mar. 11, 1961; (7) children--Katha-
rine Bennett, Edith Evans; (8) Direct mail, sales promotion & public
relations for major U.S. corporations 1959-72. Research and Teaching Assistant, U.C. Berkeley, 1970-72; Assistant Professor, Williams College, 1972-present; summer theatre critic, Manchester
(Vt.) Journal, 1973-present; (15) Mem. American Theatre Assn.,
Modern Language Assn; (16) Independent; (21) Petersburg Rd., Williamstown, Ma. 01267, Ph. 413-458-5209; (22) Williams College,
Williamstown, Ma. 01267, Ph. 413-597-2186; (24) 8-10 plays and
musicals.

Williamstown's "Juno" Is Uncomfortable and Unsatisfying
(by Edith Notman, Manchester Journal, August 15, 1974)

Note to the Williamstown Theatre Festival; Whoever had the
bright idea of doing Sean O'Casey's "Juno and the Paycock" as
a musical deserves a big bouquet of the prettiest poison ivy to
be found in Berkshire County.

In its original form, "Juno" is O'Casey's bitter celebration
of life among Ireland's urban poor during the civil war of the
1920's. We watch as the Boyles--parents, son and daughter--
are destroyed by their Dublin tenement world and their own
limitations. Politics, unwise love, liquor, social aspirations
and grinding poverty are all factors, but the fundamental responsibility rests with the family itself.

As a theatre piece, the Williamstown version of the play has
been doubly misconceived. It indicates little understanding of
the nature of musical comedy, it mutilates the original play almost beyond recognition, and the result is not satisfying as
either musical or play.

It is important to remember that the emotional range of drama set to music is limited. That is why we normally refer to
"musical comedy" rather than "musical play." The emphasis
is on style, not content, and even a serious musical is held
back from involvement with the characters by the form itself.

The musical comedy form is simply not suited to the presentation of the extreme states of emotion needed for the full development of a dramatic character.   For instance, pauses for songs make virtually impossible the concentration needed to represent extremes of emotion on stage.   Therefore, the stress falls on comedy.

The exceptions prove the rule.   Brecht's "Threepenny Opera" demands not emotional but intellectual rapport.   We are expected to become involved with the social problem, not with the characters.   A serious musical like Stephen Sondheim's "Company," to take another example, also distances us from the characters to focus on the situation.

But "Juno and the Paycock" is not suited to this treatment. It is a play centering squarely on human beings, but the brilliant character studies which make the original play memorable, are largely lost in the musical.   Also lost is the almost Shakespearean sense of many lives and events contributing to the whole fabric of human existence.

The chief fault is with the adaptation, by Richard Maltby, Jr. and Geraldine Fitzgerald.   Furthermore, Marc Blitzstein's pert, cheerful little melodies and his and Mr. Maltby's lyrics are not suited to a play with any pretense at seriousness.

The lyrics particularly do not serve the play well.   They run to such rhymes as, "I've got more than double / my share of trouble," which isn't much of a start to an act which ends not only in the final destruction of the family's hopes for a better future, but also in the death of one of its members.

In the musical, unlike the play, the characters are all depicted as victims.   The mother, Juno, as played by Miss Fitzgerald, is a refined woman who borders on the saintly.   In fact, she is also a sharp tongued, disagreeable scold who must bear some of the responsibility for what befalls her family.

In the original, it is easy to understand why the work-shirking husband and Peacock of the title, Captain Jack Boyle, gets back at his wife by taking every opportunity to run off to the neighborhood pub with his sidekick, Joxer Daly.   But here Captain Jack and Joxer (played with relish by Milo O'Shea and Emery Battis) are little more than skillfully done comic turns. The musical does not permit us to take them seriously, even though the consequences of Jack Boyle's irresponsibility are profoundly serious.

The son Johnny, well played by David Clennon, is shattered in body and mind as a result of his IRA activities.   He appears before us as a one-armed, shivering wreck who is hardly the stuff of which musicals are made.

The character of the daughter, Mary (Suzanne Lederer) is
similarly fragmented. Though she is given sweet love songs to
sing, she is also depicted as a tough, insensitive street girl
whose attempts to extracate herself from her tenement existence
result in disaster for her.

My strongly negative feelings are directed against the script,
not the actors. These are good performances in a bad cause,
and the smaller parts are also well done. Arvin Brown has directed with his usual skill, and the setting, costumes and lighting, by David Jenkins, Bill Walker and Richard Devin are nicely
suited to the milieu of the play.

What is wrong is the whole idea behind the project, which
has resulted in an evening that is both uncomfortable and unsatisfying. Good drama often makes us uncomfortable--Shakespeare's
tragedies are the standard examples--but at the same time it is
deeply satisfying. Entertainment may not be satisfying in any
significant way, but at the same time it should not make us uncomfortable, as the musical version of "Juno and the Paycock"
does.

"Private Lives" a Delicious Soufflé at Williamstown
(by Edith Notman, Manchester Journal, August 22, 1974)

The Williamstown Theatre Festival's version of Noel Coward's "Private Lives," directed by Nikas Psacharopoulos, is a
souffle of a production, light and delicious despite its failure to
rise to its full potential.

It is a funny, funny play about impossibly urbane people who
express themselves in an unending stream of Cowardly bon mots.
(Enraged husband; "certain women are like gongs--they should
be struck regularly.") And if the enthusiastic reaction of the
first-night audience was any indication, the fact that the play's
British precision has been considerably blunted by American
heartiness does not spoil the fun, for the play is simply too
good to spoil.

Many of the opening night problems were obviously the result of under-rehearsal, and these should disappear in a few
days. Furthermore, even though the style and pace needed to
realize the play fully were evident only fitfully, and even though
there are awkwardnesses in this staging that have no place in a
professional production, the play itself overcomes these handicaps.

Consider the potentialities of the situation. A man and woman, divorced five years earlier and newly embarked on second
marriages, find themselves sharing a terrace in adjoining honeymoon suites at a Deauville resort.

Each has chosen a second spouse who is precisely the

opposite of the first, but old love quickly rekindles and the two flee their new marriages. Secluded in Paris, the debate on how best to break the news to the other two that, just married, they want divorces.

Discussion leads to bickering, then to arguments, and they come to blows just as the rejected pair arrive with their own confession to make. After another act of twists and turns, the plot is neatly tied up, tongue stylishly in cheek.

Marjorie Kellogg's sets, which appear to have been constructed mainly from orange and lemon sherbert, look good enough to eat. Rita Bottomley's costumes carry through the airy elegance in concept, but unfortunately several of the women's outfits fit rather poorly. Richard Devin was the capable lighting designer.

The cast is a good one. John Cunningham plays Elyot Chase, the role Coward wrote for himself, and he seems most comfortable in the uncomfortable position of a newlywed newly enamored of his ex-wife. He also comes closest to capturing the play's style.

Virginia Vestoff plays his ex-wife, Amanda Prynne, a human battering ram with the heart of a top sergeant, packaged as an elegant redhead.

Anne Toomey and David Ackroyd play Sibyl Chase and Victor Prynne. Ackroyd, though clearly miscast, does a creditable job. He is all earnest incomprehension, trying desperately to behave properly in a totally improper situation.

Miss Toomey is a former member of the apprentice company who has advanced quickly into major roles, and though she gives this one a game try, she hasn't yet enough authority for it. Additionally, I think, she has been directed into a worldly manner foreign to the character, who is the most innocent of the four.

Suzanne Gilbert appears as the French maid who disapprovingly provides coffee and rolls to the menage.

A year after his death, Coward's plays are enjoying a wave of popularity, and "Private Lives" is probably his most acclaimed play. The popularity is deserved, for in a theatrical climate that all too often cheats the audience with cheap tricks, Coward was not only a superb craftsman but also a meticulously honest one, a playwright who promises no more than he delivers and who delivers what he promises, with authority and wit.

NOURSE, Joan Thellusson; (2) Theater Critic; (3) b. New York City

Feb. 17, 1921; (4) d. Charles and Mary (FitzPatrick) Thellusson; (5) B.A. Manhattanville Col., major subj.: English, 1942; M.A., Fordham U., major subj.: English Drama, 1944; Ph.D. Fordham U., major subj.: Modern Drama, 1948; (6) m. Philip E. Nourse, Feb. 6, 1954; (7) children--William Philip, Kathleen Mary-Elizabeth; (8) English Instructor, Hunter Col., 1948-52; Drama Critic, The Catholic News, 1952- ; The Tablet, 1953-75; The Monitor, 1954- ; The Advocate, 1955-75; The Long Island Catholic, 1958- ; The Catholic Transcript, 1957- ; The Catholic Universe-Bulletin, 1971-74; (9) Professor of English, Seton Hall U., 1959- ; Co-author with Philip E. Nourse, The Happy Faculty, produced by The Blackfriars Guild, 1968; author, Lib Comes High, produced by The Blackfriars Guild, 1970; (15) Awards Committee, The Outer Critics Circle, 1955- ; Mem. Modern Language Association of America, 1948- ; (16) Democrat; (17) Roman Catholic; (20) Author, with A. A. Norton of A Christian Approach to Western Literature, 1963 and Literary Craftsmanship, 1965; author of Monarch Notes on My Antonia, 1964, The Crucible, 1965, Death of a Salesman, 1965, and Major Barbara, 1965; (21) 780 Riverside Drive, New York, N.Y., Ph. 212-WA 6-3691; (22) Seton Hall University, South Orange, N.J. 07079, Ph. 201-SO 2-9000; (23) Circulation: 230,000, general readership; (24) All Broadway shows, most Off-Broadway, some Off-Off-Broadway.

Power of Suggestion Key to "Old Times"
(by Joan T. Nourse, Catholic Transcript, December 3, 1971)

A stroll down memory lane with Harold Pinter can be a risky business. For while we do live in the present, he insists that our relationships with others depend largely upon our assumptions about the past.

So if these are disturbed or left open to doubt, the sense of loss may be shattering. Not that a Pinter play is ever going to come out with some astounding revelation in the Holmes tradition. There'll be only clues, no solution. But even hints can be destructive.

Set in a stark converted farmhouse designed by John Bury, "Old Times" introduces a charming sophisticate, Anna (Rosemary Harris), arriving from overseas to visit her former roommate, Kate (Mary Ure), and the latter's movie-director husband Deeley (Robert Shaw).

The two women have not seen each other for 20 years, and Deeley seems good-naturedly curious about the newcomer. No great concern, just polite interest. And after one of Kate's casseroles, they all talk about what London was like two decades ago, the movies they went to, the parties where they might have met, while now and then Deeley and Anna recall snatches of former hits like "Lovely to Look At" or "They Can't Take That Away from Me."

All very amiable over a drink. Quite civilized. But hard, somehow, on the nerves.

For what wounds is not so much what is said as what is un-
said. Pinter's specialty is, after all, the pause or the "silence."
And despite our almost irresistible urge to conjure up explanations, fill in the blanks, chances are the questions here are
more important than the answers.

The marriage of Deeley and Kate appears to be reasonably
stable, if not overly passionate. Making films, he's often away
on location. And she's given to long solitary walks along the
beach.

They're congenial enough, though. They get along.

Then enter Anna. And the speculation starts. How strong
was the attachment between her and Kate?

Did Deeley actually encounter Anna in that earlier era and
choose the wrong girl? For that matter, has he ever possessed
the heart of the woman he once wanted so fiercely?

Rejection is always a painful experience. But just who was
rejected?

And so it goes. The play is splendidly acted by its cast of
three, and Peter Hall has directed for quietly compelling effects.
But our reactions to this type of work will probably be favorable
only if we're willing to settle for the power of suggestion.

Nothing much overt is going to happen, and precious few of
the trio's recollections will be clear or complete enough for us
to get the picture. All we can do when the speech breaks occur
is either try to figure out what's going on in the character's
psyche or simply accept his agitation as fact, for what it's worth.

What Pinter does, he does remarkably well. The problem
of whether or not he does enough, hinges upon our willingness
to accept enigmatic theatre as truly mirroring a less and less
intelligible world.

Best and Worst of Human Nature
(by Joan T. Nourse, Catholic News, December 12, 1974)

The Island

Like Solzhenitsyn's "The First Circle," this harrowing South
African two-character play reveals at once both the worst and
the best that can be said of human nature. Dealing with two
black political prisoners on a bleak prison island near Cape
Town, playwright Athol Fugard and his actor-collaborators John
Kani and Winston Ntshona give us first of all some appalling indications of the cruelty with which those in power can treat helpless individuals at their mercy. But they also show how splendidly the spirit of man can rise above the most dreadful depriva-
tions.

Using their own first names, the two able performers make it evident from the start that they are re-creating an intensely felt, very personal experience. Not that they themselves have ever been sent to the actual notorious Robben Island. But they've known well those who have been, and the threat of it has long hung over them in their homeland.

Purely physical torture does not seem to be a major issue here, at least not in old melodramatic forms like rack and thumbscrew. What these men suffer is rather the deadening tedium of long sentences, an agonizing separation from wife and children, grueling labor in the blazing sun, minimal creature comforts, and a harsh regimen designed to inflict continual insult to individual dignity.

Yet, as Fugard and his friends maintain, some do survive with amazing courage and resilience. They argue and make jokes. They share memories and fragile hopes. They even find solace in art. Here the two manage somehow to put on a truncated version of "Antigone," thus identifying their torments with those of all who throughout history have dared raise a protest against governments that choose to ignore man's inalienable rights.

As in their companion piece, "Sizwe Banzi Is Dead," these talented visitors from South Africa are giving us disturbing glimpses of just what it can mean to be a proud people subjugated by discriminatory laws. But their plays also serve, as did "Antigone" in its time, to remind us that those ruling oppressively can never rest wholly secure so long as there remains one eloquent rebel to cry out for justice.

The Wager

In his first new work since "When You Comin' Back, Red Ryder?" New Mexico professor Mark Medoff again suggests that our young American intellectuals are a confused, disheartened, even desperate lot. His two California graduate students, who share an apartment, are in some ways contrasting personalities. But they're similar in that both lack a clear system of values that might give meaning to their lives.

The title derives from a bet made by one of them, the scholarly, introverted Leeds (Kristoffer Tabori) that the other Ward (Kenneth Gilman) an arrogant, womanizing athlete, can't seduce a young faculty-wife neighbor without being shot by her husband. Ward takes the bet because lately his triumphs in the love game have been so easy that any excitement would be a nice novelty. As for Leeds, who normally shies away from involvement, romantic or otherwise, the wager grows out of his disgust at Ward's callous self-indulgence and thinly disguised hope that some retribution will strike.

The lady in question, ironically named Honor (Linda Cook),
seems at first to present no challenge. Bored after several
dull years of marriage, she offers little resistance. But is she
really having an affair to assert herself as a person? Or is
she merely trying to infuriate the uptight Leeds? And as the
liaison becomes obvious, what of her bewildered mate, Ron
(John Heard)? Can he possibly appeal to their common recollections of good times? Or were they all wishful thinking on
his part? And should he get violent, what good would that do?

Like Mr. Medoff's earlier hit, this drama has more questions than answers. And again, the lines are witty, with the
acting very good indeed. If the professor is right, though,
our privileged young are in far worse shape spiritually than
those poor, beaten-down black prisoners on "The Island."

NOVICK, Julius: (2) Theatre Critic: (3) b. New York City, Jan. 31,
1939; (4) s. Solomon J. and Ethel (Lerner) N.; (5) B.A. in English,
Harvard, 1960; Fulbright Scholarship, University of Bristol (England),
1960-61; D.F.A. in drama, Yale, 1966; (6) Single; (8) Theatre critic,
The Village Voice, 1958 to date; Instructor in English and later As-
sistant Professor of English, New York University, 1966-72; Associ-
ate Professor of Literature, State University of New York College
at Purchase, 1972 to date; (9) Apprentice (actor-crew member), New
York Shakespeare Festival, summer 1957; actor, Group 20 Players,
Wellesley, Mass., summer, 1958; visiting lecturer, Drama Division,
Juilliard School, 1968-71, dramatic critic, WNDT-TV, Channel 13,
New York City, 1968-70; visiting faculty member, Critics Institute,
O'Neill Memorial Theatre Center, Waterford, Connecticut, 1971 to
date; dramaturg, City Center Acting Company, 1971-73; (14) Special
Award, New England Theatre Conference, October 1969; Special
Mention, Sang Prize Competition for Critics of the Fine Arts, March,
1968; (15) Mem. American Theatre Critics Association, American
Theatre Association; (16) Democrat; (17) Agnostic; (20) Book, Beyond
Broadway: The Quest for Permanent Theatres (Hill and Wang, 1968,
1969); contributed articles and reviews to The New York Times
("Arts and Leisure" section and "Book Review"), The Encyclopedia
Britannica Book of the Year, Harper's Magazine, Harper's Bazaar,
Vogue, The Nation, The Humanist, etc.; (21) 3 Washington Square
Village, New York, N.Y. 10012, Ph. 212-GR 3-5927; (22) SUNY-
Purchase, Purchase, N.Y. 10577, Ph. 914-253-5044; (23) Circula-
tion: 150,000 (Village Voice); (24) 50-60.

<u>No Play's Like "Holmes"</u>
(by Julius Novick, Village Voice, November 21, 1974)

The reign of Queen Victoria--when piano-legs were sometimes swathed in cloth because naked legs, even wooden ones,
were too shocking to be left exposed--is often remembered with
distaste as, psychologically speaking, the Great Age of Repression. But what we repress is what makes us nervous, uneasy,
frightened: what we are not sure we are capable of dealing
with. So Victoria's reign, when so much in us that is potentially frightening seems to have been so securely buttoned up, is

also, retrospectively at least, remembered with nostalgia as the
Great Age of Security.   That is why we delight--why some of
us delight--in Gilbert and Sullivan, in the novels of Trollope,
and in the early episodes of the televised version of "The Forsythe Saga." Nanny ruled in the nursey, and Queen Victoria--
Supernanny--reigned in Buckingham Palace: stern, strong maternal angels symbolizing Repression and Security both.   And a
whole society sometimes seems to have been governed by Hilaire
Belloc's adjuration:

> Be Sure to take Good Hold of
> Nurse.
> For Fear of meeting Something
> Worse.

But "Something Worse" was there, all the same.   What is
repressed does not simply vanish, it sinks down; it lies latent;
it lurks.   Beneath the bland delights of middle-class Victorianism lurked the whole underside of human personality, a teeming
jungle of horrors: it has lately been asserted that Jack the
Ripper was really a member of the Royal Family.   For Dickens,
the great city of London was the symbol of these horrors--these
impulses, these passions--the city, and particularly the fog, fed
then by coal smoke, which used to shroud the city far more
thickly than ever it does now: the fog, when impulses, passions,
desires that were hidden in the full Victorian sunshine could
emerge, and work.

Sir Arthur Conan Doyle took over this symbology with all
its fascination--the fearful and the forbidden are always fascinating, if we can stand them--and placed two irresistible figures
at its center.   One is Doctor Watson, who expresses our fascination while he soothes our fears with his sturdy, four-square
normality, who at the same time stands for us (we are normal
too) and allows us, in his wonderful obtuseness, a sense of superiority (we are not quite so normal as that).   And the other
of course is Sherlock Holmes, cocaine addict, amateur violinist,
and consulting detective.   Holmes is a little frightening himself:
he is not quite human in his incredible skill and his iron self-
repression, yet this very self-repression--the cocaine is an important clue--implies unplumbed gulfs within.   At the same time,
Holmes is wonderfully reassuring, a symbol of control, of man's
power--our power--to descend into the most terrible depths of
the fog, confront and conquer what is found there, and return to
the surface smiling, unruffled, and supremely in charge.   He is
Queen Victoria's true deputy, her invincible general in the war
on the inner frontier.   At his side we are as safe, really, as
we were when holding the hand of Nurse--but the excitement is
terrific.

One of the chief delights of the Holmes stories is their controlled extravagance, the delicate way in which Conan Doyle balances them on the very edge of self-parody.   This delicate

balance, however, is obviously very susceptible to being unbal-
anced when other hands apply themselves to the Holmesian
oeuvre, and that, regrettably, is what has happened in the case
of the Royal Shakespeare Company's large and lavish production
entitled "Sherlock Holmes," which has now been exported to our
shores.

This "Sherlock Holmes" has been directed by Frank Dunlop
in a vein of deliberately preposterous exaggeration. The actors
are too busy striking attitudes and being picturesque to get very
much pressure of intent and urgency behind what they say and
do. Much of the time their subtext seems to be, "Isn't this
delicious nonsense?"--and so it might be, if only they would not
insist on it so much. The performances undercut themselves.

The real Holmes, if I may be allowed that paradox, was an
exquisite master of understatement: it is no coincidence that
his most famous comment on his own feats of deduction is the
dismissive adjective, "Elementary." Watson speaks of his
"cool, nonchalant air." But John Wood's Sherlock Holmes stands
stiffly and speaks portentously, emphasizing everything that can
be emphasized, belting key lines out to the audience, understat-
ing nothing. Even his appearance is an exaggeration: Holmes
is supposed to be pale and thin, but Mr. Wood comes in looking
as though he had been dead for several years.

Philip Locke as Professor Moriarty, "the Napoleon of
crime," ia also tall and thin, with staring eyes, mouth turned
down at the corners, and curly white hair fringing a bald pate.
He moves and speaks with an odd sort of jerkiness, as if he
were an android that had something slightly wrong with its
plumbing. He looks like an Archbishop of Canterbury gone mad;
most of all he reminded me of the Wizard of Oz. But what he
lacks almost entirely is the one thing a Moriarty most needs:
menace. Like Mr. Wood's Holmes, Mr. Locke's Moriarty is
very vividly outlined; but it is hard to feel very much sense of
life-and-death conflict when neither of the two parties seems to
be really in earnest.

Mr. Dunlop's production has other weaknesses. He employs
a dramatization written originally by Conan Doyle himself, rewritten by the American actor William Gillette, and first produced in 1899. It is not a very good dramatization; one can
see why Conan Doyle was minded to wash his hands of it. It is
based primarily on "A Scandal in Bohemia" and "The Final Problem," the first story in "The Adventures of Sherlock Holmes"
and the last in "The Memoirs of Sherlock Holmes," and the two
are unconvincingly mixed together. Irene Adler, the beautiful,
brilliant, sophisticated prima donna and international adventuress
("To Sherlock Holmes she is always the woman"), is changed
into a soppy, victimized girl named Miss Faulkner. And though
the authentic Holmes was a man of monkish temperament ("He
was, I take it, the most perfect reasoning and observing machine

that the world has seen, but as a lover he would have placed
himself in a false position. He never spoke of the softer passions, save with a gibe and a sneer."), the play ends, shamefully, with Holmes and this Miss Faulkner in one another's arms.

I do not want to overstate the case; this "Sherlock Holmes"
is still quite tolerably entertaining. Though the sets by Carl
Toms are not as lovingly evocative as one might hope (visually
speaking, Victorianism is a matter of detail), still the production
is pleasing in its lavishness--especially the billows and billows
of good thick fog that cover the set-changes. The acting, though
wrongly conceived, is very skillful; these people are not the
Royal Shakespeare Company for nothing. There are some laughs,
a few mild thrills, and at least some sharp reminders of the
real Sherlock Holmes to be had. The thing was a hit in London,
a hit in Washington, and will probably be a hit in New York; it
has that aura about it. But there is another aura--the authentic
aura of 221B Baker Street--that it lacks.

Scenes from Another Marriage
(by Julius Novick, Village Voice, March 19, 1975)

"So you're the little lady who started this big war," said
Abraham Lincoln to Harriet Beecher Stowe, and one is tempted
to think of Ibsen in the same terms. Of course, just as "Uncle
Tom's Cabin" did not really start the Civil War, so "A Doll's
House" did not really start the War for Sexual Liberation. Like
Ms. Stowe, Ibsen just articulated very strongly what many people were thinking and feeling--and what a great many other people were ready to think and feel, given a little encouragement.
And now people seem to be ready all over again, readier than
they ever were in Ibsen's own time. All those women in Park
Slope I was reading about in The Voice a couple of weeks ago,
who it seems are leaving their husbands and their brownstones
in droves in search of self-fulfillment, are the direct spiritual
descendants of Nora Helmer, Ibsen's heroine, who walked out
on her husband and her doll's house and slammed the door behind her with a slam that, as James Gibbons Huneker said, was
heard 'round the world.

And heard not only by women. (Ibsen himself denied that
he was a feminist.) The point of the play is that our duty to
others is less important than our duty to ourselves, a point applicable to men as well as women--and men as well as women
have listened to it, and women as well as men have been left,
like Torvald Helmer in the play, shattered and bewildered in an
empty house. (For every gain--and the domestic liberation that
"A Doll's House" furthered is a great gain--brings losses along
with it.) Again these things used to happen before "A Doll's
House," and they happen today, irrespective of "A Doll's House,"
but it was Ibsen, more than anyone else, who popularized the
morality of self-realization that justified them. So that now,
among "enlightened" people (Voice readers, Voice writers),

everybody is a Nora, men and women alike. There are hardly
any Torvalds left, so that the Noras have no one to leave but
each other. Which they do.

"A Doll's House" is a great symbol but aside from being
a great symbol it is not a particularly good play. To force
Nora Helmer to see that she has not known what kind of man
her husband was, to make her realize how she has been living,
and to motivate her to turn her back on the doll's house, Ibsen
invented a rather old-fashioned, rather creakily elaborate plot
about forgery and blackmail. In the current revival at the Vivian Beaumont, there are some dry stretches as Ibsen gets his
machinery revved up, before the suspense takes over--and even
thereafter I was impatient sometimes: I wanted to see more of
this marriage, not to be deflected onto other matters. Still, the
marriage is there--in the play, and, oddly but not uninteresting-
ly distorted, in the production--the marriage that stands for so
many marriages, and affairs, and cohabitations, and "primary
relationships." When Liv Ullmann as Nora said, "Does it occur
to you that this is the first time that we two, you and I, man
and wife, have ever had a serious talk together--" I wanted to
shout, "I've been having them for years, and I'm not even married! And they're awful!" But necessary. I am intensely suspicious of the morality of self-realization--I have been hurt by
it--but I think "A Doll's House" has done good work for us by
encouraging lovers to talk to each other.

Of course, as the play is not just a play but a symbol, so
this production is not just a production but a celebrity occasion.
Not that many people want to see "A Doll's House"; not all that
many people perhaps, want to see Liv Ullmann; but it seems as
if everybody wants to see Liv Ullmann in "A Doll's House."
And yet, Norwegian though she is, and talented though she mani-
festly is, she is not ideally cast as Nora Helmer. She is very
beautiful, and she is intelligent about being beautiful, and so she
is very good in those scenes where Nora, hardly knowing what
she is doing, uses her beauty to manipulate men. She dances
the tarantella--Ibsen's image of the wife as sexual plaything and
possession, whose job is to be provocative on cue--with a powerfully ironic come-hither smile plastered onto her face. There
is a wonderful moment in the third act, when, her independence
rising in her, she shouts at her husband "Stop! Leave me alone!
I won't have all this!"--and then bursts into shocked laughter,
incredulous at her own daring. And she is powerful again a little later, standing silently, wrapped in a black cloak, waiting
for Torvald to realize that something important has happened to
her. Her fear as the blackmail-plot closes its web around her
is sometimes affecting, but what she lacks, for the most part,
is the vital gift of vulnerability. She is too powerful. It is hard
to escape the feeling that this crisis in her life, which is supposed to be so shattering (to her, and in a different way to us),
doesn't matter all that much because whatever happens, she can
take care of herself.

Opposite her as Torvald is Sam Waterston, an actor whose special gift is for developing nuances of vulnerability. He is a comically pathetic paterfamilias: how this Torvald enjoys exercising his little authority! (And how finely Mr. Waterston shows him enjoying it.) And how touching he is at the end, crushed and left, crying "Nora!" as if something had been torn out of him.

But this Nora and this Torvald make a strangely ill-assorted couple. She is obviously bigger, older, and stronger than he is; the relationship that is supposed to prevail throughout most of the play--he the mature, protective father-husband, she the cuddly, chirpy child-wife--seems a preposterous fantasy, doggedly maintained by both of them in spite of the obvious fact that she could annihilate him at any moment with one sweep of her paw. All this is not implausible--stranger relationships have been known--but it does undercut Ibsen's basic assumption that Torvald has been in some way victimizing Nora. Nobody, but nobody, could victimize this Nora--especially this Torvald. And so the sympathy goes to him; he becomes a foolish but likeable neurotic, deserted by his magnificent, implacable wife because of some abstruse point of principle. All of which is not without its own significance and interest (it will presumably appeal to the men in the audience, especially to those who love implacable women)--but it is somewhat at odds with the play.

(There should be a paragraph in here somewhere, just for the record, about the supporting cast. Michael Granger has some touchingly sardonic moments as Dr. Rank, Torvald's friend, who is in love with Nora and dying, in highly Ibsenesque fashion, of some loathsome, inherited disease. Barbara Colby as Nora's old-friend Kristine and Barton Heyman as Krogstad the blackmailer manage to make something believable and gently appealing out of the scene in which Ibsen rather arbitrarily pairs them off.)

But the evening belongs to Miss Ullmann, for all her stolidity (as the director, Tormod Skagestad, recognizes by letting her have center stage apparently whenever she wants it). Her presence makes the occasion an Occasion, charges it with special excitement, and somehow sets the seal on the fact that the play's time has come.

OGDEN, Jean Custer; (2) Entertainment Critic; (3) b. Chicago, Ill., June 22, 1926; (4) d. Robert J. and Lillian (Custer); (5) B.A. Douglass College, New Brunswick, N.J., 1973, major subj.: History, Political Science, Journalism; (6) m. William N. Ogden, Aug. 15, 1952; (7) children--Bruce, Laurie; (8) Sales promotion 1944-51, Public Relations 1956- , Feature writing and theatre reviewing 1968- ; (9) Drama critic, Somerset Messenger Gazette and Radio station WBRW (Somerville, N.J.); (15) Charter member of N.J. Drama Critics' Association; (16) Republican; (17) Protestant; (19) Raritan

Valley Country Club (Raritan, N.J.); (20) Newspaper and radio entertainment reviews and features, N.Y. and N.J. productions; (21) 94 East Spring St., Somerville, 08876, Ph. 201-725-7290; (22) Promedia, Inc. (p. r.) Box 991, Somerville, Ph. 201-725-7686, Somerset Messenger Gazette, E. Main St., Somerville, Ph. 201-722-3005, Station WBRW, Box 1170, Somerville, Ph. 201-725-1170; (23) Gazette circulation: 20,000, WBRW listenership: 75,000 all mainly in Somerset County; (24) prof. and comm. theatre productions--150 annually, films--50, dance and other entertainment--25.

Foothill Suffers Setback Updating "Born Yesterday"
(by Jean Ogden, Messenger Gazette, June 13, 1974)

The Foothill Playhouse is taking liberties with Garson Kanin's comedy, "Born Yesterday," and they are not all for the best. World War II has been updated Viet Nam, and immortal bubblehead Billie Dawn has been revamped with an ever-so-smart Sassoon haircut and an ever-so-uncharacteristic suburban matronliness.

Kanin's story of a bully of a small town junk dealer who turned his scrap into millions and makes a dumb chorine his mistress and unwitting cover for his questionably overlapping corporations was originally set in 1945; Harry Brock's traffic was in World War II surplus, and Billie's type was the kick line floradora who wore anklestrap stilts and a simple expression.

What Brock coveted was raw-knuckled status, what Billie knuckled under for was mink and expensive hotel suites. It was cutie and the beast in the social climbing 40s, and updating its naivete to the super-con 70s is like reading Grimm's fairy tales to Judge Sirica.

The human nature may be the same, but the methods are child's play after 30 more years of practice.

So why doesn't Foothill director Virginia Schwartz just let funny bygones be history and 40s villains and victims be comic forerunners, and leave it to the audience to make whatever relevant connections it will with today's Harrys and Billies?

After speaking of today's Billies, they may be a little more aware of their rights and somewhat more confident about their native intellect, but regardless of liberation and social acceptance any woman that a Harry Brock could take out of the chorus line with promises of mink and trinkets and then slap around for eight years is not going to look and act like a Somerset Hills housewife on a convention.

There are some isolated nice moments in Susan Schwirck's performance as Billie. The finger counting during the famous gin rummy game is a good dumb blonde move. But for the most part, they are scattered over a very surface interpretation that doesn't move, talk or dress like a show girl who came out of the back row of "Anything Goes."

If, as Kanin says, the proper study of dumb blondes is dumb blondes, then we really need a reasonably authentic example for the research.

Arsene Gautier, as Harry, is closer to the role. He is burly and loud and capable of volcanic expansiveness and anger, but his acting is so tentative that Harry is more of a bore than a horrendously comic slob.

Besides being a very funny criticism of underhanded business practices, "Born Yesterday" is an endearing, and as it turns out for Harry, expensive Liza Doolittle romance.

In order to impress the senator he has bought and the Washington, D. C. , he plans to corner, Harry hires a writer to educate Billie in the social and intellectual niceties. Somewhere between Thomas Paine's essays and Saint-Saen's music, she grows wise to Harry's shady tactics, falls in love with her teacher and the two threaten to put Harry out of business if he doesn't reform.

"Born Yesterday" is a light and clever comedy wrapped around a serious intent, and it makes its ethical points best with light but crucial humor. Played more like political melodrama at the Foothill, it loses a good deal of zest.

In the supporting cast, Jim Corre, as the writer, is too smug to be loved by the ingratiating Billie; Daniel Carlson is an adequate Hood Friday for Harry; Geoff Hamer a humorless Senator Hedges, and Joan Lonsdorf an incomprehensibly arch senator's wife. Why she equates a lockjawed delivery with an upper class attitude is a mystery director Schwartz should have solved before opening night. Bill Smith is an attentive hotel manager.

Leaving Don Soderlund for the last but not the least mention. . . .

On Stage
(by Jean Ogden, over WBRW radio, Somerville, N.J. ,
November 30, 1974)

Brooklyn's Chelsea Theatre, an innovative producing company always on the lookout for new ideas, new plays and new people, has a Manhatten annex on West 43rd Street in the shell of an old church for some of its more unusual experimentations.

Presently the San Francisco Mime Company and the Madhouse Company of London, two groups as different as Karl Marx and the Marx Brothers, are being exposed to the New York theatre going public there, in the case of the Madhouse the exposure is literal, and they are both most unusual experiences.

The Mime Company is not as you would expect from the name a pantomime troupe, they are very vocal thespians who do street theatre in and around their California homebase as well as tour college campuses. They do political satire, pool their meagre resources in the communal company, and are in the East at the invitation of the Chelsea to raise funds and show off their considerable acting and interpretive skills.

The Mimes have brought two political pieces with them, Bertold Brecht's "The Mother" and their own "Great Air Robbery."

I saw "The Mother" last week, and although I wouldn't recommend it for someone looking for a light evening, I would certainly recommend it for anyone who appreciates a wry twist to revolutionary drama.

The Mimes manage to make Marxist propaganda not only relevant, there's an unmistakable scent of Chavez, lettuce and grapes in the Russian workers' movement, they make it entertaining. Brecht's work is almost charming without losing its polemic, and the Mimes, interchanging roles handily, singing propagandist songs and rolling out quotations from Richard Nixon to Mayor Dailey as ironic commentary on the action, are beguilingly critical of oppression.

While the Mimes are committed to political expression, their theatre mates in the Chelsea's downstairs cabaret are committed to madness, and the audience gets into the act willing or not.

The Madhouse Company of London is a small troupe of zanies for whom nothing is too vulgar and with whom no one is safe. Their nightly entertainment is a grab bag of ridiculous stunts, some inside, some outside the theatre and you'd better go along. If you're in the mood to be impossibly silly, they're a riot. If you have an ounce of sense, they're raunchy.

Drinks and munchies are sold to get you through the night. However, several drinks before you go will hardly prepare you for the bad taste of the Madhouse.

O'HAIRE, Patricia, New York Daily News, 220 East 42 St., N.Y., N.Y. 10017, Ph. 212-682-1234.

OLIVER, Edith; (2) Theater reviewer; (3) b. New York City, Aug. 11, 1913; (4) d. Samuel and Maude (Biow) Goldsmith; (5) Horace Mann School, 1931, student, Smith College 1931-33; (8) Author radio program, Take It Or Leave It, 1940-52; member editorial staff New

Yorker, 1947- ; Off-Broadway reviewer, 1961- , New Yorker; dramaturg Eugene O'Neill Theater Center, 1971-74; (22) New Yorker Magazine, 25 West 43 St. , New York, N. Y.   10036.

OPPENHEIMER, George; (2) Drama Critic; (3) b. New York, Feb. 7, 1900; (4) s. Ida (Adler) and Julius Oppenheimer; (6) Single; (8) Advertising--publicity manager, Alfred A. Knopf, 1921-25; co-founder Viking Press 1925-33; worked on motion picture scenarios 1933-49; Daily drama critic, Newsday, 1955- ; Sunday drama critic Newsday 1973- ; (13) WW I, Officers Training at Camp Zachary Taylor; WW II, made training films at First Air Force Unit; joined staff of Lord Louis Mountbatten in India and Ceylon 1943-44; (16) Democrat; (17) Jewish; (20) Short stories for Cosmopolitan, Colliers, Saturday Evening Post; author of comedy, "Here Today" 1932; co-authored comedy "A Mighty Man Is He," 1957; ed. The Passionate Playgoer, 1958; ed. Well, There's No Harm in Laughing, 1972; The Best in the World, with John K. Hutchens, 1973; The View of the Sixties (Memoirs), 1966; TV Series, Topper, 1953; (21) 15 East 64 St. , New York City, N. Y. 10021; (23) Newsday circulation: 60,000; (24) 48 Sunday articles, 125 or more daily articles.

Shakespeare with and without Trimmings
(by George Oppenheimer, Newsday, August 31, 1968)

In my memory the first Shakespeare production that broke sharply away from tradition was a "Hamlet" in which Mary Ellis, Basil Sidney and the rest of the cast were garbed in modern clothes.   It caused quite a stir in its day (1925) as did Orson Welles' Mercury Theater version of "Julius Caesar" (1937) with Hitlerian brownshirts dominating the scene.

As time went on more and more directors and producers sought ways of changing the tried and true but overly familiar treatments of these classics.   Sometimes the results were more than justified.   I can think of few Shakespearean productions as fresh and imaginative as Tyrone Guthrie's "Troilus and Cressida," laid at the time of World War I with Priam as an approximation of the Kaiser, Helen of Troy a beer-drinking Brunnhilde and the Greek heroes transformed into so many warring Huns.

More recently Peter Brook, who has a tendency to alter the intent of a playwright, even so great a one as Shakespeare, to suit his own whims of staging, gave us a strange but haunting "King Lear," in which Paul Scofield was so fine a Lear that the author emerged not too battle-scarred.   In Stratford, Conn. , there was quite a charming "Much Ado About Nothing" with Katharine Hepburn as Beatrice and Alfred Drake as Benedick, set in Texas in the days of the caballeros and from what I hear, there is a splendid "As You Like It" now in London in which male and female characters alike are played by men.   In Shakespeare's time the women's parts were played by boys but these actors are more matured. These are only a few of the successful instances of discarding the old moulds.

Of late, however, the Shakespeare syndrome has become more and more frenetic. Even when the treatment claims to be traditional, there is an urge toward novelty at any cost that too often ruins effect with affectation. In his most recent staging of "Romeo and Juliet" in Central Park, Joseph Papp has dispensed with the balcony and, in so doing, destroyed one of the greatest love scenes in all of dramatic literature. Gerald Freedman at the same location jumped two plays ahead of "Henry IV, Part I" when he had Prince Hal recite "Once more into the breach, dear friends" from "Henry V" for reasons best known to himself. As for Mr. Papp's staging of "Hamlet" last season, one woe did tread upon another's heels. Hamlet was discovered shaving himself with an electric razor in the rear of the house, his father's ghost did a ventriloquist act in long underwear, the "to be or not to be" soliloquy was delivered in a Puerto Rican dialect and Ophelia went mad with a male chorus joining in.

This last presentation pledged allegiance to the ideas of Polish critic Jan Kott, who is dedicated to knocking the Bard down to size. With his "Shakespeare Our Contemporary," Mr. Kott wrote a fascinating but spurious book that has tempted too many directors to emulate him and distort poor Will into the jagged shape of our times. Director John Hancock was another who followed Kott's precepts and staged "A Midsummer Night's Dream" as a surrealistic nightmare that successfully eliminated all magic and transformed the lovely fairy tale into a monstrosity.

There are and should be an infinite number of interpretations of Shakespeare's plays. "Twelfth Night" has been turned into a rock 'n roll musical, "Your Own Thing," and is an irreverent delight. There are rumors of "Othello" also becoming a musical (with no credit to Verdi) and others will follow in the footsteps of Rodgers and Hart, who did no harm at all to "The Comedy of Errors" with their enchanting "Boys from Syracuse." I recall seeing in Munich some years ago an amalgam of "Henry IV, Parts 1 and 2" and "Henry V," cut to fit one evening's entertainment, in which jokes were interpolated. There was also the time when Mary Pickford and Douglas Fairbanks Sr., then married, made a film of "The Taming of the Shrew" and gave credit for "additional dialogue" to a Hollywood writer whose career was not furthered by this gesture. Shakespeare, on the other hand, survived.

There are those who demand that his plays should be done traditionally. I am not among them. Neither am I with those who scoff at conventional treatment, no matter how well acted and staged. (The best "Hamlet" I ever saw was a conventional one with John Barrymore triumphant as the melancholy Dane.)

This summer the Stratford company in Connecticut is presenting
a sturdy "Richard II" with Donald Madden a fine doomed Richard,
a properly pastoral "As You Like It" in addition to a mod
"Love's Labour's Lost" (which I have not seen).   Since its first
summer, when "The Tempest" and "Julius Caesar" seemed less
Caliban and Cassius than Balaban and Katz this company has
improved mightily, hewing far closer to tradition than to novelty,
but still willing to try the latter.   At times it has fallen into
traps with a "Troilus" ill fitting into our Civil War period and
an unconsciously camp "Midsummer Night's Dream," but at
other times it has shown, among its works, a fine "King Lear"
with Morris Carnovsky in the title role and a superior "Coriolanus" with Philip Bosco.   And let me not forget another Stratford (in Ontario, Canada) and its superb "Antony and Cleopatra"
with Christopher Plummer and Zoe Caldwell.

In other years in the Park Gerald Freedman has staged the
best "Comedy of Errors" I have yet to see (and I am not forgetting the English production by the Royal Shakespeare Company) and a well-directed version of that blood bath, "Titus
Andronicus." Joseph Papp has followed suit with a number of
directorial successes, including a lusty "King John."

Yet, with all the fine directors and actors, traditional or
not, panoplied or simple, as great an evening as I have spent
with Shakespeare was Sir John Gielgud's "Ages of Man."   He
appeared in evening clothes on a stage bare except for a lectern,
played various Shakespeare roles and made them come to life
as few full productions have done.   He needed no props and no
Kotts, only a text and a talent that was born to speak these
words.

The next time a director is tempted to impose new forms
on Shakespeare simply because the old forms seem to him outmoded, let him buy the L. P. recording of Sir John's "Ages of
Man" and listen to it carefully.   He may well find that the novelty he is seeking in Shakespeare is already there.

Ah, a Portrait of Happier Days
(by George Oppenheimer, Newsday, October 3, 1975)

Eugene O'Neill wrote two plays that were set in the home
of his youth in New London.   One is a stark tragedy, "Long
Day's Journey Into Night"; the other, the only comedy he ever
wrote, "Ah, Wilderness!"   As Arthur and Barbara Gelb wrote
in their excellent biography, "O'Neill," the two plays "may be
regarded as two sides of the same coin--one a benign glimpse
of what the O'Neill family, at its best, aspired to be, and the
other, a banefully heightened picture of what it was at its worst."

"Ah, Wilderness!" is now being revived at the uptown Circle
in the Square for a limited engagement.   It comes to us from
the admirable company, the Long Wharf in New Haven, and is

staged in fine fashion by its director, Arvin Brown. Forty-five
years have passed since I saw the original production with
George M. Cohan in the role of the paterfamilias of the Harris
family. It was the first play that Cohan ever did that was not
of his own making. I remember thinking then that it was overly
sentimental. Now, for me at least, it possesses far more genuine sentiment than sentimentality and emerges as a nostalgic,
sunny glimpse into an America of much happier and better days.

It is a family portrait, the central figure of which is Richard
Miller, an attractive teenager in the year 1906. Richard is a
rebel, albeit a lovesick one, since the reactionary father of his
beloved disapproves of him heartily. Believing himself to be
jilted, Richard goes on his first fling to a disreputable inn, gets
drunk, almost has an affair and ends up with a severe hangover
and an even worse case of remorse.

Grouped about Richard are Nat, his newspaper father; Essie,
his loving mother; Mildred and Tommy, two younger children;
Arthur, his older brother; Lily, his maiden aunt, and Uncle Sid,
who is something of a rip.

Richard Backus plays Richard and confirms my faith in him
as one of the first young actors on our stage. That lovely actress, Geraldine Fitzerald, is his mother. It may be remembered that she also played, and played superbly, the tortured
mother some seasons ago in "Long Day's Journey." Here, she
is warm and funny and altogether enchanting. Teresa Wright, another favorite actress, is fine as the spinster aunt, and so, too,
are William Swetland as the father, John Braden as the bibulous
uncle and Paul Rudd (doubling as the chauffeur in TV's "Beacon
Hill") as the older Yalie brother.

Despite my objections to the stage of Circle in the Square,
which seems better suited to a 440-yard dash or other athletic
contests than a play, I had a fine time at "Ah, Wilderness!"
and so, I strongly suspect, will you.

I wandered far off Broadway recently to see "Summer Brave"
by William Inge at the Eisenhower Theater in Washington's Kennedy Center and was richly rewarded. Inge wrote four plays,
"Come Back, Little Sheba," "Picnic," "Bus Stop" and "The
Dark at the Top of the Stairs," that were all critical and financial successes and were made into films. Although he continued
to write, he never achieved anything like this success again.
In 1973, at the age of 60, he took his life.

"Summer Brave" is "Picnic," renamed and revised by the
author shortly after the original production that won the New York
Drama Critics' Circle and Pulitzer Prize awards for 1953.

Inge wrote of the revised version, "I feel that it is more
humorously true than 'Picnic' and it does fulfill my original

intentions." The main difference between the two plays is that Madge, the small town belle, no longer goes away with the shiftless Hal with whom she has had her first affair.

Watching again, after a lapse of 22 years, it seemed a truer and more honest ending and a better play. Much of this may well be due to the production, with its lovely setting by Stuart Wurtzel that captures so well the feel of a small Kansas town, its lighting by David Segal, who contrives to make a sunset altogether real, and the faithful period costumes of Donald Brooks. Above all is the cast, under the loving and superlative direction of Michael Montel, who matches the skill of Joshua Logan, the director of the original.

And what a cast he has assembled. Alexis Smith sheds her glamor to play Rosemary, the schoolteacher starved for romance and longing for an escape from her sexless life. Her scene with the colorless bachelor (sensitively played by Joe Ponazecki) is a triumph of acting. No less good is Nan Martin as the mother of two girls, working hard to makes ends meet. The pretty daughter is Madge, in the attractive and appealing person of Jill Eikenberry, while Sheila K. Adams makes much of the younger, less attractive, but brighter daughter, Millie.

A relative newcomer, the personable young Ernest Thompson, has the difficult role of Hal--sympathetic despite his boasting, his fecklessness and his flagrant sex appeal. Martha Greenhouse is fine as the neighbor lady who hires Hal and so, too, is Peter Weller as the rich boy who loves but loses Madge. For the rest, every one of the small roles is well played under the knowing direction of Montel.

It is not sure yet whether or not "Summer Brave" will be brought to Broadway. It richly deserves to be.

OSGOOD, Richard E.; (2) Movie and theater critic (retired); (3) b. Boston, Apr. 16, 1901; (4) George E. and Bertha B. Osgood; (5) Delbert Moyer Staley's College of the Spoken Word, 1920; (6) m. Anne Piper, Feb. 14, 1943; (7) children--Stella Bartlett Kirby and William Estey Osgood; grandchildren-Kristine and Kraig Kirby; (8) Stage Actor (using name Elmer Cornell) 1920-1931, 20 plays, 12 in New York, by George S. Kaufman, Marc Connelly, Sidney Howard, George Abbott, John V. A. Weaver, Patterson McNutt and others, with Madge Kennedy, Nance O'Neil, Lynn Fontanne, James Gleason, George Abbott, Roberta Arnold, Wallace Ford, Nydia Westman, Una Merkle, Fredric March, Augustin Duncan, Louise Closser Hale, Donald Meek, J. C. Nugent, Ralph Morgan, Spencer Tracy, John Cromwell, Pauline Lord, Elsie Ferguson, Bette Davis, etc.; Radio debut, Feb. 4, 1928, True Story Hour. Others: Harbor Lights, Empire Builders, True Detective (The Shadow), Light Opera Series, etc; Author of Royal Romance series purchased by WNAC-WAAB in Boston for Yankee Network. Dramatic Director, Yankee Network,

1932-33. Author play, No-Account, produced by Louise Galloway in summer stock, 1933, and optioned by William A. Brady but not produced in New York; joined WXYZ, Detroit, October, 1935; researched and wrote and broadcast Factfinder, "Eyes on Tomorrow," March of Victory and In Bold Relief series over regional network (Michigan, Ohio, Indiana) all for one sponsor (Hickok Oil Corporation) 1936-51; newscaster, 1949-63; Began Show World program, Mar. 6, 1938 and commenced critical coverage of movies and stage plays soon after, continuing until retirement, January, 1971; (10) Helped Greater Detroit Motion Picture Council create Youth Film Forum for high school students, now participated in every year by students within forty-mile radius of Detroit; hosted summer "Green Room" series, University of Detroit, 1966 and 1967; (12) President Detroit Local of AFTRA several terms; President Franklin Knolls Improvement Association, several terms; currently Vice President of the Detroit Council of Churches and member of the Board of Manager of the Radio and TV Division of the Council; (18) 3rd degree Mason; (17) Presbyterian; (20) Now researching, writing and transcribing five 3-minute stories about People Behind the Things for Henry Ford Museum and Greenfield Village used by 500 radio stations; also Bicentennial TV spots, America's Family Album (as above). Now finishing book, Station Break, 50 Years Inside a Radio Station; (21) 32575 Nottingham Knoll, Farmington Hills, Michigan 48024.

"Illya Darling"
(by Dick Osgood, Detroit Free Press, February 26, 1967)

After the Manos Hadjidakis brand of music (which is very, very good) has been introduced by half a dozen musicians hanging precariously from the flies; after the waterfront of Piraeus, Greece, has materialized through the complicated scenic machinations of Oliver Smith; after Jules Dassin has re-introduced his plot of the pursuit of reason, ancient Grecian culture and philosophy (Orson Bean) versus the contemporary pursuit of life, love and physical pleasure (Melina Mercouri) ...

After all this, which takes a little time, "Illya Darling" bursts into life at the Fisher Theater with as vigorous a lot of male dancers as you'll find this side of--well--this side of Athens.

And throughout the evening, when the spirit of things begins to sag, choreographer Onna White puts these men to work and all is well.

Don't get me wrong. Melina Mercouri is a living goddess. Hers is a strong, open-faced talent working hard to adapt itself to a new area. That thousand-watt smile reaches beyond a voice that seems to have blown a fuse. To get the words requires concentration. But the magic is there even if the magician is not relaxed.

Bean has worked out a neat, clear-cut characterization. He

can be heard, and his performance seems ready for the Broadway plunge.

There is a rich human texture to the show, an occasional drag that can be overcome, and a star's voice that could stand an electronic boost--or a smaller theater. But from here, "Illya" looks, sounds, and feels like a new darling for Broadway.

Show World
(by Dick Osgood, over WXYZ radio, Detroit, June 5, 1968)
[Note: This was the day Robert Kennedy was assassinated.]

Good evening, ladies and gentlemen. This seems too sad an evening to be relaying show world news and gossip. Yet it may be an appropriate hour to wonder what part the world of entertainment may be playing in sickening minds to such a degree of hatred and violence as to prompt attempts to murder temperate and sensible men. Let's think about this for a minute after reminding you for the Metropolitan Exhibitors of Detroit that Paul Newman's comedy, "The Secret War of Harry Frigg" opens tonight at the Washington Royal Oak, and at these drive-ins: Algiers, Belaire, Dearborn, Michigan and West Side. "Madigan," a police drama starring Richard Widmark, Henry Fonda and James Whitmore, continues at the Palms, Birmingham, Royal, Wyandotte-Annex and all Cinemas ONE.

Shakespeare's "Hamlet," is his advice to the players, referred to acting "whose end, both at the first, and now, was, and is, to hold as 't were, the mirror up to nature--to show virtue her own feature, scorn her own image, and the very age and body of the time his form and pressure."

Now mind you, Shakespeare said this is the job of the actor --not the purpose of entertainment. If this famous speech is interpreted to mean that entertainment, generally, should reflect life as it is--and this interpretation IS sometimes made to excuse what one encounters in entertainment--then one can suggest that the man basically in control, the producer, may aim his mirror in whatever direction he chooses, to reflect whatever phase of life or nature he pleases. This, long before the actor takes over. And there can be little argument other than that producers today too often choose to reflect moral breakdown.

Sexual promiscuity is enlarged and glamorized. Violence is common in entertainment, and the results of violence are shown in detail. A number of foreign countries bar American films-- not because of sex--but because of violence. Scenes of violence are considered more dangerous in their influence upon those who see them than sequences of bedroom activity. It seems to me even more harmful than the sex and violence per se, is the casual spirit in which these things are often presented. So often the approach is flip, humorous, indifferent. Too often the attitude toward evil is one of acceptance; too often those who stand

for virtue are made fun of. James Stewart told us several
years ago that it's easier to dramatize the negative. It's easier
to make evil people attractive in entertainment. To make a good
character interesting takes more doing.

And you often hear that sex and violence are better box office. But Walt Disney seems to have founded a financially successful enterprise with the clean entertainment. And Disney was
not alone. "Around the World in 80 Days," "This Is Cinerama,"
"Cinerama Holiday," "Sound of Music," "My Fair Lady," "Lil-
lies of the Field," "Ben Hur," "The Ten Commandments,"
"Thoroughly Modern Millie" and others buried in memory were
enormously successful at the box office. These are times for
a re-examination of our morals, for a re-statement of what is
right and what is wrong. These are times for a return to the
principles upon which Americans built a great nation. Perhaps
writers should do more--than reflect. Perhaps it has become
the duty of producers and directors of stage, screen and television entertainment to inspire man to a new decency and
strength of character. This observer is no crusader, but recent events indicate the time has come to aim the mirror in
such a direction as to once more show virtue her own image,
to accentuate the positive and eliminate the negative--in entertainment as well as in our daily lives. Example: "Yours, Mine
and Ours"--a comedy with Lucille Ball and Henry Fonda at the
Adams, Dearborn, Gateway, Norwest, Royal Oak, Terrace,
Woods and Wyandotte-Main. I keep an open Bible in my desk
drawer. I opened the drawer this morning to get a pen. And
just as I heard a neuro-surgeon make his statement following
the operation on Robert Kennedy, my eyes fell upon these words
in the Seventh Psalm: "Oh let the wickedness of the wicked
come to an end; but establish the just." Good night.

PAINE, Canio Francis; (2) Theatre critic, Broadway columnist; (3)
b. Naples, Italy, Mar. 28, 1920; (4) s. Giuseppe Palladino and Maria (Russo); (5) B.A. Sofia U., Japan, Bus. Admin. 1955, Texas
Tech, Texas, Journalism; (6) m. Louise Barilla, Sept. 9, 1946; (7)
children--Richard, Karen; (8) Theatre Critic, Broadway Columnist,
Entertainment Editor, Staten Island Register 1965-present, also published in nine New York and New Jersey newspapers as Broadway
columnist; (9) Stage Actor, "Life and Times of Josef Stalin," Brooklyn Academy of Music 1973, Motion Picture Actor, "The Retaliator"
1974, Playwright, "Woman of Destiny" unproduced musical; (10) Mbr.
Boy Scouts of America Executive Board, Past Area Gov. Toastmas-
ter International; Mbr. Advisory Board Richmondtown Prep School,
S. I. , N. Y. , Past President Granite Manor Civic Association; (13) Major, U.S.A.F. 1943-65; (15) Mbr. Drama Desk of New York, Editor
Drama Desk News, Mbr. Outer Critics Circle; (16) Democrat; (17)
Catholic; (21) 118 Roman Avenue, Staten Island, N.Y. 10314; Ph.
212-698-2898; (22) Staten Island Register, 2100 Clove Road, Staten
Island, N.Y. 10305, Ph. 212-447-4700; (23) Circulation: audience
reached approximately 5 million readers in New York, New Jersey
and Pennsylvania (10 newspapers); (24) 60 plays and musicals, 5

operas, 5 dance, 25 nightclubs and miscellaneous.

"The Ritz" Lays it on and "Seascape" Intrigues
(by Canio Paine, Staten Island Register, February 6, 1975)

Bring your Turkish towels to the Longacre Theatre for it
has been transformed into The Ritz, a continental bathhouse.
Consider the bathhouse, the Big Apple phenomenon as the meeting place for New York's gay crowd.

Consider also Jack Weston as a "balding, middle-aged fat
man" who seeks refuge in the baths from his nefarious brother-
in-law, Jerry Stiller. Then consider a splash of wonderfully
unintelligible song, dance and patter from the bath's own Googie
Gomez (Rita Moreno), assorted strange characters, amateur
night and you have The Ritz, baths, of course, a hilarious new
comedy by Terrence McNally.

The ingenious three-storied set designed by Lawrence King
and Michael H. Yeargan complete with steam room, massage
parlor and other accoutrements, gives the characters of the play
plenty of romping room where they prance, wisecrack and swish
their way through the side-splitting two act comedy.

Jack Weston's Gaetano Proclo is thoroughly flustered by the
place until he teams up with F. Murray Abraham's swishy Chris
and Stephen Collins as Carmine (Stiller). Vespucci's falsettoed
detective proves to be an unknown ally in disguise. Under Robert Drivas' fast moving direction everyone on stage had as
much fun as the audience. Mistaken identity, The Andrews Sisters and a lecherous "chubby chaser " combined to make The
Ritz thoroughly entertaining fare. I laughed myself silly.

Edward Albee's Seascape at the Shubert Theatre is a most
intriguing play with the cogent message that evolution is a never
ending process ad infinitum.

Alone, picnicking on a deserted beach, Nancy and Charlie
(Deborah Kerr and Barry Nelson) now grandparents, feel that
they have earned the right to do whatever they please. Nancy
expresses a desire to hop from beach to beach around the world
and Charlie just wants to stay put and rest. During this repartee, two lizards rise from the sea. Leslie and Sarah (Frank
Langella and Maureen Anderman) and, in a critical moment of
encounter, four startled creatures face one another.

Overcoming their fright and belligerence, a guarded friendly
atmosphere prevails as their different life styles are discussed
by the foursome with evolution the conversational theme. Finally convinced that there is more to life than merely existing under the sea, Leslie asks, no, demands that he and Sarah be
taught this new human life style.

Directed by the author with intelligent humor and sympathy, Seascape is an escape from reality that at times evokes hearty laughter. The outstanding portrayals of the four member cast especially Frank Langella as Charlie the lizard and Albee's imaginative ploys makes this intriguing comedy with its subtle seriousness a most delightful theatrical evening. I liked it very much and after seeing the play, I wondered about my own personal life style. Fred Voelpel's magnificent lizard costumes are truly amazing and James Tilton has literally transformed the Shubert stage into a realistic beach and sand dune. Nice to have Deborah Kerr back on Broadway--she's been away much too long!

Scott Great in Miller Classic
(by Canio Paine, Home Reporter and Sunset News, July 4, 1975)

An impressive cast headed by George C. Scott as Willy Loman makes Arthur Miller's "Death of a Salesman" at the Circle in the Square Theatre, an unforgettable dramatic experience meriting the standing ovations accorded George C. Scott, its star and director.

A classical play of an aging tired salesman who, beset by financial worries, filial disappointment, personal frustrations and the loss of his job, chooses death as the answer to all his problems, is given character, strength, credibility and sympathetic understanding by George C. Scott's superb portrayal of the hopeful salesman, loving husband and dominant father. James Farentino is also outstanding as the son originally headed for football fame but at age 34, is still unmarried and unable to find his place in life. Deeply moving, "Death of a Salesman" is a dramatic insight into family love, friendship, aspirations, failures and the changing world as it affects the life and eventual death of a salesman.

The cast is an exceptional one with noteable performances turned in by Teresa Wright as Linda Loman, understanding wife and mother; Harry Keitel as Happy, the youngest of Willy's two sons who views life through rose colored glasses; Chuck Paterson, next door neighbor and school chum of Biff (James Farentino) and Dotts Johnson, next door neighbor and Willy Loman's only true friend. Marjorie Kellog's scenery is very effective and Thomas Skelton's lighting sets the proper moods. See it for its outstanding performances, dramatic impact and excellent theatre.

PATE, Bob, Jacksonville Journal, 1 Riverside Ave., Jacksonville, Fla. 32203, Ph. 904-791-4111.

PATRICK, (John) Corbin; (2) Theater critic, arts and entertainment editor; (3) b. Tell City, Ind., April 22, 1905; (4) s. Norman E. and Ethel (Corbin) P.; (5) Student, Notre Dame U., major subj:

journalism, 1922-25; B.A. Butler U., major subj: English, 1927;
(6) m. Miriam L. Clapham, Nov. 15, 1930; (7) children--Nancy D.,
John C.; (8) Editorial staff, Indianapolis Star, 1925- ; drama dept.,
1927- ; music and movie critic, asst. drama critic, 1927-41; drama
critic, dept. head, 1941- ; editorial page columnist, 1944-70; (9-19)
Mem. Indpls Sesquicentennial Comm., 1969-70; board of directors
Community Concerts Assn., Metropolitan Arts Council (1965-74);
board of directors, treasurer Hoosier Salon Patrons Assn., Inc.,
(1970-). Member National Screen Council, Sigma Delta Chi, Indianapolis Press Club (pres. 1939-41), Society of American Travel
Writers, Society Friends of Music of Indiana University, Indianapolis
Museum of Art, American Theater Critics Assn. (founding member),
International Skal Clubs (associate), Society of Indiana Pioneers, Indiana Museum Society; (21) 6829 Willow Road, Indianapolis, Ind.;
(22) Indianapolis Star, 307 N. Pennsylvania St., Indianapolis, Ind.;
46206, Ph. 317-633-9269; (23) Circulation: 224,630 (Daily), 364,954
(Sunday); (24) 65 plays and musicals, 35 motion pictures, 10 dance,
25 concerts, 6 operas.

Galvin's "The Dungeon" Is Play of College Life
(by Corbin Patrick, Indianapolis Star, June 6, 1975)

We have here an actor-manager and playwright, a theatrical
jack of all trades, in the old tradition of Dion Boucicault.

His name, as if you didn't know, is W. Randolph Galvin and
he presented his latest opus, "The Dungeon," for a small but
select audience at the Showcase in Talbott Village last night.

In this one he deals with the problem of the college girl who
thinks she is pregnant, but isn't. The action takes place in a
basement apartment, somewhere off campus. That, and the fact
a trap is set on the premises for a rat called George, helps explain the title.

It's a play replete with Galvinesque aphorisms bound together
by a series of amusing sequences in a plot that takes a rather
surprising turn in Act III.

Measuring Galvin's stride from "The Immaculate Misconception," the first of his own works premiered at his Black Curtain Dinner Theater, it's a long step forward.

We'll remember it for its number of clever scenes more
than for its total dramatic impact, and for the excellent work of
the cast of three players who give it life and zest--P. Bradley
Armacost and Roger Wooden as the rival roommates and Sandra
Tonne as the girl who must choose between them.

Armacost, seen most recently in "Star Spangled Girl," contributes another fluently athletic performance as the cynical and
flamboyant Hal, combining elements of Tarzan and Cyrano, not
to mention Douglas Fairbanks I and Galvin himself, in his portrayal.

Wooden, a veteran of "Godspell" and other Black Curtain productions, plays the noble youth, his adversary, with a becoming luminosity. His guy is almost too good to believe, but Wooden makes him credible. Miss Tonne, last seen in another Galvin premiere, "Bantry," is altogether delightful in a high-spirited performance of the play's only feminine role--more would only gum up the works.

The way it begins in Act I, you may think Hal is trying to palm off Ellen (she's the girl) on Ron (he's Wooden) to avoid the responsibilities that seem likely to result from his affair with her.

In Act II, sure enough, Ron and Ellen get together, passionately, only to be discovered by Hal, who apparently couldn't care less.

Two of the play's most entertaining scenes are in this act: the candlelight party, a pleasant bit of makebelieve featuring Ron and Ellen, and Hal's mock Sherlock Holmes routine in reconstructing the situation by deduction when he surprises them.

Hal, you realize, has feelings that run deeper, when he begins to rave and rant in Act III. Meanwhile, Ron is rising to his full stature. They plead their cases with Ellen as the judge. In the end, however, Ron is the best judge. The question is who is trapped.

Plays are usually considered works in progress, rewritten rather than written, until they reach their ultimate destination, which in the case of "The Dungeon" is off-Broadway New York.

It needs finishing and clarifying touches, more bite perhaps, but it's much farther on its way than "The Immaculate Misconception," which Galvin did offer in New York, only to find that it's a different turf. But he keeps trying and improving and developing a style and we have a feeling that someday he will make it.

"The Dungeon," with its small cast and economical staging, certainly has possibilities. Audiences in the 98-seat Showcase should find it diverting.

CTS Ending Season with "Iguana"
(by Corbin Patrick, Indianapolis Star, June 9, 1975)

The venturesome repertory group conducted by Dr. Alfred R. Edyvean at the Christian Theological Seminary is closing its season next weekend with an enterprising production of Tennessee Williams' powerful drama, "Night of the Iguana."

It's a play of conflict and compassion among characters who meet in a seedy resort hotel on the edge of a tropical rain forest somewhere on Mexico's Pacific Coast, near Acapulco.

What makes it a bold undertaking for CTS is the fact its nominal hero is a defrocked cleric whose weaknesses are drink and women and who rails against the "establishment" god, created in their own image by "cruel, senile delinquents."

He is given a glimpse of the love and truth he seeks in God by a middle-aged gentlewoman from New England who finds the Costa Verde Hotel at the end of a long journey for herself and her invalid, 97-year-old grandfather, "the world's oldest practicing poet."

The warmth and understanding, the spiritual values, of their friendship are contrasted with the ex-reverend's more earthy attachment to Maxine, recently widowed, the owner of the Costa Verde.

It's a somewhat lurid "fantastic allegory on the tragi-comic subject of human existence," as the playwright himself said in another connection.

Dr. Edyvean and his excellent company handle its more combustible elements with dignity and discretion. While it's not as steaming as the memorable performance of the Morris Street Players a few years ago, this one makes its point, and makes it well.

Steven D. Miller, last seen as Becket in "Murder in the Cathedral," displays remarkable versatility as the Rev. Shannon, quite a different role. Edith Bruce is amiable, but tough under pressure, as Maxine, the proprietor of the hotel--the action takes place on its veranda.

Jackie Pitman plays Hannah, the good influence, with becoming sweetness and nobility--she needs only to project her voice a little more at times. James B. Conkle, as Nonno, the grandfather, and Freda Coleman, as Shannon's nemesis, a belligerent member of the tour group he is conducting, are good in other important roles.

Some deletions have been made, and some parts dropped. But then Williams himself revised it several times before it reached Broadway in 1961.

PEET, Creighton; (2) Writer, Theatre and Movie Critic; (3) b. New York City, 1903; (4) s. William Creighton Peet and Jane (Boyse); (5) English major, Univ. of Pa., and Univ. of Colorado; Columbia Univ. School of Journalism; B. Lit.; (6) m. Bertha Anne (Houck), 1934; (7) children: one son, Creighton Houck; (8) Film critic, New York Post, 1929, N.Y. drama critic, L.A. Daily News, Sunday edition Norfolk Virginia Pilot, (1924-1973); weekly critical theatre reviews, From New York for 94 community theaters, 177 schools and universities, 49 individuals, and 19 miscellaneous people, (1924-1973) for varying periods; film critic New York Evening Post, (1927-29); free lance writer The New Yorker, Scribner's, This Week magazine, Herald Tribune, The Outlook, Literary Digest, Forum; (15) Mem. Outer Circle, Delta Psi; (19) Columbia Univ. Club, Saint Anthony Club; (20) w. 12 hard cover books for young people, (Harper's, Franklin Watts), chiefly with photos by the author, some translated into Japanese, French, and Spanish; (21) 300 East 34th St; New York, N.Y. 10016, Ph. 212-679-1377; (22) 22 East 17th St., New York, N.Y. 10003, Ph. 212-WA 9-2090.

"Home"
(by Creighton Peet, From New York, November 23, 1970)

"Home," David Storey's quiet but strangely moving play just over from London, is certainly an important and memorable piece of dramatic writing. And the performances of Sir John Gielgud and Sir Ralph Richardson, growing on you as they do, are nothing less than overwhelming.

The stage is bare except for two white chairs, a small white iron table, a flagless flagpole and a short balustrade. When two well-dressed gentlemen--Gielgud and Richardson, walk in, meet, and sit down to chat about trivialities, they might be in a formal park. They are Harry and Jack, of necessity daily companions, you gather. It is some little time before you understand about them and the two noisy, chattering cockney women who pass by, and soon join them. These two have neither their reticence nor their dignified and compelling sadness. Soon you are reminded of Pinter, but there is a basic difference. Much of Pinter always remains a mystery, while after a time you conclude that all these people are inmates of a mental home. In fact one of the women cheerfully recalls the final incident which got her "put away." She murderously assaulted the milkman when he presented a bill, and then wrecked the house. The other woman who is forever complaining about her feet, slyly asks Jack if he got his for following little girls in the street. Neither of the men answers any such questions, but many times, in quieter moments, they can be seen weeping. We never know the nature of the behavior which brought these men here, but we are extraordinarily aware of their unspoken anguish. Now their lives have become quite unraveled. There is nothing to fear or to hope for. They are beyond hatred or even animosity. But at an especially disturbing moment one of the women reaches out and holds Gielgud's hand in a gesture of sheer compassion.

While the women too have moments of silence, you feel that something of the men's distress is due to finding themselves in the company of women who do not even understand the big words they use. However, the men never condescend or patronize them. You may see this as a slight touch of upper-class British snobbery--but certainly there are many such situations where it is impossible to choose your friends. Oddly enough there is some quiet humor in "Home."

The performances of Gielgud and Richardson are as nearly perfect as any I can recall. With amazing underplaying they make these brief scenes both touching and important. This is the kind of quiet, untheatrical acting we almost never see in America. "Home" is as timeless as man himself, and it may well remain a permanent part of our dramatic literature. We should give thanks to producer Alexander H. Cohen who was courageous enough to bring this important and intellectually stimulating play to New York for a few weeks. It will be at the Morosco Theatre until Jan. 9th.

Joyce Carol Oates is undoubtedly a talented lady who has won a great many awards and scholarships for her novels and short stories, but I must confess that her play "Sunday Dinner" at The American Place Theatre left me and the other newspaper writers quite baffled as to its deeper meaning. Outwardly we see a dreadful, dismal family having Sunday dinner in its dreadful, dismal home after its weekly trip to the cemetery to visit mother's grave. They all make a big thing of being simple, honest, respectable people, but after they have taken in and fed a blind old man who says he is a census taker and who asks them some irrelevant questions, they go to pieces. Each member confesses to dark and hidden sins--all but the youngest brother who commits his offense right then and there. He doesn't believe the old visitor is really blind, so he gouges his eyes out with a teaspoon. Now he, too, feels weighted down with guilt. People do think of the nicest things to put in their plays! "Sunday Dinner" lasts just an hour-- plenty long enough.

The strike of 200 off-Broadway actors and stage managers, now in its second week, is more complicated than simply the differences over money. It gets down to the theatre itself versus a living wage. Many managers, including Richard Barr, producer, and president of the League of New York Theatres, say that off-Broadway actors are not supposed to live on their salaries alone. Up to now this salary started at from $75 to $150 a week, depending on how much a show was earning. Currently the League is offering $90 to $165, while Equity is demanding $125 to $265. All these figures are minimums.

Mr. Barr holds that off-Broadway is a training ground for actors and that $90 a week should be enough for them "to get by economically." Actually, many actors in the little houses have regular jobs on the side, and the lucky ones work in TV soap operas or commercials. And others, of course, get more than the minimums.

But there is another matter which concerns the theatre everywhere in America. This is that if off-Broadway salaries rise substantially, these little theatres will be in exactly the

same position as the big establishment houses. Producers will
stage only shows they feel confident will earn a profit. In the
past producers did experimental productions on which they expected to take a loss. Mr. Barr said he had backed 50 off-
Broadway shows only three of which made money. "I use the
money I make on Broadway," he added. This is fine for the
well-off Mr. Barr, but young actors get pretty hungry. So it
gets down to this: we can only have experimental, adventurous
theatre if we underpay our actors. Quite a problem.

"A Midsummer Night's Dream"
(by Creighton Peet, From New York, February 1, 1971)

The stage is the inside of a box with three dazzlingly white
walls, blank except for two doors at the back. On the floor are three
or four large white pillows, and hanging in midair are two trapezes.

Soon the actors in floor-length blue, red, green, and yellow
satin robes appear and begin to speak the lines of Shakespeare's
"A Midsummer Night's Dream" with wonderful clarity and simplicity. Vanished are all the props associated with this play for
generations--the palace, the forest, the mossy banks, the gauzy
fairy wings, the realistic costumes.

This transformation is the work of Britain's Peter Brook,
probably the most original and inventive director now working
anywhere in the world. Originally done in London for the Royal
Shakespeare Company, this "Dream" is now on Broadway with
its original cast for a short run. Never sacrificing the play or
its poetry, it is impudent, bawdy, and has a joyous sense of
fun which absolutely delights audiences. It was brought to this
country by David Merrick.

The action is physical, even athletic, and early in the play
all the actors are equipped with short lengths of plastic hose
(much like that on hair dryers) which they whirl round and round
over their heads, producing weird whistling tones--the sound of
magic taking hold. Soon Theseus and Puck swing themselves up
and sit on the trapezes, and we become aware of a walkway and
railing running around the tops of the white walls. Here, other
actors move about, casually leaning on the railing to watch the
action on the stage below, like passengers on an ocean liner.
From time to time Theseus and other characters do a little jug-
gling, balancing metal plates on short wands. When characters
chase each other about they use almost invisible ladders hidden
in cracks in the walls to race to the upper level, and then down
again. Other times they swing about on the trapezes or sit in
plastic bucket seats which lift them high into the air, or climb
down a rope hanging in Mr. Brook's gymnasium, all the while
speaking Shakespeare's lines and enjoying themselves immensely.
You soon get into the spirit of the evening, and realize this is
nothing but a fantastic party in which all the dialogue was written by Shakespeare, no less, and spoken by such superb actors

as Alan Howard (who plays Theseus/Oberon) and Sara Kestelman (Hippolyta/Titania).

Once the action has moved into the enchanted forest, things really get wild, Puck (John Kane) smirking with pleasure as he drops enchanted potions into sleeping eyes. Later, the actors on the upper walkway shower the stage with small paper plates. Many fall into the audience which whirls them back at the actors. Eventually we come to the familiar scene in which Titania, queen of the fairies, awakens after magic drops have been put in her eyes, to discover she is passionately in love with Bottom, whose head has been changed to suggest an ass. Audiences have been enduring this silly business for generations, but here the reason for her interest is made bawdy clear.

Speaking with drama reporters at lunch some days after the opening, director Brook and his actors said they felt that "stripping away" all the settings and costumes inherited from the 19th century had been a tremendous help to this production. As for the white walls, Mr. Brook explained their virtue was "nothingness." A bare stage exposing brick walls and heating pipes would have been a joyless background, while the brilliantly lighted white walls give the excitement scene designer Sally Jacobs wanted.

This production was rehearsed eight weeks, he said, starting with many readings of the play, and at all times actors were encouraged to suggest and develop their own ideas. "Anything is possible," Mr. Brook said, "when actors are permitted to express their feelings about a role." During the discussion one of the actors confessed, "At times I wanted to bend the play my way, while Peter (Mr. Brook) wanted the play to drift through our minds." Mr. Brook added, however, a director's role was to maintain some established things.

"At the same time," he said, "when a director imposes his style too strongly on a play it can be a reduction of it. Any play has several themes--you try to capture the greatest number of these you can. But instead of saying 'either/or' you replace them with a greedy 'both.'"

Mr. Brook recalled that the temptation to indicate the darkness of night and the heavy fog mentioned in the text of Shakespeare's play had been very great, "and at one point we had Puck blowing cigarette smoke through cracks between the walls." This would have been quite in keeping with the other unorthodox devices used in this production. However, both he and the rest of the cast realized that if they made one concession to this kind of realism, many others would soon follow, and in a short while they would be right back with the Victorian settings and costumes of seventy-five years ago. So they have left the blazing white lights full up all through the forest scenes of darkness.

While Mr. Brook has staged a great deal of his work for the Royal Shakespeare Company which has a very handsome subsidy from the British Government, he is becoming restive. "Modern people cannot live in the past," he said. Accordingly he is now organizing an International Center of Theatre Research in Paris, and hopes to get financing for this from America as well as Britain and France.

PENNINGTON, Ron; (2) Theatre Critic; (3) b. Topeka, Kansas, May 5; (4) s. Glen and Lucile (Englert) P.; (5) Northwest Missouri State College/the University of Missouri at Kansas City, major subj.: Theatre Arts, English; (6) Single; (8) Assistant Editor/Production Manager, Hurst House Publications, 1962-64; Assistant to the Promotion Manager, The Kansas City Star, 1964-68; Staff Reporter/Film Critic, Boxoffice Magazine, 1968-69; Hollywood Editor/Film Critic, Quigley Publications, 1969-71; Theatre Critic/Staff Reporter, The Hollywood Reporter, 1971- ; (9) Actor, Dancer, Choreographer, Assistant Director, Stage Manager, Set Designer, Backstage Crew, etc. for various regional and community theatres in Kansas City area from 1961-69; Soloist, The Kansas City Civic Ballet and The Kansas City Modern Dance Company, 1967-69; Actor, various theatre workshop productions in Los Angeles, 1969-71; Appeared in films "Terror from the Stars," "High School Caesar," "Punishment Park" and "Blacula"; (15) American National Theatre and Academy; The Los Angeles Drama Critics Circle; American Theatre Critics Association; (22) The Hollywood Reporter, 6715 Sunset Blvd., Hollywood, Calif. 90028; (23) Readership, 65,000; (24) 150 plays and musicals, 40 television; 30 nightclub, 15 films

Shubert Theatre: Seascape
(by Ron Pennington, Hollywood Reporter, April 4, 1975)

A new Edward Albee play is almost always an event and his latest work, "Seascape," which opened a limited engagement at the Shubert Theatre Wednesday, is certainly no exception.

It's an entertaining, intelligent and thought-provoking work that should be seen by everyone who is the least bit concerned about the present state of the American theatre. Even those who are not concerned should find this superior production highly enjoyable.

"Seascape," in a sense, is a much more gentle and readily accessible play than many of Albee's earlier works. It opens with a middle-aged couple lounging on a beach, discussing their past life together, their old dreams and current ambitions. Suddenly--or not quite so suddenly because Albee has subtly prepared us for this--two lizard-like creatures appear and the second act is devoted to an examination of evolution and the point at which man really began to rise above his fellow creatures.

On the surface, it is a deceptively simple play once the audience accepts the fact that these early evolutionary creatures can talk. But, as usual, Albee passes out several fascinating ideas and suppositions, many of which he does not follow through but which remain to tantalize the audience's imagination long after the final curtain has come down. As with Albee's earlier plays, much will be written about the meaning and implications of "Seascape."

One can argue that it is a rather contrived work in that the lizards have enough of a vocabulary to carry on an intelligent conversation with the humans but, when Albee has a point on which he wants to elaborate, they suddenly, for no other reason, do not understand the key words. True, the playwright is often quite obvious in imposing himself on the materials but his use of language in exploring old cliches and new conceptions is so commanding as to make it all acceptable.

For this production, Albee has also found the perfect director--himself. The two things that make the play work so well are its theatricality and its comedy. It is really a very funny play and instead of trying to absorb it at the time one should just sit back and enjoy. Anything else will come later.

Albee, both as a playwright and as a director understands this thoroughly and he has done an admirable job in keeping the mood properly light and brisk.

He is also fortunate enough to have an excellent cast working for him. It's difficult to imagine anyone but Deborah Kerr playing the role of the wife. The first act depends almost entirely on this character and Ms. Kerr, with her marvelous sense of comedy and expression, makes it work perfectly. It's an engagingly buoyant and fascinating performance. Barry Nelson is also excellent as her husband, expressing the role with just the right amount of charm and personality.

While Ms. Kerr beautifully carries the first act, Frank Langella dominates the second act with his truly sensational portrayal of the male lizard. Langella, darting around the stage in quick, reptilian movements, amazingly and believably embodies the qualities of an early evolutionary creature. Maureen Anderman turns in a surprisingly touching performance as his submissive and curious mate.

The lizard costumes by Fred Voelpel are extraordinary and the set and lighting by James Tilton are equally impressive. Tilton has created an imposing, realistic sand dune setting and his lighting is so natural that one can almost feel the heat of the summer sun.

UCLA: Edward II
(by Ron Pennington, Hollywood Reporter, May 2, 1975)

Anyone who is interested in classical theatre--from either

a performance or an audience standpoint--should rush to UCLA's Royce Hall Saturday night when the City Center Acting Company of New York will repeat its brilliant production of Christopher Marlowe's seldom performed "Edward II."

According to a program note, this is the first professional production of this classic to be presented in America. In a way, it's possible to see why past generations have ignored the play (which was first performed around 1592) because of its dark themes of homosexuality and the overwhelming, corrupting influence of absolute power.

But the time for this play (considered by many to be Marlowe's masterpiece) seems to be now and director Ellis Rabb and the excellent CCAC ensemble have met the challenge to create one of the most exciting, vital and intriguing theatrical events imaginable.

Rabb concentrates on the dark, destructive aspects of these characters and how they are slowly consumed by the cancer of unbridled influence and power. It's interesting that Edward (played with exceptional sensitivity, determination and conviction by Norman Snow) emerges as the most sympathetic and least malignant of all these characters.

Rabb's staging is fantastic in its theatrical impact as he probes the decaying psyches of these people and the grotesque deeds into which ambition and power pushes them. It is in no way a cautious production and Rabb pulls no punches in playing both the mental and physical perversions of these characters.

The ensemble work of this well-trained company is of the highest level and every role is carefully developed and drawn with convincing authority.

The physical production is also most exciting, with costumes by Nancy Potts that are perfectly in tune with the production and lighting by David F. Segal that adds greatly in terms of focus and effect.

Bob James' music nicely underscores and often heightens the tension, although Royce Hall occasionally defeats the sound and several times the dialogue is garbled and impossible to understand.

PETERSON, Maurice; (2) Theater and Film Critic; (3) b. Manhattan, Feb. 19, 1952; (4) s. Pierce and Lucille (Jones); (5) B.A. Columbia U., major subj.: English, 1973; (6) Single; (8) Theater and Film Critic, The Columbia (Univ.) Spectator, 1971-72; Film Department Editor, The New York Metropolitan Review, 1971-71; Theater and Film Critic, Essence Magazine, 1971-present; (9) Co-Directed with brother, Gregory Peterson and acted in the following short films:

"Joan of Arc," 1966* (*indicates direction only); "Sunset Blvd." 1967; "Coming Soon ... Vertigo"* (presented on Metromedia Television); "Passionella" 1967; "Race" 1969; Actor in stage production of "Dark of the Moon," at Camp Lexington for the Performing Arts, 1968; Technical Director for "Meet Mr. Dickens" at the Royal Playhouse, NYC, 1968; Co-producer of Film Festival "Movies by Young Filmmakers," at Library and Museum of Performing Arts at Lincoln Center, 1969; Leading Man in One-Act Play, "Chezz," by Gregory Peterson, presented in workshop at Columbia, 1972; Leading Man (Billy Jester) in Columbia Players production of the musical, "Little Mary Sunshine," 1972, studied acting and direction with Donald Pace at Barnard College, 1972; studied and performed in choreography workshops with Janet Soares, Barnard College, 1972-73; performed with James Cunningham and the Acme Dance Company, 1973; studied acting and directing and performed in workshop productions with Luz Costanos, Barnard, 1973; acted in "Visions of New York," a theatrical collage conceived and directed by Mary Bush, Barnard, 1973; Publicist for 20th Century-Fox's "Claudine," 1973; acted in film short, "Streak Poker," by Gregory Peterson, 1974; wrote, produced and acted in one-act play, "The Felt Is Green," presented at The Library and Museum of Performing Arts at Lincoln Center, 1974; music columnist for Unique New York (mag.), 1974-present; Producer and Host of Cable Television series, "New York Now," covering theater and arts events and celebrities, 1974-present; (13) no military experience; (14) Cash Award and Citation from New York Metropolitan Museum of Art for film, "Passionella," 1968; Seymour Brick Award for Playwriting at Columbia University, 1973; (15) Member New York League of Theaters and Producers 1974-present; The Theater Forum, 1975-present; (16) US Citizen; (17) Believe in faith; (18) Favorite: Howard Johnson's Motor; (19) Mickey Mouse; (20) Cont. Articles to: Village Voice; Andy Warhol's Interview; Show Magazine; After Dark; The New York Times; Plays: "Fantasm," produced by Columbia Players, 1972; "The Felt Is Green," produced at Lincoln Center, 1974; "Love Talk," 1973 (Seymour Brick Award); Screenplays "Oreo," 1970; "The Soul Truth," 1974; "Jamaica," (treatment) 1974; (all yet to be produced) and "Come to the Table," (with J.V. Means), being readied for production by Table Associates, 1975; (21) 324 West 84 St. #62, New York, N.Y., 10024, Ph. 212-787-7039; (22) c/o Essence Magazine, 300 East 42 St., New York, N.Y., 10017, Ph. 212-687-2100; (23) Circulation: 450,000, audience: 1,800,000; (24) Approx. 60 plays and films per annum, plus 12 theater and film personality interviews.

"Raisin": A Play with Nine Lives?
(by Maurice Peterson, Essence, December 1973)

When the late Lorraine Hansberry's A Raisin in the Sun opened in 1959, it chronicled the spirit of the great age of liberalism, integration, passive resistance and Martin Luther King, Jr. Times certainly have changed. Yet, the new musical adaptation of Ms. Hansberry's play, Raisin, shows that her work has not faded with the years. If anything, the power of her words has grown.

A contemporary drama in its original Broadway form, Raisin is now a period piece about three generations of a Black family living together in a Chicago ghetto tenement. All of the family members have dreams which can come true with the benefits from the recently deceased grandfather's life insurance policy. Grandmother Lena and mother Ruth, want a new house so that grandson Travis can grow up away from rats and roaches. Daughter Beneatha has her heart on medical school, and Walter Lee, husband, wants to invest in a liquor store. Trouble comes when the only house they can afford is in a white neighborhood, and when Walter Lee, at sight of the first tenable project of his life, gets carried away by ambition. The tension among the family members mounts as, all of a sudden, it seems that all their dreams will be deferred, as they have been generation upon generation before. But, true to the Black lifestyle and human spirit, they ultimately stay together and find the way to go forth.

The non-musical, A Raisin in the Sun is not a light comedy; it is a strong and moving drama, rich with a full range of emotional nuances. It was complete, and tampering with it by adding songs, dances and production numbers could have resulted in a skeletal disaster on the order of last season's Seesaw (miserably adapted from The Apartment). But in their adaptation, Robert Nemiroff and Charlotte Zatzberg, Judd Woldin (music) and Robert Brittan (lyrics) have remained completely faithful to the original, retaining all its poignance and insight. Perhaps they were too faithful, because the least successful aspect of the show is its music.

Woldin and Brittan, a white team, only seldom come close to capturing Blackness in their rhythms, melodies and words. This critic would much have preferred to see Raisin treated more like Aint Supposed to Die a Natural Death than Funny Girl. They certainly don't display the gift of George Gershwin, whose adaptation of Porgy and Bess so transcends its precursor that hardly anyone remembers it was originally a straight, dramatic play. Gershwin had a gift for making fluid transitions from dialog to song, but in Raisin--especially in the first act--one often feels the characters saying, "OK everybody, let's stop here and sing!"

Their attempts at capturing the flavor of the fifties is also slipshod. They come close in numbers like "Booze," but even that is ruined by a line with the slogan, "Put a tiger in your tank," which was not popularized by Madison Avenue until the sixties. There are some excellent numbers, including "You Done Right," "Not Anymore" and "Measure the Valleys," but, at best, they only sustain a mood established perfectly well by the dialog.

That the show still comes across as powerfully as it does is only testament to the talent of Lorraine Hansberry, and to the cast, which received a standing ovation at every performance it played in Washington, D. C. 's Arena Stage. I saw it there, before it opened in Philadelphia and on Broadway. As it was playing in the round, without scenery and with completely different staging of movements and dance numbers than it has on the proscenium stage, there is little more I can note here than those performances, and they were inspired to say the least.

The original performances of A Raisin in the Sun were excellently recorded in the film version, so these cast members have the task of standing in the mountainous shadows of Claudia McNeil, Ruby Dee, Diana Sands, Lou Gossett, Douglas Turner Ward and Sidney Poitier. With perhaps only one or two exceptions, the acting in this company equals that of the original, and where it doesn't, those performers more than make up for it with their singing. Special mention must go to Ralph Carter (Travis), who, at age 11, has more stage magnetism than most stars thrice his age; Ernestine Jackson (Ruth), who carries such tension and frustration in her posture and facial expressions that she tells a whole story just by standing on stage. When she finally breaks down and vows to scrub every kitchen in Chicago, if necessary, to buy a clean home of her own, you sympathize enough to want to scrub them for her; and Virginia Capers (Lena), whose towering strength as a singer and actress drives home every pound of sorrow, struggle and hope written into Lorraine Hansberry's original script. In the end, it is Ms. Caper's portrayal of determination, faith and love that captures the essence of the Black experience and the beauty of human nature. Hers is the performance that can move you to tears and, at the curtain, make you stand and cheer. After 23 years of relative obscurity in show business, this role should make Virginia Capers a star in the most honorable sense of the word.

Of course, no single performer could come across so well without the overall orchestration of the play by the director, Donald McKayle. Although his choreography was diffused by the awkward arena stage--a problem which should not exist on Broadway--the show is not dependent on flashy production numbers. The play didn't suffer at all for their lack.

Even after a flat season for musicals, with even the year's best, Pippin and A Little Night Music, coming across just as fluffy entertainment, Raisin is just what we need to restore faith in legitimate theater. It deeply moves its audience, providing enlightenment as well as entertainment with an intimacy that only the theater can offer. As the "Great White Way" fades, more and more certainly becoming "The Fabulous Invalid," Raisin is all the more rare an experience, one that should not be missed by anyone.

Spotlight on Jane White
(by Maurice Peterson, Essence, April 1975)

Most actresses interpret the classics occasionally, but Jane

White has so many classical credits that you would think she
had a passion for them. The ancient characters--Helen of Troy
and Clytemnestra--as well as Shakespeare's Kate the Shrew have
all come to life in her personage. And in 1965, she was
awarded the coveted Obie Award for her portrayals of Volumnia
in Coriolanus and the French princess in Shakespeare's Love's
Labors Lost. Actually, her pursuit has been due not so much
to her attraction to the classics as to her repulsion from the
popular milieu. For contemporary theater, it seems she presents a "casting problem." Her skin is too light for her to
play Blacks, and she's not white enough to play whites. So, for
Jane White, the classics have become a creative asylum. Soon
after her opening at New York's Roundabout Theater in Ibsen's
Rosmersholm, I met with Jane White and we discussed the dilemma that has also afflicted the careers of Ron O'Neal, Ellen
Holly and many other actors. The Smith College graduate had
her first Broadway success playing a Black woman in Strange
Fruit, a 1946 drama in which she starred opposite Mel Ferrer.
Strange Fruit was one of the rare plays of its day to deal with
the human elements of racial prejudice.

"Eleanor Roosevelt even wrote a special article about it,"
she recalled. "People were very excited that, finally, the
American theater was going to have something to say about
Black/white relations." She went from that success, naturally,
to calls for other Black roles.

Then came the rub. "People would not believe I was Black.
They'd think it was a white girl onstage and that the message
was not being stated clearly. So, I got fired from a couple of
things."

The only roles producers and audiences seemed to accept
her in were Polynesians, Mexicans and Puerto Ricans. So, for
the ten years following Strange Fruit, Jane White went through
what she calls "my tropic period."

Later, the role of the mad wife in Jane Eyre was the first
to afford her a departure from literal Black or white, and the
success of Once Upon a Mattress set her firmly on the path of
classics. The Broadway musical was not itself classical, but
by playing a medieval queen to Carole Burnett's princess, she
paved the way to her many subsequent successes in the acting
field that allows deviation in color. "It's like singing in the
opera. Audiences are willing to accept it because there's a removal from reality."

Black roles have crept into Jane White's repertoire, and
she has cherished them. She appeared on The Edge of Night
(a television soap opera) as Nurse Holiday, and was the madam
in Klute. She starred as the evangelist in the Rome, Paris and
NET television productions of Trumpets of the Lord. On Broadway, that role was played by the then little-known Cicely Tyson,

her direct opposite on the light meter. They played the same
role once, but the likelihood of their even being considered for
the same role again, outside of classics, is infinitesimal.

"And so I have strangely enough gotten off into this area of
the classics, and I am hardly ever playing Black women. I do
use my own Black experience and heritage to fulfill those women, however," she explains. "Maybe when this country grows
up a bit more and realizes that Black people come in all sizes
shapes and colors, then I'll have a more diversified career.
But I don't know if I'll live that long. In the meantime, I have
a craft. I am an artist and I want to be able to function."

Theater: Last April, James Earl Jones stated in this column that he was "committed to the communication of pain."
Emotional pain, that is, especially that which is derived from
the inability to express one's needs. Having had a speech problem for several years of his childhood, he has invaluable insights to the role of the inarticulate, dimwitted Lennie in John
Steinbeck's Of Mice and Men. That role, he later confided,
was his dream to play. Now, on Broadway, his dream has
come true, and the performance may prove to be the crowning
achievement of his entire life's work.

Originally produced in 1937, Of Mice and Men is a simple,
stark tragedy of stifled lives on a barren terrain, in which the
friendship of two farmhands is the only beautiful thing. Kevin
Conway is Jones' perfect counterpart as the feisty, fast-thinking
George, and Pamela Blair, as Curley's seductive wife, is a
captivating beauty for Jones' beast. This production is one of
the best dramas of the season, certainly the most compelling.

Other excellent stage presentations are: In Praise of Love,
a charming, conventional love story; The Hashish Club, an audacious attempt to convey the viewer on a theatrical, acid trip
that is fresh, funny and thoroughly enjoyable; and All Over Town,
Cleavon Little's first Broadway appearance since Purlie. Dustin Hoffman's direction of Murray Schisgal's new comedy is
crazy, and they've got people laughing all over town!

Film: The great disaster pictures are back, and with a
vengeance. Not only does Earthquake show you in authentic detail how it will look when Los Angeles crumbles, the new dimensional effect, "Sensurround," shakes you up so that you can
feel it too. It's a blast with the grandest special effects of all
time. You'll suddenly find yourself with a whole new perspective on the mere troubles of inflation.

And you aint seen bad news until you've watched Jennifer
Jones fall out of a scenic elevator, or a ballroom full of men
get flushed away by a million gallons of water in Towering Inferno. Earthquake may be the biggest, but Towering Inferno
is by far the classiest disaster picture so far. I must admit

that after being rattled to the bone in Earthquake, I was somewhat disappointed not to have been smoked, heated and drenched
at Towering Inferno.

Anyone who saw how Mel Brooks ravaged the western genre
with Blazing Saddles should be prepared for his thirties science
fiction. The damage is Young Frankenstein, his most cohesive,
stylish and lunatic movie of all. With Gene Wilder as the grandson destined to fulfill the family legacy and Peter Boyle as the
lovable monster, Young Frankenstein is for the entire family.

Stardust is for more mature audiences. A Star Is Born is
here reincarnated in rock music rather than the movie scene,
and it's still a winner.

PETRYNI, Michael, Arizona Republic, P.O. Box 1950, 120 East
Van Buren St., Phoenix, Ariz. 85001

PLAUT, Jonathan; (2) Theater and Film Critic; (3) b. New York
City, February 27, 1936; (4) s. Abraham and Beverly (Carlson) P.;
(5) B.S. Pennsylvania State U., major subj.: engineering, 1957;
J.D. Georgetown U. Law School, 1961; LL.M. New York U., major subj.: Law, 1966; M.A. New York U., major subj.: Cinema,
1970; (6) m. Anne Friedberg, March 29, 1958; (7) children--David
Lawrence, Jeffrey Benjamin, Joshua Andrew; (8) Film Critic Summit Herald and other newspapers in New Jersey, Pennsylvania and
Michigan, 1966- ; theater critic Summit Herald and other New Jer-
sey newspapers, 1970- ; teacher of film and theater related courses
in Ridgewood, Madison, and South Orange-Maplewood School Sys-
tems, 1966- ; Lecturer, Kent Place School, 1973- ; Board of
Judges, American Film Festival, 1970 and Cine, 1973- ; organizer
Springfield Film Festival, 1971, 72, 73, and Allied-Morristown
Film Series, 1973, 74; (10) Member, U.S. Dept. of Commerce
Committee on Cultural Aspects, 1962, 63; (11) Chairman, Union
County New Democratic Coalition Caucus, 1968; member, Summit
Civil Rights Commission; (16) Democrat; (17) Jewish; (20) Contri-
bute articles to The American Scholar, Scene, Filmograph, Film
Comment; (21) 3 Ashland Road, Summit, N.J., Ph. 201-273-9217;
(22) Summit Herald, 22 Bank Street, Summit, N.J. 07901, Ph. 201-
277-4000; (23) Circulation: newspapers, 25,000; (24) 20 theater reviews, 50 motion picture reviews, 5 miscellaneous.

"Measure for Measure"
(by Jon Plaut, Summit Herald, July 1974)

To say that the New Jersey Shakespeare Festival opening
production for the 1974 summer season at their Drew University
Theater of William Shakespeare's "Measure for Measure" is not
a complete success is not to condemn or belittle it.

"Measure for Measure" is a difficult, minor play. It is a

comedy of morals and manners, and writers who came later, such as Oscar Wilde, must have been influenced by it. But Moliere may be the better example, for there is a kind of desperation, of wildness, of humor, in "Measure for Measure," which makes the play both funny and serious, both touching and grotesque, and both subtle and grossly farcical at the same time.

To the New Jersey Shakespeare Festival Company's credit, their production of "Measure for Measure" deals strongly with the play on its own terms, but the theatrical innovation which is so prominent lessens character development and finally must be relied upon to hold the audience's attention.

"Measure for Measure" concerns a dukedom (set in this production in Victorian Vienna) from which the duke has taken temporary leave and placed an austere aide, Angelo, in charge. Angelo condemns Claudio, a young man, to death for getting a woman with child, and his sister Isabella (a novitiate) pleads for his life with Angelo. Angelo falsely consents to spare Isabella's brother if she will submit to him. The duke, disguised as a friar, oversees all this, and the neat ending is predictable, but welcome since the play runs down somewhat.

Shakespeare has the foibles and moral hypocrisies of men in society as a subject of "Measure for Measure. "

Director Paul Barry seeks to reach to that in his "Measure for Measure" by framing the play within the boundaries of the raucous and bawdy humor within it. Not a simple comedy, then, this "Measure for Measure" employs slapstick and unpretentious farce as its tools. And for the most part that works as it should, although the posturing and pratfalls for laughs sometimes becomes too studied an attempt at freshness. For example, Angelo's funny but exaggerated nonsense movements while he sexually pursues Isabella (while she pleads for her brother's life) are too much. Neither Margery Shaw (Isabella) nor J. C. Hoyt (Angelo) are fully comfortable with the frantic actions posed against their serious lines.

John Capodice works hard and shows a great deal of frenzied charm as the duke. Margery Shaw (who was so outstanding in last year's production of "Summer and Smoke") is less at home in her role; because, I think, her nervous energy is not fully harnessed to the wildly comic form in which this serious play is staged. Miss Shaw's talents are undeniable, however, and she may work into the role as the season progresses. The rest of the cast is competent, although there is a good deal of exaggerated performance dwelling on idiosyncracies. Of course, this is what the director called for, and may be what "Measure for Measure" requires (although I am not convinced).

Paul Barry has shown flair and originality in Shakesperian productions, and the New Jersey Shakespeare Festival, with its commitment to do serious works imaginatively, is off to a good, if not perfect, start.

"Scenes from a Marriage"
(by Jon Plaut, Summit Herald, June 1974)

Ingmar Bergman's "Scenes from a Marriage" is superlative and proves once again his absolute and unfailing mastery of motion picture art. "Scenes from a Marriage" must be put at the very top of Bergman's staggering output of masterwork films.

Edited by Bergman into a movie from his serialized production for Swedish television, "Scenes from a Marriage" picks up and follows the lives of its married and then divorced couple (Liv Ullmann and Erland Josephson) over a ten-year period. Except for a brief but very effective appearance by Bibi Andersson as a beautiful, sensitive and embittered woman on her way to divorce, as well as a few other minor characters, the film focuses exclusively on the husband and wife, and their relationship.

Bergman has always been the most subtle of directors. Even in his earlier days, when his films (such as "The Seventh Seal") were heavy with germanic symbolism, he created sharply defined characters. And since "Shame" and "Persona," and especially "The Passion of Anna" and "Cries and Whispers," he has molded (from each screenplay, the unrivaled camera work of Sven Nykvist, his gifted actresses, and his own unparalleled film art) the finest and most detailed women ever created for the screen.

In "Scenes from a Marriage," the woman and her husband are clearly drawn, and yet as in the best in life they are ambiguous and ever changing. They grow, and they are diminished. They reach greater understanding, and they delude themselves. They are alternately (and sometimes at the same time) happy, morose, ambitious, content, violent, disappointed, lustful, selfish, generous and just about every other emotion, feeling, quality and capacity known to men and women.

Some of the film is very bitter, but the capacity for growth and the anticipation for the future keeps "Scenes from a Marriage" essentially optimistic. The manner in which Bergman draws the viewer into personalizing these lives (similar in its soap opera technique to the BBC "Upstairs/Downstairs") and the truly brilliant acting maintain the film not only as high art, but perfectly realized entertainment.

The performance by Liv Ullmann is not to be believed. Surely, it is one of the great works in all of film or stage acting craft. The enlarging and engaging woman that Miss Ullmann fashions with her small gestures, her many different moods, her marvelous voice, her changing physical appearance, and her insight into the character and partnership with Bergman is a new height for her already unequaled work.

There is, for example, a moment at the end of the first half of "Scenes from a Marriage" in which Miss Ullmann covers her face with her hands in an agony which each person in the audience was experiencing with her. Bergman has just been particularly unremitting with his closeup photography in exposing the psychic violence done on the woman before us (from that experience, she is to grow, and grow, and grow). Rooted as I was before this woman with her feelings so completely exposed, I wanted to avert my eyes. Not from distaste, or displeasure, but because Mr. Bergman and Miss Ullmann had so completely taken hold of me as to make me a part of the experience on the screen.

"Scenes from a Marriage" is a collaboration of acting and cinematic genius.

PLUTZIK, Roberta; (2) Theater critic; (3) b. Rochester, N.Y., March 5, 1948; (4) d. Hyam and Tanya (Roth); (5) B.A. U. of Rochester, major subj.: English and History; (6) m. Neil Baldwin, September 12, 1971; (7) children--none; (8) Daily feature writer, TV critic, assistant theater and film critic, Rochester Democrat and Chronicle, 1971-72; Theater and film critic, Buffalo Courier Express, Birmingham, England, 1967-68; freelance script-reader, Metro-Goldwyn-Mayer, 1970; freelance script-reader, Sterling Lord Literary Agency, 1970; Critic Fellow, Eugene O'Neill National Critics' Institute, Waterford, Conn., 1974; (14) Buffalo Newspaper Guild, Rookie-of-the-Year, 1972; (15) National Theater Critics' Assn., Charter Member; Buffalo Newspaper Guild, Editor, Page One Magazine 1975; (17) Jewish; (21) 369 Pennsylvania St., Buffalo, N.Y. 14201; (22) Buffalo Courier-Express, 787 Main St., Buffalo N.Y. 14240; (23) Circulation: weekday, 135,000; Sunday, 400,000; (24) one hundred plays and musicals; one hundred motion pictures; twenty-five rock concerts; thirty television; ten miscellaneous; frequent features on entertainment subjects.

Capote Adaptation Superb
(by Roberta Plutzik, Buffalo Courier Express, October 6, 1973)

There are no buses or trains to Noon City, or past it to another country, Skully's Landing. Yet a boy is seen going thataway, down its overgrown paths of mystery. If he is unequipped for its revelations, he will learn.

The adaptation of Truman Capote's first novel, "Other Voices, Other Rooms," published when he was 23 in 1948, opened Thursday at the Studio Arena Theater.

Hopes for it in this community have been borne out: Anna Marie Barlow's adaptation is incredibly true to its source, just as it is entirely able to stand alone. The performances almost all are superb; Melvin Bernhardt's direction is smooth and diverting.

Though the people behind the effort still may be saying "give us another week," "Other Voices, Other Rooms" looks, feels and resounds more completely than any recent Studio production first night.

Joel Knox is 13. His mother is dead in New Orleans. A finely printed letter arrives asking Joel to come home to a father he does not remember.

Nobody is there to meet him in Noon City but old Jesus Fever (Avon Long, making him likably wry and withered). They make the trip to the Landing ("The Skulls," one man calls it). It is an overgrown weedpatch of a place oozing mystery, fear, sadness. Joel meets a menagerie:

Amy, his father's wife, a weary, youngish woman in dismal gray, left hand shrouded by a glove, her voice nervous, then shrill, always on guard; Randolph, the "poor cousin" prone to attacks of asthma; Zoo, a bony black girl with backwoods common sense and emotion, and fine lungs--the cook; Idabel and Florabel, young neighbor twins, the first rough and boyish seeming--a "gangster"--the other petite, an aspiring actress; Little Sunshine, a maker of potions in a forest hermitage.

And there is a white-wigged lady of dream. Joel sees her--he is sure of it, then not so sure--peering from the house. She is as elusive as his father, as complicated as Randolph.

They are like nobody Joel has ever met, stranger than the magician at the Nemo theater where he would go in New Orleans. "Try to be happy here," the fat, sickly, pale-white Randolph tells Joel, "Try just a little to like me."

It is hard, these appeals coming from all directions, pulling at a boy. David Aaron, the found star of the play, was plucked from an open audition going on in the same building in New York as the "Voices" tryouts and cast in a role 10 years his junior. Aaron is just right, though, his body, compact as it is, set in kid's slouch and a boy's baggy clothes. Aaron's secret is his delicate measuredness--never does he strive for more than the essential, the distilled reaction, so that he can finish the play strong, untired, convinced, "I am me, I am me. We're the same, I am me."

A measure of Ms. Barlow's respect for the novel is her direct transposition of some of the essential speeches. The audience seemed, in its quiet, to understand the point of Randolph in his silk pajamas, chubby feet stuck into slippers, going on and on about a prize fighter named Pepe Alvarez who stole his heart; and about all the weariness inside.

A few scenes--the transition and treatment of Joel's lengthy illness, and the journey to the Cloud Hotel--work less well, seem on the brink of falling together.

John Harkins is a complete Randolph--no less praise would be apropos. Subject to all the cruelty he can measure up against himself, he hovers like a wounded bird. "Everything in this house is a joke played on myself, by myself," he tells Joel, who must try to understand.

The characters in this tiny world, all bent, still are surprisingly diverse, "What we want most in the world is to be held and told everything--everything--will be all right," Randolph says. Yet how does each want this love? Joel must learn.

Idabel, this "Pretty Boy Floyd, as she is tagged, prefers punches to kisses, or so she says. Bumped and battered inside and out, wearing dark glasses so things will be prettier, Swoosie Kurtz' performance is natural, comic, memorable.

Zoo, her throat bearing the scar of a madman's knife, dreams of snow in Washington, D. C., and of a true man. Lynn Thigpen is a sight in her men's shoes, her rhinestone earrings and her lace on prayer meetin' day. Her wide arms can hold all of us, we feel.

Miss Wisteria, the country fair midget grasping poignantly for little boys not yet grown, leaves us with the sad echoes of her dreams; Yvonne Moray, in her first dramatic role, is as Joel says of her hands, "like little jeweled butterflies."

"Other Voices, Other Rooms" is set forward on the SAT thrust stage, in a many-leveled design too completely detailed with the dull, tarnished rag and wood remains of the past, hindered perhaps by lighting which remains an eerie but not fantastical complement to the set. Music by James Reichert is moody; his sound effects are particulary wide-ranging.

Bernhardt's staging and Barlow's script building, building to Joel's quiet, final ascension of the stairs of Skully's Landing, knowing he can finally reach the top, make us think of the Broadway possibilities of "Other Voices, Other Rooms." They should be pursued.

"Antony, Cleopatra" Pitfalls Avoided; Acting Is Excellent
(by Roberta Plutzik, Buffalo Courier-Express, June 11, 1976)

Today "Antony and Cleopatra," the Shakespearean tragedy, more often is called a "problem play." One of the problems is that it is rarely produced.

Reasons why include its abrupt changes of temperament and its loose construction built upon short scenes involving masses

In the play's favor are a challenging female role and a captivating subject, one of the world's favorite love stories.

The Stratford Shakespeare Festival opened its new "Antony and Cleopatra" Wednesday at the Festival Theater under the direction of Robin Phillips, who best responds to challenge.

It is a challenge to do "Antony and Cleopatra" even half well. For all its romantic resonance and sustained poetical sense, it stands ready to divert good intentions.

Phillips' position was advantageous to start, having Maggie Smith, who could not be better as Cleopatra, and Keith Baxter, as the doomed Antony, the Roman warrior torn between duty to homeland and the lure of foreign love.

The play-maze is confronted and admirably avoided for the most part in the production, though for the viewer unfamiliar with the complexities of the story--the shifts, sometimes unmerciful, between the Egyptian court and the Roman encampments--the going will be rough.

The first act alone runs almost two hours.

But Phillips has a graceful way on stage, as he has shown with this year's "Hamlet" and last season's "Measure for Measure." He digs for the humanity of characterization, a welcome change from Shakespearean recitation with lots of bluster but little heart.

So this "Antony and Cleopatra" moves as quickly and unobtrusively through scenes of political explication as it can without the cutting of those scenes altogether.

The large cast comes and goes every which way across the stage in great white waves and more times than one could count, but never sounds like a thundering herd. The play, without fuss, finds a rhythm that supports and connects changes of place and time.

If the confrontations between Octavius Caesar and once-ally and friend Antony will seem extended and without particular joy, the production is genuinely affecting in its telling of Antony's need for Cleopatra, and hers for him.

It begins before the play opens, when Antony, in a triumvirate with Octavius and Lepidus for rule of the Roman Empire, comes upon Cleopatra of Egypt and lets slide his care of things political. The physical attraction is greater.

Cleopatra, knowledgeable in love, does all in her power to

command Antony's senses. She is selfish for him, and she makes him selfish. Octavius won't stand for it. Antony's descent is set in motion.

Shakespeare is clear to support none of these characters. Octavius (Alan Scarfe), the businessman, is bloodless. The lovers are moody, prone to thunderous fights followed by childlike embrace. Antony takes his own pulse, registering the shame, fear and recognition of defeat ("I have lost my way forever," he tells his men).

The lovers' well-known suicides are grippingly played out without hystrionic padding.

Actor Baxter isn't always clear to hear in moments of rage leading to the suicides from the balcony or the orchestra. Still, when he is heard he is quite marvelous as Antony spreads himself thin in confusion and a lover's haste for companship and nothing else.

He approaches the warrior's slipping away almost off-handedly, flicking a wrist as if to whisk away a bad dream.

Maggie Smith exudes femaleness in the role. Hers is a Cleopatra as dynamo, knowing her own mind very well, but needing companions (she embraces her maids for dear life)-- and Antony.

Her death, fast upon Antony's own, is a silent, wrenching moment. She presses the viper to her breast, swoons, pales and is gone. The massive festival stage seems small in the moment.

Daphne Dare's set and costume designs are simple and complimentary. Gil Wechsler's lighting task in this rambling play is well executed, as is the larger effort.

But if you come to "Antony and Cleopatra," read the play first. It should make the difference.

POLLACK, Joe; (2) Theater-film critic, columnist; (3) b. Brooklyn, N.Y., Feb. 3, 1931; (4) s. Samuel H. and Hannah (Weisman) P.; (5) B.J., U. of Missouri, 1952; (6) m. Carol Atchison, Dec. 1, 1964; (7) children (by former marriage)--Wendy Leah, Dara Rebecca, Sharon Merrill; (8) Assistant sports editor, Jackson (Miss.) Daily News, 1952; sports editor, Columbia (Mo.) Missourian, 1954; sports and feature writer, St. Louis Globe-Democrat, 1955-61; public relations director, St. Louis Football Cardinals, 1961-72; critic-feature writer, St. Louis Post-Dispatch, 1972- ; (13) Cpl., U.S. Army, 1952-53; (15) Member Sigma Delta Chi, Kappa Tau Alpha, U.S. Pro Football Writers Assn.; (16) Democrat; (17) Jewish; (19) Club: St. Louis Press; (20) Contribute articles and book reviews to wide

variety of publications; (21) 7553 Cromwell Drive, St. Louis, Mo.
63105, Ph. 314-862-3321; (22) St. Louis Post-Dispatch, 900 North
12th Blvd., St. Louis Mo. 63101, Ph. 314-621-1111; (23) Circulation:
320,000 daily, 800,000 Sunday; (24) 75 plays and musicals, 125 motion pictures, 150 books.

Loretto-Hilton Performs Shaw
(by Joe Pollack, St. Louis Post-Dispatch, December 2, 1974)

The bright, sardonic, pungent wit of George Bernard Shaw
is a welcome part of any theater season, and the great iconoclast's presence gleams smartly through the Loretto-Hilton Repertory Theater production of "Caesar and Cleoptra," which
opened a three-week run Friday night.

Rome and ancient Egypt, spiced with wry--and astonishingly
current--comment on his own world and times, proves once
again that while great ships founder on mighty icebergs, great
men founder on smaller icebergs, wrapped neatly in the soft
warmth of a women.

Cleopatra was such, and Francesca James gives a dazzling
performance as the fabled Egyptian queen. From the young girl
hunting a pet cat and huddling in fear before a Sphinx to the woman who can order assassination without a second thought
is a great distance, and Miss James covers it in outstanding style, so softly that she seems to move on the little
cat feet of Carl Sandburg's fog.

She achieves it almost like one's own children, so quietly
that the transition isn't noticed until suddenly there is an adult
sitting across the dinner table, where yesterday was an infant
in a high chair.

Miss James takes the play away from Caesar with delightful
deftness and real skill, and although she is always Shaw's Cleopatra, she truly fits the Cleopatra about whom Shakespeare
said, "Age cannot wither her, nor custom stale her infinite variety."

It is childlike when Cleopatra refers to Caesar as "good old
king," with the accent on the middle word, and it is childlike
when she teases Caesar about his bald spot, but Cleopatra always knows what she is doing, and what she is saying. She is
an alive, exciting--often frightening--woman as played by Miss
James.

Although there are great differences between Shaw's Caesar
and Shakespeare's Caesar, not to mention Plutarch's Caesar, it
is difficult to see Brendan Burke as the all-conquering Roman
Hero. Burke is splendid as the sardonic, reasoning Caesar,
disappointing as the dominant, ruling Caesar.

There is unevenness to the portrayal that falls short too often to be completely successful.

The supporting cast is generally excellent, with Lewis Arit, Robert Darnell, Arthur A. Rosenberg and Henry Strozier leading the way.

Rosenberg is perfect, in white tie and tails, as the great god Ra, that veteran of crossword puzzles, who leads the audience into the play with a prologue of commentary about ancient Egypt and turn-of-the-century England. He orchestrates the curtain call in delightful manner as well.

Strozier is Shaw, in the person of Brittanus, secretary to Caesar and commentator on manners and morals. It is a meaty role, and Strozier plays it under good control and with the proper manner. He is very good, as is Lewis Arit as Apollodorus, the Sicilian rug merchant whose foppishness acts as a delightful counterpoint to the goings-on about him and who reminds everyone that "when a stupid man is doing something he is ashamed of, he always declares that it is his duty."

Darnell's performance as Rufio is excellent, his rugged honesty and faith a constant throughout the evening. Margaret Winn is patrician and nasty as Ftatateeta, the queen's servant, and Kevin Lorin Pawley delivers brightly as Ptolemy, Cleopatra's brother and rival for the throne.

Director Davey Marlin-Jones decided to do the play in semi-modern dress, and it is most effective once one recovers from the shock of seeing Cleopatra in a pantsuit. Sigrid Insull's costumes carry the theme through very well and John Kavelin's ambitious set works effectively.

If there is an over-all shortcoming, it is that the company again showed an occasional tendency to rush its lines, as it did a year ago in "Henry V." Maybe it's the bumpiness of the trans-Atlantic crossing, but neither Shaw nor Shakespeare reach the Loretto-Hilton unsmudged.

English, as written by both men, becomes a rich and beautiful language, and the words should be enjoyed and examined and loved, not stepped on in the quest for the next line. In the many moments when the actors treat their words with the proper reverence, all the Shavian wit and wisdom makes for glorious theater.

The play will run through Dec. 21, with the company turning to an American playwright, Arthur Miller, for its next offering, "The Crucible," beginning on Jan. 3. Shaw fans will have another chance this month when "Don Juan in Hell," originally written as the third act of "Man and Superman," arrives Dec. 30, for a week-long run at the American Theater.

Play at American Theatre Mourns Passing of Heroes
(by Joe Pollack, St. Louis Post-Dispatch, December 10, 1974)

The physical bleakness of New Mexico and the emotional bleakness of so many Americans are mirrored in dark accuracy by Mark Medoff's "When You Comin' Back, Red Ryder?" a somber song to the present and the recent past that opened a weeklong run at the American Theatre last night.

Medoff's drama, well-acted and uncomfortably biting, is strong, modern American writing, reminiscent of "Easy Rider" in some of its attitudes, "American Graffiti" in some others.

It is not a pretty story, yet it shows excellent writing and acting--which are, in the final analysis, what theater is all about.

The drama mourns the passing of the traditional American hero, as epitomized by Red Ryder and so many others. In their symbolic death, Medoff finds a loss of conscience, of history lesson-taught values, of the American dream. Still, Teddy, Medoff's antihero, played with a striking viciousness by the author himself, is a capitalist of the "Easy Rider" school, carrying a load of dope from Mexico to California.

On a quiet Sunday morning, Teddy and his traveling companion stop in a 24-hour cafe, just off the super-highway, and Teddy proceeds to terrorize the inhabitants--a woman violinist and her husband who also are passing through, a young man and young woman who work at the cafe and a man who owns the filling station-motel across the road.

Teddy starts slowly, with idle conversation and easy wisecracks. He builds gradually to threat and real power, to total command over the other people, whom he proceeds to degrade and humiliate, sharply reading their weaknesses and exploiting them to perfection.

And, in their degradation, the others find some lost facets of their own personalities, facets that have begun to gleam before the end of the play and which will blaze more sharply in time to come.

Medoff's performance is startling. He is totally unpleasant, snarling and sardonic, and he comes across with tremendous effectiveness.

So does Elizabeth Sturges, the dumpling of a waitress who created the role of Angel in New York. Pudgy and shapeless, her hair stringy and her voice strident and whining, she displays no likable traits and yet she becomes winningly lovable. Miss Sturges gleams brightly--even more brightly than her shiny nose.

Joe Kennedy is outstanding as Stephen Ryder, who would be called Red. Filled with cowardly braggadocio, he threatens mightily until faced with reality, when he crumbles like a damp paper bag.

Camilla Hawk and David Whitaker are effective as the violinist and her husband. Otto L. Schlesinger adds a dimension as the kindly motel owner.

Medoff tripled in brass as director of the road company, and handles it well.

James E. Maroneck's cafe setting is realistic, but could have been a touch more flyspecked.

The play will run through Saturday, with curtain at 8 p.m. and matinees Wednesday and Saturday at 2. The American then will be dark until Dec. 30 when Ricardo Montalban, Edward Mulhare, Kurt Kasznar and Myrna Loy will open a one-week engagement of "Don Juan in Hell."

PORTMAN, James Bickle; (2) Theatre Critic and Fine Arts Writer; (3) b. North Battleford, Saskatchewan, Oct. 6, 1935; (4) s. Herbert Gordon and Margaret (Bickle) P.; (5) B.A. U. of Manitoba (St. John's College) major subj.: English, 1957; (6) m. Barbara Ruth Musselwhite, March 31, 1967; (7) children--Elizabeth Anne, Margaret Michelle; (8) Staff writer, Winnipeg Free Press, 1954-56, Staff writer, Calgary Herald, 1957-58, Theatre Critic, 1959-60, 1962-71, Entertainment Editor and Theatre Critic, 1972-75, Theatre Critic and Fine Arts Writer, Southam News Services (representing 14 Canadian dailies), 1975- ; (9) Canada Council critic-at large, 1975; (15) Member Associated Canadian Television and Radio Artists (ACTRA); (17) Anglican; (20) Contributed articles to Canadian Theatre Review, Performing Arts in Canada Magazine, Time and Tide (British), Prism (British), Toronto Star Weekly, Anglican World (British); regular contributor to the Canadian Broadcasting Corporation; (21) 10635 Oakmoor Way S.W., Calgary, Alberta, Ph. 403-281-0573; (22) 502 Herald Building, 206 7th Ave. S.W., Calgary, Alberta T2P OW8, Ph. 403-269-6211; (23) Total combined circulation: 1.5 million; (24) 50 plays and musicals, 75 motion pictures, 40 miscellaneous.

It's Easy to Admire this Production, but Not to Like It
(by Jamie Portman, Calgary Herald, March 1, 1975)

It's easier to admire the Stratford Festival's production of The Two Gentlemen of Verona than it is to like it.

As one of the two debut productions unveiled to us by Robin Phillips in his new capacity as Stratford artistic director, it is not without interest.

There is no denying the intelligence of Phillips' approach to one of the most neglected of Shakespeare's plays. One must also commend the general excellence of the new "young" company assembled by Phillips for Stratford's current Western Canadian tour.

Nevertheless, there is little that is endearing in this version of The Two Gentlemen--apart, perhaps, from the presence of an uninhibited mongrel named Crab.

Crab's enjoyable turns on stage provoked the most perceptible response from the tiny audience attending the play's opening performance Friday afternoon in the Jubilee Auditorium. But Crab is matching wits with another accomplished scene-stealer in the person of Eric Donkin.

Donkin, a Stratford veteran and an old favorite of Theatre Calgary audiences, plays the dog's master, a servant called Launce who maintains a despairing fidelity to his capricious pet and who, in so doing, comments obliquely on the somewhat more tenuous relationships and loyalties floating about him.

Indeed, Donkin's sturdy comic philosopher offers one of the few solid bastions in a production generally awash in ambiguity.

The ambiguity is in identities and relationships rather than in plot--and it's deliberate. We get it at the very beginning when the maddeningly elusive strains of "Who Is Silvia?" waft about the stylized stage tableau, the purpose of which is to introduce us to the characters. It is a production in which shadow is as key a factor as substance.

On the surface, we seem to have an adolescent yarn about two friends, Valentine and Proteus. Valentine leaves Verona to seek his fortune in Milan where he falls in love with Silvia. Proteus follows his friend to Milan where he, too, falls under Silvia's spell, and as a result forgets his fidelity to his true love, Julia, who has followed him to Milan disguised as a page.

That's what seems to be happening. But the sensibilities which Phillips brings to bear on this play of Shakespeare's apprenticeship create undercurrents. A contemporary motif whispers a bleak decadence with its starkly geometric set and muted colors. Even the emotional flow is muted and cooled so much that it threatens to turn to ice and certainly turns those of us in the audience into cool appraisers of the fortunes and follies of the characters on stage.

The society Phillips offers us is rich, leisured, rather parasitical. The beach scenes indolently symbolize the most fashionable and most exclusive of the European resorts. Antonio, father of Proteus, is played by Graeme Campbell as a cigar-smoking, casually sinister millionaire. Silvia's father, the Duke of Milan, emerges in the characterization of Douglas Chamberlain as a sophisticated, self-satisfied university don, insulated in his cocoon against the baser intrusions of life. Even a relatively minor role like that of Julia's maid gets unexpected treatment; in Gale Garnett's performance, this character becomes a wordly-wise cynic who knows all about the good life and what it exacts.

The central characterizations are less provocative. Stephen Russell reveals Valentine's insecurities but also a rough and ready honesty. Nicholas Pennell, very good indeed, is fascinating as the fair-weather friend, Proteus, the deceptive surface charm of his characterization giving way to reveal the moral--indeed metaphysical--ambivalence underneath. Jackie Burroughs, in voice and demeanor, is a true enchantress in the role of Silvia. As for Mia Anderson's Julia, she is best in her scenes as a page boy; at other times she tends to be awkward, mannered and flat.

The impersonation of a page boy by a woman is the most obvious indicator of sexual ambivalence for a director who's seeking out such things. But this concern is reflected elsewhere in Phillips' production, as it explores the differences between love and friendship--between men and women, men and men and women and women, and the complications which may arise from failure to understand and define these relationships.

All of which means that you're also finding the production concerned with broader questions of identity--more specifically with the question of "role-playing" in one's life.

Phillips has clearly modelled this Canadian production on his 1970 staging of The Two Gentlemen of Verona for Britain's Royal Shakespeare Company. What we have is an ultimately bleak and enervating experience. The clowning is subdued, the psychological implications deliberately heightened. Within the context of Phillips' approach to the play, he makes the whole thing work, even the normally unworkable final scene. But the memories that linger are the awful grayness of the background, the metallic-colored costumes, the blank and sightless sunglasses concealing God knows what truths in the eyes of the characters.

It's a production you can admire, even respect. It's imaginative and provocative. But, in the final analysis, it's a sterile theatrical encounter.

TV Jamie Boy Mild Compared to Stage Original
(by Jamie Portman, Calgary Herald, April 15, 1975)

While the politicians on Parliament Hill continue their frenzied yelping over CBC Television's recent production of You're Gonna Be Alright, Jamie Boy, Vancouver's enterprising Arts Club Theatre has gone ahead and staged David Freeman's controversial play in its original version.

The politicians should shut up and examine the script before it was cleaned up--yes, cleaned up--for television. If their sensibilities were scorched by what they saw in the living room, they would be positively frazzled by what transpires in the stage version.

In the Vancouver production, the obscenities flew thick and fast, but I doubt if anyone in attendance was corrupted by the experience. After a while, one becomes immune to this sort of thing.

There's no denying that Freeman's play constitutes a raw slice of naturalistic theatre, and that it unrepentantly wrings comedy out of some of the most tragic of human situations. There's no denying either that, given the type of family he was writing about, the impact of his play would have been blunted had he been more fastidious with his dialogue.

The fact of the matter is that Freeman's play is a merciless examination of the slob mentality. The household he depicts is lower middleclass, and he has no intention either to sentimentalize its inhabitants or to commit the other error of patronizing them via sociological slumming.

Freeman even shuns compassion. The play's two most attractive characters--the Jamie Boy of the title and his sister Carol--demand our approval because they bolt the family circle, but the clear implication is that they would be dolts to do otherwise.

After all, Jamie Boy is recovering from one nervous breakdown and destined to have another if he stays around Dad any longer. As for Carol, she's finally become pregnant by husband Fred, a sub-level specimen if there ever was one. She not only wants to reject the baby, but she wants to reject Fred as well.

Those of us concerned about the apparent moral ambiguities of Freeman's position mustn't fall into the trap of suggesting that Fred and Carol see a marriage counsellor or that the Dinsdale family have a talk with their clergyman.

This sort of solution is not merely beyond the reach but outside the experience of a family like the Dinsdales, and that's another reason why You're Gonna Be Alright Jamie Boy is a play of unusual, if unsettling, significance.

One might argue that, given an absence of moral certainties and an uprooting of traditional beliefs, families like the Dinsdales are inevitable. But if you prefer to set aside the metaphysical and theological aspect and opt for the straight sociological route, you still find a great deal of provocative matter in this play.

It's been suggested in some quarters that Freeman was lambasting the so-called television-viewer's mentality with this work. That's true, but only to a point.

Certainly, there's a great potential for pungent social commentary in a situation which offers us the spectacle of a family getting together for a night of tv viewing, indulging in arguments over whether they will watch Mod Squad, the hockey game or Chariots of the Gods, and getting into further childish hassles over who will end up with the most tempting tv dinners.

There are no books visible in the living room and at one point Jamie Boy is mocked by his father for reading the poetry of Yeats.

The Dinsdales--or at least some of them--represent the horrendous fulfillment of Marshal McLuhan's non-linear predictions, as they sit gawping at the tv screen.

But Freeman has more on his mind than a mere satirizing of the type of person who spends night after night watching pap on television. He goes much further. He shows us what happens to such a family when the television set breaks down and its members have to fall back on each other's company. That's when the fur starts flying and the wounds start opening. The sardonic implication seems to be that at least television can function as an anaesthetic for such people and make it possible to tolerate one another.

But there's another abrasively fascinating aspect to all this, and it comes to the fore when the play is done on stage and when it gets a production as good as that provided by the Arts Club Theatre last week.

You watch Gregory Reid, so persuasive as the coarsely stupid father, and you watch Doris Chillcott flapping frenziedly about as his loyal but equally mindless wife, and you're in a type of Archie Bunkerland. But it's not a laundered Archie Bunkerland in which oafs, bigots and ignoramuses are made lovable and in which crudity is prettified as a vehicle for mass entertainment. Freeman slices mercilessly through the veneer to reveal what he considers to be the real thing--and the real thing, he suggests, is not very pleasant.

In the process, of course, he is scrutinizing yet another aspect of television and what it does to people--i. e. here it tells lies about ourselves and therefore helps us feel better--but his unerring ear for credible dialogue and sharp instinct for situation--also results in joltingly effective entertainment. It may not be tea-party conversation, but the play isn't tea-party fare.

Bill Millerd's Arts Club Theatre production didn't make for particularly subtle viewing, but Jamie Boy isn't really a

particularly subtle play. One could argue that the stridency
quotient was too high at the beginning and that the production had
trouble establishing a rhythm during the first half hour. Even
so, it was an evening of considerable substance. In addition to
the work of Reid and Chillcott as the parents, there was an effective demonstration of yahoo insensitivity from Terry David
Mulligan as the son-in-law, plus fine work from Brent Carver
as the beleaguered Jamie Boy, too sensitive to the nuances of
family relations for his own good, and the fascinating Pia Shan-
del who made the most of a succession of astringently funny one-
liners in her performance as the sister.

PROBST, Leonard; (2) Drama Critic NBC News; (3) b. Brooklyn,
June 10, 1921; (4) s. Alexander and Edith (Weichert) Probst; (5)
B.A. UCLA, major subj.: philosophy and English; (6) m. Bethami
Gitlin, May 11, 1943; (7) children--Kenneth Andrew, Katharine
Nicole; (8) United Press Hollywood 1945-48, as a reporter, 1949
drama critic Los Angeles Mirror, 1950-51, roving reporter CARE
Europe. 1952 Press Chief, Geneva, United Nations High Commissioner for Refugees, 1953-57, Bureau Chief UP Geneva, later Dublin, UP reporter Paris and later London, 1957 CBS News writing
Walter Cronkite news show, 1957-76 NBC News, 1959 drama critic
radio, 1960-69 drama critic WNBC-TV show, 1971-72 Byline reporter on Today, WNBC-TV arts editor, 1971; (15) Vice President Drama Desk, Tony Committee, 1972-74 theatre annual Funk and Wag-
nals, 1972-76 Faculty member New School for Social Research teaching Theatre Criticism, conducting series "Performers on Performing,
Conversations with Leonard Probst," 1965 member Eugene O'Neill
Theatre, Waterford, Conn. at first conference, returning as Critic
in seminars; (13) United States Naval Reserve, 1941-44, Lt. (j.g.); (19)
Brooklyn Heights Casino Tennis Club; (20) Cont. articles to New
York Times Sunday Section on Arts, TV Guide, Atlantic Monthly,
Village Voice, House Beautiful and Saturday Review; (21) 266 Henry
Street, Brooklyn, N.Y. 11201; (22) NBC News, 30 Rockefeller Plaza,
N.Y. 10020; (24) More than one hundred plays off and on Broadway
per year for 15 years. Reviews now carried on NBC News Network
Radio.

"Streamers"
(by Leonard Probst, over NBC television, New York, May 28, 1976)

The best new American play this year--in my view--is
"Streamers," by David Rabe, directed by Mike Nichols, and now
playing at the small 300-seat theatre at Lincoln Center for the
Performing Arts in New York.

The play is about random violence. It is set in an Army
barracks in Virginia in 1965 ... "Streamers" completes David
Rabe's trilogy on the Vietnam war.

The play is delicate ... performed like a fragile poem ...
every bit real and every bit--in the end--bloody and angry.

It is the story in a sense of how any of us can be streamers, how symbolically we lose our parachute, when we are hurtling to the ground without control ... help ... or understanding. A most powerful, brilliant and brutal play. I don't like brutal plays. But "Streamers" is something special.

"Godspell"
(by Leonard Probst, over NBC television, New York, June 23, 1976)

"Godspell" cast a spell when it opened Off-Broadway in 1971; I doubt it will cast a spell now on Broadway in 1976.

It is the Gospel according to St. Matthew, acted out by ten teenagers. The set is a city playground at night. The message is love. The story is the Bible the way the People's Bicentennial Commission might do it; with love, rock music, jokes, irreverent asides, and dressed in counter-culture costumes.

What stands up best is the music and lyrics by Stephen Schwartz. The now popular ballad "Day by Day," and rock tunes such as "Save the People" and "Prepare Ye the Way of Our Lord."

The attack of the show is the counter-culture of the 1960's. The show is now too young to be nostalgic and too old to be fresh.

PROCTOR, Roy, Richmond News Leader, 333 East Grace St., Richmond, Va. 23219, Ph. 804-649-6000.

QUARM, Joan Helana Phelan; (2) Drama Critic, Assoc. Prof. English, University of Texas at El Paso, Director El Paso Gilbert and Sullivan Company, adviser Adobe Horseshoe Dinner Theater and Upstairs Theater Downtown board; (3) b. Bristol, England, Feb. 24; nat. US citizen, New York, 1946; (4) d. Samuel George and Mary Phelan (O'Phelan) deceased; (5) M.A. San Francisco State U., major subj.: Drama, 1966; B.A. Reading U., major English and Educ.; (6) Divorced; (7) children--Susanna Rosemary (m. Terry Gardner), T. Michael (m. Martha Serfontein), Robin Anthony, Christopher Noel, Nicholas Jonathon; (8) Faculty, A.S. Neill's Summerhill, England, 1942; British Council's St. Julian's School, Portugal, 1945; Asst. Ed. Clarence Streit's "Freedom and Union," Washington, D.C., 1948; teacher, Cerro de Pasco Copper Corp. school, Morococha, Peru, S.A., 1949; English professor, UTEP, 1957-present; Arts Critic, "El Paso Herald-Post," (Scripps-Howard) 1961-present; (9) Founder La Oroya Little Theater, 1950, director-actor there; co-founder and namer of El Paso's The Theater, 1962, Festival Theater, 1964, and Gilbert and Sullivan Company, 1971, directed 8 productions of it to date; dir. many plays, six grand operas for community-university opera company here, incl. "Faust," "Tosca," "Madame Butterfly," "Carmen"; dir. 2 army contest musicals at Ft. Bliss; now (1975)

prod. dir. forming a rep. company at the Adobe Horseshoe; series
four radio lectures and readings on the Brontes, 1975, book reviews,
and many roles in civic theater, including Mother Courage, Martha
("Virginia Woolf") Juno, Fraulein Schneider (Musical "Cabaret");
joined Actors Equity Union, 1973, resigned 1975 because of restric-
tive rules; (14) Awarded personal grant from Nat. Found. Arts and
Humanities 1968 to research bilingual theater on border, founded and
for 3 years directed Los Pobres, as a result, turned it over to
Chicano director I trained, after tr. "El Censo," by Emilio Carbal-
lido, writing and producing "Las Bodas de Luis Alonzo," perf. at
SW Theater Conference, Lubbock, 1970; (15) Member National Critics
Inst. , O'Neill Playwrights Conference, Waterford, Conn. , 1973; (20)
Various articles and poems in little-known journals; (21) 1520 Upson,
El Paso, Tex. 79902, Ph. 915-532-4010; (22) UTEP English Dept. ,
University Ave. , El Paso, Tex. 79999, Ph. 915-747-5731; or "El
Paso Herald-Post," Newspaper Building, Kansas and Main, El Paso,
Tex. 79999; (23) Circulation: 47,000; (24) I also regularly review films,
concerts and operas, do some book and art reviews.

A Sparkling Carmen
(by Joan Quarm, El Paso Herald-Post, August 9, 1975)

"Carmen" seems to be one of the more controversial productions of the Santa Fe opera this summer, yet when I saw and
heard it on Aug. 2, it had much to recommend it.   First, Ann
Howard, in her opening performance of the title role, was a
Carmen to be praised and remembered.   She is a big, earthy,
rounded girl, of considerable beauty and sexuality.   She has a
big, beautiful voice, which is as sensuous as her big beautiful
mouth.   She is an actress of power and passion.

This physical detail must be stressed because without feline
seductiveness and female peasant strength, Carmen cannot be
made to come alive.   She has to be the one wildcat of the cigaret factory whom every man in Seville knows and would know
better.   She has to be fully aware of her power, to make an
audience fully aware of it, and to flaunt it at every step.   Ann
Howard leaves no doubt in any mind that Don Jose and Escamillo and all the rest are pawns before her.   So is the listener.

We were also fortunate to hear Brent Ellis, in his first appearance as Escamillo: a comparatively minor role, which he
played proudly and well.   Mr. Ellis has one of the most musical tenors among the Santa Fe artists, and one of the most attractive stage personalities, also.   His difficult knife-fight with
Don Jose was a little miracle of apparent ease.

I also enjoyed Jack Trussel's performance as moody,
doomed Don Jose, the army corporal who gives up home, sweetheart, career, and the last vestige of respectability, out of devouring passion for Carmen.   His descent to ragged murderous
rage is close to great tragedy.   He would be a tragic hero, indeed, if he were less stupid, more likeable, more a power than

the toy Carmen throws away broken. Mr. Trussel made all this very clear, and his voice, again, is more than equal to the challenge the demanding role presents.

Strong supporting singers, such as Sarah Beatty and Faith Esham, whose Tarot-card trio with Carmen was warmly, rightly applauded; Joanna Bruno, whose Micaela solos received the nearest thing to an ovation we saw this year at Santa Fe; and William Dansby, as Zuniga, were joined by an excellent chorus. "Carmen" sounded fine.

What, then, caused all the discussion? It was certainly not the opening set, to anyone familiar with the white light of the Spanish sun, which in summer takes all color out of things it touches. The street outside the cigaret factory winds uphill from the square, with odd forms and angles, distorted like a Goya satirical drawing. The place promises trouble, and trouble soon arrives.

Nor did the earth colors of the costumes distress me at all. They are fitting to the elemental theme of the libretto, and a rest from the customary bright colors of most designers. Suzanne Mess designed interesting costumes which complement Rouben Ter-Arutunian's interesting, unusual scenery: Spain affected by Morocco, particularly in the Inn scene of Act Two, with its oriental rugs in place of ordinary furnishings.

I grew tired, for the second evening in a row, of peering through gloom, at the Inn and Mountain Pass scenes, both of which, of course do take place at night. The darkness need hardly be literal, however, for audiences really want to see, as well as hear an opera. This is Director Bliss Hebert's season of semi-darkness, it appears, for his "La Vida Breve" was similarly afflicted.

"Carmen" was efficiently directed, but without much originality of staging. The bullfight procession in Act Four was a complete failure, since far too many soldier-extras were in the crowd watching for the army participants to make any display. Also, a minor point, but irritating: it was careless to use only boy children in that crowd, as though the entire city of Seville was devoid of little girls.

Again, why the entire city had to empty itself for each aria or duet was a puzzle. People do pass by when others are talking, or even singing in the foreground. Finally, the death scene aroused no real fear or pity. It should have done so. The orchestra, conducted by John Crosby himself, sparkled. "Carmen" plays again on Aug. 15, 21 and 23, at 9 p. m.

Lynn Redgrave Is Always Wonderful to See Perform
(by Joan Quarm, El Paso Herald-Post, September 16, 1975)

Lynn Redgrave is always wonderful to see onstage, and a

preview of her latest play in Los Angeles last weekend only confirmed the fact. Daughter of one of Britain's most distinguished acting familes, Miss Redgrave is more at home onstage than most of us are anywhere in this world. She wears her talent lightly, as if it were inevitable: which, given her background, it probably is.

The show which opens at the Huntington Hartford Theater in Hollywood tonight was completely ready when the first of its previews was run on Friday. Called "The Two of Us," by Michael Frayne, it is a series of four independent one-act plays, linked only in the dominant man-woman theme. That provides as much variety as men and women in the various conditions of love, and as wide a range of comedy and tragedy.

Comedy is predominant. With the exception of the wry "Mr. Foot," which ends the evening, these are vignettes about the funny side of love, which range from mildly humorous to utterly farcical. The audience responded to each as it touched on personal experience. Each was graced by Lynn Redgrave as the woman.

It took two actors to play the men, since one was English and the other American: John Tillinger and Roy London, respectively; but Lynn Redgrave not only took all four ladies' parts, but played the Americans so well that American friends in the business (Dana Andrews and his wife, Mary Todd, to be exact) commented on her perfect speech. Her native British English was naturally flawless.

The first scene was set in a luxury hotel in Venice, where a young American couple was attempting to recapture the bliss of their honeymoon there. Unfortunately for bliss, the yells of their baby tore through the night every time they shut the perambulator back into a roomy closet, and attempted to sleep. Anyone who has ever stayed in a hotel with a crying baby knows the agony and despair. Rarely do any of us have such brilliant dialogue to help us through the night.

"The New Quixote," which followed, took us to a Greenwich Village apartment, whose owner, Gina, awoke with a hangover and loss of memory about the young man who had stayed the night. He, poor boy, saw the post-party incident as a great love, while she attempted vainly to get rid of him. Again, Lynn Redgrave, now older, tougher, yet unexpectedly vulnerable, gave us ridiculous reality, but here was a touch of tenderness as well. Not so with "Chinamen." This is the funniest play since Joe Orton stopped living and writing. It deals with the most horrid dinner party to be imagined in a hostess' worst nightmares.

Miss Redgrave and Mr. Tillinger played not only the hosts, but also assorted guests, in a series of dazzling quick-changes. Faced with the horror of having invited a newly-divorced husband together with his ex-wife and her new boyfriend, the hosts do everything possible to keep them apart. Alone in the kitchen, the lonely ex-husband becomes steadily drunk. Alone in the sitting room, the other guests become sleepy, while host and hostess invent a hundred ridiculous situations. Directed with lightning speed by John Clark, this was the most popular of the quartet, and the most virtuoso for both actors.

Finally, at last allowed to sit down a little, Lynn Redgrave played an older woman whose husband hardly communicated except by irritated wavings of his foot, as he sat cross-legged and reading. The armchairs were on separate islands, spotlit; and the terrible loneliness of an empty marriage was too poignant to be comic. We almost resented being sent away thinking. It was an unkind twist at the last.

QUILL, Gynter Clifford; (2) Amusements Editor; (3) b. Waco, Tex., April 26, 1915; (4) s. Martin B. and Nora (Rossing) Quill; (5) B.A. Luther College, major subj.: History, English, 1937, graduate study National U. of Mexico, U. of Texas; (6) m. Ruth Moen, Aug. 23, 1939; (7) child--Clifford Moen Quill; (8) Teacher, Big Spring, Tex., public schools 1938-39; teacher Decorah, Ia., public schools 1939-42; Robstown, Tex., public schools 1942-43; reporter Waco Tribune-Herald 1944, Amusements Editor 1945- ; (10) Member Waco-McLennan County Library Commission 1969- (chairman 1973); Chairman, Advisory Council of Central Texas Library System 1972- ; (14) Distinguished Critic Award by Southwest Theatre Conference 1971; (16) Democrat; (17) Lutheran; (20) Cont. articles to The Best Plays (The Burns Mantle Theater Yearbook, ed. by Henry Hewes, Otis Guernsey); The Family Weekly; Randolph-Macon alumnae magazine; (21) 1608 North 15-A St., Waco, Tex. 76707, Ph. 817-753-7905; (22) Waco Tribune-Herald, 900 Franklin Ave., Waco, Tex. 76703, Ph. 817-753-1511; (23) Circulation: 58,000; (24) 60 plays, musicals, concerts.

Last Yelvington Drama Is Super
(by Gynter Quill, Waco Tribune-Herald, September 16, 1973)

Ramsey Yelvington's last play, "The Folklorist," is also one of his best plays in a canon that number at least 16 when the prolific Texas playwright-historian-academician and folklorist himself died of a heart attack near his Wimberley home last July.

The drama of a West Texas family torn apart by cultural conflicts, some of them indigenous and some of its own making, was then in a pre-premiere run at Southwest Texas State University at San Marcos, where he was an instructor and playwright-in-residence.

It was given its official premiere there last week, with direction by his daughter, Harriet Smith, a drama instructor in

New Braunfels and one who knows and obviously is keenly sensitive to the drives and urgencies that motivated her father in all that he did.

Mr. Yelvington is best known for his "Texian Trilogy" of the Independence period. But when he went outside Texas history for his material he was best in just this sort of play. His forte was in people living and working together, people of different social and economic status but, though they may not be aware of it at first, united by common bonds of humanity.

Sometimes they have to learn that, to be taught it the hard way, with force, with conflict against nature and--for better drama--against each other.

That is a universal truth, a universal problem. Mr. Yelvington applied it to Texans, usually West Texans of mixed cultural heritage, because that is the area and people he knew best and especially loved. And, for him, among them the problems are better defined and answers more difficult to find and then to accent.

In "The Folklorist" he teases the interest at the beginning, hinting at conflict rather than punching it, then letting it unfold peripherally.

A man, a father, a wealthy rancher near Uvalde, has died. His son, living estranged in Washington because of his radical ideas of humanity and his dangerous militancy, is notified that day. The funeral is set for tomorrow because it is not expected that he will attend.

But he will. It is fitting. Also, he is glad the old man, the stern old Baptist is dead and can no longer flay him with questions about his state of grace. And for Phelps Britten, on that same day contemplating suicide, it is at least a temporary reprieve.

His girl friend, the even more militant Marta Cassavetes, puts another finger on the Yelvington theme with her own domestic situation. Her father is Mexican and Catholic. Her mother, whose funeral in Monterrey she attended and then was sent back to school in New Orleans, was a Jewess. She, too, has known a divided family.

She will go with him to Texas but, he insists, no farther than San Antonio, must not go to the ranch with her inflammatory political concepts.

Young Britten had told Marta that his is a close family but it isn't. Roma, the old man's second wife, is an Indian with a Mexican name, Roma Garcia, and though the Anglos all say there are good Mexicans the burden of proof is on them.

Phelps' older sister, Adele, recently elected county tax collector with the help of Will Breeding, the county strong man, soon lets her bitchiness break through the early veneer of hospitality toward him.

Vinnie, his younger sister, is married to Sam McLaughlin, one of the more vocal class-conscious conservatives, resenting any movement toward equality or fair play. It's too much like Communism, and that is why Phelps is so hated around Uvalde.

Warren and that bunch in Washington are held responsible for Anglos carrying guns for the first time in many years. And Phelps is responsible for his father's suicide and the thinly veiled threats against the old man's life.

At the very lightest, he is faulted for not staying at home, raising a family and keeping up the family's holdings and traditions.

The real fear, and what Phelps says is inevitable, is that the lands will be cut up and sold, much of it to Mexicans who soon will outvote the Anglos and control the country "which our people won and pioneered."

But, in goading Phelps, they and he bring some other skeletons out of the family closet, and in the gush of bile and hatred he resolves to remain there if only to spite the others. "I find there's nothing like a trip home to regain one's perspective, to see one's whole life clearly."

But that is not to be. There is no place there for him after the near riot, which even he thinks disgraceful, that mars the burial service, with a shouting, honking band of intruders led by Marta.

Nor does the tragedy for Phelps end at the ranch.

The theme is unity, or reunity, realized dramatically only in contradictions, that must take off from fragmentation, a condition that Mr. Yelvington has said he purposely exaggerated in order to make his point.

But he did not find it necessary, in that, to make his characters caricatures. They are all real people we know or know of. The venom, the unreasoning hatreds within and without the family, the refusal to try to find a common ground, and the bald hypocrisy are unfortunately real aspects of the human condition.

And Mr. Yelvington was the son of a Baptist minister and the temptation to sermonize is more than he can resist. But he does it gracefully, without forcing it outside the context of his drama, chiefly through Will Breeding, a strong force in the community without whose approval few Anglos move.

Breeding is not happy with the march of time in a direction that he mistrusts, but he counsels strongly against saying "Never." There is in him, the pragmatist, a somewhat kindred spirit with Phelps, the idealist, but only somewhat, stopping short of surrendering his birthright.

And Phelps can echo, with loud moans, the reading by old Rev. Pruitt of Paul's word to the Galatians about the fruit of the spirit being love, joy, peace, longsuffering, gentleness, goodness and faith.

Mr. Yelvington wrote his play with the new island theater at SWTSU in mind. Not many others have the facilities to mount it as he saw it--a large and deep main stage and side stages to accommodate the large central set of multi-level ranch house flanked by a fenced yard, the little chapel and the adjoining family burial ground. And in front of that, and removed when not used for the opening and closing scenes, is the balcony of Phelps' Washington apartment.

With all that there is a massive and intricate light plot to illuminate the points of action and veil, or show dimly, others to make subtle visual comments.

Demands on the players are not beyond the reach of good drama students--and Dr. James Barton of the drama department has 150 majors and 60 minors to select from this year--but firm control is a vital factor that Harriet Smith brings to it. What easily unbridled excesses could do to Mr. Yelvington's really very sensitive piece of craftsmanship is a thought to make one shudder.

Good news for those who remember his "A Cloud of Witnesses" which had its premiere in Baylor Theater in 1954 and was staged as "The Drama of the Alamo" for a number of summers at San Jose Mission in San Antonio, is that Dr. Barton will revive it again next spring.

For a number of people, including one who has seen every Yelvington play that was produced, that one-third of the Texian Trilogy is the finest thing he has done.

There is still one other that has not been mounted, "The Marble Horseman," a story of George Washington at Yorktown, which he was asked to write for a band of Virginians who planned and then abandoned an annual outdoor pageant on the order of Paul Green's "The Lot Colony."

That is scheduled at SWTSU for next year, or perhaps the following one, in celebration of the Bicentennial.

Baker's Play About Jack Ruby One of His Most Exciting Works
(by Gynter Quill, Waco Tribune-Herald, May 18, 1974)

"Jack Ruby, All American Boy," is one of the most visually stunning things Paul Baker has done at Dallas Theater Center and one of the most exciting and gripping, not for the suspense of wondering what will happen, for we know that, but for the immediacy not of time but of person.

We are involved in it, recalling the events and where we were and what we were doing at the moment, but more because we are, in a purposely disturbing sense, one with Jack Ruby.

In the script by John Logan, a member of the professional company, in association with Baker, we are a part of him and he is a part of us, mercurial and hard though he was, for Jack Ruby is not an island unto himself.

His milieu unfolds in Peter Wolf's set, we are drawn into it and find it different from our own only on the surface and in its trappings, a mawkish, garish club with strip teasers and drunks and gawkers and hecklers.

Ruby's mind, personality, hopes and fears, are peeled bare for us by script and action and we find them so much like our own in their basics that the play is provocative and disturbing.

No more can Jack Ruby be dismissed as some other unfortunate guy light years removed from us, an egotistical punk, lewd, conniving and insane. Aspirations and gut reactions parallel our own.

But why call him "All American Boy?" Ruby is more than an individual and the play is about more than Ruby. It is, as Baker says, about the American Dream, the one Ruby had-- recognition as a person- the one we all have, which differs from his only in the manner of implementation. In that respect, it is easy to identify with him.

It is about the world that created Jack Ruby and the world that he created for himself, in which he was a man of popularity, idolatry, one of "class."

And it was a world that was shattered by those shots fired in Dealy Plaza and against whose violator he had to lash out in blind fury.

Peter Wolf's magnificent set, surrounded by winking lights and tall ladders and flanked by small side stages on which peripheral things are frequently happening, is more than an area in which to act. There is, principally, Ruby's Carousel Club with its atmosphere that many do not know but was the life he breathed and it is a set of symbols, that also have utility, of

many levels and steps and ladders by which Ruby climbed, struggling to realize his dream.

It is used to unfold, also, more than the events of Nov. 22
and Nov. 23, 1963, in which to focus on the things that made
Ruby what he was, a Chicago ghetto world pervaded by fear and
abuse for being born a Jew, as our own environment and relation
to it and reactions spurred by heredity shape us.

The story is told in vignettes and bits of film, events momentous and trivial but all meaningful, and part of it as a sort
of "This Is Your Life." The assassination is treated dramatically but as something Ruby did not see. His breakdown is shown
graphically, and the murder of Lee Harvey Oswald takes a page
from the movie "Bonnie and Clyde" and Baker's own W. C.
Brann killing, with long, exaggerated, torturing slow motion.

Logan can provide a solid, well motivated script, Wolf can
provide an excellent setting, and Baker can put it and those kaleidoscopic effects together and give it all a uniform sense of
direction, but Ken Latimer is needed to bring Jack Ruby to life,
give him breath and spirit and make the audience see and feel
and empathize with that unlovable but tragic little man's yearning to be somebody.

There is a very large supporting cast representing a cross-
section of Dallas, but the standouts are Randy Moore playing
many roles--barker, tour guide, night club comic, salesman,
doorman, banker, news announcer, Western Union clerk and
master of ceremonies--and a genuine strip teaser, Chastity Fox,
who choreographed the play, trained the girls for their roles
as part of Ruby's "family" and was so important to him, and
does her specialty spectacularly.

RAIDY, William A., Long Island Press, 92-20 168th St., Jamaica,
N.Y. 11404.

RAND, Sumner G., Jr.; (2) Theater Critic and Staff Writer; (3) b.
Orlando, Fla., Aug. 20, 1923; (4) s. Sumner G. and Mary A. (Hol-
loway); (5) B.A. College of William & Mary in Virginia, major subj.:
European History, 1947; M.A. Harvard U. Graduate School of Arts
& Sciences, European History, 1948; (6) Single; (8) Staff Writer, Or-
lando Sentinel Star, Assistant City Editor, 1950-60, Drama Editor
1950-75; (9) Apprentice, Priscilla Beach Theater, Mass., Summer
1946; Actor, William & Mary Theatre, President, Dramatic Club,
College of William & Mary, 1946-47; Actor: Orlando Players Little
Theater 1950-65, Orange Blossom Playhouse 1952 & 1955, Rollins
College Annie Russell Theater 1955 & 1959; (10) Orlando Jaycees
Board of Directors 1953-58; Orlando Players Little Theater Board
1949-53; Loch Haven Park Board 1965-75; (13) U.S. Army 1943-45;
(14) Purple Heart, Presidential Unit Citation; (16) Democrat; (17)

Episcopalian; (19) Phi Beta Kappa, Omicron Delta Kappa, Phi Delta
Theta (honorary theatrical society); (21) 4880 S. Fern Creek Drive
(P. O. Box 142), Orlando, Fla. 32802, Ph. 305-851-7098; (22) Orlando Sentinel Star, 633 N. Orange Ave., Orlando, Fla. 32802, Ph.
305-423-4412; (23) Circulation: over 200,000; (24) 70 plays, musicals, motion pictures and attractions.

Stoppard Wordy but Well-Acted
(by Sumner Rand, Sentinel Star, October 26, 1974)

"Enter A Free Man," the first production of the season for
the Florida Technological University Theater, reenforces director
David Mays' penchant for taking lesser known but highly interesting works and bringing them before the public.

Tom Stoppard, the young British playwright who wrote "Enter A Free Man" in 1968 originally for television, has become
much better known since then for "Rosencranz and Guildenstern
Are Dead" and last season's "Jumpers."

Noted mainly for his nimble displays of verbal wit and his
facile imagination, Stoppard can seem intolerably wordy to some,
his plays short on action and long on windy discourse.

Until one discerns where what little plot there is is head-
ing--and that isn't until the second half--"Enter A Free Man"
does produce almost a soporific effect as the exasperating "hero" rambles along at great length to his pub cronies about his
"inventions" and his daughter complains bitterly to her long-
suffering, infinitely patient mother about his daydreaming and
inability to supplement the family income.

Stoppard's use of a cleverly contrived flashback technique
in this first act that comes full circle almost sends the audience
home midway thinking the play is over and that nothing other
than a vignette of middle-class life in England is intended.

Direction suddenly appears in the second act, as it becomes
apparent the mother is holding this family together and there is
something endearing about the hopelessly impractical, bumbling
husband. The strong emotional scenes in this act are well
handled by Mary Monroe as the mother and Tara Buckley as the
daughter.

The high-flown rhetoric and curious delivery adopted by
Doug Emerson in the role of the "inventor" George Riley in the
first act fall into place as applicable to the sort of dream world
in which he lives. He's sort of a Don Quixote madman-saint
figure whom his wife has always understood and made allowances
for and whom his daughter comes around to after she also has
had her illusions shattered.

It is also a very long, very difficult part, for a young actor,

and, while Emerson is not always convincingly the age he is
playing, the portrait he presents is, in the end, affecting.

As the cronies who lead Riley on in the pub, Jeff King,
Michael Carlson, Dennis Hill and Joy Jones, along with pubkeep-
er Chuck Aitken, provide good support. No one in the cast,
with the possible exception of Hill, attempts a British accent,
perhaps wisely, although many expressions used are typically
English.

The FTU Science Auditorium stage severely handicaps the
staging of the play, since the two separate playing areas--Riley's
home and the pub--are practically on top of one another.

"Enter A Free Man" is more accessible to the average theatergoer than Stoppard's more recent successes, which have
been almost too dazzling in their display of verbal gymnastics
and intellectual puzzles, leaving some audience members bewildered.

There are clear indications of this later development in the
current offering, but no one should have any difficulty understanding "Enter A Free Man," except possibly for the ironic
title. Tonight's is the final performance of three.

"Bacchae" Has Meaning Today
(by Sumner Rand, Sentinel Star, December 6, 1974)

The Rollins Players employ many techniques of modern
staging to make presentation of a Greek tragedy from the Fifth
Century B. C. highly effective theater for a contemporary audience.

In addition, Euripides, whose "The Bacchae" is being presented in the Annie Russell Theater tonight and Saturday and
next Thursday through Saturday nights, is somewhat more accessible to modern audiences than the other two giants of Attic
tragedy--Aeshylus and Sophocles--as he lived at a time when
older values were beginning to collapse, an era comparable to
ours.

He could view the ancient myths--in this case one of the
legends of Dionysius--with more detachment and even bring a
measure of psychological insight into his characterizations.

"The Bacchae" deals with the fury of Dionysius when his
godhood is flouted by Pentheus, the King of Thebes. As a punishment against Pentheus, the god inspires the Theban women
with Bacchic frenzy, sending them into wild and secret revelries
in the mountains.

In the grip of this frenzy Pentheus' mother, Agave, sees
her son as a lion and, with her women, slaughters him, literally

tearing him to pieces and bearing his head back to Thebes as a trophy. Dionysius appears and pronounces banishment on all the royal line.

Director Robert O. Juergens and his staff have marshalled all the considerable facilities of the Annie Russell Theater to provide a theatrically viable offering--a handsome setting and costumes by Dale Amlund, dramatic lighting by James Dooley and, particularly, a goose-pimple raising electronic score that's large on percussive effects.

The writhing and shrieks of the bacchantes and maenads and the gory remains of Pentheus that are brought on stage at the end--the Greeks fortunately had a convention of relating rather than showing violent deaths--may disturb the more squeamish, but they are probably true to the emotions of horror and pity Euripides sought to arouse and purge.

An interesting approach to representation of the god Diony-sius, whose essence included both masculine and feminine ele-ments, is Juergens' employment of two actors--William McNulty and Robin Jewell--who sometimes speak simultaneously, some-times break up the lines between them and quite realistically give the appearance of merging as one takes his or her place in front of the other, who vanishes offstage.

No choreographer is listed, but much of the movement in the presentation has a ritualistic look, a reminder that early drama originated from the dance. And much of the choral--or synchronized--speech of the bacchantes is almost musical, de-livered with changes in pitch, and not always intelligible.

There is one unintentionally funny--perhaps because anachro-nistic--line in the translation, though, when Pentheus remarks, "I go to my reward." He and the playwright mean it in one sense--to get a peek at the women in their revelry--but it has come to have another sense in the Christian world, and those who are familiar with the tragedy know Pentheus is unwittingly predicting his death.

The performance is really sort of heroic declamation and mime more than acting in the modern sense. While the exces-ses of Greek tragedy no longer seem to have the power to move modern audiences short of a Laurence Olivier gouging out his eyes as Oedipus, the Rollins production is still most effective theater.

REED, Rex; (2) Author, critic; (3) b. Fort Worth, Tex. , Oct. 2, 1938; (4) s. Jimmy M. and Jewell (Smith) Reed; (5) B.A. Louisiana State U. 1960; (8) Film critic, Holiday, Women's Wear Daily, 1968-71; music critic Stereo Review 1968-75; syndicated columnist Chica-go Tribune - New York Times syndicate, 1971-75; film critic New

York Daily News, 1971-75; (9) Appeared in film Myra Breckenridge
1970; (20) Author of: Do You Sleep In the Nude? 1968; Conversations
in the Raw, 1969; Big Screen, Little Screen, 1971; People Are Crazy
Here, 1974; (22) New York Daily News, 220 East 42 St., New York,
N. Y. 10017.

"A Doll's House"--Cramped Quarters for Liv
(by Rex Reed, Sunday News, March 16, 1975)

Liv Ullmann, as everyone knows, is a great film actress.
Everything she does shines with an inner radiance that lights up
the screen. Now she has conquered New York with her first
appearance on an American stage, playing the indefatigable Nora
in Ibsen's "A Doll's House" for Joe Papp's American Shakespeare
Festival at Lincoln Center. The production that surrounds
her is mediocre at best, sometimes downright lousy, but Liv Ullmann cuts through its colorless banality like a laser beam. She
is the best thing to happen to the New York scene since Nureyev
defected.

"A Doll's House" is a clumsy, dated antique, and I have
slept through more revivals of it than almost anything else I can
think of. Last year, there were two movie versions with Claire
Bloom and Jane Fonda, and I guess since the role of Nora provides relentless excitement for actresses brave enough to meet
its challenges, we'll keep getting new versions of "A Doll's
House" as long as we have women who want to play it.

The commercial benefits from women's lib are making themselves known. The entire Liv Ullmann engagement was sold out
before it even opened. And there is the reward of seeing a
great actress at the top of her form, so I guess we should be
grateful for small favors.

The play, about a wife and mother who walked out on her
husband and three children after eight years of subjugated role-
playing to find a newly liberated life within herself, might have
shocked the 19th century society it was fashioned for, but it now
happens every day, and the shock value is decidedly dead. It
isn't even very pungent propaganda for women's lib, but it is a
plum pudding for actresses, and Liv Ullmann devours it.

The problem is that when you have a great Nora and the
rest of the cast is only of community theater quality, the entire
production is thrown off balance. Liv Ullmann is a great Nora:
desperate, frightened, spoiled, possessed of a childlike purity
and little-girl silliness that come more from her sociological
background than from physical characteristics. Ullmann gives
us a frivolous, foolish victim whose instincts seem destined to
drive her sensible, up-tight husband mad, nibbling forbidden
macaroons, childishly prying her husband's fingers apart to pull
money from them, flattering his ego with her dependence, cozily
obscured in her role as a mindless Victorian kitten.

But all is not peachy in Nora's doll house. She has forged her father's name to a loan and now, after his death, she is being blackmailed by the man who loaned her the money. Instead of making a clean break, she sinks into lies and deceit and mistake piling on mistake, growing harder and colder as her problems increase, destroying her husband's reputation and future, jeopardizing her own marriage. Once the contract is destroyed, the husband forgives her, chalking it up to her feminine vulnerability and stupidity--but the pain and damage have already set in.

The play at this point becomes a reckoning--Nora speaks her mind as an oppressed woman and declares her independence, closing that final door. This total character reversal, and the scorching scene that reveals it, come so fast it has never made sense to me. This is Ibsen's fault, not Liv Ullmann's, for she plays the final scene with smoldering power and keen insight. But Tormod Skagestad's plodding direction doesn't help. He shows no hints of self-doubt along the way to make the trip more believable, and the rest of the cast is so dull and one-dimensional that the joy we feel for Nora's final, sudden and coolheaded bid for freedom seems to come from other reasons. We are happy she's fleeing a sinking ship. It's not the marriage; it's the whole play.

Ibsen's implausible subplot of love between Nora's friend Kristine and the evil blackmailer, Krogstad, as well as the talky exposition scenes in which the characters tell us what they know about each other, are better resolved in the Joseph Losey film version with Jane Fonda. Sam Waterston, an actor whose popularity among directors and casting agents has yet to be explained, is much too young to play Liv Ullmann's husband, and he is too inexperienced to find the key to rounding out the role. He is boorish without being sympathetic and is so overshadowed by his co-star that his only way of grasping attention is to fly into rages when his authority is challenged.

Waterston is a competent actor, but he's in over his head in Liv Ullmann's company. Barbara Colby, as Kristine, is alarmingly Daitch-Shopwell in her suburban appearance and delivery, and Michael Granger, as the kindly family friend dying of a mysterious disease, is embarrassingly inept in all departments. This might just be the worst supporting cast any actress has been saddled with since Tallulah Bankhead, as Cleopatra, rowed down the Nile and got sunk by a chorus of barge slaves wearing Man-Tan and ankle bracelets.

But it is still Liv Ullmann who opens and closes all the doors in "A Doll's House." "No man would sacrifice his honor for love," says her husband. "Millions of women have," she replies soberly. At this point, the audience should rise as one, with joy and understanding and pride, like a blind person seeing the sun for the first time. Ullmann has been directed to deliver the line like she knew it all the time, strapped to a chair with no aid from her director or her cast. There's an inner passion missing. Still, she's a superb actress fighting overwhelming odds to stay that way, and once she shuts that final door it's difficult to imagine anyone entering it again once she's gone.

"Goodtime Charley," the new musical about Joan of Arc and her dauphin who became Charles VII of France, is a hapless, hopeless disaster all the more lamentable because it exploits the charm and talent of Joel Grey without knowing what to do with either.

The role is a natural. With his leprechaun bounce and his wall-to-wall energy, he's perfect as the elfin king for whom "life is like oatmeal--cold and full of lumps." Fey and frightened of shadows, bossed and bullied by all who think him a fool, declared a bastard by his monstrous mother and expected to live up to the insanity of his ancestors, Charley is out of sorts with times in which he's living. He doesn't want to be grand or powerful. He just wants to be liked--a philosophy he echoes in the evening's most plaintive song, "Goodtime Charley." ("It's my life to dance to, just give me the chance to," sings Joel Grey, and you care, you care.)

But the turbulence of the era won't concede. There's Joan of Arc to deal with--historically and histrionically. Ann Reinking, with her dancer's thighs and her plain, bony face and her round, piercing eyes, is too peculiar and too robust to be very appealing, sympathetic or believable as Joan. We've seen too many great ones. She lacks the most important quality Joan must possess--vulnerability. This is a maid of Orleans who talks like James Cagney, sings through her nose like the clanging of a kitchen utensil and acts like a zombie. Give Joan a musical number, give her a fan dance, give her a polka--she'll survive it all if you like her and feel moved by her. But Miss Reinking's Joan is too cool, too tough, too self-servicing. She's a stiff.

They really should've reversed the roles. With his shaved wisps of hair and bangs, Joel Grey looks more like Joan of Arc than she does. Miss Reinking is big enough and bold enough to play the king. Neither of them is well-served by Sidney Michael's book or the score by Larry Grossman and Hal Hackady. The story has been reduced to vaudeville vulgarity. The scene in which Joan meets Charley's mother has the Queen Mother saying, "Eat a little something." The general who frames Joan sings, "Oh what I did--to that poor kid," in a church confessional with a mincing Archbishop Regnault de Chartres. Onna White has staged some energetic dances with her usual imagination and flair, and there are songs about poxes, plagues and famines. But a musical about Joan of Arc with an incompetent Joan of Arc is an eyebrow-raising affair, and this one is so lifeless there were times I couldn't get my eyes open at all.

Last and definitely least, there's "The Rocky Horror Show," which has arrived from London rather circuitously by way of Los Angeles, in a haze of noise and body odor. The show is a horror, all right, but any resemblance between this trash and anything resembling talent, freshness and originality is purely coincidental.

As you enter, a stoned usherette sings a brainless ditty about Saturday afternoon, science-fiction double features at the movies. Then some semblance of a hackneyed plot rises from the grave like Lugosi's corpse: Two kids have a flat tire on a stormy night. Following a lonely road, they reach a nearby castle for help ("There's a light over at the Frankenstein place," sings the Day-Glo glitter chorus.)

The inhabitants pour forth like a toilet in need of repair. An evil villain lurks over the young couple in the form of a tattooed drag queen in Cuban heels, fox furs and a leather jockstrap, singing, "I'm Just a Sweet Transvestite Transsexual Transylvanian. " There are assorted delivery boys frozen in refrigerators right out of "The Texas Chainsaw Massacre," tap-dancing lesbian maids, a hunchback, a naked Frankenstein-monster beach boy, electronic gadgets called "sonic transeducers," deaths by laser-beam torture, and simulated nudity and sex that is enough to make you gag.

The rock score is beneath contempt, the acting is a disgrace, and the entire evening gave me a headache for which suicide seemed the only possible relief. Wiping the whole rotten experience out of my mind forever seems, on second thought, a safer solution.

There is some talk of making this swill a hit in New York, where, it is hoped, the mindless lengths to which New York audiences will go to be humiliated and insulted by amateurs will assure it of instant box-office durability. I've got news for the mousebrains responsible for "The Rocky Horror Show": We've already seen it all. The cockettes did it better, and they were laughed out of town before the sun went down.

Britain: As Welcome as the Flowers in May
(by Rex Reed, Sunday News, May 18, 1975)

Political and economic shock waves may be rocking England in the grip of recession, taxes, strikes and unemployment, but the theater in London is jumping. I don't know how they do it, but the British are people with amazing resilience in times of stress. They hang on like leaves defying an autumn wind. The cynics warn of disaster and depression, but the man on the street talks of saving the mallards on Cambridge Lake, while the letters columns in the local newspapers offer helpful hints on how to store up on canned fruit. Remarkable. And, I might add, a refreshing change of pace from the complaints at home.

If, as it is rumored, people turn to entertainment to forget their problems, the proof is currently available in London. It is impossible to get tickets to most shows, and there are plenty to see. Jean Simmons is riding on a crest of triumphant glory in the London production of "A Little Night Music." Few Broadway musicals make successful crossings to London, but this one has not only kept its reputation intact but picked up some additional charm and brilliance along the way. One London critic gushed that it is "America's answer to the crown jewels."

It is certainly one of the rare and exemplary works of art the American theater has ever created, and in its soaring and sophisticated new London production, it reaches even greater heights of wit, style, literacy and good taste than it seemed to have on Broadway. Set at the turn of the century in the castles and birch trees of Sweden, its sets dazzle, its dance movements bewitch and its songs enthrall. London audiences seem to appreciate instinctively the subtle nuances of Stephen Sondheim's flawless lyrics even before they are sung, where Broadway rubes seemed disappointed because the score was too musically complex to hum along with. Simply everything about "A Little Night Music" seems to have improved, like the ripening of a peach.

Hermione Gingold's Grandmother Gargoyle, looking like a Lewis Carroll playing card, is more acid than before, charging the lushness and beauty around her with added humor. Joss Ackland, a fine British actor, gives just the right lumpiness to the stuffy lawyer. The sets are sumptuous, the costumes move as lyrically as the music, and Harold Prince's knowing direction is much in evidence throughout. But what really lifts this production to dizzying elevations of elegance is the presence of Jean Simmons, making her first appearance in her home town in 25 years.

It has been a royal homecoming. She is enchanting. As the glamorous Desiree, it is at last possible to see in her performance why so many brigands drew so many swords and fought so many duels for her affections. She's a prize worth coveting. The way she sings "Send in the Clowns" gives the show its emotional center. The way she looks leaves the audience breathless. And the way she acts is exhilarating. A great star, often criminally misused and lately shamefully neglected in films, in a great theater piece that matches her artistry. Altogether, a show touched from all angles by the rarity of genius.

There's genius, too, in Harold Pinter's new play, "No Man's Land," at the Old Vic, another puzzling examination of human imagination by England's master of architectural rhetoric. "No Man's Land" is almost plotless, concentrating not on actions or deeds but on conversation in a reunion between a rich old reclusive alcoholic (Sir Ralph Richardson) and a seedy, failed poet (Sir John Gielgud), who invades the former's protective sanctuary to rekindle old times and even old scores.

They were friends at Oxford. The rich man seduced the
poor man's wife. The menacing atmosphere heightens the tension, but it is merely a setting for a literary canasta and, as
an audience, we wait for answers that never come while the
actors meld, raise the ante and refuse to go out.

Nothing much is ever learned from the play, and I don't
much care. What is unquestionable is the wisdom and beauty of
Pinter's dialogue, the haunting hush of Peter Hall's meticulous
direction and the mastery of Richardson (majestic, bullying and
dominant) and Gielgud (crumpled, furrowed and regal). These
are two of England's finest knights, and rearely have they appeared so dauntless.

The most controversial play in London is "Kennedy's Children," a savage and disturbing examination of the people who
embraced the 1960s with love and peace, and got nothing in return but heartbreak. It's set in a lower East Side bar on a
rainy February afternoon in 1974 and consists of soliloquies delivered to the audience by five of the patrons--once full of idealism, loud and clear about everything from cafeteria sit-ins to
Castro's Cuba, their voices now stilled through shock and disillusionment. The characters are metaphors. The play is a
polemic. The message is a terrifying indictment of America.
To an American, the characters are almost hopeless cliches.

We've seen them all in countless plays and films: the plain
Jane who made the Kennedys into storybook heroes; the asp-
tongued homosexual who saw in the '60s a courageous tempo and
in the Camelot of the Kennedys a peaceful kingdom to be a minority in without fear of rejection; the tough, burned-out radical
hippie; the all-American Vietnam veteran who came home shaking,
stuttering and shell-shocked, the voluptuous showgirl who wanted
to be Marilyn Monroe. These were the prototypes who lived
through the fads and no longer care. Everything they believed
in died and withered away with the deaths of Bobby, JFK, Martin Luther King and Marilyn Monroe. These are the ones who
fought so hard and are now too weak, tired and hungry to care.
"What a joke," says the hippie. "We marched in every march
since we were babies, and all we did was make Jane Fonda famous." The role is played by Deborah Norton, and she is devastating.

"Kennedy's Children" is a sensation here, but I have serious
doubts about its commercial and artistic success in America.
One of the Kennedy family, Jean Kennedy Smith, was dispatched
to London to see the play and report to the Kennedy Center in
Washington for a possible production there. She was appalled
and deeply offended by it. Luckily, the trustees of the Kennedy
Center overruled her, sent other observers and have now decided
to present the play there.

It won't satisfy every taste, but it is a very interesting and effective play, and there are moments when it strikes a blow to the heart with instant, penetrating truths.   For anyone who lived through the '60s and finds disenchantment with the way so much idealism turned out, "Kennedy's Children" plows familiar soil, but I've never seen the material so freshly presented.   It forces one into a dead reckoning with the truth, and that fulfills one of the noblest aims of theater.

In a less interesting context, I have also seen the new mystery chiller by Anthony Shaeffer called "Murderer." It's a disappointing follow-up to his intricate "Sleuth," but a much more commercially viable project for Broadway than "Kennedy's Children." The first act opens with an amateur crime buff chopping up a corpse with a hatchet and pitching the remains into a furnace.

Not a bad beginning, with interminable talk about famous murder cases along the way.   There's a drowning in a bathtub of boiling steam and the inevitable plot twist at the end, but "Murderer" is dramatically anemic in the melodrama department.   Robert Stephens gives an energetic performance as the foolish murderer with ambitions of becoming as famous as Jack the Ripper in the annals of crime, and he drags his corpse up and down a flight of stairs in an ornately designed antique shop setting with genuine relish.

It's the play, with its silly climax, that falls to pieces, that fails.   For bloodthirsty appetites it's pretty weak tea.

British appetites, while I'm on the subject, have always been decidedly kinky.   What other explanation, then, for the cultish interest in the plays of Joe Orton?   The Royal Court is in the midst of a Joe Orton season, with such glittering talents as Lindsay Anderson, Albert Finney and Malcolm McDowell contributing their time and energy to a hopeless celebration.

Orton was a terrible writer whose slim plays dealt with homosexuality, sado-masochism and violence.   He was never much of a success until he was savagely murdered by his girl friend. The scandalous headlines died, but his memory is being kept alive by a new generation of enthusiasts who are just now discovering the merits of black comedy.   It's a bit like discovering swinging London a decade after the Beatles and Stones left town.

I saw the season's opening production, "Entertaining Mr. Sloane," and I still don't know what the fracas is about.   Its horrendous story--a predatory brother and sister feast sexually on their young hustler lodger who has murdered their father-- is not very amusing, but Beryl Reid is giving a bravura performance as the addled, frustrated sister who should not go unrewarded.   Malcolm McDowell makes an angelic-looking villain with peroxided curls and skin-tight leather pants, and the boarding house in the middle of a garbage dump is so perfect you can al-

most smell rancid butter on the cabbage-rose wallpaper. I guess
you have to be English. The audience was certainly doubled
over with hilarity. I have personally never had much fun laughing at graffiti.

Elsewhere, Mia Farrow is making a movie musical of "Peter Pan" with a score by Anthony Newley and Leslie Bricusse,
and Danny Kaye as Captain Hook. Norman Jewison is readying
a powerful film about a deadly futuristic sport called "Rollerball"
(I saw the first rough cut and predict it will be one of the year's
most hotly discussed films). Montserrat Caballe is knocking
them dead at Covent Garden, and David Hockney, the bleached-
blond painter who keeps the art world on its toes, has just
shocked London with pornographic sets for Stravinsky's opera,
"The Rake's Progress." It's something to write home about.

REISS, Alvin; (2) Staff Writer; film and drama reviewer, Medford
(Oregon) Mail Tribune; (3) b. Fort Sill, Okla., Oct. 31, 1932; (4)
s. Clarence G. and Mabel A. (Craig); (5) Attended U. of Oregon
and Southern Oregon State College, no degrees; (6) m. Audrey Spencer, Sept. 1, 1951, d. 1974; (7) children--daughters Belinda, Karen;
(8) Since 1952 have held variety of jobs including clerical positions
with Union Pacific and Denver and Rio Grande Western Railroads;
radio announcer-writer-producer for KBOY-FM, Medford, Ore. News
announcer and news director for KYJC radio, Medford, Ore., 1969-
73; Staff Writer for Mail Tribune 1969--(concurrent with radio through
June, 1973); (9) Acted briefly with University Theater, University of
Oregon, 1950. Acted with community theater, Medford, Ore. 1958-
61; playwriting (see #20) Special radio assistant to Oregon Shakespearean Festival, 1969; (15) Poetry Society of America; (20) Author
of several short stories, essays, and poems; (22) Mail Tribune, Medford, Ore., P.O. Box 1108, 97501, Ph. 503-779-1411; (23) Circulation:
25,600 daily; 27,800 Sunday; (24) About 40 films, 12 plays, 12 miscellaneous: nightclub acts, etc. also personality interviews and film location coverage.

"Henry" Production Better than Play
(by Al Reiss, Mail Tribune, June 22, 1975)

At the Oregon Shakespearean Festival in Ashland the current
repertory production of "Henry VI, Part One" is much better
than the play itself.

The festival stages one history play a season (with some exceptions) in the chronological order of the events they depict, not
in the order of their writing. Last year the festival omitted
"Henry VI, One." "Henry V" was presented in 1973. For
awhile there was talk in the administrative offices of presenting
a special, original work combining parts of "Henry VI." To the
Oregon Festival's credit, and validating its claim of presenting
the entire Shakespearean canon, "Henry" won.

But Henry is not exactly a winner among the Bard's work.
Scholars differ about the authorship of the first part of "Henry
VI." Some credit most of the writing to Robert Greene and
George Peele, allowing some scenes and revisions contributed
by Shakespeare.

The writing is inconsistent in its verse structure and fact.
This does not consider historical discrepancies, which can be
forgiven for the sake of drama. But, within the play, for example, Henry Beaufort, Bishop of Winchester (played by Jeff
Brooks) is referred to as cardinal in an early scene by the Duke
of Gloucester (Todd Oleson): "Under my feet I'll stamp thy
cardinal's hat."

Much later in the play an English nobleman expresses surprise that Winchester has been elevated to cardinal. A costuming question arises in the later scene when Brooks, as Winchester, is wearing white robes, a papal color, rather than the cardinal's red.

"Henry VI Part One" is generally recognized to have been
written after parts two and three, and revised in 1599, about the
time of the first staging of "Henry V." Part one begins, literally, on the coffin of the dead Henry V. The glories that Henry
the Fifth brought England died with him. The young king, Henry VI, is a boy incapable of ruling. France, conquered by Henry V, is in rebellion, and England is falling into civil strife.

Director Will Huddleston has skillfully blended these elements
through the talents of actors, technicians and an austere staging
concept. Even though there are some flaws, the result is good
theater.

The two outstanding performances in the play are by Eric
Booth Miller as Lord Talbot, a fighter for the English cause
in France, and Randi Douglas as Joan of Arc, also called La
Pucelle.

This play was written from the English point of view, not
the French. Joan, the warrior woman is not treated as a saint;
but quite the contrary. Ms. Douglas interprets Joan as assured,
even arrogant, as she offers her sword to Charles, the French
King (William Moreing). Then, in a scene of devil-consorting,
she is wanton and supplicant. Finally, being burned as a witch,
she is raving. Ms. Douglas captures it all.

Talbot is drawn as valiant and shrewd. He wins on the
battlefield and in an encounter with the Countess of Auvergne
(le Clanche du Rand), a meeting that is dramatic, not historical.
When Talbot is finally slain, with his son, Miller plays this
scene, as others, fully.

The play has scenes that seem only prologues for what will

follow in parts two and three. Vernon and Basset (Neil Savage and John Caldwell) representing the houses of York and Lancaster presage the War of the Roses with a garden argument in which they select red or white flowers to wear, indicative of their views. The Lancaster-York battles carry through parts two and three and into "Richard III."

Another scene inserted for dramatic purpose, and for later reference, is the capture of Margaret, daughter of the Duke of Anjou, by the Earl of Suffolk. Suffolk wants the Frenchwoman for his mistress in England. To have her near, he plans to arrange a marriage between her and Henry, the weak young King of England. Margaret is prominent and manipulative in Part Two of "Henry VI."

Although Peter Silbert looks mature for the role of Henry, his acting conveys the indecisive nature the part requires.

Michael Keys Hall and Carmi Boushey are Suffolk and Margaret.

One of the very strong aspects of the play is the sword battles. David Boushey has choreographed these into some of the most intricate to appear on the Ashland stage in a long while.

"Henry VI, Part One" is largely a series of battle scenes separated by anti-French polemic and groundwork for succeeding plays. Still, it deserves inclusion in the production canon, particularly from a theater which is basically educational in its identity. The Oregon Shakespearean Festival presents the play very commendably this summer.

"Night" Does Honor to O'Neill, Festival
(by Al Reiss, Mail Tribune, June 22, 1975)

The Oregon Shakespearean Festival sought, this year, to honor America's great playwright, Eugene O'Neill with a production of his autobiographical "The Long Day's Journey into Night."

The festival not only does much honor to O'Neill, but to itself. For a span of three hours (it seems much shorter) five gifted actors form a compelling ensemble that binds the audience to the lives of the Tyrone family in a way that is at once brutal and poignant.

In their individual ways James and Mary Tyrone and their two sons, Jamie and Edmund, slice at each other as relentlessly as the sun peels minutes from the day. Yet there was a time when each felt love for at least one of the others. Pervading the play is the compassion the author feels for his characters. They are not personae, but real people limned through the perspective of art, so that they touch something in the lives of the audience as they unfold the misfortunes of their own.

Michael Kevin Moore is cast as James Tyrone, a 65-year-old actor whose career brought him fame, respect and money, but not enough by his standards.

Jean Smart, a newcomer to the festival, is James' wife, Mary, who traded her Catholic faith for the more immediate sacrament of morphine.

William M. Hurt portrays Edmund Tyrone, the younger of the adult sons, a failed poet dying of consumption.

Denis Arndt is Jamie, the alcoholic who cannot resolve the love-hate relationship he holds toward others in the family.

These four are so matched in their abilities and so complete in fulfillment of their roles it is impossible to say that one excels another. The play is superbly cast and directed by Jerry Turner, producing director of the festival.

Katherine James is Cathleen, a serving girl in the Tyrone house. Her portrayal complements the rest.

Richard Hay's set and Steven Maze's lighting immediately draw us into the Tyrones' summer house on the Connecticut coast in 1912. On this particular August day, the morning begins brightly enough with James sitting on the porch to enjoy an after breakfast cigar while he talks with his wife.

The lightness between them is obviously forced. From that point, they and their sons retreat into single and collective darkness, mostly of their own making.

The play is constructed so that it is often a dialogue between two people. At times, although two are on the stage, one engages in what amounts to a soliloquy. This may be a monologue of self-deception, as midway in the play when Mary talks with Cathleen.

The Tyrones snipe at each other from safe distances: Jamie from behind alcohol; James from the viewpoint of the career sacrifices he made; Edmund from inside his illness. Mary's trick is to pretend to blame herself for some misfortune while she is actually placing it on another. Speaking to James of a child who died in infancy, she says, "If I hadn't left him at my mother's to join you on the road ..." blaming her husband for his life as a traveling actor.

The Tyrones continually throw the past at each other. Mary refuses to forget so she can magnanimously forgive. But their reliving of their past transports them, and the audience outside the Connecticut summer home, into a larger world. One of the play's very beautiful passages is Edmund's recollection of an experience at sea, on a sailing ship.

Another suggestion of a larger, unseen world, is the sound of foghorns punctuating the Tyrones' night conversation, linking them to others who are also drifting through gray isolation.

This is the first O'Neill the festival has attempted. It is an admirable success. In all its facets, it is perhaps the finest, best realized drama to be produced in the Angus Bowmer Theatre since that structure opened, six seasons ago.

REYNOLDS, Linda Melick; (2) Theater and Film Critic; (3) b. Summit, N.J., Feb. 18, 1952; (4) d. George and Florence (Bevins) Melick; (5) B.A. in English, Douglass College, M.A. in Theater Arts, Rutgers U.; (6) m. William P. Reynolds, May 25, 1974; (8) Staff Writer, Somerset Spectator, 1975-76, Theater and Film Critic, Somerset Spectator 1975- ; (9) Costume Assistant, George St. Playhouse, New Brunswick, 1975; (20) Cont. articles to Woodbridge News Tribune, Review of Books and Religion; (21) 309 Central Ave., Edison, N.J. 08817, Ph. 572-6885; (22) Somerset Spectator, Rutgers Plaza, Somerset, N.J. 08873, Ph. 247-7997; (23) Circulation: 3,600; (24) 50 plays and films annually.

"Red Ryder" Performances Inspired
(by L. Melick Reynolds, Somerset Spectator, 1975)

In our cities and towns, the lawless are criminals; on the stage, their counterparts are gangsters, villains, bad guys.

The difference goes beyond mere terminology. Criminals are sadistic and overly ambitious while gangsters, villains and bad guys are Sadism and Excessive Ambition in the form of a character. From Little Caesar to the Sundance Kid, they represent these impulses in us, in our society. That is why, even though we find them unforgivably despicable, we like them.

Teddy in Mark Medoff's biting "When You Comin' Back, Red Ryder?" is no exception. As we believe in the stage illusion, Teddy horrifies us with his sheer brutality. But, at the same time, the stage character who can't fire real bullets at us fascinates for two full hours. Indeed, the Villagers' powerful production of this play holds us as captive an audience as Teddy holds his with a gun.

But Teddy is no simple bad guy. In the 50's when values started getting jumbled, his prototype was born in the film "Rebel Without a Cause." So, too, unlike our simple horse thieves and blackmailers, Teddy has no apparent cause for his aggression.

The scene: a sleazy, sleepy roadside diner in New Mexico, Sunday before 7 a.m.; two young employees, the crippled owner of the motel-gas station across the street, and a well-to-do tourist couple exercising social behavior fitting the time and place. Enter: a barrel-chested young man--ears looped with gold, hair meaningfully long; this being the late 60's--behind, a jean-clad young woman. Campus envoys.

His face frozen, menacing. Sweaty silence. Then, an explosion of genuine laughter. Geniality? Perhaps. Egotistical delight in his immediate control of the situation? Yes.

Dawn has brought a snotty college grad who slowly spits up his increasingly sinister entrails. It seems he can't decide which torture is best--or worst--physical or psychological. And so, twisting clever phrases and others' arms left and right, he inflicts both upon his captive audience.

A small-time dope smuggler, Teddy needs cash but his reign of terror does little to meet this need. Like Charlie Manson, he rationalizes his violence screaming he is a "disaffected" youth of American society. He condemns a counterfeit society in which the only heroes are paper and cardboard--Red Ryder in comic strips, Bob Richards on Wheaties boxes, to name a few.

The Red Ryder in this play is a case in point. The cowboy's namesake, a diner employee, is a skinny nervous kid, ironically branded with the tattoo "Born Dead," who can't get it together to leave this godforsaken outpost.

Teddy so humiliates and degrades him that Red, for the first time in his life, acts assertively, aggressively, threatening Teddy with a knife and finally, at the end of the play, leaving town. The wife grows a backbone, too, to survive the ordeal, and gains a new independence from her spineless husband.

You see, Teddy is not only a demon, he is an exorcist of sorts. He rips out the submerged truth about each character and flails it in their own faces, the ugly hidden tumor it has become. And, as quickly as he has come on a clod of desert dust, he is gone--an anti-climax to the suspense thriller the play starts but never finishes. The question remains, was Teddy's presence therapeutic or merely malignant?

At the hands of director Tony Adase, this random menace that blooms red into violence makes the production a unique blend of Harold Pinter and Sam Peckinpah. The excellent ensemble of actors generates an electrical current that grips but, because the play ultimately cops out, energizes little in us.

As Teddy, Richard Barranger has impressively sunk his teeth into the very meat of this raucous ruffian. The performance is on par with his portrayal of McMurphy in last season's "One Flew Over the Cuckoo's Nest" which won him a New York Daily News acting award.

Indeed, all the performances are inspired--Red played by Len Rusay, Angel by Beverly Gorelick, Lyle by Bill Smith,

Clarisse by Jane Tamm Bendavid, Richard by Donald L. Bumgardner and, last but not least, Cheryl, Teddy's reluctant and deeply disturbed Moll, by Sheila Condit. One wishes Medoff had been when he finished off his play.

Behind the Parlor Doors
(by L. Melick Reynolds, Somerset Spectator, 1976)

An elegant ice blue drawing room in a townhouse in Victorian Washington Square is not the most likely place to find a web of seething emotions trapping its inhabitants.

More likely are the steamy New Orleans of Tennessee Williams' "A Streetcar Named Desire" or the mistcaught moors of Emily Bronte's "Wuthering Heights."

Yet the drawing room of Dr. Sloper, M.D. is a perfect hiding place for the secret desires of the widower, his daughter and an ambitious suitor in "The Heiress." In that room, beneath rich gowns and cut-away coats, behind masks of wit and social grace, passions are twisted into ugly desires.

The McCarter Theater production of the Ruth and Augustus Goetz play is a masterful blend of what is on the surface of things and what is within. It is at once a witty comedy of manners and a sobering drama of manipulators and their victims.

Based on the Henry James novel "Washington Square," "The Heiress" is essentially the story of an ugly duckling. Only the duckling--Catherine Sloper played by Maria Tucci--isn't really ugly at all. Dressed in a succession of jewel tone gowns that hint at her wealth's extent, she is striking. (So was Olivia De Haviland in the movie version.)

Catherine's ugliness is a reflection of her father's attitude toward the daughter who was the cause of his beloved wife's death in childbirth.

On the face of it, Sloper seems only disappointed in Catherine's lack of 19th century woman's color and charm. Jack Gwilliam's Sloper, however, proclaims his daughter's dull conversation, awkwardness and tin ear with all the triumph of diagnosing a difficult medical case. It was he who undermined her self-confidence all along.

And so the score is evened, the taste of revenge is bittersweet. But there is one more matter to take care of before this pillar of the community can order himself to his own deathbed.

A prince charming has come courting the heiress and Catherine steps all over her crinolines at the chance to gain the love her father has never given her.

But Sloper is convinced the young man is seeking to fill his shoes in a very different manner. Morris Townsend wants position, wealth and security, the doctor instructs, chopping logic in the witty and wry manner of Sherlock Holmes.

And who can be sure that Townsend's motives, or those of any future suitor, for that matter, are not these?

Sadly, the shoes do not all fit and the ice blue room becomes a cold tomb for dashed dreams.

Michael Kahn has guided his cast to an elegant and explosive production. To those who missed Kahn's WNET television production of Eugene O'Neill's "Beyond the Horizon" on January 14 or who are otherwise unfamiliar with his work, "The Heiress" is an excellent introduction to this talented man who is artistic director of both the McCarter Theater and the American Shakespeare Theater at Stratford, Connecticut.

RHINEHART, Raymond Patrick; (2) Theatre Critic; (3) b. Jersey City, N.J., June 7, 1942; (4) s. Reginald Willard and Emmy W. (Taube) R.; (5) B.A. Brown U., major subj.: English lit., 1962; M.A. and Ph.D. Princeton U.; English Ren. lit., 1969; (6) Single; (8) Instructor, U. Va. 1965-68; instructor, Hofstra U., summer 1968; asst. professor, Va. Commonwealth U. 1968-73; exhibition director and lecturer for Va. Museum, "The American Scene," "Landscape," 1974- ; drama critic, Richmond Mercury, 1974- ; free-lance writer and lecturer, poet; (9) NEA Poets in the Schools, 1974- ; (14) Phi Beta Kappa; magna cum laude; Wilson Fellow; Fellow in Cooperative Program in the Humanities, UNC, Chapel Hill, 1971; (15) MLA, AAUP, SAMLA, Southeastern Renaissance Conference, Renaissance Soc. of Am.; (16) Independent; (17) Episcopalian; (20) Cont. articles to Interiors, Richmond Magazine, Renaissance Papers 1975; (21) 2 N. Plum St., Richmond, Va. 23220, Ph. 804-359-1469; (22) Richmond Mercury, 16 E. Main St., Richmond, Va. 23219, Ph. 804-644-2366; (23) Audience: 25,000; (24) 70 plays and musicals, 10 misc., 10 book reviews.

Battered but Not Bruised
(by Raymond P. Rhinehart, Richmond Mercury, September 25, 1974)

One of the most pervasive fictions around is that proposition that unhappiness is not a necessary function of life, but rather the result of negative forces exerted on otherwise happy, good-natured men. If, for example, a cutting insult slips out, it is quickly covered by the familiar explanation, "I was not myself." Therefore, it follows that unhappiness can be warded off or exorcised. But what happens when in the act of exorcism it is revealed that to be human is to suffer?

Eugene O'Neill's Long Day's Journey into Night has the smell of mortality in every scene. The actor-businessman James

Tyrone and his wife Mary are spending the summer somewhere
on the New England coast. They have with them their two sons
Jamie and Edmund. But far from being a light and airy summer home, the house is an armed camp.

James is preoccupied with real estate speculation: there
can never be enough security to ward off the terror of the poor-
house. His eldest son Jamie is a failure, a failure even at being a cynical rake, the only role he throws himself into with
any passion. On the other hand, quiet, sensitive Edmund, so
like his mother, has begun to show promise of becoming a writer.
He also shows signs of being tubercular. Unable to bear the
growing awareness of her youngest son's serious condition, Mary
Tyrone anesthetizes the pain of her painful circumstances and
drifts off into a fogbank of morphine where she finds the careless
innocence of her childhood.

As the action begins, the temptation is to take sides: if
James Tyrone were not so cheap; if Jamie were not so anxious
to have his cynicism confirmed; if Mary would only give up her
infatuation with her lost virginity; if Edmund had not come down
with consumption. Yet O'Neill has not written melodrama.
Each character (with the possible exception of Edmund) in turn
alienates us. Each is tormentor and tormented. Everyone is
to blame, yet no one is to blame. And in the confusion the play
deliberately engenders, moral absolutism is abandoned; in its
place comes compassion if not understanding. Each character
becomes important not because anyone is heroic or villainous,
but quite amazingly because each is nothing more than human,
all too human.

To put this another way, the source of the play's overwhelming impact is not the admittedly unusual circumstances the four
main characters find themselves in, but their extraordinarily ordinary personalities. As such, O'Neill's play sets up rather
formidable obstacles that should intimidate most actors and directors. There is fundamentally very little action. The dialogue is necessarily mundane. And as the title warns, the play
is a test of endurance for actors and audiences alike. Nevertheless, the roles, particularly that of Mary Tyrone, are marvelous acting vehicles. Unfortunately the actors at Barksdale
are seldom up to the exhausting demands that O'Neill's play
makes.

The difficulty with this current production is apparent right
from the beginning. As the lights come up on Lyde Longaker's
set (in the main a resonably faithful translation of O'Neill's own
directions, except for the oriental rugs which are far too rich
for that household), James Tyrone (Mallory Freeman) and his
wife, Mary (Lalla Rolfe), enter from the dining room. What
we see is a man who looks and sounds much too old and fragile
to be the lusty, vigorous Irish peasant that the play calls for.
James Tyrone should be an aging but still great bull of a man

who can elicit admiration from the servant girl, Cathleen. He
is a man capable of exquisite spontaneous tenderness, but more
typically gives vent to towering, somewhat theatrical rages.
Mallory Freeman has none of this energy or deep tenderness
for that matter. Extreme emotional agitation is conveyed by a
curious hunting after words and phrases, curious because it is
not always clear whether Freeman is actually trying to recall
his lines or has for some mysterious reason been directed by
Muriel McAuley to speak his lines thus.

Furthermore, Freeman's Tyrone never develops, which again
seems more a function of miscasting than poor direction. In
fact, once in his robe in the second half of the play, Freeman
looks as if he has somehow stumbled out of a Noel Coward play
into O'Neill.

In the case of Lalla Rolfe's Mary Tyrone, the director's responsibility is more clear. The role itself is easily the most
difficult in the play. Despite her deep resentment toward her
family and occasional fits of anger, she is required to portray
throughout what O'Neill calls her "most appealing quality," "a
shy convent-girl youthfulness she has never lost--an innate unworldly innocence."

Now if there is an emotion almost impossible to communicate successfully, it has to be "unworldly innocence." It is a
pose that is hedged in on all sides by the dull, the flat, the
colorless. Perhaps it is no accident that the appropriate English
adjective "simple" is itself likewise slippery. And all too often
Miss Rolfe slides into a rather two-dimensional portrayal of the
character. She tries so hard to master the necessary inflections
of this subtle role that she comes off studied and mechanical.
Only when the script allows her to abandon this pose, as in the
first scene of Act II where she turns on her husband, does a
real and credible character emerge.

Miss Rolfe's predicament is unneccessarily aggravated by her
pacing. The pianist Arthur Schnabel once remarked that the most
important element of music is silence. This holds equally true
for O'Neill's play, for between sentences and individual words
there are, as it were crucial "rests" that must be observed if
the action is not to be chaotic.

For example, at the very end of the play, Edmund makes
one last desperate effort to reach his mother by telling her he
has consumption. O'Neill's stage directions read: "For a second he almost breaks through to her. She trembles and her
expression becomes terrified. She calls distractedly, as if giving
a command to herself"--"No!"

Clearly the silent "action" that precedes her cry is the most
important element of the scene. Miss Rolfe, as elsewhere, jumps
into the line before it has had a chance to breathe.

Robert Albertia's Jamie suffers from a similar lack of breath in the first two acts at least. He looks much more like what O'Neill had in mind than his "father": there is the requisite over-ripe, city slicker air about him. But he speaks too rapidly. The lines pull him along. Fortunately the play calls for him to be drunk in the last two acts. And with vino comes the missing veritas. Albertia now speaks slowly, deliberately-- has time, in other words, to act. In fact, the most effective moments of this production are those scenes where Albertia is on the stage alone with Matt Costello. There the play shows signs of life.

Which brings us to the last of the four main characters, Edmund. In the wrong hands, Edmund can come off pathetic rather than sympathetic. After some initial nervousness, Costello settled fairly comfortably into his role and gave the most consistently satisfying performance of the evening.

The servant girl, Cathleen, though admittedly a relatively minor role nevertheless can be in its own way quite effective. She is common, a little vulgar and a lot coquette. In short, she is a comic character. Gina Vetter's conception of her, however, is curiously up-tight. She moves so stiffly that Miss Vetter appears to be trapped in her costume.

In the final moments of the action as his mother enters in a drug-induced trance, Edmund breaks out bitterly: "The Mad Scene. Enter Ophelia!" Jamie jumps up and slaps Edmund across the mouth with the back of his hand. The blow last Friday night was a very obvious stage slap. As such, it was an unintentional but appropriate metaphor for a production that left the audience battered but not bruised as O'Neill had intended.

Staging Marital Infidelity
(by Raymond P. Rhinehart, Richmond Mercury, March 12, 1975)

Is the institution of matrimony morally and economically untenable? Are wives by day little more than expensive live-in domestics, by night, sleep-in whores?

Such questions are today the cliches of militant feminists. But they are somewhat unexpected in a 50-year-old comedy of manners by a confirmed bachelor no less, Somerset Maugham-- as unexpected as the unorthodox cynical answers Maugham's wit provides. And judging by the laughter last week at Kennedy Center, despite the somewhat creaky well-made plot of "The Constant Wife," the apparently cool advocacy of marital infidelity still strikes a responsive chord.

But apparent is the key word here. For there is vitriol in Maugham's wit for husbands, too. Constance, the play's heroine, remarks:

"The modern wife is nothing but a parasite." Can it be that the irony cuts in both directions, that Constance is Maugham in chemise and petticoat? It's this well-intentioned ambiguity, this refusal to declare for either side in the constant battle of husbands and wives that make a revival of Maugham's play more than a nostalgic exercise.

Yet it takes an intelligent production too. And happily director John Gielgud's hand is as deft as Maugham's wit is pointed. Despite the timelessness of the issues involved, Gielgud wisely locates the action in the London of the late 1920's. Here, the repartee, the studied elegance of a self-confident upper-class sounds natural rather than precious or/arch. Stage movement is likewise well-conceived. The long-legged strides, the toss of a head, the cocktails and the angle of a cigarette beautifully define the terribly clever Smart Set.

Beatrice Dawson's costumes are similarly elegant animations of dusty copies of "Vogue," and Alan Tagg's tasteful set is liberated from an old copy of "Town and Country."

As for the cast, it is usually good when it is not excellent. Ingrid Bergman's Constance Middleton radiates a self-confidence alarming to anyone in her path. Miss Bergman is even master of a bandaged, broken foot--the result of a fall in Los Angeles. If she is forced to sit most of the time, no matter. The animation of her face and the sparkle of Maugham's dialogue set the stage alive with motion.

Sometimes too much motion, however, as Bergman does tend to speak too rapidly. As a result, she stumbled over her lines several times last Wednesday night. Maugham's irony needs time to breathe. And Constance should be thinking, not reciting on her feet.

Delphi Lawrence gamely plays the thankless role of Constance's pallid younger sister Martha, a girl who, as even her own mother remarks, has "come out and gone in again." Miss Lawrence is convincingly tiresome without being a bore, a perfect foil not only for Constance, but also Constance's widowed business friend, the smart Barbara Fawcett (Marti Stevens). The only complaint I have with Miss Stevens' vigorous performance is that Maugham did not give her enough lines.

What sets the play into motion and the Middleton household on its ear is a certain Marie-Louise Durham, who had laid claim to an awkward double role as Constance's best friend and her husband John's mistress. Constance spends the first half of the evening trying to ward off the well-intentioned efforts of her friends to tell her what she already knows. Carolyn Lagerfelt's reading of Maugham's rather mindless flapper _femme fatale_ is perhaps too high-pitched and wide-eyed. There ought to be some sensuousness within this Kewpie doll.

By contrast the John Middleton Jack Gwillin sketches out has far too little color. His voice has a washed-out, air-brushed quality, and his movement around stage has the specific gravity not so much of his medical profession, but granite. It is true that the men in this play are scarcely more than walking aphorisms. But the role of John Middleton ought to have at least as much life as Donald Silber brings to Marie-Louise's husband, Mortimer, or Paul Harding inspires in Constance's once and future lover Bernard Kersal.

The brightest star in this constellation turns out to be Brenda Forbes. As Constance's mother, Miss Forbes delivers the vast store of her wisdom with a dry straight-forwardness that has no patience with the cant of polite conversation:

"... when women are alone together I don't see why they shouldn't tell the truth now and then. It's a rest from the weary round of pretending to be something that we quite well know we're not."

Unfortunately, this production is playing a limited and already sold-out engagement of three weeks.

RICH, Alan; (2) Theater & Music Critic; (3) June 17, 1924; (4) s. Edward and Helen (Hirshberg); (5) B. A. Harvard, pre-med, 1945; M. A. , U. of California at Berkeley, music, 1952; (8) Program Director, Pacifica Foundation, 1953-61; Associate Music Critic, New York Times, 1961-63; Chief Music Critic, Herald Tribune, 1963-67; Contributing Editor, Time Magazine, 1967-68; Music and Theater Critic, New York Magazine, 1968- ; (9) Instructor, U. of Calif. , Berkeley, 1953-57; Instructor, New School of Social Research, N. Y. C. 1970-74; Artist-in-Residence, City College, New York, 1974-75; (14) Traveling Fellowship, U. of Calif. , 1952-53; four Deems Taylor Awards, ASCAP (two in 1970, one in 1973, one in 1974); (15) N. Y. Music Critics Circle, 1961-65; N. Y. Drama Critics Circle 1974- ; (16) Democrat; (20) Books: Careers and Opportunities in Music, 1964. Music, Mirror of the Arts, 1969. Contributed articles to Saturday Review, Show Opera News, Play Bill, etc. ; (21) i13 River Road, Grand-view-on-Hudson, N. Y. 10960, Ph. 914-358-2393; (22) New York Magazine, 755 Second Ave. , N. Y. 10017, Ph. 212-986-4600; (23) Circulation: 400,000; (24) 90

Memorabilia
(by Alan Rich, New York, November 17, 1975)

The external brilliances in Travesties, its manic virtuosity of language, its diabolical manipulation of time and notion, cannot elude any visitor to Tom Stoppard's verbal prank now at the Barrymore. I suggest, however, a little pleasurable homework before you go. First, bone up on Oscar Wilde's The Importance of Being Earnest. (If you find that a chore, you might as well forget the whole thing.) Second, get hold of the

record of Luciano Berio's Sinfonia, and make your way through
the third movement. That astounding composition, about twelve
minutes in length, is a concise precursor of much that Stoppard
attempts in his play.

Berio's piece is a collage. Its foundation is a movement
from a Mahler symphony, which appears--sometimes submerged,
sometimes in the foreground--in every measure. Berio uses
that movement as a sculptor might use a pedestal, building onto
it his own complex mingling of wildly dissimilar elements: bits
from other music (La Valse, Beethoven's Pastoral, etc.), several spoken and sung texts (graffiti from Paris walls, some
Beckett, asides to the audience, etc.). Whether you hear every
note in etched clarity is less important than your hearing the
whole as an interweaving of ideas that hammer themselves into
a dramatic shape.

Stoppard's collage is, likewise, a jostling of dissimilar elements, personages related only in that they all happened to be
in Zurich in 1917: James Joyce, Vladimir Lenin, Tristan Tzara
(a founder of Dada), and a British consular flunky named Henry
Carr. As Berio uses Mahler as his objet trouvé, Stoppard uses
the Wilde play. That is because Carr's one moment of relative
glory, in a life otherwise uncrowded with incident, was his appearance as Algernon in a production of the play put together
by Joyce. That event, and the petty squabble that arose from
it, were of no importance to anyone except Carr but, as his senile memory struggles to construct a portentous memoir of that
time and that place, his thoughts take shape as scenes from
Earnest.

The scenes constantly go awry. Wilde's opening, the conversation between Algernon and his valet, gets tangled up with
Leninist revolutionary cant: Lady Bracknell's inquisition merges
into the dialectic of the Ithaca scene in Ulysses; John Worthing
is transmuted into Tzara. Out of this blur and side-slipping
something does emerge: not the memoir that Carr lacks the insight to create, but a keen portrait of Carr himself. As he retold Hamlet through the eyes of sideline observers, to the point
where we learned more about Rosencrantz & Guildenstern than
was rationally worth knowing, Stoppard achieves the considerable
miracle of forcing us to care about Henry Carr. John Wood's
stupendous performance compounds the miracle, his every movement and glance an exact reflection of Stoppard's antic, immaculate word-gaming.

Under the sheen of its immense daring, the play reveals a
touching center, a study of a useless but endearing chap frantic-
ally beating off the onrush of obscurity. His struggle is inept,
but ineptitude has been his life companion. His hilarious attempts to spy on Lenin in Zurich, whence the Russian leader had
already fled, are achingly funny. No less so are Carr's pathetic stabs at coping with intellectual life. "I don't know it," he

says of Wilde's play, "but I've heard of it and I don't like it." That philistine manifesto resounds through later scenes like a litany.

Multilayered, complex, intellectually astringent, Stoppard's play bats about a remarkable number of important ideas. Like E. L. Doctorow in his Ragtime, Stoppard involves his historical characters in a web of fictions: Joyce (who made words dance) bickering with Tzara (because he loathes the way the Dadaists make words dance); Lenin, the spirit of a progressive age, whose idea of a good evening at the theater is a performance of Camille (which might explain why the Bolshoi Opera still stages everything as if it were Camille). The very disorganization of Carr's memory becomes the play's organizing force. As the old man gabbles along, his thoughts go off in opposing directions and take on clashing tone-colors. This Stoppard translates into a broad spectrum of theater techniques: a music-hall number here, a dance there, a spy-behind-the-arras routine worthy of the Keystone Kops. Some of the casting seems to go blatantly against type: Tim Curry, late of Rocky Horror, seems a perverse candidate for Tzara until a couple of routines reveal the genius of the choice. Peter Wood, who staged Travesties last year for the Royal Shakespeare Company, here again gives the stunning conception both body and wings.

"Great days ... Zurich during the War," says Carr at the start of his last monologue. That much we know from history, and that chapter might serve for an excellent historical play. The ultimate, mind-tickling travesty in Travesties is the way history becomes vivid as anti-history. It is thinking-man's theater that makes it a privilege to think.

Kennedy's Children is also based on memory, this time horrifying, poignantly accurate. Five people sit in an East Village bar (the excellent Phebe's, and may it survive its new fame), remembering. They are unrelated; each speaks only of himself; they share nothing but geographical proximity. Yet, they also share a common origin: they are all children of the Kennedy decade, the sixties. Their visions were formed between the election of John and the murder of Robert, and each had found a way to become an active participant in his individual vision. Now the time is the present, and Robert Patrick has brought them to this bar on this afternoon to survey the collapse of their hopes.

There is no conversation, no interaction, and yet the author's splendid craft supplies an illusion of great dramatic tension. Part of this stems from his fine sense of timing, the shrewd intercutting of fragments of monologue so that words and ideas seem to circle around Santo Loquasto's beautifully observed barroom set. But more comes from the intricate counterpointing of the five characters, who have come to a point of shared disillusion, each along a separate path.

First, there is Carla. Her friends downtown, she tells us, were into the amphetamines and the peace marches, but for her the downhill progression of the sixties began with the death of Marilyn Monroe, the last star. Carla is a failed star in a time when stars were going out of style, and for her the wreckage of the decade is symbolized by the fact that the men she once cared for are now successful drag queens. The day of the play is her 26th birthday. Marilyn only began her career at 26, but Carla, before coming to the bar, has downed several dozen sleeping pills.

Wanda is the romantic. To her the Kennedy reign was Camelot. That beauty has faded, but she fights to keep its memory alive, legend merging into superstition. Rona was the flower-child, drifting from Haight-Ashbury, to New York, to Chicago in the summer of '68, protesting as long as protest made sense, but then surrendering. Mark is back from Vietnam, his mind obliterated by drugs, his speech an insane babble of Lyndon Johnson's war rhetoric and private paranoia. Sparger had spent the decade in underground theater in the Village, working in the zany, creative ferment of the Caffé Cino. His personal betrayal took place on the day that a Village Voice critic discovered the place and turned it respectable. (Robert Patrick also came out of this scene, and we may accept Sparger as his surrogate.)

Aided by Patrick's impeccable feeling for speech--brittle, urban-bitchy, intense--Clive Donner has turned this study in non-communication into powerful, communicative theater. Donner has hit upon a unique tone that strikes a fine balance between soliloquy and oratory, and has welded a consistent ensemble out of his exemplary cast.

RICHARDS, David Bryant; (2) Theater Critic; (3) b. Concord, Mass. Oct. 1, 1942; (4) s. Gordon D. Richards and Elizabeth Eddy; (5) Occidental College, French, 1964; M.A. , Middlebury College, French, 1965; M.A. , Catholic University, Speech and Drama, 1969; (6) Single; (8) Instructor of French, Howard U. , 1968-70; Theater Critic, Radio Station WGMS, Washington, D. C. , 1969-71; Article Editor, Washington Magazine, Washington Star, 1970-71; Theater Critic, Washington Star, 1971- ; (13) Member, Peace Corps, Ivory Coast, Africa, 1965-67; (14) Member Phi Beta Kappa; (15) Member American Theater Critics Association; (16) Democrat; (17) Unitarian; (20) Contributor to Otis Guernsey/Burns Mantle Theater Yearbook, 1974-75, 1975-76; (21) 1743 P. St. , N. W. ,Washington, D. C. 20036; (22) 225 Virginia Avenue, SE, Washington, D. C. 20003; Ph. 484-4320; (23) Circulation: 400,000; (24) 100 theater reviews; 50 Sunday columns (interviews, profiles, analyses, etc.)

An Explosion of Invention
(by David Richards, Washington Star, March 21, 1974)

Considering that most of the theater we see today is still
mired in the patterns and pretensions of the 1930s, "Leonce and
Lena," which opened last night at Arena's Kreeger Theater, is
a gulp of fresh air, as sweet as it is vivifying.

Not since Peter Brook introduced Shakespeare to trapezes in
"A Midsummer Night's Dream" have we had such an explosion
of theatrical invention, anarchic energy, and sheer, shimmering
pleasure. This is the sort of production that makes the scales
tumble from your eyes. It celebrates the theater as both plaything and guardian of the truth. In its marriage of metaphysics
and highjinks, it makes "Jumpers" look like a cripple.

It is the Marx Brothers, Alfred de Musset, "Marat-Sade,"
Mack Sennett, Marie Antoinette, Emmett Kelly, Max Ernst and
Victor Herbert, all rolled into one magical evening.

Romanian director-designer Liviu Ciulei, making his American directorial debut, has to be one of the truly creative spirits
working in the contemporary theater. He has taken what is
largely an unknown 19th century German comedy by Georg
Buchner, and staged it with only the most legitimate ploys of the
avant-garde, all the while remaining unimpeachably faithful to
his source.

What Buchner wrote, prior to his death at 23, was a brief,
dense script, an absurdist fairy tale, long before the absurdists
began propounding their outlandish metaphors for the boredom of
man and the hollowness of the universe.

Prince Leonce, weary of his skin, decides to escape his responsibilities in a cardboard court by fleeing into the wide, wide
world. Likewise, Princess Lena, his betrothed--seeing life close
around her like a canary's cage--slips on her own dainty traveling slippers. The two accidentally meet in some no-man's land
(all lands, Buchner implies, are no-man's land), fall in love,
and return home to solemnize the marriage. The king turns
over the reins to his son and goes off to play cards with his
cronies.

Buchner's dialogue is aphoristic and unconnected, written in
darts of poetry and illumination. Its logic is that of an unfet-
tered imagination. But in its way, it is wise to our preposterous status in a preposterous world.

Using what is really a simple scenario at his base, Ciulei has
built a gingerbread palace of wonders. The mood is sometimes
wacky and wild, sometimes poignant and unsettling, and frequently self-mocking. Unlike much experimental theater, this production knows the risk of taking itself too seriously and is generous with the winks.

On the bare Kreeger boards, Ciulei has placed a second, makeshift stage. A large eyeball gazes at us from above; off to one side, a crank-up gramophone rasps a tinny accompaniment. The cast is garbed in everything from jeans to tatty French lace, hoop skirts and tutus. These improbable masquers pull into a huddle at the start and bombard us, by way of a prologue, with lines and quick encounters from the play to come, as well as from Buchner's two other works, "Danton's Death" and "Woyzeck." As a buckshot depiction of today's world, it hits its target.

What follows is a riot of clownery (some of it involving the audience) that is unflagging in the cleverness with which it finds new life in old props, older costumes, and even older situations. Rarely has an Arena cast ever appeared quite so liberated, seizing Ciulei's suggestions and acting on them with clear comic delight.

Max Wright, looking like a cross between Caligula and a plucked turkey, is chaotically funny as the king--bathing with rubber ducks, biting the nose of a courtier, and generally putting the piston engine to shame. In an improbable lampshade of a dress, Halo Wines has irresistible charm as Lena, as does Dennis Howard, the blue-jeaned prince with the long face. Their courtship is ever so touching and innocent.

There are gorgeous performances too, by Stanley Anderson, the epicene master of ceremonies; by John Christopher Jones, as the prince's congenial sidekick, who knows that the answer to ennui lies in an up-turned bottle; and by Leslie Cass, as Lena's beak-nosed duenna. But actually, everyone is doing something, sometime, somewhere on that stage that is bound to make you blink twice, before your fancy is subjugated.

The philosphical implications of "Leonce and Lena" may tend to baffle some, but the visual aspects (all designed by Ciulei) can only delight them. Indeed, the show is primarily descriptive in thrust: with bright, bold juxtapositions, it paints an image of the world as funhouse and funny farm. We're all locked in, reason is a rusty key, and only a burst of love makes temporary sense out of the craziness.

The evening's password is unfuried on a large painted banner at the outset, "Here are the foolish silences from which we can see the hidden side of the world," it reads. All you have to do is look, listen and enjoy.

"Waiting for Godot" A Light on Our Time in Arena's Fine Revival
(by David Richards, Washington Star, March 24, 1976)

"Time has stopped," says Didi, surveying the landscape, empty of noise and emptier of life.

"Don't you believe it, sir," retorts Gogo. "Anything you

like but that."

Didi and Gogo are, of course, the two tramps of "Waiting
for Godot," Samuel Beckett's threnody for a universe on the
wane, and one of the indisputable masterpieces of the contemporary theater.

And time is indeed what it's all about--time that flashes by
so fast that birth to death might as well be a snap of the fingers; time that, paradoxically, also ticks away so arthritically
that the world seems to have been hollow for an eternity.

Probably no other 20th-century play paints our lives so
bleakly or captures so succinctly the futility with which we furnish our endless minutes and our brief days. Even hope is a
time-filler, while we wait for the mysterious Godot who is always about to show up on the scene with purpose and meaning
in his satchel, but who somehow never makes the rendezvous.

And yet this swan song for humanity, flawlessly revived last
night by Arena Stage, is written with such compassion and such
vigorous low comedy that it almost gives the lie to its basic
nihilism. We are alone, it says, drawing us into common brotherhood with Didi and Gogo. We are dying, it says, giving us a
renewed sense of life. Reason is a snare and communication a
delusion. And we understand and our thoughts are enriched.

Hooted at and howled over a mere 23 years ago, "Waiting
for Godot" has waited for us to catch up. Its seeming obfusca-
tions have revealed themselves as illuminations. What was
thought by some to be a ludicrous belittlement of mankind is now
seen as Beckett's rigorous admiration for our gallant attempts
to carry on through another nightfall.

As soon as the bright white lights go up, it is clear that
this is going to be one of Arena's very special evenings. Those
lights shine down on a yellow pine floor, an eroded boulder and
a hapless tree, designed by Ming Cho Lee to suggest both the
stark simplicity of the Kabuki theater and the polished planks of
the musical hall.

Things are immediately right. For if Beckett's play is stark,
it is also rowdy with echoes of vaudeville's baggy pants comics.
Didi and Gogo despair, but they also can't always get their shoes
off. They meditate on the point of things and they take spectacular pratfalls. They contemplate suicide, but they swap jokes as
well, munch radishes, play games with their bowler hats and,
in moments of unaccountable euphoria, tap out a little soft shoe
or sketch abortive tours jetes on the planking.

Director Gene Lesser has found a perfectly matched team in
Max Wright (Didi) and Howard Witt (Gogo)--the spindly eccentricity of the former playing grandly off the sulking petulance of the

latter. There is a scruffy razzle-dazzle to their performances, even when they're voicing variations on the same old complaints, that is triumphantly theatrical. Lesser has found the fine line between ham and pathos, and the actors seesaw adroitly the evening long.

Their waiting games are interrupted in each of the two acts by Pozzo, a rotund master of bluster and command, and Lucky, his white-haired porter tethered to the end of a long rope. Just as Didi and Gogo find themselves increasingly immobilized, Pozzo and Lucky wheeze and stomp their way across the stage on a mindless mission to nowhere. Lord and lackey? Boss and worker? Oppressor and oppressed? Yes, and more: they are a perverse embodiment of the movers, as opposed to the waiters, of the world.

Pozzo (brilliantly enacted by Mark Hammer as an oily Middle European tyrant) chats with smug authority about everything and nothing. He nibbles drumsticks from a silver platter, magnanimously casting the bones aside. Lucky dances for their entertainment (Michael Mertz' portrayal of decrepitude is amazing), only his dance is more like a clawing for fleas. So Pozzo yanks the rope around Lucky's neck and orders him to think, whereupon Lucky spews forth a torrent of gibberish.

Entertainment over, time passed, they move on. But they will return later--Pozzo blind and Lucky even more bent. Alliances have been forged; habit has soldered the chains. We all make do.

When in the second act, the four of them collapse to the floor and, like beetles on their backs, kick their limbs furiously to right themselves, you have as vivid a stage image of man's basic impotence as you'll ever see.

It may sound strange to talk of poetry in this context, but poetry it is, stripped so close to the bone you can almost taste the marrow. It is merely another of the evening's paradoxes, however, that "Waiting for Godot" has an ultimate fullness to it as a play.

Beckett's fierce creativity and Arena's matching intelligence are filling the very void they have both set out to depict.

RIDLEY, Clifford Anthony; (2) Theater Critic and Arts Editor; (3) b. New York City, March 12, 1935; (4) s. Edmund C. and Mabelle R.; (5) A.B. Brown U., cum laude, major subj.: English literature, 1956; (6) m. Sharon Krock, April 14, 1968; (7) Stepchildren--Paula Gaye and Robyn Michelle Krock; (8) Successively staff writer, city editor, managing editor, also music and drama critic, Westport (Conn.) Town Crier, 1956-61; successively feature editor, news editor, senior editor, The National Observer, 1961- ; Observer film

critic, 1966-71, arts columnist 1971-74, theater critic 1971- ; (16)
Democrat; (17) Jewish; (20) ed. anthology The Arts Explosion (Dow
Jones, 1972); (21) 1539 Live Oak Dr. , Silver Spring, Md. 20910,
Ph. 301-589-7351; (22) The National Observer, 11501 Columbia Pike,
Silver Spring, Md. 20910, Ph. 301-622-2900; (23) Circulation:
540,000; (24) 70 plays and musicals, 30 books, films, concerts, etc.

The Musical's Future: On the "Line"
(by Clifford A. Ridley, National Observer, June 14, 1975)

Nobody calls it Musical Theater 101, but that's about what
it is--three new musical evenings that suggest where the American musical has been, where it's going, and where, if you will
excuse me, it's at. The three weren't planned as a pedagogical
exercise, of course; only the roll of the Broadway dice has
joined them in such fortuitous combination. Still, here they are.
If we watch and listen, we may learn something.

The musical past, first of all? That would be embodied in
Rodgers & Hart, a delightful compendium of some 100 tunes
that Richard Rodgers and Lorenz Hart wrote during their fecund
collaboration from 1918 to 1943. The songs are sung and danced,
revue-style, by a young, energetic company of 12 (take note,
please, of the pert Ms. Jamie Donnelly and the winsome Mr.
Wayne Bryan) with nary a scrap of dialog between them, but don't
think for a moment that director Burt Shevelove--or whoever
ordered these numbers in such witty and telling counterpoint--
didn't know what he was about. The simplicity of the evening is
like the simplicity of its songs: wickedly deceptive. The studied
artlessness of Rodgers' melodies and (those incessant interior
rhymes notwithstanding) Hart's lyrics masked a joint sensibility
in which sentiment and reality existed in precarious, unpredictable alliance: Yesterday I Married An Angel, but today I'm Be-
witched, Bothered and Bewildered. Rodgers and Hart were onto
a new direction in musical comedy, and it was called honesty.

Yes, they knew how to write songs back then, but don't forget that's about all they did: The books that those songs adorned
were negligible things, no more than bridges between musical
numbers, and the staging of them was mostly rudimentary. Oklahoma! in case you've forgotten, changed all that. As the first
musical with a book that made sense, with songs that addressed
character as well as situation, with dancing that sprang from the
interior life of the show, it made the American musical comedy
the American musical play, and the form flourished for the next
two decades. Our little survey, sadly, contains no exemplar of
this musical heyday; would someone care to revive South Pacific?

Perhaps inevitably, though, the stagecraft unleashed by this
new idea of the "total musical" began to assume a life of its
own, to become not cause but effect. The apotheosis of that development is now at hand; it's called Chicago.

Chicago, subtitled "A Musical Vaudeville," is the latest creation of Bob Fosse, the director-choreographer who gave us Pippin. Oh, sure, it has a musical score and lyrics, by John Kander and Fred Ebb; they're altogether agreeable, if seldom much more. It even has a book of sorts, by Fosse and Ebb from an old play by one Maurine Dallas Watkins, which has to do with a tootsie named Roxie Hart who shoots her lover in 1920s Chicago, goes to jail, hires a smart mouthpiece, beats the rap, and emerges as half a singing duo. (The other half is Velma Kelly, who is like Roxie, only dumber.)

But make no mistake; Chicago is Bob Fosse's show, a spectacular triumph of pure stagecraft. Prison-cell bars glide across the stage; the singing shyster strips behind scarlet fans; Roxie and Velma strut in trench coats and fedoras. Why? Because it looks good--and, to be fair, does it ever. (Two numbers even succeed dramatically: Roxie at a press conference portrayed as a dummy to her lawyer's ventriloquist, and Roxie's wronged husband done up in a baggy clown outfit to sing a touching song called "Cellophane.") The spare sets, the dazzling lighting effects, the minimal costumes (at maximal cost, no doubt) ... smashing, every one. And the cast? Well, Roxie is the incomparable Gwen Verdon, all bumps and wriggles; Velma is the demonic Chita Rivera, 20,000 volts of untamed electricity; and the mouthpiece, Billy Flynn, is the engaging Jerry Orbach. Get the picture?

It all looks so good that you may overlook the fact that it's pretty much a reprise of Bob Fosse's Greatest Hits--notably Pippin, of course (observe the ragtag chorus), but also a lot of other shows stretching all the way back to The Pajama Game. Fosse's has been an odd career; the theater is supposed to have grown from vaudeville, not back to it. Yet here he is, seeking nothing more than to recapture that mythically innocent era, with his scenes announced in vaudeville-turn fashion and his band suspended in full view above the stage. It's all very disarming, but it's also pointless; today we want something more, and Chicago is empty at the center. "Why am I sitting here?" you may ask, and the play will give you back no answer but cheap, muzzy cynicism and another burst of frantic razzmatazz. For many, even at $17.50 a ticket, that will be enough. It wasn't for me.

Have we no longer a choice, then, between the musical that's all songs and the musical that's all stagecraft? Happily, we do. In attempting to reproduce 1920s Chicago not literally but as an abstraction, Bob Fosse hints at where the musical seems destined to proceed; the trouble is that he has produced a cluttered abstraction, which is something of a contradiction in terms. A Chorus Line knows better.

The new musical in Joe Papp's downtown Newman Theater transpires on a bare stage backed by an enormous mirror that now and then flipflops to black. You are eavesdropping on an audition for a Broadway musical; after early winnowing, 16 dancers remain to compete for 8 positions in the line. They array themselves across the stage, face front, to respond one by one to questions posed from the back of the auditorium by the director. And we are off and hoofing.

Think, for a moment, of a chorus line. An entity, right? A multiheaded, multilegged creature whose parts perform in perfect synchronization? Of course right, and at the end A Chorus Line gives you that image, in a stunning unison number appropriately titled "One." But until that moment the show gives you the chorus line not in long shot but in close-up; it separates those heads and limbs to reveal 16 individuated souls whose talents, motivations, backgrounds, responses, fears, and aspirations are entirely unlike. In solo musical turns and spoken monologs, in fragmented interpolations, in contrapuntal groups of two or three or four, they lay their lives before you. There is a danger in this approach: Now and then the evening turns momentarily static. But not for long.

If such a schema sounds strikingly like Life itself (and the director, who has his own hang-ups, like some quixotic God), the resemblance is not, I think, accidental. Yet A Chorus Line knows better than to insist on its larger meanings; it knows that Truth writ large derives entirely from fidelity to observed detail. Thus its characters are no mere stock types; behind every burst of braggadocio peeps a nagging hunk of insecurity, and vice versa. And thus, as in both the theater and in life, sentiment and toughness exist throughout the show in uneasy cohabitation. In this sense, at least, we are back partway to Rodgers and Hart.

Credits: The hard-headed book is by James Kirkwood and Nicholas Dante, although a lot of it is the result of improvisation by the cast. The gritty lyrics and music, both of which owe a debt to Company (as does the entire show, and what better?) are by Edward Kleban and Marvin Hamlisch. The marvelous lighting, which does so much both to isolate and unite the performers, is by Tharon Musser. The cast is exceptional all 'round; if I particularly mention Pamela Blair, Priscilla Lopez, and especially Donna McKechnie (whose solo dance is literally breath-taking), I am in no wise slighting anyone else. And the conception, direction, and choreography are by Michael Bennett, who has wrought a small miracle. Yes this is his show; but unlike Bob Fosse, he has placed his enormous talents in the service of theme and character, not of himself. God bless him.

Betrayal Haunts a Reunion: A Sad Enigma From Russia
(by Clifford A. Ridley, National Observer, June 21, 1975)

On first look, it's a paradox: The Russian theater, which of all the world's dramas may consistently have been the most

political and philosophical, has mostly flourished under conditions
of censorship and repression--first the czars', then the Soviets'.
But the paradox, as critic Andrew R. MacAndrew has pointed
out is only apparent, for "in a society with restricted freedom
of expression, art forms become the natural vehicles for voicing
dissent." Barred from framing their ideas about man and his
institutions in public statements or polemical essays, Russian
writers early discovered that otherwise unacceptable notions could
at least be suggested in the dramatic argument of a play or a
novel, that dissatisfaction with things as they were could be conveyed in the over-all impact of a story. The discovery was not
without its artistic hazards, of course, among them a certain
prolixity; the man walking through mine fields is unlikely to proceed in a straight line. But the hazards have been small price
for a tradition that addresses some of man's deepest needs with
humanity, wit, and intellectual rigor.

That the tradition continues down to the present is clear
from The Ascent of Mount Fuji, a fascinating contemporary Russian drama by Chingiz Aitmatov and Kaltai Mukhamedzhanov that
is receiving its American premiere from the Arena Stage here.
The play gathers four middle-aged men, former schoolmates,
together with the wives of three of them for a weekend camping
reunion atop a small mountain in central Asia, which one of the
wives has christened "Fuji" after the extinct Japanese volcano
to which Buddhists repair to address their consciences. The
reunionists are something of a cross section of the Soviet "middle class"--they include two teachers, a pompous scientist, a
statefarm manager, a writer, an actress, and a lady doctor--
and they are failed, unhappy creatures to the last man and woman. "Oh dreams, where has your sweetness gone?" asks one
in a lament for them all.

It is on this level of false promises and blasted lives--two
in the party are having an affair, the writer has squandered his
talent on travel articles, the scientist is a useless man, the actress despairs over not having had a child--that The Ascent of
Mount Fuji is most effective. Human heartbreak and disillusion,
after all, are the same the world over. But there is another
thread to the play, which comes gradually clearer at the prod-
ding of the old schoolteacher whom the reunionists have invited
to the mountaintop. Once, these four students were five, and
the fifth of them, a poet named Sabur, was the most talented of
all. During the war, however, when the quintet enlisted en
masse in the army, the poet wrote an unacceptably pacifistic
poem and was betrayed to the authorities by one of the others.
Although he was eventually exonerated of wrong, he has become
a broken man, a lush abandoned by his family.

So we are dealing, clearly, with questions of responsibility
and guilt--collective guilt, as it turns out, for each of these men,
in his own way, wronged their comrade in his time of need. Nor
have they yet come to terms with the incident, and in the second

of the play's three acts they rip it apart like dogs worrying a common bone. The scientist justifies the betrayal "in the interests of the general good." One of the wives protests that the disputed poem was never even published; "all he did was think." Several in the group liken the relationship between the poet and the travel writer to that of Mozart and Salieri, the composer who once was alleged (in a story apparently still popular with the Russians) to have poisoned his rival. The old teacher announces that communism itself has not fulfilled her expectations.

This is fascinating stuff, but along the way it poses some problems as drama, in the way that long, on-stage discussions of offstage people and events (particularly events that occurred nearly three decades earlier) are wont to do. There are other difficulties with the evening as well: Its handling of exposition is fairly elemental, its dialog is often stilted (perhaps that is the fault of the translation by Nicholas Bethell), its shuttling of characters in and out of the others' earshot is arbitrary and awkward, and its ending is feeble and unnecessarily enigmatic. After all is said, though, you forgive these crudities and lapses in the interest of the play's search for truth--a limited truth, perhaps, but truth nonetheless. In its encompassing vision of an imperfect society peopled less by independent men and women than by role-players, The Ascent of Mount Fuji is in direct succession to the works of Gorki--he, I think, more than Chekhov-- as well as a fine, disturbing evening in its own right.

Under Zelda Fichandler's direction, the cast mostly does its material full justice. One or two seem to lose more control than the script suggests, but there are especially notable performances from Vivian Nathan, as the old schoolteacher; Dianne Wiest, as the actress; and Halo Wines, as the farm manager's dissatisfied wife. And a special word for Ming Cho Lee's mountaintop set, whose desolation mirrors the lives of those who assemble on it.

RIESEL, Victor; (2) Newspaper columnist; (8) Directs an hour-long talk show on radio; has syndicated newspaper column printed in 357 daily newspapers; appears on Metromedia's television news; (10) Consultant on foreign affairs to the American Foundation on Automation and Employment; member of the commercial panel of the American Arbitration Association; (14) Has won 22 major journalistic awards; (15) President, Past Vice-President, and member of Board of Governors of the Overseas Press Club; Vice President of the Association of Radio and Television News Analysts; (20) The Strike--For and Against, 1971, Hart Publishing Co.; (22) Field Newspaper Syndicate, 30 East 42 Street, New York, N.Y. 10017, Ph. 212-681-5560 or 401 North Wabash Avenue, Chicago, Ill. 60611, Ph. 312-321-2795; (23) Circulation: 23 million.

ROBERTS, John, New Haven Register, 367 Orange St., New Haven, Conn. 06503

ROZMIAREK, Joseph, The Honolulu Advertiser, P. O. Box 3110, Honolulu, HI 96802.

RUBENSTEIN, Nancy; (2) Theatre Reviewer/Critic; (3) b. Fall River, Mass., Feb. 8, 1929; (4) d. Ralph and Rose (Edelstein) R.; (5) B.A. Boston University--Liberal Arts; (6) m. Edwin Rubenstein, Sept. 23, 1951; (7) Son--David Alan; (8) Editor-Writer-Reviewer, Today Newspapers July 1970- ; (9) Treasurer, New Jersey Drama Critics Assn.; (10) Scout leader-past, PTA; (15) Charter Member, N.J. Drama Critics Assn.; (16) Independent; (17) Jewish; (18) B'nai B'rith Women; (19) Women's American ORT, past president, past regional vice president; Temple Menorah Woman's Club; American Assn. of University Women; (20) By-line column appears weekly; numerous feature stories; (21) 33 Meadowbrook Lane, Cedar Grove, N.J. 07009, Ph. 201-256-8436; (22) Today Newspapers, 1661 Route 23, Wayne, N.J. 07470, Ph. 201-696-3000; (23) Circulation: appx. 147,000 in 27 towns; (24) 35 plays and musicals, 5 dance, 5 miscellaneous.

"A Little Night Music" Deserves Much Praise
(by Nancy Rubenstein, Today Newspapers, January 15, 1975)

The award winning musical "A Little Night Music" opened on Friday at the Playhouse on the Mall at the Bergen Mall in Paramus, bringing its audience proof that not only does this show deserve the many praises it has received, but also proving that its star, Dorothy Collins, still has the captivating voice and the vitality that earned her fame years ago in the old "Your Hit Parade" days.

Especially outstanding are the brilliant lyrics by Stephen Sondheim. Rapid-fire, the patter-style lyrics are clever and sparkling. The chorus in this production really handles them well with expert delivery and careful enunciation and clear fine voices.

"A Little Night Music" is a musical version of "Smiles of a Summer Night," by Swedish film-maker Ingmar Bergman. It is set in the carefree early days of this century and centers about the romantic matchings and mismatchings of four couples among the silver birches surrounding a Swedish chateau on a country weekend. It is one of the few occasions in which a film becomes a theatrical production instead of the reverse, and it is an outstanding example of how effectively the switch can be maneuvered.

The comedy involves an actress, an attorney trying to renew his unrenewable life and his wife, her lover, his wife, the attorney's son and assorted other characters. Presiding over the liasons is the grandmother, capably played by Nancy Andrews in a salty, dominant manner.

Ronald Holgate, real-life husband of Dorothy Collins, plays the lawyer, Fredrik Egerman, opposite his wife and there is no question that Holgate is a star himself. His resonant voice and easy manner find him extremely well cast as the old flame of Desiree Armfeldt, seeking to recapture the love they once shared.

"Solitare is the only game that should be played honestly" declares Nancy Andrews as Madame Armfeldt, the knowing ex-mistress of assorted dukes and kings as she regally hosts her weekend guests. The proceedings follow, deceptively, as suggested by the aging grandmother.

Although Linda Byrne is a bit weak, the major roles are generally superbly played. Richard Cooper Bayne is an appealing, sympathetic Henrick, Nancy Andrew is most convincing, Ronald Holgate is strong and Dorothy Collins is delightful. "Send in the Clowns" gives her a vehicle to exhibit her talent splendidly.

Beth Fowler makes the absolute most of her role as Countess Charlotte Malcolm opposite a properly stuffy Bob Gunton as Count Carl-Magnus Malcolm.

A second round of applause should go to Dale Butler, Patti Allison, Marsha Bagwell and Donald Craig as a bright and outstanding chorus. George Martin directs this production and Frank Desmond designed the scenery, which received a spontaneous ovation from the audience especially in the banquet segment.

"A Little Night Music" is pure pleasure. After all, if 30 of Hal Prince's people turned out to see it again in this production after such a long association with it on Broadway, it just has to be great theatre.

"Fat Friend" Is Hot Hit
(by Nancy Rubenstein, Today Newspapers, February 12, 1975)

"My Fat Friend" opened on Friday, February 7 at the Playhouse on the Mall at the Bergen Mall, Route 4 in Paramus, and it just may be one of the funniest comedies ever to hit the boards. With a cast of only four performers, this great little show is punctuated with one laugh after another, and I mean LAUGH ... not smiles, not chuckles but honest out-loud laughs.

The script is by Charles Laurence imported from England with sparkling dry English wit. It is performed to perfection by all of its four players, but most especially by Brian Bedford, who employs every nuance and milks the absolute most out of every line.

The story is fairly simple. Vicky Harris, a bookshop owner

and boarding house landlady, is gorging her way toward the 200-pound plus weight bracket and has reached the stage where she can only fit into her "fat dress," an enormous tent-type affair. One of her two boarders, Henry Simpson (Brian Bedford) tries in vain to convince Vicky to diet seriously but it isn't until she meets Tom, a handsome young man who scouts new oil fields for an international company, that Vicky agrees to fight the battle of the bulge. Tom dates her despite her obesity but leaves the next day on a trip to Iran for four months and Vicky's fat fight begins.

Almost predictably, Vicky drops some 60 pounds before Tom's return and, also predictably, Tom is turned off by her new svelte figure. As Henry says "Tom is doomed to a life of hanging around outside Weight Watchers classes ... hooked on mountains of flesh."

Although the story line is light, the two-act play moves very quickly, paced by hysterical dialogue.

Stephen C. Bradbury plays Tom nicely and John Lithgow plays James. Vicky's other boarder, a ne'er-do-well author who manages the role he played so brilliantly in the Broadway production with a halting, shy Scottish accent and a boyish [manner]....

RUBIN, Joan Alleman; (2) Editor-in-chief, Playbill· Magazine; (3) b. Hanover, Penna., Oct. 1, 1931; (4) d. Richard and Katherine (Eckert) Alleman; (5) College of William and Mary, B.A.; philosophy 1953; (6) m. Robert Rubin July 30, 1955; (7) children--Thomas, and Andrew; (8) Mademoiselle Magazine--1954 to 1961 assistant to feature Ed., Assoc. Travel Ed., Career Ed.; (9) Drama Desk, member 1975 Tony Award Nominating Committee; (10) Chairman of Heart Fund, theatre division; (12) Vice-President of Film Modules, Inc.; (21) 172 Sullivan Street, NYC 10012, Ph. CA 8-7648; (22) Playbill, 151 E. 50, NYC 10022, Ph. 751-9550; (23) Circulation: 920,000 theatregoers per month; (24) Approx. 20 articles on the arts per year.

Theatregoers' Scrapbook
(by Joan Alleman Rubin, Playbill, April 1975)

No Matter What Their Passports Say Those Men Are Actors.... Two of the finest performers currently on Broadway have entered this country on passports which list them not as "actors" but as "domestics." The two are John Kani and Winston Ntshona, the young South Africans in Athol Fugard's Sizwe Banzi is Dead and The Island, playing in repertory at the Edison Theatre.

Because of South Africa's strict apartheid rules, the category of "actor" simply does not exist for black men.

Consequently, the playwright was forced to officially hire Kani and Ntshona as his garden boys.

Sizwe Banzi and The Island, which had a long run in London and now are doing very well in New York, were never performed in a real theatre in South Africa. Both plays, however, were successful in S. A. 's "underground theatre"--stores, private homes, abandoned factories--where invited interracial (illegal) audiences gather.

"Tony Book".... What dramatic play received last year's "Tony?" Who has collected the most Tony awards over the years? The answers to these and all the other "who got what when" questions can be found in a new book, The "Tony" Award, compiled by the American Theatre Wing and published by Arno Press/A New York Times Company.

The hard cover book includes the nominees in all categories, together with all the winners' names and a history of the Wing, which founded the "Tony" awards almost 30 years ago in honor of Antoinette Perry.

P. S. Just in case you can't wait until you get your copy of the book--The River Niger was last year's best dramatic play and Hal Prince has received the most Tony awards--9 (followed by Bob Fosse with 7).

The Irregulars Are Regulars At The Broadhurst.... Everybody's happy that the Royal Shakespeare Co's production of Sherlock Holmes has settled in for a long run in New York. But there's one group that finds it a special treat. That's the Baker Street Irregulars, 120 otherwise apparently sane men and women, who are a little nutty about Holmes. One "irregular," Norman Nolan, a New Jersey computer executive, told me that the group breaks into three factions--(1) Conan Doyle collectors. Mr. Nolan is definitely one--he owns an original Holmes manuscript and three rooms of Baker Street memorabilia, including a two-foot replica of Holmes' study, recreated by his artist wife. (2) Fans of the Holmes character and the Victorian era. (3) Holmes scholars. These last, Mr. Nolan said, spend a lot of time arguing about when Holmes' cocaine habit began and ended or whether Dr. Watson's war wound was in the shoulder or the leg.

At any rate, all the regulars got together a month or so ago for their annual dinner and theatre party and they went to see-- guess what? "Incredible as it may seem," said Mr. Nolan, "I didn't hear one unfavorable criticism. In fact one of our older members remembers seeing William Gillette's original production and he pronounced this one better." Many Irregulars have been back to see Sherlock Holmes more than once. Mr. Nolan has seen it twice and expects to see it several more times--"After all there are only 60 Sherlock Holmes stories and now there's this play and it's here in New York and most of us agree we can't get enough of it."

East Side/West Side.... Several years ago when four new
theatres opened on Broadway there was no end to the hoopla.
So isn't it only fair that some attention should be paid to the
very first theatre to open on Manhattan's East Side in 50 years.
The 250-seat theatre, which is complete with a full orchestra
pit, is part of Marymount Manhattan College's new educational
complex on E. 71st St. It has been designed to handle dance,
drama, film, music and opera; and though it will be used primarily as a lab/workshop for students it will also be available
next fall for bookings. Marymount's Theatre shows every promise of becoming a lively "East Side" center for the arts.

And That Ain't Chopped Liver.... Diamond Studs, that knee-
slapping, toe-tapping musical revue about Jesse James, which is
currently packing 'em in at the Chelsea's Westside Theatre, reports that its audiences consume 150 pounds of peanuts a week.
That's not bad, but Diamond Studs will have to go a long way to
match that other Chelsea Theatre production Candide. The
Broadway Theatre told us that since Candide has taken up residence there, audiences have purchased, shelled and devoured
13 tons of peanuts.

A New Moon.... Mark May 27th on your calendar and at
8:30 turn off your neighbors and turn on your television sets.
That's the night that ABC is presenting Eugene O'Neill's A Moon
for the Misbegotten, with Colleen Dewhurst and Jason Robards.
The production sponsored by the Mobil Oil Corporation is a TV
recreation of the 1973 Broadway revival for which Miss Dewhurst
won the Tony for best actress and Mr. Jose Quintero the award
for best director.

Are You Ready For Queen Victoria?.... There's a strange
and rather wonderful theatrical event at the ANTA Theatre
(through April 20). It's Robert Wilson's A Letter for Queen
Victoria. It's not really a play, since there's no plot, and it's
not really dance, since there are words. And it's not really
about Queen Victoria, although Wilson has imported his 88-year-
old grandmother from Waco, Texas, to play the title role. What
it is, is 3 hours worth of images, movement, music and words
that make no sense at all, but somehow add up to an unusual
experience if you're patient enough to sit still and let it happen.... Wilson, who created, directed and acts in the piece,
is a former architect and painter, who turned to theatre because
he found the images in his head were more vivid than anything
he could put on canvas.

Ingrid Bergman's Year.... On April 14, Ms. Bergman
opens in a limited engagement of Maugham's comedy The Constant Wife. The theatre: The Shubert. The director: John
Gielgud. The Outlook: long lines at the B.O.

Alumni Report.... Years ago, it was Professor Baker's
Workshop at Harvard which supplied the theatre with some of

its most distinguished playwrights. Then Catholic University seemed to take over as the incubator for theatrical talents--both in writing and acting. Some of its former students and teachers include: Jason Miller, author of That Championship Season; Mart Crowley, The Boys in the Band; James Rado, Hair; directors Alan Schneider and Robert Moore; Jean and Walter Kerr; Jon Voight, Bibi Osterwald, Pat Carroll.... But recently, we were told by Tony Roberts of Absurd Person Singular that his class at Northwestern ('61) includes a pretty impressive list of show business luminaries. In addition to Tony, there's Paula Prentiss, Dick Benjamin, Karen Black, Penny Fuller, Marcia Rodd, Larry Pressman, Nancy Dessault, Marshall Mason, Stewart Hagman and Ron Hussman.

Marriage on the Rocks?
(by Joan Alleman Rubin, Playbill, May 1975)

Whatever problems the institution of marriage may be having elsewhere, it seems to be keeping its good name on Broadway. Pippin ends in an ode to reluctant togetherness. Absurd Person Singular gives a glimpse of three couples who are sticking through sick and sin. In Praise of Love endorses that old fashioned romantic notion that a "good wife" always makes her husband believe he is the strong one, despite all evidence to the contrary.

And now, of course, there's Same Time, Next Year, the biggest hit in a smashing season and a play destined for longevity on Broadway and a heftier afterlife than Marley's ghost (two characters, one set, a universally appealing plot--you can expect it in stock companies, dinner theatres, community theaters for decades).

The play is about a man and woman, both married, but not to each other, who rendezvous in the same motel once each year for 25 years. (We see them in 1951, '56, '61, '65, '70, '75.) The two characters, Doris and George, played brilliantly by Ellen Burstyn and Charles Grodin, are likeable, decent people, who care for each other and for their respective spouses--each time they meet she tells him one good and one bad story about her husband; he tells her one good and one bad story about his wife. It's a warm, rewarding, safe relationship. There's never much doubt in their minds, or in the minds of the audience, that their marriages will stay intact.

In an age which glorifies "now," Same Time, Next Year stresses "now and then." The play comes on strong for the positive value of having someone who sees and loves, not only the person you are this year, but all those other people you've been along the way. Now that's a pretty conventional (really not a dirty word) notion and I was curious to see if the playwright, Bernard Slade, a former actor and television writer might (under his beard and fading California tan) turn out to be an old-fashioned man.

"I've been married 20 years ... these days some people think that's ridiculous, so I say it in a low voice," Slade told me. "I can't say I buy the abstract idea of spending all of one's life with the same person, as a matter of fact in the abstract it sounds pretty terrible. I believe my wife Jill and I have been incredibly lucky. I guess one secret to a long marriage is liking each other. The other is having a life apart from the marriage --not being thought of as a pair." (When the Slades married in the early 50's, both were actors in Canada. Ten years ago when Bernard and Jill and their two children moved to L.A., Jill went back to college. In the play Doris also returns to college where she describes herself as "the only person in the class with a clear complexion," a line Slade confesses unabashedly is Jill's.)

So we can assume that Bernard Slade knows something about marriage, and though he does not pretend to have written a play on the subject ("Same Time, Next Year is an entertainment; it sometimes embarrasses me to discuss the ideas in it"), the relationship between the two characters Doris and George appears to be more "married" than illicit. It's not the same bed we see them sharing over the years (there's no explicit sex in the play); it's one another's embarrassment, guilt, success, grief, failure, even a pregnancy--hers by her husband.

"Most people," Slade told me, "buy Erica Jong's fantasy of the 'zipless fuck,'" the faceless, nameless roll in the hay with no messy involvements. "It's a great fantasy, but it doesn't work with human beings. They come in with feelings of guilt and loyalty. They have a past as well as a present."

You began to understand that the past is important to Bernard Slade. He told me, for example, of having once been asked about his long marriage on a Canadian TV interview ... "I found myself replying, 'we have 2 dogs, one is 14-years-old and the other is 16-years old. Our car is 10-years-old. We just seem to keep things.' Afterwards, Jill asked me indignantly if I couldn't find something more positive to say, but I felt that was positive. I can understand the excitement and novelty of discovering a new person, exploring new feelings, finding out about another life; but there's a kind of shorthand that grows up in a long relationship that I value."

To illustrate his point, Bernard Slade told two stories about friends of his who had recently split with their wives. "One friend told me he'd stopped dating because he didn't think he could stand 'one more girl asking me what sign I was born under?' The other confessed that he knew he was in trouble when on the 'fourth time I told my life's story--I fell asleep.'"

In Same Time, Next Year, Bernard Slade hit on the perfect compromise--a long, nonthreatening extramarital relationship which combines continuity and novelty--"At the end of the play," Slade told me, "even though Doris and George have known each other for 25 years, they've been together for only five weeks."

It's interesting that the idea for Same Time, Next Year came out of a holiday Bernard and his wife Jill took at an isolated inn near Mendocino. "Because of its remoteness, we started to talk to each other in a new way, and I got the idea of doing a two-character play in which a man and woman are together in a hotel room and only at the end do you find out they are married." Slade later rejected this plot, partially because "Pinter had already done it." But he never gave up on his basic plan "to write a two-character play that would make people laugh and touch them too." The opportunity came when he had an "artistic and contractual disagreement" with his television studio and found himself on a plane for Hawaii. By the time the plane landed in Honolulu, Bernard Slade had an outline for Same Time, Next Year. Six weeks later he had a finished script--"Nothing ever writes itself," he said, "but this play came as close to it as possible."

One of the unexpected aspects of being the author of Same Time, Next Year is that Bernard Slade has suddenly become the recipient of all kinds of interesting confidences. Two elderly blue-haired matinee ladies told him emphatically "We've decided that if we're going to do that at our age we'd better make it once a month." A Boston Brahmin whispered to him quietly one evening, "You'd be surprised how many marriages are kept alive by an extramarital affair." And just recently Slade received an extraordinary letter from a college professor who admitted to a relationship that was in its 26th year. The professor and "his lady," each married with a number of children, agreed that, except for the obvious dramatic device of having the couple meet only once a year, Slade presented "a pretty accurate picture of what I suspect is a not uncommon situation." The professor went on to write, "You accept such a situation when you have lived with it for years and indeed there is a lurking fear on each side that the only reason you are still fond of each other is that you do not live together. It's one of those notions that no one cares to admit. At the same time everyone knows that the basic trouble with marriage is that you are stuck with a partner. It is boredom that kills marriage in the last analysis."

And in the last analysis, it's also boredom that kills the theatre. Maybe that's why we're all so grateful to Bernard Slade. Same Time, Next Year is touching, funny, occasionally sad, but never boring--not for a minute.

RUSSELL, Kathlyn Wilson; (2) Sunday supplement editor and reviewer, Escondido Times-Advocate; (3) b. Trinidad, W.I. Feb. 8, 1927; (4) d. R. Sydney and Marie (Corsbie) Smith; (5) B.A. English Lang. and Lit., Victoria College, U. of Toronto, 1950; postgraduate studies English lit. Bedford College, Univ. of London, England, 1951; (6) Divorced; (7) children--Alan, 15; Maureen, 11; (8) Staff writer and

reviewer, Trinidad Evening News, 1951 to 1953, Staff writer, entertainment editor, reviewer, Escondido (Calif) Times-Advocate 1965--
(part time staff writer previously); (9) Years of consistent attendance
at live performances in four countries, social and official contacts
with persons in the arts; (10) Member Escondido Cultural Arts Committee 1972-74; Cultural Arts Commission 1974-75; Escondido Oratorio
Association 1960-69; La Jolla Recorder Society, 1961-63; founding
member and vice chairman Escondido Regional Arts Council, 1974-
75; Escondido Democratic Club 1960-66, Treasurer North San Diego
County Press Club 1973-74; (21) 2585 Felicita Rd., Escondido, Calif.
92025, Ph. 714-745-5091; (22) 207 E. Pennsylvania Ave., Escondido
Calif. 92025, Ph. 745-6611; (23) Circulation: 29,000 daily; (24) 50-
55 plus Sunday column on the arts.

Frost Comes Alive in Palomar Production
(by Kathlyn Russell, Times-Advocate, February 6, 1975)

Robert Frost is being rediscovered as a major playwright as
well as a major poet through the presentations of a San Francisco theater group called "The Open Eye."

In a recent multimedia (meaning music, acting, dance, mime,
not film media) production at Palomar College the small company
dramatized a group of Frost's poems and a one-act play he wrote
called "A Masque of Reason."

Frost's magic as a poet is that he creates deeply-moving and
lyrical poetry out of a prosaic vocabulary while dealing with the
everyday emotions of people of the soil.

The heightened language and deep emotional values come out
of the distillation and selectivity of words and phrases to express
the personal values which everyone recognizes and identifies with
but to which the ordinary person seldom dares give expression.

These values are enhanced many times in a dramatized presentation of the poems. Never, for instance, has the "The
Death of the Hired Man" been as poignant as in this performance
when the farmer and his wife are real people. And never has
the abrasive understructure of a marriage been gashed open so
rawly as in the staged version of "Home Burial."

This is an excellent example of how refined and sensitive
theatrical productions become when a small company works together all the time. The interaction between performers, in
character and as actor to actor, is so finely-honed it carries
over easily into the audience, even in a presentation like the one
at Palomar where the relatively small audience wasn't at all sure
what it was going to see and the surroundings of a two-thirds
empty gymnasium almost were in opposition to the intimacy of
the performance.

The simple sets and basic costumes and the superiority of

the three musicians contributed to the spellbinding quality of the performance.

The cast includes John FitzGibbon, Lee McClelland, John Genke, Wendy Erdman with Dan Erkkila taking one part in the play, which is a modernized version of the aftermath of the "Job" story and involves a witty and satiric dialogue between Job and his wife (a Southern belle), God and Satan, in the most fantastic (in the sense of fantasy) costume imaginable.

If you ever get a chance to see this group again, grab it. They have some other programs and they tour. Not enough credit is given in the program to the musicians, but the same people (John Genke, Teiji Ito, Dan Erkkila) and the actors conceived, composed, directed and everything.

They use a great variety of musical styles, from avant-garde atonal to square dance and folk-rock, but always are true to Frost, not violating a single phrase or concept. It's quiet entertainment, and very moving.

"Don Juan" Hits the Mark
(by Kathlyn Russell, Times-Advocate, February 14, 1975)

The art of conversation is like the bald eagle--a disappearing national treasure, of no marketable value but a natural resource we can ill afford to be without.

The conservation of conversation is in preserves, like the theater, and has its moguls, like Tom Stoppard and Christopher Fry and, of course, George Bernard Shaw.

There is no rational defense for the survival of Shaw's preachifying episode from "Man and Superman," "Don Juan in Hell," as a popular theater piece in a day when multimedia or bust is the battle cry and people demand total titillation of the senses from the most basic entertainment forms.

Yet survive it does, like the bald eagle in spite of freeways through the mountains and DDT on the brush. People keep touring with it, reviving it in the most unlikely places, and going to see (no, hear) it although the ideas designed to make the smugly moral Victorians apoplectic have no more than a mild historical interest any more.

Or have they? There is that question, popping up again on the occasions when, as on current Thursdays, Fridays and Saturdays at the Patio Playhouse, one has an opportunity to be in the room with the entire "Don Juan in Hell" text again.

The version that opened Thursday night to a handful of the faithful or the curious is done in readers' theater, and the four dramatic readers are Stan Rubin as Don Juan, the ladies' man,

Susan Thiss as the Victorian woman incarnate, Richard Gant as the Devil and Curt Babcock as a former army officer and father to the lady.

All three have died and are in hell, with the lady as a new arrival accosted by her former lover and learning that her revered father has been in heaven but is moving to hell because heaven is so dull.

They talk--and how they talk, trading ideas and letting them develop to the end of the logical Yo-Yo string, and letting the barbs fall where they may. Not only are the romantic notions about good and evil, love and marriage, heroism and habit cut into confetti, but the case is made for the devil being too much of a romantic.

The principal points of Shaw's personal philosophy are put into the mouths of the characters without need for dramatic conventions, and although the notions may be historical, the details are remarkably fresh and stimulating.

The local readers are intelligent and personable, and seem to understand and enjoy what they're saying, which makes it possible for the audience to understand and enjoy it, too.

There are no slides on the wall or music in the background, but for a rare chance to take your wits out of cold storage and walk them around for a couple of hours, there's nothing like Shaw.

Performances are at 8 p.m. at the theater in the Vineyard shopping center and tickets may be bought at the door.

RUTH, Dan, Tampa Tribune, P.O. Box 191, Tampa Fla. 33601.

RUTH, James Richard; (2) Theater critic, performing arts columnist and staff reporter; (3) b. Lancaster, Pa., April 8, 1940; (4) s. Samuel Elmer and Julia Sophia (Weina); (5) Lampeter-Strasburg High School, academic; 1958; (6) m. Patricia Ann Banzhof, Oct. 28, 1968; (7) children--Gary Donald, Karen Lynn; (8) Editor TV Week magazine, Lancaster Newspapers, Inc., 1964-66; staff writer, Sunday News, Lancaster, Pa., 1966-69; ,theater critic, performing arts columnist, 1969-present; (9) High school and military theatrics; (10) Member, Lancaster County Citizens' Council for Venereal Disease Control, member, American Heritage Festival Friends; (13) SSgt. USAF, 1960-63; (15) National Screen Council; (16) Democrat; (17) Protestant; (20) Contributed articles to Modern Maturity Magazine, Grit; script consultant, co-author for BBC-TV documentary on military air reconaissance in England, 1962; (21) 312 Broadmoor Drive, Willow Street, Pa. 17584, Ph. 717-464-2881; (22) Sunday News, 8 W. King Street, Lancaster, Pa. 17604, Ph. 717-397-5251; (23) Circulation:

125,000; (24) 35 play and musical reviews, weekly performing arts column.

"The Crucible"
(by Jim Ruth, Sunday News, July 21, 1974)

The historic-prophetic power of Arthur Miller's "The Crucible" has been effectively captured by the American Heritage Festival players at the Fulton Opera House where the work will be performed through August in repertory alternation.

The eclipsing element of the production is Karl Eigsti's masterfully symbolic set whose bookend, shingled walls and menacing black forest background perfectly express the human elements which made the infamous Salem Witch Trials possible. Representing righteous intolerance and Pilgrim supersition, respectively, these set elements form a perfect frame for the turning of some of America's blackest pages of human history.

Written during the likewise notorious McCarthy Era of House Unamerican Activities Committee investigations, "The Crucible" is nonetheless powerful in the framework of the Watergate Era.

But "The Crucible" needs no present grounds. Superstition and self-righteousness are with us always, as are lust and the penchant for revenge.

Richard Greene, as John Proctor, forms an excellent hero, all the more sympathetic for the chinks in his moral armor. His performance reflects the depth of Eigsti's set as he progresses from earthy idealism to the brink of relinquishing his soul at the hands of the inquisition whose rule is confess or die.

Michael Lewis displays the same feeling of character dimension as Deputy Governor Danforth, stoker of "the hot fire which melts down all concealment"--the Trials. I have often seen this role portrayed but never before have I fathomed what I now take to be Miller's intended complexity of this character. He is not Villain. He is, rather, a man caught up in the frightening whirlpool of events gone out of control but tormented by a twisted obsession for Truth.

Claudia Zahn also is powerful in the role of Abigail Williams whose "whore's revenge" against one-time lover Proctor is cat-like in its menace and execution. It is entirely possible to see how this woman-child could have led rational men to believe "The powers of darkness have gathered in a monstrous attack."

That Mildred Ice should cement such a solid image of charity and compassion in such short scripted time is a tribute to the actress's skills. Her late Act II presence fills what is essentially John Proctor's scene and therefore adorns his actions with poignant credibility.

This is also the moment in which Lynn Milgrim abandons what is occasionally too limp a portrayal of the accused witch Elizabeth Proctor. When she rushes to embrace her death-sentenced husband, there is a grand power unleashed.

Lancastrian Luke Sickle too gives his role, that of the innocently drawn-in Giles Corey, the breath of believability complete with welcome humor.

Warren Kliewer as Rev. John Hale who discovers the truth behind the cries of "Witches" too late, Nancy Madden as the Proctor's girl-servant Mary Warren who is forced to join the accusers and Marcella Jordan as the condemned servant Tituba also contribute well.

It is therefore especially regrettable that in a few brief moments, William Parker should shatter the mood so carefully constructed by the others. In the role of Francis Nurse, he is totally mechanical, reducing tension to snickers.

More could also be demanded from lighting designer Mark Kruger. During Wednesday's performance, the lights appeared to be locked into full blaze, an insensitivity only a grand set such as that designed by Eigsti could have survived so well.

"The Crucible" deserves a bigger audience. I suspect that the ugliness of "The Exorcist" has kept many people at bay. That is sad. There is no comparison.

Tobacco Rd. Triumphs
(by Jim Ruth, Sunday News, July 28, 1974)

The promise of excellence which has built through the first two American Heritage Festival productions at the Fulton Opera House has culminated in an exceptional mounting of "Tobacco Road."

Jack Kirkland's celebrated stage adaptation of Erskine Caldwell's lusty novel about moral depravity among Georgia tenant farmers during the Depression is an inherently powerful vehicle. It is to director Robert Tolan's credit that nothing has escaped this tragi-comic balance in the Fulton production. What could so easily have been a depressing theatrical experience is instead a thoroughly satisfying and rewarding one.

Scenic designer Douglas Lebrecht's superior creation of the Jeeter Lester farm in the back country of Georgia must be credited along with direction and uniformly fine performances for the ultimate impact of the piece. The barren, dying tree, the deteriorating house and corn crib all reflect the past, present and future of the family itself, once strong and productive, now consumptive and ravaged by neglect, beyond salvation.

Jeeter Lester, head of the family, remains one of the most demanding roles in the theater. His dialogue is virtually non-stop, the depth of his characterization awesome. His lethargy, slovenliness, animalistic lusting and insensitivity to the needs of his wife, 17 children and his own starving mother are merely the surface trappings. There must be, if one is to find the necessary grounds for audience tolerance if not empathy, suggestions of the circumstances, and environment which have molded this man and which propel him to commit base deeds, not out of evil but out of a malignant struggle to survive the accident of his birth.

George Hall has discovered this essence. His projection may suffer under the burden of his perfect dialect and he may occasionally slump under the sheer volume of his scripted burden but his "by God and by Jesus" portrayal is a beautiful execution of a classic role.

Supportive strength abounds around him--Tim Wallace as the sadistically ignorant son Dude, Michele La Rue as the hair-lipped castoff daughter Ellie May, Lee Billington as the hot-pants preacher woman Sister Bessie, Gloria Maddox as the suffering wife Ada, Richard Greene as the love-lust-consumed Lov Bensey and Jan Renee Devereaux as the hostile object of his desires, Pearl.

Somehow, without benefit of lines, Mildred Ice towers above them all, haunting the stage and conscience as the discarded Grandma Lester. Her cowering, her mute pleas for crumbs of food and affection to sustain her failing life and the grim prophecy of her very being are masterful contributions.

"A person born on the land should stay with the land," Jeeter has proclaimed, thereby dooming the remaining members of his family to the gutting poverty of body and soul. The land, though barren and without promise of a planting stake, is all he knows. He can never own it. It owns him.

That comedy could take root in such soil is incredible but it bears much delightful fruit in the course of this production.

Tolan has orchestrated Sister Bessie's pawings of Dude and Lov's frustrated huggin' 'n a-rubbin' of Ellie May into grand burlesques, shameless exaggerations which scatter the gathering clouds of gloom.

If you have been waiting for the proper motivation through which to sample The American Heritage Festival, this is it.

RYWECK, Charles; (2) Theatre & Film Critic; (3) b. Philadelphia, Aug. 31; (4) s. Daniel and Reba (Gittelman); (5) New York U. , major subj.: Journalism; (6) m. Cecile Loberstein, Nov. 29, 1947; (7) children--Mitchell, Jonathan, Randy; (8) Staff writer, Motion Picture Daily 1943-46; staff member advertising-publicity dept., Columbia Pictures, 1946-73; Eastern editor, The Hollywood Reporter, 1973-74; Theatre-Film Critic, The Hollywood Reporter, 1973- ; (16) Democrat; (17) Jewish; (21) 67-48 212th Street, Bayside, N.Y. 11364, Ph. 212-321-1018; (22) The Hollywood Reporter, 1501 Broadway, Rm. 1710, New York, N.Y. 10036, Ph. 212-947-2470; (23) Circulation: entire Entertainment Industry; (24) 75 plays and musicals, 50 motion pictures.

The Glass Menagerie
(by Charles Ryweck, Hollywood Reporter, January 5, 1976)

Tennessee Williams' lovely, glowing early play, "The Glass Menagerie," has been given an exquisite revival at the Circle in the Square Theatre. It is Williams at his compassionate best as he glimpses a family through the diffuse filter of memory. Like many memories, which combine reality and illusion, "The Glass Menagerie" is shot through with a shimmering radiance that makes this one of the writer's truly magical works. The superb cast, which includes Maureen Stapleton, Rip Torn, Pamela Payton-Wright and Paul Rudd has been sensitively directed by Theodore Mann, the Circle's artistic director, and succeeds in transmitting the playwright's fragile work into compelling theatre.

Maureen Stapleton as Amanda, the mother, who tries to hold her brood together, is, by turns, fierce and tender. One of Williams' southern belles, she lives in the past glories of her courting days when suitors came calling, and before her husband deserted her. She tries to keep her son, Tom, tied to her until Laura, her crippled daughter, can find a husband. But she only succeeds in driving Tom away by her constant orders as to how he should conduct himself.

Rip Torn, who is the play's narrator as well, creates a full-bodied character of the son torn by internal furies. Pamela Payton-Wright, as Laura, is exceptionally fine as the cripple retreating from life into the remote world of her glass figurines and her absent father's old phonograph records. Paul Rudd, as the gentlemen caller, completes the quartet of magnificent performers. The climactic scene between Payton-Wright and Rudd, which shatters her last hope of love, is a truly enchanting scene.

The scenery by Ming Cho Lee, lighting by Thomas Skelton and costumes by Sydney Brooks, together with Craig Wasson's incidental music, help inmeasurably in creating "The Glass Menagerie's" magical mood.

Pacific Overtures
(by Charles Ryweck, Hollywood Reporter, January 15, 1976)

An innovative, precedent-shattering musical, "Pacific

Overtures" opened up new vistas in the American musical theatre as it dazzled a Winter Garden audience with the brilliance
of an exploding rocket.   It is the latest collaboration of producer-
director Harold Prince and composer-lyricist Stephen Sondheim.
Played by an Asian cast, who, in the Shakespearean tradition,
are all males, the musical daringly combines the stylized, pag-
eant-like movement of Japanese Kabuki theatre with the vigorous
vitality of the American musical.   While it doesn't succeed on
all scores (no pun intended), it is a sumptuous, visual feast of
a show to which theatregoers who are open to the unconventional
in entertainment will undoubtedly respond.

John Weidman's book concerns the opening up of Japan to
Western culture and trade by Commodore Matthew Perry's naval
expedition to the floating island empire of Nippon in 1853.   All
events are viewed through Japanese eyes (Perry's squadron of
gunboats is seen as black dragons).   The Western barbarians
(as the Americans are viewed) are met by the futile response
of the Shogun, the ruling Japanese warlord, until a humble fish-
erman who has been in America comes up with a formula that
satisfies the honor of both sides.

Weidman's book lacks, however, a central character with
whom we can identify.   And its mood, in the very short second
act, breaks sharply with the first.   And there is, inevitably, a
slackness in this second act as the Westerners flood into Japan
after Perry has broken the barriers.

Sondheim's music and lyrics are brilliantly original.   Prince's
direction has employed all the artistry of Kabuki theatre and the
percussive beat of Japanese music to create the fanciful world
of Japan's floating island.   Boris Aronson's scenic production
design is awesomely beautiful.   Florence Klotz's costumes and
Tharon Musser's lighting design contribute importantly to the
Oriental ambiance.   Patricia Birch's choreography has its inspiration in Asian rhythms.   Hugh Wheeler contributed additional
book material.

The cast is impeccable ranging from Mako, the reciter, or
narrator, to Soon-Teck Oh and Isac Sato.   The musical was presented by Prince in association with Ruth Mitchell.

SAFFORD, Edwin Ruthven III; (2) Music and gen. arts critic; (3) b.
Ogdensburg, N. Y. , June 18, 1924; (4) s. Edwin and Wilhelmina
(Emerson) R. Jr. ; (5) A. B. Syracuse U. , major: journalism-fine
arts, 1950; (6) m. Mary H. Felton, June 29, 1946; (7) children--
Emily Walker, Edwin Ruthven IV; (8) Readers Digest art dept. , various positions, magazine and Condensed Books, 1950-59; free-lance
writer, criticism and articles, 1960-66; music and gen. arts critic,
special writer Providence Journal-Evening Bulletin, 1966- ; (9) Apprentice: Mohawk Drama Festival, Schenectady, N. Y. , summer
1940; member community theater, acting, directing (once!); (10)

Member and v. pres. R.I. chapt. Episcopal Society for Cultural and
Racial Unity (ESCRU, now defunct); (13) T/5, U.S. Army, 1943-45;
(15) Member Music Critics Association, member at large bd. of
dirs. , 1971- ; (17) Episcopal; (20) Articles and criticism reprinted
in the American Musical Digest, have cont. to the Music Educators
Journal and Musical America; (21) 4 Vero Ct. , Barrington, R.I. ,
02806, Ph. 401-246-1993; (22) Providence Journal-Evening
Bulletin, 75 Fountain St. , Providence, R.I. 02902, Ph. 401-277-
7275; (23) Circulation: 206,000; (24) 40 plays and musicals, incl.
operas, 20 motion pictures, 25 dance, 75 concerts, 5 art.

Acute Acting but in "Henry" the Play's Still the Thing
(by Edwin Safford, Providence Journal-Bulletin, March 1, 1975)

It takes nothing away from direction or performances to say
that the play variously called Enrico IV, King Henry IV and at
the Lederer Theater The Emperor Henry, by Luigi Pirandello
in Eric Bentley's English version, is the first and last thing to
capture your attention.   Naturally Brooks Jone's directorial planning and Trinity Square's company contribute greatly to this reaction, but Pirandello with Bentley's assist really does reign.

Such especially is the case if ever you were caught up by
the playwright's Six Characters in Search of An Author.   That
makes you ready for his sending you one way only, at the point
when you feel fairly secure about events, to make an abrupt
shift which leaves you (sometimes laughing at his trickery) momentarily at a loss.

And the fact that your confusion lasts but a moment is simply one of the more masterful jests Pirandello uses to keep his
gears oiled.   This is manipulation of the highest order.

As King Henry IV the work had no special success a couple
of seasons back.   Under the present circumstances it is very
difficult to understand why.   There is yet another credit to
Trinity's The Emperor Henry, however inverse the compliment.

Certainly the plot intrigues.   Here you have a man of rank
who in the past has fallen from a horse, landed on his conk and
been rather out of it for a number of years.   He has assumed
the role of the Holy Roman Emperor Henry IV, who in 1077
stood in the snow as a penitent for three days at Canossa (Italy's
Ciano d'Enza) hoping for Pope Gregory VII's reprieve of excommunication.

To bolster his reconstruction of personality he has taken
residence in vaulted medieval surroundings, throne room and
all, and forced his servants to dress in the same gothic garb
he attires himself in.   You may be sure also he has extracted
royal obedience from them in act and gesture.

Pirandello deals in many layered illusion, here as elsewhere.

So enter persons from the Emperor's and the man's past, the Countess Matilda Spina and her daughter included and, yes, a psychiatrist, each from the present to assume identities of that ancient time.

Thus the mystery begins, the dazzling shifts of character and plot. Who is who? What is what? Is the man's madness fine and theirs mundane? Where will his machinations lead the pack of them?

Except, as the play says, "You can't return 900 years and not bring back a few strange experiences," it should be left to Trinity to advise you of the outcome and the crosscurrents of passion, strained allegiances, pouts and dangers which float you giddily to that outcome. Just be sure to take the trip.

Part of the reason you are told to is the, once again, visual feast at the Lederer. Robert D. Soule's castle great hall has solidity, now softly illuminated by the color of torchlight, now bright when the "electricity" is turned on in John McLain's design. The costumes by James Berton Harris have a quiet spectacle in their medieval emergence; women's modern dresses are Christian Dior, post-war new look, giving an unexpected added period dimension (seamed stockings!).

Their occupants are attractive as well. Perhaps Jan Farrand might not use her well turned ankles quite so much like a fashion model in movement as the Countess, but her tentative tremble and facial performance fill out the character. Margo Skinner, honey voiced, is her frightened doe of a daughter.

Timothy Donahue, Richard Jenkins, Daniel von Bargen and Lane Davies are appositely strapping as the Emperor's attendants. John D. Garrick the properly concerned Di Nolli. Ed Hall, the psychiatrist, has nice eyestrain as he looks for the precise description of analogical elasticity, a term Pirandello or Bentley liked enough to use twice. Richard Kavanaugh's offhanded though out of sorts Baron is contributing as well.

At this date what more can be said of Richard Kneeland? There was that touch of arbitrary chic in exposing himself on opening night (would not even a crazy wear underpants in the draughty chill of his castle?). But the actor is so complete, and you have one beautiful scene when Henry and his shuffling servant, beatified Howard London clothed as a confessor, come across their brief exchange over votive candles.

Pirandello buffs, indeed, can rejoice over Trinity's handling of their favorite. When you leave your step will be light from experiencing the treat and the treatment.

A Barn Is Born for Trinity's Uproarious "Tom Jones"
(by Edwin Safford, Providence Journal-Bulletin, March 8, 1975)

Who is left to remember putting on shows in the barn of a
boring summer afternoon, spontaneous low dramas with a sheet
or old blanket for curtain and big fights over who would play
whom? Director Larry Arrick remembers for one.

For his Trinity Square adaptation of Henry Fielding's Tom
Jones upstairs at the Lederer Theater Eugene Lee has provided
him with a barn too. It is a total environment setting in which
the audience sits on tiered wooden benches and the action, often
uproarious, flows past all about you. So it happens that you
enter physically into the 18th century.

There is a further entering, into the play itself. A group
of rustics (the program calls them peasants but that would never
do in Britain), rough of speech and tattered of dress, is casting
about for something to do. The decision is Tom Jones as a social document of protest.

Not every actor is involved all the time, even though each
has more than a single role, including animals and birds. While
not performing they lounge around the periphery, reacting to the
play much as you do. You have a double audience combining
you and them. The enmeshment is just about complete.

Arrick's approach is ballad opera in form with songs by
Barbara Damashek, the two sharing credit for lyrics. While
this poses comparisons with The Beggar's Opera and its descendant, The Threepenny Opera, it is not really bothersome. As
during the celebrated dinner scene between Tom and Mrs. Walters, which at first seems a ripoff from the movie, you finally
relax and enjoy.

At the heart of this Tom Jones you will find 18th century
English manners satirized. But superimposed upon that is the
point of how far poverty is capable of diminishing humanity, a
lesson for every age though it may not be exactly a new one
(see Brecht).

While the production is lusty, as well as a trace too long,
it has moments of contrasting beauty. A fox hunt, with actors
as hunters and their mounts, is electrifying and choreographical-
ly twice as convincing as William Dollar's ballet, The Duel.
Later there is a masked ball in what might be the Vauxhall Gardens, where a smudgy piece of canvas becomes a night-lighted
pavillion.

And the only change of James Berton Harris' wonderfully
meager costumes in these transformations is by adding a piece
of torn rag here or a swatch of lace there. You have not a
doubt that the bumpkins suddenly, briefly, are turned into people

of fashion, such bare surroundings and sham elegance to the
contrary.

Barbara Damashek's score is very derivative, sometimes
purposely so. Purcell's Sound the Trumpets is brought in consciously. Elsewhere Bernstein (the great eclectic himself),
Weill, Porter and the St. John's night brawl from Wagner's
Meistersinger drop in to pay calls on the music.

Yet the songs are decent enough and do add pleasing effects.
Accompanied variously by harpsichord, violin and percussion of
all sorts, you might mention the National Organization of Women's topical "Let's dream somewhat higher," Tom and Sophia
Western's love duet and "The Ladies of London," strongly sung
as usual by Barbara Meek.

So large a cast precludes mention of every particular player.
Robert Black, predictably maybe, has a wide-eyed though
raunchy innocence in the name role which counts for plenty.
Watch, too, as if you could avoid it, Mina Manente's Mrs. Wal-
ters, David C. Jones' Lord Fellamar, Peter Gerety's Turp
Merlyn and fox, Robert Colonna's Miss Western (in shredded
drag) and owl, Julie Miterko's Honor and Lila Daniels' Lady
Bellaston. Oops, add George Martin's Squire Western and Nancy
Nichols' Sophia.

As Tom Jones, the poor country bastard, is exiled to the
city for his irrepressible lechery, bosoms heave and there are
more slaps, tickles and couplings in the hay than you can shake
a finger at. If the play within the play loses a touch of simple
narrative, other things are gained including a mordantly surprise
ending. You will want to see the combination.

SAINER, Arthur; (2) Theatre critic; (3) b. New York City, Sept. 12,
1924; (4) s. Louis and Sadie (Sainer); (5) B.A. New York U., radio,
English and philosophy, 1946; M.A. Columbia U., English, 1948;
(6) m. Stefanie Janis, Dec. 26, 1957, later divorced; (7) No children;
(8) Editor, TV Guide magazine, 1954-60, drama critic, Village
Voice, 1961 to present, English faculty, C.W. Post College, 1963-67,
Drama faculty, Bennington College, 1967-69, Fiction-writing work-
shop, Chautauqua Writers Workshop, Summer '69, Fiction-writing
workshop, Staten Island Community College, '74-'75, Playwriting
workshop, Hunter College, Fall, 1974, Playwriting workshop, C.W.
Post College Fall '74-Spring '75, Playwriting workshop, Adelphi
University, Spring and Fall, '75; plays produced primarily Off-Off
Broadway, 1964 to present, recent productions include: "Day Old
Bread: the Worst Good Time I Ever Had," April '76, "Charley
Chestnut Rides the I.R.T." April '75, "The Children's Army Is Late,"
March '74, "The Thing Itself," November '72, "The Celebration:
Jooz/Guns/Movies/The Abyss," February '72, all at Theater for
the New City; "The Spring Offensive," produced by the Bridge Col-
lective, New York City and Ohio State U.; (10) Me. Advisory Panel,

Theatre, New York State Council on the Arts, 1975- , Advisory
board, Video program, Theatre Collection, New York, 1975- ; (11)
Political organizer, Students for (Henry) Wallace, 1948; (14) John
Golden Playwriting Award, 1946, Grant from Office for Advanced
Drama Research, 1967; (15) Founding member, Playwrights Group;
(17) Jewish; (20) "The Radical Theatre Notebook," Avon Books,
March '75, critiques of English-language playwrights for "Contemporary Dramatists," St. James Press, London, 1974, "The Sleep-
walker and the Assassin," Bridgehead Books, 1964, theatre and literary criticism for Village Voice from 1961 to present; also following published plays: "The Spring Offensive" in "The Radical Theatre
Notebook," "1 Piece Smash" in "The Scene," Vol. 2, "The Thing
Itself" in "Playwrights for Tomorrow," Vol. 6, theatre and film articles to yale/theatre, Vogue, Bennington Review, Show Business Illustrated; (21) 79 Sullivan St. , New York 10012; (22) Village Voice,
80 University Pl. , New York 10003, Ph. 212-741-0030; (23) Circulation: 150,000; (24) Approximately 100 plays reviewed per yr.

A Dream Production Falls Flat
(by Arthur Sainer, Village Voice, April 5, 1976)

Woyzeck, born the Feast of the Annunciation, common soldier, atheist, has a child by Marie without the blessings of the
Church. They name the child Christian. Woyzeck later stabs
the unfaithful Marie, and dies for his crime. Christian is left
in the care of an idiot. Or Woyzeck, on lowest rung of the
economic ladder, without "virtue" because without bread, is exploited, used as guinea pig, commits an act of desperation, is,
in Artaud's phrase, "suicided by society." Or Woyzeck, haunted
by voices, by visions of a hollow earth, sensing that the moon
is a piece of rotten wood, that the sun is a faded sunflower,
knowing that "a man with courage is a dirty dog," dies as Kafka's Joseph K. dies, "like a dirty dog." Buchner's play is at
least all these plays.

A play of victims. Victim Woyzeck, but human existence
is a victim and so are all its members. Woyzeck, perhaps
most victimized, is at the mercy of other victims, it is an element in the drama's terrible poignancy. The terrible hierarchy
of victims. Victim Marie, she's as good as the grand ladies
whose hands are kissed by gentlemen, she's not content to be
Woyzeck's domesticated frau, she has sensual longings and a
need for joy that Woyzeck can't satisfy, she exults in her ful-
some body but pays a terrible price.

I'm in an obvious minority, among my Voice colleagues and
the daily press, concerning the virtues of the current production.
Despite director Leo Shapiro's tendency to simplify what seems
to me Buchner's complex and sometimes contradictory vision--
e. g. , the deemphasizing of Woyzeck's anxiety about the Free-
masons, the deemphasizing of Marie's feelings of guilt, the cari-
caturizing of Woyzeck's oppressive superiors like the captain
and the doctor so that we don't see them as victims--despite

all this, I found Shapiro's production in all its bareness a most compelling one.

First, there is Joseph Chaikin's masterly portrayal. Joe's Woyzeck is physically like a landscape overrun by the enemy: bruised, scorched, pockmarked; the tanks of the oppressor lie heavily on this terrain, but the action is still in the present, the miraculous solidity of the man is seen to be continually wincing and recovering and wincing again from the hammered nails of--what shall we call them finally--the Others?

Joe has given Woyzeck a stutter which is sometimes evident under moments of stress. Woyzeck is a seer, without formal education, in all his animal crudity. Woyzeck's stutter, in a way, is an attempt to retreat from seeing, but the vision of calamity is so compelling that the stutter is also contrarily the breaking through to the word, the eruption of truth convulsively forcing its way through barriers of rock (attempts at unfeeling).

Joe inhabits Woyzeck's spirit with feelings of distress and compassion so harrowing that it sometimes becomes difficult to watch, to remain seated without attempting an action of some sort, and yet there's a marvelous sense of art as redemption in watching the portrayal of compassion, the portrayal of a spirit laving itself hopelessly over the human condition, the condition past sickness, past evil, and yet even in hopelessness believing and somehow knowing that hopeless sickness and hopeless evil can be transformed. In what world?

I've heard my colleagues saying that many of the other roles aren't acted but simply "read" and I wonder what they consider "acting." I like much of what I would call the "dryness" of the Shaliko production, in Christopher McCann's Andres, in James Carrington's idiot, in the multiple roles by Maria Zakrzewski and Arthur Strimling. This dryness, this lack of resonance suggests that Woyzeck's life is flying by as if in a dream. "One thing after another."

What I find a problem is the multiplicity of styles. Ron Faber is quite wonderful as the captain and Jake Dengel is charming as the doctor who has Woyzeck on a diet of peas in in the interest of science (low-keyed prophesy of Nazi experiments 100 years later), but their use of caricature deprives the play of a rich complexity. The irony of caricature isn't necessary for us to understand their incompleteness as people. For Woyzeck is also incomplete but differently so.

Woyzeck's aloneness is one of the great, barely endurable alonenesses in drama, and yet it's an affirmation, for like the crucified Jesus that figures in Woyzeck's peculiar rejection of Christianity, Woyzeck is ultimately alone not only for himself but even in his despair he is alone for us as well.

We Cease to Be Victims of the Past
(by Arthur Sainer, Village Voice, April 26, 1976)

One of the mysteries of art is its ability to transform pain into spiritual comfort, to metamorphose anguish at horrendous events into a suffusing, succoring joy. Unlike history, which mobilizes the past and turns on it a sometimes dazzling analytic searchlight, art forces a reliving of the experience; it is another kind of analysis, a re-forming of actions. In this reforming we suffuse the remembered actions with nothing less than our humanity, much as if we were tending a wounded animal or nurturing plants in a window box when the impulses of the spirit are transmitted through our fingers. We have ceased to be victims of the past and have become collaborators in a move toward transcendence: At its best the remembered actions are drained of past evil and take on a sanctity through our replaying.

These thoughts are prompted by two lovely works, Meredith Monk's "Quarry" and Margo Sherman's "If the Prophets." "Quarry," an epic opera performed by Monk, the members of The House, and several dozen additional performers, is essentially an abstraction of a Jewish coming to consciousness and a growing up both during and after the events of the Holocaust, and it is also the playing out of that Holocaust. So that the work is on several levels: the private concerns of a girl in a privileged household--but there is already anguish in these private moments--and the private concerns of several adults related to the girl, balanced against public, mass spectacles which in time envelop these private lives. And also a complicated level of time, for the girl seems both to be living through the growth of her thirties and awakening to its horrors at a later moment in history. And the work is so constructed that the spectator comes as late to the consciousness of fascist horrors as the girl does.

There is a wonderful eye for detail, both of objects and movements. The long space of La Mama Annex is intermittently drained of emptiness by domestic groupings: Orthodox Jewish couple in traditional blacks, husband poring over Scripture or perhaps Talmud; three girls at a dinner table in a bourgeois household, light source a lamp with a fat, comforting base; an older bourgeois couple, husband in maroon-colored robe, reading peacefully, wife in simple black dress and pearls, upright, dignified; another relative in long print dress, clacking heels, rehearsing for a part; and in the center the sleeping, troubled, or waking, feverish girl, watched over by comic maid, dusting, peeping out windows.

The groupings sometimes evoke a sense of ineffectuality, of giddiness, but often of devotion, in the bourgeois households to a way of material and intellectual life, or in the Orthodox setting to a Supreme Being. The girl, even less effectual and more vulnerable than the others, nevertheless seems to be in the throes of some half-understood anguish that goes past the silly whining about "My head, my ears, my eyes." She is Monk's "vessel," apprehending the beginnings of something that will later come to be understood as the fascist mining of victims, or "quarrying," and the fascist forces will be represented by grotesque or comic dictators or the supremely evil dictator in business suit, the insidious "banality" of the business suit, that eventually takes over the space, or the terrible sight of mass, choraling youth in fascist, body-building movements that choke the space.

There is so much in the Monk opera, and in fact it seems to me overproduced, but it is a work of beautiful devotion, and I haven't even begun to mention the warbles and staccato cries and other sounds that help compose this remembering of six million Jews.

In production terms, Margo Sherman's "If the Prophets" is at the opposite end of the spectrum. The entire cast is one young woman, barely moving against a simple print backdrop. In the first half of the program, Ms. Sherman performs "She Makes a Speech," a monologue by Avram Patt, and appears as an elderly Jewish woman, offering the spectator homely, comic wisdom about kinds of love, about receiving telephone calls, about visiting. It is also about survival through love.

On Saturday I made my way past a procession of merrily painted figures proceeding clownlike through SoHo. I was in a hurry to stop off at a marathon benefit for UTO, a collection of artists from theatre, film, music, and painting, whose loft at 597 Broadway had been partially gutted by fire. My friend Elizabeth Converse then told me, as I looked through UTO's block-long interior and smelt evidence of their recent catastrophe, that the procession was part of the day's entertainment.

The depth of the UTO Space is quite impressive and the plans for reopening UTO as a collectivity are ambitious. Frankly, UTO would simply be another name to me if not for the presence of my friend Converse, as she likes to call herself, former member of the Performance Group and the Bridge Collective. She's an intense and intensely interesting young presence, a fighter, a dreamer, and these words will probably embarrass her but they're true.

She tells me that UTO's going to reopen on May 7 with Philipe Doinel's Odyssey Repertory group doing "The Lower Depths." I asked Converse how Voice readers could help UTO and she said, "Just tell them to come and see the work." So I have.

SALES, Grover; (2) Theater, Film and Music Critic; (3) b. Louisville, Ky., Oct. 26, 1919; (4) B.A. U. of California Berkely, 1949,

Highest Honors in History, Graduate School, History, 1949-51; (6)
m. Georgia MacLeod, Dec. 30, 1972; (7) children--daughter, Rachel;
(8) Actor, Playhouse Rep, San Francisco, 1955-57; professional
photographer, 1962-66; Headed own theatrical publicity firm, 1956-
68; Film & Drama Editor, San Francisco Magazine 1965-75; Film
Critic, KQED-TV since 1968; Critic-at-large, City Magazine; (9) Instructor in Music and Drama, University of California Extension,
1970-73; Faculty, Critic's Institute, O'Neill Theater, Waterford,
Conn. 1967-71; (10) Founder of Third Stream Concerts, San Francisco; (13) Sgt. U.S. Army Air Corps 1942-46; (14) Special Mention,
Sang Prize for Theater Criticism, 1968; (17) Jewish; (20) Articles
appeared in San Francisco Chronicle, Holiday, Saturday Review; co-
author with wife, The Clay-pot Cookbook (Atheneum); author, The
Gospel According to John Maher (W.W. Norton, Sheldon Press, London.); (21) Box 689, Belvedere, Cal.

Jazz Is Not Gay Music
(by Grover Sales, San Francisco Magazine, November 1973)

In the late '50s--before the ascendancy of Rock and the greed
of artists' managers with their impossible-to-meet fees turned
San Francisco's historic jazz clubs into parking lots and topless
joints--the Black Hawk, Jazz Workshop and Sugar Hill were
nightly camping grounds for a black homosexual whore and would-
be entertainer immortalized in Shirley Clarke's searing documentary, Portrait of Jason. Born Aaron Paine, this fluttery and
engaging poseur called himself Jason Holliday, but the jazz crowd
called him "Jason the Faggot."

Nothing hostile or demeaning was implied by a word that
Gay Lib has come to equate with "nigger"; of all peer groups,
the jazz set has long been unrivaled for its blithe indifference
to the vagaries of human comportment. "Faggot" was not a
term of derision, but simply an identifying tag in a milieu where
the regular presence of an overt homosexual seemed as peculiar
as John Wayne at a Black Panther rally.

The yawning chasm that splits the gay world from jazz is a
territory both fascinating and unexplored. The only reference
I have found to this strange cleavage is a solitary comment 15
years ago by the astute English critic Francis Newton: "Of all
the arts in mid-20th century Britain, (jazz) is so far the one
with the overwhelmingly strongest heterosexual tradition ... in
spite of the almost unlimited toleration of jazzmen for deviations
and idiosyncrasies in other people's lives. By tradition, the
jazz musician (and by imitation the jazz fan) goes for women
just like the traditional Italian operatic tenor."

When I first grew curious about this sexual-cultural split,
I asked many great and near-great jazz musicians--provided I
knew them well enough to expect candid replies--if they knew
of any gays in jazz. Whether they came of age in the '20s or
the '60s, their answers were much the same: "No, not a one.

I guess I never really thought about it before. I understand that pianist Tony Jackson was queer (died 1921) and that piano player with Erskine Hawkins in the '40s, and maybe so-and-so, but he's an arranger ... and some people say so-and-so was bi, swung both ways, but in this business you just don't find them around."

Francis Newton's observation that "the jazzman is a keen follower of the women," and vice versa, is well known to anyone who follows the music. In any large city you could always find the most exotic and uninhibited women where jazz musicians played. The prime figures from Duke Ellington to Charlie Parker were celebrated for their almost legendary prowess. A front-rank trumpet player once insisted to me: "Man, if you're playing a dance and you point your horn at a certain chick, and play right at her all night, when the gig is over, you'll make that chick!" and I've watched him, and many others, prove this theory to be more than idle mysticism. The term "swinger," in both its musical and sexual sense, and its antonym "square" were common parlance in the jazz sub-culture decades before Playboy discovered them. Women and the joys of heterosexual congress have long been lauded in the titles of strictly jazz tunes: Juicy Lucy, Satin Doll, Poon Tang, Warm Valley, Four or Five Times, My Daddy Rocks Me. Growing up in the South to believe that jazz was low-class, vulgar music, I didn't need the Dictionary of American Slang to define the word:

"Jazz (noun) 1. (taboo) copulation: orig. southern Negro use, prob. since long before 1900. 2. animation; enthusiasm and a fast tempo; frenzy."

Ferdinand "Jelly Roll" Morton, whose nickname hardly derives from pastry, said the early black street bands in New Orleans were called "spasm bands" because the musicians were given to epileptic shakes while performing; it takes no university etymologist to see the link between jazz, spasm, orgasm and "jism"--that immemorial American vulgate for semen; In the '20s jazz was called "hot music"; Jelly Roll Morton named his band the Red Hot Peppers and an unemployed clarinetist during the Depression took an "at liberty" ad in Variety to proclaim his diversities: "read, fake, plenty hot." Since the time of Sappho, and perhaps before, "hot" had been used to denote a state of sexual excitement in any language.

Besides an absence of homosexuality, the jazz world is marked by another unique--and related--phenomenon among American males. Jazzmen embrace and even kiss on meeting, not the perfunctory pecks of powdered church ladies, but wild, gleeful bear hugs, wet smacks and cries of "baby!" Backstage at annual get-togethers like the Monterey Jazz Festival, one finds Jimmy Witherspoon and Jon Hendricks, Dizzy Gillespie and Thelonious Monk and even such notorious hostility symbols as Charlie Mingus and Miles Davis locked in loving embrace. Such open displays of intra-male affection suggest that jazz musicians may

be unusually secure about their sexual identity, or at least im-
pervious to what "uptight squares" might think. Dizzy Gillespie,
gifted in midconcert with a statue of himself, kissed the sculptor
and burst into tears: "if a man cries, a lot of people are going
to say he's a faggot, but it don't bother me ... hell, baby--I
know what I am!" Jazzmen have a saying, "If it's cool in your
mind, then it's cool." (The word does not mean indifference or
lack of commitment, but that good quality of being in control.)

A lifetime of experience and professional audience-watching
in every phase of the performing arts from ballet to burlesque
convinces me there is no gay audience for jazz. Jason aside,
gays are not found in jazz spots, concerts or festivals. Their
record libraries may include opera, baroque, and tend to bulge
with showtunes and Original Cast albums, but never any jazz except the most peripheral kind--André Previn or perhaps a Bru-
beck, but no Charlie Parker or John Coltrane. There'll be an
occasional Billie Holiday, Ella Fitzgerald or Carmen McRae, but
their attraction seems to be less as jazz singers than as overpowering matriarchal presences (like McRae, but more likely
Eileen Farrell or Ethel Merman) or disaster-identification objects
(Holiday, but more often Judy Garland). Jason adopted Holiday's
last name and once affixed himself to Carmen McRae as house
boy. An intriguing footnote is that bi-sexuality among women
singers from Bessie Smith to Janis Joplin is not uncommon, and
it's long been a jazz cliché that "girl singers," to put it kindly,
veer toward the eccentric; but the understandably minor function
of women in jazz, often forced into male-playing roles by the
nature of both the music and its environs, is too complex and
elusive to go into here.

Of all the performing arts in America, jazz alone holds no
allure for the homosexual. The preponderance of gays among
balletomanes led Oscar Levant to quip that "ballet is the faggot's
baseball." In opera, commanding bulwarks like Farrell, Schwarz-
kopf and Sills enjoy an enormous gay entourage, as do Bette Davis and the late Tallulah. The Broadway theater and especially
its musicals form an exclusive roped-off sandbox for the Boys
in the Band who venerate a glittering pantheon of brassy, leath-
er-lunged den mothers: Garland, Minnelli, Streisand, Channing,
Merman, and for young gays, a new Campop turn-on called Bette
Midler. Martin Gottfried, the perceptive drama reviewer for
Women's Wear Daily, illuminates the special appeal of the Broadway Matriarchy:

"The homosexual director will cast productions not necessarily for ability but because certain actors are either part of his
sexual set or because they represent homosexual jokes--actresses
who are unwitting parodies of women ... the female star of a
Broadway musical is often at the mercy of homosexual creators
and even audiences who, because they tend to hyperenthusiasm,
tend to adore such a woman (exactly as they do the opera diva)
which promotes the already existing vanity of the ladies and leads

them into excesses of performance and costuming. They begin
to camp . . . playing for the boys in the balcony or the chorus.
In most cases . . . these women are talented, but when they are
conned by choreographers and directors, they are made fools of
and this produces a truly vulgar and deceitful kind of theater.
Such ladies range from Judy Garland to Sophie Tucker. Musicals like Hello Dolly and Mame are built for them. Some are
clever enough to know what's happening and manage to put even
their claques on--Channing in particular," as witness the recent
Chronicle front page spread on Lorelei with photos of 100 drag
queens done up as Channing, who awarded a prize to the most likely.

Aside from a happy accident like I Can't Cope, the isolation
of a gay-dominated Broadway from jazz is total, unlike 50 years
ago when Eubie Blake and Fats Waller wrote their joyful revues
with tunes that are still around, and the scores of jazz-oriented
composers like Gershwin were kept alive by jazzmen in jam
sessions and recording studios. Broadway showtunes like I Got
Rhythm and Lady Be Good gave Louis Armstrong, Art Tatum and
Lester Young the chordal frame on which to hang some of their
most inspired improvisations. But today's musical theater,
fronted by such non-swinging parodists as Stephen Sondheim and
Al Carmines, leaves meager pickings for the jazz musician.
Miles Davis cut a jazz version of Porgy and Bess, Oscar Peterson waxed an album of My Fair Lady, but what juice could they
squeeze from dry pomegranates like Follies, Company or Promenade? They don't even try.

This divorce of Broadway from jazz is also a matter of mutual consent. To find a fanatical jazz fan at a matinee of Lorelei is as unlikely as spotting a bevy of Channing's chorus boys
at a Connonball Adderley concert. While some jazz devotees
suffer from narrow parochialism, many enjoy a remarkable
catholicity of taste; they collect Wagner and Puccini, attend ballet and symphony, read Chaucer, like Balinese music, old Scottish folk ballads and Haydn quartets. But during more than 35
years of adhesive contact with "jazz people," never have I come
across one who dug Judy Garland, nor have I flipped through a
record collection so schizoid as to give equal space to Charlie
Parker and Ethel Merman.

There are no ready-made answers to explain this split between homosexuality and jazz. To fall back on the "sinful" origins of this music is no help, since jazz issued as much from
the black church as from the cathouse, and has been heard in
our most venerable concert halls for a full generation. The
most often-heard response, "jazz is a masculine music," doesn't
tell us a thing. Another pat reply, "jazz is good-time, party-
ing, ball-all-night-long music" has a ring of truth. Jazz's
mass-pop offshoots, Rhythm n' Blues and Rock, formed
the insistent pulse throbbing under a massive sexual revolt among white youth for whom music became a more
immediate and useful language than the written or spoken word.

An extraordinary book by Ben Sidran, Black Talk, bears the provocative subtitle: "How the music of Black America created a
radical alternative to the values of Western literary tradition,"
a way of saying that The Beat has supplanted Tom Paine, Freud
and Marx as an instrument of social change.

From Tokyo to Liverpool, jazz taps the source of powerful
emotions, makes its listeners feel good, sad, exalted, airborne,
gets them to move their bodies in very special ways. Why has
this explosive music that has literally changed the lives of millions made so little impact on the gay community? What does
this split reveal about the still mysterious nature of both jazz
and homosexuality? Will Gay Lib, acting in concert with the
sexual freedom of the Rock Generation, dispel guilts and inhibi-
tions that may have kept the closet homosexual from enjoying
his body along with its most dramatic musical stimulant?

The mere raising of these questions is not, as some will
insist, an attack on gays (even though I deplore what they have
wrought on Broadway, and feel that the Gay White Way could do
with a Straight Lib Movement). These questions are asked, not
only because they are fascinating in themselves, but also in the
hope that others more qualified can come up with answers that
have so much to tell us about where America is headed.

The Nitty Without the Gritty
(by Grover Sales, San Francisco Magazine, May 1974)

GORFISM (gorf'iz əm), n. Psychiatry, a mental disorder that
impairs the ability of adults to distinguish between mature and
infantile behavior patterns; endemic to overcrowded urban centers of the post-Korean War, when large adult populations re-
gressed to the sexual, artistic and recreational appetites of pre-
school children. (After Gorf, 1974 play by Michael McClure.)

In a rare confluence of taste, the daily press, liberal "alternative" weeklies and the funky underground sex guides all got
cracking with Gorf weeks before it opened at the Magic Theatre.
Herb Caen thought it worthy of note that Gorf spelled backwards
was frog, but as Stella Brooks used to say, "obscure" spelled
backwards is "your box," and besides Gorf is about nothing as
intelligible as a retrograde frog. Every paper but The Watch-
tower treated its readers to that from-the-rear nudie shot of
gorf-star Laura Duncan, said to be the great-grand-niece of the
grand Isadora and wardrobe mistress of the Magic Theatre.
Poised astern of the nubile Ms. Duncan is playwright McClure,
spendidly bleak, enswathed in woolen scarves, full face with
destiny like Heathcliff on the moor.

Back in pre-Oh Calcutta days, McClure used The Beard to
ride the crest of an historical moment, surfing far beyond where
his natural bent for self-promotion could propel. A ten-minute
Committee skit inflated to an hour, The Beard, like Catch-22,

wasn't all that funny, but its time had clearly come, with Billy the Kid going down on Jean Harlow right on stage before an audience still agog over the pallid orgy scenes in La Dolce Vita. There wasn't much shaking on off-off Broadway in those days, with the New York Times and Village Voice reduced to making culture heroes out of such bedraggled Dantons as Julian Beck and Judith Malina, so the hungry media snapped at The Beard as a long-awaited breakthrough, and you should see what this opened up for "San Francisco's own" Mike McClure! London tours with his rickshaw hauled by Kenneth Tynan, international headlines of road companies busted for muff-diving in Stockton, contracts with Grove Press for "99 poems in beast language," and even a Guggenheim, thrusting McClure into the pantheon of Guggenheimed immortals like Ann Halprin and E. Howard Hunt (who won it as a novelist, over the likes of Truman Capote and Gore Vidal).

McClure found himself lionized as resident-playwright by Berkeley's Magic Theatre, a first-rate company of authentic talents squandered on old McClure laundry slips, Kounter Kulchur Klassics and Spider Rabbit, an unabashed nursery-school pageant and costume show hailed by the kiddies' underground press as Masterpiece of the Week. But the advance poop on Gorf gave ominous hint that, in comparison, Spider Rabbit might stand as the finest flowering of Periclean Athens. Press releases proclaimed the world premiere of a "religious, dada musical melodrama, featuring a giant penguin, naked tap-dancing stars and the authentic death cry of the giant mountain octopus, dealing with the notion of cosmic unification, an alchemical drama, like Mozart's Magic Flute turned inside out, with an accompanying orchestra of cello, piano ... and watering can."

Such prose, of course, deliberately resists analysis, as did the actual performance of the "Ur-Gorf Drama" it ballyhoos, but it must be said that few can touch McClure in whipping up casual put-ons for his gorfaudience; when it comes to titillating the most miserably educated generation spawned in the history of the Republic, McClure's got it down to a science:

1. The plotless, pointless drama is set in Thebes and Abyssinia to persuade susceptible audiences and critics that Universal Values are afoot.

2. Two characters are dressed as TV sets to suggest that somehow our wicked technocracy is being satirized.

3. A 300-pound blind lesbian motorcyclist in black leather is turned loose, affording unbridled hilarity for an audience too young to have seen Lenny Bruce and too unlettered to have read anything except The Hobbit.

4. Endless repetitions of animal grunts and shouted naughty words remind us that this is the Theater of Primal Experience,

really getting down to the gut-level Artaudian nitty if not gritty.

  5. The moving scenery is mounted on giant paper rollers
as in a Punch and Judy show, the only theater most of McClure's
audience has ever seen.

  6. Likewise, the "orchestra" is of the Quaker box top and
kazoo variety, dear to everyone's kindergarten days.

  7. Two women tap dancers in full beaver disport themselves
à la Warner Bros. musicals of the '30s, thus slaking the crowd's
perennial thirst for both nudity and period camp.

  8. As the White Rock Girl, Isadora Duncan's great grand-
niece makes a truly resplendent nude; this insures that some
semi-literate, nipple-happy copy boy elevated to Drama Critic
on a major metropolitan paper can't say anything bad about the
show.

  9. The male lead is both nude and uncircumcized, providing
exotic repulsion for San Francisco's thriving population of upwards of 500 Jews.

  Since these goings-on are beyond description, only a reprint
of McClure's "Theban Anthem" will encapsulate the elusive naivete he has poured into Gorf. What follows is a verbatim facsim-
ile, typography and all, of lyrics by a recipient of a Guggenheim
Fellowship for "Creative Writing in Poetry":

PUT YOUR FINGERS ON A STAR
or you won't get very far
but no matter who you are
YOU
GOTTA
LEARN
to take good care of yourself!
YOU MAY NOT REMEMBER
YOU'RE AN ELF
but you gotta keep tellin yourself ...
THAT YOU ARE
more than you think!
YOU ARE REAL AND SWEET
and your feet are mighty fleet
and your voice and words are neat
AND
YOU
ARE
more than you think!
BABY, YOU'RE A FAIRY AND AN ELF!

  Burma Shave. Should this not give enough insight into the
McClurian aesthetic, there's his recent cover story on Bob Dylan in Rolling Stone, wherein the author of "It's All Right, Ma,"

a lyric McClure both misreads and misquotes, is celebrated as the heir to William Blake. With the compulsive narcissism that seems never to desert him, McClure proves more revealing about McClure than Dylan. Our Guggenheim Fellow tells us he, (McClure) wrote "Come On God, and Buy Me a Mercedes Benz," that Dylan gave him an autoharp (a push-button zither for the handicapped), and that Joan Baez said McClure and Allen Ginsberg should be Dylan's conscience. To prove Dylan a master of the squelch elegant, McClure tells of a wonderous encounter with Ken Kesey, who advised Dylan, "Hey, man, you should try playing when you're high on acid." "Without a pause, Dylan said, 'I did and it threw off my timing.' There was no way," McClure marvels, "to one-up Bob or get ahead of him at any level or any time," and hot damn, son, that Dylan sure is fast with a snappy comeback.

McClure is the artistic embodiment of Gresham's Law. The trouble lies not with his studied infantilism as playwright or entertainer, but with his seduction of the media, and consequently the public which elevates this amiable mediocrity at the expense of those genuinely gifted among us. Prior to its puzzling infatuation with McClure, The Magic Theatre loomed as a reservoir of the finest acting and directing talent in West Coast off-Broadway; with Gorf, it's hard to believe this is the same company that gave us John Lion's Sheriff Bill only a few years ago. Rolling Stone, once a mindless pusher of the worst of bubblegum rock, has of late unearthed a goldmine of creative political reportage, with Watergate pieces that have become "must" reading; with McClure on Dylan, this remarkable journal slips back into gorfic infancy. The same week Gorf opened with General MacArthur fanfare, Earl 'Fatha' Hines, our resident genius of the piano, sneaked into the Miyako Hotel for two weeks unheralded by a single line in the daily press. The production of Gorf was partly funded by some rich society folk who dispensed no such largess to San Francisco's yet to be recognized Poet Laureate, Lew Welch, while he worked full time as a longshoreman. Philip Whalen, our most illustrious man of letters, now lives in anonymity at the Zen Center on Post Street and was turned down when he applied for a Guggenheim.

A copy of Gorf should be buried in a time capsule beneath the Vaillancourt Fountain. When both of these squalid objects are unearthed, our awestruck legatees will know exactly what passed for high culture in the atomic age.

SARMENTO, William Edward; (2) Theater Critic; (3) b. Lowell, Mass., 1946; (4) s. Manuel and Mary (Sheedy); (5) A.B. Boston U., major subj.: American Civilization, 1967, Ed.M. subj.: Educational Psychology, courses in drama and criticism at: Boston U., N.Y.U., U. of London; (6) single; (9) Theater Critic and Drama Editor, Lowell Sun and Sunday Sun, Lowell, Mass., 1961-75; (12) Director of Pupil Personnel Services: Tuckahoe, N.Y., 1971-75; (13) First Lieut.

U.S. Army; (16) Ind.; (17) Roman Catholic; (19) Boston University
Club; (20) Cont. articles to: Lowell Sun and Sunday Sun, Boston
Jewish Advocate, London Daily Telegraph, London Observer; (21) 500
East 77th St., New York, N.Y.; (22) Lowell Sun and Sunday Sun, Ph.
617-455-5671; (23) Circulation: 75,000; (24) 50 plays and musicals,
100 motion pictures, 25 ballets, 10 operas, 200 miscellaneous.

"A Chorus Line" Musical Worth a Trip to New York
(by William E. Sarmento, Lowell Sun, September 2, 1975)

It's a phenomenal summer on Broadway. Theaters are doing
great business. Several shows are playing to standing room only
crowds. And leading the town as the most extraordinary and
brilliant musical in ages is "A Chorus Line."

Regular readers of this column may indeed ask, "What's A
Chorus Line?" since it was not one of the many Broadway shows
I reviewed in this space this past season 'Tis true! "A Chorus
Line" opened in May at one of producer Joseph Papp's little theaters down in The Village. It became an instantaneous hit; and
because the theater in which it was playing had under 300 seats,
Mr. Papp bowing to the demand of a clamoring public, brought
the musical to Broadway at the end of July into the Shubert Theater. It has been a blockbuster there; and should run for years
and years.

So much for the background, "A Chorus Line" is the most
innovative musical since "West Side Story" almost 20 years ago.
It is the most wildly exciting musical to hit Broadway in the last
five years.

What "A Chorus Line" does is take the audience behind the
scenes of the Broadway musical stage and show us not the life
of the star and his or her friends, but rather it focuses in on
the faceless and nameless singers and dancers who usually blend
into the scenery of most big musical shows. This is their story.
A story about the hundreds of singers and dancers coming to
New York each year, hoping for any part in any show, and putting themselves through endless auditions that strip bare the very
soul of the performer. "A Chorus Line" is about just such an
audition and the two dozen or more singers and dancers putting
their talent, their dreams and their lives up for scrutiny and
evaluation. It is a musical that will lift your heart and break
your heart. It is a musical the likes of which you have never
seen before.

Utilizing the bare stage of an audition hall with only rehearsal mirrors in the background, "A Chorus Line" presents all
these singers and dancers trying to be their best. They perform.
They sing. They dance. They talk about themselves, their
background, their families, their successes, their disappoint-
ments. By the time "A Chorus Line" concludes, you know something about each performer and you are sitting there as anxious

as they awaiting the decision as to which of them has been chosen.

All the performers are terrific but let me single out Donna McKechnie about whom I wrote in this column five years ago. "She is the most exciting dancer to hit Broadway since Gwen Verdon." She is superb and if this show doesn't make her a star, I give up.

"A Chorus Line" is worth a trip to New York.

"The Norman Conquests" Are a Triumphant Triumvirate
(by William E. Sarmento, Lowell Sun, December 19, 1975)

For the first time I don't know when, a hit show has come to Broadway from London in a production that is even better than the original London version. The play or plays, as you shall soon learn, are called "The Norman Conquests"; and whereas I found them "mildly amusing" last Christmas when I was covering the new shows in London; they are now in their transplanted state wonderfully entertaining and sometimes downright hysterical. "The Norman Conquests" are a triumphant triumvirate and Broadway has three new hits. Read on, dear reader, and I shall explain.

"The Norman Conquests" is the banner under which British comedy writer Alan Ayckbourn has composed three separate and complete comedies. Their titles are: "Table Manners"; "Living Together" and "Round and Round the Garden." All three feature the same characters in basically the same situation. The trick is that the plays take place in this English country house which if you will accept the philosophy that all the world is a stage, then so too is this house. For in "Table Manners" we find our six characters in the dining room sorting out their problems. In "Living Together" we find those characters who were not on stage or who went off stage into another room of the house dealing with their problems. And in "Round and Round the Garden" all the characters who have wandered out of play one and play two into the garden to face their problems are seen. Each play is a comedy unto itself. And yet like a jigsaw puzzle, if you see all three, you are going to find even more to laugh at in each successive encounter.

The plot is simple enough, as is the case for most British farce comedies. Norman, an oversexed librarian assistant has planned a "dirty" weekend in East Grinstead with Annie, the young unmarried sister of his wife. Annie asks her brother and his busy-body wife to come to the house for the weekend to look after their sickly mother while Annie secretly goes off with Norman. Alas sister-in-law, Sarah finds out and halts the would be affair. Norman's wife is summoned from town. She is dedicated in life to her work and to getting Norman out of trouble. She dislikes her sister Sarah and her own mother. She would rather see sister Annie marry the dull veterinarian, Tom who hangs around the house curing the cat. And so they all converge on this country house for the wildest weekend the Broadway stage has seen in years.

The cast is just about magnificent. They do tend to let their British accents fall by the wayside too often, but this is a mild criticism of people who rotate in three different comedies nightly. Richard Benjamin is the amorous Norman. Paula Prentiss is the eager but not so willing Annie. Estelle Parsons is the neurotic Sarah. Barry Nelson her bewildered husband Reg. Ken Howard is the bumbling Tom. And Carole Shelly, the old true Britisher in the cast, is positively galvanizingly funny as the acid tongued wife of Norman. As directed by Eric Thompson, the cast and the plays are a joy.

Author Ayckbourn suggests that you can see the plays in any order. I beg to differ with him having seen all three now twice. If possible see them in the order I listed above. But for heaven's sake see them. "The Norman Conquests" are the three best comedies in town.

SAUNDERS, Dudley, Louisville Times, 525 West Broadway, Louisville, Ky. 40202.

SCHAU, Michael P.; (2) Editor, theatre and film critic; (3) b. St. Louis, Sept. 19, 1945; (4) s. Peter and Ruth (Froning) S.; (5) B.A. U. of Missouri, major subj.: English Lit., 1967; (6) m. Carole Beiser, Aug. 19, 1967; (8) Assoc. Editor Amusement Business magazine (Billboard Publications) 1967-69, Film Critic, Motion Picture Daily and Motion Picture Herald 1970, currently editor and entertainment critic Where magazine, New York edition; (20) Author J. C. Leyendecker 1974 and All American Girl: The Art of Coles Phillips 1975; (21) 173 Riverside Drive, New York City, N.Y. 10024, Ph. 212-877-9132; (22) Where magazine, 135 W. 50th Street, New York City, N.Y. 10020, Ph. 212-977-8395; (23) Circulation: 20,000; (24) 40 plays and musicals, 20 films, 10 miscellaneous productions, 25 free-lance book reviews.

Music with Hart
(by Michael Schau, Where Magazine, May 31, 1975)

Frankly stated, "Rodgers and Hart" has the best music of any Broadway show this season. But then, what other musical can boast ninety-eight songs by one of America's greatest songwriting teams? The title tells it: "Rodgers and Hart" is a celebration of music by Richard Rodgers and lyrics by Lorenz Hart, songs that are (to borrow Hart's own phrase) "so easy to remember, but so hard to forget."

The team, partnered from 1918 to 1943, wrote over five

hundred songs, many of them for such Broadway shows as "Babes in Arms," "The Boys From Syracuse," "On Your Toes" and "Pal Joey." The originators of this new show selected nearly one hundred to present excerpted or in total. The list is astonishing, both in terms of achievement by Rodgers and Hart, and of the evening's enjoyment.

The selections range from the familiar ("The Lady is a Tramp," "Blue Moon," "This Can't Be Love") to some less-well-known selections ("A Lovely Day for a Murder," "He and She," "Cause We Got Cake").

Director Burt Shevelove has staged the revue-type evening with an eye to showcasing the star--the music itself. Some songs have been collected into mini-vignettes, others cleverly mounted to give a new twist to a familiar lyric.

The cast of young people--six men and six women--sing, dance and act the songs which nicely cover the Rodgers and Hart territory: the songs of romance, the witty songs of "the classic battle of a him and her," wry songs of disenchantment with love, travel, New York City.

"Rodgers and Hart" mixes the sentimental and the cynical, the exuberant and the melancholy, but all in an affectionate trib-ute to the songwriters and their songs.

Next, Please
(by Michael Schau, Where Magazine, June 7, 1975)

Talented director Michael Bennett is responsible for "A Chorus Line," the new musical evening at the New York Shake-speare Festival Public Theater. Mr. Bennett must have seen the enormous theatricality and dramatic posibilities in auditions for a musical comedy chorus. He conceived, choreographed and directed this powerhouse show which takes place at the final try-out for "kids in the chorus."

And so, "A Chorus Line" is a show without a star, or more correctly, with seventeen co-stars. Some of Broadway's most talented young performers play the auditioning hopefuls. The di-rector of the show-within-the-show stands at the back of the the-atre and puts the line through its paces. Each of the seventeen gets his or her opportunity to shine somewhere during the even-ing, either in monologue or song and dance. They are indivi-duals who have in common (as the opening song tells us) the single thought: "I hope I get it; I need this job." By evening's end eight of the seventeen will be hired.

Here is a musical involving intense emotions, backstage backbiting, frustration and hope. The songs by Marvin Hamlisch and Edward Kleban cover the range perfectly. Mr. Hamlisch is best known as the multi-Oscared creator of movie music ("The

Way We Were," "The Sting"). But in this, his theatrical debut, he shows a decided flair for stage music. The James Kirkwood-Nicholas Dante book is admittedly based "on lives and experiences of Broadway dancers." The characters are fascinating and this is one of the few plays which attempts to explain what sort of people seek a livelihood in the theatre.

Michael Bennett, a former chorus boy himself, has made something special of dances in Broadway hits such as "Company," "Coco" and "Follies." His past stagings have worked such theatre magic that he seemed to be doing it with mirrors. For "A Chorus Line" mirrors are his only scenery and the effect is sensational. But then everything about "A Chorus Line" adds up to an electrifying, one-of-a-kind musical show.

SCHIER, Ernest; (2) Drama Critic; (3) b. N.Y. City, Mar. 25, 1918; (4) s. David & Celia (Reiss); (5) Autodidact; (6) m. Marjorie Poore, June 30, 1945; (7) children--Johanna, Jennifer, Harry, William; (8) Drama Critic, Washington Post, 1942-43; Drama Critic, Washington Times Herald 1946-54; Press Relations, Arena Stage, Washington, D.C. 1954-55. Film Critic, Philadelphia Daily News, 1956-58; Drama/Film Critic Evening and Sunday Bulletin, 1958 & currently; (9) Project Director, National Critics Institute, O'Neill Center, 305 Great Neck Road, Waterford, Conn. Chairman, Executive Committee, American Theatre Critics Association. Instructor in Playwriting, Villanova University; (22) Evening and Sunday Bulletin, 30th and Market Sts., Philadelphia, Pa. 19101; (23) Circulation: 700,000.

Phoenix Brings Distinction to the Zellerbach
(by Ernest Schier, Evening and Sunday Bulletin, October 19, 1972)

The New Phoenix Repertory Company has jumped right in with a major production of "The Great God Brown," one of Eugene O'Neill's most difficult plays, and brought it off with something close to astounding success.

The Phoenix, newly reorganized with Harold Prince as one of its three artistic directors, upgraded the local theater season last night and brought a new measure of distinction to Penn's Zellerbach Theater, where it has opened a three-week stand.

To judge by the performance (with Moliere's "Don Juan" still to come) the company of actors is one of the finest of any repertory in the land and they have thrown themselves, under Prince's direction, completely into the task of penetrating a play that on some levels is impenetrable.

O'Neill wrote "The Great God Brown" in 1926. In it he attempted through the use of masks worn (or carried) by the characters to deal with the conflicting natures of man, to show what went on inside as well as outside of each being, and to examine the warring drives of spiritualism and materialism.

The plot has to do with Dion Anthony (Dionysius and St. Anthony) who is a devil-may-care, regular fellow on the outside but a sensitive artistic soul behind his mask, rebelling against man's fate, searching for the meaning of life, etc.

As long as he shows his social face he is loved by Margaret, whom he marries, and his best friend, Billy Brown. Without the mask he terrifies his wife and becomes a stranger in his own home.

"The Great God Brown" begins as a simple anti-Establishment play and then goes careening off into a dozen heavy questions: the life force vs. the death wish, paganism vs. Christianity, the question of the existence of God and the quest for love. By his own judgement, O'Neill felt "The Great God Brown" missed achieving the mysticism he wanted to emphasize.

That is probably true. For two acts, "The Great God Brown" holds up remarkably well but in the third, when Dion dies of a heart attack and his friend Brown takes his place and becomes Margaret's husband, the tension fades into confusion and the metaphysics are dissolved in melodrama.

O'Neill was dissatisfied with the mask device and in this director Prince agrees. The masks in this production are only indications of the dualistic nature of Dion and Brown and the women in their lives. The approach frees the actors to do on their own the work that the masks were intended to do.

This is a measured, almost deliberate concept that Prince brings to the play and it proves also to be warmly sympathetic to O'Neill and to the play's problems of construction and meaning. It is almost entirely absorbing even when, in the final act, the action becomes not only murky but hectic.

What holds it all together is the acting, three or four performances by actors who are masterful interpreters of O'Neill. John McMartin is fine as Dion Anthony, the young man who drinks his way to oblivion, Katherine Helmond is a pea-brained Margaret, and Marilyn Sokol is splendid as Cybel, the prostitute who is a stand-in for the Mother Earth figure in O'Neill's scheme of things.

The title role belongs to John Glover, who is tall, slender and brilliant as the envious Brown who pursues success and then tries passionately to become Dion.

Glover smooths the roughness of O'Neill with his sensitive performance and develops a rhythm that is the dominating force of the play. The sets by Boris Aronson, tiny revolving floor pieces, sketch out home, office, a water front casino and other places in the play.

O'Neill has seldom been treated better than he is in this
devoted production of a flawed play.

"3 Daughters" Raps Marriage
(by Ernest Schier, Evening and Sunday Bulletin, May 18, 1976)

"The Three Daughters of Monsieur Dupont" all come to an
unhappy end, which is not surprising in light of the fact that they
were created to dramatize the oppression of women. Eugene
Brieux, who wrote the play close to the end of the last century,
was the Ibsen of France, although he did not have the talent of
Ibsen, nor could he write with the vitality, power and brevity
of Ibsen.

The Philadelphia Company has undertaken the admirable project of polishing up "The Three Daughters of Monsieur Dupont"
with a new translation by Pauline Jones, and an energetic and
sincere performance by the company. Apparently, for the sake
of scholarship, the play is offered uncut. It does tend to make
a long evening of anguished melodrama but many of the scenes
are played at a high enough level of energy to make the theater-
goer's investment in time more than worthwhile.

Brieux' drama is quite simply an attack on marriage--one
of Shaw's favorite subjects, as well--and the treatment of women
as so many chattels, chips in the game of middleclass life.

"The Three Daughters of Monsieur Dupont" could almost be
a contemporary polemic from the feminist movement.

The playwright's rhetoric matches his fervor. He is far
less interested in the interaction of character than he is in making points. This isn't always a fault. In one scene there is a
discordant symphony as the members of two families shriek out
their points of view. It is an amusing scene.

The play deals with the marriage of the youngest Dupont to
the scion of a neighboring family. On both sides the motivating
factor is greed, although the bride-to-be cherishes illusions of
motherhood and a happy family life.

She finds anything but, marriage to a man who is gross,
ignorant and insincere.

The dialog is direct and wooden. Many ideas are conveyed
several times. But there is passion to the work under the careful, sympathetic and most of all appreciative direction of James
J. Christy. He has done splendidly in sustaining the pace and
grouping the actors on the small stage in ways that continually
suggest the forces at work.

Largely, this is a good cast. John Owen is forceful as the

father caught up in a system where he thinks selling off a daughter is both moral and good business.

Majorie Murray is persuasive as the daughter who is rapidly disillusioned by marriage, and Carla Belva, in an admirable character portrait, is simply true to life as a spinster who takes conslation in religion.

Most of the performances are on the same high level, although Rosemary Seminar seems quite lost as Madam Dupont, and Peter Mattaliano does everything but twirl his moustache as the loutish young husband.

SCHOLEM, Richard Jay; (2) Theater Critic; (3) b. Sept. 28, 1931; (4) s. Charles and Evelyn (Levy); (5) B. A. Bowling Green State U. , (Ohio), major subj. : speech/drama, 1953; (6) m. Ann Fast, Aug. 22, 1954; (7) children--Robert; (8) Staff Announcer, WFOB, Fostoria, (Ohio) 1951-53, News, Sports, Sales, KGBC, Galveston (Texas) 1955-57, Critic, News, Sports, Managment, WTIG, Massillon (Ohio) 1957-1966, Radio, TV Director, Kent State U. , Kent (Ohio) 1966-67, Critic/Management, Greater New York Radio 1967-present, Drama Critic: National Public Radio 200 Station Network 1969-74; (9) Drama Student: Bowling Green State U. , Ohio, Actor, Director, Stage Hand: Bowling Green State U. , Ohio, Board Member: Huntington Arts Council, Huntington (New York) 1970-75; (10) President: American Civil Liberties Union, Suffolk Chapter, Suffolk (Long Island) 1970-73, Board Member: Suffolk County Family Services 1970-75, President: Massillon (Ohio) Urban League 1960-67, Board Member: Akron (Ohio) American Civil Liberties Union 1960-67; (13) 1st Lieutenant U. S. Air Force 1953-55; (14) Massillon (Ohio) Citywide Human Relations Award 1964, Community Service Award, Huntington Arts Council 1973, Elliott Stewart Award for the writing and directing of New York State's most outstanding Public Affairs Program 1972 (presented by New York State Broadcaster's Association), Special Citation for Distinguished Editorial Writing in New York State (presented by United Press International) 1973 and 1974, 6th Annual Elliott Stewart Award for Outstanding Broadcast Editorial Commentary (presented by United Press International); (15) Drama Critic's Outer Circle, Drama Desk; (16) Democrat; (17) Jewish; (20) 52 Broadcast editorials each year for the past 18 years, broadcast on various radio stations in Ohio and New York, many public affairs programs and series of programs including the award winning Emergency Medical Care on Long Island; (21) 7 Bayview Lane, Huntington Bay, New York 11743, Ph. 516-271-3227; (22) 900 Walt Whitman Road, Melville, New York 11746 and 509 Madison Ave. , New York, New York 10022; (23) Audience reached: 750,000; (24) 100 to 150 reviews annually.

"The Wiz"
(by Richard J. Scholem, over Greater New York Radio, January 6, 1975)

The Wiz at the Majestic Theater has a style of its own and the style is soul ... for The Wiz is a black spoof of The Wizard

Of Oz. No Judy Garland singing "Over the Rainbow" here. The music is rock, soul, gospel, rhythm and blues.

The Munchkins are jive-talking midgets. The evil witch is a black Sophie Tucker, sprouting lines that sound as if they were written by Mel Brooks. The good witch of the West refers to her as a "downer." The cowardly lion is in psycho-therapy with an owl who listens a lot, but says nothing. And, the Tinman is referred to as a "spaced out garbageman."

In short, The Wiz is a clever novelty show directed with an artful touch by Geoffrey Holder. The dances are exciting. The cast--first rate!

Stephanie Mills as Dorothy and Mabel King as Evillene, the witch, were especially commendable.

This is a flamboyant, imaginative production, sporting some of the most colorful and diverse costumes and scenery of the theater season. Weaknesses? Yes. It is far from a perfect show. The style and excitement have enough momentum to take about two hours. Unfortunately, the show runs longer. But, no matter. This is an evening of fun and light entertainment. It is, in fact, a blacktacular!

"Same Time Next Year"
(by Richard J. Scholem, over Greater New York Radio, March 14, 1975)

There are only three people to talk about in Same Time Next Year, at the Brooks Atkinson Theater, but the minute and a half I have allotted me will not be enough to properly praise this new comedy by playwrite Bernard Slade, making his Broadway debut and the show's only two performers, Ellen Burstyn and Charles Grodin. In a word, Same Time Next Year is marvelous, brimming over with life, humor, warmth and the ability to turn a laugh to a tear in an instant.

Miss Burstyn, who has received two academy award nominations and is pending another, is an Oakland housewife married at 18, living in a downtown duplex with her husband and a number of children when we first meet her in 1951 ... Mr. Grodin, a New Jersey C. P. A. similarly married, full of hangups, insecurities and guilt. The two become lovers for what initially looks like a single weekend, but they continue to meet one weekend every year. The audience sees them grow and change and interact and come to know each other inside out. They laugh and love and argue and mature through the fads and the fears of the period between 1951 and 1975. She turns from typical housewife to beatnik to businesswoman, he from C. P. A. to establishment type to cocktail lounge musician.

Mr. Slade has written us sympathetic characters, believable understandable people--a delightfully funny and warm show. He is a Canadian who has been laboring in the mundane world of television, who we hope will bring his work back to Broadway again and again.

Burstyn and Grodin are a matched pair bringing perfection to their roles. Their acting and reacting to one another is the stuff of which Tony Awards are made.

On a night like last night, all the weeks of watching dreadful theater become worthwhile for Same Time Next Year will deservedly be on Broadway in a year from now and for many to come. It's a story of real people tenderly and humorously told.

SCUDDER, Virgil Elmer; (2) News editor and arts specialist; (3) b. Vevay, Ind., Sept. 25, 1936; (4) s. Howard and Bessie (Romans) Scudder; (5) A.B., Indiana U.; major--radio & television; minor--music history, 1958; p.g. work at Montclair State College, Upper Montclair, N.J.; (6) m. Marlene Susan Shaul, Aug. 17, 1963; (7) children--Kenneth H. (b. 1967), Kathryn (b. 1969); (8) News and sports editor, WJCD, Seymour, Ind., 1958-59; News director, WSAL, Longansport, Ind. 1959-62; Cable Television management, Jerrold Electronics Corp., Philadelphia, 1962-64; News and Sports Director, WCTC, New Brunswick, N.J. 1964-69; News editor, WINS, New York, 1969-76, NBC Radio, New York, 1976- ; (9) Actor, director, Logansport Civic Players, 1959-62; (14) Ohio State University award, 1974, for excellence in coverage of the arts in New York City; New Jersey Sigma Delta Chi award, 1969, for political coverage; New Jersey Sportswriters Association citation, 1970, for sportscasting; (15) The Society of Journalists, Sigma Delta Chi; Writers Guild of America-East; American Federation of Television and Radio Artists (AFTRA); (21) 49 Essex Avenue, Metuchen, N.J. 08840, Ph. 201-549-6865; (22) WINS, 90 Park Avenue, N.Y., N.Y. 10016, Ph. 212-867-5100; (23) Circulation: 50,000 watts; (24) 75 plays and musicals, 6 concerts, 3 operas, 10 miscellaneous.

"All Over Town"
(by Virgil Scudder, over WINS radio, New York, December 29, 1974)

Murray Schisgal writes the kind of comedy you're sure you won't like. Predictable, slapdash, and just as orthodox as can be. No message that I can detect and nothing to remove it from the category of pure escapist entertainment.

Still, "All Over Town" has one great redeeming virtue--it's a very funny show. And, I guess that's all that was intended.

"All Over Town" is a sex farce based on mistaken identities. There are eleven doors and two windows, and people are popping in and out of them constantly.

But, Dustin Hoffman, in his first effort as a director, has had the wisdom to keep things moving.

And, he has a cast that can work wonders, especially leading man Cleavon Little, a stylish performer with impeccable
comic timing.

"All Over Town" is a little silly, a little dirty, and very,
very funny.

"He That Plays the King"
(by Virgil Scudder, over WINS radio, New York, April 2, 1975)

One of the great assets of New York's theatre season in recent years has been the Royal Shakespeare Company. This fine
troupe, based in Stratford-on-Avon and London, has become a
Brooklyn institution.

Ian Richardson, one of the world's greatest actors and a
Shakespearean interpreter without peer, has put together a fascinating collection of excerpts from MacBeth, Hamlet, Lear,
John, Richard II, Richard III, and Henrys the fourth, fifth, and
sixth. They comprise some of Shakespeare's most interesting
characters and challenging roles.

Richardson is joined by Mike Gwilym, Tony Church, and
Susan Fleetwood--all fine performers with distinctive styles.
Gwilym as Hamlet, Church as Lear, Fleetwood as Lady Mac-
Beth--all splendid renditions. But the evening's highlights are
a delightful courtship scene from Henry V and Richardson's
frightfully compelling Richard III.

"He That Plays the King" is not for everybody. But, for
those who admire kings, the English language, or superlative
acting, the evening is quite a treat.

SHARP, Christopher William; (2) Theater and Book Critic; (3) b. San
Francisco, Dec. 10, 1948; (4) s. William Walter and Marjory Dawn
(Wesperman) Sharp; (5) Two years undergraduate studies at Southwestern Oregon Community College and Oregon State U. (6) Single
(8) Editor of College Newspaper and Chairman of College Publications
Board, 1969-71; VISTA Volunteer, 1968-69, stationed in Orange
County, Fla; Reporter and Critic for Women's Wear Daily, 1972-
present; (9) Acted in three local plays in Coos Bay, Ore. from 1969-
71; Contributor to the Willamette Bridge, a weekly newspaper in Portland, Ore. 1971; (10) Served as a Volunteer Fireman for the city of
Eatonville, Fla. 1969; Served in a forest fire crew for the U.S. Forest Service, in Grants Pass, Ore. 1970; Volunteer for a suicide pre-
vention telephone service in Portland, Ore. 1971; Volunteer Attendant
at a charitable overnight lodge for derelicts in Portland, Ore. 1971;
Scoutmaster for a church scout troop in New York City, 1973; (11)
Coos County Delegate to the Oregon Democratic State Convention,
1970; (16) Democrat; (17) Mormon; (19) By-lined articles and reviews
have appeared in several newspapers throughout the country under
the Fairchild Syndication Services; theater reviews are collected in

"New York Theatre Critics' Reviews" published by Critics' Theatre
Reviews; (21) 154 West 75 Street, New York, N.Y. 10023, Ph. 212-
362-8122; (22) Women's Wear Daily, 7 East 12 Street, New York,
N.Y. 10003, Ph. 212-741-4048; (23) Circulation: 80,000; (24) 25
plays, 15 books, 15 miscellaneous.

"Cat on a Hot Tin Roof"

There is at least one critical advantage is seeing a brilliantly written and well-staged play for a second time: One is not
so preoccupied with the novelty of the production's technique.
There is little reason to be surprised again by interpretation.
The technique of the play is clearly subordinate to its substance.

Director Michael Kahn's version of "Cat on a Hot Tin Roof"
--staged this summer at Stratford, Conn. , and now being presented at the Anta Theater--in a wonderful example of substance
overtaking technique. This version is vintage Tennessee Williams, and if at times it seems that Maggie is mostly a mouthpiece for Williams, what the playwright says through her is chilling. It is Elizabeth Ashley who gives character to the lines that
count. Her Maggie is a cat, but closer to a wildcat than a
housecat.

In my review of the Stratford production, I mentioned that
Kahn's version stresses a close relationship between the characters and their thoughts. When originally produced, Williams'
dialog was such a novelty that the lines were presented in a
disembodied form, with many of the actors simply delivering
them directly to the audience. Here the lines are clearly a part
of the chemistry of the characters. What is interesting is that
the American Shakespeare Theater--in staging its first play by
a living American playwright--has chosen a work that comes close
to Shakespearean language. The highlights do not come in the
action--there is almost no physical action--but rather in the
poetry.

The first two acts are staged here as monologs by Maggie
and Big Daddy respectively. Brick--played by Keir Dullea--has
the difficult task of punctuating these monologs with occasional
wisecracks and sarcastic protests. His rebuttals are important
because they keep Maggie's and Big Daddy's soliloquies from
dissolving into philosophical ether. Unfortunately, Dullea gives
the impression of being a sounding board. His is the weakest
performance of all.

Although this production (which I saw in a preview) belongs
to Ms. Ashley, there are other striking performances. Fred
Gwynne as Big Daddy fills the stage with the old patriarch's
bellicose personality. Gwynne is just as effective with understatement, and funniest when he combines hyperbole with an understated delivery. Charles Siebert's Gooper is truly slimy,
yet he never disintegrates into a stereotype. Kate Reid--who

seems interested mainly in drawing laughs as Big Mama--is not on the stage long enough to ruin the play.

The lasting impression is that of Maggie's self-imposed martyrdom. Elizabeth Ashley finally becomes more than a mouthpiece for the playwright; she becomes the conscience of the play. In addition to doing everything that is required of her in this production, Ms. Ashley conveys a compelling femininity.

"Same Time, Next Year"

Bernard Slade's new comedy at the Brooks Atkinson Theater proves that good old jokes--like good old songs--seem to improve with the years. The old jokes in "Same Time, Next Year" encompass unexpected labor pains, impotence and sexual hypocrisy. In the hands of lesser actors, these good old jokes could seem like schtick; in the hands of Ellen Burstyn and Charles Grodin, the comedy glistens.

The play is about a couple who--while married to others-- have honored an annual rendezvous at a California cottage for 25 years. The affair began casually enough--after the first night in bed, the pair had to learn each other's names--but quickly the two became romantically involved. Strangely enough, they never had the opportunity to see each other more often than once a year. But the annual date is potent enough to accelerate and change the course of their lives.

Ms. Burstyn's Doris is subject to a little suspension of reality. Within five-year intervals, she changes from a rather inhibited housewife on a fling to a floozy, then from a hippie to hardnosed businesswoman. In fact, every time we see her show up for her rendezvous, her new role is as grating to our expectations as a non-sequitur. What keeps Doris from becoming unbelievable is Ms. Burstyn's gift for understatement. Her understated, even characterization smooths Doris's rocky transitions. Moreover, it's clear that Doris is a little uncomfortable regardless of what she draws from her wardrobe of affected personalities. The result of Ms. Burstyn's effort is a vulnerable and beautiful woman who is swept up but never washed up in the trends of the last 25 years.

Charles Grodin's George is as shaky as Doris is steady. While Ms. Burstyn makes her lines spiral, Grodin's lines seem to wobble. His is a lopsided comic presence on stage, and he is even more consistently funny here than he was in the film "The Heartbreak Kid." His comic sensitivity is so acute that he can give life to a line by a calculated waver of his voice. Still-life lines such as "I'm not a cab driver--I don't know how to deliver a baby" become animated by his delivery.

The first three scenes of the play take place in 1951, 1956 and 1961. The second act encompasses scenes in 1965, 1970

and 1975. Doris pretends to her husband that she is going on
a Catholic retreat so that she doesn't have to be with her mother-in-law on the latter's birthday. For this reason, Doris and
George can meet only on the birthdays of Doris' mother-in-law.

The humor in the first act is sharper than in the second,
perhaps because the first act deals with old sexual jokes that
haven't been fossilized by the movies and television shows of
the 1950s. The comedy revolves around sexual guilt, particularly George's. At one point, Doris asks George if he is Jewish. He says no, and she asks him why he is so guilty. It is
guilt that gives George continuity through his many changes, just
as Ms. Burstyn's creation of besieged innocence gives Doris a
certain constancy.

The presence of director Gene Saks is evident in the balancing act between the characters. While Grodin's comedy is more
choleric and louder than Ms. Burstyn's, at no time does one
character take over the stage at the expense of the other.

It's curious that the guest cottage where the two meet doesn't
change over the years. The constancy in the setting is obviously
intentional, but the intentions are not clear. Against the background of an unchanging setting, Jane Greenwood's costumes
seem more luminous than they should. Yet, Ms. Greenwood accomplishes the goal of every good costume director. Her clothes
express things that the characters don't talk about.

All in all, "Same Time, Next Year" is good for laughs, and
that's all anyone can want in a Broadway comedy.

SHEEHAN, David; (2) Entertainment Reporter and Critic; (5) U. of
Notre Dame, Journalism; UCLA, Theater Arts; (8) WLW-C, WTUN,
WDNU-TV, 1966-71; KNXT, Los Angeles, 1971- ; (9) Managing Di-
rector of Theater Now Troupe at Century Playhouse, 1967-71; (20)
Before I Wake, novel; pub. in Esquire, Mademoiselle, Los Angeles
Magazine; (22) KNXT, 6121 Sunset Blvd. , Los Angeles, Cal. 90028,
Ph. 213-469-1212; (24) All major movie and local stage productions,
produces 2 half-hour television specials per year.

SHERTZER, James Melton; (2) Theatre, Film, Music and Dance Critic; (3) b. Washington, D. C. , April 12, 1943; (4) s. George Monroe
and Edythe (Melton) S. ; (5) B. A. , Wake Forest U. , major subj. :
English, 1965; M. A. , Wake Forest, English, 1971; Fellow, West
Coast Institute for Dance Criticism, California State U. at Long
Beach, Summer 1972; (6) Single; (8) Film Critic, Old Gold and Black,
Wake Forest University, 1963-64; News Editor, Old Gold and Black,
1964-65; Staff Reporter and Film Critic, Winston-Salem (N. C.) Journal, 1967-71; Staff Arts Reporter, Winston-Salem Journal, 1971- ;
(9) College Theatre, Wake Forest University, 1961-62; Director of
College Union Film Series at Wake Forest University, 1963-65; (10)

Juror, Little Theatre of Winston-Salem Bicentennial Play Contest,
1975-76; (16) Democratic; (20) Unpublished M. A. thesis, "Edgar Allen Poe: Hoaxer and Practical Joker"; (21) 1615-A Zuider Zee
Drive, Winston-Salem, N. C. 27107, Ph. 919-784-0319; (22) Winston-
Salem Journal, 416-420 N. Marshall Street, Box 3159, Winston-Salem,
N. C. 27102, Ph. 919-725-2311; (23) Circulation: 100,000; (24) 28
plays and musicals; 44 motion pictures; 32 musical concerts; 44 recordings; 6 dance programs.

"Godspell" a Mire of Calculation
(by Jim Shertzer, Winston Salem Journal, February 22, 1975)

The "Godspell" According to William Dreyer and the N. C.
School of the Arts can be summed up in three words: it doesn't
work.

My first reaction to the production, which opened Thursday
night at the Agnes de Mille Theatre, was that the concept and
script were not strong enough to stand up through yet another
viewing.

The pop-rock musical based on the Gospel According to St.
Matthew has been offered here twice in the last six months
(three times counting the movie version on television), and a
large chunk of it was also in last year's N. C. Summer Festival
revue.

The show, which relies on audience surprise for much of
its effectiveness, is not one that wears well. But 15 minutes
into this staging, I realized overexposure was not the reason
for my lack of interest in the doings on stage.

The cast was simply doing John-Michael Tebelak and Stephen
Schwartz's material badly. To realize how badly, all I had to
do was think about the vital and sincere touring version here in
August and November.

Instead of radiating spontaneity, this "Godspell" was a mire
of calculation. The vaudeville routines and corny jokes came
out too tired to be funny. Most of the stage business and routines in the audience seemed sophomoric. The show's spirit of
love was poorly conveyed in cute mannerisms, and the general
mood of artifice and insincerity left even the crucifixion of Jesus
unmoving.

I had not fully appreciated before just how tough a show this
is to pull off or realized what an embarrassing, tiresome mess
the musical is with its heady pop evangelism and high spirits
rendered as windy theology and kinetic energy.

Neither director Dreyer nor much of the overly large cast
(with 14 people attending The Last Supper) seems up to the demands of the show, and the production is further weakened by
its set.

Dreyer and designer Robert Stephen Nance offer "Godspell" in a circus tent instead of the usual sparsely decorated junkyard. The set thrusts into the auditorium, with its main ring center stage and aerial bars and rings above.

There is too much to look at, and Dreyer--unsure of what to do with all the space--invariably has too much going on. It is so distracting that one quickly realizes why wise directors have played "Godspell" on an almost naked stage.

The circus setting, of course, forces the actors into circus roles. Jesus is a clown garbed in white, with a prissy neck ruffles, and the ringmaster takes the John the Baptist-Judas role. Others turn up as lion tamers, strong men, high wire artists, exotic dancers and the like, instead of the hippie types of conventional stagings.

Cast members supposedly play themselves in this show or are at least to draw from their own personalities in creating their stage characters. This is one of the most delightful facets of the show and why no two productions ought to be quite the same.

In this setting, though, the performers are carried away with their circus parts, and too little of themselves come through. Some exceptions are Judy Montgomery, Lorri Lindberg, Ramonia Kornegay and Missy Snelling, who share some measure of themselves with the audience.

Everyone else fails to open up, especially Bob McClendon, who is miscast as Jesus and cannot muster the dramatic strength to take charge of the stage and his disciples.

Musically, the show is in good hands with Brian Evans and his band. But as singers, the drama students vary. Some sing very well; others just get by and some are apparently tone deaf. "By My Side," one of the show's loveliest ballads, was sung in no less than four keys at once. Audience enthusiasm ran high at the opening. And with the entire run through March 2 sold out in advance, the show is certainly a resounding popular success. As an example of what the arts school can do, though, it is painfully disappointing stuff.

"Oh Coward!" Is Tiresome
(by Jim Shertzer, Winston Salem Journal, February 28, 1975)

Like a swank society party, "Oh Coward!," presented at Reynolds Auditorium Tuesday night by the Winston-Salem Civic Music Association, made a civilized but slightly tiresome evening.

There was plenty of individual sparkle in the more than four dozen Noel Coward songs on parade in Roderick Cook's homage to the late Englishman gifted with such an extraordinary talent to amuse.

But like champagne, the fizz began to go flat as the party wore on. Coward addicts could doubtless have gulped down several more hours with delight.

But others probably started noticing the weakesses as well as the strengths of Coward's songs (notably melodies that seldom measure up to the lyrics), as well as the weaknesses of the cast of three.

Patricia Morison, Christian Grey and Dalton Cathey waltzed engagingly through Cook's frequently imaginative staging but hardly seemed to be giving the show their all.

Grey's top-drawer delivery of "The Party's Over Now," which brimmed with urbane impishness, should not have been the standout it was. The whole show should have been similarly spirited.

As it was, the trio was content to be lightly amusing and seldom tried to be more, though some genuinely delightful moments cropped up in "The Stately Homes of England," "Uncle Harry," "Mad Dogs and Englishmen" and the gingerly risque "Let's Do It," a Coward collaboration with Cole Porter.

Miss Morison was additionally handicaped by vocal tightness, unsure pitch and weak projection that left a good half of her lyric dropping around her ankles.

Reynolds is not an ideal house for what is basically an intimate revue, and that hurt, too.

SHIPLEY, Joseph Twadell; (2) Theater critic; (3) b. New York, Aug. 19, 1893; (4) s. Jay R. and Jennie (Fragner) Shipley; (5) B.A. CCNY 1912 (Phi Beta Kappa); M.A. 1914, Ph.D. 1931 in Comparative Literature, Columbia U.; (6) m.; (7) children--Margaret (Mrs. Leslie Fiedler), Paul, John Burke, Thorne; (8) Drama critic: The Call, The Leader (daily), The New Leader (weekly), 1918-1962; Radio Station WEVD 1940- ; longest in service of all New York critics; (9) President, New York Drama Critics' Circle, 1952-54; Secretary same 1968- ; Taught literary and dramatic criticism of the graduate school, CCNY, 1928-42. Lectured in the US and 12 other countries on American life as shown in the theater; (10) President, CCNY Class Alumni, (12) Member, Cultural Advisory Board, American College in Paris; Board of Directors of Hwa Kiu University, Macao; Chinese Univ., Hong Kong. Listed in Who's Who in America, Who's Who in the Theatre (London); (14) CCNY Alumni Service Award, 1974; (15) American Advisor to Theatre des Nations. Honorary Overseas Member of the Critics' Circle, London; American Representative of the International Association of Theatre Critics; (20) Among published books: The Art of Eugene O'Neill (1928), first book on O'Neill; Guide to Great Plays; Five Major Plays of Ibsen; The Quest for Literature; Trends in Literature. Wrote and edited study guides to plays of

Shakespeare. For two years, wrote on the New York theater for the Manchester Guardian. For 8 years wrote a monthly column on the New York theater in the Paris Theatre. Articles in many periodicals in America, England, France, Pakistan, and India; (21) Oct. 1 to April 30, 29 West 46th Street, New York, N. Y. 10036, Ph. 212-246-4314; May 1 to Sept. 30, 13 Gledhow Gardens, London SW5oAY, England, Ph. 01-370-3521 (for annual survey of the European theater); (24) About 75 reviews of theater, opera, dance, per year.

Fertile Fusion of Art and Life
(by Joseph T. Shipley, New Leader, November 30, 1959)

In the theater, Nobel Prize-winner Luigi Pirandello has been the prime explorer of the tenuous border line between life and art. Art, say many critics, imitates nature. Life, say fewer but no less astute observers, strives to imitate art. Pirandello suggests that there is a haunting region where you cannot tell the two apart.

Note that he is in no way dogmatic. He does not seek to make up your mind. He shows you events and situations: you may--if you are sufficiently presumptuous--judge them. What you see in them depends upon what you may be. Pirandello will not tip the scales; as one of his titles puts it: "Right you are-- if you think you are."

Pirandello's most complete explorations of the range where art and life commingle are the well-known Six Characters in Search of an Author and the even more entertaining Tonight We Improvise. In the former, six characters, tossed aside by their author, break in upon a director and insist that their story be completed. In the latter, a company of players, told by the director to forget the script and to improvise, begin to live their parts, throw out the director, and complete their story.

Tonight We Improvise is the latest production of The Living Theater, whose repertoire has been making off-Broadway history. In a sparking translation by Claude Fredericks, deftly directed by Julian Beck, the harum-scarum incidents spin across footlights into the audience, and out into the lobby at intermission, until with theatrical assurance the author goes onstage again for a deeply moving scene--then in a sudden finale swoops back to the entanglement of life in art.

The evening begins with the director explaining to the audience that today the author is negligible. The director should dismiss the writer, set the actors rolling, and--actors planted in the audience start to heckle. Julian Beck seems a man of unstrained good will and patience; he will have the actors out, to introduce them. But the first actor he calls, Alan Ansara, objects. He has already begun to put himself into the part, he protests; he is not Alan, he is Rico. Rico is coming to life, and must neither be interrupted nor ordered about.

Somehow the players get started with the story of the La
Croce family. The engineer father is cuckolded by his bossy
wife, and dismayed by his four wanton daughters, who are giving
the young men of their Sicilian town untold pleasure, except for
jealous Rico, who wants Mommina all for himself. He marries
her, then sets her in the prison of his jealousy, shrouding her
in reproaches of her past. Rico's fancies of the things she used
to do with other men crush Mommina, despite the drab fidelity
of her wedded years. Imagination is more powerful than reality.

At the end of this story the director, whom the actors have
thrown out, pops in again and tells them they've done a good
job. At once they protest. Some demand set speeches, precise
lines to memorize: What's an actor for? And as the wrangling
begins again, the final curtain falls.

To make clear the play's Sicilian setting, we are shown a
motion picture that is a whirr of meaningless colors and lines
that would curdle the abstract blood in Cocteau's Blood of a Poet.
The boys take the La Croce girls to a show; they go off--and
come to our theater. Down the aisle they flaunt their noisy way,
looking for their seats, variously tangling themselves with our
lives in front of the travesty of Pagliacci that has somehow gotten onto the stage. During intermission, the characters of the
play are in the lobby with the rest of us. Near a drinking-foun-
tain, Rico continues his jealous quarrel with Mommina.

Other problems of art break into the story. Papa La Croce,
his shirt dyed deep with blood, interrupts his death scene to
complain that those onstage ignore his dying entrance. They
protest that they must act as they feel--no one paid any attention
to him while he was alive; why bother with him, dying?--and
several versions are proposed before the story moves on. But
before it ends, the playwright pulls 15 full minutes of sincere
and poignant emotion, as the imprisoned Mommina sets her child
on the floor and before the silent infant tries to recreate her
joyous past. Actress Judith Malina rises in this scene to deeply
moving art.

The fresh translation, the understanding direction and the
concordant company, make this the best Pirandello production
New York has seen in a score of years. There may seem a
measure of presumption in one company's pre-empting "The Living Theater" as its name, but there is no doubt that in this production art and life have made a fertile fusion.

Ionesco Turns Man Back to the Herd
(by Joseph T. Shipley, New Leader, January 23, 1961)

It is the fashion, if not indeed the fate, of our time to shake
its head over the depressing state of the world. Unfortunately
too many rest content with shaking their heads--the idea of positive action seems not to occur to them. And all the heads swing

in unison before any work that claims to show what is wrong with the world.

In the theater, such works take two main forms. They may be realistic pictures emphasizing degeneration or degeneracy, such as we are familiar with from Tennessee Williams and his brood. Or they may be symbolic representations of man's forlorn state or dismal destiny. Some of these have been quite direct, clear and forceful, like Capek's R.U.R.; more recent plays have masked their thought in modernistic devices, as in Beckett's Waiting for Godot and Ionesco's Bald Soprano. Now Ionesco has plumped for clarity in his new play, Rhinoceros.

Perhaps it is unfortunate that Ionesco has spoken clearly. He has with him the herd of headshakers, but his play is an attack upon the herd. Those that hold back, to ponder before they join, may find that what has become clear is the routine quality of Ionesco's thought and the shallow nature of its development.

Capek in 1921 was concerned with the mechanization of men, the grinding down of the individual by the machine. Ionesco today is concerned with the gregation of men, the absorption of the individual in the herd. "People who try to hang onto their individuality always come to a bad end," says Berrenger, the last human in the play, desperately trying to turn himself, as all the others have turned, into a rhinoceros.

Anthropologists tell us that primitive man existed as part of a group; consciousness of the "I" emerged only gradually from the "we." Now, many suggest, the process is reversing itself. Such is the thesis of Ionesco. Presumably for its dramatic values--though also for his clowning--he takes as his herd-symbol not the sheep but the rhinoceros.

The idea, indeed, is developed less by a thinker than by a clown. The first act is spent in largely irrelevant buffoonery. For most of the play, we are urged to laughter rather than to thought. It is only toward the very end that the basic theme is urged--and then by the wrong person.

For Berrenger, the one human who is not changed, should have been one of the first to go. He is a Caspar Milquetoast sort of fellow, lengthily troubled and apologetic because he has offended his pal, and wishy-washy in most of his actions. The play lacks point, indeed, because in the persons presented there is no valid reason for their becoming herd-creatures; this aspect of their being is not stressed. As a result, the "rhinocerization," which apparently strikes only this town, seems more like a freak pestilence than a symbolic mutation of mankind.

Details of the drama are on an equally childish level. There is a "logician" who seems to impress the folk onstage with what we called at the age of 10 "sillygisms"--such as "Fish swim.

Socrates swims. Therefore Socrates is a fish." Does Ionesco
believe he is satirizing modern thinking with repeated piddling
of this sort? What level of audience does he expect? What
level of mankind does he imply? Ionesco should have remained
behind his mask of obscurity; then the herd could have kept crying that he is profound.

The American production lacks finesse, especially in its
failure to give distinction to the minor figures, who could be
neatly differentiated types of the French middle class. In Eli
Wallach and Zero Mostel, however, it has two consummate performers. As the conceited, self-satisfied, pompous John, Zero
Mostel plays with a mobility of face and a sure deftness of gesture that convey much more than the words. His attitude commands the first act, and in the second act his transformation
into a rhinoceros, though a bit longdrawn, is a high peak of buffoonery.

Eli Wallach amusingly plays the amoeba-like Berrenger,
shifting with life's pressures, eager to please. This makes it
easy to understand how his fear of becoming a rhinoceros
changes to loneliness when he becomes the last of the humans;
he is the only one that actually tries to make himself change
into the beast. But all this makes his final rebellion less natural. His last words are that he will "never capitulate," that he
will fight to remain human. Thus the least individualistic person in the town is chosen to be the last human individual.

The trouble with most of Ionesco's plays is that we don't
understand them; the unfortunate aspect of this one is that we do.

SHIPPY, Richard W.; (2) Theater and film critic; (3) b. Kalamazoo,
Mich., May 7, 1927; (4) s. James and Emma (Williams); (5) B.S.,
Northwestern U., Evanston, Ill., maj. subj.: English Lit., history,
pol. science; (6) m. Joanne L. Griffin, Sept. 23, 1950; (7) children--
Kathleen Therese, Kevin S., Brian G. (desceased), Drew; (8) Staff
writer, Marion, Ind. Leader-Tribune, 1952-53; staff writer and asst.
sports editor, Fort Wayne, Ind., Journal-Gazette, 1953-56; staff
writer, Akron Beacon Journal, 1956-59; film and theater critic, entertainment editor, Akron Beacon Journal, 1959 to present; (9)
Scripts, magazine articles; (10) Akron Fair Housing Comm., ACLU;
(13) U.S. Army, 1944-46; (16) Democrat; (17) none; (21) 1056 Gar-
man Road, Akron, O. 44313; (22) Akron Beacon Journal, 44 E. Exchange St., Akron, O. 44328; (23) Circulation: 180,000 (500,000 potential readers); (24) Reviews annually, 40 plays and musicals, 100
films, occasional music (jazz), weekly film and theater columns,
news commentary page op ed.

The Saga of J. L. Seagull: One Flew Over a Cuckoo Mess
(by Dick Shippy, Akron Beacon Journal, December 27, 1973)

"Somewhere over the garbage scow seagulls flap.

"If gulls flap over the garbage scow, why can't I stomach this ... uh ... nonsense!"

Ah, but you can, my boy. For there's a little bit of Jonathan Livingston Seagull in all of us. That's the gospel of Richard Bach, according to Hall Bartlett.

So, shorten your wingspan, nose over into a Stuka dive and plunge right into one of the year's dullest, dippiest movies.

It is, perhaps, a paean to flight, pastoral allegory on man's striving for perfection, an ode to non-conformity. And if it's all of these, it is also a lot of droppings from a dead pigeon.

J. L. Seagull begat a movie in the sense that a best-seller, though it be a monstrous put-on, inevitably will beget a Hollywood movie. Out there, if several million people acknowledge they're reading a certain matchbook cover, someone immediately will begin work on the screenplay.

Producer-director Bartlett, not being bright enough to turn over this metaphysical mishmash to someone capable of giving it the treatment it deserves (Mel Brooks could have shipped out a dandy screenplay), collaborated with author Bach. This insured that the pin feathers would remain more or less intact.

J. L. Seagull, as book or film, is about as inspirational as Norman Vincent Peale and only a little less intellectual than "The Little Train That Thinks It Can."

Because there are camera helicopters which can swoop and soar as nimbly as J. L. Seagull while scanning the landscape below, someone will protest "But isn't it an interesting nature study!"

Well, yes, but you can accomplish the same using a goony bird as the subject.

And because Neil Diamond has contributed a score which aspires to be soaring, too (with lyrics which scan like a Rod McKuen bilious attack, to wit: "Somewhere in a painted sky where the clouds are hung for a poet's eye"), somebody is certain to say, "But isn't the music dreamy!"

Well, who needs music to lull 'em to sleep when J. L. Seagull is around, trying to exceed his own, personal Mach One (which is 62 m. p. h.)!

Let's concede, though, there are souls addicted to greeting card uplift. Wherever they are, they can glory in the following:

J. L. Seagull gets thrown out of the flock for refusing to throttle down ...

J. L. Seagull flies inland to visit new worlds--and sees his first horse ...

J. L. Seagull stops off in the desert and works up a thirst ...

J. L. Seagull discovers snow and gets frost on his fern ...

J. L. Seagull meets the Big Daddy Gull who says, "You gotta lot of promise, kid, so we're calling you up from the minors " ...

J. L. Seagull is voted into the Hall of Feathers.

Where can he go from there? I don't know, but Daffy Duck can't last forever.

Able Cast Struggles in "Father's Day"
(by Dick Shippy, Akron Beacon Journal, February 22, 1975)

Lying there on the platter, garnished with laughs, Oliver Hailey's "Father's Day" might seem to be an appetizing bit of theatrics. Doesn't it look all steamy and spicy and Who's-Afraid-of-Virginia-Woolfish!

But appearances DO deceive, as is confirmed again when you bite into Hailey's comedy-drama and find it tough, stringy, unrelievedly bitter--and mostly indigestible.

It's this insubstantial meal with which Kent State University Theater is struggling at present. It might be a heroic struggle--an able, young cast strives to turn that which is tawdry into the tangy--but it's a losing one.

Chalk up the defeat for author Hailey. Attempting to be brightly, balefully witty in a study of love, marriage and sex among the loveless, poor Oliver managed only to achieve a knee-jerk sort of anger.

There are six characters: Three divorcees and their ex-mates who come visiting one Sunday in June (guess what day). That the setting for this confrontation is the patio of a New York condominium (three deck chairs and a table of liquor bottles) guarantees this must be dialog comedy.

Among the ex-wives are an angrily caustic actress who hurls around snappish little barbs like a venomous "Mary, Mary" and who has lost her husband to "the fat girl"; an intellectual poseur (daddy was a fashionable Communist) and would-be essayist who has lost her mate to his bisexuality, and a dear, sweetly confused thing--a one-time orphan--who has just lost her partner (also an ex-waif). She doesn't know why; he just decamped.

During Act I, then, the girls sit around exchanging brittle, bitter observations on the state of men and their discards.   And there's nothing Hailey won't try here for a laugh--Kraft-Ebbing jokes, Billy Wilder jokes, New York Times jokes ("There's a homosexual on every street corner in New York, like the Times"), sex jokes and "Oh! Calcutta!" jokes ("There are no small actors, only small parts"--and that's Hailey cribbing and twisting another's line).

And so, on to Act II; enter the ex-husbands.   Not Tom, Dick and Harry, but Tom, Harold and Richard.   No matter; they're just as interchangeable.   The boys sit around talking about homosexuality (would you or wouldn't you?), about flunking the Ladies Home Journal parents' test, about vasectomy, about their sex lives with and marital breaks from the Girls of Act I.   The girls re-enter, make one last pitch (or bitch) to their exmates, the husbands depart and the discarded are left with their brave desperation.

Bob Maddox' production efficiently dispatches the mock-acid humor and compulsive scatology of Hailey's portrait, sustains the mood of bantering scorn and despair.   And the wives, particularly--Chris Gottlieb as the razor-tongued actress, Nina Bunts as the haughty intellectual and Valerie Vess as little girl lost--have been deftly deployed, poses as they may be.

But little good it does them, confronted by the author's failures.

"Father's Day" is repeated tonight (at 8) in Wright Theater (Rockwell Hall) and next Thursday through Saturday.

SHOREY, Kenneth Paul; (2) Theater and Movie Critic; (3) b. Toronto, Ontario, June 19, 1937; (4) s. Kenneth M. and Clara (Gazey); (5) Self; (6) m. Phyllis Sease, March 30, 1968; (7) children--Craig, Roberta, Bronwyn, Morgan; (8) Editorial Assistant, National Review, 1962; Research Assistant, Russell Kirk, 1962-66, Editorial Writer, The State, 1966-68, Editorial Writer, The Birmingham News, 1968-69, Assistant Editor, Open Court Publishing Co. , 1969-71, Senior Production Editor, J. B. Lippincott Co. , 1971-73, Theater and Movie Critic, The Birmingham News, 1973- ; (17) Baptist; (20) The Death of Theatre, University of Alabama Press; several hundred editorials, reviews, essays, articles in various magazines; (21) 324 Ginger Drive, Birmingham 35215, Ph. 854-2802; (22) Box 2553, Birmingham 35202; (23) Circulation: 200,000-plus; (24) 250.

"Oil Lamps" Is Coming!
(by Kenneth Paul Shorey, Birmingham News, November 17, 1974)

Oil Lamps, beginning its American Premiere run Friday at the Alabama Theatre, is one of the four or five most deeply moving, moral, sentimental/romantic films I've ever seen.   I

first saw it two years ago at the Atlanta Film Festival, sitting
in with seasoned movie buffs, many of whom had seen thousands
of movies. When it was over, no one moved, no one talked.
Some things that happen to us needn't be talked about very much,
and Oil Lamps is one of them.

Not very often, but sometimes, we're privileged to have experiences that lift us out of ourselves. Concerts, sermons,
thrilling sports events, films and personal triumphs or tragedies
can, and do, change our lives. Bang the Drum Slowly was, for
many of those who saw it, a work of philosophy; The Way We
Were touched the lives of thousands of viewers; Dr. Zhivago involved us in romance and adventure quite beyond the range of
day-to-day living.

La Strada, Elvira Madigan, The Umbrellas of Cherbourg,
Ryan's Daughter, Lady Caroline Lamb, Gervaise, Far From the
Madding Crowd, Kamouraska all have, in various ways, made
lasting impressions on the people who've seen them; and now
Cecil Brown of the Alabama is affording Birmingham the chance
to see Oil Lamps, without any help or encouragement from the
ABC Southeastern Theatre people in Atlanta. Brown has taken
a calculated risk, and for that alone he deserves the special
thanks of every serious moviegoer in Birmingham.

It's 1900, in Bohemia, and there is hope--hope for love and
decency and peace in the 20th century. With some irony, a New
Year's Eve party character tells us that the next hundred years
will be years of scientific and artistic progress; that poets and
painters and (presumably) filmmakers will be given complete
freedom to create, heh-heh, without interference.

Stepa Killian (Iva Janzurova), 30, unmarried, coquettish,
lonely, and desperately in love with life, meets her rakish cousin Paul (Petr Cepek), a childhood sweetheart of sorts, and falls
instantly in love with him again; but he scarcely knows she exists,
and is, in any case, boorish and thoughtless.

Stepa drinks beer "like a laborer," wears outlandish hats,
and likes to flirt. Paul, pensioned from the army because a
fatal illness is slowly destroying him, suddenly decides to save
his debt-ridden farm by marrying Stepa for her money--neglect-
ing to mention that he cannot have children. Stepa succumbs,
hesitantly, only to become the patient, long-suffering, decent,
loving wife of a dying, drunken clod. Ultimately, she is left
alone--a virgin, married and childless.

A sentimental tale, surely, not without flaws; and yet, an
emotionally-wrenching cinema experience that belongs with the
films mentioned above; a David Lean experience, if you like,
with some fibre and resonance added. Director Juraj Herz provides some truly cathartic moments--some I daren't describe
for fear of coloring your own impressions--and at the same time

succeeds in giving us courage. Of very few films can it be
said that we actually feel better for having seen them. Oil
Lamps is one of those very few. It speaks directly to the mind
and heart of modern man in tones we turn away from at our
cost.

It's an exquisitely careful emotional, romantic, and, yes,
political statement--on about 17 different levels--to a world hungry for new movies that do for us what some of the old movies
used to do. (Readers familiar with Paul Kletzki's Czech Philharmonic performance of Beethoven's Ninth will know precisely
what I'm talking about.) Of necessity, it's a cautious film (you
can't do just anything in Czechoslovakia nowadays, as the "Spirit
of 1900" suggests in the beginning), but unless I'm insane and
have altogether missed the mark, it's a cry for help.

Stepa, for example, at a beautifully photographed spring picnic, writes a secret message on a slip of paper (glancing directly into the camera as she does so), then folds and places the
paper into the basket of a hot-air balloon. Someone (a Czech
censor?) takes and reads, then replaces, the paper--and the
balloon ascends to the rich, soaring Lubos Fiser score and drifts
off.

Unless I miss my guess, Herz intends for us to realize that
his film itself is in the basket of the balloon. Certainly, the
image, tied to other instances of glancing directly into the camera and to the concluding image of the gate closing, is one of
the most affective cinematic coups since the burning of Kane's
sled: poetic, evocative, poignantly tear-jerking--calculated to
fix itself permanently in our minds' eyes.

Abe Fawal, the UAB lecturer in film who has worked with
David Lean, calls Oil Lamps "a stunning movie; the sort of
movie I can unreservedly urge my students to see." Robert
Whorton, formerly the manager of the Grand Bijou before it
went X, says the Fiser music soundtrack alone is worth the
price of admission. News women's writer Olivia Barton counts
it among the best films she's ever seen.

Juraj Herz (who got his start as an assistant to Jan Kadar)
is perhaps the most accomplished director Czechoslovakia now
boasts. That his films should for so long have been neglected
in this country is a sad commentary on the present complex of
producer-distributor-exhibitor relationships, and a sad commentary on the myriad blocks standing between cinema artists and
their public.

Oil Lamps is one of the most satisfying films to come out
of Europe since the early '50s. It's composed of many of the
elements that made Dr. Zhivago a commercial success, yet in
the four years since its initial release, it has only once been
shown (at the Atlanta Film Festival in 1973), and may even have

been permitted to rot in the can were it not for Cecil Brown.

Once having seen the film, Brown considered it important enough to play here on his own, thus arranging for a bona fide American premiere in Birmingham. Favorable audience response will unquestionably put Birmingham on the movie map and lift the city's sights about 300% in terms of attracting other films of comparable quality.

Oh, I don't suppose there's anything we can do for Stepa or Paul, much less for Hertz or for Czechoslovakia. (Successful, outspoken directors and other artists have an annoying habit of disappearing suddenly in Communist countries.) Oil Lamps is only a movie, after all, perhaps too sweetly weepy for some. But in a number of social and political ways, it hits, and it hits hard.

It's a picture simply to be grateful for, like a bottle of fine wine. I happen (privately) to believe it's a subversively Christian film--normative, ritualistic, and profoundly moral; fully as much an enduring work of art as The White Dawn. But then, I may be altogether mistaken.

Lenny Bombs Again!
(by Kenneth Paul Shorey, Birmingham News, March 9, 1975)

For fans of the late drug-addict "comedian" Lenny Bruce, of whom there are undoubtedly six or seven in the Birmingham area, Bob Fosse's film, Lenny (R), now at the Brookwood 1, comes as a real treat--rather like discovering a lump of perfectly preserved dinosaur dung from the year 6,000,000 B.C.

Dustin Hoffman stars with Valerie (Slaughterhouse-Five) Perrine, Jan Miner, Stanley Beck, and Gary Morton. Black and white photography is by master craftsman Bruce Surtees. The original New York play was directed by Tom (Jesus Christ Superstar) O'Horgan. Screenplay is by Julian Barry.

Hoffman's performance, as you might guess, is superb; but then, Hoffman's always good. Valerine Perrine's Honey Bruce certainly deserves some sort of award, and Bob (Cabaret) Fosse is already a director of stature, if not lively imagination.

All this out of the way, one is impelled to agree with columnist William F. Buckley when he says "Lenny Bruce was probably mad, and mad people can under certain circumstances be entertaining, in time and place. But it is mad to admire them and sick to find them enduringly funny.... Listening to Lenny Bruce is like a visit to one of those clinics where they keep two-headed children until, mercifully, they die off."

Time's Richard Schickel argues that "Bruce's use of previously forbidden words to make jokes about subjects long forbidden in public was in some small way liberating." (Nonsense. It was merely an unbuttoning.) "Bruce insisted in his routines that all of us--presidents and popes, straights and gays, celebrities and commoners--share equally in the obscene anguish of an absurd existence."

Mercy! It's a wonder we don't all just kill ourselves if life is that disgusting.

Bruce was what the late Wyndham Lewis would have called "a little squinting image of zero"--a man terminally ill with paranoia and needle wounds--who was never very well liked, for obvious reasons, and who devoted his brief hour in the limelight to offending as many people as possible.

"Don't take away my words!," he told the courts--meaning, Don't take away the only thing I've got going for me. Truth to tell, Bruce was boring. He hadn't the talent or wit of that other iconoclast, Mort Sahl; his "social comments" amounted to saying things like "Vietnam is obscene" or "Mrs. Kennedy wasn't trying to protect her husband in Dallas; she was trying to get out of the car!" He had his words, but they simply weren't enough to make him a comic--as he himself realizes in a pathetic nightclub sequence: "I'm not funny."

Neither is this film funny. It's just depressing. We admire what Dustin Hoffman is doing up there, but seriously doubt it's worth doing. Those who saw Frank Sinatra's Pal Joey back in 1957 may recall that while Sinatra's portrayal of a down-at-the-heels nightclub artist was commendably realistic, the film as a whole was blah-blah. Some here.

The TV documentary technique, coupled with the black and white photography, works subtly on the subconscious to recreate the mood of the '50s and early '60s, as though the movie had actually been made back then. All well and good from a technical point of view; but it ultimately makes one wonder why Lenny Bruce (of all people) should be considered a hero, for he really failed in his own time.

United Artists' ad slogan runs, "Lenny's Time Has Finally Come." But Lenny's time is never going to come, in fact, because Lenny was an inarticulate, stumbling mess of a man--obsessed with himself, obsessed with sex, obsessed with social issues he only dimly understood. He was an early blend of Jack Carter and Don Rickles.

Fosse and Hoffman bring him alive, all right, and Valerie Perrine is there to love him, but why? What are all these talents trying to tell us? As Buckley puts it: "If you want to say that Bruce is pathetic because he went to jail back before the Warren Court issued general instructions to protect pornographers, then I say: Thanks, but my reservoir of sympathy is otherwise spoken for."

The film, rated R for sex and language, would most certainly have been rated X in Lenny's time, had there been an MPAA Code then. Perhaps this in itself is the message of Lenny--to wit, contemporary attitudes toward obscenity have mellowed sufficiently as to make Bruce seem a tame talker by today's standards.

My standards, I'm proud to confess, are yesterday's--or, perhaps, a little bit before yesterday's--and while both pornography and obscenity have their place (as, indeed, anything within the range of possible human experience has its place), it depends a lot on who's being obscene, and for what purpose.

As a reader wrote recently, many great works of world drama have been concerned with adultery, incest, homosexuality, lesbianism, murder, and so on. But "the prime function of the artist is to instruct (It is?), and to separate what is important from what is not. Through the centuries, it would seem, human emotions, human moral values, and the conflict between emotions and morals, have given the world its masterpieces of drama."

Lenny, in Hoffman's portrayal, seems vaguely to be fighting for First Amendment privileges; but the historical Lenny occasionally had difficulty finding his way to the bathroom, and probably couldn't have read the First Amendment aloud to an audience without faltering. A laundered, spruced-up Lenny is momentarily interesting, and as cinema, perhaps, should be looked at.

Only, though, out of morbid curiosity.

SHULL, Leo; (2) Publisher, film and stage producer, columnist and author; (3) b. Milwaukee, Wis. Feb. 8, 1913; (4) s. of David Shull and his wife Anne (Rosenkrantz); (5) University of Pennsylvania (B. S. 1934), Temple University (M. A. 1936), New School for Social Research, New York Law School; (6) m. Claire Klar; (8) Produced 30 or so plays, Broadway and Off Broadway, including "Apollo of Bellac" and "The Virtuous Island," "Genius Inc Shows," "Norman Corwin Plays," "Political Revue." Published the weekly trade paper, "Show Business" since 1941; writes weekly columns for it. Also publishes 20 trade periodicals seasonally, notably "Summer Theatre Guide," "Who's Where In Show Business," "Models' Guide," "Angels," "Dancer's Guide," "Production Directory," "Casting Guide," "Show Guide," "TV-Film Producers." Operates the "Show Business Syndicate." (9) Produced political shows and pageants for Nelson Rockefeller, Lyndon Johnson, Abe Beame; (15) Founder and Member of the New York Drama Desk, Member of Dramatists Guild; (20) Published books "Playwrighting for Broadway," "How to Break into Show Business." Produced the films "New York Town," "Liza" and the weekly television "Leo Shull Show." (22) Show Business, 136 West 44th Street, New York, 10036, Ph. 212-586-6900.

Katharine Hepburn/"Matter of Gravity"
(by Leo Shull, Show Business, February 5, 1976)

(One star, namely, KH)

Wed. ... 2/4/76

Taxiing down Fifth Ave. , to the premiere of Hepburn's "A Matter of Gravity," and passing Saks Fifth Ave. , I glanced at a window and, as usual, saw a setting of an elegant room, elegant wooden manikins frozen in time and space, and heard the babble of canned voices coming from the outdoor loudspeaker, a gibberish.

Imagine my disbelief as, sitting in the theatre, the curtain went up and I found the whole wooden set, cast, and crew had been magically, instantly, transferred to the stage of the Broadhurst ... same canned gibberish, only now I too was frozen in time and space. God, how I wanted to get out, but like the other prisoners, critics, present, we couldn't break out.

All the TV broadcast reviews gave her the Hepburn hoot. DOUG WATT in the News said the "Play creaked its way laboriously,... the director, Noel Wilman, merely kept the traffic moving" (ed. note: like near Saks Vth Ave.)

Of course everyone had come to see Saint Hepburn, who, as one vice president said about slums, if you've seen one once you've seen her all. Her delirious fans, those who were not there last night, will be relieved to hear that age hasn't changed her--the same wooden acting running the gamut of A to B, as Dorothy Parker once said at an intermission, and the same cackle aged in the wood for seventy years.

BARNES: "I didn't understand it [the play]," It's about high society in England, a decaying English house, and a rich old eccentric (KH) ... the characters are all equally unlikely ... and equally disagreeable.

Variety says today, on its front page, the show has been a sellout since it began its tour last Oct. 27, playing to standees. Budget was $160,000, which was repaid, and Angels already got another 100% profit, before its NY opening.

The set by Ben Edwards was brilliant.

Author Enid Bagley has repeated her usual cast of characters: homosexuals and lesbians--apparently this is her slam at the English ruling class, which cut her all her life--and the director has cast it with his usual stock company of effete performers.

What the play is about? Read the decoding by Watts and Barnes.

*   *   *

Well, for the sake of my two friends, owners of the Broadhurst, Gerry Schoenfeld and Bernard Jacobs, whom I congratulate on their astuteness, I will say: this show will be revered by box-office treasurers unto eternity because the play is going to run forever in stock and give surcease to all male insomniacs, hereafter.

I would suggest to the hayseed theatres that if they're going to feed this corn to the $15 visitors, they should at least hand out the stuff, popped, big free bags of it.

BUSINESS REPORT:

Hepburn made a handshake deal with Whitehead and Stevens that calls for a straight Equity minimum; scale of $265 a week for Broadway and $375 on the road.

She received expenses during the tryout tour. She intends to remain for six months from the date of the road opening-- till late April. "After that, we'll see."

She wanted the backers of "A Matter of Gravity" to be repaid their investment immediately.

When she appeared some years ago at the financially-pressed American Shakespeare Festival at Stratford, Conn., she did not cash her paychecks, then toured a full season in "Measure for Measure," again not cashing her checks.

Rockabye Hamlet
(by Leo Shull, Show Business, February 19, 1976)

This musical is a huge, lavish, extravagant super-spectacle, big-time, old-time Broadway-is-Broadway show ... realllllly big.

If other producers would have spent a half million, when Joe Kipness puts his hand in, it becomes a million, and this one looks it. There is a half million in equipment--more lights on a stage than I've ever seen in my life--as Doug Watt said today, it looks like an "electrical warehouse" ... floating staircases, massive drawbridge, ramps, towering pulpits, flashing billboards the size of Times Square signs.

The dancing, singing, and athletics--swordplay, too--are also spectacular. The audience rose to its feet on opening night (Tues.), several times.

I know that Stuart Klein and Pia Lindstrom gave it raves, but Doug Watt, Clive Barnes, the boot; and I wonder if the five of us saw the same show, or don't I have 20/20 vision? I prefer the audience's optical lenses, and mine.

It depends on what kind of story-teller you are, or like to hear. Here we have a yarn-spinner interpreting Hamlet to his ilk--rock, hippies, groupies, or sound freaks--and if you take it that way, what are the two carping at, this is the way the "man" set sees the Hamlet legend, which is entrancing. The show continues the "Hair" and "J. C. Superstar" genre. They were also formless, but spectacle.

Actually, it's Gower Champion's interpretation. It's his show. The music is not very good or inventive, the lyrics--if you could hear them--were banal, but who cares what the clowns say at the circus? It's the circus, the excitement, the roar, lights, motion, gymnastics that make this show. Yes, it's gaudy, as Doug says.

It began as a radio show in Canada, grew and grew. Cliff Jones, a TV and music director, brought it into life. His music and lyrics do not match his powerhouse drive, but Champion took care of that.

The performers are super; Larry Marshall is wonderful as Hamlet; his stepfather, Alan Weeks, is heroic, dynamic; Leata Galloway, the mother, brought down the house, the most seductive beauty, exquisite singer; Beverly D'Angelo looks, moves, and sings like an angel, indeed. Exquisite, both of these ladies.

The costumes by Joseph G. Aulisi set a new high in magnificence. Lester Osterman is the principal producer, and there are five or six others.

I'm going to see the show again.

SIMON, John Ivan; (2) Film critic; (3) b. Subotica, Yugoslavia, May 12, 1925; (4) s. Joseph and Margaret (Reves) Simmon; (5) A. B. Harvard, 1946, A. M. , 1948, Ph. D. 1959; (8) Teaching fellow Harvard, 1950-53; Instructor U. of Washington, 1953-54, Massachusetts Institute of Technology 1954-55; Assistant Prof. Bard College, 1957-59; Associate Editor Mid-Century Book Society 1959-61; drama critic The Hudson Review 1960- ; drama critic Theater Arts Magazine, 1962; film critic The New Leader, 1962-73, its cultural critic 1974-75; its drama critic, 1975- ; drama critic WNET-TV, 1963; Commonweal, 1967-68; drama critic, New York Magazine, 1968-75, its film critic, 1975- ; film critic Esquire, 1973-75; guest professor University of Pittsburgh; (13) Served with USAF 1944-45; (14) Recipient George Polk Memorial award in film criticism, 1968; George Jean Nathan award for dramatic criticism, 1969-70; Literary award American Academy of Arts and Letters, 1976; Fulbright Fellow at the University of Paris, France, 1949-50; (15) Member P. E. N. , New York, Drama Critics' Circle, New York Film Critics' Circle; (20) Author: Acid Test, 1963; Private Screenings, 1967; Movies into Film, 1971; Ingmar Bergman Directs, 1972; Uneasy Stages, 1976; Singularities, 1976; (21) 200 East 36 Street, New York, N. Y.

10016; (22) New York Magazine, 755 Second Avenue, New York, N.Y. 10017.

SIMON, Richard Dages; (2) Staff writer: the Arts and Entertainment; (3) Oct. 2, 1922; (4) s. Jacob and Libby Simon; (5) Bachelor of arts, University of Chicago with a major in comparative literature; (6) Single; (8) Teacher, Paris-English School, 1950-53, public relations, Helgo Foam Rubber Company, N.Y., 1953-56, reporter, The Solano Republican, 1956-59, the Vallejo Times-Herald, 1959-65, The Sacramento Union, 1965 to present; (13) private, Army of the United States, 1942-45; (15) Director on board of the Society of Professional Journalists-Sigma Delta Chi, Sacramento chapter and Sacramento Press Club; (21) 529 San Antonio Way, Sacramento, Calif. 95819; (22) 302 Capitol Mall, Sacramento 95814, Ph. 442-7811; (23) Circulation: 100,000; (24) Approximately 100 annually in all the arts.

Rather Uneven G & S Offering
(by Richard Simon, Sacramento Union, June 1, 1975)

"An Evening With Gilbert & Sullivan," produced by the Davis Comic Opera Company, proved an enjoyable but distinctly uneven entertainment when it opened this past weekend for a four-weekend run in the Old Eagle Theater, 925 The Embarcadero.

One cannot blame G & S, for a majority of their work is uniformly brilliant. The fault, I think, lies with the Davis ensemble. The most glaring fault--and one that could easily be corrected--is the failure of director Elinor Barnes to impose a common performance style on her actors. At present, the styles range from the absolutely hammy to the polished farce associated with the D'Oyly Carte Company.

There is another fault, alas, but one beyond the control of any community theater director. And that is the wide difference in talent such a director has to work with. Here it ranges from marginal to extraordinary.

Miss Barnes made an additional problem for herself when she chose to use three continuing characters to introduce the highlights from the opera plus "Trial by Jury."

The premise was that the Old Eagle was a saloon of the period, and that the D'Oyly Carte Company was going to perform in it. To carry out the premise, Miss Barnes used performers to impersonate a bartender, a dance hall hostess and a cleaning woman responding like hicks to the news. The humor, such as it was, consisted of tripping over the pronunciation of such works as "Iolanthe" and the elaborate syntax characteristic of Gilbert's librettos.

It was all excessively arch and irrelevant, G & S undiluted is far more attractive.

Another problem--but one beyond anyone's power to do anything about--was that of movement of a chorus and principals on the postage stamp-sized stage of the Old Eagle. At times, one was painfully aware of a very tight fit. Still, Nancy Loofbourow's choreography worked reasonably well, although designed for roomier quarters.

One of the charms of the production was evident when the curtain rose on the Chorus of Peers singing their ringing march "Bow, Bow, You Lower Middle Classes." The chorus, trained by Martha Dickman, sang very well (although there were one or two, I suspect, who did not sing loudly enough to be heard).

Another asset of the production was the ringing tenor of Jack Preisss, singing "Spurn Not the Nobly Born." Jim Hutchison, baritone, managed to get through the most difficult of all G & S patter songs, "Love Unrequited," and that is an achievement in itself.

But the best singing, I think came from tenor Ivan Sandoval. It was robust and yet refined as he sang "I Have a Song to Sing, Oh," from "Yeomen of the Guard," and the counsel for the plaintiff in "Trial by Jury."

There were also stylish performances by the judge in "Trial by Jury," either Bob Schroeder or Dick Walters (the program did not specify which one was singing that night, and an inquiry on my part brought no illumination).

Perhaps the bleakest moment came from the hammy performance of either Malcolm Mackenzie or Bob Schroeder as the lascivious jailer in the "Yeomen" sequence (again the program did not help).

The most curious performance was that of Steven Watson as the romantic lead in "Trial by Jury." He did not so much act as preen. The closest thing to it I can think of is modeling for a hood ornament on a car. And when the jury lashed out at him, "Monster, Monster, Dread Our Fury," his reaction suggested "I don't care what you say about me. Just get my name right."

In contrast, Robin Treseder was a perfectly artless heroine as Angelina, suing him for breach of promise of marriage.

A mixed bag altogether.

Dan Parsons led a wind ensemble and pianist in spirited accompaniments. The costumes (all save the robes for the peers in "Iolanthe") were admirably suited to the situation and characters, and Gwen Bruch, Jacqueline LaMar and Marinka Phaff deserve credit. Ed Pinson's set--a series of panels--created no illusions and may have cramped movement by the actors.

A Balanced Evening with Coward
(by Richard Simon, Sacramento Union, June 14, 1975)

"I have only a small talent to amuse," the late Sir Noel
Coward is reported to have modestly declared shortly after he
received his knighthood from the queen.

He did himself an injustice, for his was clearly no small
talent. The statement suggests, however, his deference to the
then--and still--prevalent belief that the serious is somehow
more important than the comic.

The statement also suggests that he placed less value on his
more serious work. Theatergoers in Northern California can
arrive at their own conclusions about both the light and serious
Coward, for both are represented in an evening of two short
plays, "Noel Coward in Two Keys," on view through June 19 in
the Geary Theater here.

They are "Come Into the Garden Maud" and "A Song at
Twilight."

The comedy, "Come Into the Garden Maud," is both the
funnier and the stronger play. In it, Coward departs from his
usual preoccupation with the British upper classes to observe the
nouveau riche American.

Anyone who has ever read "Bringing Up Father" will recognize Verner and Anna-Mary Conklin. Jiggs lives again in Verner, a goodnatured businessman resigned to life with a snobbish,
arrogant and shrewish wife, Anna-Mary is all that and even
more.

She is also a woman aware of the stereotype of the Ugly
American but unable to shake off its burden.

"Come Into the Garden Maude" places them in their suite
in a luxurious Swiss hotel on the evening when Mrs. Conklin is
offering a dinner party for some minor European royalty.

A crisis develops, however. One of the guests, stricken
with a temperature of 102, cannot appear, and Mrs. Conklin is
desperate. It means 13 at the table so she relegates her husband to eating alone in their suite while the party is held downstairs.

It would simply be one such evening among many for the
complacent husband, but for the appearance of an authentic Italian princess. She proves everything the wife is not--lovable
and loving, gracious and unpretentious.

The relegation to a solitary evening upstairs provides the
opportunity for the unappreciated businessman and the princess

to enjoy a tete-a-tete and the basis for a happy ending.

It also provides Coward with a chance to make his subtle points about European and American lifestyles.

The material is provocative, but the charm of the play is heightened by the polished performances of the principals.

Hume Cronyn is extraordinary as Conklin. He reveals an unaffected simplicity as the businessman who cheerfully accepts the onus of being considered indifferent to the higher things of life as well as the onus of being expected to pay all the bills.

He also enlivens his performance with some brilliant touches --the way he nods approvingly when his hat lands exactly where he wanted it to when he threw it across the room. Also when his wife complains about 13 at the table, his droll inflection when he responds "we're in serious trouble."

Ms. Tandy (his offstage wife as well) does not cheat as Mrs. Conklin. She plays the role without sympathy, and she gives a strong performance.

Anne Baxter is perfectly engaging and seemingly artless as the Italian princess.

Joel Parks has little to do as the waiter, but he is a handsome presence.

"A Song At Twilight," although much too long and static, is an intriguing drama about an aging literary lion (supposedly Somerset Maugham).

The writer has established a facade of sexual normality for his public, and that facade is endangered when a former mistress appears on the scene.

She wants his approval to publish his love letters to her for the memoirs she is preparing. When he refuses, she reveals she has a set of love letters concerning him that she can publish--love letters from a male secretary now dead.

The implied blackmail produces an ambiguous situation, for the present wife of the author, also a former secretary, is aware of the letters. She has long remained silent in order to protect her husband.

SINGER, Deborah Anne; (2) Arts Reviewer; (3) b. Chicago, Ill., Aug. 13, 1953; (4) d. Benjamin (deceased) and Dorothy E. (Pettis); (5) B.S. Southern Illinois U. at Carbondale, major: Journalism, minor: Theater, 1975; (6) Single; (8) Advertising layout and design, Entertainment Staff Writer, Daily Egyptian, SIU, 1974-75; (9) Box

Office and House Manager, University and Laboratory Theaters, SIU, 1974; Acting: Columbia College Free Theatre, 1973; SIU Southern Players, 1974-75; Southern Illinois Repertory Dance Theater, 1974-75; (12) Member of the Faculty Appointments Committee, SIU, 1974-75; (14) Dean's list, SIU, 1973-75; Theater Department Scholarship, 1974; Illinois State Scholarship, 1974-75; (15) Member, Sigma Delta Chi; Journalism Students Association; Southern Players; (16) Independant; (17) Nonaffiliated; (21) 2449 West Foster, Chicago, Ill., 60625, Ph. 312-784-6313; (22) Daily Egyptian, Communications Bldg., SIU, Carbondale, Ill. 62901; Ph. 618-536-3311 (ext. 241); (23) Circulation: 19,500; (24) 25 plays or musicals, 20 films, 10 dance, 10 concerts, 10 records, 25 miscellaneous.

"Old Soldiers" a Hit, Miss Production
(by Deborah Singer, Daily Egyptian, December 23, 1974)

The Southern Players production of "Old Soldiers," currently in the Laboratory Theater of the Communications Building, provokes a response as varied as the two one-act plays housed within the singular title.

There are some nice moments in each play, the first titled "Armistice Day 1919," and the second titled "Old Soldiers," but there are more of them in the latter.

The superficial similarity between the plays ends with the set of the St. James Hotel, the never-appearing character of Harry and the intention of an Armistice celebration.

But the theme of mutually destructive relationships is the real common bond between the two plays. In "Armistice Day 1919," the relationship exists between Helen and Ruth, sisters who appear to have come together to celebrate the Armistice and wait for Helen's husband Harry to join them. As the play goes on what really evolves are the sick attempts of each sister to destroy the other.

But from the very beginning the play is bogged down by too much exposition and not enough action. Exposition involves the use of dialogue to explain previous action in a play. Exposition is often essential in a play and the way in which it is handled determines the response of the audience.

And in "Armistice Day 1919," the audience is left fidgeting during the long speeches of Helen, played by Margaret Richardson. Although Richardson does have some strong scenes with her sister Ruth, she flounders through two-thirds of the play that have her involved in seemingly endless monologue.

Her attempts to degrade the reputation of her sister Ruth in the eyes of a hotel desk clerk are apparently unmotivated, and becomes a transparent effort to tell the audience how she feels about Ruth.

Although Dennis Bateman as the desk clerk lightens the ponderous tone of Helen's speeches, he is primarily there to react to her sometimes unusual statements. Serving much the same purpose as the butler in an English drawing-room comedy, Bateman is never really given the chance to develop a strong relationship with any of the other characters. But he does react well, and is often funny as the confused desk clerk, Lindbeck.

Teri Brown as Ruth brings life to the play. When she enters there is finally a tangible target for all of Helen's hostility. The enmity and hate between the sisters has them locked in constant battle and the potential they have to destroy one another becomes a frightening aspect of the play.

As victory goes back and forth between the sisters, each suffers a breakdown only to be followed by a great resurgence of strength. Nobody ever actually wins the cruel game of one-upmanship and when Peter says "You're both crazy," there is a tendency to agree with him.

The destructive relationship existing in "Old Soldiers" is between two oldtime war buddies, Tom and Dick, who are sharing a rather shabby existence in a run-down version of the once elegant St. James Hotel.

A third resident of the hotel, Mr. McMurty, is a secret drinker who manages to keep his other neuroses pretty well hidden. But it just may be that his neuroses are pale in comparison to those of Tom and Dick. His only penchant, other than for drink, is for women, and at 70 odd-years-old, he manages to have one.

When McMurty tells Tom, "You've become a sour old fart lately," it is a perfect description. Tom is a hater with a Benzedrine inhaler constantly shoved up his nose. He says he hates everything and he says it loudly, but the fine characterization by John Speckhardt lets another side of this belligerent old man come through. On the inside, Tom is a lonely old man who needs others as much as he says he hates them.

The play really revolves around the relationship between Tom and Dick. Played by Rick McCormick, Dick, is a pathetic and simpering old man constantly cowed by his "best friend" Tom. When Lucille, Mr. McMurty's girlfriend tells Dick to stand up to Tom, his pain in doing so is obvious. Dick has no sense of his own worth and has seen himself only in Tom's reflection for a great many years. For him to cut their relationship is somewhat like a newborn child cutting the umbilical cord.

Unlike "Armistice Day 1919," theirs is a victory in "Old Soldiers," but a hollow one at best. Although Tom breaks down, and Dick escapes, the memories of their pitiable relationship linger on.

"Old Soldiers" will be in the Laboratory Theater through November 24. Tickets are on sale at the University Theater box office. This is the Southern Players entry into the American College Theater Festival.

"Seesaw" Production Has Its Ups and Downs
(by Deborah Singer, Daily Egyptian, February 26, 1975)

Monday night when "Seesaw" star, Jerry Ryan (John Raitt), asked Gittel Mosca (Lis Torres), "When did the pain start?"-- I would have liked to give him the answer.

It could have been something like, "When I walked into Shryock Auditorium tonight," but that wouldn't have been honest. The pain really started about 15 minutes after the "Seesaw" prologue, somewhere around the "My City" number, starring Jerry Ryan and "The Neighborhood Girls."

"The Neighborhood Girls," looking like prostitutes (intentionally?), were offensive in the extreme. With costumes that would have made creations from Frederick's of Hollywood look like the best of Edith Head, the girls try to bump and grind their way into Jerry's heart.

But their sloppily choreographed dancing wasn't enough to entice the oh-so-cool WASP, straight out of Nebraska and living in the "Big Apple" for the first time. The raucous sound of the orchestra's brass drowned out the singer's words, so they obviously weren't making a hit with Ryan that way.

As a matter of fact, very few things made a hit with Ryan. As he seemed to be so busy holding his stomach all night trying to disguise midriff bulge I'm surprised he was able to sing, much less react to anything. But he managed to do both with a minimal amount of energy and a maximum amount of his charming, toothy smiles.

If contrast was the main consideration of director Lawrence Kasha in casting the "Seesaw" leads, he couldn't have done better than putting Liz Torres opposite Raitt. Where Raitt has the flexibility of cast iron, Torres is like a blob of mercury. They are about as well-suited together as bagels and Polish ham, but so are Ryan and the "hot-blooded Biblical broad," Gittel.

Torres' performance was captivating. Actually the saving grace of the production, she offered a slightly Rhoda-ish character as the "girl who gets a nosebleed when she has to go past 14th Street." Torres with her huge expressive eyes and lithe body in her first 'Broadway' role as Gittel steals the show from veteran Raitt.

Ron Kurowski leads the company in the show's largest production number, "It's Not Where You Start," in his role as

Gittel's extremely close friend, David. As the gay choreographer who has finally been discovered and subsequently has dreams of glory, Kurowski is funny and remains somewhat subtle in his characterization. This was a nice way of handling the role because David could have turned into a sickening stereotype if not played with sensitivity.

The 14-member chorus was disappointing. Although at times some of them exhibited an ability to dance, nobody was very outstanding in the full company numbers--except for a certain dancer who used to be a member of the SIU Southern Repertory Dance Company in 1969-72. Ken Rogers (formerly known as Ken Johnson), was half of the team for a softshoe routine that was a high spot in the company's dancing.

Raitt's attempts to make the audience happy, via his solo appearance after the show singing "They Call the Wind Mariah," "Oklahoma" and "Surrey With the Fringe on Top" was more the businessman singing than the entertainer. After all, it was John Raitt Productions Inc. that brought the musical to SIU.

SLACK, Lyle; (2) Drama and Film critic; (3) b. Buffalo, N.Y., May 26, 1946; (4) s. Lyle James, Sr. and Eileen (Potratz); (5) B.A. Bloomsburg State College (Pa.) English Literature, 1968; M.A.T. Allegheny College, Political Science, 1974; (6) Unmarried; (7) child--Lyle James, III; (8) Teacher of English, Warren Area High School, Warren, Pa. 1968-69; Teacher of English and Film, Shaker Heights Senior High School, Shaker Heights, Ohio, 1969-72; copywriter, Griswold-Eshleman Co., Cleveland, Ohio; copy writer, Russell T. Kelley Co. Ltd., Hamilton, Ont.; Senior writer, McKim Advertising, Vancouver, B.C.; Freelance writer, various Canadian magazines; (11) United States Senate Intern, Office of Senator Joseph S. Clark, 1966; Candidate for the 14th District seat of the Ohio House of Representative, 1972; (15) Toronto Drama Bench; (16) Democrat; (21) 96 Dalewood Crescent, Hamilton, Ont., Ph. 416-525-8477; (22) Spectator, Hamilton, Ont., Ph. 416-522-8642; (23) Certified circ. 150,000; (24) 100 movie reviews, 50 theatre reviews, 10 music reviews.

Stratford's Second Hamlet Superior
(by Lyle Slack, The Spectator, June 1976)

The crux of Shakespeare's Hamlet has always been, of course, that there are two Hamlets, one who would revenge his royal father's death and one who is paralyzed with doubt about the right course.

Stratford has doubled the dilemma this season by giving us, literally, two Hamlets.

On Wednesday of this festive week, Richard Monette delivered up the prince of Denmark and last night Nicholas Pennell held the Avon stage as Hamlet.

Excepting the title role and that of Queen Gertrude, Hamlet's mother, who is played by Pat Galloway opposite Pennell and by Patricia Bentley-Fisher opposite Monette, they are virtually identical productions with only minor differences in staging.

Given that, it is quite remarkable, really, the difference in the result.

Nicholas Pennell's version is vastly superior, his portrayal is a strong, direct depiction and one that does not make Hamlet look either weak or rash.

That has always been the problem with this character. His father, the King of Denmark has died and his uncle, Claudius-- played miserably in both versions by Michael Liseinsky -usurped the throne, married the queen, and Hamlet cannot believe it is all the work of nature.

The spirit of his dead father comes to settle the issue one foggy night by revealing the method by which Claudius assassinated him and requesting that his son revenge the foul deed so that his spirit may rest.

Hamlet vows to do so but is not so passionate in his desire for revenge as to forget the possible consequences that may befall him if he just boldly kills the king, so he shapes a plan that requires he feign madness.

Also, for unclear reasons, Hamlet begins to have doubts about whether the apparition was genuinely his father's ghost or a demon sent by the devil to entrap him.

The tragedy thereafter is the working out of his doubts, his escape from Claudius's own trap, and his final revenge coupled by his own death.

The difficulty of this role is to lapse from sanity into feigned insanity and also into moments of real doubt and still make sense out of the character.

For us, nearly 400 years after the writing of the play, Shakespeare's elaborate and archaic tongue only compounds the problem for an actor, but both these problems Pennell masters.

With an apparently clear personal understanding of what each word and line in the drama is meant to convey, Pennell creates a cadence and delivery that lays open Hamlet's turmoil with the clarity of a modern psychological profile and the emotion of a real human being.

Monette's rendering of Hamlet, on the other hand, seems only to have emotion, for both his delivery of the difficult lines and his physical actions more frequently confuse than illuminate.

His portrayal doesn't lack conviction, and no doubt somewhere behind all the slapstick madness and unique histrionics
Monette has a master conception to which he feels he is true.

It's simply that his technique does nothing to inform us about
it.

As it happens, Pat Galloway is also a much superior Gertrude to Patricia Bentley-Fisher's queen, and in both productions,
Eric Donkin is a remarkable Polonius, authoritarian, deceitful,
aggrandizing and finally, fittingly, slain.

Both Marti Maraden as Ophelia and Richard Partington as
Laertes are fine in smaller roles, and on the whole Daphne Dare
has again designed sets and costumes that are, following the pattern of all the festival productions this season, muted, functional,
and pleasing.

Also, here as in all Robin Phillips' productions, there is a
much needed leaness in the direction, a rush and flow of people
and events that keeps these inordinately long plays from tedium.

There has been some questioning here this week at Stratford
among the critics and interested townspeople of the wisdom of the
two different Hamlets.

Whatever their reasons, it has come to a good end. Monette's exuberant misguided collage helps to make clear just how
cleanly Nicholas Pennell has etched the tragic hero.

Buffalo Bill Aimless
(by Lyle Slack, The Spectator, June 26, 1976)

It's sad to see a director with the earnest talent of Robert
Altman slowly lose a grip on his art. Buffalo Bill and the Indians (at Jackson Square) is a movie with a big subject, a big
budget and a big star, Paul Newman. Yet it suffers from the
same aimlessness that made Altman's last film, Nashville, such
an unredeemed bore.

Buffalo Bill and the Indians has an interesting point where
you can discern it. The great Indian fighter and buffalo hunter
of the American West, according to Altman's thesis, was a su-
perstar--not unlike those of today--who lost touch with his own
human flesh and began to believe all the myths about himself.

Sheltered inside the tents and corrals of his Wild West Show,
Buffalo Bill Cody reenacts for his fans the great triumphs of his
life, the slaughter of the noble prairie cattle, the rescue of
hoopskirted damsels from bloodthirsty Indians.

At first the re-enactments are embellished with heroics for
the benefit of Cody's image and the pleasure of his audience.

In the end whole episodes of gallantry are fabricated: Cody slaying the terrible Sioux warrior Sitting Bull in an elaborately staged, hand-to-hand struggle.

Embellishment and fabrication are not uncommon, Altman is saying, but Buffalo Bill is so much a victim of psychological incest that he can no longer judge reality from sham and, in fact, spends a good deal of psychic energy trying to keep out what he fears is reality.

Altman's thought, though not entirely new, is interesting and, given the number of people Hollywood and politics has yielded who came to believe themselves larger than life, it's probably a very real syndrome.

Where Altman fails is in dramatizing the point. His movie has too many characters drifting on and off the screen, too many miscellaneous conversations, too much that is enigmatic instead of direct.

Annie Oakley (Geraldine Chaplin) breezes in and out demonstrating her sharpshooting. Sitting Bull (Frank Kaquitts) arrives to silently upstage Cody at every turn while an interpreter (Will Sampson) does all the talking.

President Grover Cleveland (Pat McCormick) stops for a command performance that offers one of the film's most slyly satiric episodes, and rationed in periodically are several operatic contraltos to satisfy Buffalo Bill's more basic needs.

Ned Buntline (Burt Lancaster), the man who gave Cody his start in the business of being famous, has been shunted aside and sits in a saloon chewing on his bitterness while Nate Salsbury (Joel Grey) rushes about transposing words and reality to make sure no one punches a hole in his inflated superstar.

It's too much. Perhaps if Altman had managed a tight rope on all these characters and events, drawing them tighter and closer to his point, it could have worked. But that is not how it is.

Altman has an admirable belief in not pandering to an audience, writing his ideas in small script instead of large block letters.

In McCabe and Mrs. Miller and Images, the technique spoke with quiet strength, but in Buffalo Bill and the Indians, the writing has become nearly illegible.

SMILJANICH, Dorothy Weik; (2) Film and Theatre Critic; (3) b. Camden, N. J. , April 11, 1947; (4) s. William and Elsie Weik; (5) M. A. U. of Florida, English Literature, 1971; (6) m. Terrance A.

Smiljanich, June 15, 1969; (8) Film critic, Gainesville Sun, 1971; film and theatre critic, Clearwater Sun, 1971-73; film and theatre critic, St. Petersburg Times, 1973--to date; (9) Visiting lecturer in Mass Communications Department, University of South Florida, 1975; (15) Florida Press Club, Florida Theatre Conference; (16) Democrat; (21) 236 17th Ave. S.E., St. Petersburg, Fla. 33704; (22) St. Petersburg Times, P.O. Box 1121, or 490 First Ave. So., St. Petersburg, Fla. 33731; (23) Circulation: 190,000; (24) 50 movies; 50 plays; 25 miscellaneous articles.

Montalban Magnificent In Superb "Don Juan"
(by Dorothy Smiljanich, St. Petersburg Times, February 5, 1975)

When Ricardo Montalban strode on stage Monday night at Van Wezel Hall in Sarasota, his hands moved nervously, playing with the sleeves of his tuxedo.

But once he and the rest of the "Don Juan in Hell" cast-- Myrna Loy, Kurt Kasznar and Edward Mulhare--launched into George Bernard Shaw's philosophical diatribe against mediocrity, Montalban was amazingly in control and impassioned.

And what he said in an interview last week was true: The part is made for him.

"Don Juan in Hell" is the seldom-produced, reader's-theatre-style third act of Shaw's "Man and Superman." It pits Don Juan (in Hell) against the Devil, played masterfully by Mulhare, who creates a sympathetic and rather likeable Satan, whose chief sin the mercurial Juan identifies as being complacency and happiness.

Rounding out the cast and representing other philosophical positions are Miss Loy as Dona Ana, one of Juan's former loves, and her father, a military commander played by Kasznar.

The production is staged with great simplicity and dignity. The actors file on stage; the men in tuxedos, Miss Loy in a jeweled white gown. They begin the play, seated at microphones with great, huge books, suggesting the script itself, before them.

No one, however, so much as glances at the books, which sit, pages unturned, throughout the two-hour program as the actors turn to and engage one another, as well as the audience, in a delicious game of philosophical one-upmanship.

The acting is magnificent throughout, save for Miss Loy, upon whom at times this torturous tour of one-nighters was telling. She spoke her lines too often as if she were saying them for the thousandth time and as if they were hollow even for her.

Shay turned his great satiric wit on his own age, to criticize the foibles and follies of man, in general, and Englishmen

in particular. Many of Shaw's most pithy observations literally
go to the devil in this play and Mulhare relished every one of
them.

Whether he is observing that "An Englishman thinks he is
moral, when he's only uncomfortable," or asserting "Religion
is his excuse for hating me; law his excuse for hanging you,"
it is the devil who has much of Shaw's sympathy.

But it is Juan ultimately--life-loving, trouble-embracing
Juan--who emerges triumphant and if Shaw turned his wit against
his age, how he must have broken his heart at the stupidity of
men he loved so dearly to devote his work to their entertainment
and instruction.

O'Casey Is in Good Hands at Asolo State Theatre
(by Dorothy Smiljanich, St. Petersburg Times, April 13, 1975)

In the hands of some playwrights, the stage essentially becomes a pulpit and the play a mirror reflecting human weakness.
The gifted playwright--as Sean O'Casey most certainly was--will
also manage to so entertain his audience that before they can become defensive, they are hopelessly engaged with the material
and must follow it through to its completion, even if that end is
an indictment of themselves--as "The Plough and The Stars"
most certainly is.

There were no riots Saturday night at the Asolo State Theatre in Sarasota as there were in 1926 when the play was first
produced at the legendary Abbey Theatre in Dublin. Even the
supportive appearance of an Irishman of the ilk of William Butler Yeats could not sooth the offended Dubliners who saw in
O'Casey's tragicomedy a criticism of their most cherished ideals.

But at Asolo there was, if I gauged it correctly, a powerful impact made upon the audience by the play itself and by
some truly masterful acting (lead by Barbara Reid McIntyre and
Isa Thomas).

"The Plough and the Stars" examines the behavior and motivations of a handful of Dublin tenement dwellers during the
abortive Easter uprising of 1916. In this play, as in so much
Irish literature, it is the women who are central to the drama.
In them are to be found the most extreme examples of the characteristics which the writer wishes to explore. That is the case
here as O'Casey creates women who are both colorful, individual
characters and representatives of specific philosophical positions.

Subsequently, we find the central concerns of the play
worked out in the relationships among the women: Miss McIntyre as Nora, the clinging, devoted wife of an Irish soldier;
Miss Thomas as drunken Bessie, the bravest and best soul,
who is opposed to and ironically victim of the uprising; Bette

Oliver as Mrs. Gogan, in love with death and nursing a dying
child; and Martha J. Brown as Rosie, the barroom butterfly for
whom uprisings mean only fewer men in the tavern.

Although exposing the sunshine patriotism of his people,
O'Casey manages at the same time to pay homage to their
warmth, enthusiasm and spirit. If he condemns--and he does--
it is out of a love grown bitter by disappointment and there is
certainly nothing peevish or small about this work.

The play is in good hands with director Robert Strane, who
leads us cunningly into a feeling of good humor at the end of
act one, only to explode it with madness and death in the second
and final act.

With liberal use of the Irish green, heavy brogues affected
by the cast, and Rick Pike's careful eye in the construction of
sets (down to the rust on iron railings), "The Plough and the
Stars" comes alive. We laugh at first because it is not our
greed, our hypocrisy or our cowardice that is exposed, but O'-
Casey, Strane and company conspire together so that by the time
the play is over, the laugh has choked in our throat and an indictment of one people at one historical moment has become a
reflection of all men in all times.

SMITH, Doug; (2) Focus Editor; (3) Glen Ridge, N.J., June 27,
1935; (4) s. Joseph Jr. and Winifred (Kilroy); (5) B.A. Rider College, Trenton, N.J., major subjects: journalism and commerce
(1956); (6) m. Pauline Smith Aug. 8, 1958; (7) children--Joseph W.
III and Holly Marie; (8) Sports reporter, Jamestown (N.Y.) Post-
Journal 1948-52, sports editor Hopewell (Va.) News 1956, telegraph
editor Bloomsburg (Pa.) Press 1956-57, assistant sports editor
Jamestown (N.Y.) Post-Journal 1957-60, sports editor Warren (Pa.)
Observer 1960-61, sports reporter Erie (Pa.) Times News 1961-67,
night city editor Buffalo (N.Y.) News 1967-72, Focus editor Buffalo
(N.Y.) Courier-Express 1972-date; (9) Actor, Grand Island (N.Y.)
Theater, Niagara Falls (N.Y.) Little Theater, Courtyard Theater
and African-American Cultural Center of Buffalo, Circle Theater of
Williamsville, N.Y., 1969-date; (16) Conservative; (17) Protestant;
(20) Travel articles for New York Times, show business reports for
Variety; (21) 240 Hennepin, Grand Island, N.Y., 14072; (22) Buffalo
Courier-Express, 787 Main St., Buffalo, N.Y. 14240, Ph. 716-847-
5398; (23) Circulation: 135,000 daily, 280,000 Sunday; (24) 50 plays
and musicals, 125 movies, 15 pop music and light classical.

Musante's Purr-fect in Purple-Coated "Cat"
(by Doug Smith, Buffalo Courier-Express, March 8, 1975)

At the Studio Arena Theater, "P.S. Your Cat Is Dead!" is
a tale for two cities. Buffalonians will turn out either despite
or because of the theater's "warning" about "frank" material

and express their shock by laughing themselves almost to death; in New York, the show's next destination, there will be a lot of affirmative nods about the values of shaking off old conventions and being one's self.

Either way, "Cat" is a howling hit. The script by James Kirkwood from his own novel has the automatic feel of good TV situation comedy, but peopled with people who really develop.

The direction is top-quality with just a few draggy spots (no pun intended) and Tony Musante as the ill-fated New Year's Eve nightstalker is the funniest contemporary comic character to occupy a Buffalo stage within memory.

Now, about that "frank" material. Yes, the language does approximate that which is heard when you tromp on a stevedore's corns; yes, one male character prefers boys to girls for romance and yes, one male character plays about an hour-long scene clad in only a shirt and a scowl. As a movie, this play would be rated "R."

Yet as burglar Zito (Musante) and actor Jim Zoole (Keir Dullea) strive to outgross each other on the worst day of Zoole's life, the flow of words and glares put the audience in the position of spectator, rather than unwilling participant as in last year's mean-spirited "That Championship Season."

It becomes a pie-in-the-face contest with words subbing for lemon meringue; it may not be Noel Coward but it can be a lot of fun and these characters are pretty close to the real thing. New Yorkers will recognize them more.

The gayety, if that's the word, of burglar Zito is not central to the plot; the play might even work with a straight Zito, but the homosexual does seem the mandatory device in modern literature and here is worked for irony without excess. There may be a gay manifesto here in the eye of some beholder; I've even heard "The Odd Couple" accused of oddities well beyond dirty dishes.

The body exposure is pretty much bottoms-up, retaining some modesty, if little dignity.

Musante's task is not enviable; he has his own TV Toma image to overcome and then spends half the play tied down while guests examine him like Rabbit checking out Winnie-the-Pooh wedged in his doorway.

Withal Musante, whose character has hardly a redeeming trait, makes him both sympathetic and hugely funny, convincing Zoole that he ought to take a few chances on the hope that one might work out.

He's hardly in a position to give advice but Musante makes his man a good salesman. He's disgusting and loveable, all at once. Musante gives Zito humor and charm and, in one serious passage, pathos.

Dullea's Zoole is a basically bland character on a cataclysmic day--two firings, a breakup and the title. He flips; yet to keep the play in balance, he must be subordinate to the burglar and he does, undergoing a credible change of destiny dictated by this unlikely Fairy Godfather who comes through the skylight. I wonder if that's symbolic?

On opening night Thursday, Jennifer Warren as Zoole's examour glowingly natural one moment, gesturing like Howdy Doody the next. She looks good and I hope she steadies down.

Peter White was nicely nonplussed as her new beau, but Antony Ponzini, Mary Hamill and Bill Moor, three late visitors, were trapped in a disjointed and overlong scene that never worked. They should do their business and get out.

Vivien Matelon, British director who will guide this show on its projected Broadway opening, doubtless will have his editing pencil out. About 15 minutes should put the "Cat" in championship form.

Then, if the Studio can avoid the affront of a 15-minute-late curtain, everything will be homeward bound and smiling by 11.

At a time when TV is being thrashed for the likes of "Hot L Baltimore," the Studio would appear to be going against the trends with this "hot" property.

Perhaps so--but I think the point is being missed on TV's "Hot L," which is bad because it's not funny. "P.S. Your Cat Is Dead!" is. For the record, three early departures were noted in Thursday's S R O crowd; whether prompted by offense or a call of nature magnified by excessive laughter, I did not determine.

Top Cast Makes Audience "Godspellbound"
(by Doug Smith, Buffalo Courier-Express, April 4, 1975)

"Godspell" pulled 'em out of their pews Thursday night at the Studio Arena Theater. As one person, the multitude of 400 (about 150 were snowbound) arose in tribute at the finale in a spontaneous baptism of affection for an inexhaustible troupe and its cleverly commercialized message of love.

It's quite amazing. Consider the times. Many religious institutions are in structural and financial difficulty, vaudeville has been dead for decades and planned obsolescence makes an anachronism of anything more than two years old.

At the Studio, "Godspell" comes right out to get you. It's better than the other "Godspells" which have been available locally--including the Toronto production which ran for a year-- because the thrust stage puts the performers barely a step away from the audience.

It seems most natural, then, when even that gap is closed and the troupe tromps up and down the aisles passing out greetings or wine or, in the case of Helen Geizer, self-appointed vamp, tickling the press corps with a feather boa. Diplomatically, she touched both sides of the aisle.

That's right out of Ann Corio's handbook of good burlesque, of course, but you ain't heard nuthin' yet. "Godspell" flexes to fit the talents of the company and here those talents lean heavily toward celebrity impressions--Groucho Marx, the Lone Ranger, Ed Sullivan and Freddie Prinze, TV personality whose contemporary cop-out, "It's not MY yob," is mouthed by a backsliding disciple.

There's a lot of complex humor, much of it originating with this particular company directed by William Cox. One example should suffice. Matt Landers, who has the apparent Jesus role (no Biblical names are used) is trying to get across the turn-the-other-cheek principle. A disciple is aghast. "--Jesus Ch ..." he blurts before a colleague's hand interrupts his blasphemy.

Now Matt wants a demonstration. The disciple is slapped, hard. He raises his hand to retaliate. Matt appears again. The disciple now pretends that his raised hand clutches a telephone. "It's for you," he tells this Jesus. (Glance heavenward.) "It's your Father."

Any more would spoil it for you and they play better than they tell, anyway.

As for individuals, reportedly the cast lineup varies from night to night, so there's no telling what to expect.

Personally, I found Landers an affecting and almost puppydog Jesus, which added to the pathos of his crucifixion against a chain-link fence; just loved robust and joyful Maggie Hyatt, whose talents include sounding like a 33 rpm record played at 45; laughed at the self-effacing carryings-on of Tony Hoty and was fooled for the third time by the magical appearance of batons.

It says here that "Godspell" is not all as spontaneous as it looks; that its way was paved by "Superstar," that it reached across the generation gap by its softer approach. In the world of pop Gospel, "Godspell" is the Carpenters and "Superstar" the Rolling Stones.

Further, its distribution certainly hasn't followed its own

tenets of love and charity; the Studio Arena has been trying for
years to get this and has had to wait its turn while the money-
changers worked the bigger temples.

Thursday night, it almost seemed worth the wait. When
word gets out that The Word is In, there won't be a seat left
for "Godspell" 'til Judgment Day. Last performance is May 10.

SMITH, Helen Creeger; (2) Theater and Dance Critic; (3) b. Attle-
boro, Mass., Apr. 8, 1924; (4) d. Marion and Florence (Rader)
Creeger; (5) B.A. Allegheny College, Meadville, Pa., major subj.:
English, 1946; M.A., Syracuse U., guidance and counseling, 1948,
electives in drama criticism; (6) m. Kenneth F. Smith, July 9, 1949;
(7) children--Douglas, Gregory, Bradley, Steven; (8) Women's editor,
Caracas Daily Journal, Caracas, Venezuela, 1961-65, wrote all drama reviews; Staff writer, News Bureau, University of Miami (Fla.),
wrote all releases for school of music and school of drama, 1956-
66; English teacher, The American School, San Salvador, El Salvador, 1967-68, also director of school newspaper and free lance
writer for USIS during this period; Assistant editor, Caldwell (N.J.)
Progress, wrote all reviews, 1969-71; Family editor, Conroe (Tex.)
Daily Courier, wrote all reviews, 1971-73; Staff writer and theater/
dance critic, The Atlanta Constitution, 1973 to present; (9) Worked
with Caracas Little Theater (community group) backstage and on publicity, 1959-61; won fellowship to attend Dance Critics' Conference
in New London, Conn. in July, 1975; (10) AAUW program chairman
and vice president, Caracas, Venezuela, 1959-61; (14) Magna Cum
Laude, Phi Beta Kappa, one press association award for feature
writing, New Jersey; five press association awards for feature writing, best women's section, column in Texas; Sigma Delta Chi award
for outstanding feature series on Learning Disabilities, Georgia,
1974; (16) Democrat; (17) Protestant; (20) free lance articles for
Newark Star Ledger on outstanding women in New Jersey, 1969-71;
other articles published in Miami Herald, Miami News, Pan-Am in-
flight magazine; (21) 4062 Longview Dr., Chamblee, Ga. 30341; Ph.
404-451-7076; (22) Atlanta Constitution, 72 Marietta St., Atlanta,
Ga., 30303, Ph. 404-572-5441; (23) Circulation: 250,000 daily,
600,000 Sundays; (24) 40 plays and musicals, 10-15 dance, plus a
dozen or so features relating to performing artists.

Schizophrenic Direction Mars Albee Play
(by Helen C. Smith, Atlanta Constitution, February 7, 1975)

An Albee play is always an experience, you can count on
that. "Everything in the Garden," now playing at the Druid Cellar Dinner Theatre, is no exception.

It starts out like a Neil Simon play (a farcical look at domestic troubles) and ends up a bizarre statement of where these
troubles can lead if carried to an Albee conclusion.

This is one of the weaknesses of the play.

Maybe it only seems to start out like a Simon play because of the exceptionally light touch Stuart Culpepper, director, employs in the first act. The couple's financial troubles seem more like cocktail hour banter than the basis for the wife's decision to go off in a highly unconventional way to boost the family's resources. The dialogue is certainly not Albee at his wittiest or most biting. It's an uninspired Albee repeating himself and getting nowhere.

But don't go off bored. Things really pick up in the second act, and the stars come into their own. When Laura Whyte, as the wife who chooses afternoon prostitution as the way to ease the family budget, and Terry Beaver as the unknowing husband brought to a fury of understanding, have meat to work with, they are very good indeed. Beaver is particularly outstanding and his explosion at the end of the second act is a most convincing picture of an outraged and betrayed husband.

One of the joys of this particular production is that the supporting cast is so good. Albee gives the secondaries plenty to work with scriptwise, and when handled competently, as they are here, the resulting vignettes are quite unforgettable.

To wit: Ellen Heard, as the impeccably turned out madame who entices suburban housewives to her scheme, looks like a garden club president, and that's half the comic delight of the role. The other half is the way Miss Heard plays her ... fluttering fluff on the surface with an ironclad will below the surface.

And Lewis Fox, who plays Jack (a mixture of Greek chorus, narrator, friendly family advisor) does right well with the gimmicky role.

Jon Hayden as Roger, the young son returned home from prep school, is about as natural a picture of a middling teenager as it would be possible to find.

Culpepper, who just recently took over the job of managing director of the Druid Cellar, has put together a good cast, including the three other couples who appear in the last act. His direction seems somewhat schizophrenic, and doesn't really get off the ground until the second act. It's almost as if he didn't care very much what happened in the foundation building scene and was anxious to get on with the more bizarre and explosive moments. Culpepper has a special knack of staging these, and getting the most from his performers for the big scenes.

Although "Everything in the Garden" doesn't pack the total wallop of "Who's Afraid of Virginia Woolf," it's still an Albee play worth the seeing. It will be at Druid Cellar Wednesdays through Saturdays through Sept. 7.

"Purlie" Is Smashing Theater
(by Helen C. Smith, Atlanta Constitution, March 9, 1975)

"Purlie" is smashing theater, no matter how you look at
it ... visually, musically, or dramatically. And the cast thats
cavorting on the Alliance stage has it all together. You'd be
very foolish to miss it.

The musical "Purlie," based on the play "Purlie Victorious"
by Georgia-born author Ossie Davis, deals with the adventures
of Purlie, an itinerant young black preacher who craves a church
of his own.

He's a young man in a hurry and he's not above using every
con trick his fertile imagination can dream up to achieve his
goals. Samuel Jackson is simply top-notch in the role. His
voice is splendid, his mannerisms are charismatic, and you
know right from the very beginning that he simply can't lose.

In fact, director Joan Lewis has assembled and molded into
a sparkling whole a most remarkable cast.

In spite of the fact that the first act is a long once, it never
drags for a moment. The opening prologue is the most cheerful,
foot-stomping funeral you can imagine. You get the picture
right away that serious, even distressing, things are going to
be dealt the light, hilarious touch. That's one way to make a
point, without bitterness and rancor.

And "Purlie," certainly does make points, about the white
man's treatment of the black man, when slavery was supposedly
a thing of the past, but segregation kept it alive in a more insidious way.

There's Ol' Cap'n (Raymond Campbell), an old time rapacious
white Southern colonel, to show how it was done. Campbell's
interpretation is a caricature of a stereotype, another way of
keeping the bitterness level low, and the hope for the future
high.

For "Purlie" is a positive play, a hopeful one. It preaches
love, non-violence, understanding.

And it's a foot-stomping musical all the way from the opening number "Walk Him Up the Stairs" to the final theme song,
"The World Is Comin' To a Start." Some of the music sounds
familiar, as if you'd heard it in other musicals before, but there
are enough unique pieces to make you feel you're hearing something new and exciting. "Down Home," a duet between Purlie
and Missy (Latanya Richardson) is one of the best.

"Great White Father," sung by the most musically competent

bunch of "cotton pickers" that ever existed, is a show-stopping number, and a very witty put-down in a sly, sly way of Ol' Cap'n they're pretending to honor.

There isn't a weak member of the cast. Debbie Bowman as Lutiebelle, Purlie's love interest, pops her enormous, comical eyes to great effect, and sings out songs with great spirit.

Leon Brown as Gitlow, the apparent, but only apparent Uncle Tom, is the comic highpoint of the play, and a strong, powerful dancer in addition. Wendell Barnes plays Charlie, Ol' Cap'n's son, with the right amount of awkwardness as he tries so hard to be what his father isn't. Latanya Richardson as Missy and Kathy Boulware as Idella, the two older women in the play are delightful in their separate ways of dealing with Ol' Cap'n's tyranny.

And Charlotte Gibson, who sings a solo in the funeral scene, is one fine, vivacious singer.

SMITH, Martha Ann; (3) Arts Editor/Critic; (3) b. Morgantown, W. Va., July 22, 1949; (4) d. Clyde E. and Hilda V. Smith; (5) B.S. cum laude, West Virginia U., journalism and English; (6) Single; (8) Proofreader, Morgantown Dominion-Post, Women's Department Reporter, same publication, 1967-68, Bureau Chief, the Daily Athenaeum, 1967-70, proofreader, same publication, 1970; Correspondent, The National Observer, 1970; Staff Writer, West Virginia University News Service, 1969-70, Stringer, The National Enquirer, 1975- , Arts Columnist, State Magazine, 1971- , Arts Editor/Critic, The Charleston Gazette (W. Va.); (9) Professional organist, choirmaster, 1964-70, club and pit orchestra musician, 1964-70; Critic Fellow, National Critics Institute, 1975; (10) Advisory Board, Children's Theatre of Charleston, mem. Charleston Humane Assn.; (11) Mem. Democratic party; (12) Dramaturg, Children's Theatre of Charleston; (14) Journalism Dean's Fund Award, Board of Governor's Scholarship, named "Outstanding Woman Journalist" by Sigma Delta Chi, William Randolph Hearst Foundation interpretive writing prize, Bell Award, (National Association for Mental Health) Community Service awards, Salvation Army and West Virginia Division of Vocational Rehabilitation, Associated Press Community Service Award for distinguished writing; (15) Theta Sigma Phi; (20) Cont. articles to Appalachia Magazine, American Newspaper Publishers Assn. magazine; (21) 1423 Quarrier St., Charleston, W. Va.,25301, Ph. 304-346-9889; (22) 1001 Virginia St. E., Charleston, W. Va., 25301, Ph. 304-348-5195; (23) Circulation: 112,000; (24) 50 plays and musicals, operas, symphony orchestra, chamber music, choral concerts, 52 weekly magazine arts columns.

Appalachian Play Contains Taste, Integrity, Love
(by Martha Smith, Charleston Gazette, date unknown)

Capturing the essence of a people--heritage, culture,

personality--and following that particular people through 200 years of transition seems an impossible task for a playwright.

Yet, given the confines of a single stage setting, little more than two hours time, and a small company of actors, Romulus Linney has devised a definitive work savoring the juices and flavor of the Appalachian people.

That work, "Appalachia Sounding" was performed Wednesday night by the Carolina Readers Theatre, the professional resident company of North Carolina. The performance was staged in Morris Harvey College auditorium and was sponsored by the college and the Charleston Performing Arts Council.

To his everlasting credit, Linney does not patronize his subject matter or sink to reiterating the Saturday Evening Post concept of hillbilly speech, poverty and lethargy.

Rather, Linney treats his subject--200 years of struggle, individuality and exploitation--with respect and a dignity that doesn't dissolve into mushy whining.

His vehicle is the transition of a single family of parents, daughter, her husband and sundry neighbors from a first settlement in 1776 through the Civil War, migration to Northern factories during the Depression years, to present day absentee ownership of timber and coal. It is a vehicle that works well, largely because Linney has created his characters with multidimensional personalities. They are likable, pitiable, destestable because they are familiar. They are people we have known.

The Carolina Readers Theatre, operating on a federal grant is touring "Appalachia Sounding" throughout mountain colleges and communities. It is a fine company, professional in every respect and vastly satisfying to see and hear.

The actors do not preach from a "Montani Semper Liberi" platform. They treat their characters as gentle, loving, yet rugged people dedicated to their own little piece of mountain land.

As the patriarch--the man who decides to settle halfway up a mountain where he can live as he wishes without government, armies or preachers dictating to him--David Adamson is masterful. He conveys determination and pride without overplayed belligerence. He does not talk of pride; he exudes it.

As his wife, Barbara Lea gives the only performance that doesn't ring true. She sounds unfortunately like a New York actress striving for a regional accent (settling "rot cheer" and fetching "sprang water.")

Other performances, however, are uniformly excellent. As

the lovers, Gina McMather and E. E. Norris are well-matched. She is pretty and feisty, he is cocky and determined ("You fancy me. I know what you want and you know what I want, so how 'bout it?")

Veteran actress Marian Baer creates a half dozen different characters, each a gem. She is an old woman with superstitious cures for ailments, an eccentric ginseng collector, a neighbor who holds a corn husking party, a balladeer. Best of all, certainly, is her portrayal of a coal miner's embittered widow, a woman with the gift of second sight, who travels from mine to mine warding off evil spirits and preventing mine disasters.

Douglas R. Nielsen portrays brothers, one an opportunist, the other a victim. His personification of the exploiter, offering deals for timber, mineral and gas rights, tourist development, is beautifully done with just the right touch of shiftiness. Tastefully blended throughout the play is mountain music, expertly played on banjo, fiddle, guitar, dulcimer and mandolin by Jan Davidson and Scotty Collier.

"Appalachia Sounding" undertakes the monumental job of explaining the unbreakable bond between man and mountain. The play itself is a study in strength and surely a product of love.

Teaching an Old Show New Tricks
(by Martha Smith, Charleston Gazette, August 1976)

Those who believe you can't teach an old show new tricks are in for a wonderful surprise.

At last Saturday's opening night performance of the seventh season of Hatfields and McCoys, something approaching the phenomenal occurred. A new concept of the legendary feud has been developed by director John Benjamin, and, as a result, a sparklingly fresh study has emerged unveiling the deeply-rooted suspicions that led to hatred and slaughter.

That this was a new show, alive with creativity, energy and talent was immediately evident.

In past years, the show has relied heavily on the ability of the actor playing Devil Anse Hatfield to create the mood of a larger-than-life legend. If the actor failed, the show deteriorated into disjointed fragments.

The 1976 production offers audiences a chance to study the binding--often stifling--closeness of the two proud families. It probes the depths of the feud from jealousy to assult to murder. The tightly knit, introspective picture that Benjamin and his fine cast of performers has drawn intrigues and challenges as no other has been able to do.

Many of the show's innovations are startling. The lighting
effects, for example, are utterly breathtaking. Credit for the
spectacular design--which bathes the faded Rose Anne McCoy in
a pink glow, then splashes shockingly bright, glaring illumination
on scenes of violence--goes to Stephen R. Woodring. Because
he'd never seen Hatfields, Woodring was unprejudiced in approaching his assignment. His design treats the election day brawls as
garish arenas; the love scenes of Rose Anne and Johnse Hatfield
as soft, stolen moments; the assassination tree where three Mc-
Coys die horribly as deadly dark events shrouded in blue. The
lighting thus becomes vital, incredibly valuable to the show's
success.

That Hatfields is a triumph is undeniable. That the glory
must be shared is equally obvious. First, of course, there are
Billy Edd Wheeler's book and Ewel Cornett's score, both facing
well the test of time. Their goal is to capture a bit of Americana. Their vehicle is a reflective journey backward in time,
led by two ghostly figures representing the unrestful spirits of
those who fought the bloody battle. It is a gimmick that works
and adds fluidity as the tale unfolds.

In this particular venture, there is much that must be said
for John Benjamin's gift as a director. He is a fine actor, a
talent displayed several years in the role of Rand'l McCoy. But
he is a better director, as evidenced in consistently excellent
work as founding director of Theatre West Virginia. In this first
season directing Hatfields, Benjamin has distinguished himself.

The casting reveals keen perception of actors' abilities and
limitations. Rapport between cast and crew betrays unflagging
good humor that withstands even an opening night downpour.
Stage direction of the entire ensemble displays a flair for interpretation that rips away the play's facade, exposing both fragile beauty and devastating harshness. All these are gifts Benjamin has brought to this show.

As never before, perhaps, it is possible to grasp the essence not only of the play, but also of history itself. In one
blinding, chilling scene--"Bad Blood,"--attention focuses on a
cluster of bodies, gathered as a Greek chorus to chant the message that bad blood ran between the two mountain families, sep-
arating them more powerfully than the Tug River. It was a
lasting, destructive flow that hurtled through generations, leaving
the dead, the grieving and the vengeful.

Under Woodring's daring lighting pattern, the corps de ballet, directed by Jerry Rose, executes the "Bad Blood" theme
dramatically accompanied by the singers. By positioning the entire company at center stage, Benjamin has transformed "Bad
Blood" into the most arresting scene of the show.

The players are a good, solid company, but some give

outstanding performances. Interestingly, two women's roles emerge as unusually significant. Lisa Bansavage as Levicy Hatfield and Cheryl Stockton as Sarah McCoy project images of quiet strength and determination. Ms. Bansavage wins praise for a thoroughly credible job in a role written for an older, more seasoned actress. And accolades to Ms. Stockton who has made some thing memorable of the wailing and praying scene, beseeching God to save three sons doomed to die at the hands of Hatfield assassins. Previously, that scene tended to become tedious.

As Devil Anse, veteran actor Robert Donley accomplishes what had begun to seem impossible. He has mastered a hillbilly accent without sounding like a New York actor faking a hillbilly accent. When he says "fergit" it sounds perfectly acceptable, completely natural. A few additional words of praise to Donley who, in his first outdoor theater endeavor, was greeted opening night with torrents of chilling rain. He persevered and was in the midst of an all-important dream sequence when the show was stopped for 15 minutes. When the rain abated, Donley continued, but he gave every indication he would have done so regardless. Incidentally, he's also the first Devil Anse whose age and slow, ambling gait are authentic. His long theater credits go way back to the golden years of radio.

Portraying the tragic lovers whose romance is doomed from the outset, Barbara Kosciuk (Rose Anne McCoy) and Timothy McCusker (Johnse Hatfield) make a good match. They exude youth, beauty and confidence, three often underrated commodities.

In what may be the most daring casting, Kenneth Stuart plays Spirit McCoy, the ghost who appears to plead the case for the Kentucky clan. Stuart is black. The color of his skin, while historically incorrect, has nothing to do with the power and strength of his beautiful baritone voice, which is well suited for this important singing role. His counterpart. Spirit Hatfield, is played by Michael Farah, an excellent tenor, whose handsome appearance makes the feminine pulse quicken and the heart flutter.

Among other supporting players, Ed McClelland is splendid in multiple roles, appearing initially as the goofy son, Phamer McCoy, whose sole interest in life is shooting anything that moves, then returning as the shifty lawyer Perry Cline.

Also good in dual assignments is Jim Klawin, interpreting the intense, brooding Tolbert McCoy and, later, the demented Cap Hatfield, who rekindles the feud by horsewhipping a McCoy woman.

Ideally, certain elements of this production would be different. The Hatfield's tablecloth, for instance, wouldn't look like plastic, even if someone did want to convey an impression of genuine oilcloth. And Jim McGuire, who plays the comic figure Uncle Jim Vance, wouldn't throw away so many of his big laugh lines. Likewise, Michael Morris' characterization of Rand'l McCoy wouldn't be as flat as his singing. Rand'l, history tells us, was a thoughtful, peace-loving man, not a one-dimensional dullard. Additionally, when the two Spirits are required to speak in unison, all the words would come out together.

Regardless of these faults--and all shows have them, no matter how pleasing the total product--the 1976 version of Hatfields and McCoys is an extraordinary experience. It is a mixture of young talent and veteran performers. It is an blending of strong, sure voices (in particular, listen for soprano Donna Marie Evans). It is a demonstration by exquisitely versatile, flexible dancers.

Primarily, however, this is a show that dares to be fresh, new, bold. It is a production that demands much of its company in developing a complete family portrait illuminating all the members who were bound together by a curious mixture of love and hate peculiar to the isolated mountain country.

It is, lastly, powerful, dynamic theater that must be seen and savored, especially for persons who think they've seen it all before.

Produced by Theatre Arts of West Virginia, Hatfields and McCoys will be presented each Tuesday, Wednesday, Thursday and Saturday through Aug. 28 in Cliffside Amphitheater near Beckley.

SOBEL, Robert Murray; (2) Classical Editor, International Editor, Theater Editor; (3) b. New York City, Sept. 11, 1925; (4) s. Elias and Toby (Sobel); (5) B.A. New York U., major: journalism, 1950; (6) m. Shelly Slote, Dec. 20, 1959; (7) children--Laurence, Edward, David; (8) Reporter, copy editor, N.Y. Daily Mirror 1950-1964. News bulletin writer, New York Times (part-time), 1964 & 1965 summer; (13) Non-veteran; (15) Member Great Neck Library Music Assn.; (16) Democrat; (17) Jewish; (20) Article on Songs of the Seventies. Stories and articles on Broadway musicals for present publication; (21) 44 Baker Hill Rd., Great Neck, N.Y., Ph. 516-466-8492; (22) 1515 Broadway, New York, Ph. 212-764-7342; (23) Circulation: 35,000. Audience: record companies, dealers, radio programers, disc jockeys, talent agencies, artists and those others interested in trade aspects of music-record industry; (24) 25 musicals, 20 nightclub acts, 5 concerts, 50 record reviews.

"The Wiz"
(by Robert Sobel, Billboard, January 18, 1975)

"The Wiz" works--not in the explosive or even pounding sense, but in a stylish, spoof-sprinkled and extremely professional way.

Based on "The Wonderful Wizard of Oz," that captivating classic which became a phenomenon as a film (although a successful stage version was mounted from the book by Frank Baum), this black version meets the challenge with sauce, moxie and innovation.

However, let it be said quickly that the show (book by William F. Brown) is a bit too long and that most of the songs are a disappointment. Certainly the latter is true when compared with the ambitious and totally inventive production as a whole.

Unfortunately, the songs provide nothing new. This does not mean that the tunes (music and lyrics by Charlie Smalls) are all that bad; it's just that we look for something different to compete with or to complement the splendid mounting.

For this reason 20th Century Records, which has the album rights, may find the LP a hard sell. Nevertheless, a few of the tunes, such as "To Be Able to Feel," "No Bad News" and "Believe in Yourself," have single potential. But actually this is the kind of show which must be seen to be fully appreciated. Its visual effects, its very original choreography, its tasteful costumes, the novel staging and the rest are of superior quality.

Blessed, too, with the skilled mind of director Geoffrey Holder, who doubles in brass as costume designer, an outstanding cast headed by young Stephanie Mills as Dorothy, "The Wiz" becomes an evening to enjoy.

Miss Mills, who records for ABC/Dunhill, exhibits an extremely fine voice, with a far range, and her dancing and acting are always professional. Her role does not contain much personality, unlike the juicy film role, closeups and all, afforded to Judy Garland.

Hinton Battle's Scarecrow is a feat all by itself, as he shows a nimbleness and buoyancy that fairly jumps with its own honesty. Tiger Haynes (of "Open the Door, Richard" fame) plays the Tin Man with skill; and Ted Ross as the Lion is not only cowardly but also offers some funny moments.

The Wiz, played by Andre De Shields; Evillene, performed by Mabel King as a combination of Bette Davis, Sophie Tucker and Pearl Bailey; and Dee Dee Bridgewater (Thad Jones & Mel Lewis orchestra vocalist), portray their roles superbly as does the rest of an exceptionally talented cast.

Best of all, the show never really takes itself seriously-- except when it counts. Maybe that's why it all works so well.

"Shenandoah"
(by Robert Sobel, Billboard, January 25, 1975)

"Shenandoah" is American classical theater at its musical

best. The emphasis here is on classical, for the musical, which opened here Jan. 7, is that too-rare example of the kind of traditional theater that is conceived with skill, talent and tenderness and that reminds one of brilliant show pieces such as "Oklahoma!" and "Annie Get Your Gun."

Based on the original screenplay for the film written by James Lee Barrett, who co-authored the book, the story, very briefly, concerns a Virginia farmer's unwillingness to involve himself and his six sons and daughter in the Civil War. His is a belief based on protection rather than pacivity. And simply put, it's a story of pro-family values with an anti-war theme.

Are these concepts now considered to be old-fashioned and square? Perhaps. But the story enfolds so beautifully, embraced by songs that at once deal with these "old fashioned" values in a contemporary way that they carry out "traditional theater" to the fullest. The composer is Gary Geld; lyricist is Peter Udell, who also serves as co-author with Barrett and Philip Rose, the show's director and producer. Geld and Udell have long collaborative efforts in the recording field. (They're responsible for the Carpenters' "Hurting Each Other.") This show should establish them as one of the top teams in the theatrical field as well (they collaborated on "Purlie").

John Cullum, in the featured role of Charlie Anderson, is a talent of major proportions. His singing and acting is superb. And the other principals in the cast, including Donna Theodore, Penelope Milford, Joel Higgens, Ted Agress and Gordon Halliday, are all excellent. Robert Tucker's choreography is fine.

Although no recording for the show has been firmed, a theater spokesman said that two labels have expressed interest in securing the original cast album rights. Small wonder with such tunes as "Freedom," "Papa's Gonna Make it Alright," "Why Am I Me?" and "Violets and Silverbells," to name just a few picked at random.

SPERO, Bette; (2) Entertainment writer; (3) b. Orange, N.J., June 25, 1944; (4) d. Peggy and Leonard Cohen; (5) B.A. Georgian Court College, major: English; (6) single; (8) News reporter; feature writer, Asbury Park (N.J.) Press, 1966-70; feature writer, Newark, (N.J.) Evening News, 1970-71; feature writer, specializing in entertainment, primarily drama, pop music and film, The Daily Register (Red Bank, N.J.), 1971-74; entertainment writer and drama and pop music critic, The Star-Ledger (Newark, N.J.), 1974-75; (14) Best feature writer, 1967, N.J. Daily Newspaperwomen; (15) Sigma Delta Chi, National and N.J. Professional Chapter; (16) Independent; (20) Various feature writings contributed to and syndicated by The Associated Press; (21) 25 Wesley Street, Monmouth, Beach, N.J. 07750; (22) The Star-Ledger, Star-Ledger Plaza, Newark, N.J. 07101; (23) Circulation: daily, 360,000; Sunday, 560,000; (24) 30 plays; 15 pop music concerts.

Whole Theatre Makes "Godot" Worth the Wait
(by Bette Spero, Star-Ledger, February 10, 1975)

Perhaps not everyone has been waiting for Godot, but an enthusiastic opening night audience in Montclair was certainly glad
"he" had arrived in the guise of The Whole Theatre Company.

The Company has taken the play, which has become a classic of Samuel Beckett's body of work, and turned it into a marvelous and relevant exposition for any audience today.

Some spectators may erroneously be put off by Beckett's in-
tellectual, even esoteric reputation as a writer. But don't be!
Staying away would be a terrible disservice to the play, the
Whole Theatre Company and you yourselves.

Granted, "Waiting for Godot" may never be for the dinner
theater circuit. But there is no reason why it can't succeed anywhere else. In fact, it has--in Europe, in America, on television, in professional and amateur productions and now, in Montclair.

In rereading the play the night before the performance, I
was struck by what very good writing it is: Clever, subtle, discerning, perceptive, adroit and just downright funny.   And in
seeing the play the next night, I was struck at how exceedingly
well it played onstage.

Even Beckett himself, I think, would have been pleased at
the top-drawer job The Whole Theatre Company has done with
his play.   Director Tom Brenn has combatted what some scholars
felt was the play's dramatic drawback, its lack of action, by
drawing out very active characterizations from the players.

There is the usual stark set, consisting of a tree, but the
production seems bright and colorful and sparkling because of
the wonderfully alive portrayals of the actors.   What adds vitality too is the variety exhibited by the different characters.

The three leads, the tramps Estragon and Vladimir, and the
"master" Pozzo are excellent.   Stefan Peters and Alex Kane are
perfect foils to each other as, respectively, Estragon and Vladimir and display remarkably perfect timing in their professional,
clownlike characterizations.

Ernie Schenk's appearance as a blustery and mostly loud
Pozzo provides the play with needed excitement, preventing it
from deteriorating into an intellectual talkathon.

Jason Bosseau, as the human slave, Luck, performs very
well what would have to be considered one of the more distasteful roles in contemporary theater.   Bosseau also deserves a
hand for dramatically spitting out (nearly quite literally) what must
rank as the most difficult soliloquy ever written for the stage.

Certainly it is the most absurd.

The play consists of two acts which the tramps spend sitting about the stage, occasionally chatting in a lot of non sequiturs, twice being interrupted by Pozzo and Lucky, all while they wait for Godot. Who's Godot? Who knows?

Williams' Play Chuckles at Modern South
(by Bette Spero, Star-Ledger, March 10, 1975)

Tennessee Williams has not lost his touch. He has returned to the small circle of great American dramatists with a comedy, "Kingdom of Earth."

McCarter Theater in Princeton, with the uncanny judgment of producer Michael Kahn, has a winner in Williams' latest work. The theater, which has had a superb season so far, premiered the play Thursday to the obvious delight of a very responsive audience.

Everything about the production is excellent, starting with the author. Williams presents a compact, two-act comedy, spoofing, of course, the modern south and some of its traditional anacronisms.

The writing is succinct, funny and to the point. Even Lot, the dreamy homosexual, does not deteriorate into endless talking.

There are only three characters and they are notably related to William's characters of yore. In many respects they are more deeply developed and in tune with the foibles of more modern men.

Lot's wife Myrtle, a daffy dame who was billed as "Miss Petite Personality Plus" when she was in "show business," ranks with Williams' memorable heroines.

The difference is Myrtle is much more fun and easier to relate to than the Amandas, Blanches, or even Maggies of Williams' other plays. "Kingdom of Earth" is clearly Myrtle's show (in fact, in its original version it was called "The Seven Descents of Myrtle") and Marilyn Chris makes the most of it.

Miss Chris, a blond who looks something like one of the Gabor sisters and snaps dialogue a bit like Joan Blondell, is absolutely perfect as Myrtle. Her performance is a joy and makes the play one too.

When the show was first done a few years ago under the former title it starred Estelle Parsons and was a failure. But with extensive rewriting and a new star it is an unqualified success.

Miss Chris makes the show but the supporting actors are
not slouches either. David Pendleton as Chicken, Lot's half
brother, tinges the role of a common brute with some interesting shades of humanness.

Courtney Burr as Lot, the young man who wears ice cream
colored suits when he's not wearing his late mother's dresses,
infects his sickly bridegroom with a very skilled balance of
weakness and poignancy.

Direction by Garland Wright is up to the extremely high
standard of Kahn in every way--the best compliment we can pay
him.

Paul Zalon's set is absolutely lovely and ingenious in its
functioning. Costumes by David James, particularly those for
Myrtle, are most clever, for they tell us a lot about these
characters before they even open their mouths.

The play takes place in rural Mississippi during 1960.
First there are the newlyweds Lot and Myrtle who were married
on television after she was crowned "Queen of the Day" on a
daytime TV show.

Then there is the halfbreed Chicken who lives in the kitchen
of the old family homestead where Lot and Myrtle go for their
honeymoon. They arrive just in time for the annual flood.

That, briefly, is the skeletal outline of the latest and one
of the best plays of Thomas Lanier Williams. You can see it
at McCarter through March 16.

STADELMAN, Egon P.; (2) Managing Editor, Drama and Music Critic; (3) b. Jan 31, 1911, Berlin, Germany; (4) deceased; (5) Goethe
Gymnasium, Berlin; Friedrich Wilhelm University, Berlin; (6) Married; (8) Started 1929 as City Reporter for "Berliner Volks-Zeitung"
published by Rudolf Mosse Verlag; (13) United States Army 1942-44;
(14) Bundesverdienst-Kreuz (given by the Federal Government of the
Federal Republic of Germany 1972 for furthering German-American
cultural relations; (16) No political party, independent voter; (17)
Jewish; (20) Too numerous (since 1929!) to be listed (21) Request to
leave address and telephone unlisted; (22) 36-30, 37th Street, Long
Island City, N.Y. 11101; (23) Circulation: Approx 50,000, more on
Sundays; (24) 400-500.

Meisterwerk, meisterhaft aufgeführt: Erich Korngolds "Die Tote
Stadt" in der City Oper
(by Egon Stadelman, N.Y. Staats-Zeitung und Herold, April 9, 1975)

Erich Wolfgang Korngolds Oper "Die tote Stadt," die thre
Uraufführung gleichzeitig in Hamburg und Köln erlebte, kurz
darauf in Wien und ein Jahr später von der Metropolitan Opera
in New York mit Marla Jeritza in der Hauptrolle aufgeführt

wurde, ist musikalisch kein sonderlich originelles Werk. Korngold, der sein kompositorisches Talent schon ais Elfjähriger mit einem für drei Klaviere geschriebenen Trio bewies, und der 1957 in Hollywood starb, wo er die Musik zu vielen, zum Teil sehr berühmt gewordenen Filmen schrieb, war niemals ein Neuschöpfer. Viele seiner Werke verraten deutlich den Einflub, den andene Komponisten auf ihn ausgeübt haben. Das gilt auch für "Die tote Stadt," seine erfolgreichste Oper, die er mit 23 Jahren schrieb, und die nun von der New York City Opera von neuem zum Leben erweckt wurde. Anlehnung an Richard Straub, an Puccini, an Franz Lehar und auch an Debussy läbt sich nicht verleugnen. Es Kann aber auch nicht bestritten werden, dab die Oper auberordentlich kalngvoll ist und eine Anzahl von musikalisch sehr wirksamen Arten und Duetten bietet. Ihr Thema ist die Geschichte eines Mannes, der gegen Ende des 19. Jahrhunderts in Brügge (der "toten" Stadt) lebt, seine verstorbene Frau abgöttisch liebt und verehnt, aber dem Reiz einer leichtlebigen Tänzerin nicht widerstehen kann. In dem Roman, der Korngolds Opus zu Grunde liegt, erwürgt der Mann die Tänzerin. In der Oper dagegen erweist sich das tragische Geschehen nur als ein grauenvoller Traum.

Die Aufführung der New York City Opera ist nicht zuletzt dank der Iszenierung durch Frank Corsaro und Ronald Chase äuberst sehenswert. Mit Hllfe von wechselnden Farbphotos und Filmen, die speziell für diesen Zweck in Brügge aufgenommen wurden, und die so projiziert werden, dab sich häufig ein dreidimensionaler Effekt einstellt, werden Bildwirkungen geschaffen, die nicht allein die einzigartige Atmosphäre Brügges widerspiegeln, sondern auch dem traumhaften und häufig gespenstischen Charakter des Librettos gerecht werden. Noch mehr verstärkt wird diese Wirkung durch Tänzer, die in mehreren Szenen mit grotesken Masken auftrenten, und auch durch die sehr geschickte Verwendung von unsichtbaren Chören.

In der weiblichen Hauptrolle bot Carol Neblett, obwohl sie in ihrer Erscheinung für diese Figur nicht sonderlich geeignet ist, eine durchaus überzeugende und in gesanglicher Hinsicht sehr beachtliche Leistung, was auch für ihren Partner John Alexander zutrifft. Auch die anderen Rollen wurden durchwegs sehr gut gesungen, was insbesondere für Dominic Cosa zutrifft, der in der Kleidung eines Pierrots die mustkalisch eindrucksvollste Arie der Oper sehr wirksam zum Vortrag brachte.

Die musikalische Leistung der Oper, die auf Deutsch gesungen wunde, lag in den Händen von Imre Pallo, der vollstes Verständnis für den romantischen Charakter des Werkes bewies. Erwähnenswert ist auch die ebenso geschickte wie geschmackvolle Choreographie von Thomas Andrew.

Der enthusiastische Beifall des Publikums galt mit Recht sowohl den Darstellern als auch dem Dirigenten und überhaupt allen, die für diese Aufführung verantwortlich waren. Mag

"Die tote Stadt" auch kein Werk sein, das sich mit den Opern
der groben Meister dieser Kunstant vergleichen läbt--als mu-
sikalisches Theater verdient Korngolds Oper durchaus die Wie-
derauferstehung, die thr durch die New York City Opera zuteil
wurde.

Jugendwerk O'Neills in Neu-Aufführung: "All God's Chillun Got Wings"
im Circle in the Square Theatre
(by Egon Stadelman, N. Y. Staats-Zeitung und Herold, April 9, 1975)

Im Programmheft des Circle in the Square Theaters heibt es,
dab George C. Scott, der sich in diesem Falle als Regisseur be-
tätigte, eine besondere Vorliebe für Eugene O'Neills vor mehr
als fünf Jahrzehnten geschriebenes Drama "All God's chillun Got
Wings" hat. Diese Vorliebe ist nicht leicht zu verstehen, denn
es handelt sich dabei gewib nicht um eines der besten oder auch
nur besseren Theaterstücke O'Neills, und dab es seit 50 Jahren
nicht mehr auf einer gröberen Bühne aufgeführt wurde, ist be-
greiflich wie erklärlich: "All God's Chillun Got Wings" ist die
Geschichte einer Ehe zwischen einer weiben Frau und einem
schwarzen Mann. Beide lieben einander bis zum Ende, aber im
Unterbewubtsein der Frau bricht immer wieder ein elementarer
Rassenhab durch, und nur im Irrsinn findet sie eine Lösung
dieses Konfliktes.

Es ist keine Frage, dab O'Neill selbst das Negerproblem
als solches nicht zum eigentlichen Thema seines Dramas machen
wollte, und dab ihn im Grunde nur die Problematik einer Ehe
zweier Menschen, die nicht zueinander passen, thematisch be-
shä ftigte. Der beste Beweis dafür ist die Tatsache, dab die
beiden Personen seines Dramas die gleichen Vornamen tragen
wie seine eigenen Eltern, deren Ehe zerbrach. Dennoch über-
wiegt das Rassenproblem, und die Ant, wie es von dem Autor
behandelt wurde, wirkt im Jahre 1975 veraltet und oberflächich.

Damit soll allerdings nicht gesagt sein, dab das Stück dra-
matischer Wirkung entbehrt. Manche Szenen lassen das rein
menschliche Element packend in den Vordergrund treten, und
besonders im letzten Akt erreicht das tragische Geschehen klassi-
sches Format.

Scotts Frau, Trish Van Devere, die man zum ersten Male auf
einer Broadwaybühne sieht, spielt die Rolle der unglücklichen
Frau mit sichtlicher Sympathie für die von ihr verkörperte Figur,
aber nicht immer gelingt es ihr, so überzeugend zu Wirken, wie
man es erwartet. In der schwierigen Rolle thres Mannes bietet
Robert Christian eine eindrucksvolle Leistung. Von den anderen
Mitwirkenden sind vor allem Vickie Thomas und Tom Sminkey
zu erwähnen. Ming Cho Lee schuf ein geschicktes Bühnenbild.
George C. Scotts Regie vermochte die Schwächen des Dramas
nur teilweise zu überwinden.

Die Aufführung ist trotzdem sehenswert, sei es auch nur,

weil sie einen interessanten Einblick in die Epoche eriaubt, in der Amerikas grösster Dramatiker dieses Werk schuf.

STAFF, Charles, Indianapolis News, Indianapolis, Ind. 46206.

STASIO, Marilyn L.; (2) Theatre critic; (3) b. Boston; (5) B. A. Regis College, Weston, Mass. (cum laude); M. A. Columbia U., 1962, major subj.: Comparative Lit.; (6) m. Richard J. Hummler, 1971; (8) Entertainment Ed., Ingenue Mag.; Ed. in Chief, Brooklyn Graphic; Cue Magazine, theatre critic, 1968- ; (9) Instructor, NYU School of Continuing Ed. 1974-76; (15) Mem. N. Y. Drama Critics Circle; mem. Nominating Committee for "Tony" and "OBIE" Awards; (20) Cont. art. to Stagebill (Kennedy Center program), Playbill, Ms. Magazine, Newsday; author Broadway's Beautiful Losers, theatre book pub. by Delacorte; (22) Cue Magazine, 20 West 43 St., New York, N. Y. 10036, Ph. 212-371-6900.

Lucky Cat
(by Marilyn Stasio, Cue Magazine, April 14, 1975)

"P. S. Your Cat Is Dead!" At the Golden Theatre. Lucky us. For a while it looked as if Broadway had grown out of those insipid romantic-fantasy comedies with their old-fashioned and unreal conventions. But homosexual theatre has come out of the closet, so everybody duck. Here they come again, with a sex change.

In James Kirkwood's gay fantasy, the sweet young thing is Keir Dullea. It's New Year's Eve and the lad's girl has left him, likewise his acting job in a Broadway show. Unkindest cut of all, he's just been written out of his soap opera. And, of course his cat has died. You can really feel for the cat.

Enter romance, in the guise of Tony Musante, a mucho-macho homosexual burglar who literally drops down from heaven-- the skylight--in gay-us ex machina fashion. Making him the butt of his personal and professional frustrations, the actor trusses him to the sink, goading and humiliating him with threats that are meant to be both charming and comic. Love and fantasy will out, however, and we are left with the warm glow of knowing our hero will soon be converted to gay delights.

Baring his icy grin, Dullea is about as charming as a toad, which kills any chance that his character's sadism might pass as cute and lovable. Although Musante is disarmingly likable, his abundant acting skills can't force believability on a character who is slightly less real than Prince Charming.

Although silly and hokey, the show is actively repellent on a deeper level. It plays coy and cute about sadism; it romanticizes and thereby trivializes certain painful realities of the homosexual experience; it degrades and sneers at women. It is unfit for consumption by men or women, whatever their sexual persuasion. For picket signs, apply here.

All About Evil
(by Marilyn Stasio, Cue Magazine, June 16, 1975)

"Chicago"--At the 46th Street Theatre. Come to "Chicago" and prepare to be stripped, stroked, worked over, and wiped out. The most seductive musical since "Cabaret," it propositions you with forbidden pleasure, dangerous beauty. It's all about evil, and it's irresistible.

Director/choreographer/co-author Bob Fosse uses big, bad Chicago of the late 1920s as the focal point of his "musical vaudeville." It's the gin age, the jazz age, the age of passion murders, and Roxie Hart straddles it all. A boozing singer in a gin mill, Roxie shoots her lover and skyrockets to fame to feed the lust of a sensation-slurping public. That's the bare story; the rest is attitude.

More than anything else, it's a subversive, Brechtian attitude. We might be in Berlin, as far as the juicy moral decadence goes. (And it does go far, especially in Patricia Zipprodt's tantalizing costumes.) But sex, jazz, and gin are smallpotato sin. This is Chicago, where we sin in a big, all-American way. "In this town, murder is a form of entertainment," somebody says. And so it is. But Fosse's point is bigger; everything is a form of entertainment in America. From murder to justice to life and death, "it's all a circus, kid; it's all show business." It all has to be marketed, too, and that's what this show is about. America's cynical marketing of people and principles.

Fosse sees the process as a diabolical vaudeville show, and that's what he's put on the stage, a breathtaking show-within-a-show-within-a-nightmare. Tony Walton's slick-and-sleazy set and Jules Fisher's sinister lighting conspire to create a cabaret, where events in human lives are announced and presented as tawdry nightclub turns. Against this backdrop, Roxie's infamous career is an act, and everybody gets into it--her lawyer, feeding on the notoriety; the media, cynically making celebrities of murderers; the law, perverting justice into farce; Roxie, selling herself as a commodity; and all of us, for being ravenous consumers, demanding and swallowing reality as entertainment. As the show's last line says, "We couldn't have done it without you, folks."

The inimitable Gwen Verdon plays Roxie with brutal honesty. No sentimental slush in this classy performance; her Roxie is hard and dumb and guilty as hell. But in a sensational strut-number, "Roxie," Verdon shows us what Roxie can't see herself-- that for all her complicity in the corruption of truth, she

is still a victim, the pawn of the media, the law, the social
system and all its perverted values.

John Kander's mocking "let me entertain you" tunes, set to
Fred Ebb's heretically tough lyrics and book, force every character to make the same kind of musical revelation. Cast as a
second-string murderer, the sensational Chita Rivera dances a
frenzied "act of desperation" when she realizes that her life
hangs on her ability to give the bloodsuckers a good show. As
Jerry Orbach--who is wonderfully slippery as a oleaginous law-
yer--keeps reminding his clients: "They like it better when you
hang."

"Chicago," like I've said, is set in the '20s, and its smashing finale, "Nowadays," wonders if things will change in 50
years. If you think that's a bitter irony, then go to "Chicago";
it's your kind of town.

STATEN, Vince, Dayton Daily News, Dayton, O. 45401.

STEELE, Robert Michael (writes under the name Mike Steele); (2)
Theater and dance critic, columnist on theater, dance and visual
arts; (3) b. Chicago, Ill., Jan. 14, 1942; (4) s. Robert M. and Ruth
M. (Blume); (5) B.A. U. of Colorado, major subj: literature; grad.
work, U. of Chicago; (6) Single; (8) 1964; theater director in Illinois
and Colorado; Research fellowship, Menninger Clinic, to study aber-
rant behavior and the arts in correctional institutions; writer for
Hutchinson, Kansas, News and Topeka, Kansas, Capitol-Journal; Critic for Minneapolis Tribune since 1967; (14) Ford Fellow, O'Neill Theater Conference; Ford Fellow, American Dance Festival Critics Conference; (15) Member National Endowment for the Arts Dance Advisory Panel, 1971-74; Member Minnesota State Arts Council Advisory
Panel, 1971- ; (20) Cont. articles to Time, Newsweek, N.Y. Times;
Art in America, Landscape Architecture, Artnews, Rhode Island
School of Design Bulletin, notes for Minnesota Orchestra Symphony
Magazine, wrote Catalog of Nine Artists/Nine Spaces show for Minn.
Arts Council; others; (21) 1415 Douglas Ave., Minneapolis 55403, Ph.
612-377-1165; (22) 425 Portland Ave., Minneapolis, 55415, Ph. 612-
372-4445; (23) Circulation, 250,000 daily; 700,000 Sunday; (24) An-
nual reviews; 100 plays, 40 dance concerts, 52 columns on all arts,
20 visual art reviews, 10 opera reviews.

"What the Butler Saw"
(by Mike Steele, Minneapolis Tribune, January 29, 1976)

"People are profoundly bad," said Joe Orton, "but irresistibly funny."

Nowhere did Orton illustrate his point better than in his madhouse of a play "What the Butler Saw," now being given a splendid production at the Chanhassen Dinner Theater.

Orton's major weapon always has been outrage, very apparent in a work like "Loot," this season's big Guthrie hit. But in "Butler," his last play, Orton's angry comedy has mellowed a bit. Outrage has moved to outrageousness, anger to the high-velocity fun of farce.

We know farce is afoot when we see the set--another triumph by Chanhassen's gifted designer Tom Butsch.

Four doors are spread across the stage. If that doesn't tip off an evening of high-speed exits and entrances, mistaken identities and musical beds, nothing does.

We're not let down. And to make matters even cheerier, Orton actually sets this one in a madhouse, or at least its near brother, a psychiatrists' clinic for the mentally disturbed. Orton's specific theme, of course, is that the wrong people are holding the keys and, "If this be sanity, let me out."

This is a funny, funny play where things transpire at such speed that everyone is driven to comic lunacy. None of the characters is actually insane, yet at play's end they are all certifiably mad. No one really does anything, yet everyone expends tremendous energy trying to hide the appearances of unnatural doing.

Apparent deviations flourish, from lesbian covens to homosexuality, from transvestism (seeing her husband holding a dress, the psychiatrist's wife says, "I had no idea our marriage was teetering on the brink of fashion") to unnatural acts with fragments of a Winston Churchill statue.

The play is part Oscar Wilde, part Feydeau, and there's the problem for a director. It all moves with the crazy speed of Feydeau, but unlike his work, the text is terribly important. Things must move, yet words must be understood.

Director Gary Gisselman solves the problem most of the time. He lets everything take off freely when it can--risking, and on rare occasions going into, slapstick--yet pulls it all back to a more meticulous pace when the language counts. He plays part of it with detailed realism, but he lets the characterizations move into a more stylized and inventive exaggeration when that works best. The play's countless one-line gags explode easily, yet at the same time add up to a building comedy of situation.

The cast does extremely well. Guy Paul is at the center of things as Dr. Rance, representing the government, "your immediate superiors in madness." He stands center stage directing the madness about him, spouting a new Freudian cliche for every happening.

Henry Gardner is both sleazy and bewildered as Dr. Prentice,

oiling his way around the asylum trying to regain his drooping
dignity. Susan Osborne is superb as his wife, part looney, part
trendy, part shocked conventionality. Cynthia Carle is wonderful as the put-upon secretary, and Scott Keely and Alfred Anderson do well in the supporting roles.

"Measure for Measure"
(by Mike Steele, Minneapolis Tribune, February 6, 1976)

Shakespeare's "Measure for Measure" is a difficult, flawed
erratic play with a richness that demands patience. It's a magnificent, problematic work, sometimes dry and dull but just as
often vigorous and insightful. It's a play where no one wears
halos and the least sympathetic characters are the most moral.

It has always challenged directors, and now Michael Langham has taken up the challenge as the last play on the Guthrie
season.

He's met this formidable play with a formidable production,
the key qualities of which are clarity, atmosphere and relentless
intelligence.

The low comedy of the play has been heavily cut and is used
sparingly to buoy up the pace. The play is a bridge between
Shakespeare's lyric comedies, and his majestic tragedies, and
it's toward the latter that this production heads.

Set amidst the darkness and decay of Vienna--19th century
Vienna here, dominated by designer Desmond Heeley's evocative
iron gates and steely gray colors--we have a civilization gone
stale. The benevolent Duke of Vienna, a wise, wry but aloof
ruler, has let liberty go unchecked by law. Vice, corruption
and moral decay have set in.

Seeing this, the enigmatic duke turns the government over
to Angelo, a puritanical sort and a moralistic bore. This zealous ideologue sees only rules and not the ruled. Thus he condemns Claudio to death for making love out of wedlock to his betrothed, Juliet.

Love is condemned to death because of rigid laws, and the
very real theme of this production emerges. Can man govern
man? Can the emotional, irrational, natural behavior of man
be controlled by rational, man-made laws? Are justice and
mercy irreconcilable or is a balance possible?

This production zeroes in not only on the duality of society
but also on the duality of man. There are no straw villains or
heroes here, only, like the set, shades of gray. The duke is
wise but not far-seeing. Angelo is moral and just, but not mer-
ciful. Isabella is virtuous but narrow and so on.

The characters, then, are important models for the play's thesis, and in this unsparing, Kafkaesque production, human frailty as well as human heroism can be equally funny and disturbing.

Langham has solved some problems of this "problem play" by shearing away some of the farcical banter that always rested uneasily in this dark work. This risks making the play unrelievedly gloomy, and Langham does ask his audience to walk in darkness for a long time. But it also makes the ultimate light that much brighter, and the second and especially the third acts of this production are very bright as both saints and rascals are exposed.

The cast has responded well overall to this direction, rising to the poetry when it's there--a starker, less musical poetry than in Shakespeare's previous plays--and navigating clearly through more arid passages. The players seem equally at home dealing in human foibles or in loftier contemplations.

Ken Ruta excels as the duke, mysterious, sly, ironic and often unsure of himself in his role of absolute monarch. Patricia Conolly is tough-minded and passionate as the pristine Isabella, never starchy or precious, always crystal clear. Mark Lamos' energetic Lucio looks like nothing so much as Davies in "The Caretaker," petulant, opportunistic, gratingly funny.

Nicholas Kepros as Angelo walks a tight line between being coldly virtuous and being solid. It's an enigmatic performance that is often intriguing yet occasionally so low-keyed as to be invisible.

Other excellent performances come from Jeff Chandler as Claudio, Oliver Cliff as Elbow, Karen Landry as Mariana and Jim Baker as Pompey.

STEIN, Jerry J., (2) Theater and film critic; (3) b. Cincinnati, Nov. 8, 1941; (4) s. Edward N. and Bess L. (Leisure); (5) E., B.S., U. of Cincinnati (1968); (8) ass't TV editor, Cincinnati Post 1960-68; amusements editor, Cincinnati Post 1968-74; (9) Lecturer film seminars Xavier U., '71, '72; (15) Member advisory board Educational Film Series, in schools, contributor to Film Heritage Quarterly; (20) Contributor to int'l travel guide Businessman's Guide to Entertainment; (22) Cincinnati Post, 800 Broadway, Cincinnati, O. 45202, Ph. 513-721-1111 (Off. Hrs. 4:30 p.m.-6:30 p.m. M-F).

STEWART, Perry; (2) Theater-Film Critic; (3) b. Little Rock, Ark., Oct. 18, 1942; (4) s. Perry and Betty (Thomas) S.; (5) B.A. Texas Christian U., major subj.: Govt., 1965; (6) Unmarried; (8) Reporter Arkansas Democrat 1960-61, Copy Editor Democrat 1961-63, Copy

Editor Fort Worth Morning Star-Telegram 1964-67, Amusements columnist-critic Evening Star-Telegram 1967- ; (9) Asst. dir. "The Audition," experimental short subject, 1963 and instrumentalist on "Dinner on the Ground," folk-rock LP; (11) State committeeman, Arkansas Young Democrats 1961, Alternate Delegate Democratic District Convention (Texas) 1974; (14) Dallas Press Club Citation 1964; (16) Democrat; (17) Protestant; (20) Cont. articles to Fort Worth Magazine, TCU Fine Films; (21) 504 Virginia Place, Fort Worth, Tex., 76107, Ph. 817-738-5660; (22) Evening Star-Telegram, 400 W. 7th St., Fort Worth, Tex., 76102, Ph. 817-336-9271; (23) Circulation: 137,000 daily (e); (24) 65 motion pictures, 30 plays and musicals, 2 television, 20 night club, 12 miscellaneous.

"Lenny" Has Oscar Claim
(by Perry Stewart, Fort Worth Star-Telegram, February 19, 1975)

Perhaps when Bob Fosse and Dustin Hoffman first met to discuss the filming of "Lenny," director Fosse told his star: "Stick with me and I'll get you that Oscar."

Or perhaps it was Hoffman himself, twice nominated for an Academy Award but never a winner, who decreed that with his portrayal of "sick comic" Lenny Bruce, Oscar time had come.

At any rate, one thing is clear about the 7th Street Theater's new tenant. In an otherwise skillful, at times brilliant film, Hoffman's performance regularly grabs the viewer by the throat that seems to demand: "Gimme that--Oscar!"

Of course, there are no blanks or bleeps in "Lenny." The words Dirty Lenny used to shock audiences and outrage courtrooms of the 1950s and 1960s are spoken freely on movie screens of the 1970s. Unfilmable a decade ago, "Lenny" now carries an "R" rating.

The film follows Bruce from Baltimore days as a burlesque second banana to Catskills comer to controversial cult hero. Almost as an afterthought, "Lenny" shows the aftermath of that 1966 bathroom overdose which ended all the police hassles and the dirty words forever.

Through it all, the slick-sleazy atmosphere of night clubs and coffee houses is captured superbly by cinematographer Bruce Surtees in appropriate black and white footage reminiscent of "Mickey One."

The comedian's tragic marriage to stripper Honey Harlowe is depicted in memorable fashion by the film makers and by a honey of an actress named Valerie Perrine. Clearly, if there is an Oscar contender in this film it is she more than Hoffman or Fosse. Considerable sound and fury is spent trying to make the title character an authentic martyr. Then along comes this dumpling-faced showgirl and flat breaks your heart in scene after scene.

That theirs was a mutually destructive relationship is shown
graphically by screen writer Julian Barry, who adapted his own
Broadway play which starred Cliff Gorman. Lenny and Honey
just don't seem to be destined for happiness. There is too much
failure, too much success, too much dope and kinky group sex.

Even considering the ill-conceived "Alfredo, Alfredo," it's
hard to recall a bad Dustin Hoffman performance. "Lenny" certainly doesn't qualify. Despite flaws of over-selling, Hoffman
emerges with a fine and forceful characterization.

In Fosse's supporting cast, Jan Miner (of the TV detergent
commercials) is tough and warm and real as dancer Sally Marr,
Bruce's very untraditional Jewish mama. Stanley Beck is a likewise real, but chilling, agent type. And Gary Morton, who may
never again be known as "the guy who married Lucille Ball," is
terrific as a veteran comic-showman cast in the Milton Berle
mold.

It's an argueable point whether or not Bruce is worthy of
the sort of canonization attempted by the playwright and film
makers of "Lenny." He did perform "obscene" material back
when it wasn't fashionable. But so did Redd Foxx, and it didn't
ruin his life.

When Hoffman screams to a judge, "Don't take away my
words," it's obvious Fosse anticipated a chorus of "Right on!"
from audiences around the country. Then there is the excruciating scene when a hopelessly tripped-out Hoffman fights a narco-
tic haze, attempting to get through his night club routine.

In an interview with this column last month, Miss Perrine
pronounced the scene one of the all-time greats. Fosse obviously agreed. So did I for about four minutes.

Then I simply got bored. So, apparently, did the 7th Street
patrons who walked out on "Lenny" at the same time audiences
within the film were leaving Bruce alone with his incoherencies.

You can blame only so much of this on the actor. If, as
Newsweek magazine eulogized, "Lenny Bruce died from an overdose of police," then perhaps "Lenny," the film, suffers from
an overdose of Fosse.

Just a Trifle Entertaining
(by Perry Stewart, Fort Worth Star-Telegram, February 19, 1975)

There was a lot about the 1920s that really ought to be time-
machined back into contemporary society. Ten-cent movies,
Tiffany lamps, art deco, the Model T.

On the other hand, there are relics of the period which
ought to be left to rest in peace. Things like rolled stockings,

bound bosoms, the Volstead Act, Warren G. Harding and "The Constant Wife."

The latter, a 1926 comedy by Somerset Maugham, was the object of an elaborate London revival a few seasons ago. Ingrid Bergman played the title role, and her subsequent American tour prevented Fort Worth Community Theater from obtaining rights to produce "The Constant Wife" until now. The play opened last evening in the Scott Theater and marks the 20th anniversary of the FWCT troupe.

It appears that, apart from being a vehicle for Miss Bergman, this play was exhumed because it pointed a satirical finger at the double standard concerning marital infidelity--hence was some kind of ahead-of-its-time feminist vanguard. As for the dialogue, everyone knows yesterday's old hat is tomorrow's high camp.

Bull.

This is a silly little trifle where women drop hankies and men say things like "You're a brick."

Happily, director William Garber and a journeyman cast go a long distance toward making it an entertaining trifle. You are apt to find yourself admiring the riders even as you pity this poor dead horse of a play.

Judy Ritts and Guy Lewis, so memorable a duo in "Summer and Smoke" here in 1968, are teamed again as Maugham's proper London couple. Wed 15 years, they're the picture of upper-crust complacency.

Constance is complacent despite the fact that John is having an affair with Marie-Louise. Thank heaven, everyone struggles to keep Constance from learning the awful truth. The awful truth will out, however, and Constance's revenge is the stuff of which Doris Day-Rock Hudson movies are made.

The Ritts-Lewis magic endures on stage, but it's a sometime thing. Although both handle the mannered style adroitly, there is the feeling at times that she is playing it straight and he is toying with parody. In any case, their final scene together is a delight.

Juanita Gibbs, looking perhaps a trifle youthful to portray the mother of a 35-year-old woman, is nevertheless believeable as that male chauvinist's dream: A mother-in-law who excuses infidelity as a man's right.

Shirley Edrington, Jude Johnson, Susan Moore and Bill Scarborough chip in solid support. Director Garber takes the stage for an enjoyable scene as a gullible cuckold, and Donald Gibbs is an unflappable butler in the finest Treacher tradition.

Designer Howard Parsons evokes the period with a spacious
set, and costumer Royce Renfro has garbed the female cast
members exquisitely.

The cast members seemed under-drilled at last night's opening, but it's reasonable to assume they'll warm up, like the
weather, as the week progresses. The play will run through
Jan. 17, with a matinee on Sunday, July 11.

SULLIVAN, Daniel Joseph; (2) Theater critic; (3) b. Worcester,
Mass., Oct. 22, 1935; (4) s. John D. and Irene (Flagg) S.; (5) B.A.
Holy Cross College, major subj.: English lit., 1957. U. of Minnesota graduate school of journalism 1957-59. Indiana Graduate School
of Letters 1958. U. of Southern California program for the training
of music critics, 1964-65; (6) m. Helen Faith Scheid, 1965; (7) chil-
dren--Margaret-Ann, Benjamin, Kathleen; (8) Reporter Worcester
Telegram, 1957. Legislative columnist Red Wing, Minn., Republican
Eagle, 1959. Reporter St. Paul Pioneer Press, 1959-61. Reporter
Minneapolis Tribune, 1961-62. Theater and music critic, Minneapolis Tribune, 1962-64. Music writer New York Times 1965-66. Assistant theater critic New York Times 1966-68. Theater critic Los
Angeles Times 1969- ; (9) Wrote, performed and directed for Brave
New Workshop, Minneapolis cabaret, 1961-64. Dramaturg, Playwrights Conference, Eugene O'Neill Foundation, 1972 and 1973; (10)
Member, school board, St. James School; (14) Page One award,
Twin Cities Newspaper Guild 1960, 62; (15) Los Angeles Drama Critics Circle, President 1970; (21) 837 Third Avenue, Los Angeles
90005, Ph. 389-3336; (22) Times Mirror Square, Los Angeles 90053;
(23) 1 million; (24) 150 reviews a year, all theater or theater-re-
lated.

Eloquence of a Man Without Words
(by Dan Sullivan, Los Angeles Times, February 23, 1975)

The art of Marcel Marceau, who returns to the Shubert Theater Tuesday night for a three-week run, is often referred to as
the art of silence. It would be more accurate to say that silence
is its medium, the framing device that trains the mind on the
theatrical image more sharply than if the image were to speak.
Sometimes, it's true, Marceau uses the silence he works in to
underline a point--to amplify a sense of frustration or pathos.
(A scream is most chilling when you can't hear it.) But this is
like a painter using the whiteness of his canvas in a snowscape.
The canvas is not the painter's subject. Neither, usually, are
Marceau's sketches about silence. In fact, to the horror of the
purer-than-thou, he has performed some of them to music.

His subject is no different from the theater's usual subject:
man. But considered from a different angle. If "talking"

theater presents man as a spirit who happens to have a body--
the feeling you get from conventional plays, many of which are
as effective on the incorporeal medium of radio as on the stage--
Marceau's mime presents him as a body who happens to have a
soul. For all his refinement, Marceau's basic image of man is
animal.

Hence the extraordinary physicality of a Marceau concert,
not only in what he does but in our reaction to it. To be
"moved" in the theater means to take some character or situation, as we say, to heart. You feel it in the chest. Marceau
can do that: It is what makes him a great actor. But what
makes him a great mime is his ability to make you feel it in
the legs and the shoulders as well. When he trembles on an
imaginary high wire it is not just an extraordinary imitation;
you figuratively, are up there clinging to him. When he plants
his elbow on an imaginary mantel, you can feel your own hand
dangle.

"The dancer, the mime, the actor ... three brothers,"
Marceau tells his students. (He'll conduct classes in Los Angeles at the Actors and Directors Lab, by the way; call 652-
8149.) The mime is the middle brother, combining the kinetic
charge of the dancer and the workaday "business" of the actor
into something new and special. Not only does Marceau give an
illusion of walking upstairs so complete that we can feel the
tread under our shoes. He also makes us aware of how much
is involved when we climb a flight of stairs--the kind of insight
that usually doesn't come until you can't cope with them. Like
a great dancer, he celebrates the miracle of the body. Unlike
the dancer, the terms of his demonstration are those that everybody can understand. Most of us don't do plie's. Most of us
do climb stairs.

But there is something double going on here. For while
Marceau as performer never fails to conquer the space around
him, the character he plays often do not--they are always getting
tangled up in their feet or stuck at the top of terrifying ladders.
They are always about to go into free fall. So we have an image
of man's vulnerability produced by a man who is absolutely in
control, an image that would blur and lose its force were the
control less. It's one of the most telling examples the modern
stage offers of the difference between "life" and "art." A man
in real trouble on the stage wouldn't be half so touching. He'd
be too wrapped up in his trouble to project it clearly, and we'd
be too concerned about his suffering to take it aesthetically.
Mask or face? the old theatrical argument used to run. Why,
mask, of course, Marceau would say. How can you produce a
face without one?

Some mimes are empty masks, which is why their work
seems trivial. Marceau wants us to enjoy his technique in passing, but what he is basically projecting is his vision of human

life, a vision that doesn't change from sketch to sketch, however
the mood of the sketches varies.   It starts, as noted, with the
physical facts of the body, the weights and pulleys that help this
ingenious puppet to stand and move.   This is the point of the
"style exercises" with which Marceau commonly begins a show.

But in the longer pieces we see that the body has a resident
dybbuk--a rather bewildered one who expected something grander
than this in terms of accommodations.   Marceau's alter ego,
Bip, is always getting above his station, taking on jobs he can't
handle, messing up out of sheer pretentiousness.   He is mankind,
ludicrously stuck between apehood and angelness, not knowing
which bell to answer.   Bip has never understood why something
as mundane as the law of gravity should apply to as high-minded
a creature as himself, and that's the fun of watching him slip--
he's always so surprised.   It's Chaplin; it's us.

Carry that comic surprise farther and you get shock, which
is not funny at all.   Marceau's serious pieces are only different
in degree from his amusing ones.   Again we see man painting
himself into some kind of corner (the maskmaker frozen into his
mask) or finding himself in the grip of some indifferent natural
law (Marceau's infinitely touching birth-to-death sequence).   Man
the spirit realizing, with a gulp, that he is finally man the thing.
It is not, considered deeply, a laughing matter and Marceau
makes us consider it very deeply.   A great clown, he is also
a great tragedian.

He has been billed recently as "the world's leading nonverbal
communicator."   This trendy phrase does make a point.   By
shutting off our ears Marceau reminds us how much information
we process (in life, if not the theater) through the other senses.
By eliminating words, he reminds us how much in life is too big
for words--how at the full tide of feeling speech seems straw.
If the purpose of poetry is to slip us momentarily back to a
point on the evolutionary scale where feeling and conceptual
thought are fused--the Garden of Eden that abstract language
dried up--Marceau is one of the major poets of the century.   "I
gotta use words when I talk to you," complains somebody in a
T. S. Eliot poem.   Marceau doesn't.

When Marceau comes out on the stage he brings the past
with him, a tradition of whiteface mime that goes back to com-
media dell'arte and, before that, the Greek and Roman clowns.
What makes him modern is his psychology (Bip in a corner is
a good image of what existentialism is about) and his use of
film technique.   He understands our ability, thanks to films, to
keep up with a montage of fleeting images.   Marceau works alone
(except for his superb presenter-of-cards, Pierre Verry); but he
does not always restrict himself to playing one person.   He can
be a room full of partygoers or a park full of Sunday strollers,
not at once, of course, but so quickly that it almost seems at
once.   This demands lightning precision on his part, the skill

to draw a complete figure at one stroke (age, sex, class, even clothing), and then flick on to the next. We in turn must be watching very closely to receive the whole cast of characters, and we are somewhat surprised to find that we can. Film has acclimated us to this kind of "quick cut." It's another example of how, at a Marceau concert, we perform too. In silence, he restores us to our senses.

"Night of the Iguana"--a Revival Revisited
(by Dan Sullivan, Los Angeles Times, January 25, 1976)

Lee Strasberg has been known to tell actors fretting about how they are going to measure up in a particular role to think of it this way--the role also has to measure up to you. In CTG/Ahmanson's revival of "Night of the Iguana," the Rev. T. Lawrence Shannon and Miss Hannah Jelkes measure up to Richard Chamberlain and Dorothy McGuire quite handsomely.

I went back to see Joseph Hardy's production last weekend (it closes Saturday) and found it no less rewarding than on opening night, though the combinations were a little different. Chamberlain and Miss McGuire seemed a trace less involved than before, saving something for the evening performance, maybe (it was a Saturday matinee). On the other hand Eleanor Parker was somewhat closer to the mark as the widow Maxine Faulk, playing the aloneness now, not just the sexiness. And Raymond Massey reminded you more of a 96-year-old poet, less of Raymond Massey. As before you went home knowing you'd had a full meal.

One expects that from a vintage Tennessee Williams play-- as a cook, he always uses real butter--yet somehow this "Night of the Iguana" was a surprise. We were expecting something more steamy, less lucid, certainly less playful. Had the play itself changed since it first came out in '61--i. e. , had our perceptions of it changed--or was it the particular light shed by those particular stars?

Both, probably. As Williams remarked to a New York Times interviewer recently, the sexual side of his plays so titillated audiences in the 1950s that it was the only side they could see. From the 1970s, which have seen a lot dirtier pictures than Tennessee Williams ever drew (or would care to draw) it's clear that this playwright's basic interest has always been the human race's funny, sad attempts to signal to one another over the barricades--sex being one of them, but only one. (And in "Night of the Iguana" not the deepest-reaching one.) Modern audiences aren't uptight around these plays anymore, meaning that now we can hear what they have been saying all the time.

Another accidental reason for "Night's" delicacy and maturity catching us off guard is, maybe, our associating the title with the grossness of the on-location publicity when they were filming the movie in Mexico some years ago--all those hard-breathing

items about who was doing which to whose, while the cameras
waited. It was such a turnoff that it may well have had something to do with the rareness of "Iguana" stage productions since.
(The movie itself wasn't bad.) CTG/Ahmanson's production may
prove a rehabilitation as well as a revival.

But it's also true that Chamberlain and Miss McGuire do give
this "Night" a cool luster that it wouldn't have with other actors.
It was an unexpected pairing, but an astute one, based on somebody's realization--Hardy's?   Producer Robert Fryer's?--that
Hannah and Shannon can both be thought of as moonchildren, hence
susceptible to the kind of fine crystal ring that both Miss McGuire
and Chamberlain have as actors.

The scene everyone remembers in "Night of the Iguana" is
the one where Hannah, the virgin, talks Shannon, the seducer
of teen-agers, down from his worst freakout yet.   In the film
the image was that of a nurse (Deborah Kerr) taming a wild man
(Richard Burton).   Not so at the Ahmanson.   Miss McGuire suggests a bright, loving sister telling her bright invalid brother
some truths about himself in a language they both grew up speak-
ing--among them the truth that he's getting too much satisfaction
out of his fit to deserve an excess of sympathy from her.   From
Miss Kerr, those lines sounded like a therapeutic ploy.   Miss
McGuire obviously means them and Chamberlain plays the part
so as to convince us that she's absolutely right.   The fellow's
half a faker, though not (and we see this too) consciously so.
When he collapses the pain is real enough.   But he never collapses unless somebody's around to pick him up.

Rather than subverting the story--for Shannon's suffering is
real, his enjoyment of it not to be envied--this gives it an undercurrent of ironic comedy, a sense of seeing the man in the
round.   An earthier actor than Chamberlain would probably have
pushed Shannon's demons farther, would have tried to be hair-
raising in the part.   Chamberlain, without denying the howl,
studies the self-deception behind it and comes out with a characterization that's both original and absolutely valid--for him.
It's not the Shannon we were expecting but it's a brilliant exploration of a possible Shannon, tailored to the things Chamberlain finds in himself as a man and as a player.

A colleague was saying the other day that she'd never seen
Hannah played badly.   It is a lovely part, otherworldly, yet wonderfully human, but it could be botched by an actress of less
discrimination and grace than Miss McGuire.   A smug Hannah,
a self-righteous one, an unhealthily repressed one--these aren't
hard to imagine.   Miss McGuire has the balances of the part
just right without making us aware that there's any problem
striking them.   Shyness and toughness, delicacy and frankness,
chastity and a full commitment to life don't seem opposites or
even separate qualities here.   They are all part of a light-
footed girl from Nantucket who knows what is for her in this

world and what is not--and knows what is for you, too, if you'll listen to her (which she doesn't insist on).

What keeps the blessedness from being oppressive or cute is our awareness of Hannah's vulnerability--like so many of Williams' people she, too, has had to depend on the kindness of strangers. (And return it; Miss McGuire tells a haunting story of an encounter on a boat with a women's underwear salesman, and you can hear the silence in the theater deepen as she goes on with it, a tribute both to author and actress.)

Finally there's the humor, much less overt than in Chamberlain's bitchy Shannon, indeed so sly that one can't be absolutely sure this Hannah has a sense of humor at all (though you know Miss McGuire does). One of the biggest, nicest laughs in the show, a sign of how sensitive theater audiences are, even on Saturday afternoons, when they're really caught up in a play, comes before the underwear salesman story. Shannon has been chaffing Hannah on her lack of romantic experiences. She answers that not only has she had one, she's had two "and I'm not exaggerating!" It's not itsy-poo, it's not false-naive, it's ... you'd have to hear Miss McGuire read it to know what it is. The sum of it is an immaculate performance by an actress we're going to want to see in the older classics as well as the modern ones.

As on opening night, two supporting performances stood out-- Allyn Ann McLerie, as a disgruntled Texas schoolteacher every bit as fearsome as Shannon makes her out to be yet with her own story; and Benjamin Stewart, as the pudgy creepy man who replaces Shannon as a tour leader when it all gets too much for him. (Matt Bennett as Shannon's bus driver is fine, too.) As before you also wondered why Hardy was playing the Nazis visiting Miss Parker's hotel mostly for laughs; if that was their only function in the play, it's not likely Williams would have put them in in the first place. Finally there's H. R. Poindexter's setting, rather less ratty than the one described in the text but a good practical set for the Ahmanson, where a well-stocked stage makes one of this theater's better efforts in a long time and a welcome addition to the current Williams revival. He must be smiling. From "decadence" to a classic in 20 years.

SUSSMAN, Sharron; (2) Theatre critic; (3) b. Brooklyn, N.Y., Feb. 16, 1943; (4) d. Morris and Sylvia (Schneiderman) Silverman; (5) Attended Douglass College, Oakland City College, UC Berkeley, 1959-1964, AB in English Literature from UC Berkeley, 1964; attended College of Marin, UC Berkeley 1971-75, pre-medical; currently trying to get into medical school; (6) m. Stephen Sussman May 14, 1966; (7) children--Joshua David, Noah Daniel; (8) Systems engineer, IBM Corporation, 1965-1968; data processing freelance consultant, 1968-1971; theatre critic, Mill Valley Record, 1970-present;

psychiatric counselor, Westside Community Mental Health Center, S. F., 1974-present; (10) Marin County Emergency Medical Care Committee, parent-participatory elementary and nursery schools, Marin Women's Health Collective; (16) Democrat, formerly Peace & Freedom Party; (17) Jewish; (21) P. O. Box 92, Forest Knolls, Ca. 94933, Ph. 415-488-0522; (22) Mill Valley Record, 78 E. Blithedale Avenue, Mill Valley, Cal. 94941, Ph. 415-388-3211; (23) Circulation: 10,000; (24) 50 professional and amateur plays and musicals, occasional film, dance or miscellaneous.

"Subject Was Roses" Is One of Center's Finest
(by Sharron Sussman, Mill Valley Record, September 10, 1975)

The Subject Was Roses, Mill Valley Center for the Performing Arts' opening production for a projected season of six plays, is a solid, satisfying evening of theatre. Professional competence in acting, directing, staging and technical backup combine to bring this subtle, moving play vividly to life in a rich blend of pain and humor that will touch anyone who has ever been part of a family.

Playwright Frank Gilroy, who won a well-deserved Pulitzer Prize for Roses in 1964, as well as the New York Drama Critics' Circle award for best play of that season, has taken the commonest elements of daily life and made magic of them. The feelings that ebb and flow across the stage as young Timmy Cleary and his parents work out their agonizing, funny reunion are feelings that all of us have experienced; when they happen in real life, understanding and growth are hard to come by, and therein lies Gilroy's triumph. Roses is ostensibly a totally realistic, almost naturalistic play, but at bottom it is compounded of the most delicate artistry, leaving us with a heightened awareness of the complexities of dealing every day with the people we love.

Timmy Cleary, engagingly played by Theo Weiner, is a young veteran just returned home to the Bronx after three years of combat in World War II. The story he tells on himself--that the "bravest thing he did" as a soldier was to sleep without his boots on his first night in combat--is emblematic of his character and his personal reconciliation with the world. The guys who cracked up and didn't make it, he says, were the guys who couldn't sleep, couldn't relax. Timmy Cleary learned to relax. He can accept his mother and father, their strained relationship with each other and their competition for his love. He sees them as human beings and loves them both in spite of their obvious faults. The milieu may be Irish Catholic, but Timmy Cleary is a mensch.

Weiner has not only gotten into the head of the character, but also mastered a fair range of pure technique, which is especially apparent in the lovely way he gets drunk. He blurs gradually, letting Timmy's winning glibness and charm go sloppy and just slightly belligerent, but never to the point of grossness or ugliness. He does a splendid job with a delightful character.

Lyn Statten, new at the Center but an actress of considerable experience in several media, brings great skill, sensitivity and humor to her interpretation of the role of Nettie Cleary, Timmy's mother. Nettie is a lady, born to a family of modest but comfortable means and accustomed to a good bit of culture. Her marriage to the dynamic, aggressive, driven John Cleary, incompatible from the start, has stagnated over the years into a dead end of bitter little habits, warmed every now and then by tender memories. Timmy is the receptacle of her frustrations with John, and her hope for the future of her ideals and values. Ms. Statten is appealing even when she is being most smotheringly mothery.

John Cleary, Timmy's tough, self-made father, is beautifully played by Center veteran Mel Berman. With no outlandish accents or mannerisms to concentrate on, Berman (like Statten, a native of the Bronx) can show his skill and range as an actor as he has not done in roles less perfectly suited to him. Our hearts go out to him as he struggles with conflicting emotions of pride, jealousy, love and anger for the son who has returned as a man, and not exactly the kind of man he expected. In the reconciliation of father and son on a new and durable basis, The Subject Was Roses ends on an upbeat. There is hope as long as people can change and grow; even John and Nettie may work out a better truce in their marriage, although they have not yet done so when the curtain drops. The end of war is a fitting motif for this drama of the smaller, more satisfying aspects of human destiny.

Sean David Bennett's direction, Marc De Narie's production design, and the hard work of a large production staff are evident in the technical and dramatic seamlessness of the show. The Center's aspiration to provide high-quality community theatre for the people of Mill Valley seems very close to fulfilment after an opening like this one; the season-ticket option available this year looks like a winner. The Subject Was Roses is one of the finest all-around productions in the Center's eight-year history. It is very much worth seeing.

Williams' Work Exciting, Flawed, Up to Its Name
(by Sharron Sussman, Mill Valley Record, February 11, 1976)

It would be impossible to see This Is (An Entertainment), ACT's second, and more noteworthy world premiere of the season, without taking into account its status as a theatrical event. Even if This Is were not the new and widely publicized Tennessee Williams play, it would be hard to ignore, impossible to sleep through. The vitality of its form and language connects with ancient circuses and the best of the Mitchell Brothers (don't take your young children, by the way, unless you just love answering

questions in the middle of performances,) its exuberance transcends flaws and makes it perfectly clear--with a clarity that the
play itself does not possess--that one is in the presence of at
least the germ of something most uncommon.

More closely akin, perhaps, to Camino Real than to any of
Williams' more naturalistic work, This Is is plagued by most of
the problems one would expect in a drama that even director Allen Fletcher describes as a "dramatic poem." That label generally means the director is having more trouble with the drama
than with the poetry, and this is clearly the case with This Is.
Williams' language, elegant, witty and precise even at a press
conference, easily embraces scatology, achieving transmutations
undreamed of by those who only wanted to turn lead into gold.
Poetry is not enough onstage, though, even in the magnificently
sensuous environment created by set designer John Jensen, costume designer Robert Morgan and lighting designer F. Mitchell
Dana.

Williams' characters are gratuitously grotesque, their motivation and ultimate destiny unclear, although they are fascinating
to watch for long stretches of flamboyant self-expression. The
pace of individual segments of the action is lively and well-mod-
ulated, but the play as a whole suffers from a basic rhythm dis-
turbance--its first section leisurely and well-developed, but what
ought to be a climatic second act too brief, sketchy, and fading
into a weak and unconvincing ending.

This Is centers around the adventures--sexual, political and
intellectual--of the Countess Marguerite, one of the playwright's
most gallant and memorable heroines. She arrives at a luxury
resort hotel in an unnamed European country on the eve of revolution, trailing children, dogs, Nanny, aging husband and beauti-
ful-but-dumb chauffeur. As shells shake the chandeliers in the
lobby, the Countess cavorts with her unwillingly obedient young
lover, dismissing him when the guerrillas enter the city so that
she may greet the leader of the conquering army and become
his "woman after the mountains," seductive and soft in pink chif-
fon. The Countess lives out her fantasies, always keeping "one
moment ahead of the moment" and scorning those who, like her
husband, are impotent prisoners of custom, convention and the
ordinary passage of time.

Elizabeth Huddle is stupendous in the marathon role of the
Countess--a role which requires her presence onstage almost
constantly. She is often too much for Nicholas Cortland, who
plays both lovers (the chauffeur much better than the general,
not surprisingly. I feel as if I've spent a lot of time this ACT
season lamenting the absence of Marc Singer, who could have
done wonderful things with all the parts beautiful Nicholas looks
but cannot act). Ray Reinhardt is at his bizarre and comical
best as the cuckolded Count--a scene in which he has himself
corseted, barbered and perfumed before coming to claim his

marital rights turns into a wildly funny encounter between Reinhardt (with antlers on his head) and Rick Hamilton (with gossamer wings on his hairdresser's jacket) as the original hairdress-
ing fairy.   An enormous cast of supporting characters, virtually the entire company, fleshes out Williams' elaborately fantastic
world.   There are times, as in the lobby scenes, where grotesqueries of make-up and performance blur the line between
actors and setting--Marrian Walters and Sydney Walker as two
ancient aristocrats are on the verge of achieving scenery status
by virtue of their brilliantly stylized rendition of doddering senility.

Williams has said he considers This Is to be a "work in
progress," which is not unusual for a playwright who has consistently rewritten, retitled and adapted his work, even after
publication and performance.   It does need work, especially
structural revamping, but even in its present form it is indubi-
tably (An Entertainment) and not merely a rough draft.   Go see
it--it's exciting!

SWANK, Patsy; (2) Reporter/Producer, KERA-TV, Arts reporter,
The Nine O'Clock Report; (3) b. Sherman, Tex. , Oct. 9, 1919; (4)
d. James Fred and Sallie (Harris) Peck; (5) B.A. U. of Arkansas,
major subj. : English, 1940; (6) m. Arch B. Swank, Jr. , April 24,
1948; (7) children--Graham Gilchrist, Margaret Harris (Adame),
Sallie Elizabeth, Samuel Ford; (8) Art critic, assistant music, theater and film critic, Dallas Morning News, 1941-46; general reporter, feature writer, Dallas Morning News, 1946-48.   Southwest regional editor Living for Young Homemakers, 1957-61; regional correspondent, Time, Inc. for Life Magazine, Time Magazine, Time/
Life Books, 1961-71; (9) Charter member reporter panel Ch. 13
"Newsroom," 1970-76; (17) Protestant; (20) Co-Author (with Toni
Beck) "Fashion Your Figure," "Focus Your Figure" publ. Houghton-
Mifflin; contributed articles to Look Magazine, Show, Saturday Evening Post, D Magazine; (21) 4316 Rawlins Street, Dallas, Tex. 75219,
Ph. 214-526-1398; (22) KERA-TV Ch. 13, 3000 Harry Hines Blvd. ,
Dallas, Tex. 75201, Ph. 214-744-1300; (23) Circulation: KERA-TV,
400,000 cumulative weekly; "Newsroom" 33,000 households cumula-
tive weekly.

"Saturday, Sunday and Monday"
(by Patsy Swank, over KERA television, Dallas/Fort Worth,
October 7, 1975)

Upper middle America and upper middle Italia are separated
only by parts of two continents and an ocean, and that isn't much,
these days.

Eduardo Philip's family comedy, "Saturday, Sunday and Monday" opened last night at the Dallas Theater Center as the company's salute to the Neiman-Marcus Italian Fortnight which begins next week.   Such togetherness is fine.   Fortunately the play

can stand alone.

It is about Peppino, a rough diamond who has been somewhat smoothed by marrying Rosa, the boss's daughter, fathering
her children and.taking over as head of the family in the apartment where they have lived for many years. It has been a good
marriage, mostly, and though the children are grown, they re-
gather every Sunday. On the Saturday of this weekend, as Mama
Rosa begins to prepare the Sunday meal, the small malaises that
have bothered the union begin to gather into one big crisis. It
breaks stormily at the Sunday dinner table, and is resolved, with
honesty and tenderness, in the early hours of the Monday.

It sounds thoroughly commonplace and it is, except that it
isn't. David Healy's astute direction holds the tenuous line so
that the comedy does not loosen into farce, and the sadness
doesn't get lugubrious. Practically every one in the cast could
have been played for broad comedy. Healy doesn't let it happen.
They are funny, but they are always people, never types.

As to making Italians out of the highly middle-American Center company, Healy doesn't bother to try. A study of gesture,
yes. A slightly more than token bow to Italian accent, yes.
But mostly he relies on his people playing powerfully to each
other to spell emotions more universal than Latin.

Preston and Mary Sue Jones head the cast, as Peppino and
Rosa, and she also designed the production. Barnett Shaw is
her father, the old shop keeper who still loves to block hats;
Steve Willis is Rocco the younger son, ready to open a shop of
his own; Judith Davis is Aunt Meme who has made her own ac-
comodation to a bad marriage and Randy Moore is a funny, and
pure-hearted neighbor. There are hosts of other busy and attractive people, shooting in and out.

Healy is a former Dallasite now living in England, who returned this summer to play in the Shakespeare Festival at Fair
Park, and remained to direct this play in which he appeared in
London with Sir Laurence Olivier. He is adept at transmitting
what he seems to know well--how to pace, build and shape a
script with charm, tenderness and fun. The play will run through
November 8.

"Anna Bolena"
(by Patsy Swank, over KERA television, Dallas/Fort Worth,
November 13, 1975)

Last night was ladies' night at the opera--two contemporary
rulers of the singing business, as two historical queens of England. That translates to Renata Scotto and Tatiana Troyanos,
singing Anne Boleyn and Jane Seymour in "Anna Bolena," first
of Donizetti's "queen" operas, and second production of the current Dallas Civic Opera season at the Music Hall.

There was a brilliant guest conductor--Fernando Previtali--
and a burnished-sounding new tenor, Umberto Grilli--and smart
lights and lush costumes and that was about it for drama. But
there was plenty of action in the throats of the two queens, all
of it first class. Miss Scotto commands everything, in this first
appearance in the part, from a full-force dramatic breadth, to
the merest whisper of floated tone and limpid coloratura sweep.
Miss Troyanos has virtually the same capabilities but entirely
different color and style. Even if you get itchy, waiting through
the um-pa-pas for the anguish and madness to begin, it is worth
the vamps till ready. "Bolena" is early Donizetti, but "Lucia di
Lammermoor" is a lot closer than the distance from London to
the Scottish Highlands. The set pieces are woven with surprising,
for the period, unity into great stretches of superb ensemble
writing, in which the Civic Opera chorus is the star.

Almost you can look at this one or not; but it will command
the fullest attention of your ears.

SYNA, Seymour Meyer; (2) Theatre Critic; (3) b. New York City,
Nov. 9, 1928; (4) s. Emil and Anna (Levine) S. ; (5) A. B. U. of Arkansas, maj. subj. : Journalism, 1949; B. T. A. Pasadena Playhouse,
maj. subj. : Theatre, 1953; M. F. A. Columbia U. , maj. subj. : Dramatic Arts, 1955; Ed. D. Columbia U. , maj. subj. : Theatre Educ. ,
1969; (6) Divorced; (7) children--Deborah Ruth 15, Joshua Emil 12;
(8) Combat Correspondent, 25th Inf. Div. PIO, Korea 1952, Drama
Critic, The National Underground Press Illustrated 1969, Drama
Critic, Action World, 1970, Drama Critic, The Soho Weekly News,
1974, Drama Critic, Wisdom's Child, 1975-present, Drama Critic,
The Jewish Post & Opinion, 1976, Drama Critic, WNYC-TV (Channel 31), 1976; (9) Theatre activity includes over 100 productions as
director, actor, bus. mgr. , pub. & promo. , covering 30 years,
teaching: Bennington College, 1962-63, Baruch College, 1964-69,
C. C. N. Y. 1967-68, N. Y. Institute of Technology, 1969-73, Bronx
Comm. College, 1967-present, Adj. Assoc. Prof. , Dept. Communi-
cation Arts & Sciences; The Green Room Drama School, 1964-65,
Senior Dramatic Workshop, 1960-61, Mannhardt Workshop, 1963,
Jericho Players Workshop, 1960-62, 1964; (12) Advisory Board,
Odyssey House; (13) Pfc. U. S. Army 1951-53; (14) Winner 8th Army
New Story Writing Contest 1952, Winner Riverside Poets Contest
1955; (15) Actors' Equity Assoc. , The Drama Desk, American Na-
tional Theatre & Academy, American Theatre Assoc. , Society of
Stage Directors & Choreographers, Actors Studio Director-Playwrights'
Unit; (17) Jewish; (19) City Hall Stamp Club, Canal Zone Study
Group; (20) "The Shattered Rock," full-length play produced Pasadena
Playhouse 1950, News Stories in Pacific Stars & Stripes, Army
Times, Army Home Town News Center, Wire Services for U. S. &
Turkey, verse in Quarto, Whitney, Yerba, Doors Into Poetry, River-
side Poets, articles in This Week Magazine, Cape Cod Guide, The
Military Engineer, Players Magazine; (21) 187 Chrystie Street, New
York, N. Y. , 10002; Ph. 212-254-0256; (22) Wisdom's Child, 1841
Broadway, New York, N. Y. 10023; Ph. 212-265-3270; (23) Circulation:

135,000; WNYC-TV (Channel 31) Greater Metropolitan Area.

Ethnic Theater Flowers in New York
(by Sy Syna, Wisdom's Child, February 23, 1976)

"Within the Four Seas, all men are brothers." So goes the ancient Chinese saying which gave the Four Seas Players of Chinatown their name. The proverb is just as apt for describing the ethnic theater situation in New York.

No other city in the world has the ethnic theatre activity which New York boasts. Drama groups alone number over 75, representing 16 different ethnics. If we admit solo artists who perform dance-dramas, the number rises to near 90. With dance and music groups included, the grand total is approximately 150. And there may be more!

At this time, no complete survey of ethnic theatre activity in New York has ever been taken. For example, the Folk Festival Council has between 20 and 30 folk dance troupes affiliated with it, but it includes only groups in which ethnics dance their own dances. There are literally scores of other groups.

What is ethnic theatre anyway? Well, the word "ethnic" comes from the Greek ethnos, meaning "A nation," a people, a culture. Therefore ethnic theatre has come to mean a theatre which reflects the culture, characters, problems and values of a people. It takes varied forms.

Some ethnic theater preserves a traditional art, as Peking Opera groups do. Though composed of supposed amateurs who work in various professions, members study opera techniques for years. These Chinese groups pride themselves on the accuracy, authenticity and color of their productions. Costumes and materials are often imported from Hong Kong and Taiwan. Daniel Chi, Director of the Chinese Opera Club in America, claims that shows cost about $2,000 to mount, if costumes can be reused from inventory. If all new costumes are required, costs can run $5 to $6,000.

A Chinese Opera score sounds nonsensical to Western ears. In fact, the score of Chinese Opera is a map or guide to the movement. If an actor trails a colorful banner across the stage, it may denote the passage of years, or a change of locale. Often the characters announce who they are, or tell you what you are about to see.

These techniques represent one way of handling the key problem of all ethnic theater: language. People like the feel of their native tongue, and many theater groups don't want to lose that. It's a touch of home. On the other hand, many young people want the rooted feeling but don't know the language. It raises a tough problem, which theaters have tackled in a variety of ways--some more successful than others.

For some groups the preservation of the native tongue is a
primary purpose. The Folksbiene Theater for example, presents
Yiddish classics in Yiddish. Other groups take this process one
step further and translate world famous plays into their own language. A season for the Theater of Russian American Youth is
likely to include both a production of Ostrovosky's classic Vassil-
iza Melentyeva in Russian as well as a translation of Charley's
Aunt. Nearly all foreign language theaters print a synopsis of
the action to make it accessible to the English speaking audience.

Another standard approach is to run two productions of the
same play. Many Hispanic theatres play in both Spanish and
English on alternate nights, or run one version for several weeks
before opening the other.

At the extreme, the Diocese Players of the Armenian Church
of America played Badvi Hamar in Armenian last year, and in
English this year.

Another solution is to mix languages. Golda's, a kosher
cabaret, is running a revue called Little Tel Aviv in Hebrew.
They are also rehearsing a version for later this year which
will be primarily in English with a dash of Hebrew, Yiddish and
Russian thrown in. Other examples of this approach are more
daring. Intar, a Hispanic theater, presented Cap-A-Pie, a bilingual revue, in which the same lines were spoken in both languages, creating an interesting contrapuntal effect.

Even more striking was the production of Midsummer Night's
Dream by Tisa Chang, director of the Chinese Group at La Mama. Ms. Chang had her actors speak in either Chinese or English depending upon their fluency. The effect was dazzling,
though its success leaned heavily upon audience familiarity with
the play.

Other theatres have tried other methods of spanning the language gap. The Chinese Opera Club, which perform in Manda-
rin, has experimented with flashing subtitles on a screen--a
technique that met with resounding success on a recent college
tour.

Finally, some ethnic groups sidestep the language problem
by ignoring it altogether. The Irish Rebel Theater and the Jewish Repetory Company both work only in English though the ethnic groups they represent have another language.

The history of ethnic theatres in New York has been shaped
by two key forces. One is the arrival of a particular group
here in large enough numbers to support a theatre. Political
events in other countries often result in strong ethnic theater
fallout here. The pogroms which swept Eastern Europe in the

1880's resulted in the massive Jewish migration which led to the founding of Yiddish theatre in New York. A fresh flood of immigrants in the late 1940's resulted in an upsurge of Ukranian and Russian drama groups. Though the roots of Hispanic theater go back to 1922, recently-arrived Cuban immigrants exert an influence on Hispanic theatre far out of proportion to their number in the Spanish-speaking population.

Up through the end of World War II, the "melting pot" notion was an article of faith for newly-arrived ethnics. Their ethnic theatre helped them bridge the gap into the new culture, but it was regarded apologetically as second-rate stuff. Part of its justification was that it produced performers who later made it on Broadway. Every ethnic theatre boasted its own Paul Muni, Mei Lan-Fong or Cab Calloway.

Then, a tired Black woman in the South refused to give up her seat on a bus. The Civil Rights movement exploded over America. "Black is beautiful" became the watchword, and before long, any ethnic heritage seemed beautiful. "New York wasn't meant to be a melting pot," remarks Diane Cypkin, Jewish actress and producer. "It's a beef stew." Soon everyone was in the act.

Jimmy Olwell, for example, founded the Irish Rebel Theater because of his work in the Black Civil Rights movement on Chicago's South Side. The Black movement made him question his own Irish identity. He knew nothing of Irish music, language or culture. His desire to work with the Irish led him to the music, and ultimately to the founding of the theatre. "Being Irish" he discovered, "meant more than marching in a St. Patrick's Day Parade, getting drunk, and going around to different bars looking to get laid."

All of the new ethnic theatres share common purposes. Max Ferra, director of Intar, speaks of it in terms of ethnic pride and identity. "We want to tell our people that they are not as ugly as they think they are. Our culture is 450 years old. We need them to make it better and bigger."

Like others who want to share cultural accomplishments with a larger world, George Arkas, director of the Greek Art Theater, wants to change the public's attitude toward the image of classic theatre. "People in America think Greek tragedies are school plays. They're totally wrong. The plays are full of life and fire. Greek tragedy is written tomorrow. You can present it as avant-garde drama, and the comedies as musicals." Others point to the way ethnic theatre interprets a people to themselves and others. As Ran Avni, Director of the Jewish Repertory Theatre puts it, "Everybody associates Jewish theatre with The Dybbuk, Fiddler, Yentl. Yet there's a treasure of plays that have very direct Jewish themes. They deal with Jewish problems." Perhaps Marie Irene Fornes, a Cuban and an avant-

garde playwright, best sums up the reason for an ethnic theatre;
"Experience is universal. What is Spanish, is the way of remembering. "

The inspirational way in which these people express their
purpose makes it clear that these groups are missionaries--both
for their own ethnics, and the public at large. Miriam Colon,
director of the Puerto Rican Travelling Theatre, catches this
dimension when she recalls her student days in the drama department at the University of Puerto Rico. "We used to tour
shows to the little town squares in the countryside," says Ms.
Colon. "Then we'd play the mountain villages. The people
crowded around to see the shows. Later in New York, I and a
group of actors did The Oxcart, a play about what happens to a
Puerto Rican family that comes to New York. When we closed,
we had a company, a rehearsed play, something important to
say, and no place to say it. I remembered how we used to take
our theatre to the people, and out of those memories, we founded
the Puerto Rican Travelling Theatre. "

The missionary spirit is also evident in the way these groups
approach two interlocking problems: audience development and
the nurturing of talent. Many ethnic theatres handle the audience-
development problem by ignoring it. They simply play a limited
number of performances, restricted to a few full houses. Most
groups book the Fashion Institute Theatre for one or two evenings. Some supplement these performances with tours outside
New York to other ethnic enclaves as far away as Canada and
the West Coast.

Nonetheless, the Black Theatre Alliance identifies audience
development as a key need. In particular they recognize the
importance of building an ethnic consciousness and appreciation
in young people. Many theatres are trying to solve the young
audience problem by doing their classics in English though others
are adament about using the native tongue. Lydia Krushelnytsky,
Director of a Ukranian theater, says flatly, "There are no good
translations of Ukranian classics. "

The press, of course, plays a decisive role in audience development, yet relations between ethnic theatre and the press
vary radically. Some get coverage from their own press. The
Chinese theatre, for example, receives total support from Chinese newspapers. Sister Joanna, whose productions play only
two performances, once received a 45-installment review in a
Chinese newspaper.

At the other extreme, the Irish Rebel Theatre reports only
lukewarm response from the Irish press in New York. Olwell
explains the scanty coverage by saying, "It was the so-called
Irish leaders, the politicians and the press, that led the Irish
into giving up their culture in the first place. "

Black theatres report that coverage has improved in the Black press. The Amsterdam News now has a cultural events page which carries theatre events. Ernie McClintock of the Afro-American Studio complains, however, that though his theatre is just two blocks from the Amsterdam office, he can't get them to come over and review. "I'm not asking for any favors," he says. "They don't necessarily have to be favorable reviews. I advertise in their paper, but I never see them."

Although the lack of coverage by papers of the same persuasion can't help, the major complaint lies against the general disinterest of the English-language press--both the dailies and the weeklies. Elsa Robles, Director of Spanish Theatre Programs for the Off-Off Broadway Alliance reports that all the city's dailies have Hispanic reporters and critics capable of covering Hispanic theatre. Still, their reviewing is scant and sporadic. The weeklies are also uncooperative, partly because many of the ethnics play so few performances.

A second area of concern is recruitment and development of talents. The Four Seas Amateur Theatre in Chinatown handles the matter by running workshops in language, traditional movement such as Tai Chi Chuan, acting, costumes and scenery. Sister Joanna, the theatre's director, says "When I Came to Chinatown, I found 200 organizations in a six-block area. I tried to find a way of bringing some of these organizations together. We started a theatre." Now as many as 150 people--including professional artists--are involved in mounting a production.

Ernie McClintock runs workshops also, but he finds it frustrating. "As soon as you develop an actor to the point where he's halfway proficient," he remarks, "You lose him to Superfly." The Black Theatre Alliance, a central agency for the 25 Black theatres and six dance companies in New York published a directory of Black theatre artists three years ago and, according to Harold Youngblook, Administrative Director, there's no shortage of qualified Black theatre personnel.

Money is the third plague that besets most of these theatres. According to Elsa Robles, there isn't enough money for a state-wide publicity campaign to make Hispanics aware that their theatres need their support. Box office receipts never cover production costs. Private foundation monies, a mainstay in the past, dried up during the recession.

The key source of money for non-profit, ethnic theatres, is the government. In particular the following three groups are responsive to grant requests for ethnic theaters:

Vantile Whitefield, Director,
The Expansion Arts Program
National Endowment for the Arts
Columbia Plaza, 2401 E. St., NW

Washington, D. C. 20206
(202) 634-6010

Ellen Thurston
New York State Council on the Arts
250 W. 57th St.
397-1718 (Special Programs)

Ethnic Heritage Studies Branch
Division of International Education
Bureau of Postsecondary Education
Office of Education, Room 3907
7th and D Sts., SW
Washington D. C. 20202
(Refer to: Title IX, Elementary and
Secondary Education Act of 1965 as
amended.)

Ethnic theatre is still growing. As Dr. Nishan Parakian,
Director of the Diocese Players of the Armenian Church of America says, "People have a rage to know, a rage to participate."

Audiences for this theatre, both ethnic and general, are also
increasing. Theatres are running longer seasons with more productions. College tours are being organized for more and more
groups.

The number of festivals has grown, along with inter-ethnic
group cooperation. The Armenian Diocese has sponsored a One-
World ethnic festival for two years. Last year's festival brought
together 19 different groups. Gradually, a recognition is growing that problems of ethnic theatres are mutual.

Is ethnic theatre worthwhile? Emphatically yes! Most of
these groups started out in basements with a handful of people.
Some groups are still church-basement organizations, but most
are run by professionals whose credentials represent some of
the world's best theatre training and experience. Gilberto Zaldivar, for example, ran a professional theatre in Havana. When
Castro nationalized the theatres, Zaldivar came to New York.
His Spanish Repertory Theatre Company some years ago, staged
Hospital de Los Locos, an astonishing Spanish medieval morality
play. Set in an asylum, the play prefigured by several hundred
years the devices used in Marat-Sade. Without Zaldivar's classical knowledge, the play would probably never have been seen
by New Yorkers.

Zaldivar, Sister Joanna, Daniel Chi, Lydia Kruschelnysky,
Sayed and other ethnic theatre makers have come, literally from
all Four Seas. They work--with pride--in the rich kitchen of
their own heritage, though many of them, like Miriam Colon,
have outstanding Broadway and Hollywood credits as well. What
they place before us are their traditional dishes, made with as

much love, skill and knowledge as they can muster. We are often put off by foods which seem too exotic and strange. What we need to remember is that these foods raised a people, and will nourish us as well.

The Perils of Broadway Productions
(by Sy Syna, Wisdom's Child, May 31, 1976)

I went, all expectant, to watch my godchild graduate. I saw it falter instead. At first I sat there, fearful. Then angry. Finally, bitterly disappointed. This, dear reader, is a cautionary tale, though I'm not quite sure what the moral is.

A year and a half ago, I attended a critic's matinee at the Manhattan Theatre Club of a new play, The Runner Stumbles, by Milan Stitt. I didn't know either the author, the director, or anyone connected with the production. I was most moved by the play.

It is turn-of-the-century Michigan. A priest, Father Rivard, is on trial for the murder of a nun, Sister Rita. At the time, I wrote, "It is the story of their relationship, told piecemeal as events slip in and out of Rivard's consciousness, that is the heart of Stitt's play ... Father Rivard (is) torn apart by internal warfare.

His soul, when we meet him, is a burned-over battlefield: nothing alive left on it." Moved to tears, I wrote a glowing review (for another weekly). Some weeks later, Stitt called me and told me a remarkable story.

Only I and a Voice critic had reviewed the workshop production. The Voice critic didn't like the play, dismissing it in a few paragraphs as appealing primarily to a Catholic sensibility. Stitt told me he and Pendleton were crestfallen when they read the Voice review. However my review reassured them because, as he said, I caught not only what they were trying to do, but also the problems they sensed but hadn't yet solved in the production.

The Hartman Theatre in Connecticut had the script, but couldn't decide whether to option it for their first season. Stitt sent the Hartman people my review, and they came to New York to see the workshop production. They loved it, and optioned the play. It was produced at Hartman with essentially the same cast with one key change: Stephen Joyce, a veteran of over 100 TV shows and several Shakespeare festivals went in as Father Rivard.

Clive Barnes saw the Hartman production, was moved to tears and reviewed it. The play was optioned for Broadway, and also received film offers.

That brief history explains why I felt like a godfather at the Broadway opening. And why I felt so dismayed by what I saw. The play had become more melodramatic. At one point Sister Rita slaps Rivard. He slaps her back. At another, he starts to strangle her. There's a scuffle during a courtroom scene. It was as if both author and director felt that a Broadway stage demanded physical activity. Before, in an intimate theatre, the play had worked through feelings and relationships.

Joyce played Rivard like a small red light bulb--mostly turned off. When he was on, he showed only a cruel anger. In this production there is nothing in the character as Joyce plays him, for Sister Rita to love. It was heartbreaking to watch Donohue pour out all that sensitivity and radiance into a vacuum.

The other actors I praised before were even fuller this time: Katina Commings as a frightened and insecure farm girl; Marilyn Pfeiffer as Louise, Sister Rita's former student, now a pert and sexy young woman; Josephson Mathewson, as the Bishop's secretary, flawlessly created as a self-important thin-lipped prig. Sloane Shelton as Mrs. Shandig, the housekeeper, gave a deft country portrait of a woman, converted to Catholicism, who moves toward propriety from a deep darkness.

The play and the direction are still sensitive, but the heart of it was gone for me. I never had the sense that Joyce's Rivard is putting his conscience on trial for murdering Sister Rita's spirit, while the other trial goes on for the murder of her flesh.

I don't know what the thinking was behind Joyce's being cast. Perhaps they wanted a "star," in order to bring the play onto Broadway. Perhaps there were other factors and reasons I'm not aware of. At this writing, I haven't read any of the reactions of my colleagues across the aisle. Perhaps they loved it, and my dismay at what I saw wasn't shared by those seeing it for the first time.

Perhaps the moral of this tale is this: theatre people often pay a terrible price for space in the market place. Even critics (as well as poets) have been known to weep when "the ceremony of innocence is drowned."

SYSE, Glenna, Chicago Sun-Times, 401 North Wabash Ave., Chicago, Ill. 60611.

TAGGART, Patrick Ewing; (2) Amusements editor, critic; (3) b. Waco, Tex. July 12, 1949; (4) s. Mr. and Mrs. Patrick E. Taggart; (5) Music theory and literature, journalism, Baylor U., no degree; Critic Fellow, National Critics Institute, Waterford, Conn., 1972; (6) Single; (8) News desk assistant, Waco Tribune-Herald, Waco,

Tex. , 1971-73; Entertainment editor, Winston-Salem Sentinel, 1973-74; Amusements editor, Austin American-Statesman, 1974-present, Austin, Tex. ; (16) Democrat; (19) Phi Mu Alpha Sinfonia fraternity; (21) 500 E. Riverside, Austin, 78704; (22) Austin American-Statesman, P. O. Box 670, Austin, Tex. 78767; (23) Circulation: 100-120,000; (24) 100-150 reviews of all kinds: music, theater, film.

"Omen" Landmark
(by Patrick Taggart, Austin American-Statesman, June 30, 1976)

The ads surely have told you all you need to know about what kind of movie "The Omen" is. What you may not know--and what you may be unwilling to believe--is that this little demonic potboiler by 20th Century Fox is a pretty good movie, if for nothing other than its excellent craftsmanship on the single level of horror-thriller.

Good or not, it would still probably draw the same long lines that it has drawn in its first few days at the Village. It has been 2-1/2 years since the "The Exorcist" sent us running up the theater aisles, and I can recollect no "Exorcist" imitation that came close to that film or "The Omen." If possession has become some kind of movie genre, then "The Omen" will have to go down as one of its landmarks.

The story, by David Seltzer, is based on an interpretation of the Book of Revelations, in which the end of the world is foretold by the birth of the Anti-Christ--the son of Satan--in the form of a human.

As a human, this devilish fellow will do everything possible to divide nation against nation, man against man, until the world is his. Obviously, much of the amount of fear, humor or truth one finds in the film will depend a lot on his religious disposition.

Our action takes place in London, where ambassador Robert Thorn (Gregory Peck) and wife Katherine (Lee Remick) have just gotten settled. Their 5-year-old boy becomes the source of a lot of annoying disasters: One of his nannies hangs herself, a group of crazy baboons attacks mom's car, and the little devil himself, Peck's son, causes his mother to fall (accidentally, everybody thinks) from over a railing inside the second story of their posh country home.

A sick and rather nutty priest has tried to warn Thorn that the child is the devil's and that the boy will try to destroy his parents in order to wrest control of their wealth, and ultimately, their power in order to establish his kingdom.

It takes a lot of proof to finally convince the ambassador that his kid is a beast, proof that involves the death of his wife and photographer friend Jennings, played by David Warner.

Those deaths provide some of the most effective and outlandish special effects yet. Remick, preparing to meet her husband, falls out of a hospital window several stories high and crashes through the roof of an ambulance, landing on a stretcher inside. And Warner loses his head after a conversation with Peck in such a way that will leave most audiences gasping.

Like "The Exorcist," "The Omen" has a first-rate score and soundtrack, with the decibel level of portentious noises and music boosted to the nth degree.

It's all very well acted and handsomely filmed. It asks you to take a few things for granted, but no more than you would for, say, an episode of "Mary Hartman, Mary Hartman."

"Norman, Is That You?" Could Use Polishing
(by Patrick Taggart, Austin American-Statesman, July 27, 1976)

Ken Johnson was more nervous than usual for Friday night's opening of his production of "Norman, Is That You?" at Center Stage.

"I would never try to do a show in 2-1/2 weeks," he panted, "but if I don't pay the electricity bill they're going to cut the lights off!"

That's the way it's been at Center Stage, off and on, for a long time: A hit, pay off the bills, dry spell, desperation, and eventually another moneymaker. Somehow, Johnson's outfit manages to remain just this side of extinction.

It's a good thing, too, because it's Center Stage we can count on for such unlikely productions as "Butley," "Championship Season," or the fantastic "Moonchildren."

But I kind of doubt "Norman" is going to join that elite company. The problem isn't in the production, even though the actors were having some serious problems that opening night. "Norman's" main enemy seems to be the play itself, which is, at best, a dinner theater treatment of homosexuality.

Written around 1970 by Ron Clark and Sam Bobrick, "Norman" deals with an Ohio dry cleaner whose wife has deserted him and whose son, he discovers, is living the life of a homosexual in New York. Much of the humor relies, apparently, on the audience's sustained disbelief that all sorts of homosexual jokes and sight gags are taking place on stage, some of which are fresh, some of which are not.

So, if homosexuality doesn't strike you as the freshest or richest comedy material ever, "Norman" is likely to go on like one of those tired comedies that so frequently haunt the dinner theaters. It's a well-enough crafted play, but hardly outrageous.

I did enjoy, however, Dean Nichols' rather outrageous performance as Garson, the swishy roommate of the title character.
Whether it was character playing or a painstakingly assimilated
performance, it worked, and Nichols earned his laughs.

Jerry Rollins, as the distraught father, had possibly the
most work to do, and he did it generally well, but he would do
the production a great service if he were quicker, and if he
avoided waiting for his audience to laugh.

The whole cast seemed to be largely unaware of the audience.
Actors appeared to want to induce laughs by waiting for them,
and the result was merely wasted time. Happily, timing was
cleaned up considerably in the second act.

Stephen Hinshaw was good if a little stiff opening night as
Norman, and Kathleen Boulton was a natural laugh-getter in the
role of the hooker sent to "cure" Norman. Peggy Sackett was
okay in the part of Mrs. Chambers, a role I could have done
without altogether.

Assuming that Johnson will have whipped his production into
better shape for the second weekend than it was the first, he
will have a good show. There are some really good laughs in
there, somewhere, even if they are a little familiar.

TAKIFF, Jonathan Henry; (2) Theater critic; features writer; (3) b.
Philadelphia, March 9, 1946; (4) s. Harry and Joy (Braude); (5) B.A.
U. of Pennsylvania, major subj.: political science, 1968; M.A.
program, Annenberg School of Communications, U. of Pennsylvania,
1968-70; (6) m. Susan Schwartz, March 5, 1975; (8) Pop music columnist, The Drummer, 1968-70; Drama critic, pop columnist, features writer, Philadelphia Daily News, 1971- ; Weekend air personality, WMMR, Philadelphia, 1971- ; (9) Author, co-director, performer, "The Underground," campus-based, weekly satirical revue,
1965-68; program director, Catacomos Coffee House, 1968-70; production assistant, WCAU-TV, Summer 1968, 1969; (16) Democrat;
(17) Jewish; (21) 1720 Lombard Street, Philadelphia, Penn. 19146;
(22) Philadelphia Daily News, 400 N. Broad Street, Philadelphia,
Pa. 19101, Ph. 215-854-2648; (23) Circulation: 250,000; (24) 75
plays and musicals, 25 concerts, 15 miscellaneous.

"Gravity" Is Kate's Triumph
(by Jonathan Takiff, Philadelphia Daily News, October 28, 1975)

The legion of Katharine Hepburn fans who practically bought
out the three-week engagement of "A Matter of Gravity" even
before its opening last night will be getting what they've anticipated, more or less.

As tailored by Enid Bagnold, this comedy with grave overtones (at the Forrest) casts Miss Hepburn in a role the actress

knows and does so well that it has become her own. It is that
of a droll, eccentric grande dame, a first cousin to the "Mad-
woman of Chaillot," an outcast from mainstream society for all
the wrong reasons--for her excess of emotions, for the sharp
honesty of her acerbic wit, and "worst" of all, for her hearty
acknowledgement of traditional values in a valueless age.

To underline the theme, Miss Hepburn's Mrs. Basil is placed
in the setting of a now-crumbling English country home, and is
brought in contact with any number of lost sheep, all obviously
in need of reformation if not redemption by an older and wiser
woman. A miracle or two will happen. Not just because our
lady intellectually overwhelms their misplaced bleatings point for
point, but also because Basil/Hepburn charms the boots off the
lot--and for that matter, off every soul in the theater--with her
enormously vital personality.

"A Matter of Gravity" is not merely a vehicle for Katharine
Hepburn's talents--the animated glow of her high-cheekboned face,
the raspy barks she calls a voice, the quivery tingle of human
frailty in her movements--though the deck obviously has been
stacked in her favor by the author and director, Noel Willman.

As a "generation gap" comedy, this example is incredibly
extreme, with the younger side represented by the most unsavory,
plain unlikeable bunch of motley characters imaginable.

Mrs. Basil's insipid grandson brings on the group, purport-
edly to enlighten the old woman to contemporary mores. Included are a quarrelsome, anti-institution "Major Barbara," a
man professing an inability to love; a suicide-prone former junkie, and a totally mercenary mulatto woman, whom the grandson
marries.

With the exception of the grandson, they are all homo- or
bisexual. It's the downfall of Western Civilization!

To add a slice of metaphysical curiosity to the proceedings,
the maid Dubois defies the laws of gravity, floating in mid-air
(offstage), to the bafflement of all except Mrs. Basil, who defies
human nature in her own way; don't you know.

The cumulative effect of these startling revelations, when
tacked on to a densely packed, stream-of-consciousness style
of philosophical dialogue, makes for a first act that is simply
ghastly, a strain to follow and not the least bit amusing.

The patient does relax and improve somewhat in the second
act, as Mrs. Basil unloads both barrels of wit at the visitors
and the philosophical fog begins to clear. The third act takes
us eight years into the future, for a genuinely heart-tugging reunion and resolution.

Apart from Charlotte Jones' befuddled Dubois, and Paul
Harding's easy grace as the loveless Herbert, the supporting
characters are only vaguely etched and too broadly played. These
are Targets that probably could be shot down with paperclips.

Noel Willman's rushed direction, perhaps compounded by
opening night (world premiere) nerves, isn't helping matters
much. Ms. Bagnold has some important points to debate on
family, tradition, personal freedom, sex and love, life and death
that deserve dramatic clarification. Less could be more.

At present, the production is Hepburn's triumph alone.

This "Hedda Gabler" Ibsen Wouldn't Recognize
(by Jonathan Takiff, Philadelphia Daily News, February 9, 1976)

During the past decade, it has become popular theater sport
to revive the works of Henrik Ibsen, most specifically his 1879
drama "A Doll's House" and his 1890 creation "Hedda Gabler."
In large measure, the point of all this fuss has been to show off
that playwright Ibsen was a tradition-flaunting feminist, writing
sympathetically of women who were intelligent, sensitive and
capable, women who demanded (and deserved) a fate much better
than that they had received, as simple servants to their husbands.

But for some reason, perhaps in part premeditated, the
Philadelphia Drama Guild's current production of "Hedda Gabler,"
which runs through Feb. 22 does not serve such enlightened
ends.

To the contrary, the Hedda here brought to life by Roberta
Maxwell is strictly a bitch--cruel, calculating and vengeful. It
is not from a vantage point of pure intent, or even passion, that
she attempts to take charge of the "destiny of a man," her former lover Eilert Lovborg (John Glover). After the woman pushes Eilert to suicide, the best excuse we can fathom for Hedda is
that her egomania has stretched to the point of insanity. Even
F. Lee Bailey would be hard pressed to win an acquittal on this
defense.

Given a few more performances, this attractively mounted
production might give us more options. Roberta Maxwell, you
may have heard, was felled with a throat ailment last week,
curtailing rehearsals and forcing postponement of the official
opening at the Walnut Street Theater to Friday.

The first act seemed especially hesitant--resembling a first
walk through after blocking--with lots of lines stepped on or
swallowed. That the show did thereafter build to a strong finish,
should not be downplayed. At present, it's at least entertaining
melodrama.

The burden for improvement is equally shared among the company. James Valentine currently plays Hedda's bumbling, academician husband George in a pat, buffoonish fashion. He is a bore, to be sure, but not nearly gnawing enough to drive his wife to "desperate" distraction. Valentine needs lots more stage business from director Brian Murray--activities to underscore his distance from and lack of care for Hedda.

Nor is there currently any rationale for Hedda to be so snippish and defensive with George's Aunt Julia, at least as that character is played by Betty Leighton. The latter, in babying or over-protecting George, is simply too gushy sweet, whereas I suspect that Ibsen intended more of a negative statement, as concerns this traditional maternal stereotype.

Ibsen also gave us an archetype male chauvinist pig in Judge Brock--a chap who's hot to trot with Hedda, even ready to resort to blackmail to pull off the mission impossible. So why is Robert Gerringer's lecher such a swell guy?

At the other extreme, a much more positive model is demanded from Swoosie Kurtz, as the woman who's helping to put the ner-do-well Eilert back on his feet. Hedda is supposed to be jealous of this woman, jealous of her intelligence, motivation and potency, enough so to become a spoiler. But Swoosie is just a piece of fluff, and that doesn't jibe.

One would also hope for a hint of a warmth, of good times recalled between Roberta Maxwell's Hedda and John Glover's Eilert, when this handsome, star-crossed couple pass a bittersweet reunion. At present, there aren't any sparks, just blank stares exchanged.

TALCOVE, Rick; (2) Theater critic; (3) b. Los Angeles, Jan. 13, 1948; (4) s. Henry and Helen (Calmson); (5) B.A. of California State U., Los Angeles, major subj.: English, 1971; (8) Drama Critic, Valley News and Green Sheet, Van Nuys, Calif., 1970- ; (9) Author, What Are You Doing After the War?, Mark Taper Forum, 1972; director, Green Julia, Merle Oberon Playhouse, 1974; author, Ping-Pong, Onion Company, 1976; (15) Member, Los Angeles Drama Critics Circle, 1970- ; (20) Contribute yearly article on Los Angeles theater to Best Plays, 1971; (21) 334 North Parish Place, Burbank Calif. 91506, Ph. 213-848-9351; (23) Circulation: 275,000; (24) 100 plays and musicals.

Rehearsals Even Help Top Stars
(by Rick Talcove, Valley News and Green Sheet, November 26, 1975)

The continuing presense of Tennessee Williams--both as an artist and as an individual--establishes a positive facet on the theater scene. Williams' life, forever under scrutiny, is currently getting a thorough going-over in the playwright's own "Memoirs"

(Doubleday), about as frank a self-appraisal any writer has ever dared to publish. It's poetic, stirring, shocking and, in short, highly recommended.

On the local theater scene, Williams' last major critical and financial success "The Night of the Iguana" (1961) is being revived by the Center Theatre Group at the Ahmanson Theater.

The production isn't a disaster by any means; still, you can't help describing it as uninspired. There are some extremely good performers here--Richard Chamberlain, Dorothy McGuire, Eleanor Parker, Raymond Massey--but they're all working pretty much off the cuff under director Joseph Hardy's surface reading of the text. When a good play by Tennessee Williams fails to move you, don't blame the script!

Actually, "Iguana" may very well pull itself together just by playing nightly performances. CTG insists on opening its shows in the large Ahmanson after a mere half dozen or so previews, so these "major" productions often look painfully under-rehearsed.

In "Iguana," a defrocked-minister-turned travel-guide (Chamberlain) weighs spiritual and physical needs in a rundown Mexican hotel when confronted by two female figures, the widowed owner of the resort (Parker) and a spinster artist (McGuire), traveling with her ancient grandfather-poet (Massey).

Director Hardy is extremely competent in ushering us through the early exposition, getting the minor characters on and off (including those recurring German tourists, a bothersome Williams touch of "local color"). But when silence falls across the stage and the main characters must deal with each other, there's a hesitant, unsure manner before us.

Ms. McGuire's spinster, for instance, gets the forced optimism down right but when she relates her two rather pathetic sexual experiences to us, we're not moved or touched, just momentarily interested. This is a performance that needs shading and balance.

Chamberlain lacks the world-weariness to make us feel the anguish of Shannon, but it's an interesting exploratory performance that may gain scope and purpose as the engagement continues. Perhaps the actor suffers because his role is outshadowed by Ms. McGuire's.

Ms. Parker, a fine film actress, is not very good here. She plays the bawdy Maxine with a deep laugh and a short hairdo, but the earthiness of the part escapes her. No doubt her casting was another CTG attempt to bring back an old favorite at the expense of artful acting. Occasionally it works; this time, it doesn't.

Massey looks like a 97-year-old poet, though his line readings are perhaps a shade too eloquent for someone basically tuned-out to the role. Still, it's good to see a fine actor before us once again. Allyn Ann McLerie does well as a mannish music teacher.

H. R. Poindexter's set and lighting are lush without being overbearing while Noel Taylor's costumes look fine. Summed up, a middle-of-the-road staging of a play that deserves more artistic discipline and less star casting. When you do a William's play, the script is ultimately your star!

"Selma" Taps Black Music Stereotypes
(by Rick Talcove, Valley News and Green Sheet, November 28, 1975)

Are the best black musicals written by whites?

This question repeatedly crossed the reviewer's mind at "Selma," a vanity production by Tommy Butler (with the financial assistance of Redd Foxx) currently holding forth at the Huntington Hartford in Hollywood.

Though billed as "a joyous new musical," the evening is nothing more than a misguided though occasionally dangerous social project that has been taken much too seriously by its creator and a few influential people.

Butler's virtual one-man show (he wrote the book, music, lyrics, co-directs and stars in it) may have the grand purpose of exploring late Rev. Martin Luther King Jr. 's life in song-and-dance. However, general shabbiness of the enterprise plus underlying undercoating of hatred makes the evening futile.

Developed as a project at the Inner City Cultural Center, "Selma" takes King's life and turns it inside out. One moment we're getting homey snatches of family life ("Coretta ... Coretta, come to the phone!") and the next finds us in the middle of attempted stylization (a tap dance march to Selma).

Between, there are songs. Or rather, Butler's attempt at songs. At best, they're derivative; at worst, they're simply bad. Since it's impossible for white actors to come out in black face, we have blacks in white face. Thus a lot of hatred masquerading as satire gets thrown in the audience's face.

There is, however, something good about "Selma" and her name is Ruth Brown. Impersonating Mahalia Jackson, Ms. Brown has a stunning solo--sung a capella--that stops or rather, starts the show in its tracks. A major moment in a minor show.

It's interesting that a decidedly inferior item like "Selma" can rally support while attempts at reviving distinguished past musicals with black themes run up against constant criticism.

Last season's revival of "Porgy and Bess" by the Civic Light
Opera brought forth typical liberal protest of "Uncle Tom stereotypes," as though the residents of Cattish Row were supposed to
be Rhodescholars. Even more absurd was the attempt to dis-
credit composer George Gershwin's successful attempt at capturing the speech patterns of blacks within his folk opera framework.

It's also interesting, in regard to "Selma," that white playwrights, lyricists, and composers are supposed to stay away
from black themes; the opinion being they don't have the feeling
for subject matter.

This, of course, is patently absurd. If anything, Maxwell
Anderson and Kurt Weill's "Lost in the Stars" (based on cauca-
sion Alan Paton's novel of South Africa, "Cry the Beloved Country") gave their black characters a dignity most black writers
or composers would have considered. Anderson and Weill were
critized for making their characters too solemn, yet if they'd
put in the easy rolling-eyed chorus numbers as "Selma" does
they would have been equally censured for stooping for stereotypes.

Luckily, time is the final judge of achievement in the theater. Perhaps recent mediocre efforts like "Don't Bother Me I
Can't Cope," "Bread and Beans and Things" and now "Selma"
will be classics 30 years from now. Until then, black theater--
as with any other--can only be judged by what appears on stage,
not what the author feels in his soul.

TAYLOR, Larry; (2) Theatre critic; (3) b. Huntington Park, Cal.,
April 6, 1932; (4) s. Glenn and Marguerite (Falrey); (5) B.A. San
Jose State, major: journ. 1954; M.A. Cal. State U., Fullerton,
major: English 1968; (6) m.; (7) children--Lawrence Michael, Cecilia
Louise, Dennis Patrick; (8) Newspaper 1959-73; Teaching Cal. State
Fullerton 1973-75; currently a part-time reviewer with Orange County
Evening News; (21) 1219 Cypress Point Dr., Placentia Cal., Ph.
714-524-0985; (22) Calif. State Univ. Fullerton, Fullerton, Cal.,
Ph. 714-870-2284; (23) Circulation: 80,000 The Orange County Even-
ing News; (24) 40.

Witty Delivery--Subject to Fits
(by Larry Taylor, Orange County Evening News, April 16, 1975)

Imagine a combination of Dostoevsky and "Alice in Wonderland," with music yet, and you have "Subject to Fits," a new
play by Robert Montgomery currently being staged by the South
Coast Repertory in Costa Mesa.

In fact, the play is an adaptation of Dostoevsky's novel

"The Idiot," in which the Christlike Prince Myshkin shows the impossibility for the truly good man to survive in an evil, corrupt world. This new version carries through many of the novel's themes in spirit if not in style. Myshkin is still called an idiot because of his strange, atypical behavior. However, here the world is seen more insane with its inhabitants foolishly striving for money, power and recognition, things which are shown to have no meaning in a transitory, mortal life. Myshkin sees the foolishness of it all and continually points out the contradictions.

The play is written and delivered with much wit--the characters are extremely funny in their posturing, occasionally breaking out in operatic style songs, their lofty manner contrasting with the absurd subject matter.

Garry Bell is outstanding as the harried, epileptic Myshkin-- subject to fits throughout, everyone pulling at him to satisfy their need for money, love or advice. His epilepsy enables him to see life's meaning in those transcendent moments just prior to his fits. A central irony is seen in the Prince's quote: "Knowing the meaning of life would drive us crazy"--of course, he sees and is considered crazy.

The menagerie of characters are effectively portrayed, particularly the maniacal Lebedev (Robert L. Wright), the ruminating old man, Ivolglin (John-David Keller), the sinister Rogozhin (Art Koustik), the consumptive Ippolit (James Broess) and the beautiful, selfish Natasha (Marlene Silvers).

If the final message is oblique, we have a good time along the way and the pace never falters under David Emmes deft direction in what is essentially a talk play.

Susan Tuohy's multileveled set, draped in black cloth with an appropriate gold leaf cross pattern, works well, and Steve Ellington on organ gives excellent accompaniment, ranging from church hymns to rock. You can see this very original, very entertaining play through the next four weeks.

Hedda Gabler Is Proper Play for Great Actress
(by Larry Taylor, Orange County Evening News, April 16, 1975)

A classic play with one of the world's great actresses--this combination gives Southern Californians a unique theatre experience. The occasion is the Royal Shakespeare company's production of Ibsen's "Hedda Gabler," currently in a short stay at the Huntington Hartford Theatre in Hollywood.

As soon as Ms. Jackson comes on stage, the audience is riveted to her, such is the power of her performance. Hers is a strong willed, assertive Hedda, disdainful of the middle class life into which her marriage has forced her. She is bored with

her naive, scholarly husband, Tesman (Peter Eyre), sarcastic
with his conventional Aunt Juliana (Constance Chapman), and flirtatious with the hypocritical Judge Brack (Timothy West) who
wants to start an affair with her.

She also shows us the proper Hedda underneath, her conventional upbringing fostering the need to conform. Her frustration comes through in moments of clenched fists and deep sighs.

Jackson's Hedda is also a little psychotic. She hurls sudden insults at an innocent bystander; she feels compelled to wil-
fully destroy her former lover's life in a pique of jealousy. It
is marvelous to watch her cajole information out of her advisary,
the unwary Mrs. Elvsted (Jennie Linden) or self confidently parry
Judge Brack's advances.

But Jackson isn't the whole show. Peter Eyre is marvelous
as her tall, gangling, ineffectual, Tesman.

TAYLOR, Markland James; (2) Freelance writer; regular contributor
as theatre critic and feature writer to Sunday Arts & Leisure Section
of The New Haven Register; (3) b. Adelaide, South Australia, Jan.
29, 1936; (4) s. Walter James and Nellie Watson (Loader); (5) M. Sc.
in Comparative Journalism, Graduate School of Journalism, Columbia U. , 1963; Previous education in Australia. Studied critical writing at Graduate School of Journalism. Also studied modern drama,
theatre history and opera while at Columbia. Studied music, piano
and theory, for 14 years; (6) Single; (8) Journalist, including theater,
film and music critic, The Advertiser (morning daily), Adelaide,
South Australia, 1953-61; assistant editor, Plays and Players (London monthly theatre magazine), and contributor to Music and Musicians and Record and Recordings, 1961-62; various writing positions
after graduating from Columbia, including director of publicity, William Morris Agency, New York, 1971-73; (9) Founding member,
Younger Theatre Group, Adelaide, South Australia; (16) No political
affiliations; (17) Nominally, Episcopalian; (20) Have contributed reviews and/or feature articles on theatre, etc. to The Washington
Post (and, through its news service, to newspapers throughout the
country), This Week, Show, Entertainment World, The Hartford Courant, etc. Have had several plays (adaptations) published by Dramatic Pub. Co. Wrote and edited first annual report of Connecticut
Foundation for the Arts, 1973-74; (21) 212 Shelton Road, Monroe,
Conn. 06468, Ph. 203-261-2038; (22) Sunday Arts & Leisure Section,
the New Haven Register, 367 Orange Street, New Haven, Conn. 06503,
Ph. 203-562-1121; (23) Circulation: 140,000; (24) In the past have
reviewed films, music and records on a regular basis.

Stitt's "Runner " Uneven
(by Markland Taylor, New Haven Register, January 11, 1976)

It's easy to see why Milan Stitt wrote "The Runner Stumbles"
and why Stamford's Hartman Theater Company chose it for its

first world premiere. The murder case the play is concerned with has just the tantalizing, disturbing qualities that have turned other actual murder cases into American myth--Lizzie Borden's, to name just one.

Stitt's play, at the Hartman through Jan. 18, is based, loosely, on the trial of a priest accused of murdering a nun in an isolated Michigan community at the turn of the century. It was written out of the local myths of the murder and trial rather than actual facts, and, although Stitt has constructed his play as though it takes place in the priest's mind, it is basically realistic, set firmly in historical time and place.

The playwright has, in fact, established very well the yawningly empty lives of his people of Solon, Michigan, some 70 years ago; lives of little but cruelty. To paraphrase him, these people lived with framed photographs of dead infants in their coffins, saw no reason to chastize their children when they set fire to kittens, and took it for granted that husbands beat their wives regularly and viciously. Not a pretty time or place, and one in which the story of a nun and priest being drawn together by the force of their opposing beliefs in church and God and ultimately destroying each other seems all too natural. ("The Runner Stumbles" carries with it reminders of "The Devils," John Whiting's adaptation of Huxley's "The Devils of London.")

It is a tribute to the basic fascination of Stitt's material, factual and fictional, that at the Hartman it holds its audience despite dramatic fragmentation in the writing further fragmented by lack of direction.

I don't lay all the blame for what is wrong with "The Runner Stumbles" on director Austin Pendleton--the script itself has a curiously unfinished air about it--but he must take his share. To begin with, he has failed to give the production any sense of progression or growth so that it remains in bits and pieces rather than coming together as a whole. Also, he hasn't helped his actors to flesh out and physicalize the script (or to cope with it emotionally or intellectually) enough, so that too often his production has the static quality and low dramatic temperature of a staged reading.

To give Pendleton his due, he has kept the production as sparse, bleak and basic as the time and place in which the play is set, aided by Robert Ver-Berkmoes' entirely apt set (little more than a long, room-height interior wall, it makes the best use so far of the Hartman's vast stage by placing the playing area in front of the vaulting proscenium). But this should have been where Pendleton's direction began rather than ended.

And so the cast, not always ideally chosen, is severely handicapped. In scene after scene they just begin to establish rapport among themselves and with play and audience when the

scene ends; because the director has failed to solve the problem
of building from scene to scene, they then have to start from
scratch again. This was particularly true of the first act on
opening night. It was entirely fragmentary, apparently aimless,
and failed to build at all.

In the pivotal role of Father Rivard, Stephen Joyce, as good
a natural actor as our theater has, gives a clean, uncluttered,
deeply committed performance that, when play and direction allow, rises to heights of fervent power. But there's a flaw in
his portrayal that constantly diminishes it--he does not capture
the period of the play and simply looks, sounds and feels too
modern. This fault is compounded by the clothes he wears,
slacks, shirt and sports jacket, that look like rehearsal clothes
rather than a suitable costume; this is doubly odd because elsewhere costume designer James Berton Harris has caught the
period simply and well.

As Sister Rita, Nancy Donohue has a certain appealing quality and some bright, fresh moments in the first two acts. But
she is much too free, easy and liberated for a turn-of-the-century nun and is overmatched by the passions of the last act.
Here either a far more experienced, more charismatic actress
or a stronger director (or both) is needed.

It seems to me that Father Rivard's housekeeper, Mrs.
Shandig, should be played by an actress older than Sloane Shelton. But once that drawback is discounted Ms. Shelton's performance grows quietly stronger and stronger. It is, certainly, infinitely better than her Anna, the mayor's wife, in the
Hartman's opening production, "The Government Inspector."

James Noble (straight from Long Wharf's "The Show-Off")
is hayseedy yet astute as local lawyer Toby Felker, William
Bogert drily self-important as the Prosecutor, and Katina Cummings excellent as a grey and fearful Erna Prindle. Eren Ozker seems too old for schoolgirl (even ex-schoolgirl) Louise;
Bernard Frawley was uneasy on opening night as Monsignor
Nicholson; and Morrie Piersol's guard is a bit too obviously the
work of a student, which is what Piersol is at the Hartman
Conservatory.

The ending of the play on opening night (it may well be different by now) was a mistake, what with its out-of-character
sobbing and vision of the murdered nun.

And yet, and yet ... in spite of everything there is something in "The Runner Stumbles" that commands attention. If
playwright Stitt can bear to continue rewriting until he has hewn
the best possible play from his undoubtedly fascinating material,
and if it could then come into the hands of the ideal director
(John Dexter, say, while we're being idealists), we might hear
more of "The Runner Stumbles."

"Going Up" Is Pure Enchantment
(by Markland Taylor, New Haven Register, July 4, 1976)

Let's not beat about the bush.   The current production of
the 1917 Hirsch-Harbach musical comedy "Going Up" at the
Goodspeed Opera House is purest theatrical enchantment.   It is
all beguiling innocence (were we ever that unsullied!), all heart-
lifting joy.   And it is further proof, if needed, that Goodspeed
is the most successful, best run summer theater (or winter theater, for that matter) in Connecticut.   If you miss it, your summer will be that much duller.

Otto Harbach's book for "Going Up" is gloriously lunatic.
Based on James Montgomery's comedy "The Aviator," it gives
us a hero who's written a best-seller about aviation, but who
has never even been in an airplane, being challenged to a race
with a French aviation ace in order to win the girl.   That's it,
and it couldn't be more fun.   I refuse to refer to Bill Gile's
production of "Going Up" as a revival, it's too freshly realized.
But I would like to salute all the work that must have gone into
recreating this 1917 show, the replacing of missing parts, the
trimming, adding and rewriting, the orchestrations, all done
with great love and an unerring sense of the period, Bravo!

Director Gile, with the help of absolutely everyone, has
taken off with the fun of "Going Up" and parlayed it into rampant delight.   Gile grows with each Goodspeed production, and
by now he knows exactly how to keep a musical travelling.   "Going Up" is up on its toes the whole time, and it travels first
class.

Then there's the contribution of choreographer Dan Siretta.
His dances are masterpieces of fakery.   Not because the cast
can't dance, but because there really isn't room for real dancing on the tiny stage.

Not that you'd know from the terpsichorean miracles Siretta
and his dancers achieve.   The "Everybody Ought to Know How
To Do The Tickle Toe" production number is utterly exhilarating.

Costume designer David Toser's contributions look especially winning here; how wittily his 1919 dresses look back to the
Edwardians while looking forward to the 20s (the production's
period has been advanced two years to give it post-war ebullience).   How well made and fitted the costumes are, too.   Next,
Edward Haynes.   His lightly etched, floral-wallpapered sets open
up the stage as freely as has ever been done at Goodspeed and
his mock-up of an early airplane--when airplanes were all canvas, aluminum and lots of glue--is just dandy.   It wins round
after round of applause as it flies behind a cloud-flecked scrim,
culminating with our hero (acted and sung with disarming direct-
ness by Brad Blaisdell) grabbing his second flying lesson--how
to land--from our heroine (Kimberly Farr) as he whizzes past a
church steeple.

Speaking of Miss Farr, let me tell you that there are rewards in being a Sunday reviewer. Goodspeed does not lead a
totally charmed life, and sickness laid low a lot of the "Going
Up" cast members during rehearsals. Then musical director
Lynn Crigler (a Goodspeed treasure) was sent to his bed. Worse
was to come. Miss Farr managed to get through the first performance, but succumbed for the next two which had to go ahead
with a standby, book in hand (this must have thrown the timing
way off). I saw the fourth performance. Miss Farr and Crigler
were both there and it was well-nigh impeccable.

There's not a weakness in the cast. Miss Farr (I first noticed her with pleasure when I tore my eyes away from Vanessa
Redgrave in Circle in the Square's recent Ibsen "Lady from the
Sea") gives us a musical comedy heroine who plays it completely
straight with her audience. Here's a young lady who knows exactly what she's doing and does it with a forthright charm that's
never, never cloying. Her singing, with operatic overtones, is
just right for this 59-year-old show, and she and Blaisdell work
beautifully together.

Once again Maureen Brennan gives us a superior soubrette,
a tiny bundle of zest, and the comics--Walter Bobbie as an
early Madison Avenue type and Ronn Robinson as a silly-putty
mechanic--are expert. Thank you Bill Gile for directing so affectionately all of the comedy material, originally written for
such legendary performers as Frank Craven and Donald Meek.

Then there's Michael Tartel's French ace. Tartel does a
lovely spoof of Gallic matinee idols; he's a sort of East Haddam
Georges Guetary, and he's devastating. Everyone is so good,
but let's not forget Pat Lysinger's switchboard operator. She's
delicious, and her "Hello, Frisco, Hello" (brought in from the
1915 Ziegfeld Follies to cover a scene change) is, as Variety
might have said, socko.

Goodspeed's "Going Up," far from by the way, is the sort
of musical in which whenever characters begin to sing, a har-
monizing or whistling chorus appears out of nowhere behind
them. It's obligatory, and it serves the bouncy Hirsch score
very well indeed.

Goodspeed producer Michael Price is thinking of ending the
run of "Going Up," on August 6, two days earlier than announced.
Why? Because he feels that Goodspeed standards cannot be
maintained while closing one production on Sunday night and
opening the next on Tuesday (which, of course, leaves room for
only one dress rehearsal). That sort of thinking is just one in-
gredient of Goodspeed's secret of success.

I think I know some of the other ingredients--the right policy for the right theater, good taste, good casting, good direction, complete belief in the material being done, hard work--
but I do wish Goodspeed would impart its secret to the Westport

Country Playhouse and the American Shakespeare Theater.   Just
think what summer theater in Connecticut would be like then.
Or is that just so much wishful thinking?

TAYLOR, Robert; (2) Theater and film critic; (3) b. San Jose,
Calif. , June 1, 1940; (4) s. Robert and Esther (Allen) T. ; (5) B. A.
Calif. State U. , San Jose, major subj. : Journalism, 1961; graduate
study, Stanford U. , 1966-67; (6) Single; (8) Reporter, Fairfield
(Calif.) Daily Republic 1961-63; reporter, San Jose (Calif.) Mercury,
critic, Oakland (Calif.) Tribune, 1967- ; (9) Actor, San Jose Junior
Theater, 1954-56; actor, My Heart's in the Highlands, The World Is
Round, San Jose State, 1957-58; member, San Francisco Museum of
Art film committee, 1968; critic fellow, National Critics Institute,
Eugene O'Neill Theater Center, Waterford, Conn. , 1970; (15) Mem.
American Theatre Critics Assn. ; (21) 1539 Shrader St. , San Francis-
co, Calif. 94117; (22) The Oakland Tribune (410 13th St.), P. O. Box
24304, Oakland, Calif. , 94623; (23) Circulation: 185,000; (24) 40
plays and musicals, 70 films.

Brightest, Sunniest of Farces
(by Robert Taylor, Oakland Tribune, October 10, 1975)

If anyone thought "The Matchmaker" would survive merely
as the non-musical version of "Hello, Dolly," the ACT production brings it happily back to life as one of the brightest and
sunniest of American farces.

Thornton Wilder's play celebrates nothing more nor less
than the adventure of living.   That spirit is splendidly captured--
and radiated--in the new show which opened at the Geary this
week, celebrating just as playfully the adventure of the theater.

In a loving fashion, it also kids the bloomers off the conventional 19th century comedies animated with old misers,
scheming servants and lovestruck youths.

There's a local angle here, too.   Wilder noted in his introduction to the published script that he wrote "The Matchmaker"
to parody the stock-company plays he saw at Ye Liberty Playhouse in Oakland, during the years he was a youngster attending Berkeley High School.

The ACT production, designed by Richard Seger with costumes by Robert Fletcher, preserves that era with a white gingerbread proscenium, old-fashioned footlights, and delicate patterns and colors inspired by quilts and samplers.

Director Laird Williamson has instilled the show with just
the right balance of comic flash and sentimental affection, and
the remarkable results should bring tears of joy to audiences
who allow themselves to fall under its spell.

Williamson attracted attention as an actor last season with a brilliant bit of comic timing, playing the lunacy master in "The Ruling Class." Now he has a chance with "The Matchmaker" to show a broader range of comic skills, and he is a welcome addition to the ranks of ACT's imaginative directors.

This "Matchmaker" production owes nothing to the play's latter-day musical version, but the irrepressible Dolly Levi is still its driving force. The difference is that this Dolly is a more mellow characterization than a musical comedy lead could ever be, and Elizabeth Huddle savors all the matchmakers' warmth and charm.

She isn't chasing miserly, crochety old Horace Vandergelder just to latch onto his money. Dolly wants to set that cash free to "circulate like rain water, flowing down among the people." She can't stand to think of it lying in great piles, useless, motionless, in the bank.

So what if she makes herself look foolish? Even Vandergelder says most of the people in the world are fools, himself included. "But there comes a moment in everybody's life," she declares as Dolly and Thornton Wilder bring the farce to a close, "when he must decide whether he'll live among human beings or not--a fool among fools or a fool alone."

Everyone in "The Matchmaker" gets a chance to pass on some sampler sentiments to the audience, and for all its comic contrivances the play is rich with characters who share Wilder's humanity.

The ACT production more than matches the play's affectionate attitude toward all this foolishness. One stunning example is the farcical chase through Irene Molloy's New York hat shop, which somehow segues naturally into a charming quartet of "Tenting Tonight" before the young couples bound out for an evening at the Harmonia Gardens.

It's not a "supporting" cast, because even the smallest parts and performances are beautifully developed. Particularly notable are William Paterson as the blustering (but never heartless) Vandergelder; James Winker as his frustrated feed-and-grain store clerk; Daniel Zippi as the adorably innocent apprentice; and Deborah May and Fredi Olster as the spirited hatmaker and her wide-eyed assistant.

There are more outstanding contributions from Barbara Dirickson as Vandergelder's tearful niece; Sydney Walker (out of his clerical collar at last) as his light-footed but tipsy hired hand; Raye Birk as a flustered head waiter; and Marrian Walters as a sentimental "free spirit."

A few elements of the production have yet to fall into place, and Williamson might do a little more trimming so his audience can get home by midnight.   But his "Matchmaker" production creates such an endearing parade of characters that we wouldn't mind spending even more than a single evening with them.

New Tennessee Williams Play in Dazzling ACT Debut
(by Robert Taylor, Oakland Tribune, January 22, 1976)

Tennessee Williams' "This Is (An Entertainment)" exploded on the Geary stage in the American Conservatory Theater's premiere production Tuesday night, but what remains of it after a single dazzling performance may not insure the play's survival.

Elizabeth Huddle gives that performance as an outrageous countess, a ringmistress in a sexual circus who cracks the whip over a pair of lovers and a cuckolded husband, complete with antlers.

The style is unlike any of Williams' familiar works, taking off from the "Camino Real" fantasy into an absurdist adventureland.   The wild, opulent ACT staging by Allen Fletcher reminded me of the company's previous productions of Edward Albee's "An American Dream" and Michael McClure's "General Gorgeous."

The play is a celebration of the countess' effervescent but tenuous lifestyle: giving away rings because she doesn't want a jewel more durable than herself, smashing mirrors because "they catch light, which is exclusively mine."

I found myself awed at the challenge of Williams' sprawling work, amazed at ACT's success in putting it on the stage, and astonished at Huddle's grand, multi-faceted, almost super-human portrayal.

Huddle's countess is the culmination of four ACT seasons of remarkably wide-ranging performances.   She brings to "This Is (An Entertainment)" the bawdiness of her hooker in "The Hot l Baltimore," the conniving of her matchmaker in "The Miser," the authority of "Bernarda Alba," the sleazy glitter of her chorine in "Broadway" and the overwhelming charm of Dolly Levi in "The Matchmaker."

She and the play are flashy and fun, like the sparkler lighted by her first lover (played languidly by Nicholas Cortland, who also doubles as her second).   Mad fun until Williams has to do something with the countess, go somewhere, get serious.

As if it were a balloon inflated with the countess' breath and energy, the play reaches the bursting point and explodes. Then there is nothing, only a grinding plottiness which wears down the second act.   Whatever the energy level onstage, "This Is (An Entertainment)" is an exhausting three-hour experience for an audience.

This is, however, the first draft of a play Williams has already begun to revise. His inspiration was an old friend, a
former actress with whom he spent many summers in Italy. A
couple of years ago he began writing about her enormous vitality
and charm. "The character came first, then the play," he said
in a recent interview, but onstage, the play never comes.

There are plenty of ideas zinging around John Jensen's grandiose carousel of a setting, a hotel in an unnamed European
country during a revolution. The doddering old order is about
to be overturned; in the first scene an ancient principessa warns
that "a single night can remove one from existence."

Blackouts suggest life's final blackout; concerned about it or
not, we are told in the final dark scene that "The game plays
itself. History was fixed before it began."

For the moment that doesn't stop the countess, who is out-
racing life and death with what she calls her "spectacular velocity
through time." She confides her lusty desires to the audience,
waves away a harsh spotlight and declares breathily, "The energy crisis of this performance precludes matinee performances,
if not evenings."

It's a shame the play offers the countess (and the indefatigable Elizabeth Huddle) so little solid support. Williams may
be able to provide it for ACT's trusting performers during the
San Francisco tryout: certainly they have given him the most
spectacular production he could hope for.

TAYLOR, Sam A.; (2) Staff writer, drama and music critic, Lancaster
New Era, Lancaster, Pa.; (3) b. Randolph, Ia., Aug, 2, 1918; (4)
s. Samuel Addison and Gertrude (Gilchrist) Taylor; (5) Attended U.
of Idaho, Moscow, ID.; major in journalism, minor, theater; (6) m.
Verda Wentling, May 24, 1959; (8) Correspondent, Spokane Chronicle,
Spokane, Wash., 1946; Administrative assistant U.S. Rep. Abe Goff,
1947; News Director and program director Radio Station WCHA,
Chambersburg, Pa. from 1948-1955; Current position in Lancaster
since 1955; (9) Long list of credits in amateur as well as semi-pro
theater including "Our Town" with Victor Jory, "A Christmas Carol"
with Walter Abel, "State of the Union" with Pat Carroll. Member
Lancaster Theater Arts, Actors' Co. of Pennsylvania; (10) Former
board member Lancaster Guidance Clinic; Former board member
Lancaster Humane League; Service on various committees in connection with Symphony Orchestra, and Fulton Opera House Foundation;
(13) Military--U.S. Army 1940 to 1945. Enlisted section head Mc-
Arthur's Headquarters 1943-45; four years' service in South Pacific.
Holder of bronze star & 5 battle stars; (16) Republican; (17) Episcopalian; (18) BPOE; (19) Kiwanis; (20) Contributions to several theater
publications and periodicals over a span of years. Two short stories,
"Man" Magazine, Sydney, Australia; (21) 1307 Maple Ave., Lancaster, Pa. 17603, Ph. 717-394-3127; (22) 8 W. King St., Lancaster,

Pa. 17602, Ph. 397-5251; (23) Circulation: approx. 75,000; (24) 45 plays and musicals, three dance, 10 symphonic, 25 celebrity concerts, interviews and appearances.

Wickstrom Magnificent as King Lear
(by Sam Taylor, Lancaster New Era, March 1, 1975)

It isn't often that we sit down in the aftermath of a piece of great theater, and lead off with hosannahs for the competence of one cast member.

In fact, in our book, it is almost sacrilege to do this, but do it we must, because Gordon Wickstrom turns in the greatest performance we have ever seen on the Green Room stage in his reading of King Lear.

This is a huge mouthful for us, because we have been middle-aisling it at the Green Room for 18 years. In that time we have seen some stunning and gripping performances, but the Wickstrom interpretation of the monarch whom senility and madness mark for their own, tops any of the other efforts.

Wickstrom is a member of the faculty of the drama department at Franklin and Marshall College.

He has never appeared as an actor on the local boards before. His forte has been in the direction of a theater medium about as far from the bard as possible, contemporary plays like "Tiny Alice," and "Endgame."

He has, however, gained considerable experience, both as an actor and a director at the Colorado Shakespeare Festival.

To try and capture the scope and depth of Wickstrom's contribution to one of the Bard's deepest tragedies in words would be far too much gilt for the lily when three words--moving, magnificent, and memorable, say it all.

"King Lear" opened a 9-day run at the college playhouse last night. The full house which sat through almost three hours of Shakespearean magic unconsciously paid the production its biggest tribute--"pin drop" silence--the entire length of the play.

There's a close parallel between the pagan day setting of King Lear and the Watergate era. This simile pinpoints the fact that there's nothing new in political chicanery, or in the essential nature of man.

While Lear is the story of a great soul which didn't cleanse itself until it was past the age of "four score and upwards," it is also the tale of a pride in authority which always has the power to enforce itself against the pride of truth, which in the process begets the slow erosion of flattery and falsehood which eventually leads to its own destruction.

The whole premise has a familiar 1975 ring.

Director Ed Brubaker has not only selected a star of heavy magnitude as the centerpiece of the play, he has also chosen one of the strongest casts in his support.

This is especially true in the case of two student actors, Wayne Reno, a junior playing the bastard son of Gloucester, and Michael Shuptar, appearing as his half brother.

There's measured grace and a light touch of fey villainy in Reno's reading of the part which colors him Machiavellian, yet leaves enough naive gaps to make him believable in his chicanery.

Shuptar's interpretation of the man with pretended madness as a cloak, a naked and raving idiot who arrives to match the senile rantings of the King set against nature's boiling storm, is one of those rare theatrical treasures made even more amazing by the youth and the inexperience of the portrayer.

Shuptar has been on the F & M campus for the past four years, yet he has kept this well of talent to himself and hasn't set foot on a Green Room stage. Local audiences have lost a lot by his reluctance to appear before now, just as he is ending his college career.

Roger Rollin, a member of the English faculty, brings a studied and mature elegance, almost a tongue in cheek wit, to the part of the Earl of Kent, and David Roscher is solid as Gloucester.

Roscher tended to be part of the woodwork at opening, but his performance takes fire and flowers as the blinded wanderer.

Gail Richmond brings a catty bitchiness to the part of Goneril which is sheer delight.

What Marguerite LeBaron did to the part of Regan we honestly don't know, because we didn't understand a word she uttered.

Leslie Stainton played an honest Cordelia. In less experienced hands this part could have turned into a milksop, Goody Twoshoes effort, but the candor with which she approached the role erased any bent toward the saccharine.

One word must be said about the setting. Four towering rock pillars, in Stonehenge majesty, set on a severely raked, and stepped, stage form a more than effective setting to the action.

"King Lear" plays through March 8. Curtains are at 8 p.m., and there are still tickets remaining. Ducats won't be around long once the word gets around that top-flight Shakespeare is being performed in Lancaster.

Tuneful "Dolly" Delights Packed House at Fulton
(by Sam Taylor, Lancaster New Era, May 21, 1975)

"Holy Cabooses," Dolly's back in town!

The old girl is alive and well and prancing across the stage of the Fulton Opera House.

Dolly ankled down the red-plush stairs last night at the opening of a five-night run of the Lancaster Kiwanis-sponsored musical comedy, "Hello, Dolly!"

This tuneful version of Thornton Wilder's "Matchmaker," which had a whole parade of leading ladies during a record Broadway run, is directed locally by Dorothy Kilheffer.

Among the pluses last night was a cast which included a newcomer in the title role, some highly talented and older well-known hands, and some other newcomers to the ranks of local musical comedy.

Another plus at last night's showing was a happy audience which was in the right mood to accept anything that might have been thrown at them across the footlights.

This type of audience is the kind most actors dream about-- one that can be a psychological shot in the arm and a boost to a cast with first night doubts.

On the other side of the coin was the sparest the leanest, and the least satisfying setting ever assembled for a Kiwanis show. Nearly half of the action of the Lancaster version suffered in a back-lit, gray playing area which did absolutely nothing for mood or plot development.

In past years, we have often complained of vulgarly over-dressed stages in local productions, but this one is darned near nude.

Pacing of this show is just a shade under par, especially in a long, long first act which can be slow even under the best of circumstances.

Costuming, particularly on the distaff side of the cast, appears to be a major problem.

Aside from a dazzling wardrobe for the leading lady, and average turnouts for the featured actresses, the ladies of the chorus come up pretty frumpy and "treadle-sewing-machine" homemade by comparison.

This is literally Janet Walker's first time out in a full-scale musical effort. She comes off remarkably well in the role of Dolly, especially in the musical department.

She looks great, uses a devilish twinkle in her eye to full advantage, and "sings like a boid."

There are now rough and overblown spots in her characterization which will smooth out as the run progresses. We would say she's on her way to learning stagecraft basics at least. One or two more shows will firm up this facet of her talents.

We've seen James Willig in a lot of roles in the past several years. In that span of time we have sometimes praised and sometimes damned his efforts.

But he's hit the target this time. There couldn't have been a better characterization of Horace Vandergelter around any place than the one he conjures up in this one.

He hits the top of the cast in our book. He cracked us up (a fairly hard thing to do) with his total personification of the merchant of Yonkers.

Stan Deen ends up in a photo finish with Willig for top acting honors.

Deen has been around local productions for a long time. He directs a comprehensive and progressive drama program at Garden Spot High School, and he's the only member of the Lancaster version of "The Matchmaker" of several seasons back to translate to the present production.

He knows how to please an audience, plays it like a fine cello, tickles them under the chin, and leaves them laughing at exactly the right time as Cornelius Hackle for a totally delightful performance.

Bob Hoshour, one of Deen's students at Garden Spot, plays his mentor's sidekick, Barnaby Tucker, with a dash and a flair which reveals a lot of potential in this young man.

Gail Scheaffer exhibits a great deal of expertise for stylized comedy in her very, very funny stint as Minnie Fay, and Claudia Herr comes across in the role of Irene Molloy.

Mention must be made of the high comedy and rollicking good humor of a cameo part which was supplied by Ruth Wren as Ernestina.

In the light of some of the topflight choreography which has been blossoming on local stages, the dance routines for this one emerge pretty pallid.

"Dolly" plays through Saturday night to one of the best advance sales in the history of Kiwanis shows. As of last night, there were 42 seats left unsold for the remainder of the run. Local club members really hit the gong in their sales effort, which adds folding money to the organization's public service activities.

THOMAS, Barbara; (2) Amusements editor, theater critic, Atlanta Journal; (3) b. Montgomery, Ala., May 26, 1945; (4) d. Rex and Grace Thomas; (5) B.A. Journalism and Foreign Languages, Auburn U., 1967; (6) Married; (8) News Editor, Auburn Plainsman, 1966-67, general assignment reporter, Columbus Ledger, 1967, general assignment, school desegregation, assistant lively arts editor, Birmingham News, 1967-1973, Amusements Editor, Atlanta Journal, 1973-present; (9) Member Mayor's Ad Hoc Committee on the Arts, member Outstanding Young Women in the Arts in Atlanta, charter member, co-founder Women in Film; (14) Associated Press award for feature writing, 1970, Sigma Delta Chi award for Reporting Without a Deadline, 1970, Birmingham News "Big N" Award for creative enterprise, 1971; (15) Member, officer American Society of Journalists, charter member Georgia Communications Council, member of American Theater Critics Association, member Atlanta Press Club, former member Women in Communications; (16) Democrat; (20) Published article on Cornelia Wallace in January issue of "Cosmopolitan"; (21) 5100 Peachtree Dunwoody Road, Atlanta, Ga. 30342; (22) Atlanta Journal, 72 Marietta St., Atlanta, 30303, Ph. 404-572-5384; (23)Circulation: about one million readers on Sunday; (24) 150 theater works and musicals, 180 film reviews, 70 miscellaneous.

Wittow Dwarfs Others in "Rhinoceros"
(by Barbara Thomas, Atlanta Journal, October 18, 1974)

Frank Wittow is back on stage and the anticipation built up by his return after four years has not been exaggerated.

His Berenger in Eugene Ionesco's "Rhinoceros" is the best I've seen at Academy Theater yet and good evidence of why he's earned such a strong reputation among theater folk. He's simply a stunning performer who comes on with all the stops pulled out and hanging free. Those of us who are relative newcomers to Atlanta, who haven't seen Academy Theater in "the good old days" and who have seen Wittow only in his capacity as artistic director and not actor, have a treat in store.

Academy's decision to offer "Rhinoceros" as their season opener represents a move toward less experimental theater, toward a medium more in line with community appreciations. Although avante-garde, "Rhinoceros" is far more structured than the usually company-developed productions put on by Academy in the past.

Wittow's immense talent could be seen as a drawback in one aspect in that most of the other performers are dwarfed by comparison. "Rhinoceros" essentially becomes a one-man show, a first-rate one indeed, but performers acting with Wittow must be content to be virtually unnoticed.

Robert Moyer as Jean, Berenger's friend who turns into a rhinoceros, manages to stay in the ring with Wittow for most of the rounds, giving a good showing as the dapper-turned-pachyderm.

While "Rhinoceros" on the surface seems easily deciphered as the lure of conformism, there are volumes after volumes of discussion on what the playwright was really trying to say in his absurdist story of people turning into rhinoceroses and one weakling who becomes a hero by his inability to conform.

Martin Esslin, author of "Theater of the Absurd," says of Berenger's regret that he cannot change into a rhino at the end: "His final defiant profession of faith in humanity is merely the expression of the fox's contempt for the grapes he could not have."

Ionesco himself talks of countries without understanding "a country where art is not understood ... a country of robots ... a country without mind or spirit; where there is no humor, no laughter, there is anger and hatred. Forms of rhinoceritis of every kind are there to threaten humanity ... they lie in wait for mankind today because we have lost all feeling and taste...." [The Academy Theater shows] us a "Rhinoceros" different from most American productions. If there is a difference it is in the feeling of tragic alienation we see in Berenger, while others have showed him more of a comic figure.

The production is one to be seen this season. Call the theater at 261-8550 for reservations. Tickets are selling fast.

Directing, Acting Benefit "Holmes"
(by Barbara Thomas, Atlanta Journal, April 11, 1975)

Said Sherlock Holmes to a damsel he saved from distress: "It's far more difficult to find an interesting case than to solve one."

Applying that handy theory to the theater, writer-director Dennis Rosa no doubt found it far more difficult to find an interesting and available Sherlock Holmes story than to solve one. So he wrote an adaptation from ones already in the public domain, not to be confused with the popular version the Royal Shakespeare Company recently brought over from London.

"Sherlock Holmes and the Curse of the Sign of the Four"
premiered Thursday night at Alliance Theater and benefited from
prudent direction and reined-in performances.

Phil Pleasants is Sherlock, the cocaine addict amateur detective who refers to himself as "the last highest court of appeal,
an unofficial consulting detective." Pleasants' performance was
nicely controlled, a quality he is not always able to convey.

His straight man (the playwright's mode of explaining the
events to the audience) is Dr. Watson, played admirably by
Mitchell Edmonds.

This time Watson is lovestruck over the same distressed
damsel (Mimi Bensinger) whose ancestors have involved themselves stickily in The Agra Treasure. That brings her in contact with Holmes, and, of course, us into the theater.

It is to the credit of the director, we presume, that the dramatic archaisms--poignantly timed knocks at the door, swelled
music, lace handkerchiefs pressed over demure mouths supress-
ing gasps of horror or passion--are played up but not over done.
The play never becomes a parody of the original but at times
laughs along with it instead of at it.

Costuming and technical effects surpass the expected. There's
a scene where Holmes and Watson chase the culprits down the
River Thames in a boat, replete with jostling waves and filtering
fog. Holmes even jumps overboard in pursuit of one of the cads.

There were times in the evening, however, when listening
was a task. Affected British accents occasionally made a few
players sound as if they were speaking through a mouthful of
bananas.

The play itself was shorter than expected, with concise, if
improbable, conclusions to all the mysteries. And if you missed
any as they came along, there was the "Perry Mason" scene at
the end in which the principal characters rehash the happenings.

The playwright, whether Doyle or assorted revisionists, appeared almost to apologize for the absurd coincidences in the
play in a final monologue when Holmes says, in effect, that truth
is stranger than fiction. It's also almost as much fun.

THOMPSON, Baird M.; (2) Theatre, ballet, music critic; (3) b. Honolulu, Feb. 28, 1950; (4) s. Dr. and Mrs. William D. Thompson;
(5) B.A. Johns Hopkins University, 1971; M.S. Television and Radio,
Syracuse U., 1972; (6) Single; (8) Public Relations and Broadcast
Management; (9) Public Relations Director for Syracuse Stage (LORT);
In 1976 was executive producer of the Downtown Dinner Theatre, Inc.,
in Syracuse. Most recently, joined Players Repertory Theatre in

Miami, Fla., as an actor and audience development specialist; (10)
Consultant to community theatres, Cultural Resources Council of
Syracuse and Onondaga County; faculty member Syracuse University;
board of directors Syracuse Ballet Theatre; (12) Advisor, Metropoli-
tan School for the Arts; Advisor, Common Cause, Cortland Repertory
Theatre; (13) no military record; (15) AFTRA, Baltimore and Syra-
cuse Press Clubs; PRSA; (16) Independent; (17) Episcopalian; (19)
Johns Hopkins University Faculty Club; (20) Associate Editor, Syra-
cuse New Times, Editor Metropinion, Continuing Education for Adults
Newsletter, Empire Magazine, The Baltimore Sun; (21) 3104 Florida
Ave., Miami, Fla. 33133; (22) Syracuse Stage 820 E. Genessee St.,
Syracuse, N.Y.; Ph. 315-423-4008; (23) Circulation: 60,000; (24)
Theatre 30, Music 20, Dance 10, Opera 4, Weekly Column, 52.

"Jacques Brel" Suffers Multiple Injuries
(by Baird Thompson, Syracuse New Times, February 22, 1973)

Jacques Brel got butchered. He is not alive and he is not
well in the Syracuse Musical Theatre production currently at the
Regent Experimental Theatre.

This lovely, simple cabaret piece, which is nothing more
than an exercise in imagination and good music, loses all sense
in the way it is produced. There is really nothing commendable
about the show with the one exception of the delightful music provided by the composer. The band plays and accompanies quite
well. The musical direction of Joyce Robertson, deserves mention.

Vocally and theatrically, however, none of the five players
is right for the show. Chris Gettman is the best singer of the
bunch and her one occasion to handle comedy in "Timid Frieda"
has possibilities. Unfortunately, her interpretation of the other
songs is stilted and lacks any involvement. "Carousel" is just
plain frantic. Michael Reed, Stephen Windheim and Richard
Pugh are all adequate singers but uninspiring. One shining light
is Windheim's interpretation of the "Funeral Tango." Ceryl L.
McDermott, costumed as a bouquet of roses, came forth like
she really wanted to be somewhere else.

On the technical side, the show is messy. The lighting was
off target and unnerving with specials popping on right and left
and cues leaving singers in the dark for seconds at a time. The
final blow was throwing up a gobo (scattered light) effect for the
finale of the song "If we only have love." Tacky.

The set was simple and bland. It served as a place for the
actors to hide.

It is good to see SMT looking toward intimate small productions. Jacques Brel is a natural good choice to go for that
route. It is unfortunate that the director, Lucy Doodigian, could
not evoke any of that charisma which makes this show a unique

theatrical experience and a delightful display of some of the best music around today.

"Where's Charley?"
(by Baird Thompson, Syracuse New Times, May 24, 1973)

Where's Charley? is nothing more than a farce. As musicals go, it contains nothing but silliness and is certainly a play of little consequence. The recent Syracuse Musical Theatre production attacked Where's Charley? in just this manner. It was a fun frolic, making a good evening for actors and audience.

The quick synopsis is undoubtedly the most useful for this show: Charley is Charley, Charley is also Charley's Aunt. Let all the possible situations available capture Charley in either of his two roles and he's bound to cause hilarity. It's really an I Love Lucy comedy with a couple of good songs by Frank Loesser. "The New Ashmolean Marching Society and Students Conservatory Band" and "Once in Love with Amy" are probably the best-known.

As far as the stage production, John Kirkpatrick in the role of Charley (and Charley's Aunt) did a yeoman job. He was funny, full of energy, well-timed and always appropriate with the part(s). Erwin Vrooman, who directed the show, also played Mr. Spettigue, the villain. He had some fine moments and certainly knows that any good Snidely Whiplash meany must play broadly. Both Vrooman and Kirkpatrick have good voices for this type of musical.

The rest of the cast, with the exception of Richard Pugh as Charley's roommate, were by and large extraneous bodies with no real conception of what was going on about them. Kirkpatrick, Vrooman and Pugh were a good ensemble lead for the production and made the musical succeed despite the others.

Again, it was the large production numbers which caused problems in the performance. The choreography was just plain senseless--either according to the period, the music or the mood--and with only two dancers who could waltz on stage, one might just as well employ the ol' scissors (snip) technique. The chorus, when called upon to do anything but sing, looked out of place. Vrooman could have left them off stage entirely and saved the embarrassment for 17 nontheatrical folks.

From a technical standpoint, the show was quite good. The scenery was very simple--hopefully so SMT can move this production around. A strobe was employed during the grand finale of Act I. Strobe lights are only effective when actors know what to do when one is turned on. They did not and it looked hideous. The general lighting effects were surprisingly good consistently throughout the show--quite a change from My Fair Lady last fall. Credits to Andrew Jurick and Charlie Wilson.

<u>Where's Charley?</u> was a good choice for SMT.   It's the best
all-around show I have seen this troupe do.   I hope it remains
in the repertoire so more people can enjoy its humor and the
talents of Kirkpatrick, Vrooman and Pugh.

TITCOMB, Caldwell; (2) College professor; theatre composer and
critic; (3) b. Augusta, Me., Aug. 16, 1926; (4) s. Samuel and Lura
(Smith) T.; (5) A.B. summa cum laude, Harvard 1947; M.A. Harvard 1949; Ph.D. in music, Harvard 1952; (6) unmarried; (8) Music
faculty, Brandeis U., since 1953; chairman, School of Creative Arts
1968-70; drama and music critic, Harvard Crimson and Harvard
Summer News, since 1953; (9) Teacher of course in history & practice of drama criticism; composer of a dozen stage & film incidental
music scores since 1954; chairman, New England Theatre Conference
convention 1969; (10) Board of directors, Cambridge Civic Symphony
Orchestra (1959-68); (11) Cambridge Civic Assn., Auburndale Community Assn.; (12) Executive board/advisory council, New England
Theatre Conference, since 1960; trustee, Charles Playhouse (1966-
71); (13) Staff sgt. US Army 1944-46; Military Intelligence Reserve
1946-50; (14) Phi Beta Kappa; Schurz Prize; Detur Award; (15) New
England Theatre Conference, American Musicological Society, Society
for Ethnomusicology, College Music Society, American Assn. of
University Professors; American Guild of Organists; Assn. for Study
of Negro Life & History; NAACP, Sonneck Society, ACLU; (16) Independent; (19) Signet Society; (20) The Art of Fine Words (1965);
contributing author, several books; many encyclopedia, dictionary &
journal articles & reviews; (21) 67 Windermere Road, Auburndale,
Mass. 02166, Ph. 617-969-0742; (22) Slosberg Center, Brandeis
University, Waltham, Mass. 02154, Ph. 617-647-2557; (23) Circulation: 10,000; (24) Formerly ca. 20, currently ca. 6 (drama, music,
art, misc.).

<u>"The Country Wife" in Bright, Funny Revival</u>
(by Caldwell Titcomb, Harvard Crimson, July 6, 1973)

Cuckoldry and castration do not often go hand in hand; but
the two are paired in Wycherley's The Country Wife, which the
American Shakespeare Theatre has revived this summer.   The
play has frequently been considered the most indecent one we
have--at least until the most recent work of Arrabal.

Over the past decade the AST has deserted its titular playwright eight times, but in so doing it has never gone back beyond early Shaw.   Now it has reached back to the Restoration
comedy of manners, and decided to celebrate the 300th anniversary of the Wycherley play's first performance.

Restoration comedy is something we hear a good deal about,
but we rarely see it actually put on the boards.   I know of only
three major Eastern productions of The Country Wife in our century: 1936, with Ruth Gordon in the title role; 1957, with Julie
Harris; and the lackluster 1965 revival at Lincoln Center.

The genesis of the genre lies in the fact that, when pressure
has built up for a long time and an outlet is at last afforded,
there is likely to be an explosion. Under the intolerant Puritan
regime of Oliver Cromwell, the theatres were kept closed for
nearly two decades--"The grey Puritan is a sick man, soul and
body sick," wrote D. H. Lawrence. With the accession in 1660
of Charles II, who liked the theatre, the lid blew off, and licentiousness swept high society. The Restoration aristocrats would
have agreed with Havelock Ellis that sex is "the central problem
of life"; for them the problem was how to get as much of it as
possible.

This attitude was directly reflected in the new sexual comedy
of manners, which flourished for nearly a half century. The
marriage bond was not taken very seriously, and we got a steady
parade of adulterers, cuckolds, jealous husbands, fops, hypocritical ladies, and all manner of intrigue. A contributing factor
was the emergence for the first time of professional actresses--
to replace the young boys who had traditionally played female
roles. Thus these comedies are filled with colorful and clever
scheming women, originally portrayed by players whose morals
were often as loose in real life as on the stage.

Curiously, though, the five foremost practitioners of the
genre were far from prolific. Etherege wrote only three plays;
Wycherley, four; Vanbrugh (also renowned as an architect), three
and a half; Congreve (the most accomplished of the group), five;
and Farquhar, seven and a half. This corpus laid the foundation
and set the standard for the two supreme masterpieces of the
genre: Sheridan's The School for Scandal, a century later; and
Wilde's The Importance of Being Earnest, two centuries later.

The playing of Restoration comedy demands, above all,
style--group style. And this is something American companies
generally lack. For the current Country Wife, the AST imported the British director David Giles, best known here for having
directed the bulk of the Forsyte Saga television series. Giles
has been surprisingly effective in eliciting a creditable ensemble
performance on this side of the Atlantic. The result is a highly
entertaining show, even if it betrays some unevenness and sags
a little toward the end (the text itself sags here and there, too).
It would be unfair to demand the sustained glitter that a top
British troupe could bring to the task, and one can be grateful
for a company that comes as close as this one.

Giles faced another problem, arising from the fact that Restoration dramaturgy characteristically indulged in lavish scenery
and frequent switch of locale. The Country Wife has 12 scenes,
which shift among five different locations. If there were five
full-stage sets, it would require considerable time to change
from one to another. Yet it seemed essential to have recognizable and furnished acting areas.

The solution that designer Ed Wittstein settled on was to construct a huge fixed set made up of portions of the required locales. In the rear we see tall diagonal cutouts representing the facades of London houses. To the left we have Horner's lodging, assumed to be on the second story since it is reached by a stairwell opening up through the stage floor. It is a lived-in space, decked out with a fireplace on whose mantle sit an hourglass, an astrolabe and a drinking-mug. There are a chandelier, a terrestrial globe on a stand, a mirror, antlers on the wall, and, most appropriately, a folding screen depicting the nude mythological Leda about to be impregnated by Zeus-as-swan. Doors lead offstage to other rooms, including the hyperactive bedroom.

The middle of the stage, with fish and book wagons rolled in, becomes the New Exchange, a fashionable center of commerce; and, with the wagons withdrawn, it serves as the colonnaded piazza of Covent Garden. At the right we have Pinchwife's stylish country-house drawing-room, and a flight of stairs leading up to a bedchamber containing a large canopied bed.

With the help of Marc B. Weiss's lighting, our attention can be shifted from place to place quickly, and the play's momentum can go forward unimpeded. Aside from the solo verse Prologue and Epilogue, here omitted, the five acts of the text seem intact, and the show has a running-time of two hours and three-quarters.

In opting for this solution, however, Giles was faced with a pronounced disadvantage, which he has not been able to overcome. The individual scenes are--to use Macbeth's words, which will be spoken on this stage later in the season--"cabined, cribbed, confined, bound in." This is particularly unfortunate, because the play often requires a large number of characters to be on stage at the same time. Thus the players are denied the lebensraum that should ideally be available to them, and they often cannot help getting in each other's way.

The premise of The Country Wife is Dr. Quack's spreading around London the report that Horner, as a result of unbridled whoring in France, contracted venereal disease and was castrated by the French physician treating him. Thus Horner, horny as ever, can easily cuckold unsuspecting husbands who believe him capable only of platonic friendships. (The device of the phoney impotent comes from the ancient Roman Eunuchus by Terence, who in turn took it from a lost Greek original by Menander.)

Philip Kerr, with long-flowing locks and rich red garb, looks the proper--or, rather, improper--libertine. Wycherley made his Horner an allegro con brio role. Kerr plays it allegro all right, but his portrayal needs more brio. Still, he speaks crisply, and handles his walking-stick as though born with one.

The play's major interest attaches to Pinchwife and his young bride Margery. Wycherley, who was educated in France, modeled the pair on characters in Molière's School for Husbands and School for Wives; the jealous and overprotective Pinchwife corresponds to Sganarelle and Arnolphe, the outwitting Margery to Isabella and Agnès. Jack Gwillim's gray-bearded Pinchwife is all gruff and grum, but the part is a stock two-dimensional character that admits of little variety.

The triumph of this production is the Margery of Carole Shelley, making her AST debut. It is an unalloyed delight to follow her progress from an innocent country wife to a sophisticated cunt-ry mistress (Wycherley surely intended the punning title). Miss Shelley has the advantage of being British herself and knowing just how to deal with Margery's unrefined diction. How honestly she skips about on learning she has smitten a man at the theatre! What a laugh she elicits on exclaiming, "Oh jeminy!," when first introduced to the Horner she has heard about! How telling her little gasp on finally entering Horner's bedroom!

She is an absolute marvel in the play's most celebrated scene (again suggested by School for Husbands), in which she is forced by Pinchwife to write an odious letter to Horner from dictation and then manages to substitute another of opposite sentiment. Her pauses, her inflections, and her iterations of the simple expletive "so" are indescribably funny. One notices her sly smile on penning "For Mister Horner," one senses her giddy excitement on being able to write her own letter, one enjoys her unconscious tickling of her nose with the quill, one shares her gleeful success at hiding the dictated letter under Pinchwife's very wig. Miss Shelley gives an exhibition of consummate artistry.

Of the three town ladies with pretensions to virtue, the Lady Fidget of Christina Pickles comes off best, though more vocal modulation would help. As her sidekicks Mrs. Dainty Fidget and Mrs. Squeamish, Grayce Grant and Joan Pape provide their quota of amusement. Curt Dawson and Ronald Frazier (who likes to smoke a long clay pipe) are a trifle bland as Harcourt and Dorilant, two gallants who envy Horner's success. Rex Everhart, as Sir Jasper, is foolish enough but lacks class, and should be told that the game is blindman's-buff, not blindman's-bluff. David Rounds, with beauty spots on his right chin and left cheek, has great fun with the role of Sparkish, a fop (who has a counterpart in most Restoration comedies), wielding a lorgnon and indulging in an affected speech that suggests a male Edith Evans. These characters and all the others benefit from Jane Greenwood's gorgeous period costumes.

The more than decent production of a more than indecent play should prick the titillation of everybawdy.

"Macbeth" Intrigues the Eye, Assaults the Ear
(by Caldwell Titcomb, Harvard Crimson, July 13, 1973)

Let me confess at once that, of all plays in world literature, Macbeth is the one that enthralls me most. I do not claim it is the greatest play--or even Shakespeare's greatest play. After all, the only source is the posthumous First Folio edition, which presents difficult textual problems and is several stages removed from the dramatist's original script. On the one hand, it certainly contains some passages that were foreign interpolations; on the other, it possibly lacks one or two scenes that the Bard originally included. As it stands, it is only about half the length of Hamlet; and The Comedy of Errors is the only shorter work in the canon.

Despite the imperfect state in which the play has come to us, Macbeth surmounts all obstacles and has the power to grip you like no other. I don't mean just its ability to engage the mind; the play has an almost corporeal existence, and can seize you by the throat and wring you out.

One example of the work's appeal came in May of 1849, when on the same evening in New York City there were three simultaneous productions, starring three eminent Macbeths of the time--William Charles Macready, Thomas Hamblin, and Edwin Forrest. These performances led to what has become known as the Astor Place Riot--the worst fracas in theatrical history, besides which even the celebrated free-for-all in Paris at the premiere of Stravinsky's Rite of Spring seems pale. At the final tally in New York, 31 persons were killed and more than 150 injured. Such is the incredible power of Macbeth. Even in an age with less belief in witches than obtained in the Jacobean era, perhaps we must ascribe some of the work's power to the very supernatural that this play invokes to a larger extent than does any other in Shakespeare's output.

And now for the third time the American Shakespeare Theatre has essayed this masterwork. In 1961 Pat Hingle was woefully miscast in the title role. Six years ago John Colicos was an impressive Macbeth, but poorly supported. For me the current go-around, staged by the AST's artistic director, Michael Kahn, proved frustrating.

The new production is fascinating in concept. It is engrossing to look at, both in its shifting settings and in much of its bits of business. But while it intrigues the eye, it assaults the ear. What a shame that all the effort that went into the technical aspects is so severely scotched by the vocal ineptness of its main players!

For a drama so intentionally full of ambiguities, unusual latitude is afforded a director. Although the historical events on which the work is based lay in the 11th century, Kahn has

quite legitimately placed his characters in the time of James I.
In choosing a tale from Scottish history, Shakespeare was paying
tribute to King James, himself a Scotsman; and in giving such
a major role to the supernatural, he was honoring not only a
king deeply interested in witchcraft but one who has himself recently written a treatise entitled Daemonologie.

Kahn has further conceived the three witches--or "weird
sisters," as they are repeatedly called--as not only having their
own spooky lairs, but also as permeating regular society. Thus
they are garbed as wives of members of the court, and are
listed as Lady Angus, Lady Caithness, and an unspecified dowager. They often hover on the sidelines, and even take over the
small role assigned to Lady Macbeth's servant. It is only in
their incantatory privacy that they become obviously witchlike by
donning half-masks. (Kahn of course omits the spurious interpolations involving Hecate, the patroness of witches; less commendably, he has done a little further cutting, though the production has a running-time of only two and a third hours.)

But if Kahn emphasizes the ubiquity of the clairvoyant
witches, he has also underlined the Christian milieu in which
his characters live. In fact he has framed his production with
a mimed prologue and epilogue, both laid in church. Accompanied by the ringing of bells and the chanting of plainsong, the
show opens with King Duncan receiving communion and ends with
his son Malcolm being crowned. The officiating priest, crosier
in hand, also functions as the Old Man who talks with Ross, and
later as the Messenger who urges Lady Macduff to flee with her
children.

Furthermore, the characters frequently cross themselves.
And much is made of a crucifix from time to time; even one of
the witches wears a pectoral cross. When Macbeth sits on his
ill-gained throne and exclaims, "To be thus is nothing," he rips
the cross from his chest and throws it to the floor, whence, in
a neatly ironic touch, it is shortly picked up and handed back to
him by the First Murderer.

The costumes, by Jane Greenwood, are prevailingly black,
with white or gray trimming. The exceptions are good King
Duncan, who wears the white of purity, and, similarly, Malcolm
at his eventual coronation. After the murder of Duncan, Macbeth and his wife, in their hypocritically assumed purity, are
the next appearance of white, to be followed by their blood-red
robes in the daytime.

The raked stage is dominated by a pair of 20-foot-high steel
panels, each with a portal that can be open or shut. The insides
of the panels are serrated, so they can close together as tightly
as the vise of Destiny grips its victims. Sets of steel stairs
roll in and out. When the panels are separated, we see in back
a drop with a huge translucent circular screen, on which mobile

projections are thrown from the rear.

The settings, fashioned by Douglas Schmidt, and skilfully lit by Marc Weiss, are decidedly modern or futuristic. And electronic incidental music and odd sound effects have been devised by Pril Smiley. One might surmise that the result would be a mishmash. But the idea of putting 11th-century people dressed in 17th-century garb in 20th-century environments is perfectly viable. One of the play's major themes is the wrenching of things out of their accustomed habitats, the appearance of people in "borrowed robes," the distortion of time. And the text is full of references to strange sounds ("every noise appals," Macbeth complains).

There is a fusing of the steel of modern architecture with the armor of medieval soldiers. Even the terrible knocking at the gate is not the usual pounding on wood but instead a clanking on metal. This is a cool, gray world. The huge portraits of Duncan and later of Macbeth and his wife, which are dropped down from the grid, are not colored oils; they are stark black-and-white photographs. Touches of color in this production are rare, and thus all the more striking.

When the witches await Macbeth's first visit, the circular screen shows a sort of magnified and pulsating green organism. At "A drum! A drum! Macbeth doth come," we hear--indeed we feel--the pounding of heartbeats; but the heart, significantly, is afflicted with arrhythmia. In the scene where Ross calls attention to the solar eclipse, the circle becomes a view of the period of totality with its brightly flaming corona. When Banquo is murdered and Fleance escapes, the circle becomes a blood-red target with a bull's-eye of blue, the color of heavenly innocence.

Especially effective is Macbeth's last encounter with the witches. A green-lit trap in the stage is the cauldron in which they make their unholy brew. Simultaneously the vertical circle functions as a top view of the cauldron, changing colors constantly like a kaleidoscope. When "a baboon's blood" is added and Macbeth drinks of the brew--a fine idea--the circle turns red. Then superimposed come the three apparitions, followed by the series of eight kings as a pinwheel. It's a show of virtuosity, but it works.

Alas, when we come to the two main players, there isn't a hint of virtuosity. If the AST wanted to import someone to play just the single role of Macbeth this summer, why pick Fritz Weaver? Fifteen years ago Weaver attempted Hamlet here, without much success. He hasn't improved in the interim.

Macbeth happens to be a great military general who speaks consistently the greatest poetry of any character in the canon. In real life we don't often find military, compositional and

oratorical genius combined in one man--though we had a recent
example, starting with the same three letters, in Douglas Mac-
Arthur (the comparison shouldn't be pushed any further, needless
to say). Macbeth must start off as an admirable person, sink
into murder after murder, and bounce back somewhat at the end,
winning our pity as a tragic hero despite his crimes. Not easy,
but it can be done.

Weaver gives us a Macbeth that fails to engage interest; we just don't care a rap about the guy. Weaver has a rather unattractive voice, and doesn't use well what he has. He
fails to penetrate the sense or the rhythm of his lines. And he
has never learned how to breathe properly; so we are subjected
constantly to his whiffling, snuffling, and gasping. Here he falls
into empty ranting, there he delivers a serious line so that it
elicits a laugh. One wishes too that he didn't address his servant twice as "patch," when Shakespeare wrote "whey-face" the
second time. Wonderful word, "whey-face."

Weaver's final duel with Macduff is much too tame, particularly for those who saw Christopher Plummer's breathtaking
swordplay in Cyrano recently. At the end, he pulls out a dagger and seems about to commit suicide when he falls off a par-
apet; suicide is something no real Macbeth would entertain.

A tiny bouquet, however, for one line-reading. When Macbeth starts up the stairs to kill the king, and a bell rings, almost all editions have him say, "Hear it not, Duncan, for it is
a knell/That summons thee to heaven, or to hell." Weaver
says, "me to hell." This is an emendation I have always found
rather appealing. Aside from the internal rhyme of the contrasting pronouns, it implies that the saintly king will surely achieve
salvation and that Macbeth fully realizes the enormity of what
he is about to do. It was a pleasure to hear this reading used
on stage for a change.

Rosemary Murphy, also brought in for only one role, emphasizes the sensual side of Lady Macbeth. She enjoys wearing
a revealing gown with an open V down to the navel. She likes
physical touching; the feel of her own or Macbeth's hands running
down her skin, the tousling of Macbeth's hair with her affectionate fingers.

Vocally, however, she is not strong enough--the same fault
she showed here a decade ago when trying the not unsimilar part
of Goneril in King Lear. In talking of the murder plot, when
Macbeth asks, "If we should fail?," her reply--"We fail?"--
lacks the forceful scorn, the reassuring incredulity needed to
prop his weakening resolve. A sensual Lady Macbeth is perfectly valid, but the role requires a decided streak of masculin-
ity, such as captured so imposingly in the portrayals of Dame
Judith Anderson, Mrs. Tore Segelcke, and Siobhan McKenna.

When she comes from her bedchamber, goes through her
sleep-walking scene and returns to bed, it is not clear why Miss
Murphy enters from the right and exits to the left. Her performance will probably improve as the weeks pass, for at the
critics' opening she was not yet even secure in her lines.

Miss Murphy does have one marvelous piece of business in
her "unsex me here" soliloquy. When she summons "thick
night" and the "smoke of hell," she grabs the pointed crucifix
hanging around her neck and spits on it. At the words "my keen
knife" she inverts the cross, turning it into a lethal dagger.
This is an electrifying moment, altogether fitting for a play in
which "fair is foul" and everything is topsy-turvy.

Jack Gwillim is a kindly, virtuous King Duncan; and it is a
felicitous touch to have him embrace Macbeth before retiring to
his final sleep. Kurt Garfield's bleeding Captain sounds more
Jewish than Scottish, Theodore Sorel's Angus is poorly spoken
too, and Richard Backus' Donalbain is weak. Jeanne Bartlett
is adequate as the ill-fated Lady Macduff, and William Larsen's
old Siward is a decided asset. Macduff's son (Glenn Zachar) is
far too old; so is Fleance (Keith McDermott), who seems to be
assisted in his escape by the mysterious Third Murderer engaged to kill him (is a double agent at work here?).

Even Lee Richardson, who was so fine a Ross years ago in
a Boston production and who has played the title role at Yale
(would he were doing it here!), strikes one as curiously uninvolved. His appearances at the banquet as a ghost, however,
are cleverly managed.

Rex Everhart is splendid in his one comic cameo as the
drunken Porter. Coleridge thought this scene spurious, but it
is genuine Shakespeare and inspired dramaturgy. After murdering Duncan, Macbeth hears the chilling pounding at the gate and
has second thoughts: "Wake Duncan with thy knocking! I would
thou couldst!" How follow such a climactic moment? Shakespeare's solution was perfect. The only comparable spot I can
think of occurs in the finale of Beethoven's Ninth Symphony,
when the full chorus climaxes thrillingly with words about "standing before God," and is followed by the ludicrously syncopated
sounds of a distant street-march.

It is what Bernard Shaw called Shakespeare's "word music"
that is so lacking generally in this Macbeth, though it is there
in unsurpassed abundance in the text. The only scene placed in
England, which comes well towards the end, is the single instance where its three main participants show a full feeling for
the melody and rhythm of their lines as well as the sense.
Praise, then, for Michael Levin's Macduff, Alvah Stanley's Ross,
and, above all, Philip Kerr's Malcolm. In this colloquy these
three men talk to each other, listen to each other, and demonstrate their musicality. But it is a long, long time before we

get to this beautifully spoken scene.

In an attempt to put the disappointing performances of the two principals out of my mind as I drove home, I tried to think of players whose work I had seen but whose performances as Macbeth and Lady Macbeth I most regretted missing. I extrapolated that I would have most admired the Macbeths of Laurence Olivier and I an Keith, and the Lady Macbeths of Florence Reed and Dame Sybil Thorndike. Well, there will be more productions of Macbeth; and, unlike Macduff in the just-cited scene, I have not lost my hopes.

TITUS, Tom Warren; (2) Theater critic; (3) b. Corry, Pa., May 26, 1938; (4) s. Warren and Helen (Steele) T.; (5) various writing & theater courses, no formal degree; (6) m. Beth Ciciliot, July 12, 1970; (7) child--son, Timothy Warren; (8) Sports & Wire editor, Corry (Pa.) Evening Journal 1956-60; staff writer, Orange Coast (Calif.) Daily Pilot, 1963-65; drama critic, Orange Coast Daily Pilot, 1965- ; (9) Actor (22 roles) 1965-76, director (25 plays) 1968-76; managing director Irvine Community Theater 1972- ; (13) Sp4, U.S. Army, Korea & Japan, 1960-63; (15) Orange County Press Club, Irvine Community Theater board of directors; (16) Republican; (20) Author of play "Summer Lightning," produced Westminster Community Theater 1968; (21) 1608 Primrose St., Costa Mesa, Calif. 92626, Ph. 714-557-7297; (22) Orange Coast Daily Pilot, 330 W. Bay St., Costa Mesa, Calif. 92627, Ph. 714-642-4321, ext. 204; (23) Circulation: 45,000; (24) Approx. 50-75 plays and musicals.

"Forest" Excellent at Huntington
(by Tom Titus, Daily Pilot, March 18, 1975)

"Another Part of the Forest" at the Huntington Beach Playhouse is not merely the highest point thus far of the community theater season along the Orange Coast, it is an oasis in a desert of theatrical inconsequentia.

In a season when three or four local theaters have turned their backs on serious drama altogether, any good weighty play competently presented would be welcomed with open arms. But Alex Koba's outstanding production of Lillian Hellman's finely drawn picture of an avaricious Old South family is a good deal more than that--it is, perhaps, the most completely realized project yet mounted on the Huntington Beach Playhouse stage.

Seldom does one script offer so many opportunities for individual acting excellence, and seldom has a community theater cast taken such full advantage of them as does Koba's skillfully directed and painstakingly motivated performers. This despite two alterations in the cast during the last weekend of rehearsal.

Koba, who directed Miss Hellman's "The Little Foxes"--a play which contains many of the same characters as "Forest"--

a few seasons ago, uses his affinity with the material to maximum advantage.   Each character's subsurface traits are brought out effortlessly with few of the stagy mannerisms a less experienced cast might employ.

The machinations of Miss Hellman's totally self-serving members of a post-Civil War family, all but one grasping greedily for his or her own personal gain, are occasionally a bit overplotted, particularly in the final act.   But their characters are so well drawn in the Huntington Beach production that interest never really lags.

The crown jewel of the cast is Jean Koba as Lavinia, the slightly demented mother whose only desire is a humanitarian one.   In two beautiful and compelling monologues at the close of the first and second acts, Miss Koba captures the heart of her audience with a performance rich in heart-wrenching depth, to a degree rarely attained on a local stage.

Ray Scott as her husband, a self-made cotton tycoon whose wartime profiteering has made him an abomination in his part of the South, is strong and solid in his scenes of domination over the family.   Though he wavers a bit in the final act, Scott comes through with a splendidly drawn character.

As his daughter and personal favorite, Diane Borcyckowski is a smug, calculating and headstrong wench, stubbornly pursuing her unrequited love.   A newcomer to the local stage, Miss Borcyckowski displays enormous talent and understanding of her role.

Clark Burson plays the shrewd, business minded older brother with a strong sense of understated authority.   John Autry as the more impetuous, pugnacious younger brother turns in an excellent and highly realistic portrayal.

Another superior performance is given by Maureen Shrubsole as a giddy Southern belle battling rather weakly for her heritage in the face of changing times.   Peter McAllister as her brother, a war veteran whose thirst for battle remains unquenched, offers a fine picture of thinly controlled intensity.

Barbara Gibbs, who appears in one memorable scene as Autry's round heeled heart throb, gives another exceptional interpretation in a show replete with them.   Charles Peerenboom has a strong cameo as an infuriated neighbor, while Robert Liebovich and director Koba complete the cast as a pair of visiting musicians.

Joy Lobell's setting enriches the Old South air of the play, which is further advanced by Jean Koba, doing double duty as costume designer.   Director Koba's background music is well chosen, cresting at just the proper time in the play's climactic scenes.

"Another Part of the Forest" is a superb example of the heights community theater is capable of reaching when enough dedication and talent are present in one company.

"Witness" Uneven Show
(by Tom Titus, Daily Pilot, April 17, 1975)

A major problem in the mounting of a mystery play is the more than usual difficulty involved in sustaining that aura of "willing suspension of disbelief" without which such a production cannot truly succeed.

The Lido Isle Players encounter this and other obstacles, not all of which are surmountable, in their somewhat uneven production of Agatha Christie's courtroom thriller "Witness for the Prosecution." Its ending is a playgoers' treat, but getting there is not really half the fun.

The show is beset by a number of drawbacks, paramount among which are a circuitous, plodding script and the production's flagging pace, both of which make for an extended evening long before the play's sudden and startling finale.

The required simulation of British jurisprudence draws director Randy Keene and his cast into the trap of overdeliberate interpretation which, combined with Miss Christie's novelistic playwriting style, counterbalances the show's moments of crisp, piercing drama.

Nevertheless, some fine performances emerge from the Lido Isle production, the most impressive of which is Pat Gilchrist's excellent portrayal of the surprise witness of the title, the German-born wife of the defendant in a murder trial; Miss Gilchrist sustains both her character and a difficult accent in presenting her audience with a woman completely involved in her bizarre mission.

Myron Wilson, enacting the advocate for the defense, is a strong, commanding presence both in court and out, though one might wish for a more sharply defined presentation in these contrasting settings. Wilson stalks his courtroom quarry like a predator and his killing thrusts are deftly delivered.

As the murder suspect, Ron Long requires more depth and dimension to convincingly interpret the varied facets of his complex character. Long chooses to play the role on a single level, which detracts from his credibility late in the play.

Of the supporting cast, two superior performances stand out --Fred Marsh as the wily prosecuting attorney and Peg Reday as the murder victim's faithful housekeeper, portrayed with a strong Scottish accent. Also credible are Girard Brewer as the police inspector and J. D. Reichelderfer as Long's solicitor.

The balance of the Lido Isle company--including a judge
(Earl Hardage) who is obviously reading his lines, and badly--
fails to measure up to the ensemble performance required for
a serious play. The area of cue pickups presents a particular
problem.

Technically, the Lido Isle set is quite attractive, but the
theater group's lighting limitations are all too evident, especially in the advocate's chambers. Too often performers play long
scenes in the shadows in this setting.

TOBIN, Richard Lawrence; (2) Drama and Music Critic; Theatre
Arts Editor and "Counter Critic"; (3) b. Medford, Mass., Mar. 20,
1932; (4) s. John Joseph and Helen Virginia (Roebuck); (5) A.B. Harvard '53, Romance Languages and Linguistics; Graduate study in
Education at NYU, Univ. of Maine & Wagner College; (6) Single; (8)
Theatre Arts Editor and Counter Critic The Village Post, Coconut
Grove, Fla. , 1973 to present; Music and Drama Critic, Coral Gab-
les Times and The Guide, 1974 to present; (9) Community Theatres
in New Jersey, Staten Island, New York, Arlington and Belmont,
Mass.; Drama coach (and Latin and French teacher), private secon-
dary schools New York and Florida; Summer Stock: Tufts Arena
Theatre; The Barnstormers, Tamworth, N.H.; role of Dresden (ju-
venile lead) over 100 perfs. in "The Empty Handed Piper" Theatre
Manzini, Off-Broadway 1960; produced and directed "Shunned" Off-
Broadway 1960-61, "The Purple Canary" Off-Broadway 1963; Originated "Best of Off-Broadway Series" in 1967 at Studio M, Coral
Gables, Fla.; built the Upstage Theatre in Coconut Grove to house
the series of over 100 plays (producing, directing, acting) 1968-1973;
Organized current activity, Repertory Library Theatre, Inc. in 1971
as a non-profit, tax-exempt professional showcase "to present stimulating and unusual fare to the theatre-goer and challenging and rewarding roles to the professional actor." Major film roles: Savage
(lead) in "Shanty Tramp" (1967); Detective Crane (support) in "A
Taste of Blood" (1966); (13) U.S. Army (communications intelligence)
active duty 1951-52, discharged from reserve as 1st lieutenant 1963;
(15) Actors Equity Assn.; Screen Actors Guild; (16) Independent; (17)
Christian Scientist; (19) Harvard Club of NYC; (20) Plays: "The
Doorknob" (produced 1968); musical score for "Listen, Little Id"
(1962) rewritten and produced later as "Two Bit Promotion"; short
story: "A Very Special Valentine." In progress: "Follow the Bouncing Ball" (novel), "Enter, The Runts" (play), "Those Immortal Melodies" (review); (21) 5912 SW 42 Tr. , Miami, Fla. 33155, Ph. 305-
661-1761; (22) c/o Times/Guide, Coral Gables, Fla. 33134, Ph.
305-666-7981; (23) Circulation: 56,000; (24) 75 plays & musicals,
30 movies, 20 concerts, 10 critiques of other critics and reviewers.

Every Facet Is Polished in UM's "Company"
(by Lawrence Tobin, Coral Gables Times, April 19, 1975)

Since it ranks at the top of my list of favorite musicals I can maybe be forgiven if I approached the U of M production of "Company" with just a tad more apprehension than I might feel for any other student production of a highly complex and difficult show such as is this Stephen Sondheim chef d'oeuvre. Well, about the only thing I can complain about is that Sondheim is given short shrift in the program credits, appearing not at all on the cover and with credit inside only for the music. Let there be no mistake it was Sondheim's music and lyrics that earned Broadway's Tony Award for Hal Prince's production.

Bob Ankrom's excellent production now at the Ring (which I hope will play forever) cleared up a point for me: that it was, indeed, not just Hal Prince's imaginative staging and the contributions of his creative staff that evolved the spectacle I saw in New York a few seasons back. Here, working within an entirely different milieu Ankrom's admirable team has left no stone unturned, no corner unexamined in polishing every facet of this spectacle into a sparkling delight conveying every iota of wit and charm available in the brilliant vehicle.

In a local season to which the Ring has already made such stellar contributions this production outdoes even their own earlier efforts and for again much the same reasons: the ability of a talented director to draw much of his inspiration from the gifts of the performers without trying to force them into someone else's preconceived pattern. The artistic point of view here is fresh, vital and reveals perfectly everything the show has to offer while leaving the cast to display themselves to their best advantage.

Great credit must go to Dennis Burleson whose musical direction extended not only to achieving a beautifully balanced choral effect for the very difficult contrapuntal group numbers but also, and probably very wisely, to rearranging, simplifying the rhythmic background complications like those of "Another Hundred People" without detracting much from the effect. Sharing honors in the musical department must be Jim Ewing who for over a year now has been handling the orchestral baton for U of M musicals with increasing skill. What he has done this time is truly remarkable and deserves the gratitude of both the Drama and Music departments.

To appreciate Jerry Ross' choreography most, you have to have sat through as many overly busy, under-inspired dancing extravaganzas as I have to recognize the restraint with which he approached his assignment and full-filled it so admirably, moving the cast with apparent ease, grace and seeming expertise. Technically Ken Kurtz' lighting design was effective and well executed on Roberta Griffin's multi-level and well conceived set. Roberta

Baker's costumes were stylish within period, colorful and most important appeared comfortable for the energetic cast.

Ah yes, the cast! The plot involves the attempts of Robert's (Michael West's) married friends to get him to settle down, and starts with their surprise 30th birthday party for him. Given the gap between the cast's average student age and the mid-thirtiesish locale suggested, perhaps the greatest praise is due them as a whole for not constantly apologizing for their youth by aping approaching middle-age. At whatever age, West's boyish ingenuousness would bring out what slightly lecherous ladies like to term "the mother in them." More to the point, he's an actor of great magnetism and control whose gentle command of the stage frees an audience from any desire to speculate on this or any other "type" factor, appropriate or otherwise to the role. So also with Karen B. Miller, essaying the part of the worldly-wise Joanne. However few her years, Ms. Miller taps all the wryly sardonic humor and satire in the magnificent comic ballad "Ladies Who Lunch" and the blase, jaded torpor in the rest of the role.

Tiny Susan Amdur as Amy who's "Not Getting Married," manages to make the lyrics of that rapid fire tune more intelligible than they were in New York and we find now that Lois Sage's beautiful legit voice has a lower, equally effective, pop range and a matching comic talent. Valerie Klemow's characterization of Kathy, includes her modern dance interpretation of "Tick Tock," a highpoint in the second act, while Linda Young's Marta adds a sensuous and earthy dimension to Robert's retinue of lovelies.

Let's stop there with individual mentions. The title tells it more accurately. That's where the praise belongs. The whole "Company." See it!

"Equus" Is Fine Theater with Psychological Thrust
(by R. L. Tobin, Coral Gables Times, May 17, 1975)

It is unlikely that the management of the Coconut Grove Playhouse can produce the playwright on stage every night as they did at the opening of "Equus." But no matter. They have assembled a cast so finely honed in their roles that the genius that won Peter Shaffer this year's "Tony" award for "best play" on the merits of this work is sure to be there on stage every night for what deserves to be a record-breaking run.

The play revolves around the psychological exploration of the events that predisposed a seventeen year old lad to blind six horses and, by the author's admission, is loosely grounded in an actual occurence. It is well nigh impossible for your attention to be other than riveted on the action (though that word is something of a misnomer since there is little of it) from beginning to end as Brian Murray as Dysart the "shrink" probes and parries the cracks, crannies and defenses of the personality of his patient, Alan played by Richard Dunne.

Bringing with him an extensive background in British theatre, Murray is nothing short of brilliant in the central role while Dunne's performance in the perverse tour de force that is required of him makes it difficult to believe that his background is as limited as his credits indicate. The total excellence of the production is in no small measure due also to the smaller parts in which we find Miamian Alexander Panas turning in a thoroughly crafted performance as the stable owner along with Jack Davidson, a regular visitor to the Playhouse, creating a solidly believable hypocritical martinet of a father for the tormented youngster. Betty Miller's interpretation of the boy's mother is as anguished as could be borne even by a detached audience and Suzanne Lederer, Pauline Flanagan and Elsa Raven all contribute greatly to the perfect balance of Shaffer's unique work.

It is the form of the play which lends the magic to the evening. The action flows undisrupted and without structural juncture points, from narrative to dialogue, to dream to taped sessions, flashbacks and so on yet never with any confusion to the viewer nor even any feeling of sensationalism during a prolonged male and female nude sequence but rather a mood of honest involvement.

Director Paul Giovanni has successfully recaptured the aura of the Broadway and London productions with an assist from Richard Morse who's credited with "movement" which must refer to the very convincing equine behavior of Freddie Dawson, Jameson Parker, James Pirone, Duane Tucker, William Wright and Joel Colodner as "the horses" adorned in the same skeletal masks that were so effective in New York. Colodner's portrayal of the favorite horse "Nugget" and earlier the combination horse and rider is particularly praiseworthy.

Notwithstanding its name, theme, and general preoccupation with horses, this play makes some much broader statements than what I have said, so far, implies. There is a bold consideration of the unreasoning narrowness with which the confines of "normalcy" are delineated and a gently persuasive prod toward a more perceptive examination of "exceptional" behavior. I recommend it most highly. It is a late but very strong contender for the top slot of the South Florida theatre season.

TREVENS, Francine L.; (2) Dance and Drama Reviewer; (3) b. Brooklyn, N.Y., Aug. 2, 1932; (4) d. Philip and Celia (Cohen) Freedman; (5) U. Mass. '50-'52 liberal arts; Boston Univ. '52-'53 drama; (6) m. Bruce Trevens June 4, 1955; (7) children--Janine Robin, Melissa Trevens; (8) Edit. Asst. Jerome Press Publications 1952-'53, Edit. Asst. McFadden Publications, True Love Stories 1953-54; copy-

writer, director radio-TV commercials Allied Advertising 1955-59,
columnist, Danvers Herald, 1960-65; dance, drama and art critic,
Springfield Herald, 1965-'67, dance and drama critic, 1967-1974 at
Springfield Daily News, dance and drama reviewer Literary Tabloid
and Papers, Inc. 1975- ; (9) Best director award Hecht Community
House 1950; best director award U. Mass. competition 1951; director
Admirable Crichton Danvers High School Class Play 1966; director
Happy Time, Crucible, Danvers Community Theater 1968; Director
Come Blow Your Horn, Light Up the Sky, Cinderella, Puss 'N Boots,
Time of the Cuckoo, North Shore Theatrecrafters; producer Sunday
in New York, North Shore Theatrecrafters; (10) Writer/director
"Look/See" for World Affairs Council of Greater Springfield 1967,
Director Dunbar Community Center Players 1968-69, Springfield Bi-
centennial Theater task force 1975; (12) Launched theater drama class
at Converse St. School, directed project; (14) Boston Globe H. S.
Poetry Contest 1950, two directorial awards above; (15) Mem. Dra-
matists Guild; (16) Republican; (17) Athiest; (18) Mem. Smithsonian
Institution; (20) Contributed articles to: Dramatics, Young Miss,
Yankee, Bosarts, Dramatists Guild Quarterly, Valley Advocate, Hart-
ford and Springfield Magazines, Lady's Circle, Christian Science
Monitor, movie mags including Movieland Movie Stars, Modern
Screen, TV Picture Show, currently doing dinner theater article for
Guernsey's Best Plays 1974-75; playwrighting: Birth Trauma, toured
Netherlands with Profile Ensemble 1972-73, Birth Trauma televised
in Netherlands 1971; Applejuice, Joseph Jefferson Producing Company
Off-Off Broadway August, 1973; scenes selected from and printed in
the Scene/2 No One acting edition published by Baker's Plays 1974;
Best Life accepted for workshop Women's Interart Center, 1974;
Oneth of Impossible, Jewish Repertory Company Off-Off Broadway
April 1975; Shortages, Jedermann Stage, Hartford, Conn. April 1975;
(21) 6 Farmington Avenue, Longmeadow, Mass. 01106, Ph. 413-567-
7017; (22) same; (23) Variable, I free lance frequently and both regular publications are new with growing circulations; (24) 12 dance,
20 plays and musicals.

"Colette" Emotionless
(by Francine Trevens, Springfield Daily News, August 3, 1974)

All my life I had heard of Colette, a wild, willful wondrous
woman who was ahead of her time.

Thus, I went to the Berkshire Theater earlier this week prepared, with a great star such as Estelle Parsons playing the
lady, to see a great show. It was with disappointment that I
watched the show plod on from one emotionless scene to another.

The show opened with the only tune worth remembering in
this new musical version by the team of Elinor Jones, Harvey
Schmidt and Tom Jones.

"Earthly Paradise," which runs rather like a theme through
the tediousness of the proceedings, is an immensely singable
tune. And so much--or little--for the songs in this production.

As for the script, a collage of actual Colette writings and dramatizations of great moments in her life, there was a pretentiousness and a lack of passion that was saddening.

The only hint of feeling was between Ms. Parsons and her stage mother, Mildred Dunnock. Aside from that, there seemed to be only pretensions and pretending.

Ms. Parsons was at her best when she recited the actual lines of Colette, with a cool precise diction and temper.

Ms. Dunnock's first half dozen lines were swallowed in the wings. When her projection finally reached my fourth row seat, I found her also passionless but intelligent.

Sally Kirkland was the most able of the six person cast to portray a series of differentiated characters.

The most memorable part of the play was almost a trick--it represented a pantomime in which Colette was presumably involved as she shed husband one for two. In it, she unshed one breast, which looked like a startled animal glaring out at the world in its sudden supposedly unexpected, nudity. There was more life and amazement in that moment than in the entire play.

The script seemed not so much written as pasted together from unrelated fragments that did not build to any final moment.

"There is no virtue in happiness" quotes Ms. Parsons.

It is Colette talking.

There is also no virtue in taking a vital, vibrant woman and depicting her rather like every woman; dejected about marriage but eager to be in love, thrilled with her child but needing more, bored by domesticity, tired by travel, happy in the presence of male friends.

What happened to the uniqueness that was Colette? Was it lost in a dozen "look, look, look"'s? For thus the show opened and closed, coming full circle, from her mother showing her the wonders of life to her showing them to others.

But it is just this wonder, this open-eyed awareness, this life-loving vitality which is missing from the characterization.

"Look," and you see nothing new. Sadly sad.

Drama and Dance
(by Francine L. Trevens, Literary Tabloid, February 1975)

America, in the last few years, has had a massive awakening

to the wonders of dance--ballet, classic, modern, ethnic, inter-
pretive--you name it, some company is performing it to multi-
tudinous crowds.

In January, just in the city of New York, there were about
a dozen dance events, some that stayed the month or longer,
others that played short runs, as part of tours.

Eliot Feld's relatively young company was dancing at the
Public Theater, Charles Weidman was presenting a two act ballet to Bach at 29th Street and the Murray Louis Dance Company
held sway at N. Y. U. Auditorium, all early in the month. At
mid-month, the Pearl Lang Dance Company presented "The Possessed" a dance version of "The Dybbuk" at the 92nd Street Y,
the New York Ballet switched from "The Nutcracker" to its diversified program at Lincoln Center; a special event, "Nureyev
and Friends" held court at the vast Uris Theater, the American
Ballet Theater, celebrating its 35th anniversary presided at lavish old City Center with Mikhail Baryshnikov, six months new
to this country, gathering eager spectators, etc. Many of these
events planned tours.

There was a time when dance in America was attended by
only two types of people: those smothered in furs and diamonds
who came as much to be seen as to see, and the young, horn-
rimmed glasses and shiny-seated trousers type, who came to
see and comment critically on what was seen.

Now "everybody's doing it" or, more appropriately, watching it being done.

What has attracted all these people? A love of music? A
need to escape the pressures of our world? A new-found sense
of joy in the free movement of the body? Or the birth of the
dance superstars?

At the Uris, young and old, middle class and low brow, the
cultured effete and the gum-chewing motorcyclist, the gowned
and the bluejeaned were all in awed attendance at the biggest
superstar of dance since Nijinsky: Rudolf Nureyev.

"Look at all the people he's brought to dance, people who've
never been before," exulted Lisa Bradley of the Hartford Ballet
Company, one of Nureyev's dancing partners.

Nureyev is one paramount reason so many new people have
come to the dance--his star quality has captured their imaginations, his virility appeals even to lovers of sports.

Of course, Nureyev has not come in alone. The entire
thrust of regional dance companies, college dance organizations,
TV filming of dance, etc. cannot be laid at his talented feet.
But he certainly can take his bows for creating electric excite-

ment among those who never dreamed dance could be so dynamic. Once having seen him, many have found dance fascinating with or without this superstar.

The political overtones of another dancer having left the Kirov Ballet for our shores has also brought throngs to the American Ballet Theater to view Baryshnikov. What makes them stay, however, and return, is the American dancer and the diversified repertoire which shows that dance can talk in many languages to many people simultaneously.

In "Nureyev and Friends" the Tartar set himself a spectacular task, dancing four ballets at each performance, seven times a week for five weeks, December 16 to January 25. He also hoped to negotiate a country-wide tour of the event.

Dancing four numbers at each performance necessitated Nureyev to pace himself. As a result, the opening presentation of "Apollo" was less dynamic than it has been when danced by Jacques d'Amboise. Nureyev had been good, very good, but there'd been little of the electricity he generally generated.

In the second work, the pas de deux from "Flower Festival in Genzano," an old romantic work, the air was instantly charged, the audience electrified. Merle Park and Nureyev were scintillating together.

In Paul Taylor's "Aureole" Nureyev took the smaller male role and gave Nicholas Gunn the major one.

Gunn rose to the occasion brilliantly and both men received thunderous ovations of applause, along with the company of fine ballerinas, chiefly New York's own Carolyn Adams.

The final number was the dramatic "The Moor's Pavane" choreographed by Jose Limon and danced by Nureyev in the title role with Louis Falco, Merle Park and Lisa Bradley.

This work, based on "Othello" requires great dramatic skill and stamina, as well as supreme technique. All four dancers are constantly on stage, weaving and interweaving formalized patterns and relationships with each other.

It was magnificently rendered by them all, with bodies and faces minutely expressive of the varying demands of mood and emotions.

"Rudy worked hard to make us all the best we could be. He knew what he wanted and worked with us to get it," Miss Bradley said when complimented on her fine portrayal as the Moor's wife. She also spoke highly of John Taras who staged the entire spectacular evening.

Should "Nureyev and Friends" tour to a city near you, leap at the opportunity to see it. It is a potpourri of fine dances, expertly executed.

One reason Nureyev chose to work in the West was that he wanted to break from a strictly classical repertoire, to learn and develop through newer works. He dances often because he believes he improves the more he performs--much as an athlete feels about keeping in shape.

Inevitably, being in New York at the same time as Mikhail Baryshnikov the two friends met and dined together. Both had been mildly annoyed by the media's attempt to create a rivalry between them.

The crowds at City Center to see Baryshnikov were almost as motley as those at the Nureyev performance. Here, however, the recent Kirov ballet dancer was a member of a distinguished company and danced only one ballet at each performance.

In Dauberval's comic "La Fille Mal Gardée," which had been first presented in 1789, he danced the young lover with youthful vigor, innocence and charm. He was flighty, flirtatious, frivolous and fanciful.

The ballet however, belonged to Gelsey Kirkland as Lise. Surely she can't be merely human--she is too marvelous! This American trained ballerina who was first brought to our notice while with the New York City Ballet, is now a consummate artist.

On the same program was "Les Patineurs," which was first unveiled by Sadler's Wells in 1937. Karena Brock and Fernando Bujones were the outstanding principal dancers in this charming work.

Despite all the hullabaloo, Russian and English dancers are not necessarily any greater than our own. While the international superstar category may be saved for them, the domestic star is nevertheless proficient and versatile, and quite able to win bravos, as in the case of many of the dancers named above.

As in all endeavors, the foreign product gets more attention than the domestic by the media and the multitudes, but the discerning are aware of the advantages of both.

Dance has come of age in America precisely because American ballets have been written and danced by American talents, in conjunction with the best of other worlds.

Theater

"God's Favorite" is the latest Neil Simon play on Broadway.

It's far from my favorite of the prolific outpourings of this perennially popular playwright whose works are done at every type of theater in the nation: college, community, regional, dinner theater, traveling show, summer stock, or what have you?

I object to this modernization of the story of Job because it brings Simon full circle back to "Star Spangled Girl," a fitful piece of fluff which strained for laughs, used stock characters and situations and forgot reality, thus making it one of his least meaningful works.

Sure, many claim comedies aren't, and shouldn't be, "meaningful." Neil Simon's gift is that his generally ARE. His people usually seem real, his situations familiar, his dialogue as natural as actual talk. In more recent years, "Gingerbread Lady" and "Sunshine Boys" showed Simon could go beyond merely realistic, humanistic comedies. His plays became clever criss-crosses between drama and comedy and were all the better for it.

Finding him retrogressing to burlesque routine and formula comedy is devastating for a true fan, who exulted when "Plaza Suite" opened, to see, in the first act, that Simon was capable of writing drama, drama in which salty tears are mixed with gutsy laughter.

No longer simple Simon, he was becoming Simonspeare: half way to Shakespeare in his perception of people, his grasp of his milieu and his prolificness.

It's a shame to see him turn and become simply Simonesque--a burlesque of himself at his worst. He's reaching too hard in "God's Favorite," and comedy doesn't work well when the mechanics show.

Broadway's favorite has done himself a dis-service. Despite a stellar production, one feels he has come full circle in a descending spiral. Let's hope the next play swoops back up. Meanwhile--we can go see productions of his older works elsewhere.

TUCKER, Glenn, San Antonio Light, Broadway at McCullough, P. O. Box 161, San Antonio, Tex. 78291, Ph. 512- 226-4271.

TUMA, Mirko; (2) Drama and Music Critic; (3) b. Prague, Czechoslovakia, Aug. 10, 1921; (4) s. Rudolf and Ella (Weissberger); (5) Charles U. , Prague, major subject: comparative literature, 1946; attended courses at Sorbonne, Paris, 1950 in comparative literature; (6) Single; (8) Assistant Drama Critic, Svobodne Slovo, largest daily newspaper, Prague, 1945-1948; Secretary of the Council of Free Czechoslovakia, Paris, 1948-51; regular contributor to Radio-Diffusion

Française, articles in Le Combat; freelance writer, Radio Free Europe and Voice of America, 1952-1960; drama and music critic and assistant editor, Freehold Transcript, 1960-69; public relations, 1969-70; drama and music critic of The News Tribune of Woodbridge, N.J., 1970 to date; (9) Associate producer of Lake Hopatcong, N.J., professional summer theater, 1957; guest lecturer on drama and music criticism, Westminster Choir College, Princeton, 1962-63; (10) board of directors, Monmouth Conservatory of Music, 1966-69; periodic lecture circuit, 1970 to date; (13) spent World War II in the concentration camp Theresienstadt, 1941-45; (14) Order of Civil merits, Czechoslovakia, 1946; (15) International Pen Club, Paris branch; Drama Desk, New York City (resigned, 1975); Outer Critics Circle; New Jersey Music Critics Circle; American Music Critics Circle; (17) Jewish; (20) Ghetto of Our Days, an essay in Czech (Prague, 1946); numerous radio plays; The Exile of Don Juan, a play in three acts--Czech, 1953; Eleventh Street, poems, Czech, 1954; Ghetto, a play translated from Czech into French by Jean-Emile Danes; Rust on the Weather Vane, poems (1963-1967); Crutches of Dusk, poems (1974); A Boastful Daisy, children's book (1971); adaptation of Mozart's Bastien and Bastienne (1967); (21) 142 Pikeview Lane, Woodbridge, N.J. 07095, Ph. 201-634-2727; (22) The News Tribune, 1 Hoover Way, Woodbridge, N.J. 07095, Ph. 201-442-0400; (23) Circulation; 58,000 (ABC); (24) Approximately 250 columns, "Critics Corner"; 40% drama reviews, 30% music reviews, 5% ballet reviews, 25% critical essays on regional theater and music development; in addition, a weekly column (critical essays) in The News Tribune's "Weekend" magazine, appearing each Friday as a cultural supplement.

Bettenbender Depicts "Faust" as Circus
(by Mirko Tuma, News Tribune, December 7, 1974)

The Rutgers-Douglass Department of Theater Arts last night inaugurated its new 400-seat experimental theater on the Douglass campus with a gigantic production of Goethe's "Faust," staged by the department's chairman, and one of the country's most formidable directors, John Bettenbender.

Because of space limitations, the review of this unorthodox version of "Faust" will be published in an equally unorthodox manner, that is in three parts.

Today I will attempt to deal with Bettenbender's overall philosophic concept of "Faust," Tuesday with the physical production and Joseph Miklojcik's and Michael Tomko's mind-boggling representational pentagram set and lighting design, and Wednesday with the stunning, tour de force performance of Joseph Hart as Faust, and Avery Brooks as Mephistopheles, as well as the rest of the cast.

I have always suspected Bettenbender of being a metaphysician--a Christian existentialist, to be exact, but until last night's "Faust," I wasn't aware of his asceticism. Indeed, the man balances his thoughts, his multiawareness, and his fantastic imagination on a tightrope between the scholasticism of St. Thomas Aquinas on the one hand, and the modern redemptive spiritual quest of Bernanos and Gabriel Marcel on the other.

His concept of "Faust," moreover, is Dantean, and is even scenically designed as such. Within the universal circus--and a circus it is, with noisemakers, clowns and flying swings--there are three levels: the lower depths or the Inferno; the plateau of Man's striving, mother Earth, sweating, laughing, idea-chasing, making wars and making love--the in-between realm, the new realistic purgatory; and then there is the Empyrean, the highest heaven where the Lord chats with the devil in charmingly human terms, while the three archangels of whom one, Gabriel, is a woman, intone the sun and the glory of the "First Day" of Creation, and Love triumphs in ultimate forgiveness and ultimate redemption.

These three closely related and constantly interweaving spheres alone represent the quintessence of Goethian pantheism which is, after all, the central philosophy and the central ethic of "Faust."

And yet, while all this subtle philosophy--and theology--are ever present in Bettenbender's, his "Faust" is fantastically exciting fun-filled, fast moving and very modern theater and total environmental theater to boot.

There are undertones of the "Sturm and Drang" ("Storm and Stress") elements, throughout the production, very close to the "Urfaust" not only in the refreshingly revitalized Gretchen-Faust love story with Gretchen being indeed a child-woman, but in the representation of Faust's impatience with academic pedantry and rigidity, his burning passion for emotional experience which, within Faust's soul, transcends the tangible despite Mephisto's attempts to turn it solely into lust.

The entire Faust-Mephistopheles relationship in Bettenbender's strangely ascetic mind seems to be revolving around the Shakespearean question: "The tempter or the tempted, who sins most?" ("Measure for Measure.")

Can you imagine? In the famous first garden scene between Faust and Gretchen, the lovers do not retire into a dainty gazebo, but fall into the trap below the earth level, the threshold of hell.

Who is Mephistopheles? Indeed not the devilish devil, but a tempter, a skeptical master cynic with awful intellectual limitations and almost infantile weaknesses. He is exactly what Goethe wanted him to be: "der Schalk" or the waggish knave, the funny, ironical rascal.

He is a bit of a conman, a pimp and a pederast who is only smart, not profound, and who loses Faust's soul not as much because of the Lord's power but because of his own dopiness, which the Lord, when making the bet with him on Faust's soul, simply anticipated.

Unlike other directors, including Reinhardt and Hilar, Bettenbender doesn't succumb to the temptation of making Mephisto the central figure. The central figure is Faust.

It is not Faust's body but his soul which has aged amidst the dusty paraphernalia representing academic knowledge--the dry, gray theories which may satisfy an intellectual removed from life, but frustrate a man thirsting for life.

Again, the Faustian quest for the meaning of universal existence, rather than for a meaningful existence narrowed to oneself, is in Bettenbender's vision, pantheistic, and, eo ipso, altruistic and redemptive.

This is the reason why Bettenbender couldn't end Part I of "Faust" with the Gretchen jail scene, but with the end of Part II., giving us the same glimpse of heaven as in the prologue.

Man travels a full circle, and the climax of Love is within the spirit.

[Part II] Rutgers "Faust" Called Mind-Boggling
(by Mirko Tuma, News Tribune, December 10, 1974)

John Bettenbender's physical production of Goethe's "Faust" which opened this past weekend at the new experimental theater on the Douglass campus, is a reflection of the director's existentialist concept which I briefly analyzed in the first part of the review Saturday.

Indeed the entire theater becomes what Bettenbender calls "abstract macrocosm," in which time turns into timelessness, types into prototypes, and ideas into philosophies.

The Faust-Mephisto duel takes place on a huge three-level platform shaped as a pentagram depicting not only various regions--the Empyrean, the Purgatoric earth, and the Inferno with 11 trap doors leading to it--but also a spectrum of consciousness, or levels of being.

The super-spheric image is a circus, and men and women are merely emotional clowns and intellectual acrobats.

Joseph Miklojcik, the theater department's brilliant technical director and a scene designer in the class of Joseph Svoboda and Jo Mielziner, has conceived a superb environmental set with the audience seated on each side of the five-star-shaped platform. Two huge synchronized screens denote the scene sequence with half-surrealistic, half-Medieval slides inscribed with ornate Gothic lettering.

The fantastic lighting, with several hundred computerized light cues, designed by Michael Tomko, and Vickie McLaughlin's magnificent costumes, which are essentially Gothic, but yet transcend any period, help to create, together with Daniel Goode's mixture of traditional sacred music and electronic sounds, an atmosphere of total theater and total fantasy, capable however, of emphasizing whatever is real and all-too human.

As I said Saturday, both the production and design are mind-boggling. It is a most unconventional and yet the most Goethean "Faust" I have ever seen, despite the amusical blankverse-prose translation by C. F. McIntyre.

Although all the scenes do not work with the same perfection, aparticularly the prologue and the epilogue in heaven, the Auerbach cellar-scene, and the Valentine death scene, the production is not only a challenge to the mind, but excellent theater filled with perpetual movement and Goethe's Olympian humor. At times the audience roars with laughter.

Bettenbender goes to the core of Goethe's genius and I feel it is the first time any director has captured Goethe's poignant judgment of egotistic hedonism which was indeed a confession and severe self-judgment. Goethe, the great Don Juan of his time, has seen essential evil and ugliness in loveless sex.

This is why Bettenbender in the Walpurgis Night goes beyond Goethe's own text by turning it into a frantic orgy of blood, mammon-worship, and filth. Mephistopheles and the Evil Spirit beat the drums of terror; the Golden Calf rises from the pit, and a young virgin is sacrificed on the grotesque altar of sodomy.

For the first time, I think, the great "poodle scene" is made clear both theatrically and philosophically.

The poodle whom Faust meets during an Easter walk, doesn't just turn into Mephistopheles behind Faust's stove, but with Mephisto himself heading a wild dog pack, grows and multiplies in front of the audience, almost tearing the bewildered Doctor Faust to pieces.

The production is sheer contemporary theatrical magic which leaves the spectator shattered--laughter or no laughter--like in a Greek tragedy.

The production of Goethe's "Faust" at Rutgers is indeed Bettenbender's greatest work to date.

Tomorrow the review of performances.

[Part III] Performances Help Make "Faust" Special
(by Mirko Tuma, News Tribune, December 17, 1974)

The performances in the Rutgers-Douglass version of Goethe's "Faust" which opened the new Experimental Theater on the Douglass campus this past weekend, are, with minor exceptions, as spectacular as Bettenbender's concept of the play and its challenging production.

Bettenbender has conceived "Faust" as an ensemble work with 21 artists portraying, altogether, 75 roles. It is presentational theater at its finest, with actors, except for the devils, witches, and apes, wearing no makeup, which emphasizes human changes coming from within, including Faust's magic rejuvenation by 50 years.

In Joseph Hart, a member of the drama department's faculty, Bettenbender has an ideal Faust, an unaffected modern man rather than an orator reciting philosophical tractates. The famous first reflection monologue sets the tone. It isn't a poetic, ponderous aria of self pity, but a concrete statement of an angry and disappointed scholar for whom acquiring knowledge has become an exercise in futility.

Hart's contemporary Faust is breath-taking in its underplayed power and sensational openness.

He is totally secure on stage, and, like the rest of the cast, totally selfless and non-indulgent.

The lyrical scenes with Gretchen have poise, elegance, and wisdom, and yet it is a wisdom marred by guilt and compromise.

Hart never deviates from portraying the total man, balancing his conscience. It is a formidable performance by a first-rate artist.

Then there is, of course, Mephistopheles played by Avery Brooks, one of the most versatile, polished, skillful, and intellectually subtle actors in America today.

His Mephistopheles is a slick, charming, mordant, and slightly sleazy skeptic; the quintessence of a devil we meet daily, especially among academicians.

His voice reminds one of Paul Robeson and Morris Carnovsky, and his physical prowess and involvement of Laurence Olivier.

From his first spectacular and jovial entrance in the "heaven prologue," and the mind-boggling "poodle" scene in which he indeed turns into a dog without a touch of makeup, to the final defeat, Brooks dominates the stage like a giant, without however violating the sacred ensemble spirit.

Frankly, I have run out of superlatives.

However, Hart and Brooks are not the only greats.

There is a young student actress, Diane Nish, the most moving and authentic Gretchen I have ever seen. Goethe conceived her as an innocent not overly bright, humble teenager, and Miss Nish quite rudimentarily and naturally portrays exactly that. There is no sophistry to her, only bewilderment, awakening passion, and childlike faith.

Her "King of Thule" and the "My Peace is Gone" monologues which are pantomimed while her voice is heard over the sound system, are a major theatrical experience, and so is her final prayer, and the incredibly moving jail scene.

Miss Nish is probably not quite aware of her potential, which makes her performance so admirably refreshing.

Laura Gardner is beautifully comical, cheap, and subtle as Gretchen's neighbor Martha, and Robert Ludera is hilariously pedantic as Faust's famulus, Wagner.

It is a joy to watch Neil Cuthbert, playing the eager student, discussing with Mephisto his future career in the academia.

There is the stunning Sheryl Lee Ralph displaying her alluring attributes in a variety of ensemble parts, including the frightening high-priestess in the Walpurgis Night.

And there is the rest of the cast having their moments of glory in a glorious production which, when repeated tomorrow, Friday, Saturday and Sunday at 8 p. m. , shouldn't be missed by anyone who has any affinity and respect for the theater.

[Part I] "Mother Courage" in Revival
(by Mirko Tuma, News Tribune, February 14, 1975)

Because of its scope, and its significance in the development of regional theater in New Jersey, last night's revival of Bertolt Brecht's "Mother Courage and Her Children," directed by Michael Kahn at the McCarter Theater, will be reviewed in two parts.

Today I shall try to discuss the philosophy of this controversial work, and tomorrow the concept and the design of Kahn's production as well as the tour de force performance of Eileen Heckart in the title role; Lee Richardson and Tom Poston in the parts of the cook and the chaplain; Maria Tucci's Kattrin; and the rest of the 40-member ensemble.

Since Ibsen no other modern playwright has been analyzed as extensively as Bertolt Brecht.

The late German marxist who saw in communism the answer to all man's ills, (but who still chose the United States for his asylum from Hilter during World War II, rather than the Soviet Union,) was indeed a dialectician extraordinaire, capable of creating a cult, particular among Western liberal intellectuals who have considered flirting with revolutionary ideas from the confortable armchairs of their literary salons.

I think that Brecht has written some fine poetry (although he is neither Rilke nor the much maligned Stefan George); one powerful adaptation with Kurt Weill's brilliant score ("The Three-penny Opera,") and one interesting play-interesting because it transcends the author's propagandist intent to condemn and al-lienate--"Mother Courage."

Any director, including Kahn, must first decide whether to play "Mother Courate" as Brecht wrote it or rather as he wished he wrote it.

It is indeed difficult to build dramatic tension in most of Brecht's plays. His characters are usually black or white; they are either prototypes of the cynical villainy of the ruling class and its spineless corrupt courtiers and flunkies, with every ut-terance bespeaking one dastardly deed or another; or they are prototypes of the oppressed and brutally exploited victims, and thus, in the didactic marxist sense of course, the paragons of proletarian virtue.

There is a difference in "Mother Courage"--a remarkable difference which, ironically enough, Brecht never intended and which as a matter of fact had horrified him.

In "Mother Courage," against the truly epic panorama of a devastating religious conflict--the 30-year-war--Brecht tried to portray a shark of sharks--a conscience-void profiteer living by the war and of the war, and even indirectly sacrificing her three children to the war.

However, Brecht's Anna Fierling, the aging itinerant peddler pushing her goods in her canteen wagon from one ravaged battle-field to another, and nicknamed Mother Courage because she once risked her life in order to salvage some loaves of bread about to mold by her sheer guts--no matter how void of altru-ism--emerges as an all-too-human and, strangely for Brecht, multidimensional symbol of simple and intuitive perseverance.

The scavenger turns into a tragic heroine, a female mixture of Good Soldier Schweik and Andrew Underschaft--essentially a character evoking empathy even if not intellectual respect.

[Part II] Revival of "Courage" Theatrical Milestone
(by Mirko Tuma, News Tribune, February 15, 1975)

In addition to being a master of detail and a most sensitive ambience creator, Michael Kahn, producer-director of McCarter Theater, is a man of total intellectual integrity.

Even when he fails in his repertory selection, or in his concept of a particular work--and in my opinion he has failed, at least partially, in his first two productions this season--his errors seem as much an act of faith as his triumphs.

Kahn's revival of Bertolt Brecht's "Mother Courage," which opened at McCarter Thursday night, is indeed such a triumph, but first of all, a triumph of honesty.

As I noted yesterday, Kahn views the ambivalence of Brecht's opus, and although he uses the Berlin Ensemble version revised by Brecht in the early 1950s and emphasizes the Verfremdung (alienation), seeking programmatic aspect of the play, he has nevertheless decided to play Brecht the poet rather than Brecht the propagandist.

Into the drabness of a senseless war triggered off by a 17th Century intra-Christian dispute about indulgences and papal supremacy--drabness symbolized by a burlap backdrop with gray-rusty colors of the scarred, blood-soaked soil of Europe transformed into one giant battlefield--Kahn presents Brecht's characters not as ideological prototypes but as human beings.

Kahn's economy of scenic architecture (helped tremendously by David Jenkins' set design, John McLain's lighting and Lawrence Casey's costumes, which almost reek with sweat) is just unique.

His sudden tableaux which give an illusion a sense of reality and the starkest reality a sense of theatrical illusion both affirm and transcend Brecht's concept of epic theater. Kahn is always making--to borrow an expression from Nietzche--a "human-all-too-human" statement. His interpretation is so much better than Brecht's play itself.

Take the third scene, when Mother Courage, in order to save herself and her remaining two children, must deny her son whose dead body she pretends not to recognize.

Brecht gives no stage directions for the ensuing curtain. But Kahn lets Eileen Heckart stylize a soundless scream of horror, and once her son's body is carried away to be thrown into the carrion pit, with one of the soldiers muttering "he has no one that knows him," she faints, dropping to the floor like a piece of warped wood.

Can there be anything else left but empathy?

Miss Heckart's Mother Courage is more than a tour de force by one of America's most gifted character actresses. It is a shared experience, an emotional concerto with Courage's mixture of awareness and a basic simplicity which make her thirst for survival a matter of sheer intuition and higher logic, serving as a solo instrument amidst the orchestral cacophony of war-ridden realities.

Although she starts in a lower key, and her singing indeed is not her forte, her emotional and yet earthy crescendo and her magnificently Brechtian style of delivering her songs like a diseuse gives originality and grandeur.

The entire ensemble--with one or two exceptions--is flawless.

Lee Richardson's cook comes perhaps closest to Brecht's vision of a victim forced by society to live by a double standard. Richardson's stage presence is as powerful as are his sense of interplay and his singing.

Tom Poston is marvelously confused as the demoralized chaplain: downtrodden and grabbing at any straw to survive and fluctuating between residues of conscience and total cynicism. A masterful black comedy characterization.

The ultimate plaudits, however, go to Maria Tucci, who plays Courage's mute daughter Kattrin, the very quintessence of Comte's positivistic belief that all human beings are born good.

Miss Tucci's performance is breath-taking, all-encompassing. You can't take your eyes off her. A first rate pantomimist, her every gesture and glance are symbols of peace or peacelessness, naive hope or frustration, bewilderment or anguish.

Her death scene, when she knowingly risks her life by beating the drums to warn the citizens of Halle of the approaching enemy onslaught, is a great, unforgettably moving moment in the theater and the climax of the production.

The only flaw, I feel, is in the second Yvette scene in which the former camp harlot is transformed into a bourgeois hausfrau. Michele Shay--a fine talent and a fine singer--is too much of a caricature in this scene with the absurdity being somewhat incongruous with Kahn's essentially sombre concept.

Philip Yankee, Miss Heckert's son is real life, plays her stage son Swiss Cheese with nice youthful straightforwardness.

As Mother Courage's older son Eiliff, Charles Sweigart shows verve and flexibility. His sabre dance has panache.

The McCarter revival of "Mother Courage"--whether one

agrees with Brecht or not--is an historic milestone in the development of New Jersey's professional theater.   No one should miss it.   The play will be performed at 8:30 p. m.   tonight, at 3 p. m.   Sunday and next weekend starting Thursday.

Bravo!

VADEBONCOEUR, Miss Joan E. ; (2) Entertainment Editor, Syracuse Herald-Journal (daily) and Herald-American (Sunday); (3) b. Syracuse, N. Y. , March 21; (4) d. of E. R. and Oral Orletta Vadeboncoeur; (5) B. A.   Sarah Lawrence College 1954, specializing in theater and allied arts; (6) Single; (8) Music Editor for Herald since 1958, entertainment since 1959; (9) worked in summer stock in various capacities from 1948 through 1953; worked on one Broadway show in 1952 (assisting the producer-writer-director-star); (10) Have guest lectured at Syracuse University, Onondaga Community College.   Used to do regular TV spot on entertainment but now do only occasional because of time schedule.   Also occasional speeches to variety of groups; (12) Member of the board of trustees of Cazenovia College since 1973; (15) Member of Theta Sigma Phi and American Women in Radio-TV, Theta Sigma Phi now called Women in Communications; (21) Owahgena Road, Cazenovia, N. Y. , Ph. OL 5-3608; (22) Clinton Square, Syracuse, N. Y. , Ph. 315-473-7773 or 7774; (23) Circulation: daily 123,000; Sunday 243,000; (24) Approximately 100 movies; 50 theater; 10 dance and 24 miscellaneous.

Gibson Creates Another Hit Play
(by Joan Vadeboncoeur, Syracuse Herald-Journal, December 21, 1974)

William Gibson's story of the Nativity contains as many diverse elements of theater as it does words in its title, "The Butterfingers Angel, Mary and Joseph, Herod the Nut and the Slaughter of 12 Hit Carols in a Pear Tree. "

Gibson's friendship and respect for artistic director Arthur Storch brought Syracuse Stage the honor of presenting the play's world premiere production which opened last night in the Experimental Theater of University Regent complex.

The eminent playwright of "Miracle Worker" and "Two for the Seesaw" retells the Nativity story in contemporary, folksy style.   One official associated with the production believes it is Gibson's way of rediscovering meaning of religion.

In truth, he does strip the tale of all pomp, making it sometimes a joyous celebration, sometimes a poignant tale with even an occasional bit of buffoonery.   But not once does it register as sacrilegious.

Through the ministrations, talents and apparent loving care of Storch and a superlative company, the play moves through the rapid shifts of mood and emerges as a moving, as well as amusing, piece of theater. And playwright Gibson re-affirms his faith in the story.

The angel of the Lord is more than a butterfingers; he's a klutz. Under stress, his nose sweats and he's chided by Mary for lacking confidence. She says, "You should have confidence; after all you're an angel."

Mary's an unlikely candidate for giving birth to Jesus. An early women's liberationist, she tells the angel, "I have other plans." But, seeing her chance for achieving something more than her fellow women, she accepts.

The older Joseph has been pursuing her, but doesn't want to be just a patsy for another man's baby. Mary has the strength that he lacks.

But his essential goodness wins her over and Mary herself discovers that the miracle of birth transcends the burdensome duties of marriage and motherhood.

It begins to be played as if it were script that must be followed. Thus a gorgeous red-haired chorus girl is assigned the role of the tree. She would be the equivalent of a Follies Bergere showgirl, complete to fur coat she resists taking off. "My bark," she insists. Also, "no" is a word that's impossible for her to say until the key scene. "It always comes out 'go ahead'," she wails.

The wise men and the three brutes are played like the Three Stooges with much bumping of heads. The children may like that, even if this reviewer prefers the comedy about getting lost and having to consult a road map for directions. It provides some nice asides for the third king played by Fred Stuthman.

Partially successful, Ben Kapen's donkey which can't carry Mary draws laughs, but their dialogue about the insufficiencies of man lacks conviction and the desired satire. Here again, the tree scores as she retorts to the cow who preferred man as an ape, that she didn't like them swinging through her branches.

The ineptness of the angel brings out one of the best lines in the play. Knowing the story, the audience laughs when the angel tells Mary and Joseph he's booked the bridal suite for them in Bethlehem. It's hilarious when they arrive at the stable and when they complain to the servant girl, she replies, "Well, it's where they keep the bridles."

Not enough praise can be accorded Faith Catlin and John Carpenter, Mary and Joseph. Miss Catlin's direct approach, stubborn strength and a naivete about love are fine. Immediately, she captures the core of Gibson's work. Yet only a step behind is Carpenter, a simple, common man whose Joseph has a shining goodness.

Steve Vinovich's angel is carefully etched, conveying the warmth as well as the humor side of his character. Kelly Wood gives the tree all that any playwright could hope for in a performer.

Missing a beat or two as Herod is Tom MacGreevy, who doubles nicely as the gangster-style courier. His Herod is a preening peacock and obviously a mental case. But MacGreevy hasn't quite put at it all together for a total character.

Much of the success of the Syracuse Stage production rests with Storch. The play could be expanded to a comedy that borders on burlesque, but that would not be totally true to the spirit Gibson instilled. It could be played successfully just a little more broadly without losing the proper flavor.

But, instead, Storch has ensured that the beauty, the simplicity and the importance of the Nativity are not lost in the search for laughs. Only the "Hark the Angels" number needs additional work for its performers tend to sing it stately, as though they were singing it in church.

Julie Arenal's musical staging still is being performed with some ragged spots by the cast. But the opening "Deck the Halls" already conveys the country hoedown that is exactly the mood for the play.

Years ago, Syracuse was a tryout town--a highly discriminting one. Last night it became one again and the audience responded with an ovation. Whether the work turns into a Broadway hit should not unduly concern Gibson. He has written a small but very worthy piece that should be placed in most theaters' repertory.

Theater Opens to "Nut Show"
(by Joan E. Vadeboncoeur, Syracuse Herald-Journal, January 24, 1976)

Lizzie Borden, President Calvin Coolidge, evangelist Aimee Semple McPherson, William Randolph Hearst and John Dillinger attended last night's opening of the Carrier Theater in the Civic Center complex.

Of course, they weren't there in person but through the courtesy, conjuring and photos of Michael Brown and his "Great American Nut Show," a diverting one-man show about those five and seven others termed by Brown "marvelous misfits."

The show had been billed as irreverent satire--a misnomer. Brown is a storyteller who carefully researches his subjects, then culls the humor--ironic and natural--for his piece. He is also, to use Frank Sinatra's expression, a saloon singer. His show is ideal for the intimate, 463-seat Carrier Theater.

"Nut's" opening is deceptive, but clever. The title number, performed in contemporary style by an outlandishly dressed chorus, ends as Brown dashes off the screen and onto the stage. It is the last contemporary note of the evening until he disappears in precisely the same manner, but in reverse.

From then on it was Aimee, the evangelist, who preached joy and proceeded to take in a five-week holiday with a married man. Her carefully staged return allegedly made over miles of parched desert after escaping kidnapers, struck no one as peculiar, not even when she failed to ask for water.

If Aimee was vitality personified, President Coolidge was inertia itself. Brown's sendup song "Hooray for Coolidge" is a delightful deadpan in delivery and lyrics crusading anthem, and far superior to Aimee's.

Brown strikes the best musical notes with his poignant ballad "Seventeen Kinds of Solitaire," which capsulizes the life of wealthy recluse Ella Wendel, and "Never Alone," a sad saga melded to Siamese twins Chang and Eng.

Much in the vein of his "Lizzie Borden" hit from "New Faces of '52," which intones "You can't chop your mama up in Massachusetts," is his sprightly takeoff on Ruth Snyder, who, bored with husband and in love with another man, did away with spouse. It's not as witty as "Lizzie," but it's fun.

The closest Brown comes to satire is in the middle of his Emperor Norton the First tale. Norton, a San Franciscan, proclaimed himself ruler of the U.S. and protector of Mexico. He gave up the latter as too difficult yet managed sufficient respect that theater audiences rose from their seats on his arrival.

Two dogs whom he hated trailed him daily. Says Brown, "They knew royalty when they saw it." Other than a few like that, his jabs are gentle. He respects his subjects too much for a variety of reasons, to nail them to the wall.

Probably the least known is Starr Faithfull, a woman whose greatest claim to fame is having been the subject of two novels, one of them John O'Hara's "Butterfield Eight." His fascination with this beauty inspired a song set to her last letter. His music makes it seem more important than it really was.

Brown's real milieu is the supper club but his show works well in Carrier Theater. However, standing at a lectern is stilted. He would maintain his intimacy better had he chosen to stay at the piano or sit on the stool with the lectern beside him for referral.

The star congratulated officials and the public on the facility,

which he said was the best he'd performed in during 18,000
miles of travel.

Brief introductory remarks were made by County Executive
John H. Mulroy, Dr. Joseph Golden, executive director of the
Cultural Resources Council which manages the center, and Sheil-
ah Gibons, president of the CRC board.

Front row theatergoers included Melvin C. Holm, chairman
of the board and chief executive officer of Carrier Corp., which
made a major grant to the theater and for which the playhouse
is named.

A champagne reception followed.

VANNOY, Cheryl; (2) Tempo Editor, fine arts, entertainment; (3)
b. McAllen, Tx., June 5, 1953; (4) d. Thomas R. and Eloise (Smith)
Vannoy; (5) B.F.A., Southern Methodist U., 1974, major subj.:
journalism; (6) Single; (8) Editor, SMU Rotunda 1973-74. Joined
San Angelo Standard-Times in 1975; (10) Served as ex-officio mem-
ber of the San Angelo Civic Theatre Board, San Angelo Symphony
Board, San Angelo Entertainment Association Board. Chairman of
Fiesta Del Concho Dallas Theater Center performances, 1976; (11)
Society of Professional Journalists, Sigma Delta Chi, San Angelo
Press Club; Delta Gamma; Mortar Board; Who's Who in Colleges
and Universities; (21) 2101 W. Beauregard, Apt. C., San Angelo,
Tx. 76901, Ph. 915-949-8784; (22) 34 W. Harris, San Angelo, Tx.
76901, Ph. 915-653-1221, ext. 216; (23) 50,000 combined San Angelo
Standard and San Angelo Times and the Sunday Standard-Times; (24)
25 plays and musicals, 25 motion pictures, 6 musical concerts, five
general entertainment and miscellaneous.

"Fantasticks": ASU Play Really Fantastic
(by Cheryl Vannoy, San Angelo Times, August 7, 1975)

"Try To Remember" when a stage production swept the audience off its feet. "The Fantasticks," with a lush romantic
score and effective staging will.

The Tom Jones and Harvey Schmidt musical opened last
night at the Angelo State University Center Theatre. The first
production of the "Arts at ASU" program will play in a special
dinner theater format through Aug. 14.

The play is based on Edmund Rostand's little known work,
"Les Romanesques." It is the simple story of a boy and girl in
love. Meddling mothers act like enemies but are really hoping
for their children to wed. The play does not follow the clear-
cut happy ending until some trials and tribulations between the
lovers have occurred.

The play is constructed on a unique format, with props and

curtains changing in the full view of the audience. Mute Jan
Kearley is an excellent artist, keeping in the background, yet
providing the much needed props at the exact moment. She has
a mime scene where she is able to shine, even without using
words.

Bill Mobley is a strong character as Matt, with a beautiful,
strong voice during his musical numbers, and an easy-going
stage presence during his straight acting.

Debi Gibbs is a sweet, innocent Luisa. She fulfills the
stereotype of a sixteen-year-old "in love." El Gallo, played
by Randy Taylor, is a sizable figure on the stage, with a good
scene in the sword duel with Matt.

Mothers Ms. Hucklebee and Ms. Bellomy add to the light-
hearted entertainment with their crackling voices and little
"bouts." Jeanne Charlesworth and Charlotte Smith portray the
two gardening mothers with a special style, complete with choreography in "Never Say 'No'."

Gary Kingsolver and Michael McNabb are good additions to
the cast in their supporting roles as the aging actor and the
some-times Indian. Dying scenes are their specialty.

While "Try to Remember" is probably the best known from
the musical selections, other memorable tunes are "Soon It's
Gonna Rain" and "They Were You." Other musical selections
of note are "It Depends on What You Pay" and "Metaphor."

Orchestration for the production, under the direction of Dr.
Charles Robison, provides a lively background for the action on
stage. Suzanne Grubb assisted on the piano, Lee Robison on
celeste, Susan King on bass and John Rogers on percussion.

Lighting in the right corner of the stage was a little dim,
and in the first scene, Ms. Bellomy was hard to make out from
the audience. Luckily, most of the action was forward of the
dark spot.

The dinner theater format was well planned by community
representative for the Fine Arts, Elsa Carsner. Seating was
well-marked and the student assistants acting as waiters and
waitresses were most accommodating to the crowd. A word of
caution to smokers is to prepare for the request for no smoking
in the theater.

"Lady Liberty" Shines Bright
(by Cheryl Vannoy, San Angelo Standard, June 21, 1976)

"Lady Liberty" shines a bright patriotic torch in Fiesta del
Concho's heritage celebration.

Within the short space of an hour and a half, the Dallas Theater Center Mime Troupe presents ingeneous, humorous vignettes of Americana while still reminding the audience of more somber origins of the nation.

The production opened Sunday night to a disappointingly small crowd of 200 in Sarah Bernhardt Theater. The final performance will be at 9 p. m. tonight.

The show begins appropriately with a "Tea for Two" shuffle for two bumbling British guards, the victims of the Boston Tea Party.

Wacky, fast-paced sketches continue with Paul Revere's Ride, this time originating from the dentist's chair. Only through the determined efforts of "charming" Mrs. Murray in delaying a Redcoat is Revere's ride a success. Finally, "Super Bets" comes through with the stars and stripes, completing the fables.

The light moments prepare the audience for the balance of the program, consisting of mime with narration, slides and jazzy music. The performers weave the stories through their fluid movements, a careful mixture of clowning, dance and drama.

The complexion of the first half of the show remains light, as two young boys float down the river, baiting their hooks, puffing on a pipe and hooking a fish. "Man does fly!" as the troupe forms a sputtering airplane at takeoff.

The mime troupe convinces the total skeptic that their artform is fun, meaningful and sophisticated. They act as a unified whole, with each actor a standout in his or her own right.

San Angelo will be glad to see former ASU'er Fred Moore on stage again.

The narration of the second act provides a stirring backdrop to the performance, as the founding of the nation is explored.

An Indian shoots his prey with an invisible arrow, later sharing his kill with early settlers. The show doesn't gloss over the darker sides of the nation, as slavery, planatation life and protest were portrayed.

The whole evening leaves the audience with a great upsurge, as the movement west completes the performance.

Don't miss "Lady Liberty."

VAUGHAN, Peter, Minneapolis Star, 425 Portland Ave. , Minneapolis, Minn. 55488.

WALLACH, Allan Henry; (2) Theater Critic; (3) b. New York, N.Y.,
Oct. 23, 1927; (4) s. Julius and Beatrice Wallach (Markowitz); (5)
B.A. Syracuse U., major subj.: journalism and political science,
1951; (6) m. Shirley Meyrowitz, Nov. 26, 1953; (7) children--Jona-
than Peter, Mark David, Paul Daniel; (8) Reporter, Patchogue (N.Y.)
Advance, 1953-54, Reporter and copy editor, New Haven (Conn.)
Register, 1954-56, Reporter, Newsday, 1956-57, Copy Editor, News-
day, 1958-61, Assistant Night City Editor, Newsday, 1961-63, News
Feature Editor, Newsday, 1963-64, Entertainment Editor, Newsday,
1964-71, Drama Critic, Newsday, 1972- ; (13) Aircraft Electronics
Technician Mate 2, U.S. Navy, 1946-47; (16) Democrat; (17) Jewish;
(19) New York Drama Critics Circle, New Theater Forum, Deadline
Club, Sigma Delta Chi; (21) 64 Long St., Huntington Station, N.Y.
11746, Ph. 516-HA 1-1588; (22) Newsday, 550 Stewart Ave., Garden
City, N.Y. 11530, Ph. 516-294-3197; (23) Circulation: 450,923; (24)
150 plays and musicals.

<u>Showcase for An Actor</u>
(by Allan Wallach, Newsday, October 7, 1974)

In the seven years since Roy Dotrice first performed "Brief
Lives" in London and New York, it has become the standard
against which all other one-man shows are measured. Last
night, he returned to Broadway to show why.

Dotrice's performance as John Aubrey, the 17th-Century biographer, antiquary and man of letters, is an extraordinary
amalgam of the actor's skills. At the Booth Theater, he is
creating a portrait of a solitary old man with a lifetime of memories for company that is colored by humanity, warmth, humor,
wit and--despite the great age of his subject--the savor of life.
It is truly a one-man show for all seasons.

He emerges from sleep, his face waxen and his beard dingy-
white, to shuffle through lodgings of incredible clutter (Julia
Trevelyan Oman's canny setting), a labyrinth of tables, dressers,
piles of dusty papers, stuffed animals, carvings, game hanging
beside an oven, a suit of armor, a glowing fireplace. He turns
the act of getting dressed into an acrobat's trick, and the task
of boiling milk over a burning log into a clown's routine. He
speaks in a high-pitched voice encrusted with age, cackling with
delight over a treasured memory, pausing to direct a glare of
mock reproof at someone in the audience who happened to laugh
too quickly.

There is never a sense that this is a young man playing a
72-year-old--Aubrey's age at his death in 1697--but rather that
it is Aubrey himself sharing his reminiscences with us.

Patrick Garland, who adapted and directed "Brief Lives,"
has culled the selections shrewdly from Aubrey's "Lives of Eminent Men" (better known as "Brief Lives") and other writings.
The selections, seamlessly joined, range from stories about
the great men Aubrey had known or known about--Shakespeare,

Sir Walter Raleigh, William Harvey and others--to funny, sometimes ribald anecdotes about lesser folk, ideas on medicine and education and recollections of his own boyhood.

Aubrey had a wonderful way with a story, and Dotrice burnishes every detail to a high gloss. When the biographer wrote of Sir Walter Raleigh's execution, he noted that "he tooke a pipe of tobacco a little before he went to the scaffold ... to settle his spirits," and somehow the tiny detail makes the scene come alive. Dotrice recounts gleefully how Raleigh once angrily struck his son at the dinner table and how the younger man, not wishing to strike his father, instead hit the man seated on the other side of him, saying, "Box about: 'twill come to my father anon."

Frequently, Dotrice/Aubrey will begin by saying, "When I was a boy ..." or "In Queen Elizabeth's time ...," contrasting that time with the raucous age in which he finds himself, and the effect is as though some ancient veteran of our own Civil War had survived into the Age of Watergate to remind us of Lincoln and Sherman.

The reminiscences of Aubrey's boyhood are among the most entertaining moments in "Brief Lives." Dotrice's eyes gleam and the solitary tooth in his blackened mouth glistens at the recollection of the way a headmaster repeated a nonsense phrase like "Crinkum-crankum," or agonized over the long hair of his students. Later, as he observes how much learning dies with the death of a learned man, his expression darkens at the intimation of Aubrey's own hovering death.

Aubrey likens the biographer's skill to the art of a conjurer summoning up the dead from their graves. In summoning up Aubrey himself so vividly, Dotrice is displaying a conjurer's art to rival Aubrey's.

Revival of an Early O'Neill
(by Allan Wallach, Newsday, March 21, 1975)

Throughout his career, Eugene O'Neill kept returning obsessively to the theme of mismated people locked by love and hatred in an agonizingly destructive marriage. In one of his early plays, "All God's Chillun Got Wings," he shocked the society around him by making the marriage interracial.

Despite all the recent interest in O'Neill, the play has not received a major production since it first opened in 1924 amid a storm of protest. The Circle in the Square, which has an affinity for O'Neill dating back to its early days in Greenwich Village, has now rectified this with a revival under the direction of George C. Scott. The new production, which opened last night at the Circle's uptown theater, stars Scott's wife, Trish Van Devere, and Robert Christian as the tormented couple.

The revival reveals "All God's Chillun Got Wings" as a work that falls well short of O'Neill's major plays; it is awkwardly crafted, filled with the florid language of a bygone time and almost ludicrously melodramatic moments. But the play has considerable interest nonetheless, largely because of what it tells us about America's greatest playwright.

As his biographers have pointed out, "All God's Chillun" is a disguised treatment of the marriage of O'Neill's own parents, which he was to deal with so harrowingly in "A Long Day's Journey Into Night." In the earlier play, O'Neill even gave the man and wife the names of his parents, Jim and Ella.

Like Mary Tyrone in "Long Day's Journey," Ella in the 1924 play is a woman who suffers the condemnation of a society that rejects her for having married "beneath her." Mary, who married a matinee idol, retreats into dope addiction; Ella, who married a black man, withdraws into mental illness. And both husbands, the actor James Tyrone and the would-be lawyer Jim Harris, fail to fulfill themselves in their chosen careers.

Although he blandly denied that he was writing about "the Negro question," O'Neill was surely creating a social document that daringly showed the interconnection of social and personal concerns. But in 1924 he was not able to do this without recourse to melodrama or the intrusive use of symbols; as a result, "All God's Chillun" never achieves the power of his late masterpieces, or of Strindberg's "Dance of Death," which evidently served as its model.

In a childhood scene, young "Jim Crow" Harris shyly confesses to young Ella that he has been drinking chalk in order to become white. This desire is a refrain that runs through the play ("I've got to prove I'm the whitest of the white"). Along with Ella's pervasive shame and desperate need to assert her racial superiority, it dooms the marriage. Among the symbols are a Congo mask, representing a heritage that mocks Ella, and Jim's repeated failure to pass his bar exams, a metaphor for his futile attempt to "pass" as white.

In his new staging, Scott strikes a careful balance, toning down a few flamboyant flourishes but retaining most of the play's gaucheries. It's a pity, though, that the open configuration of the Circle in the Square stage prevented him from carrying out some of O'Neill's intentions. Among them was the use of expressionistic touches, including the shrinking of the Harrises' apartment to symbolize the trap their marriage had become. The new production takes place on handsome but far from claustrophobic sets designed by Ming Cho Lee.

Both Van Devere and Christian give strong performances, although there's little either can do about some of the built-in excesses of their roles. Van Devere moves with impressive

restraint from the early girlishness to wan defeat and ultimate
madness. Christian is forceful and assured in an equally difficult role.

It may be as hard for some 1975 theatergoers to accept the
stage devices employed by O'Neill as it is to realize that this
is a work that created a furor a half-century ago. Nevertheless,
the Circle in the Square is fulfilling its function admirably by
giving us a chance to see this imperfect play by O'Neill as he
was working his way toward his final, compulsively autobiographical statements.

WALSH, Paul; (2) Performing arts critic; (3) b. Lannon, Wis., Oct.
23, 1951; (4) s. John J. and Joan (Schumann); (5) Marquette U.,
1970-72, Arizona State University 1973-75, studies in English, aesthetics and theater; (6) m. Aila Virva Niemi, Jan. 23, 1974; (7)
daughter--Madelaine Katrine; (8) Reviewer for performing arts,
Phoenix, Arizona New Times, 1974- ; (21) 307 S. Westfall Apt. 2,
Tempe, AZ. 85281, Ph. 967-8434; (22) New Times, Box J, Tempe,
AZ. 85281, Ph. 968-6147; (23) Circulation: weekly alternative press,
30,000; (24) 15 plays, 5 dance, 5 books, 5 other.

Dancing in One Mind
(by Paul Walsh, New Times, November 13, 1974)

The stage is a black thick space, a sparse maze of indeter-
minable depth. A structure of bars and planes slashes the intensity of space on the right; a passageway of bone or pillars
to the left leads inward to other corridors. A single figure
stands in the center, a woman compressed by the weight of
darkness that pushes against her. She is motionless a long
time, terrified, bewildered, holding herself tightly. Then there
is a first twinge of motion, a held breath that rebels and mag-
nifies into a series of inner contortions twisting and taunting
and hollowing her body until it explodes in a halting, tentative
step. The space yields. In a flow of motion she dives ahead,
tunneling, winding into the depths of the labyrinthine tomb that
is the self, that is the heart, that is the place of the Minotaur.

Errand into the Maze is one of the mythic probings of Martha Graham, the extraordinary woman who gave America a dance
tradition and the world a new mode of artistic expression. It
was one of three pieces performed Thursday evening when the
Martha Graham Dance Company came to Tempe.

For decades as a dancer Martha Graham articulated the
emotions of human existence, repeated the ritual cycles of human experience, edified, terrified, and gave immortality to a
technique and a tradition aimed at revitalizing movement and
the articulation of movement in dance. As choreographer, artistic director and genetic energy behind the Martha Graham
Dance Company she continues her youthful struggle past her

eightieth year. The present tour of the Company is the expression of that energy.

On stage the woman has followed the Thesian cord to the inner confines of.the maze-space. She has accepted the errand into the maze and come to battle the Creature of Fear deep within her. A black Minotaur-figure that is this creature assaults the space. With angular movements, confined by the rigid yoke that holds his arms suspended over his head, he seeks to possess it. A violent battle of percussive leaps and thrusts hollows the space until the whole of it is within the woman's grasp and like Theseus she kills the creature, freeing herself from the maze of its control.

In her dances, Martha Graham explores the essential inner encounters of human experience. Victory promises victory; battle promises battle. The terrifying distortion of human movement, the hieroglyph of fear carved from the human form, can be recognized if we dare to look within ourselves. The dances are not pretty stories about fairy kings. They are not stories at all. They present not action but the impulse to act. Through the discipline of technique, the most significant impulses of daily life are exaggerated, exalted and given form as art. Many of the dances in the company's repertory were inspired by Greek myths, others by the ritual dances of the American Indians or the Oriental cultures, but the impulse, the deep inner insistence that seeks articulation, is from the maze of the dancer's own intense experience of life.

I had the opportunity to talk, Thursday afternoon, with Tim Wengerd, the man who that evening danced as the embodiment of fear in Errand into the Maze. I explained to Tim that I did not have the rehearsed perception of a critic; I was a member of the audience seeking after his art. We talked for two hours. He led me patiently, enthusiastically toward the magnanimous impulse of the Martha Graham genius.

I asked him about the weight of tradition the present dancers in the Company must feel with each of the pieces in their repertory. The Martha Graham Dance Company is the foundation of modern dance. Many of the greatest names in modern dance-- Erick Hawkins, Merce Cunningham, Paul Taylor--have been students of Martha Graham and danced in these roles. The female roles were created by Graham for herself. "Of course this is a weight of responsibility," Tim said. "But the real responsibility is to the Dance itself, to its articulation of inner reality. And to Martha of course and to the audience. Ultimately, the responsibility is to the performance, the vital instant of personal integration with space. I have to make that moment vibrate with life." For this, Martha Graham developed a technique of concentration and explosion which trains the dancer to force all the energy of her or his body into a sparse often violent series of contortions and releases.

Tim told me that when he was dancing with the Utah Repertory Theater his one ambition was to work with the Graham
company. He felt that her disregard for mere repertory, for
the historical collection of works, and her insistence on the passionate moment of encounter in performance was the only valid
response available for him, if his personal choice of art was to
have integrity. His eyes glowed when he told me, "Martha says
she doesn't want to be the mother of a museum."

I was impressed as he spoke, by the reverence he held for
Miss Graham. He spoke of her power to control a room by her
mere presence, just as she controlled thousands of stages for
decades when she danced. "All eyes go immediately to her ...
she has a certain infectious spirit that is often terrifying." We
find the same paradox in the Graham method of contortion and
release: an infectious spirit that confronts us with the subtle
but often terrifying reality of our encounter with life. There is
conflict inherent in the vocabulary of motion. Arms reach out,
the pelvic area retracts, space opens and closes. The body
twists against itself or against gravity. But each movement is
controlled by a deep inner motivation, by a knowledge of the
body, its possibilities and responses.

Past eighty now, Martha Graham continues her own passionate affair with life and dance. "She may well live another hundred years. If you ask her how old she is she says I'm younger
than you." She continues to choreograph, continues to direct
and inspire, continues to search into existing characters and
dances for more potent articulation of her own encounter with
life. Her lack of concern for preserving artifacts or mementos
allows her to risk her art each time the dances are remade,
allows her to give each performer the responsibility to search
out for her or himself the vital energy of the first performance.

Throughout our conversation, Martha was the first and final
point of reference. From whatever distance, I felt her magne-
tism--her genius mirrored in the dancer like the sun is transposed in a rainbow.

"Movement is cheap," Tim was saying. "There are a thousand movements everywhere. What we need is purified movement that can focus its energy." Like light through a magnifying glass, I thought, that burns a paper on a sunny day. "Movements without purpose--motivation--are empty. It is the motivation that gives them integrity. It's the same with technique.
Any technique gains its integrity only in use. What difference
does it make how high I can jump or how many turns I can do?
I know what my body can do, there's no point in doing it over
and over again. The only movement left is inward to find out
what it's about--to find out how movement is motivated in the
human experience." The articulation of the Graham vocabulary
of movement, set deep within the person, offers the opportunity
for deep communication. A Graham performance has little

concern with the flawless execution of a technique. This is why
Martha's dances reach us so intensively. Coming from within,
they seek to reveal the rich significance of human movement and
emotion--the same significance that keeps a myth from becoming
just a story told over and over again.

"Three Sisters"
(by Paul Walsh, New Times, February 26, 1975)

"I have one longing and it seems to grow stronger and
stronger--if only we could go back to Moscow." We intrude on
a dream. The action is straight, stiff, almost severe like a
turn-of-the-century brown-tint portrait. The edges are softened
and blurred, filtered through gauze scrim that adds an uncertain
haze of years and distance. We seem to watch through a cloud.

But it is not a dream. In the characters we recognize life.
It is a private place of private actions and private desperations
and our attention makes them public. And we realize as we
watch that the filmy wall drawn between us and the action is a
kind of smudged window that lets us watch dreamers stare out.

Chekhov's Three Sisters is about provincial life in the last
days of Czarist Russia. It tells of the lives of three sisters,
daughters of a military father, isolated by his death in the provincial town where he had been garrisoned. Amid the vulgar
boredom of that town their cultural brightness fades into a hope
of the future and memory of the past in Moscow. The city becomes a dream and a yearning after happiness.

Three Sisters is about aspirations and the brooding frustration of boredom, about loneliness and the impotence of a decaying
social order; and it is about daily joys and loves and the desperate need for faith in an unfocused future. But mostly it is
a drama of characters.

As a drama of characters, the play puts a great many demands on the actors: whole lives must be contained in brief
moments. This requires a deep sensitivity to the interior realities of the characters and an awareness of the rich poetic
texture woven by the interactions of these characters. Without
this sensitivity and awareness the play would distintegrate into
tedium; with it, the tension of characters and incidents blend
into a symphonic statement of deeply real and deeply human impact. The ASU production is startlingly human.

The play has no heroes; the action treats scattered lives in
scattered dreams. But several performances distinguish themselves. Patricia Bachtold is brilliant as Masha--the sister
married to a dull and pompous school teacher--carefully balancing a spirited passion for life with a pensive awareness of suffering. Robert Graybill is equally outstanding as Vershinin, the
new battery commander of the garrison and Masha's lover. His

animated gestures convince us of Vershinin's inability, despite
endless philosophical discussions, to articulate the deeply personal longings of a man who has devoted himself desperately to
faith in a distant future.

Vera Marie Badertscher brings passive strength to Olga, the
eldest sister. Kathi Platz shows the shrewd brutality of Natal-
ya's social climb countering the defeated escape of her husband,
Andrai (Fred Serdinak) and the delicate and fateful indecision of
his three sisters.

The characterizations work well despite the limitations of
age that necessarily plague university productions. The night I
saw the play, the limitations were most noticeable in moments
of the performances of Joe Kenny as Chebutykin and Melvin
Barry as Kulygin. Precision lagged in the third act and with it
the continuity of action and concentration, but these were recaptured by the fourth act and held onto through the end. The largest fault was in the gritty artificiality that turned Chekhov's
mysterious punctuations of sound--bells and music and alarms--
into irritating and cheap interruptions. But the faults are minor
and easily excused in so brilliant a play as this.

Traditionally, productions of Chekhov's plays have been concerned with creating reliable illusions of life. The effects of
the transparent wall and the portrait-like floor design of the
ASU production remind me of an impressionist painting. Reality
is cluttered. This space is controlled; this language is poetic.
Chekhov's muted genius relies on the texture of specific incidents
and sounds and motivations, turning them as symbols into a
complex fabric of poetic life. The impressionistic, geometric
treatment serves Chekhov well.

Three Sisters is a masterpiece of the theater. The ASU
production is soundly human, poetically intense. I am happy to
see it done so well. It carries the magic of a great play.

WATT, Douglas; (2) Drama Critic; (3) b. New York City, Jan. 20,
1914; (4) s. Benjamin and Agnes Rita (Neimann); (5) B.A. Cornell,
major subj. : English, concentration in Theater, 1934; (6) m. Ethel
Madsen, Aug. 13, 1951; (7) four children; (8) copy boy, The News,
1936-37, songwriter for radio show, This Mad World, WMCA,
1930's, drama reporter, 1940- , staff member The New Yorker,
1946- , member ASCAP; (13) USAAF service in WW II; (19) Dutch
Treat Club (Bd. of Govs.); (21) 27 West 86th Street, New York 10024,
Ph. 212-TR 7-2320; (22) 220 East 42d Street, New York 10017, Ph.
212-MU 2-1234; (23) Circulation: 2 million; (24) 100-150.

"Sticks and Bones" Brings the Vietnam War Home
(by Douglass Watt, The Daily News, November 8, 1971)

The specter of Vietnam comes to haunt an American household in "Sticks and Bones," a harrowing and powerful play by David Rabe that opened last night in the Anspacher Theater unit of the New York Shakespeare Festival's Public Theater complex.

It is a play written out of rage over what Rabe, himself a veteran of the war, considers our widespread complacency about the events in Indochina. But it has not been written in rage. It is, instead, a beautifully controlled and even poetic work of the imagination that becomes almost unbearably moving as it unfolds.

Rabe has chosen an "Ozzie and Harriet"-type TV family for his purposes. In fact the parents are named Ozzie and Harriet and their sons are Rick and David. They live in a cozy, tidy middle-class home with standardized furnishings and Harriet is forever trotting out milk and fudge and cake, most of which is eagerly consumed by Rick, who sings and plays the guitar and borrows the car to try out an assortment of girls.

The play begins with the good news that David is coming home from the war. But David is blind and just one of several casualties being dropped off all over the land by a symbolic sergeant major. He is also so sick at heart that he can only slowly believe that this is the family life he once left. And he has brought with him the searing memory of a Vietnamese girl he had loved and lived with and who silently and gracefully moves through the house in the person of an actress named Asa Gim.

David, you see, is a symbol, too, just like the others. But he is a symbol not only of the young men who have given their lives in Vietnam but of the entire war experience, of all the filth and killing and degradation of the human spirit. He is, in short, poison and must be gotten rid of.

And he is, but not before his poison has seeped into every corner of the house and given the jittery, temperamental, forlorn father a vision of the girl, the symbol of Vietnam. It is Rabe's ironic conclusion, though, that even this vision can be laid to rest beneath a blanket by Ozzie and Harriet and Rick and that David can be persuaded to vanish by killing himself.

The cast is excellent. Tom Aldredge is perfect as the gradually disintegrating Ozzie whose life has closed behind him like water, in Rabe's phrase. Elizabeth Wilson is splendid, as Harriet, especially in a scene in which she is debased by the relentless David and reduced to a pathetic, pleading figure. And Cliff DeYoung is wonderfully loathesome as fun-loving Rick about whom his brother observes that snakes don't know they crawl.

David Selby is commanding as David, who lies quietly in his room much of the time but who gradually and awesomely lets the poison flow as he brings the sights and sounds of the war into his home in some of the evening's most vivid writing.

Charles Siebert is fine as a confident priest summoned by
Harriet but rejected and caned by David. Hector Ellis is good
as the curt, angry sergeant major.

Jeff Blackner has staged the play superbly well in Santo Loquasto's nicely designed two-level interior and Theoni V. Aldredge has supplied appropriate costumes.

"Sticks and Bones" has strength and magnificence.

"A Chorus Line"
(by Douglas Watt, Daily News, May 22, 1975)

Yes, indeed "A Chorus Line," which has been showering
sparks on Lafayette St. for several weeks now during previews,
finally burst into full flame with last night's opening at the Public
Theater's Newman unit. Thus, this daringly simple, brilliantly
staged entertainment takes its place as the hottest new thing in
town and firmly establishes itself as the most exciting Broadway
musical in several seasons. Literally, it's Off Broadway, but
I don't see how anybody will be able to stop it from moving uptown.

Incidentally, I use the term "Broadway"--it somehow seems
necessary to add these days--not in a delimiting, patronizing
sense, but to signify the proud professionalism and excellence
that make the Broadway theater, at its best, the most exciting
there is. In fact, the spirit of "A Chorus Line" is best summed up by a dancer's remark, "I don't want to hear about how
Broadway's dyin', 'cause I just got here."

This dance musical has evolved gradually throughout the season, thanks to Joseph (Broadway Joe) Papp's hospitality, from
the germ of an idea held by Michael Bennett, who is also responsible for the entire staging. A team of book writers (James
Kirkwood and Nicholas Dante) has been called in to furnish some
dialogue, and some monologues, and a composer (Marvin Hamlisch) and lyricist (Edward Kleban) have applied some agreeable
song numbers. But "A Chorus Line" is clearly a one-man conception, sometimes autobiographical in tone, balanced on that
desperate, urgent, both insignificant and momentous time when
a new musical first goes into production and the dance director
must ruthlessly pick and choose the chorus kids, or gypsies.
That's the heart and soul of "A Chorus Line."

The format is simplicity itself. We're sitting in a theater
watching a dance director audition applicants for a new musical.
There are a couple of dozen aspirants, male and female, for
eight parts (four and four). After putting them through some
paces en masse and in small groups, the director narrows the
list down to 17, who then line up behind a white line downstage.

They remain there, more or less, for the rest of the evening.

But oh! that, "more," and oh! that "less." As the director
walks up the aisle to disappear at the back, where his amplified
and questioning voice takes on the tone of a benign deity, the
applicants are questioned one by one about their vital statistics
and their pasts. We get to know their hangups and quirks (the
men seem mostly to be homosexuals, though one brags about
some female conquests and another plays a dopey husband to a
dumb girl applicant) in monologues and songs. At the end, eight
final choices are made by the director.

But "A Chorus Line" is much more than that conveys. Bennett, who has already been responsible for the musical staging
of the decade's two outstanding musicals to date, "Company" and
"Follies," has no equal in teasing a dance number into shape,
building it from bits and pieces into a suddenly dazzling whole.

He has effected this most notably here in a show-stopping
turn ("The Music and the Mirror") by the striking Donna Mc-
Kechnie, who plays a mature featured dancer trying to land a
chorus job with a director she once lived with, and in a totally
unexpected curtain-call number after the play is over and the
stage has been blacked out. The latter, a thrilling simplifica-
tion of the "Loveland" sequence in "Follies," all at once provides a resolution and a happy ending and is guaranteed to lift
you right out of your seat after more than two hours of uninter-
rupted theatrical magic, most of it in dance form.

As for those little stories--"for the most part, based upon
the lives and experiences of Broadway dancers"--well, as you
very well know, there's a broken heart for every light on Broadway. And a laugh. And laughter and tears are what these
snippets add up to. And true or false, they prod "A Chorus
Line" into occasionally resembling a "Forty-Second Street" for
moderns. Miss McKechnie is the latter-day Ruby Keeler, of
course. Carole Bishop, the single voluptuous member of the
bunch, is dandy as a sardonic veteran of the show-biz wars.
Together with blonde and saucy Pamela Blair, who found that
silicone treatments rounded out life's hard corners, Miss Bishop provides the Ginger Rogers character, and so on. Robert
LuPone's brisk but considerate dance director and Priscilla Lopez' Diana, a singing dancer, are other major assets in a uniformly winning cast.

Hamlisch has provided a supple and nicely varied score
which, though notably lacking in the least melodic or harmonic
originality, borrows tastefully and is, happily, the obvious work
of a genuine musician, a fact resulting in some superb arrange-
ments by Bill Byers, Hershy Kay and Jonathan Tunick that are
played by a knockout 16-piece orchestra backstage. Kleban's
lyrics are articulate, expressive, uncluttered (except where intended, in an amusing duet called "Sing") and entertaining.
Their big song, which must have been played 50 times and is
used for that smashing finale, is a rhythmic, mildly sardonic

love song bearing the title "One."

Robin Wagner's stage design consists of a series of pivoting flats along the back wall, mirrors on one side and black surfaces on the other. But artless as the setting Theoni V. Aldredge's costumes and Tharon Musser's expressive lighting appear to be up to then, wait and see what all three have in store for you at the finish.

"A Chorus Line" is a splendid achievement.

WATTS, Richard; (2) Saturday Theater Critic for New York Post; (3) b. Parkersburg, W. Va., January 12, 1898; (4) s. Mr. and Mrs. S. R. Watts; (5) Educated at Columbia, class of 1921; (6) Unmarried; (8) At Columbia, ran a column of play reviews in Spectator, undergraduate college daily newspaper. First, film and then drama critic of New York Herald Tribune from 1924 to 1942. Left to join Office of War Information as U.S. press attache in Dublin and then as one of its staff in Chungking, China. On return became daily drama critic and columnist on the New York Post and this year changed to Saturday theater columnist. Annual summer world traveler, particularly in Asia and Africa, covering the Spanish Civil War and the Chinese-Japanese conflict before Pearl Harbor for the Herald Tribune; (13) In First World War joined Student Army Training Corps at Columbia; (16) Independent in politics, although chiefly voting Democratic; (17) Catholic; (21) 920 Fifth Avenue, New York, N.Y. 10021, Ph. BUtterfield 8-2109; (22) New York Post, 210 South Street, New York, N.Y. 10002, Ph. DIgby 95000; (23) Post Circulation: 600,000; (24) Now doing one theater column a week.

A Plunge to the Depths
(by Richard Watts, New York Post, October 5, 1974)

It would have been too much to expect the new theater season to continue at the peak it started on with "Gypsy" and "Cat on a Hot Tin Roof." But it is a shame it had to plunge so quickly to the depths of Eugenie Leontovich's unfortunate "Medea & Jason." Her free adaptation of Robinson Jeffers' version of Euripides' classic "Medea" did have the virtue of brevity, but that is the only kind thing I can say about a production that lacked dramatic force, dignity, eloquence, interest of any sort or acting that might at least have helped to atone in part for the presentation's other sad failings.

The choreographic adornments weren't of any assistance, either, despite the eagerness and enthusiasm the scantily clad young people of the chorus put into their dancing. They seemed nice boys and girls having classroom exercises. Indeed there were times when I thought the entire company was endeavoring to transform the tragic legend of the vengeful Medea into a comedy and not doing it very well. The program added to my bewilderment by proclaiming that the first and last scenes took

place in a modern Greek bistro. The episodes didn't remind
me of my few adventures in the nightclubs and bars of Athens.

Maria Aho, who played Medea, is an actress from Finland
and her Finnish accent may have accounted for some of the difficulties she had portraying a long and demanding role in English. Richmond F. Johnson, a genial, white-bearded man,
struck me as being such a friendly and good humored Jason that
you couldn't expect him to be dangerous to anybody, particularly
to such a spirited woman as Medea. Eugenia Leontovich has
had such a distinguished career in the theater that it is astonishing to think of her as responsible for such a disaster as "Medea
& Jason," but it is impossible to exonerate her from the guilt.

David Storey is an excellent English dramatist whose work
is also favorably known in this country. We have seen three of
his plays in New York, and all of them have possessed high
merit and have been varied in subject matter. The most interesting to me was "The Contractor," which merely showed a
group of workers putting up and taking down a tent but somehow
depicted the entire British class structure. Then there was
"Home," in which those eminent baronets, Sir John Gielgud and
Sir Ralph Richardson, touchingly portrayed old men living in a
mental institution. After that came "The Changing Room," which
gave a kind of backstage view of a British soccer team.

Having admired all of them so much, I was eager to see his
latest work, "Life Class," which dealt with a day in school with
student painters. It disappointed me greatly, seeming almost
entirely without dramatic interest, although some of the London
critics, who often puzzle me, were impressed by it. What
astonished me chiefly is that it struck me as being more like
"Butley" then a Storey drama, a similarity that was emphasized
by the fact that Alan Bates, an undeniably fine actor, played the
leading role in both dramas. And the roles he had in both
works struck me as remarkably alike, and not very rewarding.

Both times, he portrayed a teacher who was facing a crisis
in his life. On the same day he was on the verge of losing his
job and his wife deserted him. He also had to realize there
was a homosexual streak in him. He handled both parts skillfully, but why do it a second time? Incidentally, "Scapino," the
most entertaining play of last season in which the wonderful Jim
Dale gave a performance that enchanted his first-night audience
and made it eager to keep him on the stage all night, is back
in town. If you miss this second chance to see it, you will be
making a great mistake. I think you should also see "The Magic Show," in which Doug Henning outdoes even the great Hou-
dini.

"Seascape": Albee at Top of Form
(by Richard Watts, New York Post, February 8, 1975)

"Seascape" is one of Edward Albee's most brilliant and

fascinating plays and marks a fresh departure for him. It is a
kind of allegorical comedy and has a warmth of heart not always
to be found in his distinguished work. Dealing with mankind's
rise from the primordial slime, it offers us a philosophical
glimpse of evolution in addition to being characteristically witty
and richly entertaining. It has four characters, two of whom
are talking lizards, who come up from the depths to engage a
pair of humans, a somewhat surprised husband and wife, in interesting and stimulating conversation. In the course of the
discussion, they give each other a lot of excellent and valuable
advice.

Albee always begins with a great advantage. He invariably
writes such beautiful prose. No contemporary dramatist can
use the English language so gracefully, and "Seascape" is wonderfully eloquent as well as witty. I don't see how even those
who don't care for the play itself can fail to recognize that the
writing is downright superb. It has been noted that, on the
whole, the lizards have the best lines and the evening doesn't
reach its peak until they arrive. But the husband and wife
aren't neglected, and indeed they have some valuable ideas for
their--and our--undersea ancestors. At times, the discussion
seems almost Shavian, but it remains Edward Albee at the top
of his form.

The play has the additional advantage of being splendidly
staged and acted. It was directed by the author himself, and
he has done it expertly. Frank Langella and Maureen Anderman
are delightful as the lizards, although I regretted to have the
the attractive Miss Anderman so completely concealed by her
costume. The beautiful Deborah Kerr is excellent as the wife
and Barry Nelson makes one regret that his role isn't larger
because of the quiet skill of his playing. James Tilton's seashore setting is atmospheric and beautiful, and Fred Voelpel's
costumes for the lizards, complete with tails, are splendidly
imaginative. "Seascape" is the sort of magnificent new American play for which the season has been awaiting.

One curious thing about "Man on the Moon" by John Phillips,
which didn't stay with us long, is that, although it was a very
simple-minded little musical comedy, its plot was too complicated
to be explained easily. I know it had something to do with an
expedition to the moon, with a stop-over on the planet Canis
Minor and a baleful scheme to blow up the constellations, but
its details were beyond me. The villain was a sinister German
scientist named Dr. Bomb, which reminds me that Wernher von
Braun was the name of the scientist who was responsible for the
flying missiles that fell in London during the war.

The virtue was some nice songs by the author, but I am
told they were not written for "Man on the Moon" and were composed by him on earlier occasions and well-known by many members of the first-night audience. In a sullen mood some years

ago, I wrote that Andy Warhol, who is billed as producer of the show, had made a successful career boring people, and the late, unlamented show might seem to give support to my ugly theory. But to add to the complications, I now gather that the cult hero had nothing to do with "Man on the Moon" except to lend his name to it. It was directed by Paul Morrissey, who did everything possible with the material at hand. The one performer who seemed professional was Monique Van Vooren.

The latest but, I'm afraid, not the last product in this era of plays about homosexuals in the theater is "Lovers." It is a mercifully short little musical having to do with the relationships between three pairs of the set. They are assorted groups of them, ranging from two pleasantly ordinary young fellows through a couple who appear tough and masculine to an aging professor and a former student of his who have been sweethearts for years. I suppose "Lovers" celebrates their liberation from the necessity for secrecy and their right to come out into the open, which they certainly take advantage of. If it has a mission, it appears to be to fill them with pride in their difference from the norm.

There are a lot of pleasant enough songs by Steve Sterner and a book of sorts by Peter del Valle, who also directed. The love-making is not overly explicit, but it is made clear what the boys are up to. It isn't offensive or surprising to people who get around much these days, but it is, I thought, far from entertaining. Perhaps it is intended to be educational and not an evening of amusement. You learn that the set has its quarrels, jealousies and infidelities, and they don't seem to have much fun. In view of the pains and anxieties the homosexuals appear to go through, I still can't understand why they are colloquially described as "gay."

WEALES, Gerald; (2) Professor of English; (3) b. Connersville, Ind., June 12, 1925; (4) s. Frank and Mary (Burton) Weales; (5) A.B., Columbia College, 1949; A.M., Columbia U., 1950; Ph.D., Columbia, 1958; (6) Single; (8) Drama Critic, Reporter, 1965-68; Commonweal, 1968-71. (I still contribute several play reviews a year to Commonweal, but they no longer have a regular reviewer.); (13) U.S. Army, 1943-46; (14) George Jean Nathan Award for Dramatic Criticism, 1964-65; (15) P.E.N.; Authors' Guild; American Theater Critics Association; (20) Religion in Modern English Drama (University of Pennsylvania Press, 1961); American Drama Since World War II (Harcourt Brace, 1962); A Play and Its Parts (Basic Books, 1964); Tennessee Williams (University of Minnesota Press, 1965: U of M Pamphlets on American Writers, No. 53); The Jumping-Off Place, American Drama in the 1960s (Macmillan, 1969); Clifford Odets, Playwright (Pegasus, 1971). I have edited Edwardian Plays (Hill and Wang, 1962); Eleven Plays (Norton, 1964); The Complete Plays of William Wycherley (Anchor, 1966: now published by Norton); Arthur Miller, Death of a Salesman, Text and Criticism (Viking, 1967); Arthur Miller, The Crucible, Text and Criticism (Viking, 1971); with

Robert J. Nelson, Revolution and Enclosure, two volumes in a new
series, Encounters (McKay, 1975). I have also contributed essays
to a number of volumes and essays and reviews to a vast collection
of publications including, recently, Film Comment, New York Times,
Michigan Quarterly Review, The Hollins Critic, North American Review, New Republic, The Village Voice, The Ohio Review, Denver
Quarterly, The Hudson Review, The Philadelphia Bulletin; (21) 208
S. 43rd Street, Philadelphia, Pa. 19104; (22) Department of English,
University of Pennsylvania, Philadelphia, Pa. 19174, Ph. 215-243-
6326 or 7341; (24) 2 plays; 9 books in 1974, but number varies
greatly.

The Stage
(by Gerald Weales, Commonweal, January 17, 1975)

It has been obvious since the early 1960s, when The Blood
Knot made its way from Johannesburg to London and New York,
that Athol Fugard is a major dramatic talent. He is one of the
two playwrights from Africa (Wole Soyinka is the other) to make
the clearest artistic claim for a place among the world's leading
contemporary dramatists. The games that Zach and Morris play
in The Blood Knot--games that wed Samuel Beckett to the strongest kind of social comment--illustrate that Fugard is a meticulous
writer, a master of nuance, subtlety, sophistication. In celebrating Fugard's virtues as a writer, I do not want to suggest
that there is an anti-theatrical impulse in his work, for Fugard,
an actor and director as well as a writer, is a man whose effects are never literary--in the pejorative sense that theater people give to that word--but are married to character and always
character as performed. Even so, The Blood Knot, Boesman
and Lena, all Fugard's early works are so obviously playwright's
plays that it was startling news to hear that Fugard--influenced
by Jerzy Grotowski--was working with two of his actors, devis-
ing (their word) group-created plays.

Whatever doubts I may have about that form of play-making,
induced by productions in which inchoate invention outfoxed artistic control, were stilled last March when I saw an abridged
version of Sizwe Banzi Is Dead on English television. An interesting play, a good production, but it never prepared me for the
impact that Sizwe Banzi--and, even more, The Island--would
have on me in the theater. These two plays, devised by Athol
Fugard, John Kani and Winston Ntshona, with Kani and Ntshona
as the only actors and Fugard as director, are presently at New
York's Edison Theatre, and they are the most exciting things
that I have seen in any theater for a long time. I suspect that
on paper neither of these plays will approach the quality of The
Blood Knot, but the meticulousness mentioned above, the marvelous sense of nuance, is present here, now the creation of
the performers rather than the writer. Part of the force of
these plays comes from what the black actors and their white
collaborator have to say about life in South Africa, but their
triumph lies not in any social or political message, but in the

fact that they have imposed life on the stage at the Edison. It is not plot, nor situation, nor even character in the conventional sense that is communicated by these plays, but a quality of being by which Kani and Ntshona, with a look, a gesture, an altered intonation, a smile--real or artificial--can convey a place, a dream, a loss or the combination of all three that is black South Africa.

It is Sizwe Banzi, heavy with rave reviews, that is drawing the bulk of the audience to the Edison; the management must have known that would be the case since The Island gives only two performances a week. Sizwe Banzi is the lighter of the two plays, the funnier, the less painful, but it is impressive in its own way. It opens with a long comic monologue, a play within a play, in which Kani, as Styles, the photographer, recalls his years in a Ford plant (where Kani, in fact, worked) and explains the dream, for himself and his people, implicit in his photographer's shop. The portraits, the group pictures, the snaps for all occasions are testimonies to the existence of these black men and women, evidence of real faces in a society which has quit looking at men, has substituted the bewysboek for the person, the number for the individual. Styles is interrupted by a customer who wants a picture to send back home to his wife--by Sizwe Banzi, although that is not the name he uses. The play then moves back in time to the day in which Buntu (Kani, in a second role) persuades Sizwe to put his picture in the bewysboek of a man they have found dead in the street, to assume a new name and a new history, his only chance to get a job in Port Elizabeth, where a stamp in Sizwe's own book forbids him to remain. When the play moves back to the photographer's studio, to the idiotically insouciant smile on the face of the man who was once Sizwe Banzi, the play pulls to a close with an unlikely mingling of hopelessness and survival in the truth-telling lie of still another of Styles' evidential artifacts.

The Island presents two men, cellmates on Robben Island, the maximum security prison for African political offenders, trying to keep from breaking under the intense pressure, physical and psychological, to which the institution and the men who run it subject them. Never, I suppose, has a Broadway stage seen so much urine, mucus, sweat as Kani and Ntshona bring to their intensely physical performances of men barely surviving in the flesh. The shocks in the play, however, come not from the actors' discharges--that would be titillation in the Arrabal manner--but from strangely quiet moments of dramatic intensity, as when an imaginary phone call turns painfully real through the need of the prisoners to reach their families outside or when an excited laugh of expectation is clumsily stifled as one prisoner realizes that the other cannot share his hope for a shortened sentence. All through the play the two men plan--one eagerly, one reluctantly--to present Antigone at a prison concert, and the play offers their variation on Sophocles, an approximation of the original that is at once ludicrous and dignified, a powerful

denunciation of South African "law. " As both plays end, Creon
is linked again to Antigone, imaginary chains at wrist and ankle,
and the two prisoners run in tandem, a pantomime scene that
recalls the opening of The Island and reminds us that the titular
island is a metaphor for a greater enclosure than the prison itself.

My attempt to describe the two plays in conventional terms
is finally self-defeating, for they are not so much their subject
matter as they are John Kani and Winston Ntshona in action.
The best I can do is record my enthusiastic response.

WEAVER, Emmett, Post-Herald, Birmingham Post Company, P. O.
Box 2553, Birmingham, Ala. 35202.

WEBSTER, Carmen Jacqueline (Kelly); (2) Drama editor; (3) b. Hou-
ston, Tx.; (5) B. S. , College of Business and Public Administration,
New York U.; (6) m. Dr. Harry M. Kelly, 1973 (formerly m. Harold
Franklyn Webster, 1940); (8) President, Model Railroad Equipment
Corp, New York City, 1942- ; Copublisher, The News, 1950-1960;
Drama Editor, The News, 1954- ; Publisher, The News, 1960-62;
(10) Permanent Patron, Bellevue Medical Center, New York Univer-
sity; New York State Legislative Advisory Commission, 1971-72; (11)
P. R. Cochairperson, Greenburgh Republican Committee, 1954-60;
(12) Board of Directors, Myopia International Research Foundation,
Board of Directors, Futura Home Foundation; (14) Madden Memorial
Award, New York University, 1953; (15) Beta Gamma Sigma; (22)
23 West 45 Street, New York, N. Y. 10036.

"Who's Who in Hell"
(by Carmen Webster, The News, December 19, 1974)

"Who's Who in Hell" opened at the Lunt-Fontaine Theater.
This is a new comedy by Peter Ustinov, who also appears in
his first United States stage appearance in twelve years. Co-
starring with him are Beau Bridges and George S. Irving, under
the direction of Ellis Rabb. The producers are Alexander H.
Cohen and Bernard Delfont.

Mr. Ustinov is a unique theatrical entity, both as an author
and as an actor. His style in both instances in stimulating and
different. This play is no exception. The "locale," beautifully
designed by Douglas Schmidt, is the "hospitality suite in the
Great Beyond. " Awaiting consideration and entry is a President
of the United States, the First Secretary of the Communist Party,
and a young American idealist who has assassinated them both.
The assassination took place in Disney Land.

The play is most current, in that it analyzes in comic
terms the current United States-Soviet relations.

This is clearly a "political" play, in a style that we have come to associate with Mr. Ustinov. He is both funny and inoffensive, and reduces men, situations and ideas to very basic, understandable terms.

The comedy treats a serious and dramatic event in understandable and amusing human terms.

We are pressured daily with the tension and events of the day. It is difficult to find humor in the stark realities of the headlines. Mr. Ustinov has, and to a great extent he has succeeded well.

There will be those who will be offended by his humor; those who will be frightened of the treatment of so serious a subject in a comic vein; but there will be others, like myself, and hopefully you, the theatregoer, who will welcome Mr. Ustinov's latest effort in the spirit of fun.

"The Constant Wife"--Good Fun
(by Carmen Webster, Home News and Times, May 8, 1975)

Ingrid Bergman has returned to New York at the Sam Shubert Theatre, thanks to Arthur Cantor, in the W. Somerset Maugham comedy, "The Constant Wife." Also starred are Paul Harding and Jack Gwillim, with the very charming Brenda Forbes as the mother, Mrs. Culver.

Miss Bergman is not generally known as a stage actress, although she studied at the Stockholm's Royal Dramatic Theatre School. Her early practical experience was in the live theatre, but her first measure of success was in Swedish films, which led to her Hollywood and first American films. Although this is the case, she has broken the house record for a straight play in every theatre that she has played in her current tour, including the Kennedy Center Opera House in Washington.

Her performance in the instant case is less the expertise of character development, as it is a vehicle for her to display her very considerable talents as an actress per se.

W. Somerset Maugham is principally not a playwright, nor is he generally associated with comedies. The present play is no exception, and was basically designed as a vehicle for Ethel Barrymore. It works equally as well for Ingrid Bergman.

The action of the play takes place in John Middleton's house in Harley Street, London, in the late 1920's.

Mr. Middleton, a well-known Harley Street physician, is having a not-too-unknown affair with his wife's best friend. Everybody seems to know about it except poor John's wife. As the plot is unravelling, and everyone is discussing Poor John's affair, it is further complicated by the return to London of his wife's old boyfriend. The play is generally amusing and has its bright spots.

Directed by Sir John Gielgud, we can easily recognize his fine, English subtle touch.

The play certainly stands as a front-runner of the Women's Liberation Movement.

The ending, for its time was unusual. For this day and age, it is most expected.

All in all, it was good fun, and worth the effort to see.

WEINER, Bernard; (2) Drama Critic; (3) b. Pittsburgh, Pa. , Feb. 9, 1940; (4) s. Daniel & Florence Weiner; (5) B. A. U. of Miami 1962, major subj. : government; M. A. Claremont Graduate School 1964, major subj: government; Ph. D. 1966, major subj. : government; (6) Single; (8) Film-Drama Critic, University of Miami Hurricane 1960-62; Film-Drama Critic, Claremont (Calif.) Courier 1962-65; Film Critic, San Diego Magazine 1965-66; Film-Drama Critic, Northwest Passage (Seattle-Bellingham) 1969-71; Film Critic, San Francisco Fault and Overseas Weekly 1972-73; Drama-Film Critic San Francisco Chronicle 1974- ; Actor, Florida, California and Washington 1960-64; Director, 1960-68; Technical Assistant, Circle-in-the-Square, N. Y. , 1964; (10) Radical politics; (14) Various civic, playwrighting and directors' awards; (20) Ten plays, two poetry volumes, various articles, critiques in numerous local and national magazines; (21) 18 Worth Street, San Francisco 94114; (22) San Francisco Chronicle, 5th & Mission Streets, San Francisco 94119; (23) Circulation: 400,000 daily; 700,000 Sunday; (24) 150 theater, 50 film, 10 miscellaneous.

<u>Sam Shepard's Powerful Drama on Confusion</u>
(by Bernard Weiner, San Francisco Chronicle, May 6, 1975)

Sam Shepard's "Action," which had its West Coast premiere last weekend at the Magic Theater, is a brilliant, important play by a relatively young (31) but extremely mature playwright, directed with consummate skill by the author, and performed with great power.

While the play's tone and style are reminiscent of Pinter and Beckett--that is to say, of the major fountainheads of modern Western theater--"Action " speaks with a voice quite its own.

A dinner table, chairs, a blinking Christmas tree. The four characters--Lupe, Liza, Shooter and Jeep--appear to be exiles in the country, there to escape the madness of civilization. (There is reference to their living in a "post-community," post-mass entertainment era; something calamitous has occurred beyond their cabin.)

They are trying to read from a book--a Star Trek story (or a history text?)--but have, quite literally, "lost their place."

On one level, they are the countercultural youth of the '60s, who jettisoned the baggage of society's standards of procedure. As Jeep laments, more than once, in his confusion: "I have no references for this."

On another level, they represent anyone who is lost in a hard-to-fathom world, searching for guideposts, directions to move, rationales for "action."

Shooter is so scared--"my skin is all that's covering me," he says in terror--that he eventually makes his stand on an arm-chair, refusing to budge from it for fear of the consequences. (He tells the story of a man, perhaps himself, who spied on his own body, regarding it as treasonous; the body finally killed him, though the man is still walking around somewhere.)

Jeep, an ex-convict, ranges in mood from near-catatonia to violence. He seems the most flaky in his despair, yet he sees a glimmer of hope: At least each of us speaks a (note: not the) language, we hear each other, know each others' names; we may even be bringing back a bit of the sense of community, he says.

While the men flail about in their search for the hows and whys of action, Lupe and Liza carry out their "action" in quite practical ways: cooking, cleaning, hanging up the wash--that is, they simply keep on living, on another level, but in many ways just as important, maybe more.

Ebbe Roe Smith as Shooter and Jack Thibeau as Jeep are nothing short of brilliant, bringing chills to one's spine as a result of their strange moods, and yet catching all the grim humor (and there is much of it) in Shepard's script.

Ann Matthews adds a fine portrait of Lupe, and Feather Rougett handles the easy role of Liza with dispatch.

Shepard's direction is exceptionally tight and forceful; the play runs about an hour and never goes slack.

"Killer's Head," the curtain-raiser, is a slight work by Shepard, only eight minutes long; about the inside of a condemned man's head before he fries in the electric chair. James Dean delivers the unexceptional monologue about horses and trucks with a subtly-developed cadence, a la Ravel's "Bolero," that reaches moments of pure despair. Dan Swain's lighting is superb.

Shepard, a major voice in the world of avant-garde theater

in New York; moved to the Bay Area recently.   He says he's
going to direct all his plays himself from now on.

He's made a fine start with "Action" and "Killer's Head,"
and one looks forward eagerly to his doing more of his plays at
John Lion's Magic Theater.   They seem an unbeatable combination.

A Brilliant New Play
(by Bernard Weiner, San Francisco Chronicle, February 9, 1976)

"AC/DC," a brilliant play by British author Heathcote Williams, currently being given its West Coast premiere by The
Magic Theater, literally explodes its white-hot language all over
the stage--and the minds of the audience.

It is a major play that flows out of the modern theater tra-
dition--its opening line reminds one of Michael McClure, its
closing scene of "One Flew Over the Cuckoo's Nest," and between are echoes of Antonin Artaud, Anthony Burgess, Harold
Pinter, Sam Shepard and others--but one possessing a voice and
style quite its own.

John Lion's production, in traditional theater terms, could
use some trimming--but Williams' language is so fecund, so
bursting with vital imagery, that one tolerates the occasional
over-writing just to be able to hear and absorb the poetic wildness of this play's language, including some delicious erotic puns
and "12-tone dirty jokes."

This 1970 work is in two acts, "AC" and "DC," electrical
terms that refer to the play's theme of psychic overload brought
on by "media rash"--in particular by films and TV and the attendant destructive power these mediums wield on the popular
consciousness.

"AC" opens in a playland arcade at 5 a.m.   Three stoned
freaks are taking pictures of themselves performing "unnatural
acts" inside the Photomaton.   It soon becomes apparent that
two of them--Gary (John Vickery) and Melody (Suzanne Kellam)--
are content to find meaning only through sex and drugs.   Their
companion Sadie (Jessica Epstein) is after something more transcendent.

Enter the arcade's mechanic, a schizophrenic named Maurice
(John Nesci).   He gives evidence to Sadie of being onto something
worth following.   He seems to have the ability, for example, to
"demagnetize" Perowne (Christopher Brooks), another schizo who
is close to turning into a vegetable, a "media sludge," as a result of sensory "over-amping."   Sadie leaves her two stoned companions (who are operating on alternating current) to follow Maurice (who seems to have hooked into direct current).

"DC" takes place in Perowne's apartment, which is clogged
with evidence of his media obsession. In this long act, Sadie
attempts to break Perowne away from his dependence on the
very things that disturb him--and from his lover--"psychic rheo-
stat" Maurice, who she comes to see is into the same power
"validation" trips as everyone else.

In the end, by virtue of some skillful manipulation, Sadie
bests Maurice at his own game, and proceeds, literally, to open
Perowne's "third eye" (his "pineal stalk") so that he can enjoy
direct contact with the astral plane.

The ending is ambiguous. Either Sadie has given Perowne
the ultimate "hollow-out" (i. e., rubbed his brain out) or connected him to the cosmic vorp--or both. In Lion's version, a
third possibility is added: that Maurice may have won, after
all, bringing even Sadie into his schizophrenic hutch.

Each of the characters in "AC/DC" is reacting to, and trying to escape from, established Western society ("psychic capitalism") in different ways. The playwright obviously is condemn-
ing that which causes them to behave this way--a society gone
power-mad, in all senses of that term--but leaves to the audience
to decide the value of various kinds of craziness in dealing with
that monster.

Lion's direction is (as usual) exceptionally creative for the
tiny stage, and though there are a few pacing and diction lapses
and some interpretative mistakes, the acting is of uniformly high
quality--especially that of Nesci, Epstein and (though he tends
to "downplay" to the point of unintelligibility at times) Brooks.

Set-designer Jock Reynolds obviously had to compromise in
what he could physically do with the small staging area, but the
result is virtually perfect: clinical, antiseptic, scary. (However, more electronic devices are called for in Perowne's apartment.) Dan Robinson's sounds and Dan Swain's lighting also
contribute much to the power of the show.

WEIRICH, Frank, Knoxville News-Sentinel, 208 West Church Avenue,
Knoxville, Tenn. 37901, Ph. 615-523-3131.

WETZSTEON, Ross Duane; (2) Theatre Critic; (3) b. Butte, Mont.,
November 5, 1932; (4) s. Raymond and Mary Wetzsteon; (5) B.A.
Cornell U., 1954; graduate studies, Harvard University, 1954-56;
(6) Divorced; (7) child--Rachel Wetzsteon, b. November 25, 1967;
(8) free-lance writer, 1958-1964; editorial department and feature
writer, Village Voice, 1964-1970; theatre critic, Village Voice, 1967-
1971, 1975- ; executive editor, Village Voice, 1971-1975; (9) critic-
in-residence, CCNY, 1969-1971; (13) U.S. Army, 1956-1958; (14) Phi

Beta Kappa, Woodrow Wilson Fellowship; (20) Village Voice, New
York Times, New York Herald Tribune, Playboy, Plays and Players;
(21) 101 West 12th Street, New York, N. Y. 10011, Ph. 212-929-2124;
(22) Village Voice, 80 University Place, New York, N. Y. 10003, Ph.
212-741-0030; (23) Circulation: 160,000; (24) 75 plays, 10 features.

Harsh, Bitter, Brutal--the Real "Threepenny" Comes to New York
               (by Ross Wetzsteon, Village Voice, May 10, 1976)

        Joe Papp's most inspired decision in 21 years as head of
the New York Shakespeare Festival was to ask Richard Foreman
to direct "Threepenny Opera."

        Let's not underestimate the risk Papp was taking. After
all, respected as Foreman is in avant-garde circles, in his nine
years in the theatre he had yet to direct any plays other than
his own, and his approach to acting has been as idiosyncratic
as his writing style--if, indeed, one could call his plays "acted"
at all. Furthermore, "Threepenny" may well be the most beloved play in the repertory at least for New York Theatergoers, who fondly remember the charming, picturesque Blitzstein version which ran through most of the 1950s at the Theatre
de Lys.

        Well, no one is leaving the Vivian Beaumont "charmed" these
days. Foreman's production isn't peopled by Sarah Lawrence
girls delightfully pretending they're whores, it doesn't sweetly
turn into an entertainment with an occasionally mordant message,
it doesn't, in short, wink "we're only kidding." Harsh, sarcastic, bitter, and brutal, this "Threepenny" is so coldly passionate
it freezes your bones.

        No small part of Foreman's achievement is that this is a
thrilling production despite the fact that it contains only two outstanding performances, and, in nearly all the female roles, inept ones. Raul Julia's Macheath is relentlessly, hypnotically
savage--his harsh intonations, his chilling arrogance even his
toe-down-first walk convey an awesome force under obsessional
discipline. And C. K. Alexander's Peachum, plump with persistence, turns mere self-serving into the most cynical of sur-
vivals. Caroline Kava's Polly, on the other hand, seems too
sweetly ingenueish and ingratiating, and Ellen Green's Jenny--
well, I'm only guessing, but I'd imagine Foreman must want to
strangle her for such laughably anguished emoting, as if some
Borscht-Belt Barbra were auditioning for Puccini. Her rubber-
mouthed performance is a perfect example of the paradox that
overstating an emotion can create precisely the opposite effect--
or conversely, that the most powerful effects are often created
by restraint and understatement.

        Indeed, Foreman has chosen a kind of rigidly mechanical
but savagely forceful monotone as his basic performance mode,
starting from the opening hurdy-gurdy number in which windup

dolls are explicitly, and horrifically, invoked. Almost every performance is unmodulated, but far from dissipating Brecht's force, this focuses it with an acidulous intensity. Foreman's directorial vision is so evident throughout, in fact, that I'm surprised not by how much Foreman has brought to Brecht but by how much Brecht has always been present in Foreman.

Some further examples of the Foreman signature:

Voices, utterly devoid of naturalistic psychology, rather than serving as means for characters to communicate with one another, are used to directly address the audience.

Props, isolated dream-like on a bare stage, rather than serving as mere "environments," take on the potency of living characters.

Space, focused with geometric precision, rather than serving as mere "place," organizes and guides our perception of the characters' relationships. (An entire book could--and certainly will--be written about Foreman's use of space. In this particular production, nearly every moment becomes a formal tableau, with special emphasis on groupings in horizontal lines, on daring use of depth and perspective, on the resonance of the emptiness between characters. One senses direction by diagram, a closet geometry teacher in Foreman--but far from mechanizing his characters, this precision liberates his vision.)

The fundamental paradox of Foreman's directorial style, then, is that by ruthlessly simplifying--by denaturalizing, by depsychologizing, by eliminating and focusing--he forces us to perceive endless complexities. Concentration of attention, in short, leads to multiplicity of meaning. One specific example: As Polly sings the words "you have to let your feelings show," everyone on stage is frozen in an expressionless tableau, everyone but Macheath, who, at these hesitantly pleading words, slowly, ironically, ruthlessly ... tips his hat. And in that single simple gesture, I felt theatre at its most resonantly provocative.

Yes, no one is leaving the Vivian Beaumont "charmed" these days--some of the comedy may have been lost, but that "happy ending" is no longer an ironic wink of complicity, it now contains the excoriating sarcasm, the bitter sneer, the full force of Brecht's rage.

WHITE, Ron; (2) Fine Arts Editor; (3) b. San Antonio, Nov. 4, 1944; (4) s. L. V. and Madge (Clark) W.; (5) B.A., M.A., St. Mary's U., San Antonio, major subject: English, 1969, 1976; (6) m. Sue Brown, Oct. 1, 1965; (7) children--Shannon Lea, Michael Jason; (8) Advertising writer, San Antonio Light, 1963-1965; Reporter, San Antonio Light, 1965-1971; Reporter, San Antonio News, 1971-72; Fine Arts Editor, San Antonio Express and News, 1971- ; (9) Actor and director, Shoestring Players, St. Mary's University, 1963-65;

editor, The Roadrunner, house publication of San Antonio Transit
Company, 1963; stringer, Time-Life, 1971- ; correspondent, Texas
Monthly, 1973- ; (10) Member San Antonio Bicentennial Commission
Publications Committee; (11) Democratic Precinct Chairman, 1970;
(12) Mem. San Antonio Arts Council Board, 1974-75; (14) Hearst
Newspapers Honorable Mentions for Short and Humorous Writing,
1966, 1967; Robert F. Kennedy Journalism Awards, honorable men-
tion, 1971; (15) American Newspaper Guild, 1965-1971; (20) Cont.
articles to Texas Monthly, San Antonio, San Antonio Review, Texas
Southwest; Mummy, Bloody Mummy, three-act play produced Melodrama Theater, San Antonio, 1975; Robin Hood's Sherwood Scandals,
three-act play (with Tim Laughter) produced Melodrama Theater,
San Antonio and Tao, N.M. , 1975; (21) 116 E. French, San Antonio,
Tx. 78212, Ph. 512, 735-1643; (22) San Antonio Express and News,
P.O. Box 2171, San Antonio, Tex. 78297, Ph. 512-225-7411; (23)
Circulation: 150,000; (24) 75 plays, 75 motion pictures, 50 art
shows, book reviews and miscellaneous.

Theater Venture Opens Doors to "Sister George"
(by Ron White, San Antonio Express, March 16, 1975)

It was like the circus had come to town and everyone was
a kid full of excitement and joy.

But the event Sunday was better than a circus. It was the
opening of a new theater in San Antonio, and a darned good, exciting and promising theater at that.

It's the Countryside Theater, an operation in a large backroom of the San Antonio Country night club at 1122 N. St. Mary's
St. The theater retains some of the atmosphere of the nightclub--
seating at tables, drinks available--making for one of the most
confortable theaters since San Antonio Theater Club went out of
business.

But one would have been willing to endure discomfort and
even some pain to see Countryside's opening production, "The
Killing of Sister George. "

Here there is a circus atmosphere too, instilled by director
Jimmy Williams in Frank Marcus' script about an actress on a
rampage because the character she plays on a BBC radio soap
opera, Sister George, is being written out of the show violently.

Set in Sister George's rather drab apartment, the show otherwise has a circus look and feel to it. The overlarge, clownish
suits of Sister George combine with the broad, booming, thundering delivery given George by Cynthia McFarland.

Susan Droke, as George's lover, Childe, looks like a caricature of a kewpie doll at a sideshow and seeming to be about as
fragile.

The abandoned exaggeration to their performances blends in
well with Marcus' script. George and Childe's lesbian relationship is a satire of the stereotypes found in heterosexual marriages.

George rants about the apartment, striking matches on her
pants fly to light thick cigars, threatening to make Childe drink
her bath water as punishment for her indiscretions. Childe is
a parody of the mousy housewife, chattering on blithely about re-
cipes, dabbling with poetry, and bestowing motherly concern on
her family of dolls littering the apartment.

Simultaneously McFarland and Droke destroy the stereotypes
in their characters.

McFarland destroys it through the sheer excess of her bom-
bast, blowing up George into a monster of nightmare proportions,
a winner of the Miss Humanity award who beats up nuns in taxi-
cabs and pounces on Childe's every action with raging paranoia
and homicidal intent.

The lives they lead are no more real than the fabricated
characters in Sister George's soap opera. Behind the cardboard
profiles of Childe, George and the radio characters, there is
another, real vicious world, where the only thing that counts in
an absurd life--made more absurd by meaningless melodramatic
death and suffering--is the ability to survive by sacrificing others.

"Sister George" is inhabited by two other phonies. Magda
Porter, as a BBC executive, is a machine of cold and deadly
etiquette, dressed in a proper suit and white gloves, drinking
a cup of tea while she politely informs George of her upcoming
demise on the radio.

And Mary Helen Langford, as a neighboring fortune teller,
is a delightful mish-mash of temper tantrums and sentimentality,
her bra straps hanging on her shoulders and one spring of her
brain always bounching into the netherworld.

They are all brought together by Williams' fast-paced, intelligent and single-minded direction. It is a fine start for any
theater. "Sister George" will be presented Tuesday night and
Sunday through Tuesday of next week.

The Countryside Theater has plans to produce a musical this
fall and possibly Shakespeare's "The Merry Wives of Windsor"
in the fall. If its productions live up to the quality of "Sister
George," it will be a major addition to San Antonio's theater life.

Director Changes Comedy of Fools into Silly Farce
(by Ron White, San Antonio Express, June 6, 1975)

An old black man, crooning softly to himself, sweeps up the

the floor of the room in the run-down Cattleman's Hotel, a room decorated with U.S. and Confederate flags, a cross festooned with light bulbs and banners from defunct lodges of the Knights of the White Magnolia.

When the local knights arrive, bickering about a horseshoe match, the custodian is hustled out because the meeting of the Knights is no place for a black man.

Nor, as it turns out, is the meeting a place for any man who's not intellectually or emotionally crippled, a dreamer or a fool.

Preston Jones' "The Last Meeting of the Knights of the White Magnolia," which opened Tuesday at Trinity University following productions at the Dallas Theater Center and the Arena Stage in Washington, D.C., is a bitter-humorous look at the small-town world of useless men looking for a cause, an exploration of the kind of mind that makes itself important with tiles like "Grand Wizard" and "Keeper of the Mystic Mountain."

The play is the middle part of Jones' trilogy about life in the fictional, West Texas town of Bradleyville, a place where Texas myths of grandeur and glory are being replaced by a Holiday Inn.

The fictional Knights of the White Magnolia, formed in 1902 when the KKK wasn't doing a good enough job, used to have lodges all over Texas and even in Oklahoma. Now the only lodge left is in Bradleyville, with seven members meeting once a week for dominoes and booze.

But this meeting is something special because a new member--the first in five years--is going to be initiated.

The head of the lodge, L. D. --played with a fine understanding of the type of man who becomes a leader of nobodies by playwright Jones--hopes the ideals of the lodge can be revived by the new brother.

But the ideals and the initiation ceremony are lost in a book no one can find except the black custodian. And the initiation distintegrates into squabbles about rules and a bottle of whiskey.

Told in the freshly interesting setting of Jones' Bradleyville, "Knights" is a basic story of illusion and reality--the illusion of importance men acquire through meaningless rituals ... men like L. D. , who honestly can't understand why their new brother finally flees from them.

The characters have a reality they aren't aware of; they do not see themselves with the unforgiving eye of Jones.

While we laugh at them as Jones intended, there is a bitter undertone to Jones' writing, a feeling that he knows these people as bigots and haters and small minds--qualities which will never be hidden by any amount of ludicrous shenanigans.

But Jones' bitterness is kept subtly in the background. He allows himself few direct comments. Col. Kinkaid's enfeebled ramblings at times become Jones' voice--the colonel commenting endlessly, "Flap, flap, flap," as the words of the initiation rite are recited, and his vivid recollection of a WW I battle, a bloody reality that ultimately destroys the silly playing of grown men.

Director Paul Baker at times seems to be working at cross purposes with Jones' script. While Jones is wisely content with letting his characters prove themselves to be failures, Baker tries to convert them into merely farcical clowns.

Although some of the actors--Jones, Crump, Moore and Ken Latimer as a cigar-chewing misanthrope--maintain a constant quality of low-pitched reality in their performances, Baker leads others, particularly Keith Dixon as the new member and Sam Nance and John Logan as constantly bickering companions, into broad caricatures that simply do not become the play.

The initiation, which needs no special emphasis to underline its silliness other than Jones' ritual of nonsense words and ludicrous costumes, is given such a TV sitcom sense of farce that one almost loses sight of Jones' truth.

Jones has written a remarkable play of subtlety and painful honesty marred only by an ending that rambles about until it finally reaches the real end: the black custodian literally getting the last laugh at the men who hoped to keep him in his place by evoking the mystic power of the moon.

But Baker's production with a Dallas Theater center cast threatens to turn "Knights" into self-mockery. It deserves a more careful, thoughtful presentation.

WICKSTROM, Gordon M. , (2) Associate Professor of Drama, Franklin and Marshall College, Lancaster, Pa.; (3) b. Boulder, Colo. , Apr. 26, 1926; (5) B. A. and M. A. English literature, U. of Colorado, Ph. D. , Dramatic theory and criticism, Stanford U. , 1968; (6) m. Betty J. Smith, 1948; (7) children--Linnea and Maurya; (8) Teacher and director of theatre, Powell High School, Powell, Wyo. , 1950-1966. Teacher of dramatic literature, criticism, and theory and director in the Green Room Theatre at Franklin and Marshall College, 1968-77; Editor of "Theatre in Review" in Educational Theatre Journal 1971-74; Chief Regional Officer for Region II of American Theatre Association, 1975-76. Director for Colorado Shakespeare Festival, summers: 1962, 73, 75; (10) Member of theatre advisory Panel for Pennsylvania Council for the Arts 1973; President

of Theatre Association of Pennsylvania 1973; (13) USN-CB Battalions,
W.W. II; (14) Invitation from Polish Ministry of Art and Culture to
visit Poland in recognition of service to Polish Art and civilization;
(15) Member of AAUP, ATA, and TAP; (20) Cont. articles to ETJ
and to Players; (21) 1937 Temple Ave., Lancaster, Pa. 17603, Ph.
717-393-9582; (22) Franklin and Marshall College, Lancaster, Pa.
17604, Ph. 717-393-3621, ex. 414; (23) Circulation: now contributing
two or three reviews to ETJ to a present total of a dozen.

"The Sky Is Falling: A Destruction Ritual." By Ralph Ortiz.
(by Gordon M. Wickstrom, Educational Theatre Journal, January 1970)

It all began quietly, uncertainly in the sceneshop of Temple
University's new Tomlinson Theatre. Over-stuffed furniture was
destroyed, tentatively at first, by twenty-five volunteer participants in Ralph Ortiz's Destruction Ritual, The Sky is Falling.
This central event of AETA Region XIV conference puzzled,
bored, angered, and impressed an audience of theatre specialists
watching over closed circuit T.V. in the main auditorium. I
was one of a handful who witnessed the thing first hand.

On one wall were 9' X 9' slide projections on paper screens
of an injured human brain, of an open visceral cavity, and of an
ulcerated penis. Celebrants on ladders cut up these paper images
and splashed them with cups of cow's blood to the cry of "Kill
the enemy body!" This action blended into general blood throwing (twenty-five gallons were required) and breaking of eggs with
cries of "Kill the enemy fetus!" Fresh fruits and vegetables
were smashed, stomped, and put in electric frying-pans to burn
in a mixture with blood and feathers. The participants tore
their clothing to rags, but not to nudity, and burned those rags
with special irons--the accumulating odor growing, as was intended, steadily worse.

Along another wall, twenty-five headless but otherwise intact
chickens were hung as on a clothes-line. At a signal, they were
attacked, torn down, and mutilated, the celebrants using the torn
parts to beat each other. Tempo, volume, excitement mounted
toward frenzy, and the chickens (Asian enemy corpses) were
thrown exultantly against the wall.

An upright piano stood in the middle of the carnage, prepared with bags of blood and live mice inside. Ortiz now took
command. With a shining, new axe and to rhythmic shouts of
"Calley, Calley, Calley," Ortiz destroyed the piano with precision and elegance, leaving its harp swimming in blood, flat and
silent on the floor.

From the beginning, two men in gigantic, floor-length dresses stood on a ledge overhead. Large balloons secreted in their
skirts were blown up accompanied by sexual gyrations. The
celebrants on the floor below were now shouting "Fuck the enemy!" The balloons burst and the two grotesque "ladies" were

delivered of live chickens--Henny Pennys of Artaud's falling sky. These chickens were intended for sacrifice while wired to the smashed piano harp, but in Philadelphia, the SPCA heard of the plans, objected, and forced a compromise wherein these chickens were saved and "needless" killing of the laboratory mice avoided.

All the while, one participant lay in a pool of blood with his shirt previously stuffed with a complete set of animal viscera. To his cry of "Let me live!" he was abused, kicked, and ignored throughout. (It might be important to note that this actor was overcome with nausea at the end.) Blood contined to flow through the ritual, and, as Richard Schechner observed later, the brilliant color of it all was incredible--no other red like that! Perhpas it was like Vietnam.

In one corner of the room were set a hundred or more mouse traps into which two hundred mice were thrown; some died; some escaped; some were hurt and helpless. Again it may be important to note that in the aftermath (not part of the scenario) when the troop was running in orgiastic procession through the building and among the T.V. viewers, several participants remained behind and in heavy silence, slowly and with infinite tenderness set about rescuing the mice.

The ritual ran out of steam and ended in the auditorium with T.V. monitor focused on the piano harp back in the shop, and the inevitable panel discussion began. Schechner defended Ortiz by declaring mimetic theatre dead and "reactualization" the new mode. Henry Hewes spoke of the differences between ritual and theatre, and Martin Gottfried was unimpressed. Ortiz declared his aim to be "conversion" through "Paleo-logistics of visceral action"--a way of self-discovery vis-à-vis monstrous modern life--especially that violence in Vietnam. He also made it clear that his rites were meant for participation, not for observation.

Many found it easy summarily to dismiss Ortiz, but it should be remembered that such violent rituals are, in fact, "paleo-logistics" of human experience. In their primordial usages, however they were justified as efficacious magic and were obligatory for celebrant and witness: these rites expressed the community in its attempt to control life and fortune. Today there is no magic, no obligation, no community, nothing to ease our worry that Ortiz's rites are of little use and may be dangerous. Private therapy and public testimony against the war cannot replace the lost faith that once sanctified blood and violence. Authentic rite was religion and became theatre only with its displacement toward secular myth. Now theatre seems anxious to return to the sacred experience; many of us welcome the impulse, but are uncertain how it can be fulfilled.

American College Theatre Festival, VI.
(by Gordon M. Wickstrom, Educational Theatre Journal, April 1974)

Neil Cuthbert's The Soft Touch, the winner in the ACTF's

first playwriting contest, launched this year's festival with high, inventive spirit. Produced by Douglass College, Rutgers University, the play had a superior cast, sensitive, fast-paced direction by John Bettenbender, a realistic faded apartment setting by Joseph Miklojcik, and a collection of unforgettably zany characters: a tramp who delivers "magic hour" speeches to the audience, rifles food supplies, and is or is not the father of several people in the play; a husband who is constantly searching for his nympho spouse and chases her through beds, into showers, as she climbs fire escapes, and makes appropriate personal use of his bat-shaped softball trophy; a brassy-voiced, barge-like mother; a fey cat burglar; one character who plays two brothers simultaneously; and an underworld landlord with Civil War relatives. To cap it, Cuthbert's dialogue is brilliant. The only drawback to the production was the static nature of the plot, revolving around the various bizarre situations and people who move in and out of the apartment while the hero, Blinky, is trying to get to sleep.

For the second production, Frank Brink, of Alaska Methodist University, directed and performed in his Song of the Great Land (the one production held in the Concert Hall). This was presented only once and under unfortunate circumstances. By midway through the first half, a number of school groups in the audience had become so noisily inattentive that the production was halted to allow various requests for polite attention. This resulted in a second half which was, at least, audible. However, as performed by the chorale of singers, instrumentalists, and readers, the production was plagued throughout by unrelieved self-righteousness and distance. Part I reviewed Alaska's early history to the gold rush; Part II moved to the present, ending with a heavy-handed plea for ecology. The production expended most of its energy in "telling"; facts and figures, names and places rolled by without contact. Only in isolated moments were we allowed to touch any of the feelings which the readers talked about with such familiarity and at such length.

Jerry Rockwood, of Montclair State College, attempted to adapt Machiavelli's Mandrake to 1890s New York. W. Scott MacConnell's sets were alive with astigmatic pinks, greens, reds, and blues--ingeniously combining Serlio and the streets of New York. The orchestra, with honky-tonk piano, was wheeled on and off in a trolley car. Within such a world, actions and lines needed to be clear and alive; instead, speaking voices were tired monotones; singers seemed to perform on residual air; the dialogue juxtaposed a seemingly straight translation of Machiavelli with flat, realistic improvisation. Dispirited actors self-consciously played scenes which required sleight-of-hand and the ability to turn phrases. It was as if the director had read a dissertation on popular late-nineteenth-century stage practices, made a list of certain techniques, and asked his actors to do a shadow play based on the lecture.

The fourth production, Lane Bateman's <u>Lying in State</u>, was awarded honorable mention in the playwriting awards program. Two gay couples have just moved into married student housing at a university--the two males posing as the husbands, the two females as their wives. In reality, the two males are living in one unit, the two females in an adjoining one. The show proceeds with long-winded lectures among the four about their gayness, problems with "others," the appearance of a straight neighbor, the splitting of one couple with the arrival of another lover, the aging homosexual, the proud gay, the mother who appears with her wealthy redneck, fag-hating, [womanizing husband]....

WILK, Dr. Gerard H.; (2) Foreign correspondent, theater critic; (3) b. Sept. 1, 1902, Berlin, Germany; (4) s. Hugo and Doris (Lewitt); (5) Dr. of Laws, University of Göttingen, Germany; (6) m. Susan Frankl, February 16, 1949; (7) daughter--Jane Dorothy; (8) Attorney-at-Law, Berlin, Germany until 1933; Lawyer for Actors, Directors, Producers, Schiller Theater, Berlin; Immigration to Yugoslavia and Internment; attached to the U.S. Army in Italy--PWB & ISB 1943-46. In this capacity Program Officer Radio Station Salzburg, Austria 1945-56; (9) Critics and reports on the theater; Germany until 1933; in Yugoslavia 1933-41. Since 1946 reporting for various offices of the U.S. Govt. on the American Theater Scene for Germany; U.S. Information Agency until 1969; (10) Officers Cross of Merit of the Federal Republic of Germany, July 1972; (16) Ind.; (17) Congregational; (18) Overseas Press Club, Outer Critics Circle; (19) Correspondent for Cultural Affaires: Die Deutsche Bühne, Cologne; Sender Freies Berlin, West-Berlin; Der Tagesspiegel West-Berlin; Süddeutscher Rundfunk, Stuttgart-Karlsruhe, Mannheim; Heidelberg-West Germany, Contr. "Mainz-Magazine"; "Rundschau, Philadelphia," "Aufbau," New York Westdeutscher Rundfunk, Cologne; (20) Author of about 100 radio plays; (21) 74-02 Kessel Street, Forest Hills, N.Y. 11375, Ph. 212-544-1713; (22) Office address the same; (23) Listeners: about 300,000--Readers around 150,000.

Chicago ist Nicht Berlin
(by Gerard H. Wilk, Der Tagesspiegel, July 16, 1975)

O tempora mutantur--am Broadway gibt es zur Zeit ein Musical "Chicago," das eine ganze Reihe von Kritikern und anderen dazu veranlasst hat, in dieser Schau ein Abbild des Berlins der sogenannten "Goldenen Zwanziger Jahre" zu sehen. In der Mitte der zwanziger Jahre kam das Stück "Chicago," auf dem dieses Musical basiert, auch nach Berlin. Eine etwas zynische Satire auf das "Jazz-Zeitalter," die Gangster in Chicago, die Prohibition und die Korruption. Es war damals ein rauschender Efolg. Als nun der "Sitzredakteur" einer Abendzeitung (der im Jahre 1933 der Garaus gemacht wurde) in Moabit angeklagt wurde, eine prominente Persönlichkeit im öffentlichen Leben beleidigt zu haben, erklärte der Verteidiger, die Zeitung habe im berechtigten Interesse genhandelt, denn Berlin sei nicht Chicago, Der "Sitzredakteur" wurde freigesprochen, der Nebenkläger verzichtete auf Berufung.

Nun sind wir also soweit, dass, wenn Korruption und Dekadenz auf einer New Yorker Bühne erscheinen, man von dem Berlin der zwanziger Jahre spricht und sich an Brecht und Weill, Georg Grosz, das Romanische Cafe und viele Dinge erinnert, die in New York zu verklärten Legenden eines Berlins wurden, das es ja tatsächlich so nie gegeben hat.

Das Musical handeit von einer verheirateten Frau, Roxy Hart, die ihren Geliebten ermordet hat und einen völlig skrupellosen Verteidiger findet. Der fragt nicht, ob sie schuldig oder unschuldig ist, sondern lediglich, ob sie sein Honorar zahlen Könne. Er bekommt sie natürlich frei. Der Prozess macht Roxy berühmt; das bringt Geld und öffnet ihr den Weg ins Showbusiness.

Das Musical trägt in jeder Phase den Stempel von Bob Fosse, dem Schöpfer des Films "Cabaret." Bereits in diesem Film, noch mehr aber in seinem zur Zeit Karl des Grossen spielenden und seit Jahren erfolgreich am Broadway laufenden Musical "Pippin," sieht Fosse im Showbusiness eine Metapher für die verschiedensten Aspekte des Lebens. In "Chicago" nun treibt Fosse diese Versinnbildlichung auf die Spitze (und verliert dadurch an Wirkung): Er macht Mord, Bestechung zu Bestandteilen der Unterhaltungswelt. Wenn Liza Minnelli singt "Leben ist ein Cabaret," so sagt hier der Verteidiger: "Mein Metier ist Zirkus und Schau." Wer würde da nicht an Wedekinds Marquis von Keith erinnert: "Das Leben ist eine Ruischbahn ...?"

Fosse zieht sein Musical als eine Reibe von mitreissenden, manchmal geradezu umwerfenden Vaudeville-Akten auf: eine Mitgefangene Roxys, die zum Tode durch Hängen verurteilt ist, wird als Zirkusakrobatin am Trapez dargestellt; wenn der Verteidiger Roxy eintrichtert, was sie vor den Geschworenen zu sagen hat, wird daraus ein Bauchrednerakt--mit Roxy auf den Knien des Anwalts. Jeder Teil der Schau wird zu einer Sang- und Tanzszene. Der Conferencier sagt: "Meine Damen und Herren--nun ein Stepptanz." Roxy bedrängt ihren gehörnten Ehemann, Geld für den Verteidiger aufzutreiben, und vier Tänzer mit Melonen steppen im Hintergrund à la Fred Astaire ... Der Ehemann zieht sich später ein Clowsgewand an und singt-- und das ziemlich rührend--Ich bin ein Zellophan-Mann-" Die Schau ist voll von einer im amerikanischen Musiktheater unüblichen Ironie--so singt der Verteidiger, dem nur an "money" gelegen ist: "Esgibt für mich nur eins--Liebe ..." und sechs Chorgirls wedein mit Fächern.

Martin Gottfried sagt in der New Yorker "Post," Bob Fosses "Chicago" sei expressionistich und eindeutig im "deutschen Stil." Als besonderen Grund führen er und andere Kritiker an, es sei eine Schau ohne Hertz. Das Berlin der zwanziger Jahre, mit dem sich immer mehr amerikanische Publikationen und

Dissertationen beschäftigen, wird in Amerika leider durch eine
Zerrbrille gesehen, und das nicht zuletzt durch Fosses unerhört
populären Film "Cabaret." Dieser Film, viel mehr als das
gleichnamige Musical, das ihm voranging, hat Kritiker, Soziolo-
gen und andere veranlasst, sich für Berlin vor der Machtergrei-
fung" auf ihre Art zu interessieren. Was dabei herauskommt,
kann allerdings manchen Berliner bedrücken. Fosses "Chicago"
ist nicht Berlin, weder in der Mentalität noch im Milieu. Auch
steht kein Sturmtrupp ante portas. Auberdem hatte Chicago auch
nie ein Romanisches Cafe. Aber doch ist dies das erste Musi-
cal--zugegeben mit bergrenztem Erfolg--, das einen Versuch
macht, ein Urteil über unsere auf Theatralik und Sensationslust
eingestellte Zeit auszusprechen, in der Kriminelle im Schauges-
chäft zu Heroen hochgejubelt werden können.

WILLIS, John Alvin; (2) Editor, teacher; (3) b. Morristown, Tenn.
Oct. 16, 1916; (4) s. John Bradford and George Anne (Myers) W.;
(5) B.A. cum laude Milligan Col. 1938; M.A. U. Tenn. 1940; post-
grad. Ind. U. 1941; Harvard 1942; (6) m. Claire Olivier 1959 (divorced 1965); (8) Tchr. English, U. Tenn. 1938-40; actor stock,
touring cos., tv, radio 1945-55; dean, tchr. drama Natl. Acad. Theatre Arts 1947-49; tchr. English NYC public high schools 1955- ;
(13) Served to lt. USNR 1943-45; (15) Member Actors Equity Assn.,
Alpha Psi Omega, NY Drama Desk; (20) Asst. Editor: Theatre
World (1945-65), Screen World (1949-65), Opera World (1952-54),
Pictorial History of the American Theatre (1950, 1960, 1970), Great
Stars of the American Stage (1952), Pictorial History of the Silent
Screen (1953), Pictorial History of Opera in America (1954), Pictorial History of the Talkies (1958), Pictorial History of Television
(1959); Editor: Theatre World, Screen World (1965-), Dance World
(1966-); (21) & (22) 190 Riverside Drive, NYC 10024.

WILSON, Edwin; (2) Teacher and theater critic; (3) b. Nashville,
Tenn., Nov. 10, 1927; (4) s. E. E. and Catherine (Jones) W.; (5)
B.A. Vanderbilt U., maj.: English, 1950; Graduate Diploma in Eng-
lish, U. of Edinburgh (Scotland), 1951; B.F.A. Yale U. Drama
School, 1957; D.F.A. Yale Univ. Drama School, 1958; (8) Taught
theater, Hofstra Univ., 1958-60; Prod. Asst., Broadway Play, Big
Fish, Little Fish, 1961; taught at Yale Univ. Drama School, (Visit-
ing Asst. Prof.) 1961-62; Assoc. Prod., Off-Bwy play, The Good
Soldier Schweik, 1963; Prod., Off-Bwy play, The Burning, 1963;
Asst. to Prod., film, Lord of the Flies, 1961; Asst. to Prod.,
film, The Connection, 1961; Resident Director, The Barter Theater,
Abingdon, Va., 1964; Co-Prod., Off-Bwy play, Rooms, 1966; Co-
Prod., Bwy play, Agatha Sue, I Love You, 1966; teacher, Hunter
College of City Univ. of New York, 1967 to present, rank Assoc.
Prof.; Theater Critic, Wall Street Journal, 1972 to present; (20) Au-
thor: Shaw on Shakespeare (ed. and Introduction); The Theater Ex-
perience, (pub. Jan. 1976, McGraw-Hill).

The Uncluttered Style of Samuel Beckett
(by Edwin Wilson, Wall Street Journal, November 28, 1972)

It was Mies van der Rohe, the architect, who said "Less is more." He meant that the cleaner the lines of a building, the less cluttered with excessive ornamentation, the more effective it was likely to be. The same can be said of all the arts, and in theater no man has pushed the notion further than Samuel Beckett.

Best known as the author of "Waiting for Godot," Beckett is a paradoxical figure. Though an Irishman, he lives in France and even writes his plays in French, later translating them into English. A recluse himself, his plays are presented all over the world, and he is probably the most widely written-about dramatist of our time.

In striving for his own clean line, he has written a number of theater pieces in which he has deliberately stripped away many of the usual dramatic elements, thereby making us focus more clearly on those which remain. Rather than giving his characters the freedom to move about the stage which dramatic action ordinarily demands, in several plays he has totally immobilized them: in one he has characters in a trash can; in another he places them in large pottery jars; and in a third he has a woman buried in a mound of earth, up to her waist in Act 1, and her neck in Act 2. In two other plays he has taken away words rather than movement, and written what amount to pantomimes. It is as if he were tying one hand behind his back.

To go as far as Beckett does is dangerous business; the risks of static, deadly dull drama are high, and every word, every gesture must count to the full. In the past Beckett has shown he can meet this challenge, and he does so again in a new short play, "Not I," which had its world premiere last week at the small Forum Theater at Lincoln Center. The play is being presented as part of a Beckett Festival: two alternating evenings of two plays each. One bill pairs "Happy Days" (the play with the lady sitting in the mound of earth) and "Act Without Words I" (one of the pantomimes), while the other pairs "Krapp's Last Tape" with "Not I." Both bills feature Jessica Tandy and Hume Cronyn and are directed by Alan Schneider.

"Not I" takes place in an almost totally darkened theater. Before we can see anything we hear a woman's voice chattering. Gradually, almost imperceptibly, in mid-air at the rear of the stage a tiny white spotlight picks out a woman's mouth and chin-- nothing else is visible. It is she who is speaking. Then we notice, as if by accident, at the front of the stage a huge, silent puppet-like figure at least fifteen feet high outlined by a vague light from above. Across the black void, the mouth and the tall, ghostly figure face one another, and for the entire play that is all we see, except for two or three occasions when the figure,

known as The Auditor, raises his hands, perhaps in propitiation
perhaps in resignation; it is difficult to tell.

But if there is no movement, there are words, a torrent of
words pouring forth nonstop from the brightly lit mouth, for
about twenty minutes. And in that time so much happens that
it is impossible to plumb the depths of the piece in one hearing,
possibly even in two or three. But we get enough.

She is a woman revealing her present and recalling her past.
As a young girl, probably Irish Catholic, she remembers strict
religious training and snatches of pleasant moments. She continually tries to recapture an April morning in the green grass,
but it slips away like quicksilver. As a woman she is shy, and
so much is pent up inside her that once or twice a year she
rushes into the street, accosts a stranger, and showers him
with words. But it does not work; the words come so rapidly,
so incoherently, that the man does not understand. Incredibly,
in the theater, we are watching a re-enactment of this very experience.

She is also concerned about her mouth, the jaws, lips, and
tongue, which never stop and seem to work independently of her.
This, in turn, suggests her brain, which never ceases either--
dreaming at night, darting from thought to thought in the day.

The play is a genuine tour de force, and so is the acting.
Jessica Tandy, as the woman, delivers the monologue at breakneck speed, but with utter clarity and every nuance in place.
(The Auditor, played by Henderson Forsythe, never speaks.)
Thanks both to Beckett and Miss Tandy, we not only get a sense
of the woman, we become involved with her. This is another
of Beckett's attributes. He is a scout who has gone out for us
to chart unknown territory, to explore the outer limits of human
desolation and futility. But no matter how far he ventures, he
never loses touch with his own humanity, or with ours. No
writer in our day has been so unsentimental and, at the same
time, so compassionate.

This shows up clearly in "Krapp's Last Tape," which shares
the bill with "Not I." A crusty old man, played by Hume Cronyn with careful gusto, always makes a tape recording on his
birthday. We see him, alone and decrepit, on his 69th birthday, listening to a tape of thirty years before. As he hears of
past loves he longingly embraces his recording machine. The
juxtaposition of his high hopes of the past with his sordid state
of the present is as heart-rending as it is uncompromising.

Beckett's work is not easy, nor is it meant to be. But in
"Not I," the new work, he has shown once again how much he
can achieve with so little. When we add the verbal images of
the woman's monologue, which throw off a thousand sparks in
the mind, to the stark visual image of the Mouth and the Auditor

in the theater, the effect is overwhelming. In Beckett's case, there is no doubt "less is more."

There will be longer plays, and far more elaborate productions opening this season, but moment for moment and word for word, it is unlikely we will see a more significant or provocative new play all year.

Fun and Games in a Cancer Ward
(by Edwin Wilson, Wall Street Journal, October 14, 1974)

"The achievement of modern art is that it has ceased to recognize the categories of tragic and comic or the dramatic classifications, tragedy and comedy, and views life as tragicomic." These words of Thomas Mann, the German writer, are, if anything, more true today than when he wrote them some 40 years ago. In recent years, serious writers like Samuel Beckett, Harold Pinter and Eugene Ionesco have chosen tragicomedy as their chief form of expression. In tragicomedy, subjects which were never thought fit for humor--death, loneliness, and horror-- are treated comically; and at the same time, humor is taken very seriously.

The most recent example of the form is "The National Health" by British author Peter Nichols, now at the Circle in the Square Joseph E. Levine Theater. The play was done in Britain about five years ago, and produced by the Long Wharf Theater in New Haven last season. It is the latter production which has now come to New York. The title refers to Britain's government health service which provides subsidized cradle-to-grave health care for everyone. Doubtless for British audiences the title was intended to have a second meaning, referring to the spirtual health of the nation as well as the physical health of its citizens. Local references are minimal, however, and for American audiences there is no serious loss; there may even be a gain in being able to concentrate on the play's more universal aspects.

The play is set in a hospital ward whose patients have a variety of ailments, some quite painful and serious. Throughout the play life--and death--goes on: Nurses come and go, doctors make their rounds more interested in teaching interns than in watching their patients, patients suffer attacks and die, other patients come to take their places. All of this is carried out in graphic detail, with no shortage of hypodermic needles, bed pans, and catheters. In this sense the play is like other recent British plays, such as "The Contractor" and "The Changing Room," in which the emphasis is on a group of characters, rather than one or two, who are caught in a very realistic situation. In the case of "The National Health" the ensemble playing under the direction of Arvin Brown is first class, which makes the unpleasant facts of medical life all the more vivid.

So far there would not appear to be much to laugh about,
but it is against this somber hospital background that Mr. Nichols places his comedy. To begin with, there is an orderly,
a sort of master of ceremonies who talks directly to the audience
and gives humorous lectures on the proper method to shave patients prior to an operation. The orderly also switches on TV
for the patients, though here the TV is not on a screen, but on
a small stage revealed at one end of the ward where members
of the hospital staff double as the participants in a soap opera.
The soap opera is a love story of doctors and nurses and serves
as a parody of what is actually happening in the ward; it also
underlines the fact that there is some truth in the soap opera,
and a good deal of soap opera in what is going on in the hospital.

In the hospital scenes themselves, Nichols points up the incongruity of having a nurse wake a patient up to give him a
sleeping pill, or of doctors in the morning performing abortions
to prevent the unborn from living while in the afternoon they
operate on the very old to keep them alive even when they no
longer want to live, or of a woman who is a religious fanatic
and comes to deliver the message that he will have everlasting
life to a man who has just died. There are scenes, too, which
are simply comical in their own right.

Unlikely as it may seem, the blend of the comic with the
unpleasant in "The National Health" provides some of the funniest scenes of any play now in New York. This is the method
of good tragicomedy: the serious and the humorous do not ne-
gate one another, but each throws the other into bold relief.
The comedy becomes even funnier, and then there is the reversal. At "The National Health" the audience is laughing uproariously one moment, and falls into total silence the next.

The play is too long, by at least twenty minutes, with several superfluous scenes at the end, including one with a chaplain. But for much of the evening Mr. Nichols has hit the right
tragicomic note. His message is that of most tragicomic writers:
that our jokes have more meaning than they may at first suggest,
and that in such serious experiences as illness, death, and the
fear of death, human beings continue to have their humorous,
foolish moments. There is also the notion that laughter is
sometimes the only way to endure severe pain.

For many people, the modern world with its violence and
injustice appears ridiculous or absurd, and anything absurd always gives rise to laughter: the laughter of tragicomedy. But
it is not laughter which escapes from reality or evades the truth,
it is laughter which helps us face the truth, as well as bear the
pain. Mr. Nichols has provided a good example of how it works
in "The National Health. "

WINER, Linda, Room 414, Chicago Tribune, 435 N. Michigan Ave. ,
Chicago, Ill. 60611.

WISE, Morna, Record-Courier, 126 N. Chestnut St., Ravenna, O. 44266.

WOOTTEN, Dick, Cleveland Press, 901 Lakeside Ave., Cleveland, O. 44114, Ph. 216-623-1111.

WRIGHT, Jr., Frederick William; (2) Theatre and Film Critic; (3) b. Nashville, Tenn., April 21, 1940; (4) s. Frederick Sr. and Mary (Boring) W.; (5) B.A. Eckerd College, major subj.: English literature, 1964; M.A. Univ. of So. Fla., major subj.: English literature, 1971; (6) Divorced; (7) no children; (8) Deskman, St. Petersburg (Fla.) Evening Independent 1964-65, Staff Writer, St. Petersburg Evening Independent 1965-66, Feature Writer, St. Petersburg Evening Independent 1966-68, Theatre and Film Critic, St. Petersburg Evening Independent 1968- ; Visiting Instructor: Critical Writing, Univ. of So. Fla., 1974-75; (10) Mem. and former VP, Eckerd College Alumni Council; (14) Cited Second Best Columnist in Florida, Fla. Press Club, 1973; Voted First Place Straight News Writing, Florida Press Club, 1974; (15) Mem. College English Assoc., mem. Florida Psychic Society, mem. National Film Council, 1972- ; (16) Democrat; (17) Protestant; (20) Writings: 5 short stories, 14 poems, 53 free lance articles to various Sunday supplements, monthly magazines, quarterlies; (21) 1701 20th Ave. N, St. Petersburg, Fla. 33713, Ph. 813-895-3291; (22) St. Petersburg Evening Independent, P.O. Box 1121, St. Petersburg, Fla. 33731; Ph. 813-893-8247; (23) Circulation: 36,000; (24) 100 plays and musicals, 175 motion pictures, 40 television shows, 20 miscellaneous.

Farce: Asolo Erupts Like Old Unfaithful
(by Fred Wright, St. Petersburg Independent, February 14, 1975)

A whole flock of new faces adorn this season's Asolo State Theater stage as those canny, campy pro actors open their 15th season with a risque French farce, updated.

Farce is the Asolo's favorite form of comedy, so it is quite appropriate that last night's gala opening would be a George Feydeau farce, verbally modernized (1970) by Suzanne Grossmann and Paxton Whitehead, so that the result is a slightly subdued romp through various bedrooms and marriages.

This year's company, fleshed out by four new full-timers and a gaggle of Florida State University grad students, is excitingly agile, with just the right mixture of old pros and new pros and promising pros.

The farce, "There's One in Every Marriage," is ridiculously complicated, with assorted lovers seeking to commit assorted infidelities, and the plot isn't as important in a farce as the carefully controlled frenzy of characters caught with their scruples down, running from cuckolded wives or husbands, scampering about in madcap fashion.

The production, directed by Howard Millman, is one of the Asolo's better farce productions in several seasons. Credit the play's updated rewriting and Millman's sense of visual business, plus the Asolo's traditional exuberance.

Newcomer Max Gulack shares the burden of the comedy with veteran Bradford Wallace, and the two are delightful studies in contrasting acting techniques that achieve the same effect--raucous laughter.

Gulack, looking like a Dickensonian character, is a perpetual motion machine. He never stops moving or gesturing or grimacing. He is frenetic and yet thoroughly understandable, playing a roue of sorts, foolish rogue who pursues women at random, and gets his unjust deserts in the end. Gulack always seems on the verge of a nervous breakdown, yet there is a distinctive sense of control at work throughout his character.

Wallace, so popular with Asolo audiences that he gets entrance applause, plays a less physical role, a husband whose lone past infidelity comes back to haunt him. Wallace is the master of control, of the subtle style of acting. A wink serves him just as well as a grimace, a glance heaven-ward as well as a pratfall. A Chaplinesque character actor, Wallace is a solid pivot for much of the farcical frenzy.

The entire cast, though new and old, is excellent. There is such a variety of characterization, from a nervous bellboy to a wanton woman, from an exhausted lover with two too many propositions at hand to an over-protective man servant.

Director Millman has cast this showcase opener well, and his perennial sense of the visual, and of the acute timing demanded for a farce to avoid seeming out of control, make this play rich in humor and performing skills.

Indeed, a large part of this year's Asolo company gets to flex its comedic muscles, to show off its talents, to expel all that kinetic energy that builds up in a repertory company as the season debut nears.

"There's One in Every Marriage" also is a wise selection, for its mixture of traditional and contemporary makes the comedy more than the usual farce fare. The dialog is expertly modernized, and the construction of plot and events is perfectly blended to integrate conventional gimmicks with modern one-liners.

The comedy is fat with puns and verbal gymnastics, and even those people who don't particularly tune in to farces will be enchanted by this grand opening offering.

If this 1975 season can be predicted on the basis of the debut play, the year will be one of the Asolo's best. The scheduled repertory is not all that exciting on the surface, but the Asolo company, recognized nationally as one of the best rep groups in the country, is capable of turning a stew into a souffle.

Asolo: Jeeter's Family Gives Us Jitters
(by Fred Wright, St. Petersburg Independent, March 3, 1975)

John Steinbeck's "The Grapes of Wrath" tells of the solidarity and love within the bounds of poverty and squalor. Erskine Caldwell's "Tobacco Road" tells of the heredital apartheid and cold emptiness of poverty and squalor.

The region isn't important, but the commentaries are. Caldwell's "Tobacco Road," transposed to script by Jack Kirland and first performed in 1933, is now at the Asolo State Theater in a production that is acutely uncomfortable in its implications rather than its statements.

The Asolo production, guest directed by S. C. Hastie, is solidly more tragic than comic, although a contemporary audience still feels the same need of the 1930s audience to laugh at the base, coarse and almost animalistic existence of Jeeter Lester and his family. The laughter comes not so much from pure comic statement as from a kind of pathos for the characters who are taken out of time and place and thrust before us like specimens at a zoo.

Their behavior, their life-styles, their laissez-faire surrender to life are so baroquely brutal that laughter is a balm for the audience. At times, under Ms. Hastie's direction, the production reaches the near tragedy of the Greeks, except these are not high men lowered by action, but tragic characters who have known only tragedy, with sex and momentary emotional eclipses as the only digressions from poverty.

The Asolo production nonetheless carries a mixture of comic relief, thanks to Ms. Hastie's astute and often dual direction so that the entertainment is varied, and the heavy burden of tragedy is not unrelenting. She gives us, on several occasions, bits of comic business in one corner of the stage while Jeeter Lester is narrating a bit of exposition about the past of these characters and these times, and the comedy, almost in mime, is gratefully diverting without smothering the necessary facts of the monolog.

But the play really belongs to Asolo company member William Leach, who gives the character of Jeeter Lester an uncomfortable dimension of humanity, although the character is one of the basest and least glorious non-heroes of American stage. Leach's patient, detailed performance, with virtually every mannerism and gesture a fitting echo to the essential character, makes for captivating/viewing, for the action pivots about Jeeter's inaction.

And while the play is basically a one-character play, the
Asolo company fills out the production with small characterizations that enhance and entertain, even when these portrayals are
not the focus of the play. Barbara Reid McIntyre as Ada Lester is silent and strong and earth mother at times, a patient bystander to life at others.

Stephen Johnson as the doltish son, Martha J. Brown as the
scarred and scared daughter, Joan Rue as the one gem in her
mother's life, and Max Gulack as a simple man with complexly
simple needs add weight and nuance to the play, particularly Gulack, who again shows his ability to handle an unaccustomed role,
underplaying his character with almost inarticulate speech and a
shuffling way of life. But Isa Thomas, in a most unflattering
but very rich role as a man-hungry woman evangelist, perhaps
strikes the audience with the most surprises, never overplaying,
but managing to make a character that is written for comic pathos a character of variety and shades of definition.

Rick Pike's single set is rough and sure and exact, a fine
background for the slow unfolding of this slice-of-nonlife story.

Indeed, this Asolo production has excellence at every turn,
although the performance is remarkably non-physical, and intensely unsettling. These are not characters we can really enjoy
or sympathize with. They know no love, and only sex in a kind
of diverting way. They are land people, bound to the earth but
not willing to turn the earth to growth. They are characters
awaitin' God's providence, but not hurryin' any to help God along
in the salvation.

These are characters out of an unpleasant past, and sadly,
a very real and more unpleasant present. It is to the Asolo's
credit that we can watch these characters, and yet perhaps be
entertained and moved as well.

WYLDER, Robert C.; (2) Professor of English, California State University at Long Beach; play reviewer, Long Beach Independent and
Press-Telegram; (3) b. Malta, Mont. , Jan. 10, 1921; (4) s. Robert
J. and Myrtle (Monroe) Wylder; (5) B.A. 1947, M.A. 1949, Montana
State University, Ph.D. 1955, University of Wisconsin; English and
drama; (6) m. Elizabeth A. Cutts, July 1, 1944; (7) children--Mar-
tha E. , Nancy A. , Jamie R.; (8) Professor of English 1953- , play
reviewer 1958-64, 1969- ; (10) American Field Service chapter and
district officer; Citizens' Advisory Environmental Committee, Long
Beach; (13) U.S. Marine Corps Reserve, officer, 1943-46 served in
Pacific and Japan; various area and unit citations; (15) NCTE, CATE,
SCTE, ZPG, FOE, Common Cause, Sierra Club, ACLU, Long Beach
Herb Society; (16) Democrat; (17) Unitarian Universalist; (20) Textbooks, An Herb Garden of Verses, articles; author or co-author of
nine textbooks; (21) 1817 Iroquois Avenue, Long Beach, Ca. 90815,
Ph. 213-431-2737; (22) English Department, CSULB, Long Beach,

Ca. 90840, Ph. 213-498-4212; (23) Circulation: 400,000; (24) 20 plays.

Dewhurst Eclipses Robards in "A Moon"
(by Robert C. Wylder, Independent, Press-Telegram, November 29, 1974)

"A Moon for the Misbegotten," now playing at the Ahmanson, is Eugene O'Neill's last play and is by many considered one of his best. It ran for almost a year to full houses in New York before opening this week in Los Angeles. There it promises to run interminably--every night.

For "A Moon," like too many other O'Neill plays, tries to accomplish in three hours what it ought to be able to do in less than half that time. It has one act's worth of content stretched out over four acts. If its subject matter were more substantial, its character analysis more penetrating, or its dialogue more interesting it might justify its ponderous length. As it stands, it only wears down the audience in a long day's journey into ho hum.

O'Neill doesn't get much help from the top-billed player, either. Jason Robards seems to be entirely lost in the role of Jim Tyrone, the lush who will soon inherit the Hogan farm. Robards is as repetitious in his use of hand-over-face and hunched shoulder gestures as O'Neill is in his lines. Both sorts of repetition get tiresome rather early. The fact that Robards muffles many of his lines through his hands so that they cannot be understood is hardly good acting, but it doesn't seem to matter; O'Neill has him saying pretty much the same things later anyway.

Now Colleen Dewhurst, the real star of the show, is another matter. As Josie Hogan, the self-styled "great rough ugly cow of a girl," she brings to the proceedings a good deal of vitality and impeccable diction. She is the misbegotten of the title, an unusually large, plain woman who speaks roughly, fosters a reputation for promiscuity, is really a virgin, and somehow manages to love Jim Tyrone. Josie is not a wholly believable character, but Miss Dewhurst at least makes her interesting most of the time.

Tom Clancy does the same for Phil Hogan, Josie's father, a petty tyrant who by his meanness has driven his three sons from the family farm. Clancy's Hogan does not emerge as particularly mean, but he is lively and dynamic, even likable. His scenes with Josie early in the play before Tyrone shows up are the most interesting of the whole evening. Everything goes downhill from there.

Jose Quintero directed the production. Apparently he shares the playwright's conviction that heavy is profound and long is

moving. But maybe not. Maybe he was just stuck with all
those lines.

Jewish Tradition Key to Dybbuk
(by Robert C. Wylder, Independent, Press Telegram, Febru-
uary 1, 1975)

It has often been said that you don't have to be crazy to be
a psychologist, but it helps. I feel the same way about "The
Dybbuk," now playing at the Forum: you don't have to be Jewish to enjoy it, but it would help. In fact, no one without some
knowledge of the Jewish tradition is likely either to understand
it entirely or to appreciate it fully.

Taken out of its context, the content of the play isn't really
very interesting. In the first act the spirit of a young man possesses the body of the young woman he loved. In the seemingly
very long second act a rabbi struggles to exorcise the dybbuk
and to free the girl. That's it.

But put back into its context of a Jewish hassidic community
in Poland of the 1880's, that rather simple plot becomes a way
of presenting and underlining the values of the Jewish world. In
the John Hirsch arrangement of S. Ansky's original 1920 script
we find a good deal of the folklore and a good many of the folk-
ways of the community as well as numerous echoes of village
life among an oppressed people.

The sense of unity that pervades the play makes the possession of the girl not a personal but a community disaster. In a
world circumscribed by religious laws and hassidic tradition, a
disruption like the dybbuk can shatter the world. A spirit
stronger than the rabbi is a threat to man and God alike. No
wonder the villagers are shaken.

The cast bringing us the play is almost as numerous as the
villagers of Brinitz; there are almost three dozen players, of
whom a dozen or so have significant parts. All perform excellently. Nehemiah Persoff as Rabbi Azrielke dominates the stage
in the second act, bringing vitality and spiritual strength to the
almost overwhelming job of exorcising the dybbuk and conducting
the trial of the possessed girl's father.

Equally compelling is the performance of Marilyn Lightstone
as the bride possessed by the demon. Her frenzy makes the
dybbuk very real indeed. Jean-Paul Mustone plays Chanon,
whose spirit enters the girl's body, Bert Freed is Sender, the
girl's father, and George Sperdakos is the Messenger. All are
good.

Maxine Graham's simple but effective set enhances the action, producing a sense of timeliness while allowing an easy flow
of movement in time and space. Graham and Mark Negin

collaborated on the costumes, which also aid in establishing just
the right atmosphere.

Well, I can't say that I understood it all or got out of it all
I might, but I can say that it was a very interesting experience.
I'm glad I went. I wonder how my Jewish friends will react to
it. They're as far from the hassidic community as I am, I suspect.

Sholom alecheim.

YOST, Barbara, Phoenix Gazette, 120 East Van Buren Street, P.O.
Box 1950; Phoenix, Ariz. 85001.

YOUNG, (Arthur) Allen; (2) Editor and critic; (3) b. Washington,
D.C., July 4, 1918; (4) s. Arthur N. and Nellie May (Bailey); (5)
Occidental College, 1937-41; U. of Chicago, 1940-41, 1946; English,
Political Science; (6) m. Barbara Stroup, June 24, 1950; (7) children--
Sarah Abigail (Travaini); David Allen; Andrew Nichols, Elizabeth
Corlett; (8) Assistant Librarian, The Denver Post, 1947-57; Writer
and critic of music, theatre, films, The Denver Post, 1948-57; Den-
ver, 1957-59; Critic and Editor of arts pages, Cervi's Rocky Moun-
tain Journal, 1959-63; Executive Director, Young Audiences, Inc.,
Denver Chapter, 1963-72; Editorial Assistant, Rocky Mountain Medi-
cal Journal, June 73 to present; free lance writer for Opera News,
The Los Angeles Times, Time Magazine, Life Magazine; Denver-
Colorado correspondent for Musical America since 1962; columnist
on environmental subjects The Daily Journal, Denver, 1966-71; arts
critic Sentinel Newspapers, Denver area, since 1964; (9) President,
The Allied Arts, Inc.; President, The Greater Denver Council for
the Arts and Humanities, 1970-72, Board of Directors, 1969-73;
Board of Directors and program annotator, The Friends of Chamber
Music, 1966 to present; (13) T/5,802d Aviation Engineers, U.S. Air
Force, 1941-45; (14) Citation, Colorado Association of Music Clubs,
1957; (16) Democrat; (17) Episcopalian; (21) 3701 South Lincoln Street,
Englewood, Colo. 80110, Ph. 303-761-4059; (22) Sentinel Newspaper;
(23) Circulation: 70,000 (24) 40 plays and musicals; 60 concerts;
5 dance, 10 art exhibits.

DU's "Scandal" Remarkable Performance
(by Allen Young, Cherry Creek News, November 28, 1973)

Glittering style in direction, performances, costumes and
setting make Sheridan's "The School for Scandal" a remarkable
theatrical achievement.

In a time when it seems the world never stops talking, it
may take undue fortitude to accommodate such verbosity as Sheridan and his theatrical personages spout. But John Powell is
the extraordinary director capable of maintaining the broth and
frivolity of the play.

Lewis Crickard's stunning design makes superficiality the key to this production with its ornate facades and rarely opened doors.   Powell creates his characters individually and amusingly, with the weight of their characterizations completely externalized. They scintillate. They flourish. They scandalize.

The DU Professional Theater Company has developed into an ensemble that is professional in the best the word can evoke. It is a brilliant company of actors displaying prodigal abilities, among them discipline and the sense of honest interplay.

Michael Murdock is fine in his rich sense of character as Sir Peter Teazle, the comedy's most sober individual, and Michele Garrison captivates with the beauty of her speech and lively air. Sherri Felt is a charming Maria.

Gary Giem is so charming as Joseph Surface, so elegant in speech and dashing in appearance, that it is something of a blow to shift sides and favor as the better man his brother, Charles, Derrell P. Capes, a forthright and affable young man.

Ann Jacques is superior as Lady Sneerwell, Bill Brady incredibly funny as Crabtree, and William McNulty all amiable idiocy as Sir Benjamin Backbite. Jessica Richman's Mrs. Candour, Louis Malandra's sterling Rowley, and Stephen B. Scott's Sir Oliver are exceptionally strong apt characterizations.

Musical interludes by Normand Lockwood evoke the clash of the times and the elegance of period manners in their apt instrumentation and strong sense of character.

*   *   *

Constance Moffit is a rare example of the operetta singer with a genuine voice, and hers has a lovely quality that makes you wish for more from her. Her role is too silly to be true, but she brings distinction to all of it. Her hero is Joe Bellomo, a stalwart with an unusually pleasing baritone.

There are other extra dividends in the buoyant beauty of Jack Morris' tenor, the wacky wizard of Jeremy Hays, Kathy Logan's impudent princess, Steve Riley's affable singing and dancing of the show's best number, "Very Soft Shoes," and Carol Conway as a Nightingale.

Bill McHale moves them around swiftly, and the best thing to fill up the spaces in this show is McHale's expert pacing. The musical direction has less polish than we are used to hearing in Country Dinner Playhouse musical shows.

"Night Music" One of Best to Hit Town
(by Allen Young, Arapahoe Sun Sentinel, June 13, 1974)

Dazzling in its Mozartean elegance, its laughter mixed with

the rue that attends men and women in their affairs of the heart, "A Little Night Music" is one of the most beautiful shows ever to play Denver, and it is certainly one you won't want to miss.

At one point in the musical play it is asked "Where is style? Where is skill?" Between Stephen Sondheim, whose graceful waltzes and sudden eruptions of musical energy mean so much, and Harold Prince, whose staging concept is so striking, the answer, or at least one answer, has been found: right on this stage.

Perhaps trivially, perhaps aimlessly, three couples lose their loves, find new loves and arrange a more optimistic future, having looked within to find the smiles of a summer night have blessed their new understandings. A simple device which is given elaboration in the songs, movement, and interplay to reach an almost Proustian depth.

These couples wandering through endless birch groves, magically created by designer Boris Aronson, are mostly concerned with time, with present urgencies in the Now, problems that make Later seem almost a lost time, and Soon, a time to be anticipated with honest understandings.

Sondheim has far exceeded his previous work in the use of song to advance dramatic action. Tuneful and tasteful, his music has consistent superior quality. A favorite? Mine is the culminating number of the first act, an almost operatic finale, "A Weekend in the County," with "The Miller's Son" a close second.

Jean Simmons' sumptuous beauty and her clear handling of spoken and sung words were there to relish, while Margaret Hamilton's spunky Madame Armfeldt was subtly colored and lively.

George Lee Andrews, a Denver favorite from The Flaming Pit of years ago and more recently of the Country Dinner Playhouse, was splendid as Fredrik, singing smoothly, projecting a debonair yet unsettled individual.

This is a strongly cast production in which the company has not one weak link. To name a few, Mary Ann Chinn sparkled as Petra, the amorous maid whose singing of "The Miller's Son" added so much. Ed Evanko was smart and impressive as the somewhat mad military Count, while Andra Akers was superb as Charlotte.

Virginia Pulos was the immature bride, singing beguilingly, while Stephen Lehew created a funny yet moving illustration of the immature son.

The quintet which introduces the show and threads its way

through it is strongly composed of Elliott Savage, Kris Karlow-
ski, Marina MacNeal, Joe McGrath and Karen Zenker.

Richard Parrinello conducted as fine a pit orchestra as you
will ever hear.

I think this is a show that is going to be around as long as
quality, style, and skill have a place, which is to say always.

YOUNG, Mort; (2) Asst. National Editor, Hearst Newspapers; (3) b.
New York City, Jan. 2, 1933; (4) Harry & Kate (Marks); (5) B.S.,
New York U., majors: Theater, Journalism (1957); (6) m. Meredith
L. Dash, Jan. 25, 1963; (7) child--Matthew; (8) Feature-writer,
investigative reporter, L.I. (N.Y.) Daily Press, 1957-58; Freelance,
N. Africa & Mid-East, 1958-1961; N.Y. Journal-American, 1961-66;
N.Y. World Journal Tribune, 1966-67; Sr. Manager, Information
Services, editor of Pan Am Clipper, Pan American World Airways,
1967-71; Hearst Newspapers, 1971-present; (13) U.S. Army, 1953-55;
(14) James Fennimore Cooper Award for best article on the U.S.
Press, N.Y.U. (1957), N.Y. Newspaper Guild Page One Award for
Journalism (1958), Deadline Club (N.Y.) Hon. Mention, investigative
reporting (1965), Hearst Newspapers Writing Awards, 1961, '62, '63,
'65, '66; (17) Jewish; (20) "UFO-Top Secret," a Study of Air Force
Investigative Methods, Simon & Schuster, (1965); (21) Manhattan; (22)
Hearst Newspapers, 959 Eighth Ave., N.Y., N.Y. 10019; (23) 1.5
million (daily), 2.5 million (Sunday), (24) 40 plays and musicals, 10
films.

New Neil Simon Play Opens; God's, Maybe, But Not Critic's Favorite
     (by Mort Young, News American, December 15, 1974)

"God's Favorite" updates the Biblical story of Job and serves,
as well, as a pseudo-biographical portrait of its author, Neil
Simon.

Simon says that his new play, which has just opened in
Broadway's Eugene O'Neill Theater, is actually about his father,
a devoutly religious man. It is no slur at Simon to recall that
it's a wise man who knows his own father.

For this is a typical Simon formula play. That is, it's
slick, fast and would make a superior TV sitcom. Any resemblance between the characters and human beings is incidental.

A superfluously wealthy man, who came up from the slums
of New York is visited by the Devil in the guise of a messenger from God. It seems God and the Devil have bet that Joe
Benjamin, played by Vincent Gardenia can be made to renounce
God if only he is visited by sufficient and unbearable misfortunes.

The mansion burns down. The man's corrugated-carton factory burns down. The electricity, heat, gas, butcher and grocer

are cut off. Various physical ailments afflict Joe Benjamin.
Yet he will not renounce God, though he does get angry when
God blinds his erring, eldest son, David, played with wry drunk-
enness by Terry Kiser.

Well, just as in the Bible Joe--Job, get it?--the favorite of
God, is finally let off the hook. Then the Devil approaches the
eldest son with the same story--and the curtain falls on Simon's
two-act TV script of the 1974 season, presented live.

The evening resounds with inside jokes that can only be
shared by 200 million TV watchers. Brand names are dropped
right and left. Some smart manufacturer ought to put up the
money for a movie, for the advertising exposure alone.

"God's Favorite" is Simon's 14th Broadway play. It is not
his best and may well be his worst. It is overloaded with snappy
comebacks, throwaway lines and running gags.

All the old jokes you loved so much are trotted out. Now,
that's not so bad. Old jokes get old by continuing to delight the
listener. But too much of a good thing is not so good a thing.

Michael Bennett directed, "God's Favorite," keeping those
jokes and actors moving right along. Of particular charm were
the Goody Two-Shoes youngest son, played by Lawrence John
Moss, and his twin sister, played by Laura Esterman, who is
tortured by the thought that a rapist might not run his clammy
hands up and down, up and down, her body.

Maria Karnilova, a fine actress, suffers because her role
as Joe's wife requires a demeanor too dim to light up the inside of her cranium. Had her role contained lines less puerile,
less hammer-over-the-head, to suggest her dimness, Miss Karnilova would have been a force to reckon with. As it was, her
pretended stupidity wrecked all the efforts she made.

The servants, played by Roseeta LeNoire and Nick Latour,
were aptly loyal and human in their responses to their master's
predicament.

Audiences come to a Neil Simon play ready and willing to
laugh. On opening night, the audience laughed when the curtain
went up--so confident has the author made them in his ability
to tickle their funny bones.

But Simon's reference to his own father's unabridged faith
in God, as depicted in "God's Favorite," was more trite than
true to the generalities of life. Simon apparently reflected himself in the role of David, the cynic who finally accepts that there
is a God.

But this really has nothing to do with the play. And as a

TV sitcom, "God's Favorite" would be overwhelmed by "Rhoda."

Casting a Vote for James Earl Jones
(by Mort Young, Hearst Publications, December 29, 1974)

The voting for the annual Tony Awards is secret, but James Earl Jones gets this reviewer's vote right now for best stage actor of the year because of his performance as the retarded giant, Lenny, in "Of Mice and Men."

The Broadway revival of John Steinbeck's 1937 play, at the Brooks Atkinson Theatre, was a tour de force by Jones. Despite admirable performances by Kevin Conway as George and Stefan Gierasch as Candy, Jones towered above not only his fellow-actors but the play itself.

Steinbeck received the Drama Critic's Circle Award for his play. No doubt it had more impact in those Depression days, in an age closer to the throbbing poverty of migrant workers, than it has today. Were "Of Mice and Men" to come to the stage fresh now, it might be picked apart for its weak expository scenes. The best scenes are the first and last; all else seems to be pie filling.

How much more pop it ought to be nowadays, even though we seem to be diving into another depression era, but for the artistry, grace and talents of James Earl Jones. How easy it would be for a lesser actor to employ a gimmick or to concentrate on one or two accepted cliches in order to create the approximate reproduction of a retardate.

Jones, however, plays the role with innate dignity: the dignity of a child grown to mammoth proportions, with the facade of a man and of a person held to accountability as a man--but who is only a baby grown large. There is no trickery in this portrayal; there is biting truth. And accuracy.

"Tell me about the rabbits, George," had become a stock phrase that elicited at least chuckles during the years after Steinbeck's drama first appeared. Now the phrase tolls with ineffable sadness.

After the final scene, when George puts a pistol to Lenny's head and kills him, while painting Lenny's favorite dream of a little farm with a rabbit hutch and a vegetable patch, Conway and Jones embraced during the curtain call. It was just as well they did. The vision of that last image became almost unbearable, so well did these two actors evoke the trust that chained the two characters together.

It was their dream to save up enough money to buy a little land of their own, where they would have no bosses, where they could put down roots and end their wandering loneliness. Candy, an old ranch hand with only one arm, makes himself a partner of the dream. Of course, it is dashed.

Two pivotal roles are that of Curley, played by Mark Gordon, and Curley's wife--she is never named--played by Pamela Blair. When Gordon, a pint-sized bully, first appears it is hard to tell whether he is really out of breath as he should be, or merely lisping to indicate he is a crypto-homosexual. Miss Blair seems miscast, doing no justice to the role of a disillusioned, lonely wife of a bully and boor.

The only reason that these two lapses need to be mentioned is that it is impossible to understand how they, particularly Miss Blair, were chosen by the director--Edwin Sherin--at all. Perhaps, considering the effectiveness of their colleagues, they were suffering first night nerves and will improve with more time in the roles.

"Of Mice and Men" may be attended to see how Steinbeck wrote it. It can be watched to recall, as an historical curiosity, the depression days of the 1930s. But the best reason to see it is James Earl Jones. It is his masterpiece.

ZWERDLING, Allen; (2) Publisher-Editor-Theatre Critic; (3) New York City, Oct. 11, 1922; (4) s. William and Yetta Zwerdling; (5) B.S. in Education CCNY; (6) m. Shirley Hoffman, December 2, 1946; (7) children--Sherry, Jan, Gary; (8) Editor-Theatre Critic Show Business 1947-1960, Publisher-Editor-Theatre Critic, Back Stage Publications, 1960-1975; (9) Editor Army Newspaper, Players Guild of Manhattan, Stage Mgr. 1936-1941; Director Kansas City Resident Company 1946; Director American Players in Switzerland and Student Director at Zurich Schauspielhaus, 1945; (13) Army Special Services 1942-45 as Director-Actor of dozens of Army shows and editor of Army newspaper. Also scripts for army radio shows; (22) Back Stage, 165 W. 46 St., New York, N.Y. 10036, Ph. 212-581-1080; (23) Circulation: 17,000 professionals in the communications industry-stage, tv & films.

"The New Moon"
(by Allen Zwerdling, Back Stage, May 14, 1976)

The Village Light Opera Group's production of Sigmund Romberg's musical delight is just that--a musical delight. Those beautiful melodies soar through the Fashion Institute Theatre, jammed with an appreciative audience, (including this reviewer) that applauds madly as each new high note is reached.

Stage Director-Choreo William Koch and Musical Dir.-Conductor Ronald Noll are responsible for this merriment which comes about from an excellent, large orchestra and an enthusiastic cast that, above all seem to be enjoying themselves thoroughly.

With a fine cast of over 50, it is difficult to single out for high praise more than Judith Inglis the star, deservedly so too. Equally important are Barbara Munday Sabel, whose costumes outshine anything on B'way, Ron Kelson's sets and the entire technical crew under producer Judith Neale's supervision.

It's been a long time since we've enjoyed such beautiful music and such beautiful people.

"Small War on Murray Hill"
(by A. Zwerdling, Back Stage, 1976)

"Small War on Murray Hill," playing at Theatre Off Park, 28W. 35th St., NYC, was billed as "a most delightful comedy." Maybe I was in the wrong theatre. In the first act, there were two laughs from the audience--neither of them from me.

Michael Clarke, Robert Quigley and Paul Haskin made valiant, vain attempts to put some life into the production, directed by Frank Marino.

For the record, the large, ambitious cast also included Richard Vernon, Lou Miranda, James Farley III, Lars Kampmann, Woody Eney, Linda Selman, Wayne Flower, Dottie Dee, Anna Lawrence, Wanda Jean Jones and Keith Aldrich. The substantial costumes were the work of Anne De Velder.

GEOGRAPHICAL INDEX

Alphabetized by State, City, Critic's Name;
Canada is at end of sequence

Includes Newspapers, News Services, Syndicates, Agencies; and Periodicals [marked with †] in one sequence; Radio and Television Stations are listed at the end

Akron Beacon Journal (eve. & Sun.) (44 E. Exchange St., Akron, O. 44328)
Shippey, Dick

Albany Times Union (morn. & Sun.) (645 Albany-Shaker Rd., Albany, N.Y. 12201)
Kelly, Martin

Albuquerque Journal (morn. & Sun.) (Journal Publishing, Albuquerque, N.M.)
Hoffman, William

America† (weekly) (106 W. 56th St., New York, N.Y. 10019)
Hughes, Catherine

Amsterdam News (weekly) (2340 8th Ave., New York, N.Y. 10027)
Harris, Jessica

Argus (weekly) (W. H. Stewart Bldg., Seattle, Wash. 98101)
Downey, Roger
Morgan, Murray

The Arizona Republic (P.O. Box 1950, 120 East Van Buren St., Phoenix, Ariz. 85001)
Petryni, Michael

Asbury Park Press (eve. & Sun.) (Press Plaza, Asbury Park, N.J. 07712)
Africano, Lillian

Associated Press (50 Rockefeller Plaza, New York, N.Y. 10020)
Glover, William

Atlanta Constitution (morn. exc. Sun.) (72 Marietta St., Atlanta, Ga. 30303)
Smith, Helen C.

Atlanta Journal (eve. exc. Sun.) (72 Marietta St., Atlanta, Ga. 30303)
Thomas, Barbara

The Austin American-Statesman (daily & Sun.) (P.O. Box 670, Austin, Tex. 78767)
Taggart, Patrick

Backstage (weekly) (165 W. 46th St., New York, N.Y. 10036)
Zwerdling, Allen

Baltimore Sun (morn., eve., & Sun.) (501 N. Calvert St., Baltimore, Md. 21203)
Gardner, R. H.

Bergen News (weekly) (113 Grand Ave., Palisades Park, N.J. 07650)
Michaels, Jeri

Berkshire Eagle (eve., Sat. morn., no Sun.) (33 Eagle St., Pittsfield, Mass. 01201)
Bass, Milton

Bernardsville News (weekly)
(17-19 Morristown Rd.,
Bernardsville, N.J. 07924)
Crossett, D. Allen

Birmingham News (eve. & Sun.
morn.) (P.O. Box 2553,
Birmingham, Ala. 35202)
Shorey, Kenneth Paul

Black World† (monthly) (820 S.
Michigan Ave., Chicago, Ill.
60605)
Fuller, Hoyt W.

The Blade (eve. & Sun.) (541
Superior St., Toledo, O.
43604)
Dresser, Norman
Nelson, Boris

Boston Globe (morn. & eve.
exc. weekends) (135 Mor-
rissey Blvd. Boston, Mass.
02107)
Kelly, Kevin

Boston Herald-American (daily
exc. Sun.) (300 Harrison
Ave., Boston, Mass. 02106)
Norton, Elliot

Boston Phoenix (weekly) (100
Massachusetts Ave., Boston,
Mass. 02115)
Clay, Carolyn

Bridgeport Post (eve. & Sun.
morn.) (410 State St.,
Bridgeport, Conn. 06603)
Day, Richard

Buffalo Courier-Express (morn.
& Sun.) (787 Main St., Buf-
falo, N.Y. 14203)
Plutzik, Roberta
Smith, Doug

Buffalo Evening News (eve. &
weekends) (218 Main St.,
Buffalo, N.Y. 14240)
Bannon, Anthony
Doran, Terry

Calgary Herald (eve.) (206 7th
Ave., SW Calgary, Alberta
Canada)
Portman, Jamie

Capitol Newspapers Group
[Union-Star; Knickerbocker
News] (eve.) (Albany, N.Y.)
Husten, Bruce

Charleston Gazette (morn.)
(1001 Virginia St., Charleston, W. Va. 25330)
Smith, Martha

Chicago Daily News (eve. exc.
Sun.) (401 N. Wabash,
Chicago, Ill. 60611)
Jacobi, Peter
Harris, Sydney J.
Nieland, Christine
Monson, Karen

Chicago Sun-Times (morn. &
Sun.) (401 N. Wabash,
Chicago, Ill. 60611)
Christiansen, Richard
Syse, Glenna

Chicago Tribune (daily & Sun.)
(435 N. Michigan, Chicago,
Ill. 60611)
Winer, Linda
Dettmer, Roger
Cassidy, Claudia

Christian Science Monitor
(morn. exc. Sat. & Sun.)
(One Norway St., Boston,
Mass. 02115)
Eckert, Thor Jr.

Christian Science Monitor
Eastern News Bureau (588
Fifth Ave., New York,
N.Y. 10036)
Beaufort, John

Christianity & Crisis† (bi-
weekly) (537 W. 121st. St.,
New York, N.Y. 10027)
Chapin, Louis

Cincinnati Enquirer (morn. & Sun.) (617 Vine St., Cincinnati, O. 45202)
McElfresh, Tom

Cincinnati Post (800 Broadway, Cincinnati, O. 45202)
Stein, Jerry

The Cleveland Press (901 Lakeside Ave., Cleveland, O. 44114)
Mastroianni, Tony
Wootten, Dick

Columbus Dispatch (eve. & Sun.) (34 S. Third St., Columbus, O. 43216)
Fisher, Edward

The Commercial Appeal (morn. & Sun.) (495 Union Ave., Memphis, Tenn. 38101)
Jennings, Robert Maurice

Commonweal† (weekly) (232 Madison Ave., New York, N.Y., 10016)
Weales, Gerald

Critical Digest† (bi-weekly) (225 W. 34th St., Rm. 918, New York, N.Y. 10001)
Kraus, Ted M.

Cue† (weekly) (20 W. 43rd St., New York, N.Y. 10036)
Stasio, Marilyn

Daily Enterprise (daily) (Box 792, Riverside, Cal. 92502)
Foreman, Thomas Elton

Daily Oklahoman-Oklahoma City Times (Oklahoma City, Okl. 73125)
Denton, Jon

The Daily Pantagraph (daily & Sun.) (301 W. Washington St., Bloomington, Ill. 61701)
Holloway, Tony

The Daily Report (eve. & Sun. morn.) (212 East "B" St., P.O. Box 593, Ontario, Cal. 91764)
Gross, Marge

The Daily Times (eve. exc. Sun.) (126 Library Lane, Mamaroneck, N.Y. 10543)
LeSourd, Jacques

Daily Variety (morn. exc. weekends) (1400 N. Cahuenga Blvd., Hollywood Cal. 90028)
Edwards, Bill

Dayton Daily News (Dayton, O. 45401)
Staten, Vince

Denver Post (eve., Sat. & Sun. morn.) (P.O. Box 1709, Denver, Col. 80201)
Nellhaus, Arlynn
Mackay, Barbara

Des Moines Register (morn. & Sun.) (715 Locust St., Des Moines, Ia. 50304)
Bunke, Joan
Mossman, Josef

Detroit Free Press (morn. & Sun.) (321 W. Lafayette Ave., Detroit, Mich. 48231)
DeVine, Lawrence

The Detroit News (615 Lafayette Blvd., Detroit, Mich. 48231)
Carr, Jay

Dramatists Guild Quarterly† (New York, N.Y.)
Guernsey, Otis L.

Educational Theater Journal† (quarterly) (1317 F St. N.W., Washington, D.C. 20004)
Wickstrom, Gordon
Loney, Glenn

Egyptian [collegiate] (morn.
exc. weekends) (Southern
Illinois University, Carbon-
dale, Ill. 62901)
Hawley, Michael
Singer, Deborah

El Paso Herald Post (eve. &
Sun.) (401 Mills St., El
Paso, Tex. 79999)
Quarm, Joan

Encore American & Worldwide
News (bi-weekly) (515 Madison Ave., New York, N.Y.
10022)
Davis, Curt

Entertainment Eye† (6/yr.)
(70 Amsterdam Ave.,
Passaic, N.J. 07055)
Kessler, Leonard

Essence† (monthly) (300 E.
42nd St., New York, N.Y.
10017)
Peterson, Maurice

Eugene Register Guard (eve.
& Sun.) (P.O. Box 1232,
Eugene, Ore. 97401)
Bishoff, Don

Evening & Sunday Bulletin
(daily & Sun.) (30th & Market Sts., Philadelphia, Pa.
19101)
Schier, Ernest

Everett Herald (eve. exc. Sun.)
(Grand & California Sts.,
Everett, Wash. 98201)
Burley, George
Downey, Roger

Field Newspapers Syndicate
(30 E. 42nd St., New York,
10017)
Riesel, Victor

Flint Journal (daily) (200 E.
First St., Flint, Mich.
48502)
Graham, David Victor

The Florida Times-Union (1
Riverside Ave., Jackson-
ville, Fla. 32202)
Brock, Charles

Focus† (Sun. suppl.) (Sunday
Camera Mag., P.O. Box
591, Boulder, Col. 80302)
MacReynolds, Janet

Fort Worth Star Telegram
(morn., eve., & Sun.) (400
W. Seventh St., Fort Worth,
Tex. 76101)
Brooks, Elston
Eureka, Leonard
Stewart, Perry

Frederick News Post (morn.
exc. Sun.) (200 E. Patrick
St., Frederick, Md. 21701)
Lebherz, Richard

Fresno Bee (eve. & Sun. morn.)
(1626 E. St., Fresno, Cal.
93786)
Hale, David

Hamilton Spectator (eve.) (115
King St., Hamilton 20, Ont.
Canada)
Slack, Lyle

Hampshire Gazette (eve. exc.
Sun.) (16 Armory St.,
Northampton, Mass. 01060)
Hatch, Elizabeth

The Hartford Times (Hartford,
Conn. 06101)
Krieger, Robert

Harvard Crimson [collegiate]
(14 Plympton St., Harvard
University, Cambridge,
Mass. 02138)
Titcomb, Caldwell

Hearst Publications [syndicate]
(959 Eighth Ave., New York,
N.Y. 10019)
Young, Mort

Herald-American Post-Standard
(Sun.) (Clinton Sq., Syracuse,
N.Y. 13202)
Apikian, Nevert

Herald-Examiner (eve. & Sun.
morn.) (Hearst Corporations,
1111 S. Broadway, Los
Angeles, Cal. 90015)
Loynd, Roy

Herald-Journal (eve.) (Clinton
Sq., Syracuse, N.Y. 13201)
Vadeboncoeur, Joan E.

The Herald News (eve. exc.
Sat. & Sun.) (P.O. Box 1019,
Passaic, N.J. 07055)
Greatorex, Susan

Herald-Telephone (eve. exc.
Sun.) (1900 S. Walnut,
Bloomington, Ind. 47401)
Apter, Andrew

Hollywood Reporter (morn. exc.
weekends) (6715 Sunset Blvd.,
Hollywood, Cal. 90028)
Pennington, Ron
Ryweck, Charles (in N.Y.)

Home News (eve. & Sun.) (123
How Lane, New Brunswick,
N.J. 08903)
Albrecht, Ernest

The Honolulu Advertiser (P.O.
Box 3110, Honolulu, HI
96802)
Harada, Wayne
Herman, George
Rozmiarek, Joseph

The Host† (weekly) (415 E.
53rd St., New York, N.Y.
10022)
Cahn, Irving W.

Houston Chronicle (eve. & Sun.)
(Houston, Tex. 77002)
Holmes, Ann

Houston Post (morn. & Sun.)
(Houston, Tex. 77001)
Albright, William

Hudson Review† (quarterly)
(65 E. 55th St., New York,
N.Y. 10022)
Simon, John

Independent Press-Telegram
(weekends) (604 Pine Ave.,
Long Beach, Cal.)
Wylder, Robert C.

Indianapolis News (Indianapolis,
Ind. 46206)
Staff, Charles

Indianapolis Star (morn. &
Sun.) (307 N. Pennsylvania
St., Indianapolis, Ind. 46206)
Patrick, Corbin

Ithaca Journal (eve. -Sat. morn.
no Sun.) (123-125 W. State
St., Ithaca, N.Y. 14850)
MacLeod, Beatrice

The Jacksonville Journal (1 Riverside Ave., Jacksonville, Fla.
32202)
Pate, Bob

Jewish Exponent† (weekly)
1513 Walnut St., Philadelphia, Pa. 19102)
Elkin, Mike

Jewish World of Long Island
(weekly) (Box 812, Melville,
N.Y. 11746)
Calder, Ethan

Journal (morn. Sun.) (75 Fountain St., Providence, R.I.
02902)
Safford, Edwin

Journal-Constitution,(Sun.) 72
Marietta St., Atlanta, Ga.
30303)
Gray, Farnum

The Journal Herald (37 S. Ludlow St., Dayton, O. 45401)
McCaslin, Walter

Journal La Presse (750 St.
Laurent Blvd., Montreal,
Quebec, Canada)
Dassylva, Martial

Kansas City Star (eve. & Sun.
morn.) (1729 Grand Ave.,
Kansas City, Mo. 64108)
Jones, John Bush
Fowler, Giles
Kaye, Joseph

Kent News-Journal (4/week)
(704 W. Meeker St., Kent,
Wash. 98031)
Jackaway, Taffy

Knickerbocker News-Union Star
(Albany, N. Y.)
Husten, Bruce

The Knoxville News-Sentinel
(eve. & Sun.) (208 W.
Church Ave. Knoxville,
Tenn. 37901)
Weirich, Frank

Lancaster New Era (eve. exc.
Sun.) (8 W. King St., Lan-
caster, Pa. 17604)
Taylor, Sam A.

Ledger-Star (Norfolk, Va.
23501)
Bacon, Ed
Dissen, Mary

Long Beach Independent Press
Telegram (morn. -eve. -Sun.)
(Box 230, Long Beach, Cal.
90844)
Wylder, Robert

Long Island Press (92-20 168th
St., Jamaica, N. Y. 11404)
Barber, William
Raidy, William A.

Los Angeles Times (morn. &
Sun.) (Times Mirror Sq.,
Los Angeles, Cal. 90053)
Drake, Sylvie
Sullivan, Dan

Louisville Courier-Journal
(morn. & Sun.) (525 W.
Broadway, Louisville, Ky.
40202)
Mootz, William

The Louisville Times (525 S.
Broadway, Louisville, Ky.
40202)
Saunders, Dudley

Mail-Tribune (Sun. & eve. exc.
Sat.) (Box 1108, 33 N. Fir
St., Medford, Ore. 97501)
Reiss, Alvin

Manchester Journal (weekly)
(Manchester, Vt. 05254)
Notman, Edith

Matzner Suburban Newspapers
[Today; Wayne Today; West
Milford Argus] (weeklies)
(1661 Route 23, Wayne, N. J.
07470)
Rubenstein, Nancy

Memphis Commercial Appeal
(morn. & Sun.) (495 Union
Ave., Memphis, Tenn.
38101)
Jennings, Robert

Memphis Press-Scimtar (eve.)
(495 Union Ave., Memphis,
Tenn. 38101)
Howard, Edwin

Mercury (weekly) (16 E. Main
St., Richmond, Va. 23219)
Rinehart, Ray

Mesa Tribune (eve.
exc. Sun.) (P. O. Box 1547,
Mesa, Ariz. 85201)
Jones, Bill

Michigan State News [collegiate]
(Lansing, Mich.)
Grant, Darryl

Mill Valley Record (weekly)
(438 Miller Ave. , Mill Valley, Cal. 94941)
Sussman, Sharron

The Milwaukee Journal (eve. &
Sun.) (Journal Sq. , Milwau-
kee, Wis. 53201)
Drew, Michael
Noth, Dominique

Milwaukee Sentinel (morn.)
(Journal Sq. , Milwaukee,
Wis. 53201)
Joslyn, Jay

Minneapolis Star (daily) (425
Portland Ave. , Minneapolis,
Minn. 55415)
Altman, Peter A.
Close, Roy M.
Morrison, Don
Vaughan, Peter

Minneapolis Tribune (morn.)
(425 Portland Ave. , Minneapolis, Minn. 55488)
Steele, Mike

Muncie Evening Press (eve.
exc. Sun.) (High & Jackson
Sts. , Muncie, Ind.)
Loy, Bob

Nashville Banner (eve.) (1100
Broadway, Nashville, Tenn.
37202)
Morrow, Sara

The Nation† (weekly) (333 Ave.
of Americas, New York,
N. Y. 10014)
Clurman, Harold

National Observer (nat. weekly)
(11501 Columbia Pike,
Baltimore, Md. 20910)
Ridley, Clifford A.

New Haven Register (eve. &
Sun. morn.) (367 Orange
St. , New Haven, Conn.
06503)
Cochran, Marsha
Lewis, Allan
Roberts, John
Taylor, Markland

New Leader† (bi-weekly) (212
Fifth Ave. , New York,
N. Y. 10010)
Shipley, Joseph T.
Simon, John

The New Republic† (weekly)
(1244 19th St. , Washington,
D. C. 20036)
Kauffmann, Stanley

New Times (weekly-alt.) (P. O.
Box J. , Tempe, Ariz. 85281)
Walsh, Paul

New York Daily News (morn.
& Sun.) (220 E. 42nd St. ,
New York, N. Y. 10017)
Davis, James
Haun, Harry
Leogrande, Ernest
Nelson, Don
Norkin, Sam
O'Haire, Patricia
Reed, Rex
Watt, Douglass

New York Magazine† (weekly)
(755 Second Ave. , New York,
N. Y. 10017)
Rich, Alan

New York Post (210 South St. ,
New York, N. Y. 10002)
Gold, Sylviane
Gottfried, Martin
Herridges, Frances
Hodenfield, Jan
Mancini, Joseph
Newton, Edmund
Watts, Richard

New York Times (morn. & Sun.)
(229 W. 43 St. , New York,
N. Y. 10036)
Atkinson, Justin Brooks (re-
tired)
Barnes, Clive
Gussow, Mel
Kerr, Walter

The New Yorker† (weekly)
(25 W. 43rd St. , New York,
N. Y. 10036)
Gill, Brendan
Oliver, Edith

News American (eve. & Sun.)
(Lombard & South Sts. ,
Baltimore, Md. 21202)
Harriss, R. P.

The News Tribune (eve. exc.
Sun.) (1 Hoover Way, Wood-
bridge, N. J. 07095)
Tuma, Mirko

Newsday (eve.) (550 Stewart
Ave. , Garden City, N. Y.
11530)
Oppenheimer, George
Wallach, Allen

Niagara Gazette (eve. & Sun.
morn.) (310 Niagara St.
Niagara Falls, N. Y. 14302)
Branche, Bill

North Jersey Suburbanite
(weekly) (12 William St. ,
Englewood, N. J. 07631)
Daniels, Robert

Oakland Tribune (eve. , Sat. &
Sun. morn.) (401 13th St. ,
Oakland, Cal. 94612)
Taylor, Robert

On and Off Broadway† (276
First Ave. , New York,
N. Y. 10009)
Gunner, Marjorie

Orange Coast Daily Pilot
(eve. & Sun.) (P. O. Box
1560, Costa Mesa, Cal.
92626)
Titus, Tom

Orange County Evening News
(bi-weekly) (13261 Century
Blvd. , Garden Grove, Cal.
92640)
Taylor, Larry

Oregon Journal (Portland, Ore.
97201)
Marks, Arnold

The Oregonian (daily & Sun.)
(Portland, Ore. 97201)
Mahar, Ted

Orlando Sentinel Star (683 N.
Orange Ave. , Orlando, Fla.
32802)
Rand, Sumner G.

Park East (weekly) (401 E.
79th St. , New York, N. Y.
10021)
Colby, Vineta

Partisan Review†
Gilman, Richard

Paterson News (morn. & eve.
exc. Sat. & Sun.) (News
Plaza, Paterson, N. J. 07509)
McKenna, Timothy

Patriot Ledger (eve. exc.
Sun.) (13 Temple St. ,
Quincy, Mass. 02169)
Lehman, Jon

Peoria Journal Star (morn. ,
eve-Sat. & Sun.) (1 News
Plaza, Peoria, Ill. 61601)
Klein, Gerald

Performing Arts Journal†
(P. O. Box 858, Peter Stuy-
vesant Station, New York,
N. Y. 10009)
Dasgupta, Gautam

The Philadelphia Inquirer (400
N. Broad St., Philadelphia,
Pa. 19101)
Collins, William B.
Niepold, Mary Martin

Philadelphia News (eve.) (400
N. Broad St., Philadelphia,
Pa. 19101)
Takiff, Jon

Phoenix Gazette (eve. exc.
Sun.) (120 E. Van Buren St.,
P.O. Box 1950, Phoenix,
Ariz. 85004)
Masters, Les
Yost, Barbara

Pioneer Press (morn.) (55 E.
4th St., St. Paul, Minn.
55101)
Harvey, John H.

Pittsburgh Post-Gazette (morn.)
(50 Blvd. of Allies, Pittsburgh, Pa. 15222)
Anderson, George

The Pittsburgh Press (eve. &
Sun.) (34 Blvd. of Allies,
Pittsburgh, Pa. 15230)
Blank, Ed.

Playbill† (151 E. 50th St.,
New York, N.Y. 10022)
Rubin, Joan A.

The Post Herald (morn. exc.
Sun.) (Birmingham Post
Company, P.O. Box 2553,
Birmingham, Ala. 35202)
Weaver, Emmet

Poughkeepsie Journal (eve. -
Sat. Sun. morn.) (85 New
Market St., Poughkeepsie,
N.Y. 12602)
Borak, Jeffrey

Providence Bulletin (eve.) (75
Fountain St., Providence,
R.I. 02902)
Gale, William

The Real Paper (weekly) (10B
Mt. Auburn St., Cambridge,
Mass. 02138)
Friedman, Arthur

The Record (eve. exc. weekend) (150 River St., Hackensack, N.J. 07602)
Lambert, Virginia

Record Courier (eve. exc. Sun.)
(126 N. Chestnut St., Ra-
venna, O. 44266)
Wise, Morna

Record World† (weekly) (1700
Broadway, New York, N.Y.
10019)
Mayer, Ira

Richmond News Leader (333
E. Grace St., Richmond,
Va. 23219)
Proctor, Roy

Richmond Times-Dispatch
(Richmond, Va.)
Longaker, Jon Dasu

The Rochester Times-Union
(eve.) (55 Exchange St.,
Rochester, N.Y. 14614
Hansen, Linda

Sacramento Bee (eve, Sat. &
Sun. morn.) (21st & Q. St.
Sacramento, Cal. 95816)
Glackin, William C.

Sacramento Union (morn.)
(301 Capitol Mall, Sacra-
mento, Cal. 95812)
Simon, Richard

St. Louis Globe-Democrat
(morn. exc. Sun.) (12th
Blvd. at Delmar, St. Louis,
Mo. 63101)
Goddard, Bob
Hunter, Frank

St. Louis Post-Dispatch (eve.
& Sun. morn.) (900 N. 12th
Blvd., St. Louis, Mo.
63101)
Pollack, Joe

St. Paul Dispatch <u>see</u> Pioneer Press

St. Petersburg Evening Independent (eve. exc. Sun.)
(P.O. Box 1121, St. Petersburg, Fla. 33731)
Wright, Fred W. Jr.

St. Petersburg Times (morn.)
(Times Building, P.O. Box
1121, St. Petersburg, Fla.
33731)
Smiljanich, Dorothy

Salt Lake City Tribune (morn.
& Sun.) (143 S. Main St.,
Salt Lake City, Ut. 84110)
Beck, David
Forsberg, Helen
Funk, Nancy
Hudson, Roy

San Angelo Standard-Times
(morn., eve., Sun.) (34 W.
Harris Ave., San Angelo,
Tex. 76901)
Vannoy, Cheryl

San Antonio Express & News
(morn., eve., Sun.) P.O.
Box 2171, Ave. E. & 3rd
St. San Antonio, Tex. 78206
White, Ron

San Antonio Light (P.O. Box 161,
San Antonio, Tex. 78291)
Tucker, Glenn

San Diego Magazine† (monthly)
(3254 Rosecrans, San Diego,
Cal. 92110)
Bardacke, Frances

San Diego Union (morn.) (P.O.
Box 191, San Diego, Cal.
92112)
Jones, Welton

San Francisco Chronicle (morn.
exc. Sun.) (905 Mission St.,
San Francisco, Cal. 94119)
Hogan, William
Weiner, Bernard

San Francisco Examiner (eve.
exc. Sun.) (905 Mission St.,
San Francisco, Cal. 94119)
Eichlebaum, Stanley

San Francisco Magazine†
(monthly) (120 Green St.,
San Francisco, Cal. 94111)
Sales, Grover

Saturday Review† [incl. former
SR/World] (450 Pacific Ave.,
San Francisco, Cal. 94133)
Hewes, Henry

Scripps-Howard Newspapers
(Cincinnatti Post, Daily
News Tribune, 200 Park
Ave., New York City, N.Y.
10017)
Nadel, Norman

Scripps-Howard Newspapers
(News Syndicate Group, 200
Park Ave., New York, New
N.Y. 10017)
Nadel, Norman

Seattle Post-Intelligencer (morn.
& Sun.) (Sixth & Wall Sts.,
Seattle, Wash. 98111)
Hawthorne, Maggie

The Seattle Times (eve. & Sun.
morn.) (Fairview Ave. N. &
John St., P.O. Box 70,
Seattle, Wash. 98111
Johnson, Wayne

Sentinel Newspaper Group
(weeklies) (3501 E. 46th
Ave., Denver, Col. 80216)
Young, Allen

Sentinal-Star (daily) (633 N.
Orange Ave., Orlando, Fla.
32801)
Rand, Sumner

Show Business† (weekly) (136
W. 44th St., New York,
N.Y. 10036)
Shull, Leo

The Sign† (monthly) (Monastery
Place, Union City, N.J.
07087)
Griffin, Henry W.

SoHo Weekly (weekly) (111
Spring St., New York, N.Y.
10012)
Marranca, Bonnie
Merin, Jennifer

Somerset Messenger Gazette
(weekly) (P.O. Box 699, E.
Main & Warren Sts., Som-
erville, N.J. 08876)
Ogden, Jean

Somerset Spectator (weekly)
(Rutgers Plaza, Somerset,
N.J. 08873)
Reynolds, Linda

Spectator (daily) (Hamilton,
Ont., Canada)
Slack, Lyle

Springfield Daily News (eve.
exc. Sun.) (1860 Main St.,
Springfield, Mass. 01103)
Hart, Thomas
Trevens, Francine L.

Springfield Republican (Sun.
suppl.) (1860 Main St.,
Springfield, Mass. 01103)
Trevens, Francine

Springfield Union (morn. exc.
Sun.) (1860 Main St.,
Springfield, Mass. 01103)
Hammerich, Dick

Staats-Zeitung (morn. exc.
weekends) (36-30 37th St.,
Long Island City, N.Y.
11101)
Stadelman, Egon

Star-Bulletin (eve. exc. Sun.)
(605 Kapoliani Blvd.,
Honolulu, HI. 96813)
Bowman, Pierre

Star-Ledger (morn.) (Star-
Ledger Plaza, Newark,
N.J. 07101)
Spero, Bette

Staten Island Register (weekly)
(2100 Clove Rd., Staten
Island, N.Y. 10314)
Paine, Canio

Summit Herald (weekly) (22
Bank St., Summit, N.J.
07901)
Plaut, Jonathon

Summit Independent Press
(weekly) (P.O. Box 189,
Summit, N.J. 07901)
Mount, Betty

Sunday News (Sun.) (8 W. King
St., Lancaster, Pa. 17604)
Ruth, Jim

Syracuse Herald-Journal (eve.)
(Clinton Sq., Syracuse,
N.Y. 13202)
Vadeboncouer, Joan

Syracuse New Times (weekly)
(Box 95, University Sta.,
Syracuse, N.Y. 13210)
Brode, Doug
Feldman, David

Tallahassee Democrat (eve.,
Sat. & Sun. morn.) (277 N.
Magnolia Dr., P.O. Box 990,
Tallahassee, Fla. 32302)
Cook, David

The Tampa Tribune (morn. &
Sun.) (P.O. Box 191, Tampa,
Fla. 33601)
Jones, Bruce
McGovern, Bernie
Ruth, Dan

The Tennessean (morn. & Sun.)
(1100 Broadway, Nashville,
Tenn. 37202)
Hieronymus, Clara

Theater in Review†
Wickstrom, Gordon

Theatre World† (190 Riverside
Dr., New York, N. Y.
10024)
Willis, John

Time† (weekly) (Time & Life
Bldg., Rockefeller Center,
New York, N. Y. 10020)
Kalem, Theodore

The Times (bi-weekly) (4627
Ponce De Leon Blvd., Coral
Gables, Fla. 33134)
Tobin, Larry

Times-Advocate (eve. exc. Sat.
& Sun.) (P. O. Box 1477,
Escondido, Cal. 92025)
Russell, Kathlyn

Times-Dispatch (morn.) (333
E. Grace St., Richmond,
Va. 23219)
Longaker, Jon D.

Times-Guide (Wed. & Sat.)
(4627 Ponce De Leon Blvd.,
Coral Gables, Fla. 33134)
Tobin, R. Lawrence

Times Herald-Record (morn.
exc. Sun.) (40 Mulberry St.,
Middletown, N. Y. 10940)
Dulzer, Marie Ann

Times-Picayune (morn.) (3800
Howard Ave., New Orleans,
La. 70140)
Cuthbert, David
Gagnard, Frank L.

Toronto Daily Star (eve.) (One
Yonge St., Toronto MSE-
1E6, Ont., Canada)
Kareda, Urjo

Travel Trade (605 Fifth Ave.,
New York, N. Y. 10017)
Abels, Joel

Tulsa Daily World (morn. &
Sun.) (P. O. Box 1770,
Tulsa, Okla. 74102)
Butler, Ron

United Press International
(220 E. 42nd St., New York,
N. Y. 10017)
Currie, (Donald) Glenne

Valley News and Green Sheet
(334 N. Parish Pl., Bur-
bank, Cal. 91506)
Talcove, Rick

Vancouver Sun (eve.) (2250
Granville St., Vancouver
9, B. C., Canada)
Dafoe, Christopher

Variety† (weekly) (154 W. 46th
St., New York, N. Y. 10036)
Morrison, Hobe

The Village Voice (weekly) (80
University Pl., New York,
N. Y. 10003)
Brukenfield, Dick
Novick, Julius
Sainer, Arthur
Wetzsteon, Ross

The Villager (weekly) (65 Uni-
versity Pl., New York,
N. Y. 10003)
Africano, Lillian

Waco Tribune-Herald (morn.
& eve., Sat.-Sun. morn.)
(900 Franklin St., Waco,
Tx. 76703)
Quill, Gynter

Wall Street Journal (morn.)
(22 Cortlandt St., New York,
N. Y. 10007)
Wilson, Edwin

Washington Post (morn. & Sun.)
(1150 15th St., NW Washington, D. C. 20005)
Coe, Richard L.

Washington Star/News (eve. &
Sun.) (225 Virginia Ave., SE
Washington, D. C. 20003)
Richards, David

West Hartford News (weekly)
(20 Isham Rd., West Hartford, Conn. 06107)
Kloten, Edgar

Westchester Rockland Newspapers (One Gannet Dr.,
White Plains, N. Y. 10604)
Beals, Kathie
Cevetillo, Lou
LeSourd, Jacques

Where Magazine† (weekly) (135
W. 50th St., New York,
N. Y. 10020)
Klain, Jane
Schau, Michael

Winston-Salem Journal Sentinel
(morn., eve., Sun.) (416 N.
Marshall St., Winston-Salem,
N. C. 27102)
Carr, Eugenie
Shertzer, Jim

Wisdom's Child (weekly) (1841
Broadway, New York, N. Y.
10023)
Syna, Seymour

Women's Wear Daily (daily exc.
weekend) (7 E. 12th St.,
New York, N. Y. 10003)
Dibble, Peter
Kissel, Howard W.
Sharp, Christopher

Radio and Television

Greater New York Radio (509
Madison Ave., New York
N. Y. 10022)
Scholem, Richard J.

KERA-TV (3000 Harry Hines
Blvd., Dallas, Tx. 75201)
Swank, Patsy

KLEF-Radio (1401 S. Post Oak
Rd., Houston, Tx. 77027)
Black, Ira

KNBC-TV (3000 W. Alameda,
Burbank, Cal. 91505)
Barbour, John

KNXT-TV (CBS TV Stations,
6121 Sunset Blvd., Los
Angeles, Cal. 90028)
Sheehan, David

KOIN-TV (140 S. W. Columbia
St., Portland, Ore. 97201)
Kincaid, Frank

KQED-TV (1011 Bryant St.,
San Francisco, Cal. 94103)
Littlejohn, David

KSD-TV (St. Louis, Mo.)
Metz, Herbert E.

NBC-TV (30 Rockefeller Plaza,
New York, N. Y. 10020)
Howell, Chauncey
Lindstrom, Pia
Probst, Leonard

WBEN-TV (2077 Elmwood Ave.,
Buffalo, N. Y. 14207)
Freeman, Jayne

WBRW-Radio (P. O. Box 1170,
Somerville, N. J. 08876)
Ogden, Jean

WBZ-TV (Soldiers Field Rd.,
Boston, Mass.)
Mitchell, Patricia

WEVD-AM-FM Radio (1700
Broadway, New York, N. Y.
10019)
Shipley, Joseph

WFRE-FM Radio (Box 319,
Braddock Heights, Md. 21714)
Lebherz, Richard

---

*Works that are not plays or musicals are identified in brackets as:
dance, film, mime, music, opera. In addition, entries have been
made in this index of general articles on theatrical subjects, in article title with the designation "[general]" and on specific persons by
their last name with the designation "[feature]."

A Doll's House (Ibsen)--Daniels,
Bob; Jacaway, Taffy; Klein,
Stewart; Novick, Julius
Don Juan in Hell (Shaw)--Rus-
sell, Kathlyn; Smiljanich,
Dorothy
Don't Call Back [film] (O'Neill)
--Klein, Stewart
Dreyfus in Rehearsal (Grum-
berg)--Colby, Vineta
DuBarry Was a Lady (Porter)--
Cochran, Marsha
The Dungeon (Galvin)--Patrick,
Corbin
The Dybbuk (Ansky)--Bardacke,
Frances; Hirsch, Sam;
Mootz, William; Wylder,
Robert C.

Edward II (Marlowe)--Penning-
ton, Ron
Electra (Euripides)--Mackay,
Barbara
The Emperor Henry (Pirandel-
lo)--Safford, Edwin
Enemies (Gorky)--Griffin, Wil-
liam
Enter a Free Man (Stoppard)--
Rand, Sumner
Equus (Shaffer)--Bowman,
Pierre; Colby, Vineta;
Eichlebaum, Stanley; Hirsch,
Sam; Kalem, Theodore;
Kaye, Joseph; Mitchell, Pat;
Plutzik, Roberta; Simon,
John; Tobin, Richard L.
The Estate (Aranka)--Hart,
Thomas
An Evening with Gilbert & Sul-
livan [music]--Simon, Rich-
ard
Everything in the Garden (Al-
bee)--Smith, Helen
The Exorcist [film] (Blatty)--
Gardner, Rufus

Fantasticks (Jones & Schmidt)--
Vannoy, Cheryl
My Fat Friend (Laurence)--
Graham, David V.; Ruben-
stein, Nancy

The Father (Strindberg)--Klo-
ten, Edgar
Father's Day (Hailey)--Shippy,
Richard
Faust (Goethe)--Tuma, Mirko
Fiddler on the Roof--Bowman,
Pierre
The First Breeze of Summer
(Lee)--Klain, Jane; Klein-
man, Louis
The Folklorist (Yelvington)--
Quill, Gynter Clifford
Fosse, Bob [feature]--Ridley,
Clifford
The Fountain (O'Neill)--Atkin-
son, Justin Brooks
Der Freischütz [opera]--Kin-
kaid, Frank

Give Em Hell, Harry!--Bar-
bour, John; Jennings, Ro-
bert; Reiss, Alvin
The Glass Menagerie (Wil-
liams)--Ryweck, Charles
God's Favorite (Simon)--Young,
Mort
Godspell (Tebelak)--Carr,
Genie; Gross, Marge; Jaca-
way, Taffy; Probst, Leonard;
Shertzer, James; Smith,
Doug
Going Up (Hirsch & Harbach)--
Taylor, Markland
Good Evening (Cook & Moore)--
Goddard, Bob
The Good Soldier Schweik (Al-
len & Kurka)--Joslyn, Jay
Gorf (McClure)--Sales, Grover
Grease (Jacobs & Casey)--
Jacobi, Peter
Great American Nut Show
(Brown)--Vadeboncoeur, Joan

Hagar's Children (Josilovith)--
Nellhaus, Arlynn
Hair (Ragni, McDermott, &
Rado)--Howard, Edwin
Half-Eaten Heads (Duling)--
Jones, John
Hamlet (Shakespeare)--Bardacke,
Frances; Glover, William;

Lenny [film]--Shorey, Kenneth
Paul; Stewart, Perry
Leonce and Lena (Buchner)--
Richards, David
The Life and Death of King
John (Shakespeare)--Bannon,
Anthony
Light up the Sky (Hart)--Cros-
sett, D. Allen
The Lincoln Mask--Griffin,
William
A Little Night Music (Sondheim)
--Lambert, Virginia; Leon-
ard, Roy; Rubenstein, Nancy;
Young, Allen
London Assurance (Boucicault)--
Kelly, Martin
London Stage [general]--Loney,
Glenn
Long Day's Journey Into Night
(O'Neill)--Bishoff, Donald;
Funk, Nancy; Holloway, An-
thony; Rhinehart, Raymond P.
Look Back in Anger (Osborne)--
Anderson, George
The Lost Ones (Beckett)--
Maranca, Bonnie
Love From Mother (Thuna)--
Daniels, Bob
Love's Labour's Lost (Shakes-
peare)--Dresser, Norman;
Gottfried, Martin
Luther (Osborne)--Markoff,
Hildy

Macbeth (Shakespeare)--Bar-
bour, John; Foreman,
Thomas; Jones, Welton;
Longaker, Jon; Titcomb,
Caldwell
Magic Show (Randall)--Harriss,
Robert Preston
A Majority of One (Spigelgass)--
Cook, David
The Man Who Came to Dinner
(Kauffman & Hart)--Klein,
Gerald
The Many Faces of Love (Wol-
quitt)--Johnson, Wayne
Marcel Marceau [mime]--Al-
bright, William; Drake,
Sylvie; Eckert, Thor; Sul-
livan, Daniel

Martha Graham Dance Company
[dance]--Walsh, Paul
A Masque of Reason (Frost)--
Russell, Kathlyn
Mass [opera] (Bernstein)--Bor-
ak, Jeffrey; Norkin, Sam
The Matchmaker (Wilder)--
Taylor, Robert
A Matter of Gravity (Bagnold)--
Morrison, Hobe; Shull, Leo;
Takiff, Jonathon
The Me Nobody Knows (Joseph)
--Chapin, Louis
Measure for Measure (Shakes-
peare)--Doran, Terence;
Kelly, Kevin; Plaut, Jona-
thon; Steele, Mike
Medea (Euripides)--Mackay,
Barbara
Medea and Jason (Jeffers)--
Watts, Richard
The Member of the Wedding
(McCullers)--Delaunoy,
Didier
The Merchant of Venice
(Shakespeare)--Graham,
David V.
Merrill, Dina [feature]--Keogh,
Jim
A Midsummer Night's Dream
(Shakespeare)--Bone, Harold;
Peet, Creighton
The Miracle Worker (Gibson)--
Leeds, Diane
Miracles and Other Versions
(Mortimer)--MacReynolds,
Janet
The Misanthrope (Molière)--
DeVine, Laurence
Miss Julie (Strindberg)--Bannon,
Anthony
Mrs. Warren's Profession
(Shaw)--Morrison, Hobe
The Moon (Baldwin)--Nellhaus,
Arlynn
A Moon for the Misbegotten
(O'Neill)--Wylder, Robert C.
Mother Courage (Brecht)--
Crossett, D. Allen; Tuma,
Mirko
Mourning Becomes Electra
(O'Neill)--Griffin, William
Much Ado About Nothing (Shakes-
peare)--Griffin, William

Murder on the Orient Express [film] (Christie)--Metz, Herbert

Nash at Nine (Nash)--Blank, Ed
The National Health (Nichols)-- Wilson, Edwin
"New Dimension Theatre Studio Participants in Festival '70" [general]--Kessler, Leonard
Night of the Iguana (Williams)-- Patrick, Corbin; Sullivan, Daniel; Talcove, Rick
The Night That Made America Famous (Chapin)--Kleinman, Louis
Noel Coward in Two Keys-- Glackin, William; Lueloff, Jorie; Simon, Richard
The Norman Conquests (Ayckbourn)--Clurman, Harold; Sarmento, William
Norman, Is That You? (Clark & Bobrick)--Taggart, Patrick
Not I (Beckett)--Wilson, Edwin
Nureyev, Rudolf [feature]-- Trevens, Francine

Of Mice and Men (Steinbeck)-- Delaunoy, Didier; Young, Mort
Oh Coward! (Coward)--Shertzer, James
Oh Dad, Poor Dad (Kopit)-- McGovern, Bernie
Oil Lamps [film] (Herz)--Shorey, Kenneth Paul
Oklahoma (Rodgers & Hammerstein)--Marks, Arnold
Old Times (Pinter)--Drake, Sylvie; Nourse, Joan
The Omen [film] (Selzer)-- Taggart, Patrick
One Flew Over the Cuckoo's Nest (Wasserman)--Holloway, Anthony
O'Neill, Eugene [feature]-- Freeman, Charles

Other Voices, Other Rooms (Capote)--Plutzik, Roberta
Our Town (Wilder)--Foreman, Thomas; Norton, Elliot
Over Here (Holt)--Greatorex, Susan

Pacific Overtures (Sondheim)-- Calder, Ethan; Glover, William; LeSourd, Jacques; Ryweck, Charles
Papp, Joe [feature]--Hughes, Catherine
PDQ Bach: Peter Shickley [music]--Jones, William
Peer Gynt (Ibsen)--Lehman, Jon
Persson, Gene [feature]-- Marks, Arnold
The Philanthropist (Hampton)-- Dettmer, Roger
Pippin (Fosse)--Griffin, William
Play, Come and Go (Beckett)-- Maranca, Bonnie
The Plough and the Stars (O'Casey)--Smiljanich, Dorothy
Pocket Mime Theater [mime]-- Mitchell, Patricia
The Primary English Class (Horowitz)--Fratti, Mario
The Prime of Miss Jean Brodie --Gross, Marge
Prisoner of 2nd Ave. (Simon)-- Brode, Douglass
Private Lives (Coward)--Cahn, Irving; Leonard, Roy; Notman, Edith
P. S. Your Cat Is Dead (Kirkwood)--Smith, Doug; Stasio, Marilyn
I Puritani [opera]--Lambert, Virginia
Purlie (Davis)--Smith, Helen
Pygmalion (Shaw)--Friedman, Arthur

Quarry [opera] (Monk)--Sainer, Arthur

The Rainmaker--Leeds, Diane
Raisin (Hansberry)--Elkin, Mi-
chael; Peterson, Maurice
Rancho Deluxe [film] (Perry)--
Funk, Nancy
The Real Inspector Hound
(Stoppard)--Burley, George
The Rehearsal (Anouilh)--Noth,
Dominique
Rex (Rodgers)--Nadel, Norman
Rhinocerous (Ionesco)--Shipley,
Joseph Twadell; Thomas,
Barbara
Rhoda in Potatoland (Her Fall
Starts) (Foreman)--Marranca,
Bonnie
Richard III (Shakespeare)--
Eichlebaum, Stanley
The Ride Across Lake Constance
(Handke)--Gunner, Marjorie
Right You Are! (If You Think
You Are) (Pirandello)--Dow-
ney, Roger
Rigoletto [opera]--Kinkaid,
Frank
The Ritz (McNally)--Cahn, Ir-
ving; Paine, Canio
The River Niger (Walker)--
Fuller, Hoyt
Rivers, Joan [feature]--Free-
man, Jayne S.
Rockabye Hamlet (Shakespeare
& Champion)--Shull, Leo
Rodgers & Hart--Schau, Mi-
chael
Romeo & Juliet (Shakespeare)--
Atkinson, Justin Brooks
The Rules of the Game (Piran-
dello)--Brukenfield, Dick
The Runner Stumbles (Stitt)--
Taylor, Markland

Saint Joan (Shaw)--Doran, Ter-
ence; Kelly, Kevin
Same Time Next Year (Slade)--
Eckert, Thor; Kareda, Urjo;
Rubin, Joan; Scholem, Rich-
ard; Sharp, Christopher
San Francisco Mime Company
[mime]--Ogden, Jean
Sarah Bernhardt (Rich)--How-
ard, Edwin

Saturday, Sunday, and Monday
(Philip)--Swank, Patsy
Scenes from a Marriage [film]
(Bergman)--MacReynolds,
Janet; Plaut, Jonathon
The School for Scandal (Sheri-
dan)--Husten, Bruce; Young,
Allen
The Seagull (Chekhov)--Gott-
fried, Martin
Seagulls of 1933 (Salisbury)--
Edwards, William
Seascape (Albee)--Clurman,
Harold; Glackin, William;
Hughes, Catherine; Kraus,
Ted; Mangold, Elva; Pen-
nington, Ron; Watts, Richard
Seesaw (Gibson)--Loy, Robert;
Singer, Deborah
Selma (Butler)--Talcove, Rick
The Seven Descents of Myrtle
(Williams)--Jennings, Robert
Shakespeare productions [gen-
eral]--Oppenheimer, George
Shenandoah (Barrett)--Clay,
Carolyn; Lehman, Jon; So-
bel, Robert
Sherlock Holmes (Doyle)--Afri-
cano, Lillian; Beaufort, John;
Blaine, Howard; Kloten, Ed-
gar; Novick, Julius; Thomas,
Barbara
6 Rms Riv Vu (Randall)--
Greatorex, Susan; Griffin,
William
Sizwe Banzi Is Dead (Fugard
et al.)--Kaye, Joseph;
Nourse, Joan; Weales, Ge-
rald
The Skin of Our Teeth (Wilder)
--Albrecht, Ernest
The Sky is Falling (Ortiz)--
Wickstrom, Gordon
The Spotlight (on Musicals)
[general]--Holmes, Ann
The Steadfast Tin Soldier
(Grimes)--Feldman, David
Sticks and Bones (Rabe)--Watt,
Douglass
Streamers (Rabe)--Probst,
Leonard
A Streetcar Named Desire
(Williams)--Edwards,

A Streetcar (cont'd) William;
Harvey, John; Hoffman, William
Stuttgart Ballet [dance]--Herridge, Frances
Subject to Fits (Montgomery)--Taylor, Larry
The Subject Was Roses (Gilroy)--Sussman, Sharon
Sugawara Denju Tenarai Kugami [puppets]--Johnson, Wayne
Summer and Smoke (Williams)--Davis, Curtis
Summer Brave (Inge)--Oppenheimer, George

Tango (Mrozek)--Morgan, Murray
The Tempest (Shakespeare)--Jones, Welton
Ten Little Indians (Christie)--Brode, Douglass
Texas Trilogy (Jones)--Coe, Richard L.
That Championship Season (Miller)--Bardacke, Frances; McElfresh, Tom; Morrow, Sara
There's One in Every Marriage (Feydeau)--Wright, Fred
Thieves Carnival (Anouilh)--Cook, David
This Is (An Entertainment) (Williams)--Sussman, Sharon; Taylor, Robert
The Three Sisters (Chekhov)--Fowler, Giles; Gold, Sylvanie; Loy, Robert; Walsh, Paul
Threepenny Opera (Brecht)--Clurman, Harold; Moatz, William; Simon, John; Wetzsteon, Ross
The Time of Your Life (Saroyan)--Fowler, Giles
Tobacco Road (Kirkland)--Albright, William; Ruth, James; Wright, Fred
Tom Jones (Fielding)--Safford, Edwin
Tommy Allen Show (Terry)--Hawley, Michael

Tonight We Improvise (Pirandello)--Shipley, Joseph Twadell
Too True to be Good (Shaw)--Branche, Lewis
Die Tote Stadt (Korngold)--Stadelman, Egon
Travesties (Stoppard)--Rich, Alan
Treemonisha (Joplin)--Holmes, Ann
Trial of the Catonsville 9 (Davidson)--Chapin, Louis
The Trojan Women (Euripides)--Mackay, Barbara
Twelfth Night (Shakespeare)--Kareda, Urjo
Two Gentlemen of Verona (Shakespeare)--Portman, James
The Two of Us (Frayne)--Quarm, Joan

Violence and Sex in Theater/Film [general]--Osgood, Richard

Waiting for Godot (Beckett)--Hirsch, Sam; Richards, David; Spero, Bette
What the Butler Saw (Orton)--Steele, Mike
What the Wine-Sellers Buy (Milner)--Fuller, Hoyt
When Ya Comin' Back, Red Ryder? (Medoff)--Pollack, Joe
Where's Charley? (Thomas)--Husten, Bruce
White, Jane [feature]--Peterson, Maurice
Who's Afraid of Virginia Woolf? (Albee)--McElfresh, Tom; Nadel, Norman; Kissel, Howard W.
Who's Who in Hell (Ustinov)--Webster, Carmen
The Wind in the Willows (Grahame)--Hieronymus, Clara
Witness for the Prosecution (Christie)--Titus